Commentary on
MATTHEW

To the cherished memory of Gessner Harrison, M.D., for many years Professor of Ancient Languages in the University of Virginia.

At your feet I learned to love Greek, and my love of the Bible was fostered by your earnest devoutness. Were you still among us, you would kindly welcome the fruit of study, which now I can only lay upon your tomb; and would gladly accept any help it can give towards understanding the blessed Word of God, the treasure of our common Christianity, whose consolations and hopes sustained you in life and in death, and went with you into the unseen and eternal.

> *Nomen multis clarum et venerabile.*
> *Mihi adhuc magister atque pater.*

John A. Broadus

Commentary on
MATTHEW

John A. Broadus

KREGEL PUBLICATIONS
Grand Rapids, Michigan 49501

Commentary on Matthew, by John A. Broadus. © 1990 by Kregel Publications, a division of Kregel, Inc. P. O. Box 2607, Grand Rapids, MI 49501. All rights reserved.

Cover Design: Don Ellens

Library of Congress Cataloging-in-Publication Data

Broadus, John Albert, 1827-1895.
  [Commentary on the Gospel of Matthew]
  Commentary on Matthew / by John A. Boadus
     p.   cm.
  Reprint, with new introduction. Originally published: Commentary on the Gospel of Matthew. Philadelphia: American Baptist Publication Society, c1886. (An American commentary on the New Testament; v. 1).
  Includes indexes.

  1. Bible. N.T. Mathew—Commentaries. I. Title.
BS2575.3.B76   1990   226.2'.07—dc20   89-77852
                                                                CIP

ISBN   0-8254-2283-3 (pbk.)
ISBN   0-8254-2284-1 (deluxe hardback)

1 2 3 4 5 Printing/Year 93 92 91 90

Printed in the United States of America

CONTENTS

Commentary on Matthew

NOTE TO THE READER

Because of the unfamiliarity of most of us today with the Roman numeral system used throughout this book, the following conversion table may offer welcome assistance to many readers:

i 1		xxii 22
ii 2		xxiii .23
iii 3		xxiv .24
iv 4		xxv 25
v 5		xxvi .26
vi 6		xxvii 27
vii .7		xxviii 28
viii .8		xxix .29
ix 9		xxx .30
x 10		xl 40
xi 11		l 50
xii 12		lx 60
xiii 13		lxx 70
xiv 14		lxxx .80
xv 15		xc 90
xvi 16		c 100
xvii .17		cx 110
xviii .18		cxx .120
xvix .19		cxxx 130
xx 20		cxl 140
xxi 21		cl 150

PREFACE

THIS Commentary is designed primarily for persons who have no knowledge of Greek. But the effort has been made to add, *in foot-notes,* some matters interesting to scholars, in regard to Greek Grammar, and especially to Text-Criticism. These will not embarrass the general reader, being entirely detached and printed in smaller type.

The basis of the work is of course my personal study of the Greek, maintained through many years of teaching as Professor of the Interpretation of the New Testament, and renewed for this task with the help of lexicons, grammars, and concordances. I have been far from seeking novel interpretations for their own sake, but it is believed that some new light has been thrown upon a good many points.

At the same time, help has been constantly sought from ancient versions and Christian "Fathers," as well as from a wide range of later commentators. The early versions constantly employed were the Peshito Syriac, the Memphitic (Coptic), the Old Latin in various forms and Latin Vulgate, and the Gothic.[1]

The Fathers found most helpful have been Origen, Jerome, and Chrysostom, with the latter's faithful followers, Theophylact and Euthymius, and Augustine. Numerous others have of course been consulted on particular passages or questions ; and on two or three passages some contribution has been made to the history of interpretation.

Copious materials of illustration have been derived from the Jewish writings. As regards Josephus and Philo, the apocryphal and apocalyptic books, and the Mishna (chiefly in the Latin of Surenhusius), I have commonly quoted them after personal examination. For the Talmud of Jerusalem I have used Schwab's French translation so far as it has appeared. The Talmud of Babylon, the Targums, Midrashim, etc., are quoted at second hand from the extracts given by Lightfoot, Schoettgen, Wetstein, Gill, and others, including especially the recent works of Wünsche and Edersheim, who have furnished many valuable additions and correc-

---

[1] For Old Latin, besides the collections of Sabatier and Bianchini, I have been interested in the mixed text of Matthew edited by Wordsworth. Along with the common printed text of the Vulgate Latin, I have used Tischendorf's revised text of the Vulgate. The Peshito is well known to be, as regards exegesis, a delightful version. Bishop Lightfoot's article in Scrivener's "Introduction to Text-Criticism" (second and third editions) has shown the great importance of the Egyptian versions in regard to text. I can testify that with only a slender knowledge of the Coptic language one will find the Memphitic version very helpful for exegesis also, and the language very curious and interesting. The Gothic can be easily acquired by those who know English and German, and very easily if they know Anglo-Saxon. I shall be glad to answer inquiries from students, concerning books for learning Coptic and Gothic.

tions. It is hoped that the frequent references to Josephus may lead some persons to make themselves familiar with his writings, which many now unwisely neglect. The references to the Old Testament Apocrypha are not intended to treat those writings as in any sense a part of the Bible, but they are used, like the other Jewish works, to show Jewish opinion or custom, or to exemplify certain uses of language.

Many of the illustrative quotations from Greek and Latin classics are from Wetstein, others drawn from various sources.

Of all these studies the commentary aims to present only the results, and everywhere, it is hoped, in a form intelligible to the English reader.

Among modern commentators, I am of course most indebted to Meyer. Life-long study of his works, and the early adoption of similar lexico-grammatical methods of exegesis, render it difficult to determine what may have been originally due to him; special acknowledgment has been made wherever there was conscious indebtedness, and this general acknowledgment is added. I have also long found the commentaries of Bishop Ellicott a highly profitable discipline in grammatical, and those of Bishop Lightfoot in historical interpretation; and the various works of Canon Westcott have been of great assistance. Except in the case of Meyer and Alexander, I have, in preparing this work, usually taken versions, Fathers, and later commentaries in chronological order. Thus before examining recent writers I had commonly been over the same ground. The result would naturally be frequent coincidence of opinion, and sometimes included curious resemblance of expressions. Wherever any explanation or remark has been derived from older or more recent works, there is express acknowledgment. The writings of Calvin, Maldonatus, Bengel, Keim, Weiss, Lutteroth, Plumptre, Morison, and Edersheim have been very often helpful, and others that cannot be particularly named.

As to the sources of the material common to Matthew and other Gospels, no theory has been adopted. Those who hold that Matthew and Luke were built on Mark, or the like, can render this view plausible by examples selected for the purpose. But go steadily through, observing, for example, the attempts of Keim to show at every point that Mark has drawn from Matthew, and of Weiss to show that Matthew has built on Mark, and one can scarcely fail to perceive that both hypotheses break down, notwithstanding that Keim and Weiss are men of rare ability, the finest scholarship, curious ingenuity, and unhesitating freedom in manipulating the materials. Nor have the recent publications of E. A. Abbott and Rushbrooke made any very important advance upon the similar work of Ewald. As to the apparent contradictions, or "discrepancies," between Matthew and the other Gospels, I have offered such explanations as seemed reasonable, without encouraging a nervous solicitude to explain everything, where our information is limited, and the points of disagreement are such as must always arise in different reports of the same event or discourse, though each thoroughly correct.

In all such cases of uncertainty about the Greek text, as would affect the translation or interpretation, I have intended to state the preferable reading with a confidence varying according to the evidence; and in all that are of considerable interest the evidence has been more or less fully presented in foot-notes. Besides persons acquainted with text-criticism, other readers who feel curiosity in regard to the subject will be likely to examine these foot-notes; and I have endeavored to present the internal evidence, viz., the intrinsic probabilities (as to what the author wrote), and the transcriptional probabilities (as to changes likely to have been made by well-meaning students or copyists), in such terms as might be intelligible to the general reader. As it is usually much easier to state transcriptional than intrinsic probabilities, I may seem to have attached a greater relative importance to the former than was intended. In a good many cases the foot-note gives a tolerably full discussion.[1] It should be borne in mind that the reader will be able to judge more safely of such questions in proportion as he has gained experience.—The solicitude, and even alarm, which some persons feel in regard to the encroachments of text-criticism, must be regarded as without cause. Instead of shaking faith in Scripture, these researches will ultimately strengthen faith. When the shock of abandoning a familiar expression has passed, one almost invariably begins to see that the true text is best. The general teachings of the New Testament as to doctrine and duty are now known to be established independently of all passages that contain doubtful readings. And why should we wonder if it is sometimes difficult to determine the true text? There is well known to be a similar uncertainty as to the translation and interpretation of some passages. This excites no alarm or anxiety, nor should we feel disturbed about occasional uncertainty of text. And the danger of subjective bias in judging as to the text, is no greater than in regard to interpretation and translation.

The commentary is based on the Common English Version, as printed by the American Bible Society, but with constant comparison of the recent Anglo-American Revision. This revision in its English form originally constituted the basis; the common version was substituted in the office of publication, in order that the work might correspond to other volumes of the series, and the *American* form of the revision was printed instead of the English. These adaptations were carefully made by a competent hand, and will not embarrass or mislead the reader unless it be in one respect. The Revised Version seems often to be presented as a mere alternative rendering; while I am fully persuaded that it is almost uniformly superior to the Common Version, and often greatly superior. Wherever its render-

---

[1] The general contributions to text-criticism made by Westcott and Hort are invaluable, and most of their judgments as to particular passages seem to me correct. But in a number of cases I have felt bound to dissent, and to give the reasons as fully and strongly as the character and limits of this work allowed. Hence arises a certain polemical attitude towards writers to whom I feel deeply indebted and cordially grateful.—It may be well to state in a general way, that Westcott and Hort appear to me substantially right in their theory as to a "Syrian" and a "Western" type of Greek text; but their supposed "Neutral" type is by no means disentangled from the "Alexandrian." And while they have nobly rehabilitated internal evidence, building their system originally upon that basis, they seem to err in some particular judgments by following a small group of documents in opposition to internal evidence which others cannot but regard as decisive.—Where I have stated the documentary evidence, it has been taken from Tischendorf, with some additions from Westcott and Hort, and a few from my own reading. In particular, I have added, where it seemed desirable, the readings of the newly found Codex Rossanensis (Σ).

ings seem of questionable propriety, the fact is distinctly brought out in the commentary. The marginal renderings of the Common and the Revised Version are usually noticed. The early English translations are mentioned, when likely to profit the general reader, omitting points of merely philological or literary interest. These versions have been quoted from Bagster's English Hexapla, and where "early English versions" in general are referred to, only those given in that collection are meant unless the contrary is stated. Certain recent English translations are also frequently cited, particularly those of the American Bible Union, Noyes, Darby, and Davidson.

The references to all parts of the Bible are the result of painstaking examination, and the minister or Sunday-school teacher who desires to make careful study of a particular passage will find his reward in searching out all that are given. The frequent cross-references may require justification. Commentaries are chiefly used, not in the way of continuous reading, but in the study of particular sentences or paragraphs. In that case it becomes highly convenient to find references to other parts of the work, in which a word or phrase may be found specially explained, or a kindred topic more fully discussed.

The descriptions of places and sketches of personal history are given for the sake of numerous readers who have no Bible Dictionary, and because others who would not hunt up the book of reference might read the brief account here given. These articles are constructed with a special view to the illustration of the Gospels. The materials of description are drawn from many sources, notably from Robinson's "Biblical Researches," and Thomson's "Land and Book," in its earlier and its later forms; also from the recent explorations of the English and American Societies, particularly as represented by the writings of Warren, Wilson, and Conder, and of Merrill. I have of course been aided in the use of these materials by my own visit to Palestine; extracts from my journal are given in some places where the matter appeared to be interesting, and has not been found elsewhere.

Quotations from the Old Testament need special attention, for they are very numerous in this Gospel, and some of them present serious difficulty. The *form* of the quotation has been carefully compared with the Hebrew and the Septuagint, and the differences of language stated and so far as possible accounted for; the *meaning* has been still more carefully examined, so as to see how far we can perceive the ground for asserting a prophetic relation. Great pains have been taken, in these passages and everywhere, to state nothing as certain that is only probable, and frankly to recognize all difficulties.

The phrase "Homiletical and Practical" became familiar to me when translating and editing the portion thus designated of Lange (Erdmann) on 1 and 2 Samuel. There are some advantages in giving homiletical and practical remarks upon an entire paragraph, rather than upon successive verses. Yet the line cannot be sharply drawn, and much in the way of general discussion and practical observation will be found in immediate connection with the explanations. Besides detached statements of truth and suggestions of duty and consolation, I have under this head very often given *schemes* of thought, hoping that these would be more readable, and make a more lasting impression, than disconnected remarks. Where such schemes amount to plans of sermons, they may suggest to ministers the practicability of constructing, by similar methods, better sermons of their own. The *extracts* added have been rigorously limited to brief and pithy passages from the Greek and Latin Fathers, from Luther and Calvin, from Jeremy Taylor, Bishop Hall, and Matthew Henry, with some from miscellaneous sources, particularly on chap. 5-7. At the outset, a good many extracts were made from the excellent homiletical works of D. Thomas, Joseph Parker, and Bishop Ryle; but as the book was growing too large for its design, and as these works are current and not costly, it was thought best, in the final revision, to strike out most of what had been drawn from these sources. The extracts have sometimes been condensed, or otherwise slightly altered.

This commentary does not profess to be undenominational. Matters upon which our religious bodies differ have been discussed with entire frankness, but also, it is hoped, with true Christian respect and regard. After all, there are but few passages of the Gospel in regard to which evangelical opinion is seriously at variance.

The better class of Sunday-school teachers have, in preparing these expositions, been constantly before my mind. It has been interesting to observe, in the last revision, how very often my paragraphs agree with the lessons of the International Series upon this Gospel, which will extend from July 1, 1887 to July 1, 1888. The teacher who is hurried will find it easy to practice, in regard to occasional prolonged discussions, what a high literary authority has called "judicious skipping"; for as the portions explained are printed in blackfaced type, the eye will quickly pass from one word or phrase to another. Some teachers will derive useful practical instruction for their pupils from the paragraphs headed "Homiletical and Practical."

This work has been on hand more than twenty years, having been pushed forward at different periods, and for several years past with rarely interrupted application. Considerable portions have been twice or thrice rewritten. I have labored to make a clear, sound, and useful commentary, and I shall be very glad and thankful if it proves acceptable and helpful to earnest readers of the Bible.

LOUISVILLE, *November, 1886.*   J. A. B.

For various reasons, no Introduction to Matthew has been prepared. The author's views as to the origin and authority of this Gospel would be substantially the same as may be found in Salmon's "Introduction to the New Testament"; Hovey's "General Introduction"; the works of Westcott and Charteris on the "Canon of the New Testament," etc.

At the close of the volume will be found an Index of the writers quoted, with explanation of abbreviated names, and some elementary information as to the authors and their works; and a second Index of terms and topics, persons and places, of which some general account is given in the commentary upon the passages indicated.

GENERAL INTRODUCTION TO THE NEW TESTAMENT

by

Alvah Hovey, D.D., LL.D.

I.

THE CANON OF THE NEW TESTAMENT.

FOR the purposes of this Introduction it is unnecessary to give a history ot the word "canon," or even a list of the significations which it has in ancient literature. As applied to the New Testament, it means "the collection of books which constitute the original written rule of the Christian faith" (*Westcott*). If there is any standard of religious faith and practice recognized by Christians of every name as authoritative, it is this collection of books which are supposed to have been written by the immediate disciples of Christ and their associates.

It is true that Christians do not all agree in holding these books to be the *only* authoritative rule of faith and practice in matters of religion, but they all agree in holding them to be *an* original and authoritative rule, even though, as some suppose, their teaching must be supplemented by ecclesiastical tradition. It is true, again, that Christians do not all agree as to the complete inspiration and final authority of these books, but they all concede to them very high authority as the only original documents of the Christian religion now extant. It is also true that Christians do not all agree in their interpretation of these books, or in their theory as to the persons who are qualified to interpret them, but they all admit the high importance of their teaching, whenever it is ascertained.

How was the Canon of the New Testament established?

In seeking an answer to this question it will be found that the ways of God are not like our ways; for human wisdom would, doubtless, have deemed it expedient to guard against possible doubt or error in time to come by committing the closing up of the Canon to the last of the apostles. If John, residing at Ephesus in his old age, had inserted in his last book a list of the inspired writings of his contemporaries, with such a sketch of their contents as would make it easy to identify them; if he had testified that the number of such writings was then complete; and if he had joined with this statement a warning against any addition to or subtraction from the number or the teaching of these books (like that in Rev. 22 : 18, 19),—this, it may be thought, would have fixed the Canon of the New Testament beyond any possibility of doubt or debate, and this, surely, would have been a very natural course for human wisdom to take in the circumstances.

But it might have proved to be a mistake after all, giving to Christians less stable grounds for confidence than they now have. Would it not have led them to overlook all other evidence, and to depend exclusively on the witness of this apostle? Would it not have excited in critical minds suspicions of human calculation or fear, and demands for impossible proof that John himself wrote the book containing the list described, or at least the paragraph in which the list was found? Would it not have provoked the assertion that such a proceeding was unexampled and uncalled for by the circumstances of Christians at that time, since they must have known who were the writers of the Gospels and Epistles which they had received? These and similar criticisms would certainly have been made if the course suggested had been taken, even though that course was the safest and best possible in the eyes of human wisdom.

But it was not taken. The Spirit of God, who is wiser than men, and who presided over the work of the apostles, chose another way of establishing the Canon, another way of making known to Christians the authoritative documents of their religion in distinction from other books pertaining to it. And the way chosen by the Spirit was perfectly obvious and natural. It was to make use of the prudence and piety of the churches in accomplishing this work, by committing to them the writings of men who were known to be inspired teachers of Christian truth. For the prudence and piety of the churches would be morally certain to preserve these writings as a sacred trust, and to hand them down, with the names of their authors, from generation to generation as authoritative expositions of their religion.

If, for example, the churches of Philippi and Corinth received from Paul letters that were instinct with the spirit of love, wisdom, and authority—letters that praised their virtues, reproved their sins, corrected their errors, relieved their perplexities, scattered their doubts, and brightened their hopes—they would not fail to preserve these letters with the utmost care, or to leave them as precious treasures to their successors in the church. While they would be very willing to have them read and copied by disciples of Christ from other churches, they would be likely to insist upon retaining them in their own custody. And since the letters directed to a single church were few in number (rarely if ever more than two), there would never be the slightest danger of mistake as to their authorship.

Thus, by a natural process, under the control of good sense and right feeling, would nearly all the writings of "apostles" and "apostolic men" (*Tertullian*) be kept distinct from the writings of those who could not declare the will of Christ with equal authority. For example, the Epistles of Paul to the Corinthians would never for a moment be put on a level with the epistle which they received, a third of a century later, from the church in Rome, and which was written by Clement, Bishop of that church. Even if the latter were sometimes read in the church at Corinth, or were copied into the same manuscript with the former, there would be no danger of confusion. For if we look merely at the general contents of the two Epistles of Paul to "the church of God in Corinth," and of the first epistle of Clement to that church, it is manifestly absurd to ascribe them all to the same author, or to ascribe the canonical epistles to Clement and the ecclesiastical epistle to Paul. Besides, the former purport to be from the apostle, while the latter purports to be from the church in Rome. There may have been cases where the possibility of mistaking a non-apostolical for an apostolical writing is less incredible than in the case mentioned, but there were none, it is believed, where such a mistake can be regarded as probable.

And, in spite of modern doubts and denials, it is evident from a variety of circumstances that the early Christians were reasonably cautious about the sources of their knowledge. It is evident, for example, from the four great Epistles of Paul (viz. Romans, First and Second Corinthians, and Galatians), which are accepted as genuine by the boldest criticism, that special and, indeed, absolute confidence was reposed in the teaching of those admitted to be apostles (1 Cor. 12 : 28, 29; 2 Cor. 11 : 5; 12 : 11, 12; Gal. 2 : 7–9; Eph. 2 : 20; 4 : 11). They were looked upon as entitled to speak with authority on all matters relating to the person and work of Christ or the duty of his followers. Naturally, therefore, their writings would be preserved and consulted with the greatest respect. It is also evident from hints in the New Testament, and from the language of the Christian Fathers, that *along with* the teaching of the apostles was placed the teaching of their companions, such as Mark and Luke, either because their doctrine was supposed to be received directly from apostles, and to be fully endorsed by them, or because, in addition to their intimacy with apostles, they were believed to have a special gift of inspiration to qualify them for their work.

If, now, as history appears to show, the formation of the New Testament Canon was left to the prudence and piety of the early churches, several things which may be said to characterize the actual process of formation are seen to be natural, if not inevitable. A few of these may be named in this place.

1. *The Principal Reason for admitting a Book to the Canon was found in its Authorship.*—If the sacred books of the New Covenant had been selected by the apostle John, the names and relations of their writers might have been a matter of no vital importance to any one. Enlightened by the Spirit, this apostle might have discerned the pure gold of truth with no admixture of error in anonymous productions, and these productions, stamped with his approval, might have been welcomed by the churches without much desire or effort to ascertain who were their authors. The great name and authority of John would have proved sufficient for a time to satisfy reason and blunt the edge of curiosity. But if books were to be pronounced authoritative and assigned a place in the Canon by the common judgment of churches composed of uninspired men, it could only be done on the ground of confidence in their authors as men who were commissioned by the Lord to declare his truth, and assisted to do this by the Holy Spirit. And this appears to have been the principal, if not the sole, ground on which the books of the New Testament were accepted by the churches, in preference to all others, as authentic statements of fact, of doctrine, and of duty.

2. *The Formation of the Canon was a Slow but Safe Process.*—To understand this, the reader must picture to himself the condition of the churches when the last of the apostles died in Ephesus. For that condition was not such as to suggest the necessity of collecting at once the standard documents of Christianity into a single volume. Had John ever directed them to collect those documents?

Were they not doing their appointed work, each in its separate form and appropriate sphere, as they had been doing it, some for a long period already? While the apostle was living there had been no lack of authoritative instruction, and now, though he had fallen asleep, there were many still alive who had heard the gospel from his lips a thousand times, and who had perhaps enjoyed his personal friendship: could these ever forget his doctrine or manner of life? Moreover, they were all familiar, it may be presumed, with one or more of the Synoptic Gospels, as well as with that of John, and with some of the Epistles—every one written on a separate parchment, convenient for use and not too expensive for ownership. Was not this the best form in which to preserve and circulate them still? Besides, the Epistles in almost every instance were written to the Christians of a particular province or church, or to an individual saint, and must therefore have been specially adapted to the spiritual wants of those addressed: were they then equally important to others? Might it not still be wise to circulate particular books for the most part where they were most needed, some in one province and some in another, even as the apostles sent them originally, some to one province and some to another?

Such may have been the reflections of devout men at the close of the first century, if indeed the subject of a New Testament Canon engaged their attention at all. But this is very doubtful. For the perils of the times, and their own probable freedom from doubts as to the origin of standard Christian writings, may have prevented the thought of forming a New Testament Canon from entering their minds. And as the years flew by, whether red with blood or white with peace, and their struggle with Paganism and error was incessant, it is clear that there could have been little opportunity for united counsel until the reign of Constantine. Then, for the first time, would the question of making a full collection of the Sacred Scriptures of the New Covenant be likely to receive due consideration. And then it did receive suitable attention. Then the claims of certain writings that had not been received as sacred in every part of Christendom were canvassed, and the full collection of books that ought to be esteemed canonical was ascertained to the satisfaction of the churches.

3. *Partial Collections preceded the Full and Final Collection.*—That this should be the case was inevitable. Consider, first, the Gentile churches founded by Paul. Is it not certain that they would feel a special interest in the Epistles written by him, both because he was their spiritual father, and because he had respect in what he wrote to their peculiar training and condition? And along with his Epistles they would surely be anxious to possess the four Gospels and the Acts of the Apostles—the former, because they would earnestly desire to know all that could be known of their Lord's earthly life; and the latter, because they would naturally wish to trace the footsteps of Paul in bringing the gospel to the Gentiles. To these might be added in many of the churches a few other books; for example, the First Epistle of Peter and the First of John. But it need not be supposed that these productions were all bound up in the same manuscript volume, even though they were believed to be of equal and ultimate authority.[1]

---

[1] Says S. P. Tregelles: "In the reign of Trajan—*i. e.* almost immediately after the death of

Consider also the early versions of books now included in the New Testament. Whenever such a version was made, it would be likely to embrace all the books that were considered by the translator inspired and authoritative, especially if the judgment of the translator was in accord with that of the churches among whom he lived. According to this view, it is reasonable to infer from an early Syriac version, the Peshito, what were the books accepted as canonical by the Asiatic churches of the time, and from an early Latin version, made in North Africa, what were the books then received as canonical by the churches of that province, and perhaps, from a catalogue like that discovered by Muratori, what were the books regarded as canonical by the churches of Italy when it was written. Yet it must be admitted that such versions or catalogues did not include every book which was supported by good evidence. Perhaps they admitted those only that were accepted at the time by all the churches in the region where the version or catalogue was made. And as some of the books were better known in one province than in another, these versions and catalogues were not precisely alike. It is even possible that a few books were omitted from the versions because the books were supposed to be of minor practical importance. The Peshito omits the Second Epistle of Peter, the Second and Third Epistles of John, the Epistle of Jude, and the Apocalypse, but includes all the other books as commonly received without any addition (*Westcott*). It was probably made in the first half of the second century (*Id.* p. 211). The early Latin version omitted the Epistle of James and the Second Epistle of Peter; perhaps also at first the Epistle to the Hebrews, though this was soon added. After critical examination Westcott concludes that the oldest Latin version was made before A. D. 170, though how long before cannot now be discovered. It is also his judgment that the so-called " Fragment of Muratori " could not have been written much after A. D. 170, and that it recognized the same books as canonical which were inserted in the North African version.

4. *Some of the Books were Canonized on Fuller Evidence than Others.*—This results from what has been said already. If the Christian Scriptures were circulated for a considerable time in portions, according to the convenience of purchasers and readers, some of them must have been much more widely scattered and generally known than others. Merely personal letters, like the Second and Third Epistles of John and Paul's Epistle to Philemon, would be known to comparatively few, unless perhaps the Epistles of Paul were early brought together in one volume and thus circulated among the Gentile churches. In this case, the Epistle to Philemon might be generally known as a work of Paul and numbered with his other letters, though rarely quoted. The same circumstance would also account for the smaller circulation of the Pastoral Epistles to Timothy and Titus,

---

St. John, the last evangelist and the last surviving apostle—the four Gospels were collected and circulated in one volume; and as a united volume they were used in the former part of the second century by the churches in general. St. Paul's Epistles were also in the same age circulated unitedly : there may have been another collection in use omitting some of them, but this question, as well as whether the Epistle to the Hebrews belonged to this united volume, does not require to be here discussed. Of the other books of the New Testament, the greater part were in use as separate books," etc. (Horne's *Introd. to the Holy Scriptures,* vol. iv. p. 25.)

though these would be sought by the ministry for a special reason, the instruction which they give as to the qualifications and duties of pastors. Again, such a book as the Epistle to the Hebrews might be chiefly used at first by churches composed of Jewish converts, for whose special benefit it was written.

Still further: local or temporary enthusiasm for a certain doctrine might lead to a more extensive and diligent use of the book in which it was supposed to be taught than was made of other books no less interesting to-day, while local or temporary dislike of certain doctrines might lead first to neglect, and then to ignorance, of the books supposed to teach them. This was probably true of the doctrine of Chiliasm as affecting the use or neglect of the Apocalypse.

For these reasons it is plain that the evidence for the canonicity of certain books of the New Testament would appear to be less compulsory in the fourth century than that for the canonicity of others. A uniform and universal tradition would commend a large part of these Scriptures to the confidence of every upright inquirer, but other portions would be supported by testimony from certain quarters and periods only.

From this general survey of the process by which the New Testament Canon was established in the early church it is now proper to turn to a consideration of the question—

Why should this Canon of the New Testament be accepted as Trustworthy?

The first and most obvious reason for this is our confidence in the good sense and piety of those who united their voices in adopting it. But if their repute for intelligence and fairness of mind were less than it is, there are two circumstances in their favor: the matter to be determined was not likely, on the whole, to enkindle partisan strife, and the evidence on which to found their decision was much more abundant then than it is now; for, as the writings of Eusebius clearly prove, a large part of that evidence has disappeared with the numerous volumes in which it was found.

In the light of these statements, the conclusions adopted by churches and councils in the latter part of the fourth century, even though they were but a ratification or declaration of the views of Christians in different parts of the empire, are presumably correct, and should be received with confidence unless they can be proved erroneous. The "burden of proof" rests upon those who reject any portions of the New Testament as unworthy of a place in the Canon of Holy Scripture. Unless well-attested facts, inconsistent with the view that these books were written by "apostles" or "apostolic men," and were received with veneration by those to whom they were first sent, can be produced, the books are entitled to retain the high position which was then accorded to them. This state of the case should be borne in mind by every one who undertakes to review the arguments for and against the limits to the New Testament Canon which have been generally accepted by Christians since the close of the fourth century. For the judgment of men having much evidence since lost must not be set aside as of no value. To restate our position: Since the churches and councils of the fourth century fixed the limits of the New Testament Canon with the *aid of all the evidence which we now have* and *of much that has been lost,* it would be unreasonable to change those limits unless they are found to be irreconcilable with ascertained facts. Yet a brief survey of the evidence which remains will be of service to those who cannot study that evidence minutely, and perhaps of nearly equal service to persons who desire to recall the principal features of that evidence or to prepare themselves for the study of it.

FIRST PERIOD—THAT OF THE APOSTOLICAL FATHERS, TO A. D. 120.

Very little Christian literature from this period has been preserved. The peculiar relation of the apostles to Christ, and the special inspiration which guided them in their work, gave them a vast influence over those who received the gospel from their lips. Hence, naturally, the spiritual leaders of the churches, after the apostolic age, were preachers, not writers. They were simply heralds of the truth which they had received from men whom they felt to be vastly superior to themselves in knowledge and authority. Most of their own work was done with the voice, and not with the pen ; but whatever they did with the pen was chiefly done by letters of a practical character, rather than by treatises or full discussions. It is not, therefore, surprising that few exact quotations from books of the New Testament occur in their writings, or that these quotations are informal. For they probably had no occasion to enumerate the Christian books which they esteemed sacred, and little or no occasion to point out the source of any expressions which they drew from those books.

That a man bearing the name of CLEMENT was one of the early pastors of the church in Rome cannot be seriously denied ; for, according to Irenæus, who wrote within less than a hundred years of the time when Clement was supposed to have stood at the head of the Roman Church, he was the successor of Anencletus, while Anencletus was the successor of Linus, the first overseer of the church (*B.* iii. 33) ; and, according to Eusebius, Linus was Pastor in Rome from A. D. 68–80 ; Anencletus, from A. D. 80–92 ; and Clement, from A. D. 92–101 (*H. E.,* iii. 13, 15). Of the many writings once ascribed to Clement of Rome, only one is now believed to be genuine—an epistle of the church in that city to the church in Corinth—and this appears to have been written about A. D. 95. It is commonly called the "First Epistle of Clement," because there is evidence that it was written by Clement in the name and on behalf of the Roman Church, and because another production, once supposed to be a second letter, was early associated with the name of Clement and with this epistle. That production is at last ascertained to be a homily belonging to some author who lived before the middle of the second century. It is therefore probably the oldest Christian homily extant.

Of the first and genuine epistle it may be remarked—(1) That it is full of Christian thought and sentiment. One who reads it attentively will perceive that the spirit of its author was thoroughly Christian, and that he must have been at home with all the great truths of Scripture. (2) That it blends together in a very natural way the several types of doctrinal statement which have been found in the different books of the New Testament, and expresses views and feelings which would be produced in a candid mind by perusing with reverence all these books. So manifest is this that, in the language of the epistle, we seem to hear again, as it were, though in fainter tones, the voices of Christ and of Peter, of John and of Paul. (3) That many passages of Scripture are reproduced with slight changes, as if from memory, and that expressions from different books or chapters are blended together in quotation, as if they belonged to the same paragraph of the sacred record. Such a method of quotation may not be commended as scholarly or critical, but it was certainly very natural, especially if the writer supposed his readers to be familiar with the Septuagint and with the books of the New Testament.[1] (4) That it refers particularly to Paul's First Epistle to the Corinthians, probably because that Epistle was addressed to the same church when it was in somewhat similar circumstances; but the author appears to have been "well acquainted with the writings of Paul" (*Donaldson*). Important extracts are made from the Epistle to the Hebrews, though without describing the source from which they were derived. (5) That the contents and language of this epistle are accounted for by supposing that its writer knew and reverenced the Scriptures of the Old and the New Testament, while they cannot easily be accounted for if he was ignorant of any considerable part of the latter volume.[2]

The brief references in early Christian writers to IGNATIUS warrant the belief that he was for a considerable time Bishop of Antioch, and that, either about A. D. 107 or about A. D. 116, he was sent as a condemned Christian to Rome, where he suffered martyrdom. The epistles ascribed to him are preserved in three forms, the longest of which may be pronounced quite unworthy of confidence. But of the other two forms it is difficult to say which has the best claim to be regarded genuine. The tendency of criticism seems, however, to be just now more favorable to the seven epistles of the shorter recension in Greek than to the three epistles in Syriac, the latter being regarded as made up of extracts from three of the former. Without undertaking to decide between the claims of these two forms of the Ignatian letters, and without affirming positively that Ignatius wrote even the three in the form published by Cureton, it may be remarked (1) that the seven contain many more references to the New Testament than the three. But even the testimony of the seven as to the New Testament will be found to be indirect instead of direct, and implied instead of expressed. For they do not formally appeal to the sacred books of the New Covenant, but presuppose their existence by the use of words, sentences, and thoughts which those books contain. (2) The author of these epistles must have been well acquainted with the writings of Paul and of John, and by no means ignorant of other New Testament Scriptures. Charteris recog-

---

[1] " We must remember that the ancient writer had not a small, compact reference Bible at his side, but, when he wished to verify a reference, would have to take an unwieldy roll out of its case, and then would not find it divided into chapter and verse, like our modern books, but would have only the columns, and those not numbered, to guide him. We must remember, too, that the memory was much more practised and relied upon in ancient times, especially among the Jews." (Sanday, *The Gospels in the Second Century*, pp. 29, 30.)

[2] Westcott (*On the Canon of the New Testament*, p. 44) gives the following books of the New Testament as certainly or possibly referred to by Clement: Romans, Ephesians, First Timothy (?), Titus (?), Hebrews, James.

nizes citations from Matthew, John, Acts, Romans, First Corinthians, Ephesians, Philippians, First Thessalonians, First Timothy, and Revelation, and "echoes" of passages in Matthew, Mark, John, Acts, Romans, First and Second Corinthians, Galatians, Ephesians, Philippians, Colossians, First and Second Timothy, Titus, Hebrews, First and Second Peter, First and Third John, and Revelation. (3) The style of Ignatius is rugged, forcible, positive, and his spirit bold, earnest, and perhaps slightly fanatical. This is said on the assumption that the seven Vossian epistles are substantially genuine. But if it is assumed that only the three Syriac epistles are genuine, the references to the New Testament are few, though the spirit and phraseology are such as we have described, and are best accounted for by supposing Ignatius familiar with the writings of Paul and of John.

POLYCARP was the living link between the apostles—especially John—and Irenæus, a well-known bishop and writer who flourished in Gaul during the last quarter of the second century. For Polycarp was a disciple of John, and Irenæus a disciple of Polycarp. Irenæus testifies that in his youth he himself had heard Polycarp "describe his intercourse with John and with the rest who had seen the Lord," and that Polycarp "survived long, and departed this life, at a very great age, by a glorious and most notable martyrdom." According to the *Martyrium Polycarpi*—which, if not wholly authentic, appears to be founded on fact—Polycarp declared that he had served Christ eighty-six years, so that, if converted in childhood, he was probably more than ninety years old at the time of his death. But scholars are not agreed as to the date of his death, some placing it about A. D. 155, and others about A. D. 166, eleven years later. If the former date be accepted as correct, he was probably born about A. D. 63—if the latter, he may have been born about A. D. 74. In one case he was about thirty-five years old when the apostle John died; in the other, he was perhaps twenty-six years old; in either, he might have known the apostle ten or fifteen years. On the other hand, Irenæus may have been born as early as A. D. 125 or 130, and may therefore have been a hearer of Polycarp many years before leaving Asia Minor for Gaul.

In a letter to Florinus, who had, as he believed, fallen into grievous errors, Irenæus says: "These opinions, Florinus, that I may speak without harshness, are not of sound judgment; these opinions are not in harmony with the church, but involve those adopting them in the greatest impiety; these opinions even the heretics outside the pale of the church have never ventured to broach; these opinions the elders before us, who also were disciples of the apostles, did not hand down to thee. For I saw thee, when I was still a boy, in Lower Asia in company with Polycarp, while thou wast faring prosperously in the royal court and endeavoring to stand well with him. For I distinctly remember the incidents of that time better than events of recent occurrence; for the lessons received in childhood, growing with the growth of the soul, become identified with it, so that I can describe the very place in which the blessed Polycarp used to sit when he discoursed, and his goings out and his comings in, and his manner of life, and his personal appearance, and his intercourse with John and with the rest who had seen the Lord, and how he would relate their words. And whatsoever things he had heard from them about the Lord, and about his miracles, and about his teaching, Polycarp, as having received them from eye-witnesses of the life of the Word, would relate altogether in accordance with the Scriptures. To these [discourses] I used to listen at the time with attention by God's mercy, which was bestowed upon me, noting them down, not on paper, but in my heart; and by the grace of God I constantly ruminate upon them faithfully."

Moreover, in his work *Against Heresies*, Irenæus refers to him again, after speaking of the succession of Roman bishops through whom the true doctrine had been handed down to his own times: "And Polycarp also—who not only was taught by apostles, and lived in familiar intercourse with many that had seen Christ, but also received his appointment for Asia by apostles in the church that is in Smyrna, an overseer, whom also we have seen in the beginning of our life, for he remained a long time, and at an exceedingly old age, having borne his testimony gloriously and most notably, departed this life—always taught these things, which also he learned from the apostles, which also he gave to the church, and which alone are true. To these doctrines testimony is also borne by all the churches throughout Asia, and by those who have been up till this time the successors of Polycarp, who was a much more trustworthy and secure witness of the truth than Valentinus and Marcion and the rest, who held wicked opinions. Moreover, there is an epistle of Polycarp addressed to the Philippians, which is most adequate, and from which both his manner of life and his preaching of the truth may be learnt by those who desire to learn and are anxious for their own salvation " (*B*. iii. 3).

To the genuineness of this letter several objections have been urged, but these objections are greatly outweighed by the evidence in its favor; so that, whatever may be thought of ch. 13, the rest of the epistle must be accepted as the work of Polycarp. Indeed, it would be difficult to name any ancient writing which is better authenticated than this. It may therefore be used without fear as a fair sample of Christian counsel and exhortation soon after the beginning of the second century. And it is specially noticeable (1) that the tone of the letter accords with the testimony of Irenæus that its author had listened to the venerable apostle John and to others who had seen the Lord. For this experience, whether in youth or early manhood, would be likely to make a deep impression on a susceptible mind, and would be unfavorable to originality of thought or expression. (2) That the phraseology of the letter agrees with the alleged circumstances of the writer. For if Polycarp was Bishop of the church in Smyrna and a disciple of John, it is extremely probable that he was familiar with the writings of Peter, Paul, and John, all of whom had been connected, more or less closely, with the churches of Asia Minor. And the mind of the writer of this epistle evidently moved in the thoughts and language of these apostles and of Christ. (3) That a very considerable part of the letter is couched in sentences borrowed from the New Testament. These sentences are not generally quoted with an express reference to sources, but they are naturally appropriated and made the vehicle of expression, as if the writer were perfectly familiar with them, and could count upon their being recognized by his readers. Especially marked is his use of the Pastoral Epistles and of the First Epistle of Peter. Charteris finds in the letter of

Polycarp "quotations" from Matthew, Acts, Romans, First and Second Corinthians, Galatians, Ephesians, Philippians, First Thessalonians, First and Second Timothy, First Peter, First John, and "echoes" from Matthew, Acts, Romans, First Corinthians, Galatians, Ephesians, Philippians, Colossians, First Thessalonians, First and Second Timothy, Hebrews, James, First and Second Peter, First John, Jude.

Three special references may be quoted as indicative of the importance which these Fathers attached to apostolic writings. "Take up the Epistle of the blessed Paul the apostle. What wrote he first unto you in the beginning of the gospel? Of a truth, he charged you in the Spirit concerning himself and Cephas and Apollos," etc. (Clement, *1 Ep.*, ch. 47). "Ye are initiated into mysteries with Paul, the sanctified, the martyred, worthy of all blessing, in whose footsteps may I be found when I obtain God! who in every part of his letter makes mention of you in Christ Jesus." "Not as Peter and Paul do I command you; those were apostles, I am a condemned man" (Ignatius, *ad Eph.*, ch. 12; *ad Rom.*, ch. 4). "For neither I, nor any other like me, is able to follow the wisdom of the blessed and glorious Paul, who, being among you, taught accurately and firmly, in the presence of the men then living, the word respecting truth, who also departing wrote you epistles,[1] into which, if ye look diligently, ye will be able to be built up into the faith given to you" (Polycarp, *ad Phil.*, ch. 3).

Early tradition (Clement Alex., Origen, Jerome) ascribes the Epistle of BAR-NABAS to the well-known companion of Paul (Acts 4 : 36, 37); and this tradition is somewhat favored by the fact that the epistle was appended to the books of the New Testament in the Codex Sinaiticus. But there are statements in the letter itself which render it extremely doubtful whether it could have been written by a Levite and an associate of the apostles. For Jewish sacrifices and fasts are denounced (chs. 3, 4), and serious mistakes are made in speaking of the great day of atonement (ch. 7), and of the red heifer as a type of Christ (ch. 8). Indeed, it is evident that the author "was neither accurately acquainted with the text of the law, nor had [he] even seen the celebration of the day of atonement" (*Donaldson*). Moreover, it is surely very improbable that the Cyprian Barnabas would have said that Christ chose for his own apostles "those who were lawless, beyond the bounds of all ordinary sin, that he might show he came not to call the righteous, but sinners" (ch. 5).

But while the author of the epistle is unknown, competent scholars are agreed in believing that it was written in the first quarter of the second century, perhaps about A. D. 120. In studying the relation of this epistle to the New Testament it will be observed (1) That the doctrines which are taught in respect to God, Christ, salvation, and morality are in substantial agreement with those of the New Testament. The author's mistakes in explaining the Old Testament "must not," says Charteris, "cause us to forget how pure is his theology, how unfaltering is his faith in the one Almighty Maker and Ruler of all, and how his constant endeavor is to show that the Son of God was incarnate, and taught, and suffered, and died,

---

[1] On this plural see Hefele *ad loc.*

and rose, and revived, that he might be Lord of both the dead and living." (2) That in doctrine this epistle represents exclusively neither Paul nor Peter nor John, but rather all of them. Hilgenfeld maintains that his teaching is Pauline, though tending to Gnosticism. Dorner says that " with the fundamental thoughts of Peter he combats Judaism within Christianity." And Charteris remarks, " Not only does Barnabas regard Christ's incarnation in the same way as John does, but the facts of Christ's life as recorded by John seem to be the indispensable basis of his theology." All are doubtless correct; and this fact is best accounted for by supposing that Barnabas was familiar with the writings of all these apostles. (3) That this epistle first quotes a passage from the New Testament with the biblical formula, " It is written " (ch. 4; cf. Matt. 22 : 14). There is also no sufficient reason for doubting that it uses the words of Matt. 9 : 13 in ch. 5: [" In order that he might show that] he came not to call the righteous, but sinners." Several pretty distinct reminiscences of the language of the Fourth Gospel may also be traced.

Of the writer of this epistle Donaldson says : " However weak and misdirected his intellectual powers may be, and however light his head may occasionally seem, his heart always beats right. There is not one expression contrary to the soundest morality, and much that stands out in magnificent contrast to the morality of his age, even of its highest philosophers."

The Age of Greek Apologists—a. d. 120–a. d. 170.

The circumstances of Christians in this period led them to write a considerable number of books, treating a great variety of topics. But of these books many, and indeed those of the greatest value, perished in the early ages. Among these were the Diatessaron of Tatian, the Expositions of Papias, the Ecclesiastical History of Hegesippus, and the works of Melito and Apollinaris, which, it is said, ranged over the wide domain of theology, interpretation, morals, apologetics, and church polity, and which must have been much richer in materials for ascertaining what books of the New Testament were deemed authoritative than most of the works that have come down from about the middle of the second century.

But nearly all these writings were in the hands of Eusebius, and it is therefore a matter of importance to know the principles which guided him in his use of them. Fortunately, Bishop Lightfoot has discovered those principles by a careful interpretation of his " prefatory statements " and a thorough verification of the meaning assigned to them. He has thus proved " that the main object of Eusebius was to give such information as might assist in forming correct views respecting the Canon of Scripture;" that he " was therefore indifferent to any quotations or references in early Christian writings which went toward establishing the canonicity of those books which had never been disputed in the church;" and " that to this class belonged the four Gospels, the Acts, and thirteen Epistles of Paul."

Hence it is claimed that " *the silence of Eusebius respecting early witnesses to the Fourth Gospel is an evidence in its favor.* Its apostolic authorship has never been questioned by any church-writer from the beginning, so far as Eusebius was aware, and therefore it was superfluous to call witnesses" (*Cont. Review*, 1875, pp. 176–183). As regards a most important part of the whole New Testament— viz. the four Gospels, the Acts, and thirteen Epistles of Paul—he contents himself with preserving any anecdotes which he may have found illustrating the circumstances under which the books in question were written. Accordingly, the statement of Bishop Lightfoot as to the bearing of the silence of Eusebius respecting early witnesses to the Fourth Gospel may be applied to his silence respecting early witnesses to the four Gospels, the Acts, and the thirteen Epistles of Paul. That silence proves the universal reception of these books. It was useless to bring forward evidence of that which no one doubted, or, as far as his reading went, had ever doubted.

But in respect to other books of the New Testament he was careful to bring the evidence, both for them and against them, which he found in early writers. Hence we are indebted to him for several important testimonies which he selected from writings since lost, but belonging to the period of the Greek Apologists— *i. e.* A. D. 120–A. D. 170.

Thus he refers to PAPIAS, Bishop of Hierapolis in Phrygia during a considerable part of the first half of the second century, for the double purpose of declaring that he made use of certain books as authoritative which were not received with full confidence by all the churches, and of borrowing from him certain anecdotes or traditions about the origin of other books that were never doubted. Papias was a friend of Polycarp, and, according to Irenæus, a hearer of the apostle John. At any rate, he loved to converse with those who had listened to one or more of the apostles. For he says: "Unlike the many, I did not take pleasure in those who have so very much to say, but in those who teach the truth. And again, on any occasion when a person came who had been a follower of the elders, I would inquire about the discourses of the elders—what was said by Andrew, or by Peter, or by Philip, or by Thomas or James, or by John or Matthew, or any other of the Lord's disciples, and what Aristion and the presbyter John, the disciples of the Lord, say. For I did not think that I could get so much profit from the contents of books as from the utterances of a living and abiding voice."

There is no good reason to suppose that Papias meant by "books," as here used, the "Oracles of the Lord," which his work was written to interpret, or indeed any apostolical writings. It is far more probable that he had in mind books, already becoming numerous, which were filled with Gnostic speculations about the meaning of Scripture. "Papias judged rightly," remarks Lightfoot, "that any doctrinal statement of Andrew or Peter or John, or any anecdote of the Saviour which could be traced distinctly to their authority, would be far more valuable to elucidate his text than the capricious interpretations which he found in current books" (*Cont. Review*, 1875, p. 290).

According to Eusebius, Papias "has made use of testimonies from the former Epistle of John, and from that of Peter likewise." From another source we learn that he maintained "the divine inspiration" of the Apocalypse, and Eusebius represents him as saying "that there would be a certain millennium after the resurrection, and that there would be a corporeal reign of Christ on this very earth ; which things he appears to have imagined, as if they were authorized by the apostolic narratives." Probably his views of the millennium were founded on what he supposed to be the meaning of Christ's language in the twenty-fourth chapter of Matthew, in connection with the well-known passage concerning "the thousand years " in Revelation, twentieth chapter. By "the former Epistle of John " Eusebius doubtless meant his First Epistle ; for he testifies in a previous chapter that "besides the Gospel of John, his First Epistle is acknowledged without dispute, both by those of the present day *and also by the ancients.* The other two Epistles, however, are disputed " (*H. E.*, iii. 24).

Eusebius also, according to his plan, quotes from Papias certain accounts respecting the origin of two of the Gospels which that writer had received from the elders Aristion and John. Thus: "So then Matthew composed the Oracles in the Hebrew language, and each one interpreted them as he was able." This declaration obviously refers to a period that was already past when Papias wrote his " Expositions," and there is no reason to suppose that the " Oracles " composed by Matthew were known to Papias in their Hebrew form. His knowledge of their existence in that form was derived from "the elders." Nor is there any good reason to believe that the word " Oracles " was not used of historical as well as of didactic writings, being, in fact, as comprehensive as the word " Gospel." Indeed, there can be little doubt that Eusebius copied this statement, because he understood it to refer to the first draft and original form of the canonical Gospel of Matthew. Hence the Aramaic " Oracles " must have been superseded by the Greek " Gospel " before the close of the first century ; and it is difficult to believe that they contained anything essentially different from what is found in that Gospel.

Again, Eusebius quotes from Papias the following account of Mark: " And John the Elder said also this: Mark, having become the interpreter of Peter, wrote down accurately everything that he remembered, without, however, recording in order what was either said or done by Christ. For neither did he hear the Lord, nor did he follow him ; but afterward, as I said, [he heard and followed] Peter, who adapted his instructions to the needs [of his hearers], but had no design of giving a connected account of the Lord's Oracles (or discourses). So then Mark made no mistake while he thus wrote down some things as he remembered them ; for he made it his care not to omit anything that he heard, or to set down any false statement therein."

According to this tradition, received by Papias from contemporaries of the apostles, the work of Mark here referred to was a careful *memoriter* record of what Peter rehearsed in his preaching from the words and deeds of Christ. And as Peter adapted his preaching to the needs of those addressed, it could not, in the nature of the case, furnish a complete or chronological narrative of Christ's life. Are we then justified in supposing that the work of Mark, referred to in this extract, was the second of our four Gospels?

(1) That Gospel is the briefest of the four. It gives no genealogy, no account of the birth of John the Baptist or of Jesus the Christ, no outline of the longer

discourses of the Lord, and no report of many of his parables. It is certainly, then, a very incomplete narrative of the Lord's words and works, and to that extent it agrees with the tradition given by Papias. (2) That Gospel, in common with the First and the Third, appears to disregard in many cases the chronological order of events, at least as compared with the Gospel of John. This statement is not inconsistent with the conclusion of Dr. Sanday, that, "so far as there is an order in the Synoptic Gospels, the normal type of that order is to be found precisely in St. Mark, whom Papias alleges to have written not in order" (*The Gospels in the Second Century*, p. 149). For it is natural to assume, with Dr. Lightfoot, that the standard of comparison for the elders of Asia Minor in the second century was the Gospel of John. (3) Eusebius evidently supposed that the Gospel of Mark, as known to himself, was referred to in the account which Papias had from "the elders," and it is pretty safe to assume that Eusebius understood the true relevancy of that account. In any case, his view deserves most respectful consideration. (4) If "the elder" really described the origin of an "Ur-Marcus," this fact must be inferred from the contents of the Synoptic Gospels, and not from any known tradition of the second century. But the proof which is alleged for the existence of such a document seems to us unsatisfactory.

It is greatly to be regretted that the work of Papias is lost, for he lived and labored during a period from which few Christian writings have been preserved. But all have not perished, and we now turn to some that have been spared.

JUSTIN MARTYR was born in Flavia Neapolis, formerly Shechem, about the close of the first century. He appears to have had some knowledge of Christians, and especially of their fortitude under persecution, even before his own conversion, which took place when he was (probably) twenty-five or thirty years old. Having been addicted to philosophical studies before conversion, he continued to wear the philosopher's cloak after that event, and was disposed to look upon the Christian religion as a sort of divine philosophy. But he exhibited great zeal and firmness in advocating the new faith, and by intercourse with Christians in different parts of the empire he became well acquainted with their creed, worship, and manner of life. It may therefore be presumed that he was familiar with the books from which they drew their knowledge of the public ministry of Christ.

But in Justin's two Apologies, and his Dialogue with the Jew Trypho, he had no occasion to make formal references to any part of the New Testament as possessing divine authority, for neither Roman emperors nor unbelieving Jews would have any particular reverence for the names of Peter, John, and Paul. The facts of Christ's life as fulfilling the predictions of the Old Testament, together with the moral character and religious worship of Christians, would be far more likely to impress the minds of Pagan rulers and hostile Jews than would any definite appeals to the writings of the apostles. Hence, if Justin Martyr's account of events and sayings in the ministry of Jesus Christ is found to agree substantially with that which is given in the Gospels (cf. *Sanday*, pp. 91–98); if his citations from the words of Christ appear to be made, though in a free way, from the same Gospels (cf. *E. Abbott*, p. 20, *sq.*); if there is just such a difference as one might expect between his use of the Gospels in his two Apologies and his use of the same in his Dialogue with Trypho (*Westcott*); if his use of the Gospels is quite as frequent as their use in later Apologies (*e. g.* that of Tertullian); and if his language suggests an acquaintance with the vocabulary as well as with the doctrine of Paul,—it is as much as any thoughtful scholar ought to expect on the assumption that Justin knew and honored the writings of the apostles as sacred. And just these things are found to be true of his two Apologies and of his Dialogue with Trypho, a Jew.

Justin in his first Apology refers three times to *the Memorabilia of the Apostles*, stating in one place that in them were "taught all things concerning our Saviour, Jesus Christ" (I. 33), in another, that they were read, together with the writings of the prophets, in the weekly meetings of Christians (I. 67), and in another, that they "were called Gospels" (I. 66). In the Dialogue with Trypho he quotes them ten times as *the Memorabilia of the Apostles* and five times as *the Memorabilia*. An interesting passage of the Dialogue contains these words: "In the Memorabilia, which I say were composed by the apostles and those who followed them, [it is written] that *sweat as drops streamed down* as he was praying and saying, *Let this cup, if it be possible, pass away from me*" (cf. Luke 22 : 44). As he was making a quotation from Luke, it seemed proper to call attention to the fact that the *Apostolic Memorabilia* were not all written by apostles, but rather by the apostles *and their followers*.

With this statement should be compared the language of Tertullian : " We lay down, in the first place, that the Evangelic Instrument has *apostles* for its authors, on whom this charge of publishing the gospel was laid by the Lord himself; if also *apostolic men*, yet not these *alone*, but *with* apostles, and *after* apostles. . . . . In fine, of the apostles, John and Matthew implant faith in us—of their followers, Luke and Mark refresh it." As the form of Justin's explanation agrees so perfectly with the general statement of Tertullian, it cannot reasonably be denied that the interpretation of his own statement by Tertullian is a just interpretation of Justin's language also. And if so, Justin knew and received the same four Gospels which Irenæus and his contemporaries, forty years later, received, and which Tertullian and his contemporaries, fifty or sixty years later, received. It is also to be considered that Justin must have been for a long time (say twenty-five years at least) a contemporary of Polycarp, and Irenæus for the first twenty or thirty years of his life a contemporary of both Justin and Polycarp, and Tertullian for as long a time a contemporary of Irenæus. Whether Irenæus ever met Justin Martyr we have no means of knowing, but they lived in the same period long enough to transmit the traditions of that period to the next; so that we cannot assume the occurrence of any great and sudden change in the written sources of Christian knowledge which left no trace of itself in their works.

It is manifestly impossible to bring within the limits of an Introduction the critical processes by which the Memorabilia of Justin are shown to be identical with our four Gospels. But the reader will find a good illustration of them in Dr. Ezra Abbot's recent work on *The Authorship of the Fourth Gospel*. He affirms that "Justin nowhere expressly quotes the 'Memoirs' for anything which is not substantially found in our Gospels; and there is nothing in his deviations

from exact correspondence with them, as regards matters of fact or the report of
the words of Christ, which may not be abundantly paralleled in the writings of
the Christian Fathers who used our four Gospels as alone authoritative." And
after a minute examination of the evidence for this statement he concludes thus:
" It is not, then, I believe, too much to say, that the strong presumption from the
universal reception of our four Gospels as sacred books in the time of Irenæus,
that Justin's ' Memoirs of Christ, composed by apostles and their companions '
were the same books, is decidedly confirmed by these evidences of his use of the
Fourth Gospel " (p. 52).

In a valuable work by Dr. Sanday, on *The Four Gospels in the Second Century,*
he examines the quotations made by Justin, and remarks: " If Justin did not use
our four Gospels in their present shape as they have come down to us, he used
them in a later shape, not in an earlier. His resemblances to them cannot be
accounted for by the supposition that he had access to the materials out of which
they were composed, because he reproduces features which by the nature of the
case cannot have been present in those originals, but of which we are still able to
trace the authorship and the exact point of their insertion. Our Gospels form a
secondary stage in the history of the text—Justin's quotations, a tertiary. In
order to reach the state in which it [the text] is found in Justin, the road lies
through our Gospels, and not outside of them."

Besides the four Gospels, there are in Justin's Apologies and Dialogue distinct
traces of the Acts, Romans, First and Second Corinthians, Galatians, Philippians,
Colossians, Second Thessalonians, First Timothy, Hebrews, James, First Peter,
First John, and the Apocalypse. The last he ascribes to " John, one of the apostles of Christ, [who] in a revelation that was made to him prophesied that those
who believe in our Christ will live a thousand years in Jerusalem " (*Dial. with
Trypho,* ch. 81).

To the period of the Greek Apologists may also be assigned the *Second Epistle
of Clement* (a homily), which makes use of Matthew and Luke, together with the
Epistles to the Ephesians and Timothy ; the *Epistle to Diognetus,* which contains
many reminiscences of the New Testament in thought and expression, and declares that by Christians " the fear of the Law is chanted, and the grace of the
prophets is recognized, and the faith of the Gospels is established, and the tradition of the apostles is guarded, and the grace of the church has free and exulting
course " (ch. 11) ; the *Shepherd of Hermas,* which, though it makes no quotations
from Scripture, has many points of connection with the Epistle of James and the
Apocalypse, some allusions to the Gospel of John and the Acts of the Apostles,
and a few echoes of language found in First Corinthians and Ephesians ; and the
Memoirs of Hegesippus, who appears to have made use of our present Gospels,
while he took certain things from " the Gospel to the Hebrews," of which very
little is known.

To the same period should probably be assigned the Muratorian Fragment on
the Canon, the Latin version of the New Testament in North Africa, and the
earliest Syriac version.

(1) The *Fragment on the Canon,* discovered by Muratori, begins now with the

last words of a sentence which probably referred to the Gospel of Mark. It then proceeds to speak of the Third Gospel as written by Luke the physician, who did not see the Lord; of the Fourth Gospel as written by John, a disciple of the Lord, at the request of his fellow-disciples and his elders, with a reference also to his Epistles, and a quotation from the First; of the Acts of the Apostles as composed by Luke; of the Epistles of. Paul—to the Corinthians the first, to the Ephesians the second, to the Philippians the third, to the Colossians the fourth, to the Galatians the fifth, to the Thessalonians the sixth, to the Romans the seventh; also to the Corinthians and Thessalonians a second each, to Philemon one, to Titus one, and to Timothy two, on account of love and affection (thirteen in all). It then speaks of two spurious Epistles that were ascribed to Paul—one to the Laodiceans and another to the Alexandrians—and adds that one Epistle of Jude and two superscribed of John are received by catholic Christians. Finally, that "we receive also only the Revelations of John and Peter, which [latter] some of us are unwilling to have read in the church." There is, moreover, a reference to "Wisdom, written by the friends' of Solomon in his honor," which Westcott thinks may imply a lost clause mentioning the Epistle to the Hebrews as written by a friend of Paul. The same scholar discovers indications of two breaks in the Fragment where the Epistles of James, First and Second Peter, and Hebrews may have been named in the original Greek list. This is of course conjecture, but there are several peculiarities of the list as it now stands which seem to render it in a certain measure probable. At any rate, this list appears to embrace the four Gospels, the Acts, thirteen Epistles of Paul, two of John, one of Jude, and the Revelation of John. And if the two Epistles of John referred to near the end of the list are the Second and the Third, Bishop Lightfoot's conjecture that the First Epistle of John was then connected with his Gospel is extremely natural (see *Cont. Review*, 1875, p. 835), especially as the opening verse of that Epistle is quoted by the Fragment in giving an account of the origin of the Gospel. Moreover, in view of the other testimonies of this period, it is difficult to believe that the First Epistle of Peter could have been omitted from the list; and it is surely more likely that there was a reference, by way of comparison, to a book of "Wisdom, written by the friends of Solomon in his honor," than to suppose that a book with that title was reckoned among the Christian Scriptures.

(2) The *earliest Latin version* of the New Testament was prepared before A. D. 170, and, according to Mr. Westcott, "it contained the four Gospels, the Acts, thirteen Epistles of St. Paul, the three Catholic Epistles of St. John, the First Epistle of St. Peter, the Epistle of St. Jude, and the Apocalypse. To these the Epistle to the Hebrews was added subsequently, but before the time of Tertullian, and without the author's name. There is no external evidence to show that the Epistle of St. James or the Second Epistle of St. Peter was included in the Vetus Latina" (*On the Canon of the N. T.*, p. 225).

(3) The *early Syriac version*, called the Peshito, is commonly supposed to have been made in the first half of the second century, and may safely be assumed to have been in use before A. D. 170. It has all the books of the New Testament

but the Second and Third Epistles of John, the Second Epistle of Peter, the Epistle of Jude, and the Apocalypse.

Turning now to heretical leaders and writings, they will be found to furnish evidence that many books of the New Testament were received as authoritative documents in respect to the Christian religion during the age of the Greek Apologists. BASILIDES is admitted to have been a teacher in Alexandria in the reign of Hadrian (A. D. 117–137). He was therefore a younger contemporary of Polycarp and of Justin Martyr. The doctrines taught by him and by his followers are described by Hippolytus and Epiphanius, while the works of Clement of Alexandria and of Origen have occasional references to them. He appears to have accepted the historical facts recorded in our Gospels; and Westcott remarks that "in the few pages of his writings which remain there are certain references to the Gospels of St. Matthew, St. Luke, and St. John, and to the Epistles of Paul to the Romans, Corinthians, Ephesians, and Colossians, possibly also to the First Epistle to Timothy," and, still further, to the First Epistle of Peter. But he is believed to have rejected the Pastoral Epistles (unless First Timothy be an exception) and the Epistle to the Hebrews. It is noticeable also that he introduces language from the New Testament Scriptures as that "which is said" or "written," or by the phrase "the Scripture saith," using the same formulas of quotation which were commonly employed in appeals to the language of the Old Testament.

VALENTINUS, a younger contemporary of Basilides, began his career as an heretical teacher in Alexandria, but soon repaired to Rome, and made that city the centre of his activity. Irenæus says (*C. Hær.*, iii. 4, 3) that "he came to Rome during the episcopate of Hyginus (perhaps about A. D. 140), was in his prime under Pius (142–150), and lived until the time of Anicetus." Tertullian says that "he seems to use 'the whole Instrument,' yet perverting the meaning by his method of interpretation." In this way he was thought to be a more crafty assailant of Christian truth than was Marcion, who boldly mutilated the Scriptures. By "the whole Instrument" Tertullian means, of course, the books of the New Testament that were recognized as sacred in North Africa at the close of the second century—*i. e.* all the books of our New Testament save the Epistles of James and Second Peter. In the brief extracts that have come down to us from the writings of Valentinus (or of his school) there are citations from the Epistle to the Romans, the First Epistle to the Corinthians, the Epistle to the Ephesians, and references to the Gospels of Matthew, Luke, and John; also, perhaps, to the First of John and the Epistle to the Hebrews.

MARCION flourished at the same time as Valentinus. In his first Apology (A. D. 140–147) Justin declares that Marcion "had in every nation of men caused many to blaspheme" (I. 26), and also that "many had been convinced by him" (I. 58). Probably, then, he settled in Rome and began to teach his peculiar views about 138–142 A. D. He did not receive all the books of the New Testament as canonical, but constructed a Canon for himself from the Gospel of Luke and ten Epistles of Paul. This, at least, is the statement of Tertullian, Epiphanius, and Irenæus. And it appears that one of the two following hypotheses is true: Either Marcion's Gospel was formed by mutilating our Third Gospel, or our Third Gospel was formed by interpolating that of Marcion. After comparing the two, Dr. Sanday says: "The Gospel [of Marcion] stands to our Synoptic entirely in the relation of *defect*. We may say 'entirely,' for the additions are so insignificant— some thirty words in all, and those for the most part supported by other authority —that for practical purposes they need not be reckoned. With the exception of these thirty words inserted, and some, also slight, alterations of phrase, Marcion's Gospel presents simply an *abridgment* of our St. Luke." Again: "In Germany it seems to be agreed at the present time that the hypothesis of a mutilated Luke suits the dogmatic argument better than that of later Judaizing interpolations." Once more, after a careful analysis of the language of Luke's Gospel, Dr. Sanday remarks: "The total result may be summarized thus: Accepting the scheme of Marcion's Gospel given some pages back, which is substantially that of 'Supernatural Religion,' Marcion will have omitted a total of three hundred and nine verses. In those verses there are found one hundred and eleven distinct peculiarities of St. Luke's style, numbering in all one hundred and eighty-five separate instances; there are also found one hundred and thirty-eight words peculiar to or specially characteristic of the third evangelist, with two hundred and twenty-four instances. In other words, the verified peculiarities of St. Luke's style and diction (and how marked many of these are will have been seen from the examples above) are found in the portions of the Gospel omitted by Marcion in a proportion averaging considerably more than one to each verse." It is therefore evident that the three hundred and nine verses were written by Luke, and were stricken from his Gospel by Marcion; for an interpolator could not have imitated the style and vocabulary of Luke so perfectly as it is represented in these verses.

But was Luke's Gospel a new production when it was adopted by Marcion about A. D. 140? Or does the text which he uses prove upon examination to be one that had been corrupted more or less by transcription? In answer to this question Dr. Sanday, in a work distinguished for caution and moderation of statement, affirms that the textual phenomena "show that Marcion's Gospel, so far from being an original document, has behind it a deep historical background, and stands at the head of a series of copies which have already passed through a number of hands, and been exposed to a proportionate amount of corruption." Again: "I think it is a safe proposition to assert that, in order to bring the text of Marcion's Gospel into the state in which we find it, there must have been a long previous history, and the manuscripts through which it was conveyed must have parted far from the parent stem."

It may be added that Marcion appears to have treated the ten Epistles of Paul which he accepted in the same way as he treated the Gospel of Luke; that is, as far as he accepted the Epistles at all, he accepted the text as he found it, without making any changes; but from the Epistles, as from the Gospel, he omitted such verses or paragraphs as did not agree with his doctrinal opinions. (See the conclusive argument by Sanday, pp. 204–237.)

To this period also must probably be assigned the so-called "HOMILIES OF CLEMENT," a theological fiction of Judaizing tendency, though scholars are not yet agreed as to the time when it was written. Those who have given the subject most attention are, however, united in the belief that it was before A. D. 180, and the best authorities assign it to the third quarter of the second century. According to Charteris, Sanday, and others, the *Homilies* make use of every one of the four Gospels. Sanday indeed, as in the case of Justin Martyr, admits a possible alternative, saying, " Either the Clementine writer quotes our present Gospels, or else he quotes some other composition later than them, and which implies them. In other words, if he does not bear witness to our Gospels at first hand, he does at second hand, and by the interposition of a further intermediate stage." And if this second hypothesis be correct, he represents the " composition " supposed as in all likelihood a harmony of the four Gospels, and suggests that it may have been " begun, and used, and left in a more or less advanced stage, by Justin," but made public afterward by Tatian.

The evidence which has been briefly noticed does not embrace every allusion to our New-Testament Scriptures which may be found in the fragments of Christian or heretical literature that have come down to us from the age of the Greek Apologists. But it embraces the most important testimonies and allusions, and may therefore be allowed to stand for the whole in a rapid survey like the present. And if the reader will simply bear in mind these circumstances—that all the books of the New Testament were not yet probably united in a single volume ; that only brief extracts have come down to us from most of the great Christian writers of this period ; that Apologists, addressing their pagan rulers, would gain nothing by definite appeals to the writings of Matthew, John, Peter, or Paul ; that it was too early for the existence of many translations, especially of the whole New Testament ; and that heretics would be very likely to have their favorite books, rejecting or neglecting others,—he will perhaps be gratified at the amount and character of the evidence now within our reach, rather than surprised at any defects in the same which critics may be able to discover.

Having examined very closely a considerable part of the evidence—namely, that which has a natural connection with the school of John in Asia Minor— Bishop Lightfoot speaks as follows : " Out of a very extensive literature, by which this school was once represented, the extant remains are miserably few and fragmentary ; but the evidence yielded by these meagre relics is decidedly greater, in proportion to their extent, than we had any right to expect. As regards the Fourth Gospel, this is especially the case. If the same amount of written matter —occupying a very few pages in all—were extracted accidentally from the current theological literature of our own day, the chances, unless I am mistaken, would be strongly against our finding so many indications of the use of this Gospel."

FROM A. D. 170–A. D. 400.

About the year 170 A. D. the long period of historical twilight as to Christian affairs begins to give place to the dawning of a tolerably clear day. A Christian literature, composed in great measure of fragments preserved in later writings, begins to be followed by a literature embracing several treatises that have come down to us, either complete or only slightly mutilated. After the shorter works of Tatian (so far as preserved), Athenagoras, and Theophilus of Antioch we pass to the more extended productions of Irenæus, Clement of Alexandria, Tertullian, and Origen, finding conclusive evidence that many books of the New Testament were received by all the churches in Europe, Asia, and Africa as indisputably apostolic. These were the four Gospels, the Acts of the Apostles, thirteen Epistles of Paul, and the First Epistles of Peter and John. No competent scholar will deny that from this time onward these writings were esteemed sacred and authoritative by the whole Christian world, just as truly as they were so esteemed at the beginning of the present century. They were nowhere questioned, but everywhere accepted as parts of the Canon. Of the remaining books, some were received here, and others there, with absolute confidence, while none of them were received without doubt everywhere and by all. From this time forward our attention will therefore be directed more and more to the doubtful books. Yet it will be instructive to notice the manner in which the undisputed books, and especially the four Gospels, as well as the disputed books, are characterized by the leading writers.

In the following passage IRENÆUS sets forth his estimate of apostolic teaching— an estimate which was shared, without doubt, by the great body of Christians in his day: "For we have learned to know the economy of our salvation through no others but those by whom the gospel came to us; which gospel they then preached, but afterward by the will of God delivered to us in Scriptures, that it might be a ground and pillar of our faith. For it is not right to say that they preached before they had a perfect knowledge, as some dare to affirm, boasting that they are correctors of the apostles. For after our Lord rose again from the dead they indeed were clothed with power from on high, through the Holy Spirit coming upon them—were filled with the Spirit for all duties and had perfect knowledge; they went forth to the end of the earth, preaching good news of blessings to us from God, and announcing celestial peace to men, because they all and each had the gospel of God" (*C. Hær.*, iii. 1).

Of the authorship of the four Gospels he thus speaks: "Matthew indeed among the Hebrews in their own language published a written Gospel, while Peter and Paul in Rome were preaching the gospel and founding the church. And after their departure Mark himself, the disciple and interpreter of Peter, delivered to us in writing that which was preached by Peter. Moreover, Luke, the follower of Paul, put down in a book the Gospel that was preached by him. Afterward, John, the disciple of the Lord, who also leaned back on his bosom, himself published the Gospel while he was residing at Ephesus in Asia" (*ibid.*).

Of the general recognition of these Gospels even by heretics he bears witness in another place: "And so great is this firmness [of evidence] about the Gospels that even the heretics themselves bear testimony to them, and each one of them, by starting from the same, is compelled to confirm their teaching. For the Ebionites, using only the Gospel according to Matthew, are proved by that to make false suppositions concerning the Lord. But Marcion, though mutilating the Gospel according to Luke, is shown by those portions which are still preserved by him to be a blasphemer against the only existing God. Moreover, those who separate Jesus from the Christ, and say that Christ remained impassible, but Jesus only suffered, and who prefer the Gospel according to Mark, can be corrected if they read this [Gospel] with a love of truth. Also those who follow Valentinus and use most fully the Gospel according to John for the purpose of setting forth their conjunctions, are detected by this Gospel as teaching nothing rightly, as we have shown in our first book. Since, therefore, our opponents bear witness for us and use these Gospels, our proof from them is firm and true" (iii. 11, 7).

To prove that there could properly be neither more nor fewer than four Gospels, he writes thus in the next section: "Since there are four zones of the world in which we are, and four general winds, and [since] the church is scattered over all the earth, but the Gospel and Spirit of life are a pillar and ground of the church, it [the church] should properly have four pillars, breathing immortality from every side, and vivifying men afresh. From which it is evident that the Word, the Architect of all things, who sitteth upon the cherubim and holdeth together all things, having been manifested to men, gave us a gospel in four forms, but bound together by one Spirit" (iii. 11, 8).

It may also be remarked that Irenæus makes abundant use of passages from the Acts, from the Epistles to the Romans, First and Second Corinthians, Galatians, Ephesians, Philippians, Colossians, First and Second Thessalonians, First Peter, First John, and from the Apocalypse; also occasional use of extracts from First and Second Timothy, Titus, Hebrews, James, and Second John, together with the expression, *a day with the Lord is as a thousand years,* which appears to be taken from 2 Pet. 3 : 8. The only books of our New Testament which are not employed by him at all are the brief Epistle to Philemon, the briefer Third Epistle of John, and the Epistle of Jude—all of them amounting to scarcely more than an average chapter in the Gospel of Luke, and no one of them holding a prominent place among the apostolical writings or likely to be needed in refuting the strange heresies of the second century.

Such is the evidence of Irenæus to the Canon of the New Testament. And the fact must not be lost sight of that he was personally acquainted with Polycarp and his associates, the disciples of the apostle John in Asia Minor; that he was a contemporary of Justin Martyr, Tatian, Athenagoras, Theophilus of Antioch, on the one hand, and with Basilides, Marcion, Valentinus, and Celsus, on the other; that he was in most respects, if not all, a man of sober judgment, familiar with the doctrinal views of both the Asiatic and the Western churches, and that he made the heresies of the second century a subject of special investigation, comparing them with the apostolic writings, and refuting them by testimonies drawn from these writings, which were deemed authoritative by Christians throughout the known world.

CLEMENT OF ALEXANDRIA flourished about A. D. 200, and was probably a more learned man than Irenæus. He thus speaks of a treatise which he was composing (called *Stromateis,* or "Miscellanies") and of the sources of his knowledge: "Now this work is not a writing artistically composed for display, but memoranda are stored up [in it] for myself against old age as a remedy of forgetfulness, an inartistic image and rough sketch of those clear and vivid discourses which I was thought worthy to hear, and of blessed and truly remarkable men.

Of these, one, the Ionian, was in Greece, and others in Magna Græcia.   One of them was of Cœle-Syria, another from Egypt, and others in [or through] the East. Of this region that of Assyria was one, and another in Palestine, a Hebrew by descent.   When I met with the last (he was first in ability), having hunted him up concealed in Egypt, I found rest.   He, a true Sicilian bee, plucking the flowers of both the prophetic and the apostolic meadow, begat in the souls of his hearers a pure substance of knowledge.   But they, preserving the veritable tradition of the blessed doctrine directly from Peter and James, John and Paul, the holy apostles, son receiving it from father (but few are they who are like their fathers), came indeed by the will of God to deposit in us also those ancestral and apostolic seeds; and well I know that they will rejoice, not, I mean, as being pleased with this description, but with the mere preservation of truth as it was noted down " (*Miscell.*, i. 1, 11).   It is generally admitted that the person whom Clement here calls his last and ablest teacher was Pantænus, head of the catechetical school in Alexandria.   Photius represents Pantænus as a hearer of the apostles, and, as far as age is concerned, he might possibly have been so.   At any rate, he appears to have been a diligent student of the prophetic and apostolic Scriptures, and, as Westcott has said, "there is not the slightest ground for assuming any organic change in the doctrine of the Alexandrian Church between the age of the apostles and Pantænus," the teacher and predecessor of Clement.   The latter was at the head of the Christian school in Alexandria from about A. D. 189 to A. D. 202, when he was compelled to leave the city by the persecution under Severus.

Clement makes use of the four Gospels, the Acts of the Apostles, the Epistles to the Romans, the Corinthians (First and Second), the Galatians, the Ephesians, the Colossians, the Philippians, the Thessalonians (First and Second), Timothy (First and Second), Titus, Philemon, Hebrews, the First Epistle of Peter, the First of John, the Epistle of Jude, and the book of Revelation; but he appears to have no quotations from the Epistles of James, Second Peter, and Third John. Eusebius testifies that "in the work called *Hypotoposes*, Clement has given us concise explanations of the whole canonical Scripture, without omitting the disputed books: I mean the Epistle of Jude and the remaining Catholic Epistles, as well as the Epistle of Barnabas and the so-called Revelation of Peter.   Moreover, he says that the Epistle to the Hebrews is Paul's, but that it was written to the Hebrews in the Hebrew language, and that Luke, having carefully translated it, published it for the use of the Greeks."   It will be observed that although Eusebius associates the Catholic Epistles with the Epistle of Barnabas and the so-called Revelation of Peter, he yet distinguishes the former from the latter, making thereby in some sense two classes of "disputed books."   Very noteworthy is the language of Clement in respect to the Epistle to the Hebrews, though there are strong objections to his view that our Greek Epistle is a translation.

To the testimony of Clement may be subjoined that of ORIGEN, his successor after a time in the Alexandrian school, and the most learned biblical critic of the Ante-Nicene Church.   If perfect reliance could be placed on the translation of Rufinus, the following passage from his Homilies on Joshua (vii. 2) would be conclusive as to his view of the New Testament Canon: "So too our Lord Jesus

Christ, whose advent was typified by that earlier son of Nun, when he came sent his apostles as priests bearing well-wrought trumpets, the glorious and heavenly doctrine which they preached.   Matthew first sounded with priestly trumpet in his Gospel.   Mark also, Luke and John, each gave forth a strain on their priestly trumpets.   Peter moreover sounds with the two trumpets of his Epistles; so also James and Jude.   None the less does John blow the trumpet by his Epistles and Apocalypse, and Luke, by describing the Acts of the Apostles.   Lastly came he who said, *I think that God hath set forth us apostles last of all,* and thundering with the fourteen trumpets of his Epistles threw down to the ground the walls of Jericho, even all the instruments of idolatry and the doctrines of philosophy."   But it is known that Rufinus sometimes modified the teaching of Origen according to his own belief of what was true, and therefore it is possible that he has done so in this place.   Yet there is ample evidence to be found in the untranslated writings of Origen that he received all the books that were received by Clement.   He accepted our four Gospels as canonical, and rejected the authority of all others. Of the Epistle to the Hebrews he says: " If I were to express my own opinion, I should say that the thoughts are the apostle's, but the diction and composition that of some one who recorded from memory the apostle's teaching, and, as it were, illustrated with a brief commentary the sayings of his master.   It was not without good reason that the men of old time have handed it down as Paul's.   But who it was that wrote the Epistle, God only knows certainly."   He accepted the Apocalypse as an undoubted work of the apostle John (*Westcott*).   He quoted the Epistle of Jude as a work of " the Lord's brother."   He referred to " the Epistle in circulation under the name of James."   But he does not, it is said, quote the Second Epistle of Peter or the Second and Third Epistles of John, though the Second Epistle of Peter is quoted several times in the Latin version of the Homilies.

TERTULLIAN, the earliest great representative of the North African Church, was probably born in Carthage about A. D. 160, and was therefore a contemporary of Irenæus, Clement of Alexandria, and Origen.   His literary activity may be chiefly assigned to the first quarter of the third century.   He speaks of the " ancient Scripture " in contrast with the " New Testament " (*Ad Prax.*, ch. 15).   He distinguishes between " the Gospels and the apostles " (*ibid.*), meaning by the latter the writings of the apostles.   And he declares that " the gospel Instrument has for its authors apostles on whom this office of proclaiming the gospel was imposed by the Lord himself; and if also apostolic men, yet not these alone, but with apostles and after apostles " (*Adv.*, iv. 2).   Referring to the church at Rome, which he pronounces " happy, because there apostles poured forth their doctrine with their blood," he declares that " she unites in one volume the law and the prophets with the writings of evangelists and apostles, and thence drinks in her faith " (*De Præsc. Hæret.*, ch. 36).   He says that the germs of later heresies were present in the first age, and remarks that " Paul in the First to the Corinthians marks those who denied and doubted the resurrection. . . . . Writing to the Galatians, he assails those who practise and defend circumcision and the law. . . . . Instructing Timothy, he also condemns such as ' forbid to marry ' (1 Tim. 4 : 3).

. . . . Equally does he smite such as said that ‘the resurrection was already past’ (2 Tim. 2 : 3). . . . . When he mentions ‘endless genealogies’ (1 Tim. 1 : 4) Valentinus is recognized,” etc. . . . . Again, “John in the Apocalypse is commanded to chastise those ‘who eat things offered to idols and commit fornication’ (Rev. 2 : 20). But in the Epistle he calls those antichrists in a special sense who deny that Christ has come in the flesh, and who do not think that Jesus is the Son of God” (*De Præscrip. Hæret.*, ch. 33).

Tertullian recognizes in his writings the four Gospels, the Acts of the Apostles, thirteen Epistles of Paul, First Peter, First John, Jude, the Apocalypse, and (though as written by Barnabas and of second-rate authority) the Epistle to the Hebrews—*i. e.* all the books of our New Testament except the Epistles of James, Second Peter, and Second and Third John (*Charteris*).

It is important to bear in mind the localities with which these great writers must have been familiar. Irenæus, connected with Polycarp, with Pothinus, and with some of the bishops of Rome, may be said to reflect the belief of Asia Minor, Gaul, and Italy; Clement of Alexandria, the pupil of Pantænus, and Origen, the distinguished scholar who was at home both in Egypt and in Palestine, may be said to reflect the belief of Christians in Egypt, Palestine, and Greece; and Tertullian, the fiery and powerful teacher at Carthage, must be presumed to reflect the belief of the churches of North Africa, with which he was well acquainted, and of the churches in and about Rome, where many of the heretics, whom he assailed with resistless torrents of argument and denunciation, resided. Thus these writers represent, if they do not doubly or trebly represent, the several great provinces where Christians had become numerous and powerful.

Noticeable also is the high authority which these writers attribute to the Old and New Testaments. Irenæus affirms that “the Scriptures are indeed perfect, because they were spoken by the Word of God and his Spirit” (*C. Hær.*, ii. 28, 2). Clement proposes to show that “the Scriptures which we have believed were ratified by Omnipotent Authority,” and “to show from them to all the heresies that there is one God and Lord Omnipotent, who has been truly preached by the law and the prophets, and in addition to these by the blessed gospel” (*Miscell.*, iv. 1). Tertullian, by a variety of testimonies, as well as by the use which he makes of the New Testament, proves that for him its teaching is ultimate and divine. With no less reverence does Origen treat the Scriptures of the New Testament.

A few remarks may now be made in respect to the seven disputed books of the New Testament—viz. the Epistle to the Hebrews, the book of Revelation, and the Epistles of James, Jude, Second and Third John, and Second Peter.

(1) The Epistle to the Hebrews was generally received in Alexandria and the East, while it was doubted or rejected for a long time in North Africa and the West. It is found in the Peshito, but not in the Fragment of Muratori on the Canon, or in the earliest form of the Latin version. Origen ascribes it habitually to Paul, though he appears to have believed that the thoughts only were the apostle’s, while the composition was by some other person. Tertullian ascribes it to Barnabas, the companion of Paul, and claims for it no more than secondary

authority. Yet Clement of Rome was certainly familiar with it, and treated it with special respect; it is also probably referred to by Justin Martyr. Dionysius, a distinguished pupil of Origen, became president of the school at Alexandria about A. D. 231, and afterward bishop of the Christians in that city. Fragments of his letters have been preserved in which are numerous references to the New Testament, and quotations from the Epistle to the Hebrews as the "testimony of Paul." The voice of the churches of Egypt and of the East prevailed, and at last this Epistle was accepted as canonical by the churches of the West also. Its earlier and unhesitating reception in the East was probably due to the circumstance that the Hebrew Christians to whom it was first sent resided in Egypt and the East.

(2) The Apocalypse, it will be recollected, is expressly attributed by Justin Martyr to the apostle John: "A certain man among us, whose name was John, one of the apostles of Christ, predicted in a revelation given to him that those who had believed in our Christ should spend a thousand years in Jerusalem, and that afterward the universal and, to speak briefly, the eternal resurrection and judgment of all would take place together" (*Dial. c. Try.*, ch. 81). There is also satisfactory evidence that Papias was familiar with the Apocalypse, and was peculiarly interested in its Chiliastic teaching. (See *Andreas Cæs. in Apoc.*, ch. 34, Serm. 12, Edit. Morel.; *Opp. S. Chrys.*, p. 52; and Euseb., *H. E.*, iii. 39.) Among the writings of Melito, Bishop of the church in Sardis, which were known to Eusebius, was one on the Revelation of John (*H. E.*, iv. 26). Irenæus, who spent his early life in Asia Minor, ascribes the Apocalypse to John the disciple of the Lord, and a careful consideration of his language shows that by "disciple" he meant the apostle John, who was called, by way of preference, "the disciple," because he was "the disciple whom Jesus loved" (*B.*, iv. 20, 11; v. 26, 1; 30, 3; 8). This testimony is very important. Tertullian cites the Apocalypse repeatedly as a work of the apostle John (*e. g. Adv. Mar.*, iii. 14; iv. 5; *De Præs. Hæret.*, ch. 33). Clement of Alexandria and Origen both make use of it as authoritative and written by John (*Strom.*, vi. 13; *Paid.*, ii. 12; *Com. in Matt.*, t. 16, tom. iii. p. 711; *Com. in Joan.*, t. 1, also t. 2). Hippolytus does the same (*De Christo et Antichr.*, ch. 36). It is included in the Fragment of Muratori on the Canon. But for some reason it was not made a part of the Peshito; and Dionysius of Alexandria, while agreeing that it was the work of some "holy and inspired man" by the name of John, doubts whether it was written by the evangelist. It is, however, noteworthy that his reasons for doubting are not historical, but critical, or, in other words, derived from the style of the book as compared with John's Gospel and First Epistle (Euseb., *H. E.*, vii. 25). In like manner Eusebius appears to have hesitated about ascribing it to the apostle John. But it is at least possible that they were predisposed to reject the book by their strong opposition to the Chiliasm of their day. At any rate, their doubts made but a slight impression on the minds of Christians, and before the close of the fourth century the Apocalypse was everywhere received as apostolic and divine. And surely there was no lack of external evidence for the apostolic authorship of this remarkable book.

(3) The Epistle of James, like that to the Hebrews, was addressed to believing Israelites who did not reside in Palestine; and this circumstance accounts for the non-universal reception of the Epistle in the early church. "It was meant only for Jewish believers, and was not likely, therefore, to circulate widely among Gentile Christians" (Smith's *Dict. of the Bible*, p. 1208). Hence, too, it was included in the Peshito, but not in the Muratorian Canon or in most of the MSS. of the early Latin version. As might have been expected, it was received as canonical in Alexandria. Thus Origen says: "For if there may be something called faith, but existing without works, such a faith is dead, as we have read in the current Epistle of James" (*Com. in Joan.*, F. 19). Again: "As also James the apostle says, Every good gift and every perfect gift is from above, coming down from the Father of lights" (*Com. in Ep. ad Rom.*, ix.). "Eusebius tells as a matter of fact that some counted it spurious, and that there was a lack of early testimony to it; but he himself quotes it as apostolic" (*Charteris*). Athanasius, a younger contemporary of Eusebius, accepted it as inspired and canonical (*Ath. Opp.*, tom. p. 38). The objections to the letter derived from its contents are of no force, and there appears to be no good reason to doubt that the churches and their teachers were guided by sufficient evidence in assigning to this Epistle a place in the Canon of Scripture.

(4) The Epistle of Jude purports to have been written by "the brother of James," who must therefore have been well known to Christians. This James is generally believed to have been "the Lord's brother," spoken of in Gal. 1 : 19, the writer of the Epistle noticed above, and for many years the Bishop of the church at Jerusalem. The Muratorian Canon numbers the Epistle of Jude with the sacred books of the New Testament. It was also in the Old Latin version, though not in the Syriac. Clement of Alexandria appeals to it in both the *Paidagogos* and the *Stromateis* (*Paid.*, iii. 44; *Str.*, iii. 11); moreover, the Latin *Adumbrationes* found in the editions of Clement contain notes written by him on this Epistle, as well as on the First Epistle of Peter and the first two Epistles of John (*Westcott*, pp. 310, 311). Origen agrees with Clement in the use of Jude as a part of the New Testament (*Com. in Matt.*, t. 10, ch. 17, and others). Tertullian speaks of the apostle Jude as bearing testimony to Enoch or the book of Enoch (*De Cultu femin*, i. 3). Eusebius, while placing it with the disputed books, says that the Catholic Epistles, including Jude, are publicly used with the rest in most of the churches (*H. E.*, ii. eh. 23). It is considered authoritative and canonical by Athanasius, by the Laodicean Council (about A. D. 364—*Charteris*), and by Cyril of Jerusalem (*Cateches.*, iv. p. 36, *sq.*).

(5 and 6) It is difficult to see why the Second and Third Epistles of John should have been called "catholic" or "general," for they are manifestly brief letters to individuals, of no more interest to the churches than was the letter to Philemon, and of much less general significance than the Epistles to Timothy and Titus. Charteris says that they "were at an early date supposed to be general, the 'elect lady' and 'Gaius' being supposed to denote the Christian church." But the fact that they are brief personal letters accounts for their being so little known to the great body of the early Christians. The writer designates himself

"*the elder*"—a title which may have been naturally applied with special reverence to the apostle John during the last years of his life in Asia Minor, and which therefore would have been sufficiently explicit and at the same time modest on his lips. Irenæus speaks of "John's *First* Epistle" (Euseb., *H. E.*, v. 8), showing thereby that he knew of more than one, and also quotes a passage from his *Second* Epistle (v. 11), declaring that it was a "saying of John the disciple of the Lord" (*B.*, i. 16, 3). Clement of Alexandria cites the words of 1 John 5 : 16 as being in his "greater Epistle," thus intimating that he knew of a smaller one (*Strom.*, ii. ch. 15, 66). Origen says of John, who reclined on the bosom of Jesus, that "he has also left an Epistle consisting of very few lines; perhaps, too, a second and a third, since not all say that these are genuine, but both together do not contain a hundred lines" (Euseb., *H. E.*, vi. 25). Dionysius of Alexandria mentions that "a Second and a Third Epistle ascribed to John were in circulation," and in such a way as to imply his acceptance of them as works of the apostle (Euseb., *H. E.*, vii. 25). These minor Epistles appear to be recognized (one of them certainly, and probably both) in the Fragment of Muratori, and both of them were also in the earliest Latin version.

(7) The historical evidence for the genuineness of the Second Epistle of Peter is less conclusive than that for any other book of the New Testament. If genuine, its circulation must have been restricted for a comparatively long time to a small number of churches. The earliest passage manifestly based upon it appears to be in the so-called Second Epistle of the Roman Clement (ch. 16, 3), which, however, is now understood to be a Christian homily from the middle of the second century. Yet there seem to be pretty clear reminiscences of the Epistle in Justin Martyr, in the Shepherd of Hermas, and perhaps in some of the Ignatian epistles, which were written as early, at least, as A. D. 150. The same may be said of Melito of Sardis (*Charteris*, p. 314), of Theophilus of Antioch (*Ad Autol.*, ii. 9, 13), and of Irenæus (iv. 36, 4; v. 23, 2; and v. 28, 3). Clement of Alexandria is said to have written short expositions of all the Scriptures, not passing by those that are disputed—viz. Jude and the other Catholic Epistles (Euseb., *H. E.*, vi. 14). And it is surely improbable that Clement would have written even short expositions of a book which he did not esteem, in some proper sense of the words, holy Scripture. Origen appears to have looked upon the Epistle as a genuine work of Peter, though he says that it was questioned in his day (Euseb., *H. E.*, vi. 25). Eusebius, speaking as an historian, classes it with the disputed books (*H. E.*, iii. 3, 25), but Athanasius (*De S. Trin.*, Dial. i.; *Contra Arianos*, Orat. i.), Cyril of Jerusalem (*Cateches.*, iv. p. 36, *sq.*), Gregory of Nazianzus (*Carm.*, 33, v. 31), Epiphanius (*Hær.*, ii. t. 2, h. 66; iii. t. 1, h. 76), and Jerome (*De Vir. Ill.*, ch. i.; also *Ep. ad Hedib. Quæst.*, xi.), receive it as a work of the inspired apostle.

Thus slowly, and not without careful inquiry, did the several disputed books of the New Testament take their place in the Canon with other books acknowledged by all the churches from the first age. It was ascertained to the satisfaction of intelligent men, by evidence that must have been derived from the churches where these books were first known, that they were written by apostles or associates of apostles, and were therefore authentic statements of the original facts and doctrines of the Christian religion.

Meanwhile, other books, with which many Christians were particularly pleased, were associated more or less with these, and were occasionally read in certain public meetings of some of the churches. The First Epistle of Clement to the Corinthians, the so-called Epistle of Barnabas, and the Shepherd of Hermas, are perhaps the most important of these. But they seem never to have been considered of equal authority with apostolic and inspired Scripture, and they were all in due time assigned without hesitation to their true place outside the Canon.

II.

ORDER OF BOOKS IN THE CANON.

THIS has not always been the same. By the present arrangement the Historical part holds the first place, the Doctrinal part the second, and the Prophetical part the third. And to this general order there seems to be no good objection. The life and work of Jesus Christ are the logical foundation and starting-point of Christianity; hence the evangelical narratives ought to precede everything else in the Christian Canon. But the early work of the apostles—until the gospel had gained a secure foothold among both Jews and Greeks—was inseparably connected with the preaching of Jesus and with the beginnings of the Christian religion; accordingly, by common consent, the story of the Acts of the Apostles is made to follow the Gospels. With equal propriety do the Epistles, which set forth the doctrines of Christianity for the edification of believers, instructing, admonishing, and encouraging the disciples of the Lord Jesus in their conflict with evil, follow the historical books, though it is not quite so obvious what is gained by disregarding chronology in the arrangement of Paul's Epistles or by placing the Catholic Epistles after those of Paul. And as to the Apocalypse, it takes the position of a final book, partly because of its relation to the future, and partly because of the time when it was supposed to have been written—that is, near the close of the first century, and after nearly or quite all the other books of the New Testament had been given to the churches.

This is the natural order, yet in some of the manuscripts, as well as in the Complutensian edition of the New Testament (1514), the Epistles of Paul precede the Acts. In one manuscript the order is said to be this: the Acts, the Pauline Epistles, the Catholic Epistles, the Gospels. In another the Apocalypse is placed between the Acts and the Catholic Epistles. Besides these, a few instances are mentioned by Scrivener (*Introd. to the Crit. of the N. T.*, p. 67) in which the three great divisions of the New Testament do not stand in their natural order. But these instances are strictly exceptional. The general order is the following: the Gospels, the Acts, the Catholic Epistles, the Pauline Epistles, the Apocalypse.

But when we turn our attention from this general order to the arrangement of books under the first and second divisions, a certain variety appears. The four

Gospels do not always succeed one another in the order to which we are accustomed—viz. Matthew, Mark, Luke, and John. In the Codex Bezæ they stand
Matthew, John, Luke, Mark; and "this, according to Scrivener (p. 68), is the
true *Western* order, found in the copies of the Old Latin *d, e, f,* and in the Gothic
version." It may have been adopted for the purpose of giving a certain precedence to the Gospels written by apostles. In this arrangement it is easy to see
why Matthew was placed before John, for it was believed to have been written
much earlier, and it was doubtless felt to be a better connecting-link between the
old economy and the new. But it is difficult to imagine why Luke was put before
Mark. Had the order of these two been reversed, we might have surmised that
the references in Luke to the relation of Christ to *all* mankind, and the close
connection of this Gospel with the Acts, written also by Luke, had led to the
arrangement; but for the actual order it seems impossible to assign any reason.
In the Curetonian Syriac version the succession is Matthew, Mark, John, Luke;
and this certainly is preferable to the "*Western*" order, though it is perhaps less
satisfactory than that which closes with the Gospel of John. For both the doctrinal character, and the time when it was written, are valid reasons for giving
the last place among the Gospels to that of John, even as the contents and the
time of writing are valid reasons for assigning the last place in the New Testament to the Revelation by John.

   In respect to the second, or Doctrinal, part of the New Testament, which is
composed of Epistles to Christians in general, to particular churches, and to certain individuals, the principal variations have been (1) In the place assigned to
the Catholic Epistles. These were generally put *before* the Pauline Epistles in
the Greek manuscripts, but in a few instances, as stated above, they were put *after*
them. We know of nothing decisive in favor of the one order or of the other.
(2) In the place assigned to the Epistle to the Hebrews. This was frequently
placed *after* the undoubted Epistles of Paul, partly perhaps because there was felt
to be some uncertainty in respect to its origin, and partly perhaps because it was
a sort of general Epistle, and might on that account be put with those of James,
Peter, John, and Jude. But it was sometimes placed *in the midst* of Paul's Epistles, and before the personal ones, because of its great doctrinal importance and
of its somewhat general destination. The reasons for the former position seem not
inferior to those for the latter, and we may therefore be satisfied with the place
which this Epistle holds in the Textus Receptus and the Common Version.

   But would not something be gained by arranging the Epistles of Paul chronologically, beginning with First Thessalonians and ending with Second Timothy?
An affirmative answer must be made to this question. For these letters chronologically arranged would connect themselves more naturally than they now do
with the history of Paul's missionary life as related in the Acts—the letters interpreting the history, and the history interpreting the letters, and both together
giving a clearer view of the progress and conflicts of the new religion than can
be easily gained from them now. Moreover, thus arranged the Pauline Epistles
would serve as a spiritual biography of the apostle. The difference of tone between his earlier and his later Epistles would be observed by the ordinary reader

as well as by the trained scholar. The letters to the Thessalonians, the Corinthians, the Galatians, the Romans, which were composed *before* his first imprisonment in Rome, and while he was pushing forward his missionary work in every direction possible, would be perceived to differ in a perfectly natural way from the letters to the Philippians, the Colossians, the Ephesians, and Philemon, which were written *during* his first imprisonment in Rome, and after his two years' confinement at Cæsarea, while the letters to Timothy and Titus would be found in harmony with a still later period of life. Without being confident as to the mode of its production, we are, on the whole, inclined to connect the Epistle to the Hebrews with the mind of Paul as its primary source, and to assign it to the period of his confinement in Cæsarea and Rome (A. D. 59–63).

If the Catholic Epistles retain their present place between the writings of Paul and the book of Revelation, there might be some slight advantage in putting the three Epistles of John *after* the Epistle of Jude—thus: James, Peter, Jude, John. And if it were a settled result of biblical criticism that Jude was written before Second Peter, it might be still better to make the order James, Jude, Peter, John. For then the really general Epistles by James, Jude, and Peter would follow the general Epistle to the Hebrews, the order of succession in the Testament would agree with the true relation between Jude and Second Peter, and the Epistles and Apocalypse of John would appear together as a final group. But biblical scholars are by no means certain that Jude was written before Second Peter, and therefore its appropriate situation remains at present in doubt.

III.

GREEK TEXT OF THE NEW TESTAMENT.

ANY commentary worthy of the name must take account of the Greek text of the New Testament. It may expound for the most part a current version of that text, but it can never do this in a safe and satisfactory manner without comparing it with the Greek original. But that original, as it came from the hands of the apostles and their associates, is no longer in existence. How, then, can we ascertain as nearly possible what it was? If the autographs have all perished, how can we learn what they contained?

(1) From *Manuscripts* of an early age or from copies of manuscripts that were made in an early age. A few of these manuscripts, distinguished for their antiquity and importance, are written in capital letters, and are therefore called *uncials*. It is not incredible that some of the inspired autographs were in the hands of those who prepared the oldest existing manuscripts, yet there is no evidence, and but little probability, of this. A great majority of known manuscripts are written in small letters connected with one another, and are therefore called *cursives*.

(2) From *Versions* of an early age. Only those that were made during the first three centuries are of much account in establishing the original text; and of the early versions the most literal are the most useful in this respect. A free,

paraphrastic translation, however truly or idiomatically it may express the sense of the original, is of little service in revealing the inspired text.

(3) From *Quotations* made by the early Christian writers. These quotations differ in value for textual criticism according to the age in which a given writer lived, the degree of exactness with which he cited passages of Scripture, and the language which he employed. Citations of the Greek Testament by Greek writers like Origen, Athanasius, Hippolytus, Cyril would often afford decisive evidence of the text as found in the manuscripts used by them, while citations in Latin by Tertullian or Cyprian or Augustine would be less decisive in their evidence.

(4) From *Critical Editions* of the New Testament founded on a careful examination of the preceding sources. If all the best editors agree in a particular reading, there is strong reason to believe it genuine. If they differ, there is presumably some ground for doubt, and at all events a commentator is compelled to look closely at the sources of evidence. Of the critical editors, Lachmann, Tischendorf, Tregelles, Westcott and Hort, deserve special attention.

Returning to the subject of manuscripts, it may be observed that all the oldest Greek copies of the New Testament are written in uncial (or capital) letters. This form prevailed until about the tenth century. But in the ninth or tenth century cursive letters began to be used, and, with various ligatures and contractions, continued to be employed until the introduction of printing. By reason of their age, therefore, the uncial manuscripts are, as a class, of pre-eminent value; but are there any marks by which the earlier manuscripts of this class can be distinguished from the later? According to Scrivener, " persons who have had much experience in the study of manuscripts are able to distinguish [them] from one another in respect of style and character; so that the exact period at which each was written can be determined within certain inconsiderable limits" (p. 28). And after pointing out as critically as possible, by means of fac-similes and verbal notes, the changes which took place in various uncial letters of the alphabet, he sums up the results in two propositions: " *First*, that the upright square uncials are more ancient than those which are narrow, oblong, or *leaning*. *Secondly*, that the simpler and less elaborate the style of writing, the more remote its probable date" (p. 38). Of these propositions there can be no reasonable doubt, but the changes from century to century must be traced with peculiar exactness, and none but experts can speak with the highest confidence respecting them. Fortunately, however, the number of experts in this branch of learning is not likely to diminish, but to increase.

Moreover, the oldest manuscripts of the New Testament are written upon vellum—*i. e.*, speaking strictly, the delicate skins of young calves; or upon parchment—*i. e.* the skins of sheep or of goats. Indeed, the oldest are said by Scrivener to be " almost invariably inscribed on the thinnest and whitest vellum that could be procured, while manuscripts of later ages are usually composed of parchment, thick, discolored, and coarsely grained." Yet *papyrus* was a cheaper material, very generally used instead of vellum or parchment at the time when the New-Testament Scriptures were written, and " its frail and brittle quality " may perhaps account for the fact that no original manuscript of any book of the New Testament is known to be in existence.

In *form* the manuscripts commonly resemble printed books. A few only are folios, more are octavos, but the greater part are quartos, their height slightly exceeding their breadth. Many copies have two Greek columns on a page, but the Codex Vaticanus has three, and the Codex Sinaiticus four. In the early uncial manuscripts there is no space between the different words: an unbroken succession of letters must be separated by the reader into words as his eye passes along the uniform line. But "the Sinaitic and Vatican manuscripts have a single point here and there on a level with the top of the letters, and occasionally a very small break in the continuous uncials, with or without the point, to denote a pause in the sense" (*Scrivener*). Abbreviated words are somewhat frequent, but they rarely occasion any ambiguity, since they are almost never resorted to unless the words are familiar—*e. g.* Θ϶ for Θεός, κϲ for κύριος, Ιϲ for Ἰησοῦς, Χϲ for Χριστός, Πνα for Πνεῦμα.

The following manuscripts must be frequently named in the Commentary, and should therefore be briefly described:

(1) *The Codex Sinaiticus* (or ℵ) is now in St. Petersburg, and is the property of the Russian emperor. "It is made of the finest skins of antelopes, and its leaves are so large that a single animal would furnish only two" (*Cod. Fred.- Aug. Proleg.*, § i.). "It consists of 345½ leaves of vellum, 147½ of which contain the whole New Testament, the Epistle of Barnabas, and a fragment of the Shepherd of Hermas. Each page contains four columns, with 48 lines in a column." It is supposed to have been written about the middle of the fourth century—*i. e.* about A. D. 350. In 1862 the Emperor of Russia published a *fac-simile* edition of three hundred copies, edited by Tischendorf, who discovered the manuscript in the Convent of St. Catharine, at the foot of Mount Sinai, in 1844.

(2) *The Codex Alexandrinus* (or A) is in the British Museum. It is written on vellum in uncial letters. Each page has two columns of 50 lines each. The fourth volume, of 134 leaves, contains most of the New Testament, also the First Epistle of Clement of Rome, a small part of the so-called Second Epistle, and three beautiful Christian hymns. Matthew's Gospel is wanting from the beginning to 25 : 6; John's, from 6 : 50 to 8 : 52 (two leaves); and Second Corinthians, from 4 : 13 to 12 : 6 (three leaves). All the other books of the New Testament are complete. The Catholic Epistles follow the Acts, and the Pastoral Epistles that to the Hebrews. This manuscript is ascribed on good grounds to the beginning, or at the latest the middle, of the fifth century, A. D. 400–450. It is believed to have been taken from Alexandria to Constantinople by the patriarch Cyril Lucas, who sent it to Charles I., King of England, through the English ambassador, Sir Thomas Roe, about 1628.

(3) *The Codex Vaticanus* (or B) is in the Vatican Library at Rome. "All who have inspected the Codex are loud in their praises of the fine, thin vellum, the clear and elegant hand of the first penman, and the simplicity of the whole style of the work" (*Scrivener*). The New Testament fills 142 leaves (out of 759 for the whole Bible). Each of the three columns on a page has 42 lines, with 16

or 18 letters in a line—the letters being somewhat smaller than those of Codex A, and considerably smaller than those of Codex ℵ. There are no intervals between the words, and no enlarged capitals *a prima manu* at the beginning of sentences. It contains the New Testament complete to Heb. 9 : 14 by the original copyist, while the rest of Hebrews, the four Pastoral Epistles, and the Apocalypse are said to have been supplied in the fifteenth century from a manuscript belonging to Cardinal Bessarion. By general consent of critics this manuscript is assigned to the middle of the fourth century, A. D. 350. A so-called *fac-simile* of it has been published by the Roman Curia.

(4) *The Codex Ephraemi* (or C) is in the Royal Library of Paris. It is a palimpsest[1], containing fragments from all parts of the New Testament on 145 leaves, but amounting in all to less than two-thirds of the volume. About 37 chapters of the Gospels, 10 of the Acts, 42 of the Epistles, and 8 of the Apocalypse have perished. It is written on vellum, very good, but not so fine as that of Codex A and some others. It has but one column on a page, with from 40 to 46 lines in the column. The letters are a little larger and more elaborate than those of A or B. The writing is continuous, with but a single point for punctuation, and this point commonly, but not always, put on a level with the top of the preceding letter. This manuscript belongs to the fifth century (about A. D. 450), and is of " first-rate importance" as far as it goes.

(5) *The Codex Bezæ* (or D of the Gospels and Acts) is in the Library of Cambridge (England), to which University it was presented by Theodore Beza in 1581. It is a vellum manuscript, though the material is not quite as fine as that of ℵ, A, or B. The Greek text on the left of each page is accompanied by a Latin version on the right—line being as nearly opposite and parallel to line as possible. The letters are of the same size as in Codex C. Both Davidson and Scrivener say of this manuscript that " its singularly corrupt text, in connection with its great antiquity, is a curious problem which cannot easily be solved." " The best judgment of the *age* of this MS. appears to be that which assigns it to the sixth century." " Taking the peculiarities of this MS. into consideration, it may be said that its evidence *when alone*, especially in additions, is of scarcely any value as to the genuine text, but of the very greatest when corroborated by other very ancient authority " (*Tregelles*).

(6) *The Codex Regius* (or L) is in the Royal Library of Paris. It consists of 257 leaves of thick vellum, with two columns of 25 lines each on a page, and contains most of the four Gospels. It was published by Tischendorf in his *Monumenta Sacra Inedita*, 1846. Written in the eighth or ninth century, it bears a strong resemblance in its text to Codex B, to the quotations of Origen, and to the marginal readings of the Philoxenian Syriac (A. D. 616), and is therefore highly esteemed by the best critics.

The following remarks of Westcott merit attention : (1) " That B deserves the first place as an authority ; (2) That ℵ and D have much in common, and a text of very high antiquity, dating from the end of the second century ; (3) That the

---

[1] *I. e.* a Codex Rescriptus, the original writing being partially obliterated and a second treatise written over it.

characteristic readings of C and L indicate careful grammatical revision; (4) That in the Gospels A gives a revised text, the basis of the later Alexandrine text; (5) That the characteristic readings of B, of א, D, and of C L, have all more or less support in the Ante-Nicene age; and (6) That very few readings in the Gospels will stand the test which are not supported by א or B or D."

More than *fifteen hundred cursive* manuscripts of the whole or of parts of the New Testament are known to be in existence—all of them written since A. D. 900. But only a few of this great number have been thoroughly "collated." Some of these deserve notice in this place:

1. *The Codex Basiliensis* is an illuminated manuscript at Basle, ascribed to the tenth century. It has been collated by Wetstein, C. L. Roth, and Tregelles. "In the Gospels the text is very remarkable, adhering pretty closely to the uncials B L and others of that class" (*Scrivener*).

13. *The Codex Regius 50* of the twelfth century is regarded (together with 69, 124, and 346) as a transcript from a manuscript whose text was substantially the same as that of the uncial D.

33. *The Codex Regius 14* is a folio of the twelfth century, containing all the New Testament but the Apocalypse. The text is very valuable, resembling Codices B, D, L more than does that of any other cursives. "After Larroque, Wetstein, Griesbach, Begtrup, and Scholz, it was most laboriously collated by Tregelles in 1850" (*Scrivener*).

157. *The Codex Urbino-Vaticanus* of the twelfth century, pronounced by Birch the most important MS. of the New Testament in the Vatican, after B. Among the cursives it stands next in value to Codex 33.

205 and 209, belonging to the Library of St. Mark's, Venice, supposed by Burgon to be copies from the same archetype, have a text much like that of B, at least in the Gospels. They are assigned respectively to the fifteenth and to the twelfth centuries.

For a more detailed account of the manuscripts of the New Testament the reader is referred to the fourth vol. of Horne's *Introduction to the Critical Study . . . . of the Holy Scriptures,* new edition (1866), this volume being written by S. P. Tregelles; to Scrivener's *Introduction to the Criticism of the New Testament,* second edition; to *The Story of the Manuscripts,* by Rev. Geo. E. Merrill; and to *The Critical Handbook,* by E. C. Mitchell, D. D.

Passing now to a consideration of early versions as affording evidence in respect to the Greek text at the time when they were made, we cannot do better than to quote the following remarks of Tregelles: "The value of the testimony of versions to the genuine ancient text is considerable; for although they have been subjected to the same casualties of transcription as has the text of the original Greek, and though at times they have been remodelled in some sort of conformity to the Greek copies then current, yet in general they are representatives of the Greek text from which they were formed. The casualties of transmission would rarely, if ever, affect documents in different languages in a way precisely similar, and we may in this manner account for not a few divergences in the versions as they have come down to us; yet when we find an avowedly ancient translation according in peculiar readings with some of the more ancient and valuable of the ancient MSS., it is an important proof of the *antiquity* at least of such readings; and thus, if they are not genuine, the *proof* must be sought in the counter-evidence that may be adduced."

Again, he says of ancient versions: "They follow the Greek from which they were taken with an almost scrupulous exactitude, and they so often preserve even the order of the words that they can be quoted as authorities on such points. At times, of course, the translator may have failed in vigilance; he *may* have passed by words which are omitted in no Greek copy, and he may have confused the text from which he was rendering, just in the same manner as was done by Greek copyists. But the admission of all this in the fullest manner does not afford any ground for the statement that the testimony of versions is of little moment in the question of the insertion or omission of a whole clause, or that 'a version need be very literal' if it is to show whether important words were or were not recognized by the Greek text from which it was taken" (*Horne*, vol. iv., pp. 225 and 228).

But Tregelles admits that special caution is needed in the use of early versions as testimony to the early Greek text. For "a copyist of a version, if he possessed any acquaintance with the original, was in danger of *correcting* by the Greek text with which he was familiar; and thus he might introduce mixed readings: this is an addition to the usual causes of transcriptural mistake; and for all these allowance must be made. We are, however, often able to revert to *very ancient* copies of versions, and then, just as in the case with such MSS. of the originals, we are brought back to the condition of the text nearly or quite identical with that in which the translation first appeared" (*Id.*, p. 228).

Even a moderately correct version of the New Testament must be of great value as evidence—(1) As to the presence or absence of certain disputed clauses, verses, or paragraphs in the manuscript from which it was made. In this respect the evidence afforded by a version would be almost independent of its literary qualities. For a poor translation would be just as useful as a good one in answering the question, Was the doxology of Matt. 6 : 13, or the last part of Mark, 16 : 9–20, or the account of an angel troubling the waters of Bethesda, John 5 : 4, or the pericope respecting the woman taken in adultery, John 7 : 53–8 : 11, in the source from which it was made? (2) As to certain important words concerning which existing manuscripts may leave the critic in doubt. Thus, if the translator had before him a Greek text which read "God only-begotten," instead of "the only-begotten Son," in John 1 : 18, or "the Lord," instead of "God," in Acts 20 : 28, or "who," instead of "God," in 1 Tim. 3 : 16, his version, though not distinguished for accuracy, would be likely to indicate these readings.

But the present text of every early version of the New Testament has suffered so many changes by transcription and correction that a critical study of its history, by means of the most ancient copies extant and through the citations of the earliest writers who employed it, is very necessary before much reliance can be placed on its testimony as a clue to the text used by the translator. The value of an early version for critical purposes will therefore depend upon three things: (*a*) Upon the time when it was made; (*b*) Upon the literal exactness with which it reproduced the original; and (*c*) Upon the certainty with which its own primary text can now be made out. Judged by these tests, it is believed that the most important versions for critical purposes are—(1) The Old Latin and the Syriac (Peshito and Curetonian); (2) The Coptic (Memphitic and Thebaic), the Latin Vulgate, the Harclean Syriac, and perhaps the Gothic.

As we have already observed, the first Latin version was made in North Africa, and is now fitly called the Old Latin Version. It can be traced in several manuscripts, especially *a*, *b*, *c*, and the fragments of *i*, compared with quotations from the New Testament found in the writings of the Fathers who lived in North Africa—*e. g.* Tertullian, Cyprian, Arnobius, Lactantius, Augustine, and in the ancient Latin version of Irenæus *Against Heresies.* On these and similar author-ities Tregelles remarks: "In one respect the testimony of the early Latin copies can hardly be estimated too highly. The translators adhered so closely to the Greek text from which the version was formed that they practically made it their rule to follow as far as they could even the *order* of the Greek words" (*Horne*, iv., p. 256). But he distinctly concedes that "the *Versio Vetus*, as unaltered, contains both readings and corruptions which are more ancient than the time of Jerome" —readings sustained by paramount early evidence, and defects which were re-moved by the recension of Jerome. The Old Latin Version was probably in existence as early as the year 170, and perhaps much earlier. And Scrivener asserts that "although the testimony of versions is peculiarly liable to doubt and error, the Peshito Syriac and Old Latin translations of the Greek Testament stand with a few of the most ancient manuscripts of the original in the very first rank as authorities and aids for the critical revision of the text."

There has been some difference of opinion among scholars as to the critical value of the Syriac Version of portions of the New Testament, published by Dr. Cureton in 1858, as compared with the critical value of the Peshito. Dean Al-ford spoke of the former as "perhaps the earliest and most important of all the versions," and Tregelles affirms that "the readings" [of this translation are] "in far greater accordance with the oldest authorities of various kinds than is the case in the previously-known Peshito. . . . . Probably this older form of Syriac text was known to the translator of the Peshito Gospels, and from it he took much that would suit his purpose," etc. On the other hand, Scrivener uses this lan-guage concerning the Peshito: "For the present we can but assent to the ripe judgment of Michaelis, who, after thirty years' study of its contents, declared that he could consult no translation with so much confidence in cases of difficulty and doubt. While remarkable for its ease and freedom, it very seldom becomes loose or paraphrastic. The Peshito has well been called 'the queen of versions' of Holy Writ, for it is at once the oldest and one of the most excellent of those whereby God's providence has blessed and edified the church" (p. 280). West-cott classifies the Syriac Versions thus: "The Old (Curetonian) Syriac, the Vul-gate Syriac (Peshito), the Harclean Syriac," showing that he agrees with Tre-gelles and Cureton as to the comparative age of the two versions.

For the two Egyptian or Coptic versions, the Memphitic and the Thebaic, we may assume a very early origin. They may have been made before the close of the second century. This is admitted by Lightfoot, who also remarks that, " with the single exception of the Apocalypse, the Memphitic New Testament, as far back as we can trace its history, contained all the books of our present Canon ;" and from the omission of the Apocalypse he infers that the completion or codification of this version was effected about the middle of the third century, when, for a short time, doubts were entertained in Egypt concerning the authorship of the Apocalypse. The order of books in this version is given as follows: Gospels, Pauline Epistles, Catholic Epistles, Acts. " The Pauline Epistles include the Hebrews, which is placed after First and Second Thessalonians and before First and Second Timothy, as in the Greek MSS. א, A, B, C," etc. " Of all the versions, the Memphitic is perhaps the most important for the textual critic. In point of antiquity it must yield the palm to the Old Syriac and the Old Latin ; but, unlike them, it preserves the best text as current among the Alexandrian Fathers, free from the corruptions which prevailed so widely in the copies of the second century " (*Scrivener*, pp. 344, 345).

The Thebaic Version exists only in fragments, though these fragments now embrace a large part of the New Testament. In this version, as well as in the Memphitic, the Epistle to the Hebrews is evidently ascribed to Paul, for it stood between Second Corinthians and Galatians. Its textual value is pronounced by Lightfoot only second to that of the Memphitic Version, of which it is wholly independent.

These are the most important of the early versions in the matter of textual criticism, and a wise editor of the Greek Testament will be careful to consult them. Others are of less value, though not unworthy of attention in the study of doubtful passages.

Lastly, some use may be made in textual criticism of the numerous *Quotations* which are found in the writings of the Christian Fathers. But these quotations are of far less service in establishing the true text than they are in proving the existence of the New-Testament Scriptures at an early day, the respect which was paid to them by Christians, and their substantial agreement with the books we now have. In these latter respects their testimony is of the highest value: in the former respect, it must be used with very great caution, for the following reasons: (1) .The quotations of the Fathers were often made from memory. This is admitted by those most familiar with early Christian literature. Nor is it at all surprising. For if those writers were sure of the substance of a passage which they desired to use, this was generally enough for their purpose. Verbal accuracy could only be attained by consulting the manuscript in almost every instance, and this process, at once slow and laborious, was felt to be unnecessary. (2) Their quotations were in many cases made up of expressions from different parts of Scripture, loosely put together, and giving no more from the several passages than suited their immediate object. Citations thus made can be of but little service in showing what was the reading of any passage from which a particular clause had been taken. (3) Their quotations have been changed, more or less, in many instances, by copyists or editors. Perhaps the circumstance that they were loosely made has seemed to copyists and editors a reason for changing them in the interest of accuracy; but if, in doing this, they have been guided by the readings found in manuscripts of their own times, they have injured the citations for purposes of textual criticism.

Nevertheless, it is certainly possible to underrate the importance of Patristic quotations as a guide to the original text of the New Testament. For there are places, though few, where the Fathers appeal to the codices of their own early day as reading thus and so, or where they discriminate between codices, saying that many of them have a particular reading, and implying that others have it not. There are places also where they show, by exposition or by argument, what must have been the reading accepted by them, though it is doubtful to us. Especially valuable in this respect are the commentaries of Greek writers; and it is not too much to say that the works of Origen and of some others may be profitably studied with reference to ascertaining the original text of the New Testament. Yet until the writings of the Christian Fathers have been edited with peculiar care, and with the use of the earliest manuscripts preserved, they ought to be appealed to with the utmost caution.

In the light of these facts as to the sources of evidence respecting the original text of the New Testament, it is manifest that interpreters are called upon to decide for themselves what that evidence requires, at least in cases where the critical editors disagree; and the writers of this Commentary have sometimes done this. It will be observed, however, that they have proceeded in this matter with very great caution, rarely favoring a change of the text from which the Common Version was made unless that change is adopted by some of the best editors and required by early and weighty evidence. In other language, they have labored diligently to discover the pure word of God as it was delivered to early Christians by inspired men, and no less diligently to ascertain the precise meaning of that word, and to place that meaning in the clearest manner possible before the reader's mind.

As an aid to the accomplishment of this purpose it has been thought desirable to print the Revised Version (1881) side by side with the Common Version (1611) at the top of the page. For, to say nothing of improvements in translation, the Greek text adopted by the Revisers must be regarded as one of great excellence, approaching more nearly perhaps than any one yet prepared to that which existed in the autographs of the sacred writers. We shall not go too far, therefore, if we assert that the Revised Version must hold a position co-ordinate with that of the Common Version—*first*, because it represents in perspicuous English a remarkably pure text of the original; and *secondly*, because it is likely to be in the hands of a vast majority of those who read the New Testament at all.

With these remarks this Introduction might be closed. But it may not be improper to add a few words of explanation. (1) Special introductions to the several books of the New Testament will be given by the writers upon those books—the present Introduction being of a general nature, applicable to the New Testament as a collection of sacred writings, but not aiming to give all the evidence for the authorship and authority of particular books. (2) The undersigned is only responsible for the selection of the writers who prepare this Commentary, and for the general character of the Commentary itself, but not for the details of interpretation in particular passages. Yet he has in a few instances inserted brief notes over his own initials (A. H.). (3) As may be inferred from our General Introduction, due regard is paid by the writers of this Commentary to the results of modern biblical scholarship as to the authenticity, the original text, and the true meaning of the New-Testament Scriptures. (4) Yet the results of careful and critical study are presented in the clearest terms possible. Greek words are very rarely introduced; indeed, never, unless they are deemed necessary to justify the interpretation given; and, when introduced, they are carefully translated— the object of the writers being distinctly this, to render the Commentary useful to *all* who desire a knowledge of God's word. Hence the practical bearings of divine truth are often insisted upon in the Commentary.

ALVAH HOVEY.

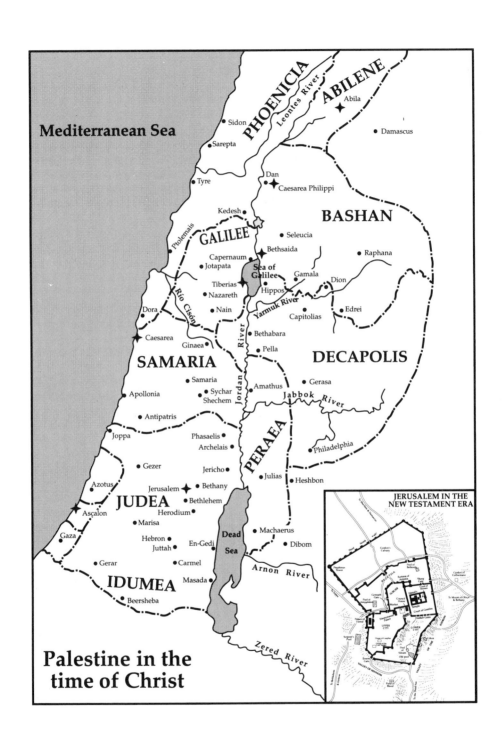

Mediterranean Sea

PHOENICIA

ABILENE

★ Abila

● Damascus

● Sidon

● Sarepta

Leontes River

● Tyre

Dan ●

Caesarea Philippi ★

Kedesh ●

BASHAN

GALILEE

● Seleucia

Ptolemais

Bethsaida ★

Capernaum ●
● Jotapata

Sea of
Galilee

● Raphana

Gamala ●

Dion ●

Tiberias ●
● Nazareth

Hippos ●

Yarmuk River

● Edrei

Río Cisón

● Nain

Capitolias ●

Dora ●

Caesarea ★

● Bethabara

Jordan River

Ginaea ●

● Pella

DECAPOLIS

SAMARIA

● Samaria

Amathus ●

● Gerasa

● Apollonia

● Sychar
Shechem

Jabbok River

● Antipatris

PERAEA

Joppa ●

Phasaelis ●
Archelais ●

● Philadelphia

● Gezer

Jericho ●

● Julias
● Heshbon

Azotus ●

Jerusalem ★ ● Bethany

JUDEA
● Bethlehem

Ascalon ●
Herodium ●

● Marisa

Dead
Sea

● Machaerus

Gaza ●

Hebron ●
Juttah ●

En-Gedi ●

● Dibom

● Gerar

● Carmel

Arnon River

IDUMEA

Masada ●

● Beersheba

Zered River

Palestine in the
time of Christ

**JERUSALEM IN THE
NEW TESTAMENT ERA**

THE GOSPEL
ACCORDING TO MATTHEW

CHAPTER I.

THE book of the generation of Jesus Christ, the son of David, the son of Abraham.

1   1 The book of the 2 generation of Jesus Christ, the son of David, the son of Abraham.

1 Or, *The genealogy of Jesus Christ*.....2 Or, *birth ;* as in ver. 18.

Ch. 1: 1-17. THE GENEALOGY OF JESUS CHRIST.

TRADITIONAL TITLE. Before the middle of the second century, we find the name **Gospel** already applied to the narratives of our Saviour's life. Justin Martyr says : "The apostles, in the memoirs made by them, which are called Gospels.'' The Greek word so rendered, which signifies "a good message," "good news," "glad tidings," is found a few times in Matthew and Mark (*e. g.*, Matt. 4: 23; 26: 13; Mark 8: 35; 16: 15) as denoting, in general, the good news of Christ's reign, and of salvation through him; and its subsequent application to our four narratives of Christ's life and teachings was natural and appropriate. The best early authorities for the text give the title in the simple form, **Gospel according to Matthew,** some of them having only "According to Matthew," where the word "Gospel" is implied, though not expressed. To say "Saint Matthew," a practice which many persons retain from Romanist usage, is useless, if not improper. No one thinks it irreverent to speak of Moses or Isaiah without any such prefix. The peculiar expression of the traditional title, "according to Matthew," implies that the gospel has been reported by different persons under different aspects, and this is the way in which Matthew has presented it. The English word "gospel" has long been supposed (it is so interpreted even in the eleventh century) to be derived from the Anglo-Saxon *godspell*, signifying good story, good tidings, and to be thus a literal translation of the Greek. But recent etymologists go far to prove, by the comparison of kindred languages, that it is from God and spell, meaning a narrative of God, and so the history of Christ. (See Skeat, "Etym. Dict. and Supplement."'

Matthew begins his Gospel with the genealogy of our Lord. Designing to prove, especially to the Jews, that Jesus of Nazareth is the Messiah, he shows *at the outset* that Jesus is a descendant of David, as it had been predicted that the Messiah would be. In order to establish this fact according to Jewish law, it must be shown that the legal father of Jesus was a descendant of David, as this genealogy does; and to give the argument greater impressiveness, he goes back to trace the descent from Abraham, the father of the Jewish race, to whose "seed" the promise was spoken (Gen. 17: 7; Gal. 3: 16). Luke, who had no special reference to the Jews, but wrote for all, gives the genealogy some distance after the beginning of his book (Luke 3: 23), and carries it up to Adam, the father of all men. (As to apparent discrepancies between Matthew and Luke, see below on v. 17). Mark, in his short narrative, gives no genealogy, but simply begins by describing Jesus Christ as "the Son of God" (Mark 1: 1). John, wishing to correct errors already rife, when he wrote, as to both the human and the divine nature of our Lord, goes back to his eternal pre-existence as the Word, his divinity and creatorship, and then states his incarnation, showing him to be not merely in appearance but in reality a man (John 1 : 1-5, 14). This comparison makes it plain that Matthew's first paragraph, indeed, his opening sentence, strikes the key-note to his treatise, which is throughout a Gospel for the Jews.

Some have supposed that the Evangelist adopted this genealogy as a whole from some public or private record existing among the Jews. There would be nothing derogatory in this idea, and the document thus adopted would have for us the sanction of inspiration as to its correctness; but it seems more natural to think that Matthew framed the list himself from the Old Testament and the Jewish records. Some of its peculiarities, *e. g.*, the incidental mention of certain females (see below), are best explained as having been introduced by him, with a special design. That the Jews did, in the first century, still possess genealogical records, at least of important families, is shown by various facts. Thus Paul asserted without reserve that he was of the tribe of Benjamin (Rom. 11: 1; Phil. 3: 5). Josephus ("Life" ⅔ 1) gives his own priestly and royal descent for several generations, and adds: "I present the descent of our family as I found it recorded in the public tablets, and to those who try to slander us I wish much joy." This unquestionable evidence made him feel perfectly secure. And in the book against Apion (i. 7) he describes the pains taken by priests residing in Egypt, Babylon, and other foreign countries, to send to Jerusalem properly certified statements as to marriages and births in their families; and declares that after any great war, such as that which had recently occurred, the surviving priests prepared new copies from the old records. The story told by Julius Africanus (Euseb. "Hist." I. 7, 13) that Herod burnt the genealogies of the Jews, in order to prevent his own inferiority as an Idumæan from being manifest, conflicts with these and all the other statements on the subject, and certainly cannot be true in its full extent. We are told that Rabbi Hillel, a contemporary of Jesus, proved from a genealogical table at Jerusalem that he was a descendant of David. ("Bereshith Rabba," f. 98, quoted by Godet, "Com. on Luke," 3: 23.) There is also a story that Domitian (A. D. 81–96) ordered all descendants of David to be slain, and certain heretics accused as such the descendants of Jude, a brother of the Saviour, who being summoned before the emperor acknowledged that they were descended from David, but stated that they lived by tilling their little farms, and showed their hands hard with toil, (from which we see, with Weiss, that the family of Jesus were still poor), so that the emperor dismissed them as persons not likely to excite revolution. (Hegesippus in Euseb. "Hist." iii. 19, 20.) On the other hand, all this is changed at the present day. The Jewish records have long since completely perished, and no Jew could now prove himself a descendant of David. If one claiming to be the Messiah should now arise, as some Jews still expect, no such evidence could be furnished as that with which Matthew here begins.

1. The opening words signify *either*, **Book of the generation,** *i. e.*, descent-book, pedigree, genealogy, thus referring only to v. 2–17 (comp. Gen. 5: 1; 11: 27), *or, Book upon the birth*, referring to the whole account of the birth of Jesus in ch. 1 and 2. (Compare the use of the same term in v. 18, there rendered 'birth'). The choice between these two meanings of the phrase must remain a matter of doubt, and is of no real importance. The view of some that "book of the generation" here denotes a history in general (as perhaps in Gen. 25: 19; 37: 2), must pretty certainly be rejected. **Jesus,** the same as Joshua (see on v. 21), is our Lord's private or personal name; **Christ** is his official name, being a translation into Greek of the Hebrew word 'Messiah,' which signifies 'anointed' and with the article, 'the anointed one.' (Comp. 1 Sam. 24: 6, 10; Psa. 2: 2; 105: 15; Isa. 45: 1; Dan. 9: 25, 26; John 1: 20, 25, 41; 4: 25, 29; Acts 4: 26). It appears in the Gospels as a *proper name* only here, together with v. 16, 18, and probably 16: 21 (comp. also v. 16, and 27: 17); Mark 1: 1; John 1: 17; 17: 3. Everywhere else in the Gospels it denotes the promised Messiah or anointed one, sometimes without reference to Jesus at all, but usually applied to him either by direct assertion or by implication. When not a proper name it commonly has the article, 'the Christ,' which is often omitted in Common English Version (see on 2: 4). In John 1: 41; 4: 25, we find Messias, a Greek form of Messiah. Whether Jesus was the Messiah, was during his ministry an open question, and the Evangelists do not, in their history of him, assume it as then settled. But after his ascension the apostles would naturally take this for granted in their expressions, and accordingly 'Christ' or 'Jesus Christ,' is very often used in the Acts and Epistles as a proper name. In like manner Matthew, Mark, and John, in writing their Gospels, use the same now familiar expression in the *introduction*, though in the body of their narrative they speak according to the state of the question when the events

2 Abraham begat Isaac; and Isaac begat Jacob; and Jacob begat Judas and his brethren;
3 And Judas begat Phares and Zara of Thamar; and Phares begat Esrom; and Esrom begat Aram;
4 And Aram begat Aminadab; and Aminadab begat Naasson; and Naasson begat Salmon;
5 And Salmon begat Booz of Rachab; and Booz begat Obed of Ruth; and Obed begat Jesse;

2   Abraham begat Isaac; and Isaac begat Jacob; and
3   Jacob begat Judah and his brethren; and Judah begat Perez and Zerah of Tamar; and Perez begat
4   Hezron; and Hezron begat [1] Ram; and [1] Ram begat Amminadab; and Amminadab begat Nahshon; and
5   Nahshon begat Salmon; and Salmon begat Boaz of

---

1 Gr. *Aram.*

---

occurred. In 16: 21 we may see a special reason, as there pointed out. And so Jesus himself, in John 17: 3, when praying in the presence of his disciples at the close of his ministry, speaks as taking his Messiahship for granted; as in Mark 9: 41, 'because ye are Christ's,' he is anticipating the future conviction of his followers. **Son of Abraham** may be in apposition either with 'David' or with 'Jesus Christ,' the Greek being ambiguous, like the English. But either sense involves what the other would express, and so both amount to the same thing: in Jesus were fulfilled the prophecies that the Messiah should descend from David and from Abraham.

2. Among the sons of Jacob, **Judas**, or *Judah*, is singled out, because he is the one from whom David and Jesus were descended; but **his brethren** are also mentioned by the Evangelist, perhaps simply because it was common to speak of the twelve patriarchs and the twelve tribes all together (Acts 7: 8, 9); or, it may be, with the design of reminding his readers that all the other tribes were of the same descent as Judah, and thus all were interested in the Messiah.

Many of the names in this list are, in the Common English Version, more or less different in form from the corresponding names in our version of the Old Testament, and throughout the New Testament the same thing frequently occurs. The New Testament writers have usually employed that form of a name which was already familiar to their readers, who were generally accustomed, Jews as well as Gentiles, to read, not the original Hebrew of the Old Testament—for the Hebrew proper was then little used in conversation (the Aramaic having largely supplanted it)—but the Greek translation known as the Septuagint. The authors of that translation often failed to express the Hebrew names in Greek as exactly as they might have done. Besides, the Greek language is in some respects less able to express Hebrew words than the English is, particularly in respect to the letter *h*, which abounds in Hebrew names, and which the Greek cannot represent at all except at the beginning of a word, or in the combinations *ch*, *th*, *ph*. Accordingly, Noah was written Noe (24: 37), Korah written Core (Jude 11), and Elisha became Eliseus (Luke 4: 27). It thus appears that not only have the names in our version of the *New* Testament undergone a two-fold change, —presenting us the English form of the common Greek form of the Hebrew words—but the difference is increased by the fact that in our version of the *Old* Testament, rendered directly from the Hebrew, we have the name often more exactly expressed than *could* be done in Greek. The writers of the New Testament gave their readers the form of the names that they were all familiar with in reading the Septuagint; so that they had the *same form* in both Testaments. And this result will be secured for English readers, if in the New Testament we should put into English letters not the Greek form of the name as there given, but the Hebrew form as it occurs in the Old Testament. Then the reader of our version, like the reader in the apostle's days, will find the name in the same form throughout his Bible, and will thus *feel* that it is the same name. There must be a few exceptions; as, for example, it would hardly be proper to write our Saviour's name Joshua, though we should thus be much more vividly reminded of the origin and associations of the name; and it is probably best to retain the Greek form, Judas, for the traitor disciple, and employ Judah for the patriarch and others, and Jude for the writer of the Epistle. But in general, the Hebrew forms can be used in the New Testament without difficulty or impropriety.

3-5. Commentators have always noticed that while this genealogy, according to custom, gives only the names of the men, it

6 And Jesse begat David the king; and David the king begat Solomon of her *that had been the wife of* Urias;

7 And Solomon begat Roboam; and Roboam begat Abia; and Abia begat Asa;

8 And Asa begat Josaphat; and Josaphat begat Joram; and Joram begat Ozias;

9 And Ozias begat Joatham; and Joatham begat Achaz; and Achaz begat Ezekias;

10 And Ezekias begat Manasses; and Manasses begat Amon; and Amon begat Josias;

11 And Josias begat Jechonias and his brethren, about the time they were carried away to Babylon;

12 And after they were brought to Babylon, Jechonias begat Salathiel; and Salathiel begat Zorobabel;

6 Rahab; and Boaz begat Obed of Ruth; and Obed begat Jesse; and Jesse begat David the king.

And David begat Solomon of her *that had been the* 7 *wife* of Uriah; and Solomon begat Rehoboam; and Rehoboam begat Abijah; and Abijah begat [1]Asa;

8 and [1]Asa begat Jehoshaphat; and Jehoshaphat be-9 gat Joram; and Joram begat Uzziah; and Uzziah be-gat Jotham; and Jotham begat Ahaz; and Ahaz be-10 gat Hezekiah; and Hezekiah begat Manasseh; and Manasseh begat [2]Amon; and [2]Amon begat Josiah; 11 and Josiah begat Jechoniah and his brethren, at the time of the [3]carrying away to Babylon.

12   And after the [3]carrying away to Babylon, Jech-·oniah begat [4]Shealtiel; and [4]Shealteil begat Ze-

---

1 Or, *Asaph*.....2 Gr. *Amos*....3 Or, *removal to Babylon*....4 Gr. *Salathiel.*

---

turns aside to make incidental mention of four women—**Thamar, Rahab, Ruth,** and the wife of Uriah—of whom three were polluted by shameful wickedness, and the fourth was by birth a heathen. This appears to have been done simply because each of the four became a mother of the Messianic line in an irregular and extraordinary way, as in re-counting a long list of names one is very apt to mention anything unusual that attaches to this or that individual. The mystical mean-ings which some find in the introduction of these names, cannot be accepted by a sober judgment; and the notion (Lange) that Tamar, for example, really acted under the impulse of a fanatical *faith,* " being resolved at all hazards to become one of the mothers of God's chosen race," is a particularly wild fancy.—The introduction of both **Phares** and **Zara,** while throughout the list only one person is usually given, is probably due to the fact that Tamar their mother has been mentioned (comp. 1 Chron. 2: 4), and that she bore them both at one birth.—There is no sufficient reason to question that the Rahab here mentioned is the famous woman of Jericho; nor that she had pursued the dis-graceful calling commonly supposed.—The length of time between Salmon and David makes it likely that some names have been here omitted (as also in Ruth 4: 21 f., and 1 Chron. 2: 11), most probably between Obed and Jesse; but this is not certain, as the general chronology of that period is doubtful, and the parents in some cases may have been ad-vanced in years when the children were born.

6. David the king is thus signalized, prob-ably as being the first of this line who attained that dignity, and he to whom the promise was made of a seed that should *reign* forever. In the second sentence of this verse, '*the king*' in

the common text is a mere addition from the first sentence, wanting in several of the best early documents.

8. Between Joram and Uzziah, three names are omitted, Ahaziah, Joash, and Amaziah (2 Kings 8: 24; 1 Chron. 3: 11; 2 Chron. 22: 1, 11; 24: 27). This was probably done to secure symmetry, by bringing the number of names in each dis-course to fourteen (see on v. 17); and these particular persons might naturally be selected for omission, because they were immediate descendants of Ahab and Jezebel.

11, 12. Here also a name has been omitted, that of Jehoiakim, who was the son of Josiah, and father of Jehoiachin, or Jeconiah (2 Kings 23: 34; 24: 6). As in v. 8, we may suppose one name to have been purposely omitted by the Evangelist, and this particular person to have been chosen because in his reign occurred the events which led to the captivity. As to the further difficulty on which some have insisted, that while we read here of **Jechonias and his brethren,** in 1 Chron. 3: 16, but one brother of his is mentioned,—it is enough to recall the familiar fact that genealogical lists such as that very often omit some of a man's children, mentioning only those which be-longed to the line of succession, or which there was some special reason for including; and so there might very well have been other brothers known from genealogies existing in Matthew's time, but whom the compiler of Chronicles had no occasion to include in his list.—The expression, **the time they were carried away to Babylon** —or, *the re-moval,* mar. of Rev. Ver.,—is of course not to be pressed as involving an exact coincidence of the two events, but to be understood in the more general way, which is natural in such cases. Josiah died some years before the removal to Babylon (2 Chron. 36). This great event was

13 And Zorobabel begat Abiud; and Abiud begat Eliakim; and Eliakim begat Azor;

14 And Azor begat Sadoc; and Sadoc begat Achim; and Achim begat Eliud;

15 And Eliud begat Eleazer; and Eleazer begat Matthan; and Matthan begat Jacob;

16 And Jacob begat Joseph the husband of Mary, of whom was born Jesus, who is called Christ.

17 So all the generations from Abraham to David *are* fourteen generations; and from David until the carrying away into Babylon *are* fourteen generations; and from the carrying away into Babylon unto Christ *are* fourteen generations.

13 rubbabel; and Zerubbabel begat Abiud; and Abiud begat Eliakim; and Eliakim begat Azor; and Azor begat Sadoc; and Sadoc begat Achim; and Achim

14 begat Eliakim; and Eliakim begat Azor; and Azor begat Sadoc; and Sadoc begat Achim; and Achim

15 begat Eliud; and Eliud begat Eleazer; and Eleazer

16 begat Matthan; and Matthan begat Jacob; and Jacob begat Joseph the husband of Mary, of whom was born Jesus, who is called Christ.

17 So all the generations from Abraham unto David are fourteen generations; and from David unto the ¹carrying away to Babylon fourteen generations; and from the ¹carrying away to Babylon unto the Christ fourteen generations.

---

1 Or, *Removal to Babylon.*

---

really a forcible transportation, but the Evangelist uses the milder term 'removal' or 'migration,' which was frequently employed in the familiar Greek translation of the Old Testament, and would be less painful to the Jewish readers he had especially in view.[1]—In making Zerubbabel the son of Shealtiel, the Evangelist agrees with Ezra 3: 2; 5: 2; Neh. 12: 1; Hag. 1: 1; 2: 2, while 1 Chron. 3: 19, makes him the son of Pedaiah, a brother of Shealtiel. The explanations of this discrepancy which have been proposed are hardly satisfactory. It is not surprising that there should be some slight differences in these lists of names which, with our imperfect information, we are now unable to explain. A nervous solicitude to explain at all hazards, is uncalled for and unbecoming.

13. The nine names from Abiud to Jacob (v. 15) are not elsewhere mentioned, as they belong to the period subsequent to the close of the Old Testament records, the "interbiblical" period. They were doubtless taken from some public or private genealogy, such as would cause the Evangelist's Jewish readers to receive them without gainsaying. The number of names being scarcely proportioned to the time over which they extend, some have thought that here also a few names may have been omitted, as in v. 8, 11.

16. The Evangelist does not connect **Joseph** and **Jesus** as father and son; but altogether departs from the usual phraseology of the genealogy, so as to indicate the peculiarity of

1 The genitive *Babulonos* specifies this as the Babylon-removal, thus distinguishing it from other removals. This is the proper force of the genitive, as the generic or specifying case. The Babylon-removal, so far as the mere form of the expression goes, might mean the removal of Babylon, the removal to Babylon, or the removal from Babylon; but the well-known historical facts left no doubt as to the real meaning. See similar uses of the genitive in 4: 15; 10: 5; John 7: 35; 10: 7.

the Saviour's birth. The name Jesus (*i. e.,* Joshua, see on v. 21), being common among the Jews (comp. Col. 4: 11; Acts 13: 6), the person here meant is distinguished as **Jesus, who is**—or, *the one*—**called Christ,** (so in 27: 17, 22, and comp. "Simon, the one called Peter," in 4: 18; 10: 2.)

17. THREE SETS OF FOURTEEN. The gathering of this long list of names into three groups of fourteen each appears to have been partly for the sake of aiding the memory, and partly in order to indicate the three great periods of the history, viz: from Abraham, the father of the nation, to "David the king" (see on v. 6), from David to the destruction of the monarchy at the removal to Babylon, and from that event to the coming of Messiah. These three periods are distinguished in many ways; among others by the form of government, which was in the successive periods a Theocracy, a Monarchy, and a Hierarchy, or government by the priests, this being for the most part the form after the return from the captivity. Finding that the names from Abraham to David amount to fourteen, the Evangelist omits some in the second period (see on v. 8, 11), and perhaps in the third also (see on v. 13), so as to leave each of these periods the same number as the first. This happened to be twice the sacred number seven, so that the whole list of names is divided into three sets of two sevens each. Similarly a Rabbinical writer says: "From Abraham to Solomon are fifteen generations, and then the moon was at the full; from Solomon to Zedekiah are again fifteen generations, and then the moon was eclipsed, and Zedekiah's eyes were put out." The omission of some names presents no difficulty, being occasionally found in Old Testament lists likewise. "It was a common practice with the Jews to distribute genealogies into divisions, each containing some favorite or mystical number, and in order to this, generations were either repeated or left out. Thus in Philo the generations from Adam to Moses are divided into two decads (sets of ten), and one hebdomad (set of seven), by the repetition of Abraham. But in a Samaritan poem the very same series is divided into two decads only, by the omission of six of the least important names." (Smith's "Dict.," Art. "Genealogy of Jesus.") We are told that the Arabians now abbreviate their genealogies in the same manner, and give the descent by a few prominent names. So, in fact, often do the English, or any other people; the object being, in such cases, not to furnish a complete list of one's ancestors, but simply to establish the descent from a certain line. Where such omissions are made in the Scripture genealogies, the usual term "begot" (or, as in Luke, "son of") is retained, and must of course be then understood not literally, but as denoting progenitorship or descent in general, a sense very common in the language of Scripture, and common throughout the East, both in ancient and modern times. (Comp. v. 1). Matthew's three fourteens have been variously made out by expositors. It seems best *either* to count from Abraham to David, from David again to Josiah, and from Jechoniah to Jesus, *or*, from Abraham to David, from Solomon to Jechoniah, as representing the time of the removal, and from Jechoniah again to Jesus. The fact that either of these modes of reckoning (and, indeed, one or two others) may be plausibly supported, concurs with the omission of some names to show that the Evangelist did not design this division to be pressed with literal exactness, but only to be taken in a certain general way, for purposes such as those above suggested.

THE GENEALOGIES OF MATTHEW AND LUKE. There is an obvious discrepancy between the two genealogies, (comp. Luke 3: 23 ff.), which has always attracted attention, and to explain which, we find various theories suggested. Most scholars at the present day are divided between two of these, and either of them is sufficiently probable to set aside *objection* to the credibility of the Evangelists on the ground of the discrepancy. The two genealogies diverge after David, Matthew's passing down through Solomon, and Luke's (which is stated in the opposite order), through Nathan, and they do not afterwards agree, unless it may possibly be in the case of Shealtiel and Zerubbabel, as these two names occur together in both lists.

1. One explanation supposes that, while Matthew gives the genealogy of Joseph, the reputed and legal father of Jesus, Luke really gives that of Mary, but simply puts her husband's name instead of hers, because it was not customary for a woman's name to appear in a genealogy, but that of her husband instead. This is a mere supposition, of course, but it is a perfectly possible and reasonable one, and it has the great advantage of showing that Jesus was not only a descendant of David legally, through his reputed father, but also actually, through his mother. There is good reason besides to believe (Luke 1: 32; Acts 2: 30; Rom. 1: 3; 2 Tim. 2: 8), that Mary was herself a descendant of David, as held by Justin Martyr,[1] Irenæus, Tertullian, and other Fathers. The fact that Elisabeth, the wife of a *priest*, was Mary's "kinswoman," (Luke 1. 36, the term denotes relationship, but without indicating its degree), is no proof that Mary was not of the tribe of Judah, since persons of the different tribes sometimes intermarried; indeed the earliest known Elisabeth, Aaron's wife, appears to have been of the tribe of Judah. (Ex. 6: 23; Numb. 2: 3.) This theory would accord with the special characteristics and manifest design of the two Gospels. Matthew, who wrote especially for Jews, gives the *legal* descent of Jesus from David, through Joseph, it being a rule of the Rabbins that "the descent on the father's side only shall be called a descent; the descent by the mother is not called any descent." Luke, who wrote without any special reference to the Jews, for general circulation, gives the *real* descent from David. In like manner Matthew mentions the angelic appearance to Joseph; Luke that to Mary. This explanation is adopted substantially, by Luther, Lightfoot, Bengel, Olshausen, Ebrard, Wieseler, Bleek (in part), Lange, Robinson, Alexander, Godet, Weiss. Andrews hesitates. (See a valuable discus-

[1] If we simply suppose that Justin adopted this theory of the genealogies, viz: that Luke gives that of Mary, there will be none of that conflict, between his statements on this subject and our Gospels, upon which the author of "Supernatural Religion" so much insists.

sion by Warfield in the "Presb. Review," Vol. II, p. 388–397).

2. Most of the Fathers, and many recent writers (as Winer, Meyer), hold that both Gospels give the genealogy of Joseph, and then attempt in various ways to remove the discrepancy, or pass it by as irreconcilable. The best explanation upon this view is that recently offered by Lord Hervey, viz.: the hypothesis that Matthew gives the line of succession to the throne, and that upon a failure of the direct line, Joseph became the next heir; while Luke gives Joseph's private genealogy, as a descendant of David by a younger line, which at this point supplied the failure in the older branch, and furnished the heir to the throne. This theory is ably advocated in Lord Hervey's volume on the Genealogies, and his article in Smith's "Dict.," "Genealogy of Jesus Christ," and is now quite popular with English writers, as Mill, Alford, Wordsworth, Ellicott, Westcott, Fairbairn, Farrar. It is altogether possible, and when presented in detail has several striking points; yet the former explanation is believed to be in some respects preferable. We are little concerned to show which of them is best, and under no obligation to prove that either of them is certainly correct; for we are not attempting to establish from the Genealogies the credibility of Matthew's Gospel. When the object is simply to *refute an objection* to that credibility, founded on an apparent discrepancy between two statements, it is sufficient to present any hypothetical explanation of the difficulty which is possible. If the explanation be altogether reasonable and probable, so much the better. And if there be two, or several, possible explanations, these reinforce each other in removing the ground for objection, and it is not necessary to choose between them.

The names Shealtiel and Zerubbabel in the genealogies need not be supposed to represent the same persons. There are various instances in the Old Testament lists, of a striking similarity between several names in lines that are unquestionably distinct.

HOMILETICAL AND PRACTICAL.

Besides the value of this genealogy, to the Jews and to us, in showing that *Jesus* was a descendant of David, as it had been predicted that *the Messiah* would be,—the apparently barren list of names might suggest much thought to a mind familiar with the Old Testament. During all this long period, the providential arrangements were going on, which prepared for the coming of the "seed" promised to Abraham. Every person in this genealogy—the wicked as well as the devout, even the woman of stained character—formed a link in the chain of providences. Through all the troubled centuries, through all the national changes, whether reigning in splendor, or dethroned and in captivity, or afterwards subsiding into insignificance under the rule of the high priests or of Herod, the appointed line was preserved; until among the rude population of an obscure village, are found the hard-working carpenter and the poor maiden, who are chosen to rear the seed of Abraham, the son of David.

V. 1. Christ, as 1) the son of Abraham (Gal. 3: 16), 2) the son of David. The Jews are the only race of mankind that can trace their origin in authentic history to a single ancestor.—V. 2 ff. The Old Testament history, 1) a history of Providence, 2) a history of Redemption; each finding its climax and consummation in Christ.—V. 3-5. The divine sovereignty and condescension, in causing the Saviour to spring from a line containing some persons so unworthy of the honor, and who reflected so little credit on their descendants. And a rebuke to that excessive pride of ancestry, to which the Jews were so prone, and which is so common among mankind in general. *Chrys.:* "He teaches us also hereby, never to hide our face at our forefathers' wickedness, but to seek after one thing alone, even virtue."—V. 7 ff. Bad men linked to good men, 1) as descendants of the good, 2) as ancestors of the good.—V. 11. The removal to Babylon, as a step in the preparation for Messiah.—V. 17. The three great periods of Jewish history before Christ, as all preparing in various ways for his coming and his work.

18-25. JESUS BORN OF A VIRGIN MOTHER.

Having presented the genealogy of Jesus, the inspired writer commences the narrative proper with matters pertaining to Jesus' birth and infancy. (1: 18, to 2: 23.) The passage now before us is designed to show that he was born of a virgin mother. Matthew does not mention the annunciation to Mary, nor the birth of the forerunner (Luke 1), but begins at the

18 Now the birth of Jesus Christ was on this wise: When as his mother Mary was espoused to Joseph, before they came together, she was found with child of the Holy Ghost.

18 Now the [1]birth [2]of Jesus Christ was on this wise: When his mother Mary had been betrothed to Joseph, before they came together she was found

---

1 Or, *Generation:* as in ver. 1....2 Some ancient authorities read, *of the Christ.*

---

time when it became apparent that Mary was with child, which would be soon after her return from the visit to Elisabeth (Luke 1 : 56).

18. The birth[1] of Jesus Christ was on this wise. It has already been intimated (v. 16) that he was not in the ordinary way the son of Joseph; and this point is now distinctly stated. **His mother Mary.** It is no doubt wisely provided that we know very little concerning the personal history of "Mary the mother of Jesus." (Acts 1 : 14.) The traditions relating to her, so highly prized by Romanists, are of no value. She was probably (see on 1 : 17) a descendant of David. We know nothing of her parents, or of any brothers; there is allusion to a sister (John 19 : 25), who is by some identified with "Mary the wife of Clopas," mentioned just after, and who upon that supposition must have borne the same name (see on 13 : 55). We are informed that Elisabeth was her kinswoman (Luke 1 : 36), so that Jesus and his forerunner were remote relatives. Mary's early home appears to have been Nazareth, and she probably lived a life of poverty and toil. As to her character, we are somewhat better informed. In Luke's narrative she appears before us as a deeply pious maiden, prompt to believe what God revealed (Luke 1 : 38, 45),. and anxious to have all difficulties in the way of her faith removed (Luke 1 : 34) ; as humbly rejoicing in the high privilege secured to her by the divine promise (Luke 1 : 46-55), and through the years which followed thoughtfully pondering the things which occurred in connection with her child.

[1] The correct text of the Greek is *genesis,* 'origin,' and so birth, rather than *gennesis,* prob. derived from *egennethe* in v. 16. A few very early versions and Fathers here omit 'Jesus,' reading simply 'the birth of the Christ,' and this is adopted by Treg., W H., and McClellan. The question is quite interesting, for the principles involved, to students of text-criticism (see Treg., Tisch., Scriv., W H.); but it does not seem allowable to leave the reading of *all* the Greek MSS. and most versions. The practical difference is not very important (see on v. 1). In the second clause omit *gar* of the common Greek text, leaving the simple genitive absolute. Matthew quite frequently employs this construction (Weiss).

(Luke 2 : 19.) The familiarity with Scripture manifested by her song of thanksgiving (Luke 1 : 46 ff.), shows how lovingly she had been accustomed to dwell on the word of God. Mary was of course not faultless, but her character was worthy of her high providential position, and she deserves our admiration and gratitude. Above all the "mothers of the wise and good" may we call her 'happy' (Luke 1 : 48), and cherish her memory. The utterly unscriptural, absurd, and blasphemous extreme to which the Romanists have gradually carried their veneration of Mary, must not drive us into the opposite extreme. The name 'Mary' is the same as Miriam, and is often written Mariam in the Greek, particularly when applied to the mother of our Lord (*e. g.,* v. 20). Its original meaning of rebelliousness was quite suitable for the sister of Moses.

Of Joseph likewise but little is known. Though of the old royal family, he appears to have been quite poor, and to have followed the lowly calling of wood-workman, probably what we call a carpenter (comp. on 13 : 55). He is here declared (v. 19, Rev. Ver.) to be a 'righteous' man, and we shall presently find him faithfully attentive to his precious charge (ch. 2); but beyond this the Scriptures give us no information (comp. at end of ch. 2).

Espoused, Rev. Ver. gives *betrothed.* So Wyc., Tyn., Gen. The Com. Ver. followed Rheims in giving "espoused," which formerly meant betrothed. It appears to have been a custom among the Jews for a betrothed maiden to remain still for some time in her father's house, before the marriage was consummated; and **before they came together,** probably refers to their coming to live in the same home, though it may be taken in the other sense, which is obvious (comp. 1 Cor. 7: 5). **She was found,** does not imply an attempt at concealment, but merely states that it was then ascertained. The expression is consistent with the view that she herself discovered the fact, and then, through information conveyed in some suitable way, it was ascertained by Joseph. The narrative is

19 Then Joseph her husband, being a just *man*, and not willing to make her a public example, was minded to put her away privily.
20 But while he thought on these things, behold, the angel of the Lord appeared unto him in a dream, saying, Joseph, thou son of David, fear not to take unto thee Mary thy wife: for that which is conceived in her is of the Holy Ghost.

19 with child of the Holy Spirit. And Joseph her husband, being a righteous man, and not willing to make her a public example, was minded to put her away privily. But when he thought on these things, 20 behold, an angel of the Lord appeared unto him in a dream, saying, Joseph, thou son of David, fear not to take unto thee Mary thy wife: for that which is

---

marked by great delicacy. A little reflection will suggest reasons why a divine revelation on the subject was made to Mary beforehand, and to Joseph only after the fact had become apparent. A different course with regard to either of them would have occasioned additional embarrassment and distress. **Ghost** is an Anglo Saxon word of the same meaning as the Latin 'Spirit,' and having the same primary sense of 'breath' (see on 16: 25). It has in modern times given way to the Latin term, and become obsolete, except (1) as denoting a spirit of a dead person supposed to become visible, (2) as used in the phrase 'to give up the ghost' (=expire), and (3) as applied to the third person of the Trinity. In this last sense our Common English Version employs it only in those passages of the New Testament in which 'holy' is prefixed, so as to make the personal designation 'The Holy Ghost'; and employs it in all such passages, except Luke 11: 13; 1 Thess. 4: 8. When used without 'holy' in the New Testament and everywhere in the Old Testament, the word is 'Spirit.' (Comp. as to 'hallow,' on 6: 9). It is to be regretted that Rev. Ver. did not uniformly adopt 'Holy Spirit,' with Amer. Revisers. Comp. on 3: 11; 12: 32; 28: 19. **Of the Holy Ghost,** (literally *out of*, marking the Holy Spirit as the source or cause of her condition), is here not meant to be understood as a part of the discovery, but is a fact appended by the narrator.—Under ordinary circumstances, Mary's condition would have involved a crime which, by the law of Moses, was punished with death by stoning (Lev. 20: 10). And a betrothed woman must be treated in this respect as if already married (Deut. 22: 23 f.).

19. From the time of betrothal the parties were legally bound to each other, so as to be called husband and wife (v. 20; Deut. 22: 24), and so that unchastity in either would be adultery. An unrighteous man would have cherished a passionate anger, and sought to punish as severely as possible. Joseph, **being a just** (Rev. Ver. *righteous*), **man,** (comp. 1

Sam. 24: 17), was not inclined to extreme severity, but was disposed to divorce her privately. (So Bleek, Grimm, Cremer). Or it may be understood thus: Joseph, being righteous (and therefore feeling that in such circumstances he could not take her as his wife), and *yet* not willing to expose her publicly,[1] was disposed to pursue a middle course, and divorce her privately. (So Meyer, Weiss, Morison.) The statement has been frequently made (so Chrysostom, Grotius), that the Greek word rendered 'righteous' may signify 'good, kind,' but it has not been shown to have that meaning anywhere in the New Test., and the common meaning gives a good sense, in either of the above ways. It would appear that the law (Deut. 22: 23 f.), was not regarded as *compelling* a husband to accuse his wife as an adulteress, and so Joseph would not be violating the law if he should avoid the extreme course, and divorce her, and this without stating his reason in the "writing of divorcement," (5: 31). Edersh. shows such a course to accord with custom and Rabbinical opinion.

20. The angel, more probably *an angel*, although the Greek might be understood as definite because of **the Lord** being appended. As to the angels, see on 18: 10. Divine communications by means of *dreams* are mentioned by Matt. in 1: 20; 2: 12, 13, 19; 27: 19; and referred to in Acts 2: 17; not elsewhere in New Test. Edersh. shows that the Jews attached great importance to dreams. There was probably something connected with such dreams as really gave divine guidance to distinguish them from ordinary dreams. Joseph is addressed as **son of David,** and thereby somewhat prepared for the remarkable disclosure about to be made. He probably knew that his was a leading branch of the royal family (see on v. 17). **Mary thy wife,**

---

[1] The earliest MSS. read *deigmatisai*, 'make her a spectacle,' the common Greek text *paradeigmatisai*, 'make her an example.' It is somewhat difficult to decide which is the correct reading, but the difference in meaning is unimportant.

21 And she shall bring forth a son, and thou shalt call his name JESUS: for he shall save his people from their sins.

21 [1]conceived in her is of the Holy Spirit. And she shall bring forth a son; and thou shalt call his name JESUS; for it is he that shall save his people from

---

1 Gr. *begotten.*

---

the betrothed woman being frequently spoken of as a wife. (Deut. 22: 24.) So as to 'Joseph her husband,' in v. 19. **Of the Holy Ghost.** Accordingly in v. 21 it is not, shall bring forth a son 'unto thee,' as was said to Zacharias, (Luke 1: 13.)

21. Jesus is the same name as Joshua, a contraction of Jehoshuah (Num. 13: 16; 1 Chr. 7: 27), signifying in Hebrew 'Jehovah is helper,' or 'Help of Jehovah.' In the later books, (*e. g.*, Neh. 7: 7; 8: 17; Ezra 2: 2, etc.), it sometimes takes the form Jeshua (Jeshuah), and this the Greek translators of the Old Testament expressed (comp. on v. 2) by Jesus. (In the Jewish books subsequent to Christianity it is frequently Jeshu). The name Joshua is everywhere in the Septuagint found in this form, Jesus, and so in the two passages of the New Testament in which Joshua is mentioned (Acts 7: 45; Heb. 4: 8). As applied to our Lord there is of course a certain modification of the idea conveyed by the name, but the leading thought is the same, viz., deliverance, salvation, and that springing from Jehovah. Like Joshua, who led Israel into the promised land, Jesus was to be the leader and ruler of his people, the "captain of their salvation" (Heb. 2: 10), under whose guidance they would be delivered from all dangers and brought safe to the rest that remaineth (Heb. 4: 9). Like the high-priest Joshua, who was associated with Zerubbabel in bringing the Jews back from the captivity (Ezra 2: 2; Zech. 3: 1 ff.), Jesus was to be the high-priest of his people. He thus answered at the same time to the civil and religious rulers of the nation, at once King and Priest. Comp. "he shall be a priest upon his throne," said of Joshua in Zech. 6: 13.[1]—Mary had also been told (Luke 1: 31 f.) that the child must be named Jesus, but without the reason for it here given. **For he shall save.** In Revised Version, *it is*

he that shall save. The word 'he' is here pretty clearly emphatic in the Greek, he himself, he and no other, though Revised Version rather exaggerates the emphasis.[1] The word rendered 'save' signifies primarily to 'preserve,' secondarily to 'deliver,' and it often conveys both ideas at the same time. It is applied to physical dangers (8: 25), death (24: 22; 27: 40, 42), disease (9: 21, 22; James 5: 15), and to sin and its consequences, which is the common use. **From their sins,** from both the *consequences* and the *dominion*, both the *penalty* and the *power* of their sins. Messiah did not come, as the Jews commonly supposed he would, simply to save his people from the dominion of foreigners; it was something deeper and higher, to save them from their sins. And not to save them *in* their sins, but *from* their sins. **His people** would to Joseph naturally mean Israel. It may have been meant to denote the spiritual Israel, including some of the nation, though not all (Rom. 9: 6, 27, 31; 11: 7), and some Gentiles. (Rom. 9: 25, 26, 30.) Or the angel may have meant simply the people of Israel, *i. e.*, the truly pious among them, not intending to exclude the Gentiles from being saved by Jesus, but confining the view at present to the salvation of the Jews. So the angel announces to the shepherds "great joy, which shall be to all the people." (Luke 2: 10, Revised Version.) Ecclus. 46: 1 says of Joshua, "Who according to his name became great for the salvation of his elect" (God's elect), which shows that the meaning of the name would be readily apprehended, and the connection in Ecclus. clearly confines the "elect" to Israel. Comp. the restriction of our Lord's ministry, and the temporary restriction of the ministry of the Twelve, to "the lost sheep of

---

[1] Other persons named Joshua or Jesus are found in 1 Sam. 6: 14, 18; 2 Kings 23: 8; Luke 3: 29; Col. 4: 11; Ecclus. Prologue and 50: 27; Josephus, "Ant." vi. 6, 6; xi. 7, 1; xii. 5, 1; xv. 3, 1. See also Bar-Jesus, Acts 13: 6. Jason, in Acts 17: 5; Rom. 16: 21 is the same name altered into a form sounding better in Greek, as Jews among us often give their names a more English shape.

[1] Winer, Fritzsche, Meyer, and others, hold that *autos* in Nom. is always emphatic. But the New Testament has some examples (see Buttmann, p. 107, Grimm II. 2) in which it cannot without great violence be so understood, and we seem compelled to admit that it is occasionally only an unemphatic 'he,' etc. (Latin *is*). It is freely so used in modern Greek (Mullach), and there is a partly similar use of *ipse* in late Latin (Rönsch). Comp. Ellicott on Col. 1: 17; Moulton's note to Winer, p. 187.

22 Now all this was done, that it might be fulfilled which was spoken of the Lord by the prophet, saying,

22 their sins. Now all this is come to pass, that it might be fulfilled which was spoken by the Lord through the prophet, saying,

---

the house of Israel." (15: 24; 10: 5, 6.) The same question as in this case arises in Acts 5: 31, Revised Version, "to give repentance to Israel, and remission of sins."

22. All this was done, etc. The statement and quotation in v. 22 f. has been understood by some expositors (Chrys., Alexander) as a part of the words of the angel. They render: 'And all this has taken place,[1] that it may be fulfilled,' etc., and the language, so far as that goes, warrants their interpretation. In 26: 56, the same form of expression is commonly referred to the speaker of what precedes, and not to the Evangelist (comp. Mark 14: 49); in 21: 4, the connection will admit of either view (see note there). In the present case, however, we should have to suppose the angel to be anticipating when he says: "All this has taken place," for most of the events to which he refers were yet future; and in 21: 4, no part of the event in question has taken place when the Saviour speaks. Matthew has not elsewhere than in these three passages the precise expression, 'all this has taken place in order that,' etc., but he remarks upon the designed fulfillment of prophecy much oftener than the other Evangelists, so that it is quite natural to refer this statement to him; which on the whole seems decidedly best. Looking back upon the events, Matthew connects them with the time at which he is writing, and thus very naturally says: 'All this has taken place that it might be fulfilled, etc. [2]

Fulfilled is the translation of a Greek word signifying to 'make full,' to 'fill up.' (So the English fill full or fulfill). It is often used in New Testament, both literally, as to fill a valley, boat, etc., and figuratively, as to fill with gladness, knowledge, etc. In a derivative sense it signifies to 'perform fully,' 'accomplish,'

being applied to a work or a duty, and to predictions, as here. This last very important use, to fulfill (a prediction), is found frequently in Matthew (1: 22; 2: 15, 17, 23; 4: 14; 8: 17; 12: 17; 13: 35; 21: 4; 26: 54, 56; 27: 9), and in John (12: 38; 13: 18; 15: 25; 17: 12; 18: 9, 32; 19: 24, 36); several times in Luke (1: 20; 4: 21; 21: 22; 24: 44), and in Acts (1: 16; 3: 18; 13: 27); once in Mark (14: 49) and in James (2: 23.) An examination of these passages would show that in general they will admit only the strict sense of fulfill, implying a real prediction, and that no one of them requires the quite different meaning attached to the term by some expositors, viz.: that while there was no real prediction, the New Testament occurrence reminded the Evangelist of the Old Testament passage, or so resembled the Old Testament occurrence as to warrant the application to it of the same language. This serious departure from the etymology and regular use of the word is supposed by such expositors to be required by a few passages in which it is difficult *for us to see* that there exists the strict relation of prediction and fulfillment. But such passages, it will be found, all admit of at least a possible explanation in consistency with the idea of a real fulfillment (see on 2: 15, 18), and we have no right to take this or any other word in a sense alien to its origin and use, unless there be found passages in which it *cannot possibly* have the usual meaning. The strict application of this rule of interpretation is here a matter of importance, as the question involved seriously affects the prophetic relation between the Old and the New Testament.

But two things are to be observed. (1) The New Testament writers sometimes quote Old Testament expressions as applicable to gospel facts or truths, without saying that they are prophecies (e. g., Rom 10: 18), and in some cases it is doubtful how they intend the quotation to be regarded. (2) It is often unnecessary, and sometimes impossible, to suppose that the prophet himself had in mind that which the New Testament writer calls a fulfillment of his prediction. Some predictions were even involuntary, as that of Caiaphas. (John 11: 50.) Many prophecies received fulfillments which the prophet does not appear to

[1] The word rendered in the Common English Version 'was done,' properly signifies to 'come to be,' 'come to pass,' 'happen,' etc., and this meaning is very important for the exact exposition of many passages in the New Testament. The student should look out for this word, and not be content to render it loosely.

[2] The peculiar idiom of the Greek makes it equally proper to render 'that it may,' or 'that it might,' according to the connection.

23 Behold, a virgin shall be with child, and shall bring forth a son, and they shall call his name Emmanuel, which being interpreted is, God with us.

23   Behold, the virgin shall be with child, and shall bring forth a son,
And they shall call his name [1] Immanuel;

---

1 Gr. *Emmanuel.*

---

have at all contemplated. But as God's providence often brought about the fulfillment though the human actors were heedless or even ignorant of the predictions they fulfilled (*e. g.*, John 19: 24), so God's Spirit often contemplated fulfillments of which the prophet had no conception, but which the Evangelist makes known. And it is of a piece with the general development of revelation that the later inspiration should explain the records of earlier inspiration, and that only after events have occurred should the early predictions of them be fully understood.

Some still insist that the phrase **that it might be fulfilled** should be rendered, or at any rate should be understood as denoting, 'so that it was fulfilled,' expressing only the *result;* but the best scholars are now very nearly unanimous in maintaining that we must hold fast, in this and all similar passages, to the established meaning of the phrase. The *design* expressed is often not merely, and in some cases not at all, that of the human agents, but the design of God in his providence. It is probably the failure to note this simple distinction—while it was clearly perceived that in some passages no such design as that stated can have been entertained by the actors themselves—that has led numerous earlier interpreters, including some of the Greek Fathers, to accept the sense of result; and the disposition to do so has doubtless been strengthened in some minds by dislike to the idea of divine predestination. Notice that the term which here precedes does not exactly signify 'was done' (which would direct our thoughts to the human actors), but, as above explained, 'has occurred,' 'has taken place,' *i. e.*, in the course of providence. (Comp. on 2: 17, and 6: 10).

23. The quotation is from Isa. 7: 14. Proposing to give Ahaz a sign of speedy deliverance from his enemies, Ephraim and Syria, the prophet speaks as here quoted, adding (Alexander's version): "Curds and honey shall he eat until he shall know (how) to reject the evil and choose the good; for before the child shall know (how) to reject the evil and choose the good, the land of whose two

kings thou art afraid shall be forsaken." A certain woman (to us unknown), then a virgin, would bear a son; and before he should arrive at the early age indicated, *i. e.*, in the course of a few years, Ahaz would be delivered from the dreaded kings of Syria and Israel by the coming of the Assyrians, who would lay those countries waste. Then Judah would prosper, and the growing child would have other food than merely curds and honey. It is not necessary to maintain that Isaiah himself saw anything further in the prediction. But as 'spoken by[1] the Lord, through the prophet,' we learn from Matthew that it also pointed forward to the birth from the more notable virgin, of one who should be not merely a pledge of divine deliverance, but himself the Deliverer; who should not simply give token by his name of God's presence to protect, but should himself be the present and manifest Deity. We need not suppose that Matthew would in argument with a Jew have appealed to this passage as by itself proving to the Jew that Jesus was the Messiah—for we have no information that the Jews understood it as a Messianic passage —but it is one of many predictions, some more and some less plain, which all combined would furnish conclusive proof. And we, who might never have perceived such a reference in the prophet's words, accept it on the authority of the Evangelist, and do so without difficulty, because we see how fully the prophetic books are pervaded by the Messianic idea. (Acts 10: 43.) 'To him all the prophets bear witness.' Some expositors of Isaiah (as Hengstenberg, Alexander) understand an *exclusive* reference to the birth of Jesus; but how could that possibly become a sign to Ahaz of his speedy deliverance from Syria and Ephraim? The Hebrew is, literally, " Behold, the maiden conceiving and bringing forth a son, and calling " etc. As the calling is future, it is natural to take the other participles as future also (Toy.) The last Hebrew verb

---

1 For the principal actor old English commonly said 'of' (same word as Latin *ab*, Greek *apo*); in modern English it is 'by.' The intermediary we now most clearly express by 'through.'

24 Then Joseph being raised from sleep did as the angel of the Lord had bidden him, and took unto him his wife:
25 And knew her not till she had brought forth her firstborn son: and he called his name JESUS.

24 which is, being interpreted, God with us. And Joseph arose from his sleep, and did as the angel of the Lord commanded him, and took unto him his
25 wife; and knew her not till she had brought forth a son: and he called his name JESUS.

---

might mean 'thou shalt call,' and so the Sept. has "Behold, the virgin shall conceive and bring forth a son, and thou shalt call," etc. Matthew has substantially the same as the Sept. (which he commonly follows, comp. on 3: 3,) only changing the last verb to 'they shall call,' *i. e.*, people shall call—he shall be so recognized. (Comp. Isa. 8: 3.) The Hebrew substantive signifies 'maiden.' No case has been found in which it *must* mean a married woman ; the only examples adduced by Gesenius and others (Prov. 30: 19; Cant. 6: 8) fail to prove the point. The Sept. here translates 'virgin,' Matthew confirms that by his authority, and all the efforts have failed to show that it is wrong.[1] **Immanuel.** One of the forms of the principal Hebrew word for God is *el ;* and *immanu* signifies 'with us.' While this was to be the actual name of the child born in the time of Ahaz, it was for Jesus not a name actually borne, but only a description of his character and position. Comp. the name Jedidiah, 'beloved of Jehovah,' which Nathan gave to Solomon at his birth (2 Sam. 12: 25), but which was not actually borne by him. Comp. also Isa. 60: 18; Ezek. 48: 35.

24. Joseph, believing and obedient, at once married his betrothed, with all the customary ceremonies, taking her to his house, where she would have his protection and tender care. They lived in Nazareth. (See on 2: 23.)

25. Till she brought forth her firstborn son. The Revised Version properly omits the phrase, 'her firstborn.'[2] Though not said here, it is said in Luke 2: 7, that he was 'her firstborn.' This phrase of Luke, and Matthew's 'till,' naturally suggest that Mary afterwards bore other children, but do not certainly prove it. The word 'till' is sometimes employed where the state of things does not change after the time indicated. Yet the examples adduced (the best are, perhaps, Ps. 112: 8; 110: 1; less apposite are Gen. 8: 7; Deut. 34: 6; 1 Sam. 15: 35; 2 Sam. 6: 23; Isa. 22: 14; 1 Tim. 4: 13) are none of them really similar to the one before us. The word will inevitably suggest that afterwards it was otherwise, unless there be something in the connection or the nature of the case to forbid such a conclusion. In like manner the dedication of the firstborn son (Exodus 13: 15) gave a sort of technical sense to the term 'firstborn,' which might cause it to be applied to an only child. Still, this would be very unnatural for Luke, writing long afterwards, and perfectly knowing that there was no other offspring, if such was the case. Combine these separate strong probabilities furnished by 'till' and 'firstborn' with the third expression 'brethren' or 'brothers' and even 'sisters' (see on 13: 55), and the result is a very strong argument to the effect that Mary bore other children. The Romanists hold marriage to be a less holy state than celibacy, and so they set aside all these expressions without hesitation. When some Protestants (as Alexander), on grounds of vague sentiment, object to the idea that Mary was really a wife, and repeat-

---

[1] This Hebrew word is *almah*. Another word, *bethulah,* generally means virgin, but in Joel 1: 8 is clearly applied to a young wife. If such an instance had been found for *almah*, it would have been claimed as triumphant proof that 'virgin' is not here a proper translation. The other Greek translations of Isaiah render by *neanis,* a young woman ; but it must be remembered that the Christians early began to use this passage against the Jews, and that of the three translators Aquila was a Jew, Theodotion a Jew or a heretic, Symmachus an Ebionite (Judaizer,) which makes their rendering suspicious. Buxtorf and Levy give no Aramaic (Chaldee) examples in which *almah* must mean a married woman. The result seems to be that *almah* does not certainly prove a virgin birth

but fully admits of that sense, which Matthew confirms.

[2] This is the reading of the two oldest (B and א), and several other important Greek MSS. (Z. 1, 33), and of the four oldest versions (old Latin, old Syriac, and the two Egyptian.) The additional words, 'her firstborn,' are obviously added from Luke 2: 7, where the text does not vary. We can see why many copies should have inserted them here, to make Matthew similar to Luke, and can see no reason why any copy should have omitted them here, when well known to exist in Luke. Observation shows that assimilation of parallel passages was almost always effected by insertion in the shorter, and the probable reason is that it would have been held irreverent by students and copyists to omit anything from the longer text.

CHAPTER II.

NOW when Jesus was born in Bethlehem of Judea in the days of Herod the king, behold, there came wise men from the east to Jerusalem,

1 Now when Jesus was born in Bethlehem of Judæa in the days of Herod the king, behold, 1 wise men

1 Gr. *Magi.*   Compare Esther 1: 13 ; Dan. 2: 13.

---

edly a mother, they ought to perceive that the Evangelists had no such feeling, or they would certainly have avoided using so many expressions which naturally suggest the contrary.

It was inevitable that Jesus should be commonly regarded as the son of Joseph (13: 55; John 1: 46), for the divine communications to Joseph and Mary could not at present be made known. Accordingly even Mary says, 'thy father and I,' and even Luke 'his parents'. (Luke 2: 41, 43, 48.)

HOMILETICAL AND PRACTICAL.

V. 18 f. The most ' highly-favored ' of all women has to bear for a time the deepest reproach a woman can suffer. (Edersh.: "The first sharp pang of the sword which was to pierce her soul.") But it proves only a step in the progress to everlasting honor.—V. 19 f. *Divine guidance in perplexity.* (1) A perplexity here of the most cruelly painful sort. (2) The perplexed man is unselfishly anxious to do right. (3) He takes time and reflects. (4) The Lord directs him. Personal righteousness and prayerful reflection will often carry us through; and the result may be the highest joy. JER. TAYLOR: "In all our doubts we shall have a resolution from heaven, or some of its ministers, if we have recourse thither for a guide, and be not hasty in our discourses, or inconsiderate in our purposes, or rash in judgment." —V. 20. *Jesus and the Holy Spirit.* (1) His humanity due to the Holy Spirit. (2) His whole life controlled by the Holy Spirit (4: 1; 12: 28; John 3: 34; Heb. 9: 14). (3) His mission vindicated and commended by the Holy Spirit. (1 Tim. 3: 16; John 16: 8-11.) (4) His work continued by the Holy Spirit (John 14: 16; 16: 13; Acts 16: 7; 'the Spirit of Christ,' Rom. 8: 9.)—V. 21. The three Joshuas.—*Our Saviour.* I. What he is. (1) God with us. (2) Born of a woman. (3) Thus the God-man. II. What he does. (1) *He* will save. (2) He will save *his people.* (3) He will save his people *from their sins.*—The gospel not merely gives us religious instruction, but makes known a personal Saviour. Its power does not reside in propositions, but in a person.—V. 22. Providence fulfilling prophecy.—V. 21-23. NICOLL: " Jesus Christ was, (1) The child of the Holy Ghost, who had existed from eternity, and now entered into the sphere of sense and time; (2) Born into the world with a distinct mission —his name was called Jesus, because he was to save."—V. 23. Mary. (1) The Mary of prophecy. (2) The Mary of history. (3) The Mary of modern fancy. See Milton's "Hymn on the Nativity," and Mrs. Browning's noble poem, "The Virgin Mary to the Child Jesus." LORIMER: "Such a mother must have exerted a marked influence on the character of her child. To question it would be to question the reality of his humanity."

The Incarnation, as to its nature, is of necessity unfathomably mysterious; but as a fact, it is unspeakably glorious, and, with the Atonement and Intercession, it furnishes a divinely simple and beautifnl solution of the otherwise insoluble problem of human salvation. Many things the world accepts and uses as vitally important facts, concerning the nature of which there may yet be questions it is impossible to answer.

Ch. 2: 1-12. THE VISIT OF THE MAGI.

Having spoken of the birth of Jesus (comp. on 1: 18,) the Evangelist now adds (ch. 2) two incidents of his infancy, viz., the visit of the Magi (v. 1-12), and closely connected therewith the flight into Egypt and return. (v. 13-23) The first tends to show that Jesus was the Messiah, and to honor him, in bringing out the signal respect paid him by distinguished Gentiles, (as often predicted of the Messiah, *e. g.*, Isa. 60: 3,) and in stating the appearance of a star in connection with his birth ; the second incident exhibits God's special care of the child. Both are connected with extraordinary divine communications (v. 12, 13, 19), designed for his protection, and with the fulfillment of prophecies concerning the Messiah, such as the birth at Bethlehem (5), the calling out of Egypt (15), the disconsolate mourners (18), and the residence at Nazareth (23). Comparing this section with Luke, ch. 2, we see that Matthew records such incidents of the infancy as furnish proofs that Jesus is the Messiah—to prove which is a special aim of his Gospel. One of these proofs, to a Jew, was the homage of Gentiles; while Luke, writing more for Gentiles, who knew that the majority of the Jews had rejected Jesus as their Messiah, mentions the recognition of the child by the conspicuously devout Jews, Simeon and Hannah.

1. The narrative goes right on. The preceding sentence ended with the name Jesus, and this begins: **Now when Jesus was born**, etc. Literally, *the Jesus*, the one just mentioned; 'this Jesus' would be too strong a rendering, but it may help to show the close connection.

Bethlehem is a very ancient but always small village, prettily situated on a hill about five miles south of Jerusalem. Its original name was Ephrath or Ephratah (Gen. 35:16, 19; 48:7), probably applied to the surrounding country, as well as to the town. The Israelites named it Beth-lehem, 'house of bread,' or, as we should say, 'bread-town,' which the Arabs retain as Beit-lahm. This name was doubtless given because of the fruitfulness of its fields, which is still remarkable. It was called Bethlehem Ephratah, or Bethlehem Judah, to distinguish it from another Bethlehem not far from Nazareth in the portion of Zabulon. (Josh. 19:15.) **Judea** here must consequently be understood, not as denoting the whole country of the Jews, Palestine, but in a narrower sense, Judea as distinguished from Galilee (see on 2:22). A beautiful picture of life at Bethlehem is found in the Book of Ruth. It was the birthplace of David, but he did nothing to increase its importance; nor did the 'Son of David,' who was born there, ever visit it, so far as we know, during his public ministry, which appears not to have extended south of Jerusalem. In like manner the present population is only about 4,000, some of whom cultivate the surrounding hills and beautiful deep valleys, while many make their living by manufacturing trinkets to sell to pilgrims and travelers. In itself, Bethlehem was from first to last "little to be among the thousands of Judah" (Micah, Rev. Ver.); yet in moral importance it was "in no wise least" among them (Matt., Rev. Ver.), for from it came forth the Messiah. The tradi-

tional localities of particular sacred events which are now pointed out there, are all more or less doubtful; but the general locality is beyond question that near to which Jacob buried his Rachel, where Ruth gleaned in the rich wheat fields, and David showed his youthful valor in protecting his flock, and where valley and hill-side shone with celestial light and echoed the angels' song when the Saviour was born.

Matthew here first mentions a place. He does not refer to a previous residence of Joseph and Mary at Nazareth (Luke 1:26, 27), but certainly does not in the least exclude it; and in fact his way of introducing Bethlehem seems very readily to leave room for what we learn elsewhere, viz., that the events he has already narrated (1:18-25) did not occur at that place.

Herod the king would be well known, by this simple description, to Matthew's first readers, who knew that the other royal Herods (Antipas and Agrippa) belonged to a later period. (Luke also, 1:5, places the birth of Jesus in his reign.) The Maccabean or Hasmonean[1] line of rulers, who had made the second century B. C., one of the most glorious periods in the national history, had rapidly degenerated, and after the virtual conquest of Judea by the Romans (B. C., 63), an Idumean named Antipater attained, by Roman favor, a gradually increasing power in the State, and his son Herod was at length (B. C., 40) declared, by the Senate at Rome, to be king of the Jews. Aided by the Roman arms, Herod overcame the opposition of the people, and in B. C. 37, established his authority, which he sought to render less unpopular by marrying the beautiful Mariamne, the heiress of the Maccabean line. Adroit and of pleasing address, Herod was a favorite successively of Antony and Augustus, and even the fascinating Cleopatra was unable to circumvent him. Amid the confusion of the Roman civil wars, he appears to have dreamed of founding a new Eastern empire; and possibly with this view he made costly presents to all the leading cities of Greece, and secured the appointment of President of the Olympic Games. Meantime he strove to please his

[1] They were called Maccabean from Judas Maccabeus, and Hasmonean or Asamonean from Chasmon, one of his ancestors.

own people, while also gratifying his personal tastes, by erecting many splendid buildings in various cities of his dominions; among others rebuilding the Temple in a style of unrivaled magnificence. That he could command means for such lavish expense at home and abroad, at the same time courting popularity by various remissions of taxes, shows that his subjects were numerous and wealthy, and his administration vigorous. But besides being a usurper,—not of the Davidic nor of the Maccabean line—supported by the hated Romans, and a favorer of foreign ideas and customs, and even of idolatry, he was extremely arbitrary and cruel, especially in his declining years. Mariamne herself, whom he loved with mad fondness, and several of his sons, with many other persons, fell victims to his jealousy and suspicion. Bitterly hated by the great mass of the Jews, and afraid to trust even his own family, the unhappy old tyrant was constantly on the watch for attempts to destroy him, or to dispose of the succession otherwise than he wished. These facts strikingly accord with the perturbation at hearing of one 'born king of the Jews,' and the hypocrisy, cunning, and cruelty, which appear in connection with the visit of the Magi. (See on v. 20, 22, and read the copious history of Herod in Josephus, "Antiquities [Ancient History] of the Jews," Book XIV.- XVIII., a history which throws much light on the New Testament times.)

The **wise men,** or *Magi* (see margin Rev. Ver.), were originally the priestly tribe or caste among the Medes, and afterwards the Medo-Persians, being the recognized teachers of religion and of science.[1] In the great Persian Empire they wielded the highest influence and power. As to science, they cultivated astronomy, especially in the form of astrology, with medicine, and every form of divination and incantation. Their name gradually came to be applied to persons of similar position and pursuits in other nations, especially to diviners, enchanters. It is used in the Greek translation of Dan. 1: 20; 2: 27; 5: 7, 11, 15, to render a word signifying 'diviner,' etc. So in the New Testament it is employed to describe Barjesus (Acts 13: 6, 8, translated 'sorcerer'), and words derived from it applied to Simon at Samaria (Acts 8 : 9, 11, 'sorceries'), who is commonly spoken of as Simon Magus (comp. also Wisdom 17: 7); and from it come our words *magic, magician,* etc. It is however probable that these magi from the East were not mere ordinary astrologers or diviners, but belonged to the old Persian class, many members of which still maintained a high position and an elevated character. (Comp. Upham.) So it is likely, but of course not certain, that they came from Persia or from Babylonia;[2] in the latter region Jews were now very numerous and influential, and in Persia also they had been regarded with special interest, as far back as the time of Cyrus. However this may be, the visit and homage of 'magi from the East' would be esteemed by the Jews, and was in fact, a most impressive tribute to the infant Messiah. The tradition that they were *kings,* found as early as Tertullian, doubtless grew out of the supposed prophecy that kings should do homage to Messiah (Psa. 68: 29, 31; 72: 10);[3] and the traditional

---

[1] The word is clearly Indo-European. The Old Persian (Zend) language has a root *maga* = greatness, evidently the same root as Latin mag-nus, Sanskrit mah-at, Greek meg-a(l)s, Gothic mik-ils, Scotch mick-le, muck-le. English much. As in Latin mag-ister is 'superior,' and hence 'instructor' (which we borrow as master, school-master), so from mag-a came mag-avash (found in the Zend Avesta), or contracted mag-ush (found in the cuneiform inscriptions), which in Syriac appears as megush, and in Greek took the form of magos; just as Korush was written Kuros, Cyrus. (Comp. Curtius Gr. Etym., Haug in Upham, Keil, Rawlinson.) Similarly the Hebrew rab, rabbi, rabboni, signifies superior, and hence teacher. It is still a question whether Rab-*mag* (Jer. 39: 3, 13) is connected with magos (see Gesen.); if so, it would combine the Shemitic with the Indo-European term for 'great one,' or it might mean the 'ruling magus.' The use of magos in the Greek of Daniel does not at all show that this word was employed among the Babylonians themselves. The argument of Zöckler (Herzog, ed. 2) that the magi existed among the early Accadians of Babylonia, is far from conclusive.

[2] 'East' is in the Greek here plural, 'eastern regions'; but it does not differ substantially (Upham wrong) from the singular (see 8: 11; 24: 27; Luke 13: 29.)

[3] Matthew can hardly have regarded their coming as the fulfillment of any *particular* prophecy, or according to his custom he would have been apt to mention it. Weiss: "The critics who maintain that he modified facts and perverted predictions in order to find varied fulfillment of Messianic prophecy, ought to account for this neglect of such notable passages as those just quoted from the Psalms."

2 Saying, Where is he that is born King of the Jews? for we have seen his star in the east, and are come to worship him.

2 from the east came to Jerusalem, saying, [1] Where is he that is born King of the Jews? for we saw his

1 Or, *Where is the King of the Jews that is born?*

number three was apparently drawn from the number of their gifts. These, with the traditional names, are of no authority, and of no consequence except as connected with modern Christian art.—**Wise men from the East.** The Greek is ambiguous, but more probably means this than "wise men came from the East." **To Jerusalem,** the capital of the country, these strangers would naturally come, as there they could most readily obtain information concerning the new-born king. (As to Jerusalem, see on 21: 10.)

2. His star. Two non-supernatural explanations have been offered. (1) One was first suggested by the astronomer Kepler (d. 1630), and is well presented by Alford (last ed.). In the year 747 of Rome there were three different conjunctions (in the constellation Pisces) of the planets Jupiter and Saturn, in May, October, and November. The astrology-loving Magi may have somehow connected this conjunction with the birth of a Jewish king; even as the Jewish writer, Abarbanel (A. D. 1453), thought the Messiah was at hand in his day because there had been a conjunction of Jupiter and Saturn in Pisces, a conjunction of which planets tradition represented as associated with the birth of Moses. It is supposed that after the May conjunction the Magi set out, and in Jerusalem saw the October or November conjunction, either of which at certain hours would have been in the direction of Bethlehem. But the Greek word is *aster*, 'star,' and not *astron*, which is used for a group of stars. The two planets cannot have "appeared as one star," for a recent English astronomer shows (Smith's "Dict.") that they were never nearer each other than one degree, which is about double the apparent diameter of the moon. Some hold that 'star' must here be taken in a general sense, denoting a group; but the distinction between the two Greek words is uniformly observed. It is also objected to this theory that other data for the time of Christ's birth would place it at least two years later than A. U. C., 747, though the conclusion from those data is not certain. Edersh. rather favors this theory, and adduces for the first

time a passage from a minor Midrash about the Messiah, to the effect that two years before his coming "the star shall shine forth in the east, and this is the star of the Messiah." But these minor Rabbinical treatises are of uncertain date, and there would be much room for suspecting that the statement in question was imitated from Matthew. (2) Some "variable stars" (see any recent work on astronomy) vary so widely as at times to become invisible and afterwards re-appear; and it has been supposed (Lutteroth) that such a disappearing and re-appearing star was seen by the Magi.—Either of these theories is in itself possible, and a reasonable natural explanation would obviously be better than the unnecessary introduction of the miraculous. But it is extremely difficult to reconcile these theories with the language of v. 9, 'the star ... went before them, till it came and stood over where the young child was.' If a heavenly body be considered as moving forward in advance of them from Jerusalem, it would be equally in advance when they arrived at Bethlehem, and in no sense standing over that place. Taking Matthew's language according to its obvious import, we have to set aside the above explanations, and to regard the appearance as miraculous; conjecture as to its nature will then be to no profit. The supernatural is easily admitted here, since there were so many miracles connected with the Saviour's birth, and the visit of the Magi was an event of great moral significance, fit to be the occasion of a miracle.

Why did they call it **his** star? Upon theory (1) we should suppose some astrological ground, as above intimated. Otherwise we are unable to explain. Some hypothetically connect it with Balaam's prophecy of a star out of Jacob (Num. 24: 17), which all the Targums refer to Messiah (Wünsche), and which on this hypothesis is supposed to have led to an eastern tradition. Others connect it with the fact attested, towards a century later than the visit of the Magi, by Josephus, Suetonius, and Tacitus, that it had long been believed throughout the East that persons sprung from Judea would gain supreme

3 When Herod the king had heard *these things*, he was troubled, and all Jerusalem with him.

4 And when he had gathered all the chief priests and scribes of the people together, he demanded of them where Christ should be born.

3 star in the east, and are come to ¹ worship him. And when Herod the king heard it, he was troubled, and

4 all Jerusalem with him. And gathering together all the chief priests and scribes of the people, he inquired of them where the Christ should be born.

---

¹ The Greek work denotes an act of reverence, whether paid to man (see ch. 18 : 26), or to God (see ch. 4 : 10).

---

power (Jos. "War," vi. 6, 4; Suet. "Vesp." 4; Tac. "Hist." v. 13); but there is in those writers nothing of a star,¹ and Suetonius and Tacitus appear to have merely borrowed from Josephus.

In the east might here mean 'at its rising'; but v. 9 leaves no doubt. **Worship.** But *do homage* is much more probably the correct rendering here (the Greek word meaning either), because there is no reason to believe that they regarded the new born king as in any sense divine, though they apparently expected his reign to influence other nations.

3. Herod was **troubled** at the idea of a rival (see on v. 1); and while many dependants of Herod would really share his feelings, being interested in the permanence of his government, all the people would be disturbed at the same time, through fear of new tyrannies and cruelties as the effect of his jealous fears.

4. As the question to be asked was a religious-political one, the king assembled all the leading students of the law to answer it. **The chief priests and scribes** might mean the Sanhedrin, as in 20: 18, the elders being here omitted, as in 27: 1 the scribes are omitted. But the word **all,** with the additional phrase **of the people,** makes it more natural to understand a general assemblage of teachers, including many scribes who did not belong to the Sanhedrin. This would accord with the idea of great uneasiness on his part; comp. the similar course of Nebuchadnezzar and Belshazzar. (Dan. 2: 2; 5: 7.) The 'chief priests' comprised the high priest at the time, any persons who had previously occupied that office (as Herod and the Romans made frequent changes), and probably also the heads of the twenty-four courses of priests (Luke 1: 8), for the language of Josephus ("Ant." xx. 8, 8; "War," iv. 3, 9) implies that the number of 'high priests' was considerable. The term 'scribes' (in the Old Testament meaning military sec-

retaries) had now for several centuries denoted those who supervised the copying of the Scriptures, which Jewish feeling required to be performed with the most scrupulous care. Their minute acquaintance with the text of Scripture would naturally lead to their being consulted as to its meaning; and in the time of our Lord they were by common consent regarded as authorized expounders of the law (hence called 'lawyers,' 22: 35), and besides answering the inquiries of individuals as to questions of truth and duty, many of them gave public instruction on such subjects, (hence called 'doctors—or *teachers*—of the law,' Luke 5: 17), particularly at the schools in the temple courts. Their instructions and practical decisions were at this time seldom the result of their own thinking, but consisted of sayings handed down from earlier teachers, or traditional decisions of tribunals in former times. (Comp. on 7: 29.) Those scribes who acted as teachers were among the persons called Rabbi. Altogether, they possessed very great influence and distinction, and some of their number were united with the 'chief priests' and the 'elders' to form the Sanhedrin (see on 26: 57, 59). Filled with ambition and vanity, they exposed themselves to the severe censure of our Lord, who gives a vivid picture of them in Luke 20: 46. Some of the scribes were Sadducees, but most of them Pharisees; and hence we frequently find the 'scribes and Pharisees' mentioned together, since the policy and the special faults which characterized the scribes extended also to all the rest of the great Pharisaic party.

Christ, literally, *the Christ*. The article should by all means be retained in the English. It is proper to use in translation the Greek word 'Christ'; but we may often see more clearly how such expressions presented themselves to the original Jewish hearers, by substituting 'the Messiah.' (Try this, *e. g.*, in

---

¹ The *position of autou*, 'his,' does not necessarily show emphasis, the star that signifies him and no other (Meyer, Weiss), for these genitive pronouns are often put before their noun, without emphasis, where

some strong word precedes on which they may lean —the matter being regulated by mere taste as to the harmonious succession of words. (See Winer, p. 155 [193].)

5 And they said unto him, In Bethlehem of Judea: for thus it is written by the prophet,
6 And thou Bethlehem, *in* the land of Juda, art not the least among the princes of Juda: for out of thee shall come a Governor, that shall rule my people Israel.
7 Then Herod, when he had privily called the wise men, inquired of them diligently what time the star appeared.

5 And they said unto him, In Bethlehem of Judæa: for thus it is written through the prophet,
6 And thou Bethlehem, land of Judah, Art in no wise least among the princes of Judah: For out of thee shall come forth a governor, Who shall be shepherd of my people Israel.
7 Then Herod privily called the [1] wise men, and learned of them carefully [2] what time the star ap-

---

1 Gr. *magi*........2 Or, *the time of the star that appeared.*

22: 42; 24: 5, 23; Mark 12: 35; Luke 24: 26, 46; John 7: 27, 31, 41, 42; Acts 17: 3; 18: 28.) As to the meaning of 'Christ,' see on 1: 1. **Should be born,** viz., according to the prophets, or any other means of knowing; where is the appointed or expected place of Messiah's birth. [1]

5, 6. They could answer without hesitation, in Bethlehem of Judea, **for thus** (to this effect, viz., that the Messiah is to be born there) **it is written** (has been written, and stands now written, is on record) **by** (properly *through*, see on 1: 22) **the prophet,** viz., Micah 5: 2. The application of this prediction to the birth of the Messiah at Bethlehem is obvious and generally admitted, and was familiar in the time of our Lord (Lightfoot, Wetstein, Wünsche, Edersh.) It is here quoted with some changes of phraseology which may be readily explained. Micah, as is often done in poetry, uses an *antique* name—Bethlehem Ephratah (Gen 48: 7; see on v. 1); Matthew takes the common Old Testament form, Bethlehem-Judah (Ruth 1: 1, etc.), though not the purely Greek form Judea, as in v. 1, 5; and prefixes 'land,' as when we say, 'Richmond, State of Virginia' (Alexander). Micah says, 'Thou art little to be among the thousands of Judah, (yet) out of thee,' etc., (Rev. Ver.), meaning that it is a small and insignificant place (see on v. 1), scarcely worthy to be numbered among the towns of Judah—yet out of it would come, etc.; while Matthew's mind turns towards the moral importance of Bethlehem as derived from this very fact, and so he puts it, 'art in no wise the least among the leaders of Judah, for out of thee,' Rev. Ver. 'Thousands' was an antique designation of the great families into which the tribes were subdivided

(Judg. 6: 15, margin; 1 Sam. 10: 19; 23: 23), and was applied by Micah to a town as the residence of such a family; while Matthew uses the more familiar term, 'governors' or 'princes,' meaning those who by birth stood at the head of the great families, and might therefore represent them or their abode. (Or Matthew's Hebrew text may, perhaps, have had a slightly different word which signifies 'leaders.') **Shall rule.** This is a general term used by Micah, but Matthew uses the specific word *shepherd, who shall shepherd my people,* which includes both governing, protecting, and feeding—a form of expression applied to kings, both in Scripture and the classics, and repeatedly used in Messianic prophecies. [2] The other slight differences require no explanation. It thus appears that the changes in phraseology which Matthew here makes in quoting do not introduce any idea foreign to the original, but bring out more plainly its actual meaning; and the same thing is true in many other New Testament quotations from the Old Testament. It was common among the Jews of that age to interpret in quoting (see Edersh., ch. 8). We see from John 7: 42 that the Jews understood this passage of Micah as Messianic; and in like manner the Targum (Toy) puts it, "Out of thee shall come forth before me the Messiah."

7 f. Then is a favorite word of transition with Matthew (2:16; 3:13; 4:1, etc.) **Privily,** or *privately.* In public, Herod doubtless affected unconcern; besides, if his inquiries should become known, the parties affected might take the alarm and escape. **What time the star appeared.** This would give some indication as to the age of the child. He therefore **inquired diligently,** or, *learned carefully,* Rev. Ver.—sought exact (or accurate)

---

[1] It is not likely that Matthew intended anything more than variety in using two words for 'born,' v. 1, 4, and v. 2.

[2] The English verb 'to shepherd' is much wanted here and in various other passages (*e. g.,* John 21: 16; Acts 20: 28; 1 Peter 5: 2; Rev. 7: 17). It is given as a

word of 'rare' use by Webster and Worcester, and is employed here by Darby and by Davidson. Though not so familiar as to suit a popular version, it may, perhaps, be allowable as a strict rendering. Rev. Ver., 'which shall be shepherd of my people.'

8 And he sent them to Bethlehem, and said, Go and search diligently for the young child; and when ye have found *him*, bring me word again, that I may come and worship him also.

9 When they had heard the king, they departed; and, lo, the star, which they saw in the east, went before them, till it came and stood over where the young child was.

10 When they saw the star, they rejoiced with exceeding great joy.

11 And when they were come into the house, they saw the young child with Mary his mother, and fell down, and worshipped him: and when they had opened their treasures, they presented unto him gifts; gold, and frankincense, and myrrh.

8 peared. And he sent them to Bethlehem, and said, Go and search out carefully concerning the young child; and when ye have found *him*, bring me word, 9 that I also may come and worship him. And they, having heard the king, went their way; and lo, the star, which they saw in the east, went before them, till it came and stood over where the young child 10 was. And when they saw the star, they rejoiced 11 with exceeding great joy. And they came into the house and saw the young child with Mary his mother; and they fell down and worshipped him; and opening their treasures they offered unto him

---

knowledge on that point. 'Diligently' in Com. Ver. was drawn from the Vulgate Latin. It is likely that when the Magi first came he had inquired why they believed the star to signify that a king of the Jews was born. And now, having learned the place and age, he takes steps to learn the person. **Go and search diligently,** or investigate accurately, the expression in v. 8 being fuller and stronger than in v. 7. He treats the matter as highly important, and he is a man who never leaves any stone unturned.

9, 10. The Magi were not well acquainted with Herod's character, and appear not to have suspected his real design; so they set about carrying out his directions. It has always been quite common in the East to travel at night. **And lo,** a phrase to call attention. The Greek word is used very often by Matt. (1: 20, 23; 2: 1, 9, 13, 19, etc.), and Luke, rarely by Mark or John. It was long ago that they saw the star in the East, and here it is again. **Went before them,** literally, *led them forward*, and the Greek has the imperfect, naturally suggesting that as they moved forward it moved also. (Comp. on v. 2). It appears to have indicated to them not merely the town —showing that the scribes were right—but the quarter of the town, if not the very house. (v. 11.) Notice the strong expression of v. 10, as to their joy.

11. The house, *i. e.*, the particular house in which he was, as referred to in v. 9, or perhaps the house over which the star stood. We are not to think here of the place in which the shepherds had found the child, on the morning after his birth. (Luke 2: 16.) It had in all probability been some time since

then: the presentation in the temple, forty days after the birth (Luke 2: 22; Lev. 12: 1-4), must have taken place before this visit which troubled all Jerusalem, and which was immediately followed by the flight into Egypt. There had possibly also been a journey to Nazareth (Luke 2: 39), and Joseph seems to have been now making Bethlehem his home. (Comp. on v. 23.)[1] To speak of a little child with his mother is so natural that no stress should be laid on the omission of Joseph, who is mentioned by Luke (2: 16) in describing the previous visits of the shepherds. Observe that it is **the child with Mary his mother.** (Comp. v. 13.) Our modern Romanists would have been sure to say, "the blessed Virgin with her child." **Fell down and worshipped,** or, *did homage.* See on v. 2.—**Presented.** *Offered*, as in all English Versions before King James, is the literal and common rendering, and more expressive of respect than "presented." The word rendered **treasures** here more probably means *treasure-chests*, or the like, *i. e.*, the vessels or packages containing the treasures. The refinements and spiritualizings of numerous ancient and modern expositors as to the number and significance of the gifts presented, are wholly unwarranted. It was, and still is, an Oriental custom and regarded as of great importance, that one must never visit a superior, especially a king, without some gift (comp. Gen. 43: 11; 1 Sam. 9: 7, 8; 1 Kings 10: 2; Psalm 72: 10); and nothing could be more appropriate, or was more customary, than gold and costly spices. **Frankincense** (English name from its giving forth its odor *freely*) is a glittering, bitter, and

---

[1] In here reading **they saw**, Com. Ver. rightly forsakes the *text* of both Stephens and Beza (who read 'found,' comp. Luke 2: 16), being guided by Stephens' statement of authorities and Beza's note. It shows the same unusual independence in 10: 10 'staves'—though wrongly there—and in a few passages of other books. (See Westcott and Abbott in Smith's Dict., *Am. ed.*, p. 2132 note).

12 And being warned of God in a dream that they should not return to Herod, they departed into their own country another way.

12 gifts, gold and frankincense and myrrh. And being warned *of God* in a dream that they should not return to Herod, they departed into their own country another way.

odorous gum, obtained by incisions into the bark of a peculiar tree. The ancients procured it chiefly from Arabia, the moderns bring it from the East Indies. **Myrrh** is the gum familiar to us, which exudes from a tree found in Arabia and Abyssinia. It was much valued by the ancients as a perfume (Psa. 45: 8; Song of Sol. 3: 6), also as a spice, a medicine, and a means of embalming. (John 19: 39).

12. Warned of God, or, *divinely instructed.* The Greek word denotes the reception of a response or communication, as from an oracle, and in the Scriptures from God, though the name of God is not mentioned. It commonly, but not necessarily, implies a previous prayer or application for direction, which may or may not have been made in this case. **In a dream.** See on 1: 20.—**Departed,** more exactly, *retired, withdrew,* as in v. 13, 14, 22. Thus the execution of Herod's deep-laid plan was delayed, and he was prevented from knowing precisely what child his jealousy should strike; while the well-meaning Magi escaped all complication with his further schemes. Their route of return may have been towards the northern end of the Dead Sea—as travelers now frequently go, leaving Jerusalem some miles to the left —or around its southern end, which would carry them far away from Herod in a few hours.

HOMILETICAL AND PRACTICAL.

1. These Magi from the East will, like the Queen of the South and the men of Nineveh (12: 41, 42), rise up in the judgment and condemn all who have had clearer light concerning the Messiah than they had, and have rejected him. 2. The 'King of the Jews' was destined to become also King of the Gentiles (Psa. 2: 6, 8), King of the world (Rev. 11: 15). 3. There were those that did not want the existing situation disturbed, even to introduce the Messianic reign. The most beneficent and indispensable changes will be opposed, and often by well-meaning people. 4. Herod inquires the teachings of Scripture only that he may work against them. By political craft and might he will make even divine predictions serve his own selfish purpose. Often now do political tricksters appeal to religious teachers to promote mere secular ends, and sometimes even at the expense of religion. 5. 'It is written.' Not only have revelations been made to men in the past, but many of them *stand on record,* "a possession forever." LUTHER: "Never mind the scribes; what saith the Scripture?" The scribes should be a warning to all religious teachers, in the pulpit, the Sunday-school, the family; they told others where to find the Saviour, but did not go to him themselves. AUGUSTINE: "They were like mile-stones; they pointed out something to travelers, but themselves remained stolid and motionless." 6. That which is materially 'little' may be morally 'by no means least.' An insignificant spot has often been the scene of events possessing the greatest importance and the highest moral grandeur. So with our little earth as the scene of redemption. 7, 8. More secret than diplomacy, deeper than the investigations of the wise, and mightier than all kingly power, is the providence of God.—'I also.' The hoary hypocrite! 9. God often overrules the errors of honest men, to lead them to truth. Astrology promoted the study of astronomy, alchemy produced the science of chemistry. The superstition of the Magi had part in their finding the Messiah. 11. The joy of beholding that which we have traveled far to find. HALL: "The east saw that which Bethlehem might have seen; ofttimes those which are nearest in place are furthest off in affection." LUTHER: "The star stood over the land of the Jews and over their heads, and they saw it not; so ever since as to the light of the gospel. The only monarch who ever deserved that man should fall down before him was a child of poverty, whose life was spent in teaching, and who died an ignominious death." Observe that they did homage to the child, not to his mother. Gifts were offered to an Oriental king, not as needed by him, but as the natural expression of reverence and love; so with our gifts to God. 12. The slightest touch of the supernatural may thwart the profoundest human sagacity. HALL: "Those sages made a happy voyage; for now they

13 And when they were departed, behold, the angel of the Lord appeareth to Joseph in a dream, saying, Arise, and take the young child and his mother, and flee into Egypt, and be thou there until I bring thee word: for Herod will seek the young child to destroy him.

14 When he arose, he took the young child and his mother by night, and departed into Egypt:

15 And was there until the death of Herod: that it

13   Now when they were departed, behold, an angel of the Lord appeareth to Joseph in a dream, saying, Arise, and take the young child and his mother, and flee into Egypt, and be thou there until I tell thee: for Herod will seek the young child to destroy him.

14 And he arose and took the young child and his

15 mother by night, and departed into Egypt; and was there until the death of Herod: that it might be fulfilled which was spoken by the Lord through

grew into further acquaintance with God.'' LUTHER : We see here how Christ has three kinds of disciples. 1. The priests and scribes, who know the Scripture and teach it to everybody, and do not come up to it themselves. 2. Herod, who believes the Scripture, that Christ is now born ; and yet goes right against it, trying to prevent what it says from being done. 3. The pious Magi, who left country and home, and made it their one concern to find Christ.

What a vast horizon opens with the beginning of the Gospels. The genealogies point back to Abraham and to Adam, and John's preface points back to eternity. The census, by order of Cæsar Augustus, reminds us of imperial Rome and all her history. The Magi, probably of Aryan descent, and full of the oldest Chaldæan learning, remind us of the hoary East. All the previous history of Western Asia and of Southern Europe stand in relation to this babe in Bethlehem. Moreover, 'the city of David,' and 'Messiah the Lord,' recall the long-cherished Messianic hope. And the angelic song treats this lowly birth as an occasion of praise in heaven and peace on earth.

13–18. THE FLIGHT INTO EGYPT.

13. Departed, withdrawn, same word as in v. 12, 14, 22. It is also employed in describing another rapid series of withdrawals, 14 : 13 ; 15 : 21.—**The**—rather *an*—**angel,** the Greek having here no article. **Appeareth in a dream,** see on 1 : 20.—**Take,** more exactly, *take along*, take with you, as in 26 : 37. —**Egypt** was at this time a well-governed Roman province, and beyond the jurisdiction of Herod. A journey of some seventy-five miles southwest, would bring Joseph to the border, towards the isthmus, and a hundred miles more would take him into the heart of the country. Besides being thus easy of access, and having in earlier days been a place of

refuge for fugitives from Judea (1 Kings 11 : 40; Jer. 43 : 7),1 Egypt was now thronged with Jewish residents. Alexander the Great, in laying out his new city of Alexandria, assigned a place to the Jews, granting them equal privileges with the Macedonians. The early Ptolemies pursued a similar course, transferring some from Palestine by force, and encouraging the immigration of others. In Egypt was made the greater part, probably the whole, of the famous translation of the Old Testament from Hebrew into Greek, commonly called the Septuagint. About 150 B. C., a separate temple was built for the Jews in Egypt, at once evincing and tending to increase their importance. Somewhat earlier began the succession of Jewish Alexandrine philosophers, the most remarkable of whom, Philo, was now twenty to thirty years old. In a treatise written about A. D. 40, he says the Jews in Egypt numbered near a million. These facts afford reasons for Joseph's being directed to flee into Egypt. At the same time all was providentially arranged with a view to the fulfillment of prophecy (v. 15). A late tradition names the village of Matarea, near Leontopolis, the site of the Jewish temple, as the residence of the "holy family." Late apocryphal writings have many marvelous stories of the flight and sojourn, and of the infancy of Jesus in general, which have passed freely into Christian art, but are otherwise unimportant. We may conjecture that the gifts of the Magi aided in the support of the refugees; a carpenter dwelling as a foreigner in a crowded country, was not likely at once to find adequate employment.

14. He arose at once, and set out **by night.** The child is named first, as the more important person, and the one endangered ; and the whole expression (here and in v. 13) reminds us that Joseph was not really his father.

15. That it might be fulfilled . . . . of

---

might be fulfilled which was spoken of the Lord by the prophet, saying, Out of Egypt have I called my son.
16 Then Herod, when he saw that he was mocked of the wise men, was exceeding wroth, and sent forth, and slew all the children that were in Bethlehem, and in all the coasts thereof, from two years old and under, according to the time which he had diligently inquired of the wise men.

the prophet, saying, Out of Egypt did I call my
16 son. Then Herod, when he saw that he was mocked of the [1] wise men, was exceeding wroth, and sent forth, and slew all the male children that were in Bethlehem, and in all the borders thereof, from two years old and under, according to the time which

---

1 Gr. *Magi.*

---

the Lord by. On 'of' and 'by,' see on 1: 22. **Have I called.** *Did I call*, is a literal translation of the Greek, and certainly better suits the statement of a remote event. The prediction quoted is from Hos. 11: 1. In form it follows the Hebrew exactly, while the Septuagint is here quite erroneous. Hosea clearly refers to the calling of Israel out of Egypt, the nation being elsewhere spoken of as God's 'son.' (Ex. 4: 22; Jer. 31: 9; comp. Wisdom 18: 13.) But there is an evident typical relation between Israel and Messiah. Thus in Isa., ch. 42 to 53, the 'servant of Jehovah' is primarily the nation, but the predictions have been more completely fulfilled in Christ, who embodied and consummated the mission of Israel. (See below, at the beginning of ch. 24, and comp. Edersh., ch. 5). In like manner here. As Israel in the childhood of the nation was called out of Egypt, so Jesus. We may even find resemblance in minute details; his temptation of forty days in the desert, resembles Israel's temptation of forty years in the desert, which itself corresponded to the forty days spent by the spies. (Num. 14: 34.) Thus we see how Hosea's historical statement concerning Israel may have been also a prediction concerning Messiah, as the Evangelist declares it was. It is not necessary to suppose that this was present to the prophet's consciousness. Exalted by inspiration, a prophet may well have said things having deeper meanings than he was distinctly aware of, and which only a later inspiration, coming when the occasion arose, could fully unfold.

16. Herod deemed that the Magi were trifling with him They got from him the information they needed, and then coolly went off without bringing back the information he required and expected. A despot easily comes to regard the slightest neglect to do his bidding as a gross insult. Already, no

doubt, designing to make way with the child, the king was now greatly incensed at this insulting neglect, and the delay it caused; and in the blind rage of a tyrant, he perpetrated an act which may seem to us not merely cruel but unnecessary, since his officers might easily have found out the child which the Magi had visited, and also ill-suited to his design, since in an indiscriminate massacre the child sought might escape. Such blind cruelty is, under all the circumstances, natural enough. And probably all this occurred within twenty-four hours, Bethlehem being only five miles off. The Magi went at nightfall, and being warned in a dream, departed during the night. As they did not return next day, Herod would send messengers to inquire, and these would report that the Magi were gone, and the child missing. Herod might conclude that the child was simply concealed in the village or its neighborhood, and so the cruel order, to be executed the same evening, would seem likely to accomplish its purpose.

All the children. Properly, *all the male children*, as in Rev. Ver., the original marking the gender.[1] **The borders.** The English word 'coasts' formerly signified borders in general; the border of the Mississippi River, for hundreds of miles from its mouth, is still called the 'coast.' The term 'borders' is often used for the territory they inclose, and here means the little district belonging to the town. **From two years old and under,** etc., does not prove, as some have inferred, that the star had appeared to the Magi two years before, or even one year. A child would be called two years old as soon as it entered the second year; and Herod would be apt to go a good way beyond the age indicated by the time of its appearance, in order to make sure.

Ecclesiastical tradition (making it fourteen

---

1 It is properly rendered in the Syriac and the Vulgate, in the Geneva and the Rheims, and by Beza. But Wyclif, through translating the Vulgate, has simply 'children,' and so Tyndale, and Cranmer, and also

Luther; and Common Version followed these. It must have been supposed that the masculine expression was meant to comprehend both sexes; but such a use can never be assumed unless the connection requires it.

17 Then was fulfilled that which was spoken by Jeremy the prophet, saying,
18 In Rama was there a voice heard, lamentation, and weeping, and great mourning, Rachel weeping *for* her children, and would not be comforted, because they are not.

17 he had carefully learned of the [1] wise men. Then was fulfilled that which was spoken through Jeremiah the prophet, saying,
18   A voice was heard in Ramah,
    Weeping and great mourning,
    Rachel weeping for her children :
    And she would not be comforted, because they are not.

---

[1] Gr. *Magi.*

---

thousand), and modern popular opinion have greatly exaggerated the number of children slain, which by any just calculation from the probable population of the little town and its district must have been very small, say fifteen, or twenty. We can thus see how little foundation there is for the objection taken by certain critics to the authenticity of this incident, on the ground that it is not mentioned by Josephus. Amid the numerous and aggravated cruelties which marked the closing period of Herod's life,[1] the massacre of a few children in an obscure village might have been easily overlooked by the historian. And when it is said that the connection of this massacre with a person supposed to be Messiah made it a prominent fact, we may reply that, supposing this connection known to Josephus (who was not born till some forty years afterwards), it would have made him all the more disposed to omit the incident, seeing that he has the impudence to represent the Messianic hopes of the nation as fulfilled in his patron, Vespasian. In like manner, when professing to state the teachings of John the Baptist, he makes no allusion to John's announcement of the coming of Messiah. (See on 3 : 2.)[2]

17, 18. Then was fulfilled. So in 27 : 9.

Everywhere else Matthew says, 'that it might be fulfilled.' In these two cases he probably felt an instinctive reluctance, in which we can sympathize, to associate directly the divine purpose with a deed of enormous wickedness. He says, in these instances, as in the others, that the event ' fulfilled' a prediction; but avoids saying, what is true in a just sense, but would seem to require explanation, that the event was providentially brought about for that purpose. **By**—or, *through*—following the correct text.[3] For the meaning of the preposition, comp. on 1 : 22. The quotation is from Jer. 31 : 15. The words **lamentation and** are here not genuine.[4]

This quotation presents serious difficulty. When Nebuchadnezzar ordered that the people should be carried into captivity, the persons selected were assembled, previous to setting out, at Ramah, which may have been Ramah in the tribe of Benjamin, about five miles north of Jerusalem (and ten miles from Bethlehem), or else some place of that name near Bethlehem (Thomson II., 28). This captivity seemed to threaten the complete destruction of the nation, with all their national hopes; and the bitter grief of the people is poetically described by representing Rachel, one of the mothers of the nation—the mother

---

[1] Besides the details given by Josephus, observe the following general statement ("Ant.," 17, 6, 1): "And despairing of surviving he grew utterly savage, acting with unrestrained anger and bitterness towards all; and the cause was his belief that he was despised, and that the nation took pleasure in his misfortunes."

[2] The Latin writer, Macrobius, an official under the Christian emperor Theodosius (5th century), among various witty sayings of the first Augustus, gives the following: "Hearing that among the boys under two years old, whom Herod, King of the Jews, ordered to be killed, his own son also was slain, Augustus said, "Better be Herod's pig than his son." (In Greek, which Augustus habitually spoke, " Better be Herod's *hyn* than his *hyion*.") The tradition associated with the jest, has obviously mingled the killing of Antipater, Herod's grown son, with the story of the children at Bethlehem. It is not at all likely that the two inci-

dents were originally connected by Augustus, who knew all about the death of Antipater and his brothers. The confusion is manifestly due to a later time, and the story of the boys under two years most probably came from Christian sources, though that question cannot be determined.

[3] Some students or copyists doubtless considered it an error of previous copyists, observing that 'the Lord' is not here mentioned, as in 1 : 22; 2 : 15, and commonly, and so altered it to 'by.' (A few MSS. have a similar change to 'by' in v. 23.) Similarly in 3 : 3.

[4] They were no doubt inserted by some, because found in the original of the prophet. Few forms of alteration in the New Testament text are more common than such assimilation of quotations to the Old Testament, it being erroneously taken for granted that the New Testament writers always quoted with verbal exactness.

19 But when Herod was dead, behold, an angel of the Lord appeareth in a dream to Joseph in Egypt,

19   But when Herod was dead, behold, an angel of the

of that tribe in whose territory the exiles were assembled—as risen from the grave, and bewailing their destruction; while the prophet comforts her with the assurance that there is hope for the future, for the people will be restored. Now, when this poetical passage is said by Matthew to be 'fulfilled' in the case of the massacre at Bethlehem, how are we to understand him? (1) If we are unable to see in the language of Jeremiah any distinct reference to this massacre, it will not follow that the Evangelist has merely made an apt quotation. He and his Jewish readers had the general conviction that everything in the history of their nation was sacred and significant. And wherever Matthew saw a resemblance between an event in the history of Israel and an event in the life of Messiah, he might consider that this resemblance was divinely designed, and wish his readers to take the same view. He may have used the word 'fulfill' in this sense, not intending to assert that there is here (as in most cases) a definite prediction, distinctly fulfilled, but only a discernible and noteworthy point in the general relation between the older sacred history and the new. Thus understood, the passage would leave the term 'fulfill' a real, though weakened sense, and we may, if necessay, regard it as similarly used in various other passages, while we must in every case inquire whether there is not a fulfillment in the complete sense of the word. (2) And may we not here trace some indications of a specific relation between the events? The massacre at Bethlehem, like the occurrence at Ramah, threatens to destroy the nation's future, which all really depends on Messiah. If the infant Messiah is slain, then is Israel ruined. Suppose only that some at Bethlehem, who had heard of the shepherds and the Magi, now despondingly believed that the new-born king was slain, and their mourning would really correspond to that mourning at Ramah, which Jeremiah poetically described. In both cases, too, the grief at actual distresses is *unnecessarily* embittered by this despair as to the future, for the youthful Messiah had not really perished, just as the captivity would not really destroy Israel. In both cases the would-be destroyer fails, and blessings are in store for the people of God. This view may seem fine-spun, and should not be too much insisted on, but it is possible. (Comp. Calvin, Fairbairn, Keil.) The poetical introduction of Rachel as representing the common grief of Israel, is only a subordinate and incidental thing, and we need not seek any special connection between Rachel personally and Herod's massacre, such as some have sought in the fact that she was buried near Bethlehem, though it would not be wholly unreasonable to regard that also as significant. The tomb of Rachel is still marked near the village, and quite probably at the real place.

19-23. JOSEPH RETURNS FROM EGYPT, AND MAKES HIS HOME AT NAZARETH.

The angel appears again, as he had promised. (v. 13.) The death of Herod (comp. on v. 1) occurred in the spring (just before the Passover) of the year of Rome 750. Josephus mentions an eclipse of the moon ("Ant.," 17, 6, 4) as taking place shortly before his death, and astronomical calculations enable us to fix the year with practical certainty. (Wieseler, Andrews, Caspari, Nicholson.) The birth of Jesus must have preceded Herod's death by several months, if not longer, and must therefore have occurred at least four years before the common Christian era, the first year of which coincides with the year of Rome 754.[1]

---

[1] Upon this nearly all scholars are now agreed, from other data as well as the death of Herod, and some suppose there is an error of as much as five or six years. Our era was determined in the sixth century. and it is not strange that an error should have been committed. The mode in which we count time, *Anno Domini*, 'in the year of our Lord.' cannot now be changed. We have simply to bear in mind that the birth of Christ actually occurred at least four years earlier than our era, and similarly as to his public ministry, and death. As he was, when he began his ministry, 'about thirty years of age' (Luke 3 : 23), this would make A. D. 26, perhaps in the autumn; and if his ministry lasted, as is probable, for three and a half years, his death occurred A. D. 30. Most books of history and tables of chronology still fail to give these dates correctly, probably from fear of confusing the popular mind. There can however be no danger of such confusion, if the simple facts, as just stated, receive the slightest attention.

20 Saying, Arise, and take the young child and his
mother, and go into the land of Israel: for they are
dead which sought the young child's life.

20 Lord appeareth in a dream to Joseph in Egypt, saying, Arise and take the young child and his mother,
and go into the land of Israel: for they are dead

The poor old tyrant died of a most loathsome
and torturing disease (see Jos. "Ant.," 17, 6,
5), in the seventieth year of his life, and the
thirty-seventh of his nominal, or thirty-
fourth of his actual reign. (Jos. "War," 1,
33, 8; "Ant.," 17, 8, 1.)

20. Take the child and go, not now 'flee,'
as before (v. 13). **They are dead.** The expression was probably suggested by Ex. 4:
19, 'For all are dead that sought thy life'
(Sept.), and so it takes a general form. There
are none now that seek the child's life—all
such are dead. This might be said (the expression being borrowed) without specific
reference to any death but that of Herod.
(So Bengel, Bleek, Keil.) It is also possible
to understand the plural as a mere general
statement of a particular fact, such as is common in all languages, and without any reference to Ex. 4: 19. (Meyer). The idea
(Euthym., Clark, Lutteroth) that Antipater
is included, who was slain a few days before
Herod's death, assumes that he had shared
his father's hostility to the child, an assumption unsupported and improbable. — To *seek
the life* of any one is a Hebrew idiom, Rom.
11: 3; Jer. 44: 30; Ex. 4: 19. **The land of
Israel** was said partly, perhaps, in contrast
to the heathen land in which they had been
sojourning, but also as a designation of the
whole country, the term 'Judea' being presently applied (v. 22) to a particular district.
'Land of Israel' is not elsewhere found in
the New Testament, but see 'cities of Israel'
in 10: 23. **But when he heard.** 'Notwithstanding,' in Com. Ver., is quite too strong for
the Greek connective.   **Judea,** always in
Matthew, Mark, and John, and sometimes
in Luke and Acts, means the southern district,
as distinguished from Galilee, Samaria, and
Perea. Elsewhere in Luke and Acts, and
always in the Epistles, it denotes the whole
country. In v. 22 the only fact of import-

ance to Joseph is that Archelaus reigns over
Judea, where he has intended to live; and
we need not suppose that 'Judea' here includes Samaria, which was also under Archelaus' dominion.[1] After many changes of his
will, Herod at the last moment divided his
dominions among three of his sons (Jos.
"Ant.," 18, 8–11). (1) Herod Antipas was
made Tetrarch of Galilee and Perea. (The
Greek word 'tetrarch' signified originally
the ruler of the fourth part of a province or
district, as in Galatia; but was applied by
the Romans in the time of our Lord to the
ruler of any considerable part of a province
or people.) He is the Herod who appears in
connection with John the Baptist and the
public ministry of our Lord (14: 1 ff). (2)
Herod Philip, Tetrarch of Iturea, Trachonitis,
and some adjacent districts, is not mentioned
in the Gospel history, except in Luke 3: 1.
It was another Herod Philip, one left in a
private station, that married their niece Herodias, and was forsaken by her for Antipas; the
daughter of this other Philip and Herodias was
Salome, the dancer, who subsequently married
Philip the Tetrarch. Among the ten wives and
numerous children of Herod the Great, the
same names frequently recur. Philip the Tetrarch is described by Josephus as a worthy
man, and a just ruler; apparently the best
man of the Herod family. Our Lord, towards
the close of his ministry in Galilee, repeatedly
retires from the dominions of the weak and
cunning Antipas to those of Philip (14: 13;
15: 29; 16: 13). (3) To Archelaus were given
Judea (with Idumea) and Samaria, making
at least one half of his father's kingdom, and
yielding twice as much revenue as both the
tetrarchies combined (Jos. "Ant.," 17, 11, 4).
Herod assigned him the title of 'king,' and
he was. saluted as such after his father's
death, and so regarded in Judea for a considerable period (Jos. "Ant.," 17, 8, 1f. and ch.

---

[1] The name 'Palestine' means land of the Philistines,
the form being a little changed in passing through the
Greek. (In Com. Ver. of Old Testament, 'Palestina'
and 'Philistia.') As the Philistines occupied the
maritime plain, the Greeks and Romans, first visiting
the towns near the coast, afterwards extended the
name of the coast to the adjacent region inland, as

they did in many other cases, and thus Palestine became a common name for the whole country, being so
used sometimes even by Philo and Josephus. Though
not found in New Testament, it has continued to rival
the name Judea to the present day. The redoubtable
Philistines still live in geography.

21 And he arose, and took the young child and his mother, and came into the land of Israel.

22 But when he heard that Archelaus did reign in Judea in the room of his father Herod, he was afraid to go thither: notwithstanding, being warned of God in a dream, he turned aside into the parts of Galilee:

23 And he came and dwelt in a city called Nazareth: that it might be fulfilled which was spoken by the prophets, He shall be called a Nazarene.

21 that sought the young child's life. And he arose and took the young child and his mother, and came

22 into the land of Israel. But when he heard that Archelaus was reigning over Judæa in the room of his father Herod, he was afraid to go thither; and being warned *of God* in a dream, he withdrew into

23 the parts of Galilee, and came and dwelt in a city called Nazareth: that it might be fulfilled which was spoken through the prophets, that he should be called a Nazarene.

9, 1-5), though the Emperor Augustus finally allowed him only the title of ethnarch (ruler of a nation or people, a rather more honorable title than tetrarch), with the promise to declare him king if he should deserve it. The expression **did reign,** or *was reigning,* i. e., was king, is thus minutely correct for the period immediately following Herod's death. It may, however, be understood as used loosely, just as 'king' is applied to any ruler, from the Roman Emperor (1 Peter 2: 13) to Herod Antipas the Tetrarch (14: 9; Mark 6: 14). So Josephus ("Life" § 1) says his own father was born "while Archelaus was reigning the tenth year." Joseph is surprised and disappointed at learning that Archelaus is appointed King of Judea, for it had been understood that Antipas was to succeed his father in the whole kingdom, and Herod made the change just before his death (Jos. "Ant.," 17, 6, 1; 8, 1; 9, 4).

On **warned** and **turned aside**, or *withdrew,* see on v. 12. **The parts of Galilee,** those parts of the country which were comprised in that district (comp. 16: 13; Acts 20: 2).

23. The town of Nazareth[1] is not mentioned in Old Testament, which is not surprising, as the Old Testament history rarely extends to any part of Galilee. Nor need we wonder that Josephus does not name it, as it was a small town remote from the principal roads, and did not fall in the way of any of the military operations which he describes. It was situated about fifty-five miles north of Jerusalem, in an elevated basin, such as is frequently found in Samaria and Galilee. This basin is about a mile long by less than half a mile wide, opening southward by a narrow and winding pass into the great plain of Esdrælon. Split a pear endwise and the lower half, with the crooked stem, will give the shape of the valley of Nazareth. The

encompassing slope is divided by depressions on its face into some seventeen distinct hills. On the western side of this elevated valley, and sloping a little way up the western hill, lies the modern town, and there is no reason to think the site has materially changed. Higher up the slope is a limestone cliff thirty or forty feet high, which (or one of the similar ones not far from it) may well have been the "brow of the hill whereon their city was built," from which the mob proposed to cast their rejected prophet (Luke 4: 29), a scene absurdly located by monkish tradition at a precipice two miles away, overlooking the plain of Esdraelon. The vale of Nazareth is green and very fertile, with many fruit trees and a fine fountain near the village, altogether presenting a beautiful scene; and from the high western hill is a view among the most extensive in Palestine, embracing Tabor and the great plain, Carmel and the blue Mediterranean, the mountain-wall east of the depressed Jordan valley, and on the north the far-off snowy summit of Hermon. Yet, as so often happens, the dwellers amid all these beauties of nature were rude, violent, and of evil repute. The question of Nathanael (John 1: 46, Rev. Ver.): 'Can there anything good come out of Nazareth?" is not sufficiently accounted for, as some have thought, by the contempt for Galilee in general which was felt by the people of Judea; for Nathanael himself lived at "Cana of Galilee" (John 21: 2), only a few miles distant. Nor can it be easily regarded as an unjust prejudice, for Nathanael was a man of singularly good character. (John 1: 47.) And so the unparalleled violence of the rabble (Luke 4: 28-30), and the persistent unbelief even on a second visit which excited the wonder of Jesus himself (Mark 6: 6), are not fully explained by the fact that he was a prophet "in his own country," but lead us to think of them as an intractable and disorderly people, deserving their bad reputation. But here lived the

---

[1] The original Aramaic form of the name was probably Nazara (see Keim).

righteous Joseph, and the meek, devout Mary ; and here "increased in wisdom and stature, and in favor with God and man" (Luke 2 : 52), the child, the boy, the youth, the man, who was in due time to come forth from this obscure village as the consolation of Israel, as the Saviour of the world.   Here he wrought (Mark 6 : 3) at the humble and laborious calling of his reputed father (see on 13 : 55); here he worshipped every Sabbath, with such worship as only the perfect could pay, in the synagogue from which he was afterwards to be rudely thrust forth ; and often, no doubt, he would climb this western hill as the sun was sinking in the Mediterranean, and look down with pure pleasure upon the beautiful valley, or far away over the magnificent prospect, and, as his human mind gradually unfolded to comprehend his mission, would think great thoughts of the kingdom that should fill the whole earth and should have no end. (See copious and pleasing descriptions in Renan and Geikie).

That he should be called, is as natural a translation of the Greek as **He shall be called,** and better suits the most probable interpretation of this passage.   The words, ' *He shall be called a Nazarene,*' are not found in the Old Testament.   The difficulty thus presented has been variously explained. (1) Chrys., Hanna, and some others, suppose a lost prophecy.   But this is a mere make-shift. The term 'the prophets' in New Testament, everywhere means the canonical prophets. (Meyer.)   Ewald's suggestion that it may be from an apocryphal book, is likewise a make-shift.   (2) Jerome, Calvin, and others, connect it with the law as to the Nazirites.   But Nazareth and Nazarene are almost certainly not derived from *nazir*, 'consecrated,' but from *netzer*, 'branch,' 'shoot,' as shown by the Syriac and the Rabbinical forms of the word Nazarene (Robinson, Evang. and Mishna); or else from some kindred word formed on the same root. (Grimm.)[1]   Moreover, Jesus was in no sense a Nazirite, being quite different, as he himself declares (11 : 18, 19), from John the Baptist.   Observe that Rev. Ver. in Num. 6 : 2; Judg. 13 : 5, etc., spells not Naza-

rite, but Nazirite, according to the Hebrew *nazir.*   (3) Fritzsche, Meyer, Bleek, Weiss, Edersh., and others, suppose a reference to Isa. 11: 1, where Messiah is called a 'branch,' Hebrew *netzer*.   An equivalent though different Hebrew word is applied to him in Jer. 23: 5; 33 : 15; Zech. 3 ; 8; 6: 12.   From the passage in Isaiah, reinforced by the others, it may have become common (Bleek supposes) to call the Messiah simply *netzer*, 'branch,' as is perhaps implied in Zech. 3 : 8.   So the prediction of the 'prophets' led to Messiah's being 'called' Netzer, and as a resident at Netzer or Natzara, Jesus was called Nazarene.   This is ingenious and may be true, though it seems far-fetched.   (4) Olshausen, Lange, Westcott (Int.), and others, understand it as referring to the various predictions (*e. g.*, Psa. 22; Isa. 53), that Messiah would be despised and reviled, as was done when he was 'called' a Nazarene.   Had he been called Jesus the Bethlehemite, it would have seemed honorable; but to be called Jesus the Nazarene, would at once awaken the contempt of the Jews, and would be a *prima facie* argument against his claims to be regarded as Messiah, the son of David; and we know that such an argument was once actually used. (John 7 : 41.)[2]   As thus understood, the passage is best translated as in Rev. Ver.   This seems, upon the whole, to be decidedly the best view.   The Mohammedans in Palestine, now commonly call Christians Nazarenes. (Thomson, II., 316.)   (5) Hengstenberg, Alexander, Ellicott, Keil, combine (3) and (4), understanding Isaiah 11: 1 to represent Messiah as "a shoot from the *prostrate* trunk or stem of Jesse, *i. e.*, as from the royal family of Judah in its humble and reduced estate." (Alex.).   But this mode of connecting the two theories appears artificial.   It is better to be content with one or the other, as either of them is quite possibly correct.   (6) Lutteroth has a new explanation : Joseph saw that a life in Bethlehem would be perilous for the child, and in order that he might live, and the prophecies concerning him as Messiah might be fulfilled, Joseph took him to dwell in Nazareth, 'because he would be called a Naza-

---

[1] McClellan begs the question, and actually translates, 'He shall be called a Nazarite.'

[2] It has been remarked that Plutarch frequently quotes Plato as saying something which cannot be found in Plato's works in so many words, but is substantially contained in various passages.   Indeed the same thing is done by many writers, and is perfectly natural.

rene,' and not a Bethlehemite, and thus would be less likely to incur hostility than if known to be from the city of David. This is quite ingenious, but strained and improbable. The translation, "because he would be called," is possible.

The plural, **by,** *through,* **the prophets,** is favorable to (4). Yet in (3) it is possible to suppose reference also to the other prophets (besides Isa. 11: 1), in which another but equivalent Hebrew word is employed. And the plural *might* be used with especial reference to a single prediction, as in John 6: 45; Acts 13: 40; 15: 15, though this is unusual, and never found in Matthew. (Comp. 26: 56.) **That it might be fulfilled,** as in 1: 22, the providential purpose.

On comparing the two first chapters of Matthew and of Luke, there appears to be some conflict as to the order of events. Not in the fact that Matthew makes no mention of the previous residence at Nazareth, which was simply not necessary to his own chief object of showing that Jesus was the Messiah. But Luke (2: 39), makes the return to Nazareth follow the presentation in the temple, thus apparently leaving no room for the visit of the Magi and the flight into Egypt. The presentation, it is true, might possibly have followed the visit of the Magi—the distance being only five miles—before Herod concluded that the Magi had mocked him. But this ill accords with the expressions of v. 13, 14, and the gifts of the Magi would, if previously received, have enabled the parents to present the regular offerings, without being restricted to those permitted to the poor. (Luke 2: 24; Lev. 12: 8.) Moreover, Luke would still seem to exclude the flight into Egypt. To meet this difficulty, some suppose that immediately after the presentation they returned to Nazareth (Luke), and having there made the necessary arrangements, removed to Bethlehem, intending to rear the child in the city of David, an intention still apparently retained by them on returning from Egypt. (v. 22.) But though tenable (adopted in Clark's Harmony), this supposition is less simple and natural than to understand that Luke, omitting all intermediate events, passes at once from the presentation in the temple to that return to Nazareth which Matthew also records. And if Luke seems to leave no room for any intervening occurrences, this arises from the necessity of the case in a brief narrative which, being compelled to omit much, must bring together events not immediately successive, and must do this without leaving a break at the point of omission, or else altogether destroy its own continuity, and become not a narrative but a mass of fragments. If Providence designed that there should be four independent Gospels, and each was to be a simple and readable story, apparent disagreements of this sort are inevitable. It follows that such cases cannot with propriety be understood as involving any real conflict. And we see that it is becoming to eschew the nervous harmonizing practiced by some, as well as the disposition of others to magnify discrepancies, and eagerly pronounce them irreconcilable.

HOMILETICAL AND PRACTICAL.

V. 13. God had promised that this child should save others (1: 21), yet now he must flee for his own life. So Paul at the shipwreck. (Acts 27: 22, 31.) The supernatural comes in only where natural powers would not suffice. The child is not preserved from Herod's designs by miracle, nor miraculously transported into Egypt, after the fashion of the legendary miracles, but there is simply a supernatural warning that he must be carried away. The revelation is not all given at once. BENGEL: "Joseph must quietly wait an uncertain time, 'till I bring thee word.'" JER. TAYLOR. "And so for all his sons by adoption, God will determine the time, and ease our pains and refresh our sorrows, and give quietness to our fears and deliverance from our troubles, and sanctify it all and give a crown at last, and all in his good time, if we but wait the coming of the angel, and in the meantime do our duty with care, and sustain our temporals with indifferency."

V. 14. HENRY: "Those that would make *sure* work of their obedience, must make *quick* work of it." V. 15. Israel and Messiah, both sojourning in Egypt—occasion in each case, and result. V. 16. Cruelty. (1) Fostered by the possession of despotic power. (2) Inflamed by fancied insult. (3) Recklessly smiting the innocent. (4) Blindly missing its object. V. 17, 18. The old, old story—the dead babe and the heart-stricken mother. 'And would not be comforted.' When we are willing to be comforted, divine comfort is not far away.

LUTHER represents the Magi in their own country as the first New Testament preachers, and the murdered innocents as the first martyrs.

V. 19 (and 13). If we wait and watch for the guidance which God has promised, it will come, and at the right time. V. 20. He that 'fled' in alarm (v. 13) now 'goes' in safety. Alas! for the human being whose death brings a feeling of relief to the innocent and the good. V. 22. Like father, like son.

V. 23. The truest greatness usually grows up in retirement, often in obscurity; and the greatest personage in history was not an exception to this rule. In our day of hot haste, and especially of youthful impatience to be at work, it is well to remember that he who knew his ministry could last but a few years, spent thirty years in the most quiet preparation.

THE YOUTH OF JESUS.

As to the Saviour's life, from the point now reached to his baptism (3: 13), we have no information in Matthew, and none in the other Gospels, save the interesting and instructive incident of Luke 2: 41-52. There we find him at the age of twelve, highly intelligent and trusted by his parents; devoted to the study of the Scriptures, showing a wonderful acquaintance with them (comp. Josephus, "Life," §2), and asking questions in the eager desire to know more; beginning to perceive that God is in some peculiar sense his 'Father,' and fond of attendance at his 'Father's house'; shrinking already from the sensation he produces, retiring into obscurity and subject to his parents; and *growing* in wisdom as he grows in stature (or age). It is a bright and inspiring glimpse, and perfectly harmonious with his character and life as a public teacher.

To meet the curiosity always felt as to his childhood and youth, a variety of marvelous stories were invented during the early centuries, which were recorded in apocryphal Gospels or passed into tradition. Though many of these are sanctioned by the Romish Church, they are often absurd, and sometimes blasphemous; and the recital of them would be to no profit, unless it were in the way of illustrating by contrast the simplicity, the reserve, the perfect good taste, of the inspired narrative.

The external conditions under which Jesus grew up, are known to us from general sources of information. His development must have been influenced by such outward circumstances as the following: (1) Home. (2) Nature (see as to Nazareth, on v. 23). His deep love of nature appears repeatedly in his public ministry. (3) The Scriptures. (4) The synagogue. (5) Labor; he was a worker in wood (Mark 6: 3), and it is stated in a very early tradition that he made "ploughs and yokes" (Justin Martyr, "Trypho," 88). It is not improbable that after Joseph's death (comp. below), the growing youth's labor aided in the support of that loved mother for whom he took pains to provide when he was about to die (John 19: 26, 27.) That he spent much time in reflection, and in prayerful communion with his Father, is naturally inferred from his course at a later period. (On this paragraph, comp. Keim and Edersheim).

Among the outward events of these twenty-eight or twenty-nine years, a few at least ought to be here recalled.

When Jesus was about ten years old, A. D. 6, such serious complaints against Archelaus were made at Rome, that he was deposed from the ethnarchate of Judea and Samaria, and banished to Vienna, in Gaul. (Jos. "Ant.," 17, 13, 2.) At that time the earlier history of Archelaus (see on v. 22) would be much talked about, and thus becoming familiar to Jesus, might have afterwards suggested the Parable of the Pounds. (Luke 19: 12. ff.) For there is a striking resemblance in many leading points: (1) Archelaus went away to Rome to receive royal power, and return to exercise it, and left his supporters in charge of his affairs. (2) The Jews hated him, and sent an embassy of fifty persons to Rome to say that they did not want Archelaus as their king. ("Ant." 17, 11, 1f.) (3) When Archelaus returned, though Augustus had enjoined moderation, he punished with great severity. (17, 13, 2.) After the banishment of Archelaus, his dominions were made a Roman province. Many of the Jews had desired this at the death of Herod, and now entreated that it be done, being weary of their weak native rulers, and expecting greater quiet and better protection for property and business under a Roman governor. Exactly similar changes, and for similar reasons, now often occur in British India, and under the Russian rule in

CHAPTER III.

IN those days came John the Baptist, preaching in the wilderness of Judea,

1 And in those days cometh John the Baptist, preach-

Central Asia, and were then taking place in other parts of the Roman Empire (*e. g.*, Tac. "Ann.," II. 42). But other Jews violently opposed such a change, clinging to the bare shadow of independence, and accounting it a sin that the people of God should be directly subject to heathen rulers, especially that they should pay them taxes. A portion of these broke out into rebellion under Judas, the Galilean or Gaulonite. (Jos. "Ant.," 18, 1; Acts 5: 37.) This movement, and other similar insurrections in following years, were easily quelled by the Romans, but the sentiment which produced them remained. (Comp. a section of the German Anabaptists, the Fifth Monarchy men in England, etc.) From it came the question, "Is it lawful to give tribute to Cesar?" (22:17.) Some of its supporters were subsequently associated as Cananites or Zelotae, including Simon, who became one of the twelve apostles. (10:4.) Degenerating by degrees into mere robbers, the men of this opinion still commanded popular sympathy, as was perhaps shown in the case of Barabbas. (27:16.) The same smouldering sentiment broke out in A. D. 66, leading (Jos. "Ant.," 18, 1, 6) to the war which ended in the destruction of Jerusalem, and in which the Zealots took a prominent part. The Roman Governors of Judea and Samaria were called procurators, the sixth of whom, Pontius Pilatus (27:2), ruled from A. D. 26 (when the ministry of John and of Jesus probably began), to A. D. 36. Meantime, the quiet dwellers at Nazareth were not directly concerned in these changes and commotions, remaining under the rule of Herod Antipas (see on v. 22), which continued to A. D. 39.

The youthful carpenter was probably in his nineteenth year (A. D. 14) when the great Emperor Augustus died, and was succeeded by Tiberius, who reigned throughout the remaining life of Jesus, and for some seven years longer (A. D. 37).

It seems nearly certain that Joseph died at some time between the visit to Jerusalem of Luke 2: 41 (probably A. D. 8), and the baptism of Christ (probably A. D. 26). Not only is he never mentioned in the history of our Lord's public ministry, but Mary is spoken of in such ways as seem to imply that she was then a widow. That several sons and daughters were born to Joseph and Mary is probable, but not certain. (Comp. on 1: 25, and 13: 55.)

A very full account of whatever will throw light on this period in the life of Christ, including the home life and school life of a Jewish child, the social influences, public worship, and religious sentiments of the time, the political changes, and the growing and shifting expectations of the Messiah, may be found in Geikie, ch. xii-xxiii, and Edersh.,ch. ix, x. See also Ewald, Keim, Hausrath, Edersheim's "Sketches of Jewish Social Life," and other writers.

Ch. 3: 1-12. MINISTRY OF JOHN THE BAPTIST.

The second great division of this Gospel comprises ch. 3: to 4: 11, and narrates the events connected with the entrance of our Lord upon his public work, including the appearance and ministry of John the Baptist (3:1-12), the baptism of Jesus (13-17), and his temptation. (4:1-11.) Here for the first time Mark (1:1-8), and Luke (3:1-18), become really parallel to Matthew; for Luke's apparently parallel matter heretofore has been entirely distinct from Matthew.

1. In those days. The Rev. Ver. has, *And in.*[1] This signifies, in the days in which Joseph and his family dwelt at Nazareth, as recorded in the preceding sentence. This event and the appearance of John are thrown together as belonging to the same period, no account being taken of the uneventful intervening time, which, in this case, was near

---

[1] The Greek has a particle of transition, *de,* which we often render 'and,' 'but,' or 'now'; and sometimes we begin more naturally without any conjunction. It is best to render it here, because the narrative seems to go right on without any marked interruption. The "Western" form of Greek text omitted the *de,* probably because it was thought there ought to be a pause.

thirty years. (Luke 3 : 23.) So Ex. 2: 11, "in those days," passes over the whole time from Moses' early youth, when his mother returned him to Pharaoh's daughter, until he was forty years old. (Acts 7 : 23.) In other cases the expression is equally indefinite, though the time passed over is shorter (*e. g.*, Isa. 38: 1; Mark 1: 9; Acts 1: 15). The same use of the phrase is found in classic writers also, where nothing is aimed at but a general designation of the time. Luke (3: 1) here gives the date of John's appearance with great particularity. Pontius Pilate became procurator A. D. 25–6. The fifteenth year of Tiberius is probably to be counted from the time when he was associated with Augustus (two years before the latter's death), which would be A. D. 12. There cannot be much doubt that John appeared in A. D. 26. **Came,** or rather, *arrives, presents himself.* The word is several times used to denote the arrival or public appearance of an official personage (comp. 1 Macc. 4: 46; Heb. 9: 11; and below, v. 13,; and it may be intended here to denote John's appearance in his official character. The Greek has here the present tense, precisely as in v. 13.

John the Baptist.—The most probable date for the beginning of the Baptist's ministry is A. D. 26, say in the spring. (Comp. on 2: 19.) The name John (Johanan = Jehovah graciously gave) had become common since the time of the popular ruler John Hyrcanus (died B. C. 106); thirteen persons of that name are mentioned in Josephus; and in the New Testament, besides the Baptist and the Evangelist, we meet with John Mark (Acts 12: 12), and John of the high-priestly family. (Acts 4: 6.) John the forerunner was well known to Matthew's first readers as the 'Baptist,' or Baptizer (comp. 14: 2, 8); we find Josephus also ("Ant.," 18, 5, 2) mentioning him as "John, who was surnamed Baptist." This name, the Baptizer, was of course given him in consequence of the remarkable rite he performed, which attracted universal attention, and was repeatedly used as the characteristic representative of his whole work (see on 21: 25).—The circumstances connected with John's birth are given only by Luke. Of his history since childhood we only know that he 'was in the deserts till the day of his shewing

unto Israel.' (Luke 1 : 80.) His father would be anxious to give to the child of such hopes the best priestly education, and it is probable that he retired to 'the deserts' after the death of his parents, who were of advanced age at the time of his birth. Such a step would be natural only when grown, or nearly so. In the wild region between Jerusalem and the Dead Sea (see below), he probably spent his time in religious meditation, ripening for his great mission. Yet that he knew human nature, and observed the men of his own time, appears from Luke 3 : 10-14. In this same wild region dwelt the Essenes (see on v. 7), and here also Josephus ("Life," 2) locates the teacher Banus, with whom he spent three years in seclusion, at a period about thirty years later than John's public appearance. It had been appointed (Luke 1 : 15) that from the beginning of John's life he should not 'drink wine or strong drink,' *i. e.*, should live as a Nazirite (Num. 6 : 1-21), implying extraordinary and lifelong consecration to God's service. A child of the mountains, and living a temperate life in the open air, he probably became strong in body, as well as 'grew strong in spirit.' (Luke 1: 80.) Comp. on v. 4. It is probable (see on v. 13) that he began his ministry when about thirty years old. "This protracted period of private discipline and preparation in the life both of Christ and his forerunner, is in striking contrast with our own impatience even under the most hurried superficial processes of education." (Alexander).—That a priest should be called to be a prophet was not strange; comp. Jeremiah and Ezekiel.—For a further account of John, see throughout this chapter, and on 4: 12; 9: 14 ff.; 11: 2-19; 14: 1-13; 17 : 10-13; 21: 25, 32. *Köhler*: "Though the historical information is very limited, there are few persons of whom we can form so clear and lively a conception. . . . An imposing figure, in whose posture and traits of countenance were depicted iron will, and deep, holy earnestness, yet without passing into hardness. In general, John may be called a classical example of the manifestation of love in the garb of severity. We cannot doubt his profound compassion for the unhappy condition of his people, sunken in sin and exposed to judgment, although it would hardly occur to us to conceive of him as weeping, like the Lord Jesus, over the coming fate of Jerusalem."

2 And saying, Repent ye: for the kingdom of heaven is at hand. | 2 ing in the wilderness of Judæa, saying, Repent ye;

Preaching. See on 4: 17. The word **wilderness** is used both in Old Testament and New Testament to denote a region not regularly built up and cultivated, portions of which were quite sterile, while other portions might be not destitute of herbage and other spontaneous productions. Such a tract was commonly used for pasturage (Psa. 65: 12; Joel 2: 22; Luke 15: 4), and sometimes contained watch-towers (2 Chron. 26: 10), settled inhabitants (Judges 1: 16), and even cities. (Josh 15: 61; Isa. 42: 11.) The 'wilderness of Judea' was a region of no very well marked boundaries, lying west of the Dead Sea, and of the extreme southern part of the Jordan, occupying about one-third of the territory of Judah (Keim), and extending up into that of Benjamin. The narrow plain of the Jordan, from the Sea of Galilee to the Dead Sea, is also called by Josephus ("War," 3, 10, 17) a desert, and de-scribed by him as parched, unhealthy, and destitute of water, except the river. (So also Thomson, II. 159 f.) Now Luke (3: 2, 3) says: 'The word of God came unto John, in the wilderness, and he came into all the country about Jordan preaching,' and John (1: 28) speaks of him as engaged in baptizing, a little later than this, at Bethany, beyond Jordan. We thus conclude that Matthew, as in many other cases, contents himself with the *general* statement that John's preaching and bap-tizing took place in the wilderness of Judea, which included the lower part of the Jordan valley, and being without definite boundaries, did not need to be carefully distinguished from the similar desert region extending far-ther up the river, into which (as we gather from the other Evangelists) John gradually moved, at length crossing the river (John 1: 28; 10: 40), and at a later period (John 3: 23), crossing back and removing to Enon, which was certainly west of the Jordan.[1] There is thus no occa-sion for inferring, as some do, from Luke's expression, that John first preached for some time in the wilderness at a distance from the Jordan, and afterwards came to the river. It should be observed that events described as occurring in 'the wilderness,' or 'the wilder-ness of Judea,' must of necessity be referred to different parts of that quite extensive dis-trict. John had probably lived (Luke 1: 80) in the southwestern part, towards Hebron; the scene of his baptizing was in the northeastern part; and the tract mentioned in John 11: 54, apparently formed the northwestern part. As to the scene of the temptation, see on 4: 1. The same Greek word is used in all the pas-sages of New Testament in which the Com. Ver. has 'wilderness' or 'desert.' (See further on 14: 13.)—John called the people away from the seats of government and of fixed social influences, into the wilder regions, where thought more readily becomes free, and where the mind is at once drawn out towards God, and driven in upon itself. (Keim.) In such a region was given the law of Moses, and pretenders to a prophetic mission, after our Lord's time, repeatedly drew crowds into the wilderness. (Acts 21: 38; Matt. 24: 26; Jos. "Ant.," 20, 5, 1; "War," 7, 11, 1.)

2. This verse gives a summary statement of the substance of John's preaching. **Repent.** To understand the precise New Testament use of this highly important term, we must dis-tinguish between the Greek word, the English (borrowed from an imperfect Latin render-ing), and the Hebrew expressions in Old Tes-tament. The Greek word here and common-ly used in New Testament (*metanoein*), signi fies to change the thought, and so to change the opinion or purpose. This inner change naturally leads to, and thus the expression may be said practically to include, a corre sponding change of the outward life, which

---

[1] Prof. Warfield (Expositor, April, 1885,) suggests that the Bethany of John 1: 28, was north of the Sea of Galilee, and so John the Baptist "traversed the whole length of Palestine, preaching repentance." But the evidence of a site called Bethany in that vicinity is very slender, and his argument from John's narrative is far from satisfactory. Jesus might easily encounter sev-eral persons from Bethsaida, and one from Cana, among the great crowds attending John's baptism, no matter where it was; for the people came from all parts of the country. And the assumption that "the third day" of John 2: 1, is to be counted not from v. 43, but from v. 35 (so as to place Jesus at Cana the day after he was with John), is arbitrary, unnatural, and in fact, when one compares the series of successive days in v. 28, 29, 35, 43, and then "the third day" in 2: 1, it seems to be out of the question. We can see no reason to believe that the Baptist ever reached Galilee.

we usually describe by the word 'reform.' A change of thought does not necessarily involve grief; and the word is sometimes used by Greek writers for a mere change of opinion or judgment, where there was no occasion for regret. But in all moral uses of the term there will of course be grief at the previous wrong course that one now determines to abandon. Whenever this Greek word is employed in New Testament (unless we except Heb. 12: 17), the reference is to changing the mind, purpose, from sin to holiness, and no one will do this who does not feel deep sorrow for the sin he has already committed. Sorrow is thus not expressed by the word itself, but in New Testament use is always suggested from the nature of the case, and thus becomes associated with the word. To repent, then, as a religious term of New Testament, is to change the mind, thought, purpose, as regards sin and the service of God—a change naturally accompanied by deep sorrow for past sin, and naturally leading to a change of the outward life. A different Greek word (*metamelesthai*), signifying to change the feeling of care or concern, to regret, is employed in 21: 29 (30), 32; 27: 3, and in Rom. 11: 29; 2 Cor. 7: 8, 10 ('repented of'); Heb. 7: 21. This regret might of course lead to change of purpose and conduct, but the term does not denote any such change, though the circumstances sometimes suggest it. It is only the first Greek word that New Testament uses to denote repenting of sin. The distinction between the two must, however, not be too strongly pressed, as shown by their use in the Septuagint (see below). A changed feeling might imply, or at least suggest, a changed purpose, and a changed purpose a changed feeling, so that both would sometimes yield substantially the same sense.

The Hebrew word for 'repent' denotes pain, grief, and sometimes suggests change of thought and purpose: the Septuagint translate it sometimes by the second and sometimes by the first of the above-mentioned Greek words.[1] It is noticeable that the prophets nowhere exhort men to 'repent' (though telling them to mourn and weep over their sins), but use the simple and practical word 'turn.' The New Testament also frequently employs this general and practical term, variously translated into English by 'turn,' 'return,' 'be converted'; and in Acts 3: 19; 26: 20, both are combined, 'repent and turn' (comp. Acts 11: 21, 'believed and turned'). It thus appears that the New Testament exhortation is substantially the same as that of the prophets (e. g., Joel 2: 12, 13; Isa. 55: 7; Ezek. 33: 11, 15; Zech. 1: 3, 4); but the New Testament term (*metanoein*) rendered 'repent' is more specific, and strictly denotes the inward change, leaving the outward change to be inferred as a consequence, or sometimes distinctly expressing it by adding the word 'turn.' In both the Old Testament and the New Testament exhortation the element of *grief* for sin is left in the background, neither word directly expressing grief at all, though it must in the nature of things always be present.

But great difficulty has been found in translating this Greek work into other languages. The Syriac versions, unable to give the precise meaning, fall back upon 'turn,' the same word as in Hebrew. The Latin versions give 'exercise penitence' (*pœnitentiam agere*). But this Latin word, penitence, apparently connected by etymology with *pain*, signifies grief or distress, and is rarely extended to a change of purpose, thus corresponding to the Hebrew word which we render 'repent,' but *not* corresponding to the terms employed in Old Testament and New Testament exhortations. Hence a subtle and pernicious error, pervading the whole sphere of Latin Christianity, by which the exhortation of New Testament is understood to be an exhortation to *grief* over sin, as the primary and principal idea of the term. One step further, and penitence was

---

[1] This Hebrew term is repeatedly applied to God, as grieving over something he had done (the Sept. using both Greek words). The people are said to 'repent' (Sept. *metamelesthai*) in Ex. 13: 17; Jud. 21: 6, 15, and in Job 42: 6; (in these the Sept. mistranslates). As applied to grieving over sin, it is found in Jer. 8: 6: 'No man repenteth of his wickedness,' and 31: 19: 'After my turning, I repent,' (in both passages the Sept. has *metanoein*). Comp. Ecclus. 48: 11. The other passages of Old Testament in which English Version represents *men* as repenting, have in the original 'turn' (1 Kings 8: 47; Ezek. 14: 6; 18: 30). But in the Apocrypha, Ecclus. 17: 24 exhorts men to turn to the Lord and forsake their sins, and says, 'Unto those that repent (*metanoein*) he grants return to him.' Wisdom 11: 24, 'Thou overlookest men's sins that they may repent.' Comp. Wisdom 12: 10, 19. Ecclus. 44: 16 speaks of Enoch as 'a pattern of repentance (*metanoia*) to the generations.' Comp. also Wisdom 5: 3.

contracted into *penance*, and associated with medieval ideas unknown to New Testament, and the English Versions made by Romanists, now represent John, and Jesus, and Peter, as saying (*pœnitentiam agite*), 'do penance.' From a late Latin compound (*repœnitere*) comes our English word 'repent,' which inherits the fault of the Latin, making grief the prominent element, and change of purpose secondary, if expressed at all. Thus our English word corresponds exactly to the *second* Greek word (*metamelesthai*), and to the Hebrew word rendered 'repent,' but sadly fails to translate the exhortation of the New Testament. It is therefore necessary constantly to repeat the explanation that the New Testament word in itself denotes simply *change of purpose* as to sin, leaving us to understand from the nature of things, the accompanying grief and the consequent reformation.[1]

But while John's exhortation is substantially the same as that of the prophets, it is enforced by a new and strong motive, the near approach of the long-expected Messianic reign. **Is at hand,** or more literally, *has come near.* (So 4 : 17; 10 : 7.) This is here mentioned by Matthew alone, who writes especially for Jews. They continually spoke of Messiah as 'the coming one' (11:3), of the Messianic period as 'the coming age' (Heb. 6:5), and John tells them that Messiah's reign has drawn near. He does not say, Repent, and so the reign will draw near, but Repent, for it has drawn near (Calvin). The word *basileia*, which everywhere in English Version is rendered **kingdom,** means (1) kingship, the possession of royal authority, *e. g.*, Rev. 11 : 15; 'the kingship (sovereignty) over the world is become our Lord's and his Christ's' ; comp. Rev. 17 : 18; Matt. 16 : 28; Ps. 22 : 28. (2) 'reign,' the exercise of royal power, or the period during which it is exercised ; (3) 'kingdom,' the subjects, the organization (12:25), or the territory. (4:8.) In the sense of the territory it is not used in New Testament concerning Messiah's kingdom, and probably not in

the sense of organization. Of the renderings kingship, reign, and kingdom, two would frequently be necessary, and sometimes all three at once, to express the full sense of the original term. As we have to choose one, the word 'reign' is in this and many other passages a more nearly adequate rendering than 'kingdom,' and less likely to mislead. **The kingdom** (*reign*) **of heaven** is an expression used more than thirty times by Matthew, though he sometimes (12: 28; 19: 24; 21: 31, 43) uses the one always found in the other Evangelists, 'kingdom (*reign*) of God.' 'Heaven' is in this phrase always plural in the Greek, 'the heavens,' an imitation of the plural (dual) form, which the word always has in Hebrew, and not differing in meaning from the singular. Heaven, regarded as the special residence of God, is sometimes very naturally used to represent God himself (*e. g.*, Dan. 4 : 26; 1 Macc. 3 : 60; Luke 15: 18, 21), just as we say, 'heaven grant,' etc., and so 'kingdom of heaven' is equivalent to 'kingdom of God.' The Jews, scrupulous about using the name of God, frequently substituted 'heaven' (*e. g.*, 1 Macc. 3: 50, 60; 4: 55), and the Talmud often has the phrase 'kingdom of heaven.' It was natural that Matthew, writing especially for Jews, should respect their feeling, and commonly use this expression.

The New Testament idea of the 'kingdom (*reign*) of God' has its roots in the prophetic writings. In Isaiah (ch. 1 : 39) and Micah, it is declared that God will raise up a righteous king, who shall deliver his people and give them prosperity (*e. g.* Isa. 9 : 6, 7; 11 : 1-10; Micah 4 : 1-8). This hope is presented with modifications by Jeremiah and his contemporaries (*e. g.* Jer. 23 : 5, 6; Ezek. 37 : 24), pointing now not to an individual king, but to a Davidic dynasty (comp. 2 Chron. 13 : 8), guiding the mission of the chosen people. But in Daniel, when Israel is fallen low, there is given assurance that "the God of heaven" will establish a universal monarchy, with "one like a son of man" as the king. (Dan. 2: 44; 7: 13, 14.) This idea must have fermented in the

---

[1] A pamphlet, by Treadwell Walden, entitled "An Undeveloped Chapter in the Life of Christ" (New York, Whittaker, 1882), is devoted to the word *metanoia*. It presents forcibly the grievous incorrectness of the translation 'repentance,' but does not show what English word or phrase could now be substituted in a popular version. The discussion is interesting and profitable. But we think the author exaggerates the importance of his theme, as monographs are apt to do, and is quite mistaken in supposing that the word expresses simply an intellectual change, a transfigured theory of moral truth.

3 For this is he that was spoken of by the prophet
Esaias, saying, The voice of one crying in the wilder-

3 for the kingdom of heaven is at hand. For this is he

---

minds of at least some Jews, till it took the form we find in the Gospels, when devout persons are not only "waiting for the consolation of Israel," and "for the redemption of Jerusalem" (Luke 2: 25, 38), but "waiting for the kingdom of God" (Luke 23: 51; 17: 20); the Baptist says, "the kingdom of heaven (God) has drawn near," as something which all will understand. The Jews of that period had many fanciful, confused, and sometimes fanatical notions in regard to the character of this expected divine reign, as shown by the book of Enoch, the Targums, and the Talmud, (see Lightfoot, Wetstein, Gill, and Drummond, "The Jewish Messiah"), but the New Testament is of course responsible only for its own use of the phrase. We see also that the statement in Daniel has, before the New Testament times, led to the belief that a "son of man," called also the Messiah, will reign in God's promised kingdom, for this is expressly asserted in the book of Enoch, (much of which was pretty certainly written before the Christian era), and the Talmud abounds in references to "King Messiah." This persuasion our Lord confirms in 13: 41; 25: 31, 34; John 18: 36. It was one great object of Matthew's Gospel to show how Jesus corrected the Jewish errors as regards the nature of the expected Messianic reign. Much error has diffused itself through the Christian world from confounding "the kingdom" with what is popularly called "the church." *Edersh.*: "We must dismiss the notion that the expression Kingdom of Heaven refers to the church, whether visible (according to the Roman Catholic view) or invisible (according to certain Protestant writers)." Comp. below on 13: 37 ff.

The statement of Josephus ("Ant.," 18, 5, 2) concerning John's teachings and baptism, is marked by his usual affectation of a philosophical tone, and his usual omission of all Messianic references: "John, who was surnamed Baptist . . . . . a good man, and one

who bade the Jews in the exercise of virtue, and in the practice of righteousness towards one another and piety towards God, to come to baptism; for that so would the baptism also appear acceptable to him, if they used it, not for the forgiveness of certain sins, but for the purification of the body, it being supposed that the soul also had previously been cleansed by righteousness." Josephus adds that the people were greatly excited by John's preaching, and that Herod imprisoned and slew him because he feared revolution—a statement which perhaps points to John's proclamation in regard to the near approach of the kingdom of God. It was natural that Josephus should omit all distinct reference to this Messianic reign, for he had long before committed himself to the essentially absurd but politic statement that the Messianic hope of Israel was fulfilled in his patron Vespasian ("War," 6, 5, 4). Both Jews and heathen constantly inclined to think that ablution was itself the means of cleansing the soul from sin; and against this notion Josephus declares that John's baptism was not expected to bring forgiveness of sins, but that the soul must have been previously cleansed by turning from sin to righteousness. Comp. Tertullian: "We are not washed that we may cease to sin, but because we have ceased: since we have already been bathed in heart."

3. This is by some expositors taken as the words of John, who certainly did on one occasion apply the prophecy to himself (John 1: 23); but here the reference is much more naturally understood as made by the Evangelist—the present tense is expressing the general fact that John is the predicted forerunner. **For** gives the reason why John appeared in the wilderness and bade the people prepare for the Messianic reign, viz., because John is the person **spoken of by**—*through*—**the prophet** ('through,' see on 2: 17), as destined to do so. **The voice of one crying,**[1] etc., Isa. 40: 3. In the Hebrew the accents indicate, and the

---

[1] Or more exactly, 'a voice of one crying.' It seems smoother in English to say 'The voice of one crying,' but the noun is not really made definite here by the succeeding genitive, for the crier is himself indefinite. A voice is heard by the prophet, a voice of a person

crying. (So Rheims, Davidson.) Darby, 'Voice of him that crieth,' errs in making the latter clause definite, for 'him that crieth' would require the article before the Greek participle.

ness, Prepare ye the way of the Lord, make his paths straight.
4 And the same John had his raiment of camel's hair, and a leathern girdle about his loins ; and his meat was locusts and wild honey.

that was spoken of through Isaiah the prophet, saying,
The voice of one crying in the wilderness,
Make ye ready the way of the Lord,
Make his paths straight.
4 Now John himself had his raiment of camel's hair, and a leathern girdle about his loins ; and his food

---

parallelism proves, that 'in the wilderness' belongs to 'prepare'; and so Rev. Ver., Isaiah. Matthew (as also Mark and Luke) follows the Septuagint in connecting that phrase with 'crying,' and in omitting the parallel phrase 'in the desert' from the next clause. This change does not affect the substantial meaning, and it makes clearer the real correspondence between the prediction and the fulfillment, 'preaching in the wilderness' (v. 1), 'crying in the wilderness' (v. 3). It might without impropriety be supposed that Matthew himself altered the phraseology to bring out this correspondence, but in many similar cases it is plain that he has simply followed the familiar Septuagint. **Prepare ye.** *Make ye ready*, was here substituted by Rev. Ver. for 'prepare,' because in the parallel passage of Mark (1: 3), the same word is translated 'make ye ready,' in order to keep it distinct from another Greek word rendered 'prepare' in Mark 1: 2. Such pains to render the same Greek word everywhere by the same English word will prove very useful in concordance work, and all minute study, but it strikes the casual reader as useless alteration of the translation.—The immediate reference of the prophecy in Isaiah is probably to Jehovah, as leading his people back through the eastern desert from their captivity in Babylon: the remote reference is to the coming of Messiah, and spiritual deliverance. Here, as often in the prophets (see on 2: 15), there is a typical relation between the history of Israel and that of Messiah.—Great public roads were rare in the East until introduced by the Romans. When an Oriental monarch was designing to journey into a certain region, he sent messengers in advance to require that a graded road should be prepared. Hence the image, here denoting spiritual preparation. Notice that in Isa. 40: 4, every part of the process of grading is mentioned.

4. And the same John had, or, '*And he, John, had*.' The difference in meaning between these renderings is unimportant. After remarking upon the prediction fulfilled in John, the Evangelist proceeds to speak

further of John himself. The clothing of **camel's hair** was a coarse cloth made by weaving camel's hair, and such cloth is still often worn in the East by the poor. There is no evidence that garments of camel-skin, like those made of sheep-skins and goat-skins (Heb. 11: 37) have ever been worn in the East (as imagined by the painters, and by Fritzsche and Smith, "Dict.," art. Camel); and the expression here distinctly forbids such a notion, being literally 'of camel's hairs' (so the Greek of Mark 1: 6, 'camel's hairs'). So Meyer, Bleek, Weiss. A **girdle** was a necessary and almost universal part of an Oriental's dress (comp. 10: 9, marg. of Rev. Ver.; Acts 21: 11), being required to bind the long, loose robe (see on 5: 40), in order to active labor, or rapid locomotion, and it was often very costly and showy (comp. Rev. 1: 13). John's girdle was made of leather, cheap and rude, as was Elijah's. (2 Kings 1: 8.) **Meat,** or *food*. The word 'meat' is used in Com. Ver. to translate several Greek words, but all of them signify food, nutriment, sustenance. This would sometimes include *flesh*, to which, in modern English, the term meat is exclusively applied. (Comp. 1 Cor. 8: 13, 'If food makes my brother sin, I will eat no more flesh.' Bib. Un. Ver.) The law of Moses (Lev. 11: 22) allowed **locusts,** at least of certain kinds, to be eaten; and a treatise in the Talmud copiously discusses the marks by which 'clean' locusts might be distinguished. To eat these is still common in the East among the poor. The heads, legs, and wings being removed, they are boiled, stewed, or roasted, and sometimes dressed with butter. They are eaten both fresh, and dried, or salted. They are very different from what we call locusts. The notion that John ate the fruit of the tree which we call locust, is utterly unwarranted, and forbidden by the Greek word. The **wild honey** is thought by some able writers (as Fritzsche, Robinson, Meyer, Bleek, Grimm, Weiss) to have been the gum exuding from a tree, but on very slender grounds (comp. Keil). Much more probably it was, as commonly supposed, the honey of wild bees, de-

5 Then went out to him Jerusalem, and all Judea, and all the region round about Jordan,

5 was locusts and wild honey. Then went out unto him Jerusalem, and all Judæa, and all the region

posited in trees, rocks, etc., such as is mentioned in Old Testament (Judg. 14:8 f.; 1 Sam. 14: 25 ff.; Ps. 81:16), and found at the present day also in the wild regions in which John lived. This was very abundant, and considered cheap and poor food (comp. Isa. 7: 15). Eustathius says (Wet.) that Pythagoras lived very poorly, often contenting himself with honey alone.

It had been predicted (Mal. 4:5 f.) that Elijah the prophet should be sent before the advent of Messiah to prepare the people for his coming. This was explained by the angel (Luke 1:17) as to be fulfilled in John, who would go before the Lord 'in the spirit and power of Elijah,' and was also declared by Jesus to have been fulfilled in John (see on 11: 14; 17: 10-13). The ministry of each consisted mainly in severe reproof and exhortation to amendment, and there was something appropriate to such a work in seclusion of life, with rude fare and coarse clothing, and in austerity of manner. "Even his appearance called men to repentance." (Theophylact). This was hardly personal asceticism, but appears to have been designed, like the numerous symbolical acts employed by other prophets, to attract attention, and give greater impressiveness, to the reformer's rebukes of a luxurious and worldly minded generation. It was what we call an "object-lesson." We may imagine the effect when Elijah suddenly issued from his retreats, and, arrayed like some Bedouin or savage Dervish of to-day, stood before a weak and self-indulgent king, with stern look and tone, and harsh words of merited reproof. And similar must have been the effect of John's appearance and known mode of life. (Comp. on 11: 8.) Elijah is described as 'an hairy man' (2 Kings 1:8), literally 'a possessor of hair,' and this is best understood as meaning that he wore a garment made of hair (margin Rev. Ver.), especially as his girdle is mentioned immediately after. This characteristic dress of Elijah appears to have been imitated by succeeding prophets; for we find in Zech. 13: 4 the prediction of a time when the false prophets would become ashamed of their impostures, and would not 'wear a garment of hair to deceive.' On the part of John, these

peculiarities were not a mere imitation of his prototype, for they had the same appropriateness and significance in both cases.—There is little propriety in the notion of some artists and writers that John was attenuated through much fasting. Doubtless he did fast (see on 9: 14), but so did many Jews, and not necessarily to attenuation. His out-door life and homely food might (see on v. 2) even promote bodily health (compare Elijah), and physical force seems naturally implied in his preaching to great crowds in the open air, and boldly facing the most jealous and powerful. John was also like Elijah in that he was not a writing prophet, but left his work to be recorded by others. (Pressensé).

5. After a general account (v. 1-4) of John's public appearance and preaching, with the fact that in him a prophecy was fulfilled, and after a description of his peculiar dress and manner of life, we have now (v. 5 f.) a general statement that the people went forth to him in large numbers and were baptized, and this is followed (v. 7-12) by a specimen of his preaching, given more in detail.

Then, Matthew's favorite term of transition, resumes the time of v. 1. 2. Not only Jerusalem, but the entire district of Judea, and **all the region round about,**—or, *the circuit of the*—**Jordan,** only part of which was included in Judea, came forth. The Hebrew phrase, 'round of the Jordan' or, 'circuit of the Jordan,' i. e., the country about the river, is inadequately rendered in Com. Ver. by 'plain' (Gen. 13: 10, 11; margin Rev. Ver. 'circle'; 1 Kings 7: 46; 2 Chron. 4: 17). The cases of its occurrence in Old Testament refer particularly, as here, to the lower part of the river, towards the Dead Sea. **All,** is of course, to be understood as an hyperbole, strongly expressing the fact that very many of the people came forth. (Comp. 8: 34.) Similar hyperbolical expressions abound in all languages and periods. We learn from John (1:35-45; 21:2), that some came from Galilee also, but this was perhaps at a later period, when John was baptizing higher up the river. The year to which John's early ministry probably belongs, A. D. 26, was a Sabbatical year (Wieseler), when the people

6 And were baptized of him in Jordan, confessing their sins. | 6 round about Jordan; and they were baptized of him

---

who strictly observed the law would have more than ordinary leisure.

It was centuries since a prophet had appeared, and the Jews had often longed for prophetic guidance. Thus Judas Maccabeus and his followers laid away the stones of the desecrated altar "until a prophet should appear to answer concerning them" (1 Macc. 4: 46); and the woman of Samaria, as soon as she perceived that here was a prophet, asked him to settle the long-disputed question concerning the proper place to worship. (John 4: 19 f.) In the time of Christ, some were expecting the personal re-appearance of Jeremiah (below, 16: 14), and many that of Elijah (John 1; 21; Luke 9: 8; Matt. 16: 14; 17: 10; 27: 49); while others were looking for the prophet like unto Moses. (John 1: 21; Deut. 18: 15, 18.) And now the report spread far and wide, that at last a prophet had come, who in dress and place of abode resembled the great Elijah, who might be Messiah, or at least a forerunner of Messiah, for he declared that the Messianic reign was near, who performed a very striking rite, and spoke severe rebukes and earnest exhortations to turn from evil ways, such as had been spoken by all the prophets, such as will always arrest the attention of mankind. No wonder the Jews, from all the country adjacent to the scene of his ministry, and for many months, continually poured forth to see and hear him, and, more or less, impressed by his announcement of the Messianic reign and his call to repentance, confessed their sins and submitted to his baptism.

6. Baptized. The Greek word *baptizo*, which we borrow, was of very common use, as is seen in every period of Greek literature, and was applied to a great variety of matters, including the most familiar acts of every-day life. It was thus a word which every Greek-speaking hearer and reader in apostolic times would at once and clearly understand. It meant what we express by 'immerse' and kindred terms,[1] and no one could then have thought of attributing to it a wholly different sense, such as 'sprinkle,' or 'pour,' without distinct explanation to that effect. The people who speak Greek at the present day wholly reject and ridicule the idea of using this Greek word in any other than its own definite and well-known sense; and the Greek Church still holds nothing to be baptism but immersion. But the newly discovered treatise called the *Didache*, or "Teaching," written some time in the second century, probably in the latter half of the century, shows that in some region of the Christian world there was a disposition to allow a substitute when water was scarce. Thus ch. 7, "Baptize . . . in living water (*i. e.* of a stream, fountain, or pool, as opposed to standing or dead water). And if thou have no living water, baptize in other water; and if thou canst not in cold, then in warm. And if thou have neither, pour water upon the head thrice." Here it is evident that baptize means only immerse, but if water be scarce, pouring may be substituted for baptizing. In like manner we find in the West, towards the middle of the third century, that in case of severe sickness some allowed pouring, and after a while some thought sprinkling sufficient, and these more convenient substitutes grew increasingly common, though often condemned by the ecclesiastical authorities, until in the thirteenth century their

---

1 *Bapto*, 'dip,' had the root *baph*, akin to *bath* in *bath-us*, 'deep' (Curtius), just as dip and deep, German *taufen* and *tief* have the same root. From *bapto*, came the verbal adjective *baptos*, 'dipt,' and from this was made the verb *bapt-izo*, as if in English we should say dipt-ize, viz., to put into a dipt condition. The usual way of bringing one into a dipt condition would be to dip him. But sometimes it might be otherwise conceived; as *e. g.*, land overflowed by water might be described as baptized, being now in, within the water, just as an object dipt would be within it. There is in language a general tendency to use stronger derivative or compound words (*e. g.*, verbs compounded with prepositions) in place of the original and simpler word, until finally the compound or derivative is no stronger in many uses than the simple word. Thus *rant-izo* means exactly the same as *raino* 'sprinkle'; comp. *statizo* and *histemi*, *kaumatizo* and *kaio*, and many similar cases. Now *baptizo* did not become exactly and uniformly equivalent to *bapto*. The sense 'dye' is confined to *bapto*, and there are various uses of *baptizo*, 'diptize' in which *bapto*, 'dip,' would be inadequate; but in many cases they are substantially equivalent, like *rantizo* and *raino*. The often repeated statement that *baptizo* is frequentative, signifying 'dip frequently,' is erroneous, and would never have been made but for a failure to perceive the etymology of the word as above given.

general use was sanctioned by the Pope. Luther and Calvin (16th cent.) both explicitly declared that the primitive baptism was immersion, and the former said it ought to be restored; but they allowed the existing practice to remain undisturbed. In the course of time many Protestants came to perceive that it was very awkward to rest their practice in this respect on the authority of the Church of Rome, and being accustomed and attached to the practice they very naturally sought countenance for it in Scripture. Such are the unavoidable defects of language, that strongly biased and ingenious minds can always cast some apparent doubt over the meaning of the plainest words; as has been done, for example, with respect to words teaching the divinity of Christ, the atonement, and eternal punishment. It is therefore not surprising that a good many able and conscientious men in Great Britain and America (very few in Germany) have succeeded in persuading themselves that perhaps, or even quite probably, *baptizo* might be understood as meaning pour or sprinkle, or purify in general, or *something* that would sanction the practice handed down from revered fathers; and that a few very bold spirits should even venture to cut the knot and assert, that not only sprinkling may be baptism, but nothing else can be. These considerations should promote charity, and may serve to explain the rise, in modern times, of so much controversy about a very plain word.

This controversy has led to a wide examination of Greek literature with reference to this term, and in all the instances of its use that have been found, whether literal or figurative, its fundamental meaning (whatever may be the particular rendering most suitable to the connection and to English idiom) is always 'immerse,' that being in the great mass of cases the only possible sense, and in all cases appropriate and natural. (See a full list of classified examples in Conant "On Baptizein," Philadelphia.) So it is defined and explained in most Greek Lexicons that are of any authority (*e. g.*, in Liddell and Scott, Grimm, Sophocles' Greek Lex. of the Roman and Byzantine periods, Boston), without a hint of any other meaning; and so it is interpreted by almost all commentators in Germany, the land of scholars, and by very many in the

Church of England. But some good Lexicons of classical Greek (as Rost and Palm) add such meanings as 'moisten,' 'drench,' 'overwhelm,' justifying them only by certain *figurative* uses of the word, in which drunkards are called 'the baptized,' or men are said to be baptized in (or with) debts, mismisfortunes, etc; some Lexicons of New Testament Greek (as Robinson) urge that in certain passages of New Testament and Septuagint (*e. g.*, Mark 7: 4; Luke 11: 38; Acts 2: 41; 10: 48; 16: 33; Judith 12: 7), the circumstances make it, in the lexicographer's judgment, unlikely that an immersion was performed; and some others (as Cremer, comp. Stephen's "Thesaurus"), suppose that the Jews came to use the Hebrew *tabal* 'dip,' and therefore used *baptizo*, as a general term for religious washing, which might then be sometimes performed in other ways. Yet all the lexicographers who thus present an additional meaning give 'immerse' as the primary and general meaning of the word. Now it is a most important principle in the interpretation of language, without the observance of which all interpretation becomes uncertain and unreliable, that whatever is the common and regular meaning of a word, as shown by its origin and general use, must be held to be its meaning everywhere, until there shall be found some passage in which it *cannot* have that sense. Upon this principle, whether formally recognized or not, scholars are constantly working. But no passage has been pointed out in which this word *must* have some other than its ordinary meaning; indeed, none in which that meaning is not both possible and appropriate. Thus the classical expressions solely relied on by Rost and Palm for another meaning, are given by Liddell and Scott (6th and 7th ed.) as examples of the primary sense 'to dip in or under water,' and compared with the English phrases 'soaked in wine,' 'over head and ears in debt,' such expressions being obviously figurative in both languages. In the passages cited by Robinson, nothing more can be claimed than that in those cases immersion would have been inconvenient or difficult, and is therefore thought unlikely; while a due consideration of Jewish scrupulosity and known customs makes immersion not only possible in such cases, but natural enough—and these passages are so explained by a multitude of German and English writers who are certainly not prejudiced in favor of immersion, for they practice sprinkling, on the authority of the church, or on the ground that it is a matter of little consequence. To the argument of Cremer that the Talmud sometimes uses 'tabal,' 'dip,' with reference to purifications in which Old Testament directed them to 'sprinkle,' (*rachatz*), and that so *tabal* and *baptizo* seem to have been employed as general terms for religious washing, however performed, it is enough to reply that the Jews had become so extremely scrupulous as frequently to employ the most complete form of purification (*tabal*) in cases in which only the less complete (*rachatz*) was required, wishing thus to make perfectly sure that no touch of impurity had failed to be removed. So already in Sirach 31 (34): 30 (Eng. Ver. Ecclus. 34: 25), 'One who immerses himself from a dead body and again touches it, what profit did he gain by his bath' (comp. Lev. 22: 4-6), in Judith 12: 7, and Mark 7: 4 (see Meyer); and so in the proselyte-immersion of a later period (see below.) This explanation is at least as probable in itself as the theory of Cremer, and accords with the well-known scrupulosity of the Jews.—It thus appears that in none of the ways mentioned is warrant found for giving *baptizo* any such meaning as pour, sprinkle, or wash religiously, or any other than its own proper and well-known sense. The argument that because baptism suggested (John 3: 25) a dispute about purification, therefore any form of purification is baptism (Ed. Beecher on "Baptism," New York), is as if from the fact that a case of yellow fever led to a dispute about malarial diseases, it should be argued that any form of malarial disease is yellow fever. Dale ("Classic Baptism," "Judaic Baptism," "Johannic Baptism," "Christic and Patristic Baptism," four separate volumes, Philadelphia), defines *baptizo* as meaning 'intuspose,' (*i. e.,* 'put within,' comp. Liddell and Scott), 'merse,' 'immerse,' and then by a novel and ingenious, but purely fanciful and unreasonable process explains it all away, and reaches the conclusion that immersion is not baptism at all.[1] Some attempt has been made to construct an argument as to *baptizo* from the word used in the Syriac New Testament, in reply to which see a tract by C. H. Toy on Amad (Louisville.) These several theories add no force to the efforts of the lexicographers above mentioned, to justify some departure from the plain and recognized meaning of this Greek word.

It was once quite generally held (see especially Lightfoot), and is still maintained by some, that John's baptism was an imitation of what is called Jewish proselyte-baptism. The resemblance between the two is but partial; for Maimonides (twelfth cent.) describes the ceremony as consisting in the person's standing in the water and dipping himself, thus making it a self-purification. Recent investigation shows that there is no ground for believing this Jewish practice of a later time to have existed, as a distinct initiatory rite, in the time of our Lord. Not only is there no allusion to such a rite in the Old or New Testament, or in the Apocryphal books, but none in Philo or Josephus, although each of these writers has various passages in which it seems almost impossible that he should have failed to mention the rite had it then existed, nor any in the early Christian Fathers, some of whom search every page of Old Testament for rites or expressions bearing any, the most fanciful resemblance to baptism. It is not mentioned in the Mishna (about A. D. 200), nor clearly referred to in any of the other Jewish writings belonging to the early centuries after Christ, the first distinct account of it being in the Babylonian Talmud (Gemara), written in the fifth century. The origin of the rite among the Jews is readily explained. When a proselyte (see on 23: 15) was received (before the destruction of the temple), he was circumcised, and then before performing his first act as a Jew, viz., offering sacrifice, he must be purified; but this purification was not distinctively initiatory (peculiar to a proselyte), for the Jewish child also must be purified after circumcision, which itself made one unclean. There were thus three acts performed in admitting a proselyte—the circumcision (which really made him a Jew), the consequent purification (which as described

---

[1] See review of Dale's different volumes in "Baptist Quarterly" (Philadelphia), by A. C. Kendrick, 1869, p. 139, J. A. Broadus, 1875, p. 245, W. H. Whitsitt, 1877, p. 175. Also H. Harvey in Bap. Rev., 1879; "Studies in Baptism" by D. B. Ford. (Boston, Young, 1879); Broadus' Tract on Immersion. (A. B. P. S., Phil.)

by Maimonides, was an immersion), and then sacrifice, in which he publicly acted as a Jew. After the temple was destroyed, the sacrifice became impossible, and then the purification became the closing, and in the case of women, the only act performed; and so it naturally attracted greater attention, and by the fifth century had come to be regarded as distinct from all other purific ions, and as possessing a very high importance, equal, if not superior, to that of circumcision. This view takes away all force from the otherwise plausible argument that the so-called prose-lyte-baptism must have been ancient, on the ground that the Jews would never have adopted it from the hated Christians; for we see that it was not so adopted at all, but was simply one of their own purifications, which from the force of circumstances came, in the course of some centuries after the destruction of the temple, to be regarded as a peculiar initiatory rite. And if later Jewish writers assert that it was ancient, even that it originated at Mount Sinai, they make the same claim for every usage existing among them, however unquestionably late in its origin ; and besides, we have seen that the essence of this practice was ancient, though it afterwards assumed its peculiar character and consequence.[1]

There is thus no reason for supposing that John's baptism was a mere modification of some existing rite. Our Lord distinctly intimated (21 : 25) that the baptism of John was "from heaven." The forerunner himself testified that God "sent" him "to baptize in water." (John 1 : 33.) *Köhler*: "So the baptism of John is a highly significant and expressive rite, which in its grand simplicity bears the distinct stamp of a divine ordering."

In Jordan. The expression thus translated affords a strong, though in itself not an absolute proof, that the action of baptizing was performed within the limits of the stream. This is the natural and regular meaning of the phrase, and must be everywhere adhered to unless there is something in the connection to forbid it. But the Greek preposition *en* is used in some connections not found in English; as, for example, we cannot say, "a city was situated in the Euxine Sea," "an ambush was laid in a river," but the Greek has these expressions, meaning that the sea or river was in a certain general sense the locality in which the city or ambush was situated, though not in the strict sense which our 'in' would indicate, seeing that such a sense is in those instances not possible from the nature of the case. So in English we say 'the man is in the mountain,' meaning not the earth composing it, but the mountain in a more general sense. Now if the action of baptizing were one which could not be performed *in* the river in the strict sense, we might understand 'in the Jordan' as meaning only in that general locality (comp. Mark 4: 1, 'in the sea'). But until it is shown that the signification of the term baptize is incompatible with the idea of its being performed strictly in the river, *i. e.*, in the water, we are bound to take the preposition in its proper and ordinary sense. Now even those who maintain that 'baptizo' is at times used with a certain latitude, generally agree that its regular and usual sense is one which does not forbid, but entirely accords with, the idea of its being performed in the water. We have therefore the natural and almost uniform use of 'in' *concurring* with the established meaning of the verb, and reinforcing the argument by which that meaning is established. (Comp. 'in water' v. 11, Rev. Ver., margin). The Rev. Ver. reads, *the river Jordan*.[2] The word Jordan, always with the article in the Hebrew and the Greek, signifies 'the descender,' and was so named from its rapid descent in a long and deep valley or

---

[1] The explanation of its rise was first given by Schneckenburger, whose excellent little work "How Old is the Jewish Proselyte-Baptism" (1828), has not been translated from the German. The most complete and satisfactory discussion of the subject is by Toy, in Baptist Quarterly, 1872, p. 301 ff. See also among many writers, Gill, "Works," Vol. II. pp. 760–799, and Leyrer (and Delitzsch) in Herzog. Recent leading writers generally concur in Schneckenburger's view, *e. g.*, Winer, Meyer, Ewald, Bleek, Cremer, Keim, Keil, Godet; on the other hand, Edersh. (App. xii.) urges that "previous to Christ, the baptism of proselytes was customary"; but he gives neither evidence nor argument for anything else than the above-mentioned purification before sacrifices, which was a matter of course. Schürer also advocates the same opinion, but presents nothing new.

[2] The word 'river' (as in Mark 1: 5) is here given by B, א. C. M. Δ. Σ. and more than thirty cursive MSS and by all the early versions except the Latin, and is adopted by Lach., Treg., Tisch., Alf., Weiss, W H. Yet while Mark would naturally tell his Gentile readers

fissure. The highest of its three principal fountains on the slopes of Hermon is seventeen hundred feet above the level of the Mediterranean ; the first lake it forms, Hûleh, has its surface only one hundred and twenty feet above the Mediterranean, while the second, the Lake of Galilee, is six hundred and eighty-two feet (Conder) *below* the level, and the third Lake, the Dead Sea, is twelve hundred and ninety-two feet below the level of the Mediterranean, besides being itself some thirteen hundred feet deep. The fissure or valley varies in width, south of the Lake of Galilee, from two to six miles, and nearer the Dead Sea it becomes fourteen miles wide (Conder). Winding about in this long, narrow valley is another depressed valley (forty to one hundred and fifty feet deeper), of several hundred yards in width ; and within this the actual bed of the river sinks deeper still. The distance *in a straight line* from its highest source to the southern end of the Dead Sea is about one hundred and sixty miles, or excluding the Dead Sea, about one hundred and fifteen miles. But so extremely crooked is the winding river that Lynch estimates it to be near two hundred miles between the Lake of Galilee and its mouth (which is sixty-five miles in a straight line), and though less crooked higher up, its whole length must be at least two hundred and seventy-five miles, not including the Dead Sea. The width and depth of course vary at different seasons, as it is swollen in February and March by the rains, and in May, the "time of harvest" (Josh. 3:15), by the melting snows of Hermon. Above Lake Hûleh it is some forty feet wide, and is deep and rapid, but fordable almost everywhere. Towards the Lake of Galilee it is about sixty feet, and easily forded at several places. For some miles below the lake Lynch found it about seventy-five feet wide, and at points ten feet deep (middle of April), but on one of the numerous rapids only eight inches deep. About five miles below the lake an important tributary enters from the east, and below this the usual depth varies from two and one half to six feet (Ritter). About half way from the Lake of Galilee to the Salt (Dead) Sea, the River Jabbok enters from the east, and smaller streams come in at various neighboring points on both sides. It here becomes from eighty to one hundred and fifty feet wide, and from five to twelve feet deep (McClintock and Crooks, "Cyc."). Near the mouth it widens to some five hundred and fifty feet, and the depth diminishes to two or three feet (Lynch). The principal *fords* are not many (though Conder collected the names of about forty in all). (1) About two miles above the mouth (Fish). Several miles higher up is the traditional place of our Lord's baptism, nearly opposite Jericho, and somewhat above this is (2) a ford used at some seasons. At the traditional place the river is, in spring (when most travelers visit it), both too deep and too swift for fording. Yet just before Easter several thousand Greek and Oriental pilgrims (in the Middle Ages there were sometimes 100,000) go to this place — men, women, and children—and immerse themselves as a sacred bath, many of them changing their garments amid the dense thickets of shrubbery which extend for some distance from the stream ; and almost every year, in the vast fanatical throng, crowding in together, some are drowned. Several miles above this place is now a ferry-boat (comp. 2 Sam. 19: 18), which is handled with difficulty, the current being in March excessively strong. (3) Ten miles below the mouth of the Jabbok is a ford now much used in going from Nabulus to Es-Salt (Van de Velde). (4) Above Jabbok is the ford of Succoth, where Jacob crossed with his family and flocks (Gen. 32: 10, 22.) (5) Near Beisan is a ford, which Robinson (III., 325) crossed with difficulty, but which, on March 24, 1871, the Modîn of Beisan said would only reach the horses' bellies. In this neighborhood Conder, in April,

---

that the Jordan was a river (like many other explanations he gives), this was quite needless for Matt., and contrary to his usage in similar cases. Translators and copyists in foreign countries would, however, think the word necessary here, even as א and Old Syriac have inserted it in John 1: 28. We thus see that Matt. is not likely to have written it and copyists would be likely to insert it. This strong union of intrinsic and transcriptional evidence might even outweigh the very strong documentary evidence in favor of the word, but for the fact that D and some copies of Old Latin *omit* 'river' in Mark 1: 5, as well as here, which indicates that the "Western" text was hostile to the word, and thus accounts for its omission in many copies of Matt. This word must therefore be accepted as a part of Matthew's text, yet not without some lingering doubt. The question has obviously no practical importance, however interesting to the textual critic.

7 But when he saw many of the Pharisees and Sadducees come to his baptism, he said unto them, O generation of vipers, who hath warned you to flee from the
wrath to come?

7 in the river Jordan, confessing their sins. But when
he saw many of the Pharisees and Sadducees coming
[1]to his baptism, he said unto them, Ye offspring of
vipers, who warned you to flee from the wrath to

1 Or, *for baptism.*

---

found twenty-one possible fords within seven
miles. About ten miles above Beisan is a
Saracenic bridge (the only one now crossing
the river), upon the road from Nabulus to
Damascus, and above it are said to be several
difficult and little-used fords. (6) Not far
below the Lake of Galilee is an important ford,
which the Jews of our Lord's time must have
constantly used in going from Galilee through
Perea to Jerusalem. At this, on March 25,
1871, the water came nearly to the root of a
horse's tail.—But in summer the river falls
much lower, and must be easily fordable at
many points.—The outer and principal part
of the Jordan valley is nearly all entirely unproductive without irrigation, justifying the
statement of Josephus that the Jordan flows
through a desert ("War," 3, 10, 7). But the
banks of the river are everywhere fringed
with trees (willow, balsam, etc.), amid which
the birds sing, and in whose pleasant shade
the multitudes could gather to hear the voice
of the new prophet. As to the scene of the
baptism of Jesus, see on v. 13.

The people received this solemn rite **confessing their sins.** The Scriptures promise
forgiveness on condition of confession (Prov. 28:
13; 1 John 1: 9), though of course this is not the
meritorious ground of forgiveness. It was required by the Mosaic Law (Lev. 5: 5; 16: 21; 26: 40;
Num. 5: 7), and is often recorded as practiced by
the penitent (*e. g*, 2 Chron. 30: 22; Psa. 32:
5; Neh. 9: 2, 3; Dan. 9: 20; Acts 19: 18). The
term here used appears to denote an actually spoken confession, and the present participle shows that it was made in immediate
connection with the act of baptism. Most
probably the confession was not made to the
multitude, but simply to John, and was not
uniform, but varied according to every man's
calling, character, etc., (comp. John's specific
exhortations to different classes, Luke 3: 10-
14). The act of submitting to baptism was itself
also (Köhler) a confession of faith, namely, of
faith in the good news of the kingdom. (Mark 1:
15; Acts 19: 4.)

We have now (v. 7-12) a specimen of John's
teachings given more in detail.

7. The Pharisees and Sadducees were
the two great parties, at once religious and
political, among the Jews at the time of
Christ. The date of their origin is unknown,
and they no doubt arose gradually. In the
centuries immediately following the return
from the Captivity there must have been various divisions of public sentiment. Some
insisted on conforming to all decisions of
tribunals and opinions of leading teachers,
others thought it enough to observe the
original directions of the law; some busied
themselves in *developing* many real or supposed germs of truth contained in the law
and the prophets, others said they wanted no
religious teaching but that of the sacred
books, especially the Pentateuch; some were
extremely zealous for their religion, and
ready to die in its defence, others were more
ready to suit their action to changing circumstances; some cherished a bitter hatred to
foreigners, others were friendly to them, etc.
Such divergencies of opinion on many questions of truth and duty would gradually associate themselves, by sympathy or antagonism,
with some one leading division, so as to form
two distinct, though at first not well defined,
parties. Then when any new religious or
political issue arose (the religious and political being always more or less blended, from
the nature of the Jewish institutions), the
mere fact that one party took one side of the
question would decide the opposite party to
take the other side. Thus by degrees the
parties became sharply defined, compact, antagonizing at all points.[1] Josephus held that
the Pharisees and Sadducees were distinct
parties in B. C. 145. ("Ant.," 13, 5, 9.) Certainly in the later years of John Hyrcanus
(died B. C. 106), they were politically antago-
nistic. ("Ant.," 13, 10, 5.) By the time of
our Lord's ministry, the division had doubtless become more pronounced. The history
of their hostility was known to run back to

---

[1] The above was written before the appearance of
Edersheim's work, and the view presented finds grati-

fying support in his elaborate discussion. (Book iii.
chap. 2.)

the Maccabean struggle, the Pharisees now representing the patriots of that time, and it had included many fierce political conflicts and wars under the successors of John Hyrcanus (" Ant.," 13, 15, 5; 13, 16, 5), which left a bitter and lasting hatred. At the time of Christ, the Sadducees were comparatively few in number, but embraced a large proportion of wealthy and influential men (" Ant.," 18, 1, 4), including many members of the Sanhedrin (Acts 5: 17), and were more likely to have the sympathy of the Roman rulers. But the Pharisees were far more numerous, and on account of the patriotic record and pious reputation of the party, possessed the sympathies and support of the people at large. Yet, while political antagonism had caused bitterness, the chief differences between the two parties had always been religious. The Pharisees held to many traditional interpretations of Scripture (e. g., 5: 21, 33, 43), some of them not merely erroneous, but subversive of its great truths, and also to many traditional rules for the conduct of life, particularly as to externals, some of these likewise tending to set aside the teachings of God's word. (15: 2 ff.) These they claimed, as most Jews have ever since done, to be of almost equal authority with the law; indeed, they were called the "oral law," and held to have been given orally to Moses at Mount Sinai, and handed down from him. About two centuries after Christ many of these traditions were written down, and form what is called the Mishna, or 'second,' i. e., the second law.[1] All these traditional interpretations and rules the Sadducees rejected, acknowledging no authority but the Scriptures, and especially 'the law,' i. e., the five books ascribed to Moses. But the interpretations of the later centuries before Christ, as received among the Pharisees, had elicited from the Scriptures various

true and important doctrines, as that of the separate existence of spirits, and a certain approach to the Christian doctrine of the resurrection from the dead (comp. on 22: 23); while the Sadducees, in avoiding traditionalism, went to the opposite extreme of rationalism, and wholly rejected these doctrines, and even the belief in angels (Acts 23: 8), though this last is so plainly and repeatedly taught in Old Testament. The Pharisees, in their fanatical zeal for the law of purifications, and the numerous rules which tradition had added, shrank from all association with "sinners," i. e., persons who notoriously violated the law (Luke 7: 39), and thought it inexcusable in Jesus to do otherwise. (9: 11; Luke 15: 2.) Thus, when they came from market, where they might possibly have touched some person or thing that was ceremonially 'unclean,' they were wont to perform a complete purification, 'immersed themselves,' before they would eat. (Mark 7: 4.)[2] This scrupulosity in separating themselves probably led to the name Pharisees, 'separaters.' The name Sadducees most likely meant 'righteous,' as denoting that they contented themselves with being simply righteous men, and did not care for newfangled beliefs and strait-laced observances.[3] Our Saviour less frequently referred to the errors of the Sadducees, great as they were, doubtless because the people in general were little likely to be misled by them; he does however caution his disciples against their doctrine (and that of the Phar.) in 16: 11. They appear 'tempting' him in 16: 1, and 22: 23. But the Pharisees had, with some exceptions (such as Nicodemus, Gamaliel, Paul), lost the true patriotism and especially the true piety which had gained their party so much popular favor, and were striving by the most shameful hypocrisy to retain an influence which they no longer deserved, and

---

[1] Commentaries upon the Mishna (with supplementary traditions also) were afterwards written, and known as Gemara, 'completion," because they completed the Mishna. The Jerusalem Gemara was written in the fourth century after Christ, and that of Babylon in the fifth century. The Mishna, with one or the other of these, is commonly meant by the term Talmud ('instruction').

[2] So, if an Egyptian touched a swine, he went to the river and 'dipped himself from it' (bapto), clothes and all (Her. II. 47).

[3] The common Jewish derivation from a supposed founder named Zadok is now almost universally rejected. Geiger's recent theory, that the Sadducees were an aristocratic, priestly class, 'the priests of the seed of Zadok' (Ezek. 43: 19), is adopted by Hausrath and Schürer, by Twisleton in Smith's Dict., Geikie, and Ginsburg in Kitto, but is extremely far-fetched, and does not explain the facts. See in opposition to it, Edersh. Vol. I. p. 322. The best recent treatises are those of Wellhausen and Montet. (See Index.)

which they abused to the worst ends; and our Lord rebuked their hypocrisy on various occasions, and unsparingly exposed it in the last public discourse of his ministry, ch. 23. The continued rivalry between Pharisees and Sadducees was the providential means of securing freedom from persecution for several years after the ascension of Christ (Acts, ch. 4-6), and was made useful even at a later time by Paul. (Acts 23 : 6.) No writings of Sadducees remain to us, and we know them, besides the few references in New Testament, only from writers who were Pharisees, viz., Josephus and the Talmud, and who may have done them scant justice. They seem to have ceased to exist soon after the destruction of the Jewish State, which was the natural fate of a rationalistic party, having little devout earnestness, and whose standing had been social and political rather than religious.

The term 'sect' applied in Eng. Ver. to the Pharisees and the Sadducees (Acts 5 : 17; 15 : 5; 26 : 5) does not, according to its present use, correctly render the Greek word nor correctly represent the facts of the case; they were parties, with the peculiarity above mentioned, that they were at the same time religious and political parties. But there was a 'sect,' in our sense, then existing among the Jews, called the Essenes, who had a strictly exclusive organization and worship, and indeed lived in seclusion, much like the monks of later times. They were few in number, having small communities scattered over Palestine, and the largest on the western shore of the Dead Sea. They were probably an offshoot of the Pharisees, whose leading views they shared. Their comparative insignificance, their never attending the temple-worship, and this apparent relation to the Pharisees, will account for the fact that they are never mentioned in N. T., nor in the Talmud, being known to us only through the writings of Philo, Josephus, and Pliny. All attempts to show that some ideas or practices were derived from them by John the Baptist or by Jesus, have proved a failure; but their teachings do throw light on the heresy Paul attacked at Colosse (see an admirable essay in Lightfoot on Colossians). Josephus says ("Ant.," 13 : 5, 9) that the Essenes were utter fatalists, the Sadducees held to extreme views of free-will, substantially reject-

ing providence, while the Pharisees occupied a middle ground, recognizing both human freedom and responsibility, and divine control.

Come—or, *coming*—**to his baptism,** that is, coming to be baptized by him.[1] The expression **many of the Pharisees and Sadducees,** with only one article, throws the two parties together as both needing sharp rebuke. (Comp. 16 : 6, 11, 12.)—What is here given as addressed to them, really applied, more or less, to the people at large, and was intended to apply to all it fitted, and Luke (3 : 7) gives it as addressed to 'the crowds that came forth to be baptized by him.' So in Matthew, the people at large are evidently addressed in what immediately follows, v. 9 ff. Perhaps also Matthew here refers to a particular case, while Luke states a general fact, as his tenses (in the Greek) may imply.—We learn from Luke 7 : 29 f., that the Pharisees and lawyers who on a certain occasion in Galilee heard the teachings of Jesus concerning John, had not been baptized by John, as the people present and the publicans had been; but this ought not to be relied on as proving that no Pharisees had been baptized by John. Only a portion of them were at all disposed to seek his baptism, and some of these were doubtless repelled by John's stern rebuke and rigorous requirements. (Comp. on 21 : 32.)

O generation, or, *Ye offspring*—**of vipers,** merely a phrase of reproach, describing them as noxious and odious, and perhaps also as insidious. (Comp. 12 : 34; 23 : 33; Isa. 14 : 29; 59 : 5; Psa. 58 : 4.) Classic writers present similar expressions. The idea that they are meant to be described as children of the devil, the old serpent, seems fanciful. **Warned,** is stronger than the original, which signifies to show secretly or partially, and thus to intimate, suggest, indicate, or more generally, to make known. **To flee from,** may either mean 'to escape,' as in 23 : 33, or to 'avoid,' 'shun,' as in 1 Cor. 10 : 14. With the former meaning it would be, 'Who intimated to you that you would escape the coming wrath?' viz., when there was so little reason to believe they would escape; with the latter: 'Who suggested to you to flee from,' etc., the surprise being that any one should take the trouble, with so little pros-

---

[1] Tisch. and W H. omit 'his,' but on insufficient grounds.

8 Bring forth therefore fruits meet for *a* repentance:
9 And think not to say within yourselves, We have Abraham to *our* father: for I say unto you, that God is able of these stones to raise up children unto Abraham.
10 And now also the axe is laid unto the root of the trees: therefore every tree which bringeth not forth good fruit is hewn down, and cast into the fire.

8 come? Bring forth therefore fruit worthy of [1]repent-
9 ance: and think not to say within yourselves, We have Abraham to our father: for I say unto you, that God is able of these stones to raise up children unto
10 Abraham. And even now the axe lieth at the root of the trees: every tree therefore that bringeth not forth good fruit is hewn down, and cast into the fire.

a Or, *answerable to amendment of life.*——1 Or, *your repentance.*

pect of any good result. The latter is the more natural sense. **The wrath to come—** or, *coming wrath.* It was expected among the Jews (as the book of Enoch shows), that in connection with Messiah's appearance there would be an outburst of God's wrath upon his enemies, *i. e.*, upon the Gentiles. But John, in accordance with the whole tenor of his teaching, describes 'the coming wrath' as threatening all God's enemies, including impenitent Jews; and this was already implied in Mal., ch. 3 and 4. Similarly Paul in 1 Thess. 1 : 10.

8. Fruits, *fruit* (singular), is the correct reading.[1] **Bring forth,** literally, *make.* The rendering 'bring forth,' common from Tyndale down, mixes the metaphors. 'Produce,' though not pleasing, would be allowable, and suits exactly in v. 10. **Therefore,** presents the exhortation as the consequence of what precedes, or is naturally supplied. "As you profess repentance and wish to be baptized, therefore produce fruit worthy of repentance, and thus prove that you really do repent." This exhortation he might naturally address to all (Luke 3 : 8), while it was especially appropriate to the Pharisees and Sadducees. It is not probable that he required them to go off and prove their repentance before he could baptize them; he only gave them a special charge.

9. A great hindrance to a true repentance on their part, was the idea generally entertained among the Jews, that all the descendants of Abraham must certainly escape wrath, would assuredly be saved (see John 8 : 33, 39). John proceeds therefore to correct this error. **Think not to say,** is an exact imitation of the Greek, and signifies either 'do not think yourselves at liberty to say,' 'warranted in saying,' (comp. Phil. 3 : 4), or more probably, 'do not think you will say,' 'do not propose to yourselves to say' (comp. Luke's 'do not begin to say'). **To say within yourselves,** corresponds to

a well-known Hebrew expression, 'to say in his heart' (24: 48; Psa. 4. 4; 10: 6; 14: 1), and is used also in 9 : 21; Luke 7 : 39, 49; Rev. 18 : 7. **We have Abraham to—**or, *for*—**our father,** with emphasis on 'father,' as shown in Greek by the order of the words. Descended as they were from Abraham, they thought themselves perfectly safe from the Messianic wrath, and in little need of repentance. One Rabbi in a Midrash even says (Wet.), "In the age to come Abraham sits beside the gates of Gehenna, and suffers no circumcised Israelite to go down"; though the Rabbi does make ingenious provision for an exception in the case of those who have sinned excessively. *Edersh:* "No principle was more fully established in the popular conviction, than that all Israel had part in the world to come, and this specifically because of their connection with Abraham. This appears not only from the New Test., from Philo, and Josephus, but from many Rabbinic passages." **I say unto you,** calls attention to what he is about to say, as being important. (Comp. on 5 : 18). **Of,** or, *out of,* as the material (translated 'out of' by Noyes and Davidson). He perhaps pointed to the loose stones lying on the river-bank. The fact that God could with such perfect ease raise up children to Abraham, and so was not dependent on *them* for the continuation of Abraham's posterity, would suggest that they might readily be set aside from enjoying the blessings promised to Abraham's descendants. So God once threatened to Moses that he would destroy the nation, and raise up a new people from him.—This representation that the Messianic blessings would not necessarily be enjoyed by all Jews as such, accords with that of John 1 : 29, that they would not be limited to Jews, but that Messiah 'takes away the sin of the world.' Comp. also Paul's argument in Gal. 3 : 7, and Rom. 4 : 16.

10. Now also, or, *already.* Not only is there a coming Messianic wrath, but already

[1] Not only is the singular best supported, but we can see how the plural might be introduced in assimilation to Luke 3 : 8.

11 I indeed baptize you with water unto repentance: but he that cometh after me is mightier than I, whose shoes I am not worthy to bear: he shall baptize you with the Holy Ghost, and *with* fire:

11 I indeed baptize you [1] in water unto repentance: but he that cometh after me is mightier than I, whose shoes I am not [2] worthy to bear: he shall baptize you

1 Or, *with*....2 Gr. *sufficient.*

there is beginning a Messianic discrimination among the descendants of Abraham. It is therefore high time to repent (Weiss). 'Also' must be omitted; it was doubtless inserted from Luke 3: 9. *Even now* translates 'now' in its emphatic position. **Is laid unto,** or, *lies at,* **the root.** Noyes. The verb is exactly 'lies.' The Greek preposition leads many to render 'is laid to the root,' *i. e.,* applied to it in actual cutting; and timber being very scarce in Palestine, it is now common to cut down a tree at the ground (Thomson, ii., 291). But the meaning more probably is that it has been brought to the tree and lies there ready for use. **Therefore,** *i. e.,* since such is the design with which the axe has been placed there. **Bringeth not forth good fruit,** is the same image as in v. 8; but instead of the specific idea of fruit appropriate to repentance, we have here the more general idea of good fruit. **Hewn down,** literally 'cut out,' viz., out of its place in the vineyard. (So Davidson). The present tenses, 'is cut out' and 'is cast,' describe the action as actually going on; the discrimination is already beginning, 'even now.' In 7: 19, the present tense denotes what is customary in the case of all such trees. **Every,** the most honored and privileged of the nation (v. 7) not excepted. There was beginning a severe scrutiny of all, and the unworthy would be utterly excluded from that share in Messiah's kingdom which the persons addressed so confidently anticipated.

At this point Luke mentions various classes as inquiring of the preacher, 'What are we to do then?' viz., by way of producing good fruit, fruit worthy of repentance; and gives some piquant and highly suggestive replies. (Luke 3 : 10-14.)

11. The idea of v. 10 is now (v. 11 f.) brought out by John more explicitly by contrasting with his own work that of the greatly superior personage who is coming after him, whose work will be far more discriminating and thorough. The most striking and characteristic thing about his own ministry being the baptism he administered (comp. on 21: 25), he

employs that in stating the contrast. And it could be very naturally thus employed, since immersion in water furnished an apt and expressive image for representing the soul as being as it were immersed in, bathed in, brought completely under the influence of, thoroughly affected by, the operations of the Holy Spirit. The risen Saviour afterwards used the same image, and made the same contrast with John's baptism, in promising to the disciples the Holy Spirit's influences, to be given after his ascension. (Acts 1: 5.) The contrast here is certainly not, as some have imagined, between John's baptism and that actually performed by Jesus, through his disciples (John 3 : 22 ; 4 : 2), for that was as much a "water-baptism" as John's. Nor does it seem proper to confine the view in any respect to the personal ministry of Jesus, but to understand a reference to the entire work of the coming Messiah, including what followed his personal ascension. This work of Messiah would differ from, and be superior to, the merely introductory work of the forerunner in the way stated.

Indeed here represents a very peculiar Greek particle (*men*) which denotes that to the clause in which it stands there will presently be opposed or contrasted some other statement (commonly introduced by 'but'). We have nothing exactly like this in English, and have to say 'indeed,' 'truly,' 'to be sure,' etc., and often we use no word, and express the idea by a mere emphasis: "*I* baptize in water . . . . but he that is coming,' etc. (Comp. especially *men,* truly, on 9: 37.) **With—**rather, *in* **water** (as given in Amer. App.), is the proper rendering of the preposition and case here employed. In a few expressions the Greek has *en,* 'in' (with its case), to denote merely the instrument or means, not merely in phrases which we can imitate, as 'In what shall it be salted?' (5: 13), 'In what measure ye measure' (7: 2), but also, in imitation of a Hebrew use, in connections where the English idiom could not employ 'in,' as 'Trample them with (in) their feet' (7: 6, see note), 'Smite with (in) the sword.'

(Luke 22: 49.) Here the action was originally conceived as in a certain sense located *in* the feet, the sword, a conception foreign to our idiom. But it must be observed that this use of the preposition is rare, and it cannot with propriety be so understood unless the connection is such as altogether to exclude the common and natural meaning. Show, on grounds apart from this expression, that baptizing, from the nature of the action, cannot have been performed 'in water' in the strict local sense, and it will be lawful to interpret the preposition (with its case) as here used in a looser local sense, denoting the instrument or means. But here the common and natural sense of the preposition exactly agrees with the nature of the action. (Comp. on v. 6, and also comp. 1 Cor. 10: 2, 'in the cloud and in the sea,' and 2 Kings 5: 10, 14.) So here Meyer, Weiss, McClellan, etc.

But we are told by some that while John (1: 26. 31, 33) has this same 'in water,' Luke, in the parallel passage to this (3: 16), and also in Acts (1: 5, repeated in Acts 11: 16), uses the simple case of the noun without any preposition (and so probably in Mark 1: 8),[1] and that this certainly means 'with water,' denoting merely an instrument, which makes it more likely that the same was meant in Matthew and John. Then it is argued that an instrument is always wielded, and *applied to* the object affected by the action, and so that "baptize with water" cannot denote an immersion. But these positions are untenable. The simple Greek case may itself mean 'in water,' that is, it may be not the instrumental but the locative case.[2] And granting it to be the instrument, an instru-

ment must be used according to its natural relation to the action. There is a curious parallel in 14: 13, 'Jesus withdrew in a boat' (*en ploio*); here, Mark 6: 32, has the simple case without a preposition (*to ploio*).[3] This also may mean 'in the boat,' but grant that it is instrumental, the way to make a boat the instrument of going across the lake is to put yourself in the boat. So the above argument from 'with water' falls to the ground.—Luke, in both the passages (3: 16; Acts 1: 5) has *en pneumati*, 'in the Spirit,' and so Mark 1: 8, the reason probably being that the local reference was obvious in speaking of 'water' as connected with baptize, but needed to be more distinctly brought out in speaking of the Holy Spirit, that the figure of immersion in the Spirit might not be overlooked.[4]

Unto repentance. The most natural way to understand this preposition (with its case), in Greek as in English, would be 'in order that you may repent.' So the same expression in Wisdom 11: 23, 'Thou overlookest the sins of men unto repentance.' The difficulty is that John's baptism evidently presupposed repentance, and was to be followed by 'fruits worthy of repentance.' Accordingly, some urge that the preposition *eis* (with its case), 'unto,' must here denote the occasion or ground of the baptizing, a meaning which it clearly has in 12: 41, and which is ascribed to it here by the Greek commentator Euthymius.[5] This, however, is a very unusual and difficult use of the preposition, though certainly possible. Others take it to mean generally, 'with reference to repentance' (so Tyndale, 'in token of'). Such a meaning the preposition with its case does somewhat frequently have,[6] and that gives here a very good sense (as it

---

[1] In Mark 1: 8, the authorities are so divided, and the probabilities of assimilation to Matt. and John or to Luke are so balanced, that it is hard to decide. But 'baptize' would naturally have suggested 'in' to the copyists (some copies have it even in Luke 3: 16), and this makes it more likely that the original text of Mark was like that of Luke (W H.) In Matt. and John, and in Acts, there is no variation in the copies.

[2] See probable examples of the locative with *baptizo*, in Conant, "on Baptizein," example 71, 78, also, perhaps, 60, 73, 76, 86. Compare Latin immergo alto, unda, etc., where the case is necessarily locative and not instrumental.

[3] Here, as in Mark 1: 8, some copies (some very good ones here) insert *en* 'in,' probably for the same reason as there, that the circumstances suggested it. John 21:

8 has a similar expression, *to ploiario* (no preposition), and without variation in the copies, and the expression in the common text of Mark is at any rate Greek, if it be not the true text.

[4] Here also (Mark) W H. omit the preposition, but with slender evidence, and apparently through their curious devotion to B.

[5] Euthymius (12th century) expressly says, " *eis metanoian* instead of *dia ten metanoian*," ('because of repentance') and argues " for he baptized them confessing, which is equivalent to repenting, because they repented. And such a baptism was a proof of repentance."

[6] See *eis*, translated *concerning*, Acts 2: 25, and such phrases as "to jeer at a man *eis* his rags" (Aristoph.), "to reproach *eis* friendship" (Xen.), "to differ from one *eis* virtue " (Plat.).

would also in Luke 3: 3; Mark 1: 4, 'unto remission of sins'). But it is best to adhere if possible to the common and most natural sense 'in order to.' And it may perhaps be so understood if we revert (Cremer) to v. 7, 8, the special occasion of what John is saying. Those whom he baptized all professed repentance, but concerning some it was very doubtful whether there was a real change of thought and purpose (see on v. 2), and he exhorts them to show by the appropriate fruits that such was the case. He might therefore say, "I baptize you in order that you may really repent," including in the one view and one expression, the primary change of purpose and the subsequent results and proof thereof. This makes the design that of John in baptizing (so Hofmann in Keil), and not exactly the design of the baptism itself (as Meyer, and many). In the parallel passages of Mark and Luke (Mark 1: 8; Luke 3: 16), this phrase, 'unto repentance,' is not given, probably because each of them had just before spoken of it as a 'baptism of repentance.' That expression (Mark 1: 4; Luke 3: 3; also Acts 13: 24; 19: 4) is still more indefinite than the other; by it the baptism is simply distinguished from other baptisms, characterized as a repentance-baptism (comp. 'Babylon—removal' 1: 11), and we are left to determine, from the nature of the case and the known circumstances, what precise relation existed between the baptism and repentance. **He that cometh after me.** Literally, *the (one) coming behind me.* The expression implies that they had heard of this coming personage before. And we know from the Talmud that the Jews frequently spoke of Messiah as *Habba*, 'the coming (one;)' (comp. 11: 3; 21: 9), perhaps originally deriving it from such expressions as Zech. 9: 9; Mal. 3: 1; Psa. 118: 26. Mark and Luke, not writing especially for Jews, do not here use this Jewish phrase. (Mark 1: 7; Luke 3: 16.) **Mightier than I,** not only superior in position, but more powerful, able to accomplish what he could not. **Not worthy to bear,** or, more exactly, in colloquial phrase, 'not fit to carry.' The word rendered **shoes** (or, *sandals*) signifies 'what is bound under,' and denotes the sole of leather, raw hide, or wood which they wore under the foot, and

which, fastened to the foot by a thong or strap, constituted its entire covering. A Bedouin from beyond Jordan may be seen to-day with just such sandals of untanned sheepskin. It was the office of the lowest menial among all the slaves of a household, to carry his master's sandals, as when he went to the bath, or to untie and remove them when he entered the house; this last being the expression given by Mark and Luke as used here or on a similar occasion. Somewhat similar among us would be the task of removing muddy over-shoes. A like menial service was that of washing the feet after removing the sandals. (Luke 7: 44; John 13: 3 ff.) We learn from Luke 3: 15 that the people were beginning to meditate whether John himself might be the Messiah, and it was partly to meet this that John told them he was so immensely inferior to the Coming One. In general, John is singularly free from self-assertion. While boldly rebuking the most influential classes (v. 7), and braving the wrath of Herod Antipas (14: 4), he speaks of himself only in the way of declaring the imcomparable superiority of the Coming One (comp. John 3: 28 ff.). Great force of character, united with great humility and modesty, must command hearty admiration. **He,** emphatic, as in 1: 21. **With the Holy Ghost and with fire.** Better, *in the Holy Spirit and fire.* Rev. Ver. The original has no article, and some propose to render 'in Holy Spirit,' *i. e.*, in holy spiritual influences. But the phrase Holy Spirit was so definite by reason of its common use, as to be for Matthew's readers virtually a proper name, so that, like other proper names, it could be used with or without the article; and it is used without the article in numerous instances, particularly when in connection with a preposition, as here. English idiom requires the article, as in many other cases where the Greek may omit it. Comp. 'holy covenant' in 1 Macc. 1: 15, and 'all Scripture' in 2 Tim. 3: 16. As to 'Ghost,' and 'Spirit,' see on 1: 18. Observe how helpful it would be to have the same word 'Spirit' here as in 3: 16, and 4: 1. This statement of John's is plainly a figure, as in v. 10, 12. To say that John's baptism was only in water, and Christian baptism is both in water and the Spirit, is curiously to mix the image and that which it signifies. But such mixing need not surprise us, for much confusion has arisen in Christian thought from the wide-spread notion of baptismal regeneration. John here says that while he immersed men in water, the *symbol* of a new and pure life, the mightier Coming One would (so to speak) immerse them in the Holy Spirit, who *really produces* such a life. Jesus did not literally immerse men in the Spirit, any more than he literally smote men with an ax (v. 10), or cleansed them with a fan. (v. 12.) *Plumptre:* " As heard and understood at the time, the baptism with the Holy Ghost would imply that the souls thus baptized would be plunged, as it were, in that creative and informing Spirit which was the source of life and holiness and wisdom." It is likewise explained as a figurative immersion by Neander, Meyer, Bleek. This figurative use of the term resembles such expressions of profane writers as 'immersed in ignorance,' 'in sorrow,' ' in debts,' as also our Saviour's description of his own dreadful sufferings as a baptism. (Luke 12 : 50.) In English too we are constantly saying, 'immersed in business,' ' plunged in despair,' 'bathed in delight,' etc.

But what is meant by the additional words, **and fire?** Observe that in the preceding verse the fire receives the unfruitful trees, and in the next verse the fire consumes the chaff. V. 11 evidently teaches the same general lesson, and it would therefore be natural to understand the fire which ends each of the three parallel sentences in essentially the same way as a fire which consumes the wicked. And notice that Luke (3 : 16) who also gives 'and fire,' has the other images of burning the unfruitful trees and the chaff (Luke 3 : 9, 17), while in Mark 1 : 8; John 1 : 33; and Acts 1 : 5; 11 : 16, where the other images are not mentioned, neither are the words 'and fire' given. This would seem to leave no doubt as to the meaning of these words. The objection is that in the other images (v. 10, 12) two classes are distinguished, and the destiny of each is separately stated; while here it is simply 'shall baptize you,' one class of persons, 'in the Holy Spirit and fire,' without even repeating the preposition before ' fire '—as if it meant one class and one destiny, though stated by means of two terms. But the 'you' whom John is addressing are not simply the believing and penitent, but the Jews in general, with special reference at

the outset (v. 7 f.) to the Pharisees and Sadducees. Now it had been predicted by Malachi (3 : 1 ff.) that the messenger of the covenant would come and purify the nation (especially the Levites, who were necessary to a bettered worship and national life), as silver is purified in a furnace; and this does not simply mean that he would purify individuals by consuming what was faulty in them, but Mal. 4: 1-3 shows it to mean that he would purify the nation by consuming the wicked individuals like 'stubble,' and then the truly righteous of the nation would rejoice and prosper. The nation would be, as it were, thrown into a furnace of fire, which would consume the wicked among them, and leave a purified nation. In like manner, John says, the mighty Coming One will 'plunge you,' the Jews whom he is addressing, 'in the Holy Spirit and fire'; some will be consumed and some preserved, a purified people. Just how far the 'Holy Spirit' in John's mouth differs from the O. T. and approaches the N. T. idea, it would be very difficult, and is not necessary, to determine. But it can scarcely be questioned that John's thought is connected with that of Malachi, and if so, the explanation just offered is in all probability correct. Comp. Bleek. More or less similar is the view of Origen, Fritzsche, Neander, de Wette, Hengstenberg, Meyer, Reynolds. — Many, however, suppose that the 'Holy Spirit' is to be taken in the strictly N. T. sense, and 'fire' is simply appended as an image of the Spirit's purifying work upon the individual, consuming his faults. So Chrys., most Roman Catholic commentators, Calvin, Olshausen, Ewald, Godet, Edersh., Morison, and a number of others. Some of these think we have a similar expression in John 3: 5, 'born of water and the Spirit,' and some refer to the tongues of fire on the day of Pentecost as an actual exhibition of the image which John here employed. Such a view disregards the striking parallelism of Matthew's three sentences, and rejects the guidance of Malachi. Our Lord promised the disciples (Acts 1 : 5) a baptism in the Holy Spirit ere many days, which was fulfilled on the day of Pentecost, and on that day appeared tongue-shaped flames sitting on their heads, and obviously symbolizing the power of speaking with other tongues. And it is maintained that this is what John

12 Whose fan *is* in his hand, and he will thoroughly purge his floor, and gather his wheat into the garner; but he will burn up the chaff with unquenchable fire.

12 [1] in the Holy Spirit and *in* fire: whose fan is in his hand, and he will thoroughly cleanse his threshing-floor; and he will gather his wheat into the garner, but the chaff he will burn up with unquenchable fire.

1 Or, *with*.

meant. But Jesus did not in his promise add 'and fire,' and there is no mention of fiery tongues in the case of Cornelius and his household, when Peter expressly recognized (Acts 11: 16) a fulfillment of the Saviour's promise. Nay, the forerunner meant something deeper and broader than the power of speaking with tongues; he was describing the great work of discrimination, by which some would be destroyed and the rest purified.

That difficulty was long ago felt as to the meaning of 'fire,' appears from its being omitted here by many late MSS., and a few late versions and Fathers; yet none of them omit it in Luke 3: 16. Wyclif and Rheims have 'in the Holy Ghost and fire.' Tyndale introduced 'with the Holy Ghost and with fire,' (altering the preposition and repeating it), followed by the other early Protestant versions, and now by Alford and Darby. 'In the Holy Spirit and fire' is the rendering of Bible Union Revision, of Noyes ('in fire') and Davidson, and Amer. App. to Rev. Ver.

12. A third image for the work of scrutiny and separation, and here expressly referred, as in ver. 11, to Messiah. **Fan,** more exactly *a winnowing-shovel;* with this the Jews threw up their wheat against the wind, which would blow away the chaff (comp. Psa. 1: 4; Dan. 2: 35; Hos. 13: 3), while the grain fell in a heap. The 'threshing-floor,' a circular space of beaten earth, was then cleaned up, and the straw and chaff sometimes burned. (See Isa. 5: 24). **Thoroughly purge,** or, *cleanse.* The examination and discrimination will be complete. The **garner,** or granary, barn, literally, *place for putting away.* The Jews often used underground granaries, cut in the solid rock, like cisterns, or vaulted and cemented. In these grain could be kept for years. The term rendered **chaff** includes also bits of straw, broken by the treading. **With unquenchable fire.** We may here render 'with fire,' instrumental, or 'in fire,' locative, just as in v. 11 and 13: 40. Comp. 'into fire,' v. 10, and Mark 9: 43. By saying unquenchable fire, he turns attention away from the

literalities of the image to the eternal things represented. So with 'eternal tabernacles' in Luke 16: 9. Rev. Ver.

Luke adds (3: 18, B. U. Ver.) that 'with many other exhortations he published the good tidings to the people,' varying his practical exhortations while adhering to the same general good news that the reign of heaven was near at hand. This statement, as shown by what follows in Luke, is designed to cover the whole period of John's ministry. In John 1: 26 f., we have two instances of testimony to Jesus after his baptism, somewhat similar to that of v. 10-12, borne before the event.

HOMILETICAL AND PRACTICAL.

The personal character of John the Baptist. (1) His courageous severity, v. 7; 14: 4. (2) His practical wisdom, Luke 3: 10-14. (3) His humility and unselfishness, v. 11; John 3: 27-30.—Religious benefits of solitude, as illustrated by the case of John.—The ministry of John. (1) Its subjects and spirit. (2) Its relation to the ministry of Jesus. (3) The great effects it produced, v. 5; 11: 11.—JER. TAYLOR: "John was like the morning star, or the blushings springing from the windows of the east, foretelling the approach of the Sun of righteousness." LUTHER: "New things. 1) A new prophet; 2) A new ceremony; 3) A new preaching; 4) A new king."—V. 2. The calls to repentance, (1) By the prophets, (2) By John, (3) By Jesus, (4) By the apostles.— The old exhortation, 'repent,' and the new motive, 'for the reign,' etc.—HENRY: "True penitents have *other thoughts* of God and Christ, and sin and holiness, and this world and the other, than they have had, and stand otherwise affected toward them. The change of the *mind* produces a change of the *way.*"— V. 3. Preparation for Christ's reign: (1) In what it consists—confessing and forsaking sins. (2) How it is exhibited, (a) by baptism, v. 6, (b) by fruit, v. 8. (3) How men are induced to make it—by the voice of one crying.—ED. IRVING: "I do therefore consider the Baptist as our pattern and permission to take strong weapons of argument and terrible de-

13 Then cometh Jesus from Galilee to Jordan. unto | 13   Then cometh Jesus from Galilee to the Jordan
John, to be baptized of him.

---

nunciation, wherewith to clear away obstructions, and make a highway for the descent of our Lord. Christ came not until the Baptist had come. The gospel of salvation cometh not until the fear of condemnation and ruin hath seized us. The Baptist rested his lever upon the instant coming of Christ, and from that fulcrum took his purchase upon the present." CHRYSOSTOM: "The Prophet and the Baptist go upon the same ideas; the Prophet says, 'Prepare ye the way of the Lord,' the Baptist, 'Produce fruits worthy of repentance.'" V. 4. The first Elijah and the second Elijah (comp. 11: 14). BENGEL: "Even John's food and raiment preached."—JER. TAYLOR: "The preacher's life is his best sermon."—ED. IRVING: "And what is there good that cometh not out of suffering? and what is there great that cometh not out of self-denial? what is there new, in knowledge or in virtue, that cometh not out of solitary thought? and what is there noble and lasting in purpose that cometh not out of long nursing and strengthening in the secret chambers of the mind?"—HALL: "Never will Christ come into that soul, where the herald of repentance hath not been before him."

V. 6. Relations between confession of sin and baptism. V. 7. The wrath to come. (1) There is still a wrath to come. (2) We ought to flee from it. (3) We ought to induce others to flee. (4) Mere alarm will not secure escape.—Coming to baptism unworthily: (1) With superficial views and impressions, v. 7. (2) With proud self-reliance, v. 9. (3) With no intention to live accordingly, v. 8. ED. IRVING: "But rougher far than hairy raiment or rocky wild was that ungentle voice which was rung among the thousands of Israel. Such a salutation as he opened with perhaps never smote the pride of any assembly, 'O generation of vipers!' It was bitterly, it was uncourtly, but oh, it was truly said." V. 8. THEOPHYLACT: "We must not only flee evil, but also produce fruits of virtue."—Christianity is positive.—V. 9. Human pride humbled by remembering divine sovereignty.—Folly of relying on a pious ancestry, when not pious ourselves. Christianity does not propose to save men by nations or by races, but individually.

V. 10-12. Christianity discriminates: (1) The righteous and the wicked living together. (2) How Christianity discriminates between them. (3) The resulting rewards and punishments. V. 10. THEOPHYLACT: "Not 'that did not produce,' but 'that does not produce'; for we must be always bearing fruit. If you showed mercy yesterday, but plunder to-day, you do not please" (God). V. 11. HENRY: "It is a great comfort to faithful ministers, to think that Jesus Christ is mightier than they, can do that *for* them, and that *by* them, which they cannot do; his strength is perfected in their weakness. . . . Those whom God puts honor upon, are thereby made very humble and low in their own eyes." V. 12. John's illustrations are all drawn from familiar objects, and mainly rural—from fruit-trees, cutting with an ax, threshing and winnowing grain, stones that lie around, a servant carrying his master's sandals, the baptism he is performing, the customs as to marriage. (John 3: 29.)—LUTHER: "Such preaching as John's does not pass away without fruits."

13-17.—BAPTISM OF JESUS.

The baptism of Jesus forms the transition from the ministry of John to that of Jesus himself. It is less fully described by Mark (1: 9-11), and Luke. (3: 21, 22.) John's Gospel gives no immediate account of it, but perhaps alludes to it afterwards. (John 3: 26.)

13. Then is a connective frequently employed by Matthew (*e. g.*, v. 5, 15; 4: 1, 5, 10, 11). In some cases it is used strictly, in others loosely, designating a period of considerable extent, like the phrase 'in those days' in v. 1, which is here used by Mark. (1: 9.) Matthew does not here mean that Jesus appeared at the moment when John was speaking the preceding words, but in general, at the time when John was engaged in baptizing and preaching, as just described. We have no means of ascertaining how long he had been thus engaged before Jesus appeared. We learn from Luke (3: 23, Rev. Ver.), that Jesus, when he began to teach, was about thirty years of age; and supposing that John

14 But John forbade him, saying, I have need to be baptized of thee, and comest thou to me?

14 unto John, to be baptized of him. But John would have hindered him, saying, I have need to be bap-

began at the same age, his ministry had already been exercised some six months. (Luke 1: 26.) But it is a mistake to say that John *must* have begun at the age of thirty, for the age fixed by the law as to Levites (Num. 4: 3, 33), was shortly afterwards lowered to twenty-five (Num. 8: 24), and by David was for a special reason further reduced to twenty (1 Chron. 23: 24-27); and so continued under Hezekiah (2 Chron. 31: 17), and after the captivity (Ezra 3: 8), and most likely in the time of Christ, when David's courses of priests were certainly maintained, and probably also his general arrangement as to Levites. Luke says it was 'when all the people were baptized' (of course a general expression, not strictly universal), which implies the lapse of at least several months, if we consider the journeys necessary. As Galilee is not mentioned in v. 5, we may suppose that the people of Galilee in general came later than those of Judea, and we should thus have an external reason also for Jesus' late arrival, besides his internal reasons. (Keim). Others from Galilee are soon after mentioned (John 1: 35-47) as disciples of John. The traditional day of our Lord's baptism is 6 January ('Epiphany,' manifestation), but that is unlikely. More probably John began in spring, and Jesus was baptized the following autumn, of A. D. 26; but no exact determination is made.

Cometh, arrives, makes his appearance, as in v. 1. **From Galilee,** *i. e.,* Nazareth (2: 22 f.), as Mark here expressly states. At Nazareth, Jesus has been living since his infancy (see above at close of chap. 2). As to Galilee, see on 4: 12. **To Jordan.** The traditional place is nearly opposite Jericho. (See on v. 6.) But the place cannot be determined. John's testimony to Jesus, apparently a few weeks later, was given at Bethany beyond Jordan (John 1: 28. Bethabara is a false reading), but we do not know where this Bethany was,

besides that John may have moved in the meantime, as he certainly moved once (John 3: 23), and probably more than once. (John 10: 40.) Conder and Geikie (comp. Stanley) think the place of our Lord's baptism was far up the river, near Bethleh m, where Conder found a ford now called Abarah, 'crossing.' This locality would suit the circumstances, but the reading Bethabara, must unquestionably be rejected. Bethany might (Köhler) very well mean 'ship-town' (*aniyah*, 'ship'), as Bethabara means 'ford-town' or 'ferry town.' A village supported by boating on the river might perish after the desolation of the country by the Romans, and so Origen could not hear of it, and avowedly changed Bethany to Bethabara. The similar name of the village near Jerusalem probably signified 'date-town,' or 'poor-town.' **To be baptized.** The construction of the original distinctly implies, what the connection also would indicate, that he came with that design. **Of him,** where modern English would say 'by.' (See on 1: 22.)

14 f. The reluctance of John to baptize Jesus, with what was said by them on the subject, is recorded by Matthew alone.[1]

But John forbade—literally, *was hindering him.* The imperfect tense is occasionally thus used to denote an attempted action, since *some* actions, *if engaged . in but not completed,* must be afterwards regarded as only attempted. This sense, in all cases, grows out of the nature of the action and the circumstances, the tense itself having the same meaning as elsewhere.[2] The verb rendered 'hinder' is compounded with a preposition, which increases its force, 'was completely hindering,' 'earnestly sought to hinder.' In the next clause, all the pronouns are emphatic: '*I* have need to be baptized by *thee,* and *thou* comest to *me!*' or, 'and comest thou to me?' an expression of surprise,

---

[1] B, ℵ and the Sahidic version, followed by Tisch. and W H., omit 'John,' and then the Greek signifies 'but he.' It is easier to explain this subsequent insertion of 'John' than its omission, and so the shorter reading is very likely correct; but the question can hardly be settled, and is practically unimportant.

[2] The rendering of Rev. Ver., 'would have hindered him,' gives the idea with tolerable success. But to call

this (Bp. Lightfoot on Revision) a "conditional sense of the imperfect" is quite unwarranted and unwise, for it is merely carrying back into the Greek a conception suggested by the approximate translation into English. It is instructive to observe how often able grammarians fall into this mistake of first translating, and then supposing the original to contain the same forms of conception as the conjectural translation.

whether it be understood as an exclamation (Euthym.), or as a question. (Comp. John 13: 6.) In like manner, John's mother had felt unworthy of a visit from the mother of her Lord. (Luke 1: 43.) It may be (Lutteroth) that as John received the confession of others, and administered to them the symbol of purification, he often remembered that he too had sins to confess and turn away from, and therefore felt on this occasion that he would gladly receive baptism from his recognized superior. There is no sufficient ground for supposing that he distinctly *expected* to receive this, but he felt the 'need' of confession, repentance, and symbolical purification. And the idea of Jesus administering baptism would not be strange, for he did afterwards baptize many, by the hands of his disciples. (John 3: 22; 4: 1 f.) The notion of some Fathers (as Chrys.) that John was afterwards actually baptized by Jesus, is not only without warrant, but seems excluded by the language of John 3: 26-28; for John's followers would in that case have expressed no surprise, and John would have settled the matter at once. (A Lapide). To understand John as here indicating the expectation that Jesus will baptize him in the Holy Spirit (Gill, others), is strangely to confound the literal and the figurative, as wild allegorizing often leads men to do. **Suffer it to be so now,** or, perhaps, 'suffer me now,' as indicated by the last clause, 'then he suffers him.' Suffer *now* that I take the position of inferiority to thee by receiving baptism at thy hands; the time has not yet come for me to assume my destined position. **Becometh us.** Some understand 'us' of Jesus alone, but against all probability, since in the preceding verse both persons were made emphatic, and since the reference to John as well as himself suits the connection. John thought it would be presumption in him, and unworthy condescension in this superior personage, if he should baptize Jesus; but Jesus declares it quite appropriate, becoming, for them both—putting the declaration, however, in the form of a general statement: for thus it becometh us **to fulfil all righteousness,** 'every (kind of) righteousness.' **Fulfil,** see on 1: 22, here signifies to perform fully. Baptism was divinely commanded (see 21: 25), and though coupled with the confession of sin and avowal of repentance, was at the

same time the expression of a readiness to welcome the approach of the reign of heaven, and of a desire to share therein. It was therefore right for all good men to be baptized; and Jesus, as a man, was under obligations to do whatever was incumbent on other good men. The remarkable relation which he and John sustained to each other and to the kingdom of heaven, did not prevent its being proper for each of them fully to perform everything that was righteous; and so in this case did not prevent its being proper that he should be baptized, and that John should baptize him. (Comp. Gill). Such seems to be the obvious and simple meaning of this expression.

But many theories have been presented as to the significance and propriety of our Lord's baptism. (1) Some hold that Jesus was baptized as a consecration to the office and work of Messiah. But was purification a consecration? It was sometimes preliminary to consecration, but the latter was effected by laying on the altar. And if the Messiah, 'the anointed,' was to be consecrated by any ceremony, it would naturally have been by anointing. (2) Others say that in baptism he was consecrated as priest. But Jesus was not literally a priest. He had no connection whatever with the priestly line, and he did not do the work of a Jewish priest. As "a priest after the order of Melchizedek" he had nothing to do with ceremonies. (3) Many have adopted the view given already by Justin Martyr ("Tryph." 88): "Jesus did not come to the river as himself needing to be baptized, or needing the Spirit's descent upon him; but just as he was born and crucified not as needing them but for the benefit of the human race, so" . . . . while men thought of him as a carpenter, "the Holy Spirit for the sake of mankind flew down upon him in the form of a dove," and a voice declared him the Son of God. (So in substance Chrys., Euthym). This view, as developed and expressed in modern theological phrase, is that he was baptized vicariously. (Comp. John 1: 29). But what Christ did for men vicariously he did because men could not do it and that they might escape the penalty of their failure; was that in any sense true of baptism? Justin's statement is in a general sense true, but the vicarious theory cannot be sustained. In

15 And Jesus answering said unto him, Suffer *it to be so* now: for thus it becometh us to fulfil all righteousness. Then he suffered him.

16 And Jesus, when he was baptized, went up straightway out of the water: and, lo, the heavens were opened unto him, and he saw the Spirit of God descending like a dove, and lighting upon him:

15 tized of thee, and comest thou to me? But Jesus answering said unto him, Suffer [1]*it* now: for thus it becometh us to fulfil all righteousness. Then he suffereth him. And Jesus, when he was baptized,

16 went up straightway from the water: and lo, the heavens were opened [2]unto him, and he saw the Spirit of God descending as a dove, and coming upon

---

1 Or, *me*....2 Some ancient authorities omit *unto him.*

---

general, we ought to beware of forcing the ideas of vicarious action and imputed righteousness upon those portions of Scripture which do not clearly present them. (4) A recent writer (Kirtley on "Design of Baptism") says that the chief object of the baptism of Jesus was to symbolize at the beginning the crowning acts of his work; that our Lord "did 'fulfil all righteousness,' actually in his work, symbolically in his baptism"; and that he "associates his followers with himself in this matter," saying, "In this ordinance it is fitting that I and my followers should fulfil all righteousness." This fancy is ingenious but far-fetched, and the latter part quite baseless. (5) The simple and natural view, for all who do not insist on carrying back the Pauline doctrine of imputed righteousness, is the one already stated. It was proper for all devout Jews to be baptized; therefore it was proper for Jesus. If one so deeply, though hitherto quietly devout, had stayed away from the ministry and baptism of the new prophet, it would have been setting a very bad example, unless explained; and explanation of his future position and work could not then be given, even if it was then entirely plain to his own mind. Notwithstanding the peculiar mission of John and Jesus, it was becoming that they should fully perform everything righteous. (So in substance, Meyer, Ewald, Bleek, Farrar, Geikie, Edersh.; Grotius already, and comp. Calvin. Davidson translates 'every duty.' Hase, Keim, and others, regard baptism in the case of Jesus as simply a *vow* of devotion to the approaching Messianic reign, which is part of the truth). A somewhat similar case occurs in 17:24 ff. Jesus there intimates that he might, as the Son of God, claim exemption from the payment of the temple-contributions, but that the rulers might make his refusal an excuse for rejecting him, and so he will do as all devout Jews do, and pay it.

16. Straightway, or, *immediately.* The stress laid on his going up immediately might

possibly be understood as meaning that whereas in that warm climate the newly baptized often stood some time in the river, waiting till others had been baptized and many could ascend together, Jesus was alone in this matter and ascended without delay. Euthymius mentions the view that others were detained by John in the water till they confessed their sins, and Jesus went up immediately because he had no sins to confess; but it would seem much more likely that the confession was made before than after the baptism. The true explanation seems to be furnished by Mark, who says (1:10), 'and straightway, coming up out of the water, he saw the heavens opened.' This makes it likely that in Matthew also the real thought is that the opening of the heavens and descent of the dove followed immediately upon the baptism. Events followed each other quickly—baptized, ascended, saw. (Keim.) The sense is brought out by putting only a comma after 'water,' and reading right on. Luke 3:21 has not the word 'immediately,' but what he says is to the same effect. **Out of,** or, *from.* This preposition does not in itself show whether he had been in the water. The correct text in Mark 1:10 is 'out of,' and does show that he had been in the water; and so in Acts 8:39. When we say that a person has just come 'from the house,' 'from the town,' we regard the house or town, so far as this expression is concerned, as the point of departure; the circumstances will usually indicate whether he was in the house or town before coming; (*e. g.*, Acts 13:13; 16:11; 25:1). So the same action is frequently described by 'from' and 'out of,' the latter expressly stating what the former leaves to be understood. Thus in 7:4, Rev. Ver.: 'Let me cast out the mote from thine eye,' (most MSS.); and in v. 5, 'out of thine eye.' In 17:18, departed, or *came forth* from him, while Mark 9:25 has 'out of him.' Comp. on 24:1. So in Tobit 6:3. 'A fish leaped up from the river, and wished to devour the lad.'

Certainly the fish had been in the river. Here in Matthew the connection and circumstances make it plain that Jesus had been in the water, and so Tyndale translated 'out of,' followed by other English versions down to the common version. Even the Rheims, abandoning Wyclif's 'fro,' and taking liberties with the Vulgate *de*, renders 'out of.' The correct *translation* in Matthew is however 'from,' and so all recent versions. But the rendering of the older versions shows that they plainly saw what the facts were. (Tyndale and his followers render similarly in 14: 13 and Luke 12: 54. *Text. Rec.*) As to the exact force of the expression 'out of' (Mark and Acts) in such a case, comp. below on 17: 9, literally, 'out of the mountain.' This means that they had been in, within, the limits represented by the mountain, though not under its soil. And so it is conceivable that 'out of the *river*,' if that were the expression here, might under peculiar circumstances be used where one had only been amid the reeds on the shore, or under the steep bank—anywhere within the space denoted by the river (comp. on 3: 6). Such an expression would be possible in such a sense, however unlikely to be used. But 'out of the *water*' must signify that the person had been within the limits denoted by the water; and the bank, though in some sense a part of the river, is in no sense a part of the water. Of course these expressions do not of themselves show that the person has been enveloped in the water; we may speak of a man as 'in the water' when he is simply standing in it. It would thus be possible—however improbable and unnatural —if we had no guide here but the preposition 'out of' in Mark and the circumstances in Matthew, to understand that Jesus merely stood in the stream and had water put upon his head. But when these expressions stand in connection with *baptizo*, which everybody agrees primarily and commonly meant 'immerse,' then the inference is inevitable. **The heavens were opened unto him,**[1] not merely signifying so that he could see into the heavens, but for him, for his benefit, so as to affect or concern him. 'Him' is naturally understood as referring to Jesus, the subject

of the preceding clause. Some writers urge that John is the subject of the preceding verses, and thus of the whole connection; but v. 16 introduces a distinct subdivision of the narrative.—Luke mentions (3: 21) that Jesus was at the time praying.—The opening of the heavens was doubtless an actual miraculous appearance, such as is frequently mentioned elsewhere. (Ezek. 1: 1; Isa. 64: 1; Acts 7: 56; Rev. 4: 1.) Mark, in his vivid way has, literally, 'he saw the heavens splitting,' in the act of parting asunder. . **And he saw,** *i. e.*, Jesus saw. Mark (1: 10) unmistakably refers the seeing to Jesus, and it is natural so to understand here. Some say that, if so, 'him' at the end of the sentence would have to be 'himself,' but this is a mistake (Winer, 151 [189]. Comp. John 1: 48). We learn from John 1: 32 that the Baptizer also saw, as it had been promised he should. Luke merely states the objective fact that the heaven opened and the Spirit descended, without saying who saw. We cannot decide whether any one else than Jesus and John saw and heard, but probably not. On the occasion spoken of in John 12: 28 ff., the people heard a sound from heaven, which they thought was thunder, but did not distinguish words. At the appearance of Jesus to Saul (Acts 9: 7; 22: 9), they that were with him saw the light and heard a sound, but did not distinguish the words. So probably here. True, the testimony as given by Matthew, 'This is,' etc., was addressed to some other than Jesus himself, but it is enough to understand that it was addressed to John, as in 17: 5 to but a few persons. John shortly afterwards (John 1: 32-34) testified to what he had seen. **Descending like a dove,** literally, *as if.* The expression leaves it doubtful whether the comparison is with the form of a dove, or with a dove's manner of descending. Precisely the same expression 'as if' is employed by Mark, Luke, and John. (1: 32.) Luke says, 'descended in bodily shape, like (*as if*) a dove,' which naturally, though not necessarily, indicates that it was in the shape of a dove. Expositors are here greatly divided. But it is certain that some bodily form was assumed. That of the gentle and guileless dove (comp. 10: 16) would be natural and

---

[1] 'Unto him' is wanting in several of the earliest and best authorities, and not found in Luke 3: 21. It might have seemed to some copyists and translators out of place, as appearing to confine the view to him. The question is difficult, and unimportant, but the expression is most probably genuine.

17 And lo a voice from heaven, saying, This is my beloved Son, in whom I am well pleased.

17 him; and lo, a voice out of the heavens, saying, [1]This is my beloved Son, in whom I am well pleased.

---

1 Or, *This is my Son ; my beloved in whom I am well pleased.* See ch. xii. 18.

---

suggestive, while a dove's *manner of descending* is hardly so peculiar and striking that a mere resemblance to it in movement would have been carefully recorded by each of the Evangelists. It seems therefore reasonable to adhere to the ancient opinion (Justin Martyr, Origen, Chrys., and others), that the Spirit descended in the form of a dove. It has been often repeated that a Rabbinical interpretation of Gen. 1 : 2, likens the Spirit of God 'brooding upon the face of the waters' to a dove. But Edersh., Vol. I., p. 287, quite explains this away, and also states that the Targum on Song 2: 12, which declares 'the voice of the turtle' to be the voice of the Holy Spirit, dates considerably later than the Talmud. So there seems to be no ground for the Jewish claim, that this appearance of a dove has earlier Rabbinical parallels. Yet if the claim were well supported, it would not be surprising. We recognize it as one of the excellencies of the Scriptures, that the form of the revelation is constantly in accordance with the modes of conception natural to man, and even sometimes conformed to the peculiar ways of thinking of the people chosen to receive it. Comp. on 7: 3-5. Morison quotes Varenius as saying, "It was not as an eagle, but as a dove; an animal corresponding among birds to the lamb among beasts." **And lighting,** or *coming,* **upon him.** It was idle to translate the plain 'coming' by 'lighting.' The Baptizer afterwards testified (John 1 : 32) that it 'abode,' or 'remained, on him,' *i. e.,* probably for some time, thus symbolizing the great fact that the Mediator was to be henceforth permanently and peculiarly in union with and under the influence of the Holy Spirit. Accordingly we find immediately after (4 : 1) that Jesus is said to be 'led up by the Spirit,' etc. (Comp. John 3 : 34.) The coming of the Spirit upon our Lord was so very peculiar in its relation to his office, that we are scarcely warranted in taking it as the ground of a petition that the Spirit would bless any ordinary baptismal occasion. Such a blessing should be fervently sought, but hardly on this ground.

17. And lo! a voice from[1]—*out of*—

heaven—rather, *the heavens,* plural, as in the preceding verse (see on v. 2). So Mark, while Luke uses the singular. We also often say 'heaven' and 'the heavens' indifferently. The Talmud has many stories of a voice from heaven, coming to decide questions, to commend certain teachers, etc., and calls it *Bath kol,* 'daughter of a voice,' perhaps meaning a faint sound as if coming from a great distance. See Lf., Gill, Wünsche. Edersh. insists that there is no real analogy between the *Bath kol* and this voice from heaven. There is no intrinsic objection to the idea of a resemblance. Here also, as in v. 16, we see that revelation adapts its choice of a form to the popular mind. Other instances of a voice from heaven, see in John 12 : 28; and to a certain extent in Matthew 17 : 5; Acts 9 : 4; Rev. 1: 10. Comp. Acts 2 : 2. **This is.** Mark 1 : 11 (according to the best authorities for the text) and Luke 3 : 22, have 'Thou art my beloved son, in thee,' etc. Of course, it cannot be that both of these are the words actually spoken. As to the authenticity of the narrative, such slight and wholly unimportant variations really confirm it, being precisely such as always occur in the independent testimony of different witnesses. As to the complete inspiration of the Scriptures, we must accept it as one of the facts of the case that the inspired writers not unfrequently report merely the substance of what was said, without aiming to give the exact words. So, for example, at the institution of the Supper (26: 26 ff.), in Gethsemane (26: 39 ff.), in the inscription on the cross (27: 37), etc. In some instances of such variation we may suppose that the exact expressions given by the different writers were all employed in the connection, but in other cases that hypothesis is unwarranted. While such facts as these should make us cautious in theorizing as to verbal inspiration, they do not require us to lay aside the belief that the inspiration of Scripture is complete, that the inspired writers have everywhere told us just what God would have us know.

The words spoken are the same that were

---

[1]Tyndale and followers translated *apo* by 'out of' in v. 16, and *ek* by 'from' in v. 17.

uttered on the Mount of Transfiguration. (17: 5; 2 Pet. 1: 17.) The person referred to was known in that case by the transfigured appearance, and here by the descent of the dove upon him. The Greek is more emphatic: 'this is my son, the beloved.'—There is no propriety in saying, with some expositors, that 'beloved' signifies 'only begotten.' As applied to our Lord, the two terms are to a certain extent equivalent, and they are sometimes confounded by the Sept. translators, but there is of course, a distinction between them. **In whom I am**—or, *was*—**well pleased,** or, 'in whom I delighted.' The tense of the verb may be understood as denoting what took place at some indefinite past time, and from the nature of the case still holds good; as in 23: 2, literally, 'The Scribes and the Pharisees sat down in Moses' seat,' and so are sitting there now—where in English we should say, 'have sat down.' (So Winer, 278 [347], Buttm., 198.) If this view be adopted, the rendering of the Common Version expresses the substantial meaning pretty well. But the Greek tense more naturally denotes some past time, to be determined from the connection, from the nature of the case, or from other teachings of Scripture. The time here referred to might be that indicated by Ps. 2: 7; by Isa. 42: 1 (which is perhaps alluded to here, and is quoted below in 12: 18); also by John 17: 24; Eph. 1: 4. In the depths of eternity, before creation began, God loved, delighted in, his Eternal Son; and now at the baptism and the transfiguration, he bears witness to him, alluding to such declarations as the above, and saying: 'This is my Son, the beloved, in whom my soul delighted.' This latter explanation is perhaps preferable, but it is hard to decide; and both agree as to the main resulting sense, that the Father delights in him now. This declaration might make more real to the human mind of Jesus that peculiar sonship to God of which he had in childhood already indicated consciousness. (Luke 2: 49.) Such a view connects itself (Calvin) with the fact that he was praying (Luke 3: 21, 22) when the voice came. It was also a commendation of him to John, who soon after bore witness before all (John 1: 34) 'that this is the Son of God'; just as at the transfiguration the voice came to the three disciples also, who were to testify at the proper time. (17: 9.)—Apocryphal writers in the second and third centuries make fanciful additions to this account, as that a great light shone round the place, that a fire was kindled in the Jordan (perhaps a fancy wrought out of 3: 11), and that the voice added, 'I to-day have begotten thee.'

HOMILETICAL AND PRACTICAL.

KEIL: "The baptism of Jesus the culmination of John's ministry, and the beginning of that of Jesus." EWALD: "The birth-hour of Christianity." Unknown in Aquinas: "As when the morning star has risen, the sun does not wait for that star to set, but rising as it goes forward, gradually obscures its brightness; so Christ waited not for John to finish his course, but appeared while he yet taught." V. 13. Importance of Baptism: Not as carrying with it regeneration, or procuring remission, but 1) an imitation of Christ's example; 2) an act of Christ's own appointment 28: 19; 3) an oath of allegiance to Christ, 'in the name'; 4) a symbol of purification from sin through Christ, Acts 22: 16; 5) a symbol of burial and resurrection in union with Christ, Rom. 6: 4. V. 14. How often are well-meant but utterly mistaken efforts made to dissuade persons from what is entirely right. Such efforts frequently proceed, as here, from the misapplication of something that is true.—John's twofold difficulty (comp. Lange); 1) to baptize the Pharisees and Sadducees, who were unworthy of his baptism; 2) To baptize Jesus, of whom his baptism was unworthy.—John's baptism highly honored: 1) It was of divine appointment, John 1: 33; 2) It gave name to his whole work, 'the baptism of John' (21: 25), John the Baptizer; 3) It was received by great multitudes; 4) Even the Saviour submitted to it; 5) Jesus baptized on like conditions, John 3: 22; 4: 1, 2; Mark 1: 14). V. 15. Here for the first time in this Gospel our Lord presents an *example* to us. Let us be careful in all that follows to seek his footsteps and learn to walk in them. (1 Pet. 2: 21; 1 John 2: 6; 1 Cor. 11: 1.)—A regard for what is *becoming* requires us not merely to consider the opinions of mankind, but our own real character and relations. To consider in this high sense what becomes us, is an exalted and inspiring view of life.   Comp. Heb. 2: 10.—

CHAPTER IV.

THEN was Jesus led up of the Spirit into the wilderness to be tempted of the devil.

1   Then was Jesus led up of the Spirit into the wilderness

Our Lord's baptism as an example: 1) It is right for those who wish to take part in the Messiah's reign to be baptized. (Jesus regarded this as a part of righteousness.) 2) The most extraordinary character and circumstances do not make it becoming to neglect this duty. 3) The mistaken opposition of devout friends should not prevent our performing it. 4) Loving obedience is apt to be followed by an approving testimony. HENRY: "They who are of greatest attainments in gifts and graces should yet in their place bear their testimony to instituted ordinances by a humble and diligent attendance on them, that they may give a good example to others." AMBROSE: "Also like a wise master inculcating his doctrines as much by his own practice as by word of mouth, he did that which he commanded his disciples to do. The Roman Cato said, 'Submit to the law which thou thyself hast enacted.'"

V. 16. GRIFFITH: "Just as the 'veil of the temple was rent in twain' to symbolize the perfect access of all men to God (Heb. 10: 19, 20), so here the heavens are 'rent asunder'(same Greek word), to show how near God is to Jesus and Jesus is to God. So in John 1: 51, Rev. Ver., 'Ye shall see *heaven opened*, and the angels ascending and descending' (to and fro between me and God), that is, You shall see that I am living in uninterrupted communication with the Father."—LUTHER: "Highest things. 1) The highest preacher, God. 2) The highest pulpit, the heavens. 3) The highest sermon: 'This is my beloved Son, in whom I am well pleased.'"

Ch. 4: 1-11. THE TEMPTATION.

The Temptation concludes Matthew's account of events connected with our Lord's entrance upon his public work (see on 3: 1, 13). That work was now about to begin, and he was doubtless meditating upon it. Some recent critics go to great lengths in speculating upon the "plan" of Jesus, at this and subsequent periods. There is little or no indication of any plan, and such unsupported speculations seem unprofitable and unwise. But his meditations in beginning his work would furnish the natural occasion for such special temptations as are here depicted. These are also recorded by Luke (4: 1-13), and briefly mentioned by Mark. (1: 12 f.)

1. Then (see on 3: 13), viz., when he had been baptized. Luke implies, and Mark states, that it was 'immediately' after the baptism. **Led up,** *i. e.,* from the valley of the Jordan (see on 3: 6) into the higher land.[1] **Into the wilderness** (see on 3: 1). Some recent writers (Stanley, Plumptre) make it east of the Jordan, but the general use of the term in the N. T. favors the common view that it was on the west. Luke's 'returned' (4: 1) also favors this view, but does not settle the question, for Jesus may have crossed below the Lake of Galilee, and come through Perea to be baptized, as the Galileans often took this route to Jerusalem. The notion that it was the wilderness of Sinai is founded only on the fact that there occurred the forty days' fast of Moses and of Elijah.—It was certainly a very retired and wild part of the 'wilderness,' for Mark says, with one of his vivid descriptive touches, 'and he was with the wild beasts.' A tradition which appears first in the time of the Crusades places it in a mountain just west of Jericho, hence called Quarantania, (a place of forty days; comp. *quarantine*, a forty days' detention). This mountain is six or eight miles from the traditional place of the baptism, and rises some fifteen hundred feet almost perpendicularly from the plain of the Jordan, which is here at its widest part. In the rocky face of the mountain are the openings of numerous artificial caves, made by monks of the Crusading period, perhaps some of them by old Jewish Eremites. But to our modern feeling it seems unlikely that our Lord withdrew to a cave, and probable that he went further away from the populous plain of Jericho. Some think (Schaff) that Quar-

---

[1] The meaning of this 'up' was obscured to early and later translators by their ignorance of the geography of Palestine. The Latin versions and the Pesh. Syriac have simply 'was led.' Tyndale gave 'ledd **awaye,**' and was followed by Cranmer and Geneva.

antania may have been the place of the *third* temptation, if not of those preceding, 'which is quite possible. After all, it may be that a special providence caused the precise locality of this and many other events in our Lord's history to be left unknown, for the purpose of restraining superstition. **The Spirit,** viz., the Spirit of God, well known and just mentioned. (3: 16.) Luke says he was 'full of the Holy Spirit.' From the time of his baptism (see on 3: 16) we find frequent statements that the God-man, the Mediator, was specially and powerfully under the influence of the Holy Spirit (John 3: 34; Luke 4: 14; Matt. 12: 28; Acts 1: 2), as had been predicted. (Isa. 42: 1; Matt. 12: 18; Isa. 61: 1; Luke 4: 18.) The term **led,** employed also by Luke, appears to denote only an internal impulse wrought by the Spirit. Mark (1: 12) expresses the same idea by a strong figure, literally, 'the Spirit casts him forth into the wilderness.' "This is the language of the prophet-paroxysm, seized with an irresistible impulse; so the 'holy men of old' were impelled by the Spirit. (Ezek. 40: 2.)" (Beecher.)

To be tempted. The Greek word signifies to try, or make trial of, to test. The motive of such testing or trial may be good or bad. (1) The object may be to ascertain character, to develop and make manifest its excellencies, or to expose its faults, that they may be mended. So in John 6: 6, 'prove'; 2 Cor. 13: 5, 'examine'; Rev. 2: 2, 'tried'; Gen. 22: 1 (God 'did tempt' Abraham; Rev. Ver., 'prove'); Ex. 20: 20, 'prove,' etc. (2) The object may be unfriendly, bad. (*a*) Men 'tempt' God, test him, in some improper way, because they lack confidence in the fulfillment of his promises or threats. So below in v. 7 (Deut. 6: 16); Ex. 17: 2, 7 (Ps. 95: 9); Isa. 7: 12; Acts 5: 9; 15: 10. (*b*) Men, or Satan and his subordinates, 'tempt' men, test them, with a view to draw out evil tendencies, and entice into sin. So here, and in 1 Cor. 7: 5; 1 Thess. 3: 5, etc. (This sense does not occur in the O. T.)[1] In all cases there is a testing, trying, and the difference lies in the nature and design of it. Our English word, 'tempt,' was formerly used in all these senses, but is now restricted to the bad sense; and

some confusion arises, for example, in the translation of James 1: 2-15, where there is a transition from the good to the bad— from 'trials' to 'temptations.' **Of the devil.** The Greek word *diabolos* (borrowed in Latin as *diabolus*, from which come Italian *diavolo*, French *diable*, English *devil*, German *teufel*, etc.), is the term regularly employed in the Sept. to translate the Hebrew name Satan. (Job 1: 6 ff.; 2: 1; 1 Chron. 21: 1; Zech. 3: 1, 2.)[2] The latter signifies 'adversary,' 'opposer,' while *diabolos* strictly signifies 'slanderer,' 'false accuser,' but in the N. T. is used as practically equivalent to Satan. So Mark 1: 13 has 'tempted by Satan,' and see below, v. 10. (Comp. 16: 23 and John 6: 70; also Rev. 12: 9.) The term 'devil' in the N. T. is strictly a proper name, as much so as Satan; his subordinates should be called 'demons,' as in the Greek (see on 8: 28). To the real existence and personality of the devil the Scriptures are fully committed. He is represented as the chief of the fallen angels (25: 41; comp. 9: 34), and through these he is able, though not omnipresent, to be carrying on the temptation of many persons at the same time. He is, of course, limited in knowledge, though immeasurably superior to man.

How could Jesus be tempted? Was it possible for him to sin? If this was in no sense possible, then he was not really tempted, certainly not 'like as we are.' (Heb. 4: 15.) But how can it have been possible for him to sin? If we think of his human nature in itself, apart from the co-linked divinity, and apart from the Holy Spirit that filled and led him, then we must say that, like Adam in his state of purity, like the angels and every other moral creature, his humanity was certainly in itself capable of sinning, and thus the temptation was real, and was felt as such, and as such overcome; while yet in virtue of the union with the divine nature, and of the power of the Holy Spirit that filled him, it was morally impossible that he should sin.—A substantially similar view is well stated by Edersheim.—Jesus was tempted on other occasions also, as is implied in Luke 4: 13,

---

[1] Alford remarks that the Greek word here employed, *peirazo,* does not have this sense in the classics. True; but the simpler and more common form, *peirao,* is repeatedly so used.

[2] Plumptre erroneously states that the Greek word is different in Zech. 3: 1, 2. In using all commentaries, including the present one, readers will find it worth while to " verify the references."

2 And when he had fasted forty days and forty nights, he was afterward an hungered.

2 ness to be tempted of the devil. And when he had fasted forty days and forty nights, he afterward

and affirmed in Luke 22: 28, and Heb. 4: 15. It has been remarked (Ullmann) that there are in the nature of things two great classes of temptations, the one to commit positive evil, and the other to shrink from what is right. In the former way Jesus was tempted here, and when the people wanted him to be king (John 6: 15); in the latter way he was tempted in Gethsemane, and when Peter tried to dissuade him. (16: 22, 23.)

Why should Jesus be tempted? We can see some of the reasons. (1) It gave proof of his true humanity, proof that he possessed a real human soul. (2) It was part of his example to us. (3) It formed part of his personal discipline (Heb. 5: 7-9); and (4) of his preparation to be a sympathizing intercessor. (Heb. 2: 18; 4: 15.) (5) It formed a part of that great conflict in which the "seed of the woman" was to "bruise the serpent's head." (Gen. 3: 15.) In this first great struggle of the conflict the destined conqueror came off completely victorious.

During the forty days (Luke 4: 2), and at other times, our Lord was doubtless tempted by suggestion to his mind, as we are; but in the three signal and final temptations here described, it seems to be distinctly declared that Satan appeared in bodily form and with actually spoken words, and this fitted the scene for distinct and impressive description. To make it a mere *vision*, is without the slightest warrant. And while it is possible to regard the history as merely a vivid description of a series of internal temptations, it does no small violence to the language and the entire color of the narrative. Note especially the correspondence of the two expressions, 'the devil leaves him,' . . . . angels came and ministered to him,' where few who believe the Bible at all will question that the angels appeared in bodily form, as on so many other occasions. The desire of many commentators to reduce the scene to internal suggestion, apparently arises from two causes. (1) Some wish to lessen the difficulties of the narrative. But those who are repelled by the idea of Satan's personal appearance will be equally reluctant to admit his personality; so that there is nothing gained, and the difficulties of the subject are in fact inherent

and have to be accepted. (2) Others wish to assimilate the Saviour's temptations to our own. (Heb. 4: 15.) But this desire is amply met by considering his temptations during the forty days and throughout his career. (See above.) Every point connected with this series of temptations has occasioned a vast amount of speculation, often of the wildest character. Yet the subject from its very nature calls for guarded interpretation, great moderation in conjecture, and willingness to remain ignorant where we have no means of knowing; and it requires to be discussed in a spirit of profound reverence and humility. Familiar as we have grown with the simple narrative, it presents one of the most wonderful, mysterious, awful scenes of the world's history. O dark and dreadful enemy, ever plotting our ruin and exulting in our woe, here thou wast completely conquered on earth, conquered by a man, and in the strength of that Spirit whose help is offered to us all.

2. It is best to understand the fasting as entire abstinence from food. The word does not necessarily mean this, nor does even the strong expression of Luke, 'he did not eat anything in those days,' for Luke uses equally strong language of Paul's companions in Acts 27: 33, where he can only mean that they had taken very irregular and inadequate food, as it were nothing at all. (Comp. below 11: 18.) Still, the literal meaning is preferable here, because there is here nothing to forbid it, because also in the corresponding cases of Moses and Elijah the fasting is usually understood to have been entire, and because we thus best see the force of the statement, 'afterwards he was hungry,' or, as Luke, 'and when they (the forty days) were completed he was hungry,' leading us to suppose that *during* the forty days he was not hungry, but supernaturally sustained. The *time* was the same as in the case of Moses (Ex. 34: 28), and Elijah (1 Kings 19: 8), and was perhaps typically related also to the forty years spent by Israel in the wilderness. (See on 2: 15). We do not know what originally caused the adoption of forty as a sacred or solemn number. (Gen. 7: 12; Deut. 9: 25; 10: 10; Ezek. 4: 6; Acts 7: 23, and often.) "Jesus had forty days before his public

3 And when the tempter came to him, he said, If thou be the Son of God, command that these stones be made bread.

3 hungered. And the tempter came and said unto him, If thou art the Son of God, command that

---

appearance; forty days, as if for preparation, before his ascension. (Acts 1 : 3.)'' (Bengel). **And forty nights,** added (by Matt. alone) perhaps because the Jews were accustomed to speak of the night and day as together constituting one period (see on 12: 40), or because they frequently fasted during the day and then ate at night (2 Sam. 1 : 12), while here it was day and night, as in Esth. 4 : 16. The design of the Spirit that he should be tempted was probably not the sole design of this retirement; our Lord, thus secluded and supernaturally sustained, doubtless spent his time in prayerful communion with his Father, as often afterwards (Luke 6 : 12 ; John 6 : 15), and probably also (see on v. 1) in meditation upon the great work he was about to commence. So Moses and Elijah, as lawgiver and reformer. Our Lord's fasting was not an act of self-mortification, if he was preternaturally sustained, and is not an example to us. To make it the authority for a regular annual "fast" of forty days by all Christians (" Lent") is wholly unwarranted, and very strange. (Comp. Alexander.)

3. Came to him—we cannot tell in what form. **If thou be**—*art*—**the Son of God.** The form of expression in Greek is most naturally understood as assuming that the supposition is fact, as shortly before declared. (3 : 17.) Wyclif 'art'; Tyndale to K. James 'be.' The Greek is not subjunctive but indicative. The tempter puts the matter in this form in order to invite Jesus to establish the fact by a miracle, and in order to intimate that he certainly has the right thus to satisfy his hunger. 'Son' is by its position in the Greek emphatic. God's ordinary creatures may suffer, they cannot help it; but if thou art his *Son*, it is unworthy of thee thus to suffer, and unnecessary—'speak, that these stones may become loaves.' It does not follow, on this view, that Satan fully understood what was involved in Jesus' being God's Son; and this ignorance will account for an attempt otherwise not only audacious but absurd. Those who prefer the view that he really doubted whether Jesus was God's Son, are at liberty so to interpret the

phrase, 'if thou art' etc., though it is a less natural and less common use. **Command,** etc.,—or, *speak that . . . may become.* (Comp. the same construction in 20: 21. [1]) Luke (4 : 3) has ' speak to this stone, that it may become a loaf,' as if pointing to a particular one. (Comp. 3 : 9; 7 : 9). 'Become' is the literal and exact translation. **These stones,** lying around, as in 3 : 9. The English word ' bread' being only used collectively, we have to introduce 'loaf,' 'loaves' to give the exact idea. (Comp. Rev. Ver. *margin,* and see on 26: 26).

This first temptation thus appears to be twofold (and so of the others); he is tempted to satisfy hunger, and in such a way as will prove him to be the Son of God. Our bodily appetites form the occasion of many of our severest temptations. Yet these appetites are not sinful in themselves; the sin consists in seeking excessive or essentially improper gratification of them, or in seeking lawful gratification by improper means. Jesus was tempted to work a miracle in order to relieve his hunger. We could not say beforehand whether this would be right, but we see throughout his history that he never performed miracles merely for his own benefit; they were all wrought to do good to others, and to attest his divine mission.—And this attestation was never given to those who asked it from improper motives. (12 : 38 ff. ; 16 : 1 ff.) He paid no heed to the taunt (27 : 40) : ' If thou be—or *art*—the Son of God, come down from the cross' (the first clause being precisely the same as here). And so he takes no notice, in replying to the tempter, of the proposition that he should by the miracle prove himself the Son of God. Nor does he condescend to refer to the attesting voice from heaven. (3 : 17.) We have no reason to believe that our Lord had ever wrought a miracle up to this time, the ' beginning of his miracles ' (John 2 : 11) taking place shortly after. He would not begin till his 'hour' had 'come.' (John 2 : 4.) The miracles of his childhood, so numerous in some apocryphal gospels, are without historical foundation, and most of them quite unworthy of him, as child or man.

---

[1] A non-final use of *hina,* see on 5 : 2

4 But he answered and said, It is written, Man shall not live by bread alone, but by every word that proceedeth out of the mouth of God.
5 Then the devil taketh him up into the holy city, and setteth him on a pinnacle of the temple,

4 these stones become ¹bread. But he answered and said, It is written, Man shall not live by bread alone, but by every word that proceedeth out of the mouth of God. Then the devil taketh him into the holy city:

1 Gr. *loaves.*

4. It is written, perfect tense, it *stands written* (so in 2: 5, and below in v. 6, 7, 10, and often). Our Lord meets every temptation by a quotation from Scripture. The Father's word was to him the sword with which he conquered the great spiritual enemy. (Eph. 6: 17.) This quotation is from Deut 8: 3, and the two below are from the same book, which is rich in spiritual and devotional matter. Notice, too, that all the passages he thus applies to himself are from precepts given to Israel in the wilderness, at the opening of the national career—there being a typical relation between Israel and the Messiah (see on 2: 15). Possibly (Godet) he had, during his retirement, been specially meditating on the account of Israel's forty years in the wilderness. This quotation agrees with the Sept., and differs from the Hebrew only in inserting ' word,' where the Hebrew has simply ' all that goes forth from the mouth of the Lord.' And this is really the meaning of the Greek, 'every word that goes¹ forth,' etc., *i. e.*, whatever he says that man shall live on. There is no propriety in understanding here a reference to the *spiritual* life as sustained by God's word, viz., by the Scriptures; the Hebrew phrase and the connection in Deuteronomy quite forbid such an idea. God fed Israel with manna, a thing unknown to them and their fathers, "that he might make thee know that man shall not live on bread only, but on all that goes forth from the mouth of the Lord shall man live"—that the support of life is not absolutely dependent on ordinary food, but it may be sustained on whatever God shall choose to say, to appoint. And so Jesus will not work the miracle to obtain ordinary food, because God can, if he should think proper, command food to be supplied him in an extraordinary way. And this appears to have been done, through angels (see on v. 11). To insist on making the passage, in spite of the connection in Deuteronomy, and here, apply also to spiritual food, as so many do, is unreasonable, and dishonoring to the Bible, which is not a book of riddles,

but given for practical instruction, and must be interpreted on principles of common sense, or it cannot be interpreted at all.—**Man shall not.** Thus he identifies himself with humanity, applying as a matter of course to himself what is true of mankind. And he conquers temptation not as God, but as man, by the power of the Spirit and of the lessons that are 'written.' **Shall not live,** viz., such is the divine plan or appointment. **By**—or, *upon*—**bread,** as that on which life rests for support. So, 'upon every word,' etc., or according to another reading 'in every word,' *i. e.*, in the use of, which amounts to the same thing. **Out of** is here literally ' through.'
5. Then, comp. on v. 1. Luke (4:5) simply connects by 'and,' and gives the two remaining temptations in the reverse order, seeming (Bengel, others) to follow the natural order of topography—first the desert, then a high mountain in the desert, then Jerusalem. Matthew's is the natural topical order, the second temptation being just the opposite of the first, and the third forming the climax. It seems natural also that the severe rebuke of v. 10, should put an end to Satan's attempts, and accordingly Luke, in the correct text, does not give it. (See also below, on v. 8.) **Taketh him**—literally, *takes him with him,* or 'along with him,' does not prove that he was carried involuntarily or supernaturally (see the same word in 17: 1; Mark 4: 36, etc.), nor does Luke's term 'led' prove the contrary. We have no means of determining the manner of going, and are left to suppose that Jesus went as men usually go, and so that the devil did likewise. The word **up,** Tyn. to King James, is not here in the Greek. **The holy city,** *i. e.,* Jerusalem, regarded as holy because the seat of the temple and its worship. Comp. Isa. 48: 2; Dan. 9: 24; Neh. 11: 1; Matt. 27: 53. Some Jewish coins were inscribed (Gill, others), 'Jerusalem the holy'; old Jewish prayers also have 'the holy city' (Wünsche), and the Arabs now call Jerusalem *El-Kuds,* 'the holy.' (As

¹ Tyndale borrowed from the Vulgate the Latin term 'proceeds,' and most English versions have followed

him, but the simple and exact English rendering is ' goes forth.'

6 And saith unto him, If thou be the Son of God, cast thyself down: for it is written, He shall give his angels charge concerning thee: and in *their* hands they shall bear thee up, lest at any time thou dash thy foot against a stone.

6 and he set him on the [1]pinnacle of the temple, and saith unto him, If thou art the Son of God, cast thyself down: for it is written,
He shall give his angels charge concerning thee:
And on their hands they shall bear thee up,
Lest haply thou dash thy foot against a stone.

---

1 Gr. *wing.*

---

to Jerusalem, see on 21: 10.) **And setteth.** Rev. Ver., *And he set.* The correct text has the past tense, but the meaning is substantially the same. **A pinnacle of the temple.**[1] Our Lord, who did not belong to the priesthood, is nowhere said to have entered the *naos*, but only went into the *hieron, i. e.*, into the courts, as other Jews did. On the inner side of the wall enclosing the great outer court ran a long portico or colonnade, the roof of which also covered the top of the wall, and sometimes was built up above the wall to a great height. The outer battlement of such a roof, rising above the outer wall, is probably what is here called 'pinnacle,'[2] and 'the pinnacle' suggests some well-known or remarkable pinnacle. It is doubtful whether this was 'the portico that is called Solomon's' (John 10: 23; Acts 3: 11), on the east side of the temple enclosure, and described by Josephus ("Ant.," 20, 9, 7) as of great height; more probably it was what he calls "the royal portico" (of Herod), on the south side, and which he represents ("Ant.," 15, 11, 5) as "one of the most remarkable works under the sun." Below the wall enclosing the temple court, there was an immense substruction extending up from the bottom of the ravine, and so deep that one could not see to the foot of it (probably the southeast corner); "on this arose the vast height of the portico, so that if one should look down from the summit of its roof, putting together the depths, he would grow dizzy, the sight not reaching into the unmeasured abyss." This high-wrought description at least presents us with a scene very suitable to the temptation in question.

6. This temptation, like the first, appears to have been twofold, appealing to a natural feeling and also to Messianic aspiration. Many persons when looking down from a dizzy height feel a strong disposition to throw themselves down; with some, the feeling is intense and almost irresistible; and it is not unreasonable, and not derogatory to our Saviour, to suppose that here also Satan tried to take advantage of a natural feeling, as he had before done with hunger. Let him throw himself down, and see if God would not protect him; and thus descending in so public a place and supernaturally protected, he would be observed, and at once hailed by the populace as 'he that should come.' This last seems to have been part of the idea presented; for otherwise why take him to the temple (Lightfoot, Lutteroth)? A precipice in the wilderness would have sufficed for the mere temptation to throw himself down; the carefully chosen place indicates that the idea was also to exhibit himself in public. *Keim:* "At the same time a test of the protection God would extend to his ambassador, and a miracle of display by which the faith of Israel might be won for God's messenger." As Jesus had in the former case fortified himself by quoting Scripture, so the tempter supports his suggestion by quoting a promise of protection amid dangers. This passage, from Psa. 91: 11 f., applies to any one who trusts in God, and by eminence to Jesus. The quotation follows Sept. and Heb., with the omission of a clause

---

[1] The N. T. has two Greek words translated 'temple.' The one (*hieron*), signifying 'sacred (place),' denotes the whole sacred enclosure, comprising the several courts (see on 21: 12), as well as the sacred house itself. This last, the sacred house, into which none but the priests entered, is designated by the other word (*naos*, rendered 'sanctuary' in 23: 35, and 27: 5, Rev. Ver.), found in Luke 1: 9, 21, 22; Matt. 23: 16-35; 26: 61 (Mark 14: 58); 27: 5, 40 (Mark 15: 29); 27: 51; (Mark 15: 38; Luke 23: 45); John 2: 19-21; Acts 17: 24; 19: 24 ('shrines'); and in every passage of the *Epistles and Revelation* in which Com. Eng. Ver. has 'temple,' except 1 Cor. 9: 13 (which has *hieron*.) *Hieron* is the word used in every passage of the *Gospels and Acts* in which Com. Eng. Ver. has 'temple,' except those just named and Luke 11: 51, (literally 'house.')

[1] The Greek word may from its use in the Sept., be readily understood to mean battlement, parapet, or the like. (Grimm, Bleek). The passage in Eus. "Hist.", ii., 23, relied on by Bible Comm., and others, to show that a pinnacle of the *naos* was here meant, is confused, and proves nothing.

7 Jesus said unto him, It is written again, Thou shalt not tempt the Lord thy God.

8 Again, the devil taketh him up into an exceeding high mountain, and sheweth him all the kingdoms of the world, and the glory of them;

7 Jesus said unto him, Again it is written, Thou shalt

8 not try the Lord thy God. Again, the devil taketh him unto an exceeding high mountain, and sheweth him all the kingdoms of the world, and the glory of

---

not important to the application ('to keep thee in all thy ways'), such an omission (Toy) as the New Test. writers often make. It is therefore not proper to say, as is often said, that Satan misquoted; it was a misinterpretation and misapplication. The expression, **in their hands they shall bear thee up,** as a mother or a nurse supports a child (Num. 11:12; Deut. 1:31; Isa. 49:22; Acts 13:18, margin; 1 Thess. 2:7), is of course figurative, referring to providential protection. Satan treats it as if we were authorized to expect its literal and supernatural fulfillment; and while there are of course limitations to such a promise (see below), he takes no account of these. Observe that the plural 'angels' renders it improper to quote this passage in support of the Jewish fancy of a guardian angel attending each individual. The passage corresponds to Heb. 1:14, where the angels are said to minister to God for the benefit of his people. 'Lest haply' is more probably the meaning here, than 'lest at any time.'

7. It is written again. What Satan had quoted is indeed found, but in another place is written that which forbids what he suggests and is seeking to justify. There is here an illustration of two important rules of interpretation: that a figurative expression must not be so understood as to bring it in conflict with unfigurative passages; and that an unlimited promise or statement must not be applied to cases forbidden by other teachings of Scripture.—This quotation is from Deut. 6:16. It follows Sept., and differs from Heb. only in using singular instead of plural ("Ye shall not," etc.), thus rendering more pointed the application to an individual.—The Greek word here rendered 'tempt' is a compound of that ordinarily used (see on v. 1), and has a somewhat more emphatic meaning; but we can hardly express the difference in a translation. To 'tempt God' is to test, or put him to the trial, in order to see whether he can and will fulfill his promises. The App. of the Amer. Revisers would here render 'make trial of.' This Ahaz (Isa. 7:12) with affected humility declined to do. Deut. 6:16, refers to the case in which the Israelites tempted Jehovah at Massah ('temptation'), by requir-

ing a supply of water to prove that he would fulfill his promise to take care of them. (Ex. 17: 2, 7. Comp. Psa. 78; 18; 95:8,9; 1 Cor. 10:9; Heb. 3:9.) Ananias and Sapphira (Acts 5:9) tempted the Spirit of the Lord, by virtually putting him to the test whether he would know and reveal their villany. Peter declared (Acts 15:10) that it would be tempting God to act as if they wanted further proof of his will that the Gentiles should not be required to bear the yoke of the ceremonial law. And so Jesus intimates that it would be tempting God to plunge voluntarily into danger, as if to make trial whether he would fulfill his promise of protection. These cases show the nature of the sin in question. Its source is in all cases unbelief. This was understood by the author of Wisdom, 1:2: "He is found by those who do not tempt him, and he manifests himself to those who do not distrust him."—It is unwarrantable to say (Alexander, others) that the passage as quoted by our Saviour has a double application, so as at the same time to rebuke Satan for tempting him. Such "double applications" of Scripture are almost always fanciful, save in the case of prophecies and types.—Throughout his ministry our Lord acted on the principle here involved. He never went voluntarily into danger, and always prudently turned away from the wrath of his enemies, save when some duty called.

8. In the third temptation Satan no longer says 'If thou art God's Son,' no longer attempts to incite Jesus to prove his Sonship or Messiahship by miracle; and as if conceding that he is Messiah and will found a kingdom, he proposes to aid him in making it a splendid earthly kingdom, in subordination to himself. That Messiah would have a magnificent earthly kingdom was the general expectation of such Jews as were now expecting Messiah at all; and the disciples clung tenaciously to this notion throughout our Lord's ministry. The tempter hopes to work upon such a conception in Jesus. *Neander:* "Herein was the temptation, that the Messiah should not develop his kingdom gradually, and in its pure spirituality from within, but should establish

9 And saith unto him, All these things will I give thee, if thou wilt fall down and worship me.

9 them ; and he said unto him, All these things will I give thee, if thou wilt fall down and worship me.

---

it at once, as an outward dominion; and that although this could not be accomplished without the use of an evil agency, the end would sanctify the means." Many a man, before and since, has with Satan's secret help surveyed the glittering spectacle of boundless dominion, and so burned with the fierce longings of ambition that he was ready for anything that would bring success. Alas! how nearly was this idea of a world-wide kingdom, held in allegiance to Satan, fulfilled by some in the Middle Ages who boasted the title of Vicar of Christ.

Here also, as in the former cases, the temptation of Jesus seems to have been twofold, appealing to a natural feeling—the love of power, the desire to rule over others—and at the same time suggesting a way in which his Messianic mission might be expeditiously carried through. **Taketh him**—or, *takes him along with him*, as in v. 5. Luke (4: 5) says, 'led him up,' Rev. Ver. What the **exceeding high mountain** was, it is quite impossible to judge. As the highest mountain on earth would no more have sufficed for a literal view of all the kingdoms of the world than the highest near to Jerusalem, there is nothing gained by going far away in our conjecture. Tradition names a mountain near Jericho (see on v. 1), but with no great probability. **Sheweth him all the kingdoms of the world.** Some understand a literal view of all the districts of Palestine. But there is no proof that the term rendered ' world' (*Kosmos*) was ever used to denote merely Palestine, though this has been often asserted; and the districts of Palestine would at that time hardly have been called kingdoms; besides that the significance of the temptation is much clearer and more striking on the other view. It is best to understand a sort of vision. It may certainly be conceived that Satan had the power, while Jesus looked round from the mountain top, to cause such a view to pass before his eyes; and Luke's phrase "in a moment of time" seems clearly to indicate that it was supernatural. *Alford:*

" If it be objected that in that case there was no need for the ascent of the mountain, I answer, that such natural accessories are made use of frequently in supernatural revelations; see especially Rev. 21: 10." *Bengel:* "Shows —to the eyes what the horizon embraced ; the rest he spoke of and perhaps pointed towards." *Keil:* " In the case of both Jesus and Satan experiences are possible which are impossible for mere man, which we cannot adequately represent to our minds, and have no right to deny." We may very well take 'all the kingdoms' as an hyperbole (comp. Ezra 1: 2), especially as many parts of the earth would present little that was glorious, or attractive to worldly ambition. **And the glory of them,** is added because their glory was especially paraded before his view. But Jesus would look beneath the glittering surface, and see hollowness, degradation, suffering, ruin. Doubtless his ardent desire to save men was not weakened by this panorama, but greatly strengthened. Throughout his subsequent ministry the idea of a glorious and all-embracing earthly kingdom was often pressed upon him by the multitude, and constantly cherished by his chosen followers, but rejected by him. How much more truly glorious the 'kingdom not of this world' (John 18: 36) which he did found ; and how blessed a thing it will be when 'the kingdom of the world is become the kingdom of our Lord, and of his Christ.' (Rev. 11: 15. Rev. Ver.)

9. All these things, the Greek placing the emphasis not so much on ' all,' as on ' these things.' The claim which Satan here implies, and in Luke 4: 6, expressly asserts, viz., that he possesses the control of the kingdoms of the world and their glory, is not wholly unfounded, for the Scriptures speak of him as the prince or god of this world. (John 12: 31; 14: 30; 16: 11; 2 Cor. 4: 4.) As to the precise nature and limitations of this power we are not informed; but it has been committed to him (Luke 4: 6), and the Revelation of John teaches that it shall one day be withdrawn. **Wilt fall down,**[1] as in 2: 11, the usual pos-

---

[1] Literally, ' if thou fall down.' This subjunctive was natural in early English (so Wyclif), and is barely possible still. To say ' if thou wilt fall down ' (Tyndale and all since) is ambiguous, seeming to introduce the element of willingness, which is not in the original. Yet it makes a smoother Eng. phrase, and so is best in a popular version.

10 Then saith Jesus unto him, Get thee hence, Satan; for it is written, Thou shalt worship the Lord thy God, and him only shalt thou serve.
11 Then the devil leaveth him, and, behold, angels came and ministered unto him.

10 Then saith Jesus unto him, Get thee hence, Satan: for it is written, Thou shalt worship the Lord thy
11 God, and him only shalt thou serve. Then the devil leaveth him; and behold, angels came and ministered unto him.

ture in the East, whether for adoration or for homage. **Worship.** See on 2: 2. There has been difference of opinion as to whether it here signifies idolatrous worship (comp. 1 Cor. 10: 20; Rev. 9: 20), or only homage as to a civil superior; but the latter, paid to Satan, would necessarily lead to the former. The tempter proposes that Jesus shall recognize the worldly power which Satan is allowed to exercise, and shall conform his Messianic reign to existing conditions by acknowledging Satan's sovereignty. Jesus was in fact to reign over this world, yet not as successor or subordinate to Satan, but by utterly overthrowing his dominion. (Comp. 12: 25, 28).

10. Get thee hence,[1] '*begone,*' or, 'away with thee,' here said in abhorrence or disgust, though sometimes in kindness (as 8: 13). **Satan,** see on v. 1. **It is written,** see on v. 4. The quotation here is from Deut. 6: 13, and follows Sept. It differs from Hebrew in introducing 'only' or 'alone,' which merely expresses what is indicated in the Hebrew by the emphasis; and also in substituting for the general term 'fear' the more specific term 'worship,' which makes more manifest the affiliation of the passage to the matter in hand. (See on 2: 6.)

11. Leaveth him. An example of what was afterwards taught by James (4: 7), 'Resist the devil, and he will flee from you.' Luke (4: 13) says, 'for a season.' Doubtless his temptations were frequently renewed throughout the Saviour's ministry (comp. on v. 1), and especially when it was about to close. (John 14: 30.) *Bengel:* "This temptation is a specimen of Christ's whole state of humiliation, and an epitome of all the temptations, not only moral but spiritual, which the devil contrived from the beginning." **Angels came;** came near to him (same term as in v. 3). **Ministered,**

or, *were ministering*—**unto him.** This word signifies to attend as a servant, wait on, etc., often with particular reference to supplying food (comp, 8: 15; 25: 44; 27: 55; Luke 8: 3; 10: 40 'serve'; 12: 37; Acts 6: 2 'serve'). And so apparently here. They waited on him as human friends might have waited on one whom they found hungry, weary, lonely. To Elijah (1 Kings 19 : 6, 7) an angel brought food *before* the forty days' fast; to Jesus at its close. He had refused to relieve his hunger by turning the stones into loaves of bread, referring to the case of Israel, to whom God supplied food in an extraordinary way; and now God makes an extraordinary provision for him. He had refused to try an experiment upon a promise of angelic help (v. 6), and now angelic help comes unsought. The term employed, 'were ministering to him,' not simply narrates the fact, but vividly describes it as going on. And so, with the baffled tempter withdrawn, and angels engaged in ministering to him, this wonderful and affecting scene comes to a close.

Our Lord is now fully prepared for his work as Messiah. At his baptism the Father gave him an extraordinary recognition and greeting. During the forty days he has doubtless reflected upon the need and the character of that saving work which he has come into the world to do. And now the tempter's proposals have familiarized his mind with the thought of three principal wrong courses which will often during his ministry be proposed to him, and which he will always instantly reject as he has done here—he will never use his supernatural powers to relieve his own natural wants, nor to make a display before man, and he will utterly avoid the favorite Jewish notion of a brilliant worldly kingdom, obtained by worldly means and used for worldly purposes.[2]

---

[1] Many MSS. and versions (some that are early) add 'behind me,' manifestly an assimilation to 16: 23, where there is no variation in the reading.

[2] The legendary temptation of Sakhya Muni (afterwards Buddha) has sometimes been likened to the temptation of Christ. Edwin Arnold, in "The Light of Asia," has borrowed phrases and ideas from the Gos-

pel, so as to give a false appearance of resemblance. When these are removed, and details which he omits are restored, the two accounts have no resemblance beyond the bare fact of a person being specially tempted when meditating a great work for the good of mankind, which is doubtless, in one shape or other, a universal experience. See Kellogg, "The Light of Asia

HOMILETICAL AND PRACTICAL.

V. 1. The occurrence of this special season of temptation immediately after our Lord's baptism and when he was about to enter on his ministry, while not wholly analogous to the case of his disciples, yet corresponds with a not infrequent experience.—ECCLUS. 2: 1: "My son, if thou art coming near to serve the Lord, prepare thy soul for temptation."—EU-THYM.: "That thou also after baptism mayst no longer lead thyself, but rather be led by the Spirit, and that if after baptism thou fallest into temptations thou mayest not be confounded."—GILL: "And so it often is, that after sweet communion with God in his ordinances, after large discoveries of his love and interest in him, follow sore temptations, trials, and exercises."—God often brings his people into temptation (6: 13), and so he brought the Captain of their salvation. (Heb. 2: 10).—MILTON (Par. Reg.):

> But first I mean
> To exercise him in the wilderness;
> There he shall first lay down the rudiments
> Of his great warfare, ere I send him forth
> To conquer sin and death, the two grand foes,
> By humiliation and strong sufferance.

Some men have fancied that they would escape temptation by fleeing to solitude—and others by seeking society; behold, Jesus is tempted both in the wilderness and in the Holy City. There is here 1) a discipline to the tempted Redeemer; 2) an example to his tempted followers, and 3) a lesson of failure to the tempter. Three distinct practical evils are prevalent as to the devil, each of which must help him. (a) Some deny his existence, *i. e.*, either his personality or his agency—which gives him an admirable opportunity to carry on his work unsuspected. (b) A few persons associate him with the sublime conceptions of Paradise Lost, and thus feel a diminished abhorrence. (c) The great mass associate him with all that is ridiculous. The instinctive desire to shake off horrible thoughts has led to this, as men joke in a dissecting-room, and it has grown customary, and gained strength from prevailing skepticism. The practice of applying ludicrous designations to the devil, and making him the point of amusing stories and jests, as well as the grotesque nursery descriptions and stories, can never fail to be very hurtful, and should be avoided and discouraged.—V. 2. GREG. NAZ., (in Wordsw.): "Christ hungered as man, and fed the hungry as God. He was hungry as man, and yet he is the Bread of life. He was athirst as man, and yet he says, Let him that is athirst come to me and drink. He was weary, and is our Rest. . . . He pays tribute, and is a King; he is called a devil, and casts out devils; prays, and hears prayer; weeps, and dries our tears; is sold for thirty pieces of silver, and redeems the world; is led as a sheep to the slaughter, and is the Good Shepherd."—EDERSH.: "Moses failed after his forty days' fast, when in indignation he cast the tables of the law from him; Elijah failed before his forty days' fast; Jesus was assailed for forty days, and endured the trial."

V. 3. The demand for special proofs of the divine mission of Christ is often made in a wrong spirit, by persons whom those very proofs would not convince; as Satan afterwards witnessed numerous miracles wrought by Jesus, but without effect.—GEIKIE: "No temptation is more difficult to resist than the prompting to do what seems needful for self-preservation, when abundant means are in our hands."—MORISON: "The prime temptation of millions, though they often realize it not, is to use improper means of making their bread." V. 4. Our Lord was 'tempted like as we are,' and he resisted like as we must. If he had wrought a miracle for his own relief, that would have been no example for us; but it was an example that he should in trying circumstances trust in God and wait—and that he should be guided and sustained by what 'is written.' If we would imitate this example, let us become thoughtfully imbued with the principles of Scripture (Ps. 119: 11), and familiar with its precepts and examples, so that they may be naturally suggested to the mind, or readily recalled, just when they are needed.—ORIGEN (Wordsw.): "He routs the tempter by what all may wield, the sword of the Spirit, which is

---

and the Light of the World," ch. iv., especially p. 145–153. Bp. Lightfoot has shown (Colossians, p. 151–157) that there is no evidence of any influence of Buddhism on the Essenes, or that Buddhism was known in Syria during the first Christian century.—The idea of a special temptation of the Messiah by Satan was quite contrary to all Jewish conceptions and expectations. See Edersh., Book iii., ch. 1.

the word of God. (Eph. 6:17.) Hence learn the value of Scripture, and the impotence of Satan against it."—STIER: "As Eve in the beginning rightly opposed the tempter with *God has said!* but alas, did not persist therein—even so now the Lord; but he hoids firm."—LIGHTFOOT: "Observe (1) That the first word spoken by Christ in his ministerial office is an assertion of the authority of Scripture. (2) That he opposeth the word of God as the properest incounterer against the words of the devil. (3) That he alledgeth Scripture as a thing undeniable and uncontrollable by the devil himself. (4) That he maketh the Scripture his rule, though he had the fullness of the Spirit above measure."—HENRY: "As in our greatest abundance we must not think to live *without* God, so in our greatest straits we must learn to live *upon* God."—There is a common saying, 'Necessity knows no law.' But it *ought* to know the law of duty.

V. 5. HENRY: "Pinnacles of the temple are places of temptation. (1) High places *in the world* are so. (2) High places *in the church* are in a special manner dangerous." V. 6. HENRY: "We must avoid going from one extreme to another—from despair to presumption, from prodigality to covetousness," etc.—LANGE: "The holiest thing may be perverted to become the most vile temptation. (1) A stay in the holy city. (2) The prospect from the pinnacle of the temple. (3) The promise contained in an inspired Psalm."— One of the subtlest and sometimes mightiest forms of temptation to a devout mind is the misapplication of Scripture, so as to give apparent warrant for doing what we incline to. We need not only to know the language of Scripture, but to understand the real meaning and legitimate application. A great aid in this is to compare other passages, as our Lord here does.—BENGEL: "Scripture must through Scripture be interpreted and reconciled."—WORDSWORTH: "The devil may tempt us to fall, but he cannot *make* us fall; he may persuade us to cast *ourselves* down, but he *cannot cast* us down."—V. 7. True faith never tries experiments upon the promises, being satisfied that they will be fulfilled as occasion may arise. We have no right to create danger, and expect Providence to shield us from it. The love of adventure,

curiosity as to the places and procedures of vice, the spirit of speculation in business, the profits of some calling attended by moral perils,—often lead men to tempt God. It is a common form of sin. (See Chalmers' Sermons on the Temptations.) GRIFFITH: "We violate the organic conditions of health, and then expect some miracle of restoration. We devote ourselves to seeming duty, labor on in what we fancy must be saintly self-sacrifice, till the brain is fevered, the strength is exhausted, and imbecility and death come in to punish the presumption of 'testing the Lord our God.' "—Jesus did afterwards work miracles equivalent to those proposed in the first and second temptations, when he multiplied food, and when he walked on the water; but in these cases he was using his supernatural power for the benefit of others.

V. 8. See Milton's description in Par. Regained, Book iii. V. 9. How often are measures adopted by preacher or church that are unworthy of Christianity, and defended only by urging that they *take*, that they *succeed*. But Christ would not rule over the world by Satan's help, and we must not seek to advance the kingdom of holiness by unholy means.— THEOPHYLACT: "Now also he says to the covetous that the world is his, so that they gain it who worship him."—SCHAFF: "Satan's greatest weapons are his half-truths, his perversions of the truth." V. 10. Often the only proper way to deal with the tempter is to bid him begone. AUGUSTINE: "It is the devil's part to suggest, it is ours not to consent."—JER. TAYLOR: "The Lamb of God could by no means endure it when tempted to a direct dishonoring of God. Our own injuries are opportunities of patience; but when the glory of God and his immediate honor is the question, then is the occasion for the flames of a clear shining and unconsuming zeal." V. 11. GROTIUS: "Formerly conqueror of our first parents and long conqueror of the human race, but now conquered by Christ, and to be conquered by Christians. (1 John 5:18.)"

GRIFFITH: "The successive temptations may be ranked as temptations to under-confidence, over-confidence, and other confidence. The first, to take things impatiently into our hands; the second, to throw things presumptuously on God's hands; the third, to transfer things disloyally into other hands than God's."

—LORIMER: "The spirit of evil takes things that are right in themselves and perverts them to our undoing; as here, the instinct of self-preservation, the feeling of self-confidence, the hope of self-aggrandizement." We can see in these temptations a *progression*. (a) The tempter *appeals to*, (1) a bodily appetite, (2) an obscure nervous feeling, (3) ambition, which is wholly of the mind. (b) He *proposes* (1) a useful miracle, (2) a useless miracle, (3) a gross sin. (c) He *seeks to excite*, (1) distrust of God, (2) presumptuous reliance on God, (3) worldly-minded abandonment of God.

12-25. BEGINNING OF OUR LORD'S MINISTRY IN GALILEE.

The third and principal division of the Gospel of Matthew, from 4: 12 to the end of chap. 18, gives an account of our Lord's ministry in Galilee. A general introduction to that account is given in 4: 12-25.

Having described the events connected with the entrance of Jesus upon his public work, it is natural that the narrative should pass to the work itself. So far as we learn from Matt., Mark (1: 14) and Luke (4: 14), this began after John the Baptist's labors were closed by his imprisonment, and its scene was Galilee and adjacent districts, until shortly before our Lord's death. Nor do they intimate that any long time intervened between the temptation and this ministry in Galilee. The Gospel of John, on the other hand, records a number of intervening events, embracing the testimony of John the Baptist to Jesus, after his baptism, and apparently after his temptation; the gaining of disciples, the marriage at Cana, and the brief residence at Capernaum (John 1: 19, to 2: 12); the first Passover of our Lord's public ministry, with the expulsion of the traders and the conversation with Nicodemus (John 2: 13, to 3: 21); the teaching and baptizing in Judea before John the Baptist's imprisonment, and the occurrences at Sychar when Jesus was on the way to Galilee. (John 3: 22 to 4: 42.) But there is here no real contradiction between John and the other Evangelists. None of them could record the whole of Jesus' public life, and each must select according to his particular design. Where events are omitted in a brief narrative, we cannot expect to find a wide break as if to invite their insertion from some other source; for this would destroy the continuity of the narrative, and greatly impair its interest and impressiveness. The story must go right on, but must not contain such expressions as would *exclude* the events it omits. This is the course which Matthew, Mark, and Luke have here pursued. They make no allusion to labors of our Lord between the temptation and John's imprisonment, but do not at all affirm that there were no intervening labors; and various facts mentioned by them (*e. g.* Luke 10: 38), really imply that our Lord had been preaching in Judea before the visit which ended in his death. What were the reasons for omitting one thing and inserting another, we may not in all cases be able to perceive. But the concurrence of the three first Evangelists in beginning their account of Christ's public ministry just after that of the forerunner closed, suggests (Ewald, Alexander), that the work of Christ then assumed in some sense a different character; the early preaching and baptizing of our Lord while the forerunner's work still went on (John 3: 22 f.; 4: 1 f.) was introductory, and his ministry now takes in some sense a higher position. The transition from the Old Dispensation to the New was in many respects gradual. Even after the ascension of Christ and the special coming of the Spirit, the Jewish Christians long continued to observe the ceremonies of the law, continued it apparently until providentially stopped by the destruction of the temple. And so the forerunner continued his preaching and baptizing side by side with that of Jesus until providentially stopped by his imprisonment. It is likely that the oral narratives commonly given by the apostles for years after the ascension were accustomed to begin their account of the Lord's ministry, as we find the three first Gospels doing, with this point at which his ministry stood out apart from that of the Baptist. But before John's Gospel was written, some persons were maintaining that the Baptist's work was designed to be permanent, and ought to be continued by his disciples; it may have been partly to correct this error that John narrates the earlier ministry of Jesus, showing that he was not a mere successor of the Baptist, but began to preach before the other ceased, and that the forerunner distinctly and repeatedly acknowledged his own inferiority, and asserted that his work was designed to be temporary. (John 1: 29-37; 3: 26 ff.)

12 Now when Jesus had heard that John was [1] cast into prison, he departed into Galilee;

12   Now when he heard that John was delivered up,

---

1 Or, *delivered up.*

If we adopt the common and probable reckoning that our Lord's public ministry occupied about three years and a half, putting his baptism some months before the Passover at which Nicodemus visited him, then the labors in Galilee and vicinity recorded by Matthew (and Mark and Luke) begin during the second year of his ministry (reckoning from Passover to Passover, because at the Passover he died), and probably in the latter part of that year; thus leaving rather less than two years for this "ministry in Galilee," which ended six months before the crucifixion.

It is evident that Matthew does not in this part of his work propose to himself a chronological account of events and discourses. He sets out with the general statement that our Lord withdrew (from Judea) into Galilee, and making Capernaum his residence and the centre of his operations, began to preach. (v. 12-17.) Then comes the fact of his calling certain persons to follow him, and unite with him in these labors. (v. 18-22.) Next a very general account of his going about all Galilee, preaching and healing, while his fame spread far and wide, and he was followed by crowds from all the adjacent regions. (v. 23-25.) The present section thus carries us into the heart of the ministry in Galilee. Afterwards we shall find that great discourse (ch. 5-7), in which our Lord set forth certain principles of the kingdom or reign he came to proclaim and establish; and then a number of miracles and discourses, such as were calculated to prove the fact that Jesus is the Messiah, and to exhibit the true nature of the Messianic reign—the twofold object of Matthew's Gospel. In all this there is no attempt at chronological order, but a grouping of the topics which is more effective for the sacred writer's object. (Comp. on 8: 1; 9: 35; 11: 2; 12: 1; 14: 1.)

12. Now when Jesus had heard, or, *and hearing.* The narrative goes right on.[1] **Cast**

into prison, or, *delivered up,*—literally, *passed on,* 'given from hand to hand.' It is a word often used in the Gospels and the Acts, sometimes correctly translated by 'deliver,'[2] often incorrectly by 'betray.' Matthew here contents himself with this general expression, without stating the circumstances of John's imprisonment, because they were familiar to his readers. Afterwards, when telling of John's death (14: 3 ff.), he states the cause of his imprisonment. According to the chronological estimates above mentioned, the imprisonment took place over twelve months after the baptism of Jesus, and thus John's preaching and baptizing continued in all about a year and a half. Henceforth, until his death, about a year later, we are to think of him as a prisoner in the Castle of Machaerus, some miles east of the northern part of the Dead Sea. (See on 14: 6.) **Departed,** *withdrew,* or, 'retired,'[3] as above in 2: 12, 13, 14, 22, and below in 12: 15; 14: 13, etc. The word does not necessarily imply danger. (See Acts 23: 19; 26: 31.) Yet the circumstances here suggest that our Lord withdrew to avoid inconvenient consequences which might follow if he remained in Judea. And this is explained by John. The Pharisees at Jerusalem had been watching the Baptist (John 1: 19 ff.), and were doubtless jealous of his influence. But of late they had heard that Jesus was making and baptizing more disciples than John (John 4: 1), and now that John was imprisoned they would be likely to turn their jealous attention to Jesus, who therefore withdrew from Judea into the remoter Galilee. It is a strange mistake to say that he wished to avoid Herod, for Judea (John 4: 3) was not in Herod's dominions, and Galilee was. Similar withdrawals by our Lord we shall find below, in 12: 15; 14: 13; 15: 21. (Comp. on 8: 4.)

Galilee, the scene of the greater part of our Lord's ministry, is wrongly conceived by

---

[1] 'Jesus' does not belong to the true text. It was probably inserted in public reading for perspicuity (as also in v. 18, 23), and so crept into the text. Some codd. of Vulgate give it even in 5: 1.

[2] Tyndale, following Wyclif, here gave 'taken,' a very poor translation of the Vulgate. Beza's note,

"*i. e.,* had been thrown into prison," appears to have been followed by the Common Version.

[3] So the Latin version and Rheims ('retired'), the Syriac ('removed'), Davidson, etc. 'Departed' comes from Tyndale.

13 And leaving Nazareth, he came and dwelt in Capernaum, which is upon the sea coast, in the borders of Zabulon and Nephthalim:

13 he withdrew into Galilee; and leaving Nazareth, he came and dwelt in Capernaum, which is by the sea,

---

many as a poor country, with a degraded population. It has always been much more fertile and beautiful than Judea, and in the time of Christ had an immense population, brave, energetic, and wealthy. (Comp. below on v. 23.) The name appears to have come from the Galil or 'circuit' of twenty cities given by Solomon to Hiram, king of Tyre (Josh. 20: 7; 1 Kings 9: 11; 2 Kings 15: 29), and was gradually extended to denote the northern part of the Holy Land in general. From its proximity to and connection with Phenicia this district would be largely occupied by Gentiles, and so was called by Isaiah, literally (9: 1) 'circuit of the Gentiles.' During and after the captivity the Gentiles became predominant. In B. C. 164, the Jews in Galilee were so few that the Maccabees carried them all away to Judea for safety. (1 Macc. 5: 23.) In the time of Christ the vast population were chiefly Jews, though several cities are expressly said (Josephus, Strabo) to have contained many Gentiles, and they were doubtless numerous elsewhere. These probably sometimes heard Jesus, who may have sometimes spoken in Greek, but there is nothing to warrant the fancy that he was a "Foreign Missionary," as habitually preaching to the heathen; and it is quite forbidden by 10: 5, and 15: 24. The constant association with Gentiles, as well as the distance from Jerusalem, may have softened the religious prejudices of the Galilean Jews, and rendered them more accessible to the new teachings. The Galileans pronounced Aramaic with some provincial peculiarities by which the people of Jerusalem could recognize them (26: 73), but this does not show them to have been ignorant. Galilee exhibited an intense activity in agriculture, fisheries, manufacturing, and trade. Besides local business, the great trade between Egypt and Damascus passed through this region. Jesus labored among an intelligent and actively busy people. The district comprised the immensely fertile plain of Esdraelon on the south; the broad, rolling uplands of the centre, rich in grass

and wheat, in bright flowers and shady trees; and the higher hills and mountains of the north, which, interspersed with deep valleys, presented the greatest variety of productions and climate. (See Josephus, Keim, Renan, Neubauer, and especially Merrill's "Galilee in the Time of our Lord," from "Biblioth. Sac." for 1874.) Three times we find our Lord described as making extensive journeys around Galilee. (4: 23; Luke 8: 1 ff.; Matt. 9: 35 ff.)

13 f. He did not make this change immediately upon reaching Galilee, but first revisited Cana (John 4: 46), and began teaching in Galilee with great acceptance (Luke 4: 15), coming presently to Nazareth. (Luke 4: 16 ff.) Being there rejected and his life attempted, he left (Luke 4: 31), and went down to Capernaum.[1] Here he would not only be more free from popular violence, but would come in contact with a much larger and more active-minded population. So Paul labored especially at Antioch, Corinth, and Ephesus, commercial centres, in which men's minds were active and ready to grasp new ideas, and from which the news would spread in every direction, and excursions could be readily made. **Came and dwelt in,** as in 2: 23. **Capernaum** was our Lord's home, the centre of his labors and journeys, for probably nearly two years. (Comp. on v. 12.) On the western shore of the Lake of Galilee (see on v. 18) there extends for some three miles an exceedingly fertile plain, called the 'Plain of Gennesaret.' (See on 14: 34.) In this plain, or a little north of it, Capernaum was situated; but the once highly exalted city has been cast down into such destruction (11: 23), that we cannot certainly determine its site. Robinson placed it at Khan Minyeh, on the northern edge of the plain, and is still followed by Keim and Conder. (Renan and Godet doubtful.) But the great majority of recent explorers prefer the view that it was at Tel Hum, two miles further up the shore. The earliest MSS. and versions give the name as Capharnaum, and the Syriac gives Capharnahum. As Ca-

---

[1] This proceeds upon the view that the visit to Nazareth in 13: 54 (Mark 6: 1) is distinct from that of Luke 4: 16, a view not certainly, but probably, correct.—Several MSS. read in this place Nazara, and that is prob-

ably the original form of the word (Keim, Grimm, Buttmann). But as Nazaret, or Nazareth, or Nazarath occurs in most passages, it seems useless to depart from the common form here.

14 That it might be fulfilled which was spoken by
Esaias the prophet, saying,
15 The land of Zabulon, and the land of Nephthalim,
by the way of the sea, beyond Jordan, Galilee of the
Gentiles;

14 in the borders of Zebulun and Naphtali: that it
might be fulfilled which was spoken through Isaiah
the prophet, saying,
15   The land of Zebulun and the land of Naphtali,
1 Toward the sea, beyond Jordan,
Galilee of the 2 Gentiles,

---

1 Gr. *The way of the sea*....2 Gr. *nations :* and so elsewhere.

---

phar in Hebrew means 'village,' Capharnahum means 'village of Nahum,' or perhaps 'village of consolation' (Origen). In
modern Arabic the word Tel denotes a hill
covered with ruins, and thus Tel Hum might
well be the modern form of village of Nahum (so Ewald, Delitzsch, and others). Moreover, the ruins at Tel Hum contain much
black basaltic rock, which is very hard to
work, and must have been brought from the
country S. E. of the lake, so that its free use
indicates a wealthy city, the most important
in the neighborhood. Now Capernaum evidently had such pre-eminence among the
cities on the northern shores of the lake, and
so it seems highly probable that Tel Hum is
the site of Capernaum.[1] At Tel Hum are the
ruins of a beautiful synagogue, the finest of
which we have any remains in all Palestine,
and this may well have been 'the synagogue'
built by the centurion. (Luke 7 : 5.) Originally
but a 'village' (Caphar), and so not mentioned in O. T., it had in N. T. times become
a 'city.' (Luke 4 : 31.) It probably had a large
fishing business (the fish were put up in salt
and transported to the interior), and general
trade on the lake, while very near it passed
the principal road from Damascus to Ptolemais, carrying the trade with Egypt. It had
a custom-house (9 : 9), and a garrison of Roman
soldiers. (8 : 9.) Our Lord had at a former
period remained here for a short time (John
2 : 12), perhaps sojourning with Peter, whom
we afterwards find living at Capernaum. (8 : 14;
Mark 1 : 29; 2 : 1.) In the synagogue at Capernaum
he delivered the great discourse of John, ch. 6
(see John 6 : 59). It was a convenient starting point for his journeys into Galilee or Decapolis, towards Tyre or Cesarea Philippi, to
Perea or Judea; and was the home to which
he constantly returned.

Borders, as in 2 : 16. The borders of **Zabulon and Nephthalim** means the borders
common to the two, the boundary between

them. For the peculiar forms of the names,
Zabulon and Nephthalim, see on 1: 2. The
Evangelist takes pains to describe the situation of Capernaum, as beside the sea (lake),
and on the boundary between these two
tribes, in order to show the minute correspondence to the prediction he is about to
quote. Matthew often introduces Messianic
prophecies as fulfilled in Jesus (1 : 22; 2 : 6, 15, 17,
23; 3 : 3), this being an evidence of his Messiahship.

14. For that it might be fulfilled by, or,
through, see on 1 : 22; and for the form of the
names Esaias or Isaiah, on 1 : 2. A providential design of Jesus' going to reside in this
region was that the prophecy might be fulfilled; there might of course be other designs
at the same time.

15 f. The Sept. translation of this passage
(Isa. 9 : 1 f.), is quite incorrect, and Matt. does
not follow the Sept., as he commonly does
where it is sufficiently accurate for his purpose. The original Hebrew contains some expressions which would be intelligible only by
consulting the connection, and these Matt.
has omitted, but without affecting the meaning of the passage, as applying to our Lord's
settlement at Capernaum. He even begins in
the middle of a sentence, taking only what
was appropriate to the matter in hand. The
prophet has spoken of great afflictions which
would befall the people at the hands of the
Assyrians and others, but which would be followed by great blessings, to be enjoyed especially by the tribes mentioned, they having
been most afflicted; and the Evangelist shows
us a remoter reference in this to the blessings
connected with the work of the Messiah, to
whom Isaiah immediately afterwards (9 : 6 f.)
makes a distinct reference. **By the way of
the sea,** omit 'by.' This might mean road
to the sea, or simply sea-road (Meyer, Weiss);
or road by the sea, meaning the great caravan
route which passed near the sea, *i. e.,* the Lake

---

[1] This view, favored by Ewald, Delitzsch, Ritter, Hausrath, Thomson, "Recovery of Jerusalem," Farrar,
Schaff, Geikie, and others, is particularly well argued

by Bartlett. None of them present the argument from
the masses of black rock, which are not found in any
other ruins in the neighborhood.

16 The people which sat in darkness saw great light; and to them which sat in the region and shadow of death light is sprung up.
17 From that time Jesus began to preach, and to say, Repent: for the kingdom of heaven is at hand.

16   The people that sat in darkness
Saw a great light,
And to them that sat in the region and shadow of death,
To them did light spring up.
17   From that time began Jesus to preach, and to say, Repent ye; for the kingdom of heaven is at hand.

---

of Galilee (see on v. 18); or road from the sea, viz., the Mediterranean (Keim). The English 'sea-road'[1] would be equally ambiguous. The most probable meaning is the second, 'road by the sea,' designating the regions adjacent to the lake. **Beyond Jordan** (see v. 25) in O. T. usually means east of the Jordan, but in some passages west of it (see Num. 32: 19; Deut. 11: 30; Josh. 5: 1; 22: 7), reminding us that Israel came first to the region east of the river. It of course depends on the writer's point of view in each case. Isaiah, having referred to the calamities which would be inflicted by the Eastern nations, might naturally for the moment speak from their point of view, and thus 'beyond Jordan' would mean west of the Jordan, and would denote the same region as the other expressions. This fits the connection, which has a series of parallel phrases. Those who prefer the more common O. T. sense of 'beyond Jordan' understand Decapolis, east of the lake, or Perea, east of the lower Jordan (see on v. 25). They then either hold that this denotes a region distinct from Galilee, or suppose that Galilee sometimes included Decapolis, etc. **Galilee of the Gentiles** (see on v. 12). The word rendered Gentiles signifies simply 'nations' (see margin of Rev. Ver.). The Israelites called all others 'the nations,' in distinction from themselves, who were the chosen people.

16. In this verse is an instance of that "parallelism" which is the peculiarity in the structure of Hebrew poetry, and consequently abounds in O. T. There are two principal varieties of it: (*a*) the second clause simply repeats, in different phraseology, the thought of the first; and (*b*) the second stands in contrast with the first. The present example belongs to (*a*), the second clause repeating first, but in stronger terms. (See other examples in 7: 6; 12: 30.) **Shadow of death,**

or, death-shade, is simply a figure for the densest darkness. (Comp. Jer. 13: 16; Amos 5: 8; Ps. 107: 10; 23: 4, see margin Rev. Ver. 'deep darkness'; even Job 10: 21.) The 'region and shadow' may be understood as equivalent by what grammarians call hendiadys to 'region of the shadow' (which is the meaning of the Heb.), or as simply expanding the idea, region of death and shadow of death. **Is sprung up,** or, *arose;* the Greek term is often used of sunrise and dawn.[2] The image seems to be that of persons who had lost their way in the dense darkness, and upon whom arose the great light of the morning. The Heb. has 'walked. . . . sat,' while Matt. says 'sat' in both cases, which with reference to the figure is an equivalent expression. Here, as so often in Scripture, darkness and light represent ignorance, sin, misery, as opposed to knowledge, holiness, happiness.— *Alexander:* "The verse in its original connection has respect to the degraded and oppressed state of the Galileans, arising from their situation on the frontier, their exposure to attack from without, and their actual mixture with the Gentiles." Matt. shows us in this language a further reference to the spiritual darkness of the Galileans of our Lord's time. All the Jews were in spiritual darkness, and the Galileans were inferior in religious privileges to the Judeans, and despised by them. (John 7: 41, 49, 52.) There is no proof that they were morally more corrupt than the Judeans. But he who came 'to seek and to save that which is lost,' fixed in this remote and despised section of the Holy Land the centre of his labors, and here chose most of the apostles who were to carry his teachings to Judea and Samaria, and the ends of the earth. (Acts 1: 8.)

17. Establishing himself in Capernaum, our Lord began to preach. **From that time** began that public ministry which Matthew proposes to describe. (Comp. on v. 12.)

---

[1] The Greek genitive is often most exactly rendered into English by means of a compound substantive (comp. on 1: 11).

[2] Literally, 'and to those sitting. . . . light arose to

them.' This repetition of the pronoun after the verb is a Hebrew idiom, natural to the Evangelist, though awkward in Greek and English.

18 And Jesus, walking by the sea of Galilee, saw two brethren, Simon called Peter, and Andrew his brother, casting a net into the sea: for they were fishers. | 18   And walking by the sea of Galilee, he saw two brethren, Simon, who is called Peter, and Andrew his brother, casting a net into the sea; for they

The English word **preach** is derived (through the French) from the Latin *predico*, which signifies to proclaim, publish, declare. The Greek word here used (*kerusso*) has the same sense, to proclaim as a crier or herald does, and in general to proclaim, publish, declare. This is the word always used by *Matthew* where the Common English Version has 'preach,' except in 11: 5, and elsewhere in N. T. it is always rendered 'preach,' except in Luke 12: 3; Rev. 5: 2, 'proclaim,' and in Mark 1: 45; 5: 20; 7: 36; 13: 10; Luke 8: 39 'publish.' But it will not do to infer that 'to preach' is always in N. T. an official function, as these facts have led some to do, because the English word is also used (in other N. T. books) to translate various other words, which carry no suggestion of a herald or other official. Thus *euangelizomai*, to bear a good message, bring good news (comp. *euangelion*, 'gospel,' introductory note to 1: 1), used once by Matt. (11: 5), and not at all by Mark or John, is a favorite word with Luke and Paul, and often rendered in Com. Ver. by 'preach,' or 'preach the gospel.' *Laleo*, to talk, speak, a very common word in that sense, is rendered 'preach' in Mark 2: 2; Acts 8: 25; 11: 19; 13: 42; 14: 25; 16: 6.[1]

Repent, etc. See on 3: 2. Our Lord begins this ministry after the imprisonment of John, with precisely the same exhortation and announcement that had been made by John. We naturally infer that his previous preaching in Judea had been to the same effect. Yet he by no means confined himself to the announcement and exhortation, but already in Judea had strongly stated to Nicodemus and to the woman of Samaria the spiritual nature of the Messianic reign. To the woman he had also declared himself the Messiah (John 4: 26; comp. John 1: 46-51), but it did not accord with his purpose publicly to declare this in Galilee. From Mark 1: 15 we see that along with the exhortation to repent he called on the people to 'believe in the gospel,' or good news, viz., in the good news he was announcing; just as

the Baptist bade them 'believe on the (one) coming after him.' (Acts 19: 4.) Thus not only repentance, but faith in the Messiah, was preached before as well as after the day of Pentecost. Then, as in the case of Abraham (Rom. 4: 11) and always, belief in God's word was the root of piety. And if the baptism of John, and that administered by Jesus through his disciples (John 4: 1 f.), was conditioned on faith in the Messiah as well as repentance, what essential difference was there between it and Christian baptism?

18. In v. 18-22 we have an account of the call of certain disciples, Simon and Andrew, James and John. The first two of these, and in all probability John also, had attached themselves to Jesus on the Jordan, soon after his temptation, as had also Philip and Nathanael (John 1: 35 ff.). From that time we find him constantly attended by persons known as 'his disciples,' at Cana (John 2: 2, 11), at Capernaum, (John 2: 12), at Jerusalem (John 2: 17, 22), in his labors in Judea (John 3: 22; 4: 2), and at Sychar. (John 4: 8; 27-33.) Supposing, as there seems reason to do, that these included some or all of the five persons above named, we conclude that upon returning to Galilee they had left Jesus, gone to their own homes, and resumed their former occupations, it being probable that he had never yet told them they were to forsake all and follow him without intermission. And it was natural enough that they should return to fishing after being so long with Jesus, even as some of them sought food in that way after his resurrection. (John 21: 1.) The training of the disciples for their work was very gradual (see on 10: 1). On the present occasion, finding the two pairs of brothers engaged in their occupation as fishermen, Jesus calls on them to attend him in his ministry, which they seem to have constantly done from this time forward. Their immediate compliance with his demand (v. 20, 22) ceases to be strange when we remember their former connection with him; and this is one of the cases in which Matthew, Mark, and

[1] *Dialegomai*, to converse, discuss, etc., *diangello*, *katangello*, to bear a message, make known, etc., *parresiazomai*, to speak without reserve, speak boldly, and *plero* to complete (Rom. 15: 19), are also occasionally rendered 'preach,' besides being frequently used in their common meanings. The words rendered 'preacher' and 'preaching,' are always from *kerusso*, except in 1 Cor. 1: 18 ('word,' *logos*.)

Luke, make statements which seem to imply a previous ministry such as was afterwards described by John. We see also from the fuller account of the circumstances given by Luke (5: 1 ff.)—for it is very unwise to assume two different calls, as Clark and others do—that a miracle was wrought which made a great impression on Peter and the rest.—Omit 'Jesus,' as in v. 12.

The Sea of Galilee has been well said to be "the most sacred sheet of water in the world," for it is intimately associated with many of the most interesting events in the life of our Lord. It is called in O. T. "the Sea of Chinnereth," or "Chinneroth" (Num. 34: 11; Josh. 12: 3), perhaps from a town of that name on its banks. (Josh. 19: 35.) In N. T. times it was commonly called "Lake of Gennesaret" (Luke 5: 1, Josephus, Strabo, etc.), as already in 1 Macc. 11: 67, "water of Gennesar," the name being probably derived from the plain on its northwestern shore (see on 14: 34). We also find in John (21: 1; 6: 1) the name "Sea of Tiberias," from the city which Herod Antipas built on the southwestern shore, and named after the emperor Tiberius, and which is at the present day the only town remaining near the lake. The name "Sea of Galilee," here and in Mark 7: 31; John 6: 1, was obviously taken from the great district on the west. In Hebrew the term rendered 'sea' was also applied to small bodies of water (as now in German a sea may be a small lake), and this unclassical use of the term is adopted in Greek by Matt., Mark, and John, but not by Luke, who says 'lake.' It is important to observe this usage; for many persons think of the *Sea* of Galilee as a large body of water, when it is only a small lake, twelve and a quarter miles long, and six and three-quarter miles in its greatest breadth. Its surface is six hundred and eighty-two feet below the level of the Mediterranean (comp. on 3: 6), so that from the hills on either side it seems sunken in a great ravine. The range of mountains which bounds the whole Jordan valley on the east, rise here just from the eastern shore of the lake (except a bit of plain at the upper and lower extremities) to the height of nearly two thousand feet. They are deeply furrowed by ravines, and have a barren and desolate appearance. The mountains on the west curve round so as to give space for the lake, and be-

sides leaving the beautiful plain of Gennesaret on the northwest, present "an alternation of soft grassy slopes and rocky cliffs." The warmth due to the great depression, and the numerous and copious springs which break out on the western side, produce a high degree of fertility, which attains its greatest richness in the plain of Gennesaret. Down the ravines on this side, as well as on the east, come rushing winds, which often lash the surface of the lake to fury (see on 8: 24). Around nearly all the western side lies a gently sloping beach, which southward is roughly strewn with stones, but in the middle and northern part is of smooth sand. The water is found, as described by Josephus, to be remarkably clear, cool, and sweet; and the lake still abounds in choice fish, which doubtless led to the name Bethsaida, house of fish, fishtown, for a town on the northeast and another on the northwest. Besides nine cities, some of them quite populous, on the western shore, there were many villages on the hill-sides. *Hanna:* "It is perhaps not too much to say that never did so small a sheet of water see so many keels cutting its surface, or so many human habitations circling round and shadowing its waves, as did the Sea of Galilee in the days of Jesus Christ." Our Lord was throwing himself into the midst of the busy world (comp. on v. 12 and 13), where great crowds would easily collect to hear and see; while whenever he wished to avoid them, he could retire from the lake-shore to the adjacent lofty hills, or cross the narrow lake to the comparative solitudes beyond. On the present occasion we think of him as going forth from Capernaum, and walking **by the sea,** along the sloping and sandy beach, until presently he sees among the busy fishermen those humble brothers whom he had chosen to follow him in labors destined to make the Sea of Galilee famous forever.

How pleasant to me thy deep blue wave,
 O Sea of Galilee!
For the glorious One who came to save
 Hath often stood by thee.

Graceful around thee the mountains meet,
 Thou calm reposing sea;
But ah! far more, the beautiful feet
 Of Jesus walked o'er thee.

Tell me, ye mouldering fragments, tell,
 Was the Saviour's city here?

19 And he saith unto them, Follow me, and I will make you fishers of men.
20 And they straightway left *their* nets, and followed him.

19 were fishers. And he saith unto them, Come ye
20 after me, and I will make you fishers of men. And they straightway left the nets, and followed him.

Lifted to heaven, has it sunk to hell,
  With none to shed a tear?

And was it beside this very sea
  The new-risen Saviour said,
Three times to Simon, " Lovest thou me?
  My lambs and sheep then feed."

O Saviour, gone to God's right hand,
  But the same Saviour still,
Graved on thy heart is this lovely strand
  And every fragrant hill.

Oh ! give me, Lord, by this sacred wave,
  Threefold thy love divine,
That I may feed, till I find my grave,
  Thy flock—both thine and mine.
                                        M'CHEYNE.

On **Simon called Peter** (as to the form of expression comp. 1: 16), and on **Andrew,** see on 10: 2. **A net** is in the original a different word from the more general term employed in v. 20 f., but without any substantial difference of meaning. The circumstances show that it was a dip-net. (Comp. on 13 : 47.) —The fact that our Lord chose 'fishermen' to receive and propagate his teachings, and not Rabbis, shows that he relied on something better than mere human learning and worldly influence, and the success of their labors is one evidence of the divine power which attends the preaching of the gospel. But this idea must not be carried too far. There is no reason at all to consider them weak men, and their position and pursuits seemed in some respects to fit them for their work. They were perhaps less prepossessed by the follies of Pharisaic tradition, and thus better prepared for receiving and transmitting new doctrine, and they were eminently men of the people. "Working men" in the East (Kitto) are often markedly intelligent, correct in language, and courteous, and it has always been a matter of course there that some such men should rise to the highest station. And it has often been seen in America that such men, when they possess real force, have greater popular influence from their ready and well-recognized sympathy with the common mind. There was afterwards added to the number of the apostles a man of lofty intellect, filled with Jewish learning, and not ignorant of Greek literature, and it is he that was chosen

to be the chief instrument of introducing the gospel among the cultivated Greeks, and to write such inspired treatises as the Epistle to the Romans, while at the same time he abhorred the idea of relying on human philosophy or rhetoric, when the excellency of the power must be of God, and not of men. In all this we see a rebuke to the presumption and exclusiveness both of learning and of ignorance. —It is not certain that any others of the twelve than the four here named were fishermen by profession. We know that Matthew was not, nor is it likely that Nathanael of Cana was. The incident in John 21: 1 ff. does not prove that to have been the proper calling of every one present. Still, it is probable that all the twelve were men in comparatively humble life, and without the learning of the Rabbinical schools. (Comp. Acts 4: 13.)

19. Follow me. This was translated *Come ye after me,* by Wyclif and Rheims, followed by Davidson, Noyes, Alford, McClellan. The entire phrase was translated 'follow me' by Tyndale, and so came into Common Version. The first term is literally ' hither,' or 'come hither,' as in 11: 28. With the addition 'after me' it implies that they were to come and follow him, viz., as his disciples (comp. Luke 9: 23; 14: 27). The same idea is presently expressed (v. 20, 22) by the simple term 'follow'; and in 19: 21, both "hither' and 'follow,' are combined. It was the practice of many of the Greek philosophers to have their pupils accompany them wherever they went, instructing them not only by elaborate discourses, but also by conversations with them, or with others in their presence. So Elijah was for some years followed (1 Kings 19: 20 f.) by Elisha, his destined successor. It is easy to see the wisdom of such a course, in these cases and in that of the Great Teacher. Similar language is found below in 9: 9; 16: 24. **Fishers of men,** as he himself had just been occupied with a thronging crowd. (Luke 5: 1.)

20-22. For explanation of their immediately obeying, see on v. 18. So Elisha left at once his numerous oxen, and followed the prophet. Peter remembers long afterwards that they 'left all' and followed Jesus (19: 27, Rev. Ver.) **And going on,** etc., or *going forward.*

21 And going on from thence, he saw other two brethren, James *the son* of Zebedee, and John his brother, in a ship with Zebedee their father, mending their nets; and he called them.

22 And they immediately left the ship and their father, and followed him.

23 And Jesus went about all Galilee, teaching in their synagogues, and preaching the gospel of the kingdom, and healing all manner of sickness and all manner of disease among the people.

21 And going on from thence he saw other two brethren, [1] James the *son* of Zebedee, and John his brother, in the boat with Zebedee their father, mending their

22 nets; and he called them. And they straightway left the boat and their father, and followed him.

23 And [2] Jesus went about in all Galilee, teaching in their synagogues, and preaching the [3] gospel of the kingdom, and healing all manner of disease and all

---

1 Or, *Jacob:* and so elsewhere....2 Some ancient authorities read, *he*....3 Or, *good tidings :* and so elsewhere.

The connection in Luke (5: 7) shows that it was only a short distance, for Peter had beckoned to James and John when he found his boat so full, and they came and filled theirs also. Probably they then brought their boat to shore at a different point, and to this Jesus advanced, and addressed to them also his call. —These two pairs of brothers, thus called at the same time, appear to have been peculiarly associated, forming the first of those quaternions, or companies of four, into which the twelve are in all the lists divided (see on 10: 2 ff). The twelve probably comprised also a third pair of brothers (Luke 6: 16), where 'brother' is more probably the meaning). **In a ship,** or the *boat*, viz., the one they kept and used. The article was duly translated, 'in the ship,' by Tyndale and Cranmer. The translators of Common Version seem to have had in general but little feeling for the article. 'Boat' (Noyes, McClellan) is necessary in modern English to express the exact idea. The Greek word means something used for sailing, and is applied to vessels of various sizes, just as the English ship and skiff were originally the same word. On the Lake of Galilee these fishing-vessels were in all probability mere boats. We cannot tell whether or not they had *sails*, which are never mentioned in the Gospels. With v. 22 compare Mark 1: 20, 'and leaving their father Zebedee in the boat with the hired servants,' Bib. Un. Ver., which indicates that this family were not in great poverty, and so the sons were not depriving their father of necessary assistance (comp. 10: 2).

23. In v. 23-25 is given a general account of our Lord's making a CIRCUIT OF GALILEE, as he did also on two subsequent occasions. (Luke 8: 1-3, and Matt. 9: 35 to 11: 1.) Particular incidents of the circuit are postponed by Matt. till after giving the Sermon on the Mount (ch. 5-7), to which this paragraph furnishes a sort of introduction.

Jesus went about. 'Jesus' should prob-

ably be omitted, as in v. 18, though the evidence is here not conclusive. 'Went about' is imperfect tense, continued or kept going. Christ's labors were incessant. **All Galilee,** (comp. on v. 12) is also a strong expression. Galilee was a small district, say seventy miles long and forty in greatest width; but Josephus declares that it had two hundred and four cities and villages ("Life," ch. 55, Whiston, wrongly, two hundred and forty), and elsewhere ("War.," 3, 3, 2) says: "The cities are numerous, and the multitude of villages everywhere crowded with men, owing to the fecundity of the soil, so that the smallest of them contains above fifteen thousand inhabitants." This is obviously an exaggeration or loose statement, as there must, in the nature of things, have been many smaller villages. But Josephus had ample opportunity to know, having been commanding general in Galilee in A. D. 66. Nearly all the people lived in cities, or villages, and (omitting those who did not) according to these two statements of Josephus there were in Galilee, thirty-five years (one generation) later than our Lord's ministry, more than three million inhabitants; an estimate which some other facts support. But few of the cities are named in the Gospels, yet quite a number in Josephus, whose military operations lead him to speak of them. At any rate, there were over two hundred cities and considerable villages, and while we must not press the phrase 'in *all* Galilee,' we perceive that this circuit by our Lord was one of great labor, and requiring much time, since to visit only half the towns at the rate of one every day, would have taken more than three months. These arithmetical estimates should however not be insisted on, save as helps to form a general conception of the labors of love our Lord performed, as he 'went about doing good, and healing all that were oppressed of the devil.' (Acts 10: 38.) Notice also the expressions which here follow: 'all manner of sickness,' '*all*

Syria,' '*all* sick people.' Of particular miracles and discourses in our Lord's ministry the Gospels give only a few examples; and it is very important to dwell on these general statements, and expand the imagination over this great extent of beneficent work. Day after day, week after week, he goes from town to town, teaching, healing. In scores of synagogues he speaks, hundreds and perhaps thousands of persons he heals; feeling fatigue like any other human being (John 4 : 6; Matt. 8 : 24; Mark 6 : 31), he toils on. **Teaching.** The constant application of 'teach' and 'teacher' to our Lord reminds us that the gospel proposes to instruct and enlighten men, in their ignorance of spiritual things—giving both information as to the facts of God's word and instruction in its principles.

Synagogues. These were of great service to Jesus, and afterwards to his apostles, in furnishing congregations already assembled in a quiet place, associated with nothing but worship. The Greek word which we borrow (*sunagoge*) signifies a collection of objects, or persons, and in the Sept. is often used for the congregation or assembly of Israel (comp. on 16 : 18), in N. T. only for a local assembly of Jews in a particular place to worship, or for the place in which they assembled. The practice of holding such meetings probably originated during the Babylonian captivity, when the people were cut off from the temple worship, and having been found pleasant and useful, was continued afterward. In the time of Christ synagogues are referred to as a thing of course in every town, not only in Palestine, but wherever there were many Jews. After the destruction of Jerusalem, in A. D. 70, the synagogues would naturally receive a further development in organization and worship, and it should not be forgotten that the accounts of these furnished by the Jewish books (see Bible Dictionaries) refer to this later time. In N. T. we find no proofs of complete organization and regular jurisdiction, but there is mention of 'rulers' or 'elders,' and of an 'attendant' (Luke 4 : 20); also of expulsion (John 9 : 22; 12 : 42; 16 : 2), by which it is sufficient to understand that they forbade the person to attend their meetings, which would also cause him to be shunned in society. The examples in Luke 4 : 21 and Acts 13 : 15 show how our Lord and his apostles

could turn the worship and Scripture reading to account. Philo says the reading and detailed exposition of Scripture was continued till late in the afternoon. Regular meetings were held in the synagogues on the Sabbath and on festival-days; whether also on the second and fifth days of the week, as at a later period, we cannot determine (see Luke 18 : 12). Nor are we informed whether extraordinary meetings could be called on other days, as when Jesus arrived in a town and wished to be heard; and we know well that our Lord would speak wherever people could be assembled in quietness, as well in the open air as in a synagogue. **Preaching,** proclaiming (*Kerusso*), see on v. 17. **Gospel** (margin of Rev. Ver. 'good tidings') see note introductory to 1 : 1. **The gospel of the kingdom** is the good news of that kingdom (or reign) of Messiah which was about to be established (see on 3 : 2 and 6 : 10). The prophets had associated ideas of joy with the coming of Messiah's reign; and now Jesus proclaims the 'good news' that it is near. See an interesting specimen of his preaching at this period in Luke 4 : 18. **Healing.** There were two great departments of his public work—to make known truth, and miraculously to relieve men's distresses. He was a Teacher and a Healer. **All manner of sickness** — or, *every kind of disease;* the word is so rendered in v. 24. **Disease**—this word differs from that above. It seems to denote *infirmity*, or such diseases as produce feebleness rather than positive suffering. The same two Greek words meaning 'disease' and 'infirmity,' are coupled in 9 : 35 and 10 : 1. The MIRACLES of Jesus cannot possibly be separated from his history or his teaching, nor can they be rejected without impeaching his character, or also declaring the Epistles of Paul, as well as the Gospels and Acts, to be so utterly untrustworthy that nothing whatever can be received upon their authority. Nay, if one denies the possibility of miracles, he need only be logical to deny the possibility of creation. If we believe that God caused these physical forces to exist, and to act according to the laws which modern science is so nobly busy in observing, where is the difficulty in believing (upon suitable testimony) that God's own spiritual influence has sometimes modified the action of these forces, without violating their nature?

24 And his fame went throughout all Syria: and they brought unto him all sick people that were taken with divers diseases and torments, and those which were possessed with devils, and those which were lunatic, and those that had the palsy; and he healed them.
25 And there followed him great multitudes of people from Galilee, and *from* Decapolis, and *from* Jerusalem, and *from* Judea, and *from* beyond Jordan.

24 manner of sickness among the people. And the report of him went forth into all Syria: and they brought unto him all that were sick, holden with divers diseases and torments, [1] possessed with demons, and epileptic, and palsied; and he healed 25 them. And there followed him great multitudes from Galilee and Decapolis and Jerusalem and Judæa and *from* beyond Jordan.

---

1 Or, *demoniacs.*

If he made them, he can do this. If ever there could be suitable occasion for miracles, it would seem to be when God " sent his Son into the world." Nor can any nobler, worthier miracles be imagined than those recorded as wrought by the Founder of Christianity. The spiritual teachings, the perfect character, and the noble miracles of Christ, all support each other, and together form the foundation of our faith and hope.

24. His fame, Rev. Ver., *the report*, literally, *hearing.* **Went throughout.** Tyndale gave the ' throughout,' which is unwarrantably strong—more strictly, *went off into.* **Syria,** Heb. ' Aram ' (whence ' Aramaic ' as a name of language) was a term of variable extent, denoting in general the country east of the Mediterranean, between Asia Minor and Arabia. In the time of the kings of Israel it signifies the kingdom of which Damascus was the capital. During the Maccabean period it is the Greek kingdom of the Seleucidæ, with Antioch as its capital. At the time of Christ, it is a Roman province of like extent, reaching from the northeast angle of the Mediterranean towards the Euphrates, and southward so as to include Phenicia and Damascus. After Archelaus was deposed, A. D. 6, Judea and Samaria became a Roman province, under the proconsul of Antioch, (see Luke 2: 2). But Galilee, and the other districts governed by Herod Antipas and Philip (see on 2: 22), were still independent of the proconsul, and not a part of Syria. We thus understand Matthew to mean that the report of Jesus' miracles of healing passed beyond the bounds of Galilee, and went far away into the districts northward. It would be folly to press the 'into' and 'all' so as to include Antioch. Mark (1: 28) says, 'into all the region about Galilee'; comp. Luke 4: 14. **All sick people,** literally, *those having* (themselves) *badly*, those who were in a bad condition; a general phrase covering all the classes presently specified. **Torments,** or

'tortures,' such diseases as occasion violent pain; a specific term, added to the general term 'diseases.' To these are further added three particular terms, denoting affections which were severe and frequent, and in themselves quite remarkable. **Possessed with devils.** *Demoniacs* (margin Rev. Ver.), see on 8: 28. **Lunatic,** *epileptic*, as in Rev. Ver. The Greek term, like the Latin word which we borrow in English, is derived from the word for moon, but was applied not to insanity, as in our use of the corresponding Latin term (lunatics), but to epilepsy, which the ancients supposed to become worse at certain stages of the moon. The sacred writer employs the familiar term, just as he speaks of sunrise, etc., without thereby making himself responsible for the idea which gave rise to it. This epilepsy might or might not be connected with demoniacal possession (see on 17: 15 ff.) **That had the palsy,** *paralytics.* The Greek word *paralusis*, signifying a loosening or relaxation, viz., of the muscles or nerves (comp. on 8: 6), was, as originally borrowed into English, contracted into ' palsy,' and denotes in Scripture all that we now mean by ' paralysis.' This full form was borrowed at a later period (comp. story and history, fancy and phantasy, etc.), and ' palsy ' is now usually confined to one kind of paralysis; that which produces an involuntary tremulous motion of some part of the body. It is to be regretted that Rev. Ver. has not here rendered by ' demoniacs' and ' paralytics.'

25. Great multitudes, rather, *crowds.* The Greek word (*ochlos*) signifies not simply a multitude (which is *plethos*, used frequently by Luke, and a few times by Mark and John, not by Matthew), but a confused crowd or throng. This meaning must be borne in mind, for such was no doubt usually the character of the crowds that followed Jesus, as so often mentioned in the Gospels; but the word should not be insisted on as necessarily having this distinctive sense in every case, for it can scarcely be so taken in Acts 1: 15. The crowds who thus **followed** Jesus were not all in any just sense his disciples. They came and went, attended him a longer or shorter time, to see his miracles and hear his teachings; sometimes many straggled away, and again they would throng around him to see some new wonder. So we must notice that *follow* means more or less in different cases. The term **people** was uselessly introduced here by Tyndale and followers.—**Galilee.** See on v. 12. The word **from** is in the original given only before Galilee, thus grouping all the other localities with it. **Decapolis** signifies a district containing ten cities (comp. Tripolis, Pentapolis), and here designates a region of somewhat indefinite extent, lying mainly on the southeast of the Lake of Galilee, but including Scythopolis (Beth-shean) on the western bank of the Jordan valley. After the Romans gained control of Palestine (beginning B. C. 63), these ten cities were allowed peculiar privileges. Ancient writers differ as to what cities formed the ten, Pliny including Damascus, which Josephus seems to exclude; perhaps the Romans made changes. One of them was Gadara, see on 8: 28. The population of these towns was very largely Gentile, and after the death of Herod the Great they were not governed by either of his sons, but belonged to the Roman province of Syria. (See Caspari.) **Jerusalem,** see on 21: 10; **Judea,** on 2: 1; **beyond Jordan** (Perea), on 19: 1.—Though Jesus had retired from Judea to Galilee, many came thence to attend him here. (Comp. on 15: 1.)

HOMILETICAL AND PRACTICAL.

V. 12. CHRYSOSTOM: " Wherefore doth he depart? Again instructing us not to meet temptations, but to give place and withdraw ourselves."—V. 13. HENRY: " It is just with God to take the gospel and the means of grace from those that slight them. Christ will not stay long where he is not welcome."—Capernaum. 1) Greatly favored as the home of Jesus. 2) Severely tested by his teachings and miracles. 3) Utterly ruined for rejecting him. (11 : 23.)—V. 15. The most destitute field will sometimes prove most fruitful.—V. 16. Darkness and light. 1) The midnight darkness of sin, ignorance, and unbelief. 2) The morning sunlight of a present gospel. 3) The noonday

brightness reached by following the path of the just. (Prov. 4: 18.) STARKE (in Lange): " Many live under the full blaze of the gospel as if they still sat in the shadow of death." —V. 17. The preaching of Jesus. 1) Its subjects. 2) Its spirit. 3) Its effects. The call to repentance has been made by all God's messengers; e. g., by the prophets ('turn ye'), by John the Baptist, by Jesus himself, by the apostles after his ascension. (Acts 2 : 38; 3 : 19; 20 : 21.) HENRY: " The doctrine of repentance is right gospel-doctrine. Not only the austere Baptist, who was looked upon as a melancholy, morose man, but the sweet and gracious Jesus, whose life dropped as a honey-comb, preached repentance; for it is an unspeakable privilege that room is left for repentance."

V. 19. Fishers of men. 1) Humble workers, but a lofty work. 2) It requires tact, perseverance, patient endurance of frequent failure. 3) He who calls us to it promises that we shall not labor in vain. [Beware of the wild fancies of certain Fathers, comparing Christians to fishes, etc., which some modern writers unwisely quote]. STARKE (in Lange): " Let none fancy that he can succeed by himself; even Christ chose assistants."—V. 21. Two pairs of brothers. Christ sanctifies and makes use of natural affections.—V. 21 f. 1) He saw, 2) He called, 3) They followed him. CALVIN: " This shows (1) the energy of Christ's voice, (2) docility and prompt obedience in the disciples."—V. 22. We also should be ready if necessary to leave business and kindred, in order to follow Jesus. (Comp. Luke 9: 57-62.) We cannot tread in his bodily footsteps; many did this with little or no profit; but by faith and loving imagination we may see him manifested (John 14 : 21-23) ; and in imitating and obeying we shall in the best sense be following him.

V. 23. ' In their synagogues.' It may be proper to preach truth even in places where others preach much error. Jesus a Teacher and a Healer; and the relations between these functions. Sin was the prime cause of disease, and special sin is often the immediate cause of particular diseases. The miracles of healing both relieved human distress, and attested the divine authority of the teaching. HENRY: " What we hear of Christ from others, should invite us to him." CHRYS.: " If we have any bodily ailment, we do and

CHAPTER V.

contrive everything to be rid of what pains us; but when our soul is indisposed, we delay, and draw back."—V. 25. It is well if crowds come to a preacher: he should then take great pains (5:1) to teach them the truth they need (5:7); but they may admire his teachings as novel and striking (7:28 f.), and yet few of them become Christians; and the fault may sometimes be wholly their own.

SERMON ON THE MOUNT.
Chap. 5-7.

GENERAL INTRODUCTION TO THE SERMON ON THE MOUNT.

The discourse in ch. 5-7 is well known by the traditional name of The Sermon on the Mount. Several general questions in regard to it require to be answered.

(1) Unity of the discourse. Some contend that we cannot, or need not, suppose Jesus to have spoken on a single occasion all that Matthew here gives, but that he has grouped together things said at different times, for the purpose of furnishing a comprehensive exhibition of our Saviour's teachings. This they argue partly from the fact that many things contained in the discourse as given by Matthew are recorded by Luke, and even by Matthew himself, as said on other occasions (see on 5: 13, 15, 18, 25, 29, 32; 6: 9, 22, 24, 25; 7: 2, 7, 17, 23), and partly from the manifest design on Matthew's part to compose not so much a chronological narrative as a historical argument, in which things are so arranged as to bring out the points he wishes to make prominent. But in grouping the miracles of ch. 8 and 9, he does not at all say that they occurred in that order, nor that the discourse of ch. 5-7 preceded them all; while he does distinctly say that this discourse was delivered on a single occasion (comp. 5: 1, and 8: 1), and if the facts were otherwise his account of the matter would be definitely erroneous, which cannot be admitted until it is proven. And as to the occurrence of similar sayings elsewhere, why may we not suppose that our Lord would *repeat* substantially the same sayings? It would have been very unnatural had he not done that which is freely practiced by all traveling teachers, and which,

apart from any question as to the speaker's resources, is really demanded by the similarity in the condition and wants of different audiences. And we have abundant evidence, from passages having no connection with the Sermon on the Mount, that he frequently made such repetitions, with greater or less variation of statement, and particularly in the case of brief, pithy sayings, such as would naturally be introduced in different connections, and of very important doctrines and exhortations, such as various audiences would alike need. *E. g.,* "He that hath ears to hear, let him hear," 11: 15; 13: 9; "Except ye become as little children," etc., 18; 3; 19: 14, and add the repeated inculcation of humility in other ways, 20: 26; John 13: 13 ff.; Luke 12: 24 ff. (Comp. also 23: 12; Luke 14: 11; 18: 14.) "If ye have faith as a grain of mustard seed," etc., 17: 20; 21: 21; Luke 17: 6. "Whosoever shall confess me," etc., 10: 32; Luke 12: 8; 9: 26. "The servant is not greater than his Lord," 10: 24; Luke 6: 40; John 13: 16; 15: 20; in the last of which passages Jesus refers to his having told them the same thing before, as he does also in John 13: 33. (Comp. John 7: 34; 8: 21.) "He that finds his life shall lose it, and he that loses his life for my sake shall find it," 10: 38, 39; 16: 24 f.; Luke 17: 33; John 12: 25. See also the image of taking up the cross and following him, in 10: 38; 16: 24; Luke 14: 27; Mark 10: 21. With such facts before us, it is manifest that the recurrence in other connections of particular ideas and expressions which appear in this discourse, is no proof that it was not all delivered on the occasion before us. Thus both the supposed reasons fail, and we have no ground for setting aside the view which an unprejudiced reader of Matthew would naturally adopt, that he has recorded what was actually spoken by Jesus as he sat on the Mount. It is not said that nothing else was spoken; and the supposition that Matthew's report is somewhat condensed (as often in the Gospels), will account for the apparent lack of connection in some places (see on 7: 1-12), and for the rapid succession of separate points, which some have thought (Bleek) that a miscellaneous out-door audience could hardly follow or retain. *Neander:* "The discourse is made up of many sententious passages, calculated separately to impress the memory of the hearers, and remain as fruitful germs in their hearts; but, on the other hand, bound together as parts of an organic whole."

(2) Is this the same discourse as that given by Luke, in 6: 20-49? They are held to be different discourses by Augustine, after him by nearly all writers till the Reformation (Bleek), and by a few writers since, as Erasmus, Doddridge, Macknight, Alexander, Lange, G. W. Clark, Coleridge, Plumptre; some of these thinking the two were delivered on the same day, and others with a longer interval. They are taken as different reports of the same discourse by Origen and Chrys., by Calvin, and by almost all recent expositors. In favor of this view are the obvious facts that the two begin and end exactly alike, and nearly everything which Luke gives is also given by Matthew; and that both are immediately followed by the record of the same events, viz., the entrance into Capernaum and the healing of the centurion's servant. The objections (well stated in Clark's Harm.) rest on supposed differences of *place, time, circumstances,* and *contents*. (a) But Luke (6:17) does not say 'stood in the plain,' but 'stood on a level place,' which might very naturally be a bit of level ground, or a narrow plain in the mountain region, exactly what is found at the traditional place (see on v. 1).[1] (b) As to the time and circumstances, Luke's discourse follows the choice of the Twelve, and Matthew's seems to come earlier, soon after the beginning of the ministry in Galilee. But Matthew's arrangement in ch. 8–13, is obviously topical rather than chronological, and so it is natural that without saying at what precise period of the ministry it was spoken, he should give at the outset this great discourse, which would set before his Jewish readers the relation of Jesus' teaching to the law of Moses, and the true nature of the Messianic reign. (See the connection traced on 4: 12.) And if the events preceding the discourse seem different in Matthew, it must be observed that he does not at all state just when the discourse was delivered. (c) As to contents, Luke omits the large portions (Matt. 5: 17-37, and 6: 1-18) which were specially important and interesting to Jews, but less so to the Gentile readers whom Luke had chiefly in view; and also omits some portions, probably because he gives substantially the same thing elsewhere, as said by our Lord on other occasions (*e. g.*, Matt. 6: 9–13; Luke 11: 2–4; Matt. 6: 25–34; Luke 12: 22–31.) We thus account for every omission of any great importance. There are various other instances also (as in ch. 10, 11, 18, 25) in which Matthew has recorded an extensive discourse of which Mark or Luke gives only a part. Some conclude from these examples that Matthew was quite in the habit of collecting into one discourse many things said at different times; but the facts do not in any of the cases require this view, and therefore do not justify it, since we must take for granted, unless the contrary has been proven, the inspired apostles' accuracy. At the same time we may suppose that Matthew has here given, at least in some places, only a summary report of what was said, for he has several times omitted matters which Luke records (*e. g.*, comp. 5: 12 with Luke 6: 23–6; 5: 47 with Luke 6: 33–35; 7: 12 with Luke 6: 31–40.) In regard to the general fact that the Evangelists sometimes differ as to details in reporting the same saying, see on 3: 17.

(3) Design of the discourse. Our Lord had been proclaiming (4:17), as John had done before him, that the *reign of heaven* was near, and that therefore the people ought to repent. In this discourse he sets forth the characteristics of those who are to be subjects of this reign and share the privileges connected with it, and urges upon them various duties. In particular, he clearly exhibits the relation of his teachings to the moral law, in order to correct any notion that he proposed to set the law aside, or to relax its rigor, when, on the contrary he came to inculcate not merely an

---

[1] The Greek word *pedinos* is commonly used with reference to a plain as opposed to a mountain (a natural opposition), but sometimes for a plain or flat valley among mountains, or a flat place on a mountain. Thus in Jer. 21: 13 Jerusalem is called 'rock of the plain,' and in Isa. 13: 2 we have in Sept. 'lift up a signal upon a level (flat) mountain ' (*ep' orous pedinou*), Heb., ' upon a bare hill,' not covered with trees. This latter passage is obscure (see Gesen., Schleus., and commentaries on Isaiah), but either this or the use in Jeremiah seems to furnish a parallel for the use in Luke.

external but a deeply spiritual morality. It is a strange fancy of some that Jesus was a revolutionary reformer, overturning existing ideas and institutions to substitute his own, when he himself expressly declares the contrary (see on 5: 17). *Neander:* "The connected system of truths unfolded in this discourse was intended to exhibit to the people the kingdom of God as the aim of the Old Dispensation; as the consummation for which that dispensation prepared the way. The Sermon on the Mount, therefore, forms the point of transition from the Law to the Gospel; Christianity is exhibited in it as Judaism spiritualized and transfigured." Regarded as addressed especially to the Twelve, it becomes the great opening lecture in a course of instruction by which they were to be fitted for their work as his witnesses and representatives; just as the farewell discourse of John 14-17 may be called (Bernard) the closing lecture. It is quite an error if men expect to find in the discourse an epitome either of Christian doctrine or of Christian ethics. Many of the distinguishing and fundamental doctrines of Christianity were never distinctly and fully taught by the Saviour himself, because men could not understand them till after the great facts on which they rest, his death, resurrection, and ascension, had taken place. And while he here teaches us many weighty and precious lessons for the proper conduct of life, they are by no means presented as a complete system of morals, but seem to be introduced chiefly as contributing to, or incidentally connected with, the discussion of his great theme, the nature and requirements of the Messianic reign. It is therefore very unwise and presumptuous to single out this one discourse and propose to live by it, in disregard of the further teachings of Christ and his apostles. True, he here gives a single precept (7: 12), which he says 'is the law and the prophets.' But that no more warrants the neglect of everything beyond this discourse, than the closing precept 'Fear God and keep his commandments, for this is the all of man,' would warrant us in neglecting the Old Testament for the one

Book of Ecclesiastes. He who spoke the Sermon on the Mount has also said, 'Except a man be born again, he cannot see the kingdom of God,' and 'even so must the Son of man be lifted up, that whosoever believeth in him should not perish, but have eternal life,' and he in departing promised his apostles the Holy Spirit to 'lead them into all the truth,' and set them before the world as authoritative teachers of Christian doctrine and duty. It is not honoring the Sermon on the Mount, or its Author, to represent this as all that men need, seeing he has given us much more.

The unrivaled beauties of our Lord's thought and style, the lofty simplicity, the charming freshness and perfect naturalness, the familiar and vivid illustration, the pointed and sometimes paradoxical and startling statement, which even when imperfectly understood could never be forgotten, the sublime elevation of sentiment, and the inimitable *tone* which marks all his teachings, shine conspicuous in this address, which is sweet to the heart of a child, and before which the noblest intellects in every age have bowed in devout admiration. Well might Daniel Webster say, in the inscription he left for his tomb, "My heart has always assured and re-assured me, that the gospel of Jesus Christ must be a divine reality. The Sermon on the Mount cannot be a merely human production."[1]

(4) Analysis. The discourse, as given by Matthew, admits of being analyzed in various ways, the connection being less obvious in some places, and the arrangement of the whole being very simple and inartificial. The following analysis may be useful, though we must take care not to draw too broadly the lines of division between the different sections.

I. Characteristics and privileges of the subjects of the Messianic reign, 5: 3-12.

II. Their influence and responsibility, 5: 13-16.

III. Relation of Christ's mission to the Moral Law, 5: 17-48.

1. This relation stated in general, 17-19.

2. Superiority of the morality he enjoined to that taught and practiced by the Scribes

---

[1] Edersh. remarks that our Lord's use of phrases and modes of teaching current at the time, renders more striking the contrast between this discourse and the Jewish contemporary teaching as to the whole spirit and tone. The supposed Rabbinic parallels are in general only superficially similar, and often exactly opposite in spirit. See examples in Edersh., Book iii., ch. 18.

AND seeing the multitudes, he went up into a mountain: and when he was set, his disciples came unto him:

1 And seeing the multitudes, he went up into the mountain: and when he had sat down, his disciples

---

and Pharisees, 20-48. Illustrated by reference to murder, etc. (21-26), adultery and divorce (27-32), oaths (33-37), requital of injuries (38-42), love of enemies (43-48).

IV. Good works to be performed out of regard to God's approval rather than man's, 6: 1-18, *e. g.*, alms-giving (2-4), prayer (5-15), fasting (16-18.)

V. Single-hearted devotion to God, as opposed to worldly aims and anxieties, 6: 19-34.

VI. Censoriousness must be avoided, 7: 1-6.

VII. Encouragement to pray to God for strength to fulfill this and all the preceding requirements, 7: 7-11.

VIII. General principle or rule, which sums up all the (moral) teachings of the discourse, and of the Old Testament, 7: 12.

IX. Concluding exhortations to practice as well as hear and profess, 7: 13-27.

Ch. 5: 1-12. THE BEATITUDES.

1. The multitudes—or, *crowds*—viz., the 'great crowds' spoken of in the preceding sentence (see on 4: 25.) The connection goes right on without any break, the paragraph of 4: 23-25 forming a sort of introduction to the discourse. (For the general connection, see on 4: 12.) On some occasion, in the course of the labors just described, occurred that which Matthew proceeds to narrate. **He went up.** Was it to avoid the crowds, as some think, or was it not rather that the presence of such crowds made it proper to address them in an extended discourse, setting forth the nature of that Messianic kingdom, or reign, which he had been declaring to be at hand? **Into a—*the*[1]—mountain.** This more probably means the mountain-region, just as persons among us who live near such a region familiarly speak of it as "the mountain"—"He isn't at home, he's gone up in the mountain." The word 'mountain' is used for a mountain-region in Gen. 19: 17, 19, 30, and elsewhere in O. T. The most common scene of all this part of our Lord's ministry was the lake-shore, and with this would easily contrast in the apostle's mind the adjacent mountain-region. So in 14: 23, 'the mountain' is the mountain-region east of the lake, near where he had just fed the five thousand, and in 15: 29, the same region further south. That such is the meaning here becomes highly probable (if we hold Luke's discourse to be the same) from Mark 3: 13, where the same expression 'he goes up into the mountain' occurs on the same occasion, —viz., the choice of the twelve (Mark 3: 13-19), which Luke (6: 17) shows to have been immediately followed by the discourse—and the preceding connection (Mark 3: 7-9) evidently makes it there mean that he goes up from the lake-shore into the mountain-region. This also best fits in Luke 6: 12. The phrase 'the mountain,' *might* mean the particular mountain near them at the time (Meyer), or the well-known mountain (De Wette), as one or the other is probably meant in Luke 9: 28, the Mount of the Transfiguration; though of this we know nothing. But the preponderance of usage and probability is for the other sense, the mountain-region. There is then nothing in the history to indicate what particular part of the adjacent mountain-region is meant. The connection in Mark, and the statement of Matt. (8: 5) and Luke (7: 1) that he afterwards went to Capernaum, show that it was on the west side of the lake; but the latter statement does not, as so often urged, show that it was *near* Capernaum. There is no important objection to the tradition placing it at the double-top mountain now called "Horns of Hattin," which (Stanley) strikingly corresponds to the circumstances, since Jesus might well have spent the night on one of the two summits, and the next morning descended to the flat space between the two, and there delivered the discourse. But the tradition is unknown to the Greek and Eastern writers, and among Latins first found in Brocardus, about A. D. 1283. (Robinson.) We can only say, therefore, that this may quite possibly have been the spot. **When he was set,** or, *had sat down,* sitting being among the Jews

---

[1] The article is here disregarded by all the early English translators, who learned Greek through the medium of the Latin, and so had little feeling for the article, which they often omit or insert in a curiously arbitrary fashion.

2 And he opened his mouth, and taught them, saying,
3 Blessed *are* the poor in spirit: for theirs is the kingdom of heaven.

2 came unto him: and he opened his mouth and taught them, saying,
3 Blessed are the poor in spirit: for theirs is the kingdom of heaven.

the customary posture for one engaged in teaching. Luke's expression (6:17) 'stood,' does not conflict with this, for that denotes simply the end of the descent, and not the posture in teaching. **His disciples.** The Greek word rendered 'disciple,' like the Latin *discipulus*, which we have borrowed, signifies a 'learner,' as opposed to a 'teacher,' and is used in that general sense in 10: 24, literally, 'A learner is not above his teacher, nor a slave above his master.' The Greeks frequently applied it to the pupils of a philosopher, as denoting those who received his instructions and were supposed to adopt his opinions. In a like sense we read of the 'disciples of the Pharisees' (22:16), and the 'disciples of John' (9:14; 11:2; 14:12; Mark 2: 18, etc.); and similarly the 'disciples' of Jesus, in the present passage, and in general, are those who habitually heard his teachings, and were supposed to receive them as true. But the term, as there used, would have a more lax and a more strict application, sometimes denoting the whole crowd of those who followed him for a while, and apparently believed his teachings (*e. g.*, John 6: 66), but commonly used of those who really did believe, and submit themselves to his authority as a teacher. In some passages (as 14: 15 ff.) the connection shows that it means 'the disciples' by excellence, viz., the Twelve. After our Lord's ascension the application of the term was very naturally widened to embrace all who received as true the teachings of the Christian religion, Christ being in reality still their teacher, though he taught through others. We cannot here understand the term as denoting all who were present and listened to his teachings, for it is nowhere used in so loose a way; it must mean his disciples, as distinguished from others who were not such. This would include the four mentioned in 4: 18 ff., but would not be confined to them. Matthew has not previously had the word, but he employs it in that general sense with which all had become familiar at the time when he wrote. From Luke 6: 12-20 we learn that, before delivering the discourse, Jesus had selected the Twelve who were to be his special attendants; but Luke also men-

tions (6: 17, literally), a 'crowd of his disciples' as present when it was spoken. Matthew does not refer to the Twelve as a body till he comes to speak of their being sent forth two and two (10: 1 ff.), just as he gives an account of John's imprisonment only in connection with the story of his death (comp. on 4: 12; 14: 3). **Came unto him,** drew near after he had thus assumed the posture of a teacher. Or, came near while the people at large stood farther off.

2. This expanded statement is in accordance with that circumstantiality in description which is characteristic of the Hebrew language and adds beauty to the Scripture narratives. It serves, in a case like this, to fix attention upon the important discourse which follows. (Comp. Job 3: 1; Acts 8: 35; 10: 34.) **Taught** is imperfect tense, and describes the teaching as in progress—you see it going on. The English 'was teaching' or 'went to teaching,' would here be too strong. **Them** refers especially to his disciples, who are especially distinguished in the preceding verse from the crowds (comp. Luke 6: 20), and are especially addressed in such passages of the discourse as 5: 11, 13–16, etc.; but that the crowds also heard would be naturally suggested by the connection, and is affirmed in 7: 28 f.

3. In v. 3–12 our Lord sets forth the *characteristics and privileges* of the subjects of the kingdom of heaven. These sentences are commonly called the "beatitudes," from *beatus*, 'blessed' or 'happy,' the word here employed in the Latin versions, and by some are called *macarisms*, from the Greek word. Some writers compare with these the benedictions of Deut. 28; but the cases are not similar. Others mark out an elaborate parallel to the giving of the Ten Commandments; but this is highly artificial, and tends to divert attention from our Lord's real design. It would be more appropriate to compare such passages as Psa. 1: 1; 31: 1 f.; 144: 15; Prov. 3: 13; Dan. 12: 12, where a character is described as well as happiness declared. The Jews expected great felicity under the reign of Messiah; witness the saying of one of them (Luke 14: 15, lit.), 'Happy he who shall eat bread in the kingdom of God.' Our Lord, by telling who are the happy in the Messianic kingdom, gives at once a very distinct glimpse into the nature and requirements of that kingdom. It is immediately seen to be quite the reverse of the carnal expectations cherished among the Jews. Not the rich, the rejoicing and proud, not conquering warriors nor popular favorites, are the happy under the Messianic reign, but *these*—the poor, the mourning and meek, the peacemakers, the persecuted. Most of these sayings are therefore striking paradoxes, and the whole forms a singularly felicitous *introduction* to his discourse, touching a chord that vibrates in all human hearts —happy, happy—instantly awakening the liveliest attention, and also conveying important instruction as to the great theme. *Luther :* "Now that's a fine, sweet, friendly beginning of his teaching and preaching. For he goes at it, not like Moses or a teacher of the law, with commands and threats, but in the very friendliest way, with nothing but attractions and allurements and lovely promises." It was also a beautifully *natural* introduction (Weiss), because he came to preach the 'good news' of the kingdom (4: 23), the fulfillment of all the Messianic hopes and promises.

Blessed. *Happy* more nearly expresses the sense of the Greek word than ' blessed.' It is rendered 'happy' in the common version of John 13: 17; Acts 26: 2; Rom. 14: 22; 1 Cor. 7: 40; 1 Pet. 3: 14; 4: 14, and the corresponding verb in James 5: 11; and this might be used almost everywhere, leaving 'blessed' to translate another term found in 21: 9; 23: 39; 25: 34, etc., and a kindred word in Mark 14: 61; Rom. 9: 5, etc. Our 'happy' could not, it is true, be applied to God, as in 1 Tim. 1: 11; 6: 15 (Bib. Un. Ver. 'blissful'), where 'blessed,' though familiar to us, is really also inadequate. But more is gained than is lost by keeping the terms distinct, for the difference is often quite important. The shock which many persons feel at the introduction of 'happy' here, is partly a reproduction of the surprise felt by our Lord's first hearers — *happy* the *poor, happy* the *mourners*, etc.—the paradox is really part of the meaning.[1] The sense is quite similar (and the same Greek word is used) in 16: 17; Rom. 4: 6-8; 1 Cor. 7: 40; James 1: 12; 1 Pet. 3: 14; Rev. 14: 13. The original has in this case no verb—not 'happy are,' but simply 'happy the poor,' etc. So in the Greek of Psa. 1: 1, etc. **The poor.** The Jews looked upon wealth, being one of the chief elements of worldly prosperity, as a sure proof that its possessor was the object of God's favor, an error which our Lord subsequently sought to correct in the parable of the rich man and Lazarus. (Luke 16: 19.) In like manner they no doubt supposed that in Messiah's kingdom the rich, the " better class," would enjoy the highest privileges. In striking opposition to these expectations, he says, 'Happy the poor, for theirs is the kingdom of heaven.' This is all that Luke (6: 20, lit.) gives; and certainly the poor were more likely to share the privileges of the Messianic reign than the rich, because more likely to be humble and looking for Messiah's coming.[2] (Comp. 11: 5; 19: 23;

[1] The distinction between *macarios* and *eulogetos* (and kindred terms) is maintained throughout the Sept. as it is in the Hebrew words. The Pesh. Syriac version of N. T. translates 'happy' here and in 11: 6; 13: 16; 16: 17; 24: 46, and uses 'blessed' for *eulogemenos* in 21: 9, etc. The Gothic likewise maintains the distinction. But the Latin versions used *beatus* for both the Greek words, probably for two reasons; (a) *beatus* really means happy as well as blessed, (b) the other Latin word *felix* had idolatrous associations, which would have made it incongruous in Scripture, somewhat as 'lucky' would be now. But this confounding of the two Greek words in the Latin versions has caused much confusion in modern European versions, and great arbitrariness of rendering in the early English versions. Tyndale used 'happy' in John 13: 17, etc., followed by Cranmer, Geneva, and King James; but Tyndale also used it in Matt. 11: 6; 16: 17; 24: 46; Gal. 4: 15; James 1: 12, 25, followed by Cranmer or Geneva, or both, but not by King James. Neither rendering is in our passage entirely satisfactory, but ' happy' best conveys the idea.

[2] Some (Gill, others) take the word *ptochos* in its common classical sense of beggar, and understand those who *come to God as beggars*. Tertullian once expresses that view: "Happy the beggars—for so requires the meaning of the Greek word." But it is very unlikely that such is here the meaning. *Ptochos* is in the N. T. the common word for poor, being found thirty-five times, while the other word *penes* is found only in 2 Cor. 9: 9 (from Sept.) and *penichros* in Luke 21: 2. In the Sept. *penes* is used nearly as often as *ptochos*, and for the most part to translate the same Hebrew words. These facts forbid insisting on the distinctive classical sense of beggar in every N. T. passage; and in the present case it seems quite inappropriate to introduce the notion that they *beg*.

4 Blessed *are* they that mourn : for they shall be comforted.

4 ¹ Blessed are they that mourn: for they shall be comforted.

---

¹ Some ancient authorities transpose ver. 4 and 5.

Luke 4: 18; Isa. 61: 1; 66: 2; James 2: 5; and below on v. 4, 5.) But while men need not, they might misunderstand or misrepresent this general term (as well as ' hunger,' ' weep,' in Luke 6: 21.) Thus the Emperor Julian mockingly said he wished to confiscate the property of the Christians, in order that as poor men they might enter the kingdom of heaven. Now Matthew's account shows that our Lord took pains to define more precisely what he meant, by saying **the poor in spirit.** Poverty, want, sorrow, do not of themselves secure spiritual blessings; these are promised to such as have the corresponding state of thought and feeling. The grammatical construction ' poor in the spirit' is the same as in ' pure in the heart.' (v. 8.) The meaning may be (Bleek) (a) ' poor in the (sphere of the) spirit,' in spiritual matters, or (b) ' poor in their spirit,' consciously poor. Probably the former is here *meant* by the phrase, while the latter thought is *suggested* by the connection. The poor, not outwardly only, but in the inner man ; not in the temporal but the spiritual sphere; and it is involved, in the nature of the case, that they are conscious of their spiritual destitution (comp. Isa. 66: 2, and contrast Rev. 3: 17). Those who in the sphere of the spirit, in the spiritual life, are destitute, and feel their need. A good example is the publican of the parable. It is quite possible for a man rich in the temporal sphere to be at the same time poor in spirit.¹ Edersh. quotes from the Mishna, " Ever be more and more lowly in spirit, since the expectancy of man is to become the food of worms," and calls it the

exact counterpart of this saying, " marking not the optimism, but the pessimism of life." **For.** It would be a little more exact to render ' because' in all the beatitudes (see on v. 12). **Theirs** has in the original an emphatic position ; it is *theirs*, they are precisely the persons who possess and enjoy the riches, dignities, privileges of Messiah's reign (see on 3: 2). Comp. James 2: 5. These privileges already belong to them, and shall henceforth be enjoyed by them—notice the future tense in the following sentences. How different is all this from worldly kingdoms. In Luke 6: 24, is recorded the opposite of this first beatitude, " Woe to you who are rich, for you have received your consolation," have all the consolation you will get.

4. The regular gradation which some endeavor to point out in the several beatitudes is artificial, if not imaginary. They are simply grouped in a natural way, and the transition from the poor to the mourners is natural enough.² Observe (Tholuck) that the three first classes, poor, mourning, meek, are all in the prediction of Isa. 61: 1–3, to which our Lord repeatedly referred as fulfilled in his ministry (11: 5; Luke 4: 17–21).

Happy they that grieve, is a very striking paradox, suited to awaken attention and lead to reflection. **They that mourn,** over any of the distresses of life, temporal or spiritual; but with the implication that if over temporal distresses, they mourn in a religious spirit. Under the reign of Messiah they shall be **comforted**—the kind of comfort corresponding of course to the kind of distress, and suited to their highest good. The second part

---

¹ Barnabas 19 : 2 has the same grammatical construction : " Thou shalt be simple in heart and rich in spirit." Many Fathers understood our Lord to mean poor by free will, contentedly or voluntarily poor, and some applied it, as most Romanists now do, to monastic vows of poverty, and the like. But ' spirit' will not yield this (Maldon. in vain quotes 26 : 41), and the able Romanist commentator Arnoldi calls it a manifestly artificial interpretation. ' Poor in intellect,' weak-minded, was another of Julian's jests, and is gravely proposed by Fritzsche and Grimm, but seems to need no refutation. Achelis makes it poor in the matter

of the Holy Spirit, poor, and thus prepared to receive the Holy Spirit, whom Messiah was to give (3 : 11), but this is extremely forced. These interpretations are instructive as showing that the expression is really difficult.

² Tisch. and others transpose v. 4 and 5, putting the meek first, according to D, Latin, Old Syriac, several Fathers. This group of " Western" authorities is now well known to contain many arbitrary alterations of the text. The design of the alteration here probably was to have the meek come next to the poor in spirit, as an appropriate sequence.

5 Blessed *are* the meek: for they shall inherit the earth.

5 Blessed are the meek: for they shall inherit the earth.

---

of Isaiah begins (40:1), with 'comfort ye my people,' and is pervaded throughout by that idea, it being distinctly declared (61:2) that Messiah is to comfort all that mourn. The later Jews caught this conception, and in the Talmud the Messiah is sometimes called Menahem, 'comforter.' At the time of his birth some truly devout ones were 'waiting for the consolation of Israel.' (Luke 2:25.) **They** is emphatic, and so in v. 5-8. In Luke 6:25 is recorded the opposite of this beatitude.

5. The sayings of this verse, and of v. 7-10, are wanting in Luke's briefer report. The expression here used is derived from Psa. 37:11. The Heb. word for **meek** and that for 'poor' are from the same root, and certainly meekness is akin to poverty of spirit. Our Lord declares that not the ambitious and arrogant, the irascible and violent, such as usually become prominent in the outbreak of revolutions, are the happy under Messiah's reign, but the meek. The term 'meek' is hard to define, in Heb., Greek, or Eng., but it includes freedom from pretension (1 Pet. 3:4,15), gentleness (11:29; James 3:13), and patient endurance of injury—where it is proper to endure. The Messianic king himself is meek (21:5), and the meek shall be his happy subjects. **Shall inherit the earth,** or, *land*.[1] It was promised to Abraham that he should 'inherit' the 'land' of Canaan. (Gen. 13:15; 15:7, etc.) This was partly realized by his descendants under Joshua. (Judges 2:6, in the Heb.) Their possession of it was always imperfect and sometimes interrupted, but still they cherished the promise made to Abraham, and hoped for its complete fulfillment. The Psalmist distinguishes two classes in Israel, the wicked and the meek; those who amid all trials meekly trust and serve God, and declares (Psa. 37:9, 11, 22, 29) that *these* shall 'inherit the land.' Isaiah promises (57:13; 60:21) that after the captivity those who trust in God shall 'inherit the land.' The apocryphal story of Tobit represents devout Jews during the captivity as cherishing the hope that the seed of the patriarchs shall 'inherit the land.' (Tob. 4:12.) And just as the 'kingdom of heaven'

(v.3) takes in our Lord's discourses a higher and more spiritual meaning, so with this phrase. The meek shall be full citizens in the Messianic kingdom (like those holding real estate), enjoying all rights and privileges. This would of course mean especially religious privileges (comp. 'inherit the kingdom,' in its full and perfected state, 25:34; 1 Cor. 6:10; 15:50; Gal. 5:21; Eph. 5:5, etc.) The explanation that Christians shall have as much of the earth as is really desirable for them is superficial, and the other, that Christianity is finally to take possession of the whole earth, is artificial. The O. T. and the N. T. usage seems to leave no doubt as to the meaning. The poor in spirit, the mourners, the meek, obviously represent kindred traits of character, and should not be conceived of as three entirely distinct classes of persons. So as to the other beatitudes.

6. Hunger and thirst. A natural and strong expression for desire, common in all languages. Luke (6:21) gives only 'hunger,' the other term merely expanding the image (comp. Psa. 63:1); and does not say for what. (Comp. above on v. 3.) **Righteousness** here must not by any means be understood of imputed righteousness, but (as even Luther admits) of personal righteousness; the being and doing what is right, as in 3:15; 5:20; Luke 1:75, etc. The attempt (Schaff and others) to make it include both ideas, is futile. It is very doubtful whether the Pauline idea of imputed righteousness occurs anywhere in the Gospels, not even in John 16:10. **Filled.** The original word is of frequent occurrence, signifying to feed, to satisfy with food, originally used of feeding animals, in later Greek of feeding men. (Comp. in 14:20; Luke 16:21; James 2:16; Phil. 4:12; Rev. 19:21.) They who hunger and thirst for righteousness shall, under Messiah's reign, be fed full, completely satisfied. It of course does not mean satisfied once for all, so as to have no desire any more. That is here true which Wisdom says in Sirach (Ecclus.) 24:21, 'They that eat me shall still hunger, and they that drink me shall still thirst.' The Scriptures teach

---

[1] 'Earth' all the early Eng. versions except Rheims, and most of the recent versions. Rheims, McClellan 'land,' Darby hesitates.

6 Blessed *are* they which do hunger and thirst after righteousness: for they shall be filled.
7 Blessed *are* the merciful: for they shall obtain mercy.
8 Blessed *are* the pure in heart: for they shall see God.
9 Blessed *are* the peacemakers: for they shall be called the children of God.

6 Blessed are they that hunger and thirst after righteousness: for they shall be filled.
7 Blessed are the merciful: for they shall obtain mercy.
8 Blessed are the pure in heart: for they shall see God.
9 Blessed are the peacemakers: for they shall be called sons of God.

that this satisfaction will be progressive in the present life, and become perfect as we enter upon the perfect world.—Observe (Tholuck) that after righteousness there follow three elements of righteousness, viz., pity, purity, peace.

7. Merciful. The original word includes also the idea of compassion, as in Heb. 2: 17; Prov. 14: 21, and implies a desire to remove the evils which excite compassion. It thus denotes not only mercy to the guilty, but pity for the suffering, and help to the needy. See Luke 3: 11; Matt. 25: 37-40; James 2: 13. To be merciful is not the *ground* of receiving mercy from God, but an occasion and condition thereof. (18: 33 f.) Comp. the relation between forgiving and being forgiven, as explained on 6: 12. The Jerusalem Talmud gives as a saying of Gamaliel, " Whensoever thou hast mercy, God will have mercy upon thee; if thou hast not mercy, neither will God have mercy upon thee."

8. Pure in heart, as contrasted with mere external, bodily purification, about which the Jews, and especially the Pharisees, were very scrupulous. (23: 25, 28.) The phrase should not be limited to the absence of unchaste feelings, but includes freedom from all the defiling influences of sin upon the inner man. *Origen:* " Every sin stains the soul." The 'heart' in Scripture use is the seat of thought and will as well as of feeling. (Comp. on 6: 21.) We must shun defiling thoughts, purposes, and feelings. Calvin here understands especially freedom from trickery and cunning. So James (4:8) says, 'Purify your hearts, ye double-minded.' A like breadth of meaning is implied in the connection of Psa. 24: 4. Comp. for various applications of the phrase, Psa. 51: 10; 73: 1; 1 Tim. 1: 5; 2 Tim. 2: 22. The meaning is thus seen to be very comprehensive, as when we speak of a pure character, pure motives, etc. There is

nothing here said as to the way in which this purity is to be obtained; that was afterwards fully revealed through the apostles. (Acts 15: 9; 1 John 1: 7, 9; Eph. 5: 26; 2 Cor. 7: 1.) **Shall see God.** The expression is derived from the usages of Oriental courts, where kings live in great seclusion, and it is a rare and distinguished privilege to be admitted into the very presence of the monarch, and see him face to face. See 1 Kings 10: 8; Esther 1: 14; Heb. 12: 14; Rev. 22: 4, and an equivalent expression in Matt. 18: 10. With the whole verse here compare Psa. 24: 3 f.: 'Who shall ascend into the hill of the Lord? or who shall stand in his holy place? He that hath clean hands and a pure heart.'—It is a kindred, but quite distinct thought that we find in 1 John 3: 2, that of the immediate perception and thorough knowledge of God in the future life, as tending to make us like him.

9. Here the contrast to worldly kingdoms, which runs through the whole passage, is particularly great. In them the highest honor and esteem are given to warriors, but under the Messianic reign to **peacemakers,** those who bring about peace between enemies. It may be taken for granted that they will be peaceable in their own disposition and conduct, will strive to maintain peace as well as to restore it when disturbed; but that is not included in the meaning of the word. *Morison:* " This delightful beatitude must have sounded like a clap of thunder over the hearts of some of those who were reveling in the imagination that the time had arrived when war to the bitter end was to be proclaimed against the surrounding principalities of the Gentiles." It is difficult to determine whether **they** is here emphatic, as it is in v. 4-8.[1] The difference would here be slight. **Called the children,** or *sons*—**of God,** as being like him (v. 45), objects of his special affection, etc. They shall not only *be* sons of God, but

[1] The external evidence for omitting *autoi* (and thus leaving 'they' without emphasis) is strong, but not conclusive. It is more probable that the word was inserted by copyists to make this like the other beatitudes than that it was omitted.

10 Blessed *are* they which are persecuted for righteousness' sake: for theirs is the kingdom of heaven.
11 Blessed are ye when *men* shall revile you, and persecute *you*, and shall say all manner of evil against you [1] falsely, for my sake.
12 Rejoice, and be exceeding glad : for great *is* your reward in heaven : for so persecuted they the prophets which were before you.

10   Blessed are they that have been persecuted for righteousness' sake: for theirs is the kingdom of
11 heaven. Blessed are ye when *men* shall reproach you, and persecute you, and say all manner of evil
12 against you falsely for my sake. Rejoice, and be exceeding glad : for great is your reward in heaven : for so persecuted they the prophets that were before you.

---

1 Gr. *lying.*

---

shall be *called* such, recognized as such in his kingdom—not merely subjects of the kingdom, but sons of the king. We need not wonder at this exalted promise to peacemakers, for theirs is a very difficult and very noble achievement. They must often be content to bear bitter complaint from both sides, must exercise great self-control, unwearied patience, and loving tact, and must be manifestly impartial and unselfish. There is no more Godlike work to be done in this world than peacemaking.

10. They which are—or, *that have been*—**persecuted,** the form of expression according with the fact that the chief rewards of such sufferers do not so much attend on the persecution as follow it. The expression obviously points forward to the persecution of his followers, but it is well to remember that at the probable time of his delivering this discourse, Jesus himself was already beginning to be bitterly hated and reviled, and his life sought. (Luke 6 : 7, 11; Mark 3 : 6.) Persecution usually involved taking away one's possessions, leaving him in poverty and want ; and so **theirs is the kingdom of heaven** is here a manifestly appropriate form of blessing, as in v. 3. Comp. Heb. 10: 34. *Chrys. :* "Although he gives different names to the rewards, yet nothing else but the kingdom does he shadow out by all these sayings." *Alexander :* "Thus, by a beautiful reiteration of his own expressions, he comes back to the point from which he started, in declaring for whose sake his kingdom was to be erected, or of whom it was to be composed. Not the rich, the gay, the fierce, the full, the cunning, the warlike, or the favorites of earthly rulers, were, as such, to be distinguished in his kingdom ; but the poor, the sorrowful, the meek, the hungry, the sincere, the peaceful, and the persecuted, who endured all this for his sake, and who

longed for spiritual no less than for secular relief." —An addition to the text, said by Clement of Alexandria to be made by some, suggests a pleasing thought: "Happy they that have been persecuted for my sake, for they shall have a place where they will not be persecuted." V. 10 f. seem to be referred to in 1 Pet. 3 : 14; 4 : 14. Various sentiments of the Sermon on the Mount are apparently alluded to by James, Paul, and Peter.

11. Here Luke (6 : 22) again comes in, having omitted what we have above in v. 5 and 7-10. V. 11 f. contain an elaboration and express application to Christ's disciples of the general declaration of v. 10. Here for the first time we have the second person. **Blessed,** or, *happy,* **are ye.** But 'ye' is not expressed by a separate Greek word, and so is not emphatic. In Luke (6 : 20 ff.) all the beatitudes given are in the second person. **When** would be more literally *whenever, i. e.,* in all cases. **They shall revile you,** (no emphasis on 'they'), is an impersonal expression, like the Eng. 'they say,' or, 'they tell me.' **And shall say all manner of evil against you,**[1] same expression in Acts 28 : 21. Luke (6 : 26) strengthens the promise by pronouncing a *woe* upon them when universally *well* spoken of. **Falsely** is omitted from the text by some critics,[2] but on insufficient authority ; and the idea it conveys would at any rate have to be supplied, from the very nature of the case. (Comp. 1 Pet. 4: 15 f.) **For my sake.** Reproaches and cruel treatment endured on some other account, however unmerited, are not here in question.

12. Closely connected with the preceding. **Rejoice, and be exceeding glad.** The first is the common word for 'rejoice' ; the second a rarer word, denoting great delight and exultation, which is used several times by Luke, John, and Peter. Both words are com-

---

[1] Many authorities add *rema,* 'every evil word' but this is probably not genuine. It makes no difference in the meaning.

[2] By D. and Old Latin (many copies), which make so many arbitrary alterations ; here probably following Luke (6 : 22), as they do twice in v. 12.

bined, as here, in 1 Pet. 4: 13; Rev. 19: 7, and together constitute a very strong expression. Luke has 'rejoice and leap (for joy).' There is a beautiful instance of the apostles rejoicing under persecution, in Acts 5: 41. **For great is your reward.** The 'for' would be more exactly rendered 'because,' as in all the other beatitudes. In the next clause is the word properly rendered 'for.' The form of expression, 'your reward,' implies a definite reward (the Greek having an article), designed for them, and kept for them **in heaven,** literally, *the heavens.* (Comp. 25: 34; Col. 1: 15; 1 Pet. 1: 4; Heb. 11: 26.) As to the plural, 'the heavens,' see on 3: 2. **For so they persecuted they,** impersonal, as in v. 11. *Alford:* "For instance, Jeremiah was scourged, Jer. 20: 2; Zechariah, son of Jehoiada, was stoned, 2 Chron. 24: 21; Isaiah, according to Jewish tradition, was sawn asunder by Manasseh." Similar reference to persecutions is made in Neh. 9: 26; Matt. 21: 35; 23: 32 ff.; Acts 7; 52: 1 Thess. 2: 15. The fact that the prophets were persecuted in like manner, furnishes a ground for assurance that the persons addressed will be rewarded. They are following the footsteps of the prophets, and shall, like them, have a great reward. (Comp. 10: 41; James 5: 10.) The reward is however not merited by the persecutions, but is a gift of God's grace.

Luke (6: 24-6) here adds four *woes,* corresponding to the four beatitudes he has recorded. If it be thought that these would not enter naturally into Matthew's connection, we have to remember that each apparently gives only a sketch of what was said. (See above, Introd. to the discourse).

It will be observed that in Matthew the word 'happy' occurs nine times; but as v. 11 is substantially a repetition of v. 10, we see that there are eight beatitudes (or macarisms). Some exclude from the count that of v. 10—as being different in tone from the others—in order to make just seven, the sacred number. But this is utterly arbitrary. In fact the eight, although following each other in a sufficiently natural order, have no stiffness of arrangement. Our Lord here, and often elsewhere, speaks with a certain rhythmical movement such as is natural to elevated sentiment; but still all is inartificial and simple.

HOMILETICAL AND PRACTICAL.

V. 1. Sermon on the Mount: (1) The preacher. (2) The hearers. (3) The sermon —its leading thoughts. (4) The effect stated, 7: 28.—STIER: "All apostolical preaching of the gospel must begin with the gracious commencement of this sermon, the conclusion of all apostolic preaching must coincide with its awful conclusion; but intermediate lies all that progressive teaching and exhortation, which through faith in its fulfiller establishes the law in the believer.—Moses, amid the awful splendors of Mount Sinai, gave a law which condemns; Christ, on the quiet mountain in Galilee, a gospel which saves." (Heb. 2: 3.)—V. 2. SCHAFF: "When the Lord opens his mouth, *we* should open our ears and hearts."—V. 3. In general, the beatitudes teach that true happiness in life depends on character rather than circumstances.—BURNS:

> It's no' in titles nor in rank,
> It's no' in wealth like Lon'on bank,
>   To purchase peace and rest.
> If happiness hae not her seat
>   And centre in the breast,
> We may be wise, or rich, or great,
>   But never can be blest.—

A homiletical classification of the beatitudes (many might of course be given): (1) The poor in spirit, the mourners, the meek. (2) The hungering, etc., and the pure in heart. (3) The merciful, the peacemakers. (4) The reviled and persecuted.—STIER: "The eight Benedictions, with their conditions, are in a certain sense found united in every child of God, and no member of this wonderful series may be altogether wanting from the time that the first poverty of spirit has received the gift of grace; yet is there an actual and gradual growth of one out of the other. And here does the law apply in all its significance, that the gift received must be preserved, exercised, and increased; and that to him only who has, shall more be given in order to his having all."

CORN. A LAPIDE: "There are three sorts of poor: (1) those who are so actually, as beggars; (2) in spirit, but not actually—as Abraham, who was rich in fact, poor in spirit; (3) both in fact and in spirit."—CHRYS.: "As pride is the fountain of all wickedness, so is humility the principle of all self-command."—STIER: "Oh, that the richly endowed and worldly blessed of our day, to whom the beginning of the Sermon on the Mount must come with the full force of most direct contrast and contradiction, would only meekly hear it."

V. 4. THEOPHYL.: "Those who mourn— always, and not simply once" (as if it were *mourned*).—V. 5. THEOPHYL.: "The meek are not those who are never at all angry, for such are insensible, but those who feeling anger control it, and who are angry when they ought to be. Meekness excludes revenge, irritability, morbid sensitiveness, but not self-defence, or the quiet and steady maintenance of rights." The Christian inheritance in the Messianic kingdom, is, like that of Israel (according to the divine plan), a gift directly from God, (Gen. 17: 8), and therefore (1) inalienable (Lev. 25: 23); (2) imperishable (1 Pet. 1: 4).

V. 7. THEOPHYL.: "Not by means of money only are you to be merciful, but also by words; and even if you have nothing, by tears."—In this world of sin and sorrow, there is frequent, nay constant occasion for being merciful in one way or another. HENRY: "A man may be truly merciful, who has not wherewithal to be bountiful or liberal." CHRYS. (condensed in Aq.): "The reward here seems at first to be only an equal return; but indeed it is much more; for human mercy and divine mercy are not to be put on an equality." SHAK.:

Mercy . . . . . is twice blessed;
It blesseth him that gives, and him that takes:
. . . And earthly power doth then show likest God's,
When mercy seasons justice.—

—But not mercy at the expense of justice, as too often in trial by jury.—V. 8. Not merely clean garments, clean person ("cleanliness is next to godliness"), hands clean from blood or pelf, but also cleanness of thought, motive, feeling.

V. 9. Peacemaking. I. Difficulties which the task involves: (1) In our own defects, (2) in the faults of the parties at variance, (3) in the foolish or wicked interference of others. II. Inducements to undertake the task. (1) Evils which flow from variance and strife. (2) Blsssed effects of reconciliation. (3) The work is Godlike, and will have God's special aid and reward.—While not expressing, this passage naturally suggests the fact that God is in Christ, reconciling the world unto himself,

and 'making peace' (Col. 1: 20, same word as here); and that we also ought to be busy in reconciling our fellow-men to God. SHAK:

God's benison go with you, and with those
That would make good of bad, and friends of foes.

CORN. A LAPIDE: "Father Gaspar so excelled in peacemaking, that the lawyers said they should die of hunger."

V. 10. The same persons who are pure in heart and peacemakers may be reviled, and that for the sake of him who was perfectly pure and the greatest of peacemakers.—V. 11. LUTHER (in Lange): "What comfort that the Son of God himself calls us blessed, let whoever may speak ill of us." (1 Cor. 4: 3-5.) —HENRY: "There is no evil so black and horrid, which at one time or another has not been said, falsely, of Christ's disciples and followers." STIER: "The daring disregard of truth with which the world is wont audaciously to calumniate the children of God, the Satanic cunning with which its lies are woven, would be altogether incredible, if it were not matter of fact." PLUMPTRE: "The witnesses for unwelcome truths have never had, anywhere or at any time, a light or easy task." GRIFFITH: "Violent outbursts, indeed, of ill-will are now but rare. Culture has softened manners, and made ferocity illbred. But the native dislike of falsehood to truth, of worldliness to godliness, of evil to good, still dwells in the heart; it oozes out in bitter, though quiet drops; it leaps forth sometimes in words which, though smoother than oil, are very swords."—V. 12. It is often a melancholy consolation in time of sore trial or temptation to remember that no trial has taken you but such as is common to man (1 Cor. 10: 13.)

13-16. INFLUENCE AND RESPONSIBILITY OF THE SUBJECTS OF MESSIAH'S REIGN.

The influence and consequent responsibility of Christ's disciples (see Analysis in the Introduction to this discourse) are here exhibited by means of two figures, salt and light. The general thought is that they have a great work to do, and persecution (v. 10-12) must not cause them to neglect it. Several of the characteristics just ascribed to them, as meek, peacemakers, persecuted for righteousness' sake, pertain to their relation to others, and qualify for useful exertions and influence.

13 Ye are the salt of the earth: but if the salt have lost his savour, wherewith shall it be salted? it is thenceforth good for nothing, but to be cast out, and to be trodden under foot of men.

13 Ye are the salt of the earth: but if the salt have lost its savour, wherewith shall it be salted? it is thenceforth good for nothing, but to be cast out and

13. As salt preserves things from corruption and decay, so it is the office of Christians to preserve the mass of mankind from utter moral corruption and ruin. Some bring in also the idea of salt as seasoning—that Christians are to save life from being stale and flat —but this seems strained, and little in harmony with the general tone of the discourse. Others say (Grimm) that salt of the *earth* must mean some saline fertilizing material, but this is forbidden by the next clause.—There is no propriety in restricting the saying to ministers, as is done by some Fathers, by Romanists in general, and by Calvin, Gill, and others. Jesus meant the 'disciples' (v. 1) as distinguished from the world in general, but not particularly the Twelve; certainly Matthew cannot have so understood, as he has not yet mentioned the Twelve; and nobody thinks the Beatitudes were addressed to the Twelve more than other disciples (notice the 'you' in v. 11, 12). A minister's calling gives him special influence, but so will another disciple's wealth, social or official position, talents, attainments, etc.—Notice (Mey.) how the expressions used for mankind correspond to the images; the salt of the *earth*, the mass of mankind to be penetrated and preserved; the light of the *world*, the expanse over which it is to shine. **Ye** is expressed in the Greek and so is emphatic (in v. 14 also). You, the often poor, persecuted (v. 10-12), are of great importance to the world, and must fulfill your duty to it. **Are.** Already true of the disciples addressed, and a permanent fact as to Christ's disciples in general.

But this high office of Christians is by no means to become an occasion for spiritual pride; rather does our Lord proceed to show the evils of failing to exert the salutary influence in question. **Have lost his** — rather

its—**savour,** *become tasteless.* For 'its' instead of the old neuter possessive 'his,' see on 24: 32. The same idea is expressed in Mark 9: 50, by 'lost his saltness.'[1] **If.** Until lately there was hardly satisfactory evidence (Schöttgen) that this ever actually happens, and commentators generally held the expression to be a mere supposition. But Maundrell's statement (about A. D. 1690) that he found south of the Dead Sea masses of salt that had become tasteless, is now supported by Thomson: "It is a well-known fact that the salt of *this country* [Palestine], when in contact with the ground, or exposed to rain and sun, does become insipid and useless. From the manner in which it is gathered, much earth and other impurities are necessarily collected with it. Not a little of it is so impure that it cannot be used at all; and such salt soon effloresces and turns to dust— not to fruitful soil, however. It is not only good for nothing itself, but it actually destroys all fertility wherever it is thrown; and this is the reason why it is cast into the street." "The sweeping out of the spoiled salt and casting it into the street, are actions familiar to all men." See more fully in vol. ii., p. 361-3. The case supposed is thus seen to be one of actual and frequent occurrence. The application is obvious. Christians must perform their function, must really serve as salt to mankind, or they will be worthless and contemptible, and that irrecoverably. Some, (Luther, etc.), understand **wherewith**[2] **shall it be salted,** impersonally, with what shall salting then be done; but this is unsuitable to the connection, for it would require the next words to declare that there is no substitute for salt. In the similar expression of Mark (9: 50) it is clearly personal; 'wherewith will you season—or, *salt*—it?' *Maldonatus:* "There

[1] Matthew's word (same in Luke 14: 34) means primarily to make foolish (comp. v. 22), and is so used in Rom. 1: 22; 1 Cor. 1: 20. A witty saying which loses the salt of wit becomes silly, and so by a reaction in the figure salt is said to be made foolish by losing its saltness. A Greek writer (Wet.) speaks of roots that are foolish, (*i. e.,* insipid) to the taster. So the Latin *fatuus* was sometimes used.

[2] "Wherewith' is literally 'in'what,' the action being conceived in such cases as located in that which is the material, means, etc., of performing it. Such uses of 'in' are found rarely in English, oftener in classical Greek, and quite frequently in Hebrew and Hebraized Greek. Comp. on 3: 11.

14 Ye are the light of the world. A city that is set on a hill cannot be hid.

15 Neither do men light a candle, and put it under a ^abushel, but on a candlestick; and it giveth light unto all that are in the house.

16 Let your light so shine before men, that they may see your good works, and glorify your Father which is in heaven.

14 trodden under foot of men. Ye are the light of the world. A city set on a hill cannot be hid. Neither

15 do *men* light a lamp, and put it under the bushel, but on the stand; and it shineth unto all that are in

16 the house. Even so let your light shine before men, that they may see your good works, and glorify your Father who is in heaven.

^a The word in the original signifieth *a measure containing about a pint less than a peck.*

is no salt for salt." Luke (14: 34) gives the same image as used in a different connection. **Good for nothing,** literally, *has no force or efficacy.* Those who employ our Lord's image here in support of the idea that the regenerate may wholly "lose their religion," ought to observe that it would also teach that they can never recover it. In this case, as in others, a view of the mournful effects which would follow utter apostasy, is employed as one means of preserving from it. Our Lord's design is not negative but positive, to arouse his disciples to watchful diligence and persevering devotion. Many of the Jews who professed to be very religious, were orthodox and scrupulous without real piety, and the subjects of the Messianic reign must not be so.

14. The same idea is here presented by a second image, which has a natural relation to the former. *Pliny* (Wet.): "To all bodies there is nothing more useful than salt and sun." **Ye,** emphatic, as in v. 13. Jesus elsewhere declares that he himself is the Light of the world. (John 8: 12; 9: 5; 12: 35; 1 John 1: 7 ff.) We of course understand that the light which his people emit is really derived from him. (Eph. 5: 8.) In Phil. 2: 15 they are compared to the heavenly luminaries; in John 5: 35 the Baptist is called, literally, 'the burning and shining lamp'—which Jesus had probably said before he spoke the Sermon on the Mount. Here Christians are the light of the world, the source of spiritual light to it, as the sun (John 11: 9) is of natural light. They are the light by means of which the world, the mass of mankind, may see the things of religion, may see the truth about God and his service. Comp. Wisdom, 4: 26. "The multitude of the wise is the salvation of the world." Ep. to *Diognetus,* 6, "What soul is in body, this are Christians in the world."—Anything that gives light will be observed, and Christians, as being the light of the world, cannot escape observation if they would. But this thought is presented more forcibly by changing the figure. **A city that is set on a hill**—or

mountain—**cannot be hid,** being thus seen distinctly, on all sides, and from a distance. Cities thus situated were not uncommon in Galilee—as in most other hilly countries in ancient times—and Jesus may perhaps have pointed to one while speaking; but it is idle to conjecture which one. The houses were often built (as they are now) of a very white limestone, which would make the city more distinctly visible. The thought plainly is, that Christians occupy of necessity a conspicuous position, and must be seen. To make it mean "the church," on Mount Zion (Stier, Keil, etc.), is utterly unnatural. There is still probably some reference to the persecutions spoken of in v. 11 f., which might make the faint-hearted desire to withdraw from observation.

15. And Christians should not wish to avoid being observed, even if they could. Such was not the divine design in making them sources of light. **Neither do men**—literally *they,* impersonal as in v. 11. **A**—*the*—**bushel,** *i. e.,* the one kept in the house. The Greek word (borrowed from Latin, as it was natural that Roman measures should become common in the provinces) denotes a measure containing about a peck; but it is better for us to retain the familiar term, the exact dimensions being of no importance to the idea, which is simply that of concealment, and is elsewhere expressed by putting the lamp under the *bed.* (Mark 4: 21.) **' Candle '** and **' candlestick '** are misleading, the thing meant being a lamp and a lamp-stand. **Giveth light**—or *shines.* The Greek word is the same as in the succeeding verse. Here, as often, the common version has obscured the connection by unnecessarily varying the terms. The fault began here with Tyndale, and was adopted by all his early successors except Rheims.—In Luke 8: 16 and 11: 33 we find the same saying (slightly varied) used on other occasions and with a different application.

16. Let your light so shine. As the lamp which is not hidden but set on the stand shines for all that are in the house, so let your light shine before men, that (in order that) [1] they may see, etc. The position of the words in the Greek (in which 'so' is the first word), shows the emphasis to be on 'so' and 'shine,' and 'so' signifies in the way suggested by the image of the preceding sentence. The incorrect position of 'so' in Com. Ver. (from Tyndale) encourages the erroneous idea that it means in such a way that (as the result) men may see, etc. **Before.** Not simply 'for men,' for their benefit, as in the preceding clause, but 'before men,' in their presence. **That they may see. . . . . and glorify.** There is no propriety in saying that this is merely equivalent to 'that seeing. . . . they may glorify.' The passage teaches us to desire and design that men may see, because thus the higher object will be secured, their glorifying God. (Comp. on 6: 1, 3, 4.) Ostentation of good works, which Jesus afterwards (6:1) so severely condemns, would be like flaunting the lamp at the door, instead of simply setting it on its appropriate stand. The shining of the light consists in **good works.** (Comp. Titus 3: 8.) In order thus to shine, the works must not merely be morally good (*agatha*, as Rom. 13: 3), but also morally beautiful (*kala*, here and in 1 Peter 2: 12), attracting the admiring attention of others. (Achelis.) He does not say 'may glorify you,' for the good works of God's children are all due to him, and hence the beholders ought not to praise them, but to glorify their Father. (Comp. 9: 8; 1 Peter 2: 12.) For the phrase **Father . . . in heaven,** see on 6: 9. *Alexander:* "Thus the Saviour winds up this division of his great discourse, by leading his disciples through the homeliest and most familiar every-day analogies of common life, to the sublime and final end of all existence."

HOMILETICAL AND PRACTICAL.

V. 13. Those whom "society" despises (v. 11) may yet be indispensable to its highest welfare. Contempt and reviling must not prevent them from striving to exert a wholesome religious influence. But if professed Christians be *useless*, then are they really despicable. Trampled on, (a) undeservedly (v. 11),

(b) deservedly. (v. 13.)—HENRY: "Let God be glorified in the shame and rejection of those by whom he has been reproached, and who have made themselves fit for nothing but to be trampled upon."—V. 14. Christians a light to the world. I. What may they show? (1) That Christianity is true. (2) That Christian piety is practicable. (3) That a life of piety is desirable. II. How may they show it? (1) By what they say—in public—private. (2) By what they do, good works. (v. 16.)—V. 14-16. Piety shining. (1) A Christian cannot escape observation if he would—a city on a hill. (2) A Christian should not wish to hide his piety —the lamp under the bushel. (3) A Christian should show piety in natural and appropriate ways—the lamp on the lamp-stand. (4) A Christian should let his piety shine with no selfish aim, but for the good of man and the glory of God.

V. 15. CHRYS.': "Nothing makes a man so illustrious as the manifestation of virtue; for he shines as if clad with sunbeams." CLEM. ALEX. (Wet.) gives a tradition that Matthias the apostle used to say that if a pious man's neighbor sin, he himself has sinned; for if he had ordered his life aright the neighbor would have been restrained by his example. —V. 16. Wrong and right ways of exhibiting good works.—TALMUD JER. (Wünsche): "It is not enough to be innocent before God, one must show his innocence before men also."— If Christians do *evil* works, men will be pretty sure to see them, and to speak against God and his cause. (Rom. 2: 24; Ezek. 36: 20.)— ROUSSEAU (Griffith) : "Ah! what an argument against the unbeliever is the *life* of the Christian! No, man is not thus of himself; something more than human is reigning here." CHRYS. : "Or if there should even be some who speak evil of thee, search into their conscience and thou shalt see them applauding and admiring thee." STIER: "The good word without the good walk is of no avail."—Men will not be saved by abstract truth, but by truth *embodied*, 1) in a personal Saviour; 2) in saved persons.

No Christian has a right to be regardless of his reputation, for not himself alone is concerned. He may imagine it matters little for him what men may think, since God knows

---

[1] Probably no one would now claim that *hopos* any_where denotes mere result or effect, as Com. Ver. makes it, the meaning being purpose or design. Another important example is in Luke 16: 26.

17 Think not that I am come to destroy the law, or | 17   Think not that I came to destroy the law or the
the prophets: I am not come to destroy, but to fulfil. |

his heart; but in so far as men do him injustice, they fail to render that glory to God which his good works ought to secure; and so, out of regard for the cause with which he is identified, he should not suffer himself to be misunderstood or misrepresented, where it can be avoided.—This passage, v. 13-16, should lead the Christian reader at once to tremble at his responsibility and to rejoice at his privilege. How much harm we do by our inconsistencies; how much good we may do, the least influential among us, by simply being what we profess to be. TYREE ("The Living Epistle"): "Of all modes of inculcating Christianity, exemplifying it is the best. The best commentary on the Bible the world has ever seen is a holy life. The most eloquent sermon in behalf of the gospel that the world has ever heard is a uniform, active piety. The best version of the written truth that has ever been made is a consistent religious example. The Christian whose light thus shines not only correctly renders, but beautifies the sacred text. . . . . While the truth is being read from the Bible, and proclaimed from the pulpit, let all the members of our churches second and enforce that truth by the silent eloquence of holy lives, and the world's conversion will move forward at home and abroad, with primitive speed."

17-26. RELATION OF CHRIST'S MISSION TO THE LAW.

Here commences the main division of the discourse, in which our Lord shows the relation of his mission to the law of Moses; and asserts that, so far from proposing to relax its restraints or overthrow its authority, he came to complete it. This portion, which is not given by Luke, extends to 5: 48 (see Analysis in Int. to ch. 5). The relation to what precedes, though not distinctly indicated, is sufficiently plain. Having set forth certain characteristics of the subjects of the Messianic reign (v. 3-12), and their influence and responsibility (13-16), he now proceeds to show that the Messianic reign will in important respects be different from what was popularly expected.

17. Think not. (For the expression comp. 10: 34; 3: 9.) The Jews were very likely to think so. The introduction of Messiah's reign was in the view of many to be a great political revolution, such as is apt to be attended by a setting aside of many institutions and laws, and a diminished regard for the restraints of morality. And it appears from later Jewish writers that some of them did in fact expect that Messiah would abrogate the law, and supported the notion by their interpretation of Jer. 31: 31. Many might also begin to think that Jesus cherished some such revolutionary design, from the fact that he had already (as we see from the order of Luke and Mark) called a publican to be one of his immediate followers, and eaten with publicans and sinners (Luke 5: 27-32), declared that he was introducing a new order of things (Luke 5: 36-39), and repeatedly disregarded the Jewish notions of the Sabbath. (Luke 6: 1-11.) These things appeared to them revolutionary, though we know they were not contrary to the real spirit and design of the Old Test. **I am come,** or, *came,* an expression frequently employed by Jesus, indicating that he had a mission (comp. 9: 13; 10: 34; 1 Tim. 1: 15, etc.), and which naturally accords with the fact of his pre-existence; but it must not be relied on as a *proof* of his pre-existence, for the same expression is applied to John (see 11: 18 f.) **To destroy.** In the physical sense, the word signifies to loose, dissolve, pull to pieces (as a bridge, wall, house), and is applied to the temple in 26: 61 and 24: 2 ('throw down'), to the body regarded as a house in 2 Cor. 5: 1, and is figuratively used in Rom. 14: 20 and Acts 5: 38 f. ('come to nought' and 'overcome'). So in Gal. 2: 18, Paul uses this word to describe Peter as having (so to speak) pulled down an old building as useless, and now gone to building it up again. In like manner here the image is most probably that of a building. There is no other example in N. T. of this precise use—pulling down, abrogating, a *law*—but it is found in 2 Macc. 2: 22, and in the classics (Grimm). A less intensive form of the same verb is employed in v. 19 ('break'), where it is contrasted with 'do,' and refers to the *practical* setting aside of the law in men's action, while here the reference is rather to the theoretical setting aside in our Lord's teaching.

The law or the prophets. This phrase was frequently employed to denote the entire

Scriptures (*i. e.*, the O. T.), the 'law' being the five books of Moses, and 'the prophets' the remainder. (See, *e. g.*, 7: 12; 11: 13; 22: 40; Luke 16: 16; John 1: 45; Acts 13: 15; 28: 23; Rom. 3: 21.) In Luke 24: 44 it is 'the law, and the prophets, and the psalms,' the last division probably including the other poetical books. In some other cases 'the law' denotes the whole (see John 10: 34; 12: 34; 15: 25; 1 Cor. 14: 21.) Observe it is 'the law *or* the prophets.' Not merely were the requirements of Moses to continue in force, (which some Jews regarded as more sacred than the rest of the O. T.), but also all that was taught by the other inspired writers, the prophets. No part of the existing Scriptures was to be set aside. And we know from Josephus and early Christian writers, that all Jews of our Lord's time would understand 'the Scriptures' or 'the law and the prophets' as meaning a well known and well defined collection of sacred books, the same as our Old Testament.

To fulfil. The word thus rendered has been explained on 1: 22. It here signifies to 'make full,' 'complete.' Comp. 23: 32, 'fill up the measure of your fathers'; Phil. 2: 2, 'complete my joy' (so in many places); Acts 13: 25, 'was completing his course'; Col. 2: 10, 'ye are complete in him'; 1 Thess. 2: 16, 'fill up their sins'; and so of completing a number, a time, etc. The idea seems to be that the law is regarded as previously incomplete, not fully developed into all the breadth and spiritual depth of its requirement; and Christ came to make it complete. The majority of expositors understand the word as denoting to fulfill by performing what the law required (comp. 3: 15; Rom. 13: 8). But does this suit the connection? (1) There is a marked contrast to 'destroy,' which term pretty clearly refers to his teaching. (2) The instances which follow throughout the chapter to illustrate this saying, are expressly examples of his teaching and not of his action; and while that which here immediately follows relates to action, it is not his action, but that which his teachings require of others. The thought is, then, not to perform by his life, but to complete by his teaching. *Luther:* "He speaks of that fulfilling which is accomplished by *teaching*, just as by 'destroy' he does not mean acting contrary to the law, but

breaking with it by his teaching," *Calvin:* "The question here is of fulfilling by teaching, not by his life." And it is interpreted in substantially the same way by Meyer, Olshausen, deWette, Ewald, Tholuck, Alford, and others. The Latin, Syriac, and Gothic versions, here use words as ambiguous as the Greek; but the Coptic word distinctly means to perfect, complete. Origen, in quoting this passage on 13: 48, takes it to mean complete. Jerome doubts; Augustine, Theophyl., Euthym., understand it in both senses at the same time, in which they are followed by various modern writers (*e. g.*, Gill, Plumptre), and some work out quite a number of distinct senses as included (*e. g.*, Chrys., Bleek, Wordsw., Clark, Schaff.) But such interpretation enfeebles the Scripture.—It has been vainly attempted to bring this saying of Jesus in conflict with what Paul teaches concerning the law. The latter treats of the law not as a rule of life, but as a means of justification; and he declares, not only that the law cannot justify now that Christ is come, but that it never was able to justify, and hence the necessity for Christ's work. "The law of the Lord is perfect," said the Psalmist, *i. e.*, free from defect or blemish, and precisely adapted to the object for which it was given; while yet for a higher and more spiritual dispensation its principles might be developed into greater completeness. This as to moral precepts, the subject of which our Lord proceeds to speak (*e. g.*, v. 31 f., and comp. 19: 8). As to types and predictions, his teachings and work completed them by presenting the full reality to which they referred; and so, as a whole, the previous revelation was 'completed' by the teachings of Christ and his apostles.—The idea still sometimes presented (mentioned as early as Calvin) that Jesus was a revolutionary reformer, setting aside the law of Moses as imperfect and effete, is contrary to the whole spirit of this passage. (1) Jesus expressly states the contrary—he came not to destroy but to complete, and completing is very different from setting aside. (2) The examples which follow in this chapter are not examples of teaching *contrary* to the law of Moses, but of going *further in the same direction.* The only saying he *condemns* is 'and hate thine enemy' (v. 43), and this was

18 For verily I say unto you, Till heaven and earth pass, one jot or one tittle shall in no wise pass from the law, till all be fulfilled.

18 prophets: I came not to destroy, but to fulfil. For verily I say unto you, Till heaven and earth pass away, one jot or one tittle shall in no wise pass away

not from the law, but a Rabbinical addition. In 19: 8 is only an apparent exception (see note there). *Chrys:* "Let us now ask those who reject the law, Is 'be not angry' contrary to 'do not kill'? or is not the one the perfecting and filling out of the other? It is manifest that the one is a completion of the other, and is the greater for this reason. For he that is not carried away into anger, will much more abstain from murder."

18. For, presenting what follows as a confirmation of what precedes. **Verily** is in the original 'amen,' a Heb. word signifying firm, faithful, reliable (comp. Rev. 3: 14), often employed in O. T. as an adverb, 'surely,' 'truly,' and then usually placed at the end of a sentence, either as endorsing its assertion ('so it is'), or expressing the wish that it may prove true ('so be it'). When thus used at the *end* of a sentence, our Eng. versions both of O. T. and N. T. retain the Heb. word Amen, and also in a few cases where with the same meaning it precedes the sentence. (Jer. 28: 6; Rev. 7: 12; 19: 4; 22: 20.) Notice particularly the *responsive* use in 1 Cor. 14: 16; Rev. 5: 14; comp. Deut. 27: 15 ff. Our Lord frequently employs the term at the *beginning* of a sentence, in the literal sense of 'surely,' 'truly,' and in these cases Eng. versions translate it 'verily' (*i. e.*, truly). In John it is always doubled, but single in the other Evangelists. Two modified forms of the Heb. word are similarly employed in Josh. 7: 20; Job 19: 5. **I say unto you,** is a formula very often employed by our Lord, with or without 'verily' (*e. g.*, v. 20, 26; 6: 2, 5, 16, 29; 8: 10, 11, etc.), and serving to call attention to what follows, as being important and certainly true, somewhat as in colloquial English we say, "I tell you," "I assure you," etc. In these cases 'I' is not separately expressed in the Greek, and consequently is not emphatic; but it is separately expressed, and therefore emphatic in v. 22, 28, 32, 34, 39, 44, where there is a contrast between his teachings and those of others.

Till heaven and earth pass away, is a proverbial expression which would popularly signify *never*, and is probably designed to be so understood here, the true limit of the law's continuance being given in the other clause, **till all be fulfilled.** In 24: 35, the same idea is expressed only the more strongly by departing from the proverb—'Heaven and earth shall pass away, but my words shall not pass away.' Comp. also Luke 16: 17. In like manner the Midrash on Genesis (Wet.) says, "Everything has its end, heaven and earth have their end, one thing being excepted which has no end, that is the law." **Jot,** in the Greek *iota*, signifies the Heb. letter *iod* (pronounced yōd), corresponding to the Eng. *i.* It is much smaller than the other Heb. letters, so that it is liable to be overlooked; and besides, in many words it can be either inserted or omitted without affecting the sound or the sense, somewhat like the *u* in favour or honour. The Midrash on Leviticus says (Edersh.) that the *iod* which was taken from the name Sarai was prefixed to that of Hoshea, making Jehoshua, Joshua. No part of the law, not the most insignificant letter, was to be set aside. And this statement is further strengthened by adding **tittle,**—in the Greek 'horn,'—denoting a very slight projection at the corner of certain Heb. letters, which distinguishes them from others that are rounded.[1] Comp. Luke 16: 17. The word 'horn' in this sense would not be understood among us, and so 'tittle' (a very small object) was wisely used by Wyclif, and retained by all subsequent translators. The whole expression has been aptly compared to our Eng. saying, "Not the dot of an *i* nor the cross of a *t.*" We also frequently employ in the same way the Greek *iota* (same as *iod*), "Every iota of it." The Rabbis have similar expressions, but they quibble about the mere words, while our Lord refers to the meaning. **In no wise,** is, in the original, merely a doubled and thus strong negative, the same as in John 6: 37. **From the law.** He does not add 'or from the prophets'; and it is of the law that he proceeds to speak in v. 19 f., and in the examples which follow; yet he had in v. 17 equally affirmed the permanence of the

---

[1] Thus ⸯ is d, ⸯ is r; ⸯ is b, ⸯ is k.

19 Whosoever therefore shall break one of these least commandments, and shall teach men so, he shall be called the least in the kingdom of heaven: but whosoever shall do and teach *them*, the same shall be called great in the kingdom of heaven.

20 For I say unto you, That except your righteousness shall exceed the *righteousness* of the scribes and Pharisees, ye shall in no case enter into the kingdom of heaven.

19 from the law, till all things be accomplished. Whosoever therefore shall break one of these least commandments, and shall teach men so, shall be called least in the kingdom of heaven: but whosoever shall do and teach them, he shall be called great in the kingdom of heaven.

20 For I say unto you, that except your righteousness shall exceed *the righteousness* of the scribes and Pharisees, ye shall in no wise enter into the kingdom of heaven.

---

prophets, and a reference to them seems to be suggested in the expression which here immediately follows. **Till all be fulfilled—** or, *come to pass.* This is not at all like the word rendered 'fulfil' in v. 17, but is the one rendered 'come to pass' in 24: 6, (see on 1: 22). Not the smallest part of the law shall pass away till everything (*i. e.,* everything it contains) shall come to pass. The things predicted in the law must all occur; the entire substance foreshadowed by any ceremony or type must have come into existence; the civil regulations for the Jewish State, after lasting while it lasts, must continue to serve as the germ and basis of much Christian legislation; the moral (ethical) precepts must be obeyed by every new generation. Not till all this has taken place, shall the least particle of the law be annulled.

19. Therefore. As all remains in undiminished force, it is a sin to violate, or to teach others to violate, one of its least commandments. **Break.** It is a compound of the word here used that is rendered 'destroy' in v. 17. This word signifies to 'loose,' and as applied to our action in regard to a law, it would mean to loose the obligation of the law, viz., by acting contrary to it, which we in English call *breaking* the law. In v. 17 it was to loose or pull down by teaching; but here the 'teach' is expressed separately, and spoken of as corresponding ('so') to the loosing. (Comp. John 1: 23; 10: 35.) **One of these least commandments.** The Jews were much in the habit (see in Wet., etc.) of classifying the various commandments as greater and less (22: 36), sometimes comparing those which they reckoned least to the smallest letters of the alphabet. Such a distinction was natural in regard to external rites, even as John (7: 37) calls the last day the 'great' day of the Feast of Tabernacles. And although they made unwarranted and artificial distinctions even among moral duties, yet the Saviour

does here clearly recognize some commandments as less important than others, while expressly declaring them to be not unimportant. So in 23: 23 (see note there) he declares ethical duties to be 'weightier' than the duty of tithing herbs. **And shall teach men so.** It is bad to do wrong, but worse if in addition we teach others to do wrong. **Called.** Not only shall *be* such, but shall be so called, *i. e.,* declared, recognized to be such. (Comp. on 5: 9.) **Least . . . great,** shall have the lowest place, or a high place, in Christ's kingdom, in point of dignity and privilege. (Comp. 11: 11; 18: 1, 5.)

20. For. This sentence gives a *proof* of the previous statement. You may readily see that he who transgresses one of these least commandments shall have a *low* place in the Messianic kingdom, *for* without a righteousness surpassing the Scribes and Pharisees, you shall have *no* place in it at all. Comp. 18: 4. **I say unto you,** see on v. 18. **Except.** *Unless* (Davidson, Darby) is better in modern English. **Righteousness.** Not imputed, but personal righteousness, as in v. 6, 10; and it must surpass that [1] of the Scribes and Pharisees both in degree and in kind, must be a more spiritual and free (James 1: 25), and a more complete righteousness, as illustrated at length in the remainder of the chapter. The Jews looked upon the Scribes and Pharisees as being eminently righteous, and doubtless did not think it incumbent on ordinary people to be as good as they were; so much the more surprising must have been this declaration of Jesus. For the Scribes, see on 2: 4; for the Pharisees, on 3: 7. Some Greek Fathers and Roman Catholic writers, with Neander, Bleek, etc., hold that he means the righteousness required by the law of Moses (which law the Scribes and Pharisees kept), thus implying that the law did not require enough; but this is strained and unnatural. **In no case.** In the Greek simply a strong negative, as in v. 18.

---

[1] Literally, 'shall exceed the Scribes and Pharisees', but this is evidently a condensed expression for 'exceed that of the S. and P.' (Winer, 245 [307], Butt. 168.)

21 Ye have heard that it was said by them of old time, Thou shalt not kill; and whosoever shall kill shall be in danger of the judgment:
22 But I say unto you, That whosoever is angry with his brother without a cause shall be in danger of the judgment: and whosoever shall say to his brother, Raca, shall be in danger of the council: but whosoever shall say, Thou fool, shall be in danger of hell fire.

21   Ye have heard that it was said to them of old time, Thou shalt not kill; and whosoever shall kill shall
22 be in danger of the judgment: but I say unto you, that every one who is angry with his brother [1] shall be in danger of the judgment; and whosoever shall say to his brother, [2] Raca, shall be in danger of the council; and whosoever shall say, [3] Thou fool,

---

1 Many ancient authorities insert *without cause*....2 An expression of contempt....3 Or, *Moreh*, a Hebrew expression of condemnation.

Enter into the kingdom of heaven is a phrase often employed by our Lord (*e. g.*, 7: 21; 18: 3; 19: 23; comp. 'enter into life,' 18: 8; 'enter into the joy of thy Lord,' 25: 21), meaning to become subjects of the Messianic reign and share its full benefits.

21 ff. Our Lord now proceeds (see Anal. at the beginning of the chap.) to illustrate the general statements of v. 17–20, by instancing various commandments of the law, with the interpretations which the Jewish teachers were accustomed to put on them, and declaring in every case that he enjoined a still stricter and more inward and spiritual morality, not merely in condemning the prevalent errors, but in more fully carrying out the spirit of the commandments themselves than had been done by the law. This was completing the law (v. 17), giving it a deeper and more spiritual application. The revelation given through Moses and the prophets, though perfectly adapted to its objects, was in various respects rudimentary, and now God's Son (Heb. 1: 2) would develop the whole into completeness. All that he teaches as to moral duties was really involved in the law, but he brought it out, so as to give a more distinct and complete exhibition of its requirements. Of the six examples thus presented, the first is the law of MURDER. (v. 21-26.)

Ye have heard, especially when listening to the reading of the law in the synagogues, with the comments and explanations made by the teachers of former generations, which, as handed down by tradition, were there repeated in connection with the reading. (Comp. John 12: 34; Rom. 2: 13.) **That it was said by** —rather *to*—**them of old time,** or *the ancients.* Every generation naturally regards

its own as modern times, and looks back to long past generations as "the ancients." The rendering 'said by' which Com. Ver. and some able commentators adopt (as Fritz., Olsh., Ewald, Keim), is possible according to general Greek usage, but is altogether opposed to the actual N. T. use (presented by Conant) of the terms and constructions which the original here employs; and the great mass of recent expositors hold to the other sense, 'said to.' [1] This will then naturally mean, said by Moses in giving the law (Ex. 20: 13; Deut. 5: 17), but may also include the old teachers in their interpretations; and a traditional addition being here given, it seems necessary to consider them included. Some of these traditional modifications (see another in v. 43) had come down through several centuries, and might thus be said to have been spoken to the ancients. And our Lord takes his examples from the law as in his day habitually heard and understood. The traditional addition in this case, **and whosoever shall kill shall be in danger of the judgment,** was probably designed by specifying the proper tribunal to indicate the appropriate penalty. 'The judgment' is generally understood to mean a local Jewish court established in every important town, in accordance with the command of Deut. 16: 18. (2 Chr. 19: 5.) It is said by Josephus ("Ant.," 4, 8, 15, comp. "War," 2, 20, 5), to have consisted of seven persons, though the Rabbins say twenty-three. It inflicted punishment, for capital crimes, by the sword.

22. But I say unto you. 'I' is here separately expressed in the Greek, and is therefore emphatic, contrasting his teachings with the law, and the traditional interpreta-

---

1 The rendering 'said by' is not in any Eng. ver. before K. J., which here (as often) followed Beza, who gives 'by,' and defends it at length in a note. Many commentators suppose this rendering to have originated with Beza, and Tholuck says it is first found in the Persian (Polyglott); it may therefore be well to state the rendering of the leading Old Latin copies as

printed by Sabatier and Bianchini. *Ab antiquis* is here given in a, b, c; *antiquis* in d, f, ff, Ambr. In v. 33, *ab antiquis* in a, c; *antiquis* in b, f, ff, g¹, h, Cyp., Hil., Aug. This *antiquis* (which is also the reading of the Vulgate) is ambiguous like the Greek, and so is the Pesh. Syriac. The Gothic gives 'to the ancients,' and the Coptic what is unmistakably equivalent thereto.

tions. The same contrast recurs in every instance throughout the series, (v. 28, 32, 34, 39, 44, and comp. on v. 18.) He "taught them as one having authority." (7: 29.) **That whosoever**—literally, *every one that*—**is angry with his brother.** The expression is somewhat different from that of the preceding verse and of the two following clauses in this verse, translated 'whosoever,' and fixes attention upon the idea that the statement applies to every single individual. The term 'brother' is probably drawn from the familiar Jewish usage of calling each other by that name (*e. g.*, in Tobit), but appears to be meant in a broader sense, as applying to any fellow-man, just as in Luke 10: 20, the Jewish restriction of 'neighbor' is corrected. The fact that all men are brothers, aggravates the guilt of that anger which our Lord condemns. **Without cause,** is omitted by some of the oldest authorities for the text,[1] and by most of the recent critics. It was probably introduced by students and copyists from a feeling that the condemnation of anger was too sweeping. But killing too is sometimes necessary and lawful, yet the commandment does not say, Thou shalt not kill without cause. The exception is to be made, in both cases, as a matter of course. **Raca** is an Aramaic word, most probably signifying 'empty' (Jerome), as if one should call another 'empty head,' equivalent to our *blockhead*. Davidson and Noyes translate it 'simpleton.' It seems to have been a common expression of contempt among the Jews, being often so used in the Talmud. **Fool,** is thought by many (as Meyer, Grimm) to be here used, as in Psa. 14: 1, and other passages of O. T., to denote a wicked man—which would make this a greater reproach than Raca. But there is no necessity for introducing that idea here; the same word occurs, in its common sense, in this discourse. (7: 26.) "Fool" is used as an expression of contempt in all languages, "evincing pride of intellect to be a universal passion." (*Alexander*.) The word rendered **council,** signifies here, as commonly in N. T., the great Senate and Supreme Court of

the nation, which the Jews (borrowing this Greek word) called Sanhedrin (see on 26: 59) ; and Darby here renders it 'Sanhedrim.' Before this highest tribunal Jesus was tried. **Hell-fire,** literally, *the Gehenna of fire.* Gehenna is from two Hebrew words, *Gei Hinnom,* signifying 'valley of Hinnom' or 'valley of lamentation,' (in 2 Kings 23 : 10, 'valley of the children—*sons*—of Hinnom' or 'valley of the sons of lamentation'). This name was applied to the valley lying immediately south of Jerusalem, employed by some of the later kings for the worship of the idol Moloch. (2 Chron. 28: 3; 33: 6; Jer. 7: 31.) Much obscurity still hangs over the character and worship of this horrid idol. Children were burned as sacrifices to him (Psa. 106: 38; Jer. 7: 31) ; but it is not certain whether they were burned alive or were first slain, the latter seeming to be implied by Ezek. 16: 20; 23: 37. Some late Rabbinical writers say that Moloch was made of brass and heated from beneath, and in its outstretched arms the infant was laid and burned to death; while drums were beaten to drown its cries, lest they should excite its father's compassion—and hence, they say, came the name Tophet (Jer. 7: 31, 32) applied to a place in this valley, the Heb. Toph signifying a drum. But this story was very likely derived from a similar practice among the Carthaginians, as related by some of the later Greek historians—the improbable idea of the drum being added, merely to account for the name Tophet. Yet whether performed in this way or not, the burning of children as a sacrifice to Moloch—prohibited already in Lev. 18: 21; 20: 2 ff.—was a horrid abomination; and when Josiah abolished it he determined to defile the valley of Hinnom (or lamentation) which had been its scene, by making it the receptacle of the carcasses of criminals and other filth from the city (2 Kings 23: 10); and this practice continued till the time of our Lord. Kimchi, an eminent Jewish scholar of the thirteenth century, says in his Commentary on the Psalms that fire was kept constantly burning in Gehinnom to consume the filth and carcasses—a statement which ac-

---

[1] Omitted by B. ℵ and several cursives, and by Vulg. and Ethiopic versions, and expressly declared by several Fathers to be wanting in "the accurate copies," or in "most of the ancient copies." It is found in Old Latin, Old Syriac, and Coptic, and is therefore a very early addition, say by middle of second century. Tyndale, following Erasmus' third ed., has no such word. Cranmer introduced it a few years later (1539). Stephens gives it in 1550.

counts for the phrase 'Gehenna of fire.' From these repulsive associations, Gehenna was very naturally employed among the Jews as a designation of the place of future torment; being so used in v. 29, 30; 10: 28; 23: 15, 33; Mark 9: 43, 45; Luke 12: 5; James 3: 6; and 'Gehenna of fire' in 18: 9; Mark 9: 47. The idea of fire is one naturally and frequently associated with future torment (comp. on 25: 41), and in this case may be regarded as suggested by the sacrificial fires in the worship of Moloch, if Kimchi's statement be considered too late to be reliable. 'Cast into Gehenna,' (v. 29. etc.), was a phrase naturally suggested by the practice of casting carcasses into the valley. The Greek is here literally 'liable into the Gehenna of fire,' *i. e.*, liable to be cast into it. Winer, 213 [267].—Another word, *Hades*, which in Com. Ver. of N. T. is often translated 'hell,' will be explained on 11: 23.

It has commonly been supposed that our Lord designed a climax in the three punishments—death by the sword, as inflicted by 'the judgment'; death by stoning, when condemned by the Sanhedrin; and 'the Gehenna of fire.' As to the latter, some have fancied an allusion to some peculiarly ignominious punishment inflicted in the valley of Hinnom, while others understand the punishment of hell, according to the general N. T. use of the term Gehenna. But it is quite difficult, indeed impossible, to make out any corresponding climax in the three offences, especially to show that calling a man 'fool' is immensely worse than calling him Raca ('simpleton'), as much worse as the difference between being stoned to death and suffering eternal perdition.[1] These difficulties are avoided by "discarding the idea of a climax altogether, and explaining the three clauses as substantially equivalent, though formally dissimilar expressions of the same idea, namely, that the law of God forbids not only murder but malignant anger, and its oral manifestations." (*Alexander*.) Our Lord is showing that he enjoins a more inward and spiritual morality than they were accustomed to; and he says that not merely is murder a crime, deserving the severe punishment which the local tribunals were wont to inflict, but that anger is a crime, and should be punished too (comp. 1 John 3: 15); and that the use of words of contempt is an offence worthy to be punished by the highest tribunal, yea, worthy of eternal perdition. Edersh. represents the sages in the Talmud as declaring that to give an opprobrious by-name, or to put another openly to shame, was one of those things which deserved Gehenna. Of course all this supposes that the anger and the contemptuous expressions are unwarranted and involve malignant feelings. A man may be justified in being angry with another under certain circumstances, as, under certain circumstances, he may be justified in killing another. In Mark 3: 5, Revised Version, Jesus is said to have looked round upon the people "with anger, being grieved at the hardening of their hearts." (comp. John 2: 15); and the apostles tell us to "be angry and sin not" (Eph. 4: 26), and to be "slow to wrath." (James 1: 19.) Yet while feelings of indignation at wrong-doing are not necessarily sinful, they are very apt to become so, and need the most careful guarding. Especially is anger likely to become sinful if not quickly repressed; and hence the injunction, "Let not the sun go down upon your wrath." (Eph. 4: 26.) Comp. *Aristotle:* "He that is angry for what he ought, and moreover as he ought, and when and as long as he ought, is commended."—And so as to using expressions of contempt. Our Lord calls the Scribes and Pharisees 'fools' in 23: 17, and uses equivalent terms in Luke 12: 20; 24: 25, one of which is also applied by Paul to the Galatians (Gal. 3: 1, 3); and the word rendered 'vain' in James 2: 20 is literally 'empty,' and exactly corresponds to Raca. Jesus even used still more opprobrious terms, 'devil,' and 'Satan.' (16: 23; John 6: 70.) It follows that the use of such terms of reproach is not essentially and necessarily wrong, but it is very apt to spring from, or to lead to, wrong feelings, and may thus constitute a great sin; it should therefore be habitually avoided, and practiced only where it is certainly deserved and would do good. On the

---

[1] Some fancy that *more*, 'fool,' though a familiar Greek word, is here really a Heb. word *moreh*, signifying 'rebel' or 'stubborn.' (See Tholuck, Alford, Stanley.) But would it not in that case have been given here in the Aramaic form, *mora*, like *raka*? And then this word is not greatly stronger than 'fool,' and would not materially lessen the difficulty.

23 Therefore if thou bring thy gift to the altar, and there rememberest that thy brother hath aught against thee;
24 Leave there thy gift before the altar, and go thy way; first be reconciled to thy brother, and then come and offer thy gift.

23 shall be in danger [1] of the [2] hell of fire. If therefore thou art offering thy gift at the altar, and there rememberest that thy brother hath aught against thee,
24 leave there thy gift before the altar, and go thy way, first be reconciled to thy brother, and then come and

---

1 Gr. *unto* or *into*....2 Gr.*Gehenna of fire.*

---

other hand, we must remember that a man might scrupulously avoid the use of the particular terms 'simpleton' and 'fool,' and still be frequently violating the spirit of our Lord's teaching.—Of course if such angry expressions as these are sinful, how much more sinful is all *cursing*, a thing wrong in itself, and for which men sometimes plead as an excuse, that they were uncontrollably angry—that is, the very sinful words are excusable because they proceed from a very sinful feeling.

23. Having thus declared that according to his teachings, the principle of the law against murder applies to anger and insult (comp. 1 John 3: 15), he adds the injunction to become reconciled to one with whom we are at variance. This should be done at once, even if it requires the interruption of a sacrifice (v. 23 f.); should be done while with a plaintiff on the way, before reaching the court. (v. 25 f.) Notice that here, (v. 23-26), the singular is used, 'thou,' whereas the plural had been employed before, and is afterwards resumed. He thus takes an individual case, as it were singling out one person and addressing him, and thereby gives greater point to the precept, just as is sometimes done by all public speakers. especially by preachers. A similar change to the singular may be seen in v. 29, 36, 39, and comp. on 6: 5.

Therefore if, presenting the injunction as an inference from, or result of, that which precedes. Since the prohibition just made extends not merely to outward acts, but to words and feelings of anger and contempt, *it follows* that one ought to seek reconciliation. **Thou bring**—or, *art offering.* This is the regular use of the term, as in v. 24. Com. Ver. here follows Geneva in rendering by 'bring,' but Tyndale, Cranmer, and Rheims, had 'offerest.' **Gift,** a general term, including all kinds of offerings. **The altar,** viz., the altar in the inner court of the temple (see on 21: 12). **And there rememberest,** there, while engaged in the most solemn act of the Jewish worship. **Brother,** see on v. 22.

Aught—or, *something*—**against thee.** The expression is no doubt purposely made general, so as to cover all cases, even the slightest; he does not say, 'is at enmity with thee,' 'is angry with thee,' but 'has something against thee.' (Comp. Mark 11: 25.) Darby, 'something,' Davidson, 'somewhat.' Men are more disposed to remember that they have something against their brother, than that he has something against them. The language implies that in the case supposed the person addressed is himself the offender. But the spirit of the precept applies just as well to cases in which we know we have done no wrong. Shall we merely be willing to be reconciled if we are approached, or are we not under obligation to go and ourselves attempt a reconciliation? A man must not sacrifice his dignity, neither must he neglect his duty.

24. Leave there. Do not merely determine that you will go and be reconciled as soon as the gift has been offered. It is comparatively easy to resolve upon performing a disagreeable duty before long; the point is to perform it at once. Leave there thy gift before the altar, and *go, first* be reconciled to thy brother, and *then* come and offer thy gift. (Or it may be, 'go first, be reconciled,' etc., as Meyer, Ewald, Bleek—the Greek being ambiguous, but the meaning in either case substantially the same.) *Alexander:* "It is evident that this is not suggested as a case at all likely to occur in real life, or even as a formal rule to be observed if it shall occur, but rather it is a strong assurance that it would be right and proper thus to act, if there were no other means of accomplishing the end required." (Comp. on v. 29.) God wished his people to show mercy, rather than to offer sacrifice. Acts of worship are very important, but even an act of worship might properly be postponed that we may re-establish friendly relations with one who has a complaint against us. It is an utter misapprehension to take this precept as indicating that there is a special propriety in seeking reconciliation before partaking of the Lord's Supper, with the practi-

25 Agree with thine adversary quickly, while thou art in the way with him; lest at any time the adversary deliver thee to the judge, and the judge deliver thee to the officer, and thou be cast into prison.
26 Verily I say unto thee, Thou shalt by no means come out thence, till thou hast paid the uttermost farthing.

25 offer thy gift. Agree with thine adversary quickly, while thou art with him in the way; lest haply the adversary deliver thee to the judge, and the judge [1] deliver thee to the officer, and thou be cast into prison. 26 Verily I say unto thee, Thou shalt by no means come out thence, till thou have paid the last farthing.

---

1 Some ancient authorities omit *deliver thee.*

---

cal inference often drawn that there is no great harm in postponing reconciliation until that solemnity is approaching. For (1) the reference is to temple-worship, and the principle would apply just as truly to any other act of public or private devotion as to the Lord's Supper. And (2) the point here is not that even though we should delay to seek reconciliation at other times, we must be certain to seek it when engaging in solemn worship; but that so great is the importance of being reconciled *at once*, whenever the offence is committed or is recalled, that even if one remembers the existence of such a personal difficulty when just engaging in worship, he would do well to suspend the most solemn service in order to go immediately and be reconciled. All the more, then, is it our duty to seek reconciliation at other times. Still, it is of course natural that we should be more likely to think of the need of forgiving and being reconciled when we engage in solemn worship, and so our Lord elsewhere says, (Mark 11: 25, Rev. Ver.): 'And whensoever ye stand praying, forgive, if ye have aught against any one.' We are not so much under greater obligation to forgive then than at other times, as more likely then to remember and realize the obligation.

25, 26. For the connection, see on v. 23. **Agree with.** Literally, *be well disposed to* (Grimm, Davidson), which suggests that we must seek to secure good will by showing good will. **Quickly,** not after a while, some of these times, but quickly. Anger is wrong, and angry difficulties should be settled at once. The **adversary** at law, in the case here supposed, is a creditor, as shown by v. 26. **While thou art in the way with him,** viz., on the way to the judge. According to the Roman law, the plaintiff could carry the accused with him before the judge; the defendant might settle the matter on any terms while they were on the way, but after the

tribunal was reached the thing must go according to law. **Lest at any time.** (*Perhaps*, or simply 'lest,' as Tyndale and Geneva, Noyes and Davidson.) You do not know but it will turn out as about to be described, and had better guard against such a result. **Deliver thee,** *hand thee over.* **And the judg̈e . . .** [1] **to the officer,** the intermediate process of trial and conviction being omitted, as a thing naturally understood. **And,** in that case, **thou be cast into prison,** an easy change of construction (as in Luke 14: 8 f., and often.) **Verily I say unto thee,** see on v. 18. **Thou shalt by no means,** or, *not,* the same strong negation as in v. 18, 20. **Farthing** represents a small Roman coin of brass, equal in value to about two-fifths of a cent, and thus double the 'mite' (Mark 12: 42), which Luke has in the other instance of our Lord's employing this image. (Luke 12: 59.) The Talmud refers to a similar counsel as proverbial: "There are men that say, while thou art in the way with thy adversary, be obedient." —Most commentators understand this language of our Lord as referring allegorically to the necessity of being reconciled to God, lest he cast us into the perpetual imprisonment of perdition; while Romanists make it a proof-text for purgatory, and some Universalists for final restoration (viz., when the debt has been paid); but the whole connection (see on v. 23) seems clearly to require that we should take it in the simple, natural sense. (So Chrys., with Theophyl., and Euthym., Jerome, Zwingli, and Calvin, and even Gill, usually so given to allegorizing.) We might say that the passage affords a good *illustration* of the spiritual truth in question, but there is no sufficient indication that our Lord here meant to teach that truth. Certainly the duty of adjusting personal difficulties, for which specific directions are afterwards given (18: 15 ff.), is one of such immense importance that we may well be content to

---

1 'Deliver thee,' after judge, is wanting in some of the earliest authorities, and is evidently an addition naturally made by copyists or students.

regard that as all the Saviour is here teaching.

V. 17, 18. The Old Testament. 1) Its teachings still instructive, whether they be historical, preceptive, ceremonial, or predictive. 2) Its precepts still binding, with the necessary adaptations to a spiritual dispensation; and its moral requirements made more searching and spiritual by the N. T. CALVIN: "It is of no little avail for strengthening faith in the gospel to be told that it is nothing else than a complement of the law."—The O. T. and the N. T. are necessary to each other, as parts of one whole. When men begin by disparaging the O. T., they will end with like views of the N. T. THEOPHYL.: "What the law sketched, Christ painted completely. The painter does not destroy the sketch, but rather fills it up." AUGUSTINE: "The New Test. lies hidden in the Old; the Old Test. lies unfolded in the New." EUTHYM.: "While the law forbids the ends of sins, Christ forbade also the beginnings. For murder is a fruit of sin; but the root of the sin is anger. And unless the root be removed, it will some time or other bear fruit." DYKES: "To the philosophic statesman, and to the religious reformer of every generation, the best recommendation of what is new will always be that it comes, not to destroy the old, but to fulfill it; to understand its spirit, to realize its purpose, to carry forward its work, and to make every change an unfolding into higher power." HENRY: "Let not the pious *fear*, nor the profane *hope*, that Christianity will destroy the law."—V. 19. All should both do and teach. 1) The professed teacher must also be a doer. 2) The humblest private Christian must not be content with doing, but also teach. CHRYS.: "For on this account he himself has set the doing before the teaching; to intimate that so most of all may one be able to teach." — Least commandments. 1) Moral precepts are more important than ceremonies. (Comp. 7: 12; 15: 11.) 2) Some ceremonies are more important than others. 3) Whatever God has commanded is important. P. ABOTH: "Be attentive to a light precept as to a grave, for thou knowest not the assigned reward of precepts." (Comp. Eph. 6: 2f. with Deut. 22: 7.) HENRY: "It is a dangerous thing, in doctrine or practice, to disannul

the least of God's commands; either to contract their extent, or to weaken the obligation of them."—Men sometimes say, as to one point or another, "Oh, this is a very unimportant matter, after all." But is it a commandment of God's word? Then beware how you disregard it.—V. 20. The Scribes and Pharisees led externally a blameless life, corrupt as they were inwardly. We ought to cherish better principles and motives than they did, but surely we ought not to fall below them in outward conduct. Shall grateful love to our Saviour fail to make Christians as "careful to maintain good works" (Tit. 3:8), as those Jews were through ostentation and self-righteousness? If content to let it be otherwise, have we reason to feel assured that we have entered into Messiah's kingdom, that we are Christ's people at all?—Our righteousness should include, not only outward acts, but also feelings. (See the examples which our Lord proceeds to give.)

V. 21. HENRY: "The law was ancient, but not antiquated."—Killing. 1) When it is lawful, and no sin. 2) When it is sinful to some extent. 3) When it is one of the greatest possible sins.—The evil of carrying concealed weapons.—Dueling.—V. 22. Anger. 1) Even when justifiable and righteous, always very apt to become sinful. 2) Sometimes such in character and degree as to share the guilt of murder. 3) Contempt for others, a milder form of anger, is often highly sinful.—TALMUD (Wün.): "Whenever a man is angry, if a wise man, wisdom leaves him; if a prophet, the prophetic gift leaves him."—HENRY: "Anger is sinful. 1) When it is without any just provocation given; 2) When it is without any good end aimed at; 3) When it exceeds due bounds."—V. 21 f. The three great departments of sin—sinful actions, sinful words, sinful feelings.—The sin of calling "bad names"; e. g., rationalist, heretic, infidel; or bigot, persecutor, proselyter, sectarian, uncharitable, illiberal; or Pharisee, hypocrite, Jesuit. In all such cases, is the epithet justly applicable, and are we applying it with a right aim and in a right spirit? Otherwise we sin. Jesus called some men fools, hypocrites, serpents, devil, Satan, when such an epithet was known to him to be deserved, and when good would come from applying it.

V. 23 f. The high duty of seeking recon-

27 Ye have heard that it was said by them of old time, Thou shalt not commit adultery:
28 But I say unto you, That whosoever tooketh on a woman to lust after her hath committed adultery with her already in his heart.

27 Ye have heard that it was said, Thou shalt not
28 commit adultery : but I say unto you, that every one that looketh on a woman to lust after her hath com-

ciliation ; thinking not merely whether you have something against others, but especially when others have something against you. To seek reconciliation is a higher duty than the most solemn act of worshsp. Life is more important than external acts of worship, and a healthy life will make worship more acceptable and profitable. Yet he does not say, Go and be reconciled *instead* of offering thy gift, but *then* come and offer. Worship without charity, charity without worship, worship *and* charity ; love God *and* thy neighbor. GRIFFITH : " There is often as much mischief done to social harmony by a proud determination not to confess ourselves in the wrong, or not to make too easy, submissive reparation for wrong, as by the actual doing of wrong." STIER : " Be reconciled, forgive or obtain forgiveness, do at least thy best, that so nothing may be set against *thy* account by the great Judge."—Rom. 12: 18, "If it be possible, so far as in you lies, live peaceably with all men." If otherwise, let it proceed from the other side.—V. 25 f. GRIFFITH : " There is a new case here. The first requirement (v. 23 f.) was, offer reparation spontaneously, *before* it is demanded of you. This second is, Yield reparation ungrudgingly, *when* it is demanded of you."—Strive to settle personal difficulties in private, without waiting for the intervention of legal processes. (1 Cor. 6: 6-8.) In like manner it is best to settle difficulties without taking them before the church. (18: 15.)—It is melancholy to see how many personal difficulties arise among men, and even among the professed followers of Christ, and how often both sides are proud and unbending, instead of acting as he here solemnly enjoins. Christian, stop a moment and think. Is there some one with whom you are at variance ? Then cease reading at this line, and prayerfully consider whether you cannot do something towards reconciliation. Make an effort, even if you have before tried in vain, an honest and earnest effort, in the fear of God; and

then return to read, with a meek and gentle spirit, these words of our Saviour.

27-32. THE LAW CONCERNING ADULTERY AND DIVORCE.

By this *second example* (see on v. 21) our Lord further illustrates and applies the statement of v. 17-20 that he does not propose to relax the requirements of the law, but enjoins a still stricter and more spiritual morality.

27. Ye have heard that it was said. See on v. 21. **By—**to—**them of old time,** is here a spurious addition from v. 21.[1] It may be noticed (Stier) that a certain variety is observed in introducing this series of examples; the full phrase of v. 21 is shortened in v. 27 and still further in v. 31 ; and then in v. 33 the full phrase is resumed, to be again shortened in v. 38 and 43. **Thou shalt not commit adultery.** (Ex. 20: 14: Deut. 5: 18.) This prohibition of a particular species of unchastity may be regarded as carrying with it in principle— like others of the ten commandments—the prohibition of unchastity in general. No addition to this commandment is said to have been made in the traditional teaching, as was done in the former case (v. 21) ; but we know that the Jewish teachers were disposed to limit the commandment to actual adultery. Jesus extends it so as to forbid dallying with the corresponding desires. He thus 'completes' the law. (v. 17.)

28. But I say. The 'I' is emphatic; see on v. 22. **To lust after her,** *i. e.,* with a view to lust after her, an intentional looking for the purpose of stimulating, and delighting in, impure desire. This, 'with a view to,' is the proper force of the Greek phrase, the same that is used in 6: 1 ; 13: 30; 23: 5. The English word 'lust' originally signified desire of any kind, good or bad (as in German now). In the Scriptures it is used only for evil desires, and at the present day is confined to one particular class of evil desires. The Greek word here used signifies 'desire' in general, and is used in a good sense in 13: 17;

---

[1] It is wanting in most of the early authorities, and is manifestly an addition by way of assimilation to v. 21, etc. Its presence in some Old Latin codices (with the Vulg.) and in the Old Syriac, shows that the addition was made early, by the middle of the second century, like many other corruptions of the text.

29 And if thy right eye offend thee, pluck it out, and cast *it* from thee: for it is profitable for thee that one of thy members should perish, and not *that* thy whole body should be cast into hell.

29 mitted adultery with her already in his heart. And if thy right eye causeth thee to stumble, pluck it out, and cast it from thee: for it is profitable for thee that one of thy members should perish, and not thy

Luke 22: 15, and some other passages. More frequently it has a bad sense, as in Mark 4: 19, etc., denoting evil desires in general (human desires being so often evil). The specific sense of sexual desire is found (in the New Test.) only here and in Rom. 1: 24, though of course included, along with other desires, in most cases of the bad sense. **Hath committed adultery with her already in his heart.** The distinction between our Lord's teachings and what they were accustomed to, is essentially the same as in v. 21 f. Jesus condemns, not merely the outward act of sin, but the cherishing of sinful desire. *Stier:* "He who experiences at a first glance this desire, and then instead of turning away and withdrawing from sin (2 Pet. 2: 14), throws a second glance with lustful intent and in order to retain and increase that impulse, *commits* the sin." As in 1 John 3: 15, 'whosoever hateth his brother is a murderer,' so here, every one that cherishes lust by a look is an adulterer. Comp. Job 31: 1; Prov. 6: 25; 2 Sam. 11: 2, 4; and 2 Pet. 2: 14, 'eyes full of adultery.' The Greek and Roman and the Jewish writers have also many sayings (see in Wet., Gill), as to the sinfulness of a lustful look.

29 f. The vigorous self-restraint which is requisite in order to avoid the sin just forbidden, suggests the idea that all our propensities must be controlled, and that the greatest possible self-denial would be far better than that suffering in hell, which must be the reward of sinful gratifications. This corresponds to the application made in v. 23, and here again the adress is to an individual, 'thou.'

Thy right eye, literally, *thy eye, the right* (eye); even an eye, even the best eye, must in such a case be given up. Comp. Ex. 29: 20; 1 Sam. 11: 2; Zech. 11: 17. The 'eye' is doubtless selected because suggested by the preceding sentence (v. 28), and also because of its general importance. **Offend thee,** or, *causes thee to stumble,* or 'to sin.' The Greek word is found in Sept., and quite often in N. T., though not found in profane Greek writers, and involves such difficulties as to justify a detailed explanation. Comp. Conant.

(1) The *noun* (*skandalon*), from which this verb is derived, denotes primarily the trapstick or trigger of a net or trap, against which the game strikes and causes the trap to fall; and derivatively, anything against which one strikes, whether a *stumbling-block*, as in Lev. 19: 14: 'Thou shalt not put a stumbling-block before the blind,' or more rarely, an *obstacle* set to hinder the progress of any one, as in the apocryphal book of Judith (5: 1) it is said the Israelites had put walls on the mountain-tops, and 'obstacles' (or 'obstructions') in the plains, to resist the progress of the invaders. From these derivative senses come several figurative uses, as to moral and religious objects: (a) A *stumbling-block*, as causing one to *fall into sin.* (Matt. 13: 41; 18: 7; Luke 17: 1; Rom. 14: 13; 1 John 2: 10; Rev. 2: 14.) (b) An *obstacle* which men strike against and stop, an *occasion of disbelief.* (Rom. 9: 32 f.; 16: 17; 1 Cor. 1: 23; 1 Peter 2: 8.) (c) An object which one strikes against and is *hurt or repelled,* so as to be displeased with it, an "offence" in the present English sense of that word. (Matt. 16: 23; Gal. 5: 11.) (By further derivation comes our English use of scandal, which word is borrowed from the Greek, but conveys a meaning no where found in Greek use.) In some cases two of these senses may be united, as the second and third in 1 Cor. 1: 23. (In Rom. 11: 9, the reference is probably not to a stumbling-block, but to the primary sense of a trap-stick or trigger, as a figure for a means of destruction). (2) In like manner the *verb* (*skandalizo*) is used figuratively in three corresponding senses: (a) To make one stumble and fall, to *cause to sin.* (Matt. 5: 29 f.; 18: 6-9; Luke 17: 2; Rom. 14: 21; 1 Cor. 8: 13; 2 Cor. 11: 29.) (b) To obstruct one's path or make him stop, to *cause one to disbelieve and reject* or forsake. (Matt. 11: 6; 13: 21, 57; 15: 12; 24: 10; 26: 31, 33; John 16: 1.) (c) To pain or displease, to *offend* in our modern sense of the word, (Matt. 17: 27; John 6: 61.) (And from this by further derivation comes our peculiar English use of the borrowed word "scandalize.") Here also, as with the noun, two or three senses may sometimes be found combined.[1]

[1] It has always been found difficult to translate the words into English. Tyndale introduced the Latin 'offend,' which might have been developed into all the senses of the Biblical Greek term, but has not been.

30 And if thy right hand offend thee, cut it off, and cast *it* from thee: for it is profitable for thee that one of thy members should perish, and not *that* thy whole body should be cast into hell.
31 It hath been said, Whosoever shall put away his wife, let him give her a writing of divorcement:

30 whole body be cast into [1] hell. And if thy right hand causeth thee to stumble, cut it off, and cast it from thee: for it is profitable for thee that one of thy members should perish, and not thy whole body go into [1] hell. It was said also, Whosoever shall put away his wife, let him give her a writing of divorcement:

1 Gr. *Gehenna.*

Thus the idea is, if thy right eye causes thee to sin. The expression is obviously designed to teach a general lesson by "assuming an extreme case," a method quite "characteristic of our Lord's teachings," (see *Alexander*, and comp. on v. 24 and v. 39). He is not presenting this as an actual case, or one likely to occur; but "if it should occur, if the only alternative presented to a man were habitual transgression or the loss of his most valuable members," then he ought to "choose mutilation rather than a life of sin; and that choice includes all minor cases, as the whole includes the part, and as the greater comprehends the less."

For it is profitable for thee. The appeal is to a man's own higher interest, which is really promoted by all the self-sacrifice and self-denial required by the word of God. **That one of thy members should perish,** or simply 'that one of thy members perish,' the old English subjunctive.[1] **Be cast,** same term as in the preceding clause. **Hell,** Gehenna, the place of torment. See on v. 22.

30. Another and entirely similar illustration of the principle in question. The repetition and reiteration of a thought, with only slight change of figure or phrase, is characteristic of the Scriptures; and it is not merely to be noted as a literary peculiarity, for the inspired writers, and the Great Teacher, employ this means of impressing upon men truths which are important and which they are unwilling to receive. So preachers are often compelled to do now; and though the fastidious may complain, as in the days of Isaiah, that they are treated too much like children (Isa. 28: 10), yet others, and perhaps the complainers themselves, often need amplification and repetition—while of course these should not be used as an expedient to disguise poverty of thought, by hammering a very little gold into a very large surface. There is something exceedingly solemn and stately in the repetition here; and in 18: 8 f., where our Lord presents the same idea in a different connection, we find the foot also introduced, as a still further amplification (comp. on 7: 9-11); it may also be noticed that there the eye is mentioned last (comp. Mark 9: 43 ff.), while here it comes first, because of v. 28. **Be cast into hell,** literally *go off*—or *away—into hell*. This reading is required by the best authorities for the Greek text; it was changed so as to be like v. 29.

31 f. The extreme facility of divorce which existed among the Jews of our Saviour's time, was the occasion, on a large scale, of the sin of adultery (v. 32); and thus the transition is very natural from the topic of the preceding

The Great Bible's 'hynder' was a failure. The Geneva took 'cause to offend,' and so Bible Un., Noyes, and Davidson. King James put this sometimes in the margin, and in the text imitated Tyndale. But this rendering has long been a stumbling-block to the general reader, and an offence to scholars. The Rev. Ver. has given perhaps the best available renderings, but various senses above described require to be carefully distinguished by the reader. The Syriac uses the same root as one which in Hebrew signifies to cause to totter, stumble, fall. The Coptic and the Latin versions here transferred the Greek word *scandalizo*, and following the Vulgate the Rheims version says 'scandalize,' which to a modern English reader is even more misleading than 'offend.' Wyclif's 'slander' is but another derivative (through the French) from the same scandalizo.

1 This use of *hina*, and the subjunctive, which is common in the Sept. and extremely so in N. T., though very rare in classic Greek, should not be called subfinal or hypotelic, for it is not at all a weakening of the telic or final sense, but is entirely independent. The clause introduced by *hina* is here really *nominative* to the verb 'is profitable' (the Greek having no equivalent for our 'it' in such expressions). So in 10: 25; 18: 6, 14. Sometimes it is *accusative*, either of the direct object (14: 36; 26: 63), or of general reference, 'as to' (8: 8); in fact the final use really belongs under this last head. And sometimes it is appositional, whether to a nominative (Luke 1: 43), an accusative (John 6: 29), or a locative (John 15: 8). Whatever special idea may arise is due to the natural relations between the matters spoken of in each case, or to the connection of the statement. Abundant examples may be found in Grimm, but wrongly classified; nor are these uses at all satisfactorily treated by Winer, or Buttmann, or Jelf. (In the similar statement of 18: 8 f. we find not *hina* and subj., but the usual classical construction, the infinitive).

32 But I say unto you, That whosoever shall put away his wife, saving for the cause of fornication, causeth her to commit adultery: and whosoever shall marry her that is divorced committeth adultery.

32 but I say unto you, that every one that putteth away his wife, saving for the cause of fornication, maketh her an adulteress: and whosoever shall marry her when she is put away committeth adultery.

verses to this, which is not to be considered a new and distinct example (see on v. 21), but another department of the same subject. Accordingly it is introduced by a simpler form of expression than in the other cases; not, 'Ye have heard that it was said,' but simply, 'And it hath been said.'

The law of Moses (Deut. 24: 1) required that if a man determined to put away his wife, he should give her a formal document to that effect. The Jews in the time of Christ were greatly at variance as to the proper cause of divorce, but most of them held that it was lawful for a man to dismiss his wife 'for every cause' (see on 19: 3), and that there was no restriction at all except that he must give her the document. Accordingly, in this case also our Lord is not setting aside the law (v. 17), nor at all conflicting with its true design. The Israelites, like other Oriental nations, had no doubt been inclined to great laxity in the matter of divorce, and Moses was not encouraging this, but to some extent restricting it (so also Henry, Achelis, Rütschi in Herzog), by appointing that a man should not send off his wife with a mere oral dismissal, which he might do in a fit of passion, but should give her a regular writing. (Maimonides gives a form in use in his day, twelfth century, see in Lightfoot or Gill.) This, especially in the earliest period, when few could write, would require a Levite to prepare it, and thus give opportunity for reflection and advice, and would besides place the rejected wife in a better position for the future, by showing that she had been a lawful wife. The document, according to the intention of the law, implied that she was innocent of adultery; for if a wife was guilty of that crime the law required that she should be put to death, and there would in that case be no need of a divorce at all. Still, it was not considered obligatory to inflict this penalty. (Comp. on 1: 19.) A further restriction upon the facility of divorce was made by the provision (Deut. 24: 2-4) that after the termination, by divorce or death, of another marriage on the part of the woman, the man who formerly divorced her could not then take her back, as this would shock the instinctive sense of propriety.—It thus appears that Jesus is here carrying out the design of the Mosaic enactment by a still further restriction in the same direction; is not abrogating the law, but completing it. (v. 17.)—According to the terms of the law, and the common usage of the Jews, only the husband could divorce; and so our Lord speaks here only of what the husband may do. But on a later occasion (Mark 10: 12), he mentions also the case of a woman's putting away her husband. It is natural that Mark rather than Matthew should record this, as it was a case much more likely to occur among Gentiles than among Jews.

32. In this verse, instead of **whosoever,** the correct text gives the slightly stronger expression, *every one who,* as in Rev. Ver., every single one, as in v. 28 (comp. on v. 22). —**But I say unto you.** 'I' emphatic, see on v. 22.—Jesus recognizes only one sufficient ground of divorce.[1] It is a part of the mys-

---

[1] The Greek term employed, *porneia* (which primarily signifies 'harlotry,' the primary signification of fornication also) is not always confined to unchastity in unmarried persons, but applied to the married also, as in 1 Cor. 5: 1 ff.; Amos 7: 17. The corresponding Hebrew word is the one always employed figuratively to denote Israel's unfaithfulness to Jehovah, her husband. Thus in Ezek. 23: 5, *Aholah* (Samaria), after "bearing sons and daughters" to Jehovah (v. 6), "played the harlot when she was mine," comp. Num. 5: 19 f. See Hosea 3: 3, and Gesen. on *zanah.* Dion Cass. says of the Empress Messalina, *kai emoicheueto kai eporneueto,* 'she both committed adultery and played the harlot.' Chrys. says here: "Do you see how this agrees with what precedes?

For he that does not look at another man's wife with unchastened eyes, will not commit *porneia*; and not committing *porneia*, he will not afford the husband occasion to cast out his wife." Chrys. certainly knew Greek, and he distinctly applies this term to the case of a married woman. So Theophyl. and Euthym. expressly, and so Origen on 19: 9. Apolinarius (in Cramer,) says, "Christ allows one to put away her that has committed fornication, because she dissolved the physical union." Jerome speaks of the wife as having "separated herself from her husband by fornication." The Peshito Syriac translates by 'adultery' in 19: 9, though not in 5: 32, and though distinguishing the two terms in 15: 19 and elsewhere. Almost all expositors have under-

tery of human nature that the connection between husband and wife produces a strange feeling of oneness. (Gen. 2 : 23 f; Eph. 5 : 28; especially 1 Cor. 6 : 15 f.) And it is only when the sacred tie which thus bound them has been broken, that either of them may lawfully form a marriage union with another person. It is not said that in such a case the husband *must* put away the offending wife, but in saying that he must not except in that case, it is implied that then he *may. Hovey :* "This crime is one which inflicts so deep a wound on the innocent party, and violates so utterly and completely the substance of conjugal duty, that it is recognized by God as a valid ground for divorce, whenever this is sought by the unoffending husband or wife." But "there are many passages of the Old Testament in which God addresses his people as an adulterous wife, whom, however, he still recognizes as his own, and strives to recover from idolatry"; and the wronged husband or wife is at liberty to exercise like forbearance.—The same rule as here is laid down at greater length in 19 : 3-9 (see notes), and repeated on a third occasion, Luke 16 : 18.—The directions given by Paul in 1 Cor. 7 : 10-16 refer to a peculiar state of things, but are in accordance with our Lord's teachings, to which Paul expressly refers. Where only one of a heathen couple had become a Christian, the apostle says it was best for them to continue together, since that might result in the salvation of the one not yet converted (1 Cor. 7 : 10, 16) ; but if the unbeliever insists on a separation, the believer is not 'under bondage,' 'enslaved' in such cases (v. 15), not compelled to live with the unbeliever, whether or no. (The word is not simply 'bound,' but 'enslaved,' and quite different from that rendered 'bound' in Rom. 7 : 2 f., which refers to the *bond* of marriage.) Yet the parties thus separated, the apostle says, must remain unmarried, and the believer must seek reconciliation. (v. 11.)—Putting together that passage and our Lord's teachings,

we learn that a husband and wife may for sufficient cause separate and live apart, but may not marry again unless the tie between them has been severed through the commission, by one or the other, of the crime our Lord mentions. If a man divorced his wife for any other cause, Jesus declares that he would be causing her to commit adultery, *i. e.*, if she should be married to another; and whosoever should marry her when divorced (or, 'marry a divorced [woman]'; it may mean either, and there is no important difference)—unless, of course, the divorce were for the sufficient cause here mentioned—would be committing adultery, as she would still be, in the view of the divine law, the first husband's wife. (Comp. Hovey on The Scriptural Law of Divorce, Am. Bapt. Pub. Soc.) It has been well remarked that as the only ground of divorce which our Lord admits is one pertaining to the essential nature of the marriage relation, no changes in the *form* of the outward union, or of the outward divorce, can make any difference in this respect.—It follows that all legislation which allows of divorce "from the bond of marriage," except for the cause here named, is contrary to Christ's teaching. It may be very well to legalize *separation*, with reference to questions of property, support, the control of children, etc., as is done in the so-called divorce "from bed and board"; and in cases where the civil law does not provide for this, but permits a complete legal divorce, it may be allowable to seek such divorce as an arrangement for separation; but still neither party has a moral right to re-marry, unless the religious union has been violated by the unchastity of one of them. In that case the innocent party has a right to full divorce and re-marriage; our Lord has said nothing as to the question whether the guilty party has a moral right to marry again. This could be true only after unquestionable repentance. Comp. the case of a man who has killed his wife. But for

---

stood the word in this passage as signifying unchastity in general. See Grot., Meyer, Weiss. As the general term it would include the case of adultery, and also that in which a wife was found to have been unchaste before marriage, which latter case the law treated as having the same guilt and requiring the same punishment as adultery. (Deut. 22 : 21 f.) Döllinger urges that this last is in Matt. the sole meaning, but unsuccessfully. Yet if the term 'adultery' had been here used, it would

have excluded this case. We thus see a reason for employing the general term, here and in 19 : 9.—' Maketh her an adulteress,' (v. 32), represents the correct Greek text. It means that if she is taken as wife by another man, her first husband has caused her to be now an adulteress, by putting her away without proper ground; and the second husband becomes an adulterer, for she is still properly the wife of the other man. The woman appears as passive.

33 Again, ye have heard that it hath been said by them of old time, Thou shalt not forswear thyself, but shalt perform unto the Lord thine oaths:

33 Again, ye have heard that it was said to them of old time, Thou shalt not forswear thyself, but shalt

---

civil government to refuse a legal divorce in cases where the Lord distinctly admits it, may be a grievous wrong to the innocent party, who is now absolved from all moral obligation to the other, and yet is not permitted by the civil enactments to marry again, if desired.— The Greek and other Oriental Churches, and most Protestant Churches, have always held that in such a case re-marriage is allowable. The Church of Rome forbids it (save by special dispensation), maintaining the perpetual obligation of what it calls the "sacrament" of marriage. The German Protestant Churches are extremely lax as to divorce—starting from a wrong interpretation of Paul's teaching, so as to make "desertion" (1 Cor. 7: 15) a ground of divorce—and that fact has embarrassed many of the ablest German commentaries upon the present passage. In some of the United States there has also been a grievous facility of divorce, against which a healthy reaction is now in several quarters arising. The new law of England allows legalized separation for various causes, and divorce proper for adultery. The State of South Carolina has no provision for legal divorce. (On the history of divorce in ancient and modern times, see Woolsey on "Divorce," New York.)

HOMILETICAL AND PRACTICAL.

V. 28. Licentious looks. How much of grievous sin is committed in this respect before him who perfectly sees the heart, and to whom impurity in the heart is as real a sin as gross acts of unchastity. Many a one would boast, like the Pharisee in the parable, of being no adulterer (Luke 18: 11), who yet has often committed adultery in the heart; and God has seen it. The principle of our Lord's teaching alike forbids anything else by which men encourage lustful feeling, as looking for that purpose at works of art, indecent dances, reading, speaking, or hearing obscene stories or obscene jests, filthy imaginations, etc.— LUTHER: "You can't prevent the devil from shooting arrows of evil thoughts into your heart; but take care that you do not let such arrows stick fast and grow there. Do as a good old man of past times has said: 'I can't prevent a bird from flying over my head, but

I can prevent him from making a nest in my hair.'"—Remember that the great means of keeping improper thoughts out of our minds, is to keep them filled with good thoughts. (Gal. 5: 16.)—V. 29. Sins of the eye. How many forms of sin are indicated or excited by *looking*. The lustful eye, the jealous eye, the envious eye, the revengeful eye, the suspicious eye—the gambler's eye, the robber's eye, the flatterer's eye. CHRYS: "For this were not to act as one hating the eye, but as one loving the rest of the body."—PHILO (in Griffith): "It seems to me that all who are not entirely uninstructed will rather blind themselves than gaze on things which are unseemly, and make themselves deaf than listen to hurtful words, and cut out their tongues than speak what ought not to be spoken." — Profitable for thee. Man has a complex nature, and the Bible, which is divinely adapted to human nature, appeals not only to conscience, the felt obligation to do right because it is right, but also to our interest in the true and high sense, our hopes and fears for time and for eternity. Scriptural self-denial is real self-interest. — V. 30. SENECA (in Griffith): "Whatever vices rend your heart, cast them from you; and if they could in no other way be extracted, the heart itself ought to be plucked out with them." DYKES: "The battle of conscience and reason and modesty against appetite, is to be fought within the heart of the tempted man, and for it help is to be found nowhere but on his knees."

33-37. OATHS.

The *third example* (see on v. 21), by which our Lord illustrates the superiority of the morality he enjoins, is the subject of Oaths. (v. 33-37.)

33. Again. With this term of transition is resumed the full phrase of v. 21. **By**—or *to*—**them of old time,** or, *the ancients.* See on v. 21 and 22. **Forswear thyself,** or *perjure thyself.* This refers immediately to Lev. 19: 12, 'Thou shalt not swear by my name falsely.' But the expression in the Third Commandment (Ex. 20: 7; Deut. 5: 11) is substantially equivalent, viz., literally, 'Thou shalt not lift up (utter) the name of the Lord thy God unto vanity (for falsehood).' **But shalt perform unto the Lord thine oaths.** This

34 But I say unto you, Swear not at all; neither by heaven; for it is God's throne:

34 perform unto the Lord thine oaths: but I say unto you, Swear not at all: neither by the heaven, for it is

---

is an addition which the Jewish teachers seem to have been accustomed to make to the commandment, corresponding to those in v. 21 and 43, and was probably derived by them from Deut. 23: 21; Num. 30: 8, where the reference is specially to vows. The verb here rendered 'perform' is translated by 'pay' in v. 26, and 18: 25–34; 'recompense' in 6: 4, 6, 18, Rev. Ver.; 'render' in 16: 27, Rev. Ver.; 21: 41; 22: 21; and signifies to give back, or to give in full, and hence to repay or to pay off.[1] The idea here is that an oath becomes a debt to the Lord, and we must be sure to pay it. This conception is especially appropriate to a vow. (Same Greek term in Deut. 23: 21; Eccl. 5: 4 f.) Comp. the representation of sin in general as a debt, in 6: 12.—The Jewish teachers correctly interpreted the law as prohibiting *false* swearing. Every assertion accompanied by an oath must be true; every promise accompanied by an oath must be kept. But this cannot be if men use many oaths; and they sought to evade the difficulty in their usual fashion by a quibble of interpretation. The Third Commandment spoke of swearing in the name of Jehovah; and the law elsewhere (Deut. 6: 13) expressly required that they should "swear by his name," i. e., not by the name of any false deity. So the Rabbis held that the law made binding only those oaths which contained some name or peculiar attribute of God, or something else that was eminently sacred. (23: 16 ff.) Other oaths, not naming or directly suggesting God, they held to be not binding. The Talmud expressly declares that such oaths as 'by heaven,' 'by the earth,' do not bind at all. And though some teachers set themselves against this (see on next verse), they were borne down by the majority. Accordingly the Jews were remarkable for their frequent use of oaths in ordinary conversation, swearing by the temple, by the altar, by the lamb, by the dishes, by the law, by Moses, by the prophets, by the life of the Rabbis, as well as the oaths here mentioned and countless others, and reckoning such oaths to be 'noth-

ing.' (See on 23: 16 ff.) So common was the practice, that even among those who became Christians it continued as a great evil; and James, writing to Jewish Christians, condemns it with special emphasis: "But above all things, my brethren, 'swear not.'" (James 5: 12; comp. James 3: 9 f.) Many of the same forms of oath are now used in Syria. (Thomson.)

34. But I say unto you. 'I' emphatic, see on v. 22. **Swear not at all.** The true way to avoid false swearing is not to swear at all; the Rabbinical distinction would not hold, for even oaths which did not contain the divine name involved some sort of reference to God which made them solemn and obligatory—otherwise they would not be used as oaths. Strike at the root of the matter; do not swear, and you will never swear falsely. In this, as in the previous examples, our Lord is enjoining, not merely an outward and literal obedience to the law, but that regard be had to the *principle* involved; and he will thus 'complete' the law. (v. 17.) The command not to swear falsely was a great restriction upon the familiar use of oaths: Jesus does not abrogate that command, but goes farther in the same direction.—Yet as the prohibition of killing and of anger is not to be taken without any exception, it being lawful to kill and to be angry, upon sufficient occasion (see on v. 22), so, we might conclude by parity of reasoning, must be the case here. And accordingly we find our Lord himself consenting to speak when *formally put upon oath* before the supreme court (see on 26: 63); and the Apostle Paul repeatedly using, where there was special occasion, such expressions as 'God is my witness,' 'I call God for a witness upon my soul,' 'Before God I lie not,' (Rom. 1: 9; 2 Cor. 1: 23; Rev. Ver., Gal. 1: 20), which are strong oaths; and the angel in Rev. 10: 6, swearing a very solemn oath. So in the O. T., men being accustomed to swear 'As Jehovah liveth,' God himself is said to swear, 'As I live' (Ezek. 33: 11); and the Epistle to the Hebrews appeals to God's oath 'by myself' (Gen. 22: 16), as given to strengthen our confidence in the faithfulness of his prom-

---

[1] Tyndale's 'perform' is retained by all early and most later English Versions. McClellan 'pay,' and so Com. Ver. in Deut. 23: 21; where Sept. has the word

here used.—Tyndale and Geneva have 'God' instead of 'the Lord,' but without authority, and their reason for introducing it does not appear.

35 Nor by the earth ; for it is his footstool: neither by Jerusalem; for it is the city of the great King.

35 the throne of God ; nor by the earth, for it is the footstool of his feet; nor [1] by Jerusalem, for it is the

1 Or, *toward.*

ise. (Heb. 6 : 13 ff.) An oath, therefore, is not inherently and necessarily wrong, and there are occasions which justify its use, as in judicial proceedings (our Lord's example), and where some very solemn asseveration in speech or writing is required by the circumstances. (Paul's example.) But as anger, even when legitimate, is in great danger of becoming sinful (see on v. 22), so with oaths, which are often administered in courts of justice with such irreverence as to be highly sinful, and which in individual assertions or promises ought to be confined to very rare and solemn occasions, and to be used, as the apostle does, in the most reverential spirit.—The object of explaining that, in this and the other examples treated by our Lord, there may be exceptions to the absolute prohibition, is not to weaken those prohibitions, but partly to exhibit their accordance with other passages which might seem to be in conflict with them, and partly to show that these are no unpractical and impracticable theories, as so many superficially consider them, but when properly understood are rules for our actual guidance in life.—The utter condemnation of all oaths, which has been made by Waldensians, Anabaptists, Mennonists, Quakers, etc., is found already in Justin Martyr, Irenæus, Origen, Chrys., Jerome, and other Fathers; yet oaths were sometimes employed by the early Christians, and gradually became common, especially after the union of Church and State. (See Smith's "Dict. Christ. Antiq.")

Neither by heaven, etc. The Jews usually maintained, as above shown, that an oath was not binding unless it contained the name of God, or mention of one of his attributes. But anything used as an oath must have some sort of relation to God, and this makes it binding, and so it ought not to be used—*i. e.*, used as if not really an oath. Comp. 23 : 2'. A few of the Jewish teachers took a similar view, one of them being recorded in the Talmud

as saying, "If a person swears another by heaven and earth, does he not also swear him by him to whom heaven and earth belongs?" But most held otherwise, as shown by Philo, the Talmud, and Maimonides (Light., Wet.). Philo states that some were in the habit of saying simply "By the," without adding anything, so as to avoid making it distinctly an oath ; and he suggests that one might add, "not indeed the supreme and revered First Cause, but the earth, the sun, the stars, heaven, the universe." And Maimonides (twelfth cent.), commenting on the Talmud, goes still further: " If any one swears by heaven, by the earth, by the sun, etc., even though it be the intention of the swearer under these words to swear by him who created these things, yet this is not an oath." We see that here, as with reference to adultery and divorce, a few of the Jewish teachers were rigorous while most were lax, and that Jesus confirms the view of the rigorous few, and goes still farther. Some fancy that this is a reproach to our Lord, as detracting from his originality. But he did something better than to be original in ethics ; for by authoritatively settling actual questions of truth and duty, he showed that the tendency of his teachings is thoroughly practical. (Comp. on 7 : 3-5, and on 12 : 10.)

V. 35 f. These are further specimens, similar to that just given, of oaths which the Jews were accustomed to use habitually as not binding, and which our Lord explains to have really a sacred element, so that such use of them is wrong. **His footstool,** or, *the footstool of his feet.*[1] This and the preceding expression are quoted from Isa. 66 : 1. 'The heaven is my throne, and the earth is my footstool.' So in Psa. 48 : 2, Jerusalem is called 'the city of the great king.'[2] These objects would never have come to be employed in strengthening an affirmation, had they not been somehow regarded in their higher char-

---

1 Tyndale shortened the phrase to ' his footstool,' and was followed by Great B., Geneva, and Com. Ver. There is of course no substantial difference, but the expression ought to be given in full. Persons who ridicule the pleonasm in Rev. Ver., ought to remember that they are ridiculing the sacred writers.

2 In ' by Jerusalem,' margin ' toward,' literally ' unto,' the preposition is not the same as in the preceding and following phrases, but the substantial meaning does not differ.

36 Neither shalt thou swear by thy head, because thou canst not make one hair white or black.
37 But let your communication be, Yea, yea; Nay, nay: for whatsoever is more than these cometh of evil.

36 city of the great King. Neither shalt thou swear by thy head, for thou canst not make one hair white or black. 1 But let your speech be, Yea, yea; Nay, nay; and whatsoover is more than these is of 2 the evil *one*:

---

1 Some ancient authorities read, *But your speech shall be*....2 Or, *evil:* as in ver 39; 6: 13.

---

acter, as related to God; and though a man swearing by them, particularly after the expression has become trite, might not have such an idea distinctly present to his mind, yet it is really and necessarily involved, when they are used in the way of an oath. *Alexander:* "He who swears by the earth either swears by God, or does not swear at all."

36. Neither shalt thou swear. The form changing to the singular, as in v. 23, thus making the application more personal and pointed. **By thy head.** A very common oath among the Greeks and Romans, as well as the Jews; probably founded on the idea that a man would stake his head upon the assertion, would be willing to lose his head if it should not prove true. But his life belongs to God and not to himself, and he is not able to change the color of a single hair of that head, which he so lightly engages to cast away. The reference is of course to the change of color in growing old, which depends on the divinely directed course of nature (Weiss). Notice that the specimens mentioned descend gradually to the lower kinds of oath, heaven, earth, Jerusalem, the head. An expression often heard among us, "by my life," or "my life on it," is sinful on the same principle as "by my head."

37. But let your communication—or—*speech.*[1] The term naturally suggests that he is now referring to the use of language in general, to ordinary conversation. The repetition, **yea, yea; nay, nay,** seems designed to indicate that the proper mode of strengthening an assertion is simply to repeat the affirmation or negation. Comp. our Lord's 'verily, verily.' Paul's expression (2 Cor. 1: 17) has a different bearing. The Rabbis frequently doubled these particles (Talmud), as we do. Edersh. says that in the Midrash on Ruth it is mentioned as characteristic of the pious, that their yea is yea, and their nay nay. James (5: 12). though manifestly referring to our

Lord's discourse, states the thing in a slightly different way. ' Let your yea be yea, and your nay, nay '; let the simple affirmation or negation suffice, without needing to be strengthened by oaths. Maimonides, "Let the disciples of the wise be always truthful and trustworthy; saying simply, yes, yes, and no, no," may have really borrowed from the New Test.; for the Jewish writers adopted whatever they approved, from any source. **Cometh of evil**—or, *is of the evil one.* The Greek is ambiguous, as in 6: 13, where see note. In this passage it is interpreted 'the evil one' by Chrys. (and his followers Theoph. and Euthym.), Zwingli, Beza, Wetstein, Fritzsche, Meyer, Keim, Grimm, Mansel, Plumptre; and 'evil' by Luther (though not in the first ed. of his trans.), Calvin, Bengel, Tholuck, De Wette, Ewald, Bleek, Stier, Weiss, Archelis, Keil. Taken in the former and somewhat more probable sense, the expression means, has its origin in Satan, as in 13: 19, 38. Taken in the other sense it means, is of evil origin. The general thought is in either case the same. The necessity, real or supposed, for using oaths, originates in evil, or in Satan; for it is due to the fact that men do not always faithfully keep their simple word. And like all the consequences of sin, this practice reacts to strengthen its source; for not only do men thereby become less careful as to the truthfulness of assertions unattended by an oath, but even oaths tend gradually to lose their solemn force by frequent, and especially by heedless and irreverent repetition (comp. on 23: 16). And so the observance of our Lord's prohibition would give to oaths a much greater value in those cases in which they are really necessary and proper. Comp. *Hierocles* (Platonist of the fifth cent.), "Reverence an oath, and be not swift to use it, that you may be accustomed to swear truly, from not being accustomed to swear." Add (Wet.) *Philo:* "Not to swear is highly becoming

---

[1] 'Communication' is from Tyndale, followed by Great B., Geneva, and Com. Ver. The Revised Ver. retains it in Luke 24: 17 (yet see margin), but has 'speech' in Eph. 4: 29; Col. 3: 8. In 1 Cor. 15: 33,

Philem. 6, the Greek is different.—The authorities for 'shall be' (margin) are few; the sense is substantially the same.

33 Ye have heard that it hath been said, An eye for an eye, and a tooth for a tooth:

38 Ye have heard that it was said, An eye for an eye

---

and advantageous, and is accordant with a rational nature, so instructed to speak truth on every occasion that words are reckoned oaths." *Epictetus:* "Avoid oaths, altogether if possible, but if not, as far as you can." *Quintilian:* "To swear at all, unless where it is necessary, is unbecoming a grave man."

HOMILETICAL AND PRACTICAL.

V. 33. Perjury—its nature, causes, evil consequences, remedies. CHRYS.: "If to swear is of the evil one, how great the penalty which *false* swearing will bring."—V. 34. Profanity—different kinds, swearing, cursing, other kinds—evils of profanity, and of all irreverence.—Cursing is always and essentially wrong, since no one has a right to imprecate eternal ruin upon another, unless by explicit divine direction, like the prophets. There is much profane language which is neither cursing nor swearing, as when one speaks in any wise irreverently of God, his word, worship, or anything sacred. Preachers often speak of God too familiarly, in public discourse and conversation. And there are phrases in which the name of God is either omitted or disguised, so that persons fancy they are not wrong, which yet involve the essence of profanity. "My gracious!" means "My gracious God." "Bless your soul," is "God bless your soul." "Zounds" is "God's wounds." One may plead that he does not mean this in using such phrases, but so could the Jews have said as to the expressions which Jesus condemns; nay, the excuse of "not meaning anything by it" is often given by persons who use profanely the most solemn oaths. Any one who observes for a little while the language of those about him, or his own language, will be apt to encounter many phrases which, though not distinctly so designed, are yet in direct violation of what our Lord has here taught, and should therefore be carefully avoided. The charge of profanity also applies to all irreverent citations or ludicrous applications of the language of Scripture, a very common fault even in Christian society. (Comp. on 12: 36 f.)—V. 37. Self-respecting veracity will command respect from others. What a compliment when it is said: His word is as good as his bond.

ÆSCHYLUS: "Not oaths gain credence for the man, but the man for the oaths." JOSEPHUS ("War.," 2, 8, 6), says of the Essenes: "Every word they say is weightier than an oath, and swearing they shun, regarding it as worse than perjury."—Habitual accuracy of statement, as opposed to prevalent exaggerations. The positive degree may really signify more than the superlative.

38-48. REQUITAL OF INJURIES AND LOVE OF ENEMIES.

The *fourth and fifth examples* (see on v. 21), by which our Lord illustrates the superiority of his teachings, are the subjects of Requital of Injuries (v. 38-42), and Love of Enemies (v. 43-48.)

38. Ye have heard that it hath been said. See on v. 21. **An eye for an eye,** etc. See Ex. 21 : 24; Deut. 19 : 21 ; Lev. 24 : 20, in which passages these expressions are coupled with various similar ones, as 'life for life,' 'hand for hand,' 'foot for foot,' the general law being that of retaliation, or, "like for like"—which was also the law of Solon, and of the Roman Twelve Tables. This careful enunciation by Moses of the law of retaliation, was doubtless designed partly to restrain men from going *beyond* retaliation, as passion often prompts one to inflict a far *greater* injury than he has received. The Jews held that this law justified personal retaliation of private wrongs, and in general justified revenge; though Moses expressly forbids revenge of private injuries in Lev. 19: 18: 'Thou shalt not avenge, nor bear any grudge against the children of thy people, but thou shalt love thy neighbor as thyself." In a rude state of society, as in the early days of California, every man takes in his own hands the punishment of wrongs done to him; and in the most civilized Christian community we are apt to find some individuals who glory in the fact that they protect and avenge themselves. The Jews would defend such a procedure on their part by misapplying to private action what was given as public law. The teachings of our Lord on this subject are therefore not in antagonism to the law of Moses, but serve to carry out more fully its spirit and design, to 'complete' the law (v. 17), as we have seen in all the previous instances.

39 But I say unto you, That ye resist not evil: but whosoever shall smite thee on thy right cheek, turn to him the other also.

39 and a tooth for a tooth: but I say unto you, Resist not [1] him that is evil: but whosoever smiteth thee

1 Or, *evil.*

---

39. But I say unto you, see on v. 22. **That ye resist not evil** (*the evil man*). The Greek is ambiguous (comp. on v. 37, and 6 : 13). If understood as masculine (Wyclif) it would not here mean 'the evil (one),' Satan, as it would in v. 37 and 6: 13—but 'the evil (man),' the bad man who harms you, as in the ways that follow. If understood as neuter (Tyndale and all other early Eng. versions), it would be evil in general. The resulting sense is substantially the same. The verb rendered 'resist' signifies to stand over against, withstand; and the idea seems to be to let evil have its course (or the evil man his course), and leave it for God to punish and control (see Rom. 12 : 19 ff. ; 1 Thess. 5: 15; 1 Pet. 3 : 9). Our Lord says not merely that we must not revenge evil, but must not resist it. The explanation of his exact meaning can be better given after considering one of the examples he presents in illustration of this general principle. These examples are four, viz., personal violence (v. 39), vexatious litigation (v. 40), public exactions (v. 41), and troublesome begging and borrowing (v. 42).

Shall smite, or, *smites.* Present tense in the better Greek text, which was readily changed by copyists to the easier future, found in v. 41. The Greek word means to smite with rods, and to smite with the palm of the hand (comp. 26: 67), colloquial Eng. 'slap.' Luke (6: 29) has the general term 'strikes.'—The change to the singular number, 'thee,' is the same that occurs in v. 23 (see note). It is here continued, as there, through the several particulars which follow (v. 40-42), and the plural is resumed with the next subject. (v. 43.) Smiting on **the right cheek** (literally *jaw*), is both an injury and an insult (2 Cor. 11 : 20), and yet to this the loving Redeemer was himself more than once subjected. (26 : 67; John 19 : 3.)—The curious have observed that one naturally smites another's left cheek first, while Jesus follows rather the general custom of speaking, by which members of the right side are first mentioned (comp. v. 29).

What are we to understand by the precept not to resist evil, or the evil man, with this and the following illustrations? There have always been some who maintained that these expressions are to be taken rigorously, as absolutely forbidding war, or any resistance to personal violence. In the early centuries some Christians positively refused to render military service, as being here forbidden. Many of the Anabaptists of Germany, in the age of the Reformation, condemned war, as did the Mennonists of Holland. In America the view is now held by the Quakers (or Friends), the Tunkers (or Dunkers or Dunkards), and the Mennonists.[1] Besides those persons who conscientiously strove to carry out the supposed teachings of the passage, there have always been others who interpreted it in the same way, and have then made it a ground either of attack upon the morality of the gospel as fanciful and unwise, or of assault upon the current Christianity as inconsistent and confessedly immoral, or else of excuse for the total failure to attempt obedience in any sense to commands which it seemed so impossible fully to carry out. On the other hand, most Christians have perceived that it could not be meant to condemn war under all circumstances, as various soldiers are referred to in the New Test., without any hint of their being required to cease to be soldiers, and as war is sometimes an inevitable necessity, to prevent yet greater evils. They have also perceived that the direction to turn the left cheek, cannot have been designed as a rule for general observance, since it would often needlessly provoke greater wrong, and seeing that our Lord himself did not turn the other cheek when smitten, but mildly and yet firmly remonstrated (John 18 : 22 f.), while Paul met the suggestion to insult him in this way with a severe rebuke (Acts 23: 3)—besides the fact that Jesus repeatedly took great pains to avoid exposing himself to personal violence, by withdrawing from places at which it was threatened. (Luke 4 : 30; John 7 : 1, 10; 10 : 39 ; Mark 9 ; 30. etc.)

---

[1] The Russian novelist Count Tolstoi, in "My Religion," 1885, puts forward this interpretation with enthusiasm as a new discovery, and glories in the thought that the course thus indicated would destroy society, which according to the Russian Nihilist view ought to be destroyed, at once and completely.

40 And if any man will sue thee at the law, and take away thy coat, let him have *thy* cloak also.

40 on thy right cheek, turn to him the other also. And if any man would go to law with thee, and take away

---

How then are we to interpret the language here employed? It is not enough to say that our Lord cannot have meant this as an absolute and general rule, for while that is plain, the question recurs, what did he mean? It will not do to declare the language merely figurative, for we have no warrant whatever for calling plain statements figurative—a process by which the most vital doctrines and precepts of Scripture might be explained away. Two remarks will help to clear up the difficulty. (1) Our Saviour's teachings in general (as well as the teachings of his apostles), are not simply didactic, but polemical, aimed at existing errors and evils; and while intended to be universal in their application, they will be understood in their exact bearing only when viewed in contrast to the wrong opinion, feeling, or practice he was especially designing in each case to correct. Many passages of Scripture fail to be rightly interpreted because this principle is not apprehended or not borne in mind. In the present case, Jesus aims to correct the revengeful spirit and practice to which the Jews were greatly addicted, and which they justified by a loose application of the law of Moses. (2) Our Lord here, as we have observed in former instances (see on v. 29, and comp. the expressions in 6: 3, 6), selects an extreme case, in order to exhibit more vividly the *principle* by which we should be guided. So far from vengeful resistance and retaliation being right, it would be better, if that were the alternative, voluntarily to submit ourselves to a yet greater wrong. Better to turn the other cheek, to give up the other garment, to double the impressing officer's requisition, than to permit ourselves to practice that passionate resistance and that revengeful retaliation to which we are all prone, and which the Jewish teachers defended. The case is an extreme one, and very unlikely to occur; but if even this would be right, rather than be revengeful, all the more is it our duty to do things less difficult, since the greater includes the less. *Dykes:* "Of course, when an instance is selected to illustrate a principle, the instance is usually an extreme or next to impossible one; both because a principle is best seen when pushed to its ultimate application, and also because there is

less chance of people blindly copying the example when its extravagance drives them to search for some inner meaning in it." On v. 24 we saw that if prompt reconciliation is so important as to make it right to interrupt a sacrifice in order to settle a difficulty just then remembered, much more is it our duty, under all ordinary circumstances, to seek reconciliation without delay. And so here. If it would be proper, were that the alternative, even to expose ourselves voluntarily to the grossest additional insult and wrong, such as is here described, rather than be revengeful, then much more is it our duty to bear wrong and insult that have already been inflicted, rather than exercise a spirit of revenge. To resist, to resent, to punish, whether in national or individual affairs, is not necessarily and inherently sinful, but is useful, when properly regulated, to society, and even to the wrongdoer himself; and so it is sometimes a duty to punish, even when we should prefer to do otherwise. But to resist or resent in a passionate and revengeful spirit is deeply sinful, and a sin to which men are so strongly inclined that it ought to be guarded against with the utmost care. And yet many professing Christians not only act when excited, but deliberately and habitually avow their intention to act, in the way which is here so pointedly condemned—more sensitive as to what the world calls insult and dishonor, than to the teachings of infinite wisdom, the solemn commands of the Divine Redeemer. O, cowardly audacity! afraid to incur the world's petty frown, and not afraid to displease God.

40. Sue thee at—or, *go to*—**law.** Some understand it to include private arbitration of difficulties, as well as suits at law—and certainly the same term does cover both in 1 Cor. 6: 1, 6—but the connection here seems to point directly and exclusively to a suit at law. We have already had a reference to legal processes in v. 25. There is a Latin proverb which resembles this saying, viz., "If one sues you for the egg, give him the hen also." **Coat.** The Greek denotes the inner garment worn by a Jew in those days, resembling what the Romans called 'tunic,' and corresponding most nearly to a long shirt, which usually reached somewhat below the knee, but in the

41 And whosoever shall compel thee to go a mile, go with him twain.
42 Give to him that asketh thee, and from him that would borrow of thee turn not thou away.

41 thy coat, let him have thy cloak also. And whosoever shall [1] compel thee to go one mile, go with him 42 twain. Give to him that asketh thee, and from him that would borrow of thee turn not thou away.

---

[1] Gr. *impress.*

more elegant article for dress occasions, reached almost to the ground. It was sometimes worn loose, but commonly confined around the waist with a girdle. (3:4.) In some cases two of these were worn (see on 10: 10), but in general only one. It is this garment of our Saviour which is said to have been without seam. (John 19:23.) The other Greek word, rendered **cloak,** is sometimes used to signify a garment in general, as in 9: 16; 17: 2; 24: 18; 26: 65; 27: 31, 35. In other cases, as 9: 20, 21; 14: 36; 21: 7, 8, it denotes the outer garment, which appears (for our knowledge of Hebrew dress is quite imperfect) to have been for some persons a loose robe, and with others a large square piece of cloth, resembling a large shawl, wrapped around the person with more or less of taste and comfort. In John 13: 4, 12, there appear to have been several garments; for Jesus would not lay aside the inmost garment. But the outer and inner garment here mentioned were commonly all, and the outer one was frequently used by the poor and travelers as a covering at night—just as shawls are used by travelers now. So the law of Moses provided (Ex. 22:26) that if it were taken in pawn, it should be returned before sunset. Such being the law, the Jewish tribunals would naturally allow the inner garment to be taken by judicial process rather than the outer one, and that will explain the order in which they are here mentioned. Luke (6:29) says nothing of a suit at law, but only speaks of taking away the garments, and hence mentions them in the order in which they would naturally be removed from the person, the outer garment first.—It is matter of common observation in all ages, that a man who is threatened with an unjust lawsuit will show a peculiar animosity, and if he thinks himself unjustly treated in the sentence, a peculiar rancor and revengefulness, declaring that he will yet make his adversary suffer for it. Rather than feel and act thus, our Lord says it would be better even voluntarily to give far more than the aggressor is awarded. (Comp. 1 Cor. 6:7.) How evil then must be this rancorous spirit, and how carefully should Christians avoid it.

41. Shall compel thee to go—or, *impress thee for*—**a mile.** "A" or *One*, is in the original emphatic by position. *Impress.* The Greek word was borrowed into Greek and Latin from the Persian, to denote a Persian practice continued by the Greek and Roman rulers who succeeded them in Western Asia. It strictly signified to make one a public courier (comp. Esther 8: 10, 14), and hence to make one temporarily perform a courier's work, or help a courier on his way, with horses or personal labors, etc.; and finally it was applied to coercing or compelling any public service, as the Roman soldiers compelled or impressed Simon to carry the cross. (27:32.) Such impressments were all the more odious to the Jews as being a subjugated people, suffering this harsh treatment from *foreign* rulers. During the great Maccabean struggle, one of the rival Syrian kings sought to conciliate the Jews by promising many exemptions, including this: "And I order that the beasts of burden of the Jews be not impressed" (same Greek word, Jos. "Ant.," 13, 2, 3.) Impressment, like a lawsuit, is apt to produce very angry and revengeful feelings; and so this illustration is parallel to the foregoing.

42. The word rendered **borrow** would in classical Greek naturally suggest interest, but the Jews were forbidden (Ex. 22: 25; Lev. 25: 37; Deut. 23:19) to charge interest against each other (see on 25: 27). Readiness to lend was strongly urged in Deut. 15: 7-11, and the idea repeated by subsequent inspired writers, as in Psa. 37: 26; 112: 5. *Henry:* "Lending is sometimes as great a piece of charity as giving, as it not only relieves the present exigence, but obliges the borrower to providence, industry, and honesty." We are here required to give, and to lend, not merely where it is pleasant to do so, but where it is unpleasant, the latter being the idea apparently suggested by the connection with what precedes. But that the injunction is not intended to be absolute and without exception, is shown by the case of God himself, who promises, in terms as unlimited as these, to give whatever we ask in the name of Jesus, and yet actually does give

43 Ye have heard that it hath been said, Thou shalt love thy neighbour, and hate thine enemy.
44 But I say say unto you, Love your enemies, bless them that curse you, do good to them that hate you, and pray for them which despitefully use you and persecute you;

43 Ye have heard that it was said, Thou shalt love
44 thy neighbour, and hate thine enemy: but I say unto you, Love your enemies, and pray for them

---

only when he sees it to be proper. To give to those who "ask amiss" (James 4: 3) would be no real kindness to them—nor in us. As in v. 45 and elsewhere, God's example explains the meaning of his precepts.

43. Here begins the fifth and last example (see on v. 21), viz., LOVE OF ENEMIES. This is closely related to the preceding. (v. 38-42.) *Stier:* "As this is to close the distinctive reference to the commandments, it is not one of the individual commandments of the Decalogue which is introduced, as the first quotations had been; but the epitome of the whole second table, as Moses had already specified it, viz., the law of *love*, of that one central disposition of mind, which should evidence itself in every good word and work."

That it hath been said. See on v. 21. **Thou shalt love thy neighbor,** is from Lev. 19: 18. But the Jewish teachers, with their customary efforts to explain away the rigorous requirements of the law (comp. the case of oaths, v. 33 ff.), here insisted upon a strict and limited sense of the term 'neighbor.' The lawyer who came to Jesus (Luke 10: 25 ff.), made it all turn upon this: I am to love my neighbor, but who is my neighbor? Our Lord's answer there shows, as he teaches here, that in the sense of the law even an enemy is our neighbor. But the Jewish teachers held that an enemy was not a neighbor, and that the command to love the latter implied permission to withhold it from the former. So as they publicly repeated and expounded the law, they would make the addition, "Thou shalt love thy neighbor—and hate thine enemy." This they would perhaps seek to justify by pointing to the severe treatment of the Canaanites which God enjoined upon Israel; but that was an exceptional case. The commandment to love the neighbor was extended in Lev. 19: 33, 34 to strangers, yet that meant strangers sojourning in Israel.—With such teachings prevalent as Jesus here describes, we can understand how the Jews came to be charged by Tacitus with "hatred to the human race." (See further on 22: 39.)

44. But I say. See on v. 21. The clauses

omitted from this verse in Rev. Ver. are wanting in the earliest manuscripts and versions, and were manifestly borrowed in later copies from Luke 6: 27 ff. They are a real part of the discourse, but not of Matthew's report of it.—This injunction finds no real parallel among the teachings of heathen sages. Those alleged have been misunderstood or over-stated. The Emperor Julian (the "apostate"), while borrowing the idea from the gospel he rejected, felt that it would sound strange to his heathen readers, for he says in one of his writings: "I would affirm, even though it be a strange thing to say, that even to one's enemies it would be right to give clothing and food."—Some urge that the Old and the New Testaments are in conflict on this point, appealing, for example, to the imprecations and expressions of hate which are found in the Psalms. But the example of God himself shows that an abhorrence of confirmed wickedness and a desire for its punishment may co-exist with pitying love and persevering kindness; and difficult as it may be for man to cherish both feelings at once, it is not more difficult than some other duties. And the Old Test. repeatedly teaches to show kindness to an enemy, as in Ex. 23: 4 f.; Lev. 19: 18; Prov. 24: 17, 29; 25: 21 f.; (comp. Rom. 12: 20); Job 31: 29; Psa. 7: 4; 1 Sam. 24: 5, while the New Test. has passages corresponding to the imprecations in the Psalms, as when Paul comforts the Thessalonians with the thought that God will terribly punish their persecutors (2 Thess. 1: 6-10), or when the martyred souls under the altar cry (Rev. 6: 10, Rev. Ver.), "How long, O Master, the holy and true, dost thou not judge and avenge our blood on them that dwell on the earth?" (See also 1 Cor. 16: 22; 2 Tim. 4: 14; Luke 18: 7.) The difference is therefore of kind, and not of degree; the law speaks more of severity, the gospel more of kindness, though neither wholly lacks that which is most prominent in the other. (Comp. on 5: 4.) Still it is notably characteristic of the gospel that it enjoins not simply justice, but love.

45 That ye may be the children of your Father which is in heaven: for he maketh his sun to rise on the evil and on the good, and sendeth rain on the just and on the unjust.
46 For if ye love them which love you, what reward have ye? do not even the publicans the same?

45 that persecute you; that ye may be sons of your Father who is in heaven: for he maketh his sun to rise on the evil and the good, and sendeth rain on the
46 just and the unjust. For if ye love them that love you, what reward have ye? do not even the [1] publi-

[1] That is, *collectors or renters of Roman taxes:* and so elsewhere.

45. His sun, reminding us by the way that God possesses and controls the sun. We commonly say "it rains," etc., but Jesus here refers the agencies of nature directly to God.[1] **Sendeth rain**—literally—*and rains.* Sunshine and rain are naturally chosen as among the chief providential blessings. (Comp. Acts 14: 17.)—One element and proof of sonship is resemblance, as it is said (Eph. 5:1), 'Be ye therefore followers (*imitators*) of God, as dear children,' and we are urged to love our enemies and treat them kindly, in order that we may be acting like our Heavenly Father, for he loves his enemies, and sends natural blessings upon them as well as upon his friends. Comp. Luke 6: 35, 'for he is kind toward the unthankful and evil.'—The same idea is presented by *Seneca :* "If you imitate the gods, give benefits even to the ungrateful; for even to abandoned wretches the sun arises, and to pirates the seas lie open." *Sirach :* "Be to orphans as a father, and instead of a husband to their mother; and thou shalt be as a son of the Highest, and thy mother shall love thee more and more." *The Talmud :* "A thousand thousand, and myriads are bound to praise thy name for every drop of rain thou sendest down upon us, because thou renderest good to the wicked."—But the love of God to his enemies is not the same as to his friends, the one being a love of compassion and benevolence, the other a love of complacency; he bestows benefits upon the wicked, he delights in the good. And in like manner we are not bidden to take admiring delight in our enemies, but to cherish no revengeful and malignant feeling towards them, and to do anything we can for their welfare— that is, of course, when it would not aid in the accomplishment of their evil designs against us. This is not inconsistent with restraining and even punishing them; for God does so with his enemies.
46. Two other reasons for loving our enemies. (1) Otherwise **what reward have ye ?**

It is implied that if we love our enemies, we have a religious reward (comp. v. 12 and 6: 1; and Luke 6: 32, 35). The Scriptures do not leave men to the mere unaided sense of duty as a motive to do right, but appeal also to their hopes and fears. Thus Moses (Heb. 11: 26, Rev. Ver.), 'looked unto the recompense of reward,' and even Jesus (Heb. 12: 2), 'for the joy that was set before him endured the cross, despising the shame.' (Comp. on 5: 29.) To say that this "vitiates morality" is to propose a philosophy of human conduct at variance with human nature. (2) **Even the publicans.** It is important to understand the odium which attached among the Jews to the office of publican. The Romans farmed out the privilege of collecting taxes, as is now done in some Oriental countries. The right to collect a particular kind or kinds of revenue in a particular province was sold at Rome to some individual or joint-stock company of the better class of citizens (*equites*), who were hence called "publicans," or collectors of the *public* revenue. These parties sent out agents who employed as subordinates either Roman citizens of the lower class, or natives of the province. The subordinates were not in Roman usage called *publicani*, but *portitores.* Yet as the same Greek word is applied to both, the Latin versions called both classes publicans, and we do likewise. The tax-gatherers we meet in the Gospel history are doubtless all of the subordinate class, even Zaccheus being probably a chief of the *portitores.* (Luke 19: 2.) Tax-collectors are in all countries apt to be unpopular, and these men were especially so among the Jews. They constantly reminded the people of their subjugation to the Romans, and a proud people, whose history told of David and Solomon and the Maccabees, could never think of this without mortification. They often practiced extortion (Luke 3: 13; 19: 8), encouraged thereto by the fact that their employers paid the government a fixed sum, and had all they could get. No native would take

[1] See Matt. 6: 26, 30, and in Gen. 2: 5; Job 36: 27; 37: 6 ff.; Psa. 104: 10 ff.

47 And if ye salute your brethren only, what do ye more *than others?* do not even the publicans so?
48 Be ye therefore perfect, even as your Father which is in heaven is perfect.

47 cans the same? And if ye salute your brethren only, what do ye more *thah others?* do not even the Gen-
48 tiles the same? Ye therefore shall be perfect, as your heavenly Father is perfect.

---

such an office if he cared much for public opinion, and those who did so were usually renegades, or very lax as to observance of the law. Accordingly, while the *publicani* at Rome, who really served the State, and sometimes advanced large sums to relieve the public finances, are highly commended by Cicero and others, we find that in all the provinces the subordinates were hated and shunned, and particularly in Palestine. The Jews classed them with heathen (v. 47 and 18: 17) and with harlots (21: 31), and one of the reproaches cast on Jesus was that he was a 'friend of publicans and sinners.' (11: 19.) Matthew was himself a publican (9: 9; 10: 3), though he may have been a man of better character than was usual among them. Matthew heard this discourse, yet Jesus did not on that account use softened expressions about the class to which he had belonged. The later Jewish writers class them with robbers and murderers, and affirm that they were not allowed to give testimony, and were excluded from the synagogues. — Our Lord is thus declaring that to love those who love us proves no higher grade of morality than that occupied by the most despised, by publicans and by heathen. (v. 47.) Luke (6: 32f.) uses the more general term, 'sinners.' In loving his friends a man may in a certain sense be loving only himself—a kind of expanded selfishness.

47. This repeats, in another form, the thought of the preceding sentence, such amplification being common in Scripture (see on v. 30), and being very effective in popular discourse. **Publicans** — rather, *Gentiles;* the reading of the earliest Greek manuscripts and versions would easily be changed to 'publicans,' to correspond with v. 46. The Jews regarded other nations with dislike and contempt, and so 'the nations' would sometimes be a term of contempt, which in English we express by 'Gentiles.' When Christianity became prevalent in the Roman Empire, the old Roman religion still survived in many remote country districts (*pagi, pagani*), and so its supporters were called 'pagans,' or in English 'heathen' (living in the heath or uncultivated country). Accordingly the same Greek word is translated 'nations' in 21: 43;

24: 7, 9, 14; 25: 32; 28: 19; and 'Gentiles' in 4: 15; 5: 47, Rev. Ver.; 6: 32; 10: 5, 18; 12: 18, 21; 20: 19, 25. A derivative was rendered in all the early English versions by 'heathen' in 6: 7; 18: 17, which gives the Christian point of view, but the Rev. Ver. restores the Jewish stand-point by rendering 'Gentiles.' (It does the same in Acts 4: 25; 2 Cor. 11: 26; Gal. 1: 16; 2: 9; 3: 8.)—To **salute** a person is a stronger mark of kind feelings according to Oriental manners than among us, their salutations being usually elaborate, and therefore given only to express high respect. Jews did not generally salute Gentiles, and Mohammedans as a rule do not salute Christians; and the Apostle John (2 John 10 f.) forbids not only hospitality but 'greeting' (same word as in James 1: 1; Acts 15: 23) to teachers of those antichristian and grossly immoral notions which prevailed. To express the importance of 'salute' in this verse, Tyndale and Geneva give a sort of paraphrase, 'if ye be friendly to your brethren only,' and Great Bible, 'if ye make much of,' etc.—Luke (6. 34 f.) here gives some other expressions which still further amplify the thoughts expressed in this and the two preceding verses. It is not difficult to understand that each Evangelist has given only a part of what was spoken.

48. Be ye perfect. *Ye shall be* (so Tyndale, Great Bible, Geneva, and Rev. Ver.), a literal translation of the Greek Future, which is in such a case substantially equivalent to an imperative. The form of expression may carry an allusion to Deut. 18: 13. **Ye** is emphatic, meaning Christ's disciples as contrasted with publicans and Gentiles. **Therefore,** presents this as a conclusion from what precedes: since you ought to be at a higher point of morality than publicans and Gentiles, and ought to be like your Father in heaven (comp. v. 45), therefore you shall be perfect, etc. **Father which is in heaven.** The reading *Heavenly Father* of many early manuscripts and versions, was easily changed to the more common 'Father which is in heaven' of v. 45; 6: 9, 14. The term rendered **perfect** is used in a variety of connections, and its precise meaning must always be determined by the particular connection. Sometimes it is simply 'complete,' without any moral element, Heb. 9: 11, and perhaps James 1: 17. In other cases it means complete in growth of body or mind, 'full-grown.' (1 Cor. 14: 20; Eph. 4: 13; Heb. 5: 14; 6: 1; 1 Cor. 2: 6.) In yet others, complete morally, as Matt. 19: 21; Col. 1: 28; 4: 12; James 1: 4, 25; 3: 2. And there are passages in which it seems to mean complete in both knowledge and moral excellence, as Phil. 3: 15, and perhaps 1 Cor. 13: 10. *Here*, it is moral perfection in general, but with specific reference to *love — i. e.*, not loving friends only, which would be an imperfect love, but loving enemies also, as our Heavenly Father does. Luke (6: 36) gives only this specific thought, 'merciful.' But it does not seem proper to *restrict* Matthew's general term to this thought alone. In all things, love included, we ought to be perfect, even as our Heavenly Father is—to be like him, and so prove ourselves to be his children. Our own minds demand a perfect standard, such as the divine nature presents; and however far we may actually fall short of attaining it, yet he who is *content* with coming short gives no evidence that he is a child of God.

Thus ends the series of striking particulars (v. 21-48) in which our Lord compares his teachings with the law and the current explanations of it, so as to show that far from designing to relax the obligations of morality, its requirements were still more stringent, extending, not merely to the outward act, but to the motive and feeling; not merely to what the letter of the law required, but to all that it designed and involved. (See on v. 17.) As this portion of the Sermon on the Mount has especial reference to Jewish ideas, Luke, who wrote not for Jews in particular (as Matthew did), but for general circulation, has given no report of it, except of what was said on the subject of love to enemies, and this he introduces as general instruction, without any allusion to the Jewish misinterpretations of the law and mistaken expectations, which with his design would have been out of place.

HOMILETICAL AND PRACTICAL.

V. 38–41. Four kinds of Retaliation. (1) Natural passion says, Requite the like, and worse. (2) The law of Moses says, Let the judge requite precisely the like. (3) Christ says, Do not (revengefully) requite the like at all—better receive the like a second time. (4) The apostle Peter says (1 Pet. 3: 9), "Not rendering evil for evil, but contrariwise blessing." This is the Christian retaliation.—Self-defense, and punishment in ways regulated by law, are not forbidden in forbidding hate and revenge. But do not "take the law in your own hands," and do not press the execution of the law in a revengeful spirit. CHRYS.: "Nothing so restrains the wrong-doers, as when the injured bear what is done with gentleness. And it not only restrains them from rushing onward, but works upon them also to repent for what has gone before, and, in wonder at such forbearance, to draw back. And it makes them more our own, and causes them to be slaves—not merely friends—instead of haters and enemies. Even as avenging oneself does just the contrary; for it disgraces each of the two, and makes them worse, and their anger it brightens into a greater flame; yea, often no less than death itself is the end of it, going on from bad to worse." STIER: "That heathenish law of honor, which will not accept the very slightest indignity, but even in the midst of modern Christendom demands the duel itself. To this 'point of honor' stands opposed the patient acceptance and endurance of insult, as the genuine Christian courage and knightly honor. Offer him the other also—that is, in thy heart, and in the disposition of thy mind; calmly and patiently wait if he may strike thee another blow, and be ready to receive that also—so far let thy spirit be from opposing. . . . . The actual turning of the other cheek might be no other than a challenge to continued sin, consequently itself sinful, and opposed to the love of our neighbor. There might even be a proud despite in it, or a mere hypocritical affectation." DYKES: "By general consent, a blow on the face is the extreme of personal insults. . . . . But the spirit of our Lord's words is not open to the suspicion of being a craven spirit. It is this suspicion, more, I fancy, than any thing else, which is apt to discredit the teaching of this text with generous men. Yet here, as always, it is sin, not love, that is the real coward. He who best obeys the rule of Jesus will be the bravest man. To curb temper; to govern the spirit

CHAPTER VI.

TAKE heed that ye do not your alms[a] before men, to be seen of them: otherwise ye have no reward of[b] your Father which is in heaven.

1 Take heed that ye do not your righteousness before men, to be seen of them: else ye have no reward with your Father who is in heaven.

a Or, righteousness....b Or, with.

of revenge, even under insult; to place what is better than life, personal honor, under the control of a love which is patient and just because it is strong—stronger than passion: this is true valor and true honor."

V. 42. Our duty to Beggars. I. *Counsels.* (1) We must not refuse all because many are impostors. (2) We should strive to ascertain who are really needy and deserving, and to inform others. (3) We must not turn beggars away simply because offensive or annoying—this would be a very petty selfishness. (4) Where there is public provision for beggars we should act in harmony with such arrangements, but cannot remit the matter wholly to them. (5) To open some means of supporting themselves is far better than to support them. II. *Motives.* (1) Humanity—they have the same nature as ourselves, essentially the same sensitive feelings, pains and pleasures, memories and hopes and destiny. (2) Piety. Grateful love to God. We are beggars, to whom he gives liberally, and we must return to him by giving to our fellowmen.—Borrowing and Lending. It is more blessed to lend than to borrow. Cautions as to borrowing—encouragements to lend. Comp. Luke 6: 35.

V. 44. CYRIL: "Let us love our enemies, not as adulterers or murderers, but as men."—CHRYS.: "Have you seen what steps he has ascended, and how he has placed us on the very summit of virtue? Look at the succession from the beginning. The first step is, not to begin injuring; the second, after injury has been begun, not to defend yourself against the injurer by like actions; the third, not to inflict on the wrong-doer that which one has suffered, but to keep quiet; the fourth, even to yield oneself to suffer evil; the fifth, to yield even more than he who did the evil wishes; the sixth, not to hate him who does these things; the seventh, even to love him; the eighth, even to do him good; the ninth, even to pray to God for him. Have you seen the height of Christian philosophy?"—Love your enemies. I. *How?* (1) Do not love

what is wrong in them, but love them notwithstanding the wrong. (2) Love them in the same way that God loves his enemies. II. *Why?* (1) Because fellow-men ('neighbors'), although enemies. (2) In order to be like God, his children. JEROME: "Many say that to love enemies is too much for human nature; but David did this to Saul and Absalom; Stephen prayed for the enemies that were stoning him; Jesus both taught and did it. 'Father, forgive them.'"—HENRY: "It was said of Archbishop Cranmer, that the way to make him a friend was to do him an ill turn; so many did he serve who had disobliged him."

V. 45. Natural blessings, as sunshine and rain. The modern phrase is that they are caused by the "laws of nature." They are caused by natural *forces*, which we perceive to act regularly, and these regular modes of acting we call laws. But who appointed the laws? Who created the forces, and made them such as to act in these regular ways? The Scriptures represent the Creator as working in the forces he has created and controls. —Sonship to God. (1) Shown by moral likeness to him. (2) In particular, by kindness to our fellow-men, even to enemies.—V. 46 f. Natural kindness and Christian kindness. Christians ought assuredly to be better than men in general. V. 48. Imitating. (1) Do not imitate the publicans and the Gentiles. (2) Imitate your Heavenly Father.—Perfection. (1) We should *wish* to be perfect—and pained with our imperfections. (2) We should *try* to be perfect—not disheartened by past failures. (3) We may *hope* to be perfect—as we pass into the perfect world.

Ch. 6: 1-4. GOOD WORKS WITHOUT OSTENTATION. I. ALMS-GIVING.

Since 5: 17 (see Analysis at beginning of ch. 5), our Lord has been showing that he requires in the subjects of the Messianic reign, a higher and more spiritual morality than that which was taught and practiced by the Scribes and Pharisees. This is continued in

2 Therefore *a* when thou doest *thine* alms, do not sound a trumpet before thee, as the hypocrites do in the synagogues and in the streets, that they may have glory of men. Verily I say unto you, They have their reward.
3 But when thou doest alms, let not thy left hand know what thy right hand doeth :
4 That thine alms may be in secret: and thy Father which seeth in secret himself shall reward thee openly.

2   When therefore thou doest alms, sound not a trumpet before thee, as the hypocrites do in the synagogues and in the streets, that they may have glory of men. Verily I say unto you, They have received their reward. But when thou doest alms, let not thy left hand know what thy right hand 4 doeth : that thine alms may be in secret : and thy Father who seeth in secret shall recompense thee.

a Or, cause not a trumpet to be sounded.

6: 1–18; and as 5: 20 introduced the first main section, (5: 20-48), so v. 1 introduces the second. (6: 1-18.) In 5: 20 it is said that their righteousness must exceed the Scribes and Pharisees; accordingly (Weiss, Lutteroth) 5: 20–48 gives examples from the teachings of the Scribes, and 6: 1–18 from the practice of the Pharisees. The general principle of verse 1 is illustrated by applying it to three exercises highly valued among the Jews (commended together in Tobit 12: 8), viz., almsgiving (v. 2-4), prayer (5-15), and fasting. (16-18.) Each of these, he says, should be performed, not with a view to human approbation and reward, but to that of God. *Calvin :* " A very necessary admonition ; for in all virtues the entrance of ambition is to be avoided, and there is no work so laudable as not to be in many instances corrupted and polluted by it."

1. Your righteousness,[1] *i. e.*, righteous actions or good deeds (as in 5: 6, 10, 20), including such as alms-giving, prayer, and fasting.[2] To **do** *righteousness* is a phrase of frequent occurrence, as in Psa. 106: 3; Isa. 58: 2; 1 John 2: 29; 3: 7, 10. **To be seen of them.** More fully rendered, ' with a view to be looked at (or gazed at) by them' ; the Greek construction is the same as in 5: 28; 23: 5, conveying distinctly the idea of purpose, design ; and the Greek verb is a strong word (the root from which comes *theatre*), and suggests the being gazed at as a spectacle. So ' hypocrite' is originally ' actor,' one who plays a part. This meaning of ' to

be seen,' is very strongly brought out by Tyndale, Great Bible, and Geneva, ' to the intent that,' etc. ; and for ' seen' Geneva says, ' looked at.' What our Lord forbids is therefore not publicity in performing good deeds, which is often necessary and therefore proper, but ostentatious publicity, *for the purpose* of attracting attention and gaining applause. This obviously does not conflict with 5: 16, where the object to be had in view is that God may be glorified, not ourselves. (See on that passage.) **No reward of**—or, *with* (comp. margin of Com. Ver.), as if laid up in God's presence for you. Comp. 5: 12, 46; 1 Pet. 1: 4.--The Greek and Roman philosophers and the Jewish writers have many maxims upon the importance of being unostentatious in virtue, especially in deeds of benevolence. A desire for the approbation of our fellowmen is not in itself wrong, and not incompatible with piety, but it should be completely subordinated to the desire that God may approve us, and that he may be glorified in us. This entire subordination is manifestly very difficult, and hence many think it easier to denounce ambition altogether, forgetting that ambition is an original principle of our nature, to destroy which would be as injurious as it is impossible. But while not inherently sinful, ambition, like anger (see on 5: 22), is exceedingly apt to become sinful, and hence the solemn warning here given.

2-4. The first of the three subjects to which our Lord applies the great principle of v. 1 is

---

[1] This (comp. Com. Ver. margin) is the reading of the three oldest uncials that contain the passage (B. א D.), of the Latin versions (nearly all copies) and Latin Fathers, and is adopted by Lach., Tisch., Treg., W H. It might easily be altered to the word meaning ' alms,' partly because that is the subject of v. 2-4, and many did not see that v. 1 presented a distinct general precept, and partly because the later Jews often used 'righteousness' as meaning alms, that being in their view the foremost righteousness. (Comp. our modern employment of ' charity' to denote simply alms-giving.) This use is seen in the Talmud, and in the frequent translations of the Hebrew word for righteousness by

' alms' in the Sept., but is not found in N. T., nor in the Hebrew O. T. ; for Gesenius' examples, Prov. 10: 2; 11: 4; Psa. 24: 5; Micah 6: 5, do not at all require or justify such a sense. But this notion of righteousness as alms, spreading among Christians, might cause ' alms' to be written in the margin of v. 1 as explaining the supposed meaning of righteousness, and then its substitution by copyists. Notice that the Oriental versions generally read alms, as the usage just mentioned would be readily adopted in an Oriental language.
[2] Several early MSS. and versions insert *de*, ' But take heed,' etc., which is adopted by Tisch., and given in brackets by W H. The question of its genuineness is

Alms-giving. (v. 2-4.) **Therefore** presents what follows as an inference from what precedes, the specific precept inferred from the general. **Thou,** see on 5 : 23 ; 6 : 5. **When thou doest,** appears to take for granted that they will do so, as likewise in v. 5 and 16. The English word 'alms' is an abridged form of the Greek word here used, *eleemosune* (comp. our adjective eleemosynary), gradually reduced to German almosen, Wyclif's alm-esse, Scotch awmous, our alms (ams). **Sound a trumpet,** is by the Greek commentators and nearly all recent writers understood as merely a figurative expression, common to many languages, for parade and effort to attract notice and applause. There is no authority for the conjecture of Calvin (mentioned as early as Euthymius) and some others (including Stier), that it was a practice among the Jews for an ostentatious alms-giver literally to sound a trumpet before him in public places to summon the needy (sounding it through another person, see margin of Com. Ver.). Lightf. sought long and earnestly for evidence of such a practice, but found none; and it is very improbable that such a thing would have been permitted 'in the synagogues.' We see much benevolence at the present day so ostentatious that the giver might very naturally be figuratively described as sounding a trumpet before him. The notion of Edersheim, "The Temple," p. 26, that the expression refers to trumpet-shaped contribution-boxes, in the temple treasury, appears extremely far-fetched and fanciful. **Hypocrites.** The word is borrowed by us from the Greek, and in classic use signified an actor, who wore a mask and played a part. This well illustrates, as it naturally led to, the sense in which the word is so often used in Scripture. As to **synagogues,** see on 4 : 23. **That they may have glory,** or, *be glorified of men,* in contrast to seeking the glory which God gives. (Comp. John 5 : 44.) **Verily I say unto you,** see on 5 : 18. **They have,** or, *have received.* So Vulgate, Wyclif; and so Com. Ver. translates the same word in Luke

6 : 24. The Greek verb is a compound, signifying to have entirely, have the whole of, have in full. The idea is that in being gazed at and glorified by men they have all the reward they will ever obtain, for they must fail of the reward mentioned in v. 1. (Comp. Psa. 17 : 14.) See the same word below in v. 5, 16. **But when thou doest alms,** the position of the words making 'thou' emphatic, in contrast to the hypocrites. **Let not thy left hand,** etc. Here, as in v. 2, we have a figurative expression. It suggests the pleasing and striking image of a man passing one who is in need, and with his right hand giving alms in so quiet a way that, so to speak, even his own left hand does not know what is going on. **That,** in v. 4, is not ' so that' but ' in order that,' expressing not simply the result, but the purpose; just as in v. 2, in 5 : 15, etc. Of course this does not require that all benevolence shall be literally secret, but that no benevolence shall be ostentatious (see on v. 1). So far from trumpeting your alms-giving before the public, do not even let it be known to yourself. **Which seeth in secret,** not exactly who sees what is done in secret, but who is present in secret and sees there. Comp. v. 6, 18, ' which is in secret.' *Calvin:* " He silently glances at a kind of folly which prevails everywhere among men, that they think they have lost their pains if there have not been many spectators of their virtues." **Reward,** *recompense,* or, *repay,* is the word explained on 5 : 33,[1] and different from the noun rendered ' reward' in v. 1 f. We are not told when or how the recompense will be given, and may understand that it will be both in time and in eternity, both in character and in felicity.

The Jews held alms-giving in the highest estimation. Thus Tobit, 12 : 8, says, "It is good to do alms rather than to treasure up gold. For alms delivers from death [a misinterpretation of Prov. 10 : 2; 11 : 4], and this will purge away every sin." Comp. Sirach 29 : 11 ff. The Talmud says that alms-giving is "more excellent than all offerings,"

---

hard to decide. If adopted, it would seem to imply the expectation that 5 : 20 and 48 would stir in the persons addressed a desire to be righteous, and so they would need the caution, "But take care," etc.

[1] 'Himself' and 'openly' are omitted by the earliest manuscripts and most of the early versions. We can

see how they may have been written on the margin, to bring out the implied contrast, and then supposed to be part of the text because quite appropriate; while if present originally, we cannot imagine why any one should have wished to omit them. So they must be rejected without hesitation.

is "equal to the whole law," will "deliver from the condemnation of hell," and makes a man "perfectly righteous." In the Talmud of Babylon, Psa. 17 : 15, is explained to mean, "I shall behold thy face on account of alms" [properly, 'in righteousness'], and the inference is drawn that "on account of one farthing given to the poor in alms, a man becomes partaker of the beatific vision." Maimonides particularizes eight degrees of alms-giving, the merit being graded according to the circumstances. In like manner the Roman Catholics attach great value to gifts and other kindnesses to the poor, believing that they atone for sins. Holding the books of Tobit and Sirach to be canonical, they find in them proof-texts for this doctrine. Add to the above Sirach 3: 30, "alms will atone for sins." In this, as in various other cases, there is reason to fear that Protestants, by a natural reaction from Romish error, fail to value an important Christian duty as they should do. See Prov. 19: 17, also the cup of cold water (Matt. 10: 42), the judgment scenes (25: 35 ff.), also 2 Cor. 9: 6 ff.; Phil. 4: 18 f.; 1 Tim. 6: 19; James 1: 27. That is a good saying of a Roman poet, "It is only the riches you give that you will always have." And see Tobit 4: 7 ff.

Some of the Jewish writers also enjoin secrecy in alms-giving. Talmud: "He that does alms in secret is greater than Moses." A Mohammedan proverb says: "Hast thou done a good deed, cast it into the sea; if the fish find it not, yet will God see it." And among the traditional sayings of Mohammed, we find, "In alms-giving, the left hand should not know what the right has given"—one of the numerous instances in which Mohammed borrowed from the Scriptures, not only the Old but also the New Testament.

HOMILETICAL AND PRACTICAL.

V. 1. VINET (in Lutteroth): "To be perfect (5: 48), it is absolutely necessary to seek the notice and aim at the approval of a perfect being." CHRYS.: "It may be, both that one doing alms [he had the wrong text] before men may not do it to be seen of them, and again that one not doing it before men may do it to be seen of them . . . . . He (Christ) defines both the penalty and reward not by the result of the action, but by the intention of the doer.—V. 1 and 5: 16. Good Works in Public. 1) Wrong motive, that men may honor us. 2) Right motive, that men may glorify God.—BOARDMAN : "Distinguish between doing right in order to help others, as when one lights a beacon in order to guide the sailor, and doing right in order to be praised by others, as when one stands in full blaze of a chandelier in order to display his own jewelry." DYKES : "The actions of piety, like its tones or its gaits, are so imitable, and the imitation is so hard of detection, that they become the invariable livery of the hypocrite. For the same reason, they seduce those who are not yet hypocrites into becoming so. When a man would increase or preserve a reputation for piety which he has once honestly enough obtained, it is fatally easy to perform pious acts, with this end in view, a little oftener or a little more ostentatiously than he would do were he only careful about serving God."

V. 2-4. Two ways of doing good, and two kinds of reward.—What is the hypocrite's reward? Praise from some of his fellow-men, with the consciousness that he does not deserve it, a perpetual dread lest they find him out, and frequent fears of that coming time when the secrets of all hearts shall be revealed.—It is not necessarily wrong to employ example and emulation in persuading men to give. (2 Cor. 8 and 9.)—Hypocrisy. 1) Its nature. 2) Its unwilling tribute to true piety —as counterfeit coin is abundant because genuine coin is so valuable. 3) Its reward. (a) the reward it may gain, (b) the reward it must miss. ROCHEFOUCAULD : "Hypocrisy is a sort of homage that vice pays to virtue." HENRY : "The hypocrite catches at the shadow, but the upright man makes sure of the substance." · ECCE HOMO : "But there are subtler forms of hypocrisy, which Christ does not denounce, probably because they have sprung since out of the corruption of a subtler creed . . . . They would practice assiduously the rules by which Christ said heaven was to be won. They would patiently turn the left cheek, indefatigably walk the two miles, they would bless with effusion those who cursed them, and pray fluently for those who used them spitefully. To love their enemies, to love any one, they would certainly find impossible, but the outward signs of love might easily be learnt. And thus there would arise

5 And when thou prayest, thou shalt not be as the hypocrites *are :* for they love to pray standing in the synagogues and in the corners of the streets, that they may be seen of men. Verily I say unto you, They have their reward.

6 But thou, when thou prayest, enter into thy closet, and when thou hast shut thy door, pray to thy Father which is in secret; and thy Father which seeth in secret shall reward thee openly.

7 But when ye pray, use not vain repetitions, as the

5 And when ye pray, ye shall not be as the hypocrites: for they love to stand and pray in the synagogues and in the corners of the streets, that they may be seen of men. Verily I say unto you, They have received their reward. But thou, when thou prayest, enter into thine inner chamber, and having shut thy door, pray to thy Father who is in secret, and thy Father who seeth in secret shall recompense thee. And in praying use not vain repetitions, as

---

a new class of actors, not like those whom Christ denounced . . . . . hoping to impose by their dramatic talent upon their Father in heaven." LUTHER: "If we cease our charitable deeds because men are ungrateful, that shows that we were not aiming to please and honor God."

5-15. GOOD WORKS WITHOUT OSTENTATION. II. PRAYER.

5. The general principle of v. 1, that good works must not be performed ostentatiously, is now applied to a second example (compare on v. 2). **And when thou prayest.** The correct text is, *and when ye pray.* It was early changed in some copies into "thou prayest," to agree with the singular verbs which precede. But throughout this passage (v. 1-18) the plural is used in the general injunctions (v. 1, 5, 16), and the singular in the pointed personal applications, (v. 2-4, 6, 17, 18). Compare on 5: 23. **Hypocrites,** comp. on v. 2. **Synagogues,** see on 4: 23. Some would take the word here in its etymological sense, as denoting "gatherings" anywhere, but there is no propriety in departing from the usual meaning. It was not wrong to pray in the synagogues, which was a common usage; but these hypocrites prayed there rather than in secret, and did so for the purpose of display. **In the corners of the streets,** they could be seen from four directions, and thus would be delightfully conspicuous. The word for "streets" is different from that of v. 3, and denotes broad, spacious streets. **To pray standing.** Three postures in prayer are mentioned in Scripture; *standing* (1 Sam. 1: 26; Mark 11 : 23; Luke 18: 11, 13), *kneeling* (2 Chron. 6: 13; Dan. 6: 10; Luke 22: 41 ; Acts 7: 60; 9: 40; 20: 36; 21: 5); and in cases of peculiar awe or distress, *prostration on the face.* (Num. 16: 22; Josh. 5: 14; Dan. 8: 17; Matt. 26: 39; Rev. 11: 16.) Standing being therefore a common posture, it is plain that this formed no part of the display, which consisted in choosing the most public places to parade their devotions. The Talmud of Babylon says that persons would sometimes stand three

hours in a public place and a praying posture (Lightf.). The excuse for such parade of devotion was found in the idea that when the hour of prayer arrived, one must pray wherever he was; so with the Mohammedans now, who may often be seen praying in the most public places. The practice of indolently sitting during prayer finds no support either in Scripture precedent (unless 2 Sam. 7: 18 be claimed as such), in the natural feeling of propriety, or in devout experience.

Verily I say unto you, see on 5: 18. **They have,** *have received*—"have in full." See on v. 26.

6. But thou, changing again to the singular number for pointed personal application (see on 5: 23). The word rendered **closet** signifies originally a store-room, and then any private or retired room. Rev. Ver., "inner chamber." It is frequently applied in the Septuagint to a bed-chamber; comp. Isa. 26: 20, "Come, my people, enter thou into thy chambers, and shut thy doors about thee: hide thyself as it were for a little moment, until the indignation be overpast." Compare also Matt. 24: 26; Luke 12: 3. The notion that our Lord designs to refer to a particular room on the top of a Jewish house, or over the main entrance of the building, is unwarranted, and unnecessarily restricts the meaning of the passage. The inner chamber may in fact often be best found in the solitude of nature, as Jesus frequently did. (Mark 1: 35; 6: 46; 14: 32.) **Shut thy door,** the word denoting that it is not only closed, but fastened, thus giving the idea of the most complete privacy. (Comp. 2 Kings 4: 33.) **In secret** our Father is present, in secret he sees, and though men will not recompense, he will. Comp. Prov. 15: 3. (**Openly** is a spurious addition, as in v. 4.)

7 f. Slightly digressing in a very natural way from the precise line of thought in v. 1-18, and resuming the plural of general address, our Lord here appends a censure of another and kindred fault in prayer, in the injunction, **use not vain repetitions.** The heathen *do :* for they think that they shall be heard for their much speaking.

8 Be not ye therefore like unto them: for your Father knoweth what things ye have need of, before ye ask him.

the Gentiles do: for they think that they shall be 8 heard for their much speaking. Be not therefore like unto them: for [1] your Father knoweth what

---

1 Some ancient authorities read, *God your Father.*

Greek has a rare word formed so that its sound shall resemble the sense (onomatopoeia), and used to express stuttering, the indistinct speech of little children, or any confused babble. This well represents the practice common in the public worship of some of the heathen, as when the priests of Baal continued from morning until noon to cry: "O Baal, hear us!" (1 Kings 18:26), and the multitude in the theatre at Ephesus for two hours shouted, "Great is Diana of the Ephesians." (Acts 19:34.) A great crowd continuing to repeat the same words, every one for himself, would make just the babbling noise which the Greek word expresses; and so would a single person, when, wearily and without interest, and as rapidly as possible, repeating the same word or phrase. Tyndale rendered "babble not much," followed by Great Bible and Geneva. The Com. Ver. rendering, "use not vain repetitions," was suggested by the commentary of Beza, whose guidance that version frequently follows. It is possible that as a stutterer often repeats the same word, the Greek word came to be used to denote idle and unmeaning repetitions in general. The idea of the heathen was that **for (in) their much speaking** they would be heard. So the Roman comic writer Terence makes one person tell another not to stun the gods with thanksgivings, "unless you judge them to have no more sense than yourself, so as to think they do not understand anything unless it has been said a hundred times." The Jews must have been inclining to the same practice, thinking that there was merit in saying over certain words of prayer many times. In Talmud Bab., R. Hanin says, "If prayer is prolonged, it will not be without effect." Another objects that it may make one sick, and a third that it may make him gloomy. Compare Mark 12: 40: "And for a pretence make long prayers." Yet Eccl. 5: 2 had pointed out the impropriety of much speaking in prayer, "Therefore let thy words be few," and the apocryphal book of Sirach (Ecclus.) (7:14) said, "Do not prattle in a multitude of elders, and do not repeat a word in thy prayer." So the Roman poet Plautus says, "Transact divine things in few words." The practice of praying a long time, as a formal observance, would naturally lead to unmeaning repetition. The Buddhist monks at the present time, will for whole days together cry aloud the sacred syllable *Um;* and some Mohammedans "turn about in a circle, and pronounce the name of God until they drop down." After a Mohammedan funeral in some countries, devout men assemble, and repeat Allah el Allah, "God is God," three thousand times. A traveler in Persia tells of a man "who prayed so loud and so long that he lost his voice, and then groaned out, in voiceless accents, the name of God fifty times." (*Tholuck.*) So in some prayers recorded in the Avesta, and in the old Egyptian writings. M. Huc tells of Buddhist students in Chinese Tartary, who will put a written prayer on a wheel, which is turned with a crank, or even by wind or water; and they believe that every revolution is a prayer, and adds to their merit. In like manner, Roman Catholics now think it very devout to repeat many times—often fifteen, and in some cases a hundred and fifty times—the Ave Maria (Hail, Mary), and the Pater Noster (Our Father, *i. e.,* the Lord's Prayer), and count the repetitions by slipping the beads of the rosary — thus employing (Tholuck) the very prayer our Saviour set in contrast to such notions and practices. This use of a rosary is a Buddhist practice, which came through the Mohammedans to the Spanish Christians. But our Father (see on v. 9) is not slow to attend, as Elijah mockingly represented Baal to be, nor unable to understand unless it is said a hundred times; he knoweth what we need, not only as soon as we ask it once, but even before we ask it. Observe, however, two things: (1) God's knowing before we ask is no reason why we should not ask. We do not pray in order to give him information, but to express our own desire, our feeling of need and dependence. Not that prayer, as many say, is designed simply to influence ourselves;

men would pray very little if they really believed that to be all. We pray, as hoping thereby to induce God to grant what we desire; and his foreknowledge and even predestination of all things is no more an objection to praying than to acting. (2) Our Saviour cannot mean that long-continued praying is in itself improper, for he himself sometimes spent a whole night in prayer (Luke 6: 12), and he spoke more than one parable to encourage perseverance in prayer; nor is it necessarily wrong to repeat the same words—a thing sometimes very natural when we are deeply in earnest — for in Gethsemane he "prayed a third time, saying again the same words." (26: 44.) The difference between these and the practice condemned is plain. Augustine justly distinguishes between much speaking in prayer, and much praying.

9. After this manner therefore pray ye, with a strong emphasis (as the Greek shows) on "ye." This injunction is presented as a consequence of what precedes. Since it is unavailing for us, and unworthy of our God, to pray as the heathen do (comp. v. 7; 5: 47), *therefore* do *ye* pray *thus.* The special (though of course not exclusive) design with which the prayer that follows is here introduced is to put in contrast with that of which he has just been speaking (v. 7) a specimen of the right kind of prayer. He thus teaches them "by example as well as by precept," to avoid the faults in question. Regarded from this point of view, we are struck with the comprehensiveness and simplicity of the prayer, truly the very opposite of "much speaking," of babbling repetitions and boisterous passion. How vast its scope, how varied its applications, how simple its language. Tertullian already observed that it is "as copious in meaning as it is condensed in expression." Yet with all this comprehensiveness, there is no propriety in gravely defending, as some do, and seeking to establish by artificial exposition, the mere rhetorical hyperbole which Tertullian adds ("On Prayer," chap. 1), that "in this prayer is comprised a compend of the whole gospel."

Substantially the same prayer is recorded in Luke 11: 2-4 as a specimen or model of prayer in general, given in response to a special request from one of the disciples. Now we know that Jesus repeated many

striking or important sayings at different times and in different connections (see General Introduction to chap. 5). There is thus no difficulty in understanding that he gave this prayer on two different occasions. They who think otherwise must either suppose that Matthew has artificially constructed this discourse out of scattered materials, or that Luke has introduced on an unreal occasion (Luke 11 : 1) what actually belonged to this discourse; and there is no sufficient ground for either supposition. Recent studies in the harmony of the Gospels (Wieseler, Clark's Harmony) make it highly probable that the occasion on which Luke gives the prayer was long after the Sermon on the Mount, during the last few months of our Lord's ministry, and away in Judea or Perea. But even if it be supposed that the prayer was given only once, it would remain true that the two Evangelists have recorded it in very different terms. Even in the common Greek Text and the Common Version, there are several different expressions; and the unquestionably correct text given in the Revised Version makes the differences quite considerable.

MATTHEW 6: 9–13.

Our Father who art in heaven,
Hallowed be thy name.
Thy kingdom come.
Thy will be done, as in heaven, so on earth.
Give us this day our daily bread.
And forgive us our debts,
As we also have forgiven our debtors.
And bring us not into temptation,
But deliver us from the evil one.

LUKE 11: 2–4.

Father,
Hallowed be thy name.
Thy kingdom come.
Give us day by day our daily bread.
And forgive us our sins;
For we ourselves also forgive every one that is
   indebted to us.
And bring us not into temptation.

If then our Lord gave the prayer on two occasions, he gave it in quite different terms, which shows, beyond all question, that it was not intended as a *form* of prayer, to be repeated in the *same words.* If, on the other hand, it be supposed that he gave the prayer only once, then the Evangelists certainly did not understand it to be a *form* of prayer, or they would not have recorded it in such different terms. There is no important difference in the *substance* of the two prayers; for the petition, "Thy will be done," etc., only brings into special prominence something that is involved in "Thy kingdom come," and the petition, "But deliver us from the evil one" only gives the other side of the foregoing, "And bring us not into temptation." There is no *material* difference in the two prayers, but there is certainly a great difference in form. It is entirely proper in praying, and indeed very desirable, to repeat any passage of Scripture that seems specially appropriate. Few passages, if any, would be so often appropriate for such a purpose as this prayer, because it is so rich and sweet, and because the Saviour expressly gave it, on both occasions, as a model of praying. But in the face of the above facts, it cannot for a moment be maintained that he has made it our duty to repeat this prayer whenever we pray, or to use these precise words from beginning to end whenever we feel moved to adopt the prayer.

The common title "The Lord's Prayer" has been in use among Christians from an early period, being found already in Cyprian, about A. D. 250, if in no earlier writer.[1] The prayer contains no allusion to the mediation of Christ, says nothing about asking in his name, for which the disciples were not yet prepared. (John 16: 23 f.) Like many other portions of Scripture, it was especially adapted to the precise times in which it was spoken, and the interpretation and applications of it must be made accordingly.

It is often asserted by modern Jews and rationalistic Christian writers that no portion of this prayer is original; for they say that all its petitions are found in the Talmud or in the liturgies now used among the Jews, and supposed by them to be ancient. Let us collect and consider the facts. They must be mainly stated at second hand; but the sources will be indicated.

"Our Father, who is in Heaven," occurs often in the Jewish liturgies. One of the Jewish prayers contains: "Let us sanctify thy name in the world, as they sanctify it in the high heavens." Among the prayers the *Kaddish* is especially valued, and has to be often recited: "Magnified and sanctified be his great name in the world which, according to his good pleasure, he created, and may he spread abroad his reign in your days; and may his redemption blossom forth, and may Messiah be at hand and deliver his people." (Wet.). And there are various other prayers that God's name may be sanctified. In the Talmud a Rabbi says: "Every prayer in which the name of God is not mentioned is no prayer." And another says: "That prayer in which the kingdom of God is not named, is no prayer." As a matter of course, the Jewish prayers often include many petitions in regard to God's kingdom, though the exact phrase, "Thy kingdom come," has not been cited, the nearest approach to it being, "Reveal the glory of thy kingdom upon us speedily." The Talmud of Bab. (Berach. f. 29 b) gives short prayers proper for time of peril, derived from several Rabbis, and among them this: "Rabbi Eliezer says, 'Do thy will in heaven above, and give place to those that fear thee below; and do what thou pleasest.'" The same treatise (f. 60 b), gives as a prayer before falling asleep: "Do not make us enter into the hand (power) of sin, nor into the hand of temptation, nor into the hand of contempt." And again (f. 16 b): "Rabbi was wont thus to pray: 'Let it be thy good pleasure to deliver us from impudent men and impudence, from an evil man and from an evil chance, from an evil affection, from an evil companion, from an evil neighbor, from Satan the destroyer, from a hard judgment, and from a hard adversary," [So Lightfoot, Wetstein, Sepp, and Wünsche, in his German translation of Talmud Bab., Vol. I., A. D. 1886. Schwab's French translation of Talmud Jerusalem has "from a corrupter," instead of "from Satan the destroyer."]

It thus appears that no parallel has been found to several important clauses of the prayer, such as "Thy will be done, as in heaven, so on earth," or the prayer for daily bread, to which nothing similar has been adduced save one of the short prayers in the Talmud, "The wants of thy people Israel are many, their thought is limited; may it please thee, O Lord our God, to give each one what he needs for nourishment, and to every crea-

---

[1] In the fourth century we find it maintained that only the baptized may repeat this prayer, some holding that the unbaptized could not properly say "Our Father," others that they could not partake of "the supersubstantial bread" in the Eucharist. (See Suicer, "Euchē.")

9 After this manner therefore pray ye: Our Father which art in heaven, Hallowed be thy name.

9 things ye have need of, before ye ask him. After this manner therefore pray ye: Our Father who art

---

ture what it lacks"—which is really no parallel at all. Nor is any parallel offered to the petition that we may be forgiven as we forgive, upon which our Lord laid special stress by repeating its thought after the close of the prayer (v. 14 f.) The nearest approach is in Ecclus. 28: 2. (See below on v. 12.)

Again, the resemblance in several cases is not very marked, as in "Thy kingdom come," "Deliver us from the evil one." The only exact parallels are to the address, "Our Father who art in heaven," and to the petitions, "Hallowed be thy name," and "Bring us not into temptation."

In all these cases of resemblance the expression is one most natural to be employed. In regard to calling God our Father, see below; and petitions as to God's name and kingdom, and as to temptations, must of course enter sometimes into Jewish prayers. What then is the amount of the charge that the prayer is not original? Some of its petitions have no parallel in Jewish literature, and others only partial parallels. And as to the resemblances, exact or partial, a little reflection shows that nothing else would have been natural. Is it reasonable to suppose that the Great Teacher would give as a model of prayer to his followers a series of petitions that were throughout such as nobody had ever thought of or felt the need of? A wise teacher links new instruction to what is already known and felt. And our Lord's ethical and devotional instructions would have been really less efficient if they had been marked by the startling originality which some have unwisely claimed for them. *Grotius:* "Our Lord was far removed from all affectation of unnecessary novelty." Those, on the other hand, who have represented this prayer as entirely wanting in originality, are refuted by the facts; for we have seen that several of the petitions are without parallel, and that the cases of resemblance are perfectly natural; while the brevity and comprehensiveness of the prayer as a whole are wonderful in the extreme. It may be added, without treating it as an important fact in the present case, that some prayers in the Jewish liturgies are unquestionably more recent than the time of Christ, (see Margoliouth, Weiss, Ebrard in

Herzog), and that even prayers and other matters in the Talmud may have been derived from the New Testament. The Rabbis borrowed freely from Greeks and afterwards from Arabians, and it is by no means so certain as some modern Jews imagine, that they did not also borrow from Jesus and his apostles. But the explanation of the matter before us is independent of that question.

The prayer naturally falls into two divisions, and it is an instructive and impressive fact that the first petitions are those which relate to God, his kingdom and his glory, and those relating to ourselves come afterwards, as being of less importance. *Bengel:* "The first three are *thy, thy, thy;* the others, *us, us, us.*" So likewise the Ten Commandments fall into two parts; the former setting forth our duty to God, the latter to our neighbor. At the present day, the prevalent tendency is to begin with human nature and wants, and to ask how Christianity suits itself to these; the Bible teaches us to think of God, and ask how we may suit ourselves to his nature and will. As we are afterwards taught to seek his kingdom first (6: 33), so here to pray first that it may come. Yet the distinction in the prayer is not absolute, since the fulfillment of the first petitions will be also for our good, and the fulfillment of the others will be also for God's glory. There has been much useless discussion in Germany as to whether the prayer contains seven petitions (the Lutheran view, following Augustine), or only six (the Reformed or Calvinian view, following Chrysostom), according as we consider verse 13 to be one petition or two. Some writers try to find in the several petitions sets of threes, as if illustrating the Trinity; but this is artificial and fanciful.

9. Our Father. The use of the plural, throughout the prayer, instead of changing to the singular, as is done in v. 2, 6, 17, evidently presents this as a specimen of *social* rather than secret prayer; and so, involves prayer for each other, and not for ourselves alone. Compare 18: 19; Mal. 2: 10. The thought of God as our *Father* is presented in some passages of the Old Test. (as Isa. 63: 16; Ps. 103: 13; Deut. 32: 6), and oftener in subsequent Jewish writings (Tobit 13: 4; Ecclus.

23: 1; 51: 10; Wisdom 2: 16; 14: 3) ; and the *later* Jews have several prayers in which God is addressed as "our Father in heaven," an idea doubtless drawn by them from the Old Test. The heathen, too, were not wholly unfamiliar with the thought. *Max Müller:* "We have in the Veda the invocation *Dyaus-piter*, the Greek *Zeu pater*, the Latin *Jupiter;* and that means in all the three languages what it meant before these languages were torn asunder—it means heaven-Father." (Boardman.) Plutarch says that the superstitious man recognizes only that which is sovereign in God, and not the fatherly; and Seneca, that God has a fatherly mind towards good men. But it is Jesus who has rendered this idea so clear and precious; distinctly comparing the feelings of human parents towards their children (7: 11), and making the great thought familiar by frequent repetition. In one sense God is the Father of all men, as in one sense all men are brothers; and so we can fitly speak of the Fatherhood of God and the Brotherhood of man; and yet it is only believers in Christ who can in the fullest sense call God Father (1 John 3: 1 ; John 8: 42), and call each other brethren. (1 John 3: 14.) **In heaven.** God, who is everywhere present, is constantly represented in Scripture as making his special abode, and the special manifestation of the presence of his glory, in *heaven.* Aristotle noticed that this idea was common to all nations. But the heathen made heaven itself, variously personified, an object of worship; while in Scripture, heaven is but the dwelling-place of God. (Comp. Plumptre.)

Hallowed be thy name. To pray that his *name*, Jehovah, by which he is distinguished from all heathen deities, and marked out as his people's God, may be *sanctified*, regarded and treated as holy (comp. Exod. 20: 8; Lev. 22: 2, 32; Ezek. 36: 23; 1 Pet. 3: 15, and contrast "despise my name" Mal. 1: 6), involves the idea of praying that God, in all his character and dealings, may be reverenced and glorified. Compare such expressions as "they that love thy name," "that know thy name" in the Old Test., and "glorify thy name" in John 12: 28; Rev. 15: 4. This idea of taking the proper name as representing the person in his entire character, is altogether natural, but was rendered peculiarly impressive to the Israelitish mind by their remark-

able reverence for the name of Jehovah—a reverence which at length became superstitious, so that the later Jews would never pronounce that proper name at all, but uttered instead of it the word Adonai, which means Lord—and this led to the translation of Jehovah in the Septuagint by Kyrios, and in the English by Lord. The Anglo-Saxon word "*hallow*," though often employed in the Old Testament, is used nowhere in the King James Version of the New Testament, except here and Luke 11 : 2. Elsewhere that version uses the Latin word sanctify. But in this familiar and cherished prayer the old Anglo-Saxon word was retained (comp. on 1: 18, as to the use of Holy Ghost). So likewise the Latin Vulgate, while translated anew from the Hebrew, retained the old Latin Version of the Psalms, as being so familiar that change would not be tolerated; and the English Book of Common Prayer, though altered elsewhere to suit the King James Version, retains still the translation of the Psalms from the Great Bible, or Coverdale.

Thy kingdom come. Of the three words, *kingship, reign,* and *kingdom,* to which the Greek word here employed is equivalent (see on 3 : 2), it would be best in this and many passages to use the second term reign, since we can use only one. The reference is plainly to that Messianic reign which all devout Jews were expecting (Mark 15: 43 ; Luke 23 : 51), and which John and Jesus had been proclaiming as now near at hand. (3 : 2; 4: 17.) The prayer that it might *come* would in the minds of our Lord's hearers refer especially to the beginning of the reign, the introduction of the kingdom (Luke 17: 20 f.); but just as in the prophetic view the whole period from the beginning of Messiah's reign to its ultimate triumph, frequently appears as a point, so in the full sense the coming of that reign or kingdom includes the idea of its complete establishment. It is therefore perfectly legitimate for us to use the petition with our minds specially directed towards the consummation of Christ's reign, the complete establishment of his kingdom, his final glorious triumph, when the kingship (sovereignty) of the world, shall become our Lord's and his Christ's. (Rev. 11: 15.) **Thy will be done** is more exactly *thy will come to pass,* 'take place,' the same verb as in 1 : 22 (see foot-note there), 5: 18; 24: 6, 34 (where it is rendered 'come

10 Thy kingdom come. Thy will be done in earth, as *it is* in heaven.
11 Give us this day our daily bread.

10 in heaven, Hallowed be thy name. Thy kingdom come. Thy will be done, as in heaven, so on earth.
11 Give us this day ¹ our daily bread. And forgive us

1 Gr. *our bread for the coming day,* or, *our needful bread.*

to pass,' in Com. Ver.), and the same expression as in 26 : 42, and Acts 21 : 14. This of course *involves* the idea that moral creatures are to *do* his will, as in 7 : 21; 12 : 50 (where the word 'do' is employed), but it expresses a more comprehensive thought. Theological writers distinguish three senses of the term *will.* God's will of *purpose* always comes to pass, in heaven, earth, and hell. But his will of *desire* does not yet always come to pass on earth as it does in heaven. He wished Jerusalem to be saved (Luke 13 : 34), and they would not. He does not "wish that any should perish, but that all should come to repentance" (2 Pet. 3 : 9), and yet many refuse to repent, and perish. He wishes "all men to be saved" (1 Tim. 2 : 4), yet many are led captive by Satan according to his own will. And God's will of *command,* how often and how flagrantly it is disobeyed; how few of his moral creatures on earth are prepared to say, " I delight to do thy will, O my God" (Psalm 40 : 8), or as Jesus said, literally, "My food is to do the will of him that sent me" (John 4 : 34); how few are joined to Christ by the fullness of that tie, "Whosoever shall do the will of my Father who is in heaven, he is my brother, and sister, and mother." (12 : 50.) **In earth as it is in heaven.** The Rev. Ver., *As in heaven, so on earth,* gives the order of the Greek, and makes a difference in the emphasis.—We ought to be continually praying this prayer. In heaven, everything takes place as God wishes, everything is perfectly pleasing in his sight. Ah ! when shall it be so on earth? When shall his reign fully come, and his will take place, 'as in heaven, (so) also upon earth?' O Lord, how long!—This impressive petition is really involved in the foregoing, simply stating separately one element of it; for when God's reign is fully come, his will must come to pass, etc. When therefore this is omitted from the prayer on the second occasion (Luke 11 : 12), we perceive that no principal thought of the prayer is thus lost. Yet this is by no means a mere repetition or expansion, for it brings into prominence one practical element of God's reign, which we ought specially to desire and aim to bring about. Some 'e. g.,'

West. and Hort's Greek Test.) would affix "as in heaven, so also upon earth," to all the three foregoing petitions, making it apply separately to each of them. This is a possible view, but not probable. (1) The words would not harmonize so well with "thy reign come," as with "thy name be sanctified," and "thy will come to pass." (2) The omission of these words in Luke 11 : 2 would thus be harder to account for.

11. Here begins the second division of the prayer, that which contains petitions for ourselves (compare on v. 9). The grammatical construction here changes. The foregoing clauses pray that something may come to pass in the course of God's providence. The succeeding clauses directly petition God to give and forgive. **Daily bread.** Bread naturally represents food in general, all that is necessary to support life, of which bread is commonly esteemed the most important and indispensable part. (Mark 3 : 20; 2 Thess. 3 : 12; Prov. 30 : 8, margin.) There seems to be no warrant for understanding the term as here including spiritual nourishment. It is altogether natural and proper to draw the *inference* that if we are bidden to ask God for bodily food, we need quite as much to ask him for that of the soul; but inference is a different thing from interpretation. *Conant:* "The beauty and propriety of this single petition for earthly good (restricted to that without which life cannot subsist), has been felt in all ages of the church." Many Fathers, and many in every age, have wrongly insisted upon "spiritualizing" the passage, as they have done with well-nigh everything in Scripture. Against the overdriven spirituality which affects to be too indifferent to earthly good to think it worth asking for, Jesus vindicates a place for earthly good in our prayers. In the present age, it is especially important to urge that men shall pray for temporal good, since so many think that the recognized presence of law in all temporal things puts them beyond the sphere of prayer; as if that would not exclude God from his universe; and as if there were not law in spiritual things also. The word (*epiousion*) rendered **daily,** is extremely rare and obscure. Origen says, that it was not found in any Greek writer or in colloquial use, but seemed to have been coined by the Evangelists. Only three senses of the term have now any advocates: (1) '(bread) for to-morrow,' and so 'daily,' Bishop Lightfoot, Meyer, Grimm, Wünsche, Nicholson, margin of Rev. Test.; (2) 'needful,' Godet, Keim, Keil, Cremer, margin of Rev. Test. (American Revisers); (3) 'supersubstantial,' Jerome in Matthew, and many Romanists. Etymological considerations[1] strongly favor (1), and render (3) practically impossible. Bishop Lightfoot, "On a Fresh Revision of the New Test." App., has conclusively shown (and McClellan and Canon Cook vainly strive to meet his facts and arguments), how strongly (1) is supported by the early versions, being uniformly given by the Old Latin (and even Jerome retains it in Luke), by both the Egyptian versions, the Old Syriac, and the "Gospel according to the Hebrews." Origen preferred (2), explaining it as meaning needful for the soul—a spiritualizing conception, which suited Origen's turn of mind and habitual methods of interpretation; and he gave this view great currency among the Greek Christians (see Suicer) and the later Syrians. Jerome, by an impossible etymology, rendered it 'supersubstantial' in Matthew, though retaining in Luke the 'daily' of the Old Latin, and is followed in both passages by Wyclif and the Rheims version. Many Romanist writers have tried to use this rendering in Matthew for the support of transubstantiation, though the Romanist prayer-books have uniformly retained 'daily.' Plumptre strangely adopts Jerome's rendering, understanding it to mean "over and above material substance" (in which a *material* word is gratuitously inserted), and thus entirely restricting the petition to spiritual bread. In (1) "Give us to-day our bread for to-morrow," would mean our daily bread, if we remember that one should not let the day close without knowing how he is to have food for the next morning. It is very difficult to see how (2) could ever have suggested the idea of daily, which is found in all the earlier versions, and often referred to by Greek Fathers (Suicer). Moreover, the idea of (2) could have been easily expressed by existing Greek words, while that of (1) would have required the coining of a Greek adjective (Origen above). The objection to (1) is that it seems to conflict with v. 34, "Be not anxious for the morrow"; but it is fairly answered that the way to prevent such anxiety is to pray that to-morrow's bread may be given us to-day, as in Phil. 4: 6, the remedy for anxiety is prayer; and if v. 34 prohibits prayer for to-morrow's bread, then (Achelis) verse 31 would prohibit prayer for any food. If we combine all the evidence, it would seem that (1) must be very decidedly preferred.[2] With this compare James 2: 15, Rev. Ver., "And in lack of daily food"; Prov. 30: 8, lit., "Feed me with my portion (or allowance) of bread"; (Acts 6: 1; 2 Kings 25: 30); also the fact that the manna was given one day's supply at a time. **This day,** or simply 'to-day.' In Luke 11: 3 it is 'day by day.' The phrase in Matthew is said by various Fa-

---

[1] *Epiousios* comes easily and naturally from *he epiousa,* 'the oncoming (day),' a very common expression for 'to-morrow' or 'next day.' As to the possible etymology for (2), and the etymological impossibility of (3), see the special treatises and the lexicons.

[2] Mr. Paspati, a Greek gentleman of Constantinople, published (Athens, 1883), a lecture on the English Revised Version, in which he says (p. 14), that the word *epiousios* "is in general use among the Greeks. Many poor people complain that they cannot gain their *epiousion* bread. *Epiousios* means whatever can sustain or maintain." Mr. Sakellarios writes from Athens (Feb. 1886), that the word "was and is used in the sense of necessary, food necessary for sustenance." Now it is well known, as above stated, that this interpretation prevailed among the Greek Fathers, and so Mr. Constantine interprets, in his Greek comm. on Matt. and Mark (Athens, 1878). So far as the word is now generally used among the Greeks in that sense, it is evidently a mere appropriation of a Scripture term as commonly understood. Mr. Paspati remarks (p. 12) upon the frequent use of Scriptural expressions among the Greeks, including phrases relating to Pilate and to Satan. There is here then no independent testimony as to the meaning of the word.—It should be added that Mr. Paspati's elucidations in general show a lack of acquaintance with scientific philology. — Warth and Löckle, *Stud. u. Krit.,* 1884, No. 4, argue that the phrase may mean *to-day's* bread, because *epiousa,* ' oncoming' (which commonly means to-morrow), is occasionally used by a person speaking at or before dawn with reference to the then approaching day. They suppose the prayer to have been designed as a *morning* prayer—and it would have to be made very early, to render such a sense possible. This view is highly ingenious, but too fine spun to be probable in so simple and general a prayer. (Rejected by Cremer, ed. 4) Moreover how would this idea be expressed in Aramaic.

12 And forgive us our debts, as we forgive our debtors.

12 our debts, as we also have forgiven our debtors.

thers (Wet.) to have led to the *daily* repetition of this prayer, which is mentioned as early as the beginning of the third century; but Luke's phrase shows that at least in the second case nothing of the sort was contemplated.

12. Debts. This term is here used for transgressions, sins. In Aramaic, the native language of our Lord and the Evangelists, the word debt (*chob*) is very often used for sin. See numerous examples from the Targums in Buxtorf. This use is perfectly natural in itself, since an obligation to God which is not duly met becomes to us a sin; compare the illustration of sin by a debt in 18: 21, 24, 28. In like manner the English word duty denotes that which is due, owed. (Plumptre.) Accordingly in v. 14 f., the same idea is represented by 'trespasses,' transgressions. And in Luke (11: 4, Rev. Ver.), the prayer reads, "And forgive us our sins; for we ourselves also forgive every one that is indebted to us." So clear is it that debts here means sins that Tyndale translates in v. 12 by trespasses and trespassers; but this is unwarranted, and was not followed by any other English translators. Observe that this petition is connected with the foregoing by **and.** The life sustained by daily bread is not enough; we need also the forgiveness of sin (Weiss); compare 'And bring,' v. 13. **As we forgive**—or, as in Rev. Ver.—*also have forgiven*—**our debtors.** This does not present our forgiveness of others as the ground of our being forgiven, nor as strictly the measure of God's forgiveness towards us (for he forgives perfectly, while everything in us is imperfect); but by comparing the forgiveness we supplicate with that we have shown, it states very impressively the idea, afterwards still further emphasized in v. 14 f., that the unforgiving cannot be forgiven. Observe that the Revised text (no doubt correct) makes it "have forgiven," already before we seek forgiveness—not a mere momentary effort at forgiveness, trumped up for the nonce. In Luke 11: 4, it is, 'For we ourselves also forgive every one that is indebted to us,' which means not simply present but habitual forgiveness, as shown by the 'every one.' Luke's term 'for' might seem to make our forgiving the ground of our

being forgiven; but it rather means that there is no unforgivingness on our part to form an obstacle to our being forgiven. Compare 5: 7; Luke 23: 34; 1 Tim. 1: 3, and the beautiful illustration in the parable of 18: 21–35. The gospel ground of forgiveness—the atonement and intercession of Christ—is of course not here stated. The disciples could not have clearly understood a reference to it until after Christ's death, resurrection, and ascension.

The Greeks and Romans admired shining instances of forgiveness, but did not venture to inculcate or seem to expect it. A Jewish sage of about B. C. 200 (Ecclus. 28: 2), urged that men must forgive if they hoped to be forgiven: "Forgive thy neighbor his wrongdoing, and then when thou hast prayed, thy sins shall be forgiven." (Compare Ecclus. 28: 1–5.) But it is Christianity that has made this a thing actual and looked for. *Ecce Homo:* "The forgiveness of injuries, which was regarded in the ancient world as a virtue indeed, but an almost impossible one, appears to the moderns in ordinary cases a plain duty . . . . . a new virtue has been introduced into human life. Not only has it been inculcated, but it has passed so completely into the number of recognized and indispensable virtues, that every one in some degree practices it, and that by not practicing it men incur odium and loss of character. To the other great changes wrought in men's minds by Christ, this is now to be added, the most signal and beneficent, if not the greatest of all." (Compare on 5: 38 f.) But, like many terms expressive of Christian duty, the word forgive has come to be often used in a weakened sense, and many anxious minds are misled by its ambiguity. If forgive means merely to "bear no malice" (Ecclus. 28: 7), to abstain from revenge, leaving that to God (Rom. 12: 19), then in that sense we ought to forgive every wrongdoer, even though impenitent, and still our enemy. But this is not the Scripture use of the word forgive; and in the full sense of the term it is not our duty, and not even proper, to forgive one who has wronged us until he confesses the wrong, and this with such unquestioned sincerity and genuine change of feeling and purpose as to show him worthy of

13 And lead us not into temptation, but deliver us from evil: For thine is the kingdom, and the power, and the glory, for ever. Amen.

13 And bring us not into temptation, but deliver us

---

being restored to our confidence and regard. Thus our Lord says (Luke 17: 3, Rev. Ver.), "If thy brother sin, rebuke him; and if he repent, forgive him." Here again the example of our Heavenly Father illustrates the command to us. He sends rain and sunshine on the evil and the good (comp. on 5: 45), but he does not *forgive* men, restoring them to his confidence and affection, until they sincerely and thoroughly repent. In judging as to the sincerity and trustworthiness of those who profess repentance, our Lord inculcated great patience, and charitable judgment. If a wrong forgiven is repeated a second or third time, we are apt to lose all patience and refuse to forgive again; but he said, "If he sin against thee seven times in the day, and seven times turn again to thee, saying, I repent; thou shalt forgive him." (Luke 17: 4, Rev. Ver.) Nay, in Matt. 18: 21 f., he makes it even "seventy times seven"—not of course as an exact limit, but as a general and very strong injunction of long-suffering and charitable judgment towards human infirmity.

13. And lead—or, *bring*—**us not into temptation.** Here again 'and,' because the forgiveness of past sin is not enough; we need also preservation from sin in future. All the early English versions have 'lead,' doubtless influenced by the Latin *inducas*. The Latin Fathers, Tertullian and Cyprian, explain it to mean 'Do not suffer us to be led,' and Augustine says (Wet.) that many so pray, and that it so reads in many (Latin) copies; but that in the Greek he has never found anything but: 'Do not bring us.' This is the uniform reading and unquestionable meaning of the Greek, and the difference is important. Men *lead* each other into temptation by offering inducements to do wrong; but the thought here is of God's so ordering things in his providence as to bring us into trying circumstances, which would put our principles and characters to the test. This providential action does not compel us to do wrong, for such conditions become to us the occasion of sin only when our own evil desires are the impelling cause. (James 1: 13-15.) The same conditions properly met would but manifest and strengthen one's piety, as when God "did prove Abra-

ham" (Gen. 22: 1, Rev. Ver.), or allowed Satan to test the fidelity and patience of Job. There is thus no contradiction between this petition and the precept (James 1: 2, Rev. Ver.), "Count it all joy when ye fall into manifold temptations." One may be tested (see on 4: 1 for the explanation of 'tempt'), either with good or with evil intent. In the evil sense, God "tempteth no man." (James 1: 13.) The humble believer, self-distrustful because conscious of remaining tendencies to sin, and weakness in restraining them, prays that God will not bring him into temptation. (Comp. 26: 41; 1 Cor. 7: 5; Gal. 5: 7.) And yet, when God sees fit, notwithstanding his prayer and effort, to bring him into temptation, he is then to rejoice (James 1: 2), because when met in the strength of the Lord, it will certainly be overcome (1 Cor. 10: 13), because it will develop his Christian character and thus prove a blessing (James 1: 3 ff.), and because it will secure for him an eternal reward. (5: 12; James 1: 12; Rom. 8: 18.) In like manner (Mansel), our Lord directed the apostles to avoid persecution (10: 23), though he had told them to rejoice when persecuted. (5: 10-12.) **But deliver us from evil,** or, *the evil one.* This is not really a distinct petition from the foregoing, but further unfolds and separately states something involved therein. When therefore it was omitted on the second occasion (Luke 11: 4), no principal thought of the prayer was lost. (Comp. above on v. 10.) The Greek phrase rendered 'the evil one' is here ambiguous, as in 5: 37, and may equally well mean evil. The same expression is certainly masculine, and means Satan in 13: 19, 38; Eph. 6: 16; 1 John 2: 13, 14; 3: 12; 5: 19 (comp. v. 18); it is clearly neuter, meaning evil in the abstract, in Luke 6: 45; Rom. 12: 9; 1 Thess. 5: 22 (and several examples of the neuter plural, 'evil things'); while the meaning is doubtful in Matt. 5: 37, 39; 6: 13; John 17: 15; 2 Thess. 3: 3. It is understood here as masculine, meaning Satan, by Tert., Origen, Cyril (Jerus.), Gregory Nyss., Chrys., Theophyl., Erasmus, Zwingli, Beza, Bengel, Fritz., Olsh., Ebrard, Meyer, Grimm, Wordsworth, Reuss, Plumptre. It is taken as neuter, meaning evil in general, by Augustine, Luther,

14 For if ye forgive men their trespasses, your heavenly Father will also forgive you:

14 from [1] the evil *one*.[2] For if ye forgive men their trespasses, your heavenly Father will also forgive

---

1 Or, *evil*....2 Many authorities, some ancient, but with variations, add, *For thine is the kingdom, and the power, and the glory, for ever. Amen.*

Melanchthon, Tholuck, Ewald, Bleek, Stier, Lange, Alford, Conant, Weiss, Cremer, Keil, Achelis. Those who object so vehemently to translating here by "the evil one" are usually influenced largely by sentiment and habit, and sometimes by skepticism as to the real personality of Satan. But the New Testament familiarly associates evil with the evil one, as its leading embodiment and central director (*e. g.*, Acts 5: 3; John 13: 27; 8: 44.) It is therefore quite impossible to escape from that idea, if we believe the Scriptures. It can never be certainly determined whether the phrase is masculine or neuter in this passage and in John 17: 15. But the more frequent occurrence of the clearly masculine use, with the tendency of the New Testament to speak rather of evil persons and evil actions than of evil in the abstract, makes it more probable that the sense is masculine in each of these interesting passages. The Revisers have bravely followed the stronger probability (putting 'evil' in the margin), though it was inevitable that there would be a great outcry. Comp. Humphrey. As to the substantial meaning, it is the same in either case, as Calvin already remarks, and in fact either involves the other.

The doxology to this prayer in Com. Ver. is beyond all question spurious,[1] and rightly omitted by Rev. Ver. We may give up the pleasing and familiar words with regret, but surely it is more important to know what the Bible really contains and really means, than to cling to something not really in the Bible, merely because it gratifies our taste, or even because it has for us some precious associations.

14 f. The fact that this alone of all the topics of the prayer is taken up a second time, and amplified by stating it both positively and negatively, ought to impress upon us very deeply the importance of forgiving if we wish to be forgiven. Comp. 18: 21–35; Mark 11: 25; Luke 17: 3 f. **For** introduces what follows as a confirmation of v. 12. **Trespasses,**

---

[1] It is wanting in the Uncial MSS. ℵ, B, D, G, and in five cursives, and many other cursives have marks in the text or notes on the margin, showing that it is doubtful; also wanting in several copies of the Old Latin, in the Vulgate, and the Memphitic. Especially remarkable is the adverse testimony of Fathers. Thus Tertullian, in his interpretation of this prayer, calls the phrase "But deliver us from evil" the *conclusion;* and not a single Latin Father who comments on the prayer has the doxology except the Anonymous comm. So with Greek commentators, except Chrysostom and his followers. Cyril of Jerusalem, in concluding his exposition, says: "'From the evil one.' And the opposing demon is evil, from whom we pray to be delivered. Then, after the completion of the prayer you say ' Amen,' sealing thereby the contents of the prayer." Gregory of Nyssa: "From the evil one who in this world possesses the power, from whom may we be delivered by the grace of Christ, because to him be the power and the glory, together with the Father and the Holy Spirit, now, and forever and ever, Amen "—these words concluding Gregory's exposition of the whole prayer. This and several similar Patristic conclusions show the origin of our familiar doxology, namely, in the custom of concluding a prayer with some form of doxology. And several early versions appear to exhibit this doxology in the process of gradual formation. Thus the Old Syriac has, "Because thine is the king-

dom and the glory for ever and ever." The Thebaic gives another independent form: "Because thine is the strength and the power for ever and ever." The "Teaching of the Twelve Apostles," chap. 8, 9, 10, "For thine is the power and the glory forever," once with this prayer, and then with *two other* prayers there proposed for use in the Eucharist. And one copy of the Old Latin: "Because thine is the power forever and ever." We are thus able to explain how the doxology came in here, if originally wanting; while if originally present, it would be impossible to account for its omission, since it is beautifully appropriate, and could not be at all objectionable either to heretics or to the orthodox. Now remembering that it is wanting in several of the earliest Greek manuscripts and earliest versions, that there is no mention of it in a number of detailed Patristic expositions of the prayer, and that we see it growing up before our eyes in the earliest versions which contain it (perhaps suggested by 1 Chron. 29: 11), we can have no doubt that the doxology is spurious. It will doubtless continue to be used in liturgies like other ancient doxologies (*e. g.*, "Glory be to the Father, and to the Son, and to the Holy Ghost: as it was in the beginning, is now and ever shall be, world without end, Amen "), but it is not a part of Scripture. Nor was it introduced into the Book of Common Prayer until the time of Charles II.

more literally *transgressions*, interprets the word 'debts' in v. 12; hence the practice of substituting this word in repeating the prayer.

HOMILETICAL AND PRACTICAL.

V. 5 f. ORIGEN: "The hypocrites wearing the mask of goodness, are actors in their own theatre, the synagogues and the corners of the streets." HENRY: "Those who would not do as the hypocrites do in their way and actions, must not be as the hypocrites are in their frame and temper. As it is a terror to hypocrites, so it is a comfort to sincere Christians, that God sees in secret."—There might be ostentation in a much less public place than the synagogue or the street, and there might be true, unostentatious prayer elsewhere than in a private room. These places merely illustrate a principle, which is to be applied according to circumstances. It is therefore a mistake to suppose that our Lord here forbids individual prayer except when in solitude. The publican of the parable prayed openly, and aloud, with striking manifestations of grief, in the court of the temple, attracting the contemptuous observation of the Pharisee, and no doubt of others; yet his prayer was acceptable. Jesus himself sometimes made private prayer in the presence of his disciples. (Luke 11: 1.) Still, literal privacy is best where it is attainable, and our Saviour frequently sought it in the open air, at early dawn, or at night. Solitude is favorable to self-examination, and to individual communion with the Father.

LANDOR: "Solitude is the antechamber of God."

YOUNG: "O lost to reason, lost to lofty thought,
　　Lost to the noblest sallies of the soul,
　　Who think it solitude to be alone!"

CHRYS.: "Some, even when their person is concealed, make themselves manifest to all by their voice."

One advantage of praying in solitude is that then we need feel no hesitation in speaking aloud, which greatly aids in restraining wandering thoughts, and attaining a deeper solemnity and emotion. Regularity in private prayer is indispensable to the attainment and maintenance of a high order of piety. It is well to lift the heart to God, even for a moment, whenever we feel special inclination or need; but at stated hours we must pray, even though we feel no inclination. Thus may we combine the advantages of regularity and impulse.—How rich the reward of regular private devotion. How it soothes the perturbed spirit, strengthens for every trial, and sweetens every pleasure. Strange and sad that one who has known the blessedness of this privilege should ever permit himself to neglect it. CHRYS.: "Let us not then make our prayer by the gesture of our body, nor by the loudness of our voice, but by the earnestness of our mind: neither with noise and clamor, and for display, so as even to disturb those that are near us, but with all modesty, and with contrition in the mind, and with inward tears." THEOPHYL.: "What, then, shall I not pray in church? By all means, but with a right intention, and without display, for it is not the place that hurts, but the manner and the aim. Many in fact, when praying in secret, are doing it to please men." EUTHYM.: "If thou wishest spectators, thou hast, instead of all, God himself." WÜRT. BIBLE (Lange): "Those brief ejaculatory prayers sent up to heaven in few words, and which may be uttered even while engaged in our daily labor, are by far the richest and best." (15: 25.)—HENRY: "Secret prayer is to be performed in retirement, that we may be unobserved, and so may avoid ostentation; undisturbed, and so may avoid distraction; unheard, and so may use the greater freedom."

V. 7. CYPRIAN: "God hears not the voice, but the heart." CALVIN: "In true prayer the tongue does not go faster than the heart; the grace of God is not attained by the empty utterance of words, but the pious heart sends forth its affections like arrows to penetrate into heaven."—To keep repeating the same thought in synonyms is a fault of the same nature as these vain repetitions, though less gross. GILL: "The omniscience of God is a considerable argument, and a great encouragement to prayer; he knows our persons and our wants beforehand; and as he is able to help us, we have reason to believe he will."

V. 9. CYRIL: "Christ commands us to pray briefly, because he knows our minds are easily led off into wandering thoughts, especially in time of prayer." QUESNEL (Lange): "A king who himself draws up the petition which is to be presented must surely take great pleasure in granting it." (Isa. 65: 24; John

16:23.) BEDA (Blyth): "A prayer sweetened by the name of Father, makes me confident of getting all I ask." MALDONATUS: "The very name of father prays for us; because it is the part of a father to provide things necessary for his children." EUTHYM.: "He that lives a bad life, and calls God his Father, lies both against God and himself." CHRYS.: "We must then pray straightway, and lift our mind on wings and exalt it above the earth and attach it to the heavens; for he commands us to say, 'Our Father who art in the heavens.'" WILLIAMS: "The opening invocation presents the *Parentage*, 'Our *Father*,' the *Brotherhood*, '*Our* Father'; and the *Home*, 'Our Father *which art in heaven*.'" GRIFFITH: "We pray for our Father's honor, dominion, service; and then for our own preservation, pardon, protection." THEOPHYL.: "For as God is blasphemed for my sake, so also for my sake he is sanctified, that is, glorified as holy."—If we wish and pray that God's name may be hallowed, we ought ourselves never to speak irreverently, either of him, or of anything that is sacred from its connection with him (comp. on 5: 33-37); and if "actions speak louder than words," it is still more important to avoid acts which would profane anything that he has made holy. Is it not polluting and blaspheming the Name of God, for people to say prayers or sing praises to him when they are grossly wicked, and have no present intention to turn from their wicked ways? (Comp. Ruskin.) No church would employ a notorious drunkard, or adulterer, or an avowed infidel, to read the Bible in public worship, because of his being a good elocutionist; why employ such a man to sing solos in praise of God because he is a good vocalist? WEISS: "The fear of God is the source of all religious life, and the antecedent condition of all that is asked for in the progress of this prayer."

V. 10. STANFORD: "Oh, it is coming! The reign of the Father is sure in due season to show itself, for no power can ever frustrate his purpose or falsify his word." WILLIAMS: "To pray for Christ's kingdom is to pray for the conversion of sinners and the edification and sanctification of disciples. It is to ask the evangelization of the Gentiles and the restoration of the Jews. It is to implore that Antichrist may fall, and the idols perish from under the whole heaven. It is to profess sympathy with all that relieves and elevates and enfranchises man; and to implore the removal of all that corrupts and debases him, and that sells him, soul and body, to the service of the Evil One. . . . . Did we but know aright the necessities of our kind, and the truest, deepest wants of our own souls, the hourly burden of intercession, from our acts, and plans, and alms, and prayers, would still be, 'Let thy kingdom come.'" MILTON: "Come forth out of thy royal chambers, O Prince of all the kings of the earth! Put on the visible robes of thy imperial majesty, take up that unlimited sceptre which thy Almighty Father hath bequeathed thee; for now the voice of thy bride calls thee, and all creatures sigh to be renewed."

CHRYS.: "He hath-enjoined each one of us who pray, to take upon himself the care of the whole world. For he did not at all say, 'Thy will be done in me,' or 'in us,' but everywhere on the earth; so that error may be destroyed, and truth implanted, and all wickedness cast out, and virtue return, and no difference in this respect be henceforth between heaven and earth." SENECA: "Let men be pleased with whatever God pleases." EPICTETUS: "Do not seek for things to happen as thou wishest; but wish for things to happen as they do happen." PYTHAGORAS: "It shows knowledge and sense if we do not strive against, and worry at, Divine Providence."—This petition means not merely resignation to God's will when painful (26:42; Acts 21:14); but we pray that God's will may come to pass, and should accordingly be striving to bring to pass whatever we believe to be his will.

V. 11. BOARDMAN: "This teaches (1) Our dependence on God—*give*; (2) Modesty in our requests—*bread*; (3) Trustfulness—*this day*; (4) Brotherhood—*us, our.*" RUSKIN: "No words could be burning enough to tell the evils which have come on the world from men's using this petition thoughtlessly, and blasphemously praying God to give them what they are deliberately resolved to steal. . . . For the man who is not, day by day, doing work which will earn his dinner, must be stealing his dinner."

V. 12. We incur debt to God by sins of omission, as truly as by sins of commission.

15 But if ye forgive not men their trespasses, neither will your Father forgive your trespasses.
16 Moreover when ye fast, be not, as the hypocrites, of a sad countenance: for they disfigure their faces, that they may appear unto men to fast. Verily I say unto you, They have their reward.

15 you. But if ye forgive not men their trespasses, neither will your Father forgive your trespasses.
16 Moreover when ye fast, be not, as the hypocrites, of a sad countenance: for they disfigure their faces, that they may be seen of men to fast. Verily I say

---

Comp. 25: 42. And as every wise business man takes distinct account of all his pecuniary debts, so we should think over and deal with our moral debts. BOARDMAN: "This is the way in which our Heavenly Father forgives us, for his Son's sake, our debts. We, finite, sinful mortals, contracted the debt in the currency of earth; the Son of God paid the debt, so to speak, in the currency of heaven." THEOPHYL. "For God takes me as an exemplar; and what I do to another, he does to me." EUTHYM.: "He makes us masters of the forgiveness of our sins." BOARDMAN: "Here is a man who has been bitterly wronged by another; he says to him, 'I forgive you this, but I cannot forget it.' He enters his closet and prays: 'Father, forgive me, as I have forgiven him! Say to me in words that thou forgivest me, but do not forget my offences! Blot them not out of the book of thy remembrance! Do to me as I do to him!' Oh, how often does this prayer, if offered sincerely, mean a curse." SENECA: "Let him easily pardon who needs pardon."

V. 13. THEOPHYL.: "Men are weak, wherefore we must not fling ourselves into temptations; but, if we have fallen into them, must pray that we may not be swallowed up."—We do very wrong when we expose servants or other dependents to temptation, by negligently giving them opportunity to defraud us, or by failing to pay them what they really need for support, or by showing them only the more forbidding aspects of our own life as professed Christians, thus inclining them to think ill of Christianity. LANGE: "Thou who temptest others to sin, who exposest thyself wantonly to temptation, or who in temptation fightest, yet not with the armor of God, why wilt thou mock God by praying, 'Lead us not into temptation?' (1 Pet. 5: 6; Eph. 6: 11.'')" ORIGEN: "Let us pray that when struck by the fiery darts of the evil one we may not be kindled: and they are not kindled who with the shield of faith quench all the fiery darts

which he sends against them." (Eph. 6: 16.) RUSKIN: "Supposing we were first of all quite sure that we *had* prayed, honestly, the prayer against temptation, and that we would thankfully be refused anything we had set our hearts upon, if indeed God saw that it would lead us into evil, might we not have confidence afterwards that he . . . . would turn our hearts in the way that they should go?" BOARDMAN: "Well may this petition take its place as the conclusion of the Pattern Prayer. The evil it deprecates is the summary of all woe on man's part: the deliverance it craves is the summary of all love on God's part." [1]

The Lord's Prayer: I. That God may be glorified. 1. His name be hallowed. 2. His reign come. 3. His will come to pass, etc. II. That we may be blessed. 1. Temporal wants. 2. Spiritual wants; (a) Forgiven our sins; (b) Preserved from temptation, and delivered from Satan.

We may imagine (Bengel) that in heaven all these petitions will be turned into praises. "God's name is sanctified: his reign is come: his will comes to pass. He has forgiven us our sins: he has put an end to temptation: he has delivered us from Satan."

16-18. GOOD WORKS WITHOUT OSTENTATION. III. FASTING.

The third application of the general principle laid down in v. 1 is to Fasting. Compare on v. 2 and on v. 5. The reference here is obviously not to general public fasts, but to voluntary individual fasting. This was common among the pious Jews, but the Pharisees had reduced it to a system (as formalists usually do with their religious observances), fasting "twice in the week." (Luke 18: 12.) The Talmud informs us that they chose the second and fifth days of the week, because of the tradition that Moses went up Mount Sinai on the fifth day, and came down on the second.

16. Be not, or more exactly, '*do not become*,' implying the assumption of such looks

---

[1] Blyth on the Lord's Prayer, re-published by James Pott, New York, contains an immense collection of quotations from ancient and modern writers, one of which has been used above.

17 But thou, when thou fastest, anoint thine head, and wash thy face;

17 unto you, They have received their reward. But thou, when thou fastest, anoint thy head, and wash

---

for the time. **Of a sad countenance.**[1] It had always been the custom among the Israelites, as among other Oriental nations, on occasions of severe personal or national affliction, to manifest their grief and humiliation by wearing sackcloth, putting ashes on the head and face, etc. (Comp. on 11: 21.) These the Pharisaic hypocrites appear to have adopted in their regular individual fasting, in order to make known the fact and gain credit for singular devoutness. The Talmud of Babylon says, " Whoever makes his face black (a common expression in the Jewish writers for fasting) on account of the law in this world, God will make his brightness to shine in the world to come." **Verily I say unto you,** see on 5: 18. **They have received,** more literally, *have in full*, 'have all of.' See on v. 2. Instead of **they may appear,** etc., (the more literal rendering), *May be seen of men* (Tyndale, Geneva), is preferred, because the former might suggest a *mere* appearance, which is not here intended. (So in v. 18.)

17. The Saviour requires his disciple to dress on a day when he was fasting precisely as on other days. So far from ostentatiously exhibiting a voluntary act of devotion, he should even purposely conceal it. But it is a gross misunderstanding to take this as an injunction to dissimulation. We cannot too often remind ourselves of the distinction between deception and concealment. **Anoint thy head.** This was an established custom among the Jews from an early period. (Ruth 3: 3; 2 Sam. 12: 20; Psa. 23: 5; 104: 15; 133: 2; Eccl. 9: 8; Matt. 26: 7; Luke 7: 46.) When in great distress, they would omit this, as in 2 Sam. 14: 2; Dan. 10: 3, and the Talmud enjoins a like course in connection with fasting. In one passage, however, we read of a man as " weeping at home, but when he went forth in public, he bathed, anointed, ate, and drank. But why did he not do it openly? God answered, Although he himself did not manifest the thing, yet I will manifest it." **But thou,** the change our Lord so frequently makes from the plural to the singular (comp. v. 2, 6, and see on 5: 23). This shows that the reference is to a case of private, individual fasting, as in v. 6 to private praying. For the various phrases in v. 18, see on similar phrases in v. 4 and 6.

As to the propriety of fasting on the part of Christians now, we see that Jesus speaks as if taking for granted that his disciples would fast. It might be said that this was in the early part of his ministry, when things were in a transition stage. But in 9: 15, he likewise takes for granted that his disciples will fast after he shall have left them. Observe, however, that it is voluntary fasting of which he is speaking, and there is no trace in the New Test. of any appointment of a particular season for fasting. Indeed, the only fast enjoined by the law of Moses was that on the Day of Atonement (Lev. 16: 29-34); all the other fasting mentioned in the Old Test., whether national or individual, was voluntary. In 9: 15, the Saviour clearly teaches that fasting is right only when one's condition makes it natural. In a time of joy, fasting would be unnatural, and could not express a genuine feeling. But persons who are in great distress are naturally inclined to abstain from eating. Now every feeling is deepened by being in any natural way manifested; and so a sincere, though less strong feeling of distress, as on account of sin, may be strengthened by abstinence from food. This may also help us for a time in fixing our attention upon worship and devout meditation. Yet fasting is not in itself a meritorious action, but is proper only so far as it is natural under the circumstances, and useful in such ways as have been indicated. Wherever this utility would be counterbalanced by injury to health, disqualification for active duties, or other grave evils, then fasting ought not to be practiced. The observance of national fasts would appear to be in like manner optional, and subject to the same conditions. As to fasts appointed by some ecclesiastial authority for regular seasons of the week or year, no Scriptural authority can be claimed for making the injunction, and such regularly recurring fasts are extremely apt to degenerate into formality (comp. Isa. 58: 3 ff.), or to encourage excesses at other times

---

[1] See the same Greek term in Luke 24: 17 (Rev. Text), and in the Septuagint of Gen. 40: 7; Dan. 1: 10.

18 That thou appear not unto men to fast, but unto thy Father which is in secret: and thy Father which seeth in secret shall reward thee openly.
19 Lay not up for yourselves treasures upon earth, where moth and rust doth corrupt, and where thieves break through and steal:

18 thy face; that thou be not seen of men to fast, but of thy Father who is in secret: and thy Father, who seeth in secret, shall recompense thee.
19   Lay not up for yourselves treasures upon the earth, where moth and rust doth consume, and where thieves [1] break through and steal: but lay up for

---

1 Gr. *dig through.*

("Mardi Gras," etc.), or to be invested with an imaginary intrinsic meritoriousness, opposed to the spirit of the gospel. The mortification of the flesh, which is sometimes urged as a benefit of regular fasting, "can be better attained by habitual temperance than by occasional abstinence." (*Alexander.*) (Compare on 4: 2 and on 9: 15.) But many Christians of the early centuries had an exaggerated conception of the importance of fasting (one of the many elements of Judaism which they imported into Christianity), and so the word fasting crept into numerous manuscripts and versions in Mark 9: 29; Matt. 17: 21 (whole verse spurious); Acts 10: 30; 1 Cor. 7: 5. (See these passages in Rev. Test.) The word is part of the genuine text in Matt. 9: 15; Luke 2: 37; Acts 13: 2 f; 14: 23.

HOMILETICAL AND PRACTICAL.

Fasting. I. *When?* (1) On public occasions, if we really feel grief, and really desire to deepen it. (2) On private occasions, if it would be natural in our providential situation (9: 15), and would be profitable. (3) In either case, only so far as compatible with health and the proper discharge of existing duties. II. *How?* (1) Without the least ostentation. (v. 1, 16.) (2) With sincere desire and earnest effort to commune with God and gain spiritual profit. (v. 18.)—Hypocrisy. I. Methods. (1) Religious observances—*e. g.*, alms-giving, fasting, prayer. (2) Religious professions. II. Rewards. (1) Glory of men (v. 2), and even this usually very partial and very transient. (2) No reward from God. (v. 1.) (3) Not even the approval of one's own conscience. (4) Aggravated punishment in eternity. (Mark 12: 40.) Comp. in general chap. 23.

CHRYS.: "And, whereas, in the matter of almsgiving . . . . . after saying, 'Take heed not to do it before men,' he added, 'to be seen of them'; yet in the matter of fasting and prayer, he made no such limitation; why was this? Because for alms-giving to be altogether concealed is impossible, but for prayer and fasting, it is possible." VINET (in Lut-

teroth): "Fasting has no value save according to the dispositions by which it is accompanied; it is good only in proportion as it is not the body alone, but the heart, that fasts."

19-34. SINGLE-HEARTED DEVOTION TO GOD, AS OPPOSED TO WORLDLY AIMS AND ANXIETIES.

Having urged that good deeds should be performed, out of regard, not for human approbation and reward, but for that of God (v. 1-18), our Lord now passes to the kindred topic of inculcating, in general, an exclusive and entire devotion to God, as opposed to worldly aims and anxieties. (v. 19-34.) (See Analysis at the beginning of chapter 5.) This section of the great discourse naturally divides itself into four parts, viz., v. 19-21; v. 22 f.; v. 24; v. 25-34. We can discern between these an internal, though not a formal connection. The sayings are gnomic in form, and only an internal connection could be expected.

19-21. He begins with the thought that as the believer's heart ought to be in heaven (which is here taken for granted), and as the heart will be where the treasure is, therefore we should treasure to ourselves treasures in heaven, not on earth; and to this he encourages by contrasting the treasures of earth and heaven as respectively perishable and imperishable. The same idea occurs in Luke 12: 33 f., as used on a different occasion. The Jews of our Saviour's age were very largely a trading people, possessing much the same characteristics as at present, and among them an uncommon love of money. What is here said was therefore especially appropriate to them, but fully applies to men of all ages. It is also naturally understood as extending to all the other objects after which men long and seek; in general, we are to have regard to, and strive to obtain, heavenly rather than earthly things (compare Col. 3: 1 ff.), because the heart will be fixed on that which we are laboring to possess.

Lay not up for yourselves—literally, *Do not treasure to yourselves treasures.* The

20 But lay up for yourselves treasures in heaven, where neither moth nor rust doth corrupt, and where thieves do not break through nor steal:
21 For where your treasure is, there will your heart be also.
22 The light of the body is the eye: if therefore thine eye be single, thy whole body shall be full of light.

20 yourselves treasures in heaven, where neither moth nor rust doth consume, and where thieves do not
21 ¹break through nor steal: for where thy treasure is,
22 there will thy heart be also. The lamp of the body is the eye: if therefore thine eye be single, thy whole

1 Gr. *dig through.*

English idiom is disinclined to this immediate repetition of the same word, and hence our popular versions express it otherwise. Jesus does not mean absolutely to forbid the accumulation of wealth. It is a peculiarity of the Hebrew style, often occurring in Scripture, to make an absolute statement (especially a prohibition), which is designed to be understood relatively. See other instances in Luke 14: 12; John 4: 21; 1 Pet. 3: 3 f. This makes the expression more striking and impressive, like hyperbolical phrases, etc., and such statements were not meant, or expected to be taken literally and absolutely, any more than hyperboles are so taken. This principle of interpretation is capable of being abused, as all others are; but it requires to be applied in such passages as the present. Verse 20 is the opposite of v. 19, expanded for greater impressiveness. Comp. v. 15, and see on 5: 30. Men lay up treasures in heaven by righteousness in general, both in doing and suffering for Christ's sake (5: 12, 46; 6: 6; 2 Cor. 4: 17); and among other things, by a right use of earthly possessions, as proposed to the rich young man (19: 21), and as taught in Luke 12: 33, and in the parable of the unjust steward. (Luke 16: 1.) Remember also the cup of cold water (10: 42), the awards of the judgment (25: 40), and the remarkable passage in 1 Tim. 6: 17-19; also Rev. 14: 13. These heavenly rewards are not deserved by our good deeds, being a gift of free grace; but God chooses to connect them with, and proportion them to, our deeds of kindness to others, and devotion to him.

Moth, rust. The garments of the Jews, as of other Oriental nations, seldom changed their fashion; and hence great store of garments, perhaps in part inherited, would often form an important item in one's possessions. (Gen. 45: 22; 2 Kings 5: 5; Job 27: 16.) These were liable to be destroyed by moth. The term rendered 'rust' signifies 'eating,' and so consumption in whatever way. It may be understood here in the general sense of whatever consumes or destroys property; or in the special sense of

rust, just as we say that rust eats. Compare James 5: 2 f., in which, as in various other passages, James seems to be referring to the Sermon on the Mount. The word rendered **corrupt**—in Rev. Ver., *consume*—is literally 'cause to disappear,' and in v. 16 is rendered disfigure. 'Corrupt' does not correctly express the idea. **Thieves.** As to the other word sometimes rendered 'thief,' but more properly 'robber,' see on 27: 38. **Break through** is literally '*dig through*,' as in margin of Rev. Ver., following Geneva and Rheims. It doubtless refers to the clay walls which many houses had (comp. Job 24: 16). "The houses in Mexico are chiefly built of *adobes* (large sun-dried bricks), and in the attack on Monterey (1846), the American troops advanced into the heart of the city by digging occasionally through the walls of courts and houses." *Gen. D. H. Hill.* It is sometimes objected that the precious metals do not rust. But they can be stolen. The **heart** is spoken of in Scripture, not according to our modern view, as the seat of the affections only, but as the seat of all the powers of the soul, both intellect, sensibilities, and will. (To speak of the *head* as the seat of intellect, is a thing unknown to the Bible.) Many passages of Scripture are popularly misunderstood, from failure to keep this usage in view. The connection in the present case leads us to think of the affections as especially meant, but not exclusively. The thoughts, as well as feelings, will be where the treasure is (comp. Col. 3: 2); and it is the power of *knowing* truth that is especially referred to in the next two verses. **Your**—R. V., *thy*—(twice) in v. 21. The singular represents the correct Greek text, which was changed to 'your' by copyists who observed the plurals of v. 19 f, and did not think of that impressive change to the singular which is so often made in this discourse (comp. v. 2, 6, 17; and see on 5: 23).

22 f. This passage is in some respects obscure, and has given commentators much trouble; but by remembering the connection,

23 But if thine eye be evil, thy whole body shall be full of darkness. If therefore the light that is in thee be darkness, how great *is* that darkness!

23 body shall be full of light. But if thine eye be evil, thy whole body shall be full of darkness. If therefore the light that is in thee be darkness, how great

and carefully noting the precise meaning of the terms, the difficulty may be cleared up. Compare Luke 11: 34-36, nearly the same passage, spoken on a different occasion. **The light**—literally, *the lamp.* The word is the same as in 5: 15, and denotes any portable light. The eye is the lamp of the body because it is that part which gives the body light, by means of which the body sees. The word **single,** or, 'simple,' represents the eye as giving one image of an object; as opposed to an eye which sees double, which gives dim, flickering images that displace one another, so that the object is not seen clearly and steadily. This last is described by a more general term as a ' bad ' eye, the Greek word commonly expressing moral evil (and the phrase is so employed in 20: 15; Mark 7: 22), but being sometimes found in the other, which is really its primary sense, as in the phrases ' bad diet,' ' bad health,' ' badness of eyes,' all employed by Plato. (Some early expositors understood it to denote moral evil here, and hence Tyndale, Great Bible, Geneva, and Darby translate ' wicked.') Many interpreters conclude that ' single' should be here understood as meaning a sound, healthy eye in general, as opposed to a bad, diseased one, which does not see well. But there is no support in Greek usage for such an interpretation of the word, and the Latin versions render it *simplex,* the Peshito gives the same sense, while the Memphitic borrows the Greek word. It is very undesirable to abandon the specific meaning of this word, which precisely suits the whole connection, and in contrast with which the general term' bad ' will naturally here take to itself a corresponding application. The ' single' eye forms but one image of its object, and does not blend that with the images of other objects; the ' bad' eye forms different images of the same thing, or blends different objects in its confused vision. So the single eye really sees; while the bad eye practically does not see at all. If the eye be single, the whole body will be ' full of light,' thoroughly light; while if the eye be bad, the whole body will be ' full of darkness,' thoroughly dark. **The light that is in thee,** the lamp of the mind, or as Plato calls it, "the eye of the soul,"

would be our inner power of perceiving truth and duty—what we commonly call reason and conscience; and would include both the natural light which these give, and their capacity to receive the light of revelation. So Philo says (following Aristotle): " For what the intellect is in the soul, that the eye is in the body." Or we might recall (Weiss) the term 'heart' from v. 21, which would then represent the mind, and amount to the same thing. Now why is it that the good eye of the illustration is specifically described as a 'single' eye? The reason lies in that general truth with which the whole connection is dealing, viz., the propriety and necessity of exclusive regard to God. Just before, we are taught to store up heavenly and not earthly treasure, that our hearts may be in heaven, not on earth. Just after, that we cannot be the servants of both God and mammon, but must serve God alone ; that we must not be anxious about temporal wants, but must seek his kingdom and the righteousness he requires, and trust his providence for the supply of temporal necessities. And so in the present passage. If the 'heart' (v. 21), the "mind's eye," the reason and conscience, is fixed partly on God and partly on mammon, sometimes on heavenly and sometimes on earthly things, then it resembles the bad eye, which mixes images of different objects, so that we really see nothing. *Epictetus* expresses a similar thought by a similar image: " If you strive after moral excellence, and yet at the same time clutch at power and pelf, you will most likely lose these last from having an eye to the former also; and most certainly you will lose the former." The *general* thought is therefore of reason and conscience darkened, blinded — as by inheritance of faults, by miseducation, by bodily excesses, by covetousness, ambition, or other strong passions—but with *special* reference here to a reason and conscience divided in aim and thus darkened. The heart must be directed with exclusive and steady gaze towards God, not distracted by worldly aims and anxieties, or we shall be sadly lacking in clear perception of truth and duty. (Comp. Olsh., Alex., Plumptre.) **How great is that**

24 No man can serve two masters: for either he will hate the one, and love the other; or else he will hold to the one, and despise the other. Ye cannot serve God and mammon.

24 is the darkness! No man can serve two masters: for either he will hate the one, and love the other; or else he will hold to one, and despise the other.

(*the*) **darkness!** 'That' is an imitation of the Latin, which has no article, and sometimes overstates its meaning by a demonstrative. In the similar passage (Luke 11: 34-36), the bright side of the illustration is finally made prominent, while here it is the dark side.

24. A further and very distinct illustration of the same great truth, viz., the duty and necessity of exclusive devotion to God. See a similar passage in Luke 16: 13, as spoken on a different occasion. **No man can serve two masters.** All difficulty or cavil about this statement, on the ground that there are circumstances in which a person might serve two masters, is at once set aside by observing that the word rendered 'serve' signifies to 'be the slave of,' a relation which necessarily implies exclusive ownership, and demands exclusive service. True, a slave might belong to two masters in partnership; but here it is obviously implied that the two are altogether opposed to each other. For the different terms rendered 'serve' and 'servant,' see on 8: 9; and for the various words rendered 'master,' see on 8: 19. The next words are not tautological, but have been thus explained (Meyer): " for either he will hate A and love B, or (on the contrary) he will hold to A and despise B." The change of the verbs in the second clause (instead of simply saying, "will love A and hate B") seems to intimate that even if he should feel no positive hatred to either of the two, he will attach himself to one, and neglect, slight, despise, the other.—Our Lord does not simply furnish the illustration, leaving it to be understood of itself, but distinctly applies it to the subject in hand. **Ye cannot serve God and mammon.** The word mammon is Aramaic, signifying wealth, riches. It is here personified, in being contrasted with God as the other of two masters; but there is no sufficient evidence that mammon was, as some assert, actually worshiped as a Syrian divinity.[1]

Milton personified Mammon as one of Satan's host. (Par. Lost, Book I.)

The Saviour does not teach that the *possession* of wealth is inconsistent with piety. He delighted in the friendship of the little family at Bethany, whom the circumstances show to have been wealthy (comp. on 26: 6), and he commended Zaccheus, who gave the half (not the whole) of his goods to the poor. But he has pronounced it an impossibility to be the servants (slaves) at once of God and of mammon. Yet this is what men are constantly attempting to do, and Christians are sorely tempted to the same course. The Israelites of Elijah's time did not avowedly renounce Jehovah, but tried to worship both him and Baal; and the prophet calls on them (1 Kings 18: 21) to decide which of the two is God, and follow him—to be one thing or the other. (Comp. another striking example in 2 Kings 17: 24-41.) So we must choose between being the servants of God and Wealth; we cannot be both. Whatever efforts we make to obtain wealth must be in entire subordination to the service of God, and, in fact, a part of that service; he alone must be Master. *Porteus:* "' Every one has his ruling passion. That of the Christian must be the love of his Maker and Redeemer." Observe carefully that the principle here presented applies not merely to those who have great possessions, but to all. "*No one* can serve two masters." The poor also are tempted to make wealth a master and an idol (Col. 3: 5), and sometimes do so as grievously as the rich.

Three reasons have thus been given (v. 19-24) why we should be exclusively devoted to God. (1) The things of the world are so perishable. (2) If our minds are directed at the same time towards earthly and heavenly things, our view becomes distracted, confused, darkened. (3) It is impossible to be God's servants and the servants of mammon.

[1] The proper spelling of the Greek, as found in nearly all MSS., would give us mamon; but it is too late to alter the English form. The etymology is most likely, as usually given, from the Hebrew *aman*, meaning that which props, supports, or that which is relied on, trusted. (See Grimm, Bleek, Tholuck, Achelis.) There is probably an allusion to this, in the common text of Mark 10: 24, B. U. Ver., " those who trust in riches "; and the words may have been omitted in a few of the earliest documents (followed by Tisch. and W H.) for the very reason that this allusion was not understood, and the words were not found in the parallel passages, Matt. 19: 23 and Luke 18: 24. The different etymology of Gesenius (Meyer, Keil), is much less probable, though it yields the same meaning, viz., wealth.

25 Therefore I say unto you, Take no thought for your life, what ye shall eat, or what ye shall drink; nor yet for your body, what ye shall put on. Is not the life more than meat, and the body than raiment?

25 Ye cannot serve God and mammon. Therefore I say unto you, Be not anxious for your life, what ye shall eat, or what ye shall drink; nor yet for your body, what ye shall put on. Is not the life more

---

25-34. Here the duty of entire and exclusive devotion to God (see on v. 1 and v. 19) is set in opposition to worldly anxieties, which are shown to be both unnecessary, unavailing, and unbecoming; to spring from unbelief, and augment the ills of life; and it is added that by following the other course we shall gain, without anxiety, the very objects in question. The paragraph is found in Luke 12: 22-31, with slight variations, as on a later occasion repeated to the disciples in the hearing of a new audience. This passage "is one of the beauties of Scripture. Had it no other recommendation than its felicity of illustration and its graces of composition, it would deserve our warm admiration; and indeed it has received the tribute of admiration from men who were only in pursuit of literary beauties. But it has higher qualities of excellence than these; it speaks to the understanding, and the heart, on themes of deep and universal importance."—*John Harris.*

25. Therefore, viz., because of the truth he has been enforcing (in v. 19-24, but with special reference to v. 24), that single-hearted devotion to God is proper and needful. Consuming anxiety about the necessaries of life, instead of trusting God, betrays the same worldly-minded and ungodly feeling that is seen in the slave of mammon. Trust in God would prevent all such worldly anxieties. So the suffering Hebrew Christians, who had been plundered of their possessions (Heb. 10: 34), are urged to be free from the love of money, on the ground that God has promised never to fail nor forsake his people. (Heb. 13: 5 f.) Food and clothing are the most urgent wants of our earthly condition; and if we ought not to be anxious about these, much less should we be anxious about other things. **Take no thought** —or, *be not anxious*—**for your life**—'Take no thought' was a good rendering when King James' version was made (so also in 1 Sam. 9: 5), for in Bacon, Shakspeare, and other writers of that period, 'thought' is used as including the idea of anxiety, as when a person is said to have died of thought. Tyndale and the

succeeding English versions translate 'be not careful' in this passage, but 'take thought' or 'take careful thought' in v. 27, 31, and 'care,' in v. 27, 34. The Greek verb used throughout this passage is also found (besides Luke 12: 22-26) in 10: 19; Luke 10: 41; 1 Cor. 7: 32; Phil. 2: 20 and 4: 6, and a few other passages; and the corresponding substantive in 13: 22; 2 Cor. 11: 28 (Rev. Ver.) "anxiety for all the churches," 1 Pet. 5: 7 (Rev. Ver.), "casting all your anxiety upon him, because he careth for you" (where careth is a different verb); Ecclus. 30: 24, "anxiety brings old age before the time." These passages show that the word sometimes expresses a lawful feeling of intense concern, which is directed towards proper objects, kept within due bounds, and stimulates efforts to do our duty; and that this feeling becomes wrong when misdirected—or when existing in greater measure than is expended upon action, and so eating like an acid into the soul—especially when it is a feeling which springs from lack of trust in God, this last being the idea of the present connection. The term *care* is used by us in a similar twofold sense, expressing sometimes a right and sometimes a wrong feeling. Our Lord of course does not mean that we are to exercise no forethought, and put forth no effort. Trust in God by no means implies the lack of these. Augustine refers to a sect in his time who called themselves Euchites, or Prayer-men, because they simply prayed for everything they wanted, without laboring to attain it. This grievous folly has been reproduced by some well-meaning persons in the present generation.

The first consideration by which Jesus seeks to restrain from the anxiety just forbidden is an argument from the greater to the less. (v. 25.) If God has given us the greater, viz., life, the body, is he likely to withhold the less, viz., the food and the raiment? **Life** is the word which often denotes 'the soul,' but in many other cases, as here, simply the vital or animating principle (comp. on 16: 25), to sustain which there is need of food.[1] **Meat**—lit. as in Rev. Ver., *the food.* The word 'meat'

---

[1] Some early authorities omit ' or what ye shall drink,' and W H. place these words in brackets; but the omission is readily explained by desire to assimilate the pas-

sage to Luke 12: 22 (where also some early documents *insert* the words by way of assimilation to Matthew).

26 Behold the fowls of the air: for they sow not, neither do they reap, nor gather into barns; yet your heavenly Father feedeth them. Are ye not much better than they?
27 Which of you by taking thought can add one cubit unto his stature?

26 than the food, and the body than the raiment? Behold the birds of the heaven, that they sow not, neither do they reap, nor gather into barns; and your heavenly Father feedeth them. Are not ye of
27 much more value than they? And which of you by being anxious can add one cubit unto [1]the

---

1 Or, *his stature.*

---

formerly signified food, but is now restricted to a particular kind of food.

26. The second consideration is an argument from the less to the greater, and this applied first to food (v. 26), and afterwards to clothing. (v. 28 to 30.) **Behold the fowls of the air**—or, as in Rev. Ver., *the birds of the heaven*, birds that fly free in the sky, and over which men exercise no care. (Comp. 8: 20; 13: 32; Gen. 1: 26.) 'Fowls' formerly signified birds in general, but is now restricted to a certain variety of domesticated birds. Instead of the general term 'birds,' the similar discourse in Luke 12: 24, has the specific term 'ravens.' As sowing, reaping, and gathering into barns are the three leading processes of agriculture, we thus have it very strongly affirmed that the birds perform no part whatever of the work which men have to perform in order to obtain their food. Of course we know that the birds exert themselves; God does not feed them in idleness. But they find their food without any of our elaborate processes. The inserted 'yet' in the Com. Version enfeebles the simple and beautiful expression. **Are ye not**, better, *not ye ;* the 'ye' being expressed in the original, and thus shown to be emphatic. **Much better.** *Of much more value,* as Com. Ver. translates the same Greek phrase in 10: 31. The conclusion that much more will God feed those who are greatly more important than the birds, is here left to be understood, but in the similar argument of v. 30 is stated. The Mishna says, "Have you ever seen brutes or birds that had any trade? and yet they are nourished without trouble."

27. Before passing to the argument as to raiment (v. 28-30), our Lord pauses to add another remark to the effect that it is quite *unavailing* for us to be anxious about food. The general meaning is plain, but the ablest scholars of every period have been divided in opinion as to whether the leading term of the sentence here signifies stature or age. Its primary meaning and usual sense in Greek writers is the latter (so in John 9: 21; Heb.

11: 11); but it is sometimes used in the former sense (Luke 19: 3, and probably in Luke 2: 52; while Eph. 4: 13 may be understood either way.) The Septuagint uses it seven times in the sense of age, and only once in that of stature. The early versions, Latin, Peshito, Memphitic, Gothic, give 'stature,' and so do most of the Fathers, followed by all the early English versions. Yet the American Revisers translate 'the measure of his life,' with 'stature' in the margin; and this sense of 'age' is more appropriate to the connection. The object of the sentence is to show that it is in vain to be anxious about food. (v. 25 f.) Now few men are anxious to obtain food that they may increase their stature, but all men that they may prolong their life. This also best suits the expression in Luke 12: 26, "If then ye are not able to do that which is least," since a cubit added to one's life would be very little, while a cubit (about nineteen inches) added to the stature would be an enormous addition. It is objected that 'cubit' is nowhere in Scripture found in this metaphorical application to the duration of life; but it is supported by the analogous expression in Psa. 39: 5, "Thou hast made my days as hand-breadths; and mine age is as nothing before thee"; also by the expression of a Greek poet, "For a cubit's time we enjoy the bloom of our youth"; compare also (Achelis) Job 9: 25, and the Greek phrases "a span of life" and "a finger-long day." In this state of things it is not strange that the great mass of recent commentators prefer the sense 'age.' Morison urges that we *can* add to our life by carefulness; "otherwise the medical profession is an absurdity." But our efforts to do this are fruitless without God's blessing. He thinks the idea is that we cannot enlarge ourselves into giants; but this overlooks Luke 12: 26. Still, the other sense will yield the same general meaning for the passage. With all our anxiety about food, we cannot (apart from God's blessing) make the smallest addition to our life—or to our stature.

28 And why take ye thought for raiment? Consider the lilies of the field, how they grow; they toil not, neither do they spin:
29 And yet I say unto you, That even Solomon in all his glory was not arrayed like one of these.
30 Wherefore, if God so clothe the grass of the field, which to day is, and to morrow is cast into the oven, *shall he* not much more *clothe* you, O ye of little faith?
31 Therefore take no thought, saying, What shall we eat? or, What shall we drink? or, Wherewithal shall we be clothed?

28 measure of his life? And why are ye anxious concerning raiment? Consider the lilies of the field, how they grow; they toil not, neither do they spin:
29 yet I say unto you, that even Solomon in all his
30 glory was not arrayed like one of these. But if God doth so clothe the grass of the field, which to-day is, and to-morrow is cast into the oven, *shall he* not
31 much more *clothe* you, O ye of little faith? Be not therefore anxious, saying, What shall we eat? or, What shall we drink? or, Wherewithal shall we be

---

28. In v. 28–30, the argument from the less to the greater is urged with reference to raiment. **The lilies of the field,** like 'the birds of the heaven,' are those which grow wild without human care, and thus all the more strikingly display the care of God. We cannot determine the kind of lily meant, and the argument holds for the plainest flower as well as the most gorgeous. The writer observed in Palestine lilies of a dark violet color, looking like violet velvet, and these might very naturally have suggested a king in his rich purple robes. Solomon's Song (5: 13) indicates colored lilies, and Dioscorides speaks of purple lilies (Smith's Dict.). Tristram describes purple flowers, which he says would be popularly called lilies. The various attempts made to "spiritualize" this reference to the lily, are, as usual, wholly unwarranted and out of place. They who are not satisfied with the simple beauty of our Lord's teaching, but must be seeking some mystical meaning which they think more pleasing and instructive, are truly attempting "to gild refined gold, to paint the lily."

29. Solomon in all his glory, does not directly mean in glorious apparel, but in all the glory of his royal station, wealth, and fame, which involved the use of beautiful garments.

30. If God so clothe—translate, *clothes*—indicative mood, assuming it as a fact that he does. **The grass of the field.** The term rendered grass includes weeds and flowers. All these wither very rapidly in the East, especially when a hot south wind is blowing (comp. Psa. 90: 6); and owing to the scarcity of fuel, this dried vegetation is still often used to heat ovens for baking bread. **The oven.** This (Smith's Dict.) was a large jar made of clay, wider at the bottom. It was heated by placing the fuel within, and the ashes being removed through a hole at the bottom, the flat cakes of bread were spread both on the inside and the outside, and thus baked. Sometimes it was not a movable jar, but a fixture; and the primitive contrivance was probably a hole in the earth, with compacted sides. **O ye of little faith,** represents a single compound adjective, somewhat like *little-believing*, used also in 8: 26; 14: 31; 16: 8; in all cases with reference to distrust of God's protection, providential or miraculous. Unbelief is the root of the anxiety our Lord is here rebuking, as it is of every other sinful feeling; and thus we see one of the ways in which unbelief leads to unhappiness. In Talmud of Babylon, R. Eliezer says: "Whoever has a mouthful yet remaining in his basket, and says, 'What shall I eat to-morrow,' belongs to the number of those who have little faith."

31, 32. Therefore, viz., in view of the argument just adduced. On the ground of this, the prohibition of v. 25 is repeated, and the succeeding verses append further considerations to the same effect. In v. 32 there seem to be two distinct reasons for avoiding this anxiety: (1) The Gentiles (or heathen) seek after all these things, and it is unworthy of God's people to be like them (comp. on 5: 47); (2) our Heavenly Father knows that we have need of all these things, and we may be sure he will not fail to supply our need. Some think, however, that the second clause furnishes the ground of the first; and explain by supplying a thought, thus: The heathen seek after these things, because ignorant that God knows and cares for their wants; but do not imitate them, for your Heavenly Father knoweth, etc. (Comp. v. 7 f.) But it is very rarely well to explain "for" by a supposed ellipsis, and the former explanation seems preferable. Luke 12: 30 has 'but,' which gives the same idea a little differently. The verb rendered **seek** is a compound of that in v. 33, and denotes an over-intense or anxious seeking. **All these things**—all the things of the class to which these (food and raiment)

32 (For after all these things do the Gentiles seek:) for your heavenly Father knoweth that ye have need of all these things.
33 But seek ye first the kingdom of God, and his righteousness and all these things shall be added unto you.
34 Take therefore no thought for the morrow: for the morrow shall take thought for the things of itself. Sufficient unto the day *is* the evil thereof.

32 clothed? For after all these things do the Gentiles seek; for your heavenly Father knoweth that ye
33 have need of all these things. But seek ye first his kingdom, and his righteousness; and all these things
34 shall be added unto you. Be not therefore anxious for the morrow: for the morrow will be anxious for itself. Sufficient unto the day is the evil thereof.

---

belong, everything of this kind, *i. e.*, all temporal wants.

33. But seek ye, etc. Do not, like the heathen, seek these things, but *seek first his kingdom, and his righteousness, and these things* (emphasis here on 'these things') *shall all be added unto you.* Our Lord does not simply command us to avoid worldly anxiety, but gives us something positive to do instead, as a means of precluding it. So in Phil. 4: 6, Rev. Ver.: "In nothing be anxious; but in everything . . . . let your requests be made known unto God. And the peace of God . . . . shall guard your hearts," etc. So likewise above in v. 20 we are to lay up treasures in heaven, instead of laying them up upon the earth. 'His kingdom.' This evidently means the kingdom of our Heavenly Father, who is mentioned in the preceding sentence. But the Greek phrase is not so entirely explicit as the Com. Version; so some one put the word God in the margin, to explain what was meant, and it crept into the text.[1] So likewise in Luke 12: 31. Seek *first* his kingdom, and there will be no need of afterwards anxiously seeking food and raiment, etc., for they will be added, not indeed without seeking, but without anxious seeking; and so there will in this way be no occasion left for anxiety about them. Wünsche quotes from the Talmud: "If a man occupies himself always with the law, the Eternal supplies his wishes and needs." Our Father's kingdom is here the Messianic kingdom or reign (see on 3: 2; 6: 10). To seek this kingdom is to endeavor to become admitted into it, and share the privileges and duties of its subjects. But not leaving us altogether to our own conclusions as to what is involved, the Saviour here adds (not in Luke 12: 31) one point more specifically,

and his righteousness. This means that personal righteousness which our Father requires in the subjects of the Messianic reign, which they ought to hunger and thirst after (5: 6); which ought to exceed that of the Scribes and Pharisees (5: 20), extending not merely to outward acts, but to the inner life of purpose and desire (5: 21-48); which ought to be practiced, not with a view to the praise of men, but to the approval and rewards of the Father in heaven. (6: 1-18.) We must not introduce here the idea of *imputed* righteousness, which is foreign to the tone of this discourse, and does not distinctly appear anywhere in the Gospels, being chiefly set forth in Paul's Epistles to the Galatians, Romans, and Philippians. The great fact of imputed righteousness must have existed from the beginning of human repentance and forgiveness, but it does not follow that the idea was always revealed.

This saying sums up the great principles of the whole passage, v. 19-34, viz., things spiritual first, and things temporal will follow. He does not forbid our desiring or seeking temporal good; but says it must always be held as secondary and subordinate, to be obtained as a minor consequence of the pursuit of a higher aim. (Comp. Mark 10: 30; 1 Kings 3: 11-13.) In like manner the sayings in 5: 48 and 7: 12 form, as it were, a summing up of what precedes them.

34. This section of the discourse now ends with a renewed injunction not to be anxious, founded on the whole previous discussion (**therefore**), and directed especially to anxiety for to-morrow. It is concerning the future that we are most likely to be anxious, and to-morrow is the nearest future; and yet there is special reason for avoiding this, since to-morrow will have its own anxieties, and if

---

[1] The word God is omitted by B אֵ., three cursives, some copies of the old Latin, and of the Vulgate, the Memphitic and Æthiopic, and by one or two Greek Fathers. We readily see how the word came in, and cannot imagine why any one should have wished to exclude it. This consideration makes the evidence sufficient for omitting it. Tyndale and Geneva have 'kingdom of heaven,' which is here found only in one cursive and three Greek Fathers. Whence did they derive it?

we anticipate them, we uselessly add to the burden of to-day. Whether to-morrow's anxieties will be proper or improper, is not here the question; they will be felt then, and so should not be borrowed to-day. The **shall** of Com. Version is somewhat misleading; the Greek is a simple future, and in this connection merely predicts. **For the things,** etc., better as Rev. Ver., *for itself.* 'For the things of itself' represents a very feebly supported reading of the Greek. **Sufficient unto the day is the evil thereof.** This means not moral evil, the ordinary sense of the term, but natural evil, *i. e.*, suffering, trouble, etc., as in Amos 3:6; Eccl. 7:14; 12:1; Luke 16:25; also in 1 Macc. 7:23; 10:46.

A Jewish writer (Wet.) says, "Be not anxious about what is coming, before it takes place; for there is enough of vexation in its own hour." All men observe the folly of borrowing trouble from the future, and yet we continue to do it, and even to have a large part of our distresses spring from the dread of future evil, which likely enough will never come. A French proverb says, "The worst misfortunes are those which never arrive"; and a homely English proverb, "Never cross a bridge till you get to it." *Anacreon:* "I care for to-day; who knows to-morrow?" *Horace:* "What is to be on to-morrow avoid inquiring. Whatever sort of day fortune shall give, count it gain." But there is a broad distinction between our Saviour's teaching and such Epicurean counsels. They mean that it is foolish to harass ourselves about an unknown and uncertain to-morrow, and so we must simply enjoy to-day; he, that we ought to trust in the protection and blessing of our Heavenly Father, and thus, while not heedless of the future, we may be free from anxiety about it. They say, "To-morrow depends on chance; therefore try to forget it, and enjoy life to-day." He says, "To-morrow and all its wants will be provided for by your Heavenly Father; therefore think of it without anxiety, and try to do right and please God to-day." On the other hand, our Lord's teaching is very different from fatalism. He does not say, the morrow is fixed by fate, and you cannot help yourself, but speaks of the personal God, our Father, who cares for us (1 Pet. 5:7), and will supply our wants.

HOMILETICAL AND PRACTICAL.

V. 19-21. Laying up treasures in heaven. 1) Meaning. 2) Motives. (a) These treasures are imperishable; (b) Thus our heart will be in heaven. A Roman poet says: "A cunning thief will break your chest and carry off your money . . . . . whatever is given to friends is beyond the reach of chance." A Jewish writer tells of a king, who was reproached for expending in time of famine the treasures of his fathers, and who replied, "My fathers collected treasures on earth, but I in heaven." AUGUSTINE: "Why do you lay up where you may lose; and where, if you do not lose, you cannot always stay? There is another place to which I will remove you. Let what you have go before, and fear not lest you lose it; I was the giver, I will be the guard." EUTHYM.: "That which is distributed among the poor, where is it treasured up? In heaven. How? The rewards of all this are there stored up and kept safe." CALVIN: "If honor is thought to be the *summum bonum*, then men's minds must be wholly possessed by ambition; if money, then avarice will at once become sovereign; if pleasure, then nothing can prevent men from degenerating into brutal indulgence."

V. 22-23. Blindness. I. Lamentable evils, (1) of bodily, (2) of spiritual blindness. II. Responsibility. (1) Blindness of the body is usually a misfortune. (2) Blindness of the soul always involves guilt. III. Cure. (1) In physical blindness, cure seldom natural. (2) In blindness of the soul, cure always supernatural. (3) Yet this cure may be sought from God, and means employed for promoting it. STIER: "In a certain sense and measure, indeed, must our eye, from the very beginning, be singly fixed upon God, his kingdom, and his righteousness, upon the treasures in heaven; but is it not consummate holiness when this is perfectly realized, and there is no oblique or other regard?"

V. 24. The service of Mammon. I. Nature. (1) What it is not. (2) What it is. II. Temptations. (1) For personal gratification—of appetite, taste, social and other ambition—love of possession—love of power. (2) For benefit of others—our families—the needy around us—the great good one hopes to do *after a while.* III. Some of the ways in which men try to serve Mammon and serve God also. IV.

The two hopelessly incompatible. Compare serving Jehovah and Baal. (1 Kings 18: 21.) Whenever trying to do both, a man is, in fact, only serving Mammon—not at all serving God, and not in the highest sense benefiting himself. "Religion must be everything, or it is nothing."

A Roman writer speaks of one who did not own riches, but was owned by riches; by title a king, but in mind a miserable slave of money. SENECA: "Wealth is the slave of a wise man, the master of a fool." PLUTARCH speaks of Pelopidas as relieving the needy, that he might appear to be truly master of wealth, not slave. PLATO: "To prize wealth, and at the same time largely acquire wisdom, is impossible, for a man necessarily disregards the one or the other." DEMOPHILUS (Wet.): "For the same man to be a lover of riches and a lover of God, is impossible." LUTHER: "To have money and property is not a sin, only you must not let it be your master, but you must be *its* master." CHRYS.: "How then, saith one, did Abraham, how did Job, obtain a good report? Tell me not of them that are rich, but of them that serve riches. Since Job also was rich, yet he served not Mammon, but possessed it and ruled over it, and was a master, not a slave." ACHELIS: "The servant of Mammon estimates persons and things according to their money value; he regards loss of money as the highest loss, gain of money as the highest gain, and money as the highest aim of life." LUTTEROTH: "A man will obey the master he loves; God, if he loves God more than money; money, if he loves money more than God."

V. 25-34. Anxiety about temporal wants. I. Reasons for avoiding anxiety. (1) Apart from God, it is futile, v. 27. (2) Trusting in God, it is needless; (a) If he cares for the life and the body, he will care for the food and raiment, v. 25; (b) If he feeds his birds, he will feed his children, v. 26; (c) If he clothes the lilies, he will clothe human beings, v. 28-30. (3) It makes God's people no better than heathen, v. 31 f. (4) It is adding to-morrow's evils to those of to-day, v. 34. II. Means of avoiding anxiety. (1) Remember that our Heavenly Father knows our temporal needs, v. 32. (2) Seek spiritual good as supreme, and temporal good will, with due exertion on our part, but without anxiety, be amply supplied, v. 33. A lesson from the birds and the lilies, v. 25 f. and 28 f.—V. 32. God's children should be better than the heathen. (1) Why? (2) In what respect?

V. 25. CHRYS.: "He that formed the flesh that is nourished, how will he not provide the nourishment?"—V. 26. CHRYS.: "Even though it is theirs by nature, yet possibly we too may attain it by choice. For neither did he say, 'Behold, how the birds fly'—which were a thing impossible to man; but that they are fed without being anxious, a kind of thing easy to be achieved by us also, if we will. And this they have proved, who have accomplished it in their actions." QUESNEL (in Lutt.): "Nobody ever saw an earthly father feed his birds, and abandon his children, and shall that be believed of the Heavenly Father?" BENGEL: "Not *their* Father, but *your* Father." EUTHYM.: "So the Old Scripture, when wishing to hit men hard, sends them to the bee and the ant. . . . . What then? Must we not sow? He did not say, 'Do not sow;' but, 'Do not be anxious.'" LUTHER: "We are commanded (Gen. 1: 28) to have dominion over all creatures, and yet we behave so shamefully that a feeble sparrow must stand in the gospel as doctor and preacher for the wisest of men, and daily hold forth before our eyes and ears, teaching us to trust God, though we have the whole Bible and our reason to help us."—V. 28. Our Lord's manner of teaching is remarkable for the frequency with which he draws illustration from the objects of nature, the pursuits of common life, and the ordinary experiences of mankind. Every preacher of the gospel, and religious teacher of the young, should be a close observer of common things, that he may be better qualified to imitate this example of the Great Teacher.—V. 31. THEOPHYL.: "He does not forbid eating; he forbids saying, 'What shall we eat?'" LUTHER: "The Lord says, 'Be not careful; working is your business, caring is mine!'"—V. 32. EUTHYM.: "But if we do not even surpass the heathen, though commanded to surpass the Scribes and Pharisees (5: 20), what punishment shall we not deserve? . . . . So the cause of your anxiety ought to be the cause of your freedom from anxiety. The more necessary these things are, the more cheerful ought you to be. For what *father* will endure not to supply his children's necessities?"

V. 33. Which first, spiritual or temporal

CHAPTER VII.

JUDGE not, that ye be not judged.
 2 For with what judgment ye judge, ye shall be judged: and with what measure ye mete, it shall be measured to you again.

1, 2 Judge not, that ye be not judged. For with what judgment ye judge, ye shall be judged: and with what measure ye mete, it shall be measured unto you.

---

good? I. Suppose we seek the temporal first. (1) We shall be constantly less inclined to seek the spiritual. (2) We shall be constantly less prepared to find it. (3) Soon all temporal good must be abandoned, and for us there will be no spiritual good forever. II. Suppose we seek the spiritual first. (1) We shall not seek it in vain. (Comp. 7: 7.) (2) We shall obtain temporal good also, not without seeking, but without anxious seeking. V. 34. To-morrow. 1) We must not forget to-morrow, thinking only of to-day. The importance of to-day for civilized man is felt to lie largely in yesterday and to-morrow. 2) We must not presume on to-morrow, for we know not what morrow a day may bring forth. (Prov. 27: 1.) 3) We must not be anxious about to-morrow, but let each day bear its own sufficient burden. 4) We shall best provide for to-morrow, by faithfully performing the duties of to-day. 5) Trusting God for to-day, why can we not trust him for to-morrow?—V. 33. EUTHYM.: "For we have not come into existence that we may eat and drink and wear, but that we may please God, and enjoy everlasting blessings." THE-OPHYL.: "It is enough for thee that thou art afflicted for to-day; but if thou shalt be anxious for to-morrow, when wilt thou have leisure for God?" TALMUD (Wünsche): "Be not anxious for to-morrow, for thou knowest not what to-day brings forth; perhaps to-morrow will not find thee, and so thou hast troubled thyself about a world which does not pertain to thee." ANTONI-NUS: "Cast the future upon Providence, and direct your present care solely towards piety and justice." HENRY: "The conclusion of this whole matter then is, that it is the will and command of the Lord Jesus, that his disciples should not be their own tormentors, nor make their passage through this world more dark and unpleasant by their apprehensions of troubles, than God has made it by the troubles themselves." CHRYS.: "Let us not suppose his injunctions are impossible; for there are many who duly perform them."

Oh, sweet, sustaining trust in God, that can enable us to bear present ills without repining, and to look at the unknown future without fear; that can reconcile contentment with aspiration, and blend activity with repose; that can discern everywhere in nature and providence the proofs that all things are indeed working together for our good! Lord, increase our faith.

7: 1-12. REBUKE OF CENSORIOUSNESS; ENCOURAGEMENT TO PRAYER; AND THE GOLDEN RULE.

It has been thought by some writers that there is no connection between the early part of this chapter and the preceding topics. But as we have found connection throughout all the previous portion of the discourse, and as v. 13-27 obviously form a conclusion to the whole, it seems most probable that v. 1-12 also stand in some natural relation to the remainder. That such a relation does exist, would appear to be shown by the following view: In the whole discussion of 5: 20-48 and 6: 1-18, our Lord is contrasting the morality he enjoins upon the subjects of the Messianic reign with the teachings and practice of the Scribes and Pharisees. Various errors and evils common among the Jews, and conspicuous in their sanctimonious teachers, are there noticed and rebuked, not with the formal order of a methodical discourse, but still with the same general design manifestly pursued throughout. But the great principle stated and applied in 6: 1-18, viz., that good works should be performed (not ostentatiously, as the hypocrites did, but) out of regard for God only, admitted of a more extensive and varied application, which he proceeds to make in v. 19-34. From this partial digression, he now returns to rebuke another fault often committed among the Jews, particularly the formalistic Pharisees (Luke 18: 11), and to which all men are sadly liable, viz., that of passing harsh judgment upon others. (7: 1-5.) As it is hypocrisy (6: 2, 5, 16) to make a display of righteousness, so (Weiss) it is hypocrisy (7: 5) to assume the right to judge others, and correct their faults. Then in v. 6 our Lord adds a caution against the opposite extreme. Now to avoid both extremes in this respect, and in all respects to conform to those genuine and spiritual principles of morality which have been laid down throughout the discourse, is a task more difficult than we can in our own strength perform. Accordingly, with reference not only to the immediately preceding injunctions, but to the whole discourse, he adds (v. 7-11) an encouragement to pray to God. At the same time the expressions are put into the most general form, so as not to be confined to the idea of praying for strength to perform the duties enjoined in this discourse, but to encourage to prayer in general. (Comp. the relation of James 1: 5 to what precedes it.) Finally, he sums up all that he had been teaching throughout the discourse concerning duties to other men, compressing all into the one general precept of v. 12, which is declared to embody the essence of the entire Scriptures (Old Test.).

If this view be correct, it is not strange that we find no *conjunction* at the beginning of v. 1 and v. 7, since in each case, while there is an internal connection between the topic introduced and the previous portions of the discourse, there is no strong external connection with what immediately precedes, such as would require to be stated by a conjunction. See similar cases at 5: 13, 17; 6: 19; 7: 13. In v. 6 we might expect a conjunction, because of its close relation to the preceding verses; but observe that the expressions here assume the form of apophthegms, which are usually stated (*e. g.*, in the Book of Proverbs) without connectives, leaving it to the reader to discern their internal relation. So at 6: 22, 24. As to 'therefore' in v. 12, see below.

1, 2. The word rendered **judge** has sometimes the stronger meaning of 'condemn,' and many would so translate here. But that clearly does not suit v. 2, and we must retain the rendering 'judge,' while at the same time perceiving that the connection and the nature of the case suggest the idea of harsh, censorious judgment. Men are not likely to err in judging too favorably, nor to be restrained by the prospect of being too favorably judged themselves. In the report of the discourse given by Luke (6: 37) the idea of condemnation is distinctly stated, but by an additional word.

The judging thus forbidden manifestly does not refer to official judgments in courts, any more than 'swear not' prohibits oaths in court (see on 5: 34); nor to the formation of opinions concerning the character and conduct of others, which is always a right, where we have the means of judging, and commonly a duty, provided we strive to "judge righteous judgment." (John 7: 24.) To understand that we are never, under any circumstances, to express or to form an opinion concerning others, would conflict with v. 16, 20 below, and numerous other passages (*e. g.*, 1 Thess. 5: 21), and with the example of our Saviour and the apostles, in continually exposing and reproving error and evil. The application often made of this saying, by persons who do not wish their ruinous heresies or flagrant crimes to be condemned, is thus seen to be unwarranted. The reference is to the sadly common practice of officiously and presumptuously undertaking to pass judgment upon others, a judgment so often unfounded, unjust, or unkind. Persons most inclined to hypocritical display, like the Pharisees, would be most likely to judge others severely (Luke 18: 9-11), but all mankind are greatly given to censoriousness, and so there is no need for the supposition of some writers that our Lord here addressed himself directly to certain Pharisees, supposed to have attracted attention at this point of the discourse by their expressions or looks of derision (as in Luke 16: 14).

Some explain **that ye be not judged** (v. 1), and **ye shall be judged** (v. 2), as referring to the judgment which our *fellow-men* will pass upon us, if we are censorious. But if so, we might with impunity (Achelis) judge very pious people, who would not judge us in the same way. To understand it of God's judgment agrees with the view of the whole discourse, which teaches us in everything to have regard to that requital of reward or punishment which we are to expect from God; and the idea that God will deal with us as we deal with others, accords with the sentiment of 5: 7, B. U. Ver., "Happy are the merciful, for they shall obtain mercy," and of 6: 15, "But if ye forgive not," etc. (Compare 18: 35.) The impersonal form of the expression, not telling who will thus judge, but leaving it to the conscience to say for itself who

3 And why beholdest thou the mote that is in thy brother's eye, but considerest not the beam that is in thine own eye?
4 Or how wilt thou say to thy brother, Let me pull out the mote out of thine eye; and, behold, a beam *is* in thine own eye?
5 Thou hypocrite, first cast out the beam out of thine own eye: and then shalt thou see clearly to cast out the mote out of thy brother's eye.

3 And why beholdest thou the mote that is in thy brother's eye, but considerest not the beam that is
4 in thine own eye? Or how wilt thou say to thy brother, Let me cast out the mote out of thine eye;
5 and lo, the beam is in thine own eye? Thou hypocrite, cast out first the beam out of thine own eye; and then shalt thou see clearly to cast out the mote out of thy brother's eye.

that Judge will be, heightens the solemnity of the passage. Of course it is not meant that the mere absence of judging will of itself alone prevent our being judged by God on other grounds (comp. on 6: 12). This passage seems to be alluded to by James (2: 13; 4: 12), who repeatedly makes allusion to this discourse. The phrases, **with what judgment,** and **with what measure,** are literally 'in what judgment' and 'in what measure,' see on 3: 11. The 'again' of Com. Ver. represents a feebly-supported reading of the Greek. The saying, 'With what measure ye measure it shall be measured to you,' is also found in Mark 4: 24, as used on a different occasion. It must have been a proverbial saying at that time, for it occurs very often in the Talmud. As to our Lord's use of current sayings, see on v. 3-5. For other passages which forbid harsh judging, see Gal. 6: 1-5; Rom. 2: 1-3; 14: 3 f; 1 Cor. 13: 7. This sin grows in evil times, for instance, during a war or a pestilence, as rapidly as selfishness does. Everybody is busy finding fault, and few take time to notice the deeds that are praiseworthy. The practice is not only sinful in itself, but promotes other sins; for many a man will expend so much conscientiousness upon the severe condemnation of others' faults, that he has not enough left for his own; nay, will even think that having passed merited condemnation upon wrong-doing in others, he is thereby more at liberty to do wrong himself. We ought to judge ourselves strictly, and judge others leniently. A Roman writer states it well: "I think him best and most faultless, who pardons others as if he himself sinned every day, yet abstains from sins as if he pardoned no one."

Luke (6: 38-40) gives some additional sayings here, which Matthew omits; each has given only a sketch of the discourse. See Introduction to chap. 5.

3-5. Another instance of that change to the singular number by which the address is made more personal and pointed, see on 5: 23 and 6: 6. The word rendered **mote** denotes any dry twig, splinter, bit of straw, or other trash, being applied by a classic writer to the materials of which birds build their nests. This, which is the sort of thing likely to get into the eye, naturally suggested a **beam** as the contrasted term. The latter expression is of course eminently hyperbolical, resembling those in 19: 24; 23: 24; John 21: 25; Rom. 9: 3, etc. In the present case, no one has any difficulty; but in some others, many stumble at the hyperbole, from the failure to consider that such expressions are constantly and naturally employed in the language of common life, especially among the Orientals. **Considerest not,** does not set the mind on, think about. The ground of censure is not that one sees another's fault, however small, but that while seeing that, he does not think about his own fault, even though great. **Or how wilt thou say,** viz., with what sort of face will you say it, how feel at liberty to say it? Comp. John 6: 42; 8: 33. In Luke 6: 42 it is a still stronger expression, "Or how canst thou say," etc. **Brother** was used by Jews as it is by Christians, in addressing one another; this is a seemingly kind, fraternal proposal. **Pull** —or *cast*—**out** represents the same Greek word throughout v. 4 and 5. The Com. Version has here indulged its passion for varying the translation. See on 25: 46. **The beam,** the definite beam that is assumed to be in his eye.[1] The word **hypocrite** (v. 5.), has been explained on 6: 2. Its use here indicates that the person thus acting is esteemed as not simply self-deceived, really unaware of the beam in his own eye, but as *pretending* to be free from fault; and with this accords the 'considerest not' in v. 3. Indeed, self-deception

---

[1] The Greek text followed in the Com. Version ought to have been translated 'from' in v. 4, the preposition being *apo* in v. 4, while it is *ek* both times in v. 5. Comp. on 3: 16. Recent critics read *ek* in v. 4, on the authority of ℵ and several cursives. But it is very likely that *apo* was changed to *ek* by way of assimilation to v. 5. Of course there is no substantial difference.

6 Give not that which is holy unto the dogs, neither cast ye your pearls before swine, lest they trample them under their feet, and turn again and rend you.

6   Give not that which is holy unto the dogs, neither cast your pearls before the swine, lest haply they trample them under their feet, and turn and rend you.

rarely, if ever, exists, without some measure of hypocrisy, and *vice versa*. **See clearly,** is in the Greek a compound of the verb rendered 'beholdest' in v. 3. The idea is that correcting our own faults will not only render it less unsuitable for us to correct those of others, but will put us in better condition to do so. Ministers are by their calling especially required to "reprove and rebuke," and hence a special reason why they should seek to be blameless themselves. But of course it is not meant that no man must ever point out another's fault, or attempt to aid him in correcting it, until he has fully succeeded in correcting every similar fault of his own. This would prevent all efforts of the kind, since the truly humble Christian will never make sure that he is *wholly* free from any one fault whatsoever.

A remarkable instance of condemning the misconduct of others, while ignoring similar and far greater misconduct of our own, is seen in the history of David. (2 Sam. 12.) This tendency of human nature is so obvious, that it must have attracted attention in all ages and nations. *Horace:* "While you see your own faults with eyes bleared and unanointed, why is it that in the faults of your friends, your vision is as sharp as an eagle's?" *Seneca:* "You observe the pimples of others, when yourselves overgrown with a vast number of ulcers." The illustration our Lord uses is found several times in the Talmud; *e. g.*, "I wonder whether there is any one in this generation who is willing to receive reproof. Nay, if one says to another, 'Cast out the splinter from thine eye,' he will reply, 'Cast out the beam from thine eye.'" The same image occurs (Gesen.) in Arabic poetry. It is therefore probable that this was a proverb already current among the Jews when our Saviour used it. The same thing he appears to have done in v. 2, 6, 12; in 13: 57, (comp. John 4: 44); Acts 26: 14; and avowedly in Luke 4: 23. (Comp. as to the use of parables, on 13: 3.) The admirable wisdom with which he derived his beautiful illustrations from the most familiar objects in nature and relations of life, is here further seen in his using current popular sayings, which all would understand and feel the force of. So Paul quoted Greek poets. (Acts 17: 28; 1 Cor. 15: 33; Titus 1: 12.) Our Lord was thus acting out his own subsequent direction, bringing forth out of his treasure things new and old. (13: 52.) Originality is often a great source of power, but more good can sometimes be done, a deeper practical impression produced, by adopting ideas and expressions which are already familiar. (Comp. on 6: 9.)

6. This presents, in the form of an apophthegm, and so without any external mark of connection with what precedes (see at the beginning of this chapter), a caution against the opposite extreme to what he has just been rebuking. We must not judge others, but we must not heedlessly expose sacred things to persons wholly wanting in appreciation, and sure to reject them. These two extremes of unwise action often meet (Schaff); those who judge most harshly are often most easily imposed on. **Dogs** have always been regarded in the East with great abhorrence, not being usually kept at home, and so not evincing the strong attachment to owners which so interests us, but running wild in troops about the streets, where they devour carcasses and offal. Howling and fighting over their horrid food, they inspire intense disgust; and so they are generally associated in Scripture with ideas of reproach, contempt, or loathing. (1 Sam. 17: 43; 24: 14: 1 Kings 14: 11; 21: 19; 2 Kings 8: 13; Job 30: 1; Prov. 26: 11; Eccl. 9: 4; Isa. 66: 3; Matt. 15: 27; Phil. 3: 2; Rev. 22: 15.) So the Mohammedans now call Christians dogs. **That which is holy,** correctly renders the general and abstract expression of the original. This would include the shew-bread, or any form of food which had been offered on the altar, but especially suggests the flesh of sacrifices (called "holy flesh" in Hag. 2: 12; Jer. 11: 15), which it would have been a great profanation to throw to the dogs, like flesh torn by wild beasts. (Ex. 22: 31.) **Neither cast your pearls.** In the Talmud (Wünsche) a good thought is often called a pearl. (Comp. 13: 45 f.) **Before swine,** or, *the swine*, with the article, like 'the dogs,' meaning the class of creatures.

7 Ask, and it shall be given you ; seek, and ye shall find ; knock, and it shall be opened unto you:
8 For every one that asketh receiveth ; and he that seeketh findeth ; and to him that knocketh it shall be opened.

7   Ask, and it shall be given you ; seek, and ye shall
8 find ; knock, and it shall be opened unto you: for every one that asketh receiveth ; and he that seeketh findeth ; and to him that knocketh it shall be opened.

As the two kinds of animals were regarded with like feelings (comp. 2 Peter 2: 22), it is best to understand here a mere repetition under another image, after the manner of the Hebrew parallelism. (See on 4: 15.) The distinction some make between the dogs and the swine, as representing essentially different kinds of persons, is scarcely warranted. And so the notion of some (even Achelis) that the trampling applies to the swine, and the turning and rending to the dogs, is now commonly rejected, as making the sentence excessively artificial, and as requiring 'or turn.' Better take both as referring to the swine, conceived as wild and savage. It was not necessary to explain to Jews that giving any sacred thing to the dogs would be a horrid profanation.

What, then, do we learn from this saying? It is a warning against mistaken zeal in trying to make converts, or to correct men's faults. We must not judge (v. 1-5), but we must deal with men according to their character. Efforts to convert a drunken man, or one who has just been pouring out foul obscenity, would come under this head. Some persons do harm by expressing, in mixed society, those intimate feelings of personal Christian experience with which only the devout can sympathize. Perhaps this last is intimated by the expression **your pearls,** those precious truths which have become yours. But especially may we connect this verse with v. 5, and learn that in undertaking to correct men's faults, we must exercise discretion, lest we do harm rather than good (comp. Prov. 9: 8). Yet this precept, like those which precede, must not be pushed too far. Persons from whom a hasty judgment might least expect it, sometimes welcome gospel truth, as did publicans and sinners, and the robber on the cross. Often our only means of deciding wisely is to make the trial, and then continue our labors or not, according to the results and prospects. (10: 12-14; Acts 13: 46.) *Ryle:* "We are most of us far more likely to err on the side of over-caution than of over-zeal. We are generally far more disposed to remember the 'time to be silent' than the 'time to speak.'" Especially must we not be too solicitous to

avoid injury to ourselves, which is a matter of minor importance compared with insult to the sacred and precious truth we present. Here again (see on v. 3-5), our Lord has probably adopted a proverbial saying, since we find in the Talmud, "Do not cast pearls to swine, nor deliver wisdom to him who does not know its worth." Still, there can be little doubt that the Rabbis of later centuries borrowed striking sayings from the New Test., as they had long done from the Greeks, and afterwards did from the Arabians.

7, 8. To avoid both the extremes pointed out in v. 1-5 and v. 6, is a difficult task. We must all find it very hard to be at once charitable and watchful, hoping for the best, yet on our guard against the worst, judging no one, yet knowing men's characters and dealing with them accordingly. Well may we rejoice to find that the next words are a most affecting encouragement to prayer. Thus may we be enabled to perform these difficult duties and all the others enjoined in the discourse. Indeed, the language is so general as to hold good of prayer under all circumstances and for all objects. Similar examples of a passage specifically applying to what precedes, but having also a much wider general application, may be found in 5: 48 ; 6: 9; 7: 12; in James 1: 5, where he means especially wisdom to bear trials, but not that exclusively ; also in Gal. 6: 7, and many other passages of Paul's Epistles.

Knowing that men find it hard to pray in reality and with faith, Jesus condescends to encourage us by much repetition. **Ask, seek, knock,** are here practically equivalent, the repetition being made for the sake of impressiveness; all refined distinctions between them are out of place. Afterwards (v. 8) the threefold promise is repeated by thrice asserting the general fact that so it always is. And still further encouragement is given in the succeeding verses. What pains the Saviour takes to make us pray! And his word is crowded with gracious invitations and precious promises, such as ought to conquer all our unbelief, and fill us with joyful trust in coming to God. Of course these unqualified promises

9 Or what man is there of you, whom if his son ask bread, will he give him a stone?

10 Or if he ask a fish, will he give him a serpent?

11 If ye then, being evil, know how to give good gifts unto your children, how much more shall your Father which is in heaven give good things to them that ask him?

9 Or what man is there of you, who, if his son shall

10 ask him for a loaf, will give him a stone; or if he

11 shall ask for a fish, will give him a serpent? If ye then, being evil, know how to give good gifts unto your children, how much more shall your Father who is in heaven give good things to them that ask

---

are subject to conditions, such as are elsewhere laid down; we must ask for proper purposes (James 4: 3), according to God's will (1 John 5: 14); see below on v. 11. In v. 8, **it shall be opened,** is in some of the oldest authorities 'it is opened.' We cannot easily decide, since the present may have been changed into the future to be like v. 7, or the future into the present to be like the other verbs in v. 8; fortunately there is no substantial difference of meaning. The same thoughts here given in v. 7-11 are found in Luke 11: 9-13, as repeated on another occasion.

9-11. For the connection, see on v. 7, 8. **Or** proposes to regard the matter in another way, to introduce a different argument. *Or,* if the preceding considerations do not fully convince, look at it thus. (Compare in 12: 29 and 20: 15.) **Or what man is there of you,** which does not mean, as some explain, if he is so much as a man, and not a brute; but, though he is only a man. With all the imperfection and evil which belong to human nature, even a man will be willing to give to his son, and will have some judgment in giving. The expression thus tends to prepare the mind for the application made in v. 11. **Will he give,** is in the Greek introduced by a particle denoting that the answer must necessarily be negative; and the broken construction of the sentence renders the expression more striking. "Who is there of you, a man, of whom his son will ask a loaf—will he give him a stone? Or also he will ask a fish— will he give him a serpent"? **Bread.** The word means either 'bread' (so all the early English versions here), or 'a loaf,' according to the demands of each particular connection; and the latter seems to fit best here. (Comp. on 26: 26.) The round, flat cakes of bread, then and now common in Palestine, resembled flat stones (comp. on 4: 3). So a **serpent** somewhat resembles a **fish.** Bread and fish were the ordinary food of those who dwelt by the Lake of Galilee. On the subsequent occasion (Luke 11: 12), an egg is added, to which a scorpion coiled might not be greatly dissimilar. Now the question is not whether the father will refuse his son's request, but whether, instead of the thing asked he will give him something similar that is useless (a stone), or hurtful (a serpent). In Luke 11: 11, the expression is distinctly, "Will, *instead of* a fish, give him a serpent?" (Bib. Un. Ver.) Even an earthly parent will not be ignorant enough to make such a mistake, will not be cruel enough thus to mock his child's request. **Being evil,** in contrast with the holy God. **Know how to give,** does not simply mean are *willing* to give, but understand how to give judiciously and kindly, so that the gifts are *really* **good gifts.** Compare such expressions as, "The Lord knoweth how to deliver the godly out of temptation" (2 Pet. 2: 9); "I know both how to be abased,—or *in humble circumstances,*—and I know how to abound," *i. e.,* without being unduly depressed or elated (Phil. 4: 12); "If a man (any one) know not how to rule his own house." (1 Tim. 3: 5); also Luke 12: 55, etc.[1] The statement involves a disposition to give, and the term denotes judgment in giving; and in both respects the argument from the less to the greater holds good, **how much more** will the Father on high, who is "too wise to err, too good to be unkind," give what is really good. It is a natural extension of the same argument to say, that if we ask for something which we think to be good, but which he knows to be evil, he will withhold it, even as any judicious human parent must often do. It is really a part of the privilege of prayer, that God will withhold, if he sees best. Were this not the case, the wisest and best persons might often be slowest to ask, for they know how often their judgment as to what was best has proved erroneous. But as it is, we may ask without apprehension for whatever we think is best, and our perfectly wise and perfectly kind Father will give that, or some-

---

[1] Tyndale and the succeeding English versions render 'can give,' doubtless following Luther. The Com. Ver. wisely follows Rheims in rendering 'know how to give.'

12 Therefore all things whatsoever ye would that men should do to you, do ye even so to them : for this is the law and the prophets.

12 him?   All things therefore whatsoever ye would that men should do unto you, even so do ye also unto them : for this is the law and the prophets.

thing which he sees to be better. On the second occasion (Luke 11: 13), our Lord substitutes for the general expression 'good things,' the specific blessing 'the Holy Spirit,' which is the best of all good gifts. "In this change we may see evidence, not, as has been said, of 'a later form of Christian tradition,' but probably of a later and more spiritual teaching, addressed to more advanced disciples." (*Bib. Comm.*) As to the frequency with which Jesus speaks of God as our Father, see on 6: 9.

12. Our Lord now gives one single precept for the regulation of our conduct, a simple working rule, which is not merely a summary statement of all that he has been teaching on that subject throughout the discourse, but is expressly declared to cover the entire ground of what is required by "the law and the prophets," *i. e.*, the whole of the then existing revelation (see on 5: 17). This precept is an application of the principle, 'Thou shalt love thy neighbor as thyself,' and on that, *in conjunction with* 'Thou shalt love the Lord thy God with all thy heart,' Jesus afterwards declares that the whole law and the prophets hang. (22: 40.) It is plain therefore that he does not here mean to say that the whole requirements of the Scriptures as to *all* duties are summed up in this rule, but their whole requirements as to duties to our *fellow-men.* (Comp. Gal. 5: 14.) It is a great mistake to suppose that nothing is involved in love to God beyond love to our neighbor. **Therefore,** as an inference from what precedes. The word itself does not determine how far back its reference goes. The rule that follows is apparently given as a sort of general consequence, or recapitulatory inference, from all that he has been teaching concerning the righteousness required of his people (5: 20; 6: 1, 33), so far, of course, as pertained to their treatment of their fellow-men. He did not come to destroy the law and the prophets, but to develop and deepen and broaden them (see on 5: 17) ; and so (Weiss) he has here given one simple rule, which carries their whole contents in a compact form, ready for prompt and varied application. *Luther :* "With

these words he closes up the teachings of these three chapters, and ties them all up in a little bundle." See a somewhat similar use of 'therefore' in 6 : 34, and as to the connection here, see at the beginning of chap. 7.[1]

This simple and beautiful precept is now commonly called, from its excellence, the "Golden Rule," just as James (2: 8) calls the precept, "Thou shalt love thy neighbor as thyself," the 'royal law.' The Jewish teachers endeavored to have a special rule for every exigency of life, and have filled the Talmud with nice distinctions and wearisome details, without at last touching half the questions which must arise. The Great Teacher has furnished many particulars by way of illustration and example, but he delights to give comprehensive rules. *Harris :* "Like the few imaginary circles by which geography circumscribes the earth, he has, by a few sentences, described and distributed into sections the whole globe of duty ; so that wherever we may be on it, we find ourselves encompassed by some comprehensive maxim; and in whatever direction we may move, we have only to reflect, in order to perceive that we are receding from, or approaching to, some line of morality." It is here taken for granted, that what one wishes others to do to him is something right, such a thing as he ought to wish. Otherwise the rule would lead to folly and crime. If a man should become a criminal, he would probably wish the judge to acquit him, though guilty ; it does not follow that if the same man is a judge, he ought to let the guilty go free. When a child, one did not wish his father to restrain him; it does not follow that he must now let his own son go unrestrained. Has, then, the Saviour's rule failed here? No, it is taken for granted that the wish of our own to which he bids us conform in our treatment of others, is, or would be, a right wish under all the circumstances. I do not wish now to be treated as a child, for mine is not the character or condition of a child ; but if I were a child, and had just views and right feelings, I should wish my father not to make me my own master when unfit for it, but to restrain and discipline me,

---

[1] 'Would wish that men should do' is in Greek one of the *non-final* uses of *hina*, explained on 5: 29.

in the way that would be for my real good; and thus I ought to act towards my child.

Here again, as in v. 2, 3, 6, we find that our Lord has employed a form of statement quite similar to some sayings then already in existence. *Confucius* said (Legge's "Chinese Classics," vol. 1), "Do not unto others that which you would not they should do unto you." *Isocrates* said, "What you are angry at when inflicted on you by others, this do not do to others." A Greek biographer of Aristotle relates that, being asked how we should behave towards our friends, he answered, "As we should wish them to behave toward us." The apocryphal book of Tobit (4: 15) has "What thou hatest, do to no one." Of the great Rabbi Hillel, who was probably still living at the birth of Christ, the Talmud relates, as showing that he was kind, and not irritable and headlong like Shammai, "There is a story of a certain Gentile, who came to Shammai and said, 'Make a proselyte of me on this condition, that you teach me the whole law while I stand on one foot.' He drove him away with a long staff which he held in his hand. The man came to Hillel, and he made a proselyte of him, saying, 'What is hateful to thee, do not do to another. This is the whole law; the rest is explanation of it.'" *Philo*, who was an old man in A. D. 40, says, "One must not himself do what he hates to have done to him." *Seneca*, who died A. D. 65, says that the best way to confer a benefit is "to give as we should wish to receive."[1] It will be observed that the sayings of Confucius, Isocrates, and the three Jewish teachers are merely negative; that of Seneca is confined to giving, and that of Aristotle to the treatment of friends. Our Lord makes it a rule for positive action, and towards all men; and declares, as Hillel had done, that it is a summary of the entire Scriptures. It is a part of his wisdom that he frequently adopts modes of thought and expressions already well known among men, or which had occurred to some thoughtful mind; while in many cases, as here, he gives them a new or a wider application. (Comp. on v. 5, and especially on 6: 9.) The real novelty of Christian Ethics lies in the fact that Christianity offers not only instruction in moral duty, but spiritual help in acting accordingly.—In Luke (6: 31), this precept is given in a different part of the Sermon on the Mount. Luke's brief sketch omits very much of the discourse, and to prevent what he gives from being a mere collection of fragments, he must of necessity connect passages which have some natural relation. Accordingly, this saying there follows the injunction, "Give to every one that asketh thee," etc. The phrase, **for this is the law and the prophets,** is omitted by Luke, precisely as he omits the extensive portion from Matt. 5: 13 to 6: 18, because it was suited especially for Jews, whom Matthew had peculiarly in view, but Luke had not. (See Int. to chap. 5.)

HOMILETICAL AND PRACTICAL.

V. 1 f. Mutual misjudgments: 1) Between new converts and old disciples. 2) Between church officers and church members. 3) Between representatives of rival societies, journals, or institutions of learning. 4) Between professed Christians and non-professors. 5) Between all persons who judge each other at all.—We are apt to be very severe in judging faults to which we are not specially exposed. The drunkard is harshly condemned by a man who is too cold-blooded or too stingy to become a drunkard; stinginess is harshly condemned by one who finds it easier to be lavish than economical.—

> "Compound for sins they are inclined to,
> By damning those they have no mind to."

A preacher is apt to illustrate only by accounts of wrong-doing *elsewhere.*—MISHNA: "Do not judge your neighbor till you have put yourself in his place." BRAUNE (in Stier): "Judging others is the foul stain of social life." ACHELIS: "This judging rests upon two evil factors, the want of love to others, and the assumption of God's prerogative." HENRY: "He who usurps the bench, shall be called to the bar." CHRYS.: "'That is,' saith Christ, 'it is not the other that thou condemnest, but thyself, and thou art making the judgment-seat dreadful to thyself, and the account

[1] In Acts 15: 20 and 29, the negative precept, "and whatever you do not wish to happen to you, do not do to another," is interpolated by D, several cursives, Thebaic, Æthiopic, Irenæus (Latin), and in the second case also by the Harklean Syriac and Cyprian, a "Western" interpolation. The so-called "Teaching of the Apostles" gives the same (ch. 1), followed by the so-called "Constitutions of the Apostles," vii. 2.

strict.' . . . . He is not overthrowing reproof nor correction, but forbidding men to neglect their own faults, and exult over those of other men.'' DYKES: ''To take one's self for a Christian, and yet be ignorant of the extent of one's own guilt and evil-heartedness, is to be exactly in that state of blind conceit which qualifies a man for the *role* of a heartless and reckless, and utterly unrighteous judge. . . . . We have to live with one another; and the kindly thoughts of others about ourselves is as the breath of life to us. . . . . There are some people who always suspect base reasons for whatever looks generous, and exult in exposing them to view; but we are not apt to conclude that such men's own motives are the purest, or their own life the sweetest in the world.'' PLUMPTRE: '' Briefly we may say, (1) Judge no man unless it be a duty to do so. (2) As far as may be, judge the offence, and not the offender. (3) Confine your judgment to the earthly side of faults, and leave their relation to God, to him who sees the heart. (4) Never judge at all without remembering your own sinfulness, and the ignorance and infirmities which may extenuate the sinfulness of others.''

V. 3-5. The mote and the beam. 1) We must by no means let both remain. 2) We cannot really cast out either, if wholly careless about the other. 3) Casting out the beam will make us more clear-sighted, more sympathetic, and more skillful, in casting out the mote, (not simply seeing the mote, v. 3; but seeing to cast it out, v. 5). 4) For help in casting out both, ask, and it shall be given you, v. 7.—V. 1-5. Efforts to correct the faults of our brethren. 1) With no harsh, undiscriminating judgment of their faults. 2) With no real or apparent assumption of being without fault ourselves. 3) With clear perception, heightened by experience in correcting our own faults. 4) With sympathetic and fraternal kindness.—V. 3. What we need here is not ''to see oursels as others see us,'' but to see ourselves as we see others.—V. 4. CICERO: '' It is the part of folly to see other people's faults and forget our own.'' EUTHYM. : '' The healer ought to be healthy.'' —Proposing to cast out the mote without thinking of the beam, is (DYKES), 1) a blunder, 2) an hypocrisy. RADER (in Cor. a Lap.): '' A crooked measuring-rule makes even straight things appear crooked.''

V. 6. New converts are especially prone, in their inexperienced zeal, to cast pearls before swine. In religious teaching we must avoid those who 1) will despise the holy and precious truth, and 2) will damage the teachers. Such are pretended converts, who ''join the church'' in order to get trade or to impose on charity; cases often encountered in foreign and home missions, and in all large cities. WEISS: ''Gospel truth is 1) 'holy,' as coming from God, 2) precious (pearls, comp. 13: 45).'' DYKES : ''We often stultify our attempts to reform the vicious and brutal by plans which look charitable, but are simply childish, winking at the darker facts of human character. . . To select the fit occasion and discover the wise method; to adapt truth to the evil state of the hearer, and win for it a willing ear; to be cautious without being timid, and faithful but not indiscreet; this asks for a certain nice tact . . . . a wisdom into which there enter several elements, but of which one element usually is a spiritual gift from the Father of lights.''—We have frequent occasion to remember the proverb, '' Speech is silvern, but silence is golden.''

V. 7-11. To avoid censoriousness, and yet not cast pearls before swine, ask, and it shall be given you. To refrain from worldly anxieties, because trusting in God (6: 19-34), ask, and it shall be given you. To eschew ostentation and all self-seeking in good works (6: 1-18), ask, and it shall be given you. To attain the profound spiritual righteousness which Jesus teaches and requires (5: 17-48), ask, and it shall be given you. To be indeed the salt of the earth and the light of the world (5: 13-16), ask, and it shall be given you. To find blessing in the trials of life (5: 3-12), ask, and it shall be given you. If we do not possess God's spiritual blessings, it must be because we do not ask. One may be a truly industrious man, and yet poor in temporal things; but one cannot be a truly praying man, and yet poor in spiritual things. CHRYS.: ''And if thou dost not receive straightway, do not even thus despair. For to this end he said, *knock*, to signify that even if he should not straightway open the door, we are to continue there.'' LUTHER: '' Hast thou here the consoling promise and rich assurance he gives, as showing that prayer has something in it, and is precious in God's sight, since Jesus so earnestly exhorts to it, so kindly invites, and

13 Enter ye in at the strait gate: for wide *is* the gate, and broad *is* the way, that leadeth to destruction, and many there be which go in thereat:
14 *a* Because strait *is* the gate, and narrow *is* the way, which leadeth unto life, and few there be that find it.

13 Enter ye in by the narrow gate: for wide [1]is the gate, and broad is the way, that leadeth to destruc-
14 tion, and many are they that enter in thereby. [2]For narrow is the gate, and straitened the way, that leadeth unto life, and few are they that find it.

a Or, *How.*——1 Some ancient authorities omit, *is the gate*....2 Many ancient authorities read, *How narrow is the gate, etc.*

assures us that we shall not ask in vain; even if we had no other ground or inducement than this rich and loving word, it ought to be enough to draw us and drive us to prayer."—V. 9-11. EUTHYM.: "He that asks must both be a son, and must ask what it becomes the father to give, and is profitable for the son to receive." AUG.: "The Lord is good, and often does not give what we should wish, in order that he may give what we should wish still more." ACHELIS: "If the son asks for a stone or serpent, thinking it to be a loaf or fish, the father's love will give the real good. Paul asked thrice that the thorn might be removed, and afterwards learned that the Master had done for him something far better. (2 Cor. 12: 8, 10.") DYKES: "Here, in these simple, homely, human words of Jesus, we have surely all the philosophy of prayer which Christian hearts require . . . . all genuine intercourse betwixt child and parent must have two sides: while it is on the child's side, the freest and most unlimited expression of such things as a child's heart can long for, or a child's judgment discern to be good, it is on the parent's side the freest and most voluntary determination to give only what a riper judgment knows to be best, and all that a larger heart yearns to bestow."

V. 12. How to treat others. 1) Worldly pride and honor will say, Treat them as they have treated us—return a kindness, revenge an injury. 2) Jesus says, Treat them as we should wish them to treat us—forgive, forbear, make the best of the past, hope for the best in future.—To carry out this rule requires imagination, sympathy, unselfishness.—RYLE: "The Golden Rule settles a hundred difficult points, which in a world like this are continually arising between man and man. It prevents the necessity of laying down endless little rules for our conduct in specific cases. It sweeps the whole debatable ground with one mighty principle."—LUTHER: "All the teachings of these chapters he here ties up in a little bit of a bundle, that every one may place in his bosom. And certainly it is a fine thing that Christ sets before us precisely our-

selves for an example. Thou thyself art thy master, doctor, and preacher."

13-29. SERMON ON THE MOUNT. CONCLUDING EXHORTATIONS TO PRACTICE AS WELL AS HEAR AND PROFESS. EFFECT PRODUCED.

The Sermon on the Mount is now drawing to a close. Its leading thoughts have been presented, and there has been a general encouragement to seek help from God, and a general rule for regulating our conduct, which covers the whole ground of the discourse. It is manifest to every hearer or reader that the requirements which have been made are very rigorous, in their profound spirituality and vast compass. Our Lord does not soften this rigor at all, but goes on to declare that the way pointed out by him is indeed one hard to find and follow, and that there is great danger of being deceived by false guides, and of self-deception; yet he does not present these facts as an excuse for shrinking back, nor even say that in spite of these things we must make the effort, but urges the very difficulties as a reason for going forward. We cannot drift with the crowd, without purpose or effort, through the narrow gate; to act thus would lead through the wide gate to destruction. Heedfully and diligently we must go in through the narrow gate, along the straitened and difficult way, which leads to life. *Gloss.* (in Aquinas): "Though it be hard to do to another what you would have done to yourself, yet so must we do, that we may enter the strait gate."

We may mark, as containing distinct though closely-related topics, v. 13 f.; 15-20; 21-23; 24-27; and the concluding statement in 28 f. The apophthegmatical form of expression, which we have already noticed at v. 1, 6, 7, is continued, and hence there is no conjunction connecting v. 13 with what precedes, while the general relation of the thoughts is obvious, as just pointed out.

13, 14. **Enter ye in,** viz., into life (v. 14), as in 18: 8 f.; 19: 17; or, into the Messianic kingdom, as in 5: 20; 7: 21; 18: 3; 19: 23 f. The comparison of 19: 17 with 19: 23 shows that the two expressions are equivalent. See also 25: 21-23. **At the strait**—or *through the narrow*—**gate.** The English word 'strait' is derived (through the French) from the Latin *strictum*, and is thus a different word from straight, which is an old form of stretched. The two are popularly confounded in quoting this passage, "The straight and narrow way," although it is not at all said that the way is straight. The word 'strait' is now little used except in Geography, and in such phrases as strait-laced and strait-jacket. **For wide is the gate.** It is quite possible that 'the gate' should here be omitted (as in margin Rev. Ver.).[1] There would be nothing lost from the substantial meaning (see below). The word rendered **broad** is a peculiar and strong term, 'broad-spaced,' 'spacious,' describing the way as having plenty of room in it. **Destruction.** The Greek word is translated (Rev. Ver.) 'perdition' in John 17: 12; Phil. 1: 28; 3: 19; 1 Tim. 6: 9; Heb. 10: 39; Rev. 17: 8, 11; 'destruction' in Rom. 9: 22; 2 Pet. 2: 1, 3, Rev. Ver.; 3: 16. **Go in**—or—*enter in*, same Greek word as at the beginning of the sentence. **Thereat,** literally, 'through it,' would more naturally make us think of passing through the gate, but would also apply to the way or road, as in 'pass along through that road.' (8: 28.) Instead of **because** (v. 14), there is much authority for a reading which would mean 'how,' (*ti* instead of *hoti*) making it an exclamation, 'How narrow is the gate!' It is extremely difficult to decide which is the correct reading.[2] As to the sense, 'because' would make this a reason why many enter the broad road, and an additional reason (comp. 'for,' v. 13) for the opening in-

junction to enter in by the narrow gate. The rendering in the Common Version 'because' (the Greek word in the text followed being the same as in 'for,' v. 13) obscures the fact that these are two parallel reasons for the injunction. The reading 'how' does not present this formally as a reason, but states solemnly and impressively the fact, which he designs to act as a motive for entering in by the narrow gate. An impassioned exclamation would here be less strange than it might at first sight appear, because the fact that so few are saved might well awaken profound emotion in the Saviour's bosom.[3] The word rendered **narrow,** or in Rev. Ver. *straitened*, signifies pressed, pressed together, cramped; a Greek writer uses it when he describes one as occupying "a straitened cell"; so it implies not merely that the road is narrow, but, as it were, cramped, confined, so that there is difficulty in passing along it. This word is thus the precise opposite of the term 'spacious,' applied to the other road. In the one, men can wander heedlessly, and roam about at pleasure in the broad spaces; the other requires to be pursued with great care and exactness. **Life** is here first used, as meaning spiritual and eternal life, in our Lord's Galilean ministry; but previously in his early Judean ministry. (John 3: 15 f; 4: 14, 36.) **Leadeth** is literally *leadeth away*, perhaps implying a long course. Though the expressions in v. 14 are precisely parallel to those in v. 13, there is a striking exception at the close; he does not say, 'few are those that enter in through it,' but 'few are those that find it.' Our attention is thus strongly called to the fact that this narrow gate and way is likely to be overlooked, and so it should be

---

[1] The omission in v. 13 is supported by ℵ and the Old Latin, and "*many* Greek and Latin Fathers, early and late"; in v. 14 the evidence for omitting is weaker. The state of the evidence is readily explained by the supposition that 'the gate' is genuine in **v. 14** and spurious in v. 13, and is not easily explained otherwise. W H. adopt this view in text and Appendix. Tisch. bracketed in both places.

[2] The evidence for *hoti* being B ℵ X, many cursives, a few Latin copies, Egyptian, and Origen, is considered decisive by W H. (according to their theory as to B ℵ) so that they do not even mention the other reading. Yet the latter, besides the support of all other uncials (C and D are here wanting), numerous cursives, nearly all Old Latin and the Vulgate, Old Syr., Pesh. and Harklean, other versions and various Fathers, has

strongly in its favor the internal evidence. If *ti* was the original reading, it was quite unusual in such a connection and looked strange, and so might very easily have been changed into the familiar *hoti*. But why should *hoti* be changed into *ti*? It is very difficult to suppose the change accidental. The *repetition* of *hoti* in the successive clauses gives but slight trouble as to the sense; and even if there was trouble, it would be at once greatly increased by changing to *ti*, which would here have so rare and strange a use. In the present state of Text-criticism, the question can hardly be settled.

[3] 'How' would be a very unusual meaning of *ti*, but not unexampled, see Grimm, and Moulton in Winer, p. 562; a corresponding Hebrew word is repeatedly employed in that sense.

carefully searched for and diligently entered.

Is the narrow gate at the beginning of the way or at the end of it? Many have taken the former view, understanding by the gate conversion, or the beginning of the Christian life, and by the way its subsequent prosecution. (So Bunyan, in Pilgrim's Progress.) A larger number of expositors urge that it is more natural to conceive of a road leading to a gate, by which we enter the city; and they quote (Wet.) as similar in expression and sentiment the saying of *Cebes* (pupil of Socrates): "Do you see a certain little door, and a certain road before the door, which is not much crowded, but very few are journeying on it? . . . . This is the road that leads to true instruction." But it is also easy enough to conceive of a gate opening into a spacious avenue, and a smaller one into a narrow path, which conducts to the mansion. There is a much more serious objection than this to the common view. If passing through the narrow gate is conversion, to what does passing through the wide gate correspond? There is no marked transition made by all unconverted persons from one state to another, which can be compared to passing through a gate into a new road. If, on the other hand we understand the gate as at the end of the way, why is it put first in the statement? The difficulties on both sides are thought to be obviated by the following explanation: Our Lord, on a subsequent occasion (Luke 13: 24), uses the simple image of entering the narrow gate, expressions similar to which are common in Jewish and classical writers. But here he expands the image, representing not only a narrow gate, but a narrow and difficult road, and so as to the wide gate and spacious road. We have thus no occasion carefully to mark off the gate, as lying either at the beginning or the end of the road, but both together serve to set forth more strongly than the simple idea of a gate would do, the comparative ease of reaching perdition, and the difficulty of reaching life. (So, in substance, Chrys., Jerome, Tholuck, Weiss, Keil.) And accordingly 'enter in through it' (v. 13.) and 'find it' (v. 14) need not be specially assigned to the gate or the way, being applicable to either, and thus to both. If 'the gate' be omitted after 'wide' in v. 13 (see above), there will, according to this view, be nothing lost of the substantial meaning. Achelis takes 'find it' as meaning find life, which is grammatically possible, but does not suit the connection; and to find a road is, in itself, a much more natural expression than to find life. It is misleading interpretation to say (Plumptre) that Christ himself is here the way and the gate, because of John 14: 6; 10: 7. Must a familiar image be supposed to have everywhere in the Bible the same application?

The comparative ease and difficulty of the two gates and ways may be regarded as due both to external influences and to ourselves. Men in general do not interrupt our progress to destruction, but much of their influence tends to make it easier; the crowd are going that way, and mankind have a deplorable tendency to follow the crowd. (Comp. Ex. 23: 2.) At the same time, our sinful propensities are numerous and powerful, and incline us in that same direction. On the other hand, the way to life is fenced in on either side by God's requirements (Deut. 5: 32; Prov. 4: 27; Isaiah 30: 21), while sometimes persecutions (1.Pet. 4: 17f.), and always the thousand forms of temptation, unite with our own sinful reluctance to do right, and make the gate very narrow, the way exceedingly straitened. None the less is it true that Christ's people are the happy ones (5: 3-12), that wisdom's "ways are ways of pleasantness" (Prov. 3: 17), and that God's "commandments are not grievous" (1 John 5: 3); because all this refers to such as are born again, and holds good of them just in proportion as they are deeply pious. (John 14: 15-17.) See interesting parallels to this image of the gate and the way in Ecclus. 21: 10; 2 Esdras 7: 6-14. Images somewhat corresponding are also quoted from *Hesiod :* "Evil we may seize upon even in multitudes with ease; the way to it is smooth, and it lies very near. But the immortal gods have placed sweat at the entrance to virtue, and long and straight is the path to it, and rough at first; but when you come to the summit, then it grows easy." *Pythagoras* (Corn. a Lap.) said "that at first the path of virtue is narrow and confined, but afterwards it becomes wider by degrees; the way of pleasure, on the other hand, is not wide at the beginning, but afterwards it becomes more and more straitened." *Philo :* "A road worn by men and beasts, and suited

15 Beware of false prophets, which come to you in sheep's clothing, but inwardly they are ravening wolves.

15   Beware of false prophets, that come to you in sheep's clothing, but inwardly are ravening wolves.

for riding horses and driving chariots, is very similar to pleasure; while the ways of prudence and temperance, and the other virtues, even if not impassable, are yet wholly unworn, for small is the number of those who walk on them."

15. Beware of false prophets. In your efforts to find and enter the narrow gate, the straitened way, beware of those who would mislead you. Alas! it is not enough that we have personally so much difficulty in finding the way to life, and that so many set us a bad example; there are others who deliberately attempt to lead us astray. For the term 'prophets,' see on v. 22. There were already false teachers among the Jews, sanctimonious (6: 2) and hypocritical. (John 10: 1, 10.) And our Lord may be referring immediately to these (Weiss); but he is also preparing for the future, as he will do still further near the close of his ministry. (24: 11, 24.) So we find Paul speaking of hypocritical false teachers as early as A. D. 50 (Gal. 2: 4), warning the Ephesian elders in A. D. 58 against grievous wolves (Acts 20: 28-31), and a ·few years later giving many such warnings in the Pastoral Epistles; as Peter and John also do in their Epistles. Few things are so painful to the teacher of truth as to know that others will be busily teaching the same persons ruinous error. **In sheep's clothing** means, of course, clothed like sheep, looking like sheep, just as in Æsop's fable of the wolf in sheep's clothing. The idea of some that it means clothed in woolen garments, resembling a supposed style of garment worn by prophets, is unfounded, and very nearly ridiculous. **Ravening,** rapacious, snatching at everything to devour it. (John 10: 12.) *Henry:* "Every hypocrite is a *goat* in sheep's clothing, but a false prophet is a *wolf* in sheep's clothing; not only not a sheep, but the worst enemy the sheep have, that comes not but to tear and devour, to scatter the sheep, to drive them from God and from one another into crooked paths."

16-20. Our Lord here shows how these false teachers may be detected, viz., **by their fruits. Know** is in the Greek a compound, meaning recognize, or fully know. **Ye shall know** (in Greek simply the future tense) is

here not a command, but an assurance. **Do men gather,** literally, *they,* precisely like our impersonal expressions, "they say," etc. (Comp. on 5: 10.) The Greek introduces the question by a particle which strongly implies that the answer must be negative. James (3: 12) uses the same image, probably having this passage in mind; for, as already remarked, he often refers to the Sermon on the Mount. **Even so** (v. 17), *i. e.,* as we do not gather one kind of fruits from another kind of tree, so it is also true that fruits are good or bad according as the tree is sound or unsound. Here, and in v. 18, the original is plural, 'good fruits,' 'bad fruits'; in v. 19 it is singular—mere variations for the sake of variety. **Corrupt** is, literally, *decayed,* rotten, and then unsound in general—a tree in a decayed or unhealthy condition, such that its sap is diseased, and it cannot produce good fruits. V. 17 states the actual fact of nature; v. 18, that it cannot be otherwise, from the constitution of things; v. 19 that men are accustomed to act accordingly; v. 20 is a repetition of what was said in v. 16, made for the sake of greater impressiveness, and presented as a conclusion from what has been said in v. 16-19. A good many copies of the Greek introduce v. 19 by 'therefore,' and v. 15 by 'but'—from not perceiving the apophthegmatical character of the style. With v. 18 comp. 12: 33, where the same image is employed by our Lord in another connection; with v. 19 compare the words of John the Baptist in 3: 10, which many present had probably heard him speak. **Hewn down** (v. 19) is literally, *cut out, i. e.,* from its place in the orchard. It is a matter of common observation that men do actually cut out and burn trees that do not produce good fruit.

There has been much discussion as to whether the 'fruits' by which we are to judge, represent the *life* or the *teachings* of the teachers in question. The latter view prevailed widely until Bengel, and the passage was freely used as authority for punishing heretics. By comparing the whole connection, especially the phrases, '*doeth* the will' (v. 21), '*work* iniquity' (v. 23), '*doeth* them' (v. 24), we see the application here is to their works, their life. On the

16 Ye shall know them by their fruits. Do men gather grapes of thorns, or figs of thistles?
17 Even so every good tree bringeth forth good fruit; but a corrupt tree bringeth forth evil fruit.
18 A good tree cannot bring forth evil fruit, neither *can* a corrupt tree bring forth good fruit.
19 Every tree that bringeth not forth good fruit is hewn down and cast into the fire.
20 Wherefore by their fruits ye shall know them.
21 Not every one that saith unto me, Lord, Lord, shall enter into the kingdom of heaven; but he that doeth the will of my Father which is in heaven.

16 By their fruits ye shall know them. Do *men* gather
17 grapes of thorns, or figs of thistles? Even so every good tree bringeth forth good fruit; but the corrupt
18 tree bringeth forth evil fruit. A good tree cannot bring forth evil fruit, neither can a corrupt tree
19 bring forth good fruit. Every tree that bringeth not forth good fruit is hewn down, and cast into the
20 fire. Therefore by their fruits ye shall know them.
21 Not every one that saith unto me, Lord, Lord, shall enter into the kingdom of heaven; but he that doeth

---

other hand, in Luke's sketch of the discourse (Luke 6: 43), the special application is to the idea that as a good tree produces good fruits, etc., so a good man will put forth good teachings, and these will have a good effect upon his pupils, and a bad man the reverse; and similar is the application when our Lord uses the image again. (12: 33.) May it not be that he here indicated an application both to their life and the character and effect of their teachings; and that Matthew's incomplete sketch gives prominence to the one, Luke's to the other? (There seem to be several such cases in the two reports of this discourse.) In both respects false prophets would pretend to be members of the flock; making great pretence both to a holy life and to sound teaching. But *is* their life holy, *is* their teaching sound, and does it make their pupils wiser and better? Those tests will show what they are inwardly and really. *Jerome:* "For it behooves the servants of God that both their works should be approved by their teaching, and their teaching by their works." It is not meant that every separate item of false teaching will be attended by some distinct evil practice; their evil conduct in general will show them to be bad men, and so to be unsafe teachers. When some teachers of ruinous heresy are men of scrupulous conduct and pleasing general character, and even very devout, this may usually be ascribed to their religious education and early habits, or to the religious atmosphere they breathe, or to a real piety which their theories cannot destroy in them, however hurtful to othere.

21. The test of false prophets, their fruits (v. 16, 20), naturally leads to the kindred thought that the followers of the true prophet, the Saviour himself, will be known not by their professions of devotion to him, but by their fruits, their doing the will of his Father. That this is true in general is strikingly shown by declaring (v. 22 f.) that even many

who have prophesied and wrought miracles by his name, will be finally rejected as having never really been his people. Much more, then, is that possible and likely in the case of such as have given less evidence of really being his followers. This passage (v. 21-23) is thus seen to be naturally suggested by the preceding warning against false prophets, but to be widened into a solemn admonition to all, as to the danger of self-deception; and this again will naturally lead to the conclusion in v. 24–27. **Not every one,** but only some of them, only those of them who do the will of God. (Comp. Luke 9: 59, 61.) **Lord, Lord,** the repetition expressing earnestness in addressing him, which might, of course, be either real or assumed. Similarly in v. 22; 25: 11, and compare "Master, Master" in Luke 8: 24. For the exact meaning of 'Lord' see on 8: 19. It conveys the idea of rightful master, ruler, sovereign. If we call Jesus 'Lord,' and do not what he says (Luke 6: 46), or, what is the same thing, do not the will of God, it is a flagrant inconsistency—to pretend that he is our Master, and yet not obey him. **Enter into the kingdom of heaven,** see on 5: 20. The kingdom of heaven is here understood with reference to its consummation, its eternal, glorious rewards. (See on 3: 2.) **He that doeth the will of my Father.** This is the first time in the Galilean ministry that Jesus speaks of God as his Father. It is previously found only in Luke 2: 49; John 2: 16. Comp. as to 'life,' in v. 14. 'Will' is here especially what God requires; and to 'do' the will of God is to obey his commands. So also in 12: 50 and 21: 31. In 6: 10, the idea is quite different, viz., literally, 'Let thy will (desire, wish) come to pass.' In 1 Cor. 12: 3, Rev. Ver., Paul declares that "no man speaking in the Spirit of God saith, Jesus is anathema; and no man can say, Jesus is Lord, but in the Holy Spirit." He evidently supposes the utterance to be a sincere one,

22 Many will say to me in that day, Lord, Lord, have we not prophesied in thy name? and in thy name have cast out devils? and in thy name done many wonderful works?

23 And then will I profess unto them, I never knew you: depart from me, ye that work iniquity.

22 the will of my Father who is in heaven. Many will say to me in that day, Lord, Lord, did we not prophesy by thy name, and by thy name cast out demons, and by thy name do many [1] mighty works?

23 And then will I profess unto them, I never knew

---

[1] Gr. *powers.*

---

while the Saviour is here speaking of persons with whom it is all talk and outside. Distinct from both these cases is the future universal confession of Phil. 2: 11.

22, 23. For the connection see on v. 21, at the beginning. **In that day,** the well-known day, often spoken of, and familiar to the minds of all. It is a phrase frequently employed by the O. T. prophets to designate the time of Messiah in general; as used in the N. T., it looks especially to the consummation of Messiah's kingdom (comp. on 6: 10), and thus denotes the day of judgment (see Luke 10: 12; 2 Thess. 1: 10; 2 Tim. 1: 12, 18; 4: 8; Rev. 16: 14). Our Lord here begins to educate his hearers to that conception, as in like manner he thus early intimates that he is to be the Judge, an idea brought out more fully in John 5: 22, 27; Matt. 25: 31 ff. Throughout the discourse it is evidently assumed that he is the Messiah, though not expressly so declared, and it is therefore not strange that he should assume to be the final judge. Similar is the **Lord, Lord,** as addressed to him; for this cannot be here the mere polite form of address (8: 6; Acts 16: 30), since (Achelis) no one could imagine that he would be saved for merely speaking politely to Jesus. Here is a touch of the 'authority' which so impressed his hearers. (v. 24.) **Have we not prophesied.** The Hebrew word which we render 'prophet' signifies one who speaks under a divine influence, speaks as he is moved to speak by a divine power, and so is the ambassador of God to men, the revealer and interpreter of his will. To foretell things future was thus only a part of the prophet's office; he was the inspired and authoritative religious instructor of the people, whether as to things past, present, or future. The Greek word *prophetes* which we borrow, is now explained as meaning not one who *foretells*, but (Liddell & Scott) one who *for*-tells, who

speaks *for* God, or (Grimm, Cremer) one who speaks *openly*, an interpreter (of the Deity); it thus corresponds closely to the Hebrew word. To prophesy in the New Test., is always to speak by divine inspiration, though not always concerning the future. It is a mistake to say that it sometimes signifies merely to teach. Even in 1 Cor. 14: 1 ff., the apostle is not contrasting the gift of tongues with ordinary teaching, but with inspired teaching in the common language. In the present passage it is evident that to prophesy is regarded as a remarkable thing. **In—or *by* —thy name,** is the simple instrumental (wrongly called dative) case of the noun without a preposition.[1] 'Thy' is emphatic in the original. It was by means of *his* name that they performed these wonders, and this is repeated three times; surely then *he* would not reject them. Comp. Acts 3: 16; 19: 13; which last shows that the name of Jesus was sometimes actually called out. For the Scripture use of the word 'name' see on 28: 19; as to casting out demons, see on 8: 28. **Wonderful works.** *Mighty works* is better. Tyn. has 'miracles,' followed by Great Bible, Gen., Rheims. It would be better to render this word (powers) uniformly by 'miracles,' as Com. Ver. nearly always does in the Acts and Epistles. Comp. on 12: 38. **Profess,** see on 10: 32. They were professing to have been his followers, and he will, on the contrary, profess—openly and plainly declare—that such they never really were. The Rev. Ver. here rightly retains 'profess' (instead of 'confess'), as also in Titus 1: 16; might it not better have done likewise in Heb. 4: 14; 10: 23? (Compare below, on 14: 7). **I never knew you.** The word rendered 'never' is very strong, not even at any time, nearly equivalent to our "never, never." 'Knew,' *i. e.*, as mine, as my people. So in 25: 12, where the bridegroom says to the fool-

---

[1] This construction is not elsewhere found with this word in the New Test. (Mark 9: 38 has a preposition in the correct text), and appears to have been borrowed from Jer. 27: 15. The Gothic takes pains to express it here like the Greek, without a preposition, which it regularly employs where the Greek does. The Latin has inserted 'in.'

24 Therefore whosoever heareth these sayings of mine, and doeth them, I will liken him unto a wise man, which built his house upon a rock :

24 you : depart from me, ye that work iniquity. Every one therefore who heareth these words of mine, and doeth them, shall be likened unto a wise man, who

ish virgins, 'I know you not'; John 10: 13, Rev. Ver., 'I know mine own, and mine own know me'; Gal. 4: 9, Rev. Ver., 'To know God, or rather to be known of God'; 1 Cor. 8: 3, Rev. Ver., 'If any man loveth God, the same is known of him'; Amos 3: 2, 'You only did I know, out of all the families of the earth.' Here, as constantly in Scripture, God is spoken of in language derived from men. A man knows some persons, and does not know others; and only the former can enjoy any privileges which may pertain to his acquaintance. Suppose a prince to have formerly sojourned in a distant province, and now to ascend the throne. Various persons come from that province, claiming to have been his acquaintances, and hoping to enjoy the advantages of a residence at court. But among them are some whom he repulses, saying, "I never knew you." They may insist upon various things as showing that they were his acquaintances, and rendered him important service; but he replies, "I never at any time knew you—go away from me." Such is the kind of image here involved in the Saviour's language. (Comp. 25: 31, 41; 2 Tim. 2: 19.) And not in all the passages above quoted, nor elsewhere, is there occasion for the oft-repeated arbitrary notion derived from the Fathers, that 'know' conveys the additional idea of approve or regard. The Bible is simply speaking of God after the manner of men, and using the term to denote acquaintance, together with all its pleasures and advantages. **Depart from me,** comp. 25: 41; Luke 13: 24. **Ye that work iniquity,** is quoted from Psa. 6: 8. The Greek word signifies transgression of law, or lawlessness, and the same phrase occurs in 1 John 3: 4. Whatever the talk of these men, their doings were wicked; they did not do the will of God (v. 21), did not bring forth good fruits (v. 18), did not work the righteousness he required. (5 : 20; 6 : 33.) And Jesus not only does not know them now, he never did know them, not even when working miracles by his name. Some translate, 'Because I never knew you, depart from me,' etc. The Greek will bear this rendering, but less naturally, nor does it suit so well the connection and the general tone of the passage.

It need not surprise us to find that men whom Jesus 'never knew' yet claimed to be workers of miracles. In some cases, no doubt, the claim was without foundation. But Balaam was, for a season, truly inspired as a prophet, though he was very wicked, and died in his iniquity. Judas doubtless wrought miracles, as well as his associates, when they were sent out to preach and heal. (10 : 4-8.) Comp. also the supposed case in 1 Cor. 13 : 2. It is hardly probable that the person spoken of in Luke 9: 49 (Mark 9 : 38 f.) was really a Christian, though he was helping the Saviour's cause. Yet below, in 17: 19, the failure of the disciples to work a miracle is ascribed to their 'little faith'; and the sons of Sceva (Acts 19 : 14) failed, not from lack of power in the name they spoke, but because they themselves were unsuitable persons. We perceive therefore that wicked men were sometimes allowed to work miracles (comp. also the Egyptian magicians, Ex. 7 : 12, 22), but that some required great faith, and even special preparation by prayer. (Mark 9 : 29.) These facts do not take away the evidentiary power of miracles. (John 3 : 2.) The miracles, the character of those who wrought them, and the nature of their teachings, all three concurring, confirmed each other. But if men could speak by inspiration and work miracles without being truly pious, how great the danger that one may be a fervent and successful preacher, and yet not a Christian. Many take success as a divine attestation to them and their work; but it is not a certain proof (comp 1 Cor. 9: 27); nor does an apparent want of success certainly prove the opposite. We cannot question that the preaching of Judas had some good results, as we sometimes see happening now, with men who afterwards show that they never were really Christians. Observe that the persons described in this passage carry self-delusion into the other world, even to the Day of Judgment. So in 25: 44.

24. We have now (v. 24-27), in the shape of an inference from what has been said, a general conclusion to the whole discourse. Since professions will be of no avail, unless one does the will of God (v. 21-23), **therefore** whoever hears these words and *does* them, will be a

25 And the rain descended, and the floods came, and the winds blew, and beat upon that house: and it fell not: for it was founded upon a rock.
26 And every one that heareth these sayings of mine, and doeth them not, shall be likened unto a foolish man, which built his house upon the sand:
27 And the rain descended, and the floods came, and

25 built his house upon the rock: and the rain descended, and the floods came, and the winds blew, and beat upon that house; and it fell not: for it was
26 founded upon the rock. And every one that heareth these words of mine, and doeth them not, shall be likened unto a foolish man who built his house upon
27 the sand: and the rain descended, and the floods

prudent man, and whoever neglects the doing will be a fool. Jesus knows that many will treat him as Ezekiel was treated. (Ezek. 33 : 31 f.) **These sayings of mine** refers immediately to the Sermon on the Mount, but of course the same holds true of his other sayings (comp. Luke 6 : 47.) **And doeth them**, comp. 'doeth the will' in v. 21, 'work iniquity' in v. 23, and 'fruits' in v. 16. James refers to this passage in his Epistle. (1 : 22-25.) The Mishna, Aboth: "To learn is not the main thing, but to practice." **I will liken,** etc., or, *he shall be likened.* It is hard to decide between this reading of the Greek, and that of the Com. Ver. There is of course no substantial difference.[1] It does not mean, as some explain, that he will be made like at the Day of Judgment (comp. the futures in v. 22 f.), but either 'will be like' in character (as in 6: 8), or, will be compared in the teaching of Jesus, and in the estimation of those who learn his teaching; comp. Luke 6: 47, 'I will show you to whom he is like'; comp. also Matt. 11: 16; Mark 4: 30; Luke 13: 18; Lam. 2: 13. **Wise** is more exactly 'sensible,' 'prudent,' as in 10: 16; 25: 2; Luke 16: 18. **Upon a rock.** Rather, *the rock*, as in v. 26, 'upon the sand.' In a limestone country like Galilee, it is only necessary to dig some distance, and you are apt to find a stratum of solid rock. It is very common in that region now to dig down to the rock, and lay the foundation of a house on it. Comp. the expressions in Luke's sketch of the discourse, 'dug, and went deep, and laid a foundation upon the rock' (Luke 6: 48); comp. also Eph. 3: 18, literally, 'rooted and foundationed in love.' It is idle to say that 'the rock' here means Christ, because he is elsewhere often called a rock. Must the image of a rock always mean the same thing? The thought here obviously is that a man rests his salvation on a good foundation by actual obedience, and not

mere profession; by not simply hearing the Saviour's teaching, but acting it out in character and life.—Observe that this passage is really a parable. Comp. on 13: 10.

25. Throughout verses 24–27 the symmetrical structure of sentence, and the exact correspondence between the two comparisons, give a solemn dignity and impressiveness to this striking conclusion. Many writers distinguish the rain as affecting the roof, the floods the bottom, and the winds the sides of the house; but it cannot be that these are meant as *distinct* assaults upon it, for the power of the roof to resist rain would not depend on the solidity of the foundation. We must understand this as simply a detailed description of the overthrow. The rain descended, and (in consequence thereof) the rivers came (mountain torrents, rushing down the ravines, and swelling up to the site of the house), and these washed around the building, and would have washed the earth from under its foundations, had they rested mainly on the loose surface of the ground, and then the winds would have blown it down; but this house did not fall, for its foundation was laid upon the rock. **Beat upon** is, literally, 'fell upon' or 'fell against,' as when a man hurls himself headlong against something.[2] There may be (McClellan) a play upon the words, 'fell upon that house, and it fell not.' **Founded,** was derived by Com. Ver. from the Romish versions, and is better than the 'grounded' of Tyndale and his successors. The exact meaning would be expressed by 'foundationed,' if we had such a word. Some elements of the illustration our Lord here employs, may be found in Prov. 12: 7; Isa. 28: 16 f.; Ezek. 13: 10–16.

26, 27. Here the phraseology exactly corresponds to v. 24, 25, except **beat upon,** here literally, *smote upon,* which is a mere va-

[1] For ' shall be likened,' B. ℵ Z, a dozen or more cursives, the Vulgate, Sahidic, Armenian, some Fathers. The old Latin copies and the two Egyptian versions are divided. All the Syriac versions agree with C. L. and the other uncials, most cursives, and some Fathers, in supporting 'I will liken him.' It is much more prob-

able that this was changed into the other to suit v. 26, than contrariwise to suit 11: 16 and Luke 6: 47. Thus internal evidence is here again opposed to the authority of B. ℵ, and others.

[2] Comp. the same Greek word in Mark 3: 11.

the winds blew, and beat upon that house; and it fell: and great was the fall of it.

28 And it came to pass, when Jesus had ended these sayings, the people were astonished at his doctrine:

came, and the winds blew, and smote upon that house; and it fell: and great was the fall thereof.

28 And it came to pass, when Jesus ended these words, the multitudes were astonished at his teach-

---

riation of the expression, without substantial difference. **The sand** refers to the loose surface of the ground, or perhaps to the sand accumulated in some part of a mountain ravine, which looks smooth and firm, but is liable to be swept away by the next flood. **Great.** The foundation being swept away, the whole house would fall in one mighty crash and complete wreck.

This beautiful illustration makes its own impression : he who hears the words of Christ, and does them, is safe against all the evil influences of the world, safe forever; he who simply hears, and does not do, is doomed to fail of salvation, and be crushed in utter destruction. To find some special spiritual meaning in every particular, as "the rain of temptation," "the floods of persecution," "the wind of divers and strange doctrines," is pure fancy-work. The Mishna, Aboth, has a somewhat similar illustration: "A man who has good works, and learns the law much, to what is he like? To a man that builds with stones below, and afterwards with bricks; and though many waters come and stand at their side, they cannot remove them out of their place. But a man who has no good works, and learns the law, to what is he like? To a man that builds with bricks first, and afterwards with stones; and though few waters come, they immediately overturn them." Again: "A man richer in learning than in good works is like a tree with many branches and few roots—the first wind overthrows it; but a man whose actions are greater than his learning is like a tree with few branches and many roots—all the winds of the world may storm against it, but cannot move it from its place." There is mournful danger in every age, that men will hear Christ's servants preach, and will themselves read in his written word, and stop at that, without doing according to what they read or hear. As the

Lord's Prayer is often used in the way of that "vain repetition" to which it was given as a contrast and corrective, so this closing illustration is often greatly admired by persons who hear and do not. It is a most momentous question for every one of us, Am I doing the sayings of the Lord? *Colton* ("Lacon"): "Men will wrangle for religion ; write for it; fight for it; die for it; anything but—*live for it.*"

28 f. Concluding remarks of the Evangelist as to the effect of this great discourse. **These sayings,** viz., the whole discourse, as in v. 24-26. **The people,** more exactly, *the crowds,* the same term as in 5 : 1, and naturally leading the mind back to the state of things described before the opening of the discourse. Com. Ver. obscures this link of connection in the narrative, as it so often does, by unnecessary variation of the rendering where the original has the same word (comp. everlasting and eternal for the same Greek word in 25 : 46). **Were astonished.** We may suppose that at the close of the discourse expressions of astonishment broke forth among the hitherto silent crowds. *Stier:* "But, alas ! the mere 'were astonished' in which the whole terminated with regard to most, transmits to us a melancholy example of that hearing and not doing, with warning against which the sermon closed." In Mark 1 : 22 ; Luke 4 : 32 ; and in Matt. 22 : 33 (13 : 54) we have the same expression used with reference to the effect of our Lord's teaching on other occasions. **At his doctrine**—or, *teaching.* The English word 'doctrine' ought to be still a correct rendering here, but in present use it suggests exclusively the thing taught, and not also the act or manner of teaching.[1] It is evident that both ideas are here present, as shown by the reason for astonishment given in the next verse. *Bengel:* "You would wonder why, in this discourse, Jesus has not spoken more

---

[1] Humphrey says the Rev. Ver. has endeavored to render *didache* uniformly by 'teaching' and *didaskalia* by 'doctrine.' This is generally a proper distinction, but the Rev. Ver. has not been able to carry it through, for in Rom. 16 : 17 and 1 Tim. 4 : 13 the renderings are interchanged; and in fact the distinction is not

absolute either between the two Greek or the two English words. In this passage 'teaching' is much better, because it includes both the manner and the matter, both the substance and the tone, and doubtless both contributed to the astonishment.

29 For he taught them as *one* having authority, and not as the scribes.

29 ing: for he taught them as *one* having authority, and not as their scribes.

clearly concerning his own person. But (1) he has so excellently set forth the teaching itself, that they would thence form an estimate of the excellence of the teacher. (2) His person was now sufficiently manifest. (3) In the discourse itself, he sufficiently intimates who he is, viz., ' the coming one,' the Son of God, the Judge of all." (5: 11, 17, 22 ; 7 : 21 ff.) **Taught.** The imperfect tense of the Greek does not here denote *habitual* teaching, but simply describes him as engaged in teaching. **Authority** is the proper meaning of the word. In some cases authority carries with it the necessary power; but the term does not directly mean power. The same word will meet us in 8: 9; 9: 6, 8; 10: 1; 21: 23, 24, 27; 28: 18. In all these Rev. Ver. properly translates by ' authority,' except 9: 6, 8, and there places it in the margin. **The Scribes.** *Their Scribes* is the correct reading; and the expression resembles 'Scribes of the people' in 2: 4. The Scribes (see on 2: 4) made it their business simply to state, to explain, and to apply the teachings of the Old Testament, together with the decisions of Jewish tribunals, and the sayings of famous teachers in past generations, as handed down by tradition. Seeing that for several centuries no prophet had appeared, it was very proper that they should confine their religious ideas to the authority of the Old Test. ; but, in addition to this, they tied themselves to past teachers, and instead of forming their own opinions as to the meaning of Scripture, were always quoting some Rabbi of former generations. All this appears plainly from the Talmud; *e. g.*, "R. Eliezer boasted that he had never said anything which he had not heard from his teacher." Thus the Scribes could not speak as instinct with the conviction of ascertained truth, could not speak with the dignity and strength of assured personal knowledge. Our Saviour spoke as no other teacher would have a right to do, as himself possessing ' authority' to declare, on his own responsibility, what was true and right. Even the prophets usually prefixed to their utterances, "Thus saith the Lord"; while the words of Jesus are, "Verily I say to you." (See on 5: 18, 22.) And he quietly asserts the tremendous fact that men's future destiny will depend on their relation

to him (v. 23), on their doing his words. (v. 24.) His mode of teaching being thus in contrast with that proper for uninspired men, and even with that of the prophets, the contrast must have been all the more striking when it was compared with such teaching as the multitudes were accustomed to hear from 'their scribes.' Many persons are found now who teach precisely as these scribes did, not merely going back to Scripture as the final authority for all religious truth—which is what they ought to do—but going back to "the Fathers," or to some great teacher or convocation of the last three or four centuries, as authority for the correct interpretation and just application of Scripture. It is the part of wisdom, as well as of modesty, to give no small weight to the opinions of men whose abilities, learning, and piety have made them illustrious; but if a man is not accustomed to come for himself to the Bible, and form his own judgment of its meaning, his teachings, whatever else they may possess, will have little of living power to sway men's souls.

HOMILETICAL AND PRACTICAL.

V. 13 f. The broad road : 1) Men are in it without finding or entering; 2) They pursue it without difficulty or effort; 3) They have plenty of company ; 4) But it leads them to perdition.—LUTHER : " What makes the way so narrow ? Nothing but the world, the flesh, and the devil." SCHAFF : " Contrasts : The narrow and wide gates; the straitened and broad ways; the good and corrupt trees, with their fruit; saying and doing; active in Christ's name, yet working iniquity ; the rock and the sand; standing the storm, and falling in the storm; teaching with authority, and teaching as their scribes." CHRYS. : " For the way is strait, and the gate narrow, but not the city. Therefore must one neither look for rest here, nor there expect any more aught that is painful." STIER : " The narrow way to life is broad enough for men who carefully, steadily walk in it. That is the *consolation*, which even this rigorous saying contains. What more is wanting than a way wherein I may have room, and a gate that will let me through?" DYKES: " Amid the endless varieties to be found in life's broad road, there is but this single mark by which to recognize all travelers : they take the path which seems right in their own eyes." (Comp. Prov. 14: 12.) HENRY: "No man, in his wits, would choose to go to the gallows, because the way to it is smooth and pleasant, nor refuse the offer of a palace and a throne, because the way to it is rough and dirty ; yet such absurdities as these are men guilty of in the concerns of their souls." CALVIN: "Whence comes it that men knowingly and willingly rush headlong to ruin with a feeling of security, unless it is from thinking they are not perishing so long as they are perishing in a great crowd?" STIER: "The foolish world, indeed, loves the wide and the broad, and the numbers—delights in the majorities." THOMAS: "Man will follow the multitudes as the tides follow the moon. The social force of numbers has ever been against holiness in the world." DYKES: "The mass of one's neighbors is large enough to generate a public opinion against which it is hard to contend. Among the crowds who affect no Christian isolation or peculiarity, there are so many whom, on other grounds, one must love and venerate, that it is hard always to feel sure that one is right, and they all wrong . . . . To sensitive natures with a broad humanity, there is even a fixed pain in being profoundly out of harmony with the bulk of their fellow-men. . . . The isolation of the true Christian is, in our age, more an inward than an outward isolation."—Some may like to illustrate the two ways by the well-known story of the Choice of Hercules.

V. 15-20. Two methods of testing a religious teacher. 1) By the effect of his teachings upon his own character and life ; 2) By the effect of his teachings upon those who receive them. ST. BERNARD (Lange): "False teachers are sheep in clothing, foxes in cunning, wolves in cruelty." CHRYS.: "Let us not be troubled when we see many heretics and hypocrites even now. Nay, for this too Christ foretold from the beginning." DYKES: "When the path he leads in is discovered to be so strait and steep, it presently begins to be said, or imagined, that life may be had on easier terms. The original gospel of the King undergoes some modification. Teachers who profess to teach still in the name of Jesus point men to a path which looks deceptively like the narrow way, and appears

to conduct to a similar issue; only it is not so narrow—and it does not really lead to life." DRÄSEKE (Lange): "The desire to appear good : 1) Its nature ; 2) Its origin ; 3) Its moral character; 4) Its unavoidable dangers." —V. 21-23. Lost notwithstanding : 1) Loud professions; 2) Great advantages; 3) Striking performances; 4) Persistent self-delusions.— One may have (1) much outward knowledge of Jesus, (2) much outward activity, apparently, in his service, (3) yet have no interior relation to him at all, and (4) be at last ignominiously disavowed. CHRYS: "Better surely to endure a thousand thunderbolts, than to see that face of mildness turning away from us, and that eye of peace not enduring to look upon us."

V. 22 f. BIB. COMM: "The spirit of the warning extends far beyond the extraordinary cases actually mentioned, and applies to all those in all ages who, whether teachers or hearers, nominally profess Christian doctrine without holiness of life."—V. 21-27. THOMAS: "Four kinds of religion : (1) The religion of profession, v. 21. (2) The religion of merit, v. 22. (3) The religion of hearing, v. 26. (4) The religion of doing, v. 24."

V. 24-27. A religious teacher is apt to have two great causes of grief: that so many will not hear him at all, and that so many who hear, and perhaps admire, will not do. (Comp. Ezek. 33 : 31 f.) PARKER : "(1) All men are building. (2) All builders have a choice of foundations. (3) All foundations will be tried. (4) Only one foundation will stand." DYKES : "The whole drift and movement of this long discourse has carried us forward with it to one most weighty practical conclusion—that, after all, he only is a Christian who does what Christ bids him."—V. 27. Hark to the mighty crash in every age and every land, of religious constructions that fall for lack of foundation ! *Reflections :* "This is the conclusion of the Sermon on the Mount, and we are left with an impression of fear; it began with blessings, but its end is stern and severe."

V. 28 f. The moral teachings of Jesus, 1) Commend themselves to us as containing the highest human wisdom — surpassing ancient sages and modern philosophers; 2) Come to us with superhuman authority—that of him who is the Son of God (v. 21), and will

CHAPTER VIII.

WHEN he was come down from the mountain, great multitudes followed him.
2 And, behold, there came a leper and worshipped him, saying, Lord, if thou wilt, thou canst make me clean.

1 And when he was come down from the mountain, 2 great multitudes followed him. And behold, there came to him a leper and worshipped him, saying,

---

be our judge (v. 22); 3) Are embodied in an actual character—the peerless character of the Teacher himself; 4) Bring with them the offer of help in living up to them—that of the Holy Spirit. (Luke 11 : 13.)—Distinguishing features of Christ's ministry. (1) Those which cannot be imitated—his originality, miracle-working, authority. (2) Those which must not be imitated—his positiveness, self-assurance, self-representation. (3) Those which should be imitated—his naturalness, variety, suggestiveness, catholicity, spirituality, tenderness, faithfulness, devoutness.

In our devotional study of this great discourse, we should not be thinking too much of its special adaptation to the Jews, but should read it as addressed to ourselves. Imagine that you stand amid the crowd and listen, and ever and anon his mild eye falls upon you. Hear him telling you who are the happy under his reign, and how great, if you are one of his, is your responsibility as the salt of the earth and the light of the world. Hear him explaining how spiritual and rigorous is that morality which he requires of you, in all your relations and duties; enjoining that your deeds of righteousness shall not be performed ostentatiously, but with supreme regard to God, and that, serving God and trusting his care, you need not be anxious about the things of this life. Listen closely, and humbly, while he rebukes censoriousness, while he encourages to prayer, while he urges the danger lest you fail to be saved, and looking you solemnly in the face declares that you must not merely hear these words of his, but do them. And then turn thoughtfully away, with the "Golden Rule" hid in your heart, and the gracious assurance ever sounding in your ear, "Ask, and it shall be given you."

Ch. 8: 1-17. A GROUP OF MIRACLES.

In chap. 8: 1 to 9: 34, we find a group of remarkable miracles. Having completed his sketch of the Sermon on the Mount, the Evangelist returns to the state of things described before its introduction. (4: 23-25.) Our Lord was making a circuit of Galilee, followed by "great multitudes" (4: 25); on some occasion during the journey, moved by the presence of such crowds (5: 1), he went up into the mountain, and addressed to the disciples and them a long discourse (chap. 5 to 7), designed to set forth the nature of the Messianic reign, and correct many Jewish errors concerning it. When he had finished this and descended, "great multitudes" still followed him. And now having given this great specimen of our Lord's teaching, the Evangelist proceeds (8: 1, to 9: 34) to group some striking examples of his miracles, which show that if he *taught* as one having authority (7: 29), he *acted* in like manner; and which threw light on the nature of his work as Messiah. In connection with these miracles, Matthew also gives an account (9: 9-17) of his own call to follow Jesus. When we compare the Gospels of Mark and Luke, we find several of these miracles, and the attendant sayings, introduced there in such connections as to show that they did not occur in the precise order in which they are here mentioned. Some of them appear to have taken place before the delivery of the Sermon on the Mount, though during this journey about Galilee (see on 5: 1), and others at various subsequent times in the course of our Lord's labors in Galilee. They are grouped by Matthew without any particular regard to the chronological order, but in such a way as to promote the special design of his historical argument. Following upon these examples of our Lord's teaching (chap. 5-7), and his miracles (chap. 8, 9), we shall find (chap. 10), an account of his sending forth the Twelve, that they likewise may teach and work miracles. (See on 9: 35).

The three first miracles here grouped involve the healing of very grievous diseases—leprosy, paralysis, severe fever.

I. 2-4. HEALING OF A LEPER; also given, with some additional particulars, in Mark 1: 40-45; Luke 5: 12-16.

2. And, behold. This expression by no means necessitates the supposition that the in-

3 And Jesus put forth *his* hand, and touched him, saying, I will; be thou clean. And immediately his leprosy was cleansed.

3 Lord, if thou wilt, thou canst make me clean. And he stretched forth his hand, and touched him, saying, I will; be thou made clean. And straightway

---

cident occurred just after the close of the Sermon on the Mount. From the connection in Mark and Luke, it seems very likely, though not certain, that it preceded the delivery of that discourse. As to the locality, Luke tells us that it was 'in one of the cities,' *i. e.*, of Galilee. **There came** *to him.* The words 'to him' represent a slight correction of the common Greek text. **A leper.** The horrible disease of leprosy appears to have been particularly common among the Egyptians and the Israelites. The climate of Egypt was suited to aggravate the disease, and it may be that the Israelites there acquired a constitutional tendency to it, as supposed by Strabo and Tacitus. Various questions concerning leprosy still remain quite unsettled. The Greek word (*lepra*), from which our word is borrowed, was derived from *lepis*, 'a scale,' thus signifying the scaly disease. Among the many kinds of leprosy which seem to have existed in ancient and in modern times, that of the Bible appears to have been *not* the elephantiasis, or knotty leprosy, now often seen in Palestine, but the "white leprosy." It began with a small spot, scab, or swelling, lying lower than the surface of the skin, and the hair within it turning white. This would spread, and raw flesh would appear. In bad cases, large portions, and sometimes the whole of the body would assume a chalky whiteness; the nails, and sometimes the hair, fell off, and in some varieties the senses became blunted, and highly offensive pus gathered on the hair and flowed from the nose. But it is not certain that all these symptoms pertained to the Bible leprosy. It does seem nearly certain that, while hereditary, often for several generations, it was *not* a contagious disease, at least not in ordinary cases. The law of Moses treated it (Lev., ch. 13 and 14) as an extreme form of ceremonial defilement. When the disease spread over the whole person, the sufferer was pronounced clean (Lev. 13: 12-17), and could freely associate with others; which appears to be conclusive proof that it was not contagious. The regulations requiring a leper to keep away from others, to cry "Unclean, unclean," etc., simply meant that one who touched a leper would become ceremonially unclean, as if he had touched a dead body, or a person having a running issue. (Lev. 15: 5.) All these things were to be regarded as symbolically teaching the dreadful pollution of sin, and the need of purification; and no such symbol could be more impressive than a disease so hideous. The purifications when a leper had recovered (Lev. 14) were quite similar to those prescribed for other kinds of grave ceremonial defilement. Leprosy was incurable by any known remedies, but would sometimes wear itself out in the course of time, in the individual, or in his descendants.

Worshipped. Comp. on 2: 2. He cannot have meant worship as of God, but a deeply reverential salutation. Luke (5: 12) says he "fell on his face and besought him." Matthew's imperfect tense depicts him as engaged in this reverential act. In like manner, **Lord,** the word used in the Sept. for Jehovah, which in the Epistles commonly means Jesus and appears there to recognize his divinity, was also used in Greek (and still is) as a common form of address, and is properly translated "sir" in 13: 27; 21: 30; 27: 63, and often. What precise amount of respect it is to be understood as expressing in any case, must be determined from the connection. (See on v. 19.) **If thou wilt, thou canst make me clean.** He called the healing a *cleansing,* because the disease had the appearance of a defilement, and made one ceremonially unclean. He did not say, "If thou *canst,*" like the despairing father (Mark 9: 22); his only question was as to the Lord's willingness. (Comp. below, 9: 28.) His language will express what is often felt by persons asking spiritual blessings; yet as to these we *ought* to have no doubt, either of the Saviour's power or his willingness.

3. Put—or *stretched*—**forth his hand,** the circumstances minutely detailed, after the characteristic Hebrew style (comp. on 5: 2). 'Put forth,' Tyndale, etc., is too feeble; Rheims already has 'stretched forth.' The word 'Jesus' is wanting in several of the earliest MSS. and versions, and obviously was added in others to remove an apparent obscurity. So also in v. 5, 7. **And touched him.** This must have startled the be-

4 And Jesus saith unto him, See thou tell no man; but go thy way, shew thyself to the priest, and offer the gift that Moses commanded, for a testimony unto them.
5 And when Jesus was entered into Capernaum, there came unto him a centurion, beseeching him,

4 his leprosy was cleansed. And Jesus saith unto him, See thou tell no man; but go, shew thyself to the priest, and offer the gift that Moses commanded, for a testimony unto them.
5 And when he was entered into Capernaum, there

holders, for he seemed to be incurring ceremonial defilement; yet Jesus by touching did not receive defilement, but imparted cleansing. **I will, be thou clean.** "A ready echo to the leper's mature faith. His own saying contained the words of the desired response." (*Bengel.*) Every other worker of miracles in the Old or the New Test. constantly ascribes the power and the glory to another; Jesus alone uses such expressions as 'I will, be thou clean,' 'I charge thee, come out of him,' 'I say unto thee, arise.' (Comp. on 5: 22.) There has been much discussion upon the question whether all who received bodily healing from Jesus, also received spiritual blessings. It seems plain that in many instances such was not the case; in others, the circumstances naturally lead us to think that the faith in his power to work miracles was also attended by faith in his power to forgive sins (comp. on 9: 2). Whether that was true of the leper here mentioned, we have no means of deciding.

4. See thou tell no man. Why this prohibition? Partly, perhaps, (as some think), in order that the man might hasten to Jerusalem, and let the priests declare him healed before they should hear of the miracle, as otherwise they might, through jealousy of Jesus, pretend that the cure was not real and complete. But similar prohibitions are found in 9: 30; 12: 16; 16: 20; 17: 9, etc., and there must have been some general reason. There was danger that the people would become greatly excited, upon hearing of his miracles, with the idea that he was about to set up a splendid earthly kingdom, according to their erroneous notions of Messiah's work (John 6: 14 f.), and would thus arouse the hostility of the Jewish rulers and that of the Roman authorities, and interfere with his freedom in teaching. We see from Mark 1: 45 (Luke 5: 15) that by failing to regard this prohibition the cleansed leper actually caused a serious interruption of our Lord's labors. The exceptional case of Mark 5: 19; Luke 8: 39, proves the rule. Jesus there specially bids a man to publish what had been done for him;

but there was in that region (southeast of the lake) no danger of a great popular excitement in favor of making him a king, but on the contrary a very unfavorable sentiment towards him, which it was desirable to correct. At a later period we find our Lord making a series of distant journeys, for the same purpose of preventing excitement among the people, as well as for other reasons (see on 14: 13, and comp. on 4: 12). We also see from 12: 16-21, that his unostentatious and quiet course of action was predicted. **Shew thyself,** with emphasis on 'thyself,' as seen from its position in the Greek (comp. Mark 1: 44); no mere report could convince a priest—the man must show himself. **For a testimony unto them.** This is connected not with **Moses commanded,** but with what precedes. 'Them' cannot refer to the priests, for they must decide that the man was healed before he could offer the gift. It must refer to the people in general, as suggested by 'tell no man,' and implied in the whole connection. Such uses of 'them,' denoting persons or things only implied in the connection, are common in N. T. Greek (Buttm., p. 106), and indeed in the colloquial usage of all languages. The sacrifice, made after the regular examination by the priest (Lev. 14), would be a testimony to the people that the leper was thoroughly healed, and thus that the miracle was real; perhaps also a testimony (Chrys.) that Jesus observed the law of Moses, which they were already beginning to accuse him of disregarding. (Comp. 'for a testimony' in 10: 18; 24: 14, Rev. Ver.) For general remarks on the miracles, see on 4: 24.

II. **5-13.** Healing the Centurion's Servant; described also in Luke 7: 1-10. The language of Luke 7: 1 makes it plain that this occurred shortly after the delivery of the Sermon on the Mount.

And when Jesus,—or, *when he,* omitting the word 'Jesus,' as also in v. 3. **Into Capernaum,** now his place of residence. See on 4: 13. **A centurion.** This was the title of one of the officers of a Roman legion, who commanded a hundred men, but had a more

6 And saying, Lord, my servant lieth at home sick of the palsy, grievously tormented.

6 came unto him a centurion, beseeching him, and saying, Lord, my [1] servant lieth in the house sick

---

1 Or, *boy.*

---

responsible and dignified position than our captain. It cannot be determined whether this centurion was in the service of Herod Antipas, Tetrarch of Galilee (see on 2: 20), who would doubtless have his forces organized after the Roman fashion, and sometimes commanded by Roman officers, or whether he was connected with a Roman garrison of Capernaum, such as the Romans frequently maintained in nominally independent districts. He was a heathen, but a lover of the Jews, and had shown it by building the synagogue in which they then worshiped (Luke 7: 5); probably that large synagogue the foundations of which are now seen at Tel Hum. (See on 4: 13.) There were numerous instances of intelligent and right-minded heathen who, when brought in contact with the Jews, felt the superiority of their religion; e. g., Cornelius. (Acts 10: 1.) This centurion at Capernaum had probably known of the healing of the nobleman's son (John 4: 46 ff.), which took place there some time before, and this with other accounts of Jesus, had led to the full belief that he could heal his servant. **There came unto him.** Luke (7: 3 ff.) says that he sent the elders of the Jews, and afterwards some friends. Matthew omits these details, and represents the centurion as doing himself what he did through others. In like manner Mark (10: 35) represents James and John as presenting to Jesus their ambitious request, without any mention of their mother, whom Matthew (20: 20) declares to have come with them and acted as spokesman. In John 3: 22, we read that Jesus 'baptized'; in John 4: 1 f., this is explained to mean that his disciples baptized. So in John 19: 1, it is said that Pilate 'took Jesus and scourged him,' which of course he did not do with his own hands, but through his attendants. Comp. also 14: 10 with Mark 6: 27; and see on 14: 19. Similar forms of statement are common among us, both in literature and in the language of common life; and there is a familiar law maxim, *Qui facit per alium, facit per se:* he who does a thing through another does it himself.

6. Lord (see on v. 2), simply a very respectful address. **My servant** is, in Greek, clearly definite, and may mean either the only servant he possessed, or the only one he had with him at Capernaum, or the one that was then exclusively occupying his mind. 'Servant' (*pais*) is literally 'boy,' which term was used for a servant of any age, among the Hebrews, Greeks and Romans, as it was also used in the Slave States of this country;[1] comp. the French *garçon.* (See further on 12: 18.) The Rheims version here translates

---

[1] Seven different Greek words are in the N. T. rendered 'servant,' as follows: (1) *Diakonos,* an attendant, waiter, as at table (John 2: 5, 9),and sometimes a servant in general: rendered 'servant' in 22: 13; 23: 11; 'minister' (originally a Latin word of corresponding signification) in 20: 26, and often in the Epistles. This word we have borrowed as *deacon,* just as we borrow *bishop* from *episkopos.* (2) *Therapon,* a waiting-man, attendant, used in Heb. 3: 5, comp. common text of Matt. 24: 45. (3) *Huperetes,* a rower, sailor, and in general a hand, an underling, agent, attendant, inferior officer, etc.; rendered 'servant' in 26: 58 (Rev. Ver. 'officer'), in 5: 25. These three terms might be applied either to a slave or to a free man. (4) *Oiketes,* a house-servant (*oikos,* 'house'), domestic; used in Luke 16: 13; 1 Peter 2: 18, etc. These might be slave or free, but were usually slaves. (5) *Pais,* a child, boy or girl, and also servant, as above explained; rendered 'servant' in v. 6, 8, 13, also in 12: 18; 14: 2, and 'child' in 2: 16; 17: 18, (Rev. Ver. 'boy'); 21: 15. As applied to servants this term seems to have always meant slaves; 14: 2 may be compared with 18: 3. (6) *Doulos,* bondman, slave.

This always means a slave, though often used figuratively, as 'slaves of God,' 'slaves of Jesus Christ.' It is rendered 'bond' or 'bondman' in 1 Cor. 12: 13; Gal. 3: 28; Eph. 6: 8; Col. 3: 11; Rev. 6: 15; 13: 16; 19: 18. Where it is rendered 'servant' the Rev. Ver. usually puts 'bond-servant' in the margin. (7) *Misthios* and *Misthotos,* a hireling, hired man, rendered 'hired servants' in Mark 1: 20; Luke 15: 17, 19, and 'hireling' in John 10: 12 f. This would naturally be a free man. The English word servant is borrowed from the Latin *servus,* which means a bondman, just as *doulos* does. But it has come in English to have a much wider use, denoting either bondmen or hired attendants. 'Slave' is derived from the Slavic or Sclavonic race, many of whom were reduced to servitude in the southeast of Europe, as early as the eighth century. The strong dislike to slavery at the present day has associated degrading ideas with this term, so that we could hardly employ it now for the figurative uses of *doulos;* although the devout McCheyne writes to a friend that "it is sweet to think of ourselves as the slaves of Christ."

7 And Jesus saith unto him, I will come and heal him.
8 The centurion answered and said, Lord, I am not worthy that thou shouldest come under my roof: but speak the word only, and my servant shall be healed.
9 For I am a man under authority, having soldiers under me: and I say to this *man*, Go, and he goeth; and to another, Come, and he cometh; and to my servant, Do this, and he doeth *it*.
10 When Jesus heard *it*, he marvelled, and said to them that followed, Verily I say unto you, I have not found so great faith, no, not in Israel.

7 of the palsy, grievously tormented. And he saith
8 unto him, I will come and heal him. And the centurion answered and said, Lord, I am not [1] worthy that thou shouldest come under my roof: but only say [2] the word, and my [3] servant shall be healed.
9 For I also am a man [4] under authority, having under myself soldiers: and I say to this one, Go, and he goeth: and to another, Come, and he cometh;
10 and to my [5] servant, Do this, and he doeth it. And when Jesus heard it, he marvelled, and said to them that followed, Verily I say unto you, [6] I have not

---

1 Gr. *sufficient*....2 Gr. *with a word*....3 Or, *boy*....4 Some ancient authorities insert, *set :* as in Luke vii. 8....5 Gr. *bondservant*
6 Many ancient authorities read, *With no man in Israel have I found so great faith.*

'boy'; Wyc. supposed it to mean 'child,' as all the early English versions wrongly supposed in Acts 3: 13, 26; 4: 27, 30. Luke (7: 2) has the term *doulos*, 'slave,' which is also used by Matthew in v. 9. It is idle for Weiss to take *pais* as here meaning 'son,' from his mere passion for multiplying discrepancies.

Luke says (7: 2) 'who was dear unto him.' Josephus tells us that the Roman soldiers were followed by many servants, who "in peace constantly engaged in the warlike exercises of their masters, and in war shared their dangers." So a "Confederate" officer and the slave who attended him in camp would often risk their lives for each other, while his other slaves at home usually took the most faithful care of his wife and children. **My servant**—*boy*—**lieth,** literally, *is prostrate*, 'bed ridden.' **Sick of the palsy**—*a paralytic* (see on 4: 24). **Grievously tormented,** or, 'terribly tortured.' Some diseases then classed as paralysis produce violent pain. Compare the case in 1 Macc. 9: 55 f. Luke adds (7: 2 B. U.) that he was 'about to die.'

7-9. Jesus saith, or, *he says*, Jesus omitted, as in v. 3, 5. **I will come,** with some emphasis on 'I.' This proposition, being reported to the centurion, brought out his humility and faith. A similar effect was produced on the Syro-Phœnician mother by refusal. (15: 26.) **Worthy,** literally, *not fit for thee to enter*,[1] etc. He may have meant (Edersh.) that he was Levitically unfit, that to enter his home would render a Jew ceremonially unclean; but the additional and stronger expression in Luke 7: 7 leaves no doubt that he was also humbly thinking of his moral unworthiness. **Speak the word,** or, more exactly, speak 'with a word' (Rev. Ver. margin). So the nobleman's son there at Capernaum had been healed with a word when at a distance. (John 4: 50.) The centurion proceeds to illustrate the power of a word of command, by referring to his own experience as an officer and a master. **For I also am a man**[2] **under authority . . . and I say,** etc. It is plain that 'under authority' is opposed to 'having under myself soldiers' (Rev. Ver.)—notice the 'myself.' He is a subordinate commander, accustomed both to obey and to be obeyed, and he is confident that in like manner one word of command from Jesus will cure disease. There is involved a sort of personification of the disease, as in Luke 4: 39, 'he rebuked the fever.' But what is the force of 'also'? (Com. Ver. followed Geneva in neglecting 'also,' which was given by Tyn., Great Bible, Rheims). The centurion evidently means that his case is like that of Jesus in regard to the word of command. Some think (Humphrey) that he regarded Jesus as under divine authority, while having power over disease. Or it may be that 'also' refers to the latter part of the statement: for I also am a (subordinate) commander, and my word of command is obeyed. **To my servant,** *slave* (see on v. 6). We cannot tell whether he meant the particular servant that was sick, or the servant to whom he spoke in any case.

10. Marvelled—or—*wondered*. Here he

---

[1] For this nonfinal use of the Greek particle that follows, see on 5: 29. Comp. the classical construction with 'fit' (viz., the infinitive) in 1 Cor. 15: 9.

[2] The margin of Rev. Ver. here follows W H. in mentioning that some ancient authorities (B א and some others) insert 'set.' But this evidently is an interpolation from Luke 7: 8, and so should not have been mentioned. If genuine here, what ground can be suggested for its omission by almost all documents? It is wrong to follow B and א against the clearest internal evidence, especially when with internal evidence began the whole line of argument by which W H. have established the great general excellence of their text.

11 And I say unto you, That many shall come from the east and west, and shall sit down with Abraham, and Isaac, and Jacob, in the kingdom of heaven.

11 found so great faith, no, not in Israel. And I say unto you, that many shall come from the east and the west, and shall [1] sit down with Abraham, and Isaac,

---

[1] Gr. *recline*.

---

wondered at faith; on another occasion (Mark 6 : 6), at unbelief. We need not speculate about his wondering, nor weaken the statement by attempted explanations. Jesus wondered as a man, while as God nothing could be wonderful to him. It is only the same difficulty that we meet with in such facts as his growing in wisdom, and his not knowing the day and hour. **Verily I say unto you,** see on 5 : 18. **I have not found so great faith,[1] no, not in Israel.** A similiar case of great faith on the part of a heathen is found in 15 : 22 following. We feel sure that a person with such beautiful humility and such faith in the power of Jesus to work miracles, must have possessed, or would soon come to possess, faith in his power to forgive sins also. (Comp. on v. 3.) What our Lord thus strongly commends is not his humility, but that faith which is the root of every thing spiritual. (Comp. 15 : 28; Luke 18 : 8.) Observe that he does not express surprise at finding so great faith in a *soldier*. There is no warrant in Scripture for the notion of incompatibility between piety and the soldier's life.

11. And I say unto you (see on 5 : 18), repeating the solemn affirmation of the preceding sentence, because he was about to say what the Jews would be slow to believe, and what was of the greatest importance. **From the east and west** (comp. Isa. 45 : 6), from the farthest parts of the earth in every direction, from the remotest Gentile nations. Here is already an intimation that Christianity will spread to all nations. **And shall sit down,** literally *recline* (see margin Rev. Ver.), *i. e.,* at table. The custom of the Persians, which spread to the Greeks and Romans, had also been adopted by the Jews, viz., to lie on a couch while eating. This was placed beside the table, and on it the person reclined leaning on his left elbow, so as to take food from the table with his right hand, while the feet extended obliquely to the outside of the couch. Thus the feet could be washed while one was reclining (Luke 7 : 38; John 13 : 4 f.); a man could

lean his head back upon the breast, or lie "in the bosom" of one who reclined behind him. (John 13 : 23, 25; 1 : 18; Luke 16 : 23.) This luxurious mode of eating had not been the usage of their ancestors (see Gen. 27 : 19; Judges 19 : 6; 1 Sam. 20 : 24 f., where the Hebrew determines it to have been really sitting); and the prophet Amos (6 : 4, 7), rebukes it as a part of the wicked luxury of the people, that they stretched themselves at their banquets. But in the time of our Lord it had become the universal custom, certainly at all formal meals, and to do otherwise would have seemed singular. Wherever in the N. T. 'sit,' 'sit down,' etc., are used with reference to eating, or where the phrase is 'sit at meat,' etc., the Greek always has some word denoting 'to recline'; and it is to be regretted that Rev. Ver. did not place this in the text rather than in the margin. Wyc., Tyn., and Great Bib. had 'rest,' Geneva and Rheims 'sit down.' **With Abraham, Isaac, and Jacob.** The Jews considered that their descent from these patriarchs made it certain that they would share with them the blessings of the Messianic reign; and the Rabbinical writings show that splendid entertainments, enjoyed with the patriarchs, belonged to their conception of the Messianic felicity. Here, as so often, our Saviour adapted himself to the common modes of expression. See the same image in Luke 14 : 15; 16 : 23, the parables concerning feasts, and in Rev. 19 : 9. It was specially appropriate in the present case; the Jews would not at all eat with Gentiles; yet it is here declared that many Gentiles from every direction will recline at table with the great patriarchs, while Jews themselves shall be cast out. This had been foreshadowed by the prophets, but Israel was too blind now to see it. The Talmud says (Schoettgen): "In the future world I will spread for you a great table, which the Gentiles will see and be ashamed." Luke does not give this saying of our Lord with reference to the centurion, but in 13 : 39 he gives the same image as introduced on a

---

[1] The marginal reading of Rev. Ver. has considerable support, especially in versions, and some transcrip-

tional probability; there would be no substantial difference in meaning.

12 But the children of the kingdom shall be cast out into outer darkness: there shall be weeping and gnashing of.teeth.

13 And Jesus said unto the centurion, Go thy way; and as thou hast believed, *so* be it done unto thee. And his servant was healed in the selfsame hour.

14 And when Jesus was come into Peter's house, he saw his wife's mother laid, and sick of a fever.

12 and Jacob, in the kingdom of heaven: but the sons of the kingdom shall be cast forth into the outer darkness: there shall be the weeping and gnashing

13 of teeth. And Jesus said unto the centurion, Go thy way; as thou hast believed, so be it done unto thee. And the [1] servant was healed in that hour.

14   And when Jesus was come into Peter's house, he

---

1 Or, *boy.*

---

different occasion. As to the phrase, **kingdom of heaven,** see on 3 : 2. It must here refer to the future state.

12. But the children—*sons*—**of the kingdom.** By a Hebrew idiom a variety of ideas of intimate relation or close connection are expressed by the use of 'son' or 'child'; *e. g.,* in Old Test. 'sons of Belial (wickedness)', as it were born of wickedness, deriving their very nature from wickedness. So with 'children of disobedience' (Eph. 2 : 2, Rev. Ver.), and 'children of obedience.' (1 Pet. 1 : 14, Rev. Ver.) In 'children of wrath' (Eph. 2 : 3), 'children of cursing' (2 Pet. 2 : 14, Rev. Ver.), we have a very strong expression of the idea that these persons are by their very nature objects of wrath, of a curse. 'The sons of this world' (Luke 16 : 8, Rev. Ver.) are wholly devoted to this world, as it were with a filial devotion. (See also on 9: 15; 11 : 19; 13 : 38; 23 : 15, and comp. 1 Macc. 4 : 2.) 'The sons of the resurrection' (Luke 20 : 36, Rev. Ver.) are those who partake of it. And so 'the sons of the kingdom' here are the persons who are considered as having a right to its privileges by reason of their birth. Our Lord tells the Jews that strangers to the kingdom would come and enjoy its privileges, while its own sons would be cast out. **Into** (*the*) **outer darkness.** The image is derived from a brightly lighted mansion during an evening entertainment. Persons expelled from the house would find themselves in the darkness without. So in 22: 13; 25 : 30, and comp. 'the blackness of darkness forever' in Jude 13; 2 Pet. 2: 17. **There shall be** (*the*) **weeping and** (*the*) **gnashing of teeth,** while within is the feast of the soul, and the song of the blest. Why '*the* weeping'? Probably the idea of these as belonging to the punishment of Gehenna was familiar to our Lord's hearers. The same expression occurs six times in Matthew (see 13 : 42, 50; 22 : 13; 24 : 51; 25 : 30), and in Luke 13 : 28; always with the article, and always associated with the idea of future punishment. (Comp. Buttm., p. 88.) Bengel understands it to be

the weeping by eminence, and adds: "In this life sorrow is not yet sorrow."

13. Go thy way, *go along* (comp. v. 4), said here in kindness and encouragement; quite otherwise in 4 : 10. **So be it done unto thee,** more literally, *so let it happen to thee,* 'come to pass for thee,' the term explained on 6 : 10. His faith was great, and so should the blessing be. Our Lord frequently (not always) required faith in order to the reception of his miracles of healing, where there was a person capable of exercising it. But the healing cannot with any show of propriety be considered the effect of imagination, excited by credulous faith, as in some apparent cures at the present day, for in this and various other cases it was not the sufferer that believed, but some other person—and sometimes a person at a distance. (15 : 28; John 4: 53.) Moreover our Lord wrought miracles upon the dead, and upon inanimate nature, where such an explanation would be out of the question. **In the selfsame**—or, *in that* —**hour,** with some emphasis on 'that.'

III. **14-17.** HEALING OF PETER'S MOTHER-IN-LAW, and of many others. From the parallel accounts in Mark 1: 29-34; Luke 4: 38-41, it appears that this took place before the delivery of the Sermon on the Mount, and upon a Sabbath-day, after leaving the synagogue in Capernaum. Matthew groups these miracles with little concern for exact time and place. (See on v. 1.) **Peter's house,** at Capernaum, see Mark 1 : 21, 29. Andrew lived with his brother, and James and John accompanied Jesus on a visit to them. Peter and Andrew were natives of Bethsaida (John 1 : 44), but had removed to Capernaum. (See the town described on 4 : 13.) It seems strange that Romanists can so insist on the celibacy of the clergy, when Peter himself, of whom the Pope is imagined to be the successor, was a married man, and not only at this time but long after, when at the height of his apostolic labors; and 'the rest of the apostles' were likewise, except Paul.

15 And he touched her hand, and the fever left her: and she arose, and ministered unto them.
16 When the even was come, they brought unto him many that were possessed with devils: and he cast out the spirits with *his* word, and healed all that were sick:
17 That it might be fulfilled which was spoken by Esaias the prophet, saying, Himself took our infirmities, and bare *our* sicknesses.

15 saw his wife's mother lying sick of a fever. And he touched her hand, and the fever left her; and she
16 arose, and ministered unto him. And when even was come, they brought unto him many [1] possessed with demons: and he cast out the spirits with a
17 word, and healed all that were sick: that it might be fulfilled which was spoken through Isaiah the prophet, saying, Himself took our infirmities, and bare our diseases.

1 Or, *demoniacs.*

(1 Cor. 9: 5.) **Sick of a fever.** Malarial fevers are common, from the marshes near the mouth of the Jordan. (Thomson, Geikie.)

15. It seems from Mark 1: 30, and Luke 4: 38, that the family requested Jesus to heal her. **And he touched her hand.** Our Lord several times wrought miracles without touching, and even at a distance, as in the healing of the centurion's slave in the preceding verses; but he usually performed some act, such as touching the person, taking him by the hand, etc., which would make it evident to all concerned that he was the cause of the miraculous cure. **And ministered unto them**—literally, as in best texts, *waited on him.* The verb is explained on 4: 11, and the Greek tense denotes that the action was *continued.* 'Them,' found in some early documents, is a manifest assimilation to Mark and Luke, where companions of Jesus are mentioned. The service would consist in supplying food, and any other needed attentions—a natural way for a woman in her home to express her gratitude. *Jerome:* "That hand ministered, which had been touched, and healed." (Comp. Luke 10: 40, where the same word is rendered 'serving.') A severe fever (Luke 4: 38) always leaves a person very weak; but so complete was the miraculous healing, that she was at once prepared for active exertion. *Wordsworth:* "In the case of Christ's miracles, it was with diseases as with the sea. After the storm there is a swell, before the sea sinks into a calm. But Christ reduced the fury of the sea by a word to perfect calm, as he did the rage of the fever to perfect health."

16. This miracle became noised abroad, and only deepened the impression produced by the casting out of the unclean spirit that same day in the synagogue. (Mark 1: 21-28.) So that all the people became anxious to bring their demoniac or diseased friends to seek like miraculous relief. But the Jews were too scrupulous to do this on the Sabbath day. **When the even was come** (comp. 14: 15).

Luke yet more definitely, 'when the sun was setting.' The Jewish day was reckoned as beginning and ending at sunset; so they came the moment the Sabbath was past. Matthew says nothing to show why they waited till evening; he is simply throwing together a number of miracles without giving all the circumstances of their occurrence. It is not to be inferred that Jesus himself shared these scruples about healing on the Sabbath, a thing which he had just done (Mark and Luke), and repeatedly did afterwards. **Possessed with devils,** much better, *demoniacs* (as in margin Rev. Ver.), see on v. 28 and 4: 24. The Evangelist has already mentioned in general (4: 24) that Jesus healed all the demoniacs that were brought to him during this circuit of Galilee. **With his** (*a*) **word,** just as he had 'with a word' healed the centurion's slave. (v. 8.) **All that were sick,** a general expression embracing every class of diseases, as in 4: 24. *Kitto:* "The sun which had set upon an expectant crowd of miserable creatures, arose next morning upon a city from which disease had fled." Our Lord's miracles were very numerous. Those particularly described by the Evangelists are only specimens, and we are repeatedly told in passing, of his healing very many persons and of many diseases. Simply to read the statements in 4: 24; 9: 35; 11: 4 f.; 12: 15; 14: 35; 15: 30; 19: 2, would be apt greatly to enlarge one's idea of the extent of his labor of beneficence in this respect.

17. That it might be fulfilled. This naturally means that the events in question had been actually predicted in the prophecy quoted, and had taken place in the arrangements of Providence in order that the prediction might be fulfilled. (See on 1: 22; the particle rendered 'that' is not the same here as there, but has practically the same force.) **By Esaias.**—More exactly *through*, as in 2: 5, 17; 3: 3; 4: 14, the idea being by the Lord through the prophet, as fully expressed in 1: 22; 2: 15. 'Isaiah,' instead of 'Esaias,'

see on 1: 2. It is only Matthew that here refers to the fulfillment of a prediction, this
being the sixth prophecy which he cites as
being fulfilled in Jesus. (Comp. 1: 23; 2: 5,
15, 23; 4: 14.) **Himself took our infirmities and bare our sicknesses.** The quotation is from Isa. 53: 4, rendered in Com.
Eng. Ver., 'He hath borne our griefs and
carried our sorrows.' The whole passage in
Isaiah (52: 13 to 53 : 12) unquestionably refers to
Christ's suffering for men as their substitute.
(Comp. 1 Pet. 2: 24.) There is thus difficulty
in perceiving the ground of the Evangelist's
application of this prophecy to our Lord's healing diseases. The original of Isaiah literally
means 'Our diseases he took, and our pains
he bore,' with slight emphasis both times on
'our' and 'he,' the word 'pains' comprising
both bodily and mental distresses. As to the
words, Matthew has thus exactly followed the
Hebrew (the hypothesis of his following an
oral Aramaic version is believed to be without
adequate support), departing from the Sept.,
which here renders, "He bears our sins, and
is pained about us." But how as to the meaning? Christ took upon himself, and thus took
away from us, sin and all the distresses produced by sin. These distresses were divinely
appointed punishments of sin, and we may
suppose that but for Christ's atoning work,
God's justice would not have allowed them to
cease. For believers in Christ, diseases and
various mental sufferings do indeed still continue, yet not as punishments, but to discipline them for their good. What our Saviour
suffered, in his life of humiliation and his
death of agony, was not, as the prophet says
men would think it was, the penalty of wrong-
doing on his own part, but was the taking on
himself of our sin, and all our consequent
woe. Of course he did not endure the precise
and identical sufferings, temporal or eternal,
which we should otherwise have borne, but
what he suffered in our stead made it right
that we should be relieved, to some extent
even in this life, and completely in eternity,
of all the consequences of our sins. His taking away bodily diseases was thus not only a
symbol (Meyer), but in some sense a part of
his taking away sin. The matter may also be
viewed as *Plumptre* does: "He himself
'took' and 'bore' the sufferings which he removed. He suffered with those he saw suffer.

The power to heal was intimately connected
with the intensity of his sympathy, and so
was followed (as analogous works of love are
followed, in those who are most Christ-like in
their lives), by weariness and physical exhaustion. What is related by St. Mark and
St. Luke of our Lord's seeking out the refuge
of solitude at the earliest dawn of the day
that followed, is entirely in harmony with the
view thus suggested."

HOMILETICAL AND PRACTICAL.

V. 2 f. This suggests by analogy the need
and the means of spiritual healing. Four
questions as to our salvation : 1) Is Jesus able
to save? 2) Is Jesus willing to save? 3) Do
we need to be saved? 4) Do we wish to be
saved? Only the last question is really doubtful, and that depends on ourselves.—V. 4. Do
not make loud professions of what Christ has
done for you, but prove it by acting according
to God's law. Schaff remarks that it is possible to make too much of the miracles—"a kind
of materialism, no less than the denial of the
possibility of such miracles."

V. 5 ff. The centurion. 1) His munificent
gift to the people of God. (Luke 7 : 5.) 2) His
affectionate kindness to a servant. (v. 6; Luke 7 : 2.)
3) His poor opinion of himself. (v. 8.) 4) His
great faith in Jesus. (v. 8, 10.) 5) The exact and
immediate answer to his petition. (v. 13.)—The
three believing centurions. 1) This centurion at
Capernaum. 2) The centurion who had charge
of the crucifixion (27: 54.) 3) The centurion
Cornelius. (Acts 10: 1.)—A deeply pious soldier.
HALL: "Even the bloody trade of war yielded
worthy clients to Christ."—Kindness to a
servant. HALL: "Had the master been sick,
the faithfulest servant could have done no
more. He is unworthy to be well served, that
will not sometimes wait upon his followers.
Conceits of inferiority may not breed in us a
neglect of charitable offices. So must we look
down upon our servants here on earth, as that
we must still look up to our Master which is
in heaven."—V. 7. Developing faith. By refusing all that was asked (15: 24); 2) By offering
more than was asked; 3) By granting just
what was asked.—V. 8. It was no feigned
humility with which the centurion spoke.
He deeply felt himself unworthy of the presence and society of the Great Teacher. Yet the
Jewish elders thought him worthy. (Luke 7 : 4.)

18 Now when Jesus saw great multitudes about him, he gave commandment to depart unto the other side.
19 And a certain scribe came, and said unto him, Master, I will follow thee whithersoever thou goest.

18 Now when Jesus saw great multitudes about him, he gave commandment to depart unto the other 19 side. And there came [1] a scribe, and said unto him, [2] Master, I will follow thee whithersoever thou goest.

1 Gr. *one scribe*....2 Or, *Teacher.*

They who most deserve the esteem of others are apt to have the humblest opinion of themselves; not because ignorant of any excellencies they may have attained, but because more accustomed to dwell on their faults, and more absorbed in the desire to correct them. A man may be conscious of his powers and attainments, may rejoice in his achievements, may be pleased that men praise him, and at the same time be truly humble, and full of gratitude to him who has given it all. This is difficult for human weakness, but so much the more earnestly and prayerfully must it be sought. "What is the first thing in religion? Humility. And what is the second thing in religion? Humility. And what is the third thing in religion? Humility."—HALL: "Many a one, if he had been in the centurion's coat, would have thought well of it; a captain, a man of good ability and command, a founder of a synagogue, a patron of religion; yet he overlooks all these, and when he casts his eye upon the divine worth of Christ and his own weakness, he says, 'I am not worthy.' While he confessed himself unworthy of any favor, he approved himself worthy of all." EDERSHEIM: "Here was one who was in the state described in the first clauses of the Beatitudes, and to whom came the promise of the second clauses; because Christ is the connecting link between the two." CHRYS.: "For because he made himself out unworthy, even to receive Christ into his house, he became worthy both of a kingdom, and of attaining unto those good things which Abraham enjoyed."—V. 9. Obeying and commanding. HALL: "Oh that I could be but such a servant to mine Heavenly Master! Alas! every one of his commands says, 'Do this,' and I do it not; every one of his inhibitions says, 'Do it not,' and I do it. He says, 'Go from the world,' I run to it; he says, 'Come to me,' I run from him. Wo is me! this is not service, but enmity."—V. 10. Jesus wondering: 1) At the great faith of a heathen; 2) At the unbelief of his fellow-townsmen. (Mark 6: 6.) Believing heathen still often shame those reared in Christian lands.

V. 15. What can we do for Jesus, who has done so much for us? We cannot now minister to him in the way of personal attention, but 1) We can bring others to be his followers (John 1: 41); 2) We can minister to his suffering brethren (25 : 40); 3) In general, we can show our love by keeping his commandments. (John 14: 15.)—V. 17. STEINMEYER: "As a parable shows on earthly grounds the reflex of a higher truth, in order to serve as a means of explaining the latter, so a miracle which relieves an earthly pain is the symbol of the help within reach for a deeper need. Our Lord cures the sick of the palsy; but the first words of the narrative point most expressly to a higher region. He gives sight to him that was born blind; but the concluding words of the history exclude the thought of a mere deed of compassion."

18—9 : 1.—STILLING THE TEMPEST, AND HEALING THE DEMONIACS.

To the miracles already adduced (see on v. 1), Matt. now adds two which are very remarkable. It is evident from Mark 4: 35 ff., and Luke 8 : 22 ff., that they occurred after the delivery of the parables in chap. 13, and apparently in the evening of the same day on which those parables were delivered. Matt. is giving a *group* of miracles in chap. 8 and 9.

18. Great multitudes, literally, *many crowds,* as in 4: 25; 8: 1, etc. **Unto the other side,** i. e., of the Lake of Galilee; literally, *into the beyond.* The region east of the lake and of the lower Jordan was commonly called by the Jews 'The Perea,' i. e., 'The Beyond (region),' see on 4: 25 and 19: 1. We cannot suppose he sought escape from personal annoyance or discomfort. The fanatical excitement of the people (chap. 12 and 13) was rising too high (comp. on 8: 4); there was less opportunity to do real good by his teachings when the crowd became so great as to produce confusion and disturbance; and in general, it was his plan to diffuse his labors throughout the country. Mark's phrase (4 : 35), 'when the even was come' (comp. Matt. 8: 16), *might* include the late afternoon (see on 14: 15). It is thus not certain, though probable, that the stormy passage was after night-fall.

19. While they were preparing to cross the

20 And Jesus saith unto him, The foxes have holes, and the birds of the air *have* nests; but the Son of man hath not where to lay *his* head.

20 And Jesus saith unto him, The foxes have holes, and the birds of the heaven *have* [1] nests; but the Son

---

1 Gr. *lodging-places.*

---

lake, there occurred the conversation mentioned in v. 19-22. Mark has no mention of this. Luke (9: 57 ff.) gives similar conversation as taking place at a much later period, on the final journey from Galilee to Jerusalem, six months before the crucifixion. (See below, on 19: 1.) Perhaps our Lord repeated these sayings, as he often did. (See Introduction to chap. 5.) Or it may be supposed that either Matthew or Luke has transposed these sayings from another time, as neither gives any distinct expression of connection. **And a certain scribe came;** literally, 'one scribe' (margin Rev. Ver.), perhaps designed to intimate that, while most of Jesus' followers were men of private station and in humble life, here was *one* of the teachers, a Rabbi. But in many languages the numeral 'one' came at length to be used as what grammarians call the indefinite article; *e. g.*, German *ein;* English *an, a,* from Anglo-Saxon *an,* Scotch *ane;* French *un,* from Latin *unus;* and so in modern Greek; and it may be that we ought so to understand here (see Winer, p. 117 [145]), and in 19: 16; 21: 19. There is a similar question as to a few uses of the Hebrew word for 'one.' As to the Scribes, see on 2: 4. **Whithersoever thou goest,** (comp. Rev. 14: 4), not merely now, across the lake, but always and everywhere. This Scribe was already in a broad, general sense, a 'disciple' of Jesus—as is implied by 'another' in v. 21 —but wished to be one of his constant followers.

The various words which the Common Version renders **master** are as follows: *Kurios,* usually rendered 'Lord,' whether as applied to God, to the master of a slave, or to any person in respectful address, equal to 'Sir.' (See on v. 2.) It is rendered 'master' in 6: 24; 15: 27; and really signifies master in several passages in which it is rendered 'Lord,' as in 18: 25 ff.; 24: 45 ff.; 25: 18. *Despotes,* strictly the *master* of a slave, and rendered by that term in 1 Tim. 6: 1 f., etc., is not found in the Gospels. *Rabbi,* originally signifying a superior (*rab,* 'great,' like *mag—ister* from *mag—nus*), was the common Jewish word for a teacher. It was primarily

my rab, 'my teacher,' used only in addressing him, but afterwards also in speaking of him, like Monsieur, Monsignore. A strengthened form was Rabboni, expressing the profoundest respect. (Mark 10: 51; John 20: 16.) It is frequently retained without translation, but is by Com. Ver. rendered 'master' in 26: 25, 49. (Rev. Ver., Rabbi.) *Epistates,* literally, 'one set over,' variously used in the classics, in New Test. always a teacher, and found only in Luke. (5: 5, etc.) *Kathegetes,* leader, guide, instructor, only in 23: 10. *Didaskalos,* literally and strictly *teacher,* is so rendered in John 3: 2, and wherever it is used in Acts and the Epistles (except James 3: 1, 'masters'), and rendered 'doctor' (a Latin word, meaning teacher) in Luke 2: 46. Everywhere else in the Gospels the Com. Ver. renders it 'master,' used like schoolmaster. In the Gospels 'master' always represents *some* word denoting a 'teacher,' except in 6: 24; 15: 27; Mark 13: 35; Luke 14: 21; 16: 13. In like manner our missionaries among the heathen are constantly addressed by the people as "Teacher."

20. The birds of the air, or *heaven,* as in 6: 26. **Nests** should be *habitations* or 'haunts,' the word meaning simply a dwelling-place (Rev. Ver., margin); and nests being actually occupied only during incubation. The birds that fly free and wide in the heaven have some regular place to which they come to spend the night. A kindred verb in 13: 32 is rendered 'lodge.' Various Fathers wildly allegorize the foxes and the birds (see Aquinas, Cat. Aur.). **Hath not where to lay his head,** *i. e.,* no fixed habitation. It does not so much denote extreme poverty and discomfort, as the fact that his life was a wandering one. He had friends, at whose houses he was always welcome, and hospitality was often tendered him by others. But frequently journeying far and wide over the country, even as now he was about to cross the lake into a wild, inhospitable region, his life was one of peculiar trial and self-denying toil, and if the Scribe proposed to follow him wherever he went, he must make up his mind to follow a homeless wanderer, and so to

21 And another of his disciples said unto him, Lord, suffer me first to go and bury my father.

21 of man hath not where to lay his head. And another of the disciples said unto him, Lord, suffer me first

---

endure many hardships. Euthymius (comp. Chrys., Jerome) supposes the Scribe to have thought that large pay was received for the miracles of healing, which we know that Jesus told the Twelve they must perform gratis. (10:8.) More likely the Scribe was thinking of a temporal Messianic reign, with which the teacher was somehow connected, and which would bring its subjects power and wealth. We see from this incident how careful our Lord was to warn men beforehand what they were to expect in entering upon his service (comp. Luke 14: 28-33). And although it is not now the duty of all his followers to spend their lives in wandering labors, it is still the duty of every one to "renounce himself, and take up his cross," and in the highest sense to "follow" Jesus. We are not informed whether the Scribe determined, notwithstanding the warning he had received, that he would still follow the Teacher; one would hope that he did, and would rather infer so from the Evangelist's silence, seeing that on other occasions (*e. g.*, 19: 22; John 6: 66) the turning back of various apparent disciples is distinctly recorded; also from the association with the person next mentioned. Expositors have perhaps been severe in their judgment, in taking it for granted that the Scribe's motives were mercenary, and that he turned back at once. He was over confident, and the kind Teacher warned him to count the cost. **The Son of man.** This remarkable expression was no doubt founded on Dan. 7: 13, "I saw in the night visions, and behold, there came with the clouds of heaven one like unto a son of man," Rev. Ver., a passage which the Jewish writers agree in referring to the Messiah. The so-called "Book of Enoch" frequently speaks of the coming Messiah as the Son of man. We learn from John 12: 34 that the Jews understood this phrase to mean the Messiah; and from Luke 22: 69 f. that they saw little difference between calling him the Son of man and the Son of God. Our Lord's frequent use of the phrase (more than seventy times) constitutes an oft-repeated claim to be the Messiah (*e. g.*, 24: 30; 26: 64); it was also probably designed to render prominent the great fact that he was genuinely and thoroughly a man, a fact

which believers in his divinity sometimes fail to appreciate. The phrase is never applied to him by any other than himself, except in Acts 7: 56, and perhaps in Rev. 1: 13; 14: 14. As the Hebrew phrase originally suggested human feebleness and frailty (as in Psa. 8: 4; 146: 3), it may have seemed on that account less appropriate to the now exalted and glorified Redeemer. The many attempts to explain the phrase 'Son of man' in some other sense than as denoting the Messiah, are well stated and briefly refuted in Meyer.

21. And another of his disciples. Both he and the Scribe must have been disciples only in the wider sense of the term (see on 5: 1). Tyndale and Geneva translate "another that was one of his disciples," thus excluding the Scribe, but that is a forced rendering. There is a tradition (Clem. Alex.) that this second man was the apostle Philip, but we have no means of deciding. Conjectures, such as that the Scribe was Judas Iscariot and the other Thomas (Lange), or that they were Thomas and Simon Zelotes (Keim), are simply idle. Why will commentators and preachers waste time in such baseless and useless guess-work? Luke 9: 59, represents the man as called on by our Lord to follow him, and replying with the request that he might first go and bury his father; Matthew does not mention such a call. The man's request pertained to a matter which the Jews reckoned of great consequence. Thus in Tobit 6: 15, Tobias fears that he will die and be the death of his parents, and says, "they have no other son to bury them." It is natural to suppose that this man's father was already dead, and it was the custom to bury the dead very soon; but it was also customary (Lightfoot) to observe thirty days of special mourning, and we cannot decide whether the man meant to include that time. Elisha's somewhat similar request of Elijah was not denied (1 Kings 19: 20); and the man might well have thought himself justified in asking leave to go home first. Yet a highpriest or a Nazirite was required by the law to avoid the dead body of even father or mother. (Lev. 21: 11; Num. 6: 6 f.); and one of the late Jewish commentaries says (Wet.) that "when the study of the law and the necessity of burying

22 But Jesus said unto him, Follow me; and let the dead bury their dead.
23 And when he was entered into a ship, his disciples followed him.
24 And, behold, there arose a great tempest in the sea, insomuch that the ship was covered with the waves: but he was asleep.

22 to go and bury my father. But Jesus saith unto him, Follow me; and leave the dead to bury their own dead.
23 And when he was entered into a boat, his disciples
24 followed him. And behold, there arose a great tempest in the sea, insomuch that the boat was

---

the dead conflict, care of the dead takes precedence; but that if there is a sufficient number of persons in attendance, the student must not leave the law." V. 22. **Let the dead bury,** or, as in Rev. Ver., *Leave the dead to bury* (so Darby, Davidson), the Greek being stronger than 'let the dead bury.' **To bury their** (*own*) **dead.** This cannot mean let the dead bury each other, *i. e.*, let them remain unburied, for that is a forced explanation and an idea unworthy of our Lord. We must understand the dead spiritually and the dead literally, as in Rev. 3: 1. (Comp. John 11: 25 f.) Such a play upon words is natural and pleasing to the Oriental mind, and different forms of it occur frequently in Scripture, including many passages where it cannot be preserved in translation. (Comp. on 16: 25.) The idea here is that there were enough of those who were spiritually dead to perform all the offices of affection to the dead, and so Christ's followers were at liberty to devote themselves to their own far higher work. (Comp. 10: 37.) In Luke's account (9: 60, Bib. Un. Ver.), we have the addition, 'but go thou and announce the kingdom of God.' It does not follow that Jesus would require all his followers, under all circumstances, to neglect the burial of their dead, in order that they might work exclusively at spreading the gospel; any more than he extends to every one the command laid upon the rich young ruler, to sell all he had and give to the poor. (19: 21.) But we can easily conceive of circumstances now, in which it would be proper to hold in abeyance the strongest promptings of natural affection, in order to do our duty to Jesus; just as a soldier may see his brother fall at his side in a charge, and yet sometimes cannot pause to care for him, but must rush on. **Their own dead.** In Gen. 23: 4, 6 we have the expressions 'my dead, 'thy dead,' and similar expressions are common now. So Jesus means to say that the dead in such a case

are not yours, but belong to the spiritually dead, and should be buried by them. Here, as in v. 20, we are not informed whether the man at once followed Jesus, but it would seem probable that he did. Luke 9: 60 f., adds a third case.

23. MIRACLE OF STILLING THE TEMPEST (v. 23-27.) Comp. Mark 4: 36 ff. ; Luke 8: 22 ff. **Into a ship** [1]—or, *the boat*, probably a boat suited to fishing, and without sails (see on 4: 21). It is called '*the* boat,' most likely as being the one prepared in pursuance of his order to go across (v. 18); perhaps it was a boat kept for their regular use. We ought to translate 'boat' and not 'ship.' See on 4: 21. **His disciples followed him,** some in the same boat, and others in additional boats mentioned by Mark. (4: 36.) These little fishing craft were very numerous on the lake. (John 6: 23 f.) The 'disciples' are most naturally understood here as including not merely the Twelve (who as shown by the order of Mark and Luke had been selected before this time) but others of his followers, who could be called disciples in the more general sense of the term. (See on 5: 1.)

24. And, behold, an expression much used by Matthew in calling attention to what follows as wonderful. **Tempest.** The word in the original denotes a shaking or shock, and is usually applied to an earthquake, both in the classical writers and in the New Test. (*e. g.*, 24: 7; 27: 54; 28: 2), but here used for a mighty storm, such as would shake men's dwellings, and seem to make the very earth tremble. Luke (8: 23) tells us yet more distinctly, 'and there came down a storm (another and more common word) of wind upon the lake,' viz., down the ravines on its sides, as often happens (see description of the lake on 4: 18). *Bartlett* witnessed a precisely similar occurrence: " All the day there had not been a breath of air, the sultry heat had been that of a furnace; but now a cool breeze

---

[1] Some early documents here omit the Greek article, leaving the expression equivalent to 'into a boat'; and so W H. and Rev. Ver. But those documents have

probably imitated Luke 8: 22, and it is more likely correct to retain the article.

25 And his disciples came to *him*, and awoke him, saying, Lord, save us: we perish.
26 And he saith unto them, Why are ye fearful, O ye of little faith? Then he arose, and rebuked the winds and the sea; and there was a great calm.

25 covered with the waves: but he was asleep. And they came to him, and awoke him, saying, Save, 26 Lord; we perish. And he saith unto them, Why are ye fearful, O ye of little faith? Then he arose, and rebuked the winds and the sea; and there was a

came off the table land, and rushing down the ravines that descend to the lake, began to ruffle its placid bosom. As it grew darker, the breeze increased to a gale, the lake became a sheet of foam, and the white-headed breakers dashed proudly on the rugged beach; its gentle murmur has now changed into the wild and mournful sound of the whistling wind and the agitated waters. Afar off was dimly seen a little barque struggling with the waves, and then lost sight of amidst the misty rack." As the lake is far below the level of the Mediterranean, the air is often greatly heated and ascends rapidly; and into the vacuum comes rushing down the cold air from the eastern and western table lands.—(*Thomson.*) **The ship**—*boat*—**was covered,** or, 'was becoming covered,' the form of the Greek verb denoting an action in progress; so also in Mark (4:37), and Luke (8:23.) **But he was asleep**—*sleeping*—the Greek indicating some emphasis on 'he,' *i. e.*, he, for his part. Mark, who so often gives piquant details, adds 'on the cushion,' *i. e.*, the one they had in the boat, as a part of the couch in the stern on which he was lying. This makes a picture: Jesus sleeping with his head on the cushion, while the storm howled, the boat was tossed to and fro, the billows broke over and were rapidly filling it—soundly and quietly sleeping. The order of Mark and Luke make it appear that this was on the evening which followed the blasphemous accusation of chapter 12, and the great group of parables in chapter 13. After a day of such mental strain, the Saviour would naturally be exhausted. Probably also it was night. (See on v. 18.)

25. The disciples—or, *they*—**came.** 'His disciples' was an unnecessary addition of the copyists. So with **us; read Save, Lord, we perish.** Mark (4:38) has literally 'Teacher' (*didaskalos*); Luke (8:24) has 'Master, master' (*epistates*), see on v. 19. It is often evident that the Evangelists have not undertaken to give the exact words used. (See on 3:17.) The peril must have been really very great; "for these men exercised to the sea many of

them from their youth, and familiar with all the changes of that lake, would not have been terrified by the mere shadow of a danger."— *Trench.* Luke (8:23) says expressly, and they "were in jeopardy." 'Save' here of course means save our lives, not referring to the salvation of the soul. If the language is by us applied to the latter, it is very appropriate, but such application is made on our own authority.

26. Why are ye fearful, more exactly, *cowardly*, which expresses the force of the Greek term according to its use in the classics and in the Septuagint. In the New Test. it is found only here (including Mark 4:40) and in Rev. 21:8, or kindred forms in 2 Tim. 1:7; John 14:28, in all which cases the idea of unworthy and discreditable fear is appropriate. **O ye of little faith,** see on 6:30. Faith makes men courageous, and the disciples were discreditably timid, cowardly, because they had so little faith. This is often understood to mean faith in Jesus, but does it not rather mean a lack of faith in the providence of God their Heavenly Father, as in 6:30? **Then he arose and rebuked.** He first rebuked the disciples while still lying on the couch, and afterwards arose and rebuked the winds and the sea. This expression involves an obvious personification (comp. Ps. 106:9; Nahum 1:4); and Mark (4:39) gives the words addressed to the sea, as if speaking to a person, or to some fierce monster. Those words might be rendered 'Be silent, hush'; but the latter word is literally 'be muzzled,' applicable to a furious beast. **A great calm,** just as there had been 'a great tempest.' (v. 24.) Here was 'a greater than Jonah.' (12:41.) How perfectly was the Saviour's humanity manifested even when he exercised more than human power. Wearied, in body and in mind, by his labors during the day (see on 13:1), he is sleeping on the cushion; the next moment he rises, and speaks to the winds and the waves with the voice of their Creator. So he wept in human sympathy with the sisters of Lazarus, just before he spoke the word that brought him to life.

27 But the men marvelled, saying, What manner of man is this, that even the winds and the sea obey him!
28 And when he was come to the other side into the country of the Gergesenes, there met him two possessed with devils, coming out of the tombs, exceeding fierce, so that no man might pass by that way.

27 great calm. And the men marvelled, saying, What manner of man is this, that even the winds and the sea obey him?
28 And when he was come to the other side into the country of the Gadarenes, there met him two [1] possessed with demons, coming forth out of the tombs, exceeding fierce, so that no man could pass by that

1 Or, *demoniacs.*

---

27. And the men marvelled. 'The men' is a general term for the persons present, including such as were disciples (comp. 14: 33), and also very possibly some men employed in the boats. (Mark 4: 36.) **That even the winds and the sea obey him,** a thing they had not previously witnessed, which would therefore seem to them more remarkable than that diseases obeyed him. Doubtless also this would especially strike men whose lives had been spent as sailors and fishermen, and who had so often seen exhibited the terrible power of the stormy sea. *Stier:* "This *empire over nature* is a new thing which Matthew has to record concerning Jesus. His narrative of selected miracles in chapters eight and nine rises through a gradation of importance; cleansing of the leper (a great thing even to begin with)—healing at a distance by his word, 'Be it done'—commanding the wind and the sea—saying to the devils 'go'—*forgiving the sins* of the paralytic (more indeed than saying arise! or, go hence! more than ruling the sea)—finally giving life to the dead."

28. Healing of the two demoniacs. (8: 28 to 9: 1.) Comp. Mark 5: 1–21; Luke 8: 26–40. If the preceding miracle shows our Lord's command of the forces of nature, that which follows exhibits his power over evil spirits. *Trench:* "And Christ will do here a yet mightier work than that which he accomplished there; he will prove himself here also the Prince of peace, the bringer back of the lost harmony; he will speak, and at his potent word this madder strife, this blinder rage which is in the heart of men, will allay itself; and here also there shall be a great calm." *Theophyl.:* "While the men in the boat are doubting what manner of man this is, that even the winds and the sea obey him, the demons come to tell them."

To the other side, viz., of the lake, as in v. 18. The point reached was below the middle of the lake; and as they had probably come from the vicinity of Capernaum, the voyage would be eight or ten miles. **Into the country of the Gergesenes.** The text of this and the parallel passages (Mark 5: 1; Luke 8: 26) is greatly confused, some documents for each of the three passages reading each of the three words, Gadarenes, Gerasenes, Gergesenes. The best documents, however, give Gadarenes in Matthew, and Gerasenes in Mark and Luke. *Thomson,* Vol. II. p. 353–5, found a village called Gersa, about the middle of the eastern shore, with ancient tombs in the adjacent mountain, and near the village found a steep place exactly suiting the story of the swine. So also Wilson, McGarvey, and Merrill. We thus account for the name Gerasenes entirely apart from the large city of Gerasa, which was some thirty miles away. Gadara was a well-known city lying a few miles southeast of the lake, the ruins of which are still extensive and striking. The country immediately around a city usually belonged to it, and was called by its name; we have only to make the very natural supposition that the village of Gerasa (Khersa) belonged to the territory of Gadara, and we see how the people may be called both Gerasenes and Gadarenes. The name Gergesenes, which might be introduced by students or copyists, is thought by some to have arisen from the Girgashites. (Gen. 10: 16; Deut. 7: 1; Joshua 3: 10) Origen says there was a city called Gergesa near the lake, and Euseb. ("Onom.") says the same, but may have derived it from Origen. The form Gergesa may possibly have been merely a different pronounciation of Gerasa, the r of the latter taking a rattling, guttural sound like that of the strong Ayin, which in modern Arabic sounds much like our *rg*.[1] But however that may be, the genuine names Gadarenes and

---

[1] This suggestion is supported by the statement of Thomson (part II, ch. 25) that when he asked the Bedwin for Gergesa, they invariably said it was at Gersa (or Khersa), seeming to pronounce the words alike. But Thomson omits this statement in ed. 2. Experts in Arabic visiting the lake ought to determine how the Bedwin really pronounce the name of the ruins. Eusebius ("Onom." ed. Lagarde, p. 242) remarks that Ger-

Gerasenes, and all the circumstances, are exactly explained by the discovery of Khersa; and in this case, as in many others, current research in text-criticism and Biblical geography is clearing up a once celebrated difficulty. **There met him two.** Mark and Luke mention only one. It is an obvious explanation to suppose (so already Chrys. and Aug.) that one was more remarkable and prominent than the other. Mark and Luke give more details than Matthew does, and in so doing might naturally take only the more conspicuous case, to render the description more vivid. In 20: 30 also Matt. has two blind men, Mark and Luke but one. *Robinson* ("Harmony"): "A familiar example will illustrate the principle. In the year 1824, Lafayette visited the United States ; and was everywhere welcomed with honors and pageants. Historians will describe these as a noble incident in his life. Other writers will relate the same visit as made, and the same honors as enjoyed, by two persons, viz.: Lafayette and his son. Will there be any contradiction between these two classes of writers? Will not both record the truth ?"

Two possessed with devils—*demoniacs*—literally, ' demonized (persons.') It has always been a matter of dispute whether the demoniacal possessions so often mentioned in the history of our Lord are to be understood as real. Yet it would seem that there ought to be no doubt of their reality, when one considers the following facts : (1) The Evangelists constantly speak of them as real. (2) Jesus himself is recorded as speaking of them in the same way; and even as speaking *to* the evil spirits (Mark 1 : 25) ; and this not merely before the multitude, but in private conversation with his disciples he says, ' This kind can come out by nothing, save by prayer.' (Mark 9: 29, Rev. Ver.) (3) Jesus argues upon the assumption of their reality. (Luke 10: 17-20.) When the seventy rejoiced that even the demons were subject to them by his name, he said to them, 'I beheld Satan fallen as lightning out of heaven'; that is, he connected their expulsion of demons with the downfall of Satan's

power. (4) The demoniacs speak with superhuman knowledge, acknowledging Jesus to be the Son of God. True, he repressed this testimony (Mark 1 : 34; Luke 4: 41), doubtless because his enemies would otherwise have been ready to charge that the expulsion was a thing arranged between him and Satan for the purpose of deceiving the people ; even as we find that, without any such excuse, they did repeatedly say that he cast out demons by league with Beelzebub (see on 12: 24). But though the testimony was repressed, it showed superhuman knowledge. These four facts would seem to put the matter beyond question. But there are *objections* to the reality of the possessions, which are apt to perplex the enquirer. (1) The symptoms, it may be said, often resemble those of certain bodily and mental diseases, such as epilepsy and insanity. Now it is perfectly conceivable that the possessions might produce insanity and nervous diseases ; it may be also that persons having such affections became thereby more liable to be taken possession of by evil spirits. This probable relation between them will account for the fact that possessions are often mentioned in connection with various diseases of body or mind, and yet are always distinguished from them. (See 4: 24; 8: 16; Mark 1: 34.) Also for the use of the term 'heal' with reference to demoniacs. Also for the people's saying, as a familiar phrase, 'Thou hast a demon' (John 7: 20; 8: 48-52; 10: 20), where we should say, "You are deranged." The possessed were virtually deranged, whether as effect or occasion of the possession, so as to be the sport of delusive fancies; and notice that in John 10: 20 the two are both stated as if distinct: 'He has a demon and is mad'! Thus there is in all this no reason to depart from the plain declarations of Scripture. And the entrance of the evil spirits into the herd of swine is here in point. It might be possible that swine should have physical symptoms resembling insanity, but we could not account for these being suddenly *transferred* to them from men. (2) The Evangelists and Jesus, in speaking of these possessions as real, are held to be simply

---

gesa is said to be Gerasa. If the native pronunciation contains the rattling sound, it will then be probable that Gergesenes is the original form, changed to Gerasenes because Gerasa was a familiar name. But in any case, we have now a place called Gergesa or Gerasa, beside the lake, and adjacent to the territory of Gadara, and this accounts for the narrative, the various readings in Matt., Mark, and Luke, and the statements of Origen and Eusebius.

employing popular phraseology without endorsing it; as when Scripture writers speak of the sun as rising, standing still, etc. And if Jesus addresses the spirit, bidding it come out, etc., he is supposed to be merely humoring the fancy of the deranged person in order to cure him. But if the belief in demoniacal possessions was erroneous, how far-reaching was that error, and how important, especially in that age of great superstition. As to humoring, etc., the wisest authorities upon the treatment of the insane now say that that is not the best course; they do not contradict so as to exasperate, but neither do they confirm in delusive fancies—they try to divert attention. Thus we should have Jesus adopting a very questionable mode of treatment, which would encourage a most injurious error, when he was able to heal in any way he pleased. See too (Trench), how distinctly false his sayings would become. We speak of *lunatics*, using the popular term without meaning to endorse the idea in which it had its origin, that such persons are powerfully affected by the moon (in Latin *luna*); but suppose one addressing the moon, bidding it cease troubling the man, etc., that would be falsehood; and in our Lord's case such gratuitous deception is incredible. (3) Why should these possessions occur only about the time of our Lord's sojourn upon the earth? It is not absolutely certain that they do not always exist; and mere uncertainty on that point destroys the force of the objection, as an objection. But we can see a reason why they should occur only then; or should then be especially manifested and recognized. The Eternal Word was then manifesting himself in the flesh; and thus the great struggle which is always going on was brought out into visible appearance, so as to exhibit in a visible and striking way the absolute powerlessness of the evil spirits to contend against God. (Comp. at the beginning of chap. 4, as to the appearance of Satan in bodily form.) (4) The thing itself is so hard to understand. But this might be expected in such a subject. And can we understand the union of the divine and human nature in the person of Jesus; the action of the Holy Spirit on the human spirit; or the connection of our own mind and body? Yet none the less are all these facts.

It appears then that the demoniacal posses-

sions are to be received as a reality. And thus regarded they are not only wonderful, but instructive. The expulsion of the evil spirits by Jesus and his apostles, was a signal exhibition of the beneficent character of the gospel and of the Saviour; a striking proof of his divine mission; and an impressive manifestation of that victory over Satan by our Lord, which is real already, and shall in due time be complete. Finally, we thus vindicate as correct the plain, obvious meaning of Scripture statements, which, seeing that the Scriptures were written for the *people*, is a matter of great importance.—The Gospel of John does not mention the casting out of demons by Jesus (though it refers to the popular belief in demoniacal possessions, John 7: 20; 8: 48-52; 10: 20 f.). But we must remember that John mentions very few incidents of our Saviour's ministry, usually such only as formed the occasion of some remarkable discourse. Demoniacal possessions are not mentioned in the Old Test. nor the Apocrypha, nor (Edersheim) in the Mishna, yet are repeatedly mentioned in Josephus ("Ant.," 6, 8, 2; 6, 11, 3; 8, 2, 5; "War," 7, 6, 3). But the popular Jewish views were quite different from those of the New Test. (Edersh. App. XVI.) (As to 'devil' and 'demon,' see below on v. 31.)

Coming out of the tombs. Driven from the town by the fears of the people or by their own frenzy, the poor demoniacs would find the caves, or chambers hewn in the rock, and appropriated to the dead, a convenient and perhaps congenial abode; though no Jew in his right mind would dwell in a tomb, which would make him in the ceremonial sense perpetually unclean. Such rocky tombs still abound in the mountains lying east of the southern part of the lake. Luke (8: 27) seems in Com. Ver. to contradict Matthew's statement, saying, 'There met him out of the city a certain man,' but the correct rendering of Luke is, 'there met him a certain man out of the city,' viz., a man who was a citizen of the city. **So that no man might pass by that way,** viz., along the road that passed near the tombs, and led from the place at which the boat had landed towards the city. The unfortunate men had first rushed forth to meet Jesus and his followers, precisely as they had often done to others who came along the road. Mark and Luke give many addi-

29 And, behold, they cried out, saying, What have
we to do with thee, Jesus, thou Son of God? art thou
come hither to torment us before the time?
30 And there was a good way off from them a herd
of many swine feeding.
31 So the devils besought him, saying, If thou cast
us out, suffer us to go away into the herd of swine.

29 way. And behold, they cried out, saying, What
  have we to do with thee, thou Son of God? art
  thou come hither to torment us before the time?
30 Now there was afar off from them a herd of many
31 swine feeding. And the demons besought him,
  saying, If thou cast us out, send us away into the
32 herd of swine. And he said unto them, Go. And

tional particulars concerning the more conspicuous demoniac whom they describe.

29. And, behold, calling special attention, as in v. 24, 32, 34, and very often in Matthew. **What have we to do with thee,** literally, ' *What* (is there) *to us and thee,*' a phrase found in Hebrew, Greek, and Latin (Buttm., p. 238), and which obviously means, what have we in common, what have we to do with each other? It would express a severe rebuke (2 Sam. 16: 10; Ezra 4: 3), or a mild repulse (John 2: 4), according to the circumstances, the relation of the parties, and the manner of utterance. **Thou Son of God.** The name Jesus was wrongly inserted here in many documents, by way of assimilation to Mark and Luke. It is evident that the men spoke what the evil spirits thought and felt. We cannot determine just how much these dark beings did feel. It is likely that they very imperfectly understood what was involved in calling Jesus the Son of God; and the same was probably true of Satan, their chief (comp. on 4: 3). Mark (3: 11 f.) declares this testimony to have been given in all cases, but he may be referring only to a particular period of our Lord's ministry. **To torment us before the time.** The word rendered 'time' means ' occasion,' 'season,' etc, (See on 11: 25.) The evil spirits were persuaded that a worse torment than they had ever endured awaited them at some future period, and they shrank from the thought that the Son of God might be about to inflict such aggravated torment by anticipation. We are told in Jude 6 that this future occasion is "the judgment of the great day," after which time Satan and his agents "shall be tormented day and night forever and ever." (Rev. 20: 10.)—There are striking contradictions in the conduct of the demoniacs; they came forth fiercely to meet Jesus and his followers; as they drew near they ' ran and worshipped him' (Mark 5: 6); and now they speak words of dread and dislike. Such self-contradictions, such sudden changes of feeling, would seem perfectly natural for one possessed by an evil spirit; at one moment he expresses his own

feeling of distress and need, at another he speaks for the dreadful being who occupies and controls him.

30. A good—*long*—**way from them,** the same Greek term as in Luke 15: 20 and Acts 22: 21. The old Latin and the Vulgate, followed of course by Wyclif and Rheims, have ' not a long way ' probably to avoid a supposed conflict with Mark (5: 11) and Luke (8: 32), who say 'there was *there* a herd,' etc. Tyndale and his followers, accustomed to read the Vulgate, seem to have had the same fear, so that while following the Greek in omitting 'not' they yet softened the expression into 'a good way.' But 'a long way' is obviously a relative expression, signifying a greater or less distance according to circumstances. Matthew apparently wished to show that the herd was too far off to be frightened by the demoniacs. Absurd as such a fancy might seem there have not been wanting "rationalists" of recent times to say that the "maniacs" ran in among the herd, and terrified them into a stampede (see even Ewald); or that the convulsions and cries attendant upon their healing had that effect. Mark and Luke simply tell us that the herd was *there*, without saying that it was near or far away; and Mark, according to his custom of giving descriptive details, adds ' near the mountain,' that is, the mountain range which runs along near the eastern side of the lake. (See on 4: 18.) **A herd of many swine.** Mark says they were 'about two thousand.'

31. And the devils (*demons*) **besought him.** The word 'devil' (see on 4: 1) is a contraction of *diabolos*, the Greek name of him who is in the Hebrew called Satan. This Greek word is applied in Scripture only to Satan, never to his subordinates, who are described by *daimon*, from which we derive demon, demoniac, etc., or *daimonion*, a diminutive form with equivalent meaning. The term ' devil ' has become familiar to English usage as denoting either Satan or one of his subordinates, and the *English* Revisers of 1881 were unwilling to abandon it; while the *American* Revisers preferred ' demon,' which

32 And he said unto them, Go. And when they were come out, they went into the herd of swine: and, behold, the whole herd of swine ran violently down a steep place into the sea, and perished in the waters.
33 And they that kept them fled, and went their ways into the city, and told every thing, and what was befallen to the possessed of the devils.
34 And, behold, the whole city came out to meet

they came out, and went into the swine: and behold the whole herd rushed down the steep into the sea, 33 and perished in the waters. And they that fed them fled, and went away into the city, and told every thing, and what was befallen to them that 34 were [1] possessed with demons. And behold, all the city came out to meet Jesus: and when they saw

---

1 Or, *demoniacs.*

---

is certainly much better; for sometimes it is important to distinguish between the two words. Matthew speaks of the demons without intimating whether there were simply two, one in each possessed person, or more. Mark and Luke say that the more conspicuous person declared himself possessed by a *legion* of demons, and the full Roman legion of that day amounted to six thousand men. The correct reading here is not **suffer us to go away,** resembling Luke 8: 32, but *send us away,* resembling Mark 5: 12.

32. Go—or, *go along*—'away with you,' the same word as in 4: 10; 5: 24, 41; 8: 4, 13. **The whole herd.** Some copyists made the useless addition 'of swine.' **A steep place,** literally, *the precipice*—i. e., the one leading from the plain on which they were feeding, into the sea. **And perished.** The word is really 'died' (so Geneva, Rheims, Darby, Davidson), and there was never anything gained by substituting Tyndale's 'perished.' Swine are extremely averse to entering deep water, and require to be forced into it; so there could be no mistake here as to the cause. The fact that irrational animals were thus possessed by the evil spirits shows that the possession of men cannot have been merely a matter of imagination or insanity. (See on v. 28.)

The question has often been raised, How was it right for our Lord to destroy so much valuable property? We need not have recourse to the supposition that the owners were Jews, whom the law forbade to eat swine and the Scribes forbade to keep them, and that so their property was confiscated. It is enough to say that the Saviour was acting in the exercise of Divine Sovereignty. *Stier:* "The question why our Lord permitted the demons to enter the swine, is already answered by another question—Why had the Lord permitted them to enter the men?" *Godet:* "It is one of those cases in which the power, by its

very nature, guarantees the right." All the other miracles of Jesus, save this, and the destruction of the fig-tree (see on 21: 19), were purely beneficent in their character and tendency. Moreover the important lessons we may learn from this extraordinary occurrence, the light it sheds on the reality of demoniacal possessions, will amply account for the destruction of property.

It has also been inquired why the demons, after earnestly begging permission to take refuge in the swine, should immediately cause them to destroy themselves. It may be supposed that in their malignity they took delight in doing any harm, even destroying property. Theophylact and Euthymius think they wished to destroy the swine for the purpose of prejudicing the owners against Jesus—a result which actually followed.

33. And they that kept—i. e., *fed*—them. The word is rendered 'feed' in the parallel passages of Mark and Luke, and everywhere else in the New Test., and it was very little worth while for the King James Version, in its passion for variety (and following Great Bible) to employ here another word, 'kept.' **Went their ways into the city,** viz., Gerasa (Khersa, see on v. 28.) **And told every thing, and what was befallen,** etc. —literally, *and the (things) of the demonized,* what had happened to them. The first thing reluctantly told would be the loss of the swine, the rest being secondary in the view of the swine-herds.

34. And, behold, for this too was wonderful. (Comp. v. 24, 29, 32.) **The whole city,** an obvious and natural hyperbole, such as we frequently employ. (Comp. on 3: 5.) Luke (8: 34, 37) adds that the swine-herds had carried the news, not only into the city, but into the fields, and that all the multitude of the surrounding country of the Gerasenes came forth. **That he would depart[1] out**

---

[1] This is a nonfinal use of *hopos,* corresponding to a common New Test. use of *hina* (see on 5: 29), and found in Homer (Goodwin's "Moods and Tenses.")

Jesus: and when they saw him, they besought *him* that he would depart out of their coasts.

A ND he entered into a ship, and passed over, and came into his own city.

him, they besought *him* that he would depart from their borders.

1   And he entered into a boat, and crossed over, and

---

of their coasts. 'From' and not 'out of,' see on 3 : 16. 'Borders' rather than 'coasts,' as in 2: 16, Rev. Ver. ; 4: 13. 'Depart' is not the word commonly thus rendered, but signifies literally, to remove, transfer oneself. Why did they wish him to leave? Partly, no doubt, because their property had been destroyed, and they feared other losses, partly also (see already Theod. Mops., Jerome, in Cat.), because their conscience was aroused by such an exhibition of divine power, and conscious of guilt they felt uneasy in his presence. Compare the feelings of Peter after the miraculous draught of fishes (Luke 5 : 8), and contrast the conduct of the Samaritans of Sychar. (John 4 : 40.) While meekly retiring at the request of the frightened people, he left them efficient teachers in the men who had been dispossessed (Luke 8 : 38 f.); and he afterwards revisited their country. (15 : 29.)—This miracle forms the most instructive and impressive instance of demoniacal possession found in the Gospels. The whole scene appears before us with a vivid and terrible reality.

Ch. 9 : 1. This sentence is the end of the narrative beginning with 8 : 18, and should by all means have formed a part of the preceding chapter. Comp. on 10: 1. Mark (5 : 18 ff.) and Luke (8 : 38 f.) relate that when Jesus had entered the boat, the man who had been delivered begged to go with him, but was sent back to tell what God had done for him. (Comp. on 8 : 4.) **Passed over, and came into his own city,** viz., Capernaum. (See on 4 : 13.) Chrys. remarks (Cat.), "For Bethlehem bore him, Nazareth reared him, Capernaum was his residence."

HOMILETICAL AND PRACTICAL.

V. 19 f. The Scribe : 1) Willing, (a) to accept the teachings of Jesus, (b) to share his fortunes. 2) Warned, to count the cost of following him ; comp. Luke 14: 28-33. 3) Went on, notwithstanding. So let us suppose he did, and so let us do.—Ministers and churches ought to note the Saviour's example in regard to this Scribe, and declare plainly to all who propose to be his followers, what it is they are undertaking. In dealing with a *Scribe*, with

any person of superior cultivation and position, we are in danger of too readily taking for granted that he understands the whole matter. RYLE: "Nothing has done more harm to Christianity than the practice of filling the ranks of Christ's army with every volunteer who is willing to make a little profession, and talk fluently of his experience." STIER: "Nothing was less aimed at by our Lord than to have *followers*, unless they were genuine and sound ; he is as far from desiring this as it would have been easy to attain it."—V. 20. Jesus the wandering missionary.—V. 21 f. Even the strongest natural feelings must sometimes give way to Christian duties. Even sacred natural duties may have to be disregarded for Christ's sake. How much less then should any ordinary matters turn us away from spiritual thoughts or activities. THEOPHYL.: "We must honor our parents, but honor God still more highly." LUTTEROTH: "What good thing could be accomplished on earth if affections must override obligations?" HENRY: "An unwilling mind never lacks an excuse. Many are hindered *from* and *in* the way of serious godliness, by an over-concern for their families and relations."

V. 23. BENGEL: "Jesus had a traveling school ; and in that school the disciples were much more solidly instructed than if they had lived under a college roof without any anxiety and temptation."—V. 24. Contrast Jesus and Jonah sleeping amid a storm. CHRYS.: "Their very alarm was a profitable occurrence, that the miracle might appear greater, and their remembrance of the event be rendered lasting. . . . Therefore also he sleeps; for had he been awake when it happened, either they would not have feared, or they would not have besought him, or they would not have even thought of his being able to do any such thing. Therefore he sleeps, to give occasion for their timidity, and to make their perception of what was happening more distinct."—V. 26. Stilling the tempest. 1) Jesus sleeping soundly amid the storm—after a day of great exertion and strain—the picture. 2) The disciples afraid, through lack of faith in God—they awake the sleeping Master to save them. 3) He stills the tempest by a word

CHAPTER IX.

2 And, behold, they brought to him a man sick of the palsy, lying on a bed: and Jesus seeing their faith said unto the sick of the palsy; Son, be of good cheer; thy sins be forgiven thee.

2 came into his own city. And behold, they brought to him a man sick of the palsy, lying on a bed: and Jesus seeing their faith said unto the sick of the palsy, [1] Son, be of good cheer; thy sins are forgiven.

---

1 Gr. *Child.*

(comp. Mark 4: 39), as by a word he had healed the centurion's servant. (8: 8, 13.)   4) The disciples greatly wondering that the winds and the sea obey him; we no longer wonder, but we too must obey.—All the sufferings and perils to which in God's providence we may be exposed, are trials of our faith. If we have strong faith we shall not yield to craven fear. "With Christ in the vessel, I smile at the storm." This tempest doubtless proved a great blessing to the disciples in strengthening their faith; and our trials are among our greatest blessings, if they have a similar effect.—Not in the way of exegesis, but of *illustration*, we may say that there are storms in life, stormy passions in the soul, which only Christ can calm.—V. 27. NICOLL: "It is incomplete to say that the miracles justify belief in Christ, and it is equally incomplete to say that it is belief in Christ that makes miracles credible. Christ comes before us as a whole—his person and his work. It is impossible to separate the two, and we believe in the whole—that is, in both."

V. 29. CHRYS.: "Because the multitudes called him man, the demons came proclaiming his Godhead, and they that heard not the sea swelling and subsiding, heard from the demons the same cry, as it, by its calm, was loudly uttering."—V. 31. Here was very earnest asking, but we should not call it prayer. And the thing asked was granted, as was Satan's request with respect to Job; yet it was not the prayer which God approves and accepts. Let us beware lest our supplications be sometimes the mere utterance of selfish desire, and not the prayer of a trusting, loving, devout spirit.—V. 34. LUTHER: "The mass of men would gladly hold to the gospel, if it did not touch their kitchen and income. If Jesus gives them good things, they can very well endure him; but when he inflicts damage, as here, they say, 'Begone, Jesus, gospel, and all.'" HALL: "O Saviour, thou hast just cause to be weary of us, even while we sue to hold thee; but when once our wretched unthankfulness grows weary of thee,

who can pity us to be punished with thy departure?"

---

9. 2–34. FURTHER MIRACLES, WITH CALL OF MATTHEW, AND DISCOURSE AT MATTHEW'S FEAST.

The series of miracles (see on 8: 1, 18) is now continued by giving—

I. THE PARALYTIC HEALED, 9: 2–8; comp. Mark 2: 1–12; Luke 5: 17–26. The connection in Mark renders it probable that this miracle preceded the Sermon on the Mount. We have already observed that Matthew is evidently here not following the chronological order, but grouping together certain specimens of our Lord's actions and sayings in the way best calculated to subserve his object, viz., to establish the Messiahship of Jesus, and exhibit the nature of the Messianic reign. We cannot always see the particular principle on which he groups. But in the present case Alexander has pointed out a natural relation between the events, which accounts for their being thrown together. Shortly after the miracle of the two demoniacs (8: 28-34), occurred the raising of the ruler's daughter (9: 18-26), as we learn from Mark 5: 22; Luke 8: 41. But we see from 9: 18 that the ruler came to Jesus while he was talking with the Pharisees about fasting; and that conversation occurred (v. 14) directly after what he said to the Pharisees in reply to their complaints that he had associated with publicans and sinners, at Matthew's feast. (v. 10-13.) Now this feast would naturally suggest to the Evangelist's mind his own call to follow Jesus, which led to the feast given some time after the call. (See on v. 10.) But the call occurred (v. 9) while Jesus was going away from the house at which he healed the paralytic; and this was a very important, a peculiarly instructive miracle, which it was desirable to introduce. So instead of taking up at once the raising of the ruler's daughter, Matthew first describes the healing of the paralytic (v. 2-8), and his own call, on that same day (v. 9); then passes (see on v. 10) to the feast he subsequently gave, and the conversation which ensued (v. 10-13, 14-17); and thus approaches the case of the ruler's daughter, and the other notable miracle connected therewith (v. 18-26); afterwards appending two other miracles which took place the same day. (v. 27-31, 32-34.) We may also note (Lutteroth) an internal relation between the complaint of the Scribes in v. 3, and that of the Pharisees in v. 11, culminating in v. 34; and this may have affected the grouping. That the Evangelist's mind should thus have worked according to the natural laws of suggestion, is altogether compatible with the inspiration of his narrative; for every part of the Bible bears the impress of human thinking, only preserved by the Spirit from error and guided into all truth, so that the inspired writer says precisely what God would have him say.

The scene of this miracle was in Capernaum (Mark 2 : 1, 12), and quite probably at Peter's house, which might well be our Lord's recognized stopping place. Mark and Luke, as is frequently the case, give fuller details than Matthew. Weiss holds that Matthew makes this occur on the street, and thus conflicts with Mark; but Matthew gives not the slightest hint of locality. What in the world is gained by manufacturing discrepancies?

2. And behold, see on 8: 2, 24. **They brought to him,** literally, *were bringing*, a form of expression which not merely narrates the fact, but depicts it as going on. **A man sick of the palsy,** *a paralytic*—see on 4 : 24; 8: 6. **Lying on a bed.** 'Lying' is the same word as in 8: 6, 14. The 'bed' was doubtless a thin mattress, or a well-wadded quilt, the inner material being wool. It may have been placed in the present case on a slight frame of wood, making it more comfortable and easier to carry; but it was usually for ordinary sleeping laid on the floor; while sometimes a more elevated bedstead was employed; see Mark 4 : 21, R. V., 'under a bed.' We learn from Mark and Luke that four men were bearing the paralytic on the bed, and that in consequence of the great crowd in and about the house where Jesus was, they got on the housetop, broke through the roof, and let him down on his bed into the presence of Jesus. (Comp.

Edersh.) **And Jesus seeing their faith,** that is, the faith of the bearers and the paralytic. He was more ready to work miracles for those who had faith, (see on v. 19, 28); and where forgiveness of sins was also involved, it was indispensable that the person concerned should have faith. (Comp. on 8 : 3.) 'Seeing' their faith is of course a mere vivid expression for perceiving, as when we say "I see your motive." The pains they had taken (Mark and Luke) showed their faith all the more plainly. **Son, be of good cheer.** Literally, *Be encouraged, child*, or we should better imitate the simplicity and vigor of the original by saying, 'Courage, child.' 'Child' is the literal rendering (marg. Rev. Ver., comp. Darby, Davidson), and is often used in colloquial English as an expression of familiar affection, though not now suited to an elevated style. Comp. 'daughter, v. 22. **Thy sins be**—or, *are*—**forgiven,** as correctly rendered by Com. Ver. in Luke (5 : 20.) The Greek verb is not imperative, but indicative, while the old English 'be' is used for either. The common Greek text has a perfect tense, meaning 'have been forgiven,' stand forgiven (so in Luke 7 : 47 f.; 1 John 2 : 12); Westcott and Hort have the present tense, which would cause the forgiveness to be conceived of as just then taking place; it is not easy to decide which form is the original text.[1] The position of the Greek words makes 'forgiven' emphatic. No doubt all present were much surprised, when instead of healing the bodily disease, Jesus spoke to the man thus. It seems probable that the disease had in this case resulted from some form of dissipation, such as not unfrequently produces paralysis. Comp. the man at the Pool of Bethesda (John 5 : 14, lit.), 'Thou hast become well; do not sin any more, lest something worse happen to thee.' It would not at all follow that *all* peculiar diseases and remarkable misfortunes result from some special sin— an idea prevalent among the Jews, but distinctly corrected by our Lord. (John 9 : 3; Luke 13 : 2 f.) We may not unreasonably think that the poor paralytic was troubled and dispirited, because he felt that his sad disease was the consequence and the merited punishment of his sin; so the words of Jesus, which surprised

---

[1] The perfect might have been introduced by way of assimilation to Luke 5: 20 (where there is no variation), or might have been abandoned because it is an unusual form of the verb. There is a similar difficulty in Mark 2 : 5.

3 And, behold, certain of the scribes said within themselves, This *man* blasphemeth.
4 And Jesus knowing their thoughts said, Wherefore think ye evil in your hearts?
5 For whether is easier, to say, Thy sins be forgiven thee: or to say, Arise, and walk?
6 But that ye may know that the Son of man hath power on earth to forgive sins, (then saith he to the sick of tho palsy,) Arise, take up thy bed, and go unto thine house.

3 And, behold, certain of the scribes said within themselves, This man blasphemeth. And Jesus [1] knowing their thoughts said, Wherefore think ye evil in
5 your hearts? For whether is easier, to say, Thy
6 sins are forgiven: or to say, Arise, and walk? But that ye may know that the Son of man hath authority on earth to forgive sins (then saith he to the sick of the palsy), Arise, and take up thy bed,

---

[1] Many ancient authorities read, *seeing.*

---

all the bystanders, would be to him precisely in place and full of comfort. Yet it would suffice to say (Schaff) that "the man's conscience was aroused through his sickness," without supposing the disease to have been caused by special sin.

3. And, behold, this too being remarkable (comp. v. 2). As to the **scribes**, see on 2: 4. Luke (5 : 17, Bib. Un. Ver.) mentions that there were present "Pharisees and teachers of the law (the latter being substantially the same as 'scribes'), who had come out of every village of Galilee and Judea and Jerusalem." Here was quite a crowd of critical hearers. **Said within themselves.** Comp. on 3: 9. **Blasphemeth.** The Greek word, borrowed by us, signifies to speak injuriously, or insultingly, to defame, slander, etc., as in Rom. 3: 8; 1 Pet. 4: 4; Tit. 3: 2. From this it was applied to reviling God; saying anything insulting to God, anything impious. The Scribes held Jesus to be blaspheming, because he arrogated to himself a power and right which belonged exclusively to God, viz., that of forgiving sins. This is distinctly expressed by them, in the additional words recorded by Mark and Luke, 'Who can (is able to) forgive sins but God only?' He who claimed a power peculiar to God, spoke what was injurious and insulting to God. Yet it is not wise to find here a proof of our Lord's divinity; for he speaks as the Son of man, and speaks of authority given him. (v. 6-8. comp. 28 : 18.)

4. Knowing—properly, *seeing*—**their thoughts**, like seeing their faith in v. 2.[1] Mark (2 : 8) has the expression 'perceived in his spirit that they so reasoned within themselves.' The faith of the paralytic and his bearers could be seen from their actions; but to see the unexpressed thoughts of the Scribes required superhuman perceptions. Comp.

Luke 6: 8; 9: 47; Mark 12: 15; John 2: 24 f; 4: 29. **Wherefore think ye evil in your hearts?** The 'heart,' according to Scripture use, is regarded as the seat of the thoughts as well as the affections. (See on 6: 21.) Jesus replies not only with a mild rebuke, but with a proof that he was not blaspheming.

5. For whether—or, *which*—**is easier!** It was as easy to say one as the other, viz., to say it with effect. *Euthym:* "Both were possible for God, both impossible for man." In the case of the healing they could test the reality of the power he claimed; and from this they ought to infer that he possessed the other power also, seeing that he claimed to possess it, and that one who could work a miracle ought to be believed. They had already had many proofs at Capernaum of his power to work miracles. We are often told at the present day that Jesus always relied on his teaching to convince men, and not at all on his miracles; but here he distinctly appeals to miracles as establishing the truth of his teachings.

6. The Son of man, our Lord's favorite designation of himself, see on 8: 20. **Power.** The word thus rendered is much used throughout the N. T. It signifies primarily, permission (license, privilege), then authority, (dominion, rule, etc.), and this sometimes suggests ability and power. The word very often conveys two of these ideas at once, as privilege and power (John 1: 12), authority and power. (John 19: 10.) Comp. on 7: 29; 28: 18. The Rev. Ver. has everywhere else in Matt. rendered 'authority,' and it would have been better to do so here, as is done by the American Revisers, Davidson, and Noyes. In this passage it is meant that Jesus has authority to forgive sins, and the power which such au-

---

[1] Obvious as is the meaning of this, several MSS. (including B) and several early versions took the trouble to change it to 'knowing'; this is adopted of course by W H. (who cannot forsake B), and is unwisely followed by Rev. Version. How can we account for a change of 'knowing' into 'seeing'?

7 And he arose, and departed to his house.
8 But when the multitudes saw *it*, they marvelled, and glorified God, which had given such power unto men.
9 And as Jesus passed forth from thence, he saw a man, named Matthew, sitting at the receipt of custom: and he saith unto him, Follow me. And he arose, and followed him.

7 and go unto thy house. And he arose, and departed to his house. But when the multitudes saw it, they were afraid, and glorified God, who had given such authority unto men.
9 And as Jesus passed by from thence, he saw a man, called Matthew, sitting at the place of toll: and he saith unto him, Follow me. And he arose, and followed him.

---

thority carries with it; this power is alluded to by the phrase, ' Who *can* (Mark 2: 7, Luke 5: 21), and ' Which is *easier* (v. 5, Bib. Un. Ver.). The word ' authority' is in this passage so placed as to be emphatic, 'the Son of man hath *authority*,' etc. And while they naturally thought of forgiveness of sins as performed only by God in heaven, he will show them that the Son of man hath authority **on earth** to forgive sins. Comp. the authority to judge, John 5: 27. He does not proceed to *tell* the Scribes what he will do to prove his authority, but turns to the paralytic and lets them *see*. **Take up thy bed.** Being such as described on v. 2, a man could easily take it up and carry it. **Go**, or ' go along,' not said severely, as in 4: 10, but kindly, as in 8: 13 ; the word taking color from the connection.

7 f. What a moment of suspense for all the beholders—some hoping, others fearing, that the man would indeed show himself to be healed. What a thrill must have passed through the crowd, as he arose and went off. How the Scribes must have been abashed and confounded. The paralytic went away ' glorifying God' (Luke 5: 25) ; we can imagine his feelings of joy and gratitude, when he found himself carrying the bed which had carried him, treading the earth in vigor and health again, yea, and with his sins all forgiven. The effect upon the bystanders at large is stated in v. 8. **But when the multitudes**—*the crowds* **—saw it.** ' Crowds' is the same word as in 5: 1. **They marvelled**—better, *feared*—this, and not ' wondered,' being pretty certainly the correct reading of the text.[1] They felt that alarm and painful uneasiness which is apt to be awakened in the bosom of sinful man by anything that seems to bring God nearer to him. (Luke 5 : 8 ; comp. above on 8 : 34.) But this alarm quickly passed into praise, and they **glorified God, which had given such power unto men.** (Comp. Luke 5: 26.) Regard-

ing Jesus as only a man, it was right that they should give the glory to God. (5: 16.) And they probably did not consider this authority and power as peculiar to him, but as bestowed on *men*, and possible for others also. It was true, in a sense which cannot have entered into their thoughts, that what was given to Jesus was given to mankind.

Before proceeding to further miracles, the Evangelist narrates—

II. The Call of Matthew, and Conversation at a Feast he Gave, 9: 9-17. These are also described in Mark 2: 13-22; Luke 5: 27-39.

9. And as Jesus passed forth from thence. Mark (2: 13) shows that this occurred immediately after the healing of the paralytic, as implied in Matthew's ' from thence.' **Sitting at the receipt of custom** —*custom-house* —(so translated in Rheims) probably the place for receiving tolls on the fishing and trade of the lake. The Romans laid taxes, as the Syrian kings had done before them, on almost everything. (See details in Edersh.) **Matthew.** Luke calls him ' Levi,' and Mark ' Levi, the son of Alpheus.' It had become very common for a Jew to bear two names; and probably the first readers of the different Gospels would readily understand that Levi, the son of Alpheus, was also called Matthew. (The name Matthaios, Mattai, might mean simply ' given,' like Nathan ; or else might be a contraction of Mattijah, ' gift of Jehovah,' like Jonathan, Nethaniah.) It would be natural that Matthew should give only the name by which he was known as an apostle, which Mark and Luke also give in their lists of the apostles (Mark 3 : 18; Luke 6: 15), and should avoid, as Paul did, the name associated with his former life. Some argue that this Matthew was not the Evangelist, since he is spoken of in the third person ; but it has always been common, in ancient and modern times, for

---

[1] Superficial students and copyists would fail to see the deep meaning of ' feared' in this case, and change it to the more obvious term ' wondered.' So the inter-nal probability here concurs with the testimony of the early MSS. and versions.

10 And it came to pass, as Jesus sat at meat in the house, behold, many publicans and sinners came and sat down with him and his disciples.

10   And it came to pass, as he [1] sat at meat in the house, behold, many publicans and sinners came

---

1 Gr. *reclined :* and so always.

---

writers thus to speak of themselves; and the apostle John, in his Gospel, employs elaborate circumlocutions to avoid even mentioning his own name. Luke here tells us (Luke 5:27) that Matthew was a publican, which is implied in the narratives of Matthew and Mark, and stated by Matthew in the list. (10:3) As to the publicans, see on 5:46; and as to Matthew, see further on 10:3. **And he arose and followed him.** Luke says (5:28, Bib. Un. Ver.), 'And leaving all, he arose,' etc. Matthew does not mention this, because it would have been speaking in his own praise, which the Evangelists never do. (Comp. on v. 10.) We can account for his immediately leaving all and following Jesus by the reasonable supposition that at the place of toll by the lake-side he had often seen and heard him, and had gradually become prepared in mind to obey such a call. It is even possible that he had been following Jesus before, and only now attached himself permanently to him (comp. on 4:18 ff.). At the same time we may be sure there was something deeply impressive in the Saviour's tone and look as he spoke the simple words. (Comp. John 18: 6.) Observe that while all of the Twelve seem to have been men in humble life, Matthew belonged to a class greatly despised. The Talmud (Edersh.) distinguishes custom-house officials from other tax-gatherers, and speaks of them with peculiar hate, probably because their extortions were more frequent and more manifest. This publican Matthew, and the notorious persecutor Saul, were as unlikely, humanly speaking, to become apostles of Christ as any men that could be found. Yet such has been the work of sovereign grace in every age of Christianity.

10. We have now the account of some conversation that arose while Jesus and his disciples were eating at Matthew's house, in company with many publicans and sinners. It is clear from v. 14 and Luke 5:33 that the inquiry about fasting and the Saviour's reply occurred during this meal; and from v. 18, that the ruler's request to come and raise his daughter was made while Jesus was speaking in response to that inquiry. But from Mark 5: 22 f., and Luke 8: 41 f., we see that the raising of the ruler's daughter took place after our Lord's return from Gadara, and thus at a much later period than the healing of the paralytic and the call of Matthew. We therefore conclude that the feast was actually given by Matthew a considerable time after his call, and that it is merely introduced by him, and also by Mark and Luke, in connection with the call, because it was natural to bring the two together, thereby completing at once all that had any personal relation to this apostle. It thus appears that all three put the case of Jairus' daughter in its actual chronological position, and all three bring together the call and the feast, although they were really separated by a considerable interval; the difference is, that Mark and Luke tell of the paralytic and the call at the early period when they occurred, adding the feast by anticipation, and then some time afterwards introduce the healing of Jairus' daughter, which we know immediately followed the feast; while Matthew puts the feast in its real chronological connection with the application of Jairus, and just before the feast introduces the call (which had occurred earlier) and the healing of the paralytic, which preceded the call. (Comp. on v. 2.) Any one who will take the trouble thoroughly to grasp the facts, will see that this view removes all the difficulty attendant upon harmonizing the three Gospels at this point, a thing which has often been declared impossible. We need not feel bound, nor imagine ourselves able, to remove all such discrepancies, but it is surely worth while to do so when practicable. If the nervous harmonizers stand at one extreme, the scornful despisers of harmonizing certainly stand at the other.

And it came to pass, the same word as in 1:22; 5:18; 6:10; 7:28; 8:13. **As Jesus sat at meat,** etc., better, *while he was reclining in the house,* comp. on 8:11, where the Greek word is similar and substantially equivalent. Matthew omits to mention whose house it was; probably he omitted it through modesty (comp. on v. 9), or perhaps 'the house' seemed enough in his vivid recollec-

11 And when the Pharisees saw *it*, they said unto his disciples, Why eateth your master with publicans and sinners?
12 But when Jesus heard *that*, he said unto them, They that be whole need not a physician, but they that are sick.

11 and sat down with Jesus and his disciples. And when the Pharisees saw it, they said unto his disciples, Why eateth your [1] Master with the publicans
12 and sinners? But when he heard it, he said, They that are [2] whole have no need of a physician, but

1 Or, *Teacher*....2 Gr. *strong.*

---

tion; though it is implied in the connection; Mark (2: 15) and Luke (5: 29) distinctly state that it was Levi's house, and Luke says that ' Levi made a great feast (literally 'reception') in his house.' This would indicate that he possessed some means; he seems to have sacrificed a somewhat lucrative position in order to follow Jesus. Meyer's attempt to make 'the house' here mean Jesus' own house, and thus to bring Matthew into conflict with Mark and Luke, is strained and uncalled for. Even Keim and Weiss understand it to be Matthew's house. **Behold,** see on 8: 2, 29. **Many publicans and sinners came and sat down,** or, *were reclining.* As to the publicans, see on 5: 46. The Jews were accustomed to call those persons 'sinners' who lived in open violation of the moral or ceremonial law; and they shrank from contact with all such as polluting. Matthew's previous associations had brought him into connection not only with publicans, but with all those other men, who, disregarding many of the prevailing religious observances, and feeling themselves to be objects of popular dislike, naturally flocked together. Luke's expression as to the number present is still stronger, 'a great crowd.' Mark (2: 15) mentions that these 'followed' Jesus, as if of their own accord. This is not inconsistent with the idea that Matthew invited them in, while it implies that the feast was a sort of public affair, which agrees with the fact that the Pharisees appear to have pressed in as spectators. (v. 11.) Matthew doubtless wished to show respect to his Teacher by inviting a numerous company to meet him, perhaps asking in every one who followed Jesus toward his house. At the same time he must have had some cherished friends among these despised men, some whom he knew to have better stuff in them than was generally supposed, and to have been driven by popular neglect and scorn into association with abandoned persons; and he would hope that they might be benefited by being in company with Jesus and hearing what he said. The example deserves imitation.

Imagine the character of the general conversation at this great entertainment. We should not suppose that the presence or the words of Jesus chilled the guests into a dead stillness; that he showed a lack of sympathy with the common concerns and feelings of mankind. He was not proud, haughty, and forbidding, like many of the Rabbis, but was meek and lowly, kind and gentle, and everything about him tended to attract men rather than repel. Whatever he spoke of, it would be in a spirit marked by fidelity to truth, and yet by delicate consideration for the feelings of others. And when it was appropriate to introduce distinctively religious topics, we can see with what ease and aptness he would bring them in, from striking examples in Luke 14: 7, 12, 15, 16, and John 4: 10, 16.

11. It is plain that these Pharisees were not themselves guests at the feast, for in that case they would have been doing the very thing they complained of in Jesus. Probably they pressed into the house before the feast ended, in order to hear what Jesus would be saying. In Luke 7: 36 ff. no surprise is expressed at the woman's entering the dining-room, and no objection made by the host. **Pharisees,** see on 3: 7. **Why eateth your master** (or *your teacher*, *didaskalos*, see on 8: 19), **with** (*the*) **publicans and sinners?** The two nouns with but one article present the two classes as forming but one group. According to the prevailing Jewish ideas, a Rabbi, of all men, "ought carefully to avoid all intercourse with such persons." There was not only the social objection to "keeping low company," but the constant dread of ceremonial pollution, from coming in contact with persons likely to be ceremonially unclean (Mark 7: 4); and also that feeling so natural to man, which says, "Stand back; I am holier than thou." (Isa. 65: 5.) Accordingly, our Lord was frequently met with the objection here made to his course. (11: 19; Luke 15: 2 ff.)

12 f. *He* **said,** the correct text omitting 'Jesus' and 'to them.' The disciples told their Teacher of the question which had been

13 Bnt go ye and learn what *that* meaneth, I will have mercy, and not sacrifice: for I am not come to call the righteous, but sinners to repentance.

13 they that are sick. But go ye and learn what *this* meaneth, I desire mercy, and not sacrifice: for I came not to call the righteous, but sinners.

asked. They were themselves as yet very imperfectly freed from the erroneous Jewish conceptions of the Messiah's work, and would probably find it difficult to explain why Jesus should pursue such a course. It was cunning in the Pharisees to ask them, in hope of turning them away from their Teacher. It appears from the connection, and is distinctly stated by Luke (5: 30, 31), that his reply was addressed especially to the Pharisees, with whom the question had started. This reply embraces three points: (1) an argument from analogy; (2) an appeal to Scripture; (3) an express declaration that his mission was to men as sinners, and so he was now acting accordingly. In like manner Paul, 1 Cor. 9: 7, presents first an argument from the analogy of men's common modes of action, and afterwards an argument from Scripture.—(1) **They that be whole,** or *are strong,* stout, well, comp. the connection of the English words *hale, health, whole.* Luke 5: 31 has literally, 'they that are *in health.*' **But they that are sick,** or *ill,* the same expression as in 4: 24; 8: 16. The order of the Greek words puts an emphasis on **need not.** The force of the illustration is manifest; the physician goes among the sick, and why should not the teacher of salvation go among sinners? Here is a lesson needed in every age, for we are too apt to hold ourselves aloof from the vile and disreputable, when kind and patient efforts might win some of them to better things. At the same time we must, like the physician, take great pains to avoid the contagion of the diseases we seek to cure. And if our good is evil spoken of, as happened here to our Lord, we should be careful not to afford any just occasion or excuse for such reproach. (2) The second point of his reply is an appeal to Scripture. **But go ye and learn.** The Rabbis frequently employed the same formula, "go ye and learn," indicating that one needs further reflection or information on the subject in hand. This was a severe rebuke to Scribes (Luke 5: 30) and Pharisees, who assumed and were popularly supposed to be particularly versed in Scripture. **Learn what that meaneth** (literally *is*), *i. e.,* the following saying. The passage is referred to as familiar

to them, while yet they were quite ignorant of its real meaning. The Old Test. throughout, when rightly understood, agreed with the teachings of Jesus. **I will have** (*wish, desire*) **mercy, and not sacrifice,** quoted according to the Hebrew. (Hos. 6: 6.) The Hebrew word includes the ideas of kindness and compassion toward men, and of piety towards God. So *piety* and *pity* are originally the same word. Hosea's connection shows that the word was by him taken in the widest sense, but the single idea of kindness or mercy is all that is here necessary to the connection. The absolute statement 'and not sacrifice,' is not intended to be taken literally, but as a strong expression of preference for mercy. (Comp. Luke 14: 12.) The idea is, I wish kindly feeling and conduct toward others, especially toward the needy and suffering, rather than the externals of religion—of which sacrifice was then the most important. So the Sept. translates, 'I wish mercy rather than sacrifice.' Or the passage might be expressed, I wish kindness, and I do not want sacrifice without this. The rendering 'I will have mercy,' which Com. Ver. took from Great Bible and Geneva, is very apt to mislead, because to have mercy now usually means to exercise it.—The mere externals of religion are offensive to God, where its spirit and life are absent. The Pharisees were extremely particular to avoid that external, ceremonial pollution which they might incur by mixing with the publicans and sinners, but were not anxious to show them kindness or do them good. Notice that it is Matthew only that records this argument drawn from the Old Test., just as he most frequently refers to the prophecies fulfilled in the person of Jesus; this course being natural for one who wrote especially for Jewish readers. See the same passage quoted again in 12: 7. (3) **I am not come** (see on 5: 17), **to call the righteous, but sinners.** The words 'unto repentance' are not properly a part of the text of Matthew, but they are genuine in the parallel passage of Luke, and so were actually spoken on this occasion. Such additions to one Gospel from a parallel passage in another, are often found in MSS. and versions. This third point of our Lord's reply is that his

14 Then came to him the disciples of John, saying, Why do we and the Pharisees fast oft, but thy disciples fast not?
15 And Jesus said unto them, Can the children of the bridechamber mourn, as long as the bridegroom is with them? but the days will come, when the bridegroom shall be taken from them, and then shall they fast.

14　Then come to him the disciples of John, saying, Why do we and the Pharisees fast [1] oft, but thy dis-
15　ciples fast not? And Jesus said unto them, Can the sons of the bride-chamber mourn, as long as the bridegroom is with them? but the days will come, when the bridegroom shall be taken away from them,

---

1 Some ancient authorities omit, *oft*.

---

conduct in associating with the very wicked accords with the design of his mission, '*for I came not,*' etc. The word translated 'righteous' has no article. He is not speaking of any actually existing class as righteous, but uses the term in a general way for contrast. (Comp. Luke 15: 7.) There is comfort to the burdened soul in the thought that our Lord's mission was to men as sinners, even to the most vile.

14. The inquiry about fasting, and our Lord's reply (v. 14-17), are also found in Mark 2: 18-22; Luke 5: 33-39. **Then.** The connection in Luke (5: 33) also indicates that this conversation immediately followed the preceding (for the whole connection see on v. 2). Luke represents the Pharisees, to whom Jesus had been speaking just before, as asking the question; Matthew has the disciples of John asking him, and Mark (2:18) says that *both* came and asked, and thus suggests a way in which many similar "discrepancies" may be explained. The questioners do not venture directly to find fault with Jesus himself. (Comp. v. 11.) Who are these **disciples of John,** who in respect to fasting resemble the Pharisees rather than the disciples of Jesus? It was the design of John's ministry (comp. on 3: 1) to bring men to believe on Jesus as coming, and to follow him when he came; and he took great pains to prevent the people from regarding himself as the Messiah. (John 1: 20; 3: 28-30; Acts 19: 4.) Yet there were some who, failing to follow out their master's teachings, felt jealous of the growing influence of Jesus (John 3: 26), and continued to hold exclusively to John; and in the second century we find heretics who maintained that John was the Messiah. How many there were at this time who kept themselves aloof from Jesus, and were simply disciples of John, and what were their precise views, we

have no means of determining. As to their fasting frequently, like the Pharisees (Luke 18: 12), it is enough to understand that they had not really changed from the prevailing Jewish opinions and practices. Even among the Jewish Christians addressed in the Epistle of James we find many characteristic Jewish errors and evil practices. It is possible, besides, that these disciples of John found encouragement to fasting in that self-denying mode of life which John pursued for a special reason. It seems likely from Mark 2: 18 that they were for some reason fasting at this particular time; it may have been one of their regular days of fasting, or it may possibly have been from grief at John's long-continued imprisonment.[1] *Jerome:* "The disciples of John were certainly to blame, in calumniating him whom they knew to have been proclaimed by their teacher, and joining the Pharisees whom they knew to have been condemned by John."—The strict Jews not only fasted very often, but in many cases on very trivial occasions. The Talmud of Jerus. speaks of one rabbi as fasting four-score times to see another; and of a second who fasted three hundred times to see the same person, and did not see him at last.

15. The reply of Jesus is conveyed by three illustrations. (v. 15, 16, 17.) Luke (5: 39) has a fourth. **The children** (*sons*) **of the bride-chamber.** The term 'son' is employed, as explained on 8: 12, strongly to express the idea of *intimate relation* to the object mentioned, but in what precise sense must in every particular expression be determined by the nature of the case. Here it denotes (Edersh.) the guests invited to a wedding, while "friends of the bridegroom" meant his special attendants. (See Judges 14: 11; John 3: 29.) The festivities were commonly prolonged during a week. (See on 25: 1 ff.) The

---

1 The word rendered 'oft,' literally 'much,' is wanting in B ℵ and a few cursives, and hence omitted by Tisch. and W H. One cannot readily decide whether it was omitted to agree with Mark or inserted to agree

with Luke. There is no important difference, as Matthew's expression without 'oft' naturally indicates that they were in the habit of fasting.

16 No man putteth a piece of new cloth unto an old garment; for that which is put in to fill it up taketh from the garment, and the rent is made worse.

16 and then will they fast. And no man putteth a piece of undressed cloth upon an old garment; for that which should fill it up taketh from the garment,

word rendered **can** is so placed as to be emphatic: *can* it be, in the nature of things? And the Greek has the peculiar particle which denotes that a negative answer is taken for granted. The Talmud declares that the bridegroom, his personal friends, and the sons of the bride-chamber, were free from the obligation to dwell in booths during the Feast of Tabernacles—these being unsuited to their festivities; and were not expected to attend to the stated prayers. This shows how natural and probable, according to the prevailing ideas and usages, was our Lord's illustration. Already in prophecy had the Messiah been spoken of as a bridegroom (Ps. 45, etc.); and John the Baptist had employed a figure drawn from the nuptial ceremonies as setting forth his own relation to Jesus (John 3 : 29); so that in answering John's disciples this image was all the more appropriate. **But the days will come when the bridegroom shall be taken away from them—and then shall they fast.** The term 'will come' is so placed as to be emphatic. For "when" read *whenever*, which will indicate that the time of his being taken away is uncertain; this is the first instance recorded in Matthew of our Lord's alluding to his death. Fasting is naturally and properly an expression of grief, and therefore unnatural and unsuitable at a time of great joy. Such a time was this when the disciples were delighting in their Teacher's presence. But there was coming a time when it would be natural for them to grieve, and therefore appropriate to fast. The immediate reference is to the grief which would be felt by his disciples at the time of his death. After his resurrection, ascension, and glorious exaltation, their sorrow was turned into joy again. (John 16: 22 ff.; Acts 2: 32-36; 3: 13 ff., etc.) Yet often afterwards, and often ever since, have his followers grieved over his absence and longed for his coming again; so that the time for fasting still continues. By this illustration our Lord teaches that fasting is not to be regarded or observed as an arbitrary, "positive" institution, but as a thing having natural grounds, and to be practiced or not, according to the dictates of natural feeling as growing out of the circumstances in which we find

ourselves. In some situations it is appropriate and may be made beneficial; in others, it is out of place. We have no evidence that Jesus ever fasted himself, except in the quite extraordinary case of the forty days (for 17 : 21 is a spurious passage); but we know that the apostles and other Christians of their time fasted upon special occasion. (Acts 13: 2; 14:23; 2 Cor. 11: 27.) The principle here laid down cuts at the root of fasting as a regulated observance, leaving it to be done or omitted, not indeed according to accidental or momentary impulse, but according as it is most suitable under the circumstances and likely to do good. (Comp. on 6: 16-18.)

16 f. Regulated fasting, though enjoined by Moses only on the occasion of the Day of Atonement (Luke 16: 29), yet was now frequently practiced among the Jews, and quite in accordance with the distinctive spirit of the Old Dispensation. But it did not suit the spirit of the gospel; and our Lord shows, by two homely and striking illustrations, how incongruous and injurious would be the connection with the new of what was peculiar to the old. Luke (5: 36) calls this a 'parable,' *i. e.*, comparison for the purpose of illustration. The parables of the Gospel are usually in the form of narrative, but not necessarily. (See on 13: 3.) **No man putteth,** etc.,—literally, *patches, a patch of an unfulled piece* (*i. e.*, fragment of cloth) *upon an old garment*. The word rendered garment is here naturally taken in the general sense, and not to denote simply the outer garment. (5: 40; 9: 20.) What is meant is not simply *new* cloth, for that is often used for patching, but cloth which has not been completely dressed. A part of the process of preparing woolen cloth for use consists in shrinking it, and a patch of 'unfulled' cloth, not duly shrunk, would contract the first time it should become wet, and as the older and weaker cloth all around must then give way, the result would be a worse rent. We must remember that Jewish garments of that day were usually all wool; and if unfulled, would shrink almost like our flannel. Mark's statement of the comparison (2: 21) is almost identical with this. Luke (5: 36) gives it in quite a different form, though

17 Neither do men put new wine into old bottles: else the bottles break, and the wine runneth out, and the bottles perish: but they put new wine into new bottles, and both are preserved.

17 and a worse rent is made. Neither do *men* put new wine into old [1] wine-skins: else the skins burst, and the wine is spilled, and the skins perish: but they put new wine into fresh wine-skins, and both are preserved.

---

1 That is, *skins used as bottles.*

---

the general purport is the same. **Neither do men put,** literally, *they,* the usual impersonal expression, see on 5: 11. **Into old bottles**—or, *skins.* The Greek word signifies properly and exclusively skins for containing liquids, such as the Orientals, ancient and modern, have largely employed. The skin is usually that of a goat or kid, which is tough and light. The head and feet of the animal being removed, the skin is stripped off whole. It is then sometimes tanned in a peculiar way to prevent a disagreeable taste, and the orifices are tied up, leaving one leg or the neck as the opening. The hairy side is of course outward. These skins are habitually used for transporting liquids, such as wine, water, milk, oil, and are admirably adapted to that purpose. Every traveler, in Egypt or Palestine, often sees them, and sometimes drinks water from them. They are mentioned by Homer and other classical writers, and in various passages of the Old Test. Both in ancient and modern times, larger vessels have sometimes been prepared of the skin of the ox or the camel. However preserved, these skins would of course become hard as they grew old, liable to crack and burst, through the fermentation of new wine. (Comp. Ps. 119: 83; Job 32: 19.) It is a mistake to suppose that the Jews had no other vessels for holding liquids than these skins. Vessels of metal, as gold, of earthenware, even fine porcelain, of stone, and alabaster, and of variously colored glass, were in use among the Egyptians from an early period, and most of them among the Greeks, Etruscans, and Assyrians; and the Jews, especially in New Test. times, would no doubt import and use them. (Comp. 26: 7; Jer. 19: 1; Lam. 4: 2.) This second illustration is to the same effect as that in v. 16; just as we often find a pair of parables, in chap. 13, and elsewhere. Both are drawn, as is usual in our Lord's comparisons, from matters of common observation and experience. The "spiritualizing" as to what the 'skins' represent, and what the 'wine'—what the 'garment' stands for, and what the 'patch,' is wholly unwarranted.

(See on 13: 3.) We have simply a vivid illustration of the general truth that the combination of the Old and the New Dispensations would be not merely unsuitable but injurious, tending to defeat, rather than to promote, the aims of the Messianic Dispensation. And in the second case there is added the positive statement, **but they put new wine into new bottles,** etc., showing (Meyer) that a new life needs new forms. While the principle here illustrated was introduced with regard to fasting, it is obviously of wider application, extending to everything in which the two dispensations characteristically differ; and the great mass of the Christian world, from an early period, has sadly exhibited the evil results of disregarding this principle. They *would,* notwithstanding this and numerous other warnings, connect Levitical rites with Christianity. The simple preacher and pastor must be regarded as a priest, and spiritual blessings must depend on his mediation, as if it were not true that all Christians are priests, and all alike have access through the one Mediator. The simple memento of the Saviour's death must be a sacrifice, offered by the priest for men's sins. Numerous religious festivals and stated fasts must be established and enjoined, tending to make religion a thing only of special seasons. The buildings in which Christians meet to worship must be consecrated as being holy ground, like the temple, and splendid rites, in imitation of the temple worship, must lead men's minds away from the simple and sublime spirituality of that worship which the gospel teaches. With good motives, no doubt, on the part of many, was this jumble of Judaism and Christianity introduced, and with good motives do many retain it; but none the less is it the very kind of thing the Saviour here condemned; and with results as ruinous as he declared. It is not strange that Chrysostom and his followers (Theophyl., Euthym.), and Jerome, practicing a Judaized Christianity, were unable to understand this passage.

Returning now to the series of miracles, Matthew gives—

18 While he spake these things unto them, behold, there came a certain ruler, and worshipped him, saying, My daughter is even now dead: but come and lay thy hand upon her, and she shall live.
19 And Jesus arose, and followed him, and *so did* his disciples.
20 And, behold, a woman, which was diseased with an issue of blood twelve years, came behind *him*, and touched the hem of his garment:

18   While he spake these things unto them, behold, there came [1] a ruler, and worshipped him, saying, My daughter is even now dead: but come and lay
19 thy hand upon her, and she shall live. And Jesus arose, and followed him, and *so did* his disciples.
20 And behold, a woman, who had an issue of blood twelve years, came behind him, and touched the

---

1 Gr. *one ruler.*

III. THE RULER'S DAUGHTER, AND THE WOMAN WITH A FLOW OF BLOOD, v. 18–26. This is found also in Mark (5: 22-43) and Luke (8: 41-56), who as in many other cases give various details which Matthew omits. For the general connection, see on v. 2.
While he spake (*was saying*) **these things unto them,** with emphasis on "these things." It is thus plain that the application of the ruler, which led to these two miracles, was made while Jesus was in the act of speaking to John's disciples and the Pharisees (comp. on v. 14) These miracles must therefore have taken place at Capernaum. **Behold,** something remarkable. **A certain ruler,** or, '*one ruler*' (margin Rev. Ver.), as in 8: 19. The Greek text is here greatly confused, but there is little doubt that the true reading is that of the Rev. Ver. The term 'ruler' is ambiguous, and might denote a member of the Sanhedrin, as Nicodemus is called a 'ruler of the Jews' (John 3: 1); but Mark (5: 22) says he was 'one of the rulers of the synagogue.' There were several of these, having authority over the conduct of public worship in the synagogue (Acts 13: 15), and a certain influence rather than authority over the social relations and personal conduct of the people (comp. on 4: 23). We see therefore that it was a man of importance who made this application. Luke (8: 41) gives his name, Jairus; in Old Test. Jair. **Came.** The common Greek text would make it *came in,* viz., to the scene of the preceding conversation, probably Matthew's residence; but the more probable reading (as in W H.) would mean 'came near,' 'approached.' **Worshipped him,** bowed down before him as an expression of profound respect (comp. 8: 2). **My daughter is even now dead.** Luke (8: 42, Bib. Un. Ver.) in giving the substance of what Jairus said, has it 'was dying.' Mark (5: 23, Rev. Ver.) has, 'My little daughter is at the point of death.' And then Mark and Luke inform us that while Jesus was on his way to the ruler's house, and

after the healing of the woman, messengers came meeting him to tell the ruler that his daughter was now dead; and that Jesus told him not to fear, etc. Matthew makes no mention of this message, and we conclude (Calvin) that designing a very brief account, he has condensed the incidents so as to present at the outset what was actually true before Jesus reached the house. For a similar case of condensing see on 8: 5. **But come and lay thy hand upon her.** Jairus probably thought it necessary that Jesus should be present and touch the person to be healed, as the nobleman in the same town thought (John 4: 47,49); the centurion of that town (8: 8) had a juster view.

19. In Mark (5: 24) and Luke (8: 42) we are told that a great crowd thronged around Jesus as he was going, and that Jesus afterwards inquired, when in the midst of the crowd, as to who touched him (comp. on v. 22).

20-22. On the way to the ruler's house occurred another miracle. **And, behold,** a fresh wonder. **A woman . . . . with an issue of blood twelve years.** We know nothing as to the particular nature of the hemorrhage, but the most obvious supposition is probably correct. We learn from Mark (5: 26) and Luke (8: 43) that she had been subjected to a variety of methods of treatment by numerous physicians, spending her entire estate in paying them, but instead of receiving benefit, had been growing worse—a chronic, aggravated, and unmanageable case. Strauss finds an unveracious element in the double occurrence of the number twelve in this narrative (the woman has suffered twelve years, and the maiden was twelve years old, Mark 5: 42); some of our allegorizers would find in it a deep spiritual meaning—which is the sillier notion? **Came,** etc., or *coming to him from behind,* partly, no doubt, through general timidity, partly from a reluctance to have public attention called to her peculiar afflic-

21 For she said within herself, If I may but touch his garment, I shall be whole.
22 But Jesus turned him about, and when he saw her, he said, Daughter, be of good comfort; thy faith hath made thee whole. And the woman was made whole from that hour.

21 border of his garment: for she said within herself, If I do but touch his garment, I shall be [1] made whole.
22 But Jesus turning and seeing her said, Daughter, be of good cheer; thy faith hath [2] made thee whole. And the woman was [1] made whole from that hour.

1 Or, *saved*....2 *saved thee.*

tion; and perhaps also because the law made her ceremonially unclean (Lev. 15: 25), and she was afraid of being censured and repelled if it should be known that in that condition she had come into the crowd, since any one would likewise become unclean by touching her. **Touched the hem** (*border*) **of his garment.** We know from Num. 15: 37 ff.; Deut. 22: 12, that the Israelites were directed to wear on the corners of the upper garment a fringe or tassel (we cannot certainly determine the exact meaning), with an occasional blue thread. These were designed, as being always before their eyes, to remind them continually of the commandments of the Lord, which they were solemnly bound to obey. If we think of the outer garment as merely an oblong cloth thrown around the person like a large shawl—as it undoubtedly was in many cases (see on 5: 40)—then 'tassel' is the more natural idea; and in that case '*the* tassel' would be simply the one nearest to her. The Jews attached great importance to this fringe or tassel, the ostentatious Pharisees making it very large (see on 23: 5); and it is possible that the woman thought there might be a peculiar virtue in touching this, which was worn by express divine command—though such a supposition is not necessary. See a good discussion of the probable dress of Jesus in Edersheim.

21. For she said within herself, as in v. 3. Strictly it is, *was saying; i. e.*, at the time when she pressed through the crowd and touched him. **If I may but**—better, *if I only* —**touch his garment.** The 'may' of Com. Ver. is misleading. We do not know how far this feeling of hers was mingled with superstition, but in the main her conviction was just, since Jesus commends her faith, and power did go forth from him (Luke 8: 46), the moment she touched him. It was usual in miracles of healing that some manifest connection should be established, however slight, between the sufferer and the healer, as in Peter's shadow (Acts 5: 15) and Paul's handkerchiefs. (Acts 19: 12) See also 14: 36; Mark 6: 56; Luke 6: 19.

I shall be (*made*) **whole,** literally, 'saved'; the word has been explained on 1: 21 as signifying 'preserve' and 'deliver,' and as applied to physical dangers, disease and death, as well as to sin and its consequences. What strong faith this woman possessed! And it was justified by the event; for *immediately* (Mark 5: 29) she felt the disease was indeed healed—healed by merely touching the edge of Jesus' garment, when all the skill of the ablest physicians, through all the weary years, had been unable to relieve it.

22. But Jesus turned, etc. Matthew omits the facts narrated at length by Mark and Luke, that she touched him in the midst of a great crowd, and he insisted on being told who it was that had touched him. We can see that it was not proper to let her be healed and go off, apparently without his knowledge; because this fact, as it should gradually become known, would confirm men in the superstitious notion that he performed healing involuntarily and unconsciously, as if by some magical virtue inherent in his person. His asking who it was is not inconsistent with the idea that he knew. Comp. Elisha's asking, 'Whence comest thou, Gehazi?' (2 Kings 5: 25), though well aware of all that he had done; and God's saying to Adam, 'Where art thou?' See also Luke 24: 19, where Jesus asks, 'What things?' though he must have understood what they meant. He asked the woman in order to bring her to confession, which would be a benefit to herself—preventing superstition, strengthening faith, and deepening gratitude—as well as to others. **Daughter, etc.,** or, *Courage, daughter.* Comp. on v. 2. 'Daughter,' in this figurative and kindly use, appears nowhere in the New Test., save in this narrative. (Mark 5: 34; Luke 8: 48.) **Thy faith hath made thee whole,** literally, *saved,* as in v. 21. The perfect tense vividly represents the healing as standing complete. Her faith was of course not the source of the healing, but its procuring cause, as leading her to apply to the healing power of Jesus, and as being the reason why the application

23 And when Jesus came into the ruler's house, and saw the minstrels and the people making a noise,
24 He said unto them, Give place: for the maid is not dead, but sleepeth. And they laughed him to scorn.
25 But when the people were put forth, he went in, and took her by the hand, and the maid arose.

23 And when Jesus came into the ruler's house, and saw the flute-players, and the crowd making a
24 tumult, he said, Give place: for the damsel is not dead, but sleepeth. And they laughed him to scorn.
25 But when the crowd was put forth, he entered in, and took her by the hand; and the damsel arose.

---

was successful. See the same expression used in Luke 7: 50; 17: 19; 18: 42. **Was made whole** (*healed*) **from that hour.** The healing took place at the moment of the touch; what is here said is that from that time forward she was no more sick, but well—not only delivered, but preserved. So in 15: 28; 17: 18. Eusebius ("Hist." VII. 17) gives a tradition that this woman's name was Veronica.

23-26. This resumes the narrative of v. 18 f. We learn from Mark (5: 37) and Luke (8: 51) that Jesus suffered no one to go into the house with him save Peter and James and John, and the parents of the girl. The other two occasions on which he took these three disciples only, viz., the Transfiguration and Gethsemane, were singularly solemn and momentous. What was there corresponding in this case? It was the first instance of our Lord's raising the dead. **And saw the minstrels,** etc., rather in Rev. Ver., *the flute players* (comp. Rev. 18: 22), *and the crowd making a tumult*, the same Greek word as in Mark 5: 39; Acts 17: 5; 20: 10. This last expression is confined in the original to the crowd, so that a comma is needed after 'flute players.' It was the custom in the East and still is, for the relatives and special friends of the dying person to gather round the couch, and the moment the breath ceased they would break out into loud cries, with every exclamation and sign of the most passionate grief; and unable to continue this themselves, they would hire professional mourners, especially women, who would keep up the loud, wailing cry throughout the day and night. (Comp. Jer. 9: 17; 16: 6 f.; Ezek. 24: 17; Amos 5: 16; 2 Chron. 35: 25.) Persons of wealth might afford to hire musicians also; and Jairus being a man of consideration, a ruler of the synagogue, we find that the flute players have arrived, and although but a few minutes after the child's decease, already there is a crowd present, making a tumultuous noise of lamentation. All these things are witnessed by travelers in Egypt or Palestine at the present day.

24. Is not dead, but sleepeth. Jesus speaks with reference to what he intends to do. She is going to rise up presently as one who had been asleep, so that her death will be, in the result, no death; it will only be as if she were sleeping. Likewise in John 11: 11, he speaks of Lazarus as sleeping, because he was going to awake him out of sleep. Thus there was no occasion for the noisy mourning, and the preparations for a funeral; and the crowd must withdraw. **Laughed him to scorn.** This might only mean that anybody could see she was dead (Luke 8: 53), and it seemed silly to think otherwise. But there in Capernaum, where he had wrought many miracles, it may be that they supposed he would try to heal her, and thought the attempt absurd, as she was unquestionably dead, and it was too late. It is not likely they thought he was proposing to bring the dead to life, which he had never done. Their scornful laughter shows that the people were by no means swift to believe in his miraculous powers and his divine mission; and thus renders the wondering acknowledgment, repeatedly extorted from them by facts, an evidence all the more valuable and satisfactory.

25. But when the people were put forth, or, *thrust out,* the word implying some constraint or urgency. He was as yet in the more public reception room of the dwelling. Having expelled the crowd, he (with the parents and his three followers (Luke 8: 51), went in, viz., into the inner room where the body was lying. **Took her by the hand.** Touching the dead body, like touching the leper (8: 3), or being touched by the woman with a flow of blood, would have the effect, according to the law, of producing the highest degree of ceremonial uncleanness; but in all these cases Jesus, instead of receiving pollution through the touch, imparted cleansing. Mark (5: 41) and Luke (8: 54) relate that in addition to grasping her hand he spoke, and bade her arise. Also that he charged her parents much, not to tell what had happened (comp. on 8: 4), notwithstanding which we find here that **the fame thereof went abroad into all that land,** *i. e.,* Galilee, or the parts of Galilee adjacent to Capernaum.

26 And the fame hereof went abroad into all that land.
27 And when Jesus departed thence, two blind men followed him, crying, and saying, *Thou* Son of David, have mercy on us.
28 And when he was come into the house, the blind men came to him : and Jesus saith unto them, Believe ye that I am able to do this ? They said unto him, Yea, Lord.
29 Then touched he their eyes, saying, According to your faith be it unto you.

26 And ¹ the fame hereof went forth into all that land.
27 And as Jesus passed by from thence, two blind men followed him, crying out, and saying, Have mercy on us, thou Son of David. And when he was come into the house, the blind men came to him : and Jesus saith unto them, Believe ye that I am able to do this ? They say unto him, Yea, Lord.
29 Then touched he their eyes, saying, According to

1 Gr. *this fame.*

The woman, for one reason, was required to tell ; Jairus, for another, was forbidden to tell. It cannot be that Jesus expected the matter to remain wholly unknown ; he probably wished to prevent their speaking of it at once and generally, as they would have done, because in that case there would have been too much excitement produced, by the series of extraordinary miracles then occurring in immediate succession. (Comp. on v. 28.) *Stier :* " Three awakenings from death the Spirit has caused to be recorded for us, though others may well have taken place ; and these indeed, in a remarkable and significant progression .... the maiden is here dead upon her bed, the young man at Nain was carried forth upon his bier, Lazarus had lain four days in his grave."

The series of miracles in ch. 9, and the whole group of ch. 8 and 9, ends with—

IV. Healing Two Blind Men, and a Dumb Demoniac, v. 27–34.

These miracles are not recorded by the other Evangelists.

27-31. *Healing the blind men.* **And when Jesus departed thence**—*was passing along thence*—the same expression as in v. 9. It shows that the following miracles occurred immediately after the preceding. **Followed him,** in the purely literal sense, went along behind him. They may have been sitting beside the road when he passed by, as in Luke 18 : 35-37. **Have mercy,** or, *have pity.* The word really includes both ideas, and the latter is the one here prominent. (See on 5 : 7.) By saying, **Son of David,** they declare their belief that he is the Messiah. (Comp. 22 : 42 ; 15 : 22.) The order of the Greek shows that their first thought was for mercy on themselves—very naturally. They had probably heard of Jesus' miracles, perhaps of the two wonderful works just wrought. If one inquires why they should believe him to be Messiah, while others did not, we can only reply by asking why there is a similar difference now. The Gospels frequently mention blind persons healed.

(11 : 5 ; 12 : 22 ; 15 : 30 ; 20 : 30 ; 21 : 14 ; Mark 8 : 22 ; John 5 : 3 ; 9 : 1.) Blindness is much more common in the East than among us, in consequence of abounding dust, the practice of sleeping in the open air, the sudden change from darkened houses to dazzling light without, and the fact that their head-dress does not protect the eyes.

28. Into the house, viz., the house to which he returned from that of the ruler. (v. 23.) It may have been Matthew's house (v. 10), or Peter's (8 : 14), or some other which Jesus made his usual place of abode at Capernaum. (Comp. 13 : 1, 36 ; 17 : 25.) Observe that in Capernaum occurs all that is narrated in v. 2–34, as well as in 8 : 5-22. As they followed him along the street, Jesus gave them no answer or notice ; but when he had entered the house, they approached and he spoke to them. This failure to notice them at first was doubtless designed (1) to develop and strengthen their faith (comp. 15 : 23) ; (2) to avoid the excitement which another public miracle just then might have produced among the people, already stirred by the healing of the woman, and by the rapidly spreading news of the raising of Jairus' daughter to life. (Comp. on v. 2-6.) The question, **Believe ye that I am able ?** developed into greater clearness the faith they had already shown by following and asking. In their answer, **Lord** is probably no more than a very respectful form of address. (See on 8 : 2.) Jesus was more ready to work miracles where there was faith in him. (Comp. on v. 2, 22, and 13 : 58.) But it is too much to say that he never wrought miracles without faith ; instance the widow's son at Nain, and Malchus' ear. Observe that his question was simply whether they believed that he could heal them ; his willingness remained to be seen. (Comp. on 8 : 2.)

29. Touching the eyes of the blind (comp. 20–34), was a natural and kindly act, like taking the hand of one prostrate with fever. (8 : 15.) **According to your faith be it**—*let*

30 And their eyes were opened; and Jesus straitly charged them, saying, See *that* no man know *it*.
31 But they, when they were departed, spread abroad his fame in all that country.
32 As they went out, behold, they brought to him a dumb man, possessed with a devil.
33 And when the devil was cast out, the dumb spake: and the multitudes marvelled, saying, It was never so seen in Israel.
34 But the Pharisees said, He casteth out devils through the prince of the devils.

30 your faith be it done unto you. And their eyes were opened. And Jesus [1] strictly charged them, saying, See that no man know it. But they went forth, and
31 spread abroad his fame in all that land.
32 And as they went forth, behold, there was brought
33 to him a dumb man possessed with a demon. And when the demon was cast out, the dumb man spake: and the multitudes marvelled, saying, It was never
34 so seen in Israel. But the Pharisees said, [2] By the prince of the demons casteth he out demons.

1 Or, *sternly* . . . . 2 Or, *In*.

it happen—**unto you.** (Comp. on 8: 13). An old German writer says that faith is like a bucket by which we draw from the inexhaustible fountain of God's mercy and goodness, to which otherwise we cannot penetrate; and Calvin compares it to a purse, which may itself be worthless, but filled with money makes the man rich.

30. And their eyes were opened. We have no means of judging whether this physical blessing was attended with the pardon of their sins. (Comp. on 8: 3.) The fact that they soon after disobeyed Christ's explicit and emphatic command renders it improbable that they believed unto salvation, though not impossible. **And Jesus straitly** (*sternly*) **charged them,** an unclassical, but natural sense of the Greek word, found also in Mark 1: 43. The expression implies that he would be seriously displeased if they disobeyed. As to the probable reasons for this, comp. on 8: 4; and add here that they were virtually calling him Messiah, which might excite popular fanaticism. (16: 20; John 6: 15.) He may have spoken with greater severity of manner, because a similar injunction in previous cases had been disregarded; yet it was disregarded again in this case. **Spread abroad his fame in all that country,** as in v. 26. The Com. Ver., with its passion for variety, must needs give 'land' in v. 26, and 'country' here, though the Greek has the same word and in the same connection, and though the earlier Eng. versions translate it alike in both places. Some have sought to excuse the disobedience of the two men on the ground that it was very natural, and was no doubt sincerely designed to do him honor. But still it was a fault. What can be so pleasing to him, or so conducive to his glory, as simple, unquestioning, loving obedience?

32-34. *Healing a dumb demoniac.* This is not related by the other Evangelists. **And as they went** (*were going*) **out,** namely, out of the house in which they had been healed. (v. 28.) 'They' is slightly emphatic, standing in contrast to the next person who came to be healed. **Behold,** calling attention to what follows as wonderful. **They brought to him,** *i. e.,* some persons brought; impersonal or indefinite, as in 5: 11; 9: 17, and often. **A dumb man possessed with a devil,** *a demoniac,* see on 8: 28, 31. Comp. Mark 9: 25 for a similar case. Mark 7: 32 mentions a deaf man who spoke with difficulty, and says nothing of demoniacal influence. Matt. 12: 22 gives a demoniac who was both blind and dumb. **And the multitudes,** *crowds,* as in 5: 1; 9: 8, and often. **Marvelled,** etc. *Wondered, saying, It never at any time appeared thus in Israel;* there was never such a thing seen before, in all the wonderful history of the nation. (Comp. Mark 2: 12; John 9: 32.) Probably their wonder referred not merely to this last case of the dumb demoniac, but to the series of miracles that day wrought, and, it would seem, in quick succession—the woman, the daughter of Jairus, the two blind men, and now the dumb man. The Evangelists never stop to say themselves that the miracles of Jesus were wonderful. To them these things were not astonishing now as they looked back from the time of writing their narratives, for it was a fact long familiar to their minds that he who wrought them was divine; and so they calmly tell the story of miracle after miracle, without any exclamation or remark. But it was appropriate to mention, as they often do, the wonder felt by the persons witnessing a miracle, because this was one of the evidences of its manifest reality. V. 34.[1] **But the Pharisees said,** strictly 'were saying,'

1 W. H. bracket this verse, as of doubtful genuineness. But the only evidence for omitting is that of D, two copies of the old Latin, and two Latin Fathers of the fourth century, evidence exclusively "Western," and

quite meagre. This often arbitrary "Western" type of text might easily have omitted the sentence, from the notion that such a thing occurred but once and that its true place is in 12: 24.

viz., while the people were expressing their wonder. **Through,** literally '*in*' (margin of Rev. Ver.), *i. e.,* in union with, by power derived from, **the prince of the devils,** *demons.* This insulting charge was probably made on the present occasion in the absence of Jesus, but made afterwards in his presence; see on 12: 24. **The Pharisees;** see on 3: 7. They had been finding fault with Jesus in connection with all the preceding matters for undertaking to forgive sin (v. 3), for associating with publicans and sinners (v. 11), and for not fasting (v. 14), and now their opposition grows yet more bitter and bold, when they venture upon the accusation of union with Satan. The crowds, for their part, wondered at the unparalleled event, but the Pharisees tried to explain it away, by however baseless and blasphemous a supposition. So also in 12: 23 f. They were not willing to acknowledge the truth about Jesus' miracles, for it would diminish their own consideration among the people; and so they struck out madly after some explanation or other.

Thus ends the remarkable series of miracles which Matthew has grouped (chap. 8 and 9), as specimens of our Lord's wonderful works. (Comp. on 8: 1).

HOMILETICAL AND PRACTICAL.

Ch. 9: 2-8. Sickness and sins: 1) Some kinds of sickness proceed directly from sin, and are its penalty. 2) Forgiveness of sin is far more important than cure of sickness. 3) He who could by a word heal the severest sickness can also forgive sin. 4) The usual condition of miraculous healing was faith, and faith is the indispensable condition of forgiveness (v. 2). 5) The highest ground of cheerfulness and gratitude is to have our sins forgiven (v. 3).—V. 2. Faith and healing. 1) In rare cases Jesus healed without faith, as Malchus. 2) Sometimes upon the faith of others, as the nobleman (John 4: 50), the centurion (8: 10), the Syrophœnician. (15:28) 3) Usually upon the faith of the sufferer, v. 22, 28, and often. 4) Here upon the faith both of the sufferer and of his friends.—V. 3. HENRY: "If we have the comfort of our reconciliation to God, with the comfort of our recovery from sickness, this makes it a mercy indeed to us, as to Hezekiah. Isa. 38: 17."—V. 4 f. CHRYS.:

"Jesus here does two things superhuman—seeing thoughts, and forgiving sins."—V. 6. CHRYS.: "1) Proof of the forgiveness by healing. 2) Proof of the healing, by carrying the bed."—V. 8. Comp. the effect produced at Carmel. (1 Kings 18: 39.) HENRY: "Others' mercies should be our praises."

V. 9-11. Matthew. 1) Abandoning a lucrative employment to follow Jesus in poverty. 2) Turning from a worldly occupation to follow Jesus in spirituality. 3) Bringing his former wicked companions to hear Jesus, if perchance they will follow him too. 4) Rising from despised publican to apostle and evangelist.—CHRYS.: 1) "The power of the caller. 2) The obedience of the called."—Probably prepared before hand, yet still at his old business when called.—HENRY: "As Satan chooses to come, with his temptations, to those that are idle, so Christ chooses to come, with his calls, to those that are employed."—V. 11. Jesus eating with publicans and sinners. 1) Social intercourse affords a great opportunity for doing people good. 2) The worst men must be treated with respect, if we would win them to piety; and the worst men have in them something to be respected. (HALL: "I do not find where Jesus was ever bidden to any table, and refused.") 3) A man of despised calling may become a Christian, and an eminent minister. 4) It may be lawful to associate with very wicked people, when we can be confident of doing them good, and are duly guarded against receiving injury.— V. 13. Mercy and not sacrifice. 1) Professed teachers of Scripture may greatly mistake its meaning. 2) The externals of religion are unacceptable to God, without its true spirit. 3) The spirit of Christianity teaches a kindly pity for even the grossly wicked. Jesus seemed to be transgressing the law of ceremony; the Pharisees really were transgressing the law of mercy. 4) The greatest kindness we can do to wicked people, is to lead them to be truly pious. 5) In order to reach the most degraded with Christian influences, we must treat them with courtesy and respect.

V. 14. HENRY: "False and formal professors often excel others in outward acts of devotion, and even of mortification. . . . It is common for vain professors to make themselves a standard in religion, by which to try and measure persons and things, as if all who

35 And Jesus went about all the cities and villages, teaching in their synagogues, and preaching the gospel of the kingdom, and healing every sickness and every disease among the people.

35   And Jesus went about all the cities and the villages, teaching in their synagogues, and preaching the gospel of the kingdom, and healing all

differed from them were so far in the wrong; as if all that did less than they, did too little, and all that did more than they, did too much."—V. 15. Fasting is proper only when it has a natural basis in some actual grief.— V. 16 f. Christianity and Judaism are in many respects incongruous; let us not Judaize our Christianity.

V. 18–21. Parental grief and personal suffering both leading to Jesus.—V. 20–22. The timid sufferer's faith. 1) Follows the failure of all natural efforts (Mark 5: 26) ; 2) Overcomes timidity and shame ; 3) Presses through an unfriendly throng ; 4) Brings healing instantly and permanently ; 5) Gains the Saviour's approval ; 6) Bears her away happy.—V. 23–26. The ruler's daughter. 1) The sorrowing, but believing father (v. 18). 2) The noisy mourners, loudly proclaiming her dead. 3) The silent chamber (comp. Mark 5; 40), and the young life restored. 4) The supernatural healing, followed immediately by giving natural food. (Mark 5: 43.) Comp. John 6: 12. 5) The restored life devoted, let us hope, to the good of man, and the glory of God.

V. 27. HENRY: "It becomes those that are under the same affliction, to concur in the same prayers for relief. Fellow-sufferers should be joint petitioners. In Christ there is enough for all."—V. 28. LUTHER: "Christ is rejoiced to see our faith persistent, unwearied, stiff-necked." — V. 29. HENRY: "They who apply themselves to Jesus Christ shall be dealt with according to their faith ; not according to their fancies, not according to their professions, but according to their faith."—V. 30 f. We often fail to speak for Jesus when we ought, but sometimes fail to be silent when we ought.

V. 2–34. Striking examples of belief in Jesus, and of unbelief. (1) Of belief. (a) The paralytic, v. 2; (b) The publican, v. 9; (c) The ruler of the synagogue, v. 18; (d) The long-afflicted woman, v. 21 f; (e) The two blind men, v. 28. (2) Of unbelief. (a) The scribes accusing him of blasphemy, v. 3 ; (b) The Pharisees complaining that he eats with publicans and sinners, v. 11; (c) The disciples of John, with their skeptical inquiry about fasting, v. 14; (d) The crowd at Jairus'

house laughing scornfully, v. 24; (e) The Pharisees charging league with Satan, v. 34.

9 : 35—10 : 15. MISSION OF THE TWELVE.

Our Lord here undertakes another circuit of Galilee, similar to that described in 4: 23 ff., and in connection with it he now sends out the Twelve to engage in the same work, viz., to make the same proclamation of the near approach of the Messianic reign (comp. 10: 7 with 4: 17), and to work similar miracles of healing. (10: 1, 8.) Before sending forth the Twelve, our Lord addressed them a long discourse (10: 5-42), giving them instruction not only for this mission, but for all their subsequent labors in his name; after which discourse he went to his work (11: 1), and they to theirs. (Mark 6: 12 f.; Luke 9: 6.)—Some prefer to consider this as not the record of a distinct journey, but simply a return to the general statement of 4: 23. The idea would thus be, that having given a grand specimen of our Lord's teaching (ch. 5-7), and a group of specimens of his miracles (ch. 8 and 9), the Evangelist now repeats the general description of his journeying, teaching and healing (same terms in 9: 35 as in 4: 23), and presently branches off again to describe the mission of the Twelve. But it seems more likely that this was a second and distinct journey. Indeed, Luke appears to give a third journey (Luke 8: 1-3), which a Harmony would make intermediate between the two in Matthew.—Our present section includes so much of the address to the Twelve as is given by Mark and Luke also. The remainder (v. 16-42) is given by Matthew only.

I. 9 : 35 to 10 : 1. JESUS IS MOVED TO SEND OUT THE TWELVE. While engaged in a circuit of Galilee, he is moved with compassion at the spiritual destitution of the people, and begins to prepare the Twelve for going out as teachers. The portion in v. 35-38 is found in Matthew alone, except that Mark (6: 6) says simply, 'And he went round about the villages teaching.'

35. Same as 4: 23, except that for ' went about all Galilee' we here have more particularly, **went about all the cities and** (*the*) **villages,** referring still to Galilee, as the con-

36 But when he saw the multitudes, he was moved with compassion on them, because they *a* fainted, and were scattered abroad, as sheep having no shepherd.
37 Then saith he unto his disciples, The harvest truly *is* plenteous, but the labourers *are* few;
38 Pray ye therefore the Lord of the harvest, that he will send forth labourers into his harvest.

36 manner of disease and all manner of sickness. But when he saw the multitudes, he was moved with compassion for them, because they were distressed and scattered, as sheep not having a shepherd. Then
37 saith he unto his disciples, The harvest truly is plenteous, but the labourers are few. Pray ye there-
38 fore the Lord of the harvest, that he send forth labourers into his-harvest.

a Or, *were tired and lay down.*

nection and the circumstances show. **All** is so placed in the Greek as to be confined to the cities; and he could not have visited *all* the villages. Josephus says there were in Galilee not less than two hundred and four cities and populous villages. (See on 4: 12.) The word rendered **villages** denotes properly a town without walls, as opposed to a fortified town. The larger places would of course all be fortified. We learn then that our Lord made a thorough circuit, going into *all* the large towns, and very generally into the smaller places also. He did not go only where he could have a very large congregation. For **every sickness and every disease**—*i. e.,* every kind, not necessarily every case—and for the other terms, see on 4: 23. **Among the people,** com. Greek text, is omitted on overwhelming evidence. Here again, as in 8: 16 and 4: 23, we must pause and dwell on the strong general statement, or we shall not adequately conceive of the immense extent of our Lord's work as a Healer.

36. But when he saw the multitudes—*crowds*—as in 5: 1. As there his compassion led to a long address on the Mount, so here it leads him to send out the Twelve, that they might aid in the so much needed work of teaching and healing. Similarly after the return of the Twelve. (Mark 6 : 34.) In the present case, as in 5: 1, we understand that what follows took place at some unassigned time in the course of the circuit just described. **Because they fainted,** best text, *were distressed,* or 'harassed,' 'worried,' rendered 'trouble' in Mark 5 : 35; Luke 8 : 49. The evidence for this Greek word rather than 'fainted' (com. Greek text) is ample. **Scattered,** literally, 'thrown,' 'hurled,' might mean prostrate (so Davidson), lying down, as being worn out and unable to go forward, or might mean cast off, neglected; the general conception remains the same, that of a flock worried and suffering for lack of a shepherd's care. In the East, where sheep wander freely in wild, unenclosed regions, so as to require

constant attention, this image is very striking. Meyer supposes that our Lord saw the people to be worn out with following him in long journeys, and that this suggested to him the image of a flock tired down; but the supposition seems quite improbable. (Weiss). The people were greatly in need of spiritual instruction and guidance, for those who professed to be their shepherds were not faithful and safe guides. (See the same expression in Num. 27 : 17, and comp. 1 Kings 22: 17; Jer. 50 : 6; Ezek. 34 : 5; Zech. 10 : 2.)

37, 38. He seeks to awaken a similar compassion in his followers. **Disciples,** see on 5: 1. There were probably other disciples present, besides the Twelve (10 : 1), and the exhortation to pray was addressed to them all, but only the Twelve were at that time sent forth; at a later period, seventy others. (Luke 10 : 1.) The figure of reaping a harvest he had employed before (perhaps a year before), at Jacob's well (John 4 : 35 ff.), and will use again when sending out the seventy. (Luke 10 : 2.) **Truly** represents the Greek word (*men*) explained on 3: 11, which denotes merely that this clause is set in contrast with what follows. The idea is sufficiently expressed in English by an emphatic utterance of 'harvest' and 'laborers'; it was so rendered by Tyn. and Gen. (so also Davidson), 'truly' being introduced by Great Bible. **The harvest** signifies, not (as some explain) the elect, those who will actually be saved, but men in general, who unless gathered and saved will perish like wheat that is not reaped.—This compassion for perishing men will naturally lead to prayer for laborers (v. 38), and such compassion and prayer will form the best preparation for going forth to be laborers ourselves. (10 : 1.) Any man who is called of God to devote himself to preaching the gospel will have felt something, ought to have felt much, of this pitying love for his perishing fellow men, and will have prayed much for their rescue; and those engaged in that work should be careful to maintain, as

CHAPTER X.

AND when he had called unto *him* his twelve disciples, he gave them power *a against* unclean spirits,
to cast them out, and to heal all manner of sickness
and all manner of disease.

2 Now the names of the twelve apostles are these ;
The first, Simon, who is called Peter, and Andrew his
brother; James *the son* of Zebedee, and John his
brother ;

1   And he called unto him his twelve disciples, and
gave them authority over unclean spirits, to cast
them out, and to heal all manner of disease and all
manner of sickness.

2   Now the names of the twelve apostles are these:
The first, Simon, who is called Peter, and Andrew
his brother; James the *son* of Zebedee, and John his

---

a Or, *over.*

---

long as they live, this same pity and prayer.
And not only preachers, but all Christians,
should feel as Jesus felt, and should regularly
and habitually pray this prayer. **Send forth**
is literally *cast out,* 'throw out,' or 'thrust
out,' the same word that is used in v. 33 f., in
10: 1, and above in v. 25 (where see note).
Comp. its use in Mark 1: 12; James 2: 25. It
always implies urgency, haste, constraint, or
some such idea, and here means that the
laborers should be sent out promptly, pushed
into their work. *Beza :* "For we are all very
tardy, especially in such matters." This same
word is retained when our Lord speaks to the
seventy. (Luke 10:2.)[1] Such laborers as the
Lord of the harvest does put forth, we may
endeavor, with his blessing, to train for the
better performance of their work (see on 10:
1); but they must be his laborers, not ours,
called into the work, and urged to the performance of it, by himself.

10 : 1. Having led the disciples to feel interest in perishing throngs of men, and encouraged them to pray for laborers, Jesus now
bids them go forth to labor themselves. We
ought carefully to observe the slow and gradual process by which our Lord prepared the
Twelve for their great and important life-work.
First, he called various individuals to be his disciples, as, for example, those in John 1: 35-51 ;
these went with him for a time, but afterwards
returned to their homes and their secular employments. Next, he called some to attach
themselves permanently to him, as above in
4: 18-22, stating at the time his intention to
make them fishers of men. After a while, he
selected from the general mass of his followers the Twelve, who were to be specially near
to him, and to be trained for special duties;
delivering to them, immediately after their
selection (see on 5: 1), a great discourse on the
true nature of that Messianic reign which they
were to aid in bringing about. And now, at

a still later period, when they have been long
hearing his discourses to the people, talking
with him familiarly in private, and witnessing
his multiplied miracles, he sends them forth,
two and two, to preach and heal ; but not yet
to work independently of him, for they are
only to go before and prepare the way for his
coming. After a season spent in such personal
labors, they will return, and remain long with
him, receiving further instruction, which they
will more earnestly desire and more fully appreciate, from their attempts at actual preaching. And finally, after his ascension, they
will be ready, with the Holy Spirit as their
abiding Instructor, to go and disciple all nations. After all this training they could do
nothing without the Spirit; yet, though they
were to have the Spirit, they must also have
this training—doing what they could, meanwhile, to reap the great and perishing harvest,
but devoting themselves mainly to preparation for wider usefulness in the coming years.

With v. 1-15 comp. Mark 6: 7-11; Luke 9:
1-5. **Disciples,** see on 5: 1.—**Power,** *authority,* which in such a case would carry with it
the power, see on 9: 6. As to demoniacal
possessions, see on 8: 28. These spirits are
called **unclean,** because of their own wickedness, and perhaps because their presence was
a pollution to the person possessed (comp. on
12: 43 ff.) ; and this served to distinguish
them from good or pure spirits. Sometimes
they are called 'evil spirits.' **All manner of,**
etc., *every disease and every infirmity,* comp.
9: 35; 4: 23.

II. 2-4. List of the Twelve. Matthew
has not mentioned the *selection* of the Twelve.
which took place before this. (Mark 3: 13; Luke 6: 13,
comp. on 5:1.) At the time when he wrote, the
twelve apostles were well known, and he
speaks of them accordingly: ' his twelve disciples,' 'the twelve apostles.' The number
twelve was probably chosen with reference to

---

[1] ' That he send forth' is a non-final use of hopōs, see on 5: 29.

the number of tribes (see on 19: 28). **Apostles;** the name, borrowed from Greek *apostolos,* 'one sent off,' or 'sent forth,' is here introduced by Matt. for the first time, in connection with the occasion on which they were first actually sent forth (v. 5) to labor. But our Lord gave them that name when he selected the Twelve (see Luke 6: 13). The word is translated 'one that is sent' in John 13: 16; 'messenger' in 2 Cor. 8: 23; Phil. 2: 25; everywhere else in Com. Ver. and Rev. Ver., it is 'apostle.' Jesus himself is called an apostle, *i. e.,* sent by God, in Heb. 3: 1. Our word *missionary,* derived from the Latin, likewise signifies "one sent."

Curious, and in some respects instructive results, may be obtained from a comparison of the four lists of the Twelve.

Matthew 10: 2 f.	Mark 3: 16 f.	Luke 6: 14 f.	Acts 1: 13 f.
1 Simon Peter.	Simon Peter.	Simon Peter.	Simon Peter.
2 Andrew.	James.	Andrew.	James.
3 James.	John.	James.	John.
4 John.	Andrew.	John.	Andrew.
5 Philip.	Philip.	Philip.	Philip.
6 Bartholomew.	Bartholomew.	Bartholomew.	Thomas.
7 Thomas.	Matthew.	Matthew.	Bartholomew.
8 Matthew.	Thomas.	Thomas.	Matthew.
9 James the son of Alpheus.	James the son of Alpheus.	James the son of Alpheus.	James the son of Alpheus
10 Thaddeus.	Thaddeus.	Simon the Zealot.	Simon the Zealot.
11 Simon the Canaanite.	Simon the Canaanite.	Judas the brother of James.	Judas the brother of James.
12 Judas Iscariot.	Judas Iscariot.	Judas Iscariot.	(Vacant).

We observe at once that, with all the variety in the order of succession, Simon Peter is always first, and Judas Iscariot last. Again, the first six names in Matthew, Mark, and Luke are the five earliest known converts. (John 1: 35-51), together with James, the brother of one of them; and the first four in all the lists are the two pairs of brothers whose call to follow Jesus is the earliest mentioned. (4: 18-22.) Furthermore we note in each of the lists three groups of four, headed respectively in every list by Peter, Philip, and James, which groups contain always the same four persons, though within the limits of each group the order greatly varies, except as to Judas Iscariot. It seems a natural and unavoidable inference that the Twelve were in some sense divided into three companies of four, each having a recognized leader. The foremost in *the first company,* and at the head of all the Twelve, is Simon Peter. When Matthew says, **First, Simon who is called Peter,** he cannot mean merely that this happens to be the name first mentioned by him; and there is no explanation in the fact that those are mentioned first who first came to Jesus; for then Andrew and probably John, ought to precede Peter. (John: 35 ff.) It is unquestionable that Simon Peter was a sort of leader among the Twelve. (See on 16: 18.) As regards the remaining members of the first company or group of four, we may suppose that Matthew and Luke put Andrew next to Simon because they were brothers; while Mark and Acts and Mark 13: 3 place James and John next to Simon, because they three were admitted to special intimacy and favor with Jesus, being the only persons present on several solemn occasions. (See on 17: 1.) The four who formed this first group are mentioned in Mark 13: 3 as making private inquiries of Jesus concerning the destruction of the temple, etc. In *the second company,* Matthew puts Thomas before himself (comp. Acts), while Mark and Luke place Matthew first. After Philip, Matthew, Mark and Luke put Bartholomew, probably the same as Nathanael, who was brought to Jesus by Philip. (John 1: 46 ff.) In *the third company* of four, Simon the Cananite in Matthew and Mark is obviously the same as Simon the Zealot in Luke and Acts (see below); hence Thaddeus (Lebbeus is a false reading) must be only another name of Judas the brother of James. He might naturally be put next to his brother, as by Matthew and Mark; or Luke's order may indicate that Simon the Zealot was reckoned the more important personage. Observe that there are among the Twelve three pairs of brothers—Simon and Andrew, James and John, James the son of Alpheus, and Judas the brother of James (though this last may be 'son,' see below); also that Matthew and Luke give the list in couples, and Mark (6:7) says they were sent forth 'by two and two,' and these couples would easily lead to the grouping into fours. It would be natural that in different journeyings the couples should somewhat vary, and this might perhaps account for the different order of names in the several groups of four.

Simon who is called Peter. Simon was a Greek name, but in the New Test. is pretty certainly a contraction of Simeon, which form is given in Acts 15:14, and by some authorities in 2 Peter 1:1. Simeon signified hearing. (Gen. 29:33.) Simon was a native of Bethsaida (John 1:44), a town on the Sea of Galilee, described below on 11:21. His father's name was Jonah or John (see on 16:17). He and his brother Andrew were fishermen on the Lake of Galilee. Andrew, and probably Simon also, was a disciple of John the Baptist, before coming to know Jesus. (John 1:35 ff.) Jesus gave to Simon when he first approached him, the surname of Cephas (John 1:43), which in the Aramaic language spoken by them, signified a rock or stone (Kepha, Greek form Kephas), and which was translated into the Greek Petros, signifying the same thing; hence Latin Petrus, English Peter. The Aramaic Cephas is always used by Paul (1 Cor., Gal. correct text), and nowhere else in N. T. (except John 1:43.) After following Jesus for some time, Simon appears to have returned to his business as a fisherman, and was subsequently prominent among those called to be regular attendants. (See on 4:18 ff.) The principal events of his subsequent life are given in 8:14 ff.; 14:28 ff.; 16:16; 16, 22 ff.; John 13:6 ff.; Matt. 26:33; 26:69 ff.; John 21:15 ff.; then in Acts 1:15; 2:14; 4:8; 5:3; 8:14 ff.; 10:1 ff.; 12:3 ff.; 15:7. He was an ardent and impulsive man, of great force of character, and extremely self-confident. Sad experience, through the special influences of the Sprit, wrought a great change in him, though still, the last time he appears distinctly in the N. T. history, we discern the same impulsiveness and readiness to change, as of yore. (Gal. 2:11.) He seems to have been at Babylon, where there were many Jews, at the time of writing his First Epistle. (1 Peter 5:13.) The traditions concerning his later life are very uncertain, and so as to all the apostles except John. As regards Peter's position of leader among the Twelve, see on 16:18 f.

Andrew. The name is Greek, signifying 'manly.' The facts concerning his parentage, residence, occupation, and early discipleship, have been mentioned in connection with Peter. The only other cases in which he appears are John 6:8; 12:22; Mark 13:3. The traditions concerning him are wholly unreliable. Yet he is important to us, not only as one of the inspired apostles, but as the means of bringing to Jesus his own brother Simon. All the usefulness of Simon Peter is, in one sense, due to the brother who told him of Jesus. And so, many a one in every age, little known himself, and of no marked influence otherwise, has been among the great benefactors of mankind, by bringing to Jesus some other person who proved widely useful.

James . . and John. James was probably the elder, as he is usually mentioned first, while John is sometimes put foremost, (Luke 9:28; Acts 12:2), probably because more prominent, and because alone surviving when the books were written. James is originally the same name as Jacob, 'supplanter,' being written in the Greek, Iacobos, Latin, Iacobus, then Jacopus, Jacomus, and so James. John is the Hebrew Johanan, 'Jehovah graciously gave,' see on 3:1. Their father, Zebedee, was a fisherman on the Lake of Galilee (4:21), but apparently a man of some property, as he employed hired servants (Mark 1:20), and as his wife was one of the women who contributed to the support of Jesus and his disciples (27:55 f.; Luke 8:3), and probably a man of good social position, as we find John familiarly acquainted at the house of the high priest. (John 18:15 f.) From their mother Salome (see on 27:56) was perhaps inherited the ambition (see on 20:20), and perhaps also the ardor, intensity, vehemence, and warm affection, which characterized her sons. These qualities of theirs were doubtless the ground of the name Boanerges, 'sons of thunder,' which Jesus gave to the two brothers. (Mark 3:17.) John appears to have been a disciple of John the Baptist, it being almost certain that he was the unnamed disciple of John 1:35–41.

3 Phi.ip, and Bartholomew; Thomas, and Matthew the publican ; James *the son* of Alpheus, and Lebbeus, whose surname was Thaddeus ;

3 brother; Philip, and Bartholomew; Thomas, and Matthew the publican ; James the *son* of Alphæus,

We have no account of any call of James, until the time when the two brothers, with Simon and Andrew, were called to become our Lord's constant followers (4: 21); John at least was probably with Jesus during the previous labors recorded in his Gospel. (chap. 2-4.) The peculiar temperament of the brothers appears in Mark 9; 38 ff. ; Luke 9: 52 ff. ; Matt. 20: 20 ff. After this last event, we hear nothing of James, save as present at Gethsemane, and included in the list of Acts 1: 13, until the time when Herod Agrippa I. put him to death (Acts 12 : 2), the first martyr among the apostles.

John, however, appears quite frequently, usually in immediate association with Peter, between whom and himself there was probably a special friendship. Together they were sent to prepare for the Paschal Supper (Luke 22: 8), at which John was allowed to lean on Jesus' breast, "the disciple whom Jesus loved." Together they (and James) witnessed the agony in the garden, and both followed to the trial. (John 18 : 15.) At the cross, John only of the Twelve seems to have been present, drawn by his ardent affection, and perhaps relying to some extent on his acquaintance with the high-priest for safety ; and there he received the mother of his dying friend as one of his own family. Peter and John were also together in John 20: 2 ff. ; 21 : 2 ff. ; Acts 3 : 1 ff. ; 8 : 14; Gal. 2: 9. From Rev. 1: 9 we learn that at some time he was in exile on the Island of Patmos. There seems little doubt that he spent many years in "Asia," *i. e.,* Proconsular Asia, particularly about Ephesus, and there wrote his inspired works. Several early traditions in regard to him are pleasing and probably true, particularly the story of his reclaiming the young robber, of his keeping a tame bird, of his saying, "Little children, love one another," and of his leaving a house because a noted false teacher was there. John as disciplined by grace, exhibits one of the noblest types of human character. The love with which his Epistles abound has in it nothing effeminate. He strongly condemns and severely denounces the prevailing errors and evils. He is not merely contemplative, but intensely practical ; insisting that Christian love must show itself in holiness and usefulness, or it is naught. Still vehement, uncompromising, and outspoken, the loving and beloved old man has not ceased to be the "Son of Thunder" ; but the vaulting ambition which once aspired to be next to royalty in a worldly kingdom, now seeks to overcome the world, to bear testimony to the truth, to purify the churches, and glorify God.

3. Philip. The name is Greek, signifying "lover of horses." Philip, like Peter and Andrew, was a native of Bethsaida (John 1 : 45), and one of those who left the Baptist at the Jordan to follow Jesus, his friend Nathanael, or Bartholomew, being also brought to Jesus through his influence. (John 1 : 44 ff.) The only recorded incidents of his life are given in John 6: 5 ff. ; 12: 21; 14: 8 ff. And yet he was apparently one of the leaders among the Twelve, always standing at the head of the second group of four. The traditions concerning him are quite unreliable. He must of course be distinguished from Philip the Evangelist, of whom we read in the Acts. The name **Bartholomew** is Bar Tolmai, 'son of Tolmai,' and Tolmai (perhaps 'plowman ') is an O. T. name, having in the Sept. of Joshua 15: 14 the form Tholami, and in Josephus "Ant.," 20, 1, 1, the form Tholomeus. Nathanael denotes 'God-given,' like Theodore, etc. From John 21 : 2 we naturally suppose Nathanael to have been one of the Twelve; and as it was Philip who brought Nathanael to Jesus (John 1 : 44 ff.), and Bartholomew stands immediately after Philip in the catalogues of Matthew, Mark, and Luke, we conclude that Nathanael and Bartholomew were the same person. The only fact known in his history is that he was a native of Cana. (John 21 : 2.) The traditions concerning him are of little or no value. But he stands out in conspicuous lustre from the tribute of Jesus when he first approached him, "Behold, an Israelite indeed, in whom is no guile" ! (John 1: 47.) **Thomas.** This name signifying 'twin' was sometimes translated into the Greek Didymus (John 11 : 16), which means the same thing, just as Cephas and Peter are used, or Messiah and Christ. The incidents given of his life are in John 11: 16; 14: 4 f. ; 20: 24 ff. He does not deserve to be called "doubting Thomas," in the usual sense of the phrase; he was desponding, slow to believe what he ardently desired (as he had been ready to believe the worst, John 11 : 16), but when convinced, uttering the noblest confession in the Gospels. (John 20: 28.) The traditions concerning him are uncertain. As to **Matthew,** see on 9: 9. It is a trait of humility that he speaks of himself as **Matthew, the publican ;** recalling the discreditable business which he had formerly followed, while the other catalogues make no such allusion. Eusebius says ("Hist." iii. 24, 6) that "Matthew, after first preaching to the Hebrews, when he was about to go also to other nations, committed to writing in his native tongue the Gospel according to him, thus supplying the place of his presence." Papias, who wrote about A. D. 130, says : "Matthew composed in the Hebrew language the oracles, and every one interpreted them as he was able." The term "oracles" might mean simply discourses, or might have a more general sense, including narrative, as in Rom. 3: 2. The relation of this Hebrew (Aramaic) writing to our Greek Gospel we have scarcely the means of determining. See the works on Canon and on Introduction.—The later history of Matthew is unknown ; the traditions are unreliable.

James the son of Alpheus. If we adopt the much more probable view that this James is distinct from "James the brother of the Lord" (see on 13: 55), we are left with scarcely any knowledge of this eminent apostle, the leader in the third group of four. His father's name was Alpheus or Halpheus, which was also the name of Matthew's father. (Mark 2: 14.) Clopas (John 19: 25) might be another form of the same name, but we cannot say that it was the same person. As to whether James was the brother of Judas Thaddeus, see below.

The copious accounts sometimes given of him result from identifying him with James the brother of the Lord. **Thaddeus.** This alone is the name in Matt. and Mark, according to the correct text.[1] We have seen from comparing the catalogue that Thaddeus must be only another name of 'Judas the brother of James,' as given in Luke and Acts. He was thus known as Judas the beloved, or darling. In Luke and Acts he is distinguished from Judas Iscariot by calling him 'Judas of James,' or 'James's Judas,' a form of expression which is quite common in Greek, and which usually adds the father of the person described, but sometimes another connection, such as husband, son, brother, or even friend. (See Winer, p. 190 [237].) An eminent example is that of the early Christian writer Eusebius, who, after the death of his friend Pamphilus, always called himself Eusebius of Pamphilus. If nothing were known to the contrary, we should naturally translate 'Judas son of James,' as is done by the Peshito and Thebaic versions, and by our Rev. Ver. (Luke 6: 16; Acts 1: 13.) Comp. Bishop Lightfoot on Gal., p. 256. But as the Epistle of Jude begins 'Judas, a servant of Jesus Christ and brother of James' (where brother is expressed in the Greek), we seem entirely warranted in using that fact to solve the ambiguity of Luke's expression 'Judas of James,' and understanding it to mean the brother of James; yet it is impossible to determine the question with certainty, for we cannot even be certain that the Epistle was written by the apostle Judas. The only incident in the life of Judas Thaddeus is given in John 14: 22. The traditions concerning him are worthless.

Simon the Canaanite, or Cananaean. The name Simon being very common, this apostle is distinguished from Simon Peter and others by the surname Cananaean, which in Aramaic would signify the same thing as the

---

[1] It is given by B ℵ, 2 cursives, the two Egyptian versions, the Latin Vulgate, and several copies of the Old Latin. Lebbeus alone is given by D, some Latin documents, and Hesychius, and so is a feebly supported "Western" reading. (D and some copies of the Old Latin make the same change in Mark 3: 18.) From these two easily arose "conflate" readings, "Lebbeus who was surnamed Thaddeus," "Thaddeus who was surnamed Lebbeus," etc. The name Thaddeus is usually derived from the Aramaic *thad,* the female breast, Heb. *thad,* and would thus signify cherished in the bosom,

'beloved.' Now, Jerome says that Lebbeus (which obviously comes from *leb,* heart) signifies *corculum,* sweetheart, darling. We can easily understand how the "Western" documents, so given to arbitrary changes, might change the unfamiliar Thaddeus to a word of similar meaning formed upon a very familiar root. Thus all the phenomena are accounted for, and Thaddeus alone stands as the name in Matt., as well as in Mark. The perplexity of several recent writers has arisen from taking Lebbeus to mean hearty, courageous, overlooking Jerome's definition.

4 Simon the Canaanite, and Judas Iscariot, who also betrayed him.

4 and Thaddæus; Simon the [1]Cananæan, and Judas

1 Or, *Zealot.* See Luke vi. 15; Acts i. 13.

Greek word Zelotes given in Luke and Acts, viz., 'Zealot.' Thirty years later than this, as we find from Josephus ("War," 4, 3, 9), there existed a party calling themselves Zealots, as being very zealous for the national religion and institutions. (Comp. Acts 21: 20; Rom. 10: 2.) They were accustomed to punish without trial, to "lynch" any Jew who seemed to them a traitor or violator of the law, finding precedent and sanction in the case of Phinehas. (Num. 25: 7.) This practice, as must always happen when it is continued, led finally to gross abuses and horrid cruelties, and the Zealots had no small part in the ruin of the nation. It is likely that the party already existed in the time of our Lord (having come down from Judas the Galilean), (Acts 5: 27), though on a much smaller scale than afterwards, and that Simon had at one time belonged to it, and thus acquired his surname, Zelotes or Cananaean. It is quite a mistake to confound this with Canaanite, which in Greek is materially different (15: 22); the mistake is found as early as Great Bible, "Simon of Canaan," (so in Bagster's Hexapla, both in Matt. and Mark. Bishop Lightfoot [Rev.] seems to be mistaken in ascribing the double *a* to the Bishop's Bible.) Of this apostle's history we know nothing at all. The fact that he had been a Zealot would suggest an ardent nature; it is probable that, like Paul, he showed in doing good the same fiery zeal he had shown in doing evil.

Judas Iscariot has the same surname in John 12: 4; 13: 2. His father was called Simon Iscariot. (John 6: 71; 13: 26, correct text.) Judas is a Greek form of Judah. (See on 1: 2.) The surname Iscariot is Ish-Kerioth, 'man of Kerioth,' a town in the tribe of Judah (Josh. 15: 15); it is spelled Iscarioth in the better Greek text of Mark 3: 19; Luke 6: 16. So Ish-Tob, 'man of Tob' or 'men of Tob' is in the Sept., Istob, and in Josephus Istobos. The fact that his father had the same surname quite excludes Lightfoot's fanciful etymologies from Latin *scortea*, a leathern apron, because he carried the bag, or from Hebrew *askara*, strangling. All the other disciples appear to have been Galileans (though that is not certain), and this difference might have

some effect on Judas in preventing 'full sympathy with the others. We know nothing of his early history or his call to be a disciple. It was not only a matter of divine foreknowledge that he would betray his Teacher —as all things are—but was distinctly foreseen from an early period by Jesus (John 6: 64), who in his human mind was not omniscient. (24: 36.) That a person in whom this was foreseen should be chosen one of the Twelve, is not more mysterious than a thousand other things which are done in the providence of the same Lord. *Weiss:* "The other disciples, too, were not without great weaknesses and faults of character, which were certainly no secret to Jesus . . . . . On the other hand, Judas must have possessed special endowments, for Jesus to consider it desirable to secure him as a disciple." His talent for business, with the care of the common fund, seems to have developed a ruinous avarice, even in the very company of Jesus. He shows us that the greatest outward privileges may be of no avail, and may even be perverted into a curse; and he exemplifies the gradual progress, the terrible power, and the awful results, of covetousness. It may very well be that in the beginning he was sincere and meant to be faithful; but as so often happens, his gift became his snare.—It is some relief to our distress when we see men in high places of Christian usefulness at the present day falling utterly away, to remember that it was so at the beginning, even among our Lord's chosen Twelve. Judas must have wrought miracles like the others (comp. 7: 22 f.), and his preaching must have produced effects like theirs, or the difference would have been noticed by him and them. In like manner now, a bad man sometimes preaches, and God converts souls through his instrumentality; and these, when he afterwards turns out to have been all the while a bad man at heart, may well mourn for him, but need have no fears as to the preciousness of the truths he proclaimed, or scruples as to the validity of the ordinances he administered. As to the motives of Judas in the betrayal, see on 26: 14 ff., and as to his remorse and self-destruction, see on 27: 3ff. **Betrayed,** is

5 These twelve Jesus sent forth, and commanded them, saying, Go not into the way of the Gentiles, and into *any* city of the Samaritans enter ye not:

5 Iscariot, who also [1] betrayed him. These twelve Jesus sent forth, and charged them, saying, Go not into *any* way of the Gentiles, and enter not

1 Or, *delivered him up;* and so always.

literally, *delivered up* (margin Rev. Ver.), the same word as in v. 17, 19, 21, above in 5: 25, and often, It is a part of the characteristic moderation of the Evangelists that never, except in Luke 6: 16, do they apply to Judas the harsh words betray and traitor, which have become so fixed in our usage. Comp. on 17: 22.

III. **5-15.** INSTRUCTIONS TO THE TWELVE. The remainder of chap. 10 contains the charge given to the Twelve on sending them out. (Comp. on 9: 35.) The earlier portion of this (v. 5-15), is also briefly reported by Mark (6: 8-11), and Luke (9: 3-5). The rest (v. 16-42) is found in Matthew only. (See below on v. 16.) A charge closely resembling the earlier part of this discourse was also given to the Seventy, when sent out some time later. (Luke 10: 1-16.)

5 f. These twelve Jesus sent forth; in Greek the verb from which comes *apostolos*, ' one sent off.' (See on v. 2.) We learn from Mark (6: 7) that he sent them 'two and two.' This arrangement may possibly have been suggested by the fact that there were among the Twelve two or three pairs of brothers (see on v. 2 f.), but it had also some important advantages, both as regards the apostles themselves, and as to their work. The two served as company for each other, preventing the loneliness which the apostle Paul took so much pains to avoid on his journeys. They could also relieve each other in preaching, which, in the open air, and to the crowds gathered by their miracles, would be laborious, as our Lord himself found it. And then the testimony of the two witnesses concerning the teachings and miracles of the Great Prophet who was coming after them, would be more impressive among the people than that of one alone. The Seventy also were sent forth two and two. (Luke 10: 1.) Comp. Eccl. 4: 9-12; Luke 7: 19.—How long these journeyings and labors of the six pairs of apostles continued, we have no means of ascertaining; one would conjecture a few weeks. **Way of the Gentiles,** like ' the removal of Babylon' (comp. on 1: 11), and ' the way of the tree of life,' (Gen. 3: 24), readily signifies a way leading to the Gentiles

(so rendered by Tyndale), a road to Gentile countries. (Comp. also Jer. 2: 18; Acts 2: 28; 16: 17.) In traveling on the southern border of Galilee, they would of course come near some Samaritan towns; thus we see that the language is quite precise—Do not enter a city of the Samaritans, do not go off into a road to the Gentiles.

Samaritans. SAMARIA was the district lying between Judea and Galilee. The dislike between the Jews and the Samaritans had its beginnings as far back as the earliest times of Israel in the jealousy existing between the tribes of Judah and Ephraim, which finally led to the division into two kingdoms. When the people of the Northern Kingdom (who came to be called Samaritans from the capital city, Samaria, 1 Kings 16: 24), were carried into captivity by the Assyrians, the country was partly occupied by Mesopotamian colonists, who were idolaters. These gradually coalesced with the dregs of the Israelites who had been left in the land, and with the fugitives who returned from surrounding countries, into a half-heathen nation, attempting to unite idolatry with the worship of Jehovah. When the people of the Southern Kingdom, the Jews, returned from their captivity in Babylon, and undertook to rebuild the temple at Jerusalem, the Samaritans proffered to help them; and being repulsed, as not of pure Israelitish descent, they then did all in their power to hinder the building of the temple, and the fortification of the city. A brother of the Jewish highpriest, having married a Samaritan woman, and being unwilling to put her away as required, went over to the Samaritans, and was made priest in a temple built for him on Mount Gerizim (Jos. "Ant.," 11, 8, 2), which the Samaritans from that time began to contend was the proper place for the worship of Jehovah, rather than Jerusalem. (John 4: 20.) These causes naturally led to bitter hatred between Jews and Samaritans, and they were constantly attempting to injure and insult each other, while under the dominion of the Greek kings of Syria. John Hyrcanus conquered the Samaritans, destroying their tem-

6 But go rather to the lost sheep of the house of Israel.
7 And as ye go, preach, saying, The kingdom of heaven is at hand.

6 into any city of the Samaritans: but go rather to
7 the lost sheep of the house of Israel. And as ye go,
preach, saying, The kingdom of heaven is at hand.

---

ple and capital (about B. C. 125). Pompey established their independence (B. C. 63). At the time of our Lord's public ministry, Judea and Samaria were governed by the same Roman procurator, but as distinct administrative districts; and the hatred between the two nations, cherished through centuries, and combining all the elements of race jealousy, religious rivalry, political hostility, and numerous old grudges, had become so intense that the world has probably never seen its parallel. The theory of some writers that the Samaritans were of purely heathen origin, would suppose that the entire population of the Northern people was deported by the Assyrians—a thing extremely improbable; would render the frequent claim of the Samaritans to be Jews an absurdity; and would make it difficult to account for the Samaritan Pentateuch, and the Samaritan expectation of Messiah. For the Samaritans, like the Jews, expected the Messiah (John 4: 25, 29), and something like a year before this mission of the Twelve our Lord's preaching among them at Sychar was warmly received, and many believed on him. (John 4: 39-42.) Some time after this mission he also went twice through Samaria, and spoke and acted kindly towards them. (Luke 9: 51 ff.; 17: 11 ff.) Why, then, might not the Twelve go into their cities? It is enough to reply that the Twelve had not then such feelings towards that people as would qualify them to do good there. The proposal of James and John to call down fire from heaven upon a Samaritan village (Luke 9: 52 ff.) shows that there would have been bitter controversies, with the old national hate ever ready to burst out. (Comp. Bruce, "Training of the Twelve.") In Acts 1: 8, Samaria is expressly included in the field of their appointed labors after the ascension. (Comp. Acts 8: 5.)

6. To the lost sheep, etc., comp. on 9: 36; and see the same figure employed in Isa. 53: 6; Jer. 50: 6; Ezek. 34: 5. Our Lord confined his own personal labors almost entirely to the Jews; he declares, in 15: 24, that his mission was 'to the lost sheep of the house of Israel,' the same expression as here; though at a later period he says that he has 'other sheep which are not of this fold.' (John 10: 16.) It was a part of the peculiar privileges of the Jewish nation that the gospel should be first preached to them (Luke 24: 47; Acts 13: 46; Rom. 1: 16); yet Jesus frequently intimated that these exclusive privileges could not last always. (8: 11; 10: 18; 21: 43; 22: 9; 24: 14.) By confining his labors and those of the Twelve to them he avoided exciting their prejudices, and thus deprived them of even the poor excuse for rejecting him which they would have found in his preaching freely among the Gentiles and Samaritans. Accordingly, Matthew mentions this limitation, while Mark and Luke do not. Even at a later period, Paul found it almost impossible to convince some Jewish Christians that the Gentiles were to be admitted to the privileges of the gospel, without becoming Jews. And then had the reign of Messiah been proclaimed to the Gentiles before it had been welcomed by many Jews, the former might have made it a very plausible objection to the new religion that it was not believed in at home, where it was best understood. Furthermore, as regards this mission of the Twelve, they were as yet too ignorant themselves of the true nature of Messiah's kingdom to undertake its propagation among the Gentiles; they would have introduced the current Jewish errors on the subject. Some years later, when their own course of early instruction was completed, and the Spirit was come, they were prepared to preach "repentance and remission of sins . . . unto all the nations." (Luke 24: 47, Rev. Ver.) For the present they could prepare the Jews among whom they went for the preaching of Jesus, and what they said would not strengthen, but so far as it went would rather correct the popular errors. Such a restriction of labor to the Jews is not addressed to the Seventy (Luke 10: 1 ff.), but it is really involved in the statement that they were to go where Jesus was going.

7 f. Preach, see on 4: 17. **The kingdom of heaven is at hand,** see on 3: 2. This was the same announcement that John the Baptist had made, and with which Jesus himself had begun his ministry in Galilee (comp. on 4: 17); so the Seventy likewise. (Luke 10: 9)

8 Heal the sick, cleanse the lepers, raise the dead, cast out devils: freely ye have received, freely give.
9 *a* Provide neither gold, nor silver, nor brass in your purses;

8 Heal the sick, raise the dead, cleanse the lepers, cast 9 out demons: freely ye received, freely give. Get you

---

a Or, *Get.*

Heal the sick, cleanse the lepers, raise the dead, cast out devils—*demons.* The Greek has no article. The original means, *Heal sick, i. e., persons,* etc. They were not commanded to heal all the sick they met with. Probably they restricted their miracles, as Jesus himself usually did, to those who showed desire and faith. The Seventy also were commanded to heal the sick, in every city which received them. (Luke 10: 9.) As to leprosy, see on 8: 2; and upon demoniacal possessions, see on 8: 28-31. The clause *raise dead, i. e., persons,* is not certainly genuine, but most probably.[1] **Freely** (or, *gratis*) **ye have received, freely** (or, *gratis*) **give.** The word which Tyn., etc., and Com. Ver. here render 'freely' really signifies ' as a gift,' and is exactly rendered *gratis,* by the Latin versions and Rheims. It is not opposed to the idea of giving or receiving in a stingy way, or on a small scale, but to the idea of giving or receiving for pay. Observe the force of the word, as thus explained, in Rom. 3: 24; 2 Cor. 11: 7; Rev. 21: 6; 22: 17. (Comp. Isa. 55: 1.) The Jewish exorcisers who pretended to cast out demons were no doubt accustomed to have pay; and physicians of course took pay for healing the sick. The Twelve could easily have obtained money, in large sums, for the cures they were empowered to perform. We might think it strange that they should need to be told not to do so; but they had as yet very imperfect conceptions of the nature of Christ's work, and not merely might Judas Iscariot have been glad enough to drive a brisk trade in miraculous healing for pay, but others of them might have seen no impropriety in receiving compensation for conferring such important benefits. Jesus tells them they received gratis, and must give gratis. They had not purchased the power of miraculous healing—as Simon Magus wished to do, (Acts 8: 18)—

nor obtained it by long and expensive study, and laborious practice; it was received as a gift, and must be exercised in like manner. The miracles were really credentials for their teaching, as well as indications of divine benevolence, and should be used accordingly. As to teaching, we find Micah (3: 11) making it a reproach that the heads of Israel "judge for reward, priests teach for hire, and prophets divine for money." Some of the later Jewish writers maintained very earnestly, though often on fanciful grounds, and though many rabbis acted quite otherwise, that a man ought not to teach the law for pay, but gratuitously —just as Socrates and Plato held with reference to philosophy.

9 f. While they were thus to work their miracles, and teach the people, without pay, they must, on the other hand, look to those among whom they went for food and clothing (v. 9 f.), and for a hospitable reception. (v. 11-15.) They must neither seek for gain (v. 8), nor be anxious about their livelihood, but laying aside both selfish aims and personal cares, devote themselves to their appointed task. He therefore directs them to lay in no money, whether gold, silver, or copper, no provision-bag, nor staff, nor extra clothing, nor even a loaf of bread (Mark 6: 8; Luke 9: 3); since the laborer is worthy of his sustenance. Our Lord is not giving an exact list of objects to be dispensed with, but is only illustrating the principle; and so (Lutteroth) it is not strange that the other Gospels give the details somewhat differently.

Provide neither gold, etc., or, as in Rev. Ver., *Get you no gold, nor silver, nor copper, in your girdles.* The expression involves a climax—not gold, nor yet silver, nor even copper. Mark (6: 8) mentions only copper; Luke (9: 3) only silver. ' Brass,' as in Com. Ver., a mixture of copper and zinc, is not

---

[1] It is omitted by all later uncials, and more than one hundred and fifty cursives, by the Thebaic and Armenian, some Syriac and Æthiopic codices, and some Fathers. The concurrence of B and ℵ with C and D, supported by the other versions, some fifteen cursives and various Fathers, requires us to retain the reading.

The words may have been omitted because no other passage of the Gospels ascribes to the apostles this power. Plumptre thinks they were *inserted* because of such later instances as Acts 9: 40; 20: 9 ff. The words are retained by Lachm., Tisch., Treg., W H., and Weiss.

10 Nor scrip for *your* journey, neither two coats, neither shoes, nor yet *a* staves: for the workman is worthy of his meat.

10 no gold, nor silver, nor brass in your [1] purses; no wallet for *your* journey, neither two coats, nor shoes, nor staff: for the labourer is worthy of his food.

a Gr. *a staff*....1 Gr. *girdles.*

believed to have been in use among the ancients; they made coins, and a great variety of utensils and implements, sometimes of pure copper, but more frequently of bronze, a mixture of copper and tin, and it is this that is commonly meant in Scripture by the word copper. The ' girdle ' (see on 3: 4) was often of fine materials and elegant workmanship, and made hollow so as to carry money. The word rendered ' purse ' in Luke 10: 4, is different, and denotes a small pouch, like our purse. **No scrip,** etc., or, *no bag for the road,* (traveling bag, or haversack), the word signifying a leather bag or wallet, used for carrying provisions when traveling. The English word 'scrip' was formerly used in that sense, but is now obsolete. **Two coats,** the word meaning the inner garment or long shirt, described on 5: 40. It was not uncommon to wear two of them at once, but was unnecessary; and so John the Baptist (Luke 3: 11) directed him who had two to give to him who had none. In setting out on a journey it is natural to assume additional or thicker clothing; and even this is here prohibited. (Comp. Mark 6: 9.) Or it may mean that they must not carry with them a change of clothing, but trust to obtaining it when needed. **Neither shoes,** or, *sandals.* See on 3: 11. **Nor yet staves**—better—*nor staff.* The singular is the best supported reading of the Greek text. Mark (6: 8), ' he charged them to take nothing for their journey save a staff only,' would not necessarily conflict with Matthew. The one forbids them to *procure* a staff for the purpose, the other allows them to *carry* with them one already possessed. But Luke (9:3) uses the same Greek term as Mark, they must not carry a staff, and we have to fall back upon the principle stated above; there are indeed many cases in which the Evangelists give details differently, while the substance is the same. So in Matthew they are forbidden to procure sandals, while Mark has it, ' but to go shod with sandals.' These soles of leather or raw hide, bound under the feet, would very soon wear out in traveling, and one setting out on a long pedestrian journey would naturally wish to lay in a supply of them; but the

disciples must go with those they had on. Comp. as to the Seventy Luke 10: 4. We might take for granted that these specific directions were designed only for the existing circumstances of the disciples, and were meant to be followed after the Ascension only according to the principles involved, not according to the particular details. Still more clearly is that seen in the directions of v. 11 ff., which are manifestly founded upon the peculiar usages of Oriental hospitality. And this view is established beyond controversy by Luke 22: 35 ff., where under different circumstances they are commanded to pursue an altogether different course. Yet there have not been wanting some to contend, and even persons fanatical enough to attempt carrying the idea into practice, that ministers now, and especially foreign missionaries, should always go forth in the way here directed. But our Lord himself and the Twelve with him sometimes had money, which Judas carried in a purse (John 12:6), and expended from time to time in supplying their wants and in relieving the poor. (John 13: 29.) **For the workman is worthy of his meat**—or—*sustenance,* this being the exact meaning of the word—whatever is needed to sustain life. To the Seventy he said (Luke 10:7), ' for the laborer is worthy of his hire,' and this is the form in which Paul quotes the saying. (1 Tim. 5: 18.) Aristotle says, "A slave's hire is his sustenance." (Comp. Num. 18: 31.) It was a very useless variation for Tyndale, etc., and Com. Ver., to put 'workman' here, when the same word is rendered 'laborers' just above in 9: 37 f., and also in the corresponding passages of Luke and 1 Tim. Our Lord here distinctly sets forth the same truth concerning the preacher's right to have his wants supplied by those among whom he labors, which Paul teaches in 1 Cor. 9, and 1 Tim. 5: 17 f. Some think the meaning here to be that as God's laborers they had a right to expect that *he* would give them sustenance, by his providence; but that view does not well suit the connection here, or in Luke 10: 7, nor at all accord with Paul's use of the saying in 1 Tim. See also 1 Cor. 9: 14, which seems to refer to this passage, if we

11 And into whatsoever city or town ye shall enter, inquire who in it is worthy; and there abide till ye go thence.
12 And when ye come into a house, salute it.
13 And if the house be worthy, let your peace come upon it: but if it be not worthy, let your peace return to you.
14 And whosoever shall not receive you, nor hear your words, when ye depart out of that house or city, shake off the dust of your feet.

11 And into whatsoever city or village ye shall enter, search out who in it is worthy; and there abide till
12 ye go forth. And as ye enter into the house, salute
13 it. And if the house be worthy, let your peace come upon it: but if it be not worthy, let your peace re-
14 turn to you. And whosoever shall not receive you, nor hear your words, as ye go forth out of that house or that city, shake off the dust of your feet.

there understand 'the Lord' to mean, as so often in the Epistles, the Lord Jesus.

11-13. Whatsoever city or town (*village*), see on 9: 35. Nearly all the people were gathered into cities or villages, it being unusual to live alone in the country, and indeed unsafe, from the unsettled condition of affairs and the prevalence of robbers; in fact, travelers in Palestine have to pursue a similar course now. **Inquire,** *search out,* or 'ascertain by investigation,' a stronger term than 'enquire.' **Who in it is worthy,** *i. e.,* a man of piety and hospitality, such as would make a fit associate and a willing host. **And there abide till ye go hence,** viz., forth from the city. In addressing the Seventy (Luke 10: 7), he adds 'go not from house to house.' The chief object of this injunction seems to have been to make them feel perfectly easy about the burden of entertaining them; they must not even trouble themselves to change their stopping-place in a town, with a view to divide the burden. They had a right to a support, and must go without fear to a suitable place and stay there. It would not prove a real burden to entertain two men on a hurried journey, and they would of course not go to stay with a family which they learned was very poor. We can see another advantage of this course in that they could give themselves more uninterruptedly to their public labors. *Thomson* says (Vol. ii., 407), that at the present day, "when a stranger arrives in a village or an encampment, the neighbors, one after another, usually invite him to eat with them. There is a strict etiquette about it, involving much ostentation and hypocrisy, and a failure in the due observance of such hospitality is frequently resented, and often leads to alienations and feuds amongst neighbors."—The apostles found in carrying out the directions here given, that they lacked nothing—all their wants were supplied. (Luke 22: 35.) **Into a** (*the*) **house,** *i. e.,* the one selected according to his direction. **Salute it.** The form of salutation would be readily understood, and

was stated to the Seventy (Luke 10: 5), "Peace be to this house." This was the common salutation among the Jews, *e. g.,* Luke 24: 36; John 20: 19, 21, 26; 1 Sam. 25: 6; Psa. 122: 7, 8. The Hebrew word employed, *shalom,* signified originally wholeness, soundness, and hence health, welfare, prosperity, well-being in general; and then peace, as opposed to war, because this so greatly conduces to prosperity and welfare in general. As a salutation, the term was thus an invocation of good of every kind, a benediction, a wish that one might be blessed in every respect. It is important to observe this breadth of meaning in the term, when studying various passages, such as John 14: 27; James 2: 16, and the opening and closing salutations of several of the Epistles. The same word, *salaam,* is now used by the Arabs. **If the house be worthy,** *i. e.,* of your abiding in it, as in v. 11. The emphasis in the Greek is on 'be,' and if the house *be* worthy, as you were informed. (v. 11.)—**If it be not worthy, let your peace return to you,** without having accomplished anything. (Comp. Isa. 45: 23; 55: 11.) The explanation offered by many, that he says the benediction would come back and do good to themselves, does not appear to be warranted by the usage of similar expressions, although the idea which would thus be conveyed, is itself just and Scriptural.

14 f. Out of that house or (*that*) **city.** He refers at the same time to the case of an individual refusing them hospitality, and of a community refusing to hear their message. They would turn away from an individual, shaking off the dust of their feet, if he refused to receive or hear, but would not necessarily abandon the whole community for his sake. But if a city refused to receive or hear, then they would turn away from that city, shaking off the dust of their feet. These two directions are blended in one sentence. **Whosoever** is singular here, plural in Luke 9: 5. Shaking off the dust, etc., denoted that they wanted nothing whatever to do with them, counting them vile, and all that pertained to them polluting. We find Paul doing this in Acts 13: 51; 18: 6. The Talmud represents it as common for Jews to do so when re-entering the Holy Land from a heathen country. Similar is the ancient and modern Oriental custom of removing shoes when entering a holy place. Our Lord himself had already been rejected at Nazareth (Luke 4: 16), and in the country of the Gadarenes, and was rejected afterwards at a Samaritan village (Luke 9: 52); indeed, in general, 'he came to his own, and his own received him not.' (John 1: 11.) We need not then be surprised if some reject us and our message, since it was so with Jesus, and so with the apostles, even on the Day of Pentecost. **More tolerable for the land of Sodom and Gomorrah,** comp. on 11: 22, 24. This solemn utterance is here given by Matthew only, the corresponding sentence in Mark 6: 11 being an unquestionably spurious though early addition to the text, such as we so often find made in parallel passages.

HOMILETICAL AND PRACTICAL.

Ch. 9: 36-38. What a theme for meditation is the Saviour's compassion—at once human compassion and divine—and not a mere sentiment, but leading him to corresponding action, as Teacher and as Redeemer; and also leading him to send out others to teach the way of salvation. Every one now who is truly sent forth of God to spend his life in proclaiming salvation is really a fruit of the Saviour's compassion for the perishing.—Looking over a congregation, or any crowd, do you feel a tender concern for their salvation? Thinking of the millions who are perishing, in our own and other lands, do you long for their salvation and pray for it? If not, you are not like Jesus.—The prayer for laborers ought much oftener to form a part of our public and private supplications. All Christian men and women, and boys and girls, ought to feel that they have a work to do in gathering the great harvest of souls, that waves wide and perishing over all the earth.—V. 36-38. LUTHER: "The world think nothing more trifling and despicable than the ministers of the word, or laborers in the Lord's harvest; but that is like rejoicing over their own endless misfortune."

9: 36 to 10: 5. Origin and development of a

call to the ministry. 1) Compassionate reflection upon the perishing condition of men, v. 36 f. 2) Prayer that God will send forth laborers, v. 38. 3) Conviction that we ourselves must go, v. 1, 5. HENRY: "Those who are to be ministers ought, 1) to live near to Christ; 2) to be taught by him."—V. 1. HENRY: "This was that famous jury, (and to make it a grand jury, Paul was added to it) that was impaneled to inquire between the King of kings and the body of mankind; and in this chapter they have their charge given them by him to whom all judgment was committed."—V. 2. HENRY: "Kinsmen may be dear companions in Christian labor." —V. 7 f. The relation between the supernatural and the miraculous.—V. 9–13. Hospitality to traveling preachers; comp. Heb. 13: 2; 2 John 10.—V. 12 f. The courtesies of life may be the vehicles of temporal and spiritual blessing.—V. 14 f. Dreadful guilt of rejecting the gospel. HENRY: "The best and most powerful preachers of the gospel must expect to meet with some who will not so much as give them the hearing, nor show them any token of respect."—It may be suggested that in sermons on the twelve apostles it would be well to group two or more of those concerning whom we know very little into one discourse, rather than use uncertain traditions as material.

10: 16-11: 1. FURTHER INSTRUCTIONS TO THE TWELVE.

Our Lord's instructions to the Twelve close in Mark (6: 11) and Luke (9: 5) at this point. But Matthew goes on to give much additional matter spoken on the same occasion. There are several other remarkable cases, as the Sermon on the Mount, the discourse in ch. 18, and that on the Mount of Olives (ch. 24 and 25), in which Matthew gives much more than Mark and Luke. The remainder of the present address consists of warnings as to coming persecutions, directions how to act when persecuted, and reasons why they should not shrink from duty because of danger. Some of these warnings and directions look beyond this brief mission in Galilee and on to their labors after the Ascension. In the address to the Seventy (Luke 10: 2-16) there is no such reference to future time. It was natural that he should, on first sending them out to labor, give directions which would be of service to them throughout their appointed course. *Bruce:*

15 Verily I say unto you, It shall be more tolerable for the land of Sodom and Gomorrah in the day of judgment, than for that city.
16 Behold, I send you forth as sheep in the midst of wolves: be ye therefore wise as serpents, and harmless as doves.

15 Verily I say unto you, It shall be more tolerable for the land of Sodom and Gomorrah in the day of judgment, than for that city.
16 Behold, I send you forth as sheep in the midst of wolves: be ye therefore wise as serpents, and [1] harm-

---

[1] Or, *simple.*

"It was his way on solemn occasions, to speak as a prophet, who in the present saw the future, and from small beginnings looked forward to great ultimate issues. This Galilean mission, though humble and limited compared with the great undertaking of after years, was really a solemn event. It was the beginning of that vast work for which the Twelve had been chosen, which embraced the world in its scope, and aimed at setting up on the earth the kingdom of God." The parts most peculiar to that journey apply in principle (Edersheim) to us and to all time; the parts which pointed to the remotest future applied in principle to the immediate journey about Galilee. These considerations form a sufficient reply to those who insist that Matthew has here put together matters actually spoken on different occasions at a later period. Mark and Luke give some similar sayings in the discourse on the Mount of Olives, and Matthew there omits them. It was natural that if similar things were said in different discourses an Evangelist should give them in one case and omit them in another; and it was perfectly natural that Jesus should say similar things on different occasions. On this point comp. at the beginning of ch. 5. In applying the present discourse to ourselves, allowance must be made for the difference of situation. We do not work miracles, and are not inspired; the opposition we meet is rather moral than physical; we often go to foreign countries.

I. 16-23. They Must be on Their Guard Against Coming Persecution. We have here the general intimation and counsel of v. 16; warnings as to the persecutions which awaited them (v. 17 f.), with directions as to the defence of themselves when brought before the tribunals (v. 19 f.); further statements concerning persecutions and hatred (v. 21 f.); and the direction to flee from any town in which they were persecuted into the next.

16. They are going forth into the midst of perils, and must therefore exercise a blended prudence and simplicity. These ideas are beautifully and strikingly expressed by figures. **Behold, I send you forth.** 'Behold' calls special attention to what follows. 'I' is expressed in the Greek, and therefore in some sense emphatic. The idea perhaps is that they are not going out like sheep wandering into dangers, without the knowledge of their shepherd; he himself sends them forth into the midst of these perils; and hence both a reason why they should strive to come off safe, and an encouragement to hope they would succeed. He sends them forth as **sheep,** weak and defenceless, and not only in a region where there was danger of wolves, but in the midst of wolves—the language is very strong. To the Seventy (Luke 10:3) it is still stronger; they are 'lambs.' Herodotus speaks of leaving a man as a sheep among wolves. **Be ye therefore wise** (*prudent*) **as serpents, and harmless** (*simple*) **as doves.** 'Be' is more exactly 'become,' get to be, implying that they are not so now. 'Therefore' may be taken as an inference not merely from the fact that they would be as sheep in the midst of wolves, but also from the fact that *he* sent them as sheep in the midst of wolves; there is a duty to themselves and a duty to him. 'Wise,' more exactly 'prudent' (comp. on 7:24); Latin versions *prudentes* or *astuti.* Serpents show great caution and skill in avoiding danger. The Egyptian hieroglyphics use the serpent as the symbol of wisdom. We may understand that they were to be prudent in the recognition of danger, and in the choice of means for opposing or escaping it—in general as to their behaviour when in danger. But such prudent regard for self-preservation is very apt to be accompanied, in men as in serpents, with the tricks of low cunning. This is forbidden by the other injunction. The word rendered 'harmless,' better 'simple' (margin Rev. Ver.) signifies literally unmixed, and hence pure (as pure wine, pure gold), uncorrupted, and so guileless, sincere. The Latin versions all have *simplices:* the Peshito, a word denoting whole-minded, upright, sincere; Chrys. ex-

17 But beware of men: for they will deliver you up to the councils, and they will scourge you in their synagogues;

17 less as doves. But beware of men: for they will deliver you up to councils, and in their synagogues

---

plains by simple and artless. The English use of 'simple' does not quite clearly express the idea, but it is exactly hit by the substantive 'simplicity.' The other proposed derivation, without horns, and so 'harmless,' adopted by King James, is highly improbable. The Greek word is used also in Phil. 2: 15, and Rom. 16: 19, Rev. Ver., "wise unto that which is good, and simple unto that which is evil." In our passage the word is translated 'simple' in Wyc. and Rheims, McClellan, and Davidson, and 'innocent' in Tynd., Great B., and Geneva. They were not to deserve injury, or afford any pretext for it; and were to employ no trickery or other improper means of escaping from danger. They must combine prudence and simplicity. If the dove alone were taken as model, they might become silly (Hos. 7: 11); if the serpent alone, they would become tricky. (Gen. 3 : 1.) *Stier:* "So that thy wisdom shall never degenerate into cunning, nor thy simplicity into ignorance or imprudence." *Plato:* "Knowledge without justice should be called cunning rather than wisdom." If we are to fail in either, it is doubtless better to be lacking in Christian prudence than in Christian simplicity. But the injunction is to combine both in due proportion; and the example of Jesus shows this to be possible. How prudent he was, constantly taking pains to avoid danger till his hour was come, and at the same time how innocent, guileless, and pure. Not merely in respect to persecution, but in all the dangers to ourselves and our work which throng about Christian laborers, we have constant need of prudence, united with simplicity. In a late Jewish commentary (Midrash), a Rabbi says: "God says, toward me the Israelites are simple as doves, but toward the Gentiles subtle as serpents." This may have been borrowed from the Gospels; we know that the later Jews borrowed from every direction.

17 f. With v. 17-22 comp. similar things said to the four disciples in the great discourse on the Mount of Olives (Mark 13: 9-13; Luke 21: 12-19); there Matt. does not record them. **But beware of men,** *i. e.,* of mankind in general, spoken of as hostile to them, like 'the world' in John

15: 18; 17: 14. They were few, and men were against them. **Councils** does not here mean the great Sanhedrin, as in 26: 59, but apparently refers to the smaller judicial bodies which existed in every city and village, as in 5: 22. **Synagogues,** see on 4: 23. Other allusions to scourging in the synagogues, apparently in the very place of worship, and in the actual presence of the worshiping assembly, are found in 23: 34; Mark 13: 9; Acts 22: 19; comp. Acts 26: 11. At a later period it is said that, on one occasion, the Jews sung a psalm while a man was receiving a scourging in the synagogue; and Maimonides says that the principal judge would read passages of Scripture throughout the scourging. The Jews were very scrupulous not to exceed forty stripes, according to the law which Moses made (Deut. 25: 3) to mitigate the dreadful severity of the common Oriental scourgings; and to make sure of not going beyond forty they stopped at thirty-nine. (2 Cor. 11: 24.) **And ye shall be brought** (even) **before governors and kings for my sake.** This is introduced as more important ('even') than what precedes; and it was so not merely because they would be tribunals of greater dignity, but because they could punish with death, which the Jewish tribunals at that time could not do. It was also a remarkable thing that they were to be brought, not only before the religious authorities of their own people, but before the civil authorities, the highest Roman officials. The word rendered 'governors' is a general term, which would include several kinds of Roman rulers of provinces, viz.: propraetor, proconsul (like Sergius Paulus, and Gallio), and procurator (like Pilate, Felix, Festus), and is used in the same broad sense in 1 Peter 2: 14. As to their being brought before 'kings,' we have examples in the persecutions of James and Peter by Herod Agrippa I. (Acts 12), and the appearance of Paul before his son Herod Agrippa II. (Acts 26.) The term king was also frequently applied to the Roman imperator or emperor (1 Peter 2: 13 f.), and in that sense we should have an example in Paul's trials before Nero. **For a testimony against** (to) **them and against** (to) **the Gentiles.** The Greek might mean 'against them' (Com.

18 And ye shall be brought before governors and kings for my sake, for a testimony against them and the Gentiles.

19 But when they deliver you up, take no thought how or what ye shall speak: for it shall be given you in that same hour what ye shall speak.

20 For it is not ye that speak, but the Spirit of your Father which speaketh in you.

21 And the brother shall deliver up the brother to death, and the father the child: and the children shall rise up against *their* parents, and cause them to be put to death.

18 they will scourge you; yea and before governors and kings shall ye be brought for my sake, for a

19 testimony to them and to the Gentiles. But when they deliver you up, be not anxious how or what ye shall speak: for it shall be given you in that hour

20 what ye shall speak. For it is not ye that speak, but the Spirit of your Father that speaketh in you.

21 And brother shall deliver up brother to death, and the father his child: and children shall rise up against parents, and ¹ cause them to be put to death.

---

1 Or, *put them to death.*

Ver.), but the other is a more natural meaning, and better suits the connection. ' To them' may mean the rulers just mentioned, as distinguished from the nation at large; or it more probably means the Jews, spoken of as 'they,' 'them;' as in v. 17, in 11 : 1, and often. The idea would thus be that the design of Providence in suffering the disciples to be brought before these tribunals was, that they might bear witness to rulers and people—or, more probably, to Jews and Gentiles (Phil. 1 : 13; 2 Tim. 4 : 17)—of the truths they were going forth to proclaim. (Comp. a similar expression in 8 : 4; 24 : 14.) All this we cannot understand as referring simply to their brief journey about Galilee, during which they would perhaps encounter some persecution (see on v. 23), but were certainly not brought before governors and kings. It must therefore be understood as glancing forward to persecutions they would suffer in future days, while prosecuting that mission as Christ's apostles, of which this journey would be the first stage. (Comp. on v. 16.) How plainly our Lord spoke to his followers of the perils and persecutions which awaited them in doing his work. He would have them count the cost. And they did not shrink from his service, though warned what it would cost them, being doubtless sustained by their own devotion, and by such promises as those of v. 19 and 22.

19 f. When thus called before the authorities for trial, they need not be anxiously considering as to the defence they shall make, the testimony they are to bear, for it shall be communicated to them by the Divine Spirit (v. 19), who indeed will be speaking in them as his instruments. (v. 20.) Comp. the similar promise on the Mount of Olives (Mark 13 : 11; Luke 21 : 14 f.), and on another occasion. (Luke 12 : 12.) **Take no thought,** *be not anxious,* or ' do not anxiously consider.' See on 6 : 25. They would be more likely to feel anxious what they should

say, because it was common to make very elaborate addresses and affecting appeals; and before the Roman tribunals, even to employ counsel, such as Tertullus (Acts 24 : 1), who would understand Roman law and judicial methods, and could deliver high-wrought orations. Knowing that importance was attached to such addresses, and conscious of inexperience in Roman legal procedure, the disciples might naturally feel, when they were delivered up, great solicitude; and this would be increased by the fact that they were called to present, not only a defense of themselves, but a testimony for Jesus. There was thus great comfort for them in the promise here given. As specimens of the addresses made by some of them under such circumstances, we have the speeches of Peter and Stephen before the Sanhedrin, and of Paul before Felix, Festus, and Agrippa. **How or what ye shall speak.** ' How ' suggests the general plan and delivery of their defence, and ' what ' suggests the subject matter. Comp. 'mouth and wisdom' in Luke 21 : 15; and comp. Luke 12 : 12.

20. For it is not ye that speak, etc. With the form of expression comp. Gen. 45 : 8, " It was not you that sent me hither, but God," and so Exod. 16 : 8. **Your Father,** see on 6 : 9. This was clearly a promise of special inspiration, in the highest sense and degree (comp. Ex. 4 : 12). To apply it to uninspired preachers of to-day, is unwarranted and absurd. They may expect, and should earnestly seek, the gracious aids of the Holy Spirit in their previous reflections and in their actual preaching; but they have no right whatever to expect inspiration. This promise of inspiration was repeated by our Lord in the promise of the Comforter (John ch. 14 to 16) ; and that assures us that in their *writings* also the apostles were inspired.

21 f. Not only will the public authorities

22 And ye shall be hated of all *men* for my name's sake: but he that endureth to the end shall be saved.
23 But when they persecute you in this city, flee ye into another; for verily I say unto you, Ye shall not have gone over the cities of Israel, till the Son of man be come.

22 And ye shall be hated of all men for my name's sake: but he that endureth to the end, the same 23 shall be saved. But when they persecute you in this city, flee into the next: for verily I say unto you, Ye shall not have gone through the cities of Israel, till the Son of man be come.

---

be disposed to persecute them, but men will deliver to the tribunals their own dearest kindred for being Christians, and will put them to death, and the hatred against them will be universal; yet let them endure to the end, and they shall be saved. See a similar passage in Mark 13: 12 f. and Luke 21: 16-19, as spoken on the Mount of Olives, and part of it is in this case given by Matthew also. (24: 9-13.) **And the children shall rise up against their parents, and,** literally, *put them to death,* (see margin of Rev. Ver). This doubtless means, will put them to death through the instrumentality of the authorities. But Rev. Ver. ought hardly to have followed Com. Ver. in giving a mere interpretation a place in the text, and throwing into the margin the correct translation of Tyn. and his successors, and of Davidson, Noyes, Darby. The dreadful effects of religious bigotry, as here predicted, and as so often witnessed in the world's history, should impress us with the immense power and importance of the religious principle in man; just as when a train of cars runs off the track, or a dynamite factory explodes, we see all the more clearly from the ruinous consequences the power of the forces in question, and the importance of their being properly directed and controlled. For the motive to such persecutions has usually been, not opposition for its own sake to the religion persecuted, but attachment to another religion with which it was thought to interfere. **But he that endureth to the end, shall be saved.** It seems proper here, as is manifestly necessary in the discourse on the Mount of Olives (24: 13; Mark 13: 13) to understand the assurance as having a twofold application; first, he that endures to the end of the persecutions and other evils in question shall at last be saved, delivered, from those evils; but also more widely, he that endures to the end of life's trials shall be saved, in the usual sense of attaining eternal life. The propriety of understanding a twofold allusion in such

passages, or making a varied application of them, will be discussed at the beginning of ch. 24; see also on the next verse.

23. Flee ye into another, or *the other,* *i. e.,* into the next. The particular city in which they are persecuted, and the one next in order are conceived of as forming a pair, 'this,' 'the other.'[1] In thus avoiding persecution they would be 'prudent as the serpents' (v. 16); so Paul and Barnabas acted in going from Antioch in Pisidia to Iconium, etc. (Acts, ch. 13 and 14.) **For verily I say unto you,** see on 5: 18. Some fancy that this expression in v. 15, 23, 42, marks the close of three distinct sections of the discourse; but this is supposing a very artificial use of the phrase, and if so designed, it ought also to occur in v. 33 and 35. **Ye shall not have gone over** (or, *finish*) **the cities of Israel, till the Son of man be come.** 'Not' is a strong negative, translated 'in no wise' in John 6: 37 and Heb. 13: 5, and in Matthew 5: 20; 10: 42, etc. 'Finish' (so rendered by Tyn., Gen., Rheims, and margin of Com. Ver.), in the sense of visiting them all. They must not stay in one city, vainly endeavoring to overcome opposition and persecution, but flee to the next; for there were more cities than they would be able to visit before the Son of man should come. It is quite difficult to determine the meaning of this last expression, as here employed. It has been supposed to mean: (1) Till he come and rejoin the Twelve at the end of this journey. (2) Till he make his appearance as the Messiah, distinctly present himself as such. (3) Till he come spiritually to console and support. (John 14: 23.) (4) Till he come to put an end to the Jewish institutions at the destruction of Jerusalem. (5) Till he come to judge the world. The *first* sense might at the outset strike one as natural and good, and it would be possible that he should return from the more general view of their coming labors and persecutions, to speak of the particular journey then before them; as

---

[1] The "Western" documents, with Origen and the Armenian version add "And if out of this they persecute you, flee into the other" (so W H. margin), which would be an unimportant expansion. It is difficult to decide whether it is more likely to have been inserted or omitted.

24 The disciple is not above *his* master, nor the serv- | 24   A disciple is not above his [1] master, nor a [2] servant
ant above his lord.

---

1 Or, *teacher*....2 Gr. *bondservant.*

---

in the discourse on the Mount of Olives he sometimes returns from the second topic to the first. In the mission of the Seventy (Luke 10 : 1, R. V.), it is said that he sent them 'before his face into every city and place, whither he himself was about to come.' It is natural to suppose that he was going to follow the Twelve also; and indeed he must have done so, since their work was confined to Galilee (see on v. 5), and he himself went about all the cities of Galilee. When the objection is made that it is hardly probable they were *persecuted* during this journey, one may reply that Jesus himself was persecuted at Nazareth, and seriously threatened with death at various other places. The greatest difficulty in the way of understanding the expression in this sense is that the language seems too elaborate and solemn for so simple an idea. He does not say "for you will not finish the cities of Galilee till I come," but employs the solemn phrase 'till the Son of man come,' and prefaces it by 'verily I say to you,' using also the more general term Israel. The *second* sense proposed is not supported by any similar use of the phrase elsewhere, and does not seem very appropriate to the connection. There was indeed no broadly marked epoch at which he appeared as the Messiah, and the occasional intimations of his Messiahship commenced long before the delivery of this discourse. The *third* sense is that of Chrys. and his followers, of Beza, Maldonatus; while Calvin and Bleek understand similarly his coming in the mission of the Holy Spirit. But the time of his spiritual coming would be a very vague chronological epoch; and Jesus certainly seems to be speaking of some personal coming. The *fourth* sense is accepted by many recent writers. In 16 : 28, 'the Son of man coming' unquestionably refers to the destruction of Jerusalem. The idea here would thus be that they would not reach all the Jews with their ministry before the overthrow of the Jewish institutions; and hence they must not waste time in remaining where they were persecuted. But in the discourse on the Mount of Olives (ch. 24 and 25), the coming to destroy Jerusalem and the coming at the end of the world

are constantly associated, and sometimes both referred to in the same expression. So, also, in 16: 27 f. It would, therefore, seem natural to combine with this fourth the *fifth* sense. On no occasion would there be greater propriety in employing the obscure language and perspective view of prophecy than here. He wishes to give counsel which shall apply not only to this journey, but to their labors after the Ascension, and perhaps even to the labors of his followers in all ages; and to intimate that in each of those periods there would be more to do than they could complete before the season in question would end. It may, therefore, be that the phrase was intended to include in some obscure fashion the *first*, *fourth*, and *fifth* senses. It was manifestly impossible that the Twelve should at that time understand any distinct reference to the coming to destroy Jerusalem; indeed it is not probable that they understood when he spoke of it on the Mount of Olives. It was necessary, therefore, as so often in O. T. and N. T. prophecies, to employ language which would refer to each of these at the same time; which would be understood at once as regarded the present journey, and would afterwards be viewed in its broader meaning when needed. (Comp. on v. 22, and at the beginning of ch. 24.) The notion of Origen, that Scripture has everywhere a twofold, or even threefold, sense, is now justly rejected; our present danger is that of rejecting along with it the unquestionable fact that Scripture does sometimes use language referring at once to a nearer and a remoter event.

II. 24-33. ENCOURAGEMENT TO THE PERSECUTED. The key-note is here 'fear not,' which occurs three times, in v. 26, 28, 31.

24 f. They need not think strange, or complain that they were going to be persecuted; this would only be sharing the fate of their Teacher and Master, **The disciple is not above his master** (*teacher*,) **nor the servant above his lord** (*master*), (see margin Rev. Ver.) For 'disciple' see on 5 : 1; for 'teacher' (*didaskalos*), and 'master' (*kurios*), on 8 : 19; and for 'slave' (*doulos*), on 8: 6. This saying is also given by Luke (6: 40), as used in the Sermon on the Mount; by John (13: 16), as em-

25 It is enough for the disciple that he be as his master, and the servant as his lord. If they have called the master of the house Beelzebub, how much more *shall they call* them of his household :
26 Fear them not therefore : for there is nothing covered, that shall not be revealed ; and hid, that shall not be known.
27 What I tell you in darkness, *that* speak ye in light : and what ye hear in the ear, *that* preach ye upon the housetops.

25 above his lord. It is enough for the disciple that he be as his [1] master, and the [2] servant as his lord. If they have called the master of the house [3] Beelzebub, how much more *shall they call* them of his household :
26 Fear them not therefore : for there is nothing covered, that shall not be revealed ; and hid, that shall not be known. What I tell you in the darkness,
27 speak ye in the light : and what ye hear in the ear,

1 Or. *teacher*....2 *bondservant*——3 Gr. *Beelzebul :* and so elsewhere.

ployed in another connection; and also in John 15: 20, where the application is much the same as here. The saying, "It is enough for the slave to be as his master" (comp. v. 25), occurs repeatedly in the later Jewish writings, and was perhaps proverbial when used by Jesus. (Comp. on 7: 5, 12.) There are of course exceptional cases in which a pupil does have a better lot than his teacher, or even a slave than his master ; but the general fact is as here expressed, and so the disciples need not be surprised at hearing that they would suffer the same treatment to which Jesus himself was exposed. **If they** (*i. e.*, people, the impersonal use) **called the master of the house Beelzebub,** or *Beelzebul* (see margin Rev. Ver.). 'Master' is here *despotes* (see on 8: 19), which we borrow as *despot.* The compound term of the original 'house-master' presents him as ruler of the household in general ; a man's authority over his wife and children was then scarcely less absolute than over his slaves. The Pharisees had already charged Jesus with being in league with Beelzebul (see on 9: 34; 12: 24); are we to understand here that they had actually applied the *name* to Jesus? The expression does not necessitate this supposition, but we know they had said what amounted to it, and on other unrecorded occasions they may have literally called him by that name.

26 f. With v. 26-33 comp. Luke 12: 2-9, where substantially the same things are said in another discourse. The thought of v. 26 is also found in Luke 8: 17, as introduced in yet another connection. The injunction, **Fear them not** (*i. e.*, the persecutors, v. 25, v. 16-23) is presented on the one hand as an inference from what precedes—'*therefore* do not fear,' viz., because if they oppose and persecute you, it is nothing more than your Master encounters ; and on the other hand is supported by the assurance that the truths they bear forth are destined, in spite of all op-

position, to be made known—**for there is nothing covered that shall not be revealed** (or *uncovered*); **and hid that shall not be known.** And so they must proclaim everything boldly and publicly, even what he taught them in his private instruction. (v. 27.) V. 26 might also mean, as some suppose, that the apostles, so misunderstood and persecuted, should in a coming day be differently regarded, all men then perceiving that they were the benefactors of their time; but the other view better suits the connection. The expression of v. 27 gives a different turn to the idea than that found in Luke 12: 3, but it amounts to the same thing. There is repeated mention in the Talmud of Jewish teachers as having one standing by, to whom the teacher would whisper something, and who would then proclaim it to the audience. It is likely that such a practice existed already in our Lord's time, and it may be that he here alludes to it, not as meaning that he literally did this, but as a figurative and striking way of saying that they were to keep nothing back through fear, but even his private instructions to them were to be proclaimed in the most public manner. **Upon the housetops.** The roofs of the houses were flat, and surrounded by a narrow battlement. It was common (and still is) for persons to walk on the roof, and this would naturally afford an elevated stand from which to proclaim anything to the people in the street below. Thus Josephus, having taken refuge in a house from a mob in Tarichaea, "went up on the roof, and with his right hand quieting the uproar, said," etc. ("War.," 2, 21, 5.) The Talmud represents a religious official as proclaiming from a housetop, with the sound of a trumpet, the approach of any religious festival; and the same thing is often done at the present day. Indeed, the muezzin's call to prayer, from the minaret of the mosque, is the same sort of thing.

28 And fear not them which kill the body, but are not able to kill the soul: but rather fear him which is able to destroy both soul and body in hell.
29 Are not two sparrows sold for a *ᵃfarthing*? and one of them shall not fall on the ground without your Father.
30 But the very hairs of your head are all numbered.
31 Fear ye not therefore, ye are of more value than many sparrows.
32 Whosoever therefore shall confess me before men,

28 proclaim upon the housetops. And be not afraid of them that kill the body, but are not able to kill the soul: but rather fear him who is able to destroy 29 both soul and body in ¹hell. Are not two sparrows sold for a penny? and not one of them shall fall 30 on the ground without your Father: but the very 31 hairs of your head are all numbered. Fear not therefore; ye are of more value than many sparrows. 32 Every one therefore who shall confess ²me before

---

a It is in value half-penny farthing in the original, as being the tenth part of the Roman penny. See ch. 18: 28.——1 Gr. Gehenna.
....2 Gr. in me.

---

28. Let them not fear men, but fear God. The idea of some that the phrase **Him which is able to destroy both soul and body in hell,** means Satan, is wholly unwarranted and unsuitable. God is able to destroy; he does not *wish* that any should perish. (2 Pet. 3: 9.) Jesus does not say that God will *kill* the soul, but, avoiding that term, says he will *destroy* both soul and body. For 'destroy' need not mean annihilation, but only ruin, perdition, the destruction of all that makes existence desirable. **Hell** is *gehenna*, see on 5: 22, and comp. on 5: 29. Fear is natural to man; and our Lord does not say we must root it out and have no fear, but that the less fear must give way to the greater. The gospel does not teach stoicism or self-abnegation, but appeals to the human mind according to its actual constitution. Comp. the appeal to a higher self-interest in 5: 29, and to hope and fear in v. 32 f. below. In proportion as one has a true fear of God he will feel no fear of man. It was a saying of Col. Gardiner, "I fear God, therefore there is none else that I need fear." And not only with reference to persecution or any open opposition, but to a concern for approbation or blame, does the thought of this passage apply. How much more important that we should avoid God's displeasure, than that of our fellow-men. Comp. Luke 12: 4 f.; James 4: 12. The thought occurs often in Jewish writings. In 2 Maccabees 6: 26, "For even if for the present I shall be delivered from the vengeance of men, yet neither while living nor after dying shall I escape the hands of the Almighty." In 4 Macc. 13: 14, "Let us not fear him who thinks to kill the body; for great is the danger to the soul, consisting in eternal torment to those who transgress the commandment of God." Philo says, "For men reckon the extreme penalty to be death; but in the divine court of justice this is scarcely the beginning." And the Midrash on Numbers (Wet.): "He who causes a man to sin is worse

than he who slays him: because he who slays, slays him in this world, and he has part in the world to come; but he who causes him to sin, slays him both in this world and in that which is to come."

29-31. Let them not only dread God's displeasure (v. 28), but trust in his protection; he who cares for the least objects, will not fail to care for them. Comp. 6: 26 ff., and Luke 12: 6 f. (See above on v. 26.) The word rendered **farthing,** denotes a Roman copper or bronze coin, actually equal *not* to about three farthings sterling (as in margin of Com. Ver.), or one and a half cents, but to about five-eighths of a cent (Edersh. I., 649), and frequently used to denote any trifling amount. **Fall on the ground,** viz., dead. **Without your Father,** without his agency or permission. On 'your Father,' comp. on v. 20, and see on 6: 9. The Midrash on Genesis says (Wet.), "A bird without heaven (God) is not taken, how much less so many souls of men." In v. 30 the position of the Greek words makes 'your' emphatic, and so with 'ye' in v. 31. A single hair falling from the head seems to us a matter of the most trifling consequence (comp. 1 Sam. 14: 45); but every one of them is numbered by God. (Comp. Luke 21: 18; Acts 27: 34.) A late Jewish compilation (Wet.) represents God as saying, "Do I not number all the hairs of every creature?" This was very likely borrowed from the New Test. Our Lord's line of argument here is in precisely the contrary direction to that which men often follow on this subject. They will say that no doubt God controls great matters, but that it is questionable whether his care extends to such little things as the concerns of an individual man. Jesus says, God takes care of the smallest and most trifling things, and therefore we may be sure he cares for a man, who is so much more important.

32 f. Whosoever (*every one*) **therefore** (*who*) **shall confess me.** 'Therefore' presents

him will I confess also before my Father which is in heaven.

33 But whosoever shall deny me before men, him will I also deny before my Father which is is heaven.

34 Think not that I am come to send peace on earth : I came not to send peace, but a sword.

35 For I am come to set a man at variance against his father, and the daughter against her mother, and the daughter in law against her mother in law.

36 And a man's foes *shall be* they of his own household.

men, [1] him will I also confess before my Father who 33 is in heaven. But whosoever shall deny me before men, him will I also deny before my Father who is in heaven.

34 Think not that I came to [2] send peace on the earth : 35 I came not to [2] send peace, but a sword. For I came to set a man at variance against his father, and the daughter against her mother, and the daughter in 36 law against her mother in law: and a man's foes

---

1 Gr. *in him*....2 Gr. *cast.*

---

what follows as an inference from what precedes. Since God will protect, there is no excuse for shrinking from duty through fear of men, and therefore he will confess only those who confess him. This affecting statement stands last and highest in a climax of reasons for going forward undeterred by the fear of men : *first*, the fact that if they are maltreated and slandered, it is no more than their Master himself suffered (v. 24 f.); *second*, that the truths they proclaimed are destined to be made known, and thus no opposition will prevent it (v. 26 f.); *third*, that God's wrath is more to be dreaded than man's (v. 28); *fourth*, that he who cares for trifling things will certainly care for them (v. 29-31); *finally*, that if we do not confess Christ before men he will not confess us before his Father in heaven. It is thus manifest that the confession here enjoined upon us does not consist merely in a particular ceremony, or other single act, but denotes in general that we come out as his followers, and speak and act as his, under all circumstances and at all hazards. The term rendered 'confess' [1] has been explained on 7: 23, where it is rendered 'profess'; see also 1 Tim. 6: 12. Observe that we have here a perfectly general proposition. (a) In v. 26-31 it is 'ye'; but in v. 32 f. it is 'every one' and 'whosoever.' (b) While the statement is here specially suggested by the idea of confessing Jesus when persecuted, when brought before tribunals (v. 18), yet the language is general, and doubtless intended to include every kind of confession during the whole course of life. Many who have once publicly confessed Christ, and are numbered with his people, often fail to confess him afterwards in word or deed. It is of course possible that one should show bad judgment and bad taste in announc-

ing himself a Christian where there is no occasion for it; but for every person who does this unseasonably, there are very many who shrink from such an avowal when it ought to be made, and still more fail to confess by the actions which "speak louder than words." **Will I confess,** acknowledge as mine. (Comp. 7: 23.) What a question it is, whether we are going to be confessed or denied by Jesus, before his Father in heaven. Here again, as in 7: 22 f., our Lord speaks freely of his coming exaltation as Messiah; but it is likely that the disciples at first understood it all of elevation and honor in a temporal kingdom. With v. 32 f., comp. Luke 12: 7 f. (See above on v. 26.) As to **deny,** comp. on 16: 24.

III. 34-39. PERSECUTION IS INEVITABLE. Let no one be surprised at learning that so much persecution is to be encountered by the Twelve, and by Christ's followers in general; for it was the object of Christ's mission to introduce principles which would be sure to cause divisions and conflicts among men, even within the bosom of families. His religion was so wholly opposed to the spirit of the world, that such a result was inevitable. **Think not that I am come,** (*came*) comp. on 5: 17. Here again, as so often, the Com. Ver. (but here following Tyn., Great B., and Gen.), introduces an unnecessary variation in the rendering of v. 34 f.; for in all three cases the Greek has the same form, 'I came.' Our Lord here, as in 5: 17, speaks of himself as having come among men on a special mission. The Jews were accustomed to bloody conflicts between their politico-religious parties, the Pharisees and Sadducees, and (Lightf.) between the followers of Hillel and Shammai, but they were likely to think Messiah's reign

---

1 'Confess in me' (margin Rev. Ver.), *i. e.,* 'make confession in my case' is an imitation in the Greek of an Aramaic expression, and easily returns to it in the Peshito. So 'in him will I also confess.' It signifies to

make confession in the case of, in the matter of, the person stated. Similar is Sept. 1 Sam. 16: 9, and comp. 1 John 4: 9, 16.

37 He that loveth father or mother more than me is not worthy of me: and he that loveth son or daughter more than me is not worthy of me.
38 And he that taketh not his cross, and followeth after me, is not worthy of me.
39 He that findeth his life shall lose it: and he that loseth his life for my sake shall find it.
40 He that receiveth you receiveth me; and he that receiveth me receiveth him that sent me.

37 *shall be* they of his own household. He that loveth father or mother more than me is not worthy of me: and he that loveth son or daughter more than
38 me is not worthy of me. And he that doth not take his cross and follow after me, is not worthy of
39 me. He that [1] findeth his life shall lose it; and he that [2] loseth his life for my sake shall find it.
40 He that receiveth you receiveth me, and he that receiveth me receiveth him that sent me. He that

---

1 Or, *found*....2 Or, *lost*.

---

would be a reign of peace, for so the prophets had predicted; the disciples of Christ were especially apt to think so, if they then knew of the angelic song at his birth. The gospel does tend to bring men into peace with each other, but only in proportion as they are brought into peace with God. So as to the prophecies; men will beat their swords into plow-shares, only when men ground the arms of their rebellion against God. Till then the enemies of God will be enemies of his people, and often bitter enemies. **To send** (or *cast* as margin of R. V.) **a sword upon the earth,** is a natural image; and this led to the use of the same term with peace, 'to cast peace upon the earth'; comp. Luke 12: 49, 'to (*cast*) send fire upon the earth.' When he says that he came to cast a sword, etc., to divide the nearest relatives, etc., we understand that he came for the purpose of doing a work which would inevitably lead to this; not that these evils were what he wished for. The language of v. 35 f. resembles that of Micah 7: 6, where the prophet is describing the perfidiousness and general wickedness which existed in the reign of Ahaz. It is not here quoted as a prophecy, but the same ideas and similar expressions are introduced, and describe a similar state of things. V. 35 brings up again the ideas of v. 21 above. *Plumptre* thinks the statements may have been suggested by occurrences among our Lord's followers. "Had Zebedee looked with displeasure on the calling of his two sons? . . . Were the brethren of the Lord, who as yet believed not, as the foes of a man's own household?" With v. 34 f. comp. Luke 12: 51-53, where like sentiments and expressions are found introduced on another occasion.

In such a state of division even in families, the true follower of Christ must not hesitate. Better to give up the nearest kindred (v. 37), take cross on shoulder (v. 38), and be content to lose life itself (v. 39), than to forsake Christ. The question whether one loves father or

mother more than Christ, is put to the test in any case in which the wishes of parents stand opposed to the known will of Christ. As to the duty of keeping all natural affections subordinate to our love for the Saviour, comp. on 8: 22; 19: 29. **Is not worthy of me.** On another occasion (Luke 14: 26), he uses still stronger expressions: 'If any man cometh unto me, and hateth not his father and mother . . . . he cannot be my disciple.' As to v. 38 f., see on 16: 24 f. where the same solemn truths are repeated in a different connection. The peculiar and striking expression of v. 39 was also repeated on two other occasions. (Luke 17: 33; John 12: 25.) As to our Lord's frequent repetition of striking sayings, see at the beginning of ch. 5. The apostles would readily understand the image of v. 38, since crucifixion was a common punishment for high crime (comp. on 16: 24), but they did not yet know that Jesus was to be crucified, and so this, like many other sayings of his, was not fully understood by them until later. The term **find** was obviously suggested by the contrast to **lose**; he who by yielding to persecution and failing to confess Christ has avoided the loss of his life (the natural life), shall lose his life (spiritual and eternal life); and he who has lost (margin Rev. Ver.) his natural life for Christ's sake, shall find life eternal (comp. on 16: 25). As to such uses of a word in two different senses in the same sentence, comp. on 8: 22.

IV. 40-42. THOSE WHO DO NOT PERSE-CUTE, BUT RECEIVE AND AID THEM, SHALL BE REWARDED. Having said so much about the unkind treatment his followers will often receive, Jesus returns to speak of those who will treat them kindly, and of the reward which such shall obtain. To receive them will be receiving him who sent them, yea, the Father who sent him. (Comp. a similar thought in 18: 5, and again in John 13: 20.) **Receiveth** is here meant especially of receiving into one's house (v. 14), which would not

41 He that receiveth a prophet in the name of a prophet shall receive a prophet's reward: and he that receiveth a righteous man in the name of a righteous man shall receive a righteous man's reward.

42 And whosoever shall give to drink unto one of these little ones a cup of cold *water* only in the name of a disciple, verily I say unto you, he shall in no wise lose his reward.

41 receiveth a prophet in the name of a prophet shall receive a prophet's reward; and he that receiveth a righteous man in the name of a righteous man shall

42 receive a righteous man's reward. And whosoever shall give to drink unto one of these little ones a cup of cold water only, in the name of a disciple, verily I say unto you, he shall in no wise lose his reward.

only be an act of respect to the Lord's servant, but would be helping him in his work. (Comp. 2 John 10 f.; 3 John 8.) But any other act by which one encourages and assists a servant of the Lord in his work, is of the same class, and shall in like manner be rewarded; even if it be merely giving a cup of cool water to one of the humblest disciples because he is a disciple, it shall assuredly have a reward. 'Receiveth' may perhaps also include the notion of listening to their message and accepting it as truth. He said to the Seventy (Luke 10: 16), 'He that heareth you, heareth me; and he that rejecteth you, rejecteth me, etc.' Yet the notion of hospitality and help appears at least to be the prominent one in the present discourse, as is shown by the concluding thought of the series. (v. 42.) **He that receiveth a prophet** (a person speaking by divine inspiration, see on 7: 22) **in the name of a prophet,** with reference to the name of a prophet, *i. e.*, out of regard for the fact that he bears the name of a prophet, or, as we should say, because he is a prophet; not on any other account, such as kindred, friendship, admiration of abilities, etc., but because he is a prophet; and not simply from the hope of reward, for that would not be doing it because he is a prophet. (Comp. Luke 14: 14.) **Shall receive a prophet's reward,** the Messianic, eternal reward. Since he treats kindly and helps the prophet because he is a prophet, he shall get in eternity the same sort of reward as if he had been himself an inspired teacher, because he has been helping an inspired teacher to do his work. So as to receiving any **righteous man.** Prophets and righteous men are in like manner united in 13: 17; 23: 29. We have among us no inspired teachers; but every member of a church, in so far as he encourages and assists his pastor, takes part in the pastor's labors, and shall in like proportion have the sort of eternal reward which pastors have; so in regard to missionaries, and all Christian workers. As to future rewards, comp. on 6: 1, 19. The sentiment of v. 42 is also given in Mark 9: 41, as repeated on a different occasion. **One of these little ones** refers to Christ's disciples as despised and persecuted (comp. on 18: 6 ff). To do the very smallest kindness to the very humblest disciple because he is a disciple, shall not fail of reward.

V. Ch. 11: 1. HAVING FINISHED INSTRUCTING THE TWELVE, JESUS RESUMES HIS OWN LABORS. With this concluding remark by the Evangelist, comp. 7: 28. **Departed thence.** It was somewhere in Galilee (comp. on 9: 35), but there is no intimation as to the precise locality. **To teach and preach in their cities.** He did not by any means send forth the Twelve in order to relieve himself, but immediately set out to continue his own labors. 'Preach' is the common word *kerusso*, explained on 4: 17. **In their cities,** means not the cities of the disciples, though they are the persons just mentioned, but of the people, the Jews (comp. 10: 18). This verse properly belongs to the preceding chapter, and should have been included in it. V. 2 introduces a new subject, and actually refers to a different period. As to the frequent awkwardness of our division into chapters, see on 9: 1. Matthew does not stop to say expressly that the Twelve also went forth as they were bidden, but leaves that to be taken for granted. Mark (6: 12 f.), and Luke (9: 6), state that they went forth, preaching repentance and working miraculous cures, as the Lord had directed. Nor does Matt. say anything of their return and report, which is mentioned by Mark (6: 30) and Luke (9: 10); see below on 14: 13.

HOMILETICAL AND PRACTICAL.

V. 16. LUTHER: "That's a slim affair, when sheep preach to wolves, lay down the law to them, and judge them! Better send lions. But this comes to pass, as Paul says (1 Cor. 2: 5), that your faith should not stand in the wisdom of men, but in the power of God."—Christian Prudence and Simplicity. (Sermons by JEREMY TAYLOR.)—Find examples of combined prudence and simplicity in the life of Paul and in the life of Jesus. GERHARD (Lange): "Have a serpent's eye and a dove's heart." CHRYS.: "These things have had an accomplishment, and men became prudent as serpents and simple as doves; not being of another nature, but of the same with us. Let not then any one account Christ's injunctions impracticable. For he, beyond all others, knows the nature of things; he knows that fierceness is not quenched by fierceness, but by gentleness." BRUCE: "Happy they who can be both; but if we cannot, let us at least be doves. The dove must come before the serpent in our esteem, and in the development of our character. If we invert this order, as too many do, and begin by being prudent to admiration, the higher virtue will not only be postponed, but sacrificed; the dove will be devoured by the serpent."—V. 19. CHRYS.: "It is no small consolation, that they are suffering these things both for Christ, and for the Gentiles' conviction." LANGE: "The dangers of care for oratorical finery in preaching. 1) It springs from anxiety, and *restrains* the spiritual life. 2) It manifests itself by excitement and excess, and *adulterates* the spiritual life. 3) It leads to weariness or self-seeking, and *destroys* the spiritual life."—Difference between inspiration, and the spiritual help which may now be expected.—V. 21. Christianity as awakening hatred and as promoting love.— V. 22. Unpopularity is not always alarming. It may be easier to persevere amid the world's frowns than its smiles.

V. 26. Two reasons why the Christian worker should not fear. 1) He need not be discouraged by reviling and assault, which even perfect innocence and perfect prudence did not escape. (v. 24 f.) 2) He may be encouraged by the assurance that the gospel must and will be made known. (v. 26 f.) HENRY: "There is no part of Christ's gospel that needs, upon any account, to be concealed; the whole counsel of God must be revealed. (Acts 20: 27.) In never so mixed a multitude, let it be plainly and fully delivered."—V. 28–31. Two reasons why we must do our duty notwithstanding opposition. 1) If through fear of man we shrink from duty, God will punish us. 2) If amid all opposition we persevere, God will care for us. — V. 32 f. Confession and denial. 1) We are all constantly doing one or the other. 2) There are many ways of confessing Christ, and many of denying him. 3) There are present benefits in confessing him, and present losses in denying him. 4) Life-long confession will bring eternal reward, life-long denial, eternal ruin. LUTHER: "What a great difference. 1) The confessors, we and Christ; 2) The place, earth and heaven; 3) The hearers, wretched men and God and the angels."

V. 34–36. When Christianity divides families and produces wars, this is not the fault of Christianity, but of human nature. LUTHER: "If our gospel were received in peace, it would not be the true gospel." HENRY: "They mistake the design of the gospel, who think their profession of it will secure them from, for it will certainly expose them to, trouble in this world. Christ has dealt fairly and faithfully with us in telling us the worst we can meet with in his service; and he would have us deal so with ourselves, in sitting down and counting the cost."—V. 37. Not that we should love kindred less, but Christ more.— V. 38. WILLIAM PENN: "No cross, no crown."—V. 38 f. We ought to be ready to die for Christ; *a fortiori*, we ought to be living for him. But "men are ready to argue for Christianity, ready to fight for it, even to die for it, anything rather than *live* for it."—The great paradox—losing by finding, finding by losing. Contradictions in theory may often be completely reconciled in practice.—V. 40–42. Helping the great workers. 1) We cannot all be prophets or apostles, missionaries, evangelists, eloquent preachers, etc. 2) But the greatest workers need help, and the lowliest can give it. 3) Thus sharing the blessed work, we shall share the blessed reward.

V. 24–42. THOMAS: "Encouragements to evangelical labor. 1) The cause for which the true evangelist suffers is most honorable, v. 22. 2) The example he has is most glorious, v. 24. 3) The success of the cause is most certain, v. 26 f. 4) The providential care of God over him is positively guaranteed, v. 29–31. 5) His reward will be most glorious at last, v. 32 f. 6) If actuated by the right spirit, he will find the greatest trials the greatest blessings, v. 38 f. 7) His interests are thoroughly identified with those of Christ, v. 40, 42."

CHAPTER XI.

A ND it came to pass, when Jesus had made an end of commanding his twelve disciples, he departed thence to teach and to preach in their cities.

2 Now when John had heard in the prison the works of Christ, he sent two of his disciples,

1 And it came to pass, when Jesus had made an end of commanding his twelve disciples, he departed thence to teach and preach in their cities.

2 Now when John heard in the prison the works of

Ch. 11: 2-19.—MESSAGE FROM JOHN THE BAPTIST, AND RESULTING DISCOURSE.

Having given a general account of our Lord's journeys about Galilee, with some important specimens of his teaching and his miracles (comp. on 8: 1), and having added an account of his sending out the Twelve, with much preparatory instruction, Matthew now advances to other topics. Before introducing examples of the Parables (ch. 13), he mentions a remarkable message from John the Baptist, and our Lord's discourse thereupon (11: 2-30), and then gives instances of avowed opposition to him on the part of the Pharisees. (ch. 12.) The paragraph noted above (11: 2-19) includes so much of the discourse occasioned by John's message as relates to John himself. This is also given, and with unusually little difference of phraseology, by Luke (7: 18-35); and from the connection of his narrative it appears probable (comp. Luke 7: 1, 11, 18), that this message from John was sent shortly after the delivery of the Sermon on the Mount. We have heretofore seen that the arrangement of Matthew, in chapters 5 to 13, is not chronological but topical, a course not uncommonly pursued by historians and biographers.

2 f. THE MESSAGE. **Now when John had heard in the prison.** As to John's early life and ministry, see on 3: 1 ff. It has been stated in 4: 12, that he was 'delivered up,' in the way familiar to Matthew's first readers, and afterwards described. (14: 3 ff.) He had now been confined in the Castle of Machaerus, east of the Dead Sea (see on 14: 3), for probably not less than twelve months, during which time Jesus has been pursuing his ministry in Galilee. John was allowed some intercourse with his followers (v. 2; Luke 7: 18), who brought him accounts of what was going on in the outer world. Yet this year of imprisonment must have been for him a dreary time. He had indeed been accustomed to comparative solitude for years 'in the deserts' (Luke 1: 80); but at that time life was before him with its high hopes, and he doubt-

less felt himself to be preparing for a great mission, the nature of which was gradually growing clearer to his mind. Then came some eighteen months of public labors, during which he was attended by vast crowds, and his ardent nature must have reveled in the high excitement of his work. And now he is shut up, he, a "son of the wilderness," in one of the deep, dark, and frightfully hot dungeons of Machaerus, deprived of fresh air and bodily exercise, of cheerful mental employment and opportunity to do good, and dependent for any future opportunities on the caprice of a weak king and a cruel woman. As Elijah sometimes got sadly out of heart, so John, who in many respects closely resembled him (see on 3: 4), would be likely to grow desponding, in this season of enforced idleness and uncertain danger. (Comp. the occasional depression of Moses also.) This state of things may account for the perplexity which John's message of enquiry seems to indicate. He **heard** from his disciples (Luke 7: 18), who would learn the report, circulated throughout the country (Luke 7: 17), and some of whom had at least on one occasion heard Jesus themselves. (Matt. 9: 14.)

The works of (*the*) **Christ.** Matthew's narrative usually employs our Lord's proper name, Jesus; but in introducing John's question whether Jesus was the Messiah, he implies the answer by calling him 'the Christ,' i. e., the Messiah. (Comp. on 16: 21 and on 1: 1.) For the importance of the article, 'the Christ,' see on 2: 4. His 'works' signify his general activity (which would include teaching), but especially his miracles. This seems to be suggested by the answer (v. 4 f.), which points to the things they 'hear and see,' to his miracles and the good tidings he preached. Likewise 'all these things' in Luke 7: 18, would naturally include not merely the two miracles which there immediately precede, but some account of his remarkable teachings, as in the Sermon on the Mount, which had just occurred. Even in John, who usually employs the term 'works'

3 And said unto him, Art thou he that should come, or do we look for another?

3 the Christ, he sent by his disciples, and said unto him, Art thou he that cometh, or look we for another?

---

to mean miracles (John 5: 36; 10: 38, etc.), in 9: 4, 'work the works of him that sent me,' can hardly be restricted to miraculous works. **Sent two of** (properly *by*) **his disciples** (comp. Rev. 1: 1), was in many manuscripts and versions altered into 'sent two of his disciples' (simply changing *dia* to *duo*), so as to be like Luke 7: 19. The true reading in Matt. 'by' or 'through' implies all the more strongly that John sent the message of enquiry for his own satisfaction. We still know from Luke (7: 19) that the number of messengers was two; they would be company for each other in the journey of some eighty miles, and might supplement and confirm each other's statements upon returning. (Comp. on 10: 5.) For the word **disciples**, see on 5: 1; as to the position of the disciples of John at this period, see on 9: 14.

Art thou he that should come, or *the coming (one)?* 'Thou' is expressed in the original and at the head of the sentence, so as to be strongly emphatic; and to this corresponds the emphatic position in the Greek of **another.** 'The coming (one)' had become a familiar designation of the Messiah (3: 11; 21: 9; 23: 39; John 6: 14; 11: 27; Heb. 10: 37), having probably been derived from Psa. 118: 26; Matt. 3: 1 f., etc. **Look we,** or more probably, 'are we to look,' as in Noyes and Darby, or 'shall we look' as in Tyndale and Geneva. The Greek subjunctive has in this word the same form as the indicative, and so the term is ambiguous. The Latin versions take it as indicative, and this probably influenced the Common Version, following Great Bible and Rheims. The Peshito is ambiguous, but the Memphitic is distinctly subjunctive. The majority of leading commentators take it as subjunctive (see Meyer, Weiss). The plural, 'are we to look,' means persons in general who cherished the Messianic hope. The form of John's question seems naturally to imply (Weiss) that he had regarded Jesus as the Messiah, and that he wished to learn whether he should still think so. The whole tone of the narrative, even more in Luke than Matthew, naturally suggests that John asked at least in part on his own account, to remove difficulties in his own mind. So already *Origen* (Cremer): "John's question was not

for his own sake alone, but also for the sake of those who were sent." Tertullian also three times intimates that John himself was in doubt whether Jesus was the Messiah. So among recent writers, Neander, Meyer, Bleek, Ewald, Keim, Reuss, Godet, Plumptre, Schaff, etc.

But many have thought it wholly inconsistent with John's position and previous testimony to suppose that he now felt personally the slightest doubt; and so they hold that he sent simply for the satisfaction of his disciples. So Chrys. (and his followers), with Cyril, Aug., and Jerome, followed by Luther, Calvin, and Beza, by Bengel, Maldonatus, and many others. Now, it is always desirable to accept the plain, straightforward meaning of a passage, unless there be insuperable difficulties in the way of so doing. Any one who did not know John's previous utterances would certainly understand Matt. and Luke as here implying that he sent to Jesus for his own sake as well as that of his disciples. It is very difficult to believe that John would send in his own name ('are we to look for another?') and Jesus send back the answer to him personally ('Go your way and tell John'), when it was all merely for effect upon the minds of John's followers. Theophyl. actually says that John "affects to inquire," and Euthym., "in pretence inquiring." The only reason for adopting such an interpretation is the supposition that John cannot have been in doubt after his known previous testimony. But while John knew himself to be the harbinger of Jesus (John 1: 33) and also to be the harbinger of the Messiah (John 3: 28), as indeed had been understood by his father Zachariah (Luke 1: 67-79), still it was conceivable that Jesus might *possibly* not be the Messiah. Among the various confused ideas which the Jews had developed from imperfectly understood Messianic prophecies, the notion was entertained by some that a *succession* of great personages would arise. Elijah, they generally believed, would return to life; some thought that Jeremiah also would return, and perhaps others of the great prophets; then there was 'the prophet' predicted in Deut. 18: 15, who was not universally identified with the Messiah. (See John 1: 20 f.; 7: 40 f.; Matt. 16: 14;

4 Jesus answered and said unto them, Go and show John again those things which ye do hear and see:
5 The blind receive their sight, and the lame walk, the lepers are cleansed, and the deaf hear, the dead are raised up, and the poor have the gospel preached to them.

4 And Jesus answered and said unto them, Go your way and tell John the things which ye do hear and 5 see: the blind receive their sight, and the lame walk, the lepers are cleansed, and the deaf hear, and the dead are raised up, and the poor have ¹ good tidings

---

1 Or, *the gospel.*

Luke 9: 19.) Some thought it very likely that these would come in quick succession, to herald with all the greater pomp the approach of the glorious King of Israel. Some such notion is certainly involved in the question, 'Art *thou* the coming (one), or are we to look for *another?*' Now, John would naturally share the current Jewish ideas (as the apostles did at that time), except so far as they were corrected by the special revelations given to him. These revelations, according to the whole history and manifest law of God's communications to men, extended only to the truths necessary for his own station and appointed work. There is therefore nothing surprising, and nothing derogatory to John, in the idea that amid the despondent and perplexed thoughts of a weary prisoner, he began sometimes to question whether Jesus was himself the Messiah, or only a second and greater forerunner. Points which later revelations have made clear enough to us, may easily have perplexed him. We need not suppose that he at any time wholly lost his persuasion that Jesus was the Messiah, but only that he became harassed by difficulties that he could not solve; and he shows great confidence in Jesus by referring the whole question to him. These 'works' which he heard of as wrought by Jesus were very remarkable. But how strange it was that the great worker, to whom he had himself borne testimony, did not come out publicly in the Messianic character, and have himself crowned, and reign as the Anointed King; how strange that, with the power of working such astonishing miracles, he should leave his devoted servant and herald to languish so long in this unjust imprisonment, cut off from the work in which he delighted. John was embarrassed, perplexed—perhaps (Köhler, Morison) impatient —he knew not what to think, and was weary of waiting—he would send and ask Jesus himself; and while the answer cleared up his own perplexity, as he hoped would be the case, and perhaps aroused Jesus to prompter action, it might at the same time help him in

overcoming (comp. John 3: 25-30) the obstinate hostility to Jesus which some of his disciples manifested (Comp. on 9: 14.)

4-6. THE ANSWER. **Jesus answered and said unto them.** It is of course implied that the disciples of John came and asked as directed, which Luke (7: 20) states in detail. Jesus must have been touched by this indication of perplexity and doubt on the part of his imprisoned forerunner. *Ewald:* "And surely at no moment of these years did the whole picture of all his fortunes in the many-colored past since his first meeting with the Baptist, come so freshly before his soul as now." **Go and shew John again,** carry back the message to John. 'Again' in the Com. Ver. is correct, but apt to mislead, as it might be understood to mean, 'show a second time.' **Those things which ye do hear and see,** the teachings and miracles which he proceeds to mention. Luke (7: 21) states that 'in that hour he cured many,' etc. Just before (Luke 7), Jesus had healed the centurion's servant and brought to life the son of the widow of Nain; but 'hear' seems most naturally to refer, not to the report they heard about his great miracles (Luke 7: 17), but to what they heard Jesus saying on that occasion—particularly to the fact that he was proclaiming good tidings to the poor. Jesus was not yet prepared to avow publicly, in so many words, his Messiahship (comp. on 16: 13 ff.); and John ought to be, and we may suppose was, satisfied with the evidence furnished by his working such miracles, and bringing such good tidings to the poor, as were specially predicted in connection with the Messiah.

The blind, the lame, etc. (v. 5.) The Greek has here no articles, which is appropriate and expressive, but cannot be imitated in the English idiom without awkwardness, though Davidson and Darby so translate—'blind see again and lame walk' etc., (comp. 10: 8). 'And' before **dead,** is the best supported reading; it was probably omitted in order (Weiss) to have three parallel clauses. In Isa. 35: 5 f. we read, "Then the eyes of the

6 And blessed is *he*, whosoever shall not be offended in me. | 6 preached to them. And blessed is he, whosoever

blind shall be opened, and the ears of the deaf shall be unstopped; then shall the lame man leap as an hart, and the tongue of the dumb sing." (Rev. Ver.) Here was then a literal fulfillment of a prophecy which referred also to the spiritual healing Jesus came to accomplish. In addition to the things thus predicted, Jesus was cleansing lepers, yea, and raising dead persons. The message of John came shortly after Jesus had raised to life the son of the widow at Nain (Luke 7: 11-18); and the raising of Jairus' daughter may have been, as the Harmonists think, some time earlier. Only a few specimens of our Lord's miracles are described, and it may well be that other cases of raising the dead occurred, but were not recorded. **The poor have the gospel** (good tidings) **preached to them**, doubtless refers to Isa. 61: 1, where Messiah is described as commissioned to "bring good tidings to the lowly." This last word in the Hebrew signifies those who are oppressed and afflicted, and bear it with meekness—persons lowly in condition and in spirit. For all such Messiah had good tidings (comp. on 5: 3). The Sept. renders by 'poor,' and that word is retained, as sufficiently expressing the force of the Hebrew, both in this passage of Matt. and Luke, and in Luke 4: 18. For the Greek word rendered 'have good tidings preached to them,' see on 4: 17. It here means more than what we express by "preach the gospel," signifying more generally the tidings of blessings to be enjoyed by them through Messiah's reign. The masses of mankind, poor and ignorant and suffering, received little attention from the heathen philosophers or from the Jewish rabbis. The latter often spoke of them with the greatest contempt, literally: "But this crowd (rabble), who know not the law, are accursed" (John 7: 49); and they delighted to stigmatize them as "country folks," ancient culture being almost entirely confined to cities. It was thus the more remarkable that Jesus brought tidings of good to the poor, to the suffering, despised, and lowly.

This appeal to his 'works,' as testifying in his behalf, was repeatedly made by our Lord towards the close of his ministry (John 10: 38; 14: 11; 15: 24); and indeed had already been made, at a period probably earlier than this message

of John the Baptist. (John 5: 36.) These miracles and good tidings for the lowly, showing that Jesus of Nazareth was the predicted Messiah, still stand as an evidence of Christianity. The Emperor Julian (Wet.) says scornfully, that "Jesus wrought nothing worthy of report, unless somebody thinks that to heal the lame and blind, and to relieve demoniacs, in the villages of Bethsaida and Bethany, were among the greatest works." **And blessed** (*happy*, same word as in 5: 3 ff.) **is he, whosoever shall not be offended** (*find no occasion of stumbling*) **in me.** See the same image in Isa. 8: 14. For the word meaning 'to be made to stumble,' or 'to find occasion of stumbling,' see on 5: 29; it has here the second meaning there given—whoever does not find in me an obstacle to believing, and hence reject me. Jesus was doing and saying things predicted of Messiah. But the Jews stumbled at his failure to do various other things which they expected in Messiah, and so most of them rejected him. (Comp. 13: 57; 26: 31.) John was now perplexed by the same things; and Jesus declares, 'Happy is he who shall not stumble at me.' The form of expression delicately suggests a warning, that he who does thus stumble will be anything else than happy.—This saying is clearly a part of what they were to report to John, and this best accords with the idea that the reply was meant for John's own benefit also, and not merely for his disciples. Were John's perplexities and doubts relieved by the answer sent? We are not told, but circumstances suggest that they were (Keim). John's disciples, after his death, went and told Jesus (14: 12); and subsequently we find Jesus speaking of John in a tone of high commendation (17: 12; 21: 25, 32), as indeed he proceeds to do on the present occasion, thereby showing his confidence that John is right at heart.

7-15. Testimony of Jesus to His Forerunner. John had repeatedly borne testimony to Jesus (John 1: 15, 26 f., 29-34, 35 f.; 3: 26-30), and now when he is cut off from usefulness by imprisonment, Jesus bears testimony to him. John's disciples are sufficiently devoted to him; so Jesus speaks this commendation when they are out of hearing, for the benefit of the people at large. This was grateful to

7 And as they departed, Jesus began to say unto the multitudes concerning John, What went ye out into the wilderness to see? A reed shaken with the wind?
8 But what went ye out for to see? A man clothed in soft raiment? behold, they that wear soft *clothing* are in kings' houses.
9 But what went ye out for to see? A prophet? yea, I say unto you, and more than a prophet.
10 For this is *he*, of whom it is written, Behold, I send my messenger before thy face, which shall prepare thy way before thee.

7 shall find none occasion of stumbling in me. And as these went their way, Jesus began to say unto the multitudes concerning John, What went ye out into the wilderness to behold? a reed shaken with the
8 wind? But what went ye out for to see? a man clothed in soft *raiment?* Behold, they that wear
9 soft *raiment* are in kings' houses. [1] But wherefore went ye out? to see a prophet? Yea, I say unto you,
10 and much more than a prophet. This is he, of whom it is written,
Behold, I send my messenger before thy face,
Who shall prepare thy way before thee.

---

1 Many ancient authorities read, *But what went ye out to see ? a prophet ?*

---

the people, among whom John was highly esteemed. (21 : 26.) **Began to say.** While the messengers were going, Jesus began the discourse which continued after they had disappeared. **Unto the multitudes** (*crowds,* so also Luke 7 : 24), see on 5 : 1. **Into the wilderness,** see on 3 : 1. **To see,** to behold, look at, as a spectacle; the word explained on 6 : 1. It seems to be implied that they went too much as if to look at a sort of show. (In v. 8 f. it is 'to see,' the common and simple word.) Doubtless those who went out to see and hear John were much influenced by curiosity. But what was the object of this curious gazing? Was it **a reed shaken with the wind?** Some understand Jesus to be asking whether they went merely to see an ordinary, natural object. But the phrase shaken, or 'tossed by the wind,' and the use of the singular, 'a reed,' much more naturally suggests that this is a symbol of fickleness. They did not go out to see a fickle doubter, and they must not think he is really a fickle doubter now. The perplexities and difficulties indicated by his message were not of the sort due to inconstancy, or to any weakness of character. Nor was it (comp. on 3 : 4) to see a man in **soft raiment,** *elegant clothing,*[1] such as courtiers wore; John had refused to play courtier, as all the people knew, and had gone to prison for it. We learn from Jewish writers (Jost, in Plumptre) that in the early days of Herod the Great, some Scribes who attached themselves to him, laid aside their usual plain dress, and wore the gorgeous raiment of courtiers. But John was no weakling, no self-seeker.

These introductory questions lead up to the great question, which, in the correct text,[2] has a slightly altered form. **What went ye out for to see,** etc.—Rev. Ver, *But wherefore went ye out? to see a prophet?* We learn from 21 : 26, that the masses of the people universally regarded John as a prophet; and the fact that there had been no prophet for so many weary centuries invested him with a heightened interest. Jesus says he was indeed a prophet, and something exceedingly **more than a prophet** (the word rendered 'more' is neuter gender; comp. 12: 6, 41). He was indeed an inspired man who came to speak for God (see on 7: 22), like the prophets of earlier days. He was also something more than a prophet, for he was the fulfillment of prophecy (v. 10), and he had a unique and singularly dignified position, as the immediate forerunner of Messiah, ushering in his glorious reign. *Euthym.:* "The heralds that march near the king are greater than the others. . . . And John not merely saw the predicted one, but also baptized him." *Morison:* "He not only said, *He will come:* he said, *He has come; and there he is."* Our Lord was here in fact exalting his own mission by exalting that of John. The people should hearken to him, to whom this more than prophet had testified.

10. [3]**This is he of whom it is written,** *has been written,* and now stands on record (see on 2: 5). The quotation is from Mal. 3: 1, and the literal rendering of the Hebrew is, "Behold I send my messenger, and he shall prepare the way before my face." There Jehovah speaks as if coming himself, namely,

---

1 'Raiment,' though implied, is not expressed in the earliest authorities, and was probably added from Luke 7: 25; so it is here properly placed in italics by Rev. Ver.

2 This as given in B. א Z., and others, would be easily altered to make it like v. 7 f. and Luke 7: 26.

3 'For' of the common Greek text is wanting in several of the earliest authorities. We can easily explain its insertion, but not its omission, for it expresses the real argumentative relation between the sentences. So we conclude that it was not originally in the text. In many such cases, the better we like a particular reading, the more certainly it is to be regarded as a later insertion.

11 Verily I say unto you, Among them that are born of women there hath not risen a greater than John the Baptist: notwithstanding, he that is least in the kingdom of heaven is greater than he.

11 Verily I say unto you, Among them that are born of women there hath not arisen a greater than John the Baptist: yet he that is [1] but little in the kingdom

---

1 Gr, *lesser.*

---

in the coming of Messiah. In the application here made, Jehovah addresses Messiah, as if sending a messenger before him. This is only bringing out more clearly an idea really involved in the prophecy, as the N. T. writers have in various cases done, with an obvious propriety (comp. on 2: 6). The prophecy is quoted with exactly the same variation of expression, in Luke 7: 27, and in Mark 1: 2, and the same variation is implied in the evident reference to this passage in Luke 1: 76. The most natural explanation is that in this form it was commonly given in the oral apostolical teaching. The supposition of quotation by the Evangelist from an oral Aramaic synagogue version (Toy), seems to have no clear and adequate ground, here or elsewhere. As to the image involved, that of sending forward a messenger to prepare the way for a journey, see on 3: 3, where a similar passage is quoted from Isaiah.

11. Verily I say unto you, see on 5: 18. **Among those . . born of women,** comp. Job 14: 1; Gal. 4: 4. **A greater.** Luke (7: 28) has it 'a greater prophet.' The expression obviously refers principally to his exalted position, and also, perhaps, to his faithful devotion to its duties. No person had occupied a position of higher privilege than John the Baptist, involving clearer views of truth, or greater honor in the sight of God. **Nevertheless he that is least,** literally, *less,* viz., than all others (comp. Mark 4: 31), and so equivalent to 'he that is least.' Similar expressions are found in 18: 1; Luke 22: 24, etc., and in the Sept. of Judg. 6: 15, where Gideon says, "I am the least in my father's house." The Old Latin and Vulg. (as well as the Memphitic) render 'less,' and so all the Eng. Ver. before that of King James, which may here (as so often) have followed Beza, who renders 'least.' The Peshito also translates as if it were a superlative. The rendering of the Rev. Ver. 'but little,' does not commend itself as particularly good, for the Greek either means 'least' or 'less'; the occasional rendering of the comparative, somewhat little, rather little, etc., seems to be here quite out of

place. Chrys. understands that it means Jesus, as 'less' than John, "less in age, and, according to the opinion of the multitude," which is excessively far-fetched. To refer the **kingdom of heaven** here to the future life, as many do, is entirely unsuitable. We must understand that the lowest subject of the Messianic reign is in a position of greater privilege and dignity (comp. Zech. 12: 8) than the great forerunner; or, else, perhaps (Calvin), that the lowest of all the *teachers* instructed by the Messiah himself was superior as a teacher to the forerunner.

In any case this expression implies that John was not in the kingdom of heaven. The inference is often drawn that he belonged entirely to the Old Testament Dispensation. It is frequently asserted, and by many taken for granted, that the kingdom of heaven began on the Day of Pentecost following our Lord's Ascension, and so John had no connection with it except to predict its approach. But if this be so, where did the ministry of Jesus himself belong, the early part of which ran parallel to that of John, and embodied the same announcement (4: 17; Mark 1: 15)? If John's teaching and baptizing are to be set off as essentially different in kind from Christian teaching and Christian baptism, these beginning only on the Day of Pentecost, then we have the strange contradiction that Christ himself, as a teacher and baptizer (John 3: 22; 4: 1 f.), did not belong to the Christian Dispensation. Moreover, in v. 12, and also in Luke 16: 16, our Lord speaks of the kingdom of heaven as already in actual existence, and counts John among the preachers of the kingdom of heaven, as distinct from those who merely predicted it. (Comp. Luke 17: 21; 10: 23 f.; Matt. 13: 16.) If some argue that John's baptism was not regarded by the apostles as Christian baptism, from the single and peculiar case of re-baptism in Acts 19: 1 ff., it may be answered that those persons were re-baptized because it was evident that when they previously received baptism (probably from some ignorant disciple of John), it had been without knowing what they were

12 And from the days of John the Baptist until now the kingdom of heaven[a] suffereth violence, and the violent take it by force.

12 of heaven is greater than he. And from the days of John the Baptist until now the kingdom of heaven suffereth violence, and men of violence take it by

---

a Or, is gotten by force, and they that thrust men,

---

about, without understanding the fundamental truths of the Messianic reign, as announced by John himself. As this isolated case can be accounted for in this way, and indeed in various other ways, it is quite unwarrantable to make it the proof of a radical distinction between Christian baptism and the baptism administered by John and by Christ himself.

How then are we to conceive of John's position? In some sense he belongs to the kingdom of Messiah, the Christian Dispensation, his work constituting its introductory stage; and yet his position is inferior in dignity and privilege to the least in that kingdom. His work may be compared to a landing-place in a stairway; the highest step of the lower flight, or the lowest step of the upper flight, or, whenever you choose so to regard it, higher than the highest of one, lower than the lowest of the other. Or (Chrys.), it may be compared to the hour between dawn and sunrise—part of the day, yet less light than the first moment after the sun is actually risen. The beginning of John's ministry was the dawn of the Messianic reign, whose light gradually increased throughout the ministry of Jesus; the Day of Pentecost was its sunrise, when it appeared in full-orbed beauty and brightness; its noontide glory is yet to come. In this passage, then, John's position is distinguished from that of one living when the New Dispensation should be fully established; while in other passages he is spoken of as himself belonging to that Dispensation, in its opening stage. His position was so peculiar, that it could be variously regarded, according to the point of view in each case.

12. This is connected especially with the former clause of v. 11. The importance of John is shown by a reference to the great excitement his ministry had produced among the people (comp. Josephus, "Ant.," 18, 5, 2), and which still continued, at the time when our Lord was speaking. **From the days of John the Baptist** means from the time when John was engaged in active labors, which closed with his imprisonment. These labors had probably continued about eighteen months, and from six to twelve months had elapsed since their close. **Until now** shows that the work in question was still going on, but without at all implying that it would now cease. The kingdom of heaven is here conceived of as not simply near, but in actual existence, and as having begun to exist with the beginning of John's ministry. (See on v. 11.) **The kingdom of heaven suffereth violence,** or, 'is taken by violence.' (Davidson, Darby.) The image employed appears to be not precisely that of storming a city (2 Macc. 14: 41), but that of invading and seizing a kingdom. Before the time of John many were expecting the establishment of the Messianic kingdom, but in general were quietly waiting, without any earnest efforts to prepare for it, and share its blessings. John's ministry awakened an eager expectation of its immediate appearance, and men were aroused to press into it, like invaders pressing into a country and taking possession. Our Lord described this state of things by the same striking image on a later occasion. (Luke 16 : 16.) It is appropriate and eminently desirable that both individuals and communities should become greatly aroused on the subject of religion, and be deeply in earnest about it, so as to resemble, in their pursuit of salvation, the resolution and irresistible force with which an invading army presses into a country. How it forces its way along—every obstacle is overcome, every stronghold is seized, every opposing host is broken and scattered—nothing can withstand its conquering advance. Of course the application of this is to spiritual energy, and it gives no warrant for violent bodily exercises, except in so far as these may sometimes naturally result from uncontrollable feelings of soul; but it does show the propriety of impassioned earnestness and indomitable resolution in the entrance upon, and pursuit of, a Christian life. (Comp. 7: 13; Luke 13: 24; Phil. 3: 12 ff., etc.) The period in question was the first of those seasons of widespread religious excitement which have repeatedly marked the progress of Christian history. Christianity was born in a great revival.—Weiss interprets v. 12 as said in the

13 For all the prophets and the law prophesied until John.

14 And if ye will receive *it*, this is Elias, which was for to come.

15 He that hath ears to hear, let him hear.

13 force. For all the prophets and the law prophesied

14 until John. And if ye are willing to receive [1] *it*, this

15 is Elijah, who is to come. He that hath ears [2] to

---

1 Or, *him*....2 Some ancient authorities omit *to hear*.

---

way of censure, viz., that John had introduced a hasty and stormy way of entering the kingdom of heaven, opposed to the quiet and gentle introduction of it in which Jesus was engaged. This is ingenious, but it ill suits the following connection, and the whole tone of our Lord's testimony to John.

13-15. This reference to Elijah is not given by Luke, who on the other hand makes at this point some remarks (Luke 7 : 29 f.) not made by Matthew. **For** gives a reason for the statement of v. 12. This great religious movement, men pressing with eagerness and violence into the kingdom of heaven, he has just declared to have existed from the days of John the Baptist; *for*, **until John,** until his time, the **prophets and the law** (see on 5 : 17; prophets here mentioned first, doubtless because prediction was a less prominent element of the law) **prophesied** of the Messianic reign; but this period of prophecy ended with the coming of the new Elijah, in the person of John, who was at once the last predicter of the kingdom of heaven, and the first preacher of it; and now the good news of the reign of Messiah is made known (Luke 16 : 16), and men are pressing into it with violence. *Athanasius:* "Up to John the law; from him the gospel." (Comp. on v. 12.) **And if ye will** (*are willing to*) **receive,** *i. e.*, most naturally 'to receive it,' possibly 'to receive him' (margin Rev. Ver. and Geneva). They might be slow to receive it, because it conflicted with the popular notion that Elijah in his own proper person would appear to anoint the Messiah (Justin Martyr, Trypho 8, 49); and because too, of John's present helpless captivity, which they might fancy God would not permit in the case of one sent by him on a great mission. **This is Elias**—he, and no other, the original being emphatic, as in 1 : 21

and elsewhere. As to reasons for giving the Old Test. form of the name, Elijah, rather than Elias, see on 1 : 2. **Which was for** (*that is*) **to come,** or 'that is going to come.' This was the expression used among the Jews concerning the expected coming of Elijah, and our Lord retains it, as the familiar phrase, though the coming had now taken place (so also in 17: 11). The prediction of Mal. 4: 5, " Behold, I will send you Elijah the prophet," etc., was generally understood by the Jews to mean that Elijah would come to life again, and many of the modern Jews have that expectation still. Jesus means that John had come "in the spirit and power of Elijah" (Luke 1 : 17), a similar man, and to a similar work; and this is all that the prophecy meant. (Comp. on 3 : 4; 17 : 10 ff.) John himself was asked (John 1 : 21) whether he was Elijah, and answered 'No'; but he was answering in the sense of their question—he was not Elijah come to life again. **He that hath ears [1] let him hear.** As Elijah was to be forerunner of the Messiah, and as John the forerunner of Jesus was Elijah, it followed that Jesus was the Messiah—if they had ears, and were willing to receive it. This peculiar phrase, 'he that hath ears,' etc., was repeatedly used by our Lord, especially after saying something which was important, and also likely through ignorance or prejudice not to be understood (comp. on 13 : 9, 43; 24 : 15); and it is still used in the last words he has spoken on the earth, the messages to the seven churches. (Rev. 2 : 7, 11, 17, 29; 3 : 6, 13, 22.) We can scarcely conceive how difficult it was for the Jews to accept the assertion that the prophecy of Elijah's coming was fulfilled in John the Baptist. And we have abundant need to fear lest we ourselves lack ears to hear, lack the spiritual perception and sympathy,

---

[1] 'To hear,' after 'ears,' should pretty certainly be omitted (as in Rev. Ver. marg.), following B D, 32, k ; as also in 13 : 9, following B ℵ L, and some copies of Old Latin; and in 13 : 43, following ℵ (first hand) B, some copies of Old Latin, and some of Vulgate. The fact seems clearly to be that Matt. in all three cases gives simply ' he that hath ears, let him hear,' while Mark (4 : 9, 23) and Luke (8 : 8; 14 : 35) give without variation ' he that hath ears to hear, let him hear '; and that Matthew's expression early began to be changed into the fuller form. (Comp. Rev. Ver. of 13 : 9, 43.) It is noteworthy that in all three cases B has the correct text, while its companions vary.

16 But whereunto shall I liken this generation? It is like unto children sitting in the markets, and calling unto their fellows,

17 And saying, We have piped unto you, and ye have not danced: we have mourned unto you, and ye have not lamented.

16 hear, let him hear. But whereunto shall I liken this generation? It is like unto children sitting in the marketplaces, that call unto their fellows, and say,

17 We piped unto you, and ye did not dance; we wailed,

the candor and willingness to follow truth, the readiness to let the Bible mean what it wishes to mean, which are necessary to a thorough understanding of Scripture.

16-19. BUT BOTH JOHN AND JESUS ARE REJECTED. The thought of this passage was naturally suggested by the reception which many had given to the great Forerunner, the new Elijah, and to Jesus himself. John was unsurpassed in the dignity of his position, the greatness of his work; he whom John heralded was greater still; yet both were rejected. They had different, even opposite, peculiarities and modes of life; but that willful and unreasonable generation rejected each of them, thus showing a determined and invincible opposition to the heavenly wisdom which both were seeking to inculcate, and which was justified and vindicated by its effects in all who received it.

16 f. But whereunto shall I liken this generation? Their conduct was so strange, in its inconsistent and willful opposition to the truth, that he was at a loss to find anything like it for an illustration. (Comp. Mark 4: 30; Luke 13: 18, 20; Lam. 2: 13; and the rabbis have a similar formula.) In saying 'this generation,' he does not mean all without exception, but refers to the general tone of public sentiment, and especially to the leading men, the Scribes and Pharisees who gave that tone. Luke (7: 29) informs us that of the persons present on that occasion the mass of the people and the publicans justified God, having received John's baptism; but the Pharisees and the lawyers rendered void as regarded themselves the counsels of God, not having been baptized by John. Our Lord was not yet prepared to make open discrimination among the Jews, and denounce the Scribes and Pharisees by name, as he did at a later period. (Chap 23.) **It is like unto children,** etc. There is a certain colloquial inexact-

ness in the expression, which ought not to occasion any difficulty. He does not mean that the men of this generation correspond distinctively to the children who speak, which would make John and himself answer to the parties complained of; but in general, the conduct of this generation corresponds to the case of children sitting in the market-place, some of them saying to others, etc. So in 13: 45, the kingdom of heaven is said to be like a merchant, etc., but it is not meant that the kingdom resembles the person, but that in a general way the two cases are similar. (So also in 18: 23; 20: 1.) The comparison in such cases is made somewhat loosely, and is to be understood according to the nature of the case. There is thus no need at all for the various artificial explanations by which some able expositors (as Meyer, Ewald, Keim, Weiss, Plumptre), try to work out the view that John and Jesus are the persons called to, and complained of, for not doing as the people wished. The simple and obvious application in the contrary direction is much more natural and appropriate.[1] **In the markets—** *marketplaces.* The word denotes a public square, or place of public resort in a town, such as the Greeks called Agora (the word here used), the Romans called forum, and we call place or square. In Oriental cities this place was just inside the gate. Here the citizens assembled, the judges sat, business was transacted, and markets were opened (Gen. 19: 1; Ruth 4: 1; Prov. 31: 23, etc.); and here, as a matter of course, loafers would lounge (Psa. 69: 12), and boys would gather to play. The children, *i. e.,* boys, are represented as imitating, in their play, the practice of their elders at merry-makings or funerals. **We have piped unto you,** the instrument intended somewhat resembling a flageolet. **We have mourned,** (or, *wailed*), *i. e.,* sang the funeral wail or dirge (Davidson and Noyes translate

---

[1] Some slight differences in the Greek text do not affect the substantial meaning. 'Who call .... and say' is beyond question the correct text. It is difficult to decide between 'their fellows' (*hetairois*) and 'the others' (*heterois*), like Luke 7: 32, 'one another.' The earliest authorities for the most part give *heterois,* but the other would be more easily changed into this by assimilation to Luke. The two words are pronounced exactly alike in Modern Greek, and probably were when our oldest copies were made. 'To you' is rightly omitted in the second clause.

18 For John came neither eating nor drinking, and they say, He hath a devil.
19 The Son of man came eating and drinking, and they say, Behold a man gluttonous and a winebibber, a friend of publicans and sinners. But wisdom is justified of her children.

18 and ye did not [1] mourn. For John came neither eating nor drinking, and they say, He hath a demon.
19 The Son of man came eating and drinking, and they say, Behold, a gluttonous man, and a winebibber, a friend of publicans and sinners! And wisdom [2] is justified by her [3] works.

---

1 Gr, *beat the breast*....2 Or, *was*....3 Many ancient authorities read, *children :* as in Luke vii. 35.

'sang a dirge'), such as hired mourners were accustomed to sing at a funeral. (Comp. on 9: 23.) **Lamented,** literally, 'beat yourselves,' beat the breast, as the publican smote his breast. (Luke 18: 13.) The boys had tried their comrades with notes of joy and with notes of grief, and met no response to either. *Stier :* "It cannot but be noted that the Lord, *nihil humani a se alienum putans* [deeming nothing human without interest to himself], as he took notice of the rending of mended garments (9: 16), and the domestic concerns of the children in their beds (Luke 11: 7), so also observes the children's play in the market place, and finds in everything the material for the analogies of his wise teaching." Who is not moved at the thought of the Saviour standing sometimes in the marketplace, with the busy throng around, and watching the boys at their play? This is the only place in the Bible (*Nicholson*) where any game of children is described.

18 f. Our Lord then applies the illustration. **For,** presents this as a proof of the previous statement. The case of this generation does resemble that of the children, *for* they treat John and Jesus exactly as the children's comrades treated them. **John came neither eating nor drinking,** *i. e.*, as other men do (Luke 7: 33, 'eating no bread nor drinking wine'); not sharing with men in general in their modes of life, but living apart and abstemiously. (Comp. on 3: 4.) **He hath a devil**—*demon.* See on 8: 28, 31. As one now would say, he is deranged. It is natural that such an expression should become common (John 7: 20; 8: 48), since demoniacal possessions were often found in conjunction with mental derangement, whether as causing it, or because persons were thereby rendered more suitable to be thus possessed. Demoniacs would sometimes go into a wild region, and live on such food as they could procure there (8: 28); to these the people compared John. Though "willing to rejoice for a sea-

son in his light," as "the lamp that burneth and shineth" (John 5: 35, Rev. Ver.), they were now rejecting his witness to Jesus and ridiculing his mode of life, saying, "He has a demon." On the other hand, Jesus lived among men, eating and drinking as they did. He was accustomed to drink wine, as was common, almost universal—those light and pure wines which abounded in that country, and which, taken in moderate quantity, and mixed with a double quantity of water according to custom, would stimulate about as much as our tea and coffee. He went to the houses of Pharisee and Publican, of scrupulous observers of the law and open transgressors of it, and shared their customary food and drink. And immediately they cried, **Behold a gluttonous man, and a wine-bibber!** The Greek word here used for man implies in such connections a certain contempt, as we sometimes use 'a person.' **A friend of publicans and sinners.** The emphasis is not on 'friend,' but, as the Greek order shows, separately on 'publicans' and 'sinners.' Because he ate pleasant food like others, and with no special abstemiousness, they called him a glutton. Because he sometimes drank wine as others did, he was a wine-bibber; one who drank habitually and to excess. Because he treated bad men with civility and kindness, earnestly seeking to do them good, he himself also was bad. (Comp. Luke 15: 1, 2, and see above on 9: 11.) So they talked. John was not enough like other people—a crazy sort of man. Jesus was too much like other people. Nothing could please them. **The Son of man,** see on 8: 20. **Publicans and sinners,** comp. on 5: 46.

Now, what shall be the consolation of those religious teachers who see that, do as they may, men will find fault with their conduct, and reject their message? That in which Jesus took comfort. **But wisdom is justified of her children.** '*Works*' is clearly the correct text here, 'children' in Luke 7: 35.[1]

---

1 'Works' in B (1st hand) ℵ, 124, Memphitic, the Peshito and Harklean Syriac, the Æthiopic, and some

codices of the Armenian; and Jerome and Ambrose say it so reads in some copies. Now, this might easily

Though the people in general rejected the true wisdom, yet she was justified, shown to be right, both in John's way of living and teaching and in that of Jesus, by her works—the general effects of the true wisdom in those who receive and practice it, and in particular those miraculous works which proved Jesus to be the Messiah. (v. 2, 4 f.) There is thus no great substantial difference between 'justified by her works,' as affecting those who receive her, and seen in them, and 'justified by all her children' (Luke 7: 35), recognized and appreciated by all of kindred spirit to her, all the truly wise. (Comp. the expression 'justified God' a little before, in Luke 7: 29.) The peculiarities of John and of Jesus were in each case appropriate and effective, producing such works as the truly wise must recognize to be the legitimate effects of wisdom. John's mode of life was suitable to the stern rebukes and warnings he came to proclaim (see on 3: 4); while Jesus moved freely among men, and conformed himself pleasantly to their way of living, as representing especially the kind invitations and joyful tidings of the gospel. Both methods were blamed by the people at large, but both were justified by their effects, and both were from God. And so as to the peculiarities of temperament, modes of life, and methods of working, on the part of religious teachers now. Every sort of preacher will be found fault with by the ungodly world; but every truly devout and wise preacher will be justified by the effects of his ministry.

HOMILETICAL AND PRACTICAL.

V. 2 f. The stern law that exercise is necessary to health, bodily, mental, and spiritual, enforces itself even in a case of involuntary idleness.—V. 2-6. Is Christianity divine? 1) Reasons for inquiring. (a) Christianity, as a power in the world, has to be accounted for. (b) Our own need. (c) The need of others. 2) Evidences. (a) The effects of Christianity are beneficent, to body and soul. (b) They corre-

spond to the O. T. predictions as to its character and results. 3) Occasions of stumbling. (a) Slow progress of Christianity in the world. (b) Its highest benefits are not seen and temporal, but spiritual and eternal. (c) Many faithful workers seem to fail, and are left to suffer (like John). Happy he who earnestly presses the inquiry, wisely appreciates the convincing evidences, and rises above all the obstacles. Comp. Peter (16: 16 f.), Martha (John 11: 27), Thomas (John 20: 28 f.).—V. 6. Stumbling at Jesus. CALVIN: "Every man builds for himself a heap of stumbling-stones, because men are malignantly anxious to keep aloof from Christ." PLUMPTRE: "How tenderly our Lord dealt with the impatience implied in John's question. A warning was needed, but it was given in the form of a beatitude which it was still open to him to claim and make his own."

V. 7-9. HENRY: "They who attend on the word will be called to an account, what their intentions and what their improvements were. We think when the sermon is done the care is over; no, then the greatest of the care begins."

V. 11. John the Baptist. 1) The dignity and importance of his work as a forerunner. 2) His transitional relation to the kingdom of heaven. 3) In what respects the humblest Christian now is more favored than John.— V. 11-15. John the Baptist. 1) Coming as the climax of prophecy, and the new Elijah. 2) More than a prophet, and unsurpassed among mankind, v. 9, 11. 3) Belonging to the Messianic reign, yet not enjoying its highest privileges, v. 11. 4) Awakening that Great Revival, in which Christianity was born, v. 12.—V. 14. Comparison of John and Elijah. 1) In outward circumstances and mode of life. 2) In temper and spirit. 3) In work. (a) Evils to be corrected; (b) opposition encountered; (c) good done.

V. 16 f. Those who reject Christianity are without excuse; for it sings joyous strains and mournful strains, presents a bright side to

be changed into 'children,' to conform to Luke. The transcriptional process of assimilating parallel passages, which so often exhibits itself, is here further betrayed by the fact that some cursives insert 'all' from Luke, and that א (alone) in Luke changes 'children' to 'works.' If we suppose 'children' to have been the original reading in both Gospels, it is very difficult to account for the change here into 'works.' We might

fancy that *apo*, 'from' her children, looked strange, and that 'works' was suggested by v. 2, and by the appeal in v. 4 f., but this would be a very poor explanation, while as good as any of the others that have been suggested. The change here to 'children' is one of the many early "Western" alterations, being found in D, Old Syriac, and Old Latin.

20 Then began he to upbraid the cities wherein most of his mighty works were done, because they repented not:

20 Then began he to upbraid the cities wherein most of his [1]mighty works were done, because they re-

---

1 Gr. *powers.*

---

win and a dark side to warn, calls to repentance and welcomes to faith, offers heaven and threatens hell — and they find fault still.— V. 18 f. We often see precisely the same spirit manifested now. Let a minister, or other active Christian, be grave and serious, and people will at once complain of him as sour or dull; let him be cheerful, and they will say, "Entirely too much levity." If he is careful about his affairs, they charge that he is worldly, too fond of money ; if he silently allows himself to be cheated, rather than seem to stickle for pecuniary interests, they say compassionately, "Very good sort of man, very—but doesn't know much about business —hasn't much common sense." And, alas! it still continues true that many will quite disregard the intrinsic value of the truths proclaimed, and will treat them with respect or neglect, according as they fancy or not the habits and manners of the preacher. HENRY : "It is some comfort to faithful ministers, when they see little success of their labors, that it is no new thing for the best preachers and best preaching in the world to come short of the desired end."—Christianity and social life. 1) In some respects antagonizing social usages. 2) In other respects conforming to social usages. 3) In both cases often misjudged and rejected. 4) In all cases justified by its fruits.

20 - 30. UPBRAIDING THE IMPENITENT CITIES, AND INVITING THE HEAVY LADEN. The remainder of the discourse given by Matthew as occasioned by the message from John the Baptist (11: 2), consists of two main divisions.—V. 20-24 is given also by Luke (10: 12-15) as spoken with reference to the mission of the Seventy. (Comp. Matt. 10 : 15.)— As to v. 25–30, see on v. 25. Some recent commentators coolly take for granted that Matt. has wrongly located a passage really belonging where it is given by Luke. But it is perfectly natural that a religious teacher, going from place to place, should repeat favorite thoughts. (Comp. at beginning of ch. 5.) The present passage is as appropriately connected in Matt. as in Luke.—V. 20. **Then** would naturally mean immedi-

ately or soon after what precedes, but is sometimes used quite generally. (See on 3 : 13.) The same is true of the stronger expression in v. 25, 'on that occasion,' 'at that season.' (Comp. on 12 : 1.) It is easy here to trace an internal connection. The thought of the unreasonable conduct of the people towards John and himself (v. 16-19) would naturally suggest the kindred fact that even the cities in which the greater part of his miracles occurred, were still refusing to repent. (v. 20-24.) (See further as to the connection on v. 25.) **Began** is perhaps nothing more than a touch of that circumstantiality of description for which the Hebrew style is remarkable. (Comp. on 5 : 2.) So probably in 16 : 22 : while in other cases we can see that 'begin' adds something to the sense ; as in 11 : 7; 16 : 21 ; 24 : 49; 26 : 22, 37, 74. **To upbraid,** rendered 'reproach' in 5 : 11 ; 27 : 44. This strong term, and the language of the following verses, shows that he felt not only pitying grief, but also indignation. It was not mere childish folly,—as some might perhaps have thought from v. 16,—it was a wicked and shameful thing, that they so acted. *Stier :* "Gracious as is the Son of man in his exhibition of himself as the friend of publicans and sinners (11: 19), he can also insist upon repentance, and threaten judgments upon the impenitent as severely as John himself; yea, more vigorously and severely than he, since he is himself the Judge." **Wherein most of his mighty works were done,** or 'occurred,' the word explained on 1 : 22; 5 : 18 ; 6 : 9, etc. **Mighty works,** or *miracles,* (see on 12 : 38), literally *powers,* works of power, and hence rendered by Com. Ver. 'mighty works.' But Tyndale and his followers here translated it 'miracles' (v. 20, 21, 23), and that word ought to be restored, as in Bible Un. Ver., and Noyes. **Repented,** see on 3 : 2. Our Lord's main object, in working his numerous and striking miracles, was to convince men of his divine mission, and thus induce them to repent, that they might become subjects of the Messianic reign. If they did not repent, they had witnessed his miracles in vain, yea, with aggravated guilt,

21 Woe unto thee, Chorazin! woe unto thee, Bethsaida! for if the mighty works, which were done in you, had been done in Tyre and Sidon, they would have repented long ago in sackcloth and ashes.

21 pented not. Woe unto thee, Chorazin! woe unto thee, Bethsaida! for if the [1]mighty works had been done in Tyre and Sidon which were done in you, they would have repented long ago in sackcloth and

---

1 Gr. *powers.*

---

so that they were more blameworthy than the most wicked heathen. *Bengel:* "Every hearer of the New Test. is either much happier (v. 11), or much more wretched than the men who lived before Christ's coming." 'Most of his miracles' may mean only a majority of those which occurred in that part of the country. We have no record of any miracles wrought at Chorazin or Bethsaida, though we read of many at Capernaum (see on v. 23). The great mass of the miracles are unnoticed except by some such general expression as this (comp. on 4 : 21; 8 : 16, and see John 20 : 30). That Matthew and Luke should record this saying without having described any miracles as wrought at Bethsaida or Chorazin, is really a proof (*Plumptre*) that the words are genuine, for they would not have been introduced into a pre-existing narrative without examining whether any miracles had been referred to those places.

21 f. Examples of the upbraiding. **Woe unto thee.** See in 23 : 13 ff. **Chorazin,** not mentioned elsewhere in New Test., save the similar passage in Luke 10 : 13. Eusebius and Jerome tell us that it was now deserted, and two Roman miles from Capernaum. If the latter be placed at Tel Hum, as is of late the almost universal opinion (see on 4 : 13), then there can be little doubt that Chorazin is the extensive ruin called Kerazeh, which is up among the hills, two miles from Tel Hum; and the Arabic name would be the singular form, corresponding to Chorazin, as Aramaic plural. So Wilson, Guérin, McGarvey. **Bethsaida** probably signifies ' house of fishing,' English fish-town, indicating that it began as a fishing-station. There seem to have been two places of that name on or near the Lake of Galilee. The well-known Bethsaida Julias, near to which the five thousand were fed, was on the northeastern side of the lake; in fact on the eastern bank of the River Jordan, some distance above its mouth (see on 14 : 13). The Bethsaida here and most frequently mentioned, the native place of Andrew and Peter and of Philip (John 1 : 44; 12 : 21), was in the land of Gennesaret (Mark 6 : 45, 53), on the northwestern side of the lake. (See on 14 : 34.) This fact seems to preclude the otherwise plausible suggestion of Dr. Thomson ("Land and Book"), that Bethsaida was originally on both sides of the Jordan, and that the eastern part, being (as we know) greatly favored by the tetrarch Philip, gradually drew everything away from the western part, which thus entirely disappeared. The question of its exact location depends on the extent of the land of Gennesaret, and may never be settled. But there is now little doubt that there were two towns of this name on opposite sides of the lake or the river—a thing very natural upon a lake so abounding in fish, and in districts seldom under the same rule. Observe that John 12 : 21, ' Bethsaida of Galilee,' seems clearly to indicate that there was another Bethsaida from which this needed to be distinguished. Before Reland suggested this idea (Palestina, A. D. 1714), the allusions to Bethsaida were a vexed question, and no doubt gave rise to many charges of hopeless "discrepancy" between the Gospels.

Tyre and Sidon were doubtless chosen because they lay close by, had long been famous for the splendid wickedness which so often marks commercial centres, and were intimately associated with the Baal worship which had wrought such evil in Israel. Their wickedness was often denounced by the prophets, Joel, Amos, Isaiah, Jeremiah, and particularly that of Tyre by Ezekiel, ch. 26–28. **Repented in sackcloth and ashes,** as the people of Nineveh actually did at the preaching of Jonah. (Jonah 3 : 5 ff.) The sackcloth so often mentioned in Scripture was roughly woven from the short hair of camels, cattle, etc., and was worn as an expression of great grief—sometimes instead of the ordinary garments (Jonah 3 : 6), oftener under them, next to the flesh (2 Kings 6 : 30), and loosely girt around the waist. (2 Sam. 3 : 31; Joel 1 : 8.) Sometimes the person spread it under him and sat on it (Isa. 58 : 5), or lay on it at night. (1 Kings 21 : 27.) (As to the similar coarse garments of hair, habitually worn by Elijah and some other prophets, see on 3 : 4.) On occasions of extraordinary mourning they often added ashes, which were sometimes put on the head

22 But I say unto you, It shall be more tolerable for Tyre and Sidon at the day of judgment, than for you.

23 And thou, Capernaum, which art exalted unto heaven, shalt be brought down to hell: for if the mighty works, which have been done in thee, had been done in Sodom, it would have remained until this day.

22 ashes. Howbeit I say unto you, it shall be more tolerable for Tyre and Sidon in the day of judgment, 23 than for you. And thou, Capernaum, shalt thou be exalted unto heaven? thou shalt [1] go down unto Hades: for if the [2] mighty works had been done in Sodom which were done in thee, it would have re-

---

1 Many ancient authorities read, *be brought down....* 2 Gr. *powers.*

(2 Sam. 13 : 19; Lam. 2 : 10), and at other times the mourner sat in ashes (Jonah 3 : 6), lay in them (Esther 4 : 3), even wallowed himself in them. (Jer. 6 : 26; Mic. 1 : 10.) Accordingly Job says (42 : 6), "I abhor myself and repent in dust and ashes," and Daniel prayed long (9 : 3), "with fasting and sackcloth and ashes." (Comp. above on 6 : 16.) It should be remarked that these and various other modes of manifesting grief among the Israelites (such as rending the garments, tearing the hair, etc.), were not a matter of divine appointment, but were natural to the impassioned Oriental character, and are still customary among Eastern nations.

22. But I say unto you. The connecting word rendered 'but' or 'nevertheless' (Tyndale and followers) seems to imply some such idea as this: "It is true that Tyre and Sidon did not have the opportunity of witnessing these miracles, and you may thus regard yourselves as peculiarly favored; but it shall be more tolerable even for them in the day of judgment than for you; therefore be not proud of your privilege, but tremble at your responsibility and guilt." The words **Tyre and Sidon** are so placed in the Greek as to be emphatic. The 'woe' denounced against Chorazin and Bethsaida seems to combine the ideas of temporal calamity to the cities, and future punishment to individuals, as in 3 : 10-12; but v. 22 seems to show (*Godet*) that the latter idea is the prevailing one. **Day of judgment.** This phrase appears in Matt. 10 : 15; 11 : 22, 24; 12 : 36; 2 Pet. 2 : 9; 3 : 7; 1 John 4 : 17, and comp. Acts 17 : 31; Jude 6. It is also called the day of God, of the Lord, of Christ, the last day, the day of wrath, that day (7 : 22; 1 Thess. 5 : 4), and (simply) the day (Heb. 10 : 25), also the judgment (12 : 41 f.). He who here foretells the decisions of the day of judgment will himself be the King and Judge. (7 : 22; 25 : 34.)

This declaration of Jesus was no doubt startling to the Jews, accustomed to think themselves safe for eternity because they were Abraham's descendants, and to look down with contempt upon all Gentiles. And to us, in general, there is here brought out the great truth that men's lot in the world to come will have degrees proportioned to their advantages in this world. (Comp. on 12 : 41; 23 : 13, and consult Luke 12 : 47 f.) This truth throws some rays of light athwart the dark, sad question of the fate of the heathen. Men will be judged and punished according to their opportunities of knowing truth and duty. The heathen will not be condemned for rejecting Jesus if they had no opportunity to know of him; but only for disregarding their own conscience (Rom. 2 : 14-16), the light of external nature (Rom. 1 : 20 ff.), and any true religious ideas which may in whatsoever way have reached them. On the other hand, those who know of Jesus, and live surrounded by Christian influences, and yet will not repent, incur an unspeakable aggravation of guilt and punishment. But the expression 'more tolerable,' or more endurable, easier to bear, is general and indefinite, and does not warrant any attempt to determine precise degrees of punishment.

23 f. The same thing is here said, and in yet stronger terms, of Capernaum, which was a more prosperous city than Chorazin or Bethsaida, and more favored with the Saviour's residence, miracles, and teaching. *Stier:* "To the two cities, two others are first opposed; and then one city to the one." **Capernaum,** see on 4 : 13. Numerous miracles (Plumptre) have been described as occurring at Capernaum (besides the allusion in Luke 4 : 23): the nobleman's son (John 4 : 46-54); the demoniac in the synagogue (Mark 1 : 23-28); with Peter's wife's mother, and mention of a multitude of other healings (8 : 14-17); the paralytic borne by four (9 : 2-8); Jairus' daughter and the woman with the issue of blood, together with the two blind men and the dumb demoniac (9 : 18-33); and the centurion's servant. (8 : 5-13.) **Which art, etc.,** rather, *Shalt thou be exalted unto heaven? thou shalt go down unto Hades.*[1] In the ques-

---

[1] 'Shalt thou be exalted' is the reading of B א C D L (which represent all three pre-Syrian types of text), and most of the early versions. It could easily change, by a slight alteration of two Greek words, into 'that

24 But I say unto you, That it shall be more tolerable for the land of Sodom in the day of judgment, than for thee.

24 mained until this day. Howbeit I say unto you, that it shall be more tolerable for the land of Sodom in the day of judgment, than for thee.

tion a Greek particle is used which implies that the answer must be negative. Capernaum, already prosperous, was cherishing, like Babylon (Isa. 14: 13), arrogant hopes of unlimited prosperity in future. But this expectation is delusive. The result, as in the case of Babylon (Isa. 14: 15), will on the contrary be utter destruction, as the penalty of privileges abused. The contrasted expressions 'exalted to heaven' and 'brought down to Hades' seem here to indicate the temporal prosperity and destruction of the city, as they do in the passage of Isaiah from which the imagery is derived. This destruction might have been obviated. Capernaum might have continued to exist and prosper if it had listened to the miracle-working Teacher, and repented, as even the wicked Sodom would have done. We might not be able to decide whether v. 23 indicated, besides temporal destruction of the city, the future punishment of individuals; but this thought is brought out clearly in v. 24.

Hell. The Greek word *Hades*, which etymologically means 'the unseen (land),' 'the invisible (world),' is in accordance with its classical use, and with that of the Heb. *Sheol*, employed in Sept. and New Test. to denote the receptacle of departed spirits, without reference to differences of condition between good and bad. It was conceived of as far under the ground, and so 'brought down to Sheol' (*Hades*) was contrasted with 'exalted to heaven.' (Comp. Job 11: 8; Ps. 139: 8; Amos 9: 2; Rom. 10: 6, 7.) Some have proposed to render it 'the underworld' (Bible

Un. Ver., Noyes), which, though inadequate, is perhaps the best *translation* our language now affords. The word 'hell' formerly translated Sheol and Hades, for it originally signified (Skeat), a concealed or hidden (place.) But it has come to be associated so exclusively with the idea of torment, that Rev. Ver. properly uses it only to translate Gehenna (see on 5: 22), and borrows Hades whenever that term occurs in the New Test. (So Darby, Davidson.) In like manner the Heb. Sheol, substantially equivalent to Hades, is borrowed by Rev. Ver. in many passages of Old. Test., and ought by all means (as by Amer. Revisers,) to have been used everywhere, instead of sometimes retaining 'grave' and 'hell,' which are both misleading. Hades is used in some passages of the New Test. where the connection does not suggest any idea either of happiness or misery—it is simply the abode of the departed (Acts 2: 27, 31; Rev. 1: 18); one passage has 'in Hades, being in torment.' (Luke 16: 23.) It is also employed in 16: 18 (see below), in 1 Cor. 15: 55 (common Greek text, but the correct reading is 'death' in both clauses); and in Rev. 6: 8; 20: 13 f. In 2 Pet. 2: 4, still another Greek word is used, derived from *Tartarus*, and signifying, like Gehenna, the place of torment.

24. Sodom was a still more conspicuous example than Tyre and Sidon, of wickedness and punishment. All the world knows how it was suddenly and completely destroyed. Its indescribable abominations and its terrible doom have always thrilled men with horror

was exalted'; and the former being an unexpected turn of expression, the latter is likely to have been preferred by ordinary copyists, while really the sharp and startling interrogation is much after the manner of the Great Teacher. Thus both intrinsic and transcriptional probability concur with the leading documents in supporting the former reading. The case is substantially the same in Luke 10: 15.—Whether the second clause shall read 'go down' or 'be brought down,' is a difficult question. The external evidence for the former comprises only the "Western" documents and B. In Luke 10: 15, it has only part of the usual "Western" group with B. Now the Rev. Test. concludes that this reading is right in Matthew and wrong in Luke, which would account for the phenomena thus far stated; while W H. as usual follow B,

and read 'go down' in both passages. But the imagery is evidently drawn from Isa. 14: 13-15 (see W H, Appendix), which reads 'go down,' without known variation. It is then a very natural supposition that the "Western" documents, which make so many arbitrary changes, have altered the text of Matthew and some of them that of Luke, into accordance with the Sept., a very common species of alteration. This view would doubtless be at once accepted by every one, were it not for the support of B. But W H. admit that B has some merely "Western" readings in the Epistles of Paul, and internal evidence is believed to show that the same is true in the Gospels. If this be so, the reading 'go down' should probably be rejected both in Matthew and in Luke, as a "Western" alteration. Internal evidence is in this case not clear on either side.

25 At that time Jesus answered and said, I thank
thee, O Father, Lord of heaven and earth, because
thou hast hid these things from the wise and prudent,
and hast revealed them unto babes.

25　At that season Jesus answered and said, I [1]thank
thee, O Father, Lord of heaven and earth, that thou
didst hide these things from the wise and under-

1 Or, *praise.*

whenever it has been mentioned. And yet
Sodom would have repented, and remained
through two thousand years till our Saviour's
day, had its people seen the miracles which
took place in Capernaum. (Comp. Ezek. 16:
48.) Is this a mere hyperbole, like the precept to turn the other cheek, or to go two
miles with the impressing officer? We are
hardly warranted in saying so. If then one
should ask why the messenger Jehovah, who
stayed behind with Abraham, did not go with
the two angels to Sodom, work miracles, teach
repentance, and save it from destruction, we
may see two things to reply. (1) We may
answer as Paul does in Rom. 9: 18–20, that
God is sovereign, doing what he pleases, and
always doing right. (2) We may observe
that the divine plan required that the permanent appearance of the Son of God should take
place only among the Jews, and only "when
the fulness of time was come" (Gal. 4:4), and
this divine plan, whether we can see it or
not, was doubtless best for total humanity,
and for the moral government of the universe. When the time came, many of the
Jews had been hardened by disregarding previous divine influences, so that they were
slower to believe Christ, with all his mighty
miracles, than wicked heathen cities would
have been. (Comp. John 1: 11–13.) **The
land of Sodom,** the district belonging to the
city, and not simply the city itself. (Comp.
4: 15; Acts 7: 11.) **I say unto you. . . .
than for thee.** In v. 22, each clause has the
plural, which must then refer to the people
of the two cities; therefore the opening plural
here probably refers to the people of Capernaum, and not generally to the hearers of the
discourse. If we suppose the discourse to

have been delivered at Capernaum or in the
plain of Gennesaret—which is probable, but
the point cannot be determined—then the
hearers were mainly people of those three
cities, and that would account for the ambiguity of the expression. 'Thee' of course
means Capernaum, but with reference to
the eternal destiny of its individual inhabitants. For **but** (*howbeit*), **more tolerable,** and **day of judgment,** see on v. 22.
Stier: "We read of no enmity or persecution to which he was subjected in Capernaum;
but the careless reception of his word and
works was yet worse, and more condemnable
than any eruption of malice would have
been; it bespoke that slothful, dead, impas-
sive indifference, for which nothing more
could be done."

25 f. The remaining division of the discourse given by Matthew as occasioned by the
message from John (comp. on v. 2 and v. 20),
viz., v. 25-30, consists of two distinct portions.
V. 25-27 is also given by Luke (10:21 f.), as
spoken immediately after the return of the
Seventy: v. 28-30 is found in Matt. only, but
is closely connected with the end of v. 27.

At that time, 'on that occasion'[1] (comp.
12: 1; 14: 1). This answers to 'then' in v.
20, and connects all with the message from
John the Baptist. (11:2.) Our Lord has been
speaking of the unreasonable and determined
rejection of both John and himself by the
Jews (v. 16-19), and the impenitence of even
the cities in which most of his miracles occurred. (v. 20-24.) Yet these Jews, especially the
religious teachers and other leading men,
were wise and intelligent, well acquainted
with many aspects of religious truth. It
seemed strange that they should fail to com-

[1] The word *kairos* is not adequately translated by
'time,' for it denotes the exact time, the fixed time, the
appropriate time, occasion, opportunity, season. The
Com. Ver. renders 'season' in various places, including
21:41; 24: 45; Luke 13:1 (where the phrase is similar
to this of Matt.); Acts 1: 7; 24: 25; Gal. 6: 9; and
'opportunity' in Gal. 6:10; Heb. 11: 15. It should be
rendered 'season' in many others, including 12: 1; 13:
30; 14: 1; 21: 34, and 'opportunity' in several, as
Ephes. 5: 16; Col. 4: 5, 'buying up the opportunity'

(Rev. Ver. margin). But there are some cases in which
neither season nor opportunity, nor any other term
will suit the connection, and we have to lose the peculiar color of the Greek word and content ourselves
with rendering 'time,' as in 8: 29; 16: 3 (spurious); 26:
18; yet in every case the Greek word has its own distinctive meaning, though we cannot express it. The
Rev. Ver. has translated it by 'season' in many more
places than Com. Ver., but might have done so in several others, as 13: 30.

26 Even so, Father: for so it seemed good in thy sight.

26 standing, and didst reveal them unto babes: yea, Father, ¹for so it was well-pleasing in thy sight.

1 Or, *that.*

prehend and appreciate Christ's teachings, which were understood and received by the lowly and comparatively ignorant. This is the point to which he now addresses himself. He not only submits to this state of things, but he recognizes the propriety of it, and gives thanks for it. **Answered.** By a peculiar Heb. idiom, this word is often used in the Scriptures where there is no previous question, nor even any thing that has been said by another. Yet in probably all cases, we can see something in the foregoing connection to which the words are in some sense a response, or which formed the occasion for their being spoken (comp. 17: 4; 26: 63; 28: 5). In response to, or as suggested by, the sad truths just uttered (v. 16-19, v. 20-24), Jesus states the comforting thoughts which follow. **I thank thee.** The word originally signifies to make open or full confession or acknowledgment, as above in 3: 6; derivatively, like a corresponding Heb. word, and somewhat like our phrase "to make acknowledgments," it signifies to thank and hence to praise. (Rom. 14: 9.) The early and the recent Eng. versions are here about equally divided between praise and thank. The idea seems to be, " I fully recognize the propriety of thy course, I rejoice over it (consult Luke 10: 21), and praise thee for it." **O Father.** We find a similar direct address to his Father in John 11: 41; 12: 28; Luke 23: 34. The added form of address, **Lord of heaven and earth,** is impressively appropriate. It is the Sovereign of the universe that does this; who shall hesitate to acknowledge that what he does is right? Our Lord here sets us the example of employing in prayer such names of God, and phrases descriptive of him, as are appropriate to the special subject of the prayer, or of each particular portion of it — a thing manifestly proper and important, but often neglected. **That thou hast hid these things,** viz, the things taught by Jesus, as for example, the teachings of this discourse. **From the wise and prudent**—*understanding*, or 'intelligent.' 'Prudent' was a good translation in the Latin and early English versions (though Geneva gave 'men of understanding'), but in modern English it is too restricted in

meaning (see also in Acts 13: 7; 1 Cor. 1: 19). Bible Union Ver. and Noyes give 'discerning'; Davidson retains 'prudent.' The Greek has no article, 'from wise and intelligent (persons'), comp. on 9: 13; 11: 5. The expression is general, but here applies especially to the Scribes and Pharisees, and other religious teachers (comp. on 11: 16). The reference is of course to wisdom and intelligence misused, perverted through pride, separated from a child-like spirit. **Unto babes,** literally, *infants*, those who cannot speak (comp. Rom. 2: 20). This surely does not, as some imagine, designate simply the apostles, but the disciples of Jesus in general. Those who were not wise and intelligent, but had a child's simplicity and humble docility, understood and delighted in the teachings of Jesus (comp. Psa. 19: 7; 116: 6; John 7: 48 f.; 1 Cor. 1: 26 ff.). We often now witness the same state of things. Intelligent and reflecting men frequently overlook the simple beauty and perfect fitness of the plan of salvation, which is plain enough to those who are consciously and confessedly weak, and who gladly receive the Lord's teachings without cavil or difficulty. The gospel is so intensely practical that it can be understood at the outset only by persons willing to receive it, and will be thoroughly known only in proportion as it is truly loved. Here, as everywhere, we see the adaptation of the gospel to mankind. Not all men can become wise and intelligent, but all may, by the grace of God, become babes (comp. 1 Cor. 3: 18). The most useful Christians will be those who are 'wise and intelligent,' and are *also* 'babes'—intellectual and cultivated as possible, but childlike in spirit. And when the wise and intelligent fail to discover the significance and value of Christ's teachings, it is not the fault of their intelligence, but of this lack of a right spirit. Paul says 'not *many* wise after the flesh' (1 Cor. 1: 26); there have always been some. Observe that Jesus makes acknowledgment to the Father both for hiding these things from the one class, and for revealing them to the other. We may say that the latter is the chief subject of thanksgiving, yet the former is here the immediate occasion of

27 All things are delivered unto me of my Father: and no man knoweth the Son, but the Father; neither knoweth any man the Father, save the Son, and *he* to whomsoever the Son will reveal *him*.
28 Come unto me, all *ye* that labour and are heavy laden, and I will give you rest.

27 All things have been delivered unto me of my Father: and no one knoweth the Son, save the Father; neither doth any know the Father, save the Son, and he to
28 whomsoever the Son willeth to reveal *him*. Come unto me, all ye that labour and are heavy laden,

---

introducing the topic. Meyer justly says that *both* propositions form the ground of the thanksgiving and praise, being two sides of one great truth. So in Rom. 6: 17, which is often compared with this passage.

Our Lord enters into no explanations of God's sovereign dealings with men. He simply adds, **Even so** (or *yea*) **Father,**[1] **for so it seemed good** (or, *was well-pleasing*) **in thy sight.** (Comp. Eph. 1: 5, 9; Phil. 2: 13.) 'Well-pleasing,' as in 3: 17; Luke 2: 14 (Rev. text). If with some of the ablest expositors and Rev. Ver. margin, we render 'that' instead of 'for' (the original word meaning either according to the connection), the sense is substantially the same: 'Yea, Father, (I thank and praise thee) that so it was well-pleasing in thy sight.' Notice that this is not, as often quoted, an expression of mere resignation. Our Lord acknowledges the propriety of the sovereign Father's course, and praises him for it. Whatever pleases God ought to please us.

27. Having referred to the fact that not the wise and intelligent, but babes, understand his teachings, Jesus now presents himself as Teacher; declaring that only he can give a true knowledge of the Father (v. 27), and inviting all to come and learn from him (v. 28-30). **All things were delivered to me of** (*by*) **my Father.** At some past time, not specified, say when he entered upon his earthly mission—or, perhaps, when the covenant of redemption was formed in eternity (comp. on 3: 17)—all things were committed to him, viz., all that pertains to the instruction of men in religious truth. (Comp. John 16: 15.) It is another and distinct fact that all authority in heaven and earth was given to him as the Mediatorial King. (28: 18; 1 Cor. 15: 24 f.) Jesus is the authorized instructor in the knowledge of God. **No man** (*no one*) **knoweth.** The verb is compounded with a preposition, so as to mean 'knows fully,' as in 7: 16; and

so Davidson here translates. Luke in the similar passage (10: 22) has the uncompounded verb 'know.' On the one hand, no one really and thoroughly knows the Son except the Father, so that he must not be considered a mere ordinary human teacher, and so that we need not wonder if the wise and intelligent of earth fail, in their proudly speculative and merely theoretical study, to comprehend and appreciate his teachings. (Comp. 'reveal' here and in v. 25.) On the other hand, no one knows the Father, with that real knowledge which is eternal life (John 17: 3), except the Son, and **he to whomsoever the Son will** (*willeth to*) **reveal him.** In old English 'will reveal' expressed the idea, but that phrase has become a simple future, and the Greek must now be translated 'willeth to,' 'is pleased to,' or the like. (See especially John 7: 17; 1 Tim. 2: 4; 2 Pet. 3: 9.) All their wisdom and intelligence will not avail to gain a true knowledge of the Father, unless the Son chooses to reveal him to them. To him, then, let all come. (Comp. John 8: 19; 10: 15; 14: 9; 16: 15.) *Keim:* "This self-enclosed world of the Father and the Son opens itself to the lower world, to men, only by its own free act, because it wills to open itself and to admit to companionship whom it will." *Jerome:* "It is one thing to know by equality of nature, and another by the condescension of him who reveals." On another occasion also (Luke 10: 22) he adds to his thanksgiving that the Father had hid these things, etc., the same statement as here, 'All things were delivered,' etc.; which shows that the two ideas are very closely related. The Son approves the Father's will as to hiding and revealing, and the Father has authorized him to reveal or not, according to his will. (Weiss.) Meyer says that this statement (v. 27) "bears the stamp of superhuman consciousness." Only here (with Luke 10: 22) and in Mark 13: 32 (with perhaps Matt. 24: 30) do

---

[1] Here the Greek nominative with the article is clearly used in address, and equivalent to the vocative in v. 25. This was a common *colloquial* usage in Greek, seen often (Buttmann, p. 140) in Aristophanes and the Dialogues of Plato; and accordingly it appears frequently in Biblical Greek, which rests on a colloquial basis; important examples are John 20: 28; Heb. 1: 8.

29 Take my yoke upon you, and learn of me; for I | 29 and I will give you rest. Take my yoke upon you, and learn of me; for I am meek and lowly in heart:

the three first Gospels contain the expression 'the Son.' This whole passage (v. 25-30) has often been remarked upon as resembling the Gospel of John, and suggests to us that great mass of similar sayings of Jesus which only the Fourth Gospel contains. John's mental and spiritual constitution peculiarly fitted him to be the medium of communicating to us those discourses, as may be seen from his employing in his Epistles a style which so closely resembles them. But such passages as this show that that class of ideas and expressions was not foreign to the other Gospels, and that the Jesus of the Fourth Gospel is not essentially different from the Jesus of the other three.

28-30. He stands as the Great Teacher, who alone can give true, saving knowledge of God (v. 27), whose teachings, while hid from the wise and intelligent, are revealed to babes. (v. 25.) Though rejected by many (v. 20-24), and even slandered and reviled (v. 16-19), still he stands, in the fullness of his wisdom, and the gentleness of his love, and invites all the toiling and burdened to come to him, to wear the easy yoke of his instruction, and they shall find rest for their souls. Notice how the invitation follows immediately upon the statement that no one knows the Father but the Son, and he to whomsoever the Son chooses to reveal him. To his mind there was no contradiction between sovereign, electing grace, and the free invitations of the gospel. **Come unto me,** literally, *hither to me,* the word in the original being an adverb much used in animated invitations. (Comp. 4: 19; 19: 21; 21: 38; 22: 4; 25: 34; 28: 6). It expresses lively interest on the part of the speaker, and invites them to come at once and heartily. 'Me' is not emphatic, as the original shows; the point is, I alone can give knowledge of the Father; *come* to me, and receive my instruction. **All,** together with the whole connection, suggests a general audience (Weiss); and if we understand all since 11: 2 to be one discourse, then we know that

'multitudes' were present. (11: 7.) **All ye that labor and are heavy laden,** or more literally, *all the toiling and burdened.* 'Toiling' denotes active effort to perform difficult and painful duties, while 'burdened' denotes passive endurance.[1] The Jewish teachers of the time promised rest on condition of minute attention, not only to all the ceremonies of the written law, but also to all the traditions of the elders. This was declared by Peter (Acts 15: 10) to be "a yoke which neither our fathers nor we were able to bear." And Jesus said of the Scribes and Pharisees (23: 4), "They bind heavy burdens, and grievous to be borne, and lay them on men's shoulders; but they themselves will not move them with their finger." Our Lord does not mean to *exclude* any from the privilege of coming to him, who are not toiling and burdened; but no one would care to learn from him who did not desire saving knowledge of God, or who was satisfied with the knowledge already possessed, and he addresses his invitation to those who in the nature of the case would be likely to accept it. The most natural tendency with any one who has become painfully conscious of sin, is to seek God's favor by his own doings and sufferings. **And I will give you rest.** The original makes 'I' emphatic; *he* would do what the Scribes and other Rabbis did not do. The great difference between Jesus and other religious teachers is that he can give power to be and do what he requires; we find rest not simply in the superiority of his precepts, but in the supports of his grace.

Take my yoke upon you, and learn of (*from*) **me.** Among the Jews a pupil who submitted himself to the instruction of a certain teacher was sometimes said to take his yoke. Comp. Sirach (Ecclus.) 51: 25, where Wisdom says, "I opened my mouth and spoke, acquire for yourselves without money; put your neck under the yoke, and let your soul receive instruction . . . . . see with your eye that I toiled a little, and found for myself much rest"—'toil' and 'rest' being also the same

---

[1] The Geneva version has 'all ye that are weary and laden' (instead of Tyndale's 'that labor and are laden'); this Geneva rendering is still common in religious speech and writing, having been perpetuated by traditional use, aided doubtless by a hymn of which one verse begins, "Come, ye weary, heavy-laden." (By John Hart, written in 1759.)

am meek and lowly in heart: and ye shall find rest
unto your souls.
30 For my yoke *is* easy, and my burden is light.

30 and ye shall find rest unto your souls. For my yoke
is easy, and my burden is light.

---

words as here. Comp. also Sirach 6: 24. The
later Jewish writers frequently speak of taking or rejecting the yoke of the law, the yoke
of the kingdom of heaven. (Comp. Acts
15: 10.) 'Take my yoke upon you' is therefore only a figurative way of saying, Become
my pupils (disciples), submit yourselves to
my instruction ; which is then stated again in
unfigurative terms, 'and learn from me.' To
interpret this last as meaning simply, learn
from my example, is not natural to the expression, nor appropriate to the connection.
For I am meek and lowly in heart.
'Meek' as opposed to the haughty and harsh
teachers to whom they were accustomed.
(Comp. James 1: 5.) 'Lowly (or 'humble')
in heart,' not proud and repulsive, and not
ambitious of domination over the minds of
men. Accustomed to haughtiness and pride
in their teachers (John 1: 49), his hearers might
be slow to come to him ; and he condescends
to assure them that he is meek and humble,
and they need not shrink from him. Remember also that some teachers may be outwardly
meek and humble without being so in heart.
Stier : "I am meek in heart, although I
spoke words of such stern condemnation, v.
20, 24 . . . . . I am lowly in heart, notwithstanding that I have borne witness to myself
as the Son of the Father, v. 25-27." Here
also, as in v. 26, it is possible to render 'that'
instead of 'for,' learn from me that I am
meek, etc. So the Peshito, and possibly
(though less naturally) the Latin versions;
and so Augustine interpreted, with many
Latin followers. (See Aquinas, Maldonatus.)
This, however, is an artificial interpretation,
and not suitable to the connection—which
makes it all the more natural that Matthew
Arnold should receive it. **And ye shall find
rest unto** (*for*) **your souls.** This expression
is drawn from Jer. 6: 16, according to the
Heb., not the Sept. Remember that our
Lord used two expressions from the Psalms
when on the cross (Matt. 27: 46; Luke 23: 46), and
made three quotations from Deut. during the
Temptation. (Matt. 4: 4 ff.) All religions profess
to give rest for the spirit—Christianity alone
can truly fulfill the promise. Others may give
a kind of repose, but it is that of self-

righteousness, or other self-delusion.—Christianity affords a well-founded and lasting
repose, as to our guilt, our inability to gain
God's favor, and our sinfulness of nature.
How Jesus will do this, he does not here set
forth ; indeed it could be fully understood
only after his atoning death and ascension,
and the special coming of the Holy
Spirit, and so the complete explanation of
it was left for the inspired writings of his
apostles (*e. g.*, Rom. 5: 1 ff.; 8: 1 ff.) From
them we know that our guilt may be can-
celled through the Saviour's atonement,
that we may be accepted into God's favor
through his perfect righteousness, that the
dominion of sin within us can be broken by
his regenerating Spirit, and by degrees completely destroyed by that Spirit's sanctifying
grace. Even the painful consciousness of remaining tendencies to sin need not prevent a
certain repose of spirit, since we have the
assurance of God's word that in the truly regenerate and believing soul these tendencies
shall at last be completly overcome. Yet,
even now the Saviour's invitation and promise, in the unexplained and concrete form,
brings rest and joy to many a trusting heart.
A loving reliance on the personal Jesus, a
loving submission to his authority, and obedience to his commandments, is the very essence
of Christian piety.
**For my yoke is easy, and my burden is
light.** There is no particular emphasis on
'my'; the contrast with other teachers has
been sufficiently indicated before, and is not
here expressed. 'For' presents this as a reason for what precedes, in general, but especially for the promise just given: 'Ye shall
find rest for your souls, *for* my yoke is easy,'
etc. The word rendered 'easy' means agreeable and serviceable—a yoke that does not
gall the neck, nor cramp so as to hinder the
drawing. The Latin version and Peshito
render by words signifying sweet, pleasant,
and Davidson 'good.' He requires of his
pupils only what is possible to do and bear,
so that they will actually find rest, and not be
vainly seeking it. Still we must really take
his yoke upon us—must receive his instructions, and submit to his directions—must set

ourselves to do what he bids us, whether it seems likely to be pleasing or painful. He not only teaches what to do, but can give us strength to do it. And in proportion as we do really submit, and conform and trust, we shall find his requirements "not grievous" (1 John 5:3), but helpful and pleasant. If Christ's yoke ever galls the neck, it is because we do not work steadily in it. *Augustine:* "This burden is not the weight upon one that is laden, but the wing of one that is about to fly." And if it ever feels like a weight and an incumbrance, that is when the soul has soiled this heavenly plumage with the mire of earth. It is true that the morality enjoined by Jesus was more spiritual, and thus in one sense more severe than that taught by the Scribes and Pharisees (comp. 5: 17 ff.), but a morality depending on a multitude of minute outward observances and imperfectly known traditions must necessarily be burdensome, while spiritual morality grows increasingly easy to the spiritually minded. Observe that our Lord's invitation is supported, not only by the great promise, 'ye shall find rest for your souls,' but by two encouragements; one, the personal character of the Teacher, 'meek and humble in heart'; the other, the fact that his requirements are not severe and oppressive: 'my yoke is easy, and my burden is light.'

The most exactly parallel application of this invitation now, is to persons who vainly strive in other than gospel ways to obtain salvation and find rest; as, for example, by an upright and charitable life, or by the diligent observance of religious ceremonies—toiling to make the exterior of their life correct in the sight of men and acceptable to God, while within, the pollution of sin is not removed, the power of sin is unbroken, the guilty conscience can find no true relief; so also to those who are trying to obtain rest through false religions, or perversions of the true religion, or any of the forms of would-be philosophic infidelity. All such persons, if deeply earnest in their quest, are assuredly "toiling and burdened." Oh, that they would listen to the Great Teacher! But the invitation may be naturally and reasonably extended to all who desire religious repose in the knowledge of God. Jesus, and he only, can give it, and he has left a standing invitation: "Come to me, take me as your religious Teacher, and ye shall find rest for your souls."—When we come to Jesus now, that is not a bodily removal from one place to another; for he is present whenever and wherever we seek him. But the object in coming, the feeling with which we come, may be the same now as when he was on earth. Whenever we want anything from Jesus, let us draw near to him in heart, and ask him for it as if bodily present.

HOMILETICAL AND PRACTICAL.

V. 20. Gospel-hardened! *Henry:* "He began to preach to them long before (4: 17), but he did not begin to *upbraid* till now. Rough and unpleasing methods must not be taken, till gentler means have first been used."—V. 22. Meeting the heathen on the day of judgment. 1) The doom of all will be proclaimed as a thing unalterably determined. 2) Men will be judged according to their *opportunities* in this life; and the condemnation of the impenitent from Christian countries will be unspeakably more terrible than that of the heathen.. 3) Then should we not avoid sending the gospel to the heathen? Nay, for on that principle we ought to keep our own children ignorant of the gospel, ought to wish there had *never been* any gospel. 4) Will not the heathen pour upon us deserved upbraidings because we left them in ignorance of the only true God, and Jesus Christ whom he sent (John 17: 3)?

V. 25. Mankind are prone to find fault with God's mode of procedure in every respect. All rulers are blamed; and the only perfect ruler is blamed most of all. The pious heart should sympathize with this utterance of Jesus, and make acknowledgment to the Father that he is right in all his doings. But this does not mean that we are to be indifferent to the fate of our fellow-men. This same Jesus wept over ruined Jerusalem. GREGORY THE GREAT (Aquinas): "In which words we have a lesson of humility, that we should not rashly presume to discuss the counsels of heaven concerning the calling of some, and the rejection of others; showing that that cannot be unrighteous which is willed by Him that is righteous."—The gospel offered to *all.* 1) Not all can be rich, but all may be poor, and poor in spirit. (5:3.) 2) Not all can be

CHAPTER XII.

A T that time Jesus went on the sabbath day through the corn; and his disciples were a hungered, and began to pluck the ears of corn, and to eat.

1   At that season Jesus went on the sabbath day through the cornfields; and his disciples were an hungered, and began to pluck ears of corn, and to

wise and intelligent, but all may be babes. 3) No one can commend himself to God by his natural good works, but any one may believe in Christ, and gain the gift of the Holy Spirit.—V. 25-30. Sovereignty and Invitation. 1) The sovereign Father reveals the Son only to the lowly. 2) The sovereign Son reveals the Father only to such as he chooses. 3) All who need and desire the rest-giving knowledge of the Father are invited to learn from this sovereign, yet meek and lowly Teacher.—V. 27-30. Full knowledge of God. 1) It can be had only through the Son of God. 2) It is conferred by the Son upon such only as he willeth. 3) He willeth to confer it upon all who will come and take him as religious Teacher. 4) He is a gentle Teacher, and his requirements are easy and pleasant. 5) To accept his teaching will bring rest to the soul.—V. 27 f. True knowledge of God, and true rest in God.—V. 28. ALEXANDER: "Inviting men to come to him, not in the way of speculation, but of penitent submission, not as philosophers to be enlightened, but as sinners to be saved. There is exquisite beauty in this sudden but not harsh transition from the mysteries of the Godhead to the miseries of man. The Son is the Revealer of the Father, not to stimulate or gratify a mere scientific curiosity as to the mode of the divine existence, but to bring the Godhead into saving contact with the sin-sick, ruined soul." ME-LANCHTHON (in Meyer): "In this *all* thou shouldst include thyself also, and not think that thou dost not belong therein; thou shouldst seek no other list of them that are God's." LUTHER: "They are words of majesty when he says, I will give you rest. No angel, let alone a man, would undertake to promise that."—V. 28-30. The Great Invitation. 1) The gentle Teacher. 2) The easy yoke. 3) The assured rest. CHRYSOSTOM: "Christ did not mention the gracious things only, and then hold his peace, nor the painful things only, but set down both. Thus he both spake of a *yoke*, and called it *easy;* both named a *burden*, and added that it was *light;* that thou shouldst neither flee from them as toilsome, nor despise them as over easy."

HILARY: "And what is easier than his yoke, what lighter than his burden? To become praiseworthy, to abstain from wickedness, to choose the good and refuse the evil, to love all and hate none, to gain eternal things and not be taken with things present, to be unwilling to bring upon another what yourself would find hard to endure."—To be toiling and burdened does not confer the right to come to Christ, but should produce the disposition to come. Some persons come truly to Christ without any long and conscious toiling to save themselves otherwise; such persons are not specially addressed in this particular invitation, but are amply invited elsewhere.—V. 29. We are freed from the yoke of sin by taking the yoke of Christ. HENRY: "The way of duty is the way of rest." AUGUSTINE: "Thou hast made us for thyself, and our heart is restless until it rests in thee."—V. 30. HENRY: "It is a yoke that is lined with love." AUGUSTINE: "All things are light to love." LUTHER: "Christ's burden is light because he helps us to bear it, and when it becomes too heavy for us he puts himself under the load with us. The world thinks it heavy and unbearable; but not so, for one has a good comrade. You two can easily bear a load, though one by himself cannot."

Ch. 12: 1-21. JESUS IS ACCUSED OF BREAKING THE SABBATH.

Pursuing his treatment of successive topics, connected with our Lord's life and labors (comp. on 11: 2), the Evangelist now speaks (ch. 12) of the *opposition* he encountered. This subject has been several times already briefly alluded to (9: 3, 11, 14, 34; 10: 25; 11: 19), but is here treated at length, various instances of opposition being stated, with our Lord's reply in each case. First, we have two instances of their charging him with violating the Sabbath, viz., because the disciples plucked ears of grain on the Sabbath (v. 1-8), and because he healed the withered hand on the Sabbath. (v. 9-13.) At this, the indignation of the Pharisees became so violent that it was necessary for Jesus to withdraw, in which withdrawal the Evangelist points out the fulfillment of another prophecy. (v. 14-21.) Next, we have their charge that he cast out demons by league with Beelzebub. (v. 22-37.) Then, the demand for a "sign." (v. 38-45.) And finally, an instance of opposition even from his nearest relatives. (v. 46-50.) The fact that these last cases (v. 22-50) occurred on the same day on which he afterwards spoke the great series of Parables in ch. 13 (see on 13: 1), may account for Matthews's introducing the whole subject of opposition just at this point of his treatise. Our present section comprises the two accusations of violating the Sabbath and the immediate consequences. We shall see that this belongs much earlier in the history than the remaining instances.

I. 1-8. THE DISCIPLES PLUCK EARS OF GRAIN ON THE SABBATH. Comp. Mark 2: 23-28; Luke 6: 1-5. **At that time** (*season*), the same expression in Greek as in 11: 25. It does not necessarily show that what follows took place on the same day with what precedes, but only that it belongs to the same general period of time. (Comp. on 3: 1, and contrast 13: 1.) At that period, viz., while Jesus was engaged in journeying about Galilee, teaching and healing (see on 4: 23 and 9: 35), occurred the events now to be narrated. The order of Mark, who is usually chronological, supported by that of Luke, places these first instances of opposition in the early part of the Galilean ministry, before the Sermon on the Mount. The standing grain shows the time of year, between Passover and Pentecost.[1] As it thus followed a Passover, the question arises to which of the Passovers mentioned in the Fourth Gospel we must refer it. Now, it cannot have been that of John 2: 13, after which Jesus tarried in Judea (John 3: 22), with so extensive results of his ministry (John 4: 1) as to require at least several months. To place it just after the Passover of John 6: 4, a year before the crucifixion (Edersh., ch. 35), is to disregard altogether the order of Mark and Luke, for this supposes that Mark 2: 23 f.

follows Mark 6: 31 ff., and Luke 6: 1 ff. follows Luke 9: 10 ff. But if we suppose the feast of John 5: 1 to be a Passover, (as most of the Harmonies do), all fits exactly. This is long enough after the beginning of our Lord s ministry for the hostility to have become acute; these instances of opposition on the ground of Sabbath-breaking in Galilee correspond to one during the just preceding Passover in Jerusalem (John 5: 10), in both cases awakening a desire to put him to death (John 5: 18; Matt. 12: 14); and the order of Mark and Luke is conserved. Of course it is possible that the Passover here in question should be one not mentioned in the Fourth Gospel; but the other supposition is far more probable.

Through the corn (or, *grain-fields*), literally, *through the sown* (places), which Tyndale and his followers rendered 'through the corn,' while in Mark 2: 23 and Luke 6: 1, they make it 'corn-fields,' though the Greek is the same. The word 'corn,' in various European languages, is applied to bread-stuffs in general, especially to that most used in the particular nation, whether wheat, barley, rye, or oats. In England it means especially wheat, while in America it has become confined to maize, which our English ancestors called Indian corn. Besides this and the parallel passages, we find Tyndale and followers using 'corn' in Mark 4: 28; Acts 7: 12, where the Greek has the common word for 'wheat,' so translated by them all in Matt. 3: 12; 13: 25, and wherever else in New Test. it occurs. In John 12: 24 'a corn of wheat' (Com. Ver.) means a grain of wheat (Rev. Ver.), as in barley corn. Why Rev. Ver. should not here say 'grain-fields' and 'ears of grain' (Noyes, Bible Un. Ver.) and 'wheat' in Mark 4: 28; Acts 7: 12, is hard to tell. Among the Jews the lands of different owners were not usually separated by fences, but only by stones set up at intervals as landmarks (Deut. 19: 14), and the roads were not distinct from the fields, as commonly among us, but ran right through them, as Southern planta-

---

[1] In Luke 6: 1 W H. and Rev. Ver. omit 'second-first,' but transcriptional probability is very strongly in favor of retaining this otherwise unknown and very obscure compound word. Meyer's theory of its origin, adopted by W H., is possible, but far from probable. The question of its genuineness is quite hard to solve, and its discussion belongs to a commentary on Luke;

fortunately, it is of no historical importance, for the standing grain sufficiently shows the time of year. The most probable interpretation of the 'second-first Sabbath' makes it mean the first Sabbath after the second day of the Passover festival, when the sheaf of grain was presented, after which day the new harvest could be eaten. (Lev. 23: 5-15.)

2 But when the Pharisees saw *it*, they said unto him, Behold, thy disciples do that which is not lawful to do upon the sabbath day.
3 But he said unto them, Have ye not read what David did, when he was a hungered, and they that were with him;

2 eat. But the Pharisees, when they saw it, said unto him, Behold, thy disciples do that which it is not
3 lawful to do upon the sabbath. But he said unto them, Have ye not read what David did, when he was an hungered, and they that were with him;

---

tation paths often do, so that the grain grew up to the edge of the path (comp. on 13: 4); the same thing is seen in Palestine to-day. **Disciples,** see on 5: 1. **Began to pluck the ears of corn** (*grain*), either wheat or barley, probably the latter, if it was just after the Passover. Luke 6: 1 adds, 'rubbing them in their hands,' a thing familiar to every one who has been much in harvest fields. **Began to pluck,** and presently the Pharisees interfered, and tried to stop it.

2. These Pharisees (comp. on 3: 7) were making a short Sabbath day's journey, about one thousand yards, through the same grain-fields. **Behold,** calling his attention to something important. **Thy disciples do that** (*are doing*). Mark (2:24) makes it a question addressed to him, and Luke (6:2) a question addressed to the disciples. In many cases the Evangelists do not undertake to give the exact language employed, but only the substance of it (comp. on 3: 17). **Which is not lawful to do upon the Sabbath.** It was expressly permitted to do this in general (Deut. 23:25), and such things are still common in Palestine, but the Jews maintained that it should never be done *on the Sabbath*. For that day they numbered each distinct act that could be called work as a separate sin, requiring a separate sin-offering; to pluck the ears was one act, to rub out the grains was a second (comp. Edersh., ch. 35). As to the numerous and often absurd Rabbinical regulations for the Sabbath, see Edersh., Appendix 17, Geikie, ch. 38.

3 f. Our Lord's reply to this censure of the disciples and himself contains, as here reported, four distinct arguments, v. 3 f., v. 5 f., v. 7, and v. 8. A fifth argument is given in this connection by Mark 2: 27, a sixth below in v. 11 f., a seventh (probably just before at Jerusalem) in John 5: 17, and an eighth (much later) in John 7: 22 f. The first argument is an appeal to *history*, viz., to the conduct of David (1 Sam. 21:1-6), which these Pharisees would admit to have been justifiable. The point of the argument is, that *necessity* would justify a departure from the strict law as to things consecrated. **And they that**

were with him may be connected either with 'did,' or with 'was hungry,' and there is no substantial difference. The participation of David's followers is unmistakably indicated in 1 Sam. 21: 4 f.; our Lord brings it out clearly in order to make the case more obviously parallel to that of himself and his followers. **The house of God,** meaning the tabernacle. (Ex. 23: 19; Judg. 18: 31; 1 Sam. 1: 7, 24; 3: 15; 2 Sam. 12: 20; Ps. 5: 7; comp. 2 Cor. 5: 1.) **Shewbread,** literally, *loaves of the setting-out,* loaves that were set out, the common Septuagint' expression, in Heb. usually 'bread of the face, *i. e.,* placed before the face of Jehovah. For the law about this, see Lev. 24: 5-9. Twelve very large loaves of bread were placed on a small table (at a later period, two tables, 1 Chron. 28: 16), which sat on the right side of the holy place to one entering. When the Sabbath came, new loaves were substituted, and the old ones eaten, there in the holy place, by the priests, the descendants of Aaron—for this offering was to be regarded as peculiarly sacred. (Lev. 24: 9.) David was fleeing southward from Gibeah, Saul having determined to slay him, and came to Nob, just north of Jerusalem, where the tabernacle then was. Having left in great haste, without food, he deceived the high-priest by saying that the king had sent him on a secret and urgent mission, and thereby induced him, as there was no other bread on hand, to bring some of the shew-loaves, which had been removed from the table, but not yet eaten. It seems likely, from 1 Sam. 21: 5 f., though not certain, that the bread had been changed on that day, which was therefore the Sabbath. This would give additional appositeness to the illustration, but the point of the argument does not depend on it. Our Lord makes no allusion to the deception practiced by David, which any one would agree was wrong. The sole point he makes is, that for David and his attendants (Luke 6: 4) to eat the hallowed bread was justifiable, on the ground of necessity—a view in which all his hearers would concur. Kimchi, a celebrated Jewish commentator of the thirteenth century, on 1 Sam. 21: 5, main-

4 How he entered into the house of God, and did eat the shewbread, which was not lawful for him to eat, neither for them which were with him, but only for the priests?

5 Or have ye not read in the law, how that on the sabbath days the priests in the temple profane the sabbath, and are blameless?

6 But I say unto you, That in this place is *one* greater than the temple.

7 But if ye had known what *this* meaneth, I will have mercy, and not sacrifice, ye would not have condemned the guiltless.

4 how he entered into the house of God, and [1]did eat the shewbread, which it was not lawful for him to eat, neither for them that were with him, but only for the priests? Or have ye not read in the law, how that on the sabbath day the priests in the temple profane the sabbath, and are guiltless? But I say unto you, that [2]one greater than the temple is here.

7 But if ye had known what this meaneth, I desire mercy, and not sacrifice, ye would not have con-

---

1 Some ancient authorities read, *they did eat.*...2 Gr. *a greater thing.*

---

tains that in case of hunger the shew-bread might be eaten by those who were not priests; not only that which had been removed from the table, but that which was upon it; yea, even when there was none to put in its room. And if the law about the hallowed bread might be set aside by necessity, so might the law about the hallowed day. The disciples really needed food. Mark (2: 27) here records our Lord's adding the general principle, 'The Sabbath was made for man, and not man for the Sabbath.' It came into existence for the benefit of mankind, and so it may be temporarily set aside by any imperative necessity. (Comp. 2 Macc. 5: 19.)

5 f. A *second* ground of justification for the disciples was drawn, not from sacred history, but from the *law.* (Num. 28: 9, 10, 18, 19.) Here as in 5: 17, Jesus shows (Weiss) that he is not abrogating or violating the law, for he justifies his course out of the law itself. **Or,** introducing another argument, as in 7: 9. **Have ye not read,** as in v. 3 (comp. v. 7); 19: 4; 21: 16, etc., reproaches them with ignorance of Scripture. **Temple** is here the general term *hieron,* 'sacred (place),' including the whole consecrated enclosure—buildings, courts, and all (see on 4: 5), thus applying equally well to the tabernacle and to the Temple. The priests were directed to offer certain sacrifices in the sacred place on the Sabbath—more, in fact, than on other days—though to do so required the slaying of animals and other acts prohibited on the Sabbath, and which under any other circumstances would 'profane the Sabbath.' This was right, because the temple with its sacrifices was of higher importance than the Sabbath, and would override the requirements of its sanctity. **Blameless,** or, *guiltless,* both in v. 5 and v. 7, or else 'blameless' in both, the Greek word being the same in both verses, and the verbal connection being of some importance.

Our Lord argues that the same principle applies to the case in hand, and still more strongly, because here, he solemnly tells them, is **one**—or, *something*—**greater than the temple.** The correct reading makes the Greek word not masculine, 'a greater (man),' but neuter, 'a greater (thing),' comp. v. 41, and 11: 9. This peculiar form of expression may have been intended to render the statement less distinctly offensive to Jewish prejudices, but it unquestionably asserts a superior dignity and importance connected, in whatever way, with him and his mission. The temple was superior to the Sabbath, and there was that here which was superior to the temple; much more, then, might the usual law of the Sabbath be set aside without blame, when it became necessary for his disciples in his service. This argument would be best appreciated by Jewish readers, and is given by Matthew only. On a later occasion, our Lord drew a similar argument from circumcision. (John 7: 22 f.) The principle he here lays down would show the propriety, even upon grounds of Old Test. law, of all such active exertions on the Sabbath as are really necessary in attending upon and conducting religious worship. (V. 8 goes further still.)

7. A *third* point in the defence is drawn from a *prophet,* as the others had been from history and law. This again is given by Matthew only, who has Jewish readers especially in mind. **But if ye had known what this meaneth**—literally—*what is, i. e.,* what means, see on 9: 13. These Pharisees, many of them Scribes, did know what the passage was in its words, but did not know what it was in its true meaning. The quotation, from Hos. 6: 6, has been explained above on 9: 13. The idea here may be thus expressed: "If you knew that God desires kindness and good-will to men, rather than sacrifice, you

8 For the Son of man is Lord even of the sabbath day.

8 demned the guiltless. For the Son of man is lord of the sabbath.

---

would not have condemned the guiltless." It is implied that if they really knew the meaning of the passage, they would have acted according to it. Only those who are willing to obey Scripture, fully comprehend its spiritual instruction (comp. John 7: 17). The disciples are 'guiltless,' just as the priests in the temple are, because they are busy in connection with something even greater than the temple. And if these Pharisees were disposed, according to the prophet's words, to treat their fellow-men kindly and fairly, rather than to make piety consist exclusively in outward observances, they would not have condemned them (comp. 23 : 23).

8. This gives a *fourth* defence of the disciples, in the shape of a reason for declaring them 'guiltless.' Acting under their Master's authority, they had a right to do what would not usually be proper on the Sabbath, *for* he is Lord of the Sabbath. (**Even** is genuine in Mark and Luke, but not in Matt.) This statement carries higher the idea of v. 6. There he declared the presence of something superior to the temple, and a *fortiori*, to the Sabbath; here he says that the Messiah is Lord of the Sabbath, having full authority to control and regulate it as he may see proper. In both cases it is implied that the speaker is the person referred to, but it is not distinctly stated, because the time for publicly taking such a position has not yet come. **The Son of man,** see on 8: 20. If the inspired apostles of Jesus afterwards changed the day to be observed, and absolved Christians from all particular Mosaic as well as traditional rules concerning the manner of observing it, they were not going beyond the authoritative control over the Sabbath which their Master himself had claimed.

As a *sixth* point, our Lord now shows (v. 9-13) that it is also proper to depart from the strict observance of the Sabbath, when requisite to the *relief* of a suffering fellow-man, or even a suffering brute. These two instances have led to the familiar saying, derived from the Westminster Catechism, that we may do on the Sabbath "works of necessity and mercy." Another example of healing on the Sabbath had occurred, apparently just before, leading to a *seventh* argument (John 5 : 9, 17); and yet

other instances are recorded in Mark 1: 21, 29 f. ; Luke 13: 10 ff. ; 14: 3 ; John 9: 14 ff. This frequent departure from what the Jews thought to be proper on the Sabbath, with the pains here taken to explain and defend his course, was doubtless designed by our Lord as a part of his general undertaking to teach them a more spiritual interpretation and observance of the law (comp. on 5: 17-21). In order to this he showed, by word and deed, the error and folly of that rigid formalism with which they insisted so much on the minute and literal observance of all its outward requirements, regardless of its true spirit and real design. He has here said nothing at all calculated to impair the sanctity of the Sabbath. On the contrary, as "the exception proves the rule," his argument that there are peculiar circumstances in which its observance should be set aside, necessarily involves the idea that in general it should be observed. The Sabbath seems to have been enjoined upon our first parents as soon as they were created ; it and the institution of marriage form the only relics that remain to us of the unfallen life in Paradise. The command to hallow it was included among the Ten Commandments, the moral law which is of perpetual obligation. The very term " *Remember* the Sabbath-day to keep it holy " (Ex. 20 : 8), seems to treat it as not something new, but an already existing institution ; and it appears from the history of the first fall of manna (Ex. 16 : 5, 22-30) that the people were previously acquainted with the Sabbath and that some of them were disposed to forget or neglect it. Recent research shows that the Babylonians before the time of Abraham observed a week of seven days, ending with a rest day which they strictly kept, and which the Assyrian writers call by the name Sabbath. With this agrees the week repeatedly mentioned in Genesis, and it is now too late to say that the Sabbath was unknown till the lawgiving at Mount Sinai. In the further legislation which followed the giving of the Ten Commandments, to the general idea of hallowing the day, is added the prohibition of work on the Sabbath, under penalty of death. (Ex. 31: 14; 35: 2.) To carry this out more effectually, they were prohibited to kindle a fire on that day (Ex. 35: 3),

9 And when he was departed thence, he went into their synagogue:
10 And, behold, there was a man which had *his* hand withered. And they asked him, saying, Is it lawful to heal on the sabbath days? that they might accuse him.

9 And he departed thence, and went into their syna-
10 gogue: and behold, a man having a withered hand. And they asked him, saying, Is it lawful to heal on

---

probably in order to prevent cooking, just as a double supply of manna fell on the sixth day, and none on the seventh. This regulation about making a fire being forgotten or contemned by one of the people, who was found gathering sticks on the Sabbath, he was, by divine direction, stoned to death (Num. 15: 32-36); on which occasion it was provided that the people should wear a fringe on the garment, with a riband of blue (see above on 9: 20), to remind them continually of the commandments of Jehovah, which they seemed so prone to forget. (Numb. 15: 37-41.) Now these particular regulations, being a part of the civil and ceremonial law of the Jewish people, ceased to be obligatory when the natural gave way to the spiritual Israel, through the work of Christ. But the Sabbath still remained, as it existed before Israel, and was even from the creation a day appointed by God to be holy (Gen. 2: 3), which the Mosaic law recognized at the outset, in *reminding* the people to keep it holy. After the resurrection of Christ an additional significance was given to the day, as representing not only "the completion of God's work of Creation," but also "the triumphant completion of the still more glorious work of Redemption." (*Boyce*, Catechism of Bible Doctrine.) In order to this, the day appears to have been changed by the apostles from the seventh to the first day of the week, as that on which Christ rose. (John 20: 19, 26; Acts 20: 7; 1 Cor. 16: 2; Rev. 1: 10.) This added significance and change of day did not affect the perpetual obligation to keep holy the Sabbath. But Christianity, true to its spiritual character, gives no particular precepts as to the *mode* of observing the day, and leaves us to perform the duty of keeping it holy in such methods as an enlightened conscience may deem most conformable to its twofold significance and its general design. Comp. below, "Homiletical and Practical."

II. 9-13. HEALING THE WITHERED HAND ON THE SABBATH. (Comp. Mark 3: 1-5; Luke 6: 6-10.) **And when he was departed thence, he went into their synagogue.** We should most naturally infer, had

we Matthew's narrative alone, that this incident took place on the same Sabbath as the preceding. But Luke 6: 6 says, 'on another Sabbath'; and nothing in Matthew's statement necessarily conflicts with this. The connection in Mark 3: 7 appears to show that the place was in Galilee, but it cannot be more exactly determined. 'Their synagogue' means the synagogue of the people in that vicinity. (Comp. on 11: 1.) As to the synagogues, see on 4: 23. **A man which had,** etc. *Having a withered hand* is the best supported reading. Luke adds (6: 6) that it was his right hand. We cannot determine the precise nature of the affection which caused his hand to wither. Jerome mentions that the so-called "Gospel" of the Nazarenes called him a stone-mason—which, though only a tradition, would illustrate for us the importance of his right hand. **And they asked him.** Luke states that they were the Scribes and Pharisees. He and Mark only mention that they watched him to see whether he would heal on the Sabbath; Matthew does not contradict them, but simply adds that they asked him whether it was lawful. **That they might accuse him,** probably before the 'judgment,' the local tribunal (see on 5: 21). The later Jewish writings show much discussion as to the propriety of healing on the Sabbath. All agreed that it ought to be done where life was in danger (see Wet., Wün., or Edersh.), but they of course differed much on the question what diseases could be considered as endangering life. The Talmud gives a host of directions for different cases, with many absurd distinctions; e. g., "One who has a sore throat must not gargle with oil; but he may swallow oil (for food), and if that cures him, all right." One Rabbi taught that a man might take a purgative drink, if he took it for pleasure, but must not take it for the purpose of healing. The law had said nothing about healing disease on the Sabbath, but many Rabbis took the ground that it was "work." (Ex. 31: 14.) Tyndale and followers, including our Com. Ver., have 'on the Sabbath days,' in v. 10 and 12, but the plural form

11 And he said unto them, What man shall there be among you, that shall have one sheep, and if it fall into a pit on the sabbath day, will he not lay hold on it, and lift *it* out?
12 How much then is a man better than a sheep? Wherefore it is lawful to do well on the sabbath days.
13 Then saith he to the man, Stretch forth thine hand. And he stretched *it* forth; and it was restored whole, like as the other.
14 Then the Pharisees went out, and *a* held a council against him, how they might destroy him.

11 the sabbath day? that they might accuse him. And he said unto them, What man shall there be of you that shall have one sheep, and if this fall into a pit on the sabbath day, will he not lay hold on it, and
12 lift it out? How much then is a man of more value than a sheep! Wherefore it is lawful to do good on
13 the sabbath day. Then said he to the man, Stretch forth thy hand. And he stretched it forth; and it
14 was restored whole, as the other. But the Pharisees went out, and took counsel against him, how they

a Or, *took counsel.*

of the Greek word is frequently used (Grimm) in the singular sense, as they all translate in v. 11.

11 f. He appeals not as in the former instance, to the history, the law, or the prophets, but to the course pursued by the people themselves. This argument is here given by Matthew only, but similar arguments are given by Luke (13: 15; 14: 5), as afterwards used on other occasions. Mark mentions (3: 3) that Jesus told the man to stand up in the midst, probably that the bystanders might look at him with sympathy, and thus justly appreciate the propriety of healing him. To awaken healthy feeling, is sometimes the best remedy for unreasonable prejudice. **One sheep** would be a matter of no great consequence, and yet even this the owner would lift out of a pit on the Sabbath day. In the Talmud some Rabbis maintained that it was enough when a beast fell into a pit to give it food; others said, put something under it to lie on, and if by means of this it climbs out, all right; others said, take it out with the intention of killing it, even though afterwards you change your mind and preserve it. To such silly evasions were men driven, by the attempt to convert morality into a mere system of rules. Jesus appeals to common sense, asking whether any one present would fail in such a case to preserve his property. *Edersh.:* "There could be no doubt, at any rate, that even if the [traditional] law was, at the time of Christ, as stringent as in the Talmud, a man would have found some device by which to recover his sheep." The old Roman religious law provided that on the sacred days an ox might be drawn out of a pit. **A man better**—*of more value*—**than a sheep,** see a like argument in 6: 26, and in 10: 29-31. **Wherefore,** or, 'so that,' a general inference from what precedes. **It is lawful.** The word law does not enter into the Greek expression (see also in v. 10), which

means simply it is allowable, or permissible. **To do well** (*good*) **on the Sabbath.** Com. Ver. 'to do well,' looks literal, but really gives a different sense. Wyclif used 'to do good,' Tyn., Cran., Gen., Rheims, 'to do a good deed.' In Mark and Luke he first puts this as a question, 'Is it lawful on the Sabbath to do good, or to do harm,' intimating that by delaying to heal the man he would be inflicting an injury. They made no answer, and he 'looked round about on them with anger, being grieved at the hardening of their heart.' (Mark 3 : 5.) They could not reply to his arguments, nor deny that he was right, and yet would not give up their fierce opposition. And so he looked upon them with mingled indignation and grief.

13. And it was restored in the act of stretching it forth. **Whole,** healthy, sound, well. Even from their own point of view the Pharisees must have found it difficult to call this breaking the Sabbath, for Jesus used no remedy, performed no action, simply spoke a word, and the man merely stretched forth his hand. They had hoped to make a strong case against Jesus, and being silenced by his argument and baffled by his action, they were all the more angry, 'filled with madness,' (Luke 6 : 11.)

14-21. PLOT TO DESTROY JESUS, AND HIS WITHDRAWAL. For the plot comp. Mark 3 : 6; Luke 6 : 11; the consequent withdrawal is described by Mark (3 : 7-12) with his characteristic fullness of detail. **Held a council,** rather, *took counsel,* **against him,** as the same phrase is rendered by Com. Ver. in 22: 15, and elsewhere, and a similar one in Mark 3 : 6, and as all English versions before King James rendered here. Mark tells us that the Pharisees drew into this consultation the Herodians, who were their own enemies. (Comp. on 22 : 16.) Remembering that this was before the Sermon on the Mount (see on v. 1 and v. 15), and probably almost two

15 But when Jesus knew *it*, he withdrew himself from thence: and great multitudes followed him, and he healed them all;
16 And charged them that they should not make him known:
17 That it might be fulfilled which was spoken by Esaias the prophet, saying,

15 might destroy him. And Jesus perceiving *it* withdrew from thence: and many followed him; and he healed them all, and charged them that they
17 should not make him known: that it might be fulfilled which was spoken through Isaiah the prophet, saying,

---

years before the Crucifixion, we perceive that the enmity of the leading Jews had already gone very far. A similar effort to slay him in Jerusalem and upon the same charge of breaking the Sabbath (John 5: 16-18), probably belongs in the history shortly before this effort in Galilee. (See on v. 1.) The two movements may have arisen independently, or emissaries may have been sent from Jerusalem, as was done a year later. (15: 1.) Their pretended reason for plotting his destruction was that he violated the Sabbath, and so was condemned to death by the law (Ex. 31: 14; 25: 2); the true reason seems to have been their jealousy of his growing credit among the people, and fear that he would impair their own influence. What a reproach upon human nature, to see men maintaining that it was a mortal sin to heal disease on the Sabbath, and yet foully plotting on that same sacred day, how they might destroy the innocent Teacher and Healer.

15. Learning that such was their intention, our Lord retired from that neighborhood, and when crowds gathered to him in his new position beside the Lake of Galilee, he healed them all, and charged them not to make him known (v. 16); in which course on his part the Evangelist points out the fulfillment of another prophecy. (v. 17-21.) Already in 4: 12 we have seen him withdraw from some place to avoid persecution; and there will be similar instances hereafter. (14: 13; 15: 21; 16: 5.) *Alexander:* "The retreat before his enemies was prompted not by fear, but by that wise discretion which was constantly employed in the selection and the use of the necessary means for the promotion of the great end which he came to accomplish. As it entered into the divine plan that his great atoning work should be preceded by a prophetic ministry of several years' duration, the design of which was to indoctrinate the people in the nature of his kingdom, to prepare the way for its erection, and to train the men by whom it should be organized, it formed no small part of his work to check and regulate the progress of events, so as not to precipitate the consum-

mation, but to secure and complete the requisite preparatory process." The hour was not yet come, for the Son of man to be delivered into the hands of sinners. (26: 45.) He never shrank from doing good because of the knowledge that it would provoke opposition; he simply transferred his beneficent labors to another scene, as he directed the disciples to do (10: 23). **And great multitudes—**or, *many* **—followed him.** This was early strengthened by some copyists into the familiar phrase, 'many crowds,' or 'great crowds,' as in 4: 25, and often. **And he healed them all.** Another general and comprehensive statement of his great work (comp. on 4: 23; 8: 16; 9: 35). At this period, as appears from a comparison of 12: 15 with Mark 3: 7-12, and Luke 6: 11-20, the Sermon on the Mount was delivered. We have already seen (on 4: 12, and 8: 1), that in all this portion of his Gospel, Matthew departs from the order of time, and groups his materials according to the relation of topics, as is often done by historical writers. **And** (*he*) **charged them,** the Greek word implying threats of displeasure if they should disobey him. For some general reasons why he usually prohibited persons healed from talking about it, see on 8: 4. An additional and special reason is here given, viz., **that it might be fulfilled which was spoken by** (*through*) **Esaias the prophet.** For these phrases, comp. on 1: 22, and 4: 14. It was the divine design in his teaching thus quietly and unostentatiously, that this prophecy might be fulfilled. The connection, therefore, looks especially to that part of the prophecy which is contained in v. 19 f., but the Evangelist cites a larger portion, because the remainder also found a fulfillment in Jesus. The Jews expected the Messiah to be a great conqueror, whose warlike exploits would attract universal attention; and as the character and course of Jesus were quite the reverse of all this, it was important for Matthew's purpose of convincing the Jews that he was Messiah, to point out that his action in this respect was in accordance with a Messianic prediction —all the more, as the current Sept. translation

18 Behold, my servant, whom I have chosen ; my beloved, in whom my soul is well pleased : I will put my
Spirit upon him, and he shall shew judgment to the
Gentiles.
19 He shall not strive, nor cry ; neither shall any
man hear his voice in the streets.

18 Behold, my servant whom I have chosen ;
My beloved in whom my soul is well pleased :
I will put my Spirit upon him,
And he shall declare judgment to the Gentiles.
19 He shall not strive, nor cry aloud ;
Neither shall any one hear his voice in the streets.

had so interpolated the passage, as to turn
away attention from its proper Messianic application (see on v. 18). This quotation, from
Isa. 42 : 1-4, is made by Matthew alone, being
the seventh prophecy he cites, as fulfilled in
Jesus (comp. on 8 : 17), besides the two with
reference to John the Baptist (3 : 3; 11 : 10). It
is quite characteristic of the two first Gospels,
that while Matthew alone gives the prophecy,
Mark (3 : 7-12) gives much more copious details
of the withdrawal and the healings.

18-21. This interesting quotation is partly
from the Sept., but with various alterations,
for the sake of close conformity to the Hebrew, or to bring out more clearly the Messianic application. Isa. 42 : 1-4 may be literally
translated from the Hebrew as follows : " Behold my servant, whom I will sustain ; my
chosen (one) in whom my soul delights. I
put my Spirit upon him ; he will bring forth
judgment to the Gentiles. He will not cry
out, he will not lift up (his voice), he will not
cause his voice to be heard abroad (or, 'out of
doors'). A bruised reed he will not break,
and a dim wick he will not quench. He will
bring forth judgment unto truth. He will
not grow dim [like the wick, *i. e.*, become
feeble, faint], nor be broken [like the reed,
i. e., broken down, disheartened], till he set
judgment in the earth ; and for his law (or,
'instruction') distant coasts shall wait." Now
comp. Matthew. **Behold my servant.** The
'servant of Jehovah,' in Isa. ch. 42 : 19, is primarily Israel. But here, as in Hos. 11 : 1, and
elsewhere, there is a typical relation between
Israel and Messiah (comp. above on 2 : 15);
and the 'servant of Jehovah' also means
Messiah. Some of Isaiah's expressions refer
equally well to either, Israel or Messiah ; in
others, as Isa. 52 : 13, and ch. 53, the reference to
Israel seems to sink out of sight, and to our eye
there appears nothing but Messiah. (Comp.
at the beginning of chap. 24.) The Sept.
translators, understanding Isa. 42 : 1 of Israel,
inserted the name, " Jacob, my servant. . . .
Israel my chosen." The Greek word here
rendered 'servant' in Matthew and Sept., is
pais (see on 8 : 6), which might of itself mean

either 'child' (Tyndale, Cran.), or 'servant'
(Geneva, Com. Ver.); but the Hebrew, here
and elsewhere in Isa., is *ebed*, which unam-
biguously means 'servant.' In like manner
the question is settled as to Acts 3 : 13, 26 ; 4 :
27, 30, by the manifest reference to this portion of Isa. **Whom I have chosen,** while
the Heb. has 'will sustain.' Matthew may
have purposely used the term 'have chosen'
from Isa. 43 : 10 ; 44 : 1, as better bringing out
the Messianic reference in the term 'servant
of the Lord.' It was certainly lawful for an
inspired writer to express more clearly in his
quotation an idea that was really present in
the prophet's language. (Comp. on 2 : 6.)
God will sustain this servant of his, because
he has chosen him, to perform an important
work. So as to **my beloved,** instead of Heb.
' my chosen.' The expression 'is well pleased'
reminds us of the words spoken from heaven
at the baptism and the transfiguration, which
probably alluded to this passage of Isa. (See
above on 3 : 17.) **I will put my Spirit upon
him,** *i. e.*, in a special, remarkable degree.
(Com. Isa. 61 : 1 ; Luke 4 : 18 ; John 3 : 34,
and see above on 3 : 16.) **And he shall shew**
(*will declare*) **judgment to the Gentiles.**
'Announce' or 'declare' (as in Heb. 2 : 12)
interprets the general term 'bring forth' of the
Hebrew. 'Judgment' exactly translates the
Heb. word. It might have been understood
as meaning justice and rectitude in general.
(23 : 23; Luke 11; 42.) But it is better to take
it, in the prophecy and here, as denoting the
whole body of what God declares to be just
and right. (Comp. Isa. 51 : 4.) **Strive,** or
'wrangle,' may have been chosen by Matthew to contrast Jesus with the Scribes, who
were constantly disputing and wrangling ;
perhaps also (Plumptre) to contrast him with
" false prophets and leaders of revolt, such as
Judas of Galilee had been." **In the streets,**
gives greater distinctness to the Hebrew
phrase ; he would not talk in public places,
in a way designed to attract attention. (Comp.
6 : 5.) If on such an occasion as John 7 : 37,
Jesus 'stood and cried out' in the temple
court, it was not through ostentation, but for

20 A bruised reed shall he not break, and smoking flax shall he not quench, till he send forth judgment unto victory.
21 And in his name shall the Gentiles trust.

20 A bruised reed shall he not break,
  And smoking flax shall he not quench,
  Till he send forth judgment unto victory.
21 And in his name shall the Gentiles hope.

---

the good of those by whom he would make himself heard. **A bruised reed shall he not break,** completely break, break off. **And smoking flax** (*a wick*), literally, *smoking linen.* The lamp wick was usually a strip of linen; when there was but little oil, it would burn dimly and smoke. Instead of being a harsh conqueror and monarch, Messiah would be gentle and kind; persons bowed down with conscious unworthiness, feeble as if verging toward spiritual extinction, he would not overwhelm and destroy, but would console and strengthen. **Till he send**—or *bring*—**forth judgment unto victory.** The prophecy is quoted in a condensed form. The play upon words in the Hebrew, He will not grow dim (like the wick), nor be broken (like the reed), could not be made fully intelligible in a translation without tedious circumlocution, and as that clause was not important to the present fulfillment of the prophecy, Matthew omits it. He then combines, to some extent, the two brief clauses, 'he will bring forth judgment unto truth' (*i. e.*, truthfully, thoroughly, so that the whole truth about it should be known), and 'until he set judgment in the earth' (*i. e.*, establish it), in each of which clauses the leading term is 'judgment,' *i. e.*, God's righteous requirements. The result is this expression, 'till he send forth judgment unto victory,' *i. e.*, victoriously, which includes the two notions of its being fully manifested and fully established. The Evangelist thus avoids complexity, and comprises the whole in one simple expression. 'Send forth' is literally *thrust forth*, cast abroad, the word explained on 9: 38; and its notion of forcible action fits the following term victory. Messiah will overcome all obstacles and opposition, and victoriously pro-

claim and establish God's word. **And in his name shall the Gentiles trust,** or *hope.*[1] (Comp. Rom. 15: 12.) Here the Evangelist follows the Sept., which was sufficiently accurate for his purpose (comp. on 3: 3); nay, which states more clearly than the Heb. expressions a notion specially appropriate to the gospel, and which the Heb. really contained. The Heb. word rendered 'isles' or 'coasts' is frequently used for distant lands in general (Isa. 41: 1, 5; 49: 1; 51: 5), so that 'nations,' or Gentiles (see on 4: 15), is in such a case equivalent to it. The Heb. 'shall wait for his law' meant shall confidently expect or hope for his instruction. (Isa. 1: 10 Prov. 1: 8; 4: 2; 7: 2.) (Comp. Toy on Quotations.) The Sept. substituted 'name' and Matt. retained it, since 'hope in his name' amounted to much the same thing as 'wait for his instruction,' both denoting dependence on him. *Alexander:* "As the first part of the prophecy was cited as an introduction, so this last part was added to give roundness and completeness to the whole quotation. At the same time these supplementary expressions, although not what the author meant especially to quote, serve the incidental but important purpose of suggesting, in the language of a prophet, the extent of the Messiah's mission and the ultimate conversion of the Gentiles." Where Matt. departs from both Heb. and Sept. it is surely quite as easy to refer the changes to the inspired Evangelist himself, as to a hypothetical oral Aramaic version used in the synagogue. (Toy.)—With this prophetic description of Messiah, comp. what Jesus says of himself in 11: 29. How different was his quiet course of life from the turbulent violence of those pretended Messiahs, who frequently involved the nation in confusion and distress.

---

[1] There is an intimate connection between the ideas of hope and trust, though really quite distinct, and the words are often confounded in popular speech. Tyndale, Cran., Gen., and King James (*not* Wyc., nor commonly Rheims) seem to have thought 'hope' often an inadequate translation of the corresponding Gr. word, so that they commonly render by 'trust' (as here), and even by 'believe' in 1 Cor. 15: 19 (T. C. G.) and 1 Tim. 4: 10. (T. C.) The *noun* they all regularly translate 'hope,' except 'trust' in 2 Cor. 3: 12 (T. C. G.), and in

Heb. 10: 23, where Com. Ver. actually has 'faith,' though all the others there have 'hope.' The popular phrase "profession of faith" is perhaps founded on this erroneous translation of Heb. 10: 23. In like manner 1 Pet. 3: 15 is often *quoted* 'a reason of the faith that is in you,' though it is really 'hope.' The Rev. Ver. has rendered both noun and verb by 'hope' in all cases, sometimes 'set your hope,' or the like. Examine especially Luke 24: 21; John 5: 45; 1 Tim. 6: 17; Heb. 10: 23; 1 Pet. 3: 5.

HOMILETICAL AND PRACTICAL.

In the Christian world at the present day, we may find two extremes in respect to the observance of the Sabbath, as well as to many other things. Some act as if the Mosaic regulations for the manner of observing the Sabbath were still in force, and so they are excessively strict, and unwisely scrupulous. Others imagine that when the civil and ceremonial law ceased to be binding, the Sabbath also ceased to be obligatory, and so they come to hold very loose notions as to abstaining from ordinary employments on the Lord's Day. One class incline to condemn all enjoyment on the Sabbath, at home or abroad; the other class are in danger of making it a day of mere idleness and festivity. Some make no distinction between the Jewish Sabbath and the Christian; others, in urging that the Lord's Day is wholly different from the Jewish Sabbath, forget that it is nevertheless the same as the primeval Sabbath, with only an additional significance and a change in the day of the week. It is a day "hallowed" by divine appointment—distinguished from other days, and set apart to sacred uses; a day of rest from ordinary toils, bodily and mental, of worship and other distinctively religious employments. In an age when reading occupies so large a part of civilized life, it would certainly seem important to abstain on the Lord's Day from secular reading, especially since we have so rich a store of properly religious literature. In deciding how far to deny ourselves exercise, society, table luxuries, and the like, we must have regard both to the objects of the day, to our own bodily, mental, and spiritual health, and to the influence of our example. As regards children, it is extremely important to afford them interesting and appropriate employment, and pleasant food, so that they may not find the day wearisome and disagreeable. In general it should be remembered that most of us are far more likely to be too lax than too stringent, that we gravitate much more powerfully towards self-indulgence than self-denial.

V. 2. HENRY: "It is no new thing for the most harmless and innocent actions of Christ's disciples to be evil spoken of and reflected upon as unlawful, especially by those who are zealous for their own inventions and impositions."—V. 5. HENRY: "Ignorance of the meaning of the Scripture is especially shameful in those who take upon them to teach others."—V. 8. Christ is Lord of the Sabbath, and the Christian Sabbath is the Lord's Day. Rev. 1: 10.

V. 1-8. The ceremonial and the moral elements of Christian piety. 1) Ceremony must yield to necessity, v. 3 f. 2) Worship is superior to any sacredness of place or time, v. 5 f., comp. John 4: 21. 3) Kindly and just judgment of others is more acceptable to God than are ceremonial observances, v. 7. 4) Christ is above all ceremonies, v. 8.—V. 9-14. Baffled disputants. 1) They seek to entrap the Teacher with a question, v. 10. 2) They are unable to answer his argument, v. 11 f., comp. Matt. 3: 6. 3) They can find no fault with his action, v. 13. 4) Therefore they plot to kill him.—V. 13. GODET: "Like every call addressed to faith, this command contained a promise of the strength necessary to accomplish it, provided the will to obey was there. He must make the attempt, depending on the word of Jesus, and divine power will accompany the effort." THEOPHYL.: "Many now also have their hands withered—that is, not compassionating and not communicating; but whenever they hear the gospel word, they stretch forth their hands to give."—V. 15. THEOPHYL.: "Plunging into danger is not pleasing to God."

V. 19 f. The quiet and gentle character here ascribed to Messiah by the prophet, corresponds to what Jesus said of himself, meek and lowly and rest-giving, 11: 29.—V. 18-20. A prophetic picture of the Saviour. 1) A chosen and beloved servant of God, v. 18. 2) Specially endued with the Spirit of God, v. 18. 3) Quiet in teaching, and compassionate to the timid and distressed, v. 19 f. 4) Destined to be victorious in proclaiming God's righteousness, and winning the nations to himself, v. 18, 20, 21.

22-37.—THE BLASPHEMY AGAINST THE SPIRIT.

In the course of those labors in Galilee of which the Evangelist has just given a general account (v. 15 f.), there occurred the events narrated in the remainder of ch. 12, followed by other events on the same day. (See on 13: 1.) This was a good deal later than the two Sabbaths of v. 1-13. Between that time and this, the Sermon on the Mount was delivered. (See

22 Then was brought unto him one possessed with a devil, blind, and dumb: and he healed him, insomuch that the blind and dumb both spake and saw.

23 And all the people were amazed, and said, Is not this the Son of David?

24 But when the Pharisees heard *it*, they said, This *fellow* doth not cast out devils, but by *a* Beelzebub the prince of the devils.

22 Then was brought unto him[1] one possessed with a demon, blind and dumb: and he healed him, insomuch that the dumb man spake and saw. And all

23 much that the dumb man spake and saw. And all the multitudes were amazed, and said, Can this be

24 the son of David? But when the Pharisees heard it, they said, This man doth not cast out demons,

a Gr. *Beelzebul,* and so v. 27....2 Or, *a demoniac.*

on v. 15, and comp. Mark 3: 19.) Consulting unity of topic rather than chronological order, Matthew throws together these several instances of opposition to Jesus. Our present section treats of the blasphemous accusation; the other cases of opposition will follow. Luke 11: 14-23 describes a similar blasphemous accusation, probably belonging to the ministry in Judea and Perea, during the six months preceding the crucifixion. (Wieseler, Clark.)

Then, not necessarily on the same day as the preceding, but some time more generally, at the same period (see on 3: 13; 11: 20); here it means, at the time when he was engaged in the labors of v. 15 f. **One possessed,** etc., (*a demoniac*) **blind and dumb,** see on 8: 28, where it has been remarked that various bodily affections were frequently connected with the demoniacal possessions, whether as cause or effect. **Insomuch,** etc., *so that the dumb man spake and saw* is the correct text.[1] **And all the people** (crowds), same word as in 5: 1, and often. Jesus was in a house, and the throng was so great that he and his disciples could not even eat bread. (Mark 3: 20.) **Is** (omit **not**) **this the son of David?** meaning the Messiah, see on 9: 27. The Greek has an interrogative particle which uniformly implies that a negative answer is expected, as in 7: 16; 11: 23, and it is quite erroneous to render 'Is not this,' etc., as in Tyndale, Cran., Gen., and in all the recent editions of Com. Ver., while the two earliest editions, A. D. 1611 and 1613, give it without the 'not'; found already in Hammond, 1659 (Trench on Rev.). It is true that sometimes the speaker may intend to intimate that perhaps the answer ought to be affirmative, as here and in John 4: 29 (Winer, p. 511 [642]); but the *form* of expression is otherwise, and it ought to be translated accordingly. Colloquial English.

could give it quite exactly. "This is not the Messiah, is it?" Eng. Rev. give "Is this," Am. Rev., "Can this be the son of David," as in John 4: 29. The miracle suggested to the crowds the idea that Jesus might be the Messiah; yet surely, they would think, it cannot be so, since he does not appear and act as Messiah will do, viz., as a mighty conqueror and splendid monarch. Observe that the miracle suggested the possibility that he was the Messiah; and in v. 38, some of the Pharisees express their wish to see a 'sign' from him, after it had been intimated (v. 28) that he was the Messiah. So the Jews did expect the Messiah to work miracles, though Maimonides (twelfth cent.) declares that no miracles are to be expected from the Messiah, perhaps departing from the older view in order to secure an argument against Jesus.

24. But when the Pharisees heard it. Mark (3: 22) describes them more particularly as 'the scribes that came down from Jerusalem.' They had no doubt come to Galilee for the purpose of observing the miracles and teaching of Jesus, and seeking to prevent the people from believing on him. (Comp. on v. 14 and 15: 1.) The Scribes usually belonged to the great Pharisee party, comp. v. 38, and see on 2: 3. These men set about their work very vigorously. They saw that if his miracles were recognized the people would believe that he was sent from God (John 3: 2), and then all his teachings must be received as true, and all his claims admitted as just. They could not question the reality of the healing, nor ascribe it to mere human agency; they therefore resorted to the absurd idea of a league with Satan, though Jesus was really destroying Satan's work. 'Heard it,' viz., the inquiry made among the crowds. **This fellow doth not cast out devils** (*the demons*), **but by** (*in*) **Beelzebub, the prince**

[1] So א B. D., Old Latin (some copies), Old Syriac, Memph., Æth. This was easily altered into 'the blind and dumb man,' as in most documents and Common Text, or 'the dumb and blind man,' as in many documents: while Old Latin (most copies) and Latin Vulgate omit both terms, and read simply 'so that he spake and saw.' These variations are instructive to the student. The first reading accounts for all the others.

25 And Jesus knew their thoughts, and said unto them, Every kingdom divided against itself is brought to desolation; and every city or house divided against itself shall not stand:

25 but [1] by Beelzebub the prince of the demons. And knowing their thoughts he said unto them, Every kingdom divided against itself is brought to desolation; and every city or house divided against itself

1 Or, *in.*

of the devils (*demons*). 'This' corresponds to the inquiry of v. 23; there is nothing to authorize the contemptuous term 'fellow' of Com. Ver. 'Demons,' and not 'devils,' see on 8: 31. 'In' rather than 'by,' see on 9: 34; so also in v. 27 f., 'in Beelzebub,' 'in whom,' 'in the Spirit of God' (so Wyclif and Rheims in all these expressions), everywhere denoting intimate union. 'Beelzebul' is unquestionably the proper form of the name,[1] though it might not be worth while now to attempt a change in the popular usage. The name was probably derived from Baal-zebub, the Fly-god of Ekron (2 Kings 1: 2, 3, 6, 16), but there is doubt as to the reason for changing the last letter, and for applying the name to Satan. (v. 26.) This application to Satan is not found in the old Jewish writings, and only in Matt. 10: 25; 12: 24, 27; Mark 3: 22; Luke 11: 15-19, all referring to the blasphemous accusation. Flies are often so terrible a plague in the East that we need not be surprised to find one of the forms under which Baal was worshiped to be Baal-zebub, Baal of the fly, or Lord of the fly; Sept. makes it Baal-fly. So one of the Greek titles of Zeus (Jupiter) was "he who drives off the flies." It would be very natural for the later Jews to express their abhorrence of this Philistine idol by using his name for Satan. The change of the last letter may have been merely euphonic, as Bab-el-mandeb (the strait at the entrance of the Red Sea) is often written Bab-el-mandel, and Belial is sometimes written Beliar; but more likely the change was designed to give a new meaning, which might be, according to different etymologies, (1) "Lord of dung"—as we know the Jews were fond of contemptuously punning upon the names of idols; or (2) "Lord of the house," which would agree with the image of v. 29. This name for Satan was sufficiently common to be readily understood, as appears from Mark 3: 22, 'he has Beelzebul,' like 'he has

a demon,' and from our Lord's using it in his reply, v. 27. For the other names, Satan and Devil, see on 4: 1. 'Prince' is literally 'ruler,' a general term; we do not know the precise nature of his authority over the demons, but everything indicates that it is absolute. Satan is also called 'prince of this world' (John 12: 31; 14: 30; 16: 11), and 'prince of the power of the air.' (Eph. 2: 2.) In 9: 34, Matt. has already stated that the Pharisees had recourse to this absurd charge, on occasion of a similar miracle of healing; but he did not there pause to tell how Jesus refuted and solemnly rebuked it. Luke 11: 15 ff. gives what is probably a third instance in another part of the country; it was very natural that the same class of malignant enemies, involved in the same logical difficulty, should attempt the same blasphemous explanation.

25 f. His reply divides itself into v. 25 f. (with which v. 29 is closely connected), v. 27 f., v. 30, v. 31 f., and v. 33-37. **And Jesus knew their thoughts and said,** comp. on 9: 4. 'Jesus' was an early addition to the text, being thought necessary for clearness. Such insertions of the name frequently occur. The Scribes and Pharisees appear to have made the blasphemous charge in a low tone to those around them, so that Jesus might not hear. They were at some little distance from him, in another part of the principal room or court of the house (Mark 3: 19), for Mark (3: 23) says he 'called them unto him' and replied to the charge. They were disposed to suggest their slanderous and insulting accusations in an underhand way, and he chose to reply openly. Mark says he spoke to them 'in comparisons,' literally 'parables,' see on 13: 3. Our Lord in his pitying condescension first argues calmly against their insulting charge, before proceeding to declare their awful guilt in making it. He does this, we may suppose, partly to leave the blasphemers not even a seeming excuse, and partly to pre-

[1] So in all Greek MSS. and most of the early versions. Beelzebub is found in the Old and Vulgate Syriac, the Vulgate Latin, and one or two copies of the Old Latin. The Syriac would naturally take the Hebrew form from

2 Kings 1: 2 ff., and Jerome likewise probably borrowed it from the Hebrew. The Latin Vulgate made this form familiar to Christendom. Notice that the margin of Com. Version says, Greek *Beelzebul.*

26 And if Satan cast out Satan, he is divided against himself; how shall then his kingdom stand?

27 And if I by *a* Beelzebub cast out devils, by whom do your children cast *them* out? therefore they shall be your judges.

26 shall not stand: and if Satan casteth out Satan, he is divided against himself; how then shall his kingdom stand? And if I [1] by Beelzebub cast out demons, [1] by whom do your sons cast them out? there-

---

a Beelzebul.—[1] Or, in.

---

vent the bystanders from imagining for a moment that there was any ground for the charge (comp. on v. 30). His argument from analogy does not mean that every case of internal strife or civil war will destroy a State, but that such is the tendency, and every such act, so far as it goes, contributes to that end. And observe that if this charge was accepted as applying to a single case of casting out a demon, it must be understood as extending to all cases; the whole work of Jesus in casting out demons must be ascribed to this cause, and throughout his entire ministry he would be having the help of Satan in breaking down Satan's power. That wise "prince of the demons" is too cunning to pursue so suicidal a course. **And if Satan cast out Satan.** For the prince of the demons to cast out his subjects would be virtually casting out himself, since they were doing his work. Those persons who so dislike the rendering 'deliver us from the evil one' (6: 13, Rev. Ver.) ought to notice that here and often Jesus distinctly recognizes Satan as personal.

27 f. Condescending, as he did with reference to the Sabbath (12: 3 f.), to present the argument in a variety of ways, our Lord here gives it a new and startling turn, being what logicians call *argumentum ad hominem*, an appeal to their own case. **Your children** (*sons*) means those who had been instructed by the Pharisees, like "sons of the prophets" in 2 Kings 2: 3; comp. the use of 'father' for a revered teacher in 23: 9; 1 Cor. 4: 15, and 'disciples' of the Pharisees in 22: 16. Exorcists would naturally belong to the Pharisee party, for no Sadducee would profess the expulsion of demons, since that party did not believe in spirits, evil or good. To make 'your sons' mean Christ's own apostles, as Chrys. and other Fathers, and some modern writers do, seems unwarranted and absurd, leaving the argument without force. It doubtless arose from an unwillingness to admit that the Jewish exorcists did really cast out demons, and a failure to observe that our Lord does not affirm that they did, but only argues from the point of view of the blas-

phemers. He appeals to the case of their own followers to silence them, without then stopping to examine the question whether their pretended expulsions were real. (Paul uses the same kind of argument in 1 Cor. 15: 29.) It was very common, about the time of our Lord, for Jews to profess to cast out demons. Curious accounts of the methods they employed, such as the use of a remarkable root, with incantations, which they pretended were handed down from Solomon, are given by Josephus, "Ant.," 8, 2, 5, "War.," 7, 6, 3; comp. Tobit 8: 2; Justin Martyr, Trypho, ch. 85. In Acts 19: 13 we read of strolling Jewish exorcists who thought there must be some magical charm in the name of Jesus which Paul named when working miracles, and tried to use it themselves. **Therefore they shall be your judges** ('they' being emphatic, as in 5: 4 ff.; comp. on 1: 21), *i. e.*, shall convict you either of being yourselves in league with Beelzebul, or of unreasonable and wicked conduct in accusing another of league with him for doing what they claim to do. **But if I cast out devils** (*demons*) **by the Spirit of God,** assumes that he does; and he has just shown that the contrary supposition would charge Satan with sheer folly, and would involve the accusers in self-condemnation. The chief emphasis of the sentence (according to the correct reading of the Greek) is on the words 'by the Spirit of God'; but 'I' is also emphatic, and suggests a contrast between his case and theirs. 'Spirit' has in the Greek no article, but is made definite by the appended genitive, since there is but one Spirit of God. **Then** is in the similar passage of Luke (11: 20) rendered by Com. Ver. 'no doubt'—another of the numerous unnecessary variations. So 'unto you' here in Com. Ver. and 'upon you' in Luke, are for the same Greek preposition. **Then the kingdom of God is** (or *has*) **come unto you.** Matthew here has 'kingdom of God' instead of his usual 'kingdom of heaven' (see on 3: 2), probably because of the verbal connection here between 'Spirit of God' and 'kingdom of God.' The word rendered

28 But if I cast out devils by the Spirit of God, then the kingdom of God is come unto you.

29 Or else, how can one enter into a strong man's house, and spoil his goods, except he first bind the strong man? and then he will spoil his house.

30 He that is not with me is against me; and he that gathereth not with me scattereth abroad.

28 fore shall they be your judges. But if I [1] by the Spirit of God cast out demons, then is the kingdom

29 of God come upon you. Or how can one enter into the house of the strong *man*, and spoil his goods, except he first bind the strong *man*? and then he

30 will spoil his house. He that is not with me is against me; and he that gathereth not with me

1 Or, *in.*

'has come' usually signifies to anticipate, to be beforehand, and so to come unexpectedly; and some urge such a sense here—has already arrived, when you simply thought it would come before long — has taken you unawares. But the word appears in the later Greek usage to have sometimes meant simply come, arrive, etc. (1 Thess. 2: 16; Rom. 9: 31; Phil. 3: 16.) The idea then is, the kingdom of God, the Messianic Dispensation, has made its appearance in your presence. (Comp. Luke 17: 20 f.) Here again, as in 5: 17; 7: 21-23; 12: 8, our Lord strongly intimates that he is the Messiah, yet without distinctly declaring it. The full conviction announced by the apostles in 16: 16 seems to have been then recently arrived at. But that conclusion would not preclude, it would rather pre-suppose, a previous stage of perplexed inquiry, like that of John the Baptist (11: 3), and is not fundamentally inconsistent with an early flush of delighted persuasion when some of them first met him, as recorded by John (1: 41, 49.) There is thus no such contradiction between John and the Synoptics on this point as some have imagined. Nor is it strange that Jesus should occasionally intimate his Messiaship long before he thought proper publicly to avow it. But what as to the force of the argument in this passage? How did it follow, that if he was casting out the demons by the Spirit of God, then the kingdom of God had arrived? The miracles of Jesus did not directly prove him to be the Messiah, but they proved it indirectly. This constant divine assistance in working his great series of miracles showed that he must have a divine mission, and attested all his claims as just; but he claimed to be the Messiah, as he has before intimated and intimates here; therefore the miracles proved him to be the Messiah. So Paul says he was shown to be the Son of God by the resurrection from the dead. (Rom. 1: 4.) Besides, in casting out demons, he was to that extent destroying the kingdom of Satan (v. 26), and in so far establishing the correlative kingdom of God. (Comp. v. 29.)

29. This connects itself closely with the thought of v. 25 f. **Or,** to look at the matter in another way. (Comp. 7: 9; 12: 5.) **Else** in Com. Ver. (following Cranmer, Gen.) has no representative in the original. **How can one enter**, etc. This is a general truth, with an obvious application to the matter in hand. Jesus was taking away from Satan a part of his property, in delivering the demoniacs, and this could not be unless he were at variance with Satan, and strong enough to bind him. The word translated **goods** means utensils, implements (as those for cooking, eating, sleeping), and would suggest that the demoniacs were the instruments of Satan. **Spoil,** or 'plunder,' at the end of the sentence, represents a compound word, 'thoroughly plunder.'

30. Here again, as in the preceding verses, our Lord speaks in apophthegms (Mark 3: 23), each sentence containing a distinct truth, expressed in general terms. It naturally follows that no connection between these is outwardly indicated, and we are left to see for ourselves the internal connection of the thoughts. (Comp. at the beginning of ch. 7.) The Scribes said that our Lord was in league with Satan, but in reality he is opposing and overthrowing Satan's power, binding him, as it were, and plundering his house. In this great and deadly struggle, there can be no neutrality. No man can be friends with both sides, nor be indifferent to both. It is probable that many of those present were thinking they would not take sides between Jesus and the blaspheming Scribes. To them, in the first place, this saying would come home; but it is general, and applicable to all times, and all varieties of character and conduct. The sentence contains two parallel and practically equivalent members—the Hebrew parallelism. (Comp. on 4: 16.) The image in the second member is from gathering grain in harvest, as in 3: 12; 6: 26; John 4: 36. Men often fancy that they are by no means opposing Christ's service, though not engaged in it; that they are friendly to religion in others, though not personally religious. But in the

31 Wherefore I say unto you, All manner of sin and blasphemy shall be forgiven unto men: but the blasphemy *against* the *Holy* Ghost shall not be forgiven unto men.

32 And whosoever speaketh a word against the Son of man, it shall be forgiven him: but whosoever speaketh against the Holy Ghost, it shall not be forgiven him, neither in this world, neither in the *world* to come.

31 scattereth. Therefore I say unto you, Every sin and blasphemy shall be forgiven unto men; but the blasphemy against the Spirit shall not be forgiven.

32 And whosoever shall speak a word against the Son of man, it shall be forgiven him; but whosoever shall speak against the Holy Spirit, it shall not be forgiven him, neither in this [1] world, nor in that

---

1 Or, *age.*

---

nature of the case, this is impossible. *Stier:* " Neutrality here is no neutrality, but a remaining on the side of the enemy ; indolence here is no mere indolence, but opposition ; the merely not believing and not obeying is still resistance and rejection." The gospel is of such a nature, as to its offers and its claims, that it cannot tolerate indifference. If it deserves our respect, it deserves our entire and hearty reception. If we are not yielding Christ our whole heart, we are really yielding him nothing. Professed neutrality, with real hostility of heart, may even be more offensive to him, and is sometimes more injurious in its influence, than avowed opposition.—In Mark 9: 40; Luke 9: 50 there is an expression which at first seems to contradict this, viz., ' He that is not against us is for us.' But so far is this from being the case that both sayings (*Alexander*) " may be exemplified in the experience of the very same persons. For example, Nicodemus, by refusing to take part with the Sanhedrin against our Lord, although he did not venture to espouse his cause, proved himself to be upon his side (John 7:50 f.) ; but if he had continued the same course when the crisis had arrived, he would equally have proved himself to be against him." Comp. the apparently contradictory sayings of Prov. 26; 4 f. ; Gal. 6: 2, 5 ; Rom. 3: 28, as related to James 2: 24.

31 f. Our Lord now solemnly declares that a blasphemy against the Holy Spirit is the only unpardonable sin; and it is distinctly implied that their accusation, that he cast out demons by the help of Beelzebul, was a blasphemy against the Holy Spirit, and so was past forgiveness. **Therefore,** viz., on account of all that he has been saying, from v. 25 onward. It was manifest from such analogies that their charge of league with Beelze-

bul was absurd ; and they must have known that it was not true, and that the miracle was really wrought by divine power. Jesus says it was wrought by the Spirit of God, and so their accusation was not merely an insult to a man, but a blasphemy against the Spirit of God. For this reason he solemnly tells them that such blasphemy will never be forgiven. And we can see (Edersh.) that their malignant hostility to the kingdom of heaven, as appearing in a form so contrary to what they expected and would have been willing to recognize, here reached an acme of virulence from which they went straight on to procure his death. **I say unto you,** see on 5: 18. **All manner of sin.** *Every sin* is the exact translation. With the general truth that every sin **shall be forgiven unto men,**[1] he connects the specific term **and blasphemy,** to leave no doubt that every blasphemy too (as well as every other sin) will be forgiven ; and thus brings out all the more strongly the sole exception, **but the blasphemy against the Holy Ghost** (*Spirit*) **shall not be forgiven.** This promise of forgiveness for every sin and blasphemy is of course to be limited by the conditions of repentance, etc., elsewhere laid down in Scripture, and understood in such a case without being stated. (Comp. on 7: 7 f.) ' Blasphemy ' has been explained on 9: 3 as signifying in general injurious or insulting speaking, and so with regard to God, speaking impiously. Blasphemy was considered among the Jews a very great offence. (26:65.) In v. 32 we find the general expression **speaketh against.** Here the guilt of what the Pharisees have done is shown by another contrast. **The Son of man,** see on 8: 20. Our Lord had not distinctly claimed to be more than man. To speak against him personally, regarding him simply as a man

---

1 The marginal reading in Rev. Ver. (*not* in Amer. Revisers) ' unto you men ' has no support but B, a single cursive, and a passage in Athanasius. It may not be strange that W H. should cling to B and put this in the margin; but it is strange that the revisers should follow when internal evidence yields nothing decisive. After the second ' forgiven ' many documents add ' unto men ' as in Com. text, and some add ' unto them.'

33 Either make the tree good, and his fruit good ; or else make the tree corrupt, and his fruit corrupt ; for the tree is known by *his* fruit.

33 which is to come. Either make the tree good, and its fruit good ; or make the tree corrupt, and its fruit

---

(*e. g.* 11: 19), did not involve as great guilt as to speak against the Holy Spirit, whose influences filled his human spirit (see on 3: 16; 4: 1), and gave to him, as a man, the power of working miracles. (v. 28.) In the phrase, **but whosoever speaketh against the Holy Ghost,** *Spirit*,[1] the word 'holy' is so placed in the Greek as to be emphatic. They said, 'He hath an unclean spirit' (Mark 3: 30) ; while in truth he was full of the Holy Spirit. (Yet there is no propriety in inserting the word 'holy' in v. 31, as in Com. Ver.) Their charge of league with Beelzebul was therefore not simply a slander against the man, Jesus of Nazareth, nor simply an insult to the Son of man, the Messiah, but was a blasphemy against the Holy Spirit. And it will not do to say that he was merely warning them against a possibility ; for he is surely speaking of the blasphemy they have uttered, as blasphemy against the Holy Spirit. (Comp. v. 28.) It must be observed that the Holy Spirit, the Spirit of God (v 28), here represents the Divinity in general. There is here no allusion to the peculiar gracious office and work of the Spirit in calling, renewing, and sanctifying the soul ; it is the Spirit of God as giving power to work miracles. (Comp. Acts 2: 4; 8: 14-19, etc.) These Pharisees ascribe to the influence and aid of Satan what was manifestly and unmistakably wrought by divine power ; and this was not merely an insult to a man, but was a malignant insult to God. Similar, in this particular respect, was the sin of Ananias and Sapphira, who undertook to practice a deception, not merely upon the apostles, but upon the Holy Spirit, who was well known to give them supernatural knowledge. (Acts 5: 3 ff.) Paul had blasphemed Jesus of Nazareth, and yet was forgiven, because he "did it ignorantly, in unbelief." (1 Tim. 1: 13.) He did not then believe that Jesus spoke by the Spirit of God, and therefore was not blaspheming the Holy Spirit. Afterwards he learned and taught that the Spirit of God is "the Spirit of Christ." (Rom. 8: 9.)

The conditions, then, under which this unpardonable sin of blasphemy against the Spirit of God is committed, are (1) that there shall be a work manifestly supernatural, unmistakably the work of God and not of man, and (2) that one shall, in determined and malignant opposition, insultingly ascribe to Satan this which he knows to be the work of God. Now, are these conditions ever fulfilled, except in an age of miracles? Can any other divine work, as, for instance, the conversion of a friend, or a general revival of spirituality, be so unquestionably and unmistakably the work of God, that a person ascribing it to Satan is guilty, not merely of sin, but of that flagrant and deeply malignant blasphemy against God which is unpardonable? This is the question to be decided ; and it can hardly be decided in the affirmative. As miracles continued throughout the apostolic age, this blasphemy against the Spirit may very naturally be understood to be meant by that "sin unto death" which John implies (1 John 5: 16) cannot be forgiven. Indeed, we seem compelled so to understand it, since our Lord here says that the blasphemy against the Spirit is the only form of sin that will not be forgiven. The current phrase, "the sin against the Holy Ghost," is not found in Scripture, and has been formed by combining John's expression with the passage before us. And the familiar idea of "sinning away one's day of grace" ought not to be confounded with the blasphemy here spoken of. It has already been remarked that this blasphemy does not at all refer to the gracious work of the Spirit in calling and regenerating, but manifestly and simply to his miraculous work. Through neglect of this distinction, persons often pass from speaking of blasphemy against the Spirit to discussing what is called "resisting the Spirit," without being aware that these are quite different things. Even the passage in 1 John cannot refer to a person who has resisted the Spirit till his influences are withdrawn, for no one else could decide that a man was in that condition, while the apostle

---

[1] The Rev. Ver. here changes 'Ghost' to 'Spirit' as necessary in order to agree with 'Spirit' in v. 28 and 31.

It would have been much better had the revisers everywhere made this change. (Comp. on 1: 18.)

34 O generation of vipers, how can ye, being evil, speak good things? for out of the abundance of the heart the mouth speaketh.

34 corrupt: for the tree is known by its fruit. Ye offspring of vipers, how can ye, being evil, speak good things? for out of the abundance of the heart the

intimates that the "sin unto death" can be definitely known to others, since he will not say that one who has committed it shall be prayed for.—Heb. 6: 4-8 and 10: 26 ff., relate to the sin of apostasy, and are therefore quite distinct from the blasphemy against the Spirit, though often confounded with it.

Neither in this world, neither in the world to come. This is simply a strong and expanded declaration that it will *never* be forgiven. 'World' is here not *kosmos*, the physical universe, but *aion*, a period or age. (Comp. on 25: 46.) The Jews constantly spoke of "this period" and "the coming period," as separated by the appearance of the Messiah. In the New Test. "the period to come" is usually conceived of as following the second coming of the Lord. (Comp. on 13: 22.) *Weiss:* "Neither in this world-period, *i. e.*, in the time up to the Second Coming, nor in the future world-period, which begins with the Judgment; and as the Judgment decides the eternal destiny of men, there can never in that following period be forgiveness of the sin which at the Judgment was established and subjected to punishment." Our Lord's expression *might* in itself imply that some sins not forgiven in this world will be forgiven in the world to come (Olsh.); but it does not necessarily, nor even very naturally teach this; and as the idea is unsupported by, and inconsistent with, the general teachings of Scripture on that subject, it is quite improper to base so important a doctrine as that of "a second probation" in the future life, upon the merely possible meaning of this one passage, with perhaps the addition of 1 Pet. 3: 19, according to one possible interpretation. That he only means to say it will *never* be forgiven, is confirmed by Mark 3: 29 (correct text), 'hath never forgiveness, but is guilty of an eternal sin.' Other sins may be blotted out, and, so to speak, cease to exist; but this must continue, from the time it is committed, always existing, an everlasting sin. The thought of v. 31 f. is not recorded as repeated on the similar occasion of Luke 11:

14, 23, but on yet another occasion, Luke 12: 10.

33-35. It might be said that here was only speech, only words. But the speech came from the heart, and showed the character, as the tree is known from the fruit. This unpardonable blasphemy was just what might be expected from its authors; they were bad men, and they would say bad things. The portion of the discourse in v. 33-37 is recorded by Matt. only. The terms of v. 33 are the same as in 7: 16-19, where see Notes. There the thought is that we must test character by conduct; here it is that conduct (including speech) is all the more important because it corresponds to and reveals character. There has been much discussion about the sense of **make,** some explaining it as signifying 'regard,' 'consider'; others, 'suppose to be,' etc. The idea seems to be that the fruit will be like the tree, and if you make the tree good you make its fruit good. The word 'make' is thus understood in its ordinary sense. **His,** the old possessive 'his' from it (*hyt*), see on 24: 32; modern *its*. **Generation** (*offspring*) of·vipers, the same expression as in 3: 7.[1] This was strong language and severe; but the loving Saviour did not shrink from the severest rebukes where they were needed. These would be prompted, indeed, as much by love to sinners, as by indignation at their sin. (Comp. on 5: 29.) **How can ye, being evil, speak good things?** How is it possible, in the nature of things, that you should? This is a moral, not a constitutional impossibility. **For out of the abundance of the heart,** more exactly, 'the superabundance.' The word implies excess, that the heart is full and more than full; the mouth speaks what pours forth from the overflowing heart (comp. 15: 18); and as their heart overflows with wickedness, how can it be that they should speak what is good? Comp. 1 Sam. 24: 13.— V. 35 varies the image to that of a treasure, or store, the word not necessarily indicating something precious. The good man has in him a good store, and he brings out from it good

[1] What is the propriety of saying (Weiss) that the Evangelist has manifestly taken this phrase from John the Baptist's discourse? What objection can there be to believing that Jesus used the same phrase? Such arbitrary dicta are far from giving real support to a theory.

35 A good man out of the good treasure of the heart bringeth forth good things: and an evil man out of the evil treasure bringeth forth evil things.
36 But I say unto you, That every idle word that men shall speak, they shall give account thereof in the day of judgment.
37 For by thy words thou shalt be justified, and by thy words thou shalt be condemned.

35 mouth speaketh. The good man out of his good treasure bringeth forth good things: and the evil man out of his evil treasure bringeth forth evil
36 things. And I say unto you, that every idle word that men shall speak, they shall give account thereof
37 in the day of judgment. For by thy words thou shalt be justified, and by thy words thou shalt be condemned.

---

things. This of course means the store of his inner man, heart, and so the word "heart" was early added, in some quarters (as Old Syriac version), by way of explanation, being suggested by v. 34, and passed into many later documents and the Com. text. **Bringeth forth** is literally *casts out*, throws out, the word explained on 9: 38, and here perhaps implying that the evil things are, as it were, involuntarily thrown out, "as a fountain doth its waters, by a natural and necessary ebullition" (*Barrow*). The fact that men speak good or evil according to their nature, by no means frees them from guilt. This ought to be understood from general principles; but our Lord leaves no room for uncertainty on the subject, for he proceeds to declare that words, even idle words, must be answered for.

36 f. But (*and*) **I say unto you,** solemnly introducing an important saying (as in v. 31), see on 5: 18. Though they spoke so heedlessly the most blasphemous words, and doubtless thought, as men are apt to do, that what one *says* is of little importance, yet he assures them that men shall give account for **every idle word.** 'Idle' exactly renders the original term, which signifies 'not working,' and hence inefficient, useless, etc.— words not intended to produce any effect. **In the day of judgment,** see on 11 : 22. In v. 37, **by thy words,** is literally *out of thy words*, as a thing proceeding from their words, a result or consequence of them. Of course he does not mean that it will proceed from their words alone; every one admits the fact as to actions, and words are here the subject of remark. The repetition of 'by thy words' makes the statement more weighty and impressive. Words are important because they reveal character (v. 33, 35), and because they powerfully affect others. The only sin declared to be unpardonable is a sin of speech (v. 31 f.) ; and, on the other hand, "if any man offend not in speech, the same is a perfect man, and able also to bridle the whole body." (James 3: 2.) Speech is indeed one of the grand distinctions of human beings, and a mighty

power for good or evil. But this passage must not be understood as condemning all light pleasantries of conversation; it simply declares that the idlest nothings we ever utter are included within the range of accountability to God. We must therefore see to it that our pleasantries are not essentially untruthful, that they are free from malice and impurity —in a word, that they are innocent and helpful. (Comp. on 5 : 37.)

HOMILETICAL AND PRACTICAL.

V. 23. Different effects produced by the outward evidences of Christianity. 1) Many half convinced that it is divine, but mainly inclined to reject it, v. 23. 2) Some persuading themselves and others that it is not divine, that its effects are to be otherwise explained, v. 24. 3) Some trying to play neutral, v. 30. 4) Some requiring further evidence, suited to their own notion, v. 38. 5) Some rejoicing to believe and ready to obey, v. 49 f.—V. 24. Anything to explain away the divine power of Christianity; anything, though it be absurd, insulting, blasphemous. —V. 25 f. The forces of evil in the world do not act at hazard, nor by blind fate, but are directed by a lofty and shrewd intelligence.— V. 26. Satan and his kingdom. 1) There is a *personal* spirit of evil. 2) He has a kingdom. 3) The demons are his subjects, and are striving to make men his subjects forever. 4) Jesus opposes and shakes Satan's kingdom. (Comp. Luke 10: 17-19.)—V. 30. We must be definitely Christ's friends, or we are definitely his enemies. Vinet, "Gospel Studies," preaches from this text on "The Intolerance of Christianity," and from Luke 9: 50 on " The Tolerance of Christianity."—V. 31. Gladly, in several recorded cases, the Saviour said, "Thy sins are forgiven thee." Sorrowfully he says that this sin "shall not be forgiven."—V. 33. HENRY: "Unless the heart be *transformed*, the life will never be thoroughly *reformed*."—V. 34. A heart overfull of evil, a mouth overflowing with evil.— V. 37. CHRYS.: "Wherefore not the slan-

38 Then certain of the scribes and of the Pharisees answered, saying, Master, we would see a sign from thee.	38 Then certain of the scribes and Pharisees answered him, saying, ¹ Master, we would see a sign

1 Or, Teacher.

dered, but the slanderers, have need to be anxious and to tremble. For the former are not constrained to answer for themselves, touching the evil things which are said of them, out the latter for the evil they have spoken; and over these impends the whole danger.''—V. 36 f. Speech. 1) It is a peculiarity of human beings, and a great power in human life. 2) It reveals character, v. 35. 3) We are accountable not only for purposely wicked, but for idle speech, v. 36. 4) Speech will help to determine our eternal future. DODDRIDGE: '' Discourse tending to innocent mirth, to exhilarate the spirits, is not idle discourse; as the time spent in necessary recreation is not idle time.''

38-50. TWO OTHER CASES OF OPPOSITION TO JESUS.

These two instances of opposition belong together (v. 46), and clearly seem to have followed immediately upon the blasphemous accusation. The word **then** (v. 38) does not certainly prove this (comp. v. 22), but there is an obvious internal connection; and notice that in Mark (3: 31) the coming of the mother and brethren immediately follows the blasphemous accusation, and the house and the multitude correspond. (Mark 3: 20; 3: 31 f.)

I. 38-42. THE SCRIBES AND PHARISEES ASK A SIGN. Comp. Luke 11: 29-32, which probably refers to a subsequent occasion, in Judea or Perea. (See above on v. 22.)

38. Answered. This was their response to the severe and solemn words he had just spoken. (v. 31-37.) **Certain of the Scribes and Pharisees** (comp. on v. 24) did not concur with those he had reproved in ascribing his miracles to Beelzebul (comp. Luke 11: 15 f.), but they intimated that the miracles he had wrought were insufficient to satisfy them of his divine mission, and as he had impliedly claimed to be the Messiah (v. 28) they would like to see him present a **sign**¹ such as they would admit to be unmistakable. Their language was respectful, but their design was bad, as appears from our Lord's reply; and Luke declares on the similar occasion that they did it 'tempting him.' (Luke 11: 16.) **Teacher,** *didaskalos*, see on 8: 19. **We would** (*wish to*) **see,** as in 16: 24.

All we are here told is that they asked to see a 'sign'. Luke (11: 16) says that on the similar occasion 'they sought of him a sign

---

¹ There are three Greek words used in the New Test. to denote what we commonly and loosely call '' miracles.''

1. *Teras* signifies something portentous, suited to excite astonishment or alarm. The New Test. has it only in the plural, and always in connection with 'signs.' It is uniformly translated in Com. Ver. 'wonders.' (Comp. 24: 24.) 2. *Dunamis* strictly signifies power, whether physical or moral, whether natural, acquired, or bestowed, and is often translated 'power,' (*e. g.*, 22: 29; 24: 29 f.; 26: 64, and in Rev. Ver. 14: 2.) It is in Com. Ver. translated 'miracle' in Mark 9: 39; Acts 2: 22; 8: 13; 19: 11; 1 Cor. 12: 10, 28, 29; Gal. 3: 5; Heb. 2: 4. Of these passages Rev. Ver. gives 'mighty work' in Mark 9: 39; Acts 2: 22, 'powers' in Heb. 2: 4, and retains 'miracle' in the rest, always putting 'power' in the margin. So Com. Ver. gives 'wonderful works' in 7: 22 (Rev. Ver. 'mighty works'), and 'mighty works' in 11: 20-23; 13: 54, 58; 14: 2; Mark 6: 2, 5, 14; Luke 10: 13; 19: 37, which Rev. Ver. retains, except that in Mark 6: 14 it changes to 'powers,' as in Matt. 14: 2. And yet in all these places except Mark 6: 2 it was already rendered 'miracles' by Tyndale, Cran., Gen., and Rheims. So Noyes, except in Mark 6: 14. This confusion might be almost entirely corrected by uniformly

rendering this word 'miracle' wherever it denotes a deed of supernatural power; since our word miracle, although in its Latin origin signifying a wonder, is now regularly used in the general sense of a supernatural deed. 3 *Semeion*, a 'sign,' that by which something is signified or known, is used of things not supernatural in 16: 3; 26: 48; Luke 2: 12; 2 Thess. 3: 17 ('token.') In all other passages it denotes some more or less distinctly supernatural event. It is usually translated 'sign.' But Com. Ver. has 'miracle' in Luke 23: 8, John 2: 11, 23; 3: 2; 4: 54; 6: 2, 14, 26; 7: 31; 9: 16, 10: 41; 11: 47; 12: 18, 37; Acts 4: 16, 22; 6: 8; 8: 6; 15: 12; Rev. 13: 14; 16: 14; 19: 20; and 'wonder' in Rev. 12: 1, 3; 13: 13. In all these passages Rev. Ver. has given 'sign,' except Luke 23: 8; Acts 4: 16, 22, where it retains 'miracle,' placing 'sign' in the margin. In these last cases miracle seems in English a better word, but the other would suffice, and Rev. Ver. has often sacrificed much more than this to preserve uniformity of rendering. The Bible Union Revision renders uniformly the first word by 'wonder,' the second by 'miracle,' the third by 'sign.' This uniform rendering would make the important subject of miracles in the New Test. appreciably plainer to the English reader.

39 But he answered and said unto them, An evil and adulterous generation seeketh after a sign; and there shall no sign be given to it, but the sign of the prophet Jonas:
40 For as Jonas was three days and three nights in the whale's belly; so shall the Son of man be three days and three nights in the heart of the earth.

39 from thee. But he answered and said unto them, An evil and adulterous generation seeketh after a sign; and there shall no sign be given to it but the
40 sign of Jonah the prophet: for as Jonah was three days and three nights in the belly of the [1]whale; so shall the Son of man be three days and three

---

1 Gr. *sea monster.*

---

from heaven.' And on another occasion (Matt. 16:1), it is likewise 'a sign from heaven.' Moses gave manna from heaven, Joshua made the sun and moon stand still, Samuel caused thunder and hail in time of harvest, Elijah brought down fire from heaven, and rain at his word, Isaiah (speaking for Jehovah) bade Ahaz ask for a sign, "either in the depth, or in the height above." Some such sign as these the Scribes and Pharisees probably wanted. They may have taken literally the prediction of Joel 2: 30. (Acts 2:19.) Comp. below on 24: 30.

39, 40. An evil and adulterous generation, viz., one which has forsaken Jehovah, and demands a sign such as itself may dictate. 'Adulterous,' when thus figuratively employed, is usually applied in Old Test. to idolatry (Isa. 57:3; Ezek. 16:15; Hosea 3:1, etc.), but it is applicable also to any sin by which the nation forsook her divine husband. (Comp. James 4: 4, Rev. Ver.) The Jews had never been generally idolatrous since their return from the Babylonian captivity, but they were God-forsaking and wicked. **And there shall no sign be given to it.** Our Lord wrought many miracles, and these actually were, and ought to have been considered, signs of his divine mission, as Nicodemus early recognized. (John 3:2, Rev. Ver., 'signs.') But when with a blending of idle curiosity and unbelief, they asked him to furnish a special 'sign' (and of the precise kind that suited their fancy), he would not do it. So likewise in 16: 4, also at Nazareth (Luke 4:23 ff.), and before Herod. (Luke 23:8 f.) **But the sign of the prophet Jonas.** Jonah instead of Jonas, see on 1: 2. **For as Jonas was three days and three nights in the whale's belly,** or, in the belly of the 'huge fish.' The Greek word is used for any huge sea-creature, by Homer once for a seal, at a later period for the whale, the shark, the dog-fish, etc. The Hebrew simply says 'a great fish,' and the Greek term does not enable us to say what kind of fish it was. It was translated 'whale' because that is the largest of the huge creatures denoted by the Greek word; but the rendering was unfortunate, for the whale has not a throat sufficiently large to swallow a man, and this fact has given rise to some sneers from skeptics of the lower grade. The shark or the dog-fish could readily swallow a man, and entire human bodies have sometimes been found in the stomach of fishes of this kind. The prophet's preservation was obviously miraculous; but it is useless to make the mere deglutition a miracle, when the language does not really so indicate. **So shall the Son of man,** *i. e.*, the Messiah, see on 8: 20. **In the heart of the earth.** This expression was probably used with reference to that of Jonah 2: 3, 'heart of the seas'; comp. Deut. 4: 11, 'unto the heart of heaven,' Psa. 46: 2, 'in the heart of the seas,' (all these passages in Rev. Ver. and margin of Com. Ver.) The reference is to our Lord's interment, and the passages compared show that there is no propriety in insisting, as many do, that the language is too strong for that simple idea, and must therefore be referred to what is called his "descent into Hades." **Three days and three nights.** See Jonah 1: 17. Our Lord was actually in the grave less than thirty-six hours, but it began before the close of Friday, and closed on the morning of Sunday, and according to the mode of counting time among the Jews, this would be reckoned three days, both the first and the last day being always included. (Comp. on 17: 1, and on 27: 63 f.) The only difficulty is, that he not merely says "three days," but "three days and three nights," when he spent only two nights in the tomb. But the Jews reckoned the night and day as together constituting one period, and a part of this period was counted as the whole. Lightfoot quotes from the Jerusalem Talmud two Rabbis as saying, "A day and a night make an Onah, and a part of an Onah is as the whole." There was no way to express in Greek this period of twenty-four hours, except by day and night

41 The men of Nineveh shall rise in judgment with this generation, and shall condemn it: because they repented at the preaching of Jonas; and, behold, a greater than Jonas *is* here.

41 nights in the heart of the earth. The men of Nineveh shall stand up in the judgment with this generation, and shall condemn it: for they repented at

(or night and day) as here, or by the late and extremely rare Greek compound 'night-day' (*nuchthemeron*) used in 2 Cor. 11 : 25. It was natural to choose here the former phrase (even if we suppose the other known to Matthew), in order to state more strongly the similarity of the two cases. We find a parallel use in 1 Sam. 30: 12 f., where it is first said that the Egyptian had eaten nothing "three days and three nights," and then, " my master left me because three days ago I fell sick." So also in Esther 4: 16; 5: 1. Some have inferred from this passage of Matthew that Jesus must have remained seventy-two full hours in the grave; but some of the expressions used in speaking of his resurrection absolutely forbid this. See on 27: 63. The only sign which should be given to that wicked generation was 'the sign of Jonah the prophet,' a sign resembling the miracle which occurred in the case of Jonah, viz., the resurrection of Jesus after being three days in the tomb. Jonah's miraculous deliverance from the belly of the fish would naturally be made known by him to the Ninevites, in accounting for the zeal with which he proclaimed his message (comp. Luke 11 : 30; 'Jonah was a sign to the Ninevites'), and would contribute to their reception of his message. And so the resurrection of Jesus was to be a sign to that generation, which ought to conquer the unbelief of the most perverse, and did conquer in many cases. (Acts 2: 32 ff.; 4: 33; Rom. 1: 4.) Jesus makes a similar obscure allusion to his resurrection in John 2: 21, in which case also he had been asked for a 'sign.' (John 2: 18.)[1]

41. By a natural association of ideas, our Lord passes to say that the men of 'this generation' are acting much more wickedly than did the Ninevites. It was a sublime spectacle when the whole population of that vast heathen city, the proud king, the nobles and all, down to the very humblest, repented at the preaching of Jonah. (Jonah 3: 5-10.) This repentance, both in the grief, the reformation, and the prayer for forgiveness, must have been genuine, for otherwise God would not have regarded it, nor would Jesus have appealed to it here. Subsequent generations relapsed into idolatry, but so it often was with Israel. **Shall rise,** more literally, *stand up,* and Rev. Ver. so renders, in order to leave room for the idea of standing up to bear witness, as in Matthew 14: 57. But this is the common term for the resurrection, more common than the literal ' be raised' of v. 42, and does not probably mean anything else in the present case. **In** (*the*) **judgment,** see on 11: 22. **With this generation,** *i. e.,* along with, in company with. **And shall condemn it,** show its guilt and desert of condemnation, by the contrast between its conduct and their own. (Comp. 11: 22-24.) **Repented,** the verb corresponding to *metanoia* (see on 3: 2), denoting not merely regret, but change of mind. Tyndale, Cran., Gen., " amended." **At the preaching,** or proclamation, the word being derived from the verb *kerusso,* explained on 4: 17. The preposition rendered 'at' is *eis,* usually rendered 'into' or 'unto,' and often denoting design or aim. It cannot possibly have that sense here, for certainly the Ninevites did not repent *in order that* Jonah might preach. It clearly introduces the occasion or ground of the repenting [2] (Winer, p. 397 [495]) ; and

[1] Dr. Hort says (W H., App., p. 282) that in this passage " it is difficult to believe that all the words as they stand have apostolic authority." Dr. Toy (Quotations p. XXVIII.) holds it probable that Jesus said only what is recorded in Luke 11: 30, and the rest in Matthew was added by "the oral tradition." Why not then refer to another similar passage, Mark 8: 12, " There shall no sign be given unto this generation," and conclude that Jonah was not really mentioned by Jesus at all? Why draw one conclusion and not the other, except because the miracle of the great fish does not please the critics? Bleek attempts an argument to prove that Luke's account is alone authentic; but he is amply refuted by Weiss. In fact (though we need not urge it), does not Luke's own language really rest on the resemblance of the three days and three nights? How else (Weiss, Godet) did Jonah 'become' a sign to the Ninevites? and why else does Jesus say in Luke that the Son of man 'shall be' a sign, instead of ' is '?

[2] The Old Latin gives here in some of its forms the word-for-word translation *in prædicationem,* while other forms and the Vulgate have *in prædicatione.* The Peshito has ' *in,*' *i. e.,* on the ground of.

42 The queen of the south shall rise up in the judgment with this generation, and shall condemn it: for she came from the uttermost parts of the earth to hear the wisdom of Solomon ; and, behold, a greater than Solomon *is* here.
43 When the unclean spirit is gone out of a man, he walketh through dry places, seeking rest, and findeth none.

42 the preaching of Jonah; and, behold, [1] a greater than Jonah is here. The queen of the south shall rise up in the judgment with this generation, and shall condemn it ; for she came from the ends of the earth to hear the wisdom of Solomon ; and, behold, 43 [1] a greater than Solomon is here. But the unclean spirit, when [2] he is gone out of the man, passeth through waterless places, seeking rest, and findeth

---

1 Gr. *more than*....2 Or, *it.*

---

so it may possibly have the same force in 3: 11 and Acts 2: 38. **And behold,** calling attention to something important. **A greater** —or *more*—**than Jonah is here.** The word is neuter, not 'a greater (man),' but '(something) more.' (Comp. on 11: 9; 12: 6.) If more than Jonah was here, then the men of this generation were under greater obligation to repent than the Ninevites, and all the more guilty for not repenting. Some records of buried Nineveh have been recently exhumed, and the world eagerly reads their strangely recovered history ; let us not forget that the Ninevites of Jonah's day will rise up in the judgment and condemn all those of every age who hear the preaching of the gospel and will not repent. *Weiss :* "If John already was more than a prophet (11: 9), why should not the mightier one to whom he pointed (3: 11) be beyond comparison more than Jonah?" Wherever the gospel of Jesus is really preached, the same thing holds true ; for the gospel, when spoken by the humblest follower of Christ, has higher claims to be believed and heeded than had the solemn warning of Jonah. This reply of our Lord somewhat resembles that made at Nazareth. (Luke 4: 23 ff.) In both cases miracles were demanded, and in both the answer rebuked the arrogance of their claim by showing that God had sometimes blessed Gentiles rather than Jews.

42. Another historical instance is added, to show still further the wickedness of this generation. They not only refused to heed the *call to repentance* made by a more than prophet, but they slighted the *wisdom* taught by a more than Solomon. **The queen of the south,** called in 1 Kings 10: 1–10 'the queen of Sheba.' This people, usually called the Sabaeans, appear to have occupied a large portion of Southern Arabia. In this fertile region they grew rich by agriculture and trade, especially the great trade with India, from which country they brought spices, precious stones, etc., to supply the Western nations.

Hence came that abundance of costly articles which astonished the court of Solomon. In Joel 3: 8 the Sabaeans are called "a nation far off," and so in Jer. 6: 20, Sheba is "a far country." This corresponds with our Lord's expression, **came from the uttermost parts** (*the ends*) **of the earth** (comp. Deut. 28: 49), which, according to the knowledge of the time, would be no exaggeration as applied to the southern extremity of the Arabian peninsula. 'Ends' is literal (so Wyc., and Rheims), and simpler than 'uttermost parts' (Tyndale and followers). There were few books in the days of this queen, and the only way to get the full benefit of some famous man's wisdom was to visit and converse with him. In our day of multiplied literature, thoughtful conversation on important topics is too little practiced. **A greater** (*more*) **than Solomon is here,** as in v. 41. It must have startled the Jews very much to find Jesus quietly intimating that he was superior, not only to the prophet Jonah, but to Solomon, the magnificent monarch, the revered sage. In the case of a mere man, and a man wise and humble, such a claim would seem strange. Shall not the delicate woman, who took this long and trying journey to hear the wisdom of Solomon, condemn *us* in the day of judgment, who have the history and writings of Solomon, the life and sayings of Jesus, recorded in a book which is any hour within our reach—if we neglect to seek its treasures of wisdom?

II. **43-45.**—JESUS ILLUSTRATES THE CONSEQUENCES OF NEGLECTING HIS TEACHINGS. So on the similar occasion of Luke 11: 24–26. The illustration was doubtless suggested by the healing of a demoniac (12: 22) which had led to the foregoing discourse. *Plumptre* thinks this parable "comes in abruptly." But the wicked conduct of 'this generation' in disregarding him who is more than Jonah or Solomon (v. 41 f.) is accounted for by the parable, which is distinctly applied to them (v. 45) and gives to our Lord's imme-

44 Then he saith, I will return into my house from whence I came out; and when he is come, he findeth *it* empty, swept, and garnished.
45 Then goeth he, and taketh with himself seven other spirits more wicked than himself, and they enter in and dwell there: and the last *state* of that man is worse than the first. Even so shall it be also unto this wicked generation.

44 it not. Then [1] he saith, I will return into my house whence I came out; and when [1] he is come, [1] he findeth it empty, swept, and garnished. Then goeth [1] he, and taketh with [2] himself seven other spirits more evil than [2] himself, and they enter in and dwell there: and the last state of that man becometh worse than the first. Even so shall it be also unto this evil generation.

1 Or, *it*....2 Or, *itself.*

diate hearers a new warning. This view is made clearer by the proper reading ' but' in v. 43. For **when,** etc., read, *but the unclean spirit, when he is gone out of the man, the* spirit and *the* man, meaning a supposed or ideal individual, taken as representative of what always happens in such a case. For '*unclean*' see on 10: 1 and 8: 28. **He,** or *it*, as in margin of Rev. Ver., the Greek word for 'spirit' being neuter, and so the pronoun being neuter. (So in v. 44 and 45.) **Through dry** (*waterless*) **places,** the literal translation. It was a prevailing Jewish idea that evil spirits especially frequented desert or desolate places, see Tobit 8: 3; Baruch 4: 35. And it need not be considered merely as a Jewish notion, for it is favored by the imagery of this passage and of Rev. 18: 2. If the evil spirits that infest the earth are sometimes not occupied in possessing or tempting men, what spots would seem to be a more appropriate abode for them than parched and desolate places? As to demoniacal possessions, see on 8: 28. That demons did sometimes re-enter, after being cast out, is implied by Mark 9: 25, "Come out of him and enter no more into him." The **house** denotes the man whom he had possessed or occupied. Upon returning, the spirit finds the house unoccupied, swept, and adorned—just ready for an occupant; which, as said of the man, denotes that after being delivered from the unclean spirit he does not occupy his mind and heart with other and better things, but lives in a state of readiness for repossession. This language distinctly intimates that the possibility of demoniacal possessions depended (at least in some instances) on the moral and spiritual condition of the person, as well as on his physical and mental health. The unclean spirit, finding no rest in all his wanderings, no spot where he can be content quietly to remain, comes to re-enter his 'house'; and seeing it to be in such excellent condition for occupation, he goes after others to share it with him. **Seven other spirits,** the com-

mon, oft-recurring number (comp. Luke 8: 2, and a much greater number in Mark 5: 9.) **More wicked.** There seem then to be degrees of wickedness among the demons; just as we find in Mark 9: 29, that some were harder to cast out than others. **And the last state** (*things*) **of that man is** (or, *becomes*) **worse than the first** (*things*), i. e., his last fortunes or condition. Some propose to take the passage as a purely hypothetical illustration, derived from common fancies and modes of expression, and not implying that such a thing ever really happens as a dispossession and repossession. We have seen on 8: 28 that the demoniacal possessions must be taken as real, there being greater difficulties about any other view. And so here. The illustration is an ideal instance, as the forms of expression show, but it corresponds to and represents realities. **Even so shall it be also unto this wicked generation,** comp. v. 39; 16: 4; 24: 34. Our Lord distinctly applies his illustration to the Jewish nation of his own generation. The dispossession may refer to the great abandonment of idolatry after the captivity, and the comparatively improved religious and moral condition of the people. Then the empty, swept, and garnished stage might describe the refusal to occupy themselves with the spiritual and salutary teachings of Jesus. Or, the dispossession may refer to the great impression made by John and Jesus (11: 12), which in most of the people was proving temporary, so that in finally rejecting the Messianic reign they would become more completely than ever the subjects of Satan, and in forty years more would plunge into sore calamity and ruin. Various additional applications of the illustration might be made, as in others of our Lord's parables; but such applications are of course made by ourselves without claiming that they were contemplated by Jesus.

III. **46-50.** HIS MOTHER AND BRETHREN TRY TO SPEAK TO HIM. Comp. Mark 3: 31-35; Luke 8: 19-21. It was not enough that

46 While he yet talked to the people, behold, *his* mother and his brethren stood without, desiring to speak with him.
47 Then one said unto him, Behold, thy mother and thy brethren stand without, desiring to speak with thee.
48 But he answered and said unto him that told him, Who is my mother? and who are my brethren?

46   While he was yet speaking to the multitudes, behold, his mother and his brethren stood without, 47 seeking to speak to him. [1] And one said unto him, Behold, thy mother and thy brethren stand without, 48 seeking to speak to thee. But he answered and said unto him that told him, Who is my mother? and

---

1 Some ancient authorities omit ver. 47.

---

the leading men among his own people whom he came to save (John 1: 11) rejected him with blasphemies; but it was a part of the cruel opposition Jesus had to encounter (Heb. 12: 3), that some of his nearest kindred for a long time misunderstood him, so that his brethren taunted him (John 7: 3-5), and on the present occasion "his friends" even said he was insane, and wished to stop his teaching by force. (Mark. 3: 21.) By combining this account with that of Mark (3: 20, 21, 31) we see that Jesus and the Twelve came into a house, where a crowd assembled, so that they could not so much as eat bread, and that "his friends" (Mark 3: 21), upon hearing of it went forth to seize him, saying that he was 'beside himself.' The peculiar expression in Mark does not contain the term 'friends,' but signifies those that were of his family, or his country, or his party, etc. It cannot here mean the apostles, for they were with him in the house; and as "his mother and his brethren" presently reach the house (Mark 3: 31) desiring to speak with him, it is natural to understand that they are meant by the phrase, vaguely rendered, 'his friends.' Comp. Fritz. and Mey. (on Mark), Grimm, Winer, etc. Meantime, in the house, he healed a demoniac, and then occurred the blasphemous accusation and the discourse following. **While he was yet speaking,** his mother and brethren arrived at the house, and finding it difficult to enter because of the crowd (v. 46; Mark 3: 20), they passed in word that they were without, and were seeking to speak to him. *Seeking* is the literal and exact translation, and so Wyc. and Rheims, while Tyndale and his followers improperly rendered it by **desiring,** which fails to indicate that efforts were made. **His brethren,** see on 13: 55. On any view they were near

relatives, which is sufficient for the present passage. *Bible Com.:* "From the mention of his mother and his brethren only, it has been conjectured, with some probability, that Joseph was now dead." V. 47 must pretty certainly be omitted,[1] having been brought in here from Mark and Luke to explain the phrase 'him that told him' in v. 48. There is evidently no loss of substantial meaning.— Are we to understand that Mary wished to seize him, and thought him beside himself? She must surely have remembered what Gabriel had told her, and Simeon and Anna had said; how can she have questioned that he was the Messiah, and was to sit on the throne of his father David? Did she merely give way to the influence of the 'brethren,' or did she in fact, as many prefer to think, go along from no sympathy with their views or intentions, but in order to interpose between Jesus and their violence? Some suppose that they were only concerned about his health, from hearing that he was so thronged as to have no opportunity of taking food, and was still speaking on with solemn vehemence and consuming zeal; but this would hardly have made them venture to 'seize' him. (Mark 3: 21.) Our Lord's reply here seems to intimate that she, as well as the brethren, was unwarrantably interfering with his work, as he had gently rebuked her for doing on a former occasion. (John 2: 4.) Perhaps Mary sometimes became perplexed, as John the Baptist appears to have been (see on 11: 2),.by her son's pursuing a course so widely different from what she, in common with other Jews, expected of the Messiah; and in this frame of mind she could more easily be prevailed on by the 'brethren' to accompany them, without fully sharing either their view or their purpose.

---

1 It is wanting in ℵ (first hand), B L T, four cursives, Old Syriac, and two copies of the Old Latin. There is obvious ground for supposing it to have been inserted here from the equivalent statement which occurs without variation in Mark 3: 32; Luke 8: 20. We can see no reason why it should have been omitted, if originally present, save a possible offence at the repetition of the same words, as in v. 46; but that is a peculiarity of Hebrew style, too common in the Bible to have provoked critical excision. It is omitted in Weiss and W H.

49 And he stretched forth his hand toward his disciples, and said, Behold my mother and my brethren! 50 For whosoever shall do the will of my Father which is in heaven, the same is my brother, and sister, and mother.

49 who are my brethren? And he stretched forth his hand towards his disciples, and said, Behold, my 50 mother and my brethren! For whosoever shall do the will of my Father who is in heaven, he is my brother, and sister, and mother.

The person who told Jesus naturally thought that he would consider the claims of his mother and brothers as paramount, and would at once go forth, or cause them to be admitted. But he knew how his brothers misunderstood him, and was aware that their motive at present was not friendly. It seems to be implied that he continued his discourse, and only when this was finished, and the crowd was dispersing, went out and spoke with them. (Comp. on 13: 1.) However that may be, he took the occasion to make a most affecting declaration of his love for his disciples—for all who do the will of his Father in heaven. What he said was addressed especially to the person who spoke to him (v. 48); but also (Mark 3: 34; Luke 8: 21) to the persons present in general. **He stretched forth his hand towards his disciples** (comp. Mark 3: 34), the word here probably including other disciples as well as the Twelve (see on 5: 1). **The same** (literally *He*) **is my brother,** with emphasis on 'he,' as in 1: 21. **And sister.** Our Lord had 'sisters' in the same sense in which he had 'brothers,' probably in the most natural sense (see on 13: 56). Observe that he does not say brother, *or* sister, *or* mother (1 Tim. 5: 2), but each person is at the same time 'brother and sister and mother,' as much beloved as all these combined. Somewhat similarly Andromache says to her husband, "Hector, thou art to me father, and revered mother, and brother, and thou my blooming spouse." Luke (8: 21) only gives the general sentiment in the briefest form. And so, no doubt, many a discourse of our Lord, which of necessity is very briefly reported to us, was in the actual delivery full of such pointed interrogation and impressive repetition as we have here in Matthew and in Mark.

HOMILETICAL AND PRACTICAL.

V. 38 f. Men often demand further evidence of Christianity when they have abundant evidence but for their determination not to believe. There is a moral probation involved in believing or rejecting the gospel. (1 Cor. 1: 18-25.) HENRY: "Signs were granted to those who desired them for the confirma-

tion of their faith, as to Abraham and Gideon; but were denied to those who demanded them for the excuse of their unbelief."—V. 39. The Jews of our Lord's generation. 1) Wicked and God-forsaking, v. 39. 2) Demanding further evidence amid all his teachings and miracles, and in his own impressive presence, v. 38. 3) Grown worse since the first temporary effect of his ministry, v. 45. 4) On their way to the sin of crucifying their Messiah, and to national calamity and destruction. 5) Destined to stand ashamed at the judgment in the presence of Gentiles whom they despised, v. 41 f.—V. 39 f. Jonah and Jesus. 1) Jonah a great prophet, and Jesus more than Jonah. 2) The sign of Jonah, and the sign of Jesus' resurrection. 3) The preaching of Jonah, and the preaching of Jesus. 4) The effect of the one and of the other.

V. 42. HENRY: "The Queen of Sheba. 1) She had no invitation to Solomon, nor promise of being welcomed; but we are invited to Christ, to sit at his feet and hear his words. 2) Solomon was but a wise man; but Christ is wisdom itself. 3) The queen had many difficulties to break through—leaving her country to subordinates—a laborious and perilous journey; we have no such difficulties. 4) She could not be sure that Solomon would equal his fame; but we come to Christ upon no such uncertainties. 5) She came from the ends of the earth; but we have Christ among us, and his word nigh us. 6) It should seem the wisdom she came for was only philosophy and politics; but the wisdom that is to be had with Christ is wisdom unto salvation."

V. 43-45. Whenever a nation or an individual attempts a reformation, the evil principles and habits that are cast out must be vigorously and permanently replaced by good principles and habits, or the evil will return and be worse than ever.

V. 48. Jesus and his mother. 1) Trained by her, Luke 2: 40. 2) Subject to her, Luke 2: 51. 3) Gently rebuking her—a) Luke 2: 49; b) John 2: 4; c) Matt. 12: 48. 4) Providing for her, John 19: 26 f. 5) Loving all true Christians even more than he loved her, v. 50. EDERSHEIM: "For had he not entered into

CHAPTER XIII.

THE same day went Jesus out of the house, and sat by the sea side.

2 And great multitudes were gathered together unto him, so that he went into a ship, and sat; and the whole multitude stood on the shore.

1   On that day went Jesus out of the house, and sat by the sea side. And there were gathered unto him great multitudes, so that he entered into a boat, and

---

earthly kinship solely for the sake of the higher spiritual relationship which he was about to found? Thus it was not that Christ set lightly by his mother, but that he confounded not the means with the end, nor yet surrendered the spirit for the letter of the law of love." BENGEL: "He does not contemn the mother, but he puts the Father first." CHRYS.: "If she is nothing profited by being his mother, were it not for piety in her, hardly will any one else be saved by his kindred. For there is one only nobleness, to do the will of God. This kind of noble birth is better than the other, and more real."

FIRST GREAT GROUP OF PARABLES.

Ch. 13: 1-23.—THE PARABLE OF THE SOWER.

The Parable of the Sower, and apparently all those in ch. 13, were delivered on the same day (v. 1) with the discourse occasioned by the blasphemy against the Spirit. (See on 12: 22, 38.) Jesus went forth from the house in which the blasphemous accusation had ocurred, and sat beside the Lake of Galilee, and there spoke the parables of v. 1-35, viz., the Sower, the Tares, the Mustard-seed, and the Leaven. Then leaving the crowds and entering the house (v. 36), he added the parables of the Hid Treasure, the Precious Pearl, and the Net. (v. 36-53.) On the evening of that same day (Mark 4: 35) he went across the lake to the district of Gadara, stilling the tempest on the way, and there healed the two demoniacs— incidents which Matthew's mode of grouping topically has led him to introduce in an earlier part of his treatise. (8: 18 to 9: 1.) What a busy day was this! beginning and ending with miracles, and filled with remarkable discourses. And our Lord felt to the full, in his human nature, all that bodily and mental fatigue and prostration which such labors

must produce. Seizing upon every opportunity of doing men good, excited by a consuming zeal, yearning in unutterable pity over the perishing, oppressed by responsibilities such as no other was ever called to feel, and harassed by the most unjust and insulting accusations, he toiled on through the day, and at evening was so *tired* that he slept soundly on the cushion amid all the tossing of the waves and roar of the storm. Another example of a very busy day is pointed out in 14: 33; a third was the day of the Passion; and doubtless there were many others, it being only occasionally that the brief narratives of the Evangelists give us any complete view of his occupation throughout the day. With this section comp. Mark 4: 1-25; Luke 8: 4-18.

1 f. The house, see 12: 46, and comp. Mark 3: 20. **Sat,** the usual posture of a Jewish teacher when giving instruction. (Comp. 5: 1.) **By the sea side,** the Lake of Galilee. (See on 4: 18.) **Great multitudes,** or 'many crowds,' the same expression as in 4: 25; 12: 15, and often. These crowds so thronged around him that he could not be seen as he sat, and could not himself have any commanding view of those he addressed. When he entered the boat, probably swinging by its cable or its anchor some feet from the shore, and all the crowds stood upon the sloping and sandy beach, the situation was a beautiful one for agreeable and impressive speaking. Much less probable is Plumptre's view, that he entered a boat to prevent a "hostile attack." The precise point on the lake shore cannot be determined, but it was probably in the Plain of Gennesaret. **Ship,** or *boat,* [1] as in Latin versions, Wyc., and Rheims, rather than 'ship,' as in Tyn. and followers. (Comp. on 4: 21.) **Stood on the shore,** *beach,* the exact word for the Greek, which denotes a pebbly or sandy shore, such as the Plain of Gennesaret exhibits.

---

[1] It is probably safer to follow the text 'into a boat,' rather than the common Greek text, which ought to have been translated 'into the boat.' But the article may have been omitted by Alexandrian correctors (א B C L Z, some cursives), because no boat has been recently mentioned in the narrative. So in 8: 23 the article is omitted by א, (second hand) B C, some cursives. We could explain the article by referring to Mark 3: 9, and supposing that the boat there ordered had been kept for the use of the little company.

3 And he spake many things unto them in parables, saying, Behold, a sower went forth to sow;

3 sat; and all the multitude stood on the beach. And he spake to them many things in parables, saying,

3. He spake many things unto them in parables. The nature, design, and proper interpretation of our Lord's parables is a subject of great importance.

1. The Greek word which we borrow in the form parable signifies a *comparison*, conveying literally the notion of putting things side by side, whereby their resemblance will be perceived. A corresponding Hebrew word (*mashal*) is employed in the Old Test. to denote (1) an illustrative comparison (Ezek. 17:2; 24:3); (2) a sententious saying or apophthegm, such as frequently involves a comparison (Prov. 1:1, 6; 26:7, 9; Eccl. 12:9); (3) a current, often repeated saying of this kind, a proverb (1 Sam. 10:12; 24:13; Ezek. 12:22; 18:2, 3, etc.); (4) any high wrought expression, done into parallel clauses like a comparison, as was common in Hebrew poetry (Num. 23:7, 18; Job 27:1; 29:1; Isa. 14:4; Mic. 2:4; Heb. 2:6); (5) an obscure and deep saying (Psa. 49:4; 78:2), since pithy comparisons frequently require much reflection in order to get their full meaning. It was natural that the New Test. writers should employ the Greek word with a somewhat similar latitude of application. Accordingly we find it denoting (a) an illustrative comparison without the form of narrative (15:15; 24:32; Mark 3:23; Luke 5:36; 6:39); (b) an illustrative comparison in the form of narrative, which is the common use in the first three Gospels, and has occasioned the popular restriction of the term to our Lord's *narrative* illustrations; (c) a narrative illustration *not* involving a comparison, as the Rich Fool, the Pharisee and Publican, the Good Samaritan, the Rich Man and Lazarus; (d) a proverb (Luke 4:23), corresponding to which we find that in John 10:6 another word, which strictly denotes a proverb, is applied to an illustrative comparison; (e) a profound or otherwise obscure saying (see on 13:35, and comp. Ecclus. 38:33; 39:2 f.); (f) a symbol or image not expressed in language at all. (Heb. 9:9; 11:19.) Commonly, then, in Matthew, Mark, and Luke, (John does not employ it), the word we borrow as parable denotes an illustration, most frequently in the form of narrative, and usually, in accordance with the origin of the term, involving a comparison, though sometimes, as in (c), it is only an example of the matter in hand, a case in point.

The popular restriction of the term to narrative illustrations, is unfortunate, for there is no essential difference between these and other illustrative comparisons. (See Drummond, "Parabolic Teaching of our Lord.") Some of the narrative parables are very brief, as in v. 44 f. We are sometimes unable to decide whether the narrative is real or fictitious. But in the latter case the story is always possible, while *fables* are often impossible, representing beasts and trees as speaking, etc. The distinction some propose between parables and *allegories* is precarious. Is not the parable of the Prodigal Son an allegory?

2. Our Lord's *design* in employing these characteristic illustrations must be considered as manifold. (1) Like all other teachers, he illustrates moral and spiritual truth by comparison of things physical and social, the material for this abounding in actual analogies between the two spheres of existence. Such teaching by illustrative stories and other comparisons has from the earliest times been particularly common in the East; a few examples are found in the Old Test., 2 Sam. 12:1-14; Isa. 5:1-7, and the fables of Jotham, Judg. 9:8, and of Joab, 2 Sam. 14:5-7; and it appears from the Talmud that a like method was common among the Jewish teachers in the time of Christ, as for example (Gill) one-third of Rabbi Meir's discourses consisted of parables. In this as in other respects (comp. on 7:5), Jesus adopted such methods of instruction as were natural to men in general, and familiar to the Jews in particular. From the rhetorical point of view our Lord's illustrations are marked by exquisite simplicity and elegance, as well as the profoundest wisdom. Yet while of unequaled excellence, they do not differ in kind, but only in degree, from uninspired illustrations, and must be interpreted on the same general principles. (2) The parables also served to put truths, at first but imperfectly understood, into a compact and portable form, in which they could be easily remembered, till they should afterwards come to be understood more thoroughly. (3) They enabled the Great Teacher to state truths likely to give offence, in such a form that the enquiring and spiritually disposed could understand, while

cavilers would not see their point so as to be prematurely excited to violent hostility, and thus, while instructing some in his miscellaneous audience, he was not, in respect to others, casting pearls before swine. Sometimes, too, a man's assent might thus be gained to a principle before his prejudices were aroused, as Nathan dealt with David. (2 Sam. 12: 1 ff.) (4) In so far as parables were obscure to persons lacking in lively interest and spiritual sympathy, our Lord employed them as a *judgment* upon the willfully blind. This, though not to be reckoned his only reason for using them so frequently from this time forward, is the one which he states when questioned about the matter on the present occasion. (See on v. 10–17.) *Henry:* "A parable, like the pillar of cloud and fire, turns a dark side towards Egyptians, which confounds them, but a bright side towards Israelites, which comforts them. . . . . A parable is a shell that keeps good fruit *for* the diligent, but keeps it *from* the slothful." *Calderwood:* "There is a complete contrast between the view taken in modern times of our Lord's parables, and that taken by the audiences to which they were first delivered. Even those who are averse to accept Bible teaching have an admiration of these gospel parables; yet to those who heard them, they were the most perplexing parts of Christ's discourses." This is partly because the meaning of the parables has become comparatively plain, and partly because many skeptics now admire the Gospels regarded only as literature.

3. In the *interpretation* of parables, we have the guidance of our Lord himself, who has fully interpreted the parables of the Sower and the Tares, and, to some extent, that of the Net. Remember that our methods must apply to *all* of his illustrations, and not merely to the narratives, to which in popular usage the term parable is restricted. There are four things to be done. (1) We must make sure of understanding the language of the parable itself, and its various allusions to physical phenomena or social usages. Thus many fail to understand the wayside and the rocky ground; the treasure hid in a field; the patch of unfulled cloth upon an old garment, and the wineskins (9: 16 f.); the double invitation to a supper (Luke 14: 16 f.), etc. (2) We must ascertain what subject our Lord here designed to illustrate. Sometimes he himself states it, either before or after the parable, or else the Evangelist mentions it in recording the parable; in other cases, the connection, if carefully observed, will sufficiently indicate it, there being few instances, if any, in which we are left to infer the subject simply from the tenor of the parable itself. (3) We must consider in what light the parable presents this subject. Here it is important to regard the parable as a whole, just as we do any other illustration, and not begin by attempting to assign the meaning of particular items, without having considered the general drift. Let it be taken for granted that the Great Teacher used illustrations on common-sense principles. (4) Then it remains to determine how far the details may be understood as separately significant. In this we can have no general rule to guide us, but must study the guidance our Lord has given in his interpretations, exercise sound judgment, and endeavor to avoid both extremes. The tendency has usually been towards the extreme of giving a separate spiritual meaning to every detail. Yet Augustine already rebuked this by the remark that it is only the ploughshare that cuts the earth, while the other parts of the plough are also necessary, and, indeed, indispensable. That which is the mere filling out of the story, the mere drapery of the image, must be let alone. On the other hand, it should be remembered that our Lord has carried out his three interpretations in much detail, and we must not reduce the parable to a bare trunk, stripped of all its foliage. In some cases the resemblance or analogy is more complete than in others, and the points of contact more numerous. There may even be points in the illustration quite the reverse of the thing illustrated, as when our Lord's coming is compared to that of a thief in the night, where there is, of course, no resemblance except as to the unexpectedness of the coming; and so as to the unjust steward (Luke 16), whose conduct, while manifestly dishonest, is employed to illustrate the importance of prudent foresight and preparation for the future. *Alexander:* "As the same illustration may legitimately mean more to one man than to another, in proportion to the strength of their imaginative faculties, it

4 And when he sowed, some *seeds* fell by the way-side, and the fowls came and devoured them up:
5 Some fell upon stony places, where they had not much earth: and forthwith they sprung up, because they had no deepness of earth:
6 And when the sun was up, they were scorched; and because they had no root, they withered away.

4 Behold, the sower went forth to sow; and as he sowed, some *seeds* fell by the way side, and the birds
5 came and devoured them: and others fell upon the rocky places, where they had not much earth: and straightway they sprang up, because they had no
6 deepness of earth: and when the sun was risen, they were scorched; and because they had no root,

is highly important that, in attempting to determine the essential meaning of our Saviour's parables, we should not confound what they may possibly be made to mean, with what they must mean to attain their purpose." We may lawfully employ some detail of a parable, or even the whole (comp. on 12: 45), to illustrate some *other* truth than that to which he applied it; but it must be done avowedly upon our own authority. In general, the details of a parable must never be pressed into teaching what is contrary to the plain, unfigurative teaching of the Scriptures at large. (See on v. 20 f.) An illustration, however admirable, can only present its subject in certain aspects.

4. There are three leading *groups* of our Lord's parables. A good many isolated parables have already occurred, with or without the form of narrative, as (a) the wise and foolish builders, 7: 24–27; (b) wedding usages, patching garments, wineskins, 9: 15–17; (c) children at play, 11: 16–19; (d) the blind guiding the blind, etc., Luke 6: 39 ff.; (e) the two debtors, Luke 7: 41 ff.; (f) the evil spirit returning, Matt. 12: 43–45; and it may be observed that most of these sporadic parables refer to the reception given to Christ's teachings. Besides these, Matthew gives two leading groups: (1) The Messianic reign, its beginnings and growth, ch. 13; given about the middle of our Lord's ministry. (2) The Messianic reign, its progress and consummation; given just at the close of the ministry. (3) Between these two groups in order of time, we find a third group, given by Luke, ch. 13–19, some of which relate to the Messianic reign, but most of them to individual experiences.

The seven parables of ch. 13 are probably but a selection from the 'many things' of v. 3. Mark 4: 26–29 gives another, not mentioned by Matthew, and the language of Mark 4: 33 implies that there were many others. Like all our Lord's illustrations, the parables of this first group were drawn from familiar sources—from agriculture, fishing, and merchandise, from the preparation of bread, and

the finding of hid treasure, this last also being in the East a familiar idea.

I. 3-9. THE PARABLE OF THE SOWER. Found also in Mark 4: 3–9; Luke 8: 5–8. This and the wicked husbandmen (21: 33-45) are the only parables recorded by all three, Matthew, Mark, and Luke. We may confine ourselves here to explanation of the story itself, the interpretation belonging to v. 19-23. (See Notes there.) **Behold,** calling attention to something important. Mark (4: 3) prefixes 'Hearken.' **A** (*the*) **sower went forth to sow,** the definite article being employed to designate an ideal individual, who represents a class (comp. on 12: 43), as if in a fable we should say, "the farmer went out to look at his crops." The expression shows that this is not given as the narrative of a particular, actual occurrence. Tyndale and Cranmer gave 'the sower;' King James followed Geneva. **Some** (*seeds*) **fell by the wayside.** The roads passed right through the cultivated lands (see on 12: 1), and as he sowed the wheat or barley, some of the grains would fall on the beaten ground of the road or path, and rebounding would lie exposed on the hard surface, where the birds could readily see and devour them. (Luke 8: 5 prefixes 'trodden under foot.') It is still common in the East to see large flocks of birds following the husbandman as he sows his wheat, and eagerly picking up every grain that has not sunk out of sight. **Fowls,** rather *birds*, see on 7: 26. **Some** (*others*) **fell upon stony,** or *the rocky* (places). Palestine is a limestone country (comp. on 7: 24), and one will find places where a broad, flat, limestone rock lies just beneath the surface, with a thin layer of earth upon it. (Comp. Luke 8: 6, 13, 'the rock.') All the early English versions except Rheims gave 'stony' (ground or places), thus suggesting a soil abounding in loose stones, which really often produces good wheat; yet the Greek word was plain and unmistakable, from the same root as in 16: 18. In such places the seeds could not sink deep, and the film of earth being readily heated because of the

7 And some fell among thorns, and the thorns sprung up, and choked them:
8 But other fell into good ground, and brought forth fruit, some a hundredfold, some sixtyfold, some thirtyfold.
9 Who hath ears to hear, let him hear.
10 And the disciples came, and said unto him, Why speakest thou unto them in parables?
11 He answered and said unto them, Because it is given unto you to know the mysteries of the kingdom of heaven, but to them it is not given.

7 they withered away. And others fell upon the thorns; and the thorns grew up, and choked them:
8 and others fell upon the good ground, and yielded fruit, some a hundredfold, some sixty, some thirty.
9 He that hath ears,[1] let him hear.
10 And the disciples came, and said unto him, Why
11 speakest thou unto them in parables? And he answered and said unto them, Unto you it is given to know the mysteries of the kingdom of heaven, but

---

1 Some ancient authorities add here, and in ver. 43. *to hear:* as in Mark iv. 9; Luke viii. 8.

---

underlying rock, they would come up sooner than elsewhere, and at first would look uncommonly flourishing; but not being able to send roots deep into moist earth (comp. Luke 8. 6), when the hot, dry weather came, the stalks would soon wither, and show that the fair promise of a crop there had all been deceptive. Comp. the "grass upon the housetops," Ps. 129: 6 f. **Among**—or *upon the*—**thorns,** there being in his field some place or places specially infested with these. Persons accustomed to observe wheat-fields will remember to have seen spots where a few scattered and spindling stalks were struggling for life among the rank briers. **Into**—or *upon the*—**good ground,** free from underlying rock, and from thorns, and plowed deep. Even this would produce more in some spots than in others, according to the richness of the soil and its preparation. A crop of even thirty measures to one of seed is quite a good yield. The richer countries of the East produce very heavy crops (*e. g.* Gen. 26: 12), and some portions of Galilee have always been singularly fruitful. (Comp. on 4 : 12.) Various classical writers speak of crops as large as a hundred to one, and even two hundred or more, in very rich soil. The point of the whole story is that the same seed produced no wheat, little wheat, or much wheat, all according to the character and preparation of the soil. **Who hath ears to hear, let him hear** (see on 11: 15), would suggest to any attentive hearer that the story was meant to convey spiritual instruction, and that not all were likely to understand it.

II. **10-17.**—REASONS FOR SPEAKING IN PARABLES. Comp. Mark 4: 10–12; Luke 8: 9 f. **And the disciples came and said unto him.** They had probably been scattered among the crowds on the shore, and they now approached the boat (v. 2), and perhaps entered it, or else Jesus drew off from the crowd for a time, during which occurred this conversation with the disciples, and after-

wards resumed his discourse to the same or similar crowds. Certain it is that the reasons were given apart from the people, for Mark (4: 10) explicitly says, 'And when he was alone,' etc. It is also plain that several of the succeeding parables were addressed to 'the crowds.' (See on v. 36.) These facts can be accounted for on either of the above suppositions. The 'disciples' here are not merely the Twelve, for Mark (4: 10) says, 'They that were about him, with the twelve.' Others, therefore, of his constant companions shared the privilege of this conversation. The disciples did not see just what was meant by this story of the sower (Luke 8: 9; Mark 4: 13), though they saw that it was intended as a comparison or parable to illustrate some religious truth. And as parables in general were apt to be obscure unless the application was given, they wondered why the Teacher was employing them. Remember (Goebel) that he introduced the story of the sower without preface, and closed it without application, simply intimating that it required attention. **In parables,** is plural, while, as far as we know, only one parable had been spoken on this occasion. But the plural might be used as designating the method of instruction in general. (Comp. Mark 4: 11.) We remember also, that he had previously given scattered parables, though not without indicating the application.

It need not be supposed that our Lord meant to give what follows as his sole reason for employing parables in general. (Comp. on v. 3.) We can see a special fitness in his dwelling on this reason upon the present occasion, for it was the day on which the Scribes blasphemously accused him of league with Beelzebul (see on 12: 24 and 13: 1); and he was now surrounded by great and excited crowds, whose enthusiasm he knew was largely superficial and short-lived—rocky-ground hearers. Not very long after this

12 For whosoever hath, to him shall be given, and he shall have more abundance: but whosoever hath not, from him shall be taken away even that he hath.

12 to them it is not given. For whosoever hath, to him shall be given, and he shall have abundance: but whosoever hath not, from him shall be taken

---

(14:34-36), he had to dispel illusions among fanatical followers by the searching discourse of John 6: 26-66; and he appears (Bruce) to be in the parable of the sower commencing this work of warning and discrimination; so also on a third and much later occasion. (Luke 14:25-35.) *Godet:* "The design of Jesus is first of all to show that he is not deceived by the sight of this crowd, which is apparently so attentive; then to put his disciples on their guard against the expectations which such a large concourse might create in their minds; lastly, and more than all, to warn his hearers of the perils which threatened the holy impressions they were then experiencing." There is also in not a few of these parables, particularly in the sower, the mustard seed, and the leaven, consolation for Jesus himself in reference to the comparatively small number of true converts he was thus far making. (Comp. John 6: 37.) **Because it is given unto you,** literally, '*has been given,*' and so stands as your established privilege. **To know the mysteries of the kingdom of heaven,** *i. e.,* of the Messianic reign, see on 3: 2. The word 'mystery' does not occur elsewhere in the Gospels (except in Mark 4: 11 and Luke 8: 10, parallel to this passage), nor in the Acts, but is common in the Epistles of Paul and the Revelation. The Greek word *musterion* signifies something into which one is initiated, something hidden or secret, and known only to the initiated. It might be a very simple thing in itself, but it was a secret. Yet some of the doctrines belonging to the "Eleusinian mysteries" and other secret associations of Greek, Egypt, etc., were really profound, and difficult of comprehension, and so the word has gradually come to suggest the idea of something incomprehensible, though we still sometimes apply it to things which are merely hard to find out. But in the New Test. use, it uniformly denotes that which we could not know unless *revealed,* whether it be in its own nature simple or profound. Paul's favorite application of it is to the great fact that the Gentiles were to share in the salvation of the gospel on equal terms with the Jews, a fact always before kept in silence and

secrecy, but now manifested by God, and to be everywhere proclaimed. (Rom. 16: 25. f; Eph. 3: 4-6; Col. 1: 26 f.; 1 Tim. 3: 16.) Our Lord is in this series of parables setting forth views as to the true nature of the Messianic kingdom—such as its partial acceptance among men, its small beginnings and gradual spread, its allowing the wicked to live on in the world mingled with its subjects until the end—which the mass of the Jews were not spiritual-minded enough to comprehend, nor humble enough to receive. So he presents these views in the form of parables, which would, with the help of his explanations, make them clear to his disciples, but would leave them mysteries (secrets) to the unspiritual and unbelieving multitude. 'Secrets' is here the translation of Tyndale, Cran., and Gen. Observe that these parables carry on the work of instruction begun in the Sermon on the Mount, as to the nature of the Messianic reign. Here, as well as there, we must frequently recall the popular Jewish errors in regard to the character of that reign —errors from which the disciples themselves were not entirely free—in order to see the precise aim and point of the discourse. This is especially true in the parables of the Tares and the Net, and in those of the Mustard-seed and the Leaven. The phrase 'mysteries of the kingdom,' recorded by all three Evangelists (Mark 4: 11; Luke 8: 10), should remind us (Alexander) that this group of parables relate especially to the Messianic reign; while in so doing, they of course involve individual character and destiny.

We must not suppose that Jesus meant, like some of the Greek philosophers, to have certain (exoteric) doctrines for the masses, and certain others (esoteric) which were confined to a select few. The reverse is clearly shown by what he adds in Mark and Luke after explaining the parable of the sower, 'for there is nothing hid save that it should be manifested,' etc., Rev. Ver., (Mark 4: 21-25: Luke 8: 16-18); comp above on 10: 27, and below on v. 52. In v. 12f., he declares that he withholds some truths from the outside crowd (Mark 4: 11) because of their willful blindness. Some previous knowledge of his teachings concerning the Messianic reign was necessary in order to un-

13 Therefore speak I to them in parables: because they seeing see not; and hearing they hear not, neither do they understand.
14 And in them is fulfilled the prophecy of Esaias, which saith, By hearing ye shall hear, and shall not understand; and seeing ye shall see, and shall not perceive:

13 away even that which he hath. Therefore speak I to them in parables; because seeing they see not, and hearing they hear not, neither do they understand.
14 And unto them is fulfilled the prophecy of Isaiah, which saith,
By hearing ye shall hear, and shall in no wise understand;
And seeing ye shall see, and shall in no wise perceive:

---

derstand the hidden truths he was now revealing; not (as Meyer and Bleek strangely interpret v. 11) previous knowledge of the mysteries of the kingdom, but of his other teachings as to the kingdom. Such knowledge the unbelieving and careless had failed to obtain or refused to receive. They saw and yet did not see (v. 13), i. e., did not see the real and full meaning of his teachings. They were already becoming "gospel-hardened." **Therefore** (v. 13) or more strongly, *on this account*, refers to the general principle just stated, that he who has not shall lose even what he has; and the reason is then further presented in another form by what follows, **because they seeing see not,** etc. On this account he taught in the form of comparisons, which would be intelligible and impressive to those prepared to understand, but unintelligible to those who by their willful ignorance, neglect, and opposition, were unprepared. In Mark (4:12) and Luke (8:10) it is stated as the divine *purpose*, 'that seeing they may not see,' etc. This statement and Matthew's do not conflict with each other. That which was a natural result of their character was also a divine judgment upon them. It was not only foreseen that they would not understand these things, but designed that they should not, as a punishment deserved by their character and conduct. These people were not ignorant through lack of opportunity for gaining knowledge, but were willfully negligent, and even malignantly hostile to the truth and the Teacher. (12:24.) If we shrink sensitively from the idea that the "Lord of heaven and earth" reveals to some and hides from others, we are strangely out of sympathy with the feelings of Jesus and of Paul, who found in this idea not only occasion of resignation, but of adoration and joy. (11:25 f.; Rom. 9:18 ff.; 11:30-36.) Nor need we suppose that our Lord's object in using parables was *only* to withhold truth from the hardened as a judgment, for the shortest way to do this would have been (Chrys.) to say nothing to them at all. His

parables gave them still the opportunity to understand, if not too much hardened to do so, and were even calculated to excite their curiosity, awaken their attention, and lodge something in their mind, the spiritual meaning of which they might afterwards comprehend, if any of them should come to have a better disposition. "For the stubborn and the frivolous, this is still the only language which in a happy moment can soften and awaken them. After they have once heard it as a parable, the figure sticks to them, the mirror is ever turned towards them, and they cannot but look into it at some time or other."

The saying of v. 12 is repeated in 25:29; the word **more,** which in Com. Ver. here uselessly precedes **abundance,** is there not introduced. In Luke 8:18 (Mark 4:25) we find this same general principle given as a reason for taking heed how they hear. Perhaps our Lord stated it both at the point given by Matthew and also in his further remarks after the explanation of the parable. If this seems improbable, we must conclude that the saying was transposed either by Matthew, or by Mark and Luke, to a different connection from that in which it was spoken. As no writer could tell everything, and some relation of topics must be observed in the grouping, it would be inevitable that such transpositions of particular remarks should sometimes occur.

14 f. And in them, or *unto them* (according to the correct Greek text), so as to affect them, as applying to them. **Is fulfilled,** present tense, *is being fulfilled.* As in so many other cases, it is Matthew only who reports the citation of this prophecy. Mark (4:12) and Luke (8:10) simply represent our Lord as using expressions derived from the prophecy. **Esaias,** or *Isaiah*, see on 1:2. The citation is from Isa. 6:9 f., and exactly follows the Sept., which departs from the Heb. in only one important particular. The prophet is directed to rebuke the people for their insensibility to God's cause; and though that criminal insensibility would be increased by his

15 For this people's heart is waxed gross, and *their* ears are dull of hearing, and their eyes they have closed; lest at any time they should see with *their* eyes, and hear with *their* ears, and should understand with *their* heart, and should be converted, and I should heal them.

16 But blessed *are* your eyes, for they see: and your ears, for they hear.

15 For this people's heart is waxed gross,
And their ears are dull of hearing,
And their eyes they have closed;
Lest haply they should perceive with their eyes,
And hear with their ears,
And understand with their heart,
And should turn again,
And I should heal them.

16 But blessed are your eyes, for they see; and your

---

message, he is yet to proclaim the message. Accordingly he is told (in the Heb.), "Make the heart of this people fat, and make their ears dull and their eyes dim, lest," etc. This bids him produce the effect by his message; not that such an effect was in itself desired by him or by Jehovah, but because his message was going to be rejected and to have the effect described, and still he must proclaim it. The Sept. translators understood the Heb. differently, and rendered, "For this people's heart has been made fat, and with their ears they have heard heavily, and their eyes they have closed," etc. This, as sufficiently expressing the general idea of the passage (comp. on 3: 3), is retained by Matt. here, and also by Luke in Acts 28: 26 f. John (12: 40) refers to the same passage, and puts it, 'He hath blinded their eyes and he hardened their heart,' etc., *i. e.*, God has done so—a rendering which gives the same idea as the Heb. So likewise the expressions in Mark 4: 12 and Luke 8: 10 correspond not to the Sept., but to the Heb. The insensibility of the people may be variously conceived of, as the result of their own willful opposition, or as a judgment already actually inflicted on them by God, or as a judgment which would follow their rejection of the prophet's message. God is continually punishing men by that which is the natural result of their own misconduct in violating the natural laws which he has established. The prophet's expression 'make the heart fat' involves the image of a heart enveloped in fat, and thus less sensitive to impressions, and less lively in its movement, with a resulting dullness of the senses, so that it strikingly represents a dull, stupid, and insensible mind. We have seen on 6: 21 that the heart is constantly used in Scripture as the seat of both intelligence, sensibility, and will. "Fat as to intellect," "fat as to understanding," are phrases of classic Greek (Grimm). **Lest at any time.** *Lest haply*, or 'lest perhaps,' is a more probable rendering. The phrase expresses, not the design of the people, as some

have sought to explain it, but the divine purpose. While God might *wish* them to hear and believe and repent, even as he "wishes all to be saved" (1 Tím. 2 : 4), he did not design to bring them all to this, in spite of themselves, but it was his purpose to allow them to pursue a course which would prevent them from ever turning and being healed. **Heal** here involves the idea of forgiving their sin, and restoring them to spiritual health and the favor of God. The multiplication of similar and equivalent clauses in the passage is but the common parallelism of Hebrew poetry (see on 4: 16). **Turn again.** So Tyndale 'turn,' and Geneva 'return.' The Greek word is the same as in 12: 44, 'I will return into my house.' This is much better than the passive rendering **be converted** of Com. Ver. (comp. on 18: 3). As to the relation between 'turn' and 'repent,' see on 3: 2. A like insensibility to that which the prophet would encounter was found in the mass of our Lord's hearers (comp. John 12: 40), and in the Jews who assembled to hear Paul at Rome. (Acts 28: 25 ff.; comp. also Rom. 11: 8.) And since Matthew uses the word 'fulfil' (see on 1: 22), we understand that the language in Isaiah was designed by the Spirit of inspiration as a prediction, not merely of the reception which the prophet's message would meet with, but also of the like reception which awaited the teaching of Messiah and his servants. (Comp. on 1: 23.)

16 f. With this criminal insensibility of many among his hearers, Jesus now again contrasts the better condition and course of his disciples, as above in v. 11 f. The terms employed are suggested by the prophecy just cited. **Your,** in v. 16, is very emphatic, as shown by the position in Greek. But in the verbs, **they see** and **they hear** of v. 16, and **ye see** and **ye hear** of v. 17, the pronoun is not expressed in the Greek, and therefore is not emphatic. The disciples were **blessed,** or *happy* (which is more exact; see on 5: 3) in the fact that they saw and heard; for the things they witnessed were those to which

17 For verily I say unto you, That many prophets and righteous *men* have desired to see *those things* which ye see, and have not seen *them;* and to hear *those things* which ye hear, and have not heard *them.*
18 Hear ye therefore the parable of the sower.
19 When any one heareth the word of the kingdom, and understandeth *it* not, then cometh the wicked one, and catcheth away that which was sown in his heart. This is he which received seed by the way side.

17 ears, for they hear. For verily I say unto you, that many prophets and righteous men desired to see the things which ye see, and saw them not; and to hear
18 the things which ye hear, and heard them not. Hear
19 then ye the parable of the sower. When any one heareth the word of the kingdom, and understandeth it not, *then* cometh the evil *one,* and snatcheth away that which hath been sown in his heart. This

many prophets and righteous men (see on 10: 41) had looked forward with longing, but in vain. Here again (comp. on 12: 28) Jesus distinctly intimates that he is the Messiah. Seeing and hearing are here to be understood both of the senses and of the spirit; they saw the miracles and heard the teachings of Jesus, and they understood and appreciated their spiritual meaning. In Luke 10: 23 f., we find similar language used on a different occasion. It belongs to a class of sayings likely to be repeated. (Comp. at the beginning of ch. 5.) This congratulation was not confined to the Twelve, for others also were present. (See on v. 10.) *Olshausen:* "All the longing desires of the pious throughout the Old Test. centred in the Messiah. To behold him was the loftiest object of Old Test. hope. This blessing was granted to the disciples, and all their happiness, all their glory, consisted in this, that they were illumined by the radiance of the Sun of righteousness. The special grace thus vouchsafed is brought to their remembrance by Christ, not to exalt them above the Old Test. saints, but to lay them low before the Lord."

III. **18-23.** INTERPRETATION OF THE PARABLE OF THE SOWER. Comp. Mark 4: 14-24; Luke 8: 11-18. Our Lord's authoritative explanation of this parable and that of the Tares, furnishes us a model for the interpretation of his parables in general (comp. on v. 3),—a beautiful medium between excessive meagreness and excessive minuteness. **Hear ye therefore,** better, *then ye,* with strong emphasis on 'ye,' as distinguished from the heedless and hardened Jews to whom he gave no explanation. 'Then' presents this as a consequence of the principles just before laid down.

The idea of this parable as a whole is, that as the same grain yielded variously, according to the character and preparation of the soil which received it, so the same word of truth produces various effects according to the way in which it is received. No analogy be-

tween physical and spiritual things can ever be perfect. The soil was not responsible if it was trampled, or rocky, or thorny; but men are accountable for hearing the word improperly. This point the parable does not mean to touch, confining itself to the general idea above stated, and opening a way for the exhortation, 'take heed therefore how ye hear.' (Luke 8: 18, comp. Mark 4: 24.) **The word of the kingdom,** is the word which tells of the nature and requirements of the Messianic reign. (See on 3: 2.) Luke (8: 11) has 'word of God,' and Mark (4: 15) simply 'word.' Comp. 'gospel of the kingdom' in 4: 23; 9: 35; 24: 14. This 'word of the kingdom' means especially our Lord's own teachings; and so in 'understandeth it not' the reference is immediately to his own hearers. Yet it will not do to say that 'the sower' distinctively represents Christ; it is any one who makes known the word of the kingdom, as our Lord intimates in Mark 4: 14, 'the sower sows the word,' characterizing him not as a certain person, but as the one who does a certain work. **Understandeth it not.** *Arnot* suggests that in English as in Greek, we may express the material and the moral failure by one term, 'does not take it in.' Truth that is not understood, at least in some measure, can do men no good. There is here reference to the state of those described in v. 11-13; see the same word 'understand' in v. 13. The people were hardened into indifference, and some of them even into malignant opposition to the word, and hence they did not understand it. Christianity is so eminently practical a thing that one will not truly understand it unless he is willing to receive it. *Pascal:* "In other things, a man must know in order to love; in religion he must love in order to know." Whenever through inattention, lack of spiritual sympathy, unwillingness to receive, or opposition, men fail to 'understand' the word, it cannot benefit them. It lies for a moment on the surface of the mind, till by some one of

20 But he that received the seed into stony places, the same is he that heareth the word, and anon with joy receiveth it;
21 Yet hath he not root in himself, but dureth for a while: for when tribulation or persecution ariseth because of the word, by and by he is offended.

20 is he that was sown by the way side. And he that was sown upon the rocky places, this is he that heareth the word, and straightway with joy receiveth it; yet hath he not root in himself, but endureth
21 for a while; and when tribulation or persecution ariseth because of the word, straightway he stum-

---

the thousand evil influences which Satan and his subordinates employ, it is caught away. Often the whole impression made on some mind by a solemn sermon seems to be destroyed the instant the service is over, by an idle jest of a trifling comrade. **The wicked,** or *evil one;* see on 6: 13; 12: 45, and comp. 13: 38 f. Mark (4: 15) has 'Satan,' and Luke (8: 12) 'the devil.' It is idle to profess faith in the teaching of Jesus, and question the existence and personality of Satan. *Snatcheth away* better renders the Greek than **catcheth away ;** the idea is of suddenly and violently seizing and carrying off. **Sown in his heart,** the seat of intelligence and will, as well as of feeling; see on 6: 23. **This is he which received seed,** or *was sown—by the wayside,* comp. on v. 4. It might seem to us more natural that the different classes of hearers should be represented by different kinds of soil; but our Lord makes the seed that fell in the different places represent them, which amounts to the same thing. The comparison is a general one. The case of the seed sown beside the road, and snatched away by the birds, corresponds to the case of the hearer who does not understand the word, etc. ; and our Lord avoids circumlocution by simply comparing the hearer to the seed. (So in v. 20, 22, 23.) The rendering of Com. Ver., 'he that received seed,' is quite unwarranted; it was derived from Cranmer, while Tyn. had translated correctly ; and in Mark 4: 16, 18, the same words are correctly rendered in Com. Ver., 'they which are sown.' Some have proposed to render here 'this is that sown,' viz., the seed sown; but that seems to be forbidden by the expressions of Mark 4: 15 and Luke 8: 12. Whatever view of the phraseology be adopted, the general meaning remains the same, and is obvious to all.

20 f. Into stony, *upon the rocky (places);* see on v. 5. Like the wheat sown on a thin layer of earth spread over a rock, the gospel will produce some impression on such persons sooner than elsewhere, and the effect will look extremely promising for a time, so that people think this person will soon be a Christian, or

even that he is so already. But when persecution or any severe test of principle occurs, it is at once seen that the thing was not deeply rooted, far it perishes without having produced any real results. **Anon.** Better *straightway,* which was formerly the meaning of 'anon.' **With joy.** It is often the case that superficial and transient religious impressions produce a speedier and more boisterous joy than those which are deep and genuine. Such joy may result from general views of the beauty of piety and the blessedness of possessing it, with a self-deceived appropriation of its consolations and hopes; or from the excitement of natural feeling by touching allusions and fervid appeals; or from mere sympathy with kindred and friends; or even from utterly erroneous notions of religion, with the elation of self-righteousness and spiritual pride. See an example on a large scale in John 6: 15, 22, 66. But the deepest religious experiences may also produce, and ought to produce, a true and abiding joy. **But dureth for a while,** literally *is temporary,* the same Greek word as in 2 Cor. 4: 18, 'the things which are seen are temporal,' or '*temporary,*' and in Heb. 11: 25, literally 'to have temporary enjoyment of sin.' Such "temporary Christians" abound in times of extraordinary revival. **For,** literally, *and,* **when tribulation or persecution.** The Com. Ver. most unwarrantably translated 'for when' following Tyndale, Cran., and Gen. Such loose handling of particles was one of the gravest defects in the learning of that age. 'Tribulation' is a more general term, 'persecution' a more particular one. See the former also in 24: 9, 21, 29. The remote association of this Latin word with the process of threshing is often referred to by preachers, but the Greek word has no such association. It means simply pressure, affliction, etc. It is best translated in the New Test. sometimes by tribulation, and sometimes by affliction. The Rev. Ver. has made some good changes in both directions, *e. g.,* 1 Cor. 7: 28; 2 Cor. 1: 4, 8. **By and by,** properly *straightway,* the same Greek

22 He also that received seed among the thorns is he that heareth the word; and the care of this world, and the deceitfulness of riches, choke the word, and he becometh unfruitful.
23 But he that received seed into the good ground is he that heareth the word, and understandeth *it;* which also beareth fruit, and bringeth forth, some a hundred-fold, some sixty, some thirty.

22 bleth. And he that was sown among the thorns, this is he that heareth the word; and the care of the [1] world, and the deceitfulness of riches, choke
23 the word, and he becometh unfruitful. And he that was sown upon the good ground, this is he that heareth the word, and understandeth it; who verily beareth fruit, and bringeth forth, some a hundred-fold, some sixty, some thirty.

1 Or, *age.*

word as in v. 20 and v. 5. The person described immediately receives the word with joy, and when trouble comes, immediately he stumbles. This is a prominent feature in the characterization; but Com. Ver. has, as so often, obscured the verbal connection by employing three different terms, 'forthwith,' 'anon,' 'by and by. **He is offended,** or *stumbleth,* or 'is made to stumble.' Tyndale and Cran. give 'falleth;' it was Gen. that here introduced the unlucky rendering 'is offended.' The word has been explained on 5: 29, and has here the second sense there given; the man finds an obstacle to progress, and abandons the gospel he had apparently received. (Comp. 24: 10.) Luke (8: 13) has an equivalent expression, 'fall away.' Only when grain is produced does a crop of wheat amount to anything; only permanent piety is real piety.

22. Among the thorns, comp. on v. 7. **That heareth the word.** No further expression is here appended, such as 'understands' (v. 19, 23), or 'with joy receives it' (v. 20), but it is simply said 'hears,' the connection showing that the impression at first made is afterwards destroyed. **The care of this world.** The correct Greek text omits 'this,' as also in v. 40. For 'care' we could hardly use 'anxiety' in this place, as in 2 Cor. 11: 28, 'anxiety for all the churches,' and as the verb is translated 'be anxious' in 6: 25 (see Notes); but "worldly anxieties" will exactly express the idea conveyed. 'The world' as in 13: 39 f. and 12: 32, means the present age or world-period, with all its affairs; comp. 2 Tim. 4: 10, 'having loved this present world,' and see on 25: 46. **The deceitfulness of riches** is a stronger expression than simply deceitful riches; it presents deceitfulness not merely as a quality of riches, but as here the prominent thought; comp. 'the uncertainty of riches' (1 Tim. 6: 17. Rev. Ver.), 'newness of life' (Rom. 6: 14); also Heb. 3: 13; 2 Thess. 2: 10. Riches deceive men in many ways: as to the means of acquiring them, making things look

honest that are not so; as to the reasons why we desire them, and the objects for which we intend to use them, etc. Some professed Christians imagine that they are so absorbed in the pursuit of gain, and so reluctant to give much at present, simply from a desire to be able to do great things hereafter; when the true reason is that they love wealth. And we must remember that riches often as grievously deceive and distract those who vainly seek, as those who obtain them. "They that desire to be rich" (1 Tim. 6: 9, Rev. Ver.), may get the evil consequences without getting the wealth. Luke (8: 14) adds a third point, "and pleasures of this life." **Unfruitful.** As fruit-bearing is the test, they are thus shown to have no real piety. Alas! how often men seem deeply stirred, by the word of the gospel, and perhaps resolve that they will give heed to the message, perhaps for a while seem diligently to do so, but worldly anxieties, especially about wealth, and worldly desires (Mark 4: 19), and worldly pleasures (Luke 8: 14), soon get complete possession of the mind, and all the seeming good effect is gone, leaving the soul a very thicket of thorns. *Bruce:* "It may be asked who has a chance of bringing forth fruit unto perfection, for what character is free from thorns? But the question is not, who is free from evil desires, or from temptation to inordinate affection, but what attitude you assume towards these."

23. Into—*upon*—**the good ground,** comp. on v. 8. Good ground here stands in contrast with the three other kinds of ground, and so (Goebel) is conceived of as a soil soft, deep, and clean. **Understandeth,** see on v. 19. **Also**—better *verily,* not the word commonly rendered verily, but another, which is hard to render, but calls attention to this person, marks him out as distinctively the one who performs the action; all the others fail, this is the one that bears fruit. (Comp. Meyer, and Moulton in Winer, p. 578.) **Some a hundred-fold,** etc. Even of those who truly understand and receive the word, some exhibit better results than others. *Gill :* "The fruits of grace in believers are of the same quality, yet not of the same quantity." That which yields a less abundant harvest is still called good ground, seeing that it does produce a real crop. So the servant who made a good use of but two talents was a good and faithful servant. (25: 23.) Yet we should all desire and strive to be not merely of those who bring forth, but of those who bring forth a hundred-fold. Ambition is a worthy and noble thing, when it aims at eminent usefulness, rises above envy and jealousy, and subordinates everything to the glory of God. It has been remarked that this last class is distinctly contrasted with each of the others: they 'understand,' in opposition to the first class; they 'hold it fast in a good heart' (Luke 8: 15), in opposition to the second class; they 'bring forth fruit with patience' (Luke 8: 15) in opposition to the third class. Yet in this last case the comparison is scarcely just; for the third class did not bring forth fruit at all, as is shown by the 'unfruitful' of Matthew and Mark, and by Luke's expression (8: 14) 'bring no fruit to perfection.'

The illustration cannot touch at all points. It takes no account of the fact that the condition of the spiritual soil may be altered by divine grace—that the trampled ground can become soft, the rocky ground deep, and the thorns be rooted out. The inspired teachers in general go straight forward with the subject in hand, and towards the point in view, without pausing at every step to guard against misapprehension, or to introduce related truths; otherwise their discourse would gain no momentum, and exert no force. Other passages of Scripture will always furnish the means of preventing misapprehension or of completing the view. But, taken within the limits of its design, this parable is strikingly comprehensive. All those who hear the word to no real profit may without straining be referred to one of the three classes first given; and the fourth class comprehends various grades of actual fruitfulness.

HOMILETICAL AND PRACTICAL.

V. 2. The most spiritual preaching must not neglect to seek helpful outward conditions. Our houses of worship should be so constructed that the people may clearly see and easily hear the preacher. Many costly and handsome buildings are in these respects so extremely defective as to be an abomination. If the Master took pains in this regard, shall not we? JEROME : "A crowd is of many minds, and so he speaks to them in many parables, that each might receive appropriate instruction. He did not speak everything in parables, but many things—mingling the perspicuous with the obscure, that by what they understand they may be aroused to seek knowledge of what they do not understand."—V. 9. He that hath ears. 1) Many will not hear spiritual truths even with the outward ear. 2) None can hear spiritual truth understandingly, unless they have some desire for spiritual profit. 3) Whoever sees some meaning in spiritual teaching should earnestly seek to know more thoroughly. 4) The religious teacher must not be discouraged by the failure of some, so long as others can and do really hear. CHRYS. : "Even though the lost be more than such as receive the word, yet they were not to despond. For this was the case even with their Lord, and he who fully foreknew that these things should be, did not desist from sowing."

V. 11. Conditions of gaining a deep knowledge of Christianity. 1) A real desire to know thoroughly, comp. Heb. 6: 1. 2) Some existing knowledge as a preparation for learning more, v. 11, 12, 16. 3) Earnest effort to understand what is seen and heard, v. 13. 4) Practical conformity to the knowledge already gained, comp. John 7: 17. Christianity is intensely practical—knowing and doing must advance hand in hand.—V. 11-13. Truth is not withheld from any by arbitrary divine allotment, but as the penalty of previous neglect and hostility (12: 24); comp. Rom. 1: 28. CHRYS: "It was a voluntary and self-chosen blindness; therefore he said not, simply, they see not, but seeing they see not; for they saw even demons cast out, and ascribed it to the prince of the demons." THEOPHYL. : "To give them plain teaching would have been to cast pearls before swine." V. 14 f. A picture of many who reject God's word. 1) Slight attention, and no real understanding, v. 14. 2) Cause of this in dull torpor of thought and feeling, v. 15 a. 3) Effect in preventing them from turning and being saved, v. 15 b.—V. 17. THEOPHYL. : "In

24 Another parable put he forth unto them, saying, The kingdom of heaven is likened unto a man which sowed good seed in his field:

24   Another parable set he before them, saying, The kingdom of heaven is likened unto a man that

---

two respects the apostles excelled the prophets, in seeing bodily, and in better understanding spiritually."

V. 18-23. Even if preaching were in itself perfect, it would have a very different effect upon different classes of hearers. Our work cannot be fairly tested by its actual results, but rather by its tendencies, aims, and adaptations. Yet a religious teacher should earnestly seek for tangible results, both in winning and in building up.—CHRYS.: "Mark this, I pray thee, that the way of destruction is not one only, but there are differing ones, and wide apart from one another. Let us not soothe ourselves upon our not perishing in all these ways, but let it be our grief in whichever way we are perishing."—V. 19. The gospel not understood. I. Causes. (1) Indifference and inattention to it. (2) Prejudices which exclude it. (3) Desire to do things it forbids. (4) Insensibility through previous neglect. II. Consequences. (1) It does not reach the deeper affections. (2) It gives no impulse to the will. (3) It never touches the life. (4) It soon passes away from the memory.—V. 20 f. The temporary Christian. 1) How he receives the gospel; a) promptly, b) joyfully, c) with rich apparent effects upon life. 2) How he abandons the gospel; a) certainly before long, b) as soon as ever serious trial comes, c) without any permanent benefit to character or life.—V. 22. CHRYS.: "There is a way, if thou wilt, to check this evil growth, and to make the right use of our wealth. Therefore he said not 'the world,' but 'the care of the world'; nor 'riches,' but 'the deceitfulness of riches.' Let us not, then, blame the things, but the corrupt mind. For it is possible to be rich and not to be deceived; and to be in the world, and not to be choked with its cares." ORIGEN: "The apostle's 'anxiety for all the churches' is not 'anxiety about the world.'"—V. 23. How to treat the gospel. 1) Hear it, 2) understand and receive it, 3) act it out.

24-43. THE TARES, THE MUSTARD-SEED, THE LEAVEN.

After explaining the parable of the Sower, our Lord proceeds to utter several other parables. The first three of these were clearly

spoken on the same occasion as that of the Sower; for the 'multitudes' of v. 34 and 36 seem to be plainly the same as those of v. 2; and the 'house' of v. 36 the same as that of v. 1; the language of v. 51 and 54 makes it probable that the other three also were spoken on the same occasion. Mark (4: 26-29) has at this point another parable drawn from sowing seed, which forms a sort of pair with that of the Sower. Here then are eight parables, in four pairs, since that of the Net closely resembles that of the Tares. Keim urges that the parables of the Mustard-seed and the Leaven, asserting the victorious extension of the kingdom of heaven throughout the world, could not have been delivered in the same breath with the Sower and the Tares, which are "resigned and melancholy." But why may not the Great Teacher have naturally introduced more hopeful views for needed relief to his own mind and to his hearers? Such quick reactions of strong feeling easily occur. There is thus here no occasion for rejecting Matthew's order.

I. **24-30.** THE PARABLE OF THE TARES GIVEN. **Put he forth unto,** or *set before,* **them,** an image derived from setting food before persons, as the word is used in Mark 8: 6; Acts 16: 34; 1 Cor. 10: 27. (Comp. v. 31.) Jerome carries out the image, comparing the different parables to different articles of food, suited to one guest or another. 'Them' here means not the disciples only (v. 10), but the people in general again. (v. 34, 36.) As to the parable of the Tares (which is given by Matthew only), we must notice here the illustration itself, reserving its interpretation for the Notes on v. 37-43.

The kingdom of heaven is likened, literally, *was likened.* This kingdom or reign has been already begun, and so the resemblance may be spoken of as existing in the past. Or, we may understand it in the sense that the kingdom of heaven was likened, became like, and so is now like. Nicholson understands it to mean that some such parable as this already existed; and so in 18: 23 and 22: 2. But the phrase does not at all require such a supposition, and while Jesus used some current ideas and expressions, there is

25 But while men slept, his enemy came and sowed tares among the wheat, and went his way.

26 But when the blade was sprung up, and brought forth fruit, then appeared the tares also.

27 So the servants of the householder came and said unto him, Sir, didst not thou sow good seed in thy field? from whence then hath it tares?

28 He said unto them, An enemy hath done this. The servants said unto him, Wilt thou then that we go and gather them up?

29 But he said, Nay; lest while ye gather up the tares, ye root up also the wheat with them.

25 sowed good seed in his field: but while men slept, his enemy came and sowed [1]tares also among the

26 wheat, and went away. But when the blade sprang up, and brought forth fruit, then appeared the tares

27 also. And the [2]servants of the householder came and said unto him, Sir, didst thou not sow good seed

28 in thy field? whence then hath it tares? And he said unto them, [3]An enemy hath done this. And

29 the [2]servants say unto him, Wilt thou then that we go and gather them up? But he saith, Nay; lest haply while ye gather up the tares, ye root up the

1 Or, *darnel*....2 Gr. *bondservants*....3 Gr. *A man* that *is an enemy.*

no reason elsewhere to suppose that he borrowed an entire illustration; and this parable and that of 22: 2, are in themselves particularly unlikely to have been given by any previous teacher, being so utterly at variance with current Jewish thought and feeling. The future tense is used, shall be like (likened), in 7: 24, 26; 11: 16; 25: 1; and the present tense in 11: 16; 13: 31-52; 20: 1. **Unto a man.** The Messianic reign (3: 2) resembles not simply the man who sowed, but the parable as a whole; the comparison is simply affirmed, here and elsewhere, with reference to the leading personage of the story, or the object it is natural to mention first. Comp. v. 44, 45, 47; 18: 23; 20: 1; 25: 1. **But while men slept** (comp. Job 33: 15), viz., at night, when there was none to observe. There is no reference to any particular men as negligently sleeping; it is simply meant that the enemy selected an opportunity for *secretly* doing an injury. The word rendered **tares** has been the subject of much discussion, but it is pretty generally agreed that it denotes darnel, a plant of the same family as wheat, and not readily distinguished from it in the early stages. Jerome, who lived in Palestine A. D. 385-420, states that it was quite difficult to distinguish them until the head of the wheat appeared. Robinson, journeying in Galilee in April, 1852, says, "Our path now lay through fields of wheat of the most luxuriant growth; finer than which I had not before seen in this or any other country. Among these splendid fields of grain are still found the *tares* spoken of in the New Testament. As described to me, they are not to be distinguished from the wheat until the ear appears. The seed resembles wheat in form; but is smaller and black. In Beirût poultry are fed upon this seed; and it is kept for sale for that purpose. When this is not separated from the wheat,

bread made from the flour often causes dizziness to those who eat of it. All this corresponds with the *lolium temulentum*, or bearded darnel." So the seeds of the tares were not merely useless for human food, but noxious, which fact (Plumptre) adds to the point of the parable. Thomson, ii., p. 395, says that often "the roots of the two plants are so intertwined that it is impossible to separate them without plucking up both." The notion that the tares were a degenerate wheat, and by cultivation could be made to become wheat again, has been very pleasing to some minds, because it corresponds to the fact that wicked men are fallen and may be restored. Such a notion as to darnel appears in the Talmud, and is entertained by some persons in Palestine now; and also by some American wheatgrowers as to what they call "cheat." But (Thomson) it is not supported by adequate evidence, and the fancy may be abandoned without regret, for it would introduce an idea quite apart from the design of the parable. **Among the wheat,** in the Greek a strong expression, all through the midst of the wheat—making the separation particularly difficult. **And went his way,** *away,* so that no one knew what he had done. This practice of sowing noxious seeds in an enemy's wheatfield is said to be still found in the East, though Thomson has never been able to hear of an instance,—and is not unknown in other countries. **The blade,** the word rendered grass in 6: 30; 14: 19. **And brought forth fruit,** not here the ripe grain, but the heads containing the grain, which would show the character of the plant. **Servants,** slaves, *douloi,* see on 8: 6. **Householder,** see on 10: 25, where it is rendered 'master of the house.' **Sir,** see on 8: 2. **An enemy,** literally as in margin Rev. Ver., *a man* that *is an enemy.* **The harvest,** more exactly, *the season of harvest,* see on 11: 25. **Gather together** and **gather**

30 Let both grow together until the harvest: and in the time of harvest I will say to the reapers, Gather ye together first the tares, and bind them in bundles to burn them: but gather the wheat into my barn.
31 Another parable put he forth unto them, saying, The kingdom of heaven is like to a grain of mustard seed, which a man took, and sowed in his field:
32 Which indeed is the least of all seeds: but when it is grown, it is the greatest among herbs, and becometh a tree, so that the birds of the air come and lodge in the branches thereof.

30 wheat with them. Let both grow together until the harvest; and in the time of the harvest, I will say to the reapers, Gather up first the tares, and bind them in bundles to burn them: but gather the wheat into my barn.
31 Another parable set he before them, saying, The kingdom of heaven is like unto a grain of mustard seed, which a man took, and sowed in his field:
32 which indeed is less than all seeds; but when it is grown, it is greater than the herbs, and becometh a tree, so that the birds of the heaven come and lodge in the branches thereof.

---

in v. 30 represent different words, but amounting to the same thing; the first might be translated 'collect.' **Into my barn,** rendered 'garner' in 3 : 12.

We might suppose that so many different parables spoken on the same occasion would confuse the minds of the hearers, and thus fail to be understood or remembered. But only a part of them were spoken to the people at large (v. 36), and these not in immediate succession.   (v. 10; Mark 4 : 10.)

II. **31-33.** PARABLES OF THE MUSTARD-SEED AND THE LEAVEN. The former is found also in Mark 4 : 30-32; and both in Luke 13 : 18-21, as spoken on a later occasion. Some critics wonder why other parables were introduced between the parable of the Tares and the interpretation of it. Do not these, in correcting a common Jewish error, help to prepare the mind for understanding the important correction and instruction given by the parable of the Tares? Lutteroth suggests that the disciples, after the rebuke of Mark 4 : 13, delayed asking the interpretation to see if they could think it out; a notion which may not be wholly fanciful. Probably they did see the meaning of the parables of the Mustard-seed and the Leaven, which is comparatively obvious, and so did not ask an interpretation of them. (v. 36.) It will be found interesting to compare the four successive parables derived from the growth of seeds, viz., the Sower, the Tares, the Seed growing of itself (Mark 4 : 26-29), the Mustard-seed.

Put forth, etc. *Set before them*, see on v. 24. **The kingdom of heaven,** the Messianic reign, see on 3 : 2. **A grain of mustard-seed.** This is most likely the common mustard, which in the hot countries of the East is sometimes found eight or ten feet high. *Thomson:* "I have seen it on the rich plains of Akkar as tall as the horse and his rider." Hackett ("Illustrations of Scripture") saw stalks seven and nine feet high,

and before his eyes a bird came and perched on a branch and sung. (Comp. Clark.) Thomson, ii., p. 163, mentions one that was more than twelve feet high. Some expressions in the Talmud go beyond this, but Edersheim accounts for them as exaggerations. Maldonatus (sixteenth century) speaks of seeing great mustard-plants in Spain, with numerous birds sitting on the branches and eagerly devouring the seeds. Meyer and others think that a tree is meant, now called *Salvadora Persica*, which abounds on the shores of the Sea of Galilee. It grows twenty-five feet high, but has a small seed of pungent taste, used for the same purposes as mustard. But if a real tree were meant, it would be useless to say that it "is greater than the herbs, and becomes a tree." So we must understand the real mustard-plant. **Field,** the Greek denoting a piece of cultivated ground, whether large or small. *Less than* **all seeds** is equivalent to a superlative (as in 11 : 11). **Greatest among** — literally *greater than the* — **herbs** must be taken strictly as a comparative; it rises above its own class of plants, and becomes a tree. **The birds of the air**, or *heaven*, see on 6 : 26. **Lodge**, or 'make their habitations,' see on 8 : 20, and comp. Dan. 4 : 12; Psa. 104: 12. **The branches thereof,** rather *its branches*, see on 6 : 34. The mustard-seed seems to have been proverbially used to represent anything very small (comp. 17 : 20; Luke 17 : 6), as we find it so used (Lightf., Edersh.) in the Rabbinical writers. A Buddhist writing says (Lutteroth): "Meru, the greatest of mountains, never bows before a mustard-plant." Our Lord is of course not asserting it as a scientific fact, that this is smaller than all other seeds in the world, but is speaking popularly, this being the smallest that his hearers were accustomed to sow, or the smallest that produced a large plant.

No interpretation of this parable is given, but its application is plain from the nature of

33 Another parable spake he unto them: The kingdom of heaven is like unto leaven, which a woman took, and hid in three *a* measures of meal, till the whole was leavened.

33   Another parable spake he unto them: The kingdom of heaven is like unto leaven, which a woman took, and hid in three [1]measures of meal, till it was all leavened.

---

a The word in the Greek is a measure containing about a peck and a half, wanting a little more than a pint.——[1] The word in the Greek denotes the Hebrew seah, a measure containing nearly a peck and a half.

---

the case. It represents the growth of Christianity in the world, from small beginnings, to vast dimensions at last. Some understand it as representing also the gradual progress of piety in the individual; but the use of the phrase 'kingdom of heaven' throughout this series of parables, and in the Gospels at large, appears to confine the view to the former thought. The disciples and other Jews, clinging to the notion of a vast and splendid earthly kingdom, would think it very strange that Messiah's reign should begin so quietly, and on so small a scale; and in this parable, and that of the Leaven, our Lord wishes to impress it upon them that though small in its beginnings, the Messianic kingdom was destined to attain a vast extent. If the disciples were discouraged by the blasphemous accusation of that morning, and by the parables of the Sower and the Tares, which indicated that but few would become subjects of Christ's reign, these other two would re-assure them. And did not Jesus need to comfort *himself*, amid such small beginnings and slow progress? We see the original circumstances under which the parable was spoken well reproduced now, at the first introduction of Christianity into some great heathen nations. Not only the heathen themselves, but irreligious sailors, merchants, and travelers from our own country, often sneer at the idea that a few insignificant men, by means of so feeble a thing as preaching, should expect to change a mighty people. Yet it is from similar small beginnings that there has gradually grown up the Christianity and the civilization of Europe and America at the present time.—Some expositors, following certain Fathers, find great significance in the sharp, pungent qualities of the mustard-seed as illustrating the fact that Christianity, though small, would prove very efficacious and impressive; but this is quite beside the point of the parable; and even if any one should regard the idea as in itself worth notice, he must accept it as merely a fancy, and not as a part of the Saviour's teaching. Nor are we to find any distinct spiritual meaning in the birds lodging in the branches, which simply shows in a vivid way how large and strong the plant becomes. Several passages of the Old Test. represent an extensive kingdom by a great tree, with the birds dwelling among its branches. Ezek. 17: 22-24; 31: 3-14; Dan. 4: 10 ff.

33. The parable of the Leaven is given here by Matt. only; Luke (13: 20 f.) records it as also spoken on a later occasion. **Leaven,** see on 16: 6. **Meal,** rather what we now call 'flour,' comp. on 12: 1. **Measures.** The Greek word corresponds to a common Hebrew measure of things dry, called *seah*, holding (Josephus, "Ant." 9, 4, 5,) nearly a peck and a half *(margin);* so that 'three measures' would be rather more than our bushel; but the size varied in different parts of Palestine. (Edersh.) It contributes to the vividness of the parabolic narrative, that it does not merely say "a large quantity," but names some particular quantity; and we may infer from Gen. 18: 6; Judg. 6: 19; 1 Sam. 1: 24, that three seahs (equal to one ephah) was a quantity often taken to make up, the custom being to bake at once enough for several days. To find a special spiritual meaning in the number three, would seem to us ridiculous; yet some great men among the Fathers, and some fanciful modern expositors, have actually made it signify Jews, Greeks, and Samaritans; or Asia, Europe, and Africa (how about America, now?); or the three sons of Noah; or body, soul, and spirit, etc. So with the attempts to give separate significance to the **woman,** when it was a matter of course to speak of a woman, and not of a man, making up bread. If the **woman** here denotes "the church," what is denoted by the **man** in v. 31?—The general meaning of this parable is the same as that of the preceding. A small bit of leaven, completely hidden from view in the great mass of dough, would finally leaven the whole; and so Christianity, with its small and obscure beginnings, would pervade the whole race of mankind. There is a like gradual progress of piety in the individual, but that does not seem to be the point here in view. A slight but just distinction has been

34 All these things spake Jesus unto the multitude in parables; and without a parable spake he not unto them:
35 That it might be fulfilled which was spoken by the prophet, saying, I will open my mouth in parables; I will utter things which have been kept secret from the foundation of the world.

34   All these things spake Jesus in parables unto the multitudes; and without a parable spake he nothing
35 unto them: that it might be fulfilled which was spoken through the prophet, saying, I will open my mouth in parables; I will utter things hidden from the foundation [1] of the world.

1 Many ancient authorities omit, *of the world.*

pointed out between this parable and that of the Grain of Mustard. That represents the expansion of the Christian community into vast dimensions; this the assimilating diffusion of Christianity through the vast mass of humanity; the one is extensive, the other intensive. —Because leaven is frequently used in Scripture as the symbol of things corrupting and pernicious (16: 6; Luke 12: 1; Gal. 5: 9; 1 Cor. 5: 6; and often in Old Test.), and nowhere but here used in a good sense, some have strangely tried to interpret it here as denoting the corruptions which should arise in connection with Christianity. But can there be only one possible figurative use of an object? The lion represents Satan, and also the Saviour; but no one would fancy in the same sense. (Comp. on 3: 11.)

III. **34 f.** A PREDICTION OF SPEAKING IN PARABLES. **All these things,** with no special emphasis on 'all.' **Unto the multitudes,** or *crowds* (see 13: 2), and not merely to the disciples (comp. on v. 36). *Spake he nothing* is the correct Greek text, instead of **spake he not,** which is taken from the parallel passage of Mark. (4: 34) It must be meant simply that on this occasion he said nothing to them except in parables; we know that on other occasions, afterwards as well as before, he frequently spoke to the people in unparabolic language. 'Spake' is in Greek an imperfect, describing his practice on that occasion. — Here again, as in so many other instances, Matt. pauses to point out the fulfill-

ment in Jesus of an Old Test. prediction. **That it might be fulfilled,** see on 1: 22. This expression requires us to understand a real fulfillment of a real prediction—unless that idea could be shown to be in the given case impossible—and a fulfillment designedly brought about in the course of providence. It is difficult, in the present instance, to discern the prophetic relation, but it is not impossible. **By the prophet,**[1] more exactly *through,* comp. on 2: 5. The quotation is from Psa. 78: 2. Many of the Psalms are prophetic, and the Psalmist David is expressly called a prophet. (Acts 2: 30.) The writer of this Psalm is given by the heading as Asaph, and he in 2 Chron. 29: 30 is called the seer, equivalent to prophet. (1 Sam. 9: 9.) The Psalm relates the history of Israel, and points out its lessons; but Israel was typical of the Messiah (see above on 2: 15), and so the passage might contain a prophetic reference to him, which the inspired Evangelist informs us it did contain. He states it as a part of the divine purpose, in our Lord's adoption of the parabolic method of instruction, that there should be a fulfillment of that prophetic saying. Unless we can show that there was no such prophetic relation, we must certainly accept the Evangelist's statement. **I will utter.** The Greek word means to belch, to vomit, to pour out copious speech, and this last corresponds to the Hebrew. **From the foundation of the world.**[2] The Hebrew has a phrase usually signifying 'from antiquity,' and thus natu-

1 'Through Isaiah the prophet' is the reading of ℵ (first hand), several important cursives, one codex of the Æthiopic; it is quoted in the Clementine homilies (latter part of second century), and said by Eusebius and Jerome to have been found in some copies of the Gospel. Jerome states that Porphyry cited it as showing the ignorance of Matthew. Transcriptional probability would at once favor this, for it is easy to suppose so obvious an error to have been corrected by copyists (comp. 27: 9; Mark 1: 2). On the other hand, no prophet being named, some one might have felt moved to insert the name of the *greatest* prophet. It is also possible that some reader, observing the actual source of the quotation, might have inserted Asaph; and that then (as Euseb. and Jerome suggest) others, not having heard

of such a prophet, should change it to the somewhat similar name Isaiah. With these conflicting transcriptional probabilities, and external evidence so slender, it seems right to fall back on the intrinsic improbability (apart from all theories of inspiration) that an intelligent writer like Matt. and a special student of prophecy, would commit so manifest an error. 'Isaiah' is read by Tisch. (following ℵ) and by W H. *margin;* and strongly favored by Hort in Appendix.

2 'Of the world' should probably be omitted, with ℵ (second hand) B, two cursives, Old Syriac, some copies of Old Latin, and some Fathers. 'From the foundation' would really mean this, and 'of the world' would be easily added by copyists from 25: 34, where there is no variation of the reading.

36 Then Jesus sent the multitude away, and went into the house: and his disciples came unto him, saying, Declare unto us the parable of the tares of the field.

37 He answered and said unto them, He that soweth the good seed is the Son of man:

36 Then he left the multitudes, and went into the house: and his disciples came unto him, saying, Explain unto us the parable of the tares of the field.

37 And he answered and said, He that soweth the good

rally applying in the Psalmist's use to the early history of the nation (so Sept. 'from the beginning'); but the phrase also signifies 'from eternity,' as in Deut. 33: 27; Psa. 55: 19, and in the prophetic application might perhaps be understood in that sense, to which the Evangelist's expression is equivalent. (Comp. on 1: 23.)

IV. **36-43.** INTERPRETATION OF THE PARABLE OF THE TARES. **Sent away.** Rev. Ver. renders, *he left.* **The multitude,** *the crowds,* as in 5: 1. These or similar crowds had heard the parables of the Sower, the Tares, the Mustard-seed and the Leaven, though not the explanation of the first (see on 13: 10); also the other parable given by Mark (4: 26 ff.). Now the disciples alone are to hear the explanation of the parable of the Tares, and also to hear the three other parables that follow. **His disciples** were probably not merely the Twelve, but others also. (See on v. 10.) The name **Jesus** at the beginning of v. 36, does not appear in many of the best authorities, and was doubtless added by some early readers, because this was the beginning of a church "lesson," and so the name was apparently needed. The same thing has happened in various other passages, at the beginning of lessons. **Into the house,** probably the house mentioned in 13: 1, which may have been (Mark 3: 20) the house at Capernaum which he usually occupied, viz., that of Simon Peter. (Comp. on 4: 13 and 8: 14.) **Declare,** *explain* is doubtless the correct reading (א first hand, B, Origen,) having been changed to make it agree with 15: 15. **The parable of the tares of the field.** This designation shows that the disciples had seized the most characteristic feature of the illustration. **Answered and said,** without **unto them,** an unnecessary addition of many documents. For explanation of the terms and allusions of the parable itself, comp. on v. 24-30.

The Jews, including our Lord's disciples, would naturally think, with their rooted notions of Messiah's reign, that he would promptly destroy all those who did not submit to his authority, as was common with Orien-

tal conquerors, as David himself was known to have done. Their views and feelings are illustrated by the wish of James and John to call down fire from heaven and consume the Samaritan village, for refusing to receive Jesus. They might strengthen themselves (Weiss) in this view by supposing that the Messianic discrimination predicted by John the Baptist (3: 10-12) would be the first part of the Messianic work, and would be performed in a wholesale fashion. The contrary has already been intimated by the parable of the Sower, and by those of the Mustard-seed and the Leaven, all showing that the Messianic operation would be gradual, and upon individuals. And it is distinctly set forth by the present parable, which declares that while the Messiah does not at once destroy those who refuse him allegiance, but suffers righteous and wicked to live on together in the world, and intertwined in the relations of life (v. 29), yet he will hereafter effectually separate them, and deal with each class according to their deserts. The Messianic discrimination is to take place not at the beginning, but at the end of the present dispensation, when the unmixed wheat will be gathered into the garner, (v. 30 having the same phrase as 3: 12.) We have seen (on 3: 2) that the word rendered 'kingdom' is inadequately expressed by that one term, but includes also what we mean by 'kingship' and 'reign,' one idea or another being especially prominent in different cases. Here the kingdom of heaven (v. 24) denotes especially the Messianic reign, and the parable sets forth some things that will occur in the world in connection with that reign. But overlooking these facts, and thinking always of the kingdom as implying an organization of subjects, the Christian world has largely fallen into the habit of confounding the kingdom of heaven, here and often elsewhere, with what is popularly called "the visible church," *i. e.,* the totality of *professed* believers. Hence most expositors from an early period, have understood the parable as teaching that in "the church" we must have righteous and wicked together. The tendency to understand it in this way was strengthened by Constantine's adoption of Christianity as a plank in his political platform, leading to what in modern times we call a Church Establishment, in which all are held as church-members, and exclusion from a church, such as the New Test. sometimes enjoins (1 Cor. 5 : 4 f. ; 2 Cor. 2 : 5-8 ; Matt. 18 : 17 ff.), becomes impossible. Still a third cause affected the interpretation. When the Donatists undertook to excommunicate all persons known to be evil, and in the case of *traditores*, who had given up copies of Scripture to be burned during the persecutions, were unwilling ever to restore them to the church connection, Augustine wrote against their views a great number of treatises, in which he constantly appealed to this parable, as showing that good and evil persons must dwell together in the church. He says the Donatist bishops would reply, "It does not refer to the church; the Lord said, the field is the world, not, the field is the church." But Augustine would say that the world here means the church. They contended that the world is always used in a bad sense, quoting many testimonies from Scripture, as "If any man love the world," etc. (1 John 2 : 15.) But he replied with 2 Cor. 5 : 19, "God was in Christ, reconciling the world unto himself"; "and assuredly" (says Aug.), "God reconciles to himself nothing but the church." On one occasion Aug. actually states it as a *sign* of the church that it contains evil and good mixed together. The influence of the great Latin theologian thus made it a commonplace of Christian controversy and exposition that the parable of the Tares describes the *church* as containing good and bad, and teaches that church discipline must not attempt to have it otherwise.[1] All the commentators at the time of the Reformation, and almost all since that time, have been connected with some State Church, and would readily adopt the current interpretation, because it accorded with their education and surroundings. But this cannot be a correct view of the parable, for our Lord's interpretation, as the Donatists urged, expressly declares, "The field is the *world*." It is very true that in any church there are likely to be members who are not true Christians, and whom it is often difficult for us to detect; but Augustine's interpretation would make the parable teach that when detected, and clearly known, we must not exclude them. Now the point of the parable is not that obviously wicked men are to live on as recognized subjects of Christ's *kingdom*, regarded as a definite organization—*i. e.*, as members of his churches—but that he suffers them, under or during his *reign*, to live on in the *world*, instead of being at once destroyed, as the Jews expected. This would explain to the disciples, for example, why he who could work miracles had that morning allowed himself to be insulted and blasphemed, and had only given a solemn warning instead of blasting with instant destruction. It would also give another reason why the Messianic work was moving slowly. One reason already given was that many receive the 'word of the kingdom' improperly (parable of the Sower);

---

[1] The first statement of this interpretation we have found is in Cyprian, *Epistola* 51, "Although tares are seen in the church, that ought not to hinder our faith or our charity, nor cause us to quit the church." Tertullian, "*de Fuga in persecutione*," calls the threshing-floor of Matt. 3 : 12 the church, in which persecution discerns between the wheat of martyrs and the chaff of deniers. Origen says (on Matthew—the extant portion begins just here): "The whole world might be called (the) field, and not the church of God only ; for in all the world the Son of man sowed good seed, and the evil one the tares." Irenæus, iv. 66, refers the parable to the introduction of evil among men by Satan. Hermas, "*Simil.*" iii., iv., v., 2 and 5, gives kindred illustrations evidently founded on this parable, using the phrase, "The field is the world," and describing the presence of good and bad men together in the world. The application to the church was known to Origen, but apparently owed its wide acceptance to Cyprian, who did so much to develop the church idea. His saying is repeatedly quoted by Augustine, as high authority from a martyr. Augustine's numerous treatises and letters against the Donatists nearly all appeal to this parable, but his fullest statements are in the "*Breviculus Collationis cum Donatistis*,' and the "*Ad Donatistas post Collationem*." Optatus, whose idea of the church appears to precede that of Augustine and to have been developed independently of Cyprian, says, ("*de Schismate Donatistarum*," vii., 2), "The field is the whole world, in which is the church"—a more reasonable conception than that of Augustine.—Gregory Naz. in several hymns speaks of sowing tares on earth and in the soul, but does not refer to the church. Chrysostom (on Matthew) understands the church, arguing that the present world also is Christ's, and takes the tares to mean heretics, an idea hinted at in Basil also.—It would be well if some specialist in Church Hist. would fully work out the history of the early interpretation of this parable.

38 The field is the world ; the good seed are the children of the kingdom ; but the tares are the children of the wicked one ;
39 The enemy that sowed them is the devil ; the harvest is the end of the world ; and the reapers are the angels.
40 As therefore the tares are gathered and burned in the fire ; so shall it be in the end of this world.

38 seed is the Son of man ; and the field is the world ; and the good seed, these are the sons of the kingdom ; and the tares are the sons of the evil *one* ; and
39 dom ; and the tares are the sons of the evil *one* ; and the enemy that sowed them is the devil ; and the harvest is [1] the end of the world ; and the reapers
40 are angels. As therefore the tares are gathered up and burned with fire ; so shall it be in [1] the end of

1 Or, *the consummation of the age.*

now another reason is that while the Son of man sows wheat in the world, the devil, in the same field (the world), sows tares, all in among the wheat.

The mistaken view of this parable above condemned finds apparent support in the phrase 'shall gather out of his kingdom' (see on v. 41), and in the parable of the Net. (v. 47 ff.) Our Lord's interpretation comprises (Goebel) two distinct parts. In v. 37-39 a meaning is *separately* and briefly assigned to each leading object and person in the story. In v. 40-43, the final stage of the spiritual situation meant to be illustrated is vividly described by a *series of events.*

37-39. The Son of man, *i e.* the Messiah, see on 8: 20. **The field is the world,** here the common Greek term *kosmos,* having as broad and general a sense as our English term world. Our Lord's personal ministry was restricted to Palestine, though including some Gentiles ; but his work was to be afterwards extended into 'all the world' (Mark 16: 15), among 'all nations,' (28: 19). **The good seed,** *i. e.,* of course, the plants springing from the seed. **The children** (*sons*) **of the kingdom** (comp. on 8: 12), those who have a right to the privileges of the Messianic reign, as if they were its very offspring. But in 8: 12 the phrase represents those who were entitled, as it were, by birth, to the Messianic privileges (viz., the Jews), but many of whom would be cast out ; while here it is those who are truly the subjects of Messiah by the new birth (comp. 21: 43). And so **the children** (*sons*) **of the wicked one,** see on 13: 19 and 6: 13, are those who as closely resemble Satan, and are as completely under his control, as is the case of children towards their father. (Comp. John 8: 44 ; 1 John 5: 19.) **The devil,** see on 4: 1. Evil in the human race owes its origin to Satan. As to the reasons why God permitted its original appearance in the universe, speculation has scarcely proven satisfactory, and Scripture is silent. Some argue that the parable must refer to "the church,"

because the person who sowed the good seed is the Messiah, and the enemy sowed *afterwards ;* while in the *world* there had been sons of the evil one long *before* the Saviour's appearing. But no illustration can throw light in all directions. This parable must *of course* describe tares as sown after wheat, for otherwise the story would have been unnatural. Therefore this illustration could depict only the present and future relations of good and evil in the world, and could not bring within its horizon the past history of the human race. **The end of the world.** The Greek for 'world' is not the same as in v. 38, but the same as in v. 22 and 12: 32, which, according to Jewish usage, frequently denotes the present period, the existing condition of things, as opposed to some past or future condition of things. The word translated 'end' denotes completion or consummation (as in *margin* of Rev. Ver.) ; see the same phrase in 24: 3 ; 28: 20, and 'children of this world' in Luke 16: 8 ; 20: 34. The end or consummation of the present period or state of things will be at our Lord's second coming, which will open the new and eternal period. **And the reapers are the angels,** see on 18: 10. The Greek has here no article with 'angels' ; the Com. Ver. inserted or omitted the article with great license.—Observe that our Lord's interpretation takes no account of the men who slept (really meaning people in general, and not implying blame, see on v. 25), nor of the servants who reported what had happened ; many commentators are not content with this, and propose various interpretations, which cannot be expected to reward attention. (Comp. as to the interpretation of parables on 13 : 3.)

40-43. *Burned with fire* is a more probable translation than **in the fire** (Tyndale and followers), the form being oftener instrumental than locative. (Comp. 3: 12.) **In the end of this (**properly *the*) **world,** the word 'this' being an unwarranted addition, as in v. 22. **The Son of man . . . . his angels . . . .**

41 The Son of man shall send forth his angels, and they shall gather out of his kingdom all things that offend, and them which do iniquity ; [a]

41 the world. The Son of man shall send forth his angels, and they shall gather out of his kingdom

a Or, *scandals.*

his kingdom, suggesting the exalted dignity to which he shall attain who was once despised and rejected. (Comp. on 7 : 21 ; 10 : 32 ; 12 : 8 ; 25 : 31 ff.) The angels, who now desire to look into the things of salvation (1 Pet. 1 : 12), who rejoice over one sinner that repenteth (Luk 15 : 7), who are all ministering spirits, sent forth to do service for the sake of those who are to inherit salvation (Heb. 1 : 14), will then have assigned them the solemn task of separating the wicked from among the just, and consigning them to destruction. (Comp. 25 : 31.) And they shall gather out of his kingdom. Observe that this points forward to the time of the final judgment. The Messianic dominion will *then* be regarded as virtually extending over the whole world, like God's universal kingship or reign (Psa. 22 : 27 f.) ; the kingship of the world will be our Lord's and his Christ's (Rev. 11 : 15) ; the kingdom predicted by Daniel will be about to complete its destiny, and fill the whole earth. (Dan. 2 : 35.) All that will then be necessary to render this Messianic reign actually universal will be to gather the wicked out of the world, and as the world will then by anticipation be his kingdom, it is said that the angels ' will gather out of his kingdom,' etc. (Comp. a somewhat similar view in Meyer.) It does not follow from this anticipative expression that the wicked are *now* within his kingdom regarded as an organization apart from the world. Observe that the problem of interpretation here is to reconcile the phrase ' they shall gather out of his kingdom ' with the clear statement of v. 38, 'the field is the world.' If we understand ' his kingdom' in this case to mean what is called "the visible church" throughout its history, then we must either understand 'the world' in some strained, unnatural sense,[1] or we must utterly confound the visible church with the world ; and upon any such interpretation the inevitable result will be that the passage prohibits exclusion from a church, which as we have seen, is elsewhere distinctly enjoined. In some way, then, the phrase 'gather out of his kingdom

(reign, dominion, etc.)' must be interpreted as not meaning "the visible church," or else we bring Scripture into apparently hopeless conflict with itself. It might be enough to say that *in one sense* all the world is under the Messiah's dominion, but not in the sense that all men are really his subjects. With 'gather out of his kingdom' compare in the kindred parable (v. 49), 'the angels shall come forth, and sever the wicked from among the righteous.' In the present 'age,' or state of things, the subjects of Christ's kingdom or reign are mingled in all social and other relations with the wicked. To separate them now, and destroy the wicked—as the Jews might naturally expect of Messiah—to make now the Messianic discrimination (3 : 10-12), would be to break up the whole framework of society. But let no one imagine that this mingling will always continue ; the time is approaching when the wicked will be gathered out from among Messiah's subjects. They were never one—were always, in fact, as distinct as wheat and tares ; but they were closely united in the world, their roots intertwined, and they are to be completely separated only when human society as a whole is broken up. This is all meant not as a reason why we should refrain from putting a wicked man out of a church, but as a reason why God refrains from putting him out of the world. We repeat that if the parable did refer to the presence of unrenewed persons in a church, then it would clearly forbid any exclusion from a church— a difficulty, upon that view, which has never been satisfactorily explained. It is idle to say that the parable only forbids very *rigid* discipline. By confining our view to the natural and obvious meaning of the parable, we free ourselves from all those confused and conflicting notions on the supposed relation of its teachings to church discipline, which have almost buried, beneath a mass of unprofitable discussion, this beautiful and affecting parable of our Lord.

All things that offend, *that cause stum-*

---

[1] As when Augustine (see above) says the world means the church ; or when Calvin says the world is used by synecdoche, the whole for a part, the world thus denoting the church.

42 And shall cast them into a furnace of fire; there shall be wailing and gnashing of teeth.
43 Then shall the righteous shine forth as the sun in the kingdom of their Father. Who hath ears to hear, let him hear.

42 all things that cause stumbling, and them that do iniquity, and shall cast them into the furnace of fire: there shall be the weeping and gnashing of
43 teeth. Then shall the righteous shine forth as the sun in the kingdom of their Father. He that hath ears to hear, let him hear.

---

bling, see on 5: 29. The idea here may be, all those who cause men to sin in general, or specifically, all those who cause men to doubt and question the reality of Christ's reign, from his allowing such persons to live on in the world. **And them which do iniquity** (comp. 7: 23), this plainer and more general expression being added to the figurative and more explicit one preceding — all the stumbling-blocks, and in general, those that do iniquity. The phraseology was perhaps suggested by Zeph. 1: 3. **Into a** (*the*) **furnace of fire,** comp. 3: 11; Rev. 20: 15; Jer. 29: 22; Dan. 3: 6; and see on 5: 22. A modern traveler speaks of furnaces for punishment in Persia. 'The furnace,' the definite place of future punishment. **There shall be the weeping and gnashing of teeth** (comp. on 8: 12), departs from the image of consuming the tares, to introduce another thought of horror, and heighten the terrible picture. The use of *various* images for future punishment should prevent a crude literalism, and falls in with the important teaching that there will be degrees of punishment. (Luke 12: 47.) But the images must be understood as representing something real. Reuss, with his rationalistic freedom, justly remarks that the furnace and the gnashing of teeth stand in the same position as the shining glory of the righteous (v. 43) — both must be accepted as facts [as representing realities], or else both alike referred to the mere popular beliefs of the time; one cannot accept the Bible descriptions of heaven as representing realities, and reject those of hell. — No spiritual meaning is to be derived from 'gather up first' in v. 30, as if showing that the righteous are to witness the destruction of the wicked. Our Lord does not introduce the word 'first' into v. 41, and in the similar allusion of v. 48 the order is reversed, simply following, in each case, the obvious propriety of the figure. In like manner some expositors gravely discuss the spiritual meaning of binding in bundles, when the author of the parable has entirely omitted it from his exposition. **Shine forth as the sun,** in purity and glory; comp. Dan. 12: 3, "shall shine as the brightness of the firmament . . . as the stars for ever and ever." **The righteous** are opposed to 'those that do iniquity,' in v. 41. At present, they are often obscure and unnoticed amid the great mass of mankind, imperfectly appreciated and little honored by the world at large; but then, completely distinct and forever separate from the wicked, they shall shine forth as the sun. **In the kingdom of their Father,** the consummate and eternal state of the Messianic kingdom or reign (see on 3: 2), when Christ "shall deliver up the kingdom to God, even the Father . . . that God may be all in all." (1 Cor. 15: 24, 28, R. V.) **He that hath ears to hear, let him hear,** calling solemn attention, see on 11: 15. — We learn here that good and bad will both be found intermingled in the world until the consummation of the present age, at the second coming of Christ; which seems quite contrary to the notion of a previous millennium during which all men without exception will be faultless Christians. Comp. Luke 18: 8.

HOMILETICAL AND PRACTICAL.

V. 31 f. The slow progress of Christianity. 1) Slow because not a case of manufacture, but of growth. 2) Slow because in an unfriendly soil and clime, an exotic. 3) Slow through the fault of those who ought to tend it more carefully. 4) Slow, but sure. — V. 33. The gradual diffusion of Christianity. 1) Through different spheres of life, spiritual, moral, social, political. 2) Through successive ages of history. 3) Through various quarters of the earth. 4) Destined at last to be universal, in every sense. — V. 34. JEROME: "Even to-day, the multitudes hear in parables; the disciples ask the Saviour at home."

V. 37-43. The righteous and the wicked. 1) Dwelling in the same world. 2) Rooted together in political, social, and family life. (v. 29.) 3) Blessed with the same outward mercies. (v. 25.) 4) Sometimes confounded by superficial observers, but easily distinguished through their fruit. (v. 26.) 5) Sure to be separated in the great coming day, a) without

44 Again, the kingdom of heaven is like unto trea-sure hid in a field; the which when a man hath found he hideth, and for joy thereof goeth and selleth all that he hath, and buyeth that field.

44   The kingdom of heaven is like unto a treasure hidden in the field; which a man found, and hid; and [1] in his joy he goeth and selleth all that he hath, and buyeth that field.

1 Or, *for joy thereof.*

chance of error, b) without possibility of re-union, c) so that the one class shall burn in unquenchable fire, and the other shall shine in unsullied purity and undimmed glory for-ever.—V. 38. The sons of the kingdom. ARNOT: "For their sakes the world is pre-served now, and for their sakes it will be de-stroyed when the set time is come. The darnel is permitted to grow in its season, and in harvest is cast into the fire—both for the sake of the wheat. Because Christ loves his own, he permits the wicked to run their course in time; but because Christ loves his own, he will separate the wicked from the good at last." —V. 39. The enemy. ARNOT: " Evil does not belong originally to the constitution of man, nor has God his Maker introduced it. Our case is sad, indeed; for we learn that an enemy whom we cannot overcome is ever lying in wait, seeking how he may devour us. But what would our case have been, if evil, in-stead of being injected by an enemy from without, had been of the essence of the creature or the act of the Creator?"

THOMAS: "The mixture of the good and bad in this world is of service. (1) It is of service to the bad; it keeps them in a position of improvement. (2) It is of service to the good; holy character is strengthened and perfected by contact with palpable evil."

PARKER: "Let us remit our case to the harvest. Do not be answering the fool and the enemy now, and thus wasting opportuni-ties which ought to be usefully employed in endeavoring to do good, but wait till the har-vest. Then shall all qualities be tested, then shall every man have his proper place and standing before God."

44-53. THE HID TREASURE, THE PEARL, THE NET.

These three remaining parables of the group are found in Matthew only.

I. **44.** THE PARABLE OF THE HID TREA-SURE. The word **again** with which Com. Ver. begins is wanting here in many of the earliest documents, and was doubtless added from v. 45, 47, where the reading does not vary. This leaves it uncertain whether the

three following parables were spoken on the same occasion as the Sower and the Tares. They may have been given at some other time and place, and recorded here by way of topical grouping, as is done with the miracles in ch. 8 and 9. But the presumption in favor of the Evangelist's order is strengthened by the language of v. 51 and v. 53, and by the fact that the Tares and the Net form a pair like the other pairs of this chapter.

The kingdom of heaven, the Messianic reign, see on 3: 2. **Is like,** so in v. 45 and v. 47. Some, beginning with Origen, have insisted on the fact that in these three cases the word *parable* is not used, as it is in v. 3, 24, 31, 33, and that these are similitudes but not parables. But certainly a parable is one kind of simili-tude; and the phrase 'is like' is employed in stating the parable in v. 24, 31, 33. See also 18: 23; 20: 1, where unquestionable parables are not called by that name, and are intro-duced by this same phrase. And the point seems to be settled by v. 53, 'had finished these parables.' **Treasure hid in a** (*the*) **field,** *i. e.*, the cultivated land, the open country as opposed to the city. Palestine had passed through many revolutions, and had always been exposed to raids from wan-dering tribes around, and in many districts to plunder from robbers at home. Accordingly it was common, as is the case in all unsettled countries, for one who apprehended robbery or thievery (25: 25), or who was setting off to a distant country, to bury his money, jewelry, plate, and the like, in the earth. If the owner was killed in battle, or died in the far country, no one might know where his treasures were hid; and it became the usage that hidden valuables for which no owner appeared should belong to the owner of the land. The search for such treasures is alluded to in Job. 3: 21; Prov. 2: 4, and often in Greek and Roman writers, and is common now in Palestine. *Thomson,* ii., p. 640: " There are many per-sons digging for hid treasure all over the coun-try, and not a few spend their last farthing in those efforts." We are told that in the East men of wealth have been known to divide their

45 Again, the kingdom of heaven is like unto a mer- | 45   Again, the kingdom of heaven is like unto a man
chantman, seeking goodly pearls:

estate into three parts, one invested in trade, a second part in jewels easily kept about the person, and the remainder buried in the earth —a sad condition of affairs for the prosperity of a nation. An instance of hiding treasure occurred during the War of Secession in a South Carolina village, where the writer lived. A shoemaker, upon the approach of hostile troops, hid five hundred dollars in gold, and told his wife and a friend that he had done so, but without revealing the place, supposed to have been in some adjoining forest. In a few days he died after a brief illness, and his widow was quite unable to recover the money, which years hence some man may find "hidden in the field" where he is at work. **Found, hideth,** or *and hid, i. e.,* hid it again. **For joy,** literally *from his joy,* or less probably 'from joy thereof,' (margin R. V.). **Goeth,** the word explained on 4: 10, which perhaps here implies eager and hasty going. Notice the vivid change to the historical present— 'found and hid . . . . goes off and sells . . . . buys' It is sometimes said that this man's course was dishonest, as he ought to have revealed his discovery to the owner; if the case be so understood, we must remember that an illustration may hold good as to the thing illustrated even when the literal act is immoral, as in the case of the unrighteous steward. (Luke 16.) *Weiss:* "Jesus is not teaching how men ought to act in such a case, but is narrating a case out of ordinary life," as an illustration. But is there really any propriety in calling the man dishonest? If he paid what the land was worth on other accounts, had he not a perfect right to get the benefit himself of his good fortune, or his skill, in discovering the treasure? The transaction of the parable was entirely in accordance with Jewish law, though the apparently similar case quoted by Wet., Meyer, and many others from the Talmud, proves a failure when the connection is known. (Edersheim.)

The general idea which the parable illustrates seems to be this. If a man fully discovers and appreciates the advantages of Christ's service, he will be so anxious to make those blessings his own as to sacrifice any and everything that may be necessary for that purpose. (Comp. on v. 45 f.) It seems idle to

seek any special spiritual meaning in the rehiding, or in the field, as that it means "the church," or the Scriptures (Origen), or Christ, because of Col. 2: 3. To run through the Bible with a concordance, and wherever there is mention of a treasure or a field connect it with this illustration, is a process fatal to sound interpretation and unworthy of sober sense.

II. **45 f. PARABLE OF THE PEARL OF GREAT PRICE.** The general meaning of this parable is evidently the same with that of the preceding. It is very natural for any teacher to give two illustrations of the same truth, and was especially so for a Jewish teacher, since the more elevated Hebrew style tends always to parallelisms. **A merchantman.** The Greek word denotes not a mere shopkeeper, but one who travels to procure what he sells. **Goodly pearls,** or ' fine,' 'beautiful.' He does not want ordinary pearls, but such as are fine; so when he finds an extremely fine one, he will appreciate and desire it. One framing such an illustration now would doubtless speak of diamonds, but in ancient times these were very rare, and no merchant would have made it his business to deal in them. **One pearl of great price.** Pliny tells us (Bruce), that Cleopatra's two famous pearls were valued each at about four hundred thousand dollars of our money, and the purchasing power of money was then ten or fifteen times as great as now. It was like finding a diamond worth millions. **Sold all that he had,** not simply all his pearls, but all his possessions, as the Greek shows, and even the English in v. 44. Of course he regarded the pearl as worth much more than he gave; it was making a good investment. 'Sold' is literally 'has sold,' which gives vividness—you see the thing going on, as in 'taketh.' (Rev. 5: 7, Rev. Ver.) So this answers in some measure to the historical present of v. 44. The Mishna has a story of a man who gave his whole fortune for a pearl.

In like manner, to be a subject of Messiah's reign is so precious a privilege, that a man might willingly sacrifice everything else to obtain it; whatever pleasures, honors, possessions, or attainments it is necessary to give up he might willingly abandon—whatever efforts

46 Who, when he had found one pearl of great price, went and sold all that he had, and bought it.
47 Again, the kingdom of heaven is like unto a net, that was cast into the sea, and gathered of every kind :

46 that is a merchant seeking goodly pearls: and having found one pearl of great price, he went and sold all that he had, and bought it.
47 Again, the kingdom of heaven is like unto a [1] net, that was cast into the sea, and gathered of every

---

1 Or, *drag-net.*

---

are requisite he might make—in order to secure that which is worth so much. The Jews thought the Messianic blessings would come as a mere gift of God, without sacrifice or seeking; and Jesus corrects their error. Yet he does not mean, any more than in what he said to the rich young man (19: 21), that all his followers must actually abandon every earthly possession or pursuit; nay, piety may even contribute to the attainment of whatever else is best worth having in life. (6: 33; 1 Tim. 4: 8.) But he means that they should be willing to do so; and that his true followers actually will, whenever in his Providence it is marked out as their duty to him. Comp. Moses (Heb. 11: 24 ff.), and Paul. (Phil. 3: 7 f.)

There is a certain difference between this parable and the preceding, in that this implies a previous *seeking.* The gospel presents itself to one man while otherwise occupied (so with several of the disciples, we know), and attracts his attention by its manifest value; another, while seeking spiritual wisdom, or the highest good of life (Psa. 4: 6 f.), perceives the gospel to be the true wisdom, the supreme good. (Phil. 3: 8.) The man who finds a treasure he had not sought has the joy of surprise; he who has searched and striven, the joy of success. Observe also (Bruce) that the treasure represents piety as practically useful, the pearl as beautiful and beautifying.—Alas! how many fail to appreciate the value of this pearl, even when it is held up before their eyes; they cannot think it so valuable; they will not carefully examine, or they apply false tests. And how many, even when avowedly searching for religious truth and comfort, will buy, even at great cost, some imitation-pearl, that is really worthless.

III. **47-50.** PARABLE OF THE NET. This is to the same general effect as that of the Tares. (13: 24, 37.) Why it was separated from its companion, while the other pairs stand together, we cannot tell, unless it was for the purpose of bringing in again, at the close of the series, the solemn allusion to the final judgment. Weiss thinks the **again** shows it to be the second of a pair, as in v. 45; but the

comparison of 'another parable' in v. 24, 31, 33, will refute this notion, leaving us to understand that we have in v. 45 and v. 47 the second and third of a group. **A net,** *sagene,* a drag-net or seine (modern English form of the Greek word), drawn up on the beach. In 4: 18 ff.; Luke 5: 4 ff., the words do not determine the kind of net, but the circumstances show that it was there a dip-net, let down into deep water, and drawn up into the boat. **Gathered of every kind,** not probably species and thus symbolizing the different races of mankind (Theophyl., Meyer), but every kind as to value, both the useful and the useless. **The bad,** literally the putrid or spoilt, strictly denoting those which were dead before they were caught, and thus unfit for use; but probably designed also to include those which were worthless on any account. See the same word in 7: 17; 12: 33.

The application here is in almost exactly the same words (v. 49 f.) as in v. 40-42. It is confined to the one point that at 'the end of the world' or 'consummation of the age,' a separation will be made between good and bad, with the terrible destruction (punishment) of the bad; and it is implied that such a separation will not be made until then. This is clearly *the* lesson of the parable, and our Lord's interpretation suggests no other. If we attempt, on our own authority, not on his, to make religious application of preceding points of the parable, we must be cautious, and must assuredly avoid deriving from its supposed analogies any idea in conflict with the plain and unfigurative teaching of other passages of Scripture. (Comp. on 13: 3.) Now if we say, as many do, that the net represents "the visible church," then it is implied that good and bad must remain together in the church, without possibility of separating or distinguishing them in any single case, till the Second Coming of Christ. The parable of the Tares, upon a similar interpretation, would make church discipline wrong, because injurious; that of the Net would make it entirely impossible. But church discipline is enjoined in Scripture, as all Chris-

48 Which, when it was full, they drew to shore, and sat down, and gathered the good into vessels, but cast the bad away.

49 So shall it be at the end of the world: the angels shall come forth, and sever the wicked from among the just,

50 And shall cast them into the furnace of fire: there shall be wailing and gnashing of teeth.

51 Jesus saith unto them, Have ye understood all these things? They say unto him, Yea, Lord.

48 kind: which, when it was filled, they drew up on the beach; and they sat down, and gathered the

49 good into vessels, but the bad they cast away. So shall it be in [1] the end of the world: the angels shall come forth, and sever the wicked from among the

50 righteous, and shall cast them into the furnace of fire: there shall be the weeping and gnashing of teeth.

51 Have ye understood all these things? They say

1 Or, *the consummation of the age.*

tians recognize; shall we accept an interpretation of merely human origin, upon which the parable squarely contradicts these injunctions? And see what incongruities the interpretation will involve (Arnot). (1) The angels must be entirely distinct from those who manage "the church"; but the persons separating the good and bad fishes are not distinct from those who draw the net. (2) Augustine, and numerous modern advocates of an Established Church, urge upon Nonconformists that it is wrong to quit the church because of there being some bad fish in the net; while the fishes, good or bad, remain in the net only because they *cannot* break out. And so as to other points.

"But is it not expressly said," one might insist, "that the kingdom of heaven is like a net; and as the net gathers of every kind, must not this mean that the kingdom of heaven will contain within its limits, at least its apparent and recognized limits, both good and bad?" Answer. (a) The word rendered 'kingdom' means also what we express by 'reign' (see on 13: 37 ff.); in this sense the idea would here be not of a definite organization of persons, but of a general state of things, of what happens under the reign of Messiah; and this sense ought to be here preferred because it relieves us of the hopeless difficulties involved in the other view. (b) The opening verbal comparison of the several parables is not uniform and essential to the meaning, but incidental and varying. In v. 45 the kingdom of heaven is like a man seeking pearls, but in v. 44 it is compared, not to the finder, but to the thing found. In v. 24 it is like the owner of the field, *i. e.*, the Messiah (v. 37); but in v. 47 it is compared not to the owner of the net, but to the net. So in 22: 2, the kingdom of heaven is likened to the king who gave a marriage feast for his son, but in 25: 1 it is likened, not to the bridegroom, but to the virgins who desired to attend the feast. These and other examples show that our Lord does not in each case carefully as-

sert a special relation between the Messianic reign and this or that particular object in the parable, but means to say that something is true of the Messianic reign which resembles the case of the parable; and instead of speaking in vague terms of general comparison (as in 25: 14), he often sets out by saying that "the kingdom of heaven is like" some leading person or object of the story, or some feature that readily presents itself at the beginning. (Comp. on 11: 16.) In this parable, then, we are not at liberty to lay any stress upon the comparison of the kingdom of heaven to the net itself. The comparison is to the whole story; and its particular point is given by our Lord himself in v. 49 f.

One might incline to suppose a reference here to the unspiritual crowds who were following Jesus, many reckoning themselves his disciples, though they were not; and then an application might be proposed to similar hangers on at the present day. But fatal to this is the fact that Jesus *did* take pains, not long after the parable was spoken, to make such persons see the spirituality of true discipleship, so that they ceased following him. (John 6: 66.)

Nay, the meaning is simply that Messiah will not at once separate and destroy those persons who refuse to become his subjects, but will suffer them to live on in the world during the gradual development of his reign, until his Second Coming, and then the separation and punishment will take place. The phrases of v. 49 f. have been explained in the kindred passage, v. 40–42. The 'furnace of fire' is an image not suggested by this parable, but by burning the tares.

Some have found a mystical signification in the fact that this group contains *seven* parables (the mystical number), which they compare with the seven letters of Rev. ch. 2 and 3, and suppose to represent seven epochs in the history of Christianity. Apart from other grounds of objection to this fancy (comp. Goebel), it should be enough here to remember

52 Then said he unto them, Therefore every scribe *which is* instructed unto the kingdom of heaven, is like unto a man *that is* a householder, which bringeth forth out of his treasure *things* new and old.
53 And it came to pass, *that* when Jesus had finished these parables, he departed thence.

52 unto him, Yea. And he said unto them, Therefore every scribe who hath been made a disciple to the kingdom of heaven is like unto a man that is a householder, who bringeth forth out of his treasure things new and old.
53 And it came to pass, when Jesus had finished

that Mark (4: 26 ff.) gives an *eighth* parable spoken on the same occasion, and that these eight fall into four pairs.

IV. **51-53.** Conclusion of the Dis-course. Found in Matthew only. **Jesus saith unto them** is a spurious addition, and so is **Lord,** after **yea.** The simple **yea** or *yes* without addition was not impolite. (17: 25; Acts 22: 27.) **Have ye understood**—or *did you understand*—**all these things?** The emphasis is not so much on 'all' as on 'these things' (so in v. 34). They had not understood the parables of the Sower and the Tares without explanation; but guided by his interpretation of those two, they saw the meaning of the subsequent parables, though it is probable they often saw but dimly at first. *Morison:* " Not that we are to suppose they understood the things to their summits and their depths. Who even yet has thus exhausted or comprehended them? But they saw light streaming through them. It was light from heaven; it would increase." **Therefore,** *on this account,* a strong expression. (Alford wrong, following Euthym.) Since you have understood these new views of the Messianic reign, it follows that you, and every Scribe who like you has become a disciple to that reign, will have good store of truths to teach, of new things as well as old. If the disciples had *not* understood, it could not have been at that time said that such a store of varied instruction would be possessed by them and other teachers under the New Dispensation. **Scribe,** see on 2: 4. **That is instructed,** or, *has been discipled,* see on 28: 19. We greatly need a verb *to disciple* for both passages, and for 27: 57; Acts 14: 21, as we need a verb *to shepherd* in 2: 6; John 21: 16, etc. *Discipled* **unto the kingdom of heaven,** would be according to the correct Greek text. The Scribes held themselves as the disciples of Moses (23: 2; John 9: 28); the Christian Scribe (23: 34) has become a disciple to the Messianic Dispensation, which takes him as a pupil, and teaches him its lessons. If the Messianic reign had turned out only what the Jews expected, its Scribes would not have

been able to produce any new truths about it. The Greek might mean, though less naturally, ' discipled for the kingdom of heaven,' for its benefit or service; the expression seemed obscure, and so was altered in some documents to 'in the kingdom,' and in many to 'unto the kingdom,' meaning in order to, or in respect to (as in Com. Ver.). **Householder,** as in 13: 27; 10: 25. **Treasure,** 'treasury,' or here rather *store-house,* the term not being confined to a place of deposit for valuables (comp. on 12: 35). **Bringeth forth** is literally *throws out,* 'flings out,' as explained in 9: 38, the word appearing always to imply vigorous if not violent action. A man with ample stores flings out garments or articles of food in profusion, some recently acquired, others long on hand, each class having its peculiar value. A good housekeeper would make frequent additions to his stores, while carefully preserving the old. The Jewish Scribes gloried in teaching only old things, but the Christian Scribe learned such new lessons as these parables have just been giving, and so could fling out **things new and old.** He would now have (Meyer) the fulfillment of many old prophecies, the explanation and new extension (5: 17) of many precepts, the more correct understanding of the old Messianic hope. The expression naturally suggests to us the Old and the New Testaments, but that can hardly be regarded as here meant by our Lord. Perhaps he did also mean that the Christian Scribe must imitate his example in employing new *methods* of teaching (as parables, etc.) He here plainly shows that he did not design for the disciples to keep to themselves what had for the present been taught to them alone. (Comp. 13: 10-13.)

53. This closes the account of this series of parables. (Comp. 11: 1.) The chapter ought to have ended here, thus possessing a beautiful unity. The remaining verses have nothing to do with the group of parables, either in time, place, or topic. The other group of parables given by Matthew will be found near the close of our Lord's public ministry, in chapters 18, 20, 21, 22, and 25.

HOMILETICAL AND PRACTICAL.

V. 44. The hid treasure. 1) Piety is a treasure. 2) One should determine to make it truly and thoroughly his own. 3) He should be ready to pay the cost of procuring it, however great. 4) Well may he rejoice at the first view of it, and still more in its secured possession.—V. 45 f. The pearl of great price. 1) Piety is the most precious of all possessions, the *summum bonum*, or supreme good of life. 2) To obtain piety, we ought willingly to make all necessary sacrifices and exertions. 3) Piety is worth far more than it costs. CHRYS: "And much as he that has the pearl knows indeed himself that he is rich, but others often know not that he is holding it in his hand (for there is no corporeal bulk); just so also with the gospel: they that have hold of it know that they are rich, but the unbelievers, not knowing of this treasure, are in ignorance also of our wealth."

V. 51 f. HENRY: "It is good for us, when we have read or heard the word, to examine ourselves, or to be examined, whether we have understood it or not."—The Gospel Scribe. 1) He is a disciple to the Messianic reign, (a) learning its lessons, (b) obeying its laws. 2) He brings forth things new and old. (a) From Old Test. and New Test. (b) From former teachers and from his own thinking. (c) In old methods and in new methods. ORIGEN: "The converse must hold, whoever does not bring forth from his treasury new things and old, is not a scribe discipled to the kingdom of heaven. Therefore we must diligently study not only the Gospels, Epistles, and Apocalypse, but also the law and the prophets." CHRYS: "Let us then hear, as many of us as neglect the reading of the Scriptures, to what harm we are subjecting ourselves, to what poverty. For where are we to apply ourselves to the real practice of virtue, who do not so much as know the very laws according to which our practice should be guided?"

54-58.—JESUS VISITS HIS OWN COUNTRY.

This visit of our Lord to his own country is also given in Mark 6: 1-6. It must have been a different, though, in some respects, similar visit to Nazareth that is recorded in Luke 4: 16-31, and occurred at the very beginning of his ministry in Galilee (Luke 4: 31 coinciding in time with Matt. 4: 13). The visit described by Matt. and Luke appears to have been about a year later. Many recent commentators argue, or take for granted, that the two events were really one, and then dispute as to which occupies the more correct chronological position. But the strong probability that both Mark and Luke have followed the chronological order, as they so commonly do (at least in the early part of Luke), is here further strengthened by the great difference of circumstances in the two cases. In Luke, the synagogue address so angers the congregation that they rise up and attempt to kill him; for this there seems to be no room in Matthew and Mark. In Luke, Jesus is expected to work miracles, and openly declares that he will not; in the other case he works a few miracles, and wonders at the unbelief which prevents his doing more. It was natural that Jesus should give the acquaintances of his early life a second chance to hear, and when they did not believe, he might very naturally repeat the saying which was so readily suggested, and so strikingly appropriate (v. 57; Luke 4: 24). It is thus easier to account for the similarity of the two narratives, if distinct, than for their differences, if referring to the same event. But some critics always take for granted that two similar events or discourses must have been really the same. A little experience as missionary preachers in city and country, especially if as field-preachers or street-preachers, or in general, as "evangelists," would have taught them how natural it is to give many similar points of instruction at different times and places. (Comp. at the beginning of ch. 5, and on 15: 38.) It is impossible to say with certainty whether we have here two events or one; but the probability seems strongly in favor of the former view. It is supported by Meyer, Ewald, Wieseler, and many others.

Matthew does not here mention, though his expressions do not exclude, various occurrences which Mark's order shows to have come between the series of parables and this visit viz., the passage of the lake and healing of two demoniacs, the feast given by Matthew, the raising of Jairus' daughter, etc. These Matt., according to his topical method of grouping (in ch. 5-13), has introduced earlier. (8: 18 to 9: 34; see on 8: 18 and on 13: 1.) Some skeptical expositors insist that his expressions do exclude any intervening events.

54 And when he was come into his own country, he taught them in their synagogue, insomuch that they were astonished, and said, Whence hath this *man* this wisdom, and *these* mighty works?
55 Is not this the carpenter's son? is not his mother called Mary? and his brethren, James, and Joses, and Simon, and Judas?

54 these parables, he departed thence. And coming into his own country he taught them in their synagogue, insomuch that they were astonished, and said, Whence hath this man this wisdom, and these
55 ¹ mighty works? Is not this the carpenter's son? is not his mother called Mary? and his brethren,

---

1 Gr. *powers.*

They read it as one sentence: "He departed thence, and coming into his own country, taught," etc. The Greek might mean this, but even so, must we necessarily understand that he went off the same day, stopped nowhere on the route, and neither said nor did anything from the close of the parables beside the lake till he reached the synagogue at Nazareth? It will surely be agreed that one day may have intervened, if no more; and it so happens that one day with the preceding night would suffice for all the events mentioned by Mark as occurring in the meantime. It is wearisome to follow out such elaborate attempts to make much of "discrepancies."

In Matthew this rejection at Nazareth completes the account of opposition encountered by Jesus (ch. 12 and 13); and the parabolic teaching which was occasioned by this opposition is preceded by the interference of his kindred (12: 46 ff.), and followed by the rejection at his early home.

54. His own country must here mean the district of Nazareth, and not Galilee in general. (John 4: 43-45.) He was already in Galilee when he gave the parables. He is here in a particular city or village, having one definite synagogue. The people know his brothers by name, and declare that his sisters are all living among them. As to Nazareth, see on 2: 23; as to the synagogues, see on 4: 23. Mark (6: 2) says that this teaching was on the Sabbath, which would not be certain from Matthew's account, since they met in the synagogue also on Monday and Thursday. **And these mighty works,** or 'miracles,' the word being *dunamis*, see on 12: 38. Few or none of these were wrought at Nazareth (v. 58), but they had heard of them, and doubtless some Nazarenes had witnessed them at other points. Notice that with all their unbelief and hostility they did not question the reality of his miracles. (Comp. on 12: 24.)

55 f. Is not this the carpenter's son? Jesus was of course considered among the Nazarenes to be the son of Joseph, "and that impression was wisely permitted, because the idea of the heavenly origin of Jesus could be of use only to believers." (Olshausen.) The word rendered 'carpenter' means in general artificer, but usually denotes a worker in wood. Mark (6: 3) has it, 'Is not this the carpenter?' showing that Jesus had himself wrought at his reputed father's trade. Justin Martyr, who was reared in Samaria, affirms in his dialogue with Trypho the Jew (ch. 88), written about A. D. 150, that Jesus was a maker of plows and yokes—a tradition which may well enough be true. In laboring as a mechanic we must not fail to see that he set us an example. Belonging to a poor family, he ate not the bread of idleness, but with all the great work that lay before him, and already must have begun to press upon head and heart, he devoted himself to honest toil. It was the wise custom of the Jews that even when wealthy their sons must be taught some trade; as Paul learned tent-making, and lived to find it extremely useful. No doubt the Saviour worked diligently, a model to mechanics of never slighting work, and of always meeting engagements. And no doubt he cherished all the day long so devout a spirit as to make these homely toils a part of the life of piety.

And his brethren . . . . and his sisters. It seems impossible to determine with certainty whether we are to understand brothers in the strict sense, or half-brothers, or more loosely, near kinsmen. Each of these views has been earnestly supported from an early time. (See particularly good discussions of the whole subject in Bishop Lightfoot on Galatians, Smith's "Dict. Bible," Amer. Ed., Art. "Brothers of the Lord," Schaff in Lange on Matt., and in "Church History" 2d ed., Andrew's "Life of Christ.") The three theories are well described by Schaff as the *brother-theory*, held by many Protestants, the *half-brother-theory* prevailing in the Greek Church, and the *cousin-theory*, prevailing in the Church of Rome. 1. The most obvious view is that the 'brothers' were such in the ordinary sense, sons of Joseph and Mary. In favor of this we have the natural though not necessary meaning of three independent expressions. (a) The word 'brother' naturally means this, and ought to be so taken in any case unless the contrary can be there shown. It is used not once, but many times. And observe that here we have also 'sisters.' Moreover, it is not here Jesus' *followers* who speak of his brothers and his sisters, but the unbelieving and hostile Nazarenes, who are not likely to have employed the term in any nonnatural or unusual sense. In their mouths 'his brothers' and 'all his sisters' cannot have meant less than children of Joseph, if not of Joseph and Mary. They could easily be mistaken in calling Joseph his father, because here had been a supernatural fact of which they were not informed; but how could they be mistaken as to his brothers and sisters? (b) The phrase 'knew her not until' (1: 25), while not *necessarily* meaning that after the birth of her son they lived together in the ordinary relations of husband and wife, naturally means that, and it is highly unnatural to understand it otherwise. (c) So with 'her first-born son.' (Luke 2: 7.) The special laws as to a first-born son might possibly lead to the use of this expression, though no other children followed. But this would have been less natural for one who wrote long afterwards, as Luke did. Here then are three independent statements, each of which affords a clear and strong probability, and the combination of the three affords a very high, in fact an overwhelming probability. And how strange it would look for each of the four Evangelists, and Paul (John 7: 3 ff.; Gal. 1: 19), to use language so naturally and inevitably suggesting that Mary bore other children, if this was untrue, and a very objectionable idea.

The objections to this view are (1) sentiment. This pervades the Romanist and Greek Christian world, and extends to many Protestants. But it is a sentiment without Scriptural support, and out of harmony with the general tone of Scripture in regard to marriage. That Jesus should be born of a virgin had an obvious propriety in showing that his birth was supernatural, and helping to put him outside the line of transmitted depravity and guilt; but nothing in regard to him or his work would be affected by his mother's afterwards bearing children to her husband. (2) This view would make James his brother an 'apostle' without being one of the Twelve, see Gal. 1: 19, and comp. Acts 9: 27. But the phrase in Gal. 1: 19 does not certainly mean that James was an apostle (see *margin*, Rev. Ver.), nor does the plural in Acts. And supposing that to be meant, we must observe that 'apostle' in the New Test. is applied to others than the Twelve; clearly so in Acts 14: 14, "the apostles, Barnabas and Paul," perhaps also in 1 Cor. 9: 5 f.; Rom. 16: 7; 1 Thess. 2: 6; and the "false apostles" of 2 Cor. 11: 13; Rev. 2: 2, would have been simply ridiculed if only the Twelve had ever been called by that name. (Comp. Lightfoot on Gal.) (3) It would seem strange that Jesus on the cross should commit his mother to a friend, when she had sons. But this would hold against the other theories also, and even more strongly against the cousin-theory, for then two of her nephews were among the Twelve.

2. The half-brother-theory supposes them to be sons and daughters of Joseph by a former marriage. This leaves room for the sentiment as to Mary's perpetual virginity, and the last objection to the former view affects this in a less degree. It might also help to account for the fact that 'the brothers' were inclined to assume authority over Jesus (12: 46; John 7: 3-10); though even younger brothers are ready enough for this in the case of one whom they regard as a religious enthusiast. (Mark 3: 21.)—The objections to this theory are (1) It is a mere supposition. (2) In this case, not Jesus, but the eldest son of Joseph, would have been legal heir to the throne of David. (3) The brothers and sisters were, on this view, really no kin to Jesus. Still even Mary could say to him, "thy father and I" (Luke 2: 48), and Luke could speak of his parents. (Luke 2: 41.) (4) We must thus understand 'first-born son' in an improbable sense (see above).

3. The cousin-theory makes them the sons and daughters of Mary's sister Mary. That the term brother was sometimes used in this loose sense may be seen from Gen. 13: 8; 14: 16; 29: 12; 31: 23; Job 19: 13, and especially Job. 42: 11, where sisters as well as brothers are mentioned, and apparently mean-

56 And his sisters, are they not all with us? Whence then hath this *man* all these things?
57 And they were offended in him. But Jesus said unto them, A prophet is not without honour, save in his own country, and in his own house.

56 James, and Joseph, and Simon, and Judas? And his sisters, are they not all with us? Whence then
57 hath this man all these things? And they were [1] offended in him. But Jesus said unto them, A prophet is not without honour, save in his own

1 Or, *caused to stumble*.

ing relatives in general. And such a use of the terms is still found among Oriental nations. This theory supposes that Clopas (John 19: 25) was the same as Alpheus; it makes James the Lord's brother the same as James the son of Alpheus, and thus one of the Twelve, and 'Judas of James' (whether brother or son), another of the Twelve. This also leaves room for the sentiment involved, and accounts for Gal. 1: 19 (see above). Objections. (1) Six months before the crucifixion "his brothers did not believe on him" (John 7: 5), when according to this theory two of the four brothers had long been among the Twelve. (2) Any natural etymology of Clopas would be very different from Chalphai, Alpheus. (3) There would thus be two sisters of the same name. The notion of some that one was called Mariam, and the other Maria, is quite set aside by the actual readings of the ancient documents. (4) It would be strange that these young men, even those who were not believers in Jesus, should be mentioned so often with his mother when their own mother was alive. (5) And why should he entrust his mother to John, when among his twelve disciples were two of her nephews and familiar associates? Upon the "brother-theory" we may readily suppose that his brothers were still at the time of the crucifixion not believers, as had been the case six months before (John 7: 5); and when in Acts 1: 14 "the brothers" appear with Mary among the disciples, we may suppose that the risen Lord's appearance to James (1 Cor. 15: 7), ended all doubts with him and the other brothers. These suppositions seem not unnatural, and they account for our Lord's committing his mother to John, when her sons were not yet in sympathy with him.

The question can never be settled; but the probabilities are very decidedly in favor of the first view, that these were sons and daughters of Joseph and Mary. Thus the great and unspeakably important institution of marriage is duly honored, and Jesus, the first-born son of Mary, is in no sense dishonored. **Whence then hath this man all these things?** The astonishment of the Naza-

renes was well-founded. (Comp. also John 7 : 15.) And if Jesus is thought of as a mere man, their question remains to this day unanswered and unanswerable. In the little country of Palestine, in its least refined district, in a petty and secluded town, whose inhabitants were violent and in bad repute among their neighbors (see on 2: 23), arose a young mechanic, whose teachings, though ended by an early death, surpassed all the wisdom of India and the Chaldeans, of Egypt and Greece; and who, in the few years of his career as a teacher, founded "an empire of love," which has spread wider than any empire of earth, and seems destined to last and to grow in all coming time. Whence then had this man all these things? There is but one answer. He was a teacher sent from God; he was, then, according to his own express declaration, God's Only-begotten Son; yea, he was all that Thomas called him—for he himself commended the saying—" my Lord and my God." See Young's "Christ of History" and Schaff's "Person of Christ."

57. Offended in him, or, *caused to stumble*, as in 11 : 6, and see on 5 : 29. They found in him *obstacles* to believing. They stumbled at his humble origin, and lack of training in the Rabbinical schools, and in their blind unbelief they would not listen to his wisdom nor heed his miracles, but rejected him without further inquiry or reflection. As he had had no chance to become so wise, they concluded that his wisdom was not real. They ought to have seen that it was real, and thence concluded that it was divine. **A prophet is not without honor,** etc. It was natural that the same objection should be made by the people as on his former visit, and that he should quote the same proverb in reply. (Luke 4 : 22, 24.) The Gospel of John (4: 44) applies this saying of our Lord to a different occasion, probably as explaining why he went back to his own country of Galilee, where his labors would not be likely to produce so much undesirable excitement as they had begun to do in Judea and Samaria. In any ordinary matters, a man will be more kindly received among his

58 And he did not many mighty works there because of their unbelief.

58 country, and in his own house. And he did not many [1] mighty works there because of their unbelief.

CHAPTER XIV.

A T that time Herod the tetrarch heard of the fame of Jesus,

1   At that season Herod the tetrarch heard the report

---

1 Gr, *powers.*

---

kindred and early friends than elsewhere; but not when he appears as greatly their superior, and professes, or is popularly reported, to possess extraordinary powers. They think of him as he used to be, and are slow to believe that he has become so superior to themselves. Somewhat similar is the difficulty parents often have in believing that their children are grown and can do mature work—they keep remembering them as children. Observe that our Lord does not here formally state a universal proposition, having no exception; he merely adopts a popular saying, which generally holds true. **In his own house.** Mark adds (6: 4) 'among his own kin.' Comp. above on 12: 46. We know from John 7: 5, that 'his brethren' did not yet believe on him.

58. The people did not attempt any violence, as on his former visit (Luke 4: 28 f.), but still persisted in their unbelief, so that Jesus 'wondered because of their unbelief' (Mark 6: 6), as he had formerly wondered at the centurion's faith (see on 8: 10). **Mighty works,** or *miracles,* as in v. 54, see on 12: 38. **Not many.** The few miracles which he did work there consisted (Mark 6: 5) in healing a few sick persons. **Because of their unbelief.** As a general thing, he did not work miracles in behalf of those who put no faith in him. Religious benefit to the people, which was always his ultimate object, was impossible where they did not believe. When Mark says, 'he could there do no miracle,' we understand, not that his power to work miracles was dependent on men's faith (for he sometimes healed without their faith or knowledge, 15: 28; Luke 22: 51), but that he could not do it in consistency with his design, without violating the plan of his labors. (Comp. on 9: 28.) As to miracles of healing, we need not at all suppose that he refused to heal any who came to him; the unbelief which prevented him from working the miracles prevented the people from seeking them.

HOMILETICAL AND PRACTICAL.

V. 54-58. A prophet in his own country. 1) Jesus strives to benefit the obscure and un-

promising community among whom he had grown up. (a) A second visit, comp. Luke 4 . 16-30. (b) Wise teaching. (c) Some miracles of healing (comp. Mark 6: 5), notwithstanding the general unbelief. 2) They admire his wise teaching, and rightly think it unaccountable in an obscure mechanic. 3) They do not ask whether God has given this wisdom, whether it is Messianic teaching (comp. Luke 4: 18-21), but stumble at his known lack of Rabbinical training and worldly position, and reject him. 4) Jesus wonders at their unbelief, can do little for them by word or deed (comp. Mark), and turns sadly away—never again, so far as we know, to revisit the companions of his youth. —V. 54. "Whence hath this man this wisdom?" 1) Not from Nazareth, or Galilee. 2) Not from the Rabbis at Jerusalem. 3) Not from the adjoining countries of Asia, Africa, or Europe. 4) Not from unaided human reflection. 5) But from God.—"His sisters, are they not all with us?" 1) How little we know of many persons and things closely related to Jesus. 2) Shall we suppose that his sisters shared the unbelief of his brothers (John 7: 5)? 3) How may we become dearer to Jesus than his sisters? (12: 50.)—V. 58. "Because of their unbelief." 1) Unbelief caused the fall of man. 2) Unbelief restricted the benevolent work of the Son of God. 3) Unbelief led most of the Jews to reject him (John 1: 11; 3: 18 f.) 4) Unbelief caused him almost intolerable grief. (17: 17) 5) Oh, that instead of wonderful unbelief (Mark 6: 6), we may all have wonderful faith. (Matt. 8: 10.)

Ch. 14: 1-12. JESUS IS SUPPOSED TO BE JOHN THE BAPTIST RISEN FROM THE DEAD. ACCOUNT OF JOHN'S DEATH.

Thus far, Matthew's narrative of our Lord's ministry in Galilee, commencing with 4: 12, has to a great extent disregarded the order of time, and followed an arrangement according to topics, better suited to his object of proving to the Jews that Jesus is the Messiah, and explaining the true nature of the Messianic reign. (Comp. on 4: 12; 8: 1; 9: 35; 11: 2; 12: 1.) From this point onward, he follows the order of time, with a few slight variations in ch. 21 and 26, made for the purpose of convenience in the grouping.

I. 1 f. HEROD SUPPOSES JESUS TO BE JOHN THE BAPTIST RISEN FROM THE DEAD. Comp. Mark 6: 14–16; Luke 9: 7–9.

At that time (*season*), indefinite as in 12: 1, see on 11: 25. **Herod the tetrarch** (a term explained on 2: 19), was the son of Herod the Great (see on 2: 1), and one of the three among whom he divided his dominions. The Tetrarch's mother was a Samaritan; he was distinguished from the numerous other Herods by the name Antipas, a contraction of Antipater. He and his brother Archelaus (2: 22) had spent their youth at Rome. His tetrarchy included Galilee (see on 4: 12) and Perea (see on 19: 1), the region east of the Jordan, from the Sea of Galilee to the northern part of the Dead Sea. As Tetrarch of Galilee, he had been the civil ruler of Jesus almost from the first, and John's baptizing in Perea (John 1: 28) put him also in Herod's power. He had now been ruling about thirty-two years. His first wife was the daughter of Aretas (2 Cor. 11: 32), king of the Nabathæan Arabs, whose capital was the famous Petra, and whose dominions adjoined Perea on the south, the fortress of Machærus being on the border. (See on v. 3.) After many years Herod made proposals of marriage to his niece Herodias, sister to Herod Agrippa I. (the Herod of Acts 12), and wife of his own half-brother, Herod Philip. Her husband was not the Tetrarch Philip (see on 2: 20), who married her daughter (see on v. 6), but was another son of Herod the Great, left by him in a private station, and by Josephus called simply Herod. ("Ant." 17, 1, 2; 18, 5, 1 and 4.) The simple and natural supposition that his name was Herod Philip removes all conflict here between Josephus and the Gospels. Herodias was a woman of towering ambition, and readily accepted, if indeed she had not manoeuvred to secure, the proposals of Antipas to give her a royal station, agreeing that she would divorce her husband (comp. Mark 10: 12), while he must divorce his Arab wife. Although accustomed to incestuous marriages in this Herod family, the people must have been greatly outraged at the Tetrarch's taking the wife of his still living brother, to whom she had borne a child. Hence the effort he appears to have made to get the famous John the Baptist to endorse the marriage, which would have had a powerful effect on the popular mind. The injured daughter of Aretas escaped to her father; and some years later, disputes having arisen about boundaries, he was led by the double motive of revenge and interest to make war upon Herod. The latter's army was defeated and destroyed, and he was saved from ruin by the interference of the Romans. Josephus ("Ant." 18, 5, 2) states that some of the Jews thought the destruction of the army a judgment from God for Herod's treatment of John the Baptist, whom he proceeds to eulogize, (as quoted above on 3: 2), and says that Herod put him to death from fear that his great influence might lead to a rebellion. This account in Josephus becomes more intelligible through the facts given in the Gospels. Herod Antipas was not naturally a cruel man, but self-indulgent and unscrupulous. There were many other wicked deeds for which John felt bound to reprove him (Luke 3: 19), besides the shameful marriage. Like most weak rulers he attempted to use cunning, and Jesus afterwards called him a "fox." (Luke 13: 31 f.)—The three Herods called by that name in the New Test. may be readily distinguished by remembering that "Herod the Great murdered the infants, Herod Antipas beheaded John the Baptist, and Herod Agrippa killed James and imprisoned Peter." But we know from Josephus that many others of the family bore the name of the great founder. Thus each of the Philips mentioned above was named Herod Philip, and the Agrippa before whom Paul spoke was called Herod Agrippa, like his father who slew James.

Heard of the fame of (R. V. *report concerning*) **Jesus,** comp. on 4: 24. Herod usually resided during his latter years at Tiberias, a town on the S. W. shore of the Sea of Galilee, from which it was sometimes called Lake Tiberias (see on 4: 12, 18). We have no account of our Lord's ever visiting this town, and perhaps he stayed away to avoid exciting the hostility of Herod, who might be jealous of one beginning to be popularly regarded as King of the Jews. But his teachings and miracles had spread the report of him far and wide, till it

2 And said unto his servants, This is John the Baptist;
he is risen from the dead ; and therefore mighty works
a do shew forth themselves in him.
3 For Herod had laid hold on John, and bound him,
and put *him* in prison for Herodias' sake, his brother
Philip's wife.

2 concerning Jesus, and said unto his servants, This
is John the Baptist ; he is risen from the dead ; and
3 therefore do these powers work in him. For Herod
had laid hold on John, and bound him, and put him
in prison for the sake of Herodias, his brother

a Or, are wrought by him.

penetrated even the precincts of the court.
The recent mission of the Twelve (ch. 10) had
probably contributed to this, for both in Mark
(6: 14) and Luke (9:7) the statement follows
immediately upon the account of that mission,
which would naturally make a great stir all
over the country.   Herod paid little attention
to religious movements among his subjects,
or he would have heard of Jesus earlier; for
it had now been certainly one and a half, and
probably two and a half years (see on 12: 1)
since our Lord's baptism, and for a year or
more he had been actively at work in Galilee,
teaching and working a great number of miracles.   But it was in accordance with the luxurious and rather slothful character of the
Tetrarch, that he should be thus ignorant. It
may be (Edersh.), that as Tiberias had been
recently built (Jos. "Ant." 18, 2, 3), he was
still spending much of his time at other places,
which would partly account for his ignorance;
yet Galilee was at any rate the most important part of his dominions.

2. And said unto his servants. The
word is *pais* (see on 8: 6), literally *boy* and
thence 'servant,' and often applied to the
officers of an Oriental court (Gen. 40: 20; 1 Sam. 16:
17; 1 Macc. 1: 6, 8), just as the term *doulos* is in
18: 23, and elsewhere. We know from Luke
8: 3, that "Joanna the wife of Chuza,
Herod's steward" had, apparently some time
before this, accompanied Jesus in his journeyings, and ministered to him and his followers
from her property. It would seem more
likely that "Manaen (Menahem) the foster-
brother of Herod the Tetrarch" (Acts 13: 1), became a Christian at a later period. **This is
John the Baptist,** see on 3: 1. **He is risen
from the dead,** with emphasis on 'he'
(comp. on 1 : 21), implying that this remarkable person of whom they heard was not any-
one else than just he, come to life again. Here
is a display of philosophizing, and a touch
of guilty conscience. 'From the dead,' *i. e.*,
from among the dead.   From Mark 8: 15,
compared with Matt. 16: 6, many have inferred (even Plumptre) that Herod was a Sadducee, but without sufficient ground. It is

not likely that he intelligently and heartily
adopted the religious views of either party,
but the opinions of the Pharisees as to the resurrection (see on 3 : 7) would form a natural
basis in his mind for the notion here expressed.
This notion did not originate with Herod, but
was one of the conflicting opinions which he
heard of as expressed among the people.
(Luke 9 : 7.) Some Jews believed in a species of
metempsychosis, the soul of a righteous dead
man entering a new body born for the purpose (Josephus "War," 2, 8, 14).   But in regard to Elijah, Jeremiah, and the famous
prophets in general, it was believed that one
of them might simply come to life again, the
same in soul and body. (Luke 9 : 8, 19.) Herod
at first questioned this theory about Jesus
(Luke 9:9), but afterwards adopted it (v. 2; Mark
6: 14), and insisted on it as the only correct
view. (Mark 6: 16.) He may possibly have concluded (Lutter.) that the people would cherish
less malice against him for killing the prophet
now that he was restored to them.   At a
later period we find this notion still
maintained by some of the people. (16:14.)
Herod's desire to see Jesus (Luke 9: 9), was
perhaps partly that he might settle this question, but partly arose from mere curiosity to
see him work a miracle ; certainly the latter
was his feeling a year later. (Luke 23 : 8-11.) **And
therefore,** viz., because he has risen from
the dead, and may well thus have supernatural powers, which he did not before possess.
(John 10 : 41.) **Mighty works,** etc., or, *the powers work in him.* Perhaps the phrase 'miraculous powers' would best express the sense,
the term being *dunamis* (see on 12: 38), which
frequently means miracles, regarded as works
of power, but here denotes the powers exercised and manifested in the miraculous deeds.
Shew forth—*work*, exert themselves, operate,
produce their effect. **In him,** as the seat of
their residence and exercise.

II. **3-12.** IMPRISONMENT AND DEATH OF
JOHN THE BAPTIST. Mark 6: 16-29; Luke 3:
19 f. ; Matthew and Mark here stop to tell
about Herod's putting John to death ; and as
introductory to that, they tell of his imprison-

ment, which occurred probably more than a year earlier (see on 4: 12). Luke closes the parallel passage (9: 7-9) without describing the death of John; but in ending his account of John's early preaching, he had already mentioned in advance that Herod cast John into prison. (Luke 3: 19 f.) This return to a subject in one case, and anticipation of it in another, are both conformed to the fitness of things in historical narrative, which requires that the events to be narrated shall not always be strung along in the order of their actual occurrence, but grouped according to natural principles, or else the story will not be interesting and impressive. Mark here gives, as is characteristic of his Gospel, more minute and vivid details than the other Evangelists. **Herod had laid hold on John,** literally, *laid hold*, the writer just stating the occurrence historically, and leaving the reader to see for himself the obvious fact that this was antecedent to what he has just before narrated.[1]

Bound him and put him in prison. The place of his imprisonment and death, as we learn from Josephus ("Ant.," 18, 5, 2), was MACHÆRUS, about seven miles from the Dead Sea, on the N. E. side. Some writers wish to set aside the express statement of Josephus, and locate the narrative at some other point; but their arguments are of very little strength. Machærus was first fortified by one of the Maccabaean princes, about 100 B. C., and having been destroyed by the Roman conquerors, was rebuilt and very strongly fortified by Herod the Great. The sole ancient description of the place (Jos. "War," 7, 6) has recently been strikingly confirmed by the only full modern description (Tristram, "Land of Moab," A. D., 1873). It lies on mountains far loftier than those around Jerusalem. There are ruins of a *city*, covering more than a square mile. Beyond a valley rises a long flat ridge, more than a mile long and quite difficult of access, all of which was made a strong fortress. From this ridge rises a high, conical hill, the top of which is one hundred yards in diameter, and which was fortified as an impregnable citadel. In this citadel, besides a very deep well, and a very large and deep cemented cistern, are now found "two dungeons, one of them deep and its sides scarcely broken in," which have "small holes still visible in the masonry, where staples of wood and iron had once been fixed. One of these must surely have been the prison-house of John the Baptist." (*Tristram.*) On this high ridge Herod the Great built an extensive and beautiful palace. The vicinity of the fortress and city was remarkable for mineral fountains, bitter and sweet, hot and cold, whose mingled waters formed baths, good for various diseases, especially for strengthening the nerves. The most celebrated of these were in the valley just north of Machærus, called the *Callirrhoe* ('fair-flow'), to which Herod the Great was carried not long before his death. There were also neighboring mines of sulphur and alum. Altogether, Machærus was a delightful summer residence for the rulers, as well as a strong fortress on the boundary between Perea and Arabia. It had for a short time been subject to King Aretas (Jos., "Ant.," 18, 5, 1 in the Greek), but was now again held by Herod, who when visiting Perea would naturally be attracted by the mountain palace and the luxurious baths. We may suppose that on some former visit he summoned John, who did much of his preaching on the eastern bank of the Jordan, to come to Machærus and give an opinion about his marriage, and there left him in prison. In that remote and hopeless imprisonment, in one of those deep and dark dungeons which were so cold in winter and so hot in summer, the great Baptizer languished (see on 11: 2) for probably more than a year, until the court came again. He was allowed occasional visits from his followers, who brought him news of what was going on in the land—among other things of the works of Jesus (11: 2)—and who finally bore his headless body to the tomb.

For Herodias' sake, his brother Phil-

---

[1] This is a very common use of the Greek aorist tense. In English it may be more natural and perspicuous to use the pluperfect, but it is grammatically a very misleading practice to say that the aorist is used *for* the pluperfect. (Comp. Buttm., p. 200.) One of the commonest and gravest errors in studying the grammar of foreign languages is to make a half conjectural translation, and then reason back from our own language to the meaning of the original; or to explain some idiom of the original by the formally different idiom which is our substantial equivalent.

4 For John said unto him, It is not lawful for thee to have her.
5 And when he would have put him to death, he feared the multitude, because they counted him as a prophet.
6 But when Herod's birthday was kept, the daughter of Herodias danced *a* before them, and pleased Herod.

4 Philip s wife. For John said unto him, It is not
5 lawful for thee to have her. And when he would have put him to death, he feared the multitude, because they counted him as a prophet. But when
6 Herod's birthday came, the daughter of Herodias

a Gr. *in the midst.*

---

ip's wife, see on v. 1. **For John said unto him.** The Greek verb is in the imperfect tense, and this is carefully reproduced by the Old Latin and the Vulgate, the Memphitic, and the Peshito. Mark also (6: 18) has the same tense. It can hardly be here taken as the mere descriptive imperfect, but seems to mean that John said it repeatedly, as may also be hinted by the tense of 'being reproved' in Luke 3: 19. We are not informed how John came to give Herod his judgment, but it is likely that the Tetrarch sent for John, hoping that he would be over-awed when standing in his presence, and so would feel bound to speak favorably of the marriage—which would have a salutary effect in allaying the popular discontent. But John stood before him, apparently several times, "in the spirit and power of Elijah" before Ahab (comp. on 3: 4). Indeed, Herod and Herodias strikingly resemble Ahab and Jezebel. In his early preaching John had been equally bold, rebuking the Pharisees and Sadducees (3: 7), as fearlessly as the masses. And now he reproves Herod, not merely for the marriage, but for all his other acts of wrong-doing. (Luke 3: 19.) Every great reformer sometimes finds it necessary to be very bold and outspoken. So Luther at the Diet of Worms, and Knox before Mary Stuart; and he who was "meek and lowly" to the toiling and burdened, was stern and severe towards the hypocritical Scribes and Pharisees even when he knew they were plotting to kill him, and would eventually succeed. **It is not lawful,** strictly *it is not permissible;* thou art not at liberty, viz., because the law of Moses forbade such a marriage. (Lev. 18: 16; 20: 21.) The law required the marriage of a deceased and childless brother's wife, but here the brother was still living and had a daughter. The ground of condemnation stated (comp. Mark 6: 18), is not that she was his niece, though that too was forbidden by the law (as implied in Lev. 18: 12 f.), but his brother's wife. Nominally, she had divorced her former husband; but while the Jewish usages of that time allowed a man to divorce his wife for almost any cause (see on 19: 3), for a woman to divorce her husband (mentioned only in Mark 10: 12) was a Roman custom, which they held in great abhorrence. Jos. says ("Ant." 18. 5, 4) that "being minded to confound her country's institutions," she made this marriage.

5. He feared the multitude (or *crowd*), **because they counted him as a prophet** (comp. 21: 26, 46). 'Counted,' held, regarded, is in the imperfect tense, giving their habitual way of regarding him. 'Prophet,' see on 7: 22. Observe that it was the 'crowd,' what we call "the masses," that held this opinion; the Jewish religious rulers were quite too jealous to tolerate such an idea (21: 25-27, 32). Mark says (6: 19) literally that "Herodias had a *grudge* against him and wanted to kill him; and she could not; for Herod feared John, knowing him to be a righteous and holy man, and kept him safe. And upon hearing him he would be much perplexed, and would hear him gladly." All the verbs are here in the imperfect tense, describing actions continued or repeated from time to time. The apparent conflict between this statement and that of Matthew may be explained in various ways. We may suppose that Herod was angry at first, when John condemned his marriage, and censured all his wickedness and wanted to kill him, but fearing the masses, imprisoned him instead; afterwards, talking with John, and his wrath having cooled, he came to feel as Mark describes, and so continued during his imprisonment. Or it may be that while generally favorable to John, and disposed to "keep him safe" from the wrath of Herodias, he sometimes felt inclined to yield to her solicitations, but was then restrained by fear of the crowd. It seems plain that Herodias was watching for a chance to compass John's destruction, from the expression of Mark (6: 21), "and when a convenient day was come."

6 f. But when Herod's birthday was kept, or *came.* The correct Greek text (as in Tisch. and W H.) has a very peculiar construction, but without difference in the substantial meaning.[1] The term ' birthday ' was also sometimes applied to the anniversary of a king's accession (Edersh.), but Wieseler's extended argument for so understanding it here is quite inconclusive. It is easy to suppose that when Herod's birthday approached he was sojourning at Machærus, accompanied by leading military and civil officials of his dominions. (Mark 6: 21.) **The daughter of Herodias,** viz., of her former marriage (see on v. 1), was named Salome (Jos. "Ant." 18, 5, 4); and also apparently sometimes called Herodias, as required by the reading of the earliest and best manuscripts in Mark 6: 22, ' his daughter Herodias ' (W H. and *margin* Rev. Ver.), and supported by Origen's expression here, "the dance of Herodias." It is very easy to believe that besides the name Salome, which was common in the family (borne by Herod the Great's sister), she may have also been called by her mother's name, even as so many men of the family were called Herod. This girl subsequently married her uncle, Philip the Tetrarch (Jos., "Ant.," 18, 5; comp. on. v. 1 and on 2: 20), but the marriage did not last long, as Philip died "in the twentieth year of the reign of Tiberias" (Jos. "Ant.," 18, 4, 6), say A. D. 33 or 34. Keim has, for the sake of his theories, revived the old notion that the crucifixion occurred in A. D. 34, and the death of John only a few months earlier; but Meyer remarks that the girl's dancing is quite appropriate for A. D. 29, but not for A. D. 34, when she had been for some time married, perhaps was a widow. **Danced before them,** or *in the midst; i. e.,* of the banqueting-hall, or of the company, and so in full view of all; it is a phrase frequently used in Greek to denote publicity. We cannot readily determine just how far this act was indecorous on her part. In all Eastern countries, women being kept in great seclusion, it has always been considered extremely improper for a female to dance in public. It is very common to hire dancing-women to exhibit at entertainments (*e. g.,* the Hindoo nautch-girls), but the business is highly disreputable, and it is commonly taken for granted that they are women of bad character. True, Jewish women lived in less seclusion than in other Eastern nations, and there are instances of their taking part by songs and dancing in public rejoicings (*e. g.,* 1 Sam. 18: 6); but this was considered a religious act (comp. Exod. 15: 20; 2 Sam. 6: 21), and quite a different thing from taking the place of dancing-girls at a feast. The Romans, too, had their dancing-girls at entertainments, but regarded it as a disreputable calling. A Latin inscription says, "It was disgraceful both to dance, and for a virgin to come into the banqueting-hall to men who had drank freely." *Cornelius Nepos:* "We know that according to our manners, dancing is even put among vices." *Cicero:* "Hardly any man dances when sober (unless perchance he is crazy), whether it be in solitude or at a moderate and decorous feast "; and he mentions a Greek father who was amazed at the proposition of a drunken guest that he should send for his daughter to come in. On the whole, one must reach the conclusion that if a respectable Jewish maiden came in to dance at a feast, it would be very surprising to the guests, and could hardly fail to be regarded as very unbecoming. It was therefore a bold step which Herodias took, in sending her daughter to dance before Herod and his grandees. Would they be shocked by the immodest exposure of a princess, or would they be fascinated by the novel spectacle of a high-born and charming girl going through the voluptuous movements of an Oriental dance? The experiment succeeded. She **pleased Herod,** and all the company. (Mark 6: 22.) No doubt rapturous expressions of admiration burst from the lips of the half-drunken revelers. It is common for dancing-girls to receive presents, proportioned to the admiration their performance has excited; and Salome might naturally expect to re-

---

[1] The construction is unusual but not unexampled (Jelf. §699). The locative case gives the time of the principal action, danced ' on Herod's birthday, when it occurred.' (Comp. the locative in Mark 6: 21.) This need not be called a case absolute, though it corresponds to the Latin " ablative (locative) absolute;" and the Greek " genitive absolute " is itself also not really absolute, not cut loose from the rest of the construction, but gives some event or situation to which the principal action is specifically referred, for the indication of its circumstances. It was very natural that the unusual locative expression should be here changed to the familiar genitive construction, as we find it in many MSS. and the common Greek text.

7 Whereupon he promised with an oath to give her whatsoever she would ask.
8 And she, being before instructed of her mother, said, Give me here John Baptist's head in a charger.
9 And the king was sorry, nevertheless for the oath's sake, and them which sat with him at meat, he commanded *it* to be given *her.*

7 danced in the midst, and pleased Herod. Whereupon he promised with an oath to give her whatso-
8 ever she should ask. And she, being put forward by her mother, saith, Give me here in a charger the
9 head of John the Baptist. And the king was grieved; but for the sake of his oaths, and of them that sat

---

ceive some present on the Tetrarch's birthday. Accordingly, Herod, anxious to express his gratification, and also to play the magnificent before this grand assembly, **promised with an oath to give her whatsoever she would ask.** He even affected, petty ruler as he was, and not properly a king at all, to imitate the grandiloquence of the great Persian monarchs (Esther 5 : 3, 6 ; 7 : 2), and, with drunken dignity, swore to give her what she asked, ''unto the half of my kingdom.'' (Mark 6 : 23.) **8. And she, being before instructed** (Rev. Ver., *put forward*) **by her mother,** or 'urged on,' 'instigated.' Our early English versions, following the Vulgate, mistranslated into ' being before instructed,' and thus created an apparent conflict with Mark, who says (6 : 24) that she went out and inquired of her mother what she should ask. It is pathetic to think how many Bible students have puzzled over this manufactured difficulty.[1] We can imagine the satisfaction with which Herodias heard how well her bold scheme had succeeded, and seized the opportunity for wreaking her vengeance. The girl sympathized, and made the shocking proposal ' with haste' (Mark 6 : 25), or more exactly ' with zeal,' eagerly. **Give me here.** Mark adds 'forthwith.' Probably Salome and her mother feared that Herod would change his mind if they waited till he was sober. **In a charger,** more exactly, *upon a dish,* or 'platter' (so translated in Luke 11 : 39), and signifying a bowl or dish, usually made of wood, but upon Herod's table, probably of costlier materials. The Latin versions here have *discus,* from which we borrow disk and dish. Wyc. and Rheims have 'dish,' Tyn., Cran., and Gen.,

'platter'; King James introduced 'charger,' which was formerly used in English for a large dish. It is much better to use the homely word, which at once shows the idea to be that a dish should be taken from the table. **John Baptist's head.** This designation of John was evidently familiar to all, for it was used by Salome and by Herod, by our Lord, and the Evangelists generally, and by Josephus (see on 3 : 1).

9-11. The king. It was quite common to call a tetrarch king, as a matter of compliment (see on 2 : 20); we find this often in Josephus, as well as in the New Test. Indeed the Greek term was often applied with great latitude to any sovereign ruler, from the Roman imperator (1 Tim. 2 : 2 ; 1 Pet. 2 : 17) down to petty sovereigns like Herod. **Was sorry,** or, *grieved.* The thing would be wrong, and also unpopular. (v. 5.) But his wife ruled him, as on many other occasions. There is no good ground for the suspicion of some writers that Herod himself planned all this thing, in order to have an excuse before the people for slaying John. The idea conflicts with the language of Matthew and of Mark (6 : 20), and a drunken promise to a dancer would have seemed to the people a very poor excuse for killing a prophet. **For the oath's sake**—Rev. Ver., *his oaths,* while above in v. 7 it was 'with an oath.' Mark also (6 : 26) has here the plural. We may conclude that Herod had several times repeated his tipsy promise to the girl, with various oaths. **And them which sat with him at meat,** more exactly, *reclined with him,* the usual posture at table (see on 8 : 11). He was superstitious about his oaths, as many very wicked men are, and was ashamed not to keep the promise he had so frequently

---

[1] The rendering '*before* instructed' is not only unnecessary, but quite without warrant. The verb *probibazo* can mean instruct at all only by taking *pro* in the sense of forward, onward, to carry forward, to lead on ; and so it has to be taken in all the known uses of the verb. Liddell and Scott give ' to teach beforehand' as the meaning in Deut. 6 : 7, but the proper meaning there as shown by the connection of the Sept. and Hebrew, is simply teach. There is no authority at all in Greek

usage, for the sense 'instruct beforehand,' and the etymology forbids it. The natural meaning of urge forward, induce to a certain course (Grimm, Meyer, Weiss, etc.), is established by examples from Plato and Xenophon. The Memphitic and Peshito here render 'instructed,' 'taught.' Most copies of the Old Latin and the Vulgate, have *praemonita ;* but several copies (Sabatier, Bianchini) have simply *monita,* or *docta.*

10 And he sent, and beheaded John in the prison.
11 And his head was brought in a charger, and given to the damsel: and she brought *it* to her mother.
12 And his disciples came, and took up the body, and buried it, and went and told Jesus.

10 at meat with him, he commanded it to be given; 11 and he sent, and beheaded John in the prison. And his head was brought in a charger, and given to the 12 damsel; and she brought it to her mother. And his disciples came, and took up the corpse, and buried him; and they went and told Jesus.

---

made, and so solemnly confirmed before the assembled dignitaries. But a grossly wicked promise is better broken than kept, especially when no one will really lose thereby. As to the general subject of oaths, see on 5: 33-37.

The girl waited for her reward, and the king sent 'immediately.' (Mark 6: 27) Some argue that this term, with 'here' in v. 8, and 'straightway' in Mark 6: 25, cannot be taken literally, because the spectacle would have spoiled all festive enjoyment; but they have forgotten how Herodias' ancestor, Alexander Jannaeus, while holding a feast with his concubines, commanded eight hundred rebels to be crucified in full view, and their wives and children to be slain before their eyes. (Jos. "Ant.," 13, 14, 2.) A great feast usually began about the close of the day, and so it was probably late at night when the executioner came and awoke John and hurriedly beheaded him. After his weary imprisonment of more than a year, the Baptizer was now suddenly cut off. But his work was ended; he had come as the herald of the Messianic reign, and that reign was now being established; the answer of Jesus to his message (11 : 2 ff.) had doubtless cleared his perplexities and removed lingering doubts; there was nothing more to live for, and to die was gain. Nor is it anything very dreadful to die suddenly, if one has lived the life of faith. This murder of the greatest among the prophets in his dungeon was in itself hardly so shocking a sight, as the scene yonder in the banqueting hall. There stood the maiden, her cheek still flushed with her recent exertion, while the guests sought to drown their painful emotions in wine, and the executioner hastened on his cruel errand. When the dish was brought, with the bleeding head upon it, no doubt she took it daintily in her hands, lest a drop of blood should stain her gala dress, and tripped away to her mother, as if bearing her some choice dish of food from the king's table. It was not uncommon to bring the head of one who had been slain to the person who ordered it, as a sure proof that the command had been obeyed. When the head of Cicero was brought to Fulvia, the wife of Antony, she spat upon it, and drawing out the tongue that had so eloquently opposed and condemned Antony, she pierced it with her hair-pin, with bitter gibes. Jerome refers to this incident, and says that Herodias did likewise with the head of John. We know not his authority for the assertion, but the darling desire of the Herod family seems to have been to ape the worst follies and cruelties of the Roman nobility.

Antipas and his family are not mentioned again by Matthew, but he appears in Luke 13: 31 f. and 23: 7-12. Some ten years later, when Herodias' scapegrace brother Agrippa (the Herod of Acts 12) had, through the friendship of the Emperor Caligula, been appointed king over the former tetrarchy of Philip, this ambitious woman was consumed with envy, and gave her husband no rest until, in spite of his love of ease and his caution, he went with her to Rome, to see if he could not also be formally declared king. But Agrippa sent letters to the Emperor, accusing Antipas of treasonable correspondence with the Parthians, upon which he was deposed from office and banished to Gaul or Spain (Jos. "Ant.," 18, 7, 2; "War," 2, 9, 6), whence he never returned. The Emperor offered Herodias her freedom and her private property for her brother's sake, but she declared that she loved her husband too well to forsake him in his misfortunes; whereupon she was banished with him. One fancies it was not that she loved her husband more, but her brother less; and it may have been a trick to excite the young Emperor's sympathies.

12. There were still men who regarded themselves as distinctively John's **disciples**. (See on 9: 14.) But even those who adhered to him most tenaciously knew well how constantly he had pointed them to Jesus; and the report of the two sent by John on a mission of inquiry (11: 2) must have made its impression on them. We may therefore suppose that most of them now attached themselves to Jesus. Some, however, continued to regard John as the Messiah. Thirty years after this we meet persons at Ephesus, "knowing only the baptism of John." (Acts 18: 25; 19: 3.) In the second century we find a petty Gnostic sect who held John to be the Messiah. The Greek word translated *corpse* (Rev. Ver.) was not very often used, and was altered by many copyists into the somewhat similar word meaning **body** (Com. Ver.), (likewise in Mark 15: 45); and so *buried him* was altered into **buried it.** (Comp. on 24: 28.)

Thus ended the career of John the Baptizer. (See on 3: 1; 11: 2, 11; 17: 12 f.; 21: 25–32.) The traits which all remark as conspicuous in his character are self-denial, courage, and humility. For many years he lived a life of great hardship and loneliness, that he might be better fitted for his work as a reformer. As to his courage in speaking the truth, see on v. 4. His humility, in constantly turning away attention from himself to another (John 1: 29, 36), and his rejoicing to see that other "increase," while he himself decreased (John 3: 30), was so genuine and thorough that it seems to us a matter of course in his character. *Belfrage* (in Kitto): "In the splendor of Christ's grace and truth John was happy to be darkened, and in such fame he was content to be forgotten. Had his honors been ten thousand times brighter than they were, he would have laid them all at Christ's feet. John in his ministry was not like the evening star —sinking into the darkness of night, but like the morning star—lost to our view in the brightness of the day." In one sense (see on 11: 11), John was really the first Christian martyr—an honor usually assigned to Stephen.

HOMILETICAL AND PRACTICAL.

V. 1 f. Herod the Tetrarch's first knowledge of Jesus. 1) How ignorant is many a ruler of the great moral and religious movements going on among his subjects. 2) How quickly a man's guilty conscience will suppose any startling event to be connected with his own wrong doing. 3) How surely will superstition misinterpret the supernatural. 4) How strongly does one crime tempt to the commission of another.—V. 6. HALL: "A meet daughter for such a mother. It is not so frequently seen that the child follows the good qualities of the parent; it is seldom seen that it follows not the evil. What with traduction, what with education, it were strange

if we should miss any of our parent's misdispositions."—V. 8.—Herodias' fearful revenge. 1) As often, the offence had consisted simply in telling the truth, v. 4. 2) Delay had made the desire of revenge grow fierce, v. 5; Mark 6: 19 f. 3) The longing for revenge caused a recognized violation of decency, v. 6. 4) The demand for revenge was made with circumstances of inhuman cruelty, v. 8; Mark 6: 25. 5) The result was universal publicity as to the original crime, widespread popular reproach, and an uneasy conscience, v. 2.

V. 9. The downward progress of wrongdoing. 1) Yielding to lust and ambition, Herod forms an unlawful marriage. 2) Uneasy through popular complaint, he tries to make a prophet speak falsely. 3) Angered by the prophet's refusal, he imprisons, and wishes he could dare to kill him. 4) Won by the prophet's wisdom, he cannot preserve him from the wiles of his wife, Mark 6: 19 f. 5) Wild with drunken revelry, he makes a foolish promise. 6) Shocked and grieved at the consequent demand, he yet has not courage to refuse. PLUMPTRE: "Like most weak men, Herod feared to be thought weak." 7) Dreading reproach from the guests, he exposes himself to their utter contempt; for they perfectly understand the cause of the demand and the shame of his compliance. 8) Getting rid of the prophet, he falls a prey to superstitious fears of the prophet's rising again, v. 2. HALL: "The misgrounded sorrow of worldly hearts doth not withhold them from their intended sins. It is enough to vex, not enough to restrain them. Herod was sorry, but he sends the executioner for John's head. . . . As many a one doth good only to be seen of men, so many a one doth evil only to satisfy the humor and opinion of others."— V. 10. A remarkable death. 1) Sudden and shocking. 2) A relief from weary and hopeless confinement. 3) An occasion of everlasting disgrace to those who inflicted it. 4) To the sufferer, an introduction into eternal peace and joy.—V. 6-12. Death of John the Baptist. 1) An immodest performance charming a drunken company, v. 6. 2) A tipsy man indulging in magnificent promises, v. 7; Mark 6: 23. 3) A malignant woman seizing an opportunity for revenge, v. 8. 4) A foolish pride of consistency leads a man reluctantly to do a grossly wicked deed, v. 9.

13 When Jesus heard *of it*, he departed thence by ship into a desert place apart: and when the people had heard *thereof*, they followed him on foot out of the cities.

13 Now when Jesus heard *it*, he withdrew from thence in a boat, to a desert place apart: and when the multitudes heard *thereof*, they followed him[1] on

1 Or, *by land.*

5) After weary waiting, a sudden death, v. 10 f. —V. 12. HENRY: "When anything ails us at any time, it is our duty and privilege to make Christ acquainted with it. . . . John had long since directed his disciples to Christ, and turned them over to him, but they could not leave their old master while he lived; therefore he is removed that they may go to Jesus. It is better to be drawn to Christ by want and loss than not to come to him at all."

13-36. JESUS FEEDS THE FIVE THOUSAND, AND WALKS UPON THE WATER.

We have here three closely related events: feeding the multitude, walking on the water, healing the sick in the Plain of Gennesaret.

I. **13-21.** IN A DESERT PLACE HE FEEDS THE MULTITUDE. Recorded also in Mark 6: 32-44; Luke 9: 10-17; John 6: 1-14. This is the first time in the course of Matthew's Gospel that John has appeared as parallel. The earlier chapters of John, as indeed the greater part of his Gospel, treat of events and discourses which the other Evangelists have not described. In the present case, John wishes to record the great discourse on the bread of life (John 6: 22-71), and he therefore describes the miracle which occasioned it. **When Jesus heard of it, he departed,** as in 2: 22. What he heard may have been either the death of John (v. 12), or the fact that Herod considered him to be John risen from the dead. (v. 1 f.) It may even be that he heard both reports at the same time. At any rate, the cruel murder of John showed what Herod was capable of, and made it obviously prudent for Jesus to withdraw from his dominions, especially now, when the mission of the Twelve had spread throughout Galilee the expectation that the reign of Messiah was about to commence, which the people generally would understand to mean an earthly kingdom, established by a great conqueror who would trample down the Herodian dynasty, the Romans and all. Comp. our Lord's escape in infancy from the murderous jealousy of Herod's father, excited by a single inquiry after one born king of the Jews. (2: 1 ff.) By

crossing to the northeast of the lake, Jesus would reach a very retired and thinly settled region, belonging to the tetrarchy of Philip, who was a comparatively good ruler (see on 2: 20), and to whose dominions he retired several times afterwards. (15: 29; 16: 13.) On a former occasion (12: 15) we have seen Jesus withdrawing from the persecution of the Pharisees, as he will again do in 15: 21. On the evening of this day (v. 22) we shall find him abandoning his chosen place of retirement, to check the fanaticism of the masses. In fact, our Lord now enters upon a series of withdrawals, to avoid Herod, or the Pharisees, or his fanatical followers. In the present case there was a still further reason (Mark 6: 30 f.; Luke 9: 10), viz., to seek a place of rest for the twelve apostles, who had just returned from their novel, laborious, and very exciting mission throughout Galilee. It must have been highly exciting to the apostles to find that they could work miracles, and to proclaim with enthusiasm the near approach of the Messianic reign. (10: 7 f.) After such a strain for several weeks or months, they sorely needed rest for body and mind; and our Lord has here set us the example of paying regard to the conditions of health and vigor, in proposing an excursion into the country for rest. (Mark 6: 31.) We believe it has never been noticed that the season of these successive withdrawals was late spring and summer (from the Passover to near the Feast of Tabernacles); and that from the hot shores of the lake, far lower than the surface of the Mediterranean, he retired in each case to a mountain region—across the lake, to Tyre, to Decapolis, to Cesarea Philippi. His plan for escaping notice and obtaining rest was on this first occasion defeated, as heretofore in John 4: 6 ff., and hereafter in Mark 7: 24 f.

13. By ship, Rev. Ver. *in a boat,* comp. on 4: 21. **Into a desert place,** a thinly inhabited region (see on 3: 1), without large towns, but containing villages. (v. 15.) Luke (9: 10) shows that the region visited pertained to a city called Bethsaida, which must be distinct from the Bethsaida of 11: 21 (see note there), for the

14 And Jesus went forth, and saw a great multitude, and was moved with compassion toward them, and he healed their sick.
15 And when it was evening, his disciples came to him, saying, This is a desert place, and the time is now past; send the multitude away, that they may go into the villages, and buy themselves victuals.

14 foot from the cities. And he came forth and saw a great multitude, and he had compassion on them, 15 and healed their sick. And when even was come, the disciples came to him, saying, The place is desert, and the time is already past; send the multitudes away, that they may go into the villages, and buy

disciples recrossed the same evening to Bethsaida in the land of Gennesaret near Capernaum. (Mark 6 : 45, 53 ; John 6 : 17, 24.) Bethsaida on the eastern side of the Jordan, a mile or more above its mouth, was rebuilt and adorned by Philip the Tetrarch (Jos. "Ant.," 18, 2, 1), under the new name of Julias, in honor of Julia, daughter of Augustus ; and there Philip was afterwards buried. From the mouth of the Jordan a plain extends along the eastern shore of the lake for some three and a half miles, gradually narrowing as the lake curves towards the mountain. This plain, while not equal to that of Gennesaret on the other side, is mainly fertile, and was under careful cultivation ; but at its southern end the mountain comes so near the lake as to make a very retired locality ; and on the lower part of the mountain sides are beautiful grassy slopes, which answer to all the conditions of the narrative before us. **The people** (Rev. Ver. *multitudes*) . . . **followed him on foot.** Jesus obviously set out by boat from Capernaum, or some place in its vicinity. The excited crowds of people, seeing that the boat was going eastward, across the northern part of the lake, hurried along the shore, and passing around the upper end of the lake, reached the same locality which the boat was seeking. Nay, so eagerly did they run that at least some of them "outwent" Jesus and his disciples (Mark 6 : 33), who doubtless rowed slowly, as their object was rest, and who possibly had some distance to go after they landed. **Out of the cities.** *From* is the exact translation ; yet as they had obviously been in the cities, all the versions from Tyn. to K. James render 'out of,' precisely as in 3 : 16. These cities would include Capernaum, with perhaps Chorazin and the western Bethsaida, and of course the eastern Bethsaida, with probably others unknown to us. The crowd was very likely augmented by persons from farther north on their way to the Passover (John 6 : 4), who could be easily excited by talk about the Messianic reign. The Jordan has a ford about two miles above its mouth ; there may have been a bridge, though we have no knowledge

of it ; and there would certainly be many boats, belonging to the important city of Bethsaida Julias, which could cross the narrow river again and again in a short time.

14. And Jesus went (or, *came*) **forth.** The word 'Jesus' was introduced into many copies because this was the beginning of a church "Lesson." (See on 13 : 36.) 'Came forth' naturally means out of the boat. Hort, Introduction, § 138, thinks that this would cause 'followed' in Matthew and Luke to contradict 'outwent them' in Mark. But it is easy to understand that the crowd set out from Capernaum after the boat started, and thus were following, and yet that some of them reached the other side before the boat arrived. Of course 'came forth' might mean from some nook in the mountain, but there is nothing to suggest that idea except the supposed contradiction. John says (6 : 3, R. V.), that he 'went up into the mountain,' viz., the mountain range which skirts the eastern side of the lake. Climbing leisurely the mountain-side, and at length sitting down with his disciples for rest, he found the crowd about him continually increasing. Though they were disturbing his retirement and repose, he did not repulse or turn away from them, but 'received them.' (Luke 9 : 11.) **Moved with compassion toward them,** (comp. on 9 : 36), *i. e*, the people in general, though with special reference to **their sick.** This last word, meaning literally, 'without strength,' is not found elsewhere in Matthew (though several times in Mark), but is substantially equivalent to that used in 10 : 8 and in 25 : 36-44. We learn from Mark (6 : 34) that he also began to teach them many things, and from Luke (9 : 11) that he taught concerning the Messianic reign.

15-18. And when it was evening. The Jews were accustomed to distinguish between the first evening and the second evening. Just what the distinction was, has not been certainly determined (Edersh.) ; it is commonly supposed that the first was from about 3 P. M. to sunset, the second from sunset on into the night. In v. 23 the second evening is meant ; but here in v. 15 it is the first evening ; comp.

16 But Jesus said unto them, They need not depart; give ye them to eat.

17 And they say unto him, We have here but five loaves, and two fishes.

18 He said, Bring them hither to me.

19 And he commanded the multitude to sit down on the grass, and took the five loaves, and the two fishes, and looking up to heaven, he blessed, and brake, and gave the loaves to *his* disciples, and the disciples to the multitude.

16 themselves food. But Jesus said unto them, They have no need to go away; give ye them to eat.

17 And they say unto him, We have here but five loaves, and two fishes. And he said, Bring them

19 hither to me. And he commanded the multitudes to [1] sit down on the grass; and he took the five loaves, and the two fishes, and looking up to heaven, he blessed, and brake and gave the loaves to the

1 Gr. *recline.*

Luke 9: 12, "and the day began to decline" (Bible Union Ver). **The disciples** were here simply the Twelve. (Luke 9: 12.) **This is a desert place,** see on v. 13. **The time is now past.** The Greek expression is peculiar, and may mean either 'the time' as in Wyc. and King James, or 'the day' as in Tyn. For the origin and uses of the Greek word, see Lid. and Scott and Grimm. Some have rendered, ' The hour (for taking food) is past,' but this can hardly be correct. **May go into the villages,** small, unwalled towns (see on 9: 35), such as might well exist in the neighboring plain, and on the lower slopes of the mountain. Mark adds 'fields' or 'farms'; and Luke includes the idea of finding lodging as well as food. They did spend the night in that region. **Give ye them to eat,** with emphasis on 'ye,' as the Greek shows. Mark (6: 37) adds that the disciples asked if they must go away and buy the value of two hundred denarii in loaves. This would be about thirty dollars, and with a purchasing power at least ten times as great as now. It is not intended to intimate that the disciples had so much money, the value of two hundred days' labor (20: 2), but rather the contrary. Mark and Luke add other details, not in conflict with Matthew. But John (6: 5-9) appears at first sight to represent the matter quite differently. There, Jesus himself introduces the subject of feeding the people, speaking of it to Philip. He seems to have made this suggestion to Philip at an earlier period, when the crowd first became very large (John 6: 5), and left it to work upon his mind, in order to 'prove him' (comp. on 4: 1), viz., as to whether he would have such faith in the miraculous powers of Jesus as to think of his feeding this vast crowd by a miracle. Philip had no such thought, and said that two hundred denaries' worth of loaves would not suffice; but Andrew, who was standing by, spoke of the boy with his five barley loaves and two fishes. (John 6: 9.) Later in the after-noon, we may suppose, the Twelve came to Jesus, as narrated by Matthew, Mark, and Luke. Having heard of the conversation with Philip, they naturally mention (Mark 6: 37) the same large and round sum that he had spoken of; and the lad's supply of food some of the Twelve had by this time purchased or engaged. In this or some similar way, the apparent discrepancies may be reconciled. The loaves were probably round, flat cakes, not large (Luke 11: 5), but resembling what in many parts of this country are called "hoecakes." Fish formed an important part of the food of the people living around the lake. John (6: 9, 13) seems to take pains to say that the loaves were of barley, cheap and coarse bread. Jesus made no sumptuous feast with delicacies, but gave them homely and wholesome food.

19-21. And he commanded the multitudes to sit down, or, *recline,* the usual posture in eating, see on 8: 11. The other Evangelists show that he gave this command through the disciples; what he did through them he did himself (comp. on 8: 5). It was a pleasant season of the year, just before the Passover (John 6: 4), which was nearly the same time as our Easter. **On the grass.** John (6: 10) says there was much grass in the place, and Mark (6: 39), that it was green. Mark also says that he bade them recline ' by companies' or banqueting parties,—"and they reclined garden-beds, garden-beds, by hundreds and by fifties." Five thousand men, reclining in this orderly arrangement along the green slope of the mountain, must have spread over an extensive space, probably several acres, and as the afternoon sun shone on their bright-hued Oriental garments, they looked like beds in a flower-garden. And yonder at one end of the area, with eyes uplifted toward heaven, stands the Wonderworker, who is about to feed this vast crowd with the five loaves and two fishes now held in his hands. Nor was this arrangement

20 And they did all eat, and were filled; and they took up of the fragments that remained twelve baskets full.
21 And they that had eaten were about five thousand men, beside women and children.

20 disciples, and the disciples to the multitudes. And they did all eat, and were filled: and they took up that which remained over of the broken pieces,
21 twelve baskets full. And they that did eat were about five thousand men, beside women and children.

---

merely beautiful, but also useful. It rendered the miracle manifest, since all could see that their supply came from Jesus, and that he had only the five loaves and two fishes. It prevented selfish crowding; for so the feeble, including the women and children, had an equal chance to be supplied, and the apostles could move about among the people in an orderly manner, and furnish all alike. The number of persons present could thus be easily ascertained. To count out the groups of fifty and a hundred, and arrange them in this orderly fashion, must have required a considerable time, yet Jesus thought the matter of sufficient importance to wait till it could be done. **He blessed,** may mean either blessed God, or blessed the loaves and fishes, as in Luke 9: 16. John (6: 11) says 'gave thanks,' Rev. Ver. The same variety of phrase occurs in the parallel miracle to this (15: 36), and in the accounts of the Lord's Supper (see on 26: 26). This blessing or thanksgiving seems to have corresponded with the grace before eating, which was customary among the Jews as it is among us. **And were filled,** comp. on 5: 6. All got "as much as they would," or *wished.* (John 6: 11.) As to the mode in which the food was multiplied, we can form no conception; and it is idle to speculate concerning a matter so distinctly supernatural. Observe how readily our Lord returns from the supernatural to the natural. **The fragments,** etc., or as in Rev. Ver., **What remained over of the broken pieces.** The last Greek term is formed upon 'broke' in v. 19, and denotes not crumbs made by eaters. but a surplus of the pieces into which Jesus and the disciples had broken the food. The same expression recurs in 15: 37. The five loaves and two fishes had yielded not only enough, but much to spare. **Twelve baskets full.** The Greek word is *kophinos,* borrowed in Latin *cophinus,* and in English as coffin; Wyc. here renders 'cofyns.' It was probably an oblong basket of moderate size. A quite different Greek word is used in 15: 37; and the distinction is maintained in 16: 9, 10. We learn from the satirical allusions in Juvenal (III.

14) that the Jews of that age in Italy were in the habit of carrying a basket in traveling, probably in order to keep a supply of such food as they could eat without ceremonial defilement; accordingly we are not surprised to find baskets here, even when the owners had neglected to put food in them. Perhaps each of the Twelve took a basket and filled it, which would account for the number of baskets mentioned. This command to save the surplus, 'that nothing be lost' (John 6: 12), was suited to teach economy. It must be manifest that we have no right to waste anything, however ample our resources, when we see him who is the Lord of all, just after multiplying a little food into a vast quantity, now carefully saving the surplus pieces of coarse barley bread and fish. Thus also the disciples had constantly before them, for some days at least, a memento of the extraordinary miracle they had witnessed. Lacking in spiritual susceptibility, and living amid a succession of miracles, they needed such a reminder. (See Mark 6: 52; Matt. 16: 9.) **Beside women and children.** The number of these was probably small in proportion to the men, for otherwise Mark, Luke, and John would hardly have omitted to mention them. In John (6: 10) there is possibly an allusion to them: "Make the people recline . . . . so the men reclined." The former term is the general one, which might include women and children. Perhaps only the men were counted out in groups, the women and children being apart to themselves. (See Blunt, "Undesigned Coincidences," in Bib. Comm.)

Origen, followed by Jerome and many Fathers, runs wild in allegorizing the bread, the walking on the sea, etc. Thus Jerome says the lad with five loaves and two fishes means Moses with his five books and two tables of the law; and Origen, that the reclining by hundreds denotes consecration to the Divine Unity (the hundred being a sacred number), and reclining by fifties denotes remission of sin, through a mystical allusion to the Jubilee and the Pentecost. Such dreadful stuff from surpassingly gifted men ought to be a warning as to the perils of allegorizing. Some eminent

22 And straightway Jesus constrained his disciples to get into a ship, and to go before him unto the other side, while he sent the multitudes away.
23 And when he had sent the multitudes away, he went up into a mountain apart to pray : and when the evening was come, he was there alone.

22   And straightway he constrained the disciples to enter into the boat, and to go before him unto the other side, till he should send the multitudes away.
23 And after he had sent the multitudes away, he went up into the mountain apart to pray : and when

recent rationalists make equally ludicrous attempts to explain away this miracle and that of walking on the waves. If these lifelike narratives, given in such vivid detail by all four Gospels, could be considered to represent mere legends, then the Gospels would be nowhere worthy of confidence.

This great miracle of feeding the multitude could not fail to make a profound impression ; and the people who witnessed it took it as showing beyond question that "this is of a truth the prophet that cometh into the world" (John 6 : 14, Rev. Ver.), *i. e.*, probably the prophet predicted by Moses. (Deut. 18 : 15, 18 ; John 7 : 21, 25 ; 7 : 40 ; Acts 3 : 22 ; 7 : 37.) The Jews did not all identify 'the prophet' with Messiah ; but the persons here concerned evidently did, for they were on the point of coming and seizing Jesus to make him a king. (John 6 : 15.) It was probably their design to carry him with them to Jerusalem to the approaching Passover, and there proclaim him the anointed king, whether he consented or not. Perhaps they were all the more disposed at this time to rise against Herod and the Romans, from indignation at the recent outrageous murder of John the Baptist. (Jos. "Ant.," 18, 5, 2.)

II. **22-33.** JESUS WALKS UPON THE WATER. Found also in Mark 6 : 45-52 ; John 6 : 16-21. Luke here begins to shorten his narrative, continuing to do so up to 9 : 50. **Jesus,** or *he,* **constrained.** Here again, as in v. 14, the word Jesus was interpolated by copyists, •because a " Lesson " began at this point. 'Constrained' is more exactly rendered 'compelled,' as in Wyc., Gen. There was no use in staying there any longer. The hope of rest was gone, and the fame of this great miracle would only increase the popular excitement, and augment the danger of arousing the jealousy of his enemies. So Jesus determines to return to the west side of the lake, where we shall find him the next day busy healing the sick (v. 34), and teaching in the synagogue. (John 6 : 24, 59.) Shortly after he will with-

draw in a different direction, to the borders of Phenicia (15 : 21) ; comp. above on v. 13. For the present he wishes to be alone ; so he proceeds to break up the vast gathering, and begins by separating the disciples from the people and himself. They were naturally slow to leave the scene of so astonishing a miracle. It is also likely that they sympathized not a little with the popular disposition to coerce Jesus into assuming the crown and sceptre of Messiah. (John 6 : 15.) Possibly, too, they saw indications of the coming adverse wind, and dreaded such a storm as that of 8 : 23. Whatever was the cause of their reluctance, Jesus 'compelled them,' of course by earnestly enjoining it. **Unto the other side.** Mark (6 : 45) adds 'to Bethsaida,' and John (6 : 17, Rev. Ver.) says they 'were going over the sea unto Capernaum' ; see above on v. 13. It would seem strange to be compelled to leave the sacred spot, the interested crowds, the Master himself. So we, too, must often do what the Lord in his providence and his word clearly requires, even when it seems to us a strange and painful course. **While he sent,** etc. ; Rev. Ver., more accurately, *till he should dismiss the multitudes.*[1] This he probably did by going about among them, saying that he should do nothing more that day, and requesting them to disperse. They noticed, however, that he did not go with the disciples, and having now no occasion for anxiety about food, they spent the night in that vicinity. (John 6 : 22.) **He went up into a** (*the*) **mountain,** on the east of the lake. (John 6 : 3 ; see above on v. 14.) We may suppose that he had come down towards the shore to see the disciples off, and now 'departed again' (John 6 : 15) to the mountain, and went up into a higher and more secluded portion. Here in the mountain solitude and mild spring air he continued the greater part of the night (v. 25) in prayer. Jesus not only prayed regularly and frequently (Mark 1 : 35 ; Luke 5 : 16 ; 11 : 1), but when any special exigency in his life arose he spent

---

[1] 'Till he should dismiss' is the necessary rendering of *heos* and the *subjunctive.* So Rheims. " While he dismissed,' Tyn. and followers, would represent *heos* and the *indicative.*

24 But the ship was now in the midst of the sea, tossed with waves: for the wind was contrary.
25 And in the fourth watch of the night Jesus went unto them, walking on the sea.

24 even was come, he was there alone. But the boat [1]was now in the midst of the sea, distressed by the
25 waves; for the wind was contrary. And in the fourth watch of the night he came unto them, walk-

---

1 Some ancient authorities read, *was many furlongs distant from the land.*

---

much time in special prayer; *e. g.*, when he was about to select the twelve apostles (Luke 5: 12), and in the agony of Gethsemane. The occasion for protracted prayer in the present instance appears to have been that the strong popular desire to make him a king, together with the jealousy of Herod and of the Pharisees, increased the difficulty of his position, and made him deeply feel the need of his Father's direction and support. Through this fanatical crowd, Satan was again offering him worldly dominion upon condition of pursuing a worldly policy. (4: 8 f.) His earnest teaching throughout the day as to the Messianic reign (Luke 9: 11), had not corrected the popular misapprehensions; he could not bring the people to his views, could not conform to their views; and if he refused, they would sooner or later turn against him, and encourage the rulers to destroy him.

24 f. It seems likely from the use of 'evening' in v. 23 (Mark 6: 47; John 6: 16), and from other expressions of John, that already in the early part of the night the disciples had gone out into the midst of the lake, and there continued to be harassed by the fierce opposing wind until towards morning. **The ship** (*boat*) **was now in the midst of the sea.** John (6: 19) says they had gone 'about five and twenty or thirty furlongs,' from three to three and a half miles (the *stadion* being less than our furlong), when they saw Jesus walking, etc.[1] From the probable place of feeding the five thousand across to Capernaum (Tel Hum), is about four and a half miles. The attempt of some critics to make out an error here, by insisting that 'the midst' must mean the mathematical middle, is simply puerile. **Tossed,** literally, *tortured,* as in 8: 6, 29. While the Com. Ver. has here 'tossed,' and in Mark 6: 48 'toiling,' it translates the same word 'tormented' in 8: 6, 29. **For the wind was contrary.** John adds that it was a 'great wind.' It might seem that this statement shows they had sails, contrary to what has been said on 4: 21; but Mark says they were 'toiling' (or distressed) in rowing, for the wind was contrary,' etc.[2] Jesus *saw* them thus harassed (Mark 6: 48), but for a long time did not go to them. When they were in the former storm (8: 24), he was with them, and they only needed to awake him; but now he had compelled them to start, and had remained ashore. Thus their faith was more severely tried, and thereby in the end increased. **In the fourth watch of**

1 B, several cursives, and the Old Syriac, Peshito, and Jerusalem Syriac, the Armenian, and some other versions read 'the boat was many furlongs distant from the land' (so W H. and *margin* Rev. Ver.). The question is whether Matt. was here assimilated by copyists to John (see above) or to Mark 6: 47, 'the boat was in the midst of the sea.' It is not easy to decide this question, and it makes no substantial difference, since both expressions occur in the other Gospels. The Memphitic version was certainly conformed to John, for it reads 'about twenty-five furlongs.'

2 On March 27, 1871, the writer and a friend went in a boat from Tubariyeh (Tiberias) to the probable place of feeding the five thousand. The day was hot, and the boatmen reluctant to cross. When within a mile or two of the shore they ceased rowing and listened, and the leader said, "Bad, sir, bad." Faint in the distance, on the western side, we heard the sound of wind, rushing down the ravines. The boatmen then began to row with all their might, but before we reached land the lake was much ruffled. We went some half a mile up the nearer slopes, finding beautiful grassy spots, one

in particular, well-suited to be the scene of the miracle, and when we returned found the lake perfectly furious. From noon till nearly sunset this continued; even when the wind ceased, the billows subsided very slowly. At last the boat was pushed out from its harbor in a little crooked stream, and being borne through the surf on the shoulders of the men, we entered it and attempted to cross the lake. But the waves were still so fierce that we could make no headway against them. So the boatmen turned and kept near the shore to the mouth of the Jordan. Bursting through a wall of water caused by the lake-waves opposing the current, we remained in the river some time; and then creeping around the western shore, with the waves still troublesome, we reached Tubariyeh towards midnight. It was the same season of the year, a few days before Easter, and the same western wind was 'contrary'; but fortunately for us it blew itself out in the daytime, while we were ashore. Our rude boat, with its unskillful boatmen, could not possibly have lived if we had met the storm in the midst of the lake.

26 And when the disciples saw him walking on the sea, they were troubled, saying, It is a spirit; and they cried out for fear.
27 But straightway Jesus spake unto them, saying, Be of good cheer; it is I; be not afraid.
28 And Peter answered him, and said, Lord, if it be thou, bid me come unto thee on the water.
29 And he said, Come. And when Peter was come down out of the ship, he walked on the water, to go to Jesus.
30 But when he saw the wind boisterous, he was afraid; and beginning to sink, he cried, saying, Lord, save me.
31 And immediately Jesus stretched forth *his* hand, and caught him, and said unto him, O thou of little faith, wherefore didst thou doubt?

26 ing upon the sea. And when the disciples saw him walking on the sea, they were troubled, saying, It is
27 an apparition; and they cried out for fear. But straightway Jesus spake unto them, saying, Be of
28 good cheer; it is I; be not afraid. And Peter answered him and said, Lord, if it be thou, bid me come
29 unto thee upon the waters. And he said, Come. And Peter went down from the boat, and walked
30 upon the waters, [1] to come to Jesus. But when he saw the wind,[2] he was afraid; and beginning to
31 sink, he cried out, saying, Lord, save me. And immediately Jesus stretched forth his hand, and took

---

1 Some ancient authorities read, *and came.*   2 Many ancient authorities add, *strong.*

---

the night. The *ancient* Hebrews divided the night, probably the period from sunset to sunrise, into three watches (Judg. 7 : 19; Lam. 2 : 19; Ex. 14 : 24; 1 Sam. 11 : 11.) The Greeks appear to have had the same division. But after Pompey's conquest, B. C. 63, the Jews gradually adopted the Roman fashion of four watches (comp. Mark 13 : 35, and see Wieseler, "Synopsis," p. 371). At this season of the year, soon after the vernal equinox (John 6 : 4), the 'fourth watch' would be from about three to six o'clock. We have no means of determining more exactly the time of Jesus' coming. **Jesus went** (literally, *he came*) **unto them.** The name 'Jesus' was added by some copyists, to make the statement plainer. In like manner the common Greek text has 'came' changed to 'went away.' Mark adds, 'and he would have passed by them.' Literally, *wished to pass.* This might perhaps be understood in a weakened sense, as nearly equivalent to the phrase, 'would have passed'; but it more probably means that judging from his actions he wished to pass. Comp. Luke 24 : 28. **26 f. When the disciples saw him.** They all saw him (Mark 6 : 50); and near the boat (John 6 : 19.) **It is a spirit,** *an apparition* is the exact rendering. In Luke 24 : 37, 40, 'spirit' represents the Greek word commonly so translated. The disciples believed in apparitions, as did all the Jews (except the Sadducees), and as all nations seem naturally disposed to do. The opinions of the Twelve at that time have no authority for us, since they had many

erroneous notions from which only the subsequent inspiration of the Comforter delivered them. **Be of good cheer,** Tyn and followers, is more exactly 'courage,' as in 9 : 2, 22; weak faith made them cowardly, see on 8 : 26. Jesus spoke **straightway,** in his kind desire to free them at once from their fear. **It is I.** They would recognize his voice.

28-31. This incident is recorded by Matthew only. **Lord, if it be** (*is*) **thou.** The form of expression implies that he takes for granted it is the Lord. Instead of 'Lord' we might translate 'Master,' (Tyn., Cran.), see on 8 : 19. Seeing Jesus thus walking on the water, Peter immediately felt the desire natural to bold spirits to do anything which they see others do; and under a sudden impulse of confidence in Jesus—mingled, no doubt, with his usual self-confidence—he proposed and undertook to walk upon the water himself. We must remember that the Twelve, on their recent mission, had been empowered to work miracles. (10 : 8.) Perhaps also he was prompted by the desire to get near his loved teacher as soon as possible, as in John 21 : 7. Jesus consented to his coming. Peter would thus learn a needed lesson in the only way in which such confident spirits will learn, viz., from experience. **Walked on the water,** literally, *waters,* the plural being an imitation of the Hebrew word for water, which is used only in the plural; so in v. 28; Mark 9 : 22; John 3 : 23. **To go to Jesus.** The marginal reading of Rev. Ver., 'and came to Jesus,'[1] is

---

[1] 'And came' is the reading of B, C, Old Syriac, Armenian, Chrysostom. It is the more difficult reading, easily changed by copyists into the other, and yet not impossible, seeing that he did really come to Jesus, and was within arm's length when he began to sink. In v. 30 'strong' is not found in ℵ, B (first hand), 33, Mem-

phitic. The addition of this word would be very naturally suggested, and yet if it had been originally present we can see no reason why any copyist should have wished its omission. Therefore we may decide that it did not belong to the original text.

32 And when they were come into the ship, the wind ceased.
33 Then they that were in the ship came and worshipped him, saying, Of a truth thou art the Son of God.
34 And when they were gone over, they came into the land of Gennesaret.

32 hold of him, and saith unto him, O thou of little faith, wherefore didst thou doubt? And when they were
33 gone up into the boat, the wind ceased. And they that were in the boat worshipped him, saying, Of a truth thou art the Son of God.
34 And when they had crossed over, they came to the

very likely correct; it would make the lesson more striking, to Peter and to us, for thus his faith failed when his task was almost finished. **When he saw the wind. Boisterous,** or *strong*, is an unwarranted addition. **O thou of little faith,** see on 6: 30 and 8: 26. He does not say 'of no faith.' And he does not rebuke Peter's self-confident presumption, but his weakness of faith, just as in 8: 10, he commends the centurion's faith rather than his humility; see also 15: 28. Of course faith would have no *natural* power to keep him from sinking, as it would in swimming, because he was performing a supernatural act; God chose to put honor upon faith by enabling him to do this, so long as he did not doubt. Peter must have felt a wholesome shame and confusion at the result of his bold attempt, but the other disciples had no time to notice it, nor he himself to be greatly pained, because all were engrossed with admiration for the wonder-working power of Jesus.

32 f. And when they were come into the ship. *Gone up*, represents the correct Greek text, and not simply 'come into.' John says (6: 21) 'They were willing therefore to receive him into the ship,' or boat. At first they had feared him as an apparition; but the well-known voice, and the words and deeds of love, overcame all their fear. **The wind ceased,** and the boat which had been far out on the lake, was immediately at the land. (John 6: 21.) These things naturally made a great impression on their minds. **They that were in the ship** (*boat*) is a general expression, and might include not merely the Twelve, but other persons who aided in managing the boat; as in 8: 27. **Came and worshipped him.[1]** It is difficult to determine whether their worship or prostration (comp. on 2: 2), was simply reverence to a man, or real worship as to the Deity. And so as to the phrase **thou art the Son of God,** which here occurs for the first time in Matthew.

It seems clear that by this designation the Jews, including the disciples, meant the Messiah. (16: 16; 26: 63; 27: 40, 43, 54; John 1: 49; 6: 69.) But they appear to have had very vague ideas as to the purport of the expression. The High Priest spoke of Messiah as the Son of God (26: 63), while they by no means regarded Messiah as divine. The Jews called Jesus a blasphemer for speaking of himself as the Son of God (John 10: 33; 19: 7), but they called many things blasphemy in which there was no assumption of divinity. (Comp. on 9: 3.) This saying of the disciples shows a decided advance on that of 8: 27, but we must not press it into meaning all that *we* should mean by the same expression. Mark (6: 52) censures their astonishment at this miracle, for which the miracle of the loaves would have prepared them if their minds had not been stupid and dull. This language of Mark does not necessarily forbid the supposition that they were now convinced Jesus was divine; but it best falls in with the idea that they were at a lower standpoint.

We have thus had, v. 13-33, another interesting account (comp. on 13: 1) of a whole day in our Saviour's busy life. See "A Day in the Life of Jesus of Nazareth," in Wayland's "University Sermons."

III. 34-36. AFTER FEEDING THE FIVE THOUSAND, JESUS REVISITS THE PLAIN OF GENNESARET. Found also, with further details, in Mark 6: 53-56. **When they were gone over,** the same word as in 9· 1. **They came into the land,** etc. The general statement is first made, 'they came into (or upon) the land,' came to shore, and this is followed by the more particular statement 'unto Gennesaret.' The relation between the two clauses not being understood by some copyists or early students, it was easily changed into 'they came unto the land of Gennesaret,' as in the common Greek text and the Com. Version. Gennesaret was the name

[1] The prefixed term "came" or 'coming' of the common Greek text is wanting in some of the earliest documents, and we can more readily explain its insertion than its omission; so it is not probably a part of the text.

35 And when the men of that place had knowledge of him, they sent out into all that country round about, and brought unto him all that were diseased;
36 And besought him that they might only touch the hem of his garment: and as many as touched were made perfectly whole.

35 land, unto Gennesaret. And when the men of that place knew him, they sent into all that region round about, and brought unto him all that were sick; 36 and they besought him that they might only touch the border of his garment: and as many as touched were made whole.

---

of a plain lying on the northwest side of the lake, about three and a half miles long, and at some points over two miles wide. It is glowingly described by Josephus ("War," 3, 10, 8) as of unrivaled beauty, fertility, and variety of products; and modern travelers find his statements justified, if we make allowance for the present wretched cultivation and paucity of inhabitants. *Stanley:* "No less than four springs pour forth their almost full grown rivers through the plain; the richness of the soil displays itself in magnificent wheat fields; whilst along the shore rises a thick jungle of thorn and oleander, abounding in birds of brilliant colors and various forms." The soil is a dark loam, very rich; and by irrigation will produce three crops a year. We know of no large city in this plain. Capernaum was pretty certainly at Tel Hum, further north (see on 4: 13); and Chorazin was probably at Keraseh, up in the hills (see on 11: 21). Whether the considerable ruins in the northern angle of the plain represent the western Bethsaida, so often mentioned with Capernaum and Chorazin, we cannot determine. At the southern angle of the plain are a few huts called Mejdel, doubtless the ancient Magdala, the home of Mary Magdalene. From this remarkable plain the Sea or Lake of Galilee was sometimes called Lake of Gennesaret. (Luke 5: 1.) **Had knowledge of** (*i. e., knew*) **him,** or recognized him. Mark adds 'straightway;' they might well recognize him at once, for he had labored much in that vicinity. **All that country round about,** as in 3: 5. **All that were diseased,** or *ill,* the same phrase as in 4: 24. **That they might touch,** a non-final use of the Greek conjunction, see on 5: 29. **The hem** (or *border*) **of his garment,** see on 9: 20 f. The healing there recorded took place at Capernaum not long before, and probably encouraged the persons here mentioned. **Were made perfectly whole,** literally, *were thoroughly saved* (healed), a compound of the verb used in 9: 21. Mark (6: 54 ff.) gives further details, showing Jesus as entering into cities, villages, and country places, and every-

where healing the sick, which probably occupied several days. Weiss thinks it incredible that there were now so many sick to be healed in the region of Jesus' common residence. But he had been absent some time, on the journey about Galilee (11: 1), and the season of malarial fevers had come. For previous instances of a general statement concerning numerous miracles of healing, see 4: 23 f.; 8: 16; 9: 35.

On the morning after the five thousand were fed, they came across in borrowed boats to Capernaum, and crowded into the synagogue, where Jesus was teaching. To this idle and gaping crowd, delighted at getting plenty to eat without working, he addressed the great discourse of John 6: 26–59.

HOMILETICAL AND PRACTICAL.

V. 13 f. Jesus here an example. 1) In prudently withdrawing from danger. 2) In seeking bodily and mental rest for himself and his disciples, comp. Mark 6: 31. 3) In relinquishing needed rest in order to do men good, v. 14, comp. John 4: 6 ff.—V. 14-21. Feeding the multitude. 1) A lesson in compassion, v. 14 f. 2) A lesson in obedience, v. 16-18. 3) A lesson in order, v. 19. 4) A lesson in economy, v. 20. 5) A lesson as to the harmony of the natural and the supernatural, v. 20 f.—V. 19. HALL: "What an honor was this to thy servants, that as thou wert Mediator betwixt thy Father and men, so thou wouldst have them, in some beneficial occasion, mediate betwixt men and thee."— V. 23. Occasional seasons of retirement for long-continued prayer, whether to a private apartment, or to the solitude of nature, are much needed in this hurried age. There is something very impressive in the still depths of a forest, or the recesses of a mountain, as a scene of solitary prayer. "The groves were God's first temples"; and the noblest houses of worship cannot so powerfully appeal to our feelings of devotion. CHRYS.: "The wilderness is the mother of quiet; it is a calm and a harbor, delivering us from all turmoils."

V. 24. HENRY: "Though troubles and diffi-

CHAPTER XV.

THEN came to Jesus scribes and Pharisees, which were of Jerusalem, saying,

1 Then there come to Jesus from Jerusalem Phari-

---

culties may disturb us in our duty, they must not drive us from it; but through the midst of them we must press forward."—V. 25. "Man's extremity is God's opportunity."—V. 26. HENRY: "Most of our danger from outward troubles arises from the occasion they give for inward troubles."—V. 24-27. Danger and deliverance. 1) Perilous struggles long-continued make us deeply feel our need of help. 2) Approaching deliverance sometimes wears an alarming aspect, v. 26. 3) Divine encouragement is given "straightway," just as soon as it is really best for us, v. 27. 4) In life's worst trials, to recognize the Saviour's voice brings courage and hope. 5) Storm and struggle make us enjoy more the calm that follows, and appreciate more highly the Lord who delivers us (v. 32 f.).—V. 28-31. Walking the waves. 1) The instinct of imitation. 2) Self-appointed tests of divine presence and power. 3) Self-confidence often curiously blended with confidence in the Lord. 4) There is frequently strength enough to complete a task, and then collapse at the close, v. 29, *margin* of Rev. Ver. 5) Happy the man whose conscious helplessness leads him to cry for divine help. 6) Many an experience makes us take shame to ourselves, and give glory to God.—V. 27. HALL: "Let heaven be but as one scroll, and let it be written all over with titles, they cannot express more than 'It is I.'"—V. 28. HENRY: "The boldest spirits must wait for a call to hazardous enterprises, and we must not rashly and presumptuously thrust ourselves upon them."—V. 30. HENRY: "Looking at difficulties with an eye of sense, more than at precepts and promises with an eye of faith, is at the bottom of all our individual fears, both as to public and personal concerns. . . . . When faith is weak, prayer should be strong."—V. 31. HENRY: "Our doubts and fears would soon vanish before a strict inquiry into the cause of them."—V. 35. HENRY: "Those that have got the knowledge of Christ themselves should do all they can to bring others acquainted with him too. We can no better testify our love for our country than by pro-

moting and propagating in it the knowledge of Christ."

15: 1-20.—JESUS DISREGARDING TRADITION. This is found also in Mark 7: 1-3. When the great miracle of feeding the five thousand was wrought, the Passover was near (see on 14: 19); which, according to the view commonly held (see on 12: 1), was the third Passover of our Lord's public ministry, and one year before its close. To this last year belong half the chapters and considerably more than half the pages of Matthew's Gospel and a still larger proportion of the Gospels of Mark, Luke, and John. Jesus failed to go to this Passover because the people in Judea were seeking to kill him (as mentioned afterwards, John 7: 1), but continued his labors in Galilee, as described in general terms in 14: 35 f. The particular incident here recorded would seem to have occurred some little time after the Passover, as it would not be natural for Pharisees to leave Jerusalem shortly before the feast. The scene of this occurrence was somewhere in Galilee, apparently in the Plain of Gennesaret (14: 34-36), and probably at Capernaum, his usual place of abode. The fault-finding inquiry by the Pharisees and Scribes (v. 1 f.) is severely retorted upon them (v. 3-9), and then answered by a most important general principle, to which the special attention of all present is called (v. 10 f.), and of which the disciples afterwards seek an explanation in private. (v. 12-20.)

1. Then (see on 3: 13) does not necessarily mean at the time just before mentioned (14: 34-36), but is naturally so taken, unless there be proof to the contrary, which is not here the case. **Scribes and Pharisees,** the common order, was easily inserted by copyists in place of *Pharisees and Scribes,* the correct text. *Come from Jerusalem,* was, in like manner, changed to **which were of Jerusalem,** by inserting an apparently needed article. Jerusalem was the seat of the great schools, as well as of the temple worship, and the most eminent men were congregated

2 Why do thy disciples transgress the tradition of the elders? for they wash not their hands when they eat bread.

2 sees and scribes, saying, Why do thy disciples transgress the tradition of the elders? for they wash not

there; these persons were therefore regarded in Galilee with special reverence. Their object in coming may have been partly to satisfy curiosity about Jesus, excited by accounts given at the Passover, and partly to prevent him from gaining too much influence in Galilee. It is not unlikely that they were sent as a deputation to observe Jesus, as afterwards in Luke 11 : 54, and still later in Matt. 22: 15; comp. 12: 24 (Mark 3: 22), and the deputation sent to John the Baptist. (John 1: 19, 24.) As to the Pharisees, see on 3: 7; and as to the Scribes, on 2: 3. They begin by censuring, not Jesus himself, but the disciples. (Comp. on 9: 14.) On probably a later occasion Jesus himself excited the same complaint. (Luke 11: 38.)

2. The tradition of the elders. The word rendered 'tradition' signifies that which is passed along, or given from one to another. It is sometimes applied by Paul to teachings handed over by him to the churches for their observance. (2 Thess. 2: 15; 3: 6; 1 Cor. 11: 2.) But here and in Gal. 1: 14; Col. 2: 8, it denotes things handed down from generation to generation, which is what we mean by the similar Latin word tradition. It is a favorite evasion of Roman Catholic controversialists to confound these two senses of the term. The word 'elders' here means not officials, but the men of former times. (Heb. 11: 2, and comp. Matt. 5: 21.) The immense mass of traditions which the later Jews so reverenced, were held by them to consist partly of oral laws given by Moses in addition to the written law—which they supposed to be referred to in Deut. 4: 14; partly of decisions made from time to time by the judges (Deut. 17: 9 ff.), and which became precedent and authority; and partly of the explanations and opinions of eminent teachers, given individually or sometimes by the vote of assemblies. These oral traditions continued to accumulate after the time of Christ till they were written down in the Mishna and its commentaries. (See on 3: 7.) They were highly esteemed by all of the nation, except the Sadducees. Indeed some reckoned them more important than the writ-

ten law. The Talmud of Jerusalem says, "The words of the Scribes are more lovely than the words of the law; for the words of the law are weighty and light, but the words of the Scribes are all weighty." And the Talmud somewhere declares that it is a greater crime to "transgress the words of the school of Hillel" than the law. So again: "My son, attend to the words of the scribes, more than to the words of the law." In this as in so many respects Judaism has colored the Christianity of the Church of Rome, which teaches the observance of numerous traditions professedly coming from early times, and some of them from the apostles, though these often directly violate the spirit, and even the letter, of Scripture. Among Protestants also there is sometimes greater solicitude for the observance of custom than of Scripture; and more emphasis laid on "the rule of the church" than on the law of God. **They wash not their hands.** It is worth while to distinguish several Greek words which our English Versions render 'wash.' (1) *Nipto*, used only of washing some part of the body, as the face, hands, feet; found in 6: 17; 15: 2 (Mark 7: 3); 27: 24 (compound); John 9: 7, 15; 13: 5, 14; 1 Tim. 5: 10. (2) *Brecho*, to wet, moisten, sprinkle, and hence commonly to rain; found in Luke 7: 38, 44. (3) *Pluno*, used especially of washing clothes and the like; found in Luke 5: 2; Rev. 7: 14. (4) *Louo*, to bathe, or wash the whole body; found in John 13: 10, "he that is bathed (*louo*), needeth not save to wash (*nipto*) his feet;" also in Acts 9: 37; 16: 33; 22: 16 (compound); 1 Cor. 6: 11 (compound); Heb. 10: 22; 2 Pet. 2: 22; Rev. 1: 5, and a noun derived from it in Eph. 5: 26; Tit. 3: 5. (5) *Baptizo*, to immerse, dip (see on 3: 6), is rendered wash in Mark 7: 4; Luke 11: 38, and a noun derived from it in Mark 7: 4; Heb. 9: 10, in all which places the idea is that of immersion. Mark, who wrote especially for Gentile readers, here paused (7: 3 f.) to give details about the scrupulous and elaborate purifications of the singular Jewish people.[1]

This ceremonial hand-washing before eat-

---

[1] The law required frequent and sometimes very thorough purifications, as bathing the person, and in some cases washing beds, saddles, and vessels of every kind except earthenware, which must be broken.

3 But he answered and said unto them, Why do ye also transgress the commandment of God by your tradition?

4 For God commanded, saying, Honour thy father and mother: and, He that curseth father or mother, let him die the death.

5 But ye say, Whosoever shall say to *his* father or *his* mother, *It is* a gift, by whatsoever thou mightest be profited by me;

3 their hands when they eat bread. And he answered and said unto them, Why do ye also transgress the commandment of God because of your tradition?

4 For God said, Honour thy father and thy mother: and, He that speaketh evil of father or mother, let

5 him [1] die the death. But ye say, Whosoever shall say to his father or his mother, That wherewith thou mightest have been profited by me is given to

---

1 Or, *surely die.*

---

ing, the Rabbis tried to support by Lev. 15: 11. It very naturally arose, along with the similar washing after the meal, from the fact that the ancients habitually ate with their fingers. At a later period a third washing was practised by some persons, in the course of the meal. The Mishna (Berachoth 8, 1) mentions a difference between Hillel and Shammai as to whether one must wash the hands before or after filling the glasses. The Talmud shows that hand-washing was reckoned a matter of high importance. Some Rabbis declare the neglect of it to be as bad as licentiousness or other gross crimes. One said, "It is better to go four miles to water than to incur guilt by neglecting hand-washing"; and a story is told of the famous Rabbi Akiba that when imprisoned, and having his allowance of water reduced, he took what little there was to wash his hands before eating, instead of drinking it, saying that he had rather die than transgress the institutions of his ancestors.

3-6. Before proceeding to the great principle (v. 11) involved in his justification of the disciples for neglect of the hand-washing, our Lord retorts upon the Pharisees and Scribes their charge of "transgression." (Comp. the *ad hominem* argument in 12: 27.) **Why do**

ye also transgress, and that not a mere tradition of men, but **the commandment of God by** (*because of*) **your tradition?** 'By your tradition' does not correctly render the Greek. They had said 'the tradition of the elders,' but he says simply your tradition; no matter what was its origin, they were now making it the occasion of transgressing the law of God. This charge he proves by an example, not connected with hand-washing or other purifications, but drawn from a most sacred duty, as acknowledged by mankind, and enjoined in a peculiarly solemn command (Eph. 6: 2) of God's law. Our Lord himself declared (10: 37; Luke 14: 26) that his service is above filial duty; but (Plumptre) he claimed supernatural authority, which the Scribes did not claim. *For God said*, the true reading, was easily changed by copyists into **for God commanded, saying,** because 'the commandment' had just been mentioned. The first clause is quoted from Ex. 20: 12, the second from Ex. 21: 17, both taken from the Sept., and correctly translating the Hebrew. The second was introduced to show that this command which they practically annulled was one of the highest importance, since the penalty of its violation, among the Hebrews, was to be death without fail. Comp. very strong

---

(Lev. ch. 15.) In general, the Hebrew terms do not show how this washing of vessels, etc., was to be performed, but in Lev. 11: 32 they must be "put into water"; comp. "divers baptisms (*immersions*)," Heb. 9: 10. The scrupulous later Jews often adopted this most thorough purification even when not required by the law (see Judith 12: 7; Ecclus. 31: 30, and numerous directions in the Talmud). With this agrees Mark's statement that when they come "from the market place, except they immerse, they eat not," which may mean immerse their hands for thorough washing, as distinguished from the simpler mode of washing hands carefully described in the Talmud, but more probably means immerse themselves. So in Mishna Chagiga, 2, 5, two recent Jewish authorities differ as to whether "dipping" means washing the hands by dipping them (Wünsche, and so Edersh.), or taking a bath (Schwab,

tr. of Talm. Jerus.). Those who cannot believe that under such circumstances they would immerse the whole person might read Herodotus II., 47, who says that if any Egyptian "touches a swine in passing with his clothes, he goes to the river and dips himself (*bapto*) from it." Some early Christian students or copyists, not understanding this Jewish scrupulosity, changed *baptisontai*, 'immerse themselves,' into *rantisontai*, "sprinkle themselves;" for though found in א B, nine cursives, and the late Father Euthym., this is obviously a correction to avoid a difficulty, as is also the omission of 'couches' at the end of Mark 7: 4 by א B L Δ, three cursives, Memph. How can any one account for the *insertion* of 'couches,' and the change of 'sprinkle' to 'immerse'?—The question here is not of traditional usage or the mere *mode* of performing a ceremony, but of the principle of strict obedience to a divine command.

6 And honour not his father or his mother, *he shall be free.* Thus have ye made the commandment of God of none effect by your tradition.

6 *God;* he shall not honour his father.[1] And ye have made void the [2] word of God because of your tra-

---

1 Some ancient authorities add, *or his mother.*   2 Some ancient authorities read, *law.*

---

language on the subject in Deut. 27: 16; Prov. 20: 20; 30: 17. **He that curseth;** *speaketh evil of,* or 'reviles,' is the exact rendering; 'curses' would be a different Greek word. The Hebrew means primarily 'belittle,' 'make light of,' and derivatively 'curse.' So the command is very broad. **Let him die the death,** or better, *let him surely die* (margin Rev. Ver.), the form of expression being much used in the Old Test., and oftener denoting the certainty than the severity of the punishment. The connection here shows that we must honor parents not merely in our feelings but by our acts; see similar uses of "honor" in Prov. 3: 9; 1 Tim. 5: 3. And the Jews recognized this duty. Ecclus. 3: 8, "Honor thy father and mother both in word and deed"; *Talm. Jerus.*: "A son is bound to nourish his father, yea, to beg for him." The case here supposed is of a needy parent, requiring help from the son, which he refuses on grounds justified by tradition. **But ye say,** 'ye' being expressed in the original, and thus strongly emphatic. It is a bad position for men to occupy, when what *they* say is directly opposed to what *God* says. **By whatsoever** (or *that wherewith*) *thou mightest be* (*have been*) **profited by me,** is a general expression, covering all sorts of cases, and is often found in the Talmud (Lf., Edersh.) in connection with this same subject. **Is a gift,** or perhaps 'let it be a gift,' the Greek having no copula. 'A gift' evidently means a gift to God, and Mark (7: 11) presents the Heb. word Corban, which the Talmud shows they were accustomed to employ in such cases, denoting an offering, anything dedicated to God, or donated for the use of the temple. The Peshito has the same word in Matt., and it is used in Matt. 27: 6 to denote the 'treasury,' the aggregate of all such offerings. If a man's father or mother wanted any article from him —it might be food or clothing, or what not— he could just say, Corban, it is a gift, a thing consecrated to God (comp. Lev. 27: 9, 16), and he was then, according to the traditional rules, not only at liberty to withhold it from his parent, but solemnly bound to do so. The Mishna ("Vows," 9, 1) tells of a former dif-

cussion as to whether a vow could be set aside through regard for parents, and all but one Rabbi declared in the negative. The Jews reached this conclusion by arguing that vows, as they had respect to God, were more important than things pertaining to men; and hence that devoting a thing to God was sufficient to set aside the highest obligation, even that to one's parents. Here was a correct principle, greatly abused in the application. We learn from the Talmud, which has copious directions on this subject, that a man was not bound, after saying Corban, actually to dedicate the article in the temple, but might keep it indefinitely for his own use, or might give it to some other person, only not to the one had in mind when he made the vow. Corban might therefore be said just for the nonce, as an excuse for withholding; and with people as 'money-loving' as the Pharisees (Luke 16: 14), the license thus offered would often be shamefully abused. Even more; it appears from the Talmud that a man might not merely say Corban with reference to any particular object, but might say it once for all, as applying to everything which he possessed, and that one word spoken in passion or greed, would make it impossible that he should ever do anything for the person in question, though it were his parent. We are told of a son in Bethhoron who had taken such a vow against his father, and afterwards wishing to supply the father's need, donated his own house and dinner to a friend on condition that his father should share the dinner; but the friend immediately declared the house and meal sacred to heaven, and so the scheme failed. Mishna ("Vows," 5, 6). The Talmud mentions various ingenious expedients for evading Corban and other vows, when one afterwards changed his mind. Several Fathers state that a Jewish creditor could constrain an ugly debtor by saying "what you owe me is Corban," and so it had to be paid, as a debt to God. From all this we see how monstrous were the practices to which our Lord was referring. It is lamentable to think that they have been rivaled by teachings of modern Jesuits.

There is some difficulty as to the Greek text

7 *Ye* hypocrites, well did Esaias prophesy of you, saying,

7 dition. Ye hypocrites, well did Isaiah prophesy of you, saying,

and the meaning in the latter part of v. 5 and v. 6. The best supported text most naturally yields the meaning given by Rev. Ver., (see Moulton in Winer, p. 750); viz., you, according to your tradition, virtually say that when he has once for all made this vow he is not to honor his father.[1] The 'not' is a strong doubled negative. If 'and' be retained, then something must be silently supplied. But it cannot be as in Com. Ver., because 'honor' is certainly future. It must be somehow so: whoever says to his father or his mother, 'that wherewith thou mightest have been profited by me is given to God,' is not bound by the law, but must observe his vow in preference (comp. Mark 7: 12); what follows giving the consequence, 'and (thus) he will not honor his father,' as the law requires him to do. The general thought is the same upon both interpretations. **Have ye made void** God's authoritative word, and not merely transgressed it (v. 3).—A practice somewhat similar to this Corban vow of the Jews formerly existed in the Sandwich Islands. *Barnes:* "The chiefs and priests had the power of devoting anything to the service of the gods by saying that it was *tabu, i. e.,* consecrated to the service of religion; and no matter who had been the owner, it could then be appropriated to no other use." From this Polynesian usage comes our word *taboo*, to forbid all intercourse with a certain person or use of a certain thing.

7-9. Hypocrites, see on 6: 2. They made great pretence of devotion to God, and insisted strenuously on the externals of his service, while at heart they did not love him, and were even ready to set aside his express commands for the sake of their traditions. The persons particularly addressed were from Jerusalem (v. 1), and an early Rabbi is related to have said that "there are ten parts of hypocrisy in the world, nine at Jerusalem, and one in the whole world." This seems to be the first instance of our Lord's openly denouncing the Pharisees, as we shall often find him doing hereafter. The strong denunciations of Luke, ch. 11 and 12, are much better placed at a later period, according to the harmonistic arrangement of Wieseler, followed by Tischendorf's "Synopsis" and Clark's "Harm." (Comp. on 12: 22.) **Well,** *i. e.,* finely, aptly, with admirable appropriateness, (comp. 13: 14.) Yet our Lord does not simply say that *he* finds the words of Isaiah to his contemporaries exactly applicable to these persons, and himself makes the application, but he says, **Well did Esaias** (*Isaiah*) **prophesy concerning you.** Isaiah spoke directly to the men of his own time, but his words were also designed by the Spirit of inspiration to refer to the contemporaries of Messiah. For 'Isaiah,' instead of the changed Greek form Esaias, see on 1: 2. The citation is from Isa. 29: 13. The words in common Greek text, **draweth nigh unto me with their mouth, and** are not genuine here, but were added from the Sept.[2] Matt. quotes from the Sept. as he

[1] 'And' is omitted by א B, C, D, some other manuscripts, and several versions. The ground for hesitation is that 'and' is the *difficult* reading. But the verb 'honor' should clearly be future tense, as given by nearly the same authorities, and not subjunctive, as in the common Greek text. The future indicative after *ou me* is unclassical, though not uncommon in later Greek, and would thus be readily changed by copyists into the regular classical subjunctive, as in many other places. (Comp. 26: 35, and see Buttm, p. 213.) In this way 'honor' came into the same form as 'say,' and then it might easily occur to a copyist that these ought to be connected by 'and,' 'whosoever shall say . . . . and shall not honor.' Thus the text of the oldest authorities accounts for the other readings. 'Or his mother' (v. 6) is omitted by א B, D, and Old Syriac. The addition of this clause would be instantly suggested by the foregoing phrases (v. 4 f.), while we cannot imagine any reason for its omission if originally present. In like manner 'the word' read by B, D, and a correcter of א, and by many early versions and some Fathers would easily be changed to 'the commandment,' to suit v. 3, and this may have been changed to 'the law,' read by several documents (*margin* Rev. Ver.), because the second saying in v. 4 is not a part of the Decalogue.

[2] They are wanting in nearly all the early versions, in the earliest Greek manuscripts, and in many Patristic citations. To enlarge a quotation by bringing in something more from the Sept. was a very common and natural mode of altering the copies. The clause cannot have been omitted in Matt. by way of assimilation to Mark, for that would have led rather to its insertion in Mark, according to the custom of the copyists. Some MSS. of the Sept. omit this clause, perhaps by way of accommodation to the Gospels.

8 This people draweth nigh unto me with their mouth, and honoureth me with *their* lips; but their heart is far from me.
9 But in vain they do worship me, teaching *for* doctrines the commandments of men.
10 And he called the multitude, and said unto them, Hear, and understand:

8   This people honoureth me with their lips;
    But their heart is far from me.
9   But in vain do they worship me,
    Teaching *as their* doctrines the precepts of men.
10 And he called to him the multitude, and said unto

oftenest does, and here in v. 9 departs considerably from the Heb., which reads, "and their fear towards me is the commandment of men, (a thing) taught," *i. e.*, their piety is merely a lesson they have learned from men, and not a thing learned from and conformed to the word of God. For this the Sept. has, "but in vain do they worship me, teaching precepts of men and teachings." (As to the difference between Heb. and Sept., comp. Toy.) Matt. and Mark (7: 7) have slightly modified the Sept. into 'teaching teachings (which are) precepts of men.' This not only improves the phraseology of the Sept., but brings out the prophet's thought mere clearly than would be done by a literal translation of the Heb., for Isaiah means to distinguish between a worship of God that is taught by men, and that which is according to the teaching of God's word. As to quoting Sept. instead of Heb., see on 3: 3; and as to verbal changes to bring out the sense more plainly, comp. on 2: 6. For the different words rendered 'teaching,' see on 7: 28. Instead of **commandments,** Rev. Ver. here uses 'precepts' (as in Tyn., Cran., Gen.), because the Greek word is somewhat different from that of v. 3, though substantially equivalent. **In vain,** *i. e.*, it is not acceptable to God, nor profitable for themselves. So at the present day many persons claim a divine authority for ideas and practices which are simply of human origin (comp. on v. 2). We are not only under no obligation to conform to these, but it is our duty to oppose them wherever they tend to the violation or neglect of God's commandments. It must also be remembered that our common human nature is very prone to be intent upon the forms of religion and neglect its spirit; to honor God with the lips, while the heart is far from him.

10 f. When he retorted their question upon themselves (v. 3), it was not for the purpose of avoiding an answer, and he now publicly proclaims a principle which goes to the heart of the matter. **Called** (*unto him*) **the multitude,** or *crowd,* the mass of the people, as distinguished from the Pharisees and Scribes, who had pressed up around him. He wished all to hear what he was about to say; and in fact the crowd were more likely to receive it than the others, being less prejudiced and sophisticated. **Hear, and understand.** It was something important, and demanded attentive consideration. The disciples presently called it a 'parable' (v. 15), yet he was not now employing obscure expressions as a judgment (13: 13), but with great desire that all (Mark 7: 14) should understand. And they must not merely hear, but understand; for he will not recite decisions and opinions of the ancients, as the Scribes did, but will speak by his own authority (7: 29), directly to the understanding and conscience of the people. **Defileth a** (*the*) **man,** *i. e.*, the man concerned in any particular case. So in the second clause, and in v. 18, 20. Tyn., Cran., and Gen. give the article in v. 11 and 18, but not in v. 20; King James gives it only in v. 18. The word rendered 'defileth' is literally, *makes common.* Some kinds of food were specially set apart, as alone proper for God's chosen people, and were thus in a certain sense sacred, all other things being 'common' (Acts 10: 14); for an Israelite to partake of these forbidden things would destroy his exclusiveness, make him common. Hence 'to make common' came to mean to defile, pollute. This saying of Jesus was to the Jews in the highest degree surprising, paradoxical, revolutionary (comp. 12: 8). They saw at once that it applied not merely to hand washing, but to the whole matter of clean and unclean food, and this seemed to them one of the most vital parts of the law. So they knew not what to make of the saying, "Not what goes into the mouth defiles the man, but what comes out of it." The Pharisees stumbled at such a saying, could not admit the divine mission of one who uttered it (v. 12), and even the disciples failed to understand it. (v. 15 f.) Ceremonially, various things did defile by entering the mouth; but this was only designed to *represent* the idea of *moral* pollution, while the great mass

11 Not that which goeth into the mouth defileth a man; but that which cometh out of the mouth, this defileth a man.

12 Then came his disciples, and said unto him, Knowest thou that the Pharisees were offended, after they heard this saying?

13 But he answered and said, Every plant, which my heavenly Father hath not planted, shall be rooted up.

14 Let them alone: they be blind leaders of the blind. And if the blind lead the blind, both shall fall into the ditch.

11 them, Hear, and understand: Not that which entereth into the mouth defileth the man; but that which proceedeth out of the mouth, this defileth 12 the man. Then came the disciples, and said unto him, Knowest thou that the Pharisees were [1]offended, 13 when they heard this saying? But he answered and said, Every [2]plant which my heavenly Father planted not, shall be rooted up. Let them alone; 14 they are blind guides. And if the blind guide the

1 Gr. *caused to stumble* . . . . 2 Gr. *planting.*

of the Jews, however scrupulous about the representative purity, were careless of the inward purity. Our Lord therefore, by this saying directs attention to the internal and real impurity. Here, as with reference to the Sabbath (12:1 ff.), and to so many points in the Sermon on the Mount, he is leading the people to deeper and more spiritual views of the morality which the law designed to teach, and thus not abrogating or correcting, but 'completing' the law. (5:17.) His teachings did prepare the way for laying aside the ceremonies of the law, but this only by developing it into something higher. Accordingly, he does not abrogate the Mosaic directions about unclean food, but lays down a general principle applying to the point in hand (v. 20), and really covering the whole matter, though not now further applied. Many things taught in principle by Jesus, were to be fully developed by his inspired followers, as men should become prepared to understand them. Comp. 1 Cor. 10:31; Rom. 14:14 ff.; 1 Tim. 4:4; Tit. 1:15. Besides educating the Israelites to the appreciation of moral purity, the law about clean and unclean food was also designed to keep the chosen people separate from other nations, and so Peter was taught to set it aside when the time came for preaching freely among the Gentiles. (Acts 10:9 ff.)

12-14. This is found in Matthew only. It appears that the conversation occurred after Jesus and his immediate followers had retired from the crowd into a house. (Mark 7:17.) There had thus been a little interval since the saying of v, 11 was uttered, and the disciples had heard how the Pharisees were talking about it. They felt that the opinions of these distinguished men from Jerusalem (v. 1) were very important. **Knowest thou.** It seemed likely that he did not, or he would be hastening to explain and thus recover the sympathy of such important hearers. **Were offended** (see on 5:29), made to stumble, finding an

obstacle to their believing reception of Jesus' teachings (as in 11:6). **When they heard this** (*the*) **saying,** not that of v. 3-9 (Fritz. and others), but the great saying of v. 11, addressed to the crowd, but heard by the Pharisees also (Mey., Bleek, Weiss, and others). The Pharisees doubtless declared the saying to be in direct opposition to the law about clean and unclean food. The disciples themselves looked upon it as extremely obscure and strange (v. 15), and sympathized not a little with the prejudices involved. Our Lord's reply is to the effect that it matters not what such men think, whose authority is merely human, and who are as blind as the multitude they lead. **Every plant,** etc. Every doctrine which did not come from God, which is of merely human origin (v. 9), will lose its influence and cease to be believed. **My heavenly Father,** see on 6:9. **Let them alone,** *i. e.,* do not trouble yourselves about them, as to what they teach, or whether they approve my teaching. The Great Teacher did not expect, and did not try, to please all his hearers. Such as were blinded by prejudice, hardened in unbelief, or willful in their opposition, could only be let alone. **They be** (*are*) **blind leaders,** *guides* (oldest Greek MSS. and some versions) was easily enlarged by adding **of the blind** from the immediately following expression. 'Guides' (Rheims) is a more exact translation than 'leaders' (Wyc., Tyn., and followers). **If the blind lead** (*guide*) **the blind.** Both Greek words are singular and indefinite, 'if a blind man guide a blind man,' but the definite form makes a smoother English expression. It seems likely from Rom. 2:19, that guide of the blind was a common designation of the Rabbis. **Both shall** (*will*) **fall into the ditch** (*a pit*), the same word as in 12:11, and denoting (Liddell and Scott) a pit dug in the field to hold water, as was very common. The word is rendered 'pit' by Tyn., Cran., Gen., and Com. Ver., in

15 Then answered Peter and said unto him, Declare unto us this parable.
16 And Jesus said, Are ye also yet without understanding?
17 Do not ye yet understand, that whatsoever entereth in at the mouth goeth into the belly, and is cast out into the draught?
18 But those things which proceed out of the mouth come forth from the heart; and they defile the man.
19 For out of the heart proceed evil thoughts, murders, adulteries, fornications, thefts, false witness, blasphemies;

15 blind, both shall fall into a pit. And Peter answered and said unto him, Declare unto us the
16 parable. And he said, Are ye also even yet without
17 understanding? Perceive ye not, that whatsoever goeth into the mouth passeth into the belly, and is
18 cast out into the draught? But the things which proceed out of the mouth come forth out of the
19 heart; and they defile the man. For out of the heart come forth evil thoughts, murders, adulteries,

---

12: 11, but here they all adopted 'ditch,' probably from supposing the image to be that of the ditch beside a road. But the word does not mean ditch, and the image is that of blind persons walking in the open field, and falling into a pit—a much more serious calamity. This saying has the air of a proverb, such as our Lord repeatedly employed (see on 7: 5), and it had already been used by him in the Sermon on the Mount. (Luke 6 : 39.) Various similar sayings are found in classical writers. (Wet.)

15. Then answered Peter, not a specific reply to what Jesus had just said, but in a general sense a response, keeping up the conversation. (See on 11: 25.) Peter's expression, **declare unto us,** shows by the plural that he speaks for all, and Jesus in reply says 'ye.' (Comp. Mark 7: 17.) Peter is therefore spokesman for the Twelve, as he so often is. (See on 16: 18.) **This** (*the*) **parable;** here copyists readily changed 'the' into 'this.' The word here denotes an obscure expression. (See on 13: 13.) The reference is not to the figurative saying of v. 14, called in Luke 6: 39 a parable, but to v. 11, already spoken of in v. 12 as 'the saying.' This is plain from our Lord's reply, and confirmed by the connection in Mark 7: 15-17, who has not given the intermediate matter of Matthew v. 13 f., and with whom 'the parable' must necessarily refer to the great saying.

16-20. And Jesus (strictly *he*) **said,** the copyists inserting 'Jesus,' as in 14: 14 and often. **Are ye also,** as well as the masses and the Pharisees. **Yet.** The Greek has a strong word, not elsewhere used in the New Test., but which in later Greek has *even yet* as a well-established meaning; 'even yet,' after all the instruction you have received, comp. 16: 9; Heb. 5: 12. He had not given any instruction that we know of on this particular subject, but his teachings in ch. 5 and ch. 13, and his general influence, ought to have prepared

them to take spiritual views of things. In v. 17, **do ye not yet understand** (or *perceive*), was strengthened by copyists by introducing 'yet,' because of the expression in v. 16, and perhaps with a reminiscense of 16: 9. 'Perceive' (Tyn., Gen.) is here better than 'understand' (Wyc., Cran., Rheims, Com. Ver.), in order to distinguish from the different Greek word used in v. 10 and 16. The Jews had come very largely to confound ceremonial with moral defilement. To correct this confusion of ideas, our Lord points out that articles of food cannot really pollute, because they pass through the body and out of it, and do not 'enter the heart' (Mark 7 : 19), cannot affect the spiritual nature; but the sinful things which are uttered through the mouth, and proceed from the heart, constitute a real pollution. Comp. on v. 11. **Into the belly.** The Greek signifies the whole hollow, or internal cavity of the body, including stomach and other viscera; and the English word formerly had a similar latitude of meaning. **Into the draught** (2 Kings 10 : 27), sink, or privy (Rheims), literally, *place for sitting apart.* Mark adds (7: 19) that by this saying Jesus cleansed all articles of food, *i. e.*, declared them to be clean. (Acts 10: 15.) With v. 18 comp. on 12: 34 f. In v. 19 our Lord does not confine himself absolutely to such things as are *spoken*, in order to keep up the contrasted image, but passes to the more general notion of whatever comes forth from the heart, has its origin from within us. There is, therefore, no occasion for inquiring, as some do, how *speech* has to do with all the forms of sin here mentioned. Mark (7: 18-23) does not mention the mouth, but only the more general idea of entering and coming forth from the man, the heart. We have seen on 6: 21 and elsewhere, that the heart was conceived of by the Hebrews, and is spoken of by the Bible, as the seat of thought and volition as well as of emotion. After the general phrase **evil thoughts,** our Lord speci-

20 These are *the things* which defile a man: but to eat with unwashen hands defileth not a man.

20 fornications, thefts, false witness, railings: these are the things which defile the man: but to eat with unwashen hands defileth not the man.

---

fies violations of the sixth, seventh, eighth, and ninth Commandments in order. Mark adds some other sins not mentioned by Matt. The plural forms which Matt. has throughout (even 'false witnessings') remind us of the numerous instances and different varieties of these several sins. **Blasphemies** (see on 9: 3); a literal translation of the Greek is in Rev. Ver. 'railings.' In English we confine it to railing against God. Philo Judaeus paraphrasing Plato, says that through the mouth "mortal things go in, but incorruptible things come out. For by it enter food and drink, the corruptible body's corruptible nourishment; but through the mouth words come forth, the immortal soul's immortal laws, through which the natural life is governed."**20.** This first sums up the previous discussion, and then connects it all with the starting point in v. 1. Our Lord has now not only denounced the Pharisees as hypocrites (v. 7), but boldly antagonized their cardinal tenet of the authority of tradition. The conflict must inevitably wax fierce, and he soon begins to withdraw from their virulent opposition, and the fanaticism of his friends.

HOMILETICAL AND PRACTICAL.

V. 3-6. Two oppositions. 1) Human tradition *versus* divine commandment. (a) Men are prone to make old religious usage an authority. It can claim respect, but not obedience. (b) Men often come to take more interest in long-established usage than in the express teaching of revelation—this through personal associations and through controversial heat. (c) Men sometimes practically alter a divine commandment to make it harmonize with established custom ; the Saviour represents this as a grave sin. (v. 6.) 2) Ceremonial services *versus* moral duties. (a) Human nature naturally tends to be more interested in the external than in the moral and spiritual. Comp. 23: 23 ff. (b) To neglect a high moral duty for the sake of a mere religious usage, is to disgrace our religion.—V. 4. Honoring parents. 1) Honor them in your thoughts. 2) Honor them in your speech, v. 4. (latter part). 3) Honor them in your actions, v. 5 f.—BENGEL: "Young

people, notice." HENRY: "That which men say, even great men, and learned men, and men in authority, must be examined by that which God saith."—V. 7-9. Hypocrisy. In the days of Isaiah, and of Jesus, and in our days. 1) Two forms of hypocrisy. (a) Religious talk without religious character. (v. 8.) (b) Human precepts put in place of divine commands. (v. 9.) 2) The successes of hypocrisy. (a) It may deceive men—other persons—even the hypocrite himself. (b) It never deceives God—it is "in vain," (v. 9). —V. 10 f. Preaching to the people. 1) The common people are often more ready to receive new religious ideas than the teaching class, v. 10; comp. v. 12 ff. 2) The greatest of religious teachers had to ask special attention when giving strange and unpalatable instruction, v. 10. 3) Even he was imperfectly understood by some (v. 16), and found fault with by others. (v. 12.) 4) Yet the common people heard him gladly (Mark 12: 37), and all that the Father gave him came unto him. (John 6: 37.) HENRY: "Not only scholars, but even the multitude, the ordinary people, must apply their minds to understand the words of Christ. . . . . There is need of a great intention of mind and clearness of understanding, to free men from those corrupt principles and practices which they have been bred up in and long accustomed to; for in that case the understanding is commonly bribed and biased by prejudice."— V. 11. Many sayings of Jesus that were revolutionary at the time are now Christian commonplaces—this fact is a ground for rejoicing. —V. 11. Pollution. 1) Ceremonial defilement was but an object lesson, a symbol of polluted character; and so ceremonial purity of moral purity. 2) Evil thoughts and desires arise from a polluted nature, and their expression in speech or action pollutes the whole being, v. 18 f. 3) Evil environment endangers character, but pure character can conquer the worst environment.—V. 12-14. Blind guides. 1) Long-established religious teachers may meet new truth with blind prejudice, v. 12. 2) Highly popular religious teachings may have no divine approval or support, v. 13. 3) Greatly honored

21 Then Jesus went thence, and departed into the coasts of Tyre and Sidon.
22 And, behold, a woman of Canaan came out of the same coasts, and cried unto him, saying, Have mercy on me, O Lord, *thou* Son of David; my daughter is grievously vexed with a devil.

21 And Jesus went out thence, and withdrew into
22 the parts of Tyre and Sidon. And, behold, a Canaanitish woman came out from those borders, and cried, saying, Have mercy on me, O Lord, thou son of David; my daughter is grievously vexed with a

religious instructors may be but the blind guiding the blind, v. 14. 4) Plausible objections from distinguished sources must sometimes be quite disregarded, v. 13. CHRYS.: "It is a great evil merely to be blind, but for a man to be in such a case and have none to lead him, nay, to occupy the place of a guide, is a double and triple ground of censure. For if it be a dangerous thing for the blind man not to have a guide, much more so that he should even desire to be guide to another."—V. 16. Ignorance of Christian truth is blameworthy, 1) in any one who has opportunity to know, 2) especially in a Christian, 3) most of all in one who has long been a Christian, and has had superior advantages for learning.——V. 20. ORIGEN: "It is not eating with unwashed hands, but, if one may use so bold an expression, it is eating with an unwashed heart, that defiles a man." CHRYS.: "Even in the church we see such a custom prevailing amongst the generality, and men giving diligence to come in clean garments, and to have their hands washed; but how to present a clean soul to God, they make no account."

21-38. JESUS WITHDRAWS TO PHOENICIA.
The story of the Syro-Phoenician woman is found also in Mark 7: 24-30, in the same connection as here. Luke hastens through this part of the history, omitting various things, and stating others very briefly.

The jealousy of Herod (14: 1 f.), the hostility of the Pharisees (12: 14; 15: 1, 12; also 4: 12; John 4: 1-3), and the fanatical notions of the masses (John 6: 15), still required that Jesus should withdraw from Galilee, as heretofore in 14: 13. **Thence,** probably from Capernaum. He now set out in a different direction, towards the northwest, into Phoenicia, thus getting beyond the jurisdiction of Herod, as in 14: 13, and hereafter in v. 29, and 16: 5. **Departed,** *withdrew,* same word as in 2: 12, 22; 4: 12; 12: 15; 14: 13. **Into the coasts** (Rev. Ver. *parts*) **of Tyre and Sidon,** *i. e.,* the parts of the country, the region, belonging to those cities; so the same word in 2: 22; 16: 13; Mark 8: 10; Acts 2: 10; 19: 1; 20: 2.

'Coasts,' *i. e.,* borders (see on 2: 16), is here an utterly erroneous translation of Wyc., Tyn., and followers, due to the generally received notion that our Lord never went beyond the bounds of Palestine; the word 'parts' never means 'borders.' Still, the term looks indefinite, and Mark 7: 24 says 'borders,' as Matthew also does in v. 22; so it might seem not certain that Jesus went farther than to the boundaries of Phoenicia. But while 'borders' often denotes the territory inclosed thereby, 'parts' cannot mean simply the boundary. And the question is settled by Mark 7: 31 (correct text), 'And again he went out from the borders of Tyre, and came through Sidon to the Sea of Galilee.' (See below on v. 29.) It is then certain that our Lord went into the heathen country of Phoenicia, the nearest part of which was about thirty miles from Capernaum. This does not conflict with the fact that his mission was exclusively to the Jews (v. 24), for he did not go there to exercise his ministry (Mark 7: 24), and as soon as he had been induced to work a miracle which would attract attention and gather crowds, he went away again. He entered into a house (Mark), and wished to stay there in seclusion, just as Elijah had done in the house of a widow at Zarephath, or Sarepta, in the same country of Phoenicia. (1 Kings 17: 9 ff.; Luke 4: 26.) He probably also desired bodily and mental rest for the disciples and himself, as on the first withdrawal not long before. (Mark 7: 31.) As to Tyre and Sidon, see on 11: 21. The two cities together denote the country of Phoenicia. He was probably at first in the southern part belonging to Tyre, and afterwards went northward through the Sidon district. (Mark 7: 31.) We learn from Mark 3: 8; Luke 6: 17, that multitudes from the region of Tyre and Sidon had attended on our Lord's ministry at an early period. It was a refreshing change for him and his disciples, in the hot weather of April or May, to leave the deep basin of the lake, so far below the level of the Mediterranean, and visit the mountain region of Phoenicia. (Comp. on 14: 13.)

22 f. And behold, calling attention to

23 But he answered her not a word. And his disciples came and besought him, saying, Send her away; for she crieth after us.

23 demon. But he answered her not a word. And his disciples came and besought him, saying, Send her

---

what follows as remarkable. **A woman of Canaan.** In the earliest times the people of Phoenicia are spoken of as Canaanites (Judg. 1:3 f.), *i. e.*, as belonging to the great tribe which occupied all the low lands, and which afterwards gave its name of Canaan to the whole land. It is probable that the Jews continued to apply this name to all the inhabitants of Phoenicia, though many of the later inhabitants may have been of different origin. To Matthew's Jewish readers this word would show that she was a Gentile. Mark, having Gentile readers mainly in view, says (7: 26) that she was a Greek, *i. e.*, a Gentile, and also that she was a Syrophoenician by race, a term probably used by way of distinction from the Libyphoenicians or Carthaginians. **Came out of the same coasts,** *i. e,*, that region or territory, as in 2: 16; 4: 13; 8: 34. This means that she came, not from Galilee, but from the country of Tyre, to the place where Jesus was. Many writers, even Weiss and Edersh., understand that she came out of Phoenicia into Galilee, which they suppose Jesus had not yet left; but this arises from the persistence of the old notion that he did not really enter Phoenicia. Edersh. imagines that Jesus kept the Passover here, consequently in a Jewish house; but his chronological scheme is at this and some other points quite forced. **Cried unto him, saying,** the correct text omits 'unto him.' The word denotes loud crying. **Crieth after us,** v. 23, *i. e.*, behind us, implies that she was following them along as they walked. It is easy to suppose that while staying at the house (Mark 7: 24), Jesus and his disciples were one day taking a walk, and that she having heard about him (Mark 7: 25), followed behind and cried aloud as they went on. Tisch. reads in Mark 'came in,' but it is evidently an "Alexandrian" alteration by some early critics who thought the scene of the interview was the house, not having duly considered Matthew. **Have mercy on me,** the word including also the idea of pity, which is here the prominent idea (see on 9: 27). She makes her child's case her own. **Lord,** see on 8: 2. It is not clear whether this was an expression of high respect, or possibly of worship. She

believed him to be the Messiah, as shown by her calling him **Son of David.** (Comp. on 9: 27.) Though a heathen, and living in a heathen country, she was yet near the land of Israel, familiar with the true religion, and like the woman of Zarephath, a worshiper of the true God. Perhaps she may have previously gone, among the many from Tyre and Sidon (Mark 3: 8), and attended the ministry of Jesus in Galilee. **My daughter is grievously vexed with a devil.** '*Badly demonized*' would be a literal rendering, though the Com. Ver. gives a more familiar English expression. 'Devil,' however, should be 'demon,' see on 8: 31: as to demoniacal possessions, see on 8: 28. Mark (7: 25, Rev. Ver) uses a diminutive term, meaning 'little daughter,' which shows that she was a child.

23 f. Here is a strong contrast; she cries aloud, he is absolutely silent. His reason for not answering appears below. The effect was to develop, strengthen, and manifest her faith (comp. on 9: 28). It is often so now; if with hearty confidence in the Lord's wisdom and mercy we continue to ask, we shall at last receive whatever he sees best for us, and besides may be improved in piety by the delay. The hearer of prayer is not less designing our good when he withholds or defers than when he "hears while we are yet speaking." **His disciples,** probably the Twelve, did not understand the wisdom and love of this apparent neglect. They were probably half touched and half annoyed by her loud and persistent cries, and perhaps also were uneasy lest she should draw attention to them, when they were wishing to remain in perfect retirement. So they **came,** lit., *came near* to Jesus and begged him to **send her away, because she crieth after us.** Some have thought they wished him simply to order her off, as troublesome and likely to attract to them the attention of others. But they had never seen him dismiss a suppliant in any other way than by doing what was asked; and that they desired him to grant her request is made plain by his answer, which is a reason why he should not grant it. Observe that this was an answer to the disciples, and not addressed to the woman. It is not clear that she heard it; for the state-

24 But he answered and said, I am not sent but unto the lost sheep of the house of Israel.
25 Then came she and worshipped him, saying, Lord, help me.
26 But he answered and said, It is not meet to take the children's bread, and to cast *it* to dogs.

24 away: for she crieth after us. But he answered and said, I was not sent but unto the lost sheep of the
25 house of Israel. But she came and worshipped him,
26 saying, Lord, help me. And he answered and said, It is not meet to take the children's [1] bread and cast

1 Or, *loaf.*

ment in v. 25, 'came and worshipped him,' implies that she had been following at some little distance, as does also the loud crying of v. 22 f. **I am** (or *was*) **not sent** (Rheims), like 'I came' in 5: 17, referring indefinitely to the time when the Father sent him forth to his mission in the world; he had no commission to go to any others, even as he had given the disciples none. (10:6.) Jesus here and elsewhere speaks of himself as subordinate to the Father, with reference to his official position and work as the God-man, the Mediator (comp. on 11: 27); this does not conflict with the idea that as the Eternal Son he is very God, and equal with the Father. (John 1:1; Rom. 9:5.) **But** (or *except*) **unto the lost sheep of the house of Israel,** see on 10: 6. He doubtless healed Gentile sick when brought to him in the land of Israel (4: 24 f.; 15: 30 f.; certainly in 8: 5 ff.); but now he had gone into a Gentile country, and must avoid entering upon a general ministry there. His ministry in Israel prepared the way for a blessing to the Gentiles. (Rom. 15: 8-10.) When his work was finished, then the apostles would be his "witnesses, both in Jerusalem, and in all Judea and Samaria, and unto the uttermost parts of the earth." (Acts 1: 8.) It would have conflicted with the nature and design of Christ's mission, had he anticipated this work of the apostles, though he alluded to it as a part of his own work. (John 10: 16.) The Jewish mind required slow preparation (as the history in Acts plainly shows) for the idea that Gentiles were to share freely the benefits of the Messianic reign; and the Jews would have been irritated and utterly repelled (Lutteroth), if their Messiah had at once begun a great work among the Gentiles. Jesus was induced to make an exception to the rule by this woman's great faith and humble importunity, as the prophets had sometimes done. (Luke 4: 25-27.) There is no objection to supposing him overcome by im-

portunity. But, in fact, this was hardly an exception, for her great faith brought her in some sense within the limits of his mission. (Gal. 3: 7.) Notice that v. 23 f. is found in Matt. only, who wrote especially for Jews, and desired to show that Jesus was the Messiah. Mark's Gentile readers would not at first have understood such a saying as v. 24, and would have been repelled by it.

25-27. The woman herself now comes. **Worshipped him,** bowing before him, probably prostrating herself, but not probably as to a Deity (comp. on 2: 2; 8: 2). The Greek imperfect tense (correct text) not only states that she did this, but *describes* her as so doing. Jesus puts before her the same idea he had just stated to the disciples, that the Messianic benefits were designed for the Jews, and purposely employs harsh expressions which will develop her faith and humility. He had produced a similar effect in the centurion by an opposite course. (8: 7.) The Jews looked upon themselves as God's 'children'; and spoke contemptuously of the Gentiles as 'dogs,' unclean and vile. (Comp. on 7: 6.) The Gentiles around were accustomed to this, and therefore the expression here was not altogether so offensive and painful as it would seem to us. So the Mohammedans call Christians infidel dogs. **It is not meet,** or good, proper (*kalon*), pleasing to the sense of propriety. Wyc., Rheims, Tyn., Gen., say 'good'; Cran. gave 'mete.' The woman's reply not only shows a high degree of faith and humility, but also does credit to her shrewdness and prompt intelligence—perhaps stimulated by maternal affection and solicitude—for she gives the harshly expressed refusal an admirable turn in her favor. **Truth** (or *yes*) **Lord, yet** (*for*) **the dogs eat of the crumbs.** She does not present an idea opposed to what he had said, as the incorrect rendering of Com. Ver., 'yet,'[1] would indicate, but a confirmation of it. Yes, Lord, it is not proper to take the children's

1 Wyc., Cran., Gen., have 'for,' Rheims exactly 'for . . . also.' Tyn. gave 'nevertheless,' and so Com. Ver. 'yet.' All but Rheims overlook the 'also.' B. and

Peshito omit the 'for,' apparently because the meaning was not perceived. In Mark 7: 28 it is also omitted by several other MSS. and versions, probably for the same

27 And she said, Truth, Lord: yet the dogs eat of the crumbs which fall from their masters' table.

28 Then Jesus answered and said unto her, O woman, great *is* thy faith: be it unto thee even as thou wilt. And her daughter was made whole from that very hour.

27 it to the dogs. But she said, Yea, Lord: for even the dogs eat of the crumbs which fall from their masters' table. Then Jesus answered and said unto

28 her, O woman, great is thy faith: be it done unto thee even as thou wilt. And her daughter was healed from that hour.

---

bread and throw it to the dogs, *for* the dogs too eat of the crumbs that fall from their master's table; they also have their lowly place, 'under the table' (Mark), and their lowly portion. The Jewish people, she is aware, have a special mission in the world, and special privileges; and of these they need not be deprived by her request, for a despised Gentile also may have an humble share of Messianic blessing. He is not now healing any in Israel, and the chosen people will lose no Messianic good by this one act of pity for her. (Comp. Mald., Weiss.) *Luther:* "Was not that a master stroke? She snares Christ in his own words." In Mark, what our Lord had said to her is introduced by the words, 'Let the children first be filled;' implying that afterwards the dogs might get something. This furnished all the more natural occasion for the turn she gave to her reply. The Greek term in v. 26 f. and Mark 7: 27 f. is a diminutive, and leads us to think of smaller dogs, allowed to run freely about the house and under the table. The diminutive must have been intentionally used here, for it is found nowhere else in the Greek Bible, while the common word occurs five times in New Test., and thirty-three times in Sept. Everywhere in the Bible dogs are spoken of as objects of dislike. In Tobit 5: 16, a dog is a companion, a thing very rarely the case in the East, where dogs run wild. It is hardly proper to suppose that 'little dogs' is here a term of affection; and Weiss' notion of lap-dogs, the children's pets, is a strange anachronism.— This heroine of faith is an example to all persons who are spiritually seeking Christ. Some after awhile grow despondent, and even fretful, as if badly treated, in that they do not succeed as others do. Let them learn from her humble perseverance.

28. O woman, more expressive than simply 'woman.' **Great is thy faith.** The world is ever admiring and lauding greatness, but it is great intellect or imagination, great ambition or force of character, beauty or amiability, great learning or discoveries, possessions or conquests; here is the noblest praise for the truest greatness. The centurion's faith likewise excited the wonder of Jesus (see on 8: 10), and he too was a heathen. **Be it unto thee,** or *let it come to pass for thee;* the same phrase as in 8: 13 and 6: 10. The expression in Mark 7: 29 may have immediately followed that given in Matt. **As thou wilt.** *Trench:* "He who at first seemed as though he would have denied her the smallest boon, now opens to her the full treasure-house of his grace, and bids her to help herself, to carry away what she will. He had shown to her for awhile, like Joseph to his brethren, the aspect of severity; but, like Joseph, he could not maintain it long—or rather he would not maintain it an instant longer than was needful, and after that word of hers, that mighty word of an undoubting faith, it was needful no more." Our Lord does not speak of her humility, though so remarkable, for that was a result of her faith. Perhaps the earliest offspring of unbelief is pride (1 Tim. 3: 6), while faith at once gives birth to humility; and in both cases, the progeny reinforces the parent. So, too, her faith had led to perseverance—a perseverance which may be compared with that of Jacob, in wrestling with the same Eternal Word (Gen. 32: 24), who was now permanently incarnate as Jesus. **From that very hour,** comp. 8: 13; 9: 22.—The so-called Clementine homilies (end of second century), in telling this story, call the woman Justa, and her daughter Bernice, which names may have been either invented or traditional.

HOMILETICAL AND PRACTICAL.

V. 21. Jesus withdrawing. 1) From what? (a) From the jealousy of Herod. (b) From the machinations of the Jewish rulers. (c) From the fanatical designs of some who counted themselves his followers. 2) In what spirit? Personal prudence. Patient forbear-

---

reason. Why should it have been inserted if not originally present in either Gospel? How then should W H. bracket 'for' in Matt.? Yet it may be spurious in Mark.

The Greek word means in English either 'also' (too), or 'even,' according to the connection.

29 And Jesus departed from thence, and came nigh
unto the sea of Galilee ; and went up into a mountain,
and sat down there.
30 And great multitudes came unto him, having with
them *those that were* lame, blind, dumb, maimed, and
many others, and cast them down at Jesus' feet; and
he healed them:

29   And Jesus departed thence, and came nigh unto
    the sea of Galilee ; and he went up into the moun-
30 tain, and sat there. And there came unto him
    great multitudes, having with them the lame, blind,
    dumb, maimed, and many others, and they cast

ance. 3) Still everywhere doing good, 14: 14;
15: 28-30; 17: 18. 4) At last, when his hour
is come, he will withdraw no longer, John 12:
23.—V. 22-28. The Canaanitish woman. 1)
Believes in the Jewish Messiah, v. 22. 2)
Humbly submits to be harshly spoken to by
him, v. 26. 3) Shrewdly converts refusal
into a new plea, v. 27. 4) Gains her cause,
and wins the highest possible commendation.
v. 28.—V. 28. Great faith. 1) Seen in a
heathen; compare centurion. (8: 10.) 2) Attended by great humility (comp. Luke 18:
13), and producing great perseverance. (Comp.
Luke 18: 7). 3) Recognized and rewarded by
him who knows the heart. John 2: 24 f.—V. 22.
A mother making her child's case her own.
—V. 23. Disciples seeming kinder than their
Lord. HENRY: "There may be love in
Christ's heart while there are frowns in his
face."—V. 24. HALL: "We need no other
rule of life than the intention of our several
stations; and if he that was God would take
no further scope to himself than the limits of
his commission, how much doth it concern us
frail men to keep within compass."—V. 25.
CHRYS.: "She was the more instant. But it
is not so with us; rather, when we fail to obtain, we desist; whereas it ought to make us
the more urgent." THEOPHYL.: "Consider
that even if holy men pray for us, as the apostles did for her, yet we ourselves, praying for
ourselves, accomplish more."—V. 27. Maternal shrewdness turning the Saviour's argument against him. HENRY: "Unbelief is
apt to draw dismal conclusions even from
comfortable premises (Judg. 13: 22 f.); but faith
can find encouragement even in that which
is discouraging, and get nearer to God by
taking hold on that hand which is stretched
out to push it away."—V. 23-28. Jesus glad
to be overcome, by intercession, by personal
entreaty, by argument.

15: 29 to 16: 4.—JESUS FEEDS THE FOUR
THOUSAND, SOUTHEAST OF THE LAKE, AND
RETURNS TO GALILEE.

This is found also in Mark 7: 31 to 8: 13.
And Jesus departed from thence. We
have no means of knowing how long he

stayed in the country of Tyre; certainly not
very long, for all the journeys of ch. 15 to 18
occupied less than six months. (See on 15: 1,
and on 19: 1.) Mark (7: 31) says, in the correct text, that, 'he went out from the borders
of Tyre, and came through Sidon unto the Sea
of Galilee, through the midst of the borders
of Decapolis.' This shows that in leaving the
territory of Tyre he went northwards through
the territory of Sidon, or through the city
itself, the expression being in this case ambiguous. We have no information concerning the rest of his sojourn in Phoenicia. Next,
he must have passed eastward across the
Jordan, and then southward, until, going
through the district of the Ten Cities, Decapolis (see on 4: 25), he came to the shores of the
lake, somewhere on its southeastern border.
(For description of the Lake of Galilee, see
on 4: 18.) This region also was out of Herod's
jurisdiction, like those to which he had previously withdrawn. (14: 13; 15: 21.) The desire to
keep out of Herod's territory at that time may
have caused him to take the circuit just described, instead of going direct from Tyre
through Galilee and crossing the lake. He
appears not to have stopped in the neighborhood of Cesarea Philippi, probably through
desire to revisit the environs of the lake; but
soon the malignant attack of the Pharisees
and Sadducees will make him go away again.
(16: 4.) He was now in the vicinity of Gadara
(one of the Ten Cities), the same region in
which he had healed the two demoniacs, and
suffered the legion of evil spirits to destroy the
swine. (8: 28 ff.) This time his ministry produces a greater impression, perhaps through
the testimony of the restored demoniac. (Luke
8: 39.) Persons from Decapolis had followed
him long before. (4: 25.) **And went up into
a** (*the*) **mountain,** the mountain range
running along east of the lake. (Comp. John
6: 3.) The mountain of Matt. 5: 1 was on
the western side of the lake. The more northern part of this easterly range was the place
of feeding the Five Thousand (see on 14: 13),
and now a similar miracle is wrought on its
more southern part. **And sat down there,**

31 Insomuch that the multitude wondered, when they saw the dumb to speak, the maimed to be whole, the lame to walk, and the blind to see: and they glorified the God of Israel.
32 Then Jesus called his disciples *unto him*, and said, I have compassion on the multitude, because they continue with me now three days, and have nothing to eat: and I will not send them away fasting, lest they faint in the way.
33 And his disciples say unto him, Whence should we have so much bread in the wilderness, as to fill so great a multitude?
34 And Jesus saith unto them, How many loaves have ye? And they said, Seven, and a few little fishes.
35 And he commanded the multitude to sit down on the ground.

31 them down at his feet: and he healed them: insomuch that the multitude wondered, when they saw the dumb speaking, the maimed whole, and the lame walking, and the blind seeing: and they glorified the God of Israel.
32 And Jesus called unto him his disciples, and said, I have compassion on the multitude, because they continue with me now three days and have nothing to eat: and I would not send them away fasting, lest haply they faint in the way. And the disciples say unto him, Whence should we have so many loaves in a desert place, as to fill so great a multitude? And Jesus saith unto them, How many loaves have ye? And they said, Seven, and a few small fishes. And he commanded the multitude to sit down on the ground; and he took the seven

the usual posture of a teacher. (See on 5: 1.)

30 f. Here, seated on a point in the mountain range, probably in view of the lake, he wrought many miracles of healing, and again fed the multitudes. In this case a large proportion of those present must have been Gentiles, as the Ten Cities were more a Gentile than a Jewish district. He must have spent at least several days in this region, since it required some time for his presence to become generally known, and the Four Thousand had been 'three days' (v. 32) in close attendance on his ministry. **Great multitudes,** literally, *many crowds,* as in so many other passages. We have here another general account of numerous miracles. (Comp. 4: 23; 8: 16; 9: 35; 12: 15 f.) One of those wrought at this time and place was the healing of a deaf and dumb man, described by Mark alone. (7: 32-37.) The order of the words **lame, blind,** etc. (v. 30), varies greatly in different documents, having doubtless been affected by v. 31; but this is a matter of no consequence. The word rendered **maimed** signifies crooked, bent, contracted; it is sometimes applied to cases of mutilation, the loss of some part of the body (18: 8), which is the meaning of our word maimed, but is not often so used, and probably the best English word here would be 'crippled.' Malchus' ear (26: 51) is the only recorded instance of our Lord's miraculously restoring a missing part of the body. **And many others.** The kinds of diseases were so numerous that they could not all be named. Matthew appears to have selected those associated with predictions of Messiah. (See on 11: 5.)

Cast them down at his feet, implies not carelessness, but hurry and bustle amid the crowd of applicants. 'His feet' was easily changed by copyists into 'the feet of Jesus.' (Comp. on 14: 14.)[1] **The dumb to speak;** *speaking,* etc., is the literal translation. (So Wyc.) **And they glorified the God of Israel.** In 9: 8 it is simply 'and they glorified God.' But it was natural to mention that these heathen people glorified 'the God of Israel.'

32-38. Comp. on the similar feeding of the Five Thousand, 14: 15-21. **I have compassion,** as in 9: 36. **Three days.** They had no doubt brought some food with them, which was now exhausted. They showed great zeal to see and hear and be healed, remaining so long in the thinly inhabited region, sleeping on the ground two nights in the open air, living on the food brought with them, and slow to leave when it was gone. **And I will not** (or *am not willing to*) **send them away fasting.** ('I would not,' Rev. Ver., is hardly an improvement upon 'I will not'; it removes a possible ambiguity, but seems to suggest a condition.) Some of them were from a distance. (Mark 8: 3.) **His** (*the*) **disciples** (v. 33), 'his' being easily added from v. 32. **So much bread,** literally, *so many loaves,* for the Greek is plural. **In the wilderness,** or *a desert place,* a wild country with few inhabitants, see on 14: 13 and 3: 1. Only a region containing large towns could at short notice furnish food for such a multitude, and this wild country was a good many miles from the nearest cities of Decapolis. **A few little fishes.** The diminutive form emphasizes the

[1] 'The multitude' (v. 31) is changed in most documents into 'the multitudes,' evidently because the participle rendered 'when they saw' is plural (following a singular "noun of multitude"), and because 'great multitudes' have been mentioned in v. 30. This manifestly altered reading is given by B, which also omits 'for' in v. 27 and 'now' in v. 32—three unquestionable errors in close connection. In like manner the correct reading is, 'the multitude' in v. 35, but 'the multitudes' in v. 36, and much confusion arose in the copies.

36 And he took the seven loaves and the fishes, and gave thanks, and brake *them*, and gave to his disciples, and the disciples to the multitude.
37 And they did all eat, and were filled: and they took up of the broken *meat* that was left seven baskets full.
38 And they that did eat were four thousand men, beside women and children.

36 loaves and the fishes; and he gave thanks and brake, and gave to the disciples, and the disciples to the
37 multitudes. And they did all eat, and were filled: and they took up that which remained over of the
38 broken pieces, seven baskets full. And they that did eat were four thousand men, beside women and

---

fact that the supply was meagre; in v. 36 it is the common word for 'fishes.' Here again the people are commanded to recline on the ground, and probably in companies and rows as before (Mark 6: 39 f.), though nothing is here said of it. **Seven baskets full.** In this case the number of baskets corresponds to the number of loaves; in the previous case (14: 20) to the number of apostles. *Euthym.:* "Showing that it is easy for him to do as he wishes." In Mark 8: 19 f. our Lord seems to treat it as a matter of importance that such a quantity of broken pieces remained in each case. **Beside women and children,** mentioned by Matt. only, as before in 14: 21.

This miracle is recorded both by Matthew and Mark, and the former miraculous feeding by all four of the Evangelists. And shortly after (16: 9), we find it recorded both by Matt. and Mark that our Lord referred to the two miracles as separately teaching the same lesson. This conclusively shows that strikingly similar events did occur in our Lord's history, a thing to be remembered with reference to the two visits to Nazareth, the two instances of cleansing the temple, the two women who anointed Jesus, the parable of the pounds and that of the talents, etc, where it happens that the two events or discourses are recorded only by different Evangelists; and some expositors jump to the conclusion that they are nothing but varying and conflicting accounts of the same matter. If the feeding of five thousand with five loaves had been recorded only by one Gospel, and that of four thousand with seven loaves only by one or two others, it would have been most confidently asserted that these were the same miracle. Let us neither be nervous harmonizers, nor eager to assume that harmonizing is impossible. It is worth observing how natural in these two miracles are the points of agreement, and how striking are some of the differences. It was natural that the situation should in both cases be the wild country, where sufficient food could not be obtained from ordinary sources; that the kind of food multiplied should be that which

was common on the shores of the lake; that Jesus should 'bless' or 'give thanks' before breaking the bread, according to custom, and should distribute the food by the help of the disciples, a matter of obvious convenience and propriety. On the other hand, the precise locality in the wild country is different in the two cases; there is now, in the parched summer, no mention of reclining on the grass, as Matthew, Mark, and John, all mention in the former case, when it was spring; the supply of food is here greater than before, while the number of persons is smaller; the people here have remained three days; in the other case only one day. There is also a slight, but quite remarkable difference as to the word rendered 'basket.' This is *kophinos* in all four Gospels in the first miracle, and *spuris* (or *sphuris*) in both Gospels here; and in the subsequent mention of these miracles (16: 9 f.; Mark 8: 19 f.) it is again in both Gospels *kophinos* with reference to the first, and *spuris* with reference to the second miracle. We do not know the precise difference between the two words, but the careful observance of the distinction throughout, strikingly shows how entirely distinct the two miracles were. Origen and Chrys. suppose that the *spuris* was somewhat large, and this seems confirmed by its use in lowering Paul from the wall of Damascus (Acts 9: 25), while the *kophinos* appears to have been a small provision basket, such as a Jew on a journey commonly carried with him (see on 14: 20). The disciples may have now had these large baskets because they had been making a long journey.

The strange thing about this second miracle is the fact that the apostles do not recur (v. 33) to the former miraculous feeding, which took place but a short time before. Many critics have thought this utterly inexplicable, and on this ground have denied the reality of the second miracle, though explicitly and repeatedly affirmed. But let us remember. Our Lord had sternly rebuked the crowd who shared in the previous feeding for following him the next day with the hope of being fed

39 And he sent away the multitude, and took ship, and came into the coasts of Magdala.

39 children. And he sent away the multitudes, and entered into the boat, and came into the borders of Magadan.

CHAPTER XVI.

THE Pharisees also with the Sadducees came, and tempting desired him that he would shew them a sign from heaven.

1 And the Pharisees and Sadducees came, and trying him asked him to show them a sign from heaven.

---

again (John 6: 26), and had been much displeased at the popular determination produced by that miracle to make him a king. Nay, he had hurried the disciples themselves unwillingly away, partly, it is probable, because they sympathized with this popular design. (See on 14: 22.) In this state of things the disciples might naturally doubt whether he would repeat a miracle which had been formerly attended by such undesirable results, and might at any rate feel great delicacy about suggesting the idea that he should do so. (Comp. Mark 9: 32, "were afraid to ask him.") But as soon as he intimates such an intention, by asking how many loaves they have, they express no surprise nor doubt, but go on to carry out the details.

And he sent away the multitudes, see on 14: 22 f. **And took ship,** literally, *entered into the boat,* see on 4: 21. The boat which they were accustomed to use may have been brought from Capernaum, while they were staying here on the S. E. side. **Into the coasts of Magdala,** or *borders of Magadan.*[1] This is unquestionably the correct reading, which was early changed to Magdala, a familiar name, easily connecting itself with Mary Magdalene. The position of Magadan is unknown, as is that of Dalmanutha. (Mark 8: 10.) They appear to have been on the western side of the lake, being reached by boat from the other side, and especially because from them the party crossed to the northeastern side. (16: 5; Mark 8: 13.)

Ch. 16: 1. That which follows occurred at Magadan, somewhere on the western side of the lake. **The Pharisees also, with the Sadducees.** Here, as in 3: 7, there is but one article (literally, *the Pharisees and Sadducees*), presenting the Sadducees as accompanying the Pharisees, and perhaps as of less importance; so also in 16: 6, 11 f. The Sadducees appear only three times in the Gospel history; (1) witnessing the baptism of John, 3: 7, (2) tempting Jesus here, (3) tempting him, not at the same time with the Pharisees, but separately, in 22: 23. (Mark 12: 18; Luke 20: 27.) They are also spoken of by Jesus in 16: 6, 11 f., and are mentioned nowhere else in the Gospels. Only a few weeks before, and not more than a few miles away, Jesus had severely censured the Pharisees as hypocrites and violators of God's word (15: 6, 7) and had spoken of them as blind guides of the people, unworthy of notice. Yet the dissembled hostility here indicated was not first awakened by that censure, for they had already accused him of being in league with Beelzebub. (12: 24.) Some critics think it incredible that Sadducees should

---

[1] Magadan is read by א B, D, Old Syriac, and Jerus. Syriac, Old Latin (majority of copies), and Vulgate, and by Jerome and Augustine. The reason for changing to Magdala is obvious, while we can imagine no reason for a change in the opposite direction to an unknown name. So Herod. II. 159 (comp. Rawlinson, "Great Empires," III. 48 n.) changes Megiddo into Magdolon, a natural Greek form of Magdala. As meaning 'tower,' this word would very readily become the name of a town (Exod. 14: 2; Josh. 15: 37; 19: 38), comp. Magdala, the present capital of Abyssinia. There is now a place called Mejdel (containing a few huts), on the western shore of the Lake of Gal., which was probably the home of Mary. The Heb. Migdol, Aram. Magdala, Arab. Megdel (g, soft), are exactly characteristic forms for the three languages. Magdalan, found in C., Memph., etc., seems to have been an intermediate "Alexandrian" alteration of Magadan, and Magdala the "Syrian"

alteration. In Mark (8: 10) Dalmanutha is in a good many documents changed to Magadan, and in a few to Magdala. Caspari would identify Magadan and Dalmanutha with a Wady and town far down the Jordan valley. But in both Gospels the party came by boat to those places, and presently go from them by boat "to the other side" (northeastern side); how can these expressions suit places some twelve to twenty miles south of the lake? Canon Cook argues ("Bib. Comm.," followed by Edersh.) that Dalmanutha was not in Gal., because the Phar. came forth (Mark 8: 11) to seek a sign, viz., out of their district (Gal.) into another district. But it more naturally means, out of their town or dist. to meet him as he approached, comp. 25: 1; 26: 55; Luke 8: 35; 15: 28; John 18: 4. Nothing is known about the statement of Eus. and Jerome ("Onom.", with express reference to this passage) that "there is now the district of Magedane near Gerasa."

2 He answered and said unto them, When it is evening, ye say, *It will be* fair weather: for the sky is red.
3 And in the morning, *It will be* foul weather to day: for the sky is red and lowering. O *ye* hypocrites, ye can discern the face of the sky; but can ye not *discern* the signs of the times?
4 A wicked and adulterous generation seeketh after a sign; and there shall no sign be given unto it, but the sign of the prophet Jonas. And he left them, and departed.

2 But he answered and said unto them, [1] When it is evening, ye say, *It will be* fair weather: for the heaven is red. And in the morning, *It will be* foul weather to-day: for the heaven is red and lowering. Ye know how to discern the face of the heaven;
4 but ye cannot *discern* the signs of the times. An evil and adulterous generation seeketh after a sign; and there shall no sign be given unto it, but the sign of Jonah. And he left them, and departed.

[1] The following words, to the end of ver. 3, are omitted by some of the most ancient and other important authorities.

have come with Pharisees. But they were temporarily united by common hostility to Jesus. Comp. Herod and Pilate, Luke 23: 12, and Psalm 2: 2. **Tempting** (American Revisers would render 'trying him'), testing him (comp. on 4: 1, 7), with the hope that he will not stand the test, will not be able to show the sign; comp. 19: 3; 22: 18, 35. The Scribes and Pharisees had asked a sign from him in 12: 38, and were refused. Now the Pharisees and Sadducees make a similar demand specifically for a 'sign from heaven' (so also Mark 8: 11), and get (v. 4) exactly the same refusal as before. (12: 39.) They might be thinking of such signs as when Moses gave bread from heaven (Psalm 78: 23 ff.; John 6: 30 f.), Joshua made the sun and moon stand still, Samuel brought thunder and rain in time of harvest, Elijah repeatedly called down fire from heaven, and at Isaiah's word the shadow went back on the dial; comp. Joel 2: 30 ff. Origen conjectures that they regarded signs on earth as wrought in Beelzebul. (12: 24.) Probably some Jews really expected celestial signs of Messiah's approach; but the present request was made from bad motives. Jesus promised "great signs from heaven" in connection with his second coming (24: 29 f.; Luke 21: 11, 25; comp. Rev. 15: 1), and predicted that the false Christs would show great signs. (24: 24.)

2 f. This passage (except the opening words, **He answered and said unto them**), is quite certainly not a part of Matt. It is

wanting in a number of the earliest documents (MSS., versions and Fathers);[1] no reason can be imagined for its omission, and it may readily have come from Luke 12: 54-56, where the closing and principal expression is substantially the same, and the difference consists simply in using other signs of the weather. As the passage is retained by Rev. Ver., we mention that Wet. cites from Greek and Roman writers, these and various other signs of the weather; and that these signs hold good in England and in our country, being expressed by the saying, "Red sky at night is the shepherd's delight; Red sky in the morning is the shepherd's warning," which probably came to us from England. The *signs of the times* (*seasons*) would be the various indications then observable that the Messianic epoch was at hand, indications in the civil and religious condition of Israel, the fulfillment of Messianic prophecies, and the miracles wrought by Jesus and his followers. The other terms of the passage as inserted in Matt. call for no explanation. Even of the documents containing the passage, several of the best omit **hypocrites** (v. 3), evidently drawn from Luke 12: 56.

4. This repeats his former reply to a similar demand, 12: 38-40, and so on probably a later occasion, Luke 11: 29 f. Some critics cannot believe that Jesus would several times repeat the same thing; but see Int. to ch. 5. **Of the prophet Jonas**, or, *Jonah*. To Jonah was

---

[1] Wanting in ℵ B, V, X, Γ, and a dozen cursives, in Old Syriac, Memph. (a codex), and Armenian. Origen, the great critic, in his commentary on Matt., begins the reply of Jesus with our v. 4, making no allusion to any such passage as that in question. Jerome says, "This is not found in the majority of copies." Nobody, orthodox or heretic, could have had any objection to the passage. We cannot well suppose it omitted by assimilation to Mark (Meyer), for the copyists usually assimilated by inserting. Morison fancies it omitted by some copyist who did not find these signs of weather holding good in his locality; but this essentially im-

probable notion will not account for its absence in so many documents from different parts of the world. There is no difficulty in supposing it to have come from Luke (where all documents have the corresponding passage), when we observe that the main statement is the same, and only the particular signs of the weather have been altered by the memory of the student who first placed it on the margin of Matt., whence it would creep into the text. It is therefore quite unnecessary to suppose (Hort) a separate saying of Jesus preserved by tradition.

5 And when his disciples were come to the other side, they had forgotten to take bread.

6 Then Jesus said unto them, Take heed and beware of the leaven of the Pharisees and of the Sadducees.

5 And the disciples came to the other side, and for-
6 got to take ¹ bread. And Jesus said unto them, Take heed and beware of the leaven of the Phari-

---

1 Gr, *loaves.*

---

easily added 'the prophet' (common Greek text) from 12: 39. Mark (8: 12) records only the general refusal to give a sign, without mentioning the exception, the sign of Jonah, and states that in replying he "sighed deeply in his spirit." Jesus is beginning to find it hard to endure such perverse and malignant opposition (comp. 17: 17). **Left them and departed** (comp. 21: 17). *Bengel:* "Just severity." One of our Lord's reasons for pre-viously withdrawing from Galilee had been the hostility of the Pharisees (see on 15: 21). So now again he withdraws to the neighbor-hood of Cesarea Philippi, the region farthest removed from Jerusalem and its hypocritical and malignant parties (15: 1). It is not likely that he remained at Magadan longer than a day or two.

HOMILETICAL AND PRACTICAL.

V. 29–31. New fields and new labors ; comp. Acts 10 : 38.—V. 32. RYLE : "It is a curious and striking fact that of all the feelings expressed by our Lord upon earth, there is none so often mentioned as compassion. His joy, his sor-row, his thankfulness, his anger, his wonder, his zeal, are all occasionally recorded. But none of these feelings are so frequently men-tioned as compassion." HENRY : "Our Lord Jesus keeps an account how long his followers continue their attendance on him, and takes notice of the difficulty they sustain in it. (Rev. 2 : 2.)"—V. 33. HENRY : "Forgetting former experience leaves us under present doubts."—Ch. 16: 1. ORIGEN : "Often now also we see persons who hold the most discordant opinions in philosophy or other matters, seem-ing to harmonize that they may mock at and war against Jesus Christ in his disciples."—V. 1, 4. Signs. 1) Even our Lord's early signs convinced Nicodemus and his friends. (John 3 : 2.) 2) The many signs of the next two years did not satisfy malignant opposers (v. 1), and were even ascribed by them to Beelzebul. (12 : 24.) 3) Captious demands for special signs he al-ways refused. (v. 4 ; comp. Luke 4 : 23.) 4) Even the sign of Jonah (v. 4), when it came in his resur-rection, while a conclusive proof, was rejected

by many. (28 : 15 ; Acts 25 : 19.) 5) Even years af-terwards the Jews demanded fresh signs, but the 'called' found Christ crucified the power of God. (1 Cor. 1 : 22 ff.)

16: 5-20. JESUS WITHDRAWS TO THE NEIGHBORHOOD OF CESAREA PHILIPPI. PETER'S GREAT CONFESSION.

This is found also in Mark 8: 13–30, and the latter part in Luke 9: 18–21. Luke has passed over everything since the feeding of the five thousand, and here also is very brief. This is the last and most important of our Lord's four withdrawals from Galilee during the last six months of his ministry in that region (comp. 14: 13; 15: 21, 29), and will continue to 17: 20.

I. **5-12.** CONVERSATION ON THE WAY. **To the other side,** of the lake, as in 8: 18–28; 14: 22, always meaning the eastern side. Mark presently mentions (8: 22) that they came to Bethsaida (viz., Julias), and after-wards went to Cesarea Philippi. So the first point reached by boat was on the northeast-ern side of the lake. **Forgotten;** rather *for-got* (Wyc., Rheims), is the literal translation, natural here in English and still more so in Greek. It probably means that they forgot in preparing the boat, and on reaching the other side became aware of the forgetting; or it may mean that upon landing they forgot to supply themselves for the journey. **To take bread**—or *loaves*—except a single one (Mark), which amounted to nothing. . The seven great baskets of fragments from the miracle were probably given to the multitude for future use, or to the poor of Magadan. After dis-covering their negligence and destitution, the disciples felt an annoyance which led them to a singular blunder. Jesus meantime was think-ing of the Pharisees and Sadducees, from whose obduracy and malignity he had just with-drawn. (16 : 4.) These great politico-religious par-ties (see on 3 : 7) had immense influence. The disciples had been reared to respect them, and so Jesus takes occasion to give a warning against their teachings and influence. **The leaven of the Pharisees and of the Sadducees.** Mark has (8 : 15) 'the leaven of the Phar., and

7 And they reasoned among themselves, saying, *It is* because we have taken no bread.

8 *Which* when Jesus perceived, he said unto them, O ye of little faith, why reason ye among yourselves, because ye have brought no bread?

9 Do ye not yet understand, neither remember the five loaves of the five thousand, and how many baskets ye took up?

7 sees and Sadducees. And they reasoned among 8 themselves, saying, [1] We took no [2] bread. And Jesus perceiving it said, O ye of little faith, why reason ye among yourselves, because ye have no [2] bread? 9 Do ye not yet perceive, neither remember the five loaves of the five thousand, and how many [3] baskets

---

1 Or, It is *because we took no bread*....2 Gr. *loaves*....3 *Basket* in ver. 9 and 10 represents different Greek words.

---

the leaven of Herod.' Some have "inferred" that Herod Antipas was a Sadducee, notwithstanding in 14: 2 he expressed belief that John the Baptist was risen from the dead. But Mark has also omitted the Sadducees in 8: 11, as to asking a sign from heaven, and indeed mentions them only in 12: 18. This fact will account for his omitting them here. We thus understand that besides the Phar. and Sadd. Jesus spoke also of Herod, whose jealousy (14: 2) had been one cause of his repeatedly withdrawing from Galilee, even as now again he is going to the dominions of the tetrarch Philip. Mark's expression indicates the leaven of Herod as distinct from that of the Phar. Matthew by not repeating 'leaven,' and by having only one article (see on 16: 1), suggests something common to the Phar. and Sadd., not necessarily some common tenet or specific teaching, but a common hurtful tendency. It is therefore idle to say that Jesus is here represented as confounding the rival parties. Nor is this passage in conflict with 23: 3, for much of what the Scribes and Phar. taught was correct, and proper to be observed. Leaven was regarded in the law as symbolically impure (Exod. 34: 25; Levit. 2: 11), and hence the figure in 1 Cor. 5: 6 f. and here; see also Luke 12: 1, where it is used in a different connection, and probably on a later occasion. The disciples were in no mood for figurative and spiritual meanings of words (comp. John 4: 10 ff.; 6: 26). They took it all literally, supposing that the Master had observed their lack of bread, and was cautioning them not to purchase any loaves made with the kind of leaven used by the Phar. and Sadd. This seems to the modern mind a strange and almost impossible notion; but it was just such a matter as the Rabbis made much of. The Talmud contains discussions as to whether it was right to use Gentile leaven. (Lightf.)[1] So the

disciples reproach themselves. **Because we have taken no bread** (*loaves*), is an abrupt phrase natural to persons disconcerted. The word rendered in Com. Ver. (and Rev. Ver. *margin*) 'because' is very often the mere 'that' after a verb of saying, which in English is not used when the exact words are quoted. It is best so to understand here (Rev. Ver.) but the marginal rendering is quite possible, and is preferred by Meyer.

8-12. The Master rebukes them for supposing that he was concerning himself about kinds of food. A few weeks or months before, he had said (15: 1), "Not that which entereth into the mouth defileth the man"; how then could he be laying stress on a particular kind of leaven? And the repeated miracles of feeding vast multitudes from a very little food, and leaving a large surplus, ought certainly to have showed them that the mere lack of bread would cause him no concern. Only because they were **of little faith** (6: 30; 8: 26; 14: 31) did they imagine such a thing. Mark gives still sharper expressions. Notice the connection here between faith and spiritual perception. (v. 8 f.) With stronger faith in him they would have been lifted above temporal anxiety, and in better condition to understand his spiritual instructions. **Ye have** (v. 8) was easily changed into 'ye took' (rendered by Com. Ver. 'ye have brought'), to make it like v. 7. **Not yet,** comp. 15: 16; and Mark 6: 52. **Understand**—(or *perceive*), v. 9-11 (Tyn., Gen.,) as in 15: 17; in v. 8 it represents another word, which is awkward, but in this case cannot well be helped, for the literal 'knowing' or 'having known' would be misunderstood. In v. 11 the text in Rev. Ver., which is that of the earliest documents, seemed abrupt, and was variously changed, finally, into the form given in Com. Ver. In the true text, after rebuking them for failing

---

[1] Keim coolly sets aside the story, saying, "This gross and altogether inconceivable misunderstanding could not have occurred." One might have thought that such arrogant and superficial criticism could not have occurred, in the case of an able, learned, and earnest man.

10 Neither the seven loaves of the four thousand, and how many baskets ye took up?
11 How is it that ye do not understand that I spake *it* not to you concerning bread, that ye should beware of the leaven of the Pharisees and of the Sadducees?
12 Then understood they how that he bade *them* not beware of the leaven of bread, but of the doctrine of the Pharisees and of the Sadducees.
13 When Jesus came into the coasts of Cesarea Philippi, he asked his disciples, saying, Whom do men say that I, the Son of man, am?

10 ye took up? Neither the seven loaves of the four
11 thousand, and how many ¹baskets ye took up? How is it that ye do not perceive that I spake not to you concerning ²bread? But beware of the leaven of
12 the Pharisees and Sadducees. Then understood they how that he bade them not beware of the leaven of ² bread, but of the teaching of the Pharisees and Sadducees.
13 Now when Jesus came into the parts of Cæsarea Philippi he asked his disciples, saying, Who do men

1 *Baskets* in ver. 9 and 10 represents different Greek words....2 Gr. *loaves.*

to perceive, he repeats the counsel, in order that they might now look at it and understand; and so they did. **Understood** (v. 12), as in 15: 10, 16. **Doctrine**—literally *teaching* —see on 7: 28 and 8: 19, not simply their dogmas, as 'doctrine' would now suggest, but the whole spirit and tendency of their teaching. The Pharisees and Sadducees taught ideas concerning religious truth and duty in general, and in particular concerning the Messianic reign, which to the apostles would be misleading and corrupting. Herod represented a certain type of politico-religious opinion, accepted by the Herodians, which would also be quite misleading for proclaimers of the spiritual Messianic reign. This warning, while suggested by the recent demand of the Pharisees and Sadducees (16: 1), was a preparation for the great approaching instruction concerning Messiah's true mission.

After crossing the lake Jesus came to Bethsaida (see on 14: 13), and there healed a blind man; a very interesting case, recorded by Mark alone. (8: 22-6.)

II. **13-20.** PETER'S GREAT CONFESSION, AND OUR LORD'S SIGNAL RESPONSE. Here Luke comes in (9: 18), though both he and Mark are brief, and fail to give the *response.* The narrative in Matt. and Mark goes right on, and there is no reason to question the continuity of events. **Into the coasts** (*parts.*) Wyclif here had 'partis,' but Tyn. introduced the erroneous 'coasts,' see on 15: 21. Mark (8: 27) has the more definite expression 'the villages of Cesarea Philippi'; he was tarrying in the suburban villages. **Cesarea Philippi** was at the nothern end of Palestine, being near Dan ("from Dan to Beersheba"). It lay beside the eastern and least copious of the two chief springs of the Jordan; at the other spring, two and a half miles west was Dan; below the junction of their streams there comes in another, not mentioned by Josephus, which has flowed

many miles from far up the slope of Hermon, and is really the remotest source of the river. The town was in an elevated plain, one thousand one hundred and fifty feet above the level of the Mediterranean, and near the foot of Mount Hermon, which rises seven or eight thousand feet higher still. A mile east (McGarvey), stands "a precipitous rock, at least a thousand feet above the town," crowned by a singularly strong fortress, dating from before the time of Christ, and in its present dimensions from the Saracens and the Crusaders. Stanley and others imagine that our Lord was led by this to use the phrase, "On this rock I will build my church." The plain or terrace on which the city stood is very beautiful. *Porter:* "It is covered with oaks and olive-trees, having green glades and clumps of hawthorn and myrtle." Many travelers speak of encamping under noble shade trees just north of the town. *Tristram* (in Edersh.): "Everywhere there is a wild medley of cascades, mulberry-trees, fig-trees, dashing torrents, festoons of vines, bubbling fountains, reeds, and ruins, and the mingled music of birds and waters." The fields between and around the sources of the Jordan are very fertile, producing breadstuffs and rice; and (Keim) "in summer the whole district is a sea of flowers, whence the bees gather a rich harvest." Josephus ("Ant.," 15, 10, 3) calls the fountain Panion, showing that the Greeks here worshiped Pan, whose worship was often associated with caves and grottos; and there are Greek inscriptions on the face of the cliff to the same effect. Probably the Phoenicians had here worshiped one of the forms of Baal, for Robinson argues that here was the town of "Baal-gad, in the valley of Lebanon, under Mount Hermon." (Josh. 11:17.) Herod the Great built, near the fountain, a temple of white marble, in honor of Augustus. Philip, the tetrarch (see on 2: 20 and 11: 6), enlarged the town and called it Cesarea, in honor of

14 And they said, Some *say that thou art* John the Baptist; some, Elias; and others, Jeremias, or one of the prophets.

14 say [1] that the Son of man is? And they said, Some *say*, John the Baptist; some, Elijah; and others,

: 1 Many ancient authorities read, *that I the Son of man am.* See Mark viii. 27; Luke ix. 18.

Tiberias. To distinguish it from the great seaport it was called Ces. Philippi, "Philip's Cesarea." Some coins give it as Ces. Paneas, a name derived from Pan, and this survives in the modern Banias.[1]—Our Lord must in his youth have often gazed at Hermon from the lofty hill west of Nazareth (see on 2: 23), and so during his ministry must have looked at the snow-clad line of Lebanon from the Lake of Galilee.[2] It was doubtless a great pleasure to him and the disciples in midsummer to leave the hot shores of the lake, far below the level of the Mediterranean, and visit this cool and delightful mountainous region. There was also the advantage of being in the dominions of Philip (as in 14: 13; 15: 29), who was a comparatively just ruler, and had no such occasion for suspicious jealousy of Jesus as Herod Antipas. (14: 1 ff.) They must have remained here some weeks or even months, as the series of withdrawals (14: 13; 15: 21, 29; 16: 13) occupied nearly six months. But the matters recorded in connection with this sojourn are near together in time; for 16: 21-28 seems to occur on the same day as Peter's confession, and 17: 1-20 about a week afterwards. From 16: 13 it is natural to suppose that all this took place shortly after he reached that region, and the rest of the time remains a blank.

The inhabitants of Cesarea Philippi and vicinity were largely heathen, and while sometimes attended by crowds (Mark 8: 34), and ready to heal (17: 14), our Lord occupied himself mainly with the private instruction of the twelve disciples as to his approaching extraordinary experiences (16: 21) and the true nature of the Messianic work. His own contemplation of his approaching rejection and death was accompanied by prayer. (Luke 9: 18.) In order to prepare the minds of the disciples

for these new views of the Messianic mission, he draws from them the confession that he is the Messiah, which Peter makes as spokesman. (v. 13-15.) This occurred 'on the road' (Mark 8: 27), probably from one village to another; he had withdrawn a little, and was alone with his disciples (Luke 9: 18); afterwards he would naturally return to the road, and here came in contact with a great number of other persons. (Mark 8: 34.) In drawing out the confession, he skillfully begins with an inquiry as to popular opinion concerning him, and then advances to ask their own opinion. The former was important as to any hope of immediate general usefulness; the latter far more important as to the whole future of the Messianic movement. **Whom** (*who*) **do men say.** 'Whom' (all the early English versions) is a sort of *attraction* of the relative into the case that would be required by the nearest word, 'say.' This use of the relative is also found in Shakespeare, but abandoned in modern English. **That I, the Son of man, am?** This should read '*the Son of man is.*' The change arose from assimilation to Mark and Luke. The phrase 'the Son of man' (see on 8: 20, and comp. John 12: 23) really implied that he was the Messiah, but did not distinctly affirm it. He had already declared that the Son of man was Lord of the Sabbath (12: 8), that he had authority on earth to forgive sins (9: 6), that he shall send forth his angels for the final harvest. (13: 41.) He had also (Lutteroth) often spoken of God as his Father. (John 3: 13-18; 5: 25-27; Matt. 7: 21; 10: 32; 11: 27; 15: 13.)

14. Popular opinion varied. **John the Baptist,** see on 3: 1. This would suppose John to have risen from the dead, as Herod Antipas thought. (14: 2.) **Elias,** instead of the Hebrew form Elijah, see on 1: 2. The Jews very generally expected Elijah to come to

[1] In modern Arabic the sounds of *b* and *p* are both represented by *b* (the Arabic *p* having always the sound of our *ph* or *f*), and are often hard to distinguish. Thus Bashaw and Pasha are two European attempts to represent the same word, and Nabulus is the Arabic for Neapolis, English Naples.

[2] One afternoon in March, 1871, we stood before our tent near Tubariyeh (Tiberias), and watched a black

cloud as it came rolling up the Jordan valley and over the southern end of the lake, till it hung above us like a mighty pall. Looking northward we saw a wonderful play of jagged lightnings about the upper end of the lake, and then far in the north there gleamed out upon us the long line of Lebanon, with its snows indescribably brilliant in the evening sun. It was one of the sights of a lifetime.

15 He saith unto them, But whom say ye that I am?
16 And Simon Peter answered and said, Thou art the Christ, the Son of the living God.

15 Jeremiah, or one of the prophets. He saith unto
16 them, But who say ye that I am? And Simon Peter answered and said, Thou art the Christ, the Son of

---

life again (see on 11: 14), many supposing he would be a forerunner of Messiah. (Mal. 4:5 f.)—And those who held that Jesus was Elijah, probably thought that he was a forerunner of Messiah. **And others, Jeremias** (*Jeremiah*). 'Others' is here a different Greek word from the foregoing, and denotes (comp. Gal. 1: 6) another class or kind of persons, *i. e.*, persons who turned away from the popular expectation of Elijah. Jeremiah was in the time of our Lord greatly venerated among the Jews. They had a legend that he appeared in a vision to Judas Maccabeus and encouraged him (2 Macc. 15: 7, 13 ff.); also that when the temple was destroyed, Jeremiah hid the tabernacle, the ark, and the altar of incense in a cave of Mount Pisgah, and promised that they should one day be restored (2 Macc. 2: 4 ff.); and a very late Jewish writer says, that Jeremiah would himself appear to restore these sacred objects. Some Rabbinical writers hold Jeremiah to be the prophet promised by Moses (Deut. 18: 15). We now think of Isaiah as the great prophet, because he is so often quoted in the New Test. as predicting the Messiah; but the Jews in the time of Christ reckoned Elijah and Jeremiah as foremost. **Or one of the prophets.** There was great confusion of opinion as to the circumstances of Messiah's approach, some thinking there would be a series of forerunners (see on 11: 3). The last class here mentioned were disposed to be non-committal as to identifying Jesus with any particular ancient prophet, but thought he must be some one of them. To many minds, now that belief in a resurrection had become vivid, the idea of some former revered prophet re-appearing was more natural and credible than that of a new prophet; yet some counted John the Baptist a prophet (14: 5; 11: 9), and others already thought Jesus a new and great prophet (Luke 7: 16; John 6: 14), as many did at a later period. (John 7: 40; Matt. 21: 46.) But no class of the people at this time regarded him as being the Messiah. How could they, when in their view Messiah was to be a splendid conqueror and king?

15 f. But whom (Rev. Ver., *who*) **say ye that I am?** Observe 'ye,' plural, and by position in the Greek exceedingly emphatic—

in contrast with the discordant popular opinions. The question is addressed to all, and Peter answers as their spokesman, just as he does in many other cases. (John 6: 67-70; Matt. 15: 15 f.; 19: 25-28; Luke 12: 41; Mark 11: 20-22; Matt. 26: 40; Acts 2: 37 f.; 5: 29, etc.) *Chrys.:* "Peter, the ever fervent, the leader of the Apostolic choir (Coryphaeus)." His impulsive nature, which sometimes brought him into trouble (14: 29; 26: 51) helped to fit Peter for this post of spokesman, and a better qualification was his strong faith and ardent love for the Master. The fact that the others remained silent and left him to speak does not show that none of them fully shared his sentiments; comp. 19: 28; 26: 40; etc. **Thou art the Christ,** as in v. 20. The early Eng. versions, including the first and several succeeding editions of K. James, gave 'Christ' without the article; it is not ascertained when the article was introduced into the Com. Ver. It has also the article in the parallel passage, Mark 8: 29. For the meaning of the word 'Christ' see on 1: 1. We feel the force of it better in this and many passages of the Gospels, by using the Hebrew word Messiah (see on 2: 4). 'Thou' is expressed in the Greek, and therefore emphatic. **The Son of the living God** is a very solemn expression. The gods of the heathen were lifeless; Jehovah the God of Israel, the one true God, was *living*. So Paul at Lystra (Acts 14: 15 R. V.): "that ye should should turn from these *vain things* unto the living God." Mark (8: 29) records simply 'thou art the Christ (*Messiah*)'; Luke (9: 20) 'the Christ (*Messiah*) of God.'—The earliest disciples of Jesus, including Simon Peter, at once concluded that he was the Messiah. (John 1: 41, 49.) But he proceeded to act so differently from what they had been reared to expect of Messiah, that they would naturally become greatly perplexed about his Messiahship, even as John felt in his prison (see on 11: 3). Again and again, however, some work or word would persuade them afresh. Thus in 7: 22 he declares, "Many will say to me in that day, Lord, Lord," etc. In 11: 5 f. he refers the messengers of John to his Messianic miracles and preaching to the poor. In 14: 33 the persons in the boat say, "of a

17 And Jesus answered and said unto him, Blessed art thou, Simon Bar-jona: for flesh and blood hath not revealed *it* unto thee, but my Father which is in heaven.

17 the living God. And Jesus answered and said unto him, Blessed art thou, Simon Bar-Jonah: for flesh and blood hath not revealed it unto thee, but **my**

truth thou art the Son of God." In John 6: 69, R. V., Peter says (as spokesman): "We have believed and know that thou art the Holy One of God." (This last the copyists changed into "thou art the Christ, the Son of the living God," by assimilation to our passage of Matthew.) Now, two or three years later than their first early persuasion, they have become established in the conviction, though so in conflict with their life-long conceptions, that their Master is the Messiah. We thus see that there is no contradiction, such as many critics have alleged, between the statements of Matt., Mark., and Luke at this point, and that of John 1 : 41. Nor do we read that he had ever distinctly told the disciples that he was the Messiah, though he had said so to the woman of Samaria. (John 4 : 26, 29.) A few months later, the noble Martha, who receives scant justice in many pulpits, made the same confession for which Peter is here so commended. (John 11 : 27.) We understand the importance of this confession when we hear a Jew of the present time announce his new-found conviction that Jesus of Nazareth is the Messiah.—Does this confession of Peter represent the Saviour as divine? Not necessarily, if it stood alone without any later revelation. (Comp. on 14: 33.) But subsequent apostolic teaching, guided by the Holy Spirit, employs kindred phrases to set forth his divinity, which may therefore be regarded as implicitly contained in the language here used.

17. This response, v. 17-19, is given by Matt. only. Our Lord seems to speak joyfully. Here at last the disciples have reached the strong conviction, the clear faith, necessary to prepare them for comprehending and establishing his spiritual Messianic reign. **Blessed,** more exactly *happy*, see on 5 : 3, and comp. 11 : 6; 13 : 16. God has greatly favored him,

in bringing him to this perception and conviction, and so he is a happy man. Why does Jesus say this to Simon Peter alone, and not to all those whose opinion he had asked, and for whom Peter had spoken? Partly, no doubt, because he wishes to refer in what follows to the meaning of the name Peter, and partly because Peter is to have a certain leadership in the founding of the kingdom, and so what is about to be said will apply especially, though by no means exclusively, to him. **Simon Bar-jona.** The Hebrew Ben (Benjamin, Benhadad, etc.), and the Aramaic Bar, signifies 'son'; *e. g.*, Bar-Jesus, Barabbas (27 : 16), Bartholomew (10 : 3), Bartimeus, Barnabas, etc. Comp. John-son, Robin-son, etc., and kindred terms in many languages. The word Bar-jonah (Bar-iona in Com. Ver. is the Greek form) does not occur elsewhere in the New Testament; in John 1 : 42; 21 : 15, we find (R. V.) 'Simon, son of John,' and there is reason to suppose that Jona in Matt. is a contraction of Joana, which would be a genitive case, meaning 'of John,'[1] so that Bariona means not son of Jonah, but son of John. **Flesh and blood,** viz., humanity, on its feeble corporeal side, as distinguished from the incorporeal or spiritual side, which is relatively strong (Bleek). The phrase is found first in Ecclus. 14: 18; 17: 31; it occurs repeatedly in New Test. (Gal. 1 : 16; Eph. 6 : 12; Heb. 2 : 14, etc.), and is very common in the Talmud. The Old Test. makes a similar use of 'flesh.' (Gen. 6 : 3, etc.) **Revealed.** No one around had the fixed conviction that Jesus was the Messiah; Peter and the disciples for whom he spoke had not derived that conviction from any human teaching, nor from their own unaided reflection. **My Father which is in heaven,** see on 6 : 9. None but the Father knows the Son. (11 : 27.) To lift them out of all the perplexed conceptions due to their education and

[1] In Luke 3 : 27 Joanan (Heb. Jochanan, John) is in various documents written Jonan, and in 3 : 30 Jonam or Jonan is in some documents Joanam. So in the Sept. Joanan frequently appears as Jonan. Therefore it is quite possible that in Matt. Jona is only a contraction of Joana, which would be genitive of Joanas, a Doric form of Joannes or Joanes, and Doric forms of proper names are common in the New Test.; thus Bar-jona

would be son of John. In John 1 : 42; 21 : 15, the true text has Joanou, the Attic genitive, which was early changed by some copyists to Jona through assimilation to Matt. Bishop Lightfoot (on Rev., p. 137) gives a quotation showing that the "Gospel of the Hebrews" explained Bar-iona as a Jewish name, meaning son of John.

18 And I say also unto thee, That thou art Peter, and upon this rock I will build my church; and the gates of hell shall not prevail against it.

18 Father who is in heaven. And I also say unto thee, that thou art [1] Peter, and upon this [2] rock I will build my church ; and the gates of Hades shall not

---

1 Gr. *Petros.*   2 Gr. *Petra.*

---

environment, and fix them in the conviction that one without sceptre or army or even home, is the Messiah, required revelation from the Father (comp. John 6 : 44).

18 f. Here are four main points to be considered, (1) the rock, (2) the church, (3) the gates of Hades, (4) the keys of the kingdom, and the power to bind and loose. **And I say also unto thee,** as thou hast just said something to me which is so important. Weiss and others understand, "as the Father has given thee this great revelation, I also give thee a great distinction." But thus to contrast his gifts with the Father's would be quite foreign to the tone of our Lord's discourses ; and the emphatic position of 'unto thee' (in the Gr.) forbids such a view. **That thou art Peter,** 'thou' being expressed in the Greek, and therefore emphatic. This is not for the first time *giving* him the name, as some destructive critics hold in order to make out a contradiction between Matthew and John, but naturally implies that he has it already. (10 : 2.) He who long before gave the surname (John 1 : 42) now refers to it as significant. *Chrys :* "See throughout all, his own authority ; I say unto thee, I will build the church, I will give the keys."

A. **Upon this rock.** As Peter means rock, the natural interpretation is that 'upon this rock' means *upon thee.* No other explanation would probably at the present day be attempted, but for the fact that the obvious meaning has been abused by Papists to the support of their theory. But we must not allow the abuse of a truth to turn us away from its use ; nor must the convenience of religious controversy determine our interpretation of Scripture teaching. The other interpretations which have been proposed are, that the rock is Peter's confession (or his faith), and that the rock is Christ.

Now apart from the Romish perversion, certain other objections are made to the natural interpretation. Some hold that such a play upon words, "thou art Rock, and on this rock," is unworthy of our Lord. But there *is* a play upon words, understand as you may. It is an even more far-fetched and harsh play upon words if we understand the rock to be Christ ; and a very feeble and almost unmeaning play upon words if the rock is Peter's confession. Nor is there any real objection to supposing paronomasia. Such expressions are very common in Old Test. (*e. g.*, Gen. 17 : 5 ; 32 : 28), and in New Test., especially in Paul. See Winer, ⸶68, and Bp. Lightfoot on Revision (in Schaff on Rev., p. XV. ff.).

The fact that 'rock' elsewhere in Scripture is often applied to God and never to man (Wordsw., Alex.), may be offset by the fact that our Lord himself gave this man the name rock (John 1 : 42), and here takes pains to call him by that name, which he does nowhere else save in Luke 22 : 34 ; and perhaps even the exception is significant, for he was then predicting the shameful fall so unworthy of one whom he had named rock. Late Jewish writings (Wün.) speak of Abraham as the rock, or of the patriarchs as the rocks, on which God laid the foundation of the world.

Many insist on the distinction between the two Greek words, thou art *Petros*, and on this *petra*, holding that if the rock had meant Peter, either *petros* or *petra* would have been used both times, and that *petros* signifies a separate stone or a fragment broken off, while *petra* is the massive rock. But this distinction is almost entirely confined to poetry, the common prose word instead of *petros* being *lithos ;* nor is the distinction uniformly observed (see Lid. and Scott). It is worthy of notice, too, that Jesus himself is called *lithos* in 1 Pet. 2 : 5 ff. Again if *petros* had been used both times in the Greek, it would have meant, "thou art Peter, and on this Peter," without distinctly showing the play upon words ; and it would not have been natural for Matthew to write, 'thou art *petra*' (feminine), when he has been constantly writing the apostle's name Simon Petros (masculine). But the main answer here is that our Lord undoubtedly spoke Aramaic, which has no known means of making such a distinction. The Peshito (Western Aramaic) renders, "Thou art *kipho,* and on this *kipho.*" The Eastern Aramaic, spoken in Palestine in the time of Christ, must necessarily have said in like manner, "Thou art *kepha*, and on this *kepha*." (Comp. Buxtorf.) Beza called attention to the fact that it is so likewise in French: "Thou art *Pierre*, and on this *pierre*" ; and Nicholson suggests that we could say, "Thou art Piers (old English for Peter), and on this pier." Lightf. *supposes* (followed by Wordsw.) that "he pronounced it Cephas after the Greek manner" because he "could not have been understood if in both places he had retained the same word." How, then, has the Peshito been understood? Edersh. finds the words *petros* and *petra* borrowed in the late Rabbinical language, and thinks that Jesus, while speaking Aramaic, may have borrowed those Greek words here. But this is grossly improbable, and the suggestion looks like a desperate expedient; nor has he shown that the late Rabbis themselves make the supposed distinction between the two words.

Let it be observed that Jesus could not here mean *himself* by the rock, consistently with the image, because he is the builder. To say, "I will build, ... I am the rock on which I will build," would be a very confused image. The suggestion of some expositors that in saying 'thou art Peter, and on this rock' he pointed at himself, involves an artificiality which to some minds is repulsive. The attempts to show that the demonstrative, 'on *this* rock,' could not refer to the speaker, or could not refer to the person addressed, are alike futile.

But the great objection on the part of many to the natural interpretation is the apparent concession to Popery. Let us see how this matter stands.

The early Fathers, who are for us only very useful aids in interpretation, are for the Roman Catholic an *authority*, only second to that of Scripture. For him, though not for us, it is a grave difficulty that some of the most distinguished Fathers interpret the rock otherwise. Chrys. expressly says on our passage, "On this rock; that is, on the faith of his confession." He often elsewhere gives the same interpretation and never any other. Once he remarks, "He did not say upon Peter, for it was not upon man, but upon his faith." Maldonatus would have trouble in applying to this expression his "reverent" interpretation that those Fathers who say the church was built on the faith and confession of Peter really meant on Peter, because of his faith and confession. Chrysostom's explanation is also given by his contemporaries Gregory of Nyssa and Isidore of Pelusium, and the Latin Father Hilary, and by the later Greek Fathers Theodoret, Theophanes, Theophylact, John of Damascus. Probably these Fathers were all aware of a tendency to pervert the more natural interpretation which made Peter the rock (that of Origen, Cyprian, Basil, Gregory Naz., Ambrose, Jerome, Cyril Alex., etc.), into a support for the growing claims of the Roman Bishop. Augustine in his "Retractations" (I. 21) says that in an early work against the Donatists he stated that the church was founded on Peter as on a rock; but that very often since he has interpreted the language as meaning that the rock was Christ; and that Simon confessing him as all the church does was therefore called Peter. He adds that the reader may choose which of these opinions is more probable.[1] We repeat that Chrys., Augustine, and the rest, are notable *authorities* for the Roman Catholic, and grievously in the way of *his* building on the natural interpretation of the passage.

But grant that the rock is Peter, and consider what the Roman Catholic will then have to show in order to establish the claims of the Papacy.

1. He must show that Peter *alone* was to be the founder of Christianity. Of this there is no evidence but the obviously figurative expression before us. Against it (a) we find various express declarations, especially Ephes. 2: 20, "Built upon the foundation of the apostles and prophets," etc. (b) The *history* in

---

[1] Some other Fathers were uncertain, and have interpreted the passage differently in different writings; but most of the examples of this cited by Suicer (Thesaurus Eccles.) are misunderstood by him, and some of them mistranslated. Stier states that "Lannoy, Doctor of the Sorbonne, out of seventy-seven sayings of the most famous Church Fathers and Church writers, had found only seventeen which explain Peter himself as the rock, forty-four on the contrary understand the *faith*, and sixteen Christ himself." But such numerical statements can be but little relied on, unless one could have the citations and know something of their sources.

Acts and the Epistles is also opposed to this notion; especially in Acts ch. 15, where Peter does not at all act separately or appear to be supreme (though he is a leader), and it is really James that suggests the measure adopted by the brethren; also in Gal. ch. 2, where Peter is one of the three pillars, James being named first, and where Peter is publicly rebuked by Paul for acting contrary to his own convictions. Think of a Romish bishop rebuking the Pope to his face "before all." (c) The promise as to binding and loosing here made to Peter, is made in 18: 18 as to the action of all the apostles or any church. A partly similar promise is made in John 20: 22 f. to the ten apostles and others (as shown by the comparison of Luke). (d) This saying is omitted by Mark and Luke, though they give what precedes and what follows it. Now according to the Romanist view they have omitted the very heart of the passage, and well-nigh the most important thing Jesus ever said. Thus *H. J. Coleridge:* "This confession of St. Peter, and the magnificent blessing which it drew from our Lord, may be said to be the very central point of our Lord's ministry. All before it leads up to it, and all that follows it in some sense takes its color from it." And yet Mark and Luke have both come right up to this transcendently important saying, and then passed it by, giving the words which in Matthew immediately follow. The argument from silence must always be carefully used, but this is certainly a very strong case.

2. He must show that Peter not only was the *sole founder* of Christianity, but that he was vicegerent of God and the sovereign of all Christians. No Scripture testifies this at all, unless the present passage does; and the whole tone of the New Testament is against it. Nor do the Fathers who understand the rock to be Peter indicate the notion of his having any such position or power as the modern Pope.

3. He must show that this supposed authority of Peter's was *transmissible*, of which there is no particle of evidence in the New Test.; and it is strangely inconsistent with the very image of a corner-stone, or foundation rock, to suppose it frequently removed and a new one substituted.

4. He must show that Peter lived and died at Rome, which is probably true but not cer-

tain; and that he was, rather than Paul, the head of the church at Rome, of which there is no evidence at all, and Irenæus and Eusebius agree in making Linus first bishop of that church.

5. He must show that Peter's supposed transmissible authority was actually transmitted to the leading official of the church at Rome. Of this there is no evidence but comparatively late tradition. And against it is the general history of the earliest churches, in which the church at Rome (*e. g.*, in Clement's Ep. to the Corinthians) does indeed appear as influential (a natural thing from its being in the imperial city), but there is not the slightest indication that it was supreme, or had any sovereignty, recognized or claimed. And why should a special office or authority be transmitted to a church official at Rome rather than at Antioch or Jerusalem? Notice too (Gloag, "Exege. Studies"), that on the Papal theory the great apostle John was, after the death of Peter, completely subject to the bishop of Rome.

The Protestant reluctance to admit that the rock means Peter really plays into the hands of the Romish controversialists. It favors the impression that conceding that point would be conceding all that the Romanist claims, when, as we have seen, the hopeless burden of his argument comes afterwards. Now to take Peter as the rock is certainly the most natural and obvious meaning. And to make this the life or death issue is to give the Romanist a serious polemical advantage. In general, it is a great principle in Biblical interpretation to take the most obvious meaning of any phrase, unless it would thus yield a sense hopelessly in conflict with the unambiguous teaching of other passages.

To understand that Peter is here the rock is not forbidden by the fact that other images are drawn from the same source. In 1 Cor. 3: 10 ff., Paul speaks of himself as masterbuilder (architect), and other teachers also as builders, Christ being the only foundation. In Eph. 2: 19 ff. he makes the apostles and prophets the foundation, with Christ as cornerstone. So in Rev. 21: 14 the names of the twelve apostles are engraved on the twelve foundations of the city walls, which makes the apostles in one sense the entire foundation. In 1 Peter 2: 4 ff. all Christians are living stones built up into a spiritual house, with Christ as the chief corner stone. In the present passage Christ is the builder, and the apostles are the foundation, as represented by Peter, who spoke for the rest, and had a recognized leadership among them. There are many other cases of an image variously applied. In v. 19, Peter is promised the keys, while in Rev. 1: 18; 3: 7, Jesus has the keys. So in 5 : 14, Christians are the light of the world, while in John 9 : 5 Christ is the light of the world.—That Peter was a leader among the apostles, is seen already from his standing at the head in each of the four lists. (See on 10 : 2.) He appears as markedly prominent in Acts 1 : 15 ff. ; 2 : 14 ff. ; 2 : 37 f. ; 3 : 1 ff. (with John) ; 3 : 11 f. ; 4 : 8 ff. ; 4 : 19 (with John); 5 : 8, 15, 29; 8 : 14 (with John). Observe especially the designation of Peter to receive a special revelation and take special action concerning the Gentiles, Acts 10 : 9 ff. ; 11 : 17; 15 : 7; also the prominence of Peter and James in the decision of the conference at Jerusalem (Acts 15 : 7 ff.), where Paul says that James, Cephas, and John were reputed to be pillars (Gal. 2 : 9), an architectural image somewhat akin to that which here makes the apostles the foundation. Notice in particular that Peter was leader in converting many Jews on the great Day of Pentecost, and was also the first instrument in the conversion of Gentiles who had not become Jews. In all this there is nothing at all to show that his leadership amounted to supremacy, but in fact, much to the contrary. He appears everywhere as *primus inter pares*, the first among equals. The disciples after this time dispute who shall be greatest. (18 : 1 ; Luke 22 : 24.) In so doing they certainly did not understand that Peter was greatest, nor did Jesus intimate that in replying. We find also (Gloag) that Peter, instead of sending the other apostles is sent by them (Acts 8 : 14), and is called to account by the apostles and brethren. (Acts 11 : 1-18.) If then it be supposed that our Lord's language applies to Peter in some peculiar sense not true of the other apostles, still it cannot possibly mean that he is thereby made sovereign over the rest. Jesus here means that the apostles are the foundation on which he will build his church, and Peter is mentioned in particular because of his significant name, appropriate character, spokesmanship on this occasion, and recognized leadership in general. That the rock here means Peter is held among Protestant expositors by Bengel, Doddridge, Macknight, Fritzsche, Bleek, Meyer, De Wette, Alford, Stier, Keim, Grimm, Weiss, Geikie, Farrar, Mansel, Gloag.

B. I will build. The image is that of a house, as seen also in 'gates' and 'keys.' To build an assembly was a combination of images easy to the Jewish mind, because the *congregation* of Israel was often also called the *house* of Israel. The word **church** is used also in 18: 17, but nowhere else in the Gospels, and the discussions connected with it belong chiefly to the Acts and Epistles. The Greek word *ekklesia* signified primarily the assembly of citizens in a self-governed State, being derived from *ekkaleo*, to call out; *i. e.*, out from their homes or places of business, to summon, as we speak of calling out the militia. The popular notion that it meant to call out in the sense of separation from others, is a mistake. In a secondary sense *ekklesia* denoted any popular assembly (Acts 19 : 39.) This Greek term seems to have been applied directly to an actual congregation or assembly of Christians, what we now call a local church, as in 18: 17, and usually in the Acts and Epistles, sometimes to an (apparently) informal, unorganized meeting. (Rom. 16 : 5 ; Col. 4 : 15 ; Philem. 2.) But in the Septuagint it is often used to translate the Hebrew *qahal* (for example, Deut. 18 : 6; 23 : 1 ff. ; Judg. 21: 8; Psa. 22 : 22, etc.), which is also derived from a root meaning to call, to convoke, and so signifies a convocation, a congregation, assembly. This and another Hebrew word of equivalent meaning are used in all parts of the Old Test. to denote the congregation of Israel (comp. Acts 7 : 38; Heb. 2 : 12). In the New Test. the *spiritual* Israel, never actually assembled, is sometimes conceived of as an ideal congregation or assembly, and this is denoted by the word *ekklesia*. So in Eph. 1 : 22, and often throughout that Epistle, in Col. 1: 18, 24; Heb. 12 : 23, etc. This seems to be the meaning here. All real Christians are conceived of as an ideal congregation or assembly, and this is here described as a house or temple, built upon Peter (and the other apostles), as in Eph. 2 : 19-22, it is a temple "built upon the foundation of the apostles and prophets." There is a third use of the term *ekkle-sia*, widely diffused throughout Christendom, in which it is made to denote the aggregate of all formally professing Christians, or all outward organizations of Christians, or else some one outward organization which is alone recognized by the persons using the term as being really "the church." This aggregate of professed Christians is in modern parlance called "the visible church," as distinguished from "the invisible church," which denotes as above, the ideal assembly of real Christians. But the word is not used in the New Test. to denote a congregation, actual or imaginary, of all professed Christians, unless it be in Acts 9: 31 (correct text), and in 1 Tim. 3: 15. In the former the word probably denotes the original church at Jerusalem, whose members were by the persecution widely scattered throughout Judea and Galilee and Samaria, and held meetings wherever they were, but still belonged to the one original organization. When Paul wrote to the Galatians, nearly twenty years later, these separate meetings had been organized into distinct churches; and so he speaks (Gal. 1: 22), in reference to that same period, of "the churches of Judea which were in Christ." In 1 Tim. 3: 15, "the church" is naturally the particular local church with which one is connected. If these two passages be not relied on for the purpose, there is no New Test. authority for the sense of "the visible church," and therefore the word ought not to be so understood here. As to the English word 'church,' see on 18: 17.

C. **The gates of hell,** or *Hades.* The word Hades (see on 11: 23), denotes the invisible world, the abode of the departed. The Hebrew word Sheol has substantially the same meaning. Such was also the original sense of the English word *hell*, the hidden or unseen place (Anglo Saxon *helan*, 'to hide,' *Skeat*), which was therefore in early English a correct translation of Hades and Sheol. But it has gradually come to denote exclusively the place of torment, as so many other words have become restricted to the bad sense, and is now only a translation of Gehenna (see on 5: 22), while Hades has to be borrowed in Rev. Ver. of New Test. In Com. Ver. of Old Test., Sheol was translated either 'hell,' 'the grave,' or 'the pit.' In Rev.

Ver. the Hebrew Sheol has been often borrowed, and this ought assuredly to have been done in all cases, as urged by the American Revisers. Neither Hades nor Sheol ever denotes distinctively the place of torment. Farrar claims for this sense Luke 16: 23; 2 Pet. 2: 4; Matthew 11: 23. But in Luke 16: 23 the place of torment is *in* Hades, and so is Abraham's abode—separated by an impassable gulf, but within sight and hearing. So the rich man in torment was in Hades, but the gates of Hades (whether meaning entrance or power) cannot be distinctively the gates of the place of torment, the abode of Satan. In 2 Pet. 2: 4 the term Hades is not used, but a verb derived from the Greek word *Tartarus*, which was in Greek usage exclusively a place of torment; and this word occurs nowhere else in the Greek Bible. In Matt. 11: 23 (see note) the arrogantly aspiring city, which dreams of reaching heaven, is to be brought down to Sheol or Hades, conceived of as far underground, *i. e.*, to utter destruction; and the idea of future torment does not even enter into the connection. There is nowhere any warrant for understanding Hades as denoting distinctively the place of torment, the abode of Satan; it is the abode of the departed, and through its gates pass all who die. To argue that Abraham and Lazarus must have been in *heaven*, and therefore wholly separated from Hades, is beside the mark; for the conception of heaven as the abode of the blessed is entirely distinct from that of Hades, and the two cannot be combined into one local image.

The 'gates of Sheol' (Hades) are spoken of in Isaiah 38: 10; Wisdom 16: 13; 3 Macc. 5: 51; Psalms of Solomon 16: 2; Gospel of Nicodemus 21; and in this passage; the 'bars of Sheol' in Job 17: 16; the 'gates of Death' in Job 38: 17; Ps. 9: 14 (13); 107: 18, and the 'keys of death and of Hades' in Rev. 1: 18. So in "Iliad" IX., 312, Achilles says, "For hateful to me, like the gates of Hades, is the man who hides one thing in his breast and says another." In "Iliad" VI., 546, Tlepolemos: "But subdued by me you will traverse the gates of Hades." In "Odyssey" XI., 277, "But she went to the abode of the strong gate-keeper, Hades" (the deity presiding over that region). In Æschylus, "Agam." 1291, Clytemnestra addresses the gates of Hades, and prays that she may have a speedy and easy death. In Euripides, "Hecuba" 1, Hecuba says, "I come, leaving the hiding-place of the dead and the gates of darkness, where Hades dwells apart from the gods." It will be seen that in all the passages from Hebrew writings, and most of those from Greek writings, the gates of Hades are passed through by the dying. In the passage from Euripides a person is conceived as coming back through the gates of Hades, and there are some other passages of Greek authors to the same effect. It would be possible, though not most natural, so to understand Rev. 1: 18.

Prevail against, or 'overcome,' literally, *be strong against,* 'be too strong for.' The Greek word is found also in Luke 23: 23, and is an intensive compound of that used in Acts 19: 16. It might in the Greek grammatically refer to the rock or to the church; the connection shows plainly that the latter is meant, but there is no substantial difference. Some able commentators understand "shall not surpass it in strength," without the notion of conflict; but this is contrary to the etymology and use of the verb, and seems strained. Because 'gates' has in Greek no article, Weiss takes it to mean 'Hades-gates,' *i. e.,* gates of that class or kind shall not surpass it in strength. But the indefinite word gates is made definite by appending Hades, this being a definite and single locality—a use of the appended genitive that is quite common in the New Test. (Winer, 125 [155], Buttmann, 88, 118).[1]

'The gates of Hades shall not prevail against it' may now be seen to have three possible senses. (a) It most naturally means, according to the Hebrew uses, that the gates of Hades shall not swallow up the church. All earthly things go down through those dread gates, but Christ's church, for which he gave himself, will never cease to exist; there will always be Christians in the world. This was a bold prediction for a homeless teacher, with a handful of followers (comp. 28: 18-20). (b) Or, taking the occasional Greek, but not Hebrew use, together with the possible meaning of Rev. 1: 18, we shall have the sense, the gates of Hades shall not prevent my people from rising again (Meyer.) (c) 'Gates' may be taken, though it is an unusual sense, as a symbol of power, because strong gates completed the fortifications of a city (Gen. 22: 17; Psa. 127: 5), or because judges often sat, kings administered justice, and garrisons gathered, in the gates. Comp. "the Sublime Porte," and the European use of "Court," as connected with the court-yard of a palace. Then the expression would mean, the power of Hades shall not be too strong for my church, a sense loosely equivalent to (a.) Yet this is harsh; for while 'gates' might well represent defensive power, it is hardly congruous to take them as representing aggressive power. As to the widespread notion that it means the power of Satan, there is no authority whatever for so understanding 'the gates of Hades.' Satan rules over one part of Hades; but how can he control, or be represented by, the gates of Hades, through which the blessed pass in dying, as well as the wicked? This notion has been diffused through Christendom from two causes. The conception of heaven as the abode of the blest rapidly supplanted the idea of the blest as dwelling in Hades, and Hades came to be thought of only in the bad sense. Accordingly the Latin term *infernus* (inferni, inferna, inferi), which originally meant substantially the same as Hades, gradually became restricted in Christian usage to the place of torment (Italian *inferno,* French, *enfer,* English adjective, *infernal*), just as has happened with the English word hell. Thus in the Vulg. *portae inferorum (inferi),* like 'gates of hell' in modern English, readily came to suggest the power of Satan. The other cause is that this notion suited the conception of Christ's 'church' as a visible organization, which the power of Satan vainly strives to overthrow. (d) Ewald thinks of the gates of Hades as opening to let monsters issue from them (Rev. 9: 1 ff.), and these monsters shall not overcome the church; but this is far-fetched and highly unnatural.

The passage then seems to mean *either,* my church shall not be swallowed up in the gates of Hades (or possibly shall not be overcome

---

[1] This matter of the appended genitive, upon which Winer and Butt. make many distinctions, may be reduced to a single statement. Where the noun appended in the genitive is in its nature so related to the other noun that the complex idea becomes definite, then the speaker or writer may, if he chooses, omit the article with the first noun, and yet expect the phrase to be understood as definite.

19 And I will give unto thee the keys of the kingdom of heaven: and whatsoever thou shalt bind on earth shall be bound in heaven ; and whatsoever thou shalt loose on earth shall be loosed in heaven.

19 prevail against it. I will give unto thee the keys of the kingdom of heaven: and whatsoever thou shalt bind on earth shall be bound in heaven: and whatsoever thou shalt loose on earth shall be loosed in

by its power), shall not cease to exist—there shall always be Christians in the world; *or*, my people shall rise again. The former is much the more probable meaning, because it follows the general Hebrew usage. Then the question will turn simply on the word church (see above), whether it means an outward organization of professed Christians (or the aggregate of many such organizations), or means an ideal assembly of all true Christians.

D. **I will give unto thee the keys of the kingdom of heaven.** That copyists should prefix **and** was very natural. At first sight it seems to be required, though upon closer examination the statement is seen to be more expressive without it, as a parallel to 'I will build.' The image here changes, in part. There is still a house, but he who was before the foundation of the house now receives the keys. *Alexander:* "The abrupt transition may be urged as an objection to the supposition that the *rock* of v. 18 is Peter. It is certainly no natural association of ideas that the keys of the building should be given to the rock on which it rests. Yet it is quite as incongruous for the rock to give the keys as to receive them." He who had the keys of a city or palace determined whether any given person should enter or be shut out. (Rev. 9: 1 f.; 20: 1-3.) This would suggest a general authority and control, varying in extent according to the nature of the case. There seems to be allusion here to the high steward of the palace of David, Isa. 22: 15, 22 ; and in Rev. 1 : 18; 3: 7, a similar but spiritual function is ascribed to Jesus himself. The Talmud makes like use of the phrase. Comp. also in Luke 11: 52, "Ye took away the key of knowledge; ye entered not in yourselves. and them that were entering in ye hindered." In our passage, however the rock may be understood, all must agree that our Lord gives the keys to Peter, *i. e.*, the power of admitting (*e. g.*, Acts 11: 17), or denying admission (*e. g.*, Acts 8: 21), into the Messianic kingdom. Yet it is not given to him in any exclusive sense, for the closely connected power of binding and loosing was not long after given to any

church (18: 18), and the included power of forgiving sins was given to the ten apostles and others. (John 20: 23.) As to the 'kingdom of heaven,' see on 3: 2. There seems to be no reference here or anywhere in the use of this term to an outward organization of Messiah's subjects. His reign is a spiritual reign, and admission into his kingdom is a spiritual admission. Peter and the other apostles would admit or deny admission, as they would forgive sins or retain them, by teaching the spiritual conditions of admission or forgiveness, and by their inspired power of discerning and declaring a man's spiritual condition (*e. g.*, Acts 5: 3 ; 8: 21; 13: 10).—The legend of Peter sitting at the gate with the keys assumes that the kingdom of heaven here denotes heaven as the abode of the blest. It corresponds to, and perhaps grew out of, a Talmudic legend that Abraham sits at the door of Gehenna, and will let no circumcised person go down.

Bind and **loose,** in the Talmud and other Rabbinical writings (Lightf., Wet., Wün., Edersh.), signify to interpret and apply the law and traditions on any subject with *strictness* or with *laxity*, and hence in general to forbid or allow. The strict school of Shammai is represented as binding many things which the school of Hillel loosed. Comp. on 19: 3. In Rabbinical phrase it would be said that in Acts 15: 10 Peter advocated *loosing* what the Judaizers wished to *bind*. Diod. Sic. tells (I. 27) of an image of Isis with the inscription, "I, Isis, am the queen of all the land, and whatever I shall bind no one can loose." These uses seem to leave no doubt as to the meaning of the terms here. Our Lord declares that whatever Peter should forbid or allow, should declare to be wrong or right, would be sanctioned by divine authority, approved **in heaven.** As Peter was the spokesman of all the apostles, we should naturally understand that the same would be true of all the inspired teachings (comp. John 16: 13) ; they would have Heaven's approval. And this included forgiving or retaining sins (John 20: 23), which was promised to the apostles and others present. (Comp. Luke.) Similar in that case is the expression 'loosed us from

20 Then charged he his disciples that they should tell no man that he was Jesus the Christ.

21 From that time forth began Jesus to shew unto his disciples, how that he must go unto Jerusalem, and suffer many things of the elders and chief priests and scribes, and be killed, and be raised again the third day.

20 heaven. Then charged he the disciples that they should tell no man that he was the Christ.

21   From that time began [1] Jesus to shew unto his disciples, how that he must go unto Jerusalem, and suffer many things of the elders and chief priests and scribes, and be killed, and the third day be

---

1 Some ancient authorities read, *Jesus Christ.*

---

our sins,' Rev. 1: 5 (correct text), and the same phrase in Isa. 40: 2 (Sept.); Ecclus. 28: 2. In 18: 18 exactly the same promise as to binding and loosing is made to all the persons addressed ('ye'), meaning either the apostles in general, or more probably the action of any church. From the abuse of 16: 19; 18: 18; and John 20: 23, arose the Romish doctrine of priestly absolution, which some Protestant persuasions retain in a modified form. Ministers may teach the conditions of forgiveness, but they have no inspired power of discerning a person's spiritual condition, and their declarations of absolution are of no value beyond stating the conditions.

20. Then charged he his (*the*) **disciples.** 'His' was added by copyists, as in v. 5. The plural shows that they shared the conviction which Peter as their spokesman had expressed. **That he was Jesus the Christ.** 'Jesus' was inserted by copyists. Until their own views of his Messianic work were greatly corrected, as the Master at once began to do (16: 21), any statement by them that he was Messiah would have done harm rather than good. It would have brought him prematurely into open antagonism to the Jewish rulers, and might have awakened the fanaticism of the masses, who would take it for granted that the Messiah must collect an army for conquering, and this would have excited the jealousy of the tetrarchs and the Roman government. (Comp. on 14: 22 and 8: 4.) After he had suffered and died (Luke 9: 21 f.), they could tell everybody that he was the Messiah, and could then give correct ideas of the Messianic work.

HOMILETICAL AND PRACTICAL.

V. 6. False ideas in religion. 1) False ideas are often advocated by worthy and even distinguished people. 2) False ideas are apt to diffuse themselves through the whole mass of one's religious thinking. 3) False ideas will inevitably affect religious character and life. 4) Therefore we must beware of adopting the religious errors of eminent and admirable

persons.—The leaven of error in high places of position and culture. 1) The leaven of the Pharisees represents for us ritualism, formalism, hypocrisy. 2) The leaven of the Sadducees represents skepticism, "rationalism," "liberalism." 3) The leaven of the Herodians, secularism and the subordination of religion to politics.—V. 9. HENRY: "We are *therefore* perplexed with present cares and distrusts, because we do not duly remember our former experiences of divine power and goodness."

V. 13-17. Opinions about Jesus. 1) What men think of Jesus is a matter of great importance for their own good, and therefore of great concern to him, v. 13. 2) Men are often very ingenious in devising other theories in order to avoid a view of Jesus which offends their prejudices, v. 14. 3) Those who wish to know the truth about Jesus must be ready to break, if necessary, with popular opinion, v. 15. 4) The only true view of Jesus regards him as the Divine Redeemer, v. 16. 5) Thoroughly correct views of Jesus are drawn only from revelation, v. 17. HENRY: "It is possible for men to have good thoughts of Christ and yet not right ones, a high opinion of him and yet not high enough." —V. 17. ORIGEN: "If we say as Peter did, "Thou art the Christ, the Son of the living God," not flesh and blood having revealed it to us, but light having shone in our heart from the Father in heaven, then we also become such as Peter was, happy like him and for the same reason."—V. 18. Christ building his church. 1) The spiritual church of Christ includes all real Christians. 2) Christ himself builds his church, using his apostles as foundation, and all who believe on him through their word (John 17: 20) as materials. 3) Christ guarantees that his spiritual church shall never cease to exist—there will always be true Christians on earth.

16: 21-28. JESUS BEGINS TO FORETELL HIS DEATH.

This is also found in Mark 8: 31 to 9: 1; Luke 9: 22-27. It is closely connected with

22 Then Peter took him, and began to rebuke him, saying, Be it far from thee, Lord: this shall not be unto thee.

22 raised up. And Peter took him, and began to rebuke him, saying, [1] Be it far from thee, Lord: this

---

1 Or, *God have mercy on thee.*

Peter's great confession, and from the connection in Luke (9: 21 f.) may have been spoken immediately after. The place is in the neighborhood of Cesarea Philippi. (16: 13.)

21. From that time forth began. Being now fully convinced that he was the Messiah, the disciples must be restrained from endeavoring to carry out their erroneous notions of the Messianic reign, and could be taught more correct ideas without destroying their faith. But the instruction here *begun* had to be continued from time to time. (17: 9, 22 f.; 20: 18 f.; 26: 2, 12, 31 f.; comp. John 12: 23 ff.) Filled with the popular Jewish conceptions, it required frequent repetition to make real to their minds the amazing thought that the Messiah was to be put to death. Indeed, they were unprepared after all; their hopes were crushed by his death, and they forgot his promise of rising again. This point, at which he begins distinctly to foretell his death, constituted a new epoch (Meyer) in our Lord's ministry, like that of 4: 17, where the same expression is used, 'from that time began.' This important epoch is considerably more than six months, probably eight or nine months, before the crucifixion. It must not for a moment be supposed that Jesus only now began himself to foresee his sufferings and death. (See John 2: 19; 3: 14; Matt. 9: 15; 10: 38; 12: 40. **Jesus,** should, as in the margin of Rev. Ver., be 'Jesus Christ.' This phrase occurs nowhere else in the Gospels except in the beginning of Matt. (1: 1, 18) and Mark (1: 1), and in John 17: 3. It is here very appropriate in opening a new section of the Gospel, and when the disciples have just formally recognized Jesus as the Christ.[1] The designation 'the Christ' has been already applied by Matt. to Jesus in 11: 2; 16: 20. **How that,** obsolete; we say 'that.' **He must,** as necessary to carry out his mission and accomplish his work (26: 54; Luke 24: 26; John 3: 14.) **Go unto Jerusalem.** This is mentioned here by Matthew alone; comp. at the transfiguration, Luke 9: 31. Jesus is now at the greatest dis-

tance from Jerusalem that was possible in Palestine. At Jerusalem the opposition to him was most bitter, through the conservatism of learning and of office. (John 11: 48.) Those who had assailed him most fiercely in Galilee came from Jerusalem. (Mark 3: 22; Matt. 15: 1.) He stayed away from the last preceding Passover because the Jews at Jerusalem sought to kill him. (John 7: 1.) From this time on the thought of going to Jerusalem and facing all that awaits him, is prominent in his mind. What is to befall him cannot happen elsewhere, Luke 13: 22; comp. also Matt. 20: 18, and the parables in Mark and Luke. **And suffer many things.** So also Mark and Luke. This general expression was natural in the distance; but shortly before the crucifixion he made more specific statements, 20: 19; Mark 10: 34. **Of the elders and chief priests and scribes,** the three classes which constituted the Sanhedrin, see on 26: 59. One article for the three nouns indicates their close connection. Mark and Luke add, 'be rejected by the elders,' etc. **And be killed.** The Jews expected the Messiah to conquer and reign; there is no intimation in their interbiblical or later writings of any other persuasion, for 2 (4) Esdras 7: 28 f. is evidently a Christian interpolation, and, indeed, the original work is probably post-Christian. **The third day,** so Luke; Mark's 'after three days' is equivalent, see on 27: 62. This prediction of rising the third day had been obscurely given to his enemies, John 2: 19; Matt. 12: 40, and is now distinctly given to the disciples, and repeated on two subsequent occasions, 17: 23 (also Mark); 20: 19. (Also Mark and Luke.) He also predicts his resurrection without mentioning the three days in 17: 9 (with Mark); 26: 32 (with Mark.) Mark (8: 32) adds, 'And he spake the saying openly,' as opposed to the previous obscure expressions. The disciples evidently could not take in the idea that he was to rise again. They believed in a resurrection at the last day (John 11: 24), but that could not be meant

---

1 'Christ' is added in the first hand of ℵ and of B, and in Memphitic. The rarity of the title readily accounts for its omission by copyists, while its appropriateness here appears only to the thoughtful student.

23 But he turned, and said unto Peter, Get thee behind me, Satan : thou art an offence unto me: for
thou savourest not the things that be of God, but those
that be of men.

23 shall never be unto thee. But he turned, and said
unto Peter, Get thee behind me, Satan: thou art a
stumblingblock unto me: for thou mindest not the

---

here, for how then should he do the work of
Messiah ? They had seen persons raised from
the dead, as the daughter of Jairus and the
son of the widow of Nain ; but this was done
by Jesus, and who was to raise him? The
only way in which they could conceive of a
person's coming to life again was that some
miracle-worker should bring him to life.
They understood clearly the statement of
Jesus that he was to die; the horror of that
thought would increase their confusion of
mind, and so they did not see what his resurrection could mean (comp. on 17: 9), probably thinking it must be figurative, and
thus of little personal interest to them in
connection with the thought of his death.
This state of things appears sufficiently to
account for their failing to remember these
predictions when his death and resurrection
occurred.

22 f. Peter was probably elated by the
commendation and promises of 16: 17-19,
and his native ardor and self-confidence
thereby encouraged into an attempt to direct
the Master's conduct. **Took him,** literally,
took him to himself ; so also Mark. He drew
Jesus aside (Chrys.), to make a personal and
private remonstrance. Comp. at a later
period, John 11: 8. **Began,** seems to be here
merely a descriptive touch (see on 11: 20), not
meaning (as in v. 21) that he afterwards did
the same on other occasions, but making us
see him as he begins this utterance. **Rebuke**
implies distinctly that Jesus is in the wrong.
Peter did not appreciate the 'must' in v. 21, as
denoting a necessity of the case. He believed
Jesus to be the Messiah, and according to all
his ideas it was out of the question that the Messiah should suffer and be killed at Jerusalem.
Be it far from thee, or literally, (as Rev.
Ver., *margin*), '(God) have mercy on thee.'
The course contemplated seems so perilous or
so wrong as to excite a prayer that God will
be merciful and prevent it. Notice that the
divine name is omitted (comp. on 5: 34).

Such an expression if lightly made would be
profane, but might be properly used on adequate occasion. It is not found elsewhere in
New Test., but several times in Sept.; in 1
Chron. 11: 19, David says (Sept.), "God be
merciful to me! that I should do this," Heb.
"a profane thing to me from my God,"
equivalent to Eng. "God forbid." Comp.
also 1 Macc. 2: 21. Tyndale and Cran. render 'favor thyself;' Gen., 'look to thyself;'
Com. Ver., *margin*, 'pity thyself,' supposing
(Jerome) the Greek to mean, ' (Be) merciful
to thyself;' but the Heb. and Sept. seem to
forbid this view. The Rabbis have (Edersh.)
an equivalent phrase, 'mercy to thee.'
Comp. also Paul's favorite expression, *me
genoito,* 'may it not be,' rendered 'far be it,'
'God forbid.' **This shall not be unto thee,**
'not' being the doubled and very strong negative,[1] as in 5: 18; 10: 42; 15: 5; 18: 3; 26:
29, 35, and often. 'Never' in Rev. Ver., is
not an exact translation, for it introduces an
additional idea, as does 'in no wise,' v. 28;
John 6: 37; the Greek being simply a strong
negation. So Jelf. 749, obs. 4. Peter is sure
that this ought not to be, and is persuaded that
Jesus will follow his advice, and so it certainly
will not be. **But he turned and said,** might
mean turned sharply upon him (Alex.), or
turned away from him (Mey., Weiss); Mark,
'turning and seeing his disciples,' decides
for the latter. As Peter had rebuked him,
so he now severely rebukes Peter (Mark 8:33),
calling him 'Satan,' and using the same
phrase of repulsion and abhorrence that he
used to Satan himself in 4: 10. The ardent
disciple was playing the tempter's part, in
fact repeating Satan's temptation, in trying
to restrain the Son of God (comp. 16 : 16 with
4 : 3, 6) from going forward in his appropriate
and appointed path. So a few months earlier
(John 6:70 f.), our Lord had called Judas Iscariot
a 'devil' (*diabolos*), *i. e.,* a Satan. (See on
4 : 1.) To translate Satan by 'adversary' as
the meaning here (Mald.), is forbidden by the

---

[1] When the two negatives were united, *ou me,* it was
natural that the following verb should be in the subjunctive, agreeing with the negative nearest to it. In
later (including Biblical) Greek, the subjunctive, which

by its doubtful affirmation suggests futurity, is often
replaced by the future indicative ; thus *hina* and *ou me*
both frequently have this construction in New Test. ;
and *ean* several times. Comp. 15: 5; 18: 19; 26: 35.

24 Then said Jesus unto his disciples, If any *man* will come after me, let him deny himself, and take up his cross, and follow me.

24 things of God, but the things of men. Then said Jesus unto his disciples, If any man would come after me, let him deny himself, and take up his

---

fact that in New Test. it is always a proper name.—Alas! the rock, Cephas, has become a stone of stumbling; he who had just made the divinely-taught confession (16: 17), is now Satan, tempting him whom he had confessed. **Thou art an offence** (*a stumbling block*) **unto me** (see on 5: 29), meaning either an obstacle to going forward in duty (Mey., Alex.), or more probably, a snare, a temptation to do wrong. (Keim.) **Thou savourest** (*mindest*) represents a very expressive Greek word used often by Paul, but nowhere else in New Test. save here and Acts 28 : 22, for which we lack an exact equivalent. (a) Its leading use is most nearly expressed by 'think' and 'mind.' Thus in 1 Cor. 13 : 11, 'I thought as a child'; Acts 28 : 22, 'to hear of thee what thou thinkest,' what is thy type of religious thought; Romans 12: 16, and Phil. 2 : 2, 'be of the same mind,' think the same thing, (or the one thing.) In all such cases it suggests one's characteristic way of thinking. (b) In other uses it means to direct the mind towards, or set the mind on, some object. Thus in Col. 3: 2, R. V., 'Set your mind on the things above'; Rom. 8: 5-7, 'They that are after the flesh mind the things of the flesh,' etc. In our passage, (and Mark 8 : 33), it may signify as in (b), thou dost not direct thy mind towards the affairs (plans, interests, etc.) of God, but those of men, (so Phil. 3: 9) ; or better, as in (a), thou dost not think God's thoughts, but men's; thou hast not God's way of thinking, but that of men. Comp. Isa. 55: 8, "For my thoughts are not your thoughts," etc. According to God's purposes and predictions it was necessary that the Son of God should suffer and die before entering into his glory, Luke 24: 26; 1 Peter 1: 11. 'Savourest,' in the common and early Eng. versions, was always a defective translation, derived from the Vulgate *sapitis*, French *savourer* and *savoir* (Eng. savour), meaning think or know.

24. Then would not make us sure that it followed immediately (comp. on 3: 13), but Mark leaves no doubt: 'And he called unto him the multitude with his disciples, and said unto them,' etc. This also shows that the notable saying which follows was addressed,

not to the disciples only, but to a great throng; so Luke 9: 23, R. V., 'he said unto all.' He has come away from the place at which he had been praying alone (Luke 9: 18), and now a crowd is near; but as to persons or locality we have no information. **If any man.** Not only is Jesus himself determined to go forward in a path which leads to suffering and death, undeterred by Peter's remonstrance, and not only must his twelve disciples be willing to follow in such a path, but this holds true of any and every one who wishes to be his follower at all. **Will** (or *wishes to*) **come after me.** 'Will come' is ambiguous, and at the present day almost certain to be misunderstood; 'would come' gives a slight color not present in the original (comp. on 15: 32). As he designs to go forward like a man bearing his cross to the place of crucifixion, so any one who wishes to come along behind him must do likewise. There is here no substantial difference between 'come after' and 'follow.' The familiar use of the phrases **deny himself** and 'take up his cross,' the frequent application of them to petty actions and sufferings, has gradually enfeebled their meaning in our conception, and it requires an effort to return to their original force. The phrases (a) to deny a statement, and (b) to deny a request (both classical), have an obvious meaning; (c) to deny a person (a sense found only in New Test.), is to deny that we have the relations to him which others are supposing, or which circumstances might seem to indicate (10: 33; 26: 34), or else to· deny that one is what he claims to be, and hence to reject him (Acts 3 : 14; 7 : 35); and there are various other shades of meaning. In some of these uses the Greek has the simple verb, as here in Luke; others have it compounded with a preposition, as here in Matthew and Mark, giving a slightly increased force. (d) To deny an object or practice is to refuse, reject, or renounce it; as 'denying impiety and worldly desires.' (Tit. 2 : 12, Rev. Ver., comp. 2 Tim. 3 : 5.) (e) To deny himself, a phrase not found in classical Greek, but characteristic of Christianity, might seem to connect itself in meaning with (b); as a man denies a beggar, so he denies himself, *i. e.*, refuses to grant his

25 For whosoever will save his life shall lose it: and whosoever will lose his life for my sake shall find it.

25 cross, and follow me. For whosoever would save his life shall lose it: and whosoever shall lose his

own requests (Chrys., Mey.) This is the sense, but much weakened, in which the expression is now widely used. But does it not, as here used by our Lord, rather connect itself with (c), meaning that a man renounces himself? As the Jews denied the Messiah (Acts 3 : 14), so his follower denies self, will not have self for his ruler or his aim. He determines not to live according to his own inclinations, but to do and bear whatever may be necessary in the course he has undertaken. He must resolve to live not for pleasure, but usefulness; not for inclination, but duty; not for self, but for God. (Comp. Rom. 14: 7-9; 15 : 2 f.) Tyndale, Cran., Gen., translate 'forsake himself.' **And take up his cross.** The Jews had long been familiar with the punishment of crucifixion, which was used in Egypt and all Western Asia, and from an early time in Italy. More than a hundred years before our Lord's ministry, King Alexander Janneus crucified eight hundred rebels at Jerusalem, while he was feasting in public (Jos. "Ant.," 13, 14, 2), and even under Antiochus Epiphanes, many Jews were crucified. (13, 5, 4.) For a revolt which followed the death of Herod the Great, the proconsul Varus crucified two thousand Jews. And yet a Jewish Rabbi of to-day has said that the saying here ascribed to Jesus is an anachronism, for the disciples could not have understood an allusion to cross-bearing till after his crucifixion. It was common to make the condemned person carry to the place of execution the cross on which he was to suffer (comp. on 27 : 32); and so the disciples would readily understand the Master's allusion. He was going forward, like one marching to crucifixion, appointed to suffering and death; and any one who wished to come after him must prepare himself for the same experience. The disciples and the multitude would not necessarily infer

from this that he was to be crucified. It was not till a few days before its occurrence that he foretold the precise mode of his death. (20 : 19.) They would understand that he was *like* a person going to be crucified, and they also must be ready for suffering and death. *Chrys:* "He saith also how far one ought to renounce oneself, that is, unto death, and that a reproachful death." *Jerome:* "And follow their teacher *morientium animo.*" Jesus used the same impressive image on two other occasions. (10 : 38 ; Luke 14 : 27 ; in Mark 10 : 21, it is spurious.) It was plain enough at the time, and after he was himself actually crucified it became all the more vivid and solemn, as was the case with many other parts of his teachings. Luke 9: 23 adds 'daily.' Every day must his follower consent and determine afresh to go forward through suffering and even unto death. *Chrys:* "Bear about this death continually, and day by day be ready for slaughter." **Follow,** comp. on 4 : 19. There they were to follow with an especial view to instruction; here they must follow in a path of suffering, follow even to dying; comp. John 12: 23-26. 'Follow' is also used in Com. Ver. for another word, which Rev. Ver. more exactly renders by 'imitate,' (1 Thess. 1 : 6 ; 2 : 14 ; 2 Thess. 3 : 7, 9 ; 1 Cor. 4 : 16 ; 11 : 1 ; Eph. 5 : 1 ; Heb. 6 : 12 ; 13 : 7 ; 3 John 11), thus bringing out more distinctly the great duty of imitating Christ.

25. Notice the repeated **for** (v. 25, 26, 27), each sentence supplying that which precedes with a proof or a motive. In v. 25 our Lord passes from bodily to spiritual life, from temporal to eternal life. There is a similar transition in 'leave the dead to bury their own dead,' 8: 22; comp. John 4: 10; 6: 27. He also passes in v. 25 f., from the vital principle of the body to the immortal principle. The English word 'soul' [1] was formerly used for both of these,

---

[1] In Greek and Latin, in Heb. and in Eng. there are two sets of words, older and more recent, both derived from roots signifying to *breathe ;* (a) *psyche, anima* (*animus*), *nephesh, soul,* (b) *pneuma, spiritus, ruach, ghost.* The latter set are derived from roots still used in the same language, for even to ghost corresponds gust. The former set are from roots no longer used in the language in question to denote breath or wind, and some of them found at all only in kindred languages.

Thus *psyche* corresponds to *psucho,* ' to cool," by blowing the breath, etc. *Anima* (*animus*) corresponds to Greek *anemos,* 'wind,' Sanskrit *an,* 'to breathe,' Latin *an-helo,* 'to gasp,' breathe with difficulty. *Nephesh* answers to Arabic *naphasa,* 'to breathe.' Soul, Anglo-Saxon *sawul,* sawl, saul, Gothic saiwala, is evidently from a root sav or sva, corresponding (Toy) to Sanskrit root su, and probably to Sanskrit suka, wind. It is thus plain that the first set of terms are older. These were long used

26 For what is a man profited, if he shall gain the whole world, and lose his own soul? or what shall a man give in exchange for his soul?
27 For the Son of man shall come in the glory of his Father with his angels; and then he shall reward every man according to his works.

26 life for my sake shall find it. For what shall a man be profited, if he shall gain the whole world, and forfeit his life? or what shall a man give in exchange for his life? For the Son of man shall come in the glory of his Father with his angels; and then shall he render unto every man according to

and so in our earlier translations of Scripture, but is in other English usage now confined to the immortal principle. Thus any possible translation of the present passage into current English is necessarily defective. The Com. Ver, by changing to 'soul' in v. 26, conceals the close verbal connection between the two sentences. The Rev. Ver., by retaining the same word 'life' in both, makes it less plain to the modern reader that the reference in the second sentence is to the spiritual and eternal life. Yet the latter translation is certainly best, for it only requires the reader to observe a transition which the Greek actually makes. So in 10: 39; Luke 17: 33 (comp. Luke 14: 26); John 12: 25; and a kindred idea in Acts 14: 22; 2 Tim. 3: 12. **Will save,** or *wishes to save,* as in v. 24. Whosoever wishes to save his bodily, temporal life shall lose his spiritual, eternal life. **For my sake.** Mark, 'for my sake and the gospel's.'

26. *What shall a man be profited,* read by the earliest documents, was easily changed by copyists into **what is a man profited,** by assimilation to Luke; in Mark also the documents vary much between present and future. Either point of view is obviously possible. **And lose** (Rev. Ver., *forfeit*). The Greek verb is derived from the noun rendered 'loss' as opposed to 'gain' in Phil. 3: 7, and is itself used in Phil. 3: 8, 'I have suffered the loss of all things.' It frequently denotes a fine or forfeit (Lidd. and Scott), and so Geneva here, 'be condemned to pay his soul'; but the image here is more probably that of profit and loss in business operations, where one subtracts the total loss from the total gain to see what profit he has made. The difficulty of translating the word in this sense as distinguished from the other word 'lose' just before, may

have partly influenced the Revisers into preferring the other sense. Luke 9: 25 gives both terms, 'and lose or forfeit his own self.' And notice that Luke has 'himself' instead of 'his life'; for a man to lose his life, in the highest sense of that term, is to lose himself. Observe that the thought here is not directly of what we call the loss or perdition of a soul. The gain and loss in the great business transaction are compared, and the man's own life in the spiritual and eternal sense is the loss; what then will be the profit? In earthly business, however, one may sometimes prosper afterwards and purchase back the property he has lost; but **what shall a man give in exchange for his soul** (*life*, so as to purchase it back? *Bengel:* "The world does not suffice." The noun *antallagma* denotes that which by exchange takes the place of something else, whether as substitute (Ecclus. 6: 15; 26: 14), or as a ransom (Isa. 43: 3); here it is more generally a purchasing equivalent.

27. We see that this great balancing of accounts is not a mere figure of speech, but will actually occur. **The Son of man,** see on 8: 20. This constantly suggests that he is the Messiah (comp. on 16: 13), and indicates that he is to be the final judge, as in 7: 22, and hereafter in 25: 31, 34. **Shall come,** not the mere future tense, but a strong expression like 'is going to come,' 'is about to come,' and in the Greek made emphatic by its position at the head of the sentence; he is coming, and there is no mistake about it. This is believed to be the first distinct intimation of his second coming. **In the glory of his Father.** In the same glory amid which his Father dwells. Comp. 26: 64. This glory he had with his Father before the world was (John 17: 5); he had voluntarily left it to come

when no clear distinction was made between the vital principle of the body and the immortal principle. At a later period, when this distinction grew clearer, the second set of terms were introduced, and applied almost exclusively (*not* Psa. 104: 29; Eccl. 3: 21) to the spiritual, immortal principle, while the older terms, though now chiefly restricted to the vital principle of the body, continued to be often used in the other sense also, and were necessary when the two senses were to

be united, or there was a quick transition from the one to the other. Thus there is not an absolute distinction between the two sets of words in Scripture use, a "Biblical trichotomy," but only a generally observed practical distinction. It should be carefully noticed that 'soul' very often in Old Test. and sometimes in New Test. denotes only the vital principle of the body. Whether it means the other, or means both together, is a question for consideration in every case.

28 Verily I say unto you, There be some standing here, which shall not taste of death, till they see the Son of man coming in his kingdom.

28 his [1] deeds. Verily I say unto you, There are some of them that stand here, who shall in no wise taste of death, till they see the Son of man coming in his kingdom.

---

[1] Gr. *doing.*

---

on his present lowly mission (Phil. 2:6 ff.), but he would return to share it again, and in that glory he would hereafter come. **With his angels** (13:41; 24:31; 25:31). Luke (9:26) has an expression which implies that their encompassing glory will enhance his glory. As to the angels, see on 18:10. **According to his deeds,** or, more exactly, action, practice, course of life. (Col. 3:9 has the same word.) The expressions seem to be suggested by Psa. 62:12; Prov. 24:12, quoted in Rom. 2:6; comp. Rev. 22:12, and as to the thought, 2 Cor. 5:10. The fact of this coming retribution shows the importance of saving the soul; but there is special reference to the thought of *reward* for doing and suffering in his service (v. 24 f.). Mark 8:38 and Luke 9:26, give the additional point that when he comes he will be ashamed of every one that has been ashamed of him. Matthew has before recorded this thought as uttered on a different occasion (10:33), and so he omits it here.

28. His coming is not only certain, but near. **Verily I say unto you,** as in 5:18, introducing a very important utterance. His coming will occur before some of those present will die. **There be,** old English where we now say 'there are.' **Some** (*of those*) **standing here,** who were not only the Twelve, but a crowd. (Mark 8:34.) It is implied that not many of them would live to witness what is meant; and this shows that it was not any event very near at hand. **Shall not,** the strong double negative, as in 16:22. **Taste of death.** The image is that of a bitter cup (20:22; 26:39), which all men must sooner or later taste of, and is very common in Jewish writings. Comp. Heb. 2:9; in John 8:51 f. it is made the equivalent of 'see death' (comp. Luke 2:26). **Till they see,** naturally, though not necessarily (comp. on 1:25), implies that after the coming in question they will taste of death; and is so far an argument against understanding our Lord's *final* coming to be meant. **The Son of man coming in his kingdom,** or *kingship,* royalty—coming as king (see on 3:2). So in the robber's prayer (Luke 23:42), and comp. as to the thought, Luke

21:31. In Mark 9:1; Luke 9:27, only the coming of the kingdom is mentioned; but that implies the coming of the Messianic King, which Matt. expresses. How could Jesus say that he would come as Messianic King in the lifetime of some then present? Certain rationalizing expositors at once say that Jesus expected his final coming to judgment to take place within that period. The language would readily bear that sense, especially in such close connection with v. 27; can it fairly have any other sense? Since the Fathers of the third century a good many have referred it simply to the Transfiguration, in which Jesus appeared as the glorious king. But (a) this is a very unnatural and enfeebled sense of 'coming in his kingdom;' (b) it occurred within a week, during the lifetime not simply of 'some,' but of probably all those present; and these objections are fatal to that view. Many others content themselves with understanding a general reference to the establishment of the spiritual reign of Messiah; some say on the Day of Pentecost (Acts 2), though that occurred within less than a year and so conflicts with 'some;' others say throughout the following generation or the century. The most reasonable explanation, especially when we comp. ch. 24, is to understand a reference to the destruction of Jerusalem, forty years afterwards. This providentially lifted the Messianic reign to a new stage. It put an end to the sacrifices and the whole temple ritual, and thus taught the Jewish Christians that these need be no longer observed, and to a great extent stopped the mouths of the Judaizers who gave Paul so much trouble. The withdrawal of the Christians from Jerusalem before its destruction occasioned an alienation between them and the Jewish people at large. In general, the destruction of Jerusalem made Christianity stand out as no longer even in appearance a mere phase or mode of Judaism, but an independent and universal religion. (Comp. Bp. Lightfoot on Galatians, p. 300 ff.) The sudden transition from the final coming for judgment (v. 27) to this nearer coming at the destruction of Jerusalem, is repeatedly

CHAPTER XVII.

AND after six days Jesus taketh Peter, James, and John his brother, and bringeth them up into a high mountain apart,

1 And after six days Jesus taketh with him Peter, and James, and John his brother, and bringeth

paralleled in ch. 24; and the very phrase of v. 28 by 24: 34, "This generation shall not pass away, till all these things be accomplished." *Plumptre:* "That such words should have been recorded and published by the Evangelists is a proof either that they accepted that interpretation, if they wrote after the destruction of Jerusalem, or if we assume that they were led by them to look for the 'end of all things' as near at hand, that they wrote before the generation of them who stood by had passed away; and so the very difficulty that has perplexed men becomes a proof of the early date of the three Gospels that contain the record."[1]

HOMILETICAL AND PRACTICAL.

V. 22 f. The imperfectly instructed believer. 1) Prejudice often prevents his understanding the plain teachings of revelation. 2) Conceit often leads him to set his own judgment above God's teaching. (Comp. 1 Cor. 4: 6.) 3) Presumptuous ignorance often makes him hinder the cause he tries to help. 4) Strength of will and warmth of heart often render his ignorance more harmful. 5) Therefore his honest opinions and well-meant advice must sometimes be utterly rejected by others. 6) Further instruction and experience may make him a pillar in the church. (Gal. 2: 9.)—V. 23. BAXTER (in Morison): "Good men ofttimes do the devil's work, though they know it not."—There has always been a tendency, and especially in our day, to decide questions of religious truth and duty from the human rather than the divine point of view. The Bible is judged exclusively from its conformity to human reason and its adaptation to human wants. Well-meaning persons try to build up churches, or to further public morality, by following the dictates of worldly policy. But to think God's thoughts, to look at things so far as we may from his standpoint, is in religion the only wisdom and safety.—CHRYS.: "If the chief apostle, even before he had learnt all distinctly, was called Satan for feeling this, what excuse can they have, who after so

abundant proof deny the mystery of the cross?"

V. 24 f. Following Christ. 1) Method. (a) In self-renunciation. (b) In cross-bearing. 2) Motives. (a) The loss in following him is but temporal, the gain is spiritual and eternal. (b) The loss in refusing to follow him is remediless forever. (c) The love of Christ ("for my sake") gives patience in loss, and adds brightness to gain. CHRYS.: "If any man will. I force not, I compel not, but each one I make lord of his own choice. . . . But he that leaves the hearer to choose attracts him more. For soothing is a mightier thing than force." HENRY: "We must deny ourselves absolutely; we must not admire our own shadow, nor gratify our own humor; we must not lean to our own understanding, nor seek our own things, nor be our own end."—V. 25. CHRYS.: "On that side salvation and destruction, and on this side salvation and destruction, but how greatly the one differs from the other."—Comp. on 10: 38 f.

V. 26. Earth's greatest business transaction. 1) The greatest possible earthly gain, accompanied by the greatest possible earthly loss. 2) The loss is utterly past remedy, and will soon render the gain utterly useless. 3) In this line of business we are all engaged, and ought to consult our true profit. (Comp. 5: 29 f.)—Queen Elizabeth, when dying, said, "Millions of money for an inch of time." She had the money, but could not make the exchange.—V. 27. Christ came in lowliness, despised and rejected (Isa. 53), in the form of a servant (Phil 2: 7), to live among men and die to atone for them; he will come again in glory, and take his people to behold his glory (John 17: 24), and to share it. (Phil. 3: 21.) BENGEL: "The doctrine of the person of Christ (16: 16) is immediately followed by the doctrine of the cross (v. 24), and this by the doctrine of glory." (v. 27.)

Ch. 17: 1-13.—THE TRANSFIGURATION. This is described also in Mark 9: 2-13; Luke 9: 28-36. The scene of the Transfigu-

---

[1] We here sadly take leave of Addison Alexander, the foremost of American commentators, whose work

was interrupted at this point by death. His previous commentaries were on Isaiah, Psalms, Mark, Acts.

2 And was transfigured before them: and his face did shine as the sun, and his raiment was white as the light.

2 them up into a high mountain apart: and he was transfigured before them: and his face did shine as the sun, and his garments became white as the

---

ration is popularly supposed to have been Mount Tabor, in Lower Galilee. This opinion is expressed in the fourth century, and Origen cites from the "Gospel according to the Hebrews" a passage which probably relates to the Transfiguration, and would show that some held this view in the second century. Yet the tradition is almost certainly incorrect. The conversation (16: 21-28) which preceded the Transfiguration by six days was very closely connected (see on v. 21) with Peter's great confession, and this occurred in the district of Cesarea Philippi. It is of course *possible* that in these six days Jesus should have come back to Galilee and gone south to Mount Tabor, but we know that he was at this period keeping away from Galilee for many important reasons (comp. on 16: 5). Moreover, we find in Mark that from the place of the Transfiguration they went forth and passed through Galilee as privately as possible to Capernaum (Mark 9: 14, 30, 33), and thence went towards Jerusalem. All this leaves the hypothesis of a hasty journey to Tabor and back violently improbable. Besides, Robinson has shown that there was a fortified city on Mount Tabor at that time, which must have rendered its narrow and rounded summit anything else than a place of seclusion. In view of these facts nearly all recent writers agree that the Transfiguration must have occurred in the neighborhood of Cesarea Philippi.

1. Into a high mountain, might be any one of the numerous spurs of the Hermon range in the vicinity of the city. We can hardly suppose one of the three highest peaks of Hermon to be meant, because to climb any one of them on foot and return is a fatiguing journey of ten or twelve hours (McGarvey, Thomson). And it would be too cold to spend a night there without shelter. Conder found it very cold in a tent. **After six days.** So also Mark. Luke says 'about eight days,' *i. e.*, about a week, which was often called eight days, counting both the first and the last (see on 12: 40), just as in the French and German languages a week is frequently called "eight days," and a fortnight "fifteen days." If

Matthew and Mark say 'six days' and Luke 'about a week,' there is certainly no conflict. It is not well to suppose (Chrys., Jerome) that Matthew and Mark give only the intervening days, while Luke adds the first and last, for this is supposing them to reckon in a way quite unnatural for Heb. or Greek usage, and such artificial harmonistic hypotheses are to be deprecated. The real point to be observed is that all three Evangelists declare the Transfiguration to have occurred only a few days after the prediction that Jesus must suffer and be killed. **Jesus taketh with him,** as in 2: 13; 4: 5; 12: 45. **Peter, James, and John,** alone were also admitted to see the raising of Jairus' daughter (Mark 5: 37), and to be near the Master in Gethsemane. (26: 37.) They belonged to the first group of four among the Twelve (see on 10: 2), and were evidently received to a peculiar intimacy. The conviction wrought in their minds by what they witnessed would impart itself to all, through their tone and general influence. **Apart.** Such an unearthly, almost heavenly scene must have no unsympathizing spectators. Luke says (9: 28, Rev. Ver.) that he 'went up into the mountain to pray' (comp. above on 14: 23), and that the wonderful change of appearance took place as he was praying. We have several times found mention of special seasons of prayer at great crises of our Lord's history. (Luke 3: 21; Mark 1: 35; Luke 6: 12; Matt. 14: 23.) As the three disciples were oppressed with sleep during the scene (Luke), and his return to the other disciples was 'on the next day' (Luke 9: 37), it seems clear that the Transfiguration occurred *at night*. The shining of our Lord's face and garments, and the bright cloud, would thus be more manifest, and the whole scene more striking.

2. And was transfigured, literally, *his form was changed*, meaning however, so far as we can see, merely a change in his appearance. **Before them,** within their full view, so that they could bear witness. **His face did shine as the sun,** comp. as partially similar, Exod. 34: 29; Acts 6: 15. **And his raiment,** or, *garments*, **was**—or, *became*—**white as the**

3 And, behold, there appeared unto them Moses and Elias talking with him.

4 Then answered Peter, and said unto Jesus, Lord, it is good for us to be here: if thou wilt, let us make here three tabernacles; one for thee, and one for Moses, and one for Elias.

3 light. And behold, there appeared unto them Moses 4 and Elijah talking with him. And Peter answered, and said unto Jesus, Lord, it is good for us to be here: if thou wilt, I will make here three [1]tabernacles; one for thee, and one for Moses, and one for

---

1 Or, *booths.*

---

light ;[1] Mark, Rev. Ver., 'glittering, exceedingly white,' Luke, 'white and dazzling,' (comp. Matt. 28: 3). All this was a temporary and partial anticipation of the glory that awaited him (John 12:23; 17:5; Phil. 3:21); comp. his appearance to one of these three disciples in Patmos. (Rev. 1:13-16.)

3 f. There are here (Godet) three distinct points: the personal glorification of Jesus (v. 2), the appearance and conversation of Moses and Elijah (v. 3 f.), the theophany and divine voice (v. 5). **Moses, and Elias,** *(Elijah),* recognized at once (v. 4), and doubtless by intuition, as a part of the supernatural scene. Any question as to whether Moses appeared in a resurrection body lies beyond our knowledge and is idle. "The law and the prophets were until John; from that time the kingdom of God is preached." (Luke 16:16.) Thus the Messianic reign is distinguished from the dispensation of the law and the prophets, though not intended to abrogate them. (5:17.) Accordingly we find the founder of the law, and the great reforming prophet, coming to attend on the Messianic King; and as they disappear, a heavenly voice calls on men to hear him. The Rabbis frequently speak of Moses and Elijah together; and a writer of several centuries after Christ says they were to come together in the days of the Messiah. **Talking with him.** Luke says (9:31), "spake of his decease which he should accomplish at Jerusalem," the announcement of which, a few days before, had so startled and pained the disciples. *Plumptre:* " It is significant that the word for 'decease' *(exodos)* re-appears in this sense once only in the New Test., and then in close connection with a reference to the Transfiguration. (2 Peter 1:15.)" It is not clear whether the disciples heard this conversation; at any rate it was partly designed for the Saviour's own benefit, that he might be supported in view of the sufferings and death to which his mind was now especially turning. (Luke 12:50.) **Then answered Peter,** not an answer to something said to him, but a response to the suggestions of the situation, an utterance called forth by the impression made on his mind. (Comp. on 11:25.) **Lord.** Mark has Rabbi, and Luke *epistates,* 'master,' see on 8:19. **It is good for us to be here.** Full of strange, bewildered, but delightful feelings, Peter wanted to stay there permanently, and not have the Master go to Jerusalem for the predicted sufferings and death. Keim fancies that Peter wished to summon the other disciples and the people from every direction to witness this opening manifestation of the Messianic glory —which is pure hypothesis, but not impossible. Meyer and Weiss imagine that Peter means, "It is a good thing that we are here," so as to take the necessary steps. The Greek will bear this sense, but the tone of the narrative will not.—It was indeed good to be there, but they could not stay. Down again must Jesus and his disciples go, amid human sorrow and sin (17:15), down to witness distressing unbelief (17:17), and presently to set out on the journey towards Jerusalem and the cross. As Moses and Elijah were parting from Jesus (Luke), Peter proposed to detain them by making **three tabernacles, or** 'booths,' shelters formed of branches of trees, such as the people were accustomed to make for the Feast of Tabernacles at Jerusalem. In these their glorious Lord and his heavenly visitors might abide in comfort; as for the disciples themselves, they could remain without shelter, being accustomed to the open air in hot weather, even at night. This was a strange proposal with reference to beings come from the other world, and Mark adds, 'for he knew not what to answer; for they were (or became) sorely afraid.' *I will make,* is read by the earliest manuscripts, and was easily changed

---

[1] The "Western" type of text added a comparison to *snow* in Mark 9: 3, and substituted it for 'light' in Matt. It was doubtless derived from 28: 3; Daniel 7: 9. This addition in Mark was adopted in the "Syrian" text, and came down to our common Greek text, and Com. Ver. Being found spurious, it cannot be used, as by Stanley, in considering the question of locality.

5 While he yet spake, behold, a bright cloud overshadowed them: and behold a voice out of the cloud,
which said, This is my beloved Son, in whom I am well
pleased; hear ye him.
6 And when the disciples heard *it*, they fell on their
face, and were sore afraid.
7 And Jesus came and touched them, and said, Arise,
and be not afraid.
8 And when they had lifted up their eyes, they saw
no man, save Jesus only.
9 And as they came down from the mountain, Jesus
charged them, saying, Tell the vision to no man, until
the Son of man be risen again from the dead.

5 Elijah. While he was yet speaking, behold, a bright
cloud overshadowed them: and behold, a voice out
of the cloud, saying, This is my beloved Son, in
6 whom I am well pleased; hear ye him. And when
the disciples heard it, they fell on their face, and
7 were sore afraid. And, Jesus came and touched
them and said, Arise, and be not afraid. And lift
8 ing up their eyes, they saw no one, save Jesus only.
9 And as they were coming down from the mountain, Jesus commanded them, saying, Tell the vision
to no man, until the Son of man be risen from the

by copyists to **let us make,** through assimilation to Mark and Luke. It accords with
Peter's ardent and self-reliant character
(16:22), that he should propose to make them
himself.

5. A bright cloud. Clouds are usually
dark, but this was a cloud full of light (same
word as in 6: 22), which in the night must
have been a sublime spectacle. Comp. in Old
Test. theophanies, Exod. 33: 9; 1 Kings 8:
10. The three disciples seem to have been
outside of the luminous cloud; Luke, in the
correct Greek text, leaves this uncertain, as
Matt. does; but **a voice out of the cloud**
suggests that those who heard it were without. Matthew repeats **behold** three times in
quick succession (v. 3, 5), the events being each
very remarkable. On two other occasions a
supernatural voice bore testimony to Jesus.
(3:17; John 12:28.) The words here spoken are
the same as at the baptism (see on 3: 17), except the addition here (in all three Gospels) of
hear ye him, a solemn call to listen to his
teachings and submit to his authority. The
phrase, 'in whom I am well pleased,' is not
here given by Mark and Luke, and instead
of 'beloved' the correct Greek text of Luke
(9:35) is 'chosen.' Of course the words cannot
have been spoken in all these forms; an unquestionable proof, if it were needed, that the
Evangelists do not always undertake to give
the exact words. (Comp. on 3: 17.) The words
'hear ye him' probably refer to Deut. 18: 15,
"a prophet . . . . like unto me; unto him ye
shall hearken." It may be that Peter recalled them when he quoted that passage in
addressing the Jews. (Acts 3:22.)

6-8. This solemn voice increased the awe
and terror with which the disciples were
overwhelmed. **They fell on their face**
(comp. Deut. 5: 25 f.; Heb. 12: 19), **and
were sore afraid,** that fear which the supernatural so readily excites. (Comp. on 14: 26.)
This fear is mentioned by Mark as explaining

Peter's mental confusion and strange proposition; by Luke, as felt when they saw Jesus
with Moses and Elijah, entering the cloud;
by Matt., as felt when they heard the voice
out of the cloud. We readily understand
that it was felt throughout, and might be
emphasized at various points with equal propriety. **And Jesus came and touched
them,** as the angel touched Daniel. (Dan. 8: 18;
10: 18.) One can almost see the kindly Saviour
stooping to touch each of the prostrate forms,
so as to arouse them to attention, and saying,
Arise, and be not afraid. They looked up
(Mark, 'suddenly')—the luminous cloud
was gone, and with it the bright forms of
Moses and Elijah—**they saw no man** (or *no
one*) **save Jesus only.** This means simply
that the others were gone and Jesus was
alone; the wonderful scene was ended. It
is quite unwarrantable to "accommodate"
the words as a text in the way sometimes
adopted—trust Jesus only, obey Jesus only,
take Jesus only as prophet, priest, and king
—all correct in themselves, but by no means
here taught.

9. As they came (*were coming*) **down from
the mountain,** more exactly, *out of the
mountain.* People who live near a mountain
constantly say, "he is gone up in the mountain," "when he comes down out of the
mountain"; he is not in the earth composing
the mountain, but is in the mountain as a locality. The evidence is overwhelmingly in
favor of *ek,* 'out of,' in Matt., and probably
so in Mark 9: 9; it was changed by copyists
to *apo,* 'from,' by way of assimilation to Luke
(9:37), just as it was changed in Mark 1: 10 by
assimilation to Matt. 3: 16 (see note). This
descent in the summer morning must have
been accompanied by delightful reflections on
what they had witnessed. Here was new and
wondrous confirmation of their faith that Jesus was the Messiah. They would naturally
wish to speak of it to the other disciples and

10 And his disciples asked him, saying, Why then say the scribes that Elias must first come?
11 And Jesus answered and said unto them, Elias truly shall first come, and restore all things.

10 dead. And his disciples asked him, saying, Why then say the scribes that Elijah must first come?
11 And he answered and said, Elijah indeed cometh,

---

all the people; and were doubtless surprised and disappointed when Jesus not only said to them, but **charged them, Tell the vision,** or *sight* (Acts 7 : 31), the word meaning simply something seen, **to no man,** more exactly, *to no one*, **until the Son of man,** the Messiah (see on 8 : 20), **be risen from the dead.** He is repeating what he had said a week before (16 : 21), that he must die and rise again. But they do not understand. Mark says (9 : 10), 'They kept the saying, questioning one with another what the rising from the dead should mean.' They were familiar with the idea of a general resurrection, but could not see how the Messiah was to be killed and come to life again (see on 16 : 21). They doubtless supposed it must mean something figurative, and never thought of understanding it literally. The other disciples would naturally feel a similar difficulty concerning the prediction as made before and repeated afterwards (17 : 23; 20 : 19); but some of them mentioned that such a prediction had been made, and when the rulers heard of it, they thought only of a pretended literal resurrection, which they endeavored to prevent. (27 : 63 f.)

In considering the design of the Transfiguration, we may be aided by this fact that it was not to be made known till after the resurrection 'of Jesus, and by the question which the disciples proceeded to ask (v. 10), showing a deep conviction that he was the Messiah. The wonderful scene was suited to fix this belief so firmly in the minds of these three leading disciples that it would not be shaken by the repeated prediction, nor utterly destroyed by the heart-rending reality, of his ignominious death. Henceforth, no disappointment of their cherished Messianic expectations, no humiliation instead of honor, and death instead of triumph, could ever make them doubt that he whom they had seen in such a form of glory, and receiving such testimony, was indeed the Messiah. Even when Peter so mournfully fell, he did not utterly lose this conviction, even as Jesus said the night before, 'I made supplication for thee, that thy faith fail not.' (Luke 22 : 32, R.V.) This unconquerable conviction on the part of the three

foremost disciples would keep the rest also from wavering, though they could not be told what had occurred. When their lips were unsealed, we may be sure that they delighted to tell the sublime story, even as Peter speaks of it in glowing terms in his last Epistle (2 Pet. 1 : 16 ff.), and John perhaps alludes to it in his Gospel (1 : 14). As to the effect of the Transfiguration upon Jesus himself, see on v. 3. But why could it not be told until after his resurrection? He had forbidden the disciples to tell any one that he was the Messiah (16 : 20). An account of this wonderful scene, if given to the people in general, with their mistaken conceptions of Messiah, would only have excited fanaticism and precipitated the crisis. When his resurrection and ascension had put an end to the thought of a mere temporal kingdom, and the minds of believers had been lifted up to a just conception of their exalted Lord, then the story could be appreciated, and would do good and not harm.

10-13. His disciples, viz., the three. (Mark 9 : 2.). **Why then?** There is now no doubt that he is the Messiah. Why then, **say the scribes that Elias (***Elijah***) must first come?** The thought of Elijah had been suggested by his appearance on the Mount. The Scribes were accustomed to teach that Elijah in proper person would come before the Messiah, and prepare the way for him by a new work of reformation—thus interpreting literally the prediction of Mal. 4 : 5 (comp. on 16 : 14). Some of the Jews held that Elijah would anoint the Messiah. But here is Messiah present beyond question, and no such preparatory ministry of Elijah has occurred. They ask him therefore to explain why the Scribes say that Elijah must come before the Messiah; and this he proceeded to do. Meyer and others suppose, with far less probability, that the disciples took this appearance of Elijah on the mount to be the predicted coming, and were only perplexed that Elijah had not come *first*, but after the Messiah had appeared. **And Jesus (***he***) answered and said.** The words 'Jesus' and 'to them' are not part of the correct text; nor is 'first' in v. 11, though genuine in v. 10. **Elias (Elijah) truly shall come.** 'Indeed,' or 'truly,' expresses con-

12 But I say unto you, That Elias is come already, and they knew him not, but have done unto him whatsoever they listed. Likewise shall also the Son of man suffer of them.
13 Then the disciples understood that he spake unto them of John the Baptist.

12 and shall restore all things: but I say unto you, that Elijah is come already, and they knew him not, but did unto him whatsoever they listed. Even so shall
13 the Son of man also suffer of them. Then understood the disciples that he spake unto them of John the Baptist.

---

trast with something to follow, as in 9 : 37. That Elijah cometh is the divine arrangement, and the prediction of Scripture. (For such uses of the present tense, see Winer, p. 265 [332].) **And restore all things.** Malachi predicted (4:6) of Elijah, "he shall turn the heart of the fathers to the children," etc., viz., as a preparation for the great day of the Lord. This 'shall turn' is translated in the Sept. 'shall restore,' and hence doubtless (*Bengel, Fritz.*) the word here and in Mark (9 : 12). Elijah will effect a preparatory reformation, comp. Luke 1: 17, 'to make ready for the Lord a people prepared.' Our Lord means to say that so the prediction stands. The future tense does not appear to mean, as Chrys. and others have imagined, that there was to be some other coming of Elijah still future when our Lord was speaking. **Elias** (*Elijah*) **is come already,** comp. 11 : 14. **Whatsoever they listed,** or *wished,* the old English listed being a modified form of lusted, *i. e.,* desired. 'They' is here impersonal; a very common use in Heb. of the third person plural, like the Eng. 'they say.' The reference is to the way John had been treated by the people in general, and by Herod in particular. John was not Elijah reappearing in his own proper person, but he was Elijah in "spirit and power" (Luke 1 : 17), in character and reforming influence. (Comp. on 3 : 1.) Some of the rabbinical writers represent that Elijah will bring back the ark, the pot of manna, etc.; Jesus regards him as coming to effect a moral renovation or restoration. In Acts 3 : 21, Peter points forward to a future "restoration of all things" in connection with the second coming of the Messiah. **Likewise shall also the Son of man suffer of them,** viz., at the hands of the people, not necessarily the same persons who had maltreated John, but the same generation. He here recalls to the three the prediction of a week before, which Peter had found it so hard to bear.

HOMILETICAL AND PRACTICAL.

V. 1–8. The Transfiguration. 1) The glo-

rious appearance. 2) The holy visitants. 3) The Father's voice. 4) The effect upon the disciples. 5) The lessons for us; (a) as to the Saviour's glory, (b) his authority, (c) our service of him.—V. 3. HALL : "A strange opportunity! in his highest exaltation to speak of his sufferings; when his head shone with glory, to tell him how it must bleed with thorns; when his face shone like the sun, to tell him it must be spit upon; when his garments glistened with that celestial brightness, to tell him they must be stripped and divided; when he was seen between two saints, to tell him how he must be seen between two malefactors."—V. 4. HENRY : "We are out in our aim, if we look for a heaven here upon earth. It is not for strangers and pilgrims to talk of building. Whatever tabernacles we propose to make to ourselves in this world, we must always remember to ask Christ's leave."—V. 5. Hear him. 1) As completer of the law. (5 : 17.) 2) As last and greatest of God's messengers. (Heb. 1 : 1 f.) 3) As the suffering Saviour. (16 : 21.) 4) As destined to be the final Judge. (16 : 27.)—V. 6. HENRY : "Through the infirmity of the flesh, we often frighten ourselves with that wherewith we should encourage ourselves."—V. 8. CHRYS. : "If we will, we also shall behold Christ, not as they then on the mount, but in far greater brightness. For then, to spare his disciples, he discovered so much only of his brightness as they were able to bear; hereafter he shall come in the very glory of the Father, not with Moses and Elijah only, but with the infinite host of the angels, not having a cloud over his head, but even heaven itself being folded up so that all men shall see him sitting, and he will make answers to them by himself, 'Come, ye blessed of my Father,' 'Depart from me, ye cursed.'"

V. 9. Tell the vision to no one. 1) It is a difficult and important duty sometimes to keep silence when we burn to speak. 2) Some points of religious truth are best withheld from persons not prepared to understand. 3) Delay in telling sometimes prepares us to tell more intelligently and impressively.

14 And when they were come to the multitude, there came to him a *certain* man, kneeling down to him, and saying,
15 Lord, have mercy on my son; for he is lunatic, and sore vexed: for ofttimes he falleth into the fire, and oft into the water.
16 And I brought him to thy disciples, and they could not cure him.
17 Then Jesus answered and said, O faithless and perverse generation, how long shall I be with you? how long shall I suffer you? bring him hither to me.

14 And when they were come to the multitude, there came to him a man, kneeling to him, and saying,
15 Lord, have mercy on my son: for he is epileptic, and suffereth grievously: for oft-times he falleth
16 into the fire, and oft-times into the water. And I brought him to thy disciples, and they could not
17 cure him. And Jesus answered and said, O faithless and perverse generation, how long shall I be with you? how long shall I bear with you? bring him

---

14-20 (21). Jesus Heals the Epileptic Boy.

Mark here gives (9: 14-29) many vivid details not found in Matthew or Luke (9: 37-43).

14-16. And when they, viz., Jesus, with Peter and James and John (17: 1, 9), **were come to the multitude.** The place was near the foot of the Mount of Transfiguration (Luke 9: 37), and so pretty certainly in the neighborhood of Cesarea Philippi. (See on 17: 1.) The great picture by Raffaelle, seizing upon the close connection between the Transfiguration and this scene, has taken the artistic license of representing them as contemporaneous, the Master in glory on the Mount, the nine disciples vainly attempting to heal the demoniac boy at its foot. 'The multitude' were surrounding the nine disciples (Mark), and 'were greatly amazed,' probably at the sudden appearance of Jesus after a night's unexplained absence, and after this failure of his followers. Some think there was still a light in his countenance, as when Moses descended with dazzling face. But this would have excited a curiosity which he and the three could not gratify. (17: 9.) Mark adds that the multitude ran to him and saluted him; they were perhaps curious to know where he had been, and were doubtless eager to see whether he could heal when the disciples had failed. It was probably in regard to this point that 'Scribes' were 'questioning with them.' The fame of Jesus' numerous healings in Galilee had long ago spread far and wide. (4: 24 f.) **A man, kneeling to him,** in humility and reverence, not in worship. **Lord,** see on 8: 2. It is not clear what amount of reverence the word here expresses. **On my son,** an only son (Luke 9: 38), and still a boy. (v. 18; Mark 9: 24; Luke 9: 42.) **Lunatic,** or *epileptic,* as in 4: 24; the word does not occur elsewhere in New Test. The symptoms described, and more fully and vividly in Mark (9: 18-20), are those of epilepsy; and the boy had been so affected from childhood (Mark). The

epilepsy was in this case connected (v. 18) with possession by a demon (see on 8: 28), which might either have caused the bodily ailment, or taken occasion therefrom. In Mark (9: 17) it is called 'a dumb spirit,' indicating that the demoniacal possession had caused the child to be dumb. **I brought him to thy disciples,** the nine who had been left behind, **and they could not cure him.** Mark and Luke, 'cast it out.' They had doubtless repeatedly cast out demons during their mission in Galilee the previous winter or spring (10: 1-8), and they might have done so now but for weakness of faith. (v. 20.)

17 f. O faithless (*unbelieving*) **and perverse generation.** The terms are borrowed from Deut. 32: 5, 20; comp. Phil. 2: 15. They were not unbelieving through lack of evidence, but through *perverse* neglect or rejection of the evidence. The Greek word means thoroughly twisted, crooked, etc., and so does the Latin *perversus.* (Comp. Eng. wrong from wring.). Tyn., Cran., Gen., here render 'crooked.' The term 'generation' seems to be used generally, not meaning specifically the disciples or the Scribes, etc., as various writers have supposed. The father, the nine disciples, the crowd, the Scribes (Mark 9: 14), would all in varying degrees and ways suggest that the current generation was unbelieving and perverse. So Zwingli, Bengel, Ewald, Trench (see Morison). 'Unbelieving' does not necessarily mean that no one in the generation believed at all; the disciples had 'little faith' (v. 20), the father believed and did not believe. This prevalence of perverse unbelief made it painful to live amid such a generation, and to **suffer,** or *bear with,* them. He had shown keen distress at unbelief before, Mark 8: 12 (see above on 16: 4); Mark 3: 5 (see above on 12: 13). Our Lord's sensitiveness of feeling appears in many ways, but only here is recorded as taking the form of momentary impatience at dwelling amid such an environment; it must have been all the more distressing from the contrast with the

18 And Jesus rebuked the devil; and he departed out of him: and the child was cured from that very hour.
19 Then came the disciples to Jesus apart, and said, Why could not we cast him out?
20 And Jesus said unto them, Because of your unbelief: for verily I say unto you, If ye have faith as a grain of mustard seed, ye shall say unto this mountain, Remove hence to yonder place; and it shall remove: and nothing shall be impossible unto you.
21 Howbeit this kind goeth not out but by prayer and fasting.

18 hither to me. And Jesus rebuked him; and the demon went out from him: and the boy was cured from that hour. Then came the disciples to Jesus 20 apart, and said, Why could not we cast it out? And he saith unto them, Because of your little faith: for verily I say unto you, If ye have faith as a grain of mustard seed, ye shall say unto this mountain, Remove hence to yonder place; and it shall remove; and nothing shall be impossible unto you.[1]

1 Many authorities, some ancient, insert ver. 21, *But this kind goeth not out save by prayer and fasting.* See Mark ix. 29.

---

scene of the Transfiguration, a few hours before. **How long?** literally, *until when?* as if expecting a time of release. Yet he did bear with that generation for yet many months (see on 19 : 1), and did on this occasion, amid all the disheartening and intolerable unbelief, promptly recognize and bless a faith that was confessedly weak. This confession was made by the father in a touching dialogue recorded by Mark. (9 : 20-25.) **Bring him hither to me.** Even the disciples have been weak in faith, and what they ought to have done must be done by him. **And Jesus rebuked the devil,** literally, *him,* the demoniac, which of course means that he rebuked 'the unclean spirit' (Mark and Luke); the rebuke doubtless related to his unlawful and malignant possession. The apparent confusion of persons in speaking to the child and the demon is natural on the assumption of a real demoniacal possession, and repeatedly occurs in the Gospels. Tyn. and his followers transposed 'the devil' into the first clause. **The devil** should be *the demon,* see on 8 : 31. **Departed out of him,** *ek* and *apo* being united, comp. on 3 : 16. The dispossession caused the child frightful suffering, and presently he lay as if dead till Jesus raised him up (Mark). **The child;** *boy* is the exact translation, and more definite than 'child.' **Was cured from that very hour,** at once and permanently, as in 15 : 28; 9 : 22. Luke adds (9 : 43, R. V.), "And they were all astonished at the majesty of God." **19, 20 (21). The disciples,** viz., the nine who had tried and failed. **Apart,** Mark (9 : 28), 'when he was come into the house,'

apparently that in which he and they had been sojourning. **Why could not we cast him** (*it*) **out?** 'we' being expressed in the Greek, and thus emphatic; he had authorized them to cast out demons (10 : 1-8), and we cannot doubt they had done so. (Comp. the Seventy, Luke 10 : 17). **Because of your unbelief,** cor. text, *little faith,*[1] comp. 'ye of little faith' in 6 : 80; 8 : 26; 14 : 31; 16 : 8. To this corresponds the answer given in Mark. 'This kind can come out by nothing save by prayer,' viz., as increasing their faith and spiritual power. **For** gives a proof of the preceding statement. Your failure must have been on account of your weakness of faith, *for* a very minute faith can work a very great miracle. **As a grain of mustard seed,** often used for anything very small (see on 13 : 31); their faith must therefore have been extremely minute, being less than this. **Unto this mountain.** He probably pointed to the mountain on which he had the night before been transfigured; so in 21 : 21 it is the Mount of Olives. This faith that could remove mountains (comp. Luke 17 : 6 ; Matt. 21 : 21 f. ; Mark 11 : 23; 1 Cor. 13 : 2) was proper and possible only in those to whom it was granted to work miracles. For us to attempt such a thing is folly. **And nothing shall be impossible unto you** is of course an exaggerated expression, such as all men use, and all understand, and answers to what he had just before said to the father (Mark 9 : 23), "All things are possible to him that believeth;" comp. also Phil. 4 : 13.

21. This verse is spurious,[2] having been

---

[1] This is the reading of א B, the cursives 13, 124, 346, which are known to have been derived from one old uncial, and several other important cursives, the Old Syriac, Memphitic and Sahidic, Armenian, Æthiopic, and it is quoted in Origen, Chrys., Hilary. The word *oligopistian* is not found in the classics nor elsewhere in Biblical Greek, but sometimes employed by Greek Fathers. It was easily changed by copyists into 'unbelief (*apistian*), a familiar term, implied in v. 17, and

seeming at first more in accordance with what follows. Yet in fact Jesus has never accused the disciples of having *no* faith, but repeatedly of having little faith (*oligopistoi*). This fact is not likely to have occurred to copyists, while the other considerations are obvious.

[2] It is wanting in א (first hand) B, two copies of the Old Latin, the Old and Jerusalem Syriac, Sahidic, and a copy of Memphitic, and Æthiopic. The insertion by copyists from another Gospel is natural and very com-

22 And while they abode in Galilee, Jesus said unto them, The Son of man shall be betrayed into the hands of men:

22 And while they [1] abode in Galilee, Jesus said unto them, The Son of man shall be delivered up into

---

l Some ancient authorities read, *were gathering themselves together.*

---

added by copyists from Mark 9: 29. Already, before this was done, the passage had been enlarged in Mark by adding 'and fasting,' due to the asceticism among the early Christians. A similar addition of 'fasting' was made by copyists in Acts 10: 30; 1 Cor. 7: 5, and so came into the common text. The word fasting is genuine in Luke 2: 37; Acts 13: 2 f.; 14: 23. For our Lord's instruction as to fasting, see on 9: 15; 6: 18.

The events of 16: 13 to 17: 20 occurred within a short time, apparently little more than a week, and soon after Jesus reached the neighborhood of Cesarea Philippi. He appears to have stayed in that region, so far as our information enables us to judge, several weeks, perhaps two or three months (comp. on 16: 13), but there is no record of further sayings or doings.

HOMILETICAL AND PRACTICAL.

V. 14 f. A father's remarkable experience. 1) The distressing calamity. 2) The disheartening failure. 3) The struggling faith. (Mark 9 : 22-24.) 4) The great blessing.—V. 14. HENRY: "Sense of misery will bring people to their knees. . . . . Parents are doubly concerned to pray for their children, not only those that are weak and cannot, but much more that are wicked and will not, pray for themselves."—V. 17. The Saviour grieving at unbelief. 1) He felt an unbelieving atmosphere to be utterly uncongenial. 2) He saw clearly the perverseness and general sinfulness of unbelief. 3) He considered what blessings men were missing through unbelief. 4) He observed how attempts at usefulness were marred by unbelief. 5) He was pained by unbelief in him as a personal unkindness

and injustice. 6) He perceived that unbelief is obstinate and hard to conquer.—V. 19. HENRY: "Ministers, who are to deal for Christ in public, have need to keep up a private communion with him, that they may bewail the follies and infirmities of their public performances, and inquire into the cause of them."—V. 20. Little faith. 1) It restricts usefulness. 2) It hinders spiritual perception. (16: 8.) 3) It makes men timid amid perils. (8: 26.) 4) It leaves them consumed with temporal anxieties. (6: 30.)

22-27. RETURNING TO GALILEE, JESUS AGAIN FORETELLS HIS DEATH. HE PAYS THE TEMPLE TAX.

Here are two matters.

I. **22 f.** HE AGAIN FORETELLS HIS DEATH AND RESURRECTION. Found also in Mark 9: 30-32; Luke 9: 43-45. Mark tells how they left the place of healing the demoniac boy, near the Mount of Transfiguration, and passed through Galilee. **And while they abode,** etc.,—*were gathering themselves together in Galilee* (Rev. Ver., margin), is in all probability the true text.[1] It implies that they returned by different routes to a fixed point in Galilee. Upon reflection, this is seen to agree exactly with Mark's statement that Jesus 'wished no one to know' (comp. above on 16: 5) of the journey through Galilee, for a natural expedient to this end would be the separation of the Twelve into several parties, taking different routes. We then understand that at the rendezvous, as they were assembling, Jesus made the statement that follows. Mark's 'for' (9: 31) perhaps indicates (Alford) that he wished to pass on unnoticed, because he was engaged in privately teaching his disciples about his approaching death. Or it

---

mon, while we cannot imagine any reason for the omission of the passage if originally present in Matt., since no class of Christians in the early centuries would have objected to it. The manuscripts and versions which contain it have much verbal variation, a common thing in such borrowed passages. In Mark the sentence is found in all documents, but the words 'and fasting' are there omitted by ℵ (first hand), B, one copy of Old Latin, and apparently by Clem. (W H.) This evidence might seem slender, but there is no conceivable reason for the omission of the words by copy-

ists or students, while their insertion is explained by the asceticism prevalent among the early Christians, and is paralleled in the common text of Acts 10: 30; 1 Cor. 7: 5. So the case is clear.

1 It is the reading of ℵ B, and the cursive 1; several early versions show confusion and uncertainty in their rendering. 'Abode' represents *anastrephomenon*, and 'were gathering themselves together' is *sustrephomenon*. The latter would strike copyists as strange, and be easily changed into what seemed more simple. The case is not certain, but highly probable.

23 And they shall kill him, and the third day he shall be raised again. And they were exceeding sorry.
24 And when they were come to Capernaum, they that received *a* tribute *money* came to Peter, and said, Doth not your master pay tribute?

23 the hands of men; and they shall kill him, and the third day he shall be raised up. And they were exceeding sorry.
24 And when they were come to Capernaum, they that received ¹ half-shekel came to Peter, and

---

a Called in the original *didrachma*, being in value fifteen pence. See Ex. 30: 13, and 38: 26....1 Gr. *didrachma*.

---

may mean that he wished to avoid the fanatical multitude, who, at his last recorded visit to Capernaum, wanted to make him a king after their own notion. (John 6: 15.) **The Son of man,** see on 8: 20. **Shall be** (or *is going to be,*) the same construction as in 16: 27. **Betrayed,** or *delivered up,* **into.** So Com. Ver. rightly in Mark and Luke, though rendering 'betrayed' in Matt. (comp. on 10: 4); and we shall find similar inconsistency throughout in translating the term. The words which really mean 'betray' and 'traitor' occur only in Luke 6: 16; Acts 7: 52. **Into the hands of men.** In 20: 19 it becomes more definite, 'unto the Gentiles'; 26: 45, 'into the hands of sinners.' The idea of losing liberty and being rudely handled by other men, is always in itself painful. This being delivered into the hands of men is the new idea here added; the rest is repeated from 16: 21. (See note.) **And they were exceeding sorry,** or exceedingly grieved. Mark and Luke state that they did not understand the saying (comp. on 17: 9), and feared to ask him about it—probably with that feeling which often restrains persons from seeking more precise information that would probably but increase their distress. The three who had witnessed the transfiguration must have been better able to bear this renewed and painful announcement; but they could not tell the others what they had seen and heard.

II. **24-27.** PAYING THE TEMPLE CONTRIBUTION. Found in Matt. only, except the statement in Mark (9: 33), that 'they came to Capernaum.' This seems to have been our Lord's final visit to Capernaum, which had so long been his abode (see on 4: 13), and was probably short. (Comp. on 18: 1.) He had just come from the neighborhood of Cesarea Philippi. (See on v. 22.) **They that received the tribute money** (*half shekel*). The Greek *didrachmon*, or double drachm, was a silver coin equal to two Attic drachms, and in the times of the New Test. and Josephus was nearly equal to a half shekel, or something over thirty cents. 'Tribute money,' Cranmer and K. James, is too indefi-

nite; 'poll money,' Tyn., Gen., fails to suggest that it was a specific poll-tax for the temple. It is better in such cases to use the definite term of the original, and let this become matter of explanation. But as the Greek didrachm or double drachm is unfamiliar, it is convenient to use the half shekel, the Hebrew shekel being familiar to us from Old Test. Moses directed (Exod. 30: 11 ff.) that whenever the people were numbered, every male over twenty years old should give a half shekel, rich and poor alike, for the support of the tabernacle. Upon this Josiah based his demand for a special contribution to repair the temple. (2 Chr. 24: 6.) After the return from the captivity, Nehemiah and his followers "made ordinances"—not as being required by the law of Moses, but as a voluntary agreement—to pay *every year* the *third* part of a shekel (they were poor then), in order to provide sacrifices, etc., for the temple. (Neh. 10: 32 f.) In the Mishna, as here in Matt., we meet with a well known contribution of a half shekel. The Rabbis had kept Nehemiah's plan of making it annual, but had returned to the sum which the law of Moses required for the occasional gift, and doubtless held that they were but carrying out the law. The Mishna has a separate treatise on this subject. Priests, women, children, and slaves, were exempt, but might give if they wished. The Jews in Palestine were expected (Edersh.) to give before the time of the Passover; those in foreign countries were allowed till Pentecost or even Tabernacles, and there was a special chest in the temple for contributions due the previous year. Commissioners were sent through Palestine to collect—'they that received the half shekel,' distinct from the publicans who collected the government tax; in foreign countries the money was deposited by the leading Jews in some fortified city till it could be escorted to Jerusalem. (Jos. "Ant.," 18, 9, 1.) Cicero states that gold was, every year, in the name of the Jews, exported from Italy and all the provinces to Jerusalem, and commends Flaccus for prohibiting this exportation from Asia, *i. e.,* the region of

25 He saith, Yes. And when he was come into the house, Jesus prevented him, saying, What thinkest thou, Simon? of whom do the kings of the earth take custom or tribute? of their own children, or of strangers?

26 Peter saith unto him, Of strangers. Jesus saith unto him, Then are the children free.

said, Doth not your [1] master pay the [2] half-shekel? 25 He saith, Yea. And when he came into the house, Jesus spake first to him, saying, What thinkest thou, Simon? the kings of the earth, from whom do they receive toll or tribute? from their sons, or 26 from strangers? And when he said, From strangers, Jesus said unto him, Therefore the sons are

---

1 Or, *teacher*.... 2 Gr. *didrachma*.

---

which Ephesus was the chief city. (Cicero, "for Flaccus," 28.) Josephus says (" Ant.,"3, 8, 2) that the gift in Exod. 30: 11 was from men between twenty and fifty years old, which statement makes it likely that the age was thus limited in his times, which were those of the New Testament. After Titus destroyed Jerusalem, Vespasian decreed that the Jews everywhere "should bring two drachms every year for the temple of Jupiter Capitolinus, as before they were wont to pay for the temple at Jerusalem." (Jos. " War," 7, 6, 6.)—Quite distinct from this yearly half shekel, which was required by custom, if not by the law, were the voluntary contributions made at the temple, which varied indefinitely in amount. (Mark 12:41 ff.) Entirely distinct also was the tax (22: 17) to the Roman government in Judea and Samaria, which two districts formed at the time of our Lord's ministry a Roman province.

It is not at all clear with what design the collectors asked the question, but most likely in a reproachful tone, as if he was slighting a duty recognized by all devout Jews. **Doth not your master**—that is *teacher* (*didaskalos*, see on 8 : 19) **pay** *the half-shekel*, as everybody else does? The regular time for paying was in the spring, while it was now near the beginning of autumn. Jesus and his followers had been long absent from Capernaum, and the collectors now seized their opportunity, perhaps wishing to send up all that was behind to the Feast of Tabernacles.

25 f. Peter's ready answer, **Yes,** most naturally suggests that Jesus had paid in previous years, and so there was no doubt that he would pay now. The fact that Matt. records this incident without any explanation as to the nature and design of the contribution, is one of the many proofs that he wrote especially for Jewish readers, to whom the matter would be familiar. **Into the house,** probably the house of Peter, which Jesus usually appears to have made his place of abode at Capernaum. (comp.

on 4 : 13 ; 8 : 14). **Jesus prevented,** that is, *spake first to,* **him, saying.** The Greek means to get before, anticipate, (comp. on 12 : 28), and would be exactly translated now by 'anticipated him, saying.' Tyn. and Gen. gave 'spake first to him.' The Latin *prevent* (originally 'to come before') was introduced by Cran. and Rheims, and at that time was a good translation ; but it has now lost that meaning in Eng., and acquired a different sense, which makes it very misleading, (e. g., Ps. 119: 147 f. ; 1 Thess. 4: 15.) To avoid the word 'anticipate,' which is not used in K. James, the Rev. Ver. has returned to 'spake first to him,' a rather inadequate rendering. Jesus knew what had occurred without needing to be told. (Comp. John 1 : 48). **Custom** (rather *toll*), **or tribute.** The first Greek word denotes taxes or tribute in general, the second is the Latin word *census*, which, from meaning a registration for the purpose of taxation, might naturally in the provinces be applied to the poll-tax ; its sense here and in 22: 17. **Of their own children** (*sons*), **or of strangers?** The latter term means those of other blood, of other than the royal family. **Then are the children** (*sons*) **free,** i. e., exempt. And so the Son of God, as Peter had recognized Jesus to be (16: 16), ought to be exempted from paying tax to the temple for the support of divine worship. He uses the plural, 'sons,' because he is stating the inference from his previous argument in a general form ; but the application is obviously designed to be to himself. The Romanists in Europe have absurdly applied this to the clergy, as showing that they ought to be exempted from taxation, at any rate when it is for religious purposes. When our Lord adds, 'lest we cause them to stumble,' the plural refers not to any notion that Peter was exempt, but to the fact that Peter as well as himself had not paid ; and he proceeds to direct how Peter may pay both for the Master and himself.

27 Notwithstanding, lest we should offend them, go thou to the sea, and cast a hook, and take up the fish that first cometh up; and when thou hast opened his mouth, thou shalt find *a* a piece of money: that take, and give unto them for me and thee.

27 free. But, lest we cause them to stumble, go thou to the sea, and cast a hook, and take up the fish that first cometh up; and when thou hast opened his mouth, thou shalt find a ¹ shekel: that take, and give unto them for me and thee.

CHAPTER XVIII.

AT the same time came the disciples unto Jesus, saying, Who is the greatest in the kingdom of heaven?

1   In that hour came the disciples unto Jesus, saying, Who then is ² greatest in the kingdom of heaven?

a Or, *a stater.* It is half an ounce of silver, in value 2s. 6d. after 5s. the ounce——1 Gr. *stater.*...2 Gr. *greater.*

---

27. Lest we should offend them, or better, *cause them to stumble,* give them an occasion for objecting to my claims, and refusing to receive me. (See on 5: 29.) They would have said that he did not keep the law, did not perform a recognized duty of every Israelite, and so he certainly could not be the Messiah. **Go thou to the sea.** The preposition is that usually rendered 'into.' In a case like this it signifies into the locality represented in a general way by the sea, which would include its shores. We are not at liberty to understand it here in a stricter sense, such as would be expressed in English by 'into the sea,' because that would be manifestly inappropriate to the action which Peter was to perform, viz., catching a fish with a hook. (So in John 11: 38; 20: 1.) Wherever it would not be distinctly and decidedly unsuitable to the action in question, the natural and common sense of 'into' must be retained. (Comp. on 3: 16.) The sea was of course the Lake of Galilee, on which Capernaum was situated. (4: 13.) **Thou shalt find a piece of money,** (*a shekel,* Greek *stater,*) an attic silver coin, equal to four drachms, or two half-shekels. **For me and thee,** is strictly, 'instead of me and thee,' the notion being of *a substitution,* which was the original and proper meaning of this contribution (see Exod. 30: 11-16). Jesus never wrought a miracle for his personal benefit. If he had procured the money for this purpose in an ordinary way, it might have obscured the fact of his extraordinary position as the Messiah. Matthew probably recorded this incident to show his Jewish readers on the one hand that Jesus felt himself entitled to the respect due to the Messiah, and on the other, that he was very careful to keep the law in all respects, so that no Jew had a right to stumble at him. Our Lord's disposition to forego a privilege to which he was justly entitled, rather than that men should have an excuse for misapprehending him, was imitated by Paul (1 Cor. 9), and stands before us all as a part of the example of Christ. **A hook.** Fish-hooks are mentioned elsewhere in the Bible only in Isa. 19: 8; Amos 4: 2; Hab. 1: 15; Job 41: 1, etc., and are not now used in the Lake of Galilee. Peter had previously had experience of a miracle in catching fishes. (Luke 5: 4 ff.) Commentators compare here the story of the ring of Polycrates (Herod. III., 39-42).

HOMILETICAL AND PRACTICAL.

V. 24-27. Jesus giving for the support of the temple. 1) He takes pains to avoid being misunderstood; (a) speaking so as to prevent Peter from misunderstanding him; (b) acting so as to prevent the Jews. 2) While avowing himself the Son of God, he performs every duty of a good man (comp. 3: 15), including that of taking part in religious contributions. He relinquishes an avowed claim to exemption, lest his course should injure others. Comp. 1 Cor. 8: 13; 9: 12, 22.

Ch. 18: 1-14. THE SUBJECTS OF THE MESSIANIC REIGN MUST BE CHILDLIKE.

We are approaching the close of our Lord's ministry in Galilee. (19:1.) Convinced that their Master is the Messiah (16:16), the disciples begin to dispute which of them shall have the highest office in the Messianic kingdom, which they conceive of as secular rather than spiritual. They bring him this question, and he says at once that only by being childlike can they have any place at all in the Messianic kingdom; it follows that the childlike ought to be received for Christ's sake, and that any one incurs great guilt who causes them to sin (v. 5-9); and they must not be despised, for the Saviour and the Father are specially concerned for their salvation, v. 10-14. Comp. Mark 9: 33-50; Luke 9: 46-50.

I. 1-4. THE SUBJECTS OF THE MESSIANIC REIGN MUST BE CHILDLIKE. **At the same time,** or *in that hour,* is best taken strictly

2 And Jesus called a little child unto him, and set him in the midst of them.

2 And he called to him a little child, and set him in 3 the midst of them, and said, Verily I say unto you,

(10: 19; 26: 45), but may mean more generally, at that precise period. The time must be when Jesus was in the house at Capernaum. (17: 25; Mark 9: 33), and perhaps while Peter was gone to find the shekel. **Came the disciples unto Jesus, saying.** Luke, in his very brief account, speaks only of Jesus as seeing the reasoning of their heart. Mark says they had 'disputed one with another in the way,' apparently on the road from Cesarea Philippi to Capernaum (comp. on 17: 22), and that when Jesus asked them about it they were silent. Not knowing all the circumstances, we need not be nervously anxious to harmonize these accounts; but it is not difficult to suppose that they came intending to ask him the question, but hesitated; that perceiving their thought (Luke) he inquired, and they were at first silent (Mark), but at length spoke (Matt.). **Who,** literally, *who then,* who in the state of things present to their minds, implies some previous occurrence or conversation which led to the inquiry, and this may be the conversation to which Mark refers. **Is greatest in the kingdom of heaven,** *i. e.,* the Messianic kingdom (see on 3: 2). They were thinking of it as a temporal kingdom, in which there would of course be higher and lower officials. 'Greatest' is literally 'greater,' *i. e.,* greater than all others, comp. on 11: 11; 13: 32, and see Buttm. p. 84. Luke (9: 46) says that the point in their thoughts was 'which of them should be greatest'; but they asked the question in a more general form. Notice that the dispute closely follows a prediction that he would die (Mark and Luke), as in similar cases afterwards. (20: 20; Luke 22: 24.) Convinced that he was the Messiah (16: 16), and not understanding how he could literally rise again (see on 17: 9), their minds fastened exclusively upon the idea that somehow or other he was about to set up a Messianic kingdom. (16: 28.) And though he had recently declared it impossible to follow him save in self-renunciation (16: 24), they were intent on self-aggrandizement.

The statement in the Sermon on the Mount (5: 19) concerned a greatness which many might attain; here the question is, who shall have the single highest place. Our Lord had treated Peter, James, and John with marked distinction, in permitting them alone to witness the Transfiguration. (17: 1.) Forbidden to tell any one what they had seen (17: 9), they would naturally say so to the other disciples when asked where they and the Master had been. Besides, Peter was some time before addressed in the presence of the others in a manner which gave him special prominence. (16: 17 ff.) And just now Jesus has directed that Peter's temple-contribution shall be paid along with his own through a special miracle, taking no notice of the others. About six months later, we shall find James and John, with their mother as spokesman, actually requesting that they may have the two highest places in the kingdom (20: 20), and the other ten greatly displeased about it. And the dispute will be renewed even on the night before the crucifixion. As to the probable grounds for individual claims of pre-eminence, see on 19: 30. From all this it appears that we here reach a turning-point, the disciples beginning a contention which will be renewed unto the end.

2-4. A little child. The house was probably that of Peter (17: 25), and so the child may have been Peter's child. **Called unto him,** shows a child able to walk; it could sit by his side (Luke), yet was small enough to be naturally taken in his arms (Mark), and so young as to be appropriately a pattern, to afford an object-lesson. It cannot therefore have been personally a believer (v. 6). A late tradition makes this child Ignatius, martyred about A. D. 115, but it is without authority, and evidently arose from a fanciful misinterpretation of certain phrases in his letters. **Verily I say unto you,** indicating something very important, see on 5: 18. **Except ye be converted,** or *turn,*[1] viz., from your present sinful ambi-

---

[1] The simple Greek verb *strepho* is everywhere else in New Test., correctly translated by Com. Ver. 'turn.' The compound *epistrepho* it renders 'convert' in 13: 15 (with Mark 4: 12; John 12: 40; Acts 28: 27); Luke 22: 32; Acts 3: 19; James 5: 19 f. All the preceding English versions had given 'convert' in Luke, John, James, Acts 28: 27; in the other passages, Tyn. and one or two of his followers gave the Anglo-Saxon 'turn.' (Comp. on 13: 15 and 3: 2.) 'Turn' is in the Greek a passive form, but used in the "middle" sense, equivalent to the English active intransitive; so it is properly translated 'turn,' and not 'be turned'

3 And said, Verily I say unto you, Except ye be converted, and become as little children, ye shall not enter into the kingdom of heaven.
4 Whosoever therefore shall humble himself as this little child, the same is greatest in the kingdom of heaven.
5 And whoso shall receive one such little child in my name receiveth me.

Except ye turn, and become as little children, ye shall in no wise enter into the kingdom of heaven?
4 Whosoever therefore shall humble himself as this little child, the same is the [1] greatest in the kingdom
5 of heaven. And whoso shall receive one such little

---

1 Gr, *greater.*

---

tion and jealousy. The Latin term ' convert,' 'be converted,' formerly expressed this meaning exactly, but it has come to have an exclusively technical sense in our religious usage, which makes it quite misleading in this and some other passages. Persons long ago "converted" may often need to *turn* from some wrong practice or disposition. **And become as little children.** Like other illustrations, this must not be rigorously pressed. Little children are by no means faultless, and they sometimes plainly show envy and jealousy. But we naturally regard a little child as a pattern (*i. e.*, compared with adults) of tender affections, confiding trust, humility, docility, simplicity, readiness to believe and obey. *Chrys. :* " Both from envy the little child is pure, and from vainglory, and from longing for the first place; and he is possessed of the greatest of virtues, simplicity, and whatever is artless and lowly. . . . And the child which he set in the midst I suppose to have been a very young child indeed, free from all these passions." Origen suggests a child's readiness to cease from grief, fear, anger, and its disregard of social distinctions among its playmates. *Theophyl. :* " We must be children in humility of mind, not in childishness of thought; in being without evil, not in being without sense." **Ye shall not,** simply the strong doubled negative (see on 16: 22), **enter into the kingdom of heaven** (comp. on 5: 20). While they are disputing which is to have the highest official position in the kingdom, let them see to it that they get into the kingdom at all. This interpretation of the object-lesson is omitted here by Mark and Luke, who however give the same thought as spoken on a later occasion (Mark 10: 15; Luke 18: 17), where Matt. omits it (19: 15). Nothing is more natural than that so weighty a sentence should have been uttered on both occasions. Men had long been pressing vehemently into the kingdom (11: 12). Were the apostles at this moment still entirely out of it, still un-

renewed (John 3: 3), essentially destitute of saving faith ? They would decide this question by turning from their worldly ambition and jealousy, and becoming childlike. Judas, for example, did not do so (John 12: 4-6), for he was not a child of God, but a ' devil.' (John 6: 70 f.) **Whosoever therefore.** Since in general, they must resemble little children in order to enter the kingdom, *it follows* that whosoever **shall humble himself as this little child** is humble, will be the greatest in the kingdom. Humility is thus presented as the principal thing in a child to be imitated by Messiah's subjects, and in that the disciples had just shown themselves particularly lacking. Observe that the question was particular, ' who '; the answer is general, ' whosoever.' ' Shall humble ' is the same root as ' lowly ' in 11: 29; comp. 23: 12. ' As this little child ' humbles himself, would be grammatically possible, but is forbidden by the connection. **The same is** (*the*) **greatest,** with the article, because a definite person (comp. v. 1).

II. 5-9. THESE LOWLY SUBJECTS OF MESSIAH SHOULD BE KINDLY RECEIVED, AND SHOULD NOT BE LED INTO SIN. This is a kindred truth, suggested by the use of the little child as an object lesson. **In my name,** literally, *upon my name* (as in 24: 5; Acts 2: 38), Christ's name being the ground of the reception—receiving not on the ground of distinction, wealth, personal agreeableness, etc., but on the ground of Christ's name. (Comp. on 28: 19.) **One such little child.** So Mark, ' one of such little children.' These expressions do not refer to the literal child, but to the childlike believer. (Comp. v. 6.) *Chrys.:* " By a little child here, he mean the men that are thus simple and lowly, and abject and contemptible in the judgment of the common sort." If we bear in mind the frequent association in Scripture language of lowly spirit and lowly lot (5: 3), it will seem likely that this latter idea enters here, as it certainly does in v. 10. The reference in

6 But whoso shall offend one of these little ones which believe in me, it were better for him that a mill-stone were hanged about his neck, and *that* he were drowned in the depth of the sea.

6 child in my name receiveth me: but whoso shall cause one of these little ones that believe on me to stumble, it is profitable for him that [1] a great mill-stone should be hanged about his neck, and *that* he

---

1 Gr. *a mill-stone turned by an ass.*

Matthew and Mark then, is plainly to the lowly believer. But Luke says (9: 48, R. V.), 'whosoever shall receive this little child in my name.' Luke's account is very brief, omitting the sayings of our v. 3 and v. 4. The idea had become familiar to all Christian minds that Jesus used a little child for an object-lesson, and so it is likely that Luke meant 'this little child' representatively, the lowly believer who is like this child. *Ooster-zee* (Lange): "It is self-evident that the ex-pression is applicable, not to the child in itself, but to the child as a type of childlike minds.'' The usual interpretation is to this effect. If, however, we understand receiving this little child itself, the idea will still be to receive it, not for its own sake, but 'in my name,' and thus as the Saviour's pattern (Weiss) of what his disciples ought to be, and that involves an honest desire to be what the pattern proposes. The disciples were in a jealous mood, not dis-posed to be lowly themselves, nor to treat the lowly with kindness. Jesus teaches that his followers, though they possess no earthly grandeur, no place of power and pride, should be received in his name; that to receive the lowliest Christian in character and condition —yea, to receive a little child as his appointed pattern of such lowly character—would be receiving Christ himself; and Mark and Luke add, 'whosoever shall receive me receiveth him that sent me.' (Comp. on 10: 40 f.; 25: 40.) Receiving here seems to denote, not merely hospitality, but companionship, friend-ship, etc. Those who are not personally or socially attractive may be heartily received as Christ's representatives. Observe 'one,' to receive even a single such person is to receive Christ.

6 f. At this point, as recorded by Mark (9: 38) and Luke (9: 49), John interrupted our Lord. The idea of receiving *in his name*

suggested a recent occasion on which John and other disciples, perhaps while coming in a separate party from Cesarea Philippi (see on 17: 22), had seen a man casting out demons in the name of Jesus and had forbidden him, because he did not join them in following Jesus about. The Master's beautiful and instructive reply (with which comp. above on 12: 30), is so managed as to come natu-rally back to the subject he had just touched upon before the interruption (comp. Mark 9: 41 with 42). Perhaps Matthew's reason for omitting the incident was his anx-iety to preserve the continuity of the dis-course, v. 6 being closely connected with v. 5. In v. 5 the thought was of *receiving* one such little child; here it is that of *causing* such a one to *sin;* afterwards the discourse passes by natural association of ideas to va-rious persons and things that cause men to sin (**v.** 7-9), finally returning (**v.** 10 ff.) to another thought concerning childlike believers. **One of these little ones which believe in me** (see also in Mark 9: 42), shows that the refer-ence is certainly *not* to unconscious infants, but to childlike believers; this would seem to settle the question as to v. 5 and v. 10. Comparatively young children are sometimes believers, but infants cannot be (comp. Beza). **Offend**—or, *cause to stumble,* or to sin, see on 5: 29. **It were better** (or *is profitable*) **for him,** viz., in comparison with the fate that awaits him. So on a later occasion. (Luke 17: 2.) **A mill-stone.**[1] The ordinary mill-stone, turned by hand (24: 41), was comparatively small; here it is (Rev. Ver., margin) 'a mill-stone turned by an ass,' which would be quite large, and this makes the expression very strong. Equally strong are the phrases **drowned,** *sunk,* to the very bottom, and **in the depth of the sea,** far from the shore, where the sea is deep. Drowning was a pun-

---

1 *Mulos onikos,* 'an ass mill-stone' was by a few docu-ments here, and by many in Mark, changed to *lithos mulikos,* 'a mill-stone,' through assimilation to Luke 17: 2, where also many documents changed to *mulos onikos,* like Matthew and Mark. Such examples show the habits of copyists.—For the nonfinal use of *hina*

and the subjunctive, 'that . . . . should be hanged,' see on 5: 29. Meyer's attempt to make *hina* here ex-press purpose, only shows the impossibility of maintain-ing the ground that in the New Test. it always has that sense.

7 Woe unto the world because of offences! for it must needs be that offences come; but woe to that man by whom the offence cometh!

8 Wherefore if thy hand or thy foot offend thee, cut them off, and cast *them* from thee: it is better for thee to enter into life halt or maimed, rather than having two hands or two feet to be cast into everlasting fire.

9 And if thine eye offend thee, pluck it out, and cast *it* from thee: it is better for thee to enter into life with one eye, rather than having two eyes to be cast into hell fire.

10 Take heed that ye despise not one of these little ones: for I say unto you, That in heaven their angels do always behold the face of my Father which is in heaven.

7 should be sunk in the depth of the sea. Woe unto the world because of occasions of stumbling! for it must needs be that the occasions come; but woe to that man through whom the occasion cometh! And

8 if thy hand or thy foot causeth thee to stumble, cut it off, and cast it from thee: it is good for thee to enter into life maimed or halt, rather than having two hands or two feet to be cast into the eternal fire.

9 And if thine eye causeth thee to stumble, pluck it out, and cast it from thee: it is good for thee to enter into life with one eye, rather than having two

10 eyes to be cast into the [1] hell of fire. See that ye despise not one of these little ones; for I say unto

---

1 Gr. *Gehenna of fire.*

---

ishment common among the Greeks and Romans, the Syrians and Phoenicians, and had been once practiced, that we know of, in the Lake of Galilee, in the early part of Herod's reign. (Jos. "Ant.," 14, 15, 10.) Wicked men often think it great sport to induce a Christian to sin, especially one who seems very meek and gentle. If they can make him violently angry, or lead him into excessive levity, to say nothing of gross vices, they are prodigiously amused and gratified. Such persons ought to remember these solemn and awful words of the compassionate Saviour. **Woe unto the world because of offences,** *of occasions of stumbling* (see on 5: 29); comp. 26: 24; Luke 17: 1. *Theophyl.:* "In his philanthropy he laments over the world, as destined to be damaged by the stumbling-blocks. But why not rather help? We answer, that lamenting is a sort of help. For often those whom our exhortation did not profit, come to their senses when we lament over them." **For it must needs be.** Stumbling-blocks are a necessary part of a state of probation and corrective discipline, and God will not prevent their coming. *Beza:* "There is a distinction between necessity and compulsion." Comp. 1 Cor. 11: 19. *Chrys:* "As though a physician should say, it must needs be that this disease should come on, but it is not a necessary consequence that he who gives heed should be of course destroyed by the disease."

8 f. Having shown the guilt of causing lowly Christians to stumble, he adverts to cases in which we become stumbling-blocks to ourselves. Observe the pointed address in the second person singular, **thy,** etc.; comp. v. 15 ff., and see on 6 : 2. For v. 8 f. see on 5: 29 f., which is substantially the same. *Cut it off,* is the correct Greek text, easily changed to **cut them off.** Mark 9: 48-50 adds some kindred solemn thoughts.

III. **10-14.** THESE LOWLY CHRISTIANS MUST NOT BE DESPISED. The idea of child-like or lowly character is here connected by a natural suggestion with that of lowly station, humble circumstances. The same association of ideas is seen in 5: 3 and 11: 5, and probably above in v. 5. **Little ones** here denote, not little children, but childlike believers, as in v. 3, 6; so the Fathers, so Calvin and Beza, and nearly all modern commentators.[1] Men are very apt to despise Christians on the ground that they include so large a proportion of persons in humble life, poor, and often ignorant (1 Cor. 1: 26 ff.); and their very humility, though one of the loveliest of all human dispositions, is regarded by many proud, ungodly people as nothing but mean spiritedness. To prevent despising a single one of these little ones, lowly in character and lot, our Lord calls special attention to the reason which follows.

I say unto you, see on 5 : 18. However humble in the estimation of worldly men, believers have angels as their attendants, sent forth to serve God for their benefit (Heb. 1 : 14), and these angels of theirs enjoy in heaven the highest dignity and consideration, like persons admitted to the very presence of a monarch, and allowed, not once, but continually, to behold his face. The seclusion in which

---

1 Luther refers here to infant baptism, and holds that this child of v. 2 is said to "believe" (v. 6) because it has been circumcised and received into the number of the elect. "And so through baptism children became believers. How else could the children of Turks and Jews be distinguished from those of Christians?" Does not this involve the notion that infants dying unbaptized are lost? To find the very apostle of justification by faith saying that a little child becomes a *believer* by being baptized, is humiliating and disheartening.

11 For the Son of man is come to save that which was lost.

you, that in heaven their angels do always behold

Oriental monarchs live made this image very expressive; see 1 Kings 10 : 8 ; 2 Kings 25 : 19 ; Esth. 1 : 14 ; Tob. 12 : 15 ; Luke 1 : 19, and comp. above on 5 : 8. Surely they who have as their attendants these high and honored ministers of the court of heaven, are not to be despised, whatever may be their earthly condition.

There is in this no sufficient warrant for the popular notion of "guardian angels," one angel especially assigned to each individual; it is simply said of believers as a class that there are angels which are *their* angels ; but there is nothing here or elsewhere to show that one angel has special charge of one believer. Daniel and Zechariah speak of the angel of a particular country, as the angel of Persia, the angel of Greece ; we know nothing beyond the fact thus revealed, nothing as to the nature or extent of the protection or influence implied. But the Jews were not satisfied with this idea of national influence or guardianship, and advanced to the notion of a guardian angel for each individual, as in the beautiful story of Tobit, and in the Rabbinical writings. Comp. the Greek fancy of a guiding and protecting *daimon*, as spoken of by Socrates, and especially by Epictetus (I. 14). The disciples who were praying for Peter during his imprisonment, when the girl insisted that he was at the gate, sprang to the conclusion that he had just been put to death and this was "his angel" (Acts 12 : 15), according to a notion that a man's guardian angel was apt to appear to friends just after his death, with his form and voice. But the views of these disciples were erroneous on many subjects, and are not an authority for us unless sanctioned by inspiration. It cannot be positively asserted that the idea of guardian angels is an error, but there is no Scripture which proves it true, and passages which merely *might* be understood that way do not suffice for the basis of a doctrine. On the other hand it would appear that not sufficient importance is popularly attached to the agency of angels with reference to Christians in general. They are represented as God's messengers (both the Hebrew and Greek words signifying messenger), and his agents in both ordinary and extraordinary

matters with reference to the bodies and the souls of men. Their agency is represented as both concurring with, and controlling, the action of physical causes. They minister to God especially for the benefit of them that shall inherit salvation (Heb. 1 : 14, where 'minister for them' really meant this, but is popularly misunderstood as meaning minister to them). They protect the human servant of God when in danger and difficulty. (Psa. 91 : 11 ; Matt. 4 : 6.) They are present during our worship, and we are enjoined to preserve decorum through respect for them. (1 Cor. 11 : 10.) In the judgment they will be agents in separating the righteous from the wicked. (13 : 41 ; 24 : 31.) They can doubtless reach and affect our minds in the same way as is done by Satan and his subordinates, all of whom appear to be merely fallen angels ; but like human teachers, they can influence the mind to spiritual good only by the help of the Holy Spirit, while our fallen nature offers itself readily to the influence of the fallen angels. While avoiding all mere sentimental fancies about the angels, and everything that approaches to worshiping them (Col. 2 : 18 ; Rev. 22 : 8 f.) we may well feel for them a personal gratitude and affection, as fellow-servants of God and exalted friends to ourselves. The common notion that human beings may become angels after death, is utterly unscriptural. The redeemed in glory will "judge angels," involving superiority over them. (1 Cor. 6 : 3.) The once popular Sunday-school song, "I want to be an angel," is quite misleading. It may be added that the word 'angel' or 'messenger' has some other applications in Scripture, as to prophets (Hag. 1 : 13 ; Mal. 3 : 1), to priests (Mal. 2 : 7), and to the commissioner of God put in charge of a particular church. (Rev. 1 : 20 ; 2 : 1, etc.)

(11) 12-14. There can be no doubt that v. 11 is spurious here, being omitted by the earliest Greek manuscripts and several early versions and Fathers, and manifestly borrowed by copyists from Luke 19 : 10, where all documents contain it. In such a case there is nothing lost to Scripture as a whole. Our Lord here gives a further reason why no one should despise his believing little ones. (v. 10, 14.) One of them may seem to men as

12 How think ye? if a man have a hundred sheep, and one of them be gone astray, doth he not leave the ninety and nine, and goeth into the mountains, and seeketh that which is gone astray?

12 the face of my Father who is in heaven.[1] How think ye? if any man have a hundred sheep, and one of them be gone astray, doth he not leave the ninety and nine, and go unto the mountains, and

---

[1] Gr. Many authorities, some ancient, insert ver. 11. *For the Son of man came to save that which was lost.* See Luke xix. 10.

---

unimportant as a single sheep gone astray from a large flock; but the kindly shepherd goes after the wandering sheep, and God will take pains to save the lowliest believer. The same parabolic illustration was employed on a later occasion. (Luke 15: 4.) **How think ye,** or, *what do you think?* He appeals to their own sense of propriety and judgment of probability, comp. 1 Cor. 11: 13. **And goeth into the mountains.** The Greek of the common text is ambiguous, and might mean 'doth he not leave the ninety and nine upon the mountains and go and seek.'; and more probably correct is the reading of several early documents 'will he not leave the ninety and nine upon the mountains,' etc. Of course the substantial sense is the same. Between the readings **your Father** and 'my Father' (Rev. Ver. *margin*), it is difficult to decide, as the latter, though strongly attested, may have come from v. 10; the difference in meaning would be slight. **That** in v. 14 represents a peculiar Greek construction, explained on 5: 29. Observe '*one* of these little ones,' as in v. 12, 10, 6, 5. The application of the parable in v. 14 would be inexplicable if 'little ones' meant infants as distinguished from adults; and would be obscure if that phrase meant simply believers regarded as humble in character like little children (v. 3 f.), for such believers in no sense correspond to the straying sheep. But when there has been introduced the associated idea of lowly condition (see on v. 10), with the ignorance and grossness which so often attach to the lowest classes of men and cause them to seem of little account, not worth caring for, then the application becomes plain.

HOMILETICAL AND PRACTICAL.

V. 1. The disciples contending who shall be greatest. 1) This shows that they were like us, and so that we may become like them. 2) It was an evil hard to cure in them, and it will not easily be cured in us. 3) The Saviour took great pains to correct it in them; let us learn from the lessons he taught them, v. 2-4; Luke 18: 14; Matt. 20: 24-28; Luke 22: 24-27; John 21: 15.—V. 2-4. Our Lord's object-lessons. (Comp. the old prophets and Acts 21: 11.) 1) The scourge of cords, John 2: 15, comp. Matt. 21: 12. 2) The little child, v. 2, comp. 19: 13, 15. 3) The barren fig-tree, 21: 18 f. 4) Washing the disciples' feet, John 13: 3 ff. 5) Baptism. 6) The bread and wine.— Christians must be childlike. 1) Not in mind and speech, 1 Cor. 14: 20; 13: 11. 2) In humility and freedom from jealousy, comp. 1 Cor. 14: 20. 3) In teachableness and submission to divine authority, comp. Eph. 6: 1. VINET (in Lutter.): "While in the world the teacher says to the child, behave like a man, Jesus Christ says to the man, behave like a child." HENRY: "Humility is a lesson so hardly learned that we have need by all ways and means to be taught it. When we look upon a little child, we should be put in mind of the use Christ made of a child."—V. 4. Our Lord's lessons in humility. 1) Precepts, 20: 26 f.; 23: 12. 2) Illustrations, Luke 14: 7-11; 18: 9-14. 3) Object-lessons, v. 2-4; John 13: 3 ff. 4) His own character and example, 11: 29; Phil. 2: 8. CHRYS.: "Where envy is and love of glory, there even sincere friendship has no strength. For as those of the same craft cannot love one another with a perfect and genuine love, so is it with rivals in honor also, and with them that long for the same worldly objects."

V. 6. Leading Christians to sin. 1) Why wicked men do this. For amusement, through contempt (v. 10), to quiet their own consciences, to promote their own sinful aims. 2) How wicked men do this. By intentional example, by pretended friendship, by argument, by flattery, by ridicule, by sudden temptation of the senses, etc. 3) Wherein lies the guilt of doing this. (a) It shows delight in sin, and makes one a willing helper of Satan. (b) It shows hatred of holiness, and open hostility to God. (c) It is doing the greatest possible unkindness and injustice to a fellow-creature. (d) It reacts upon one's own soul to produce a yet more aggravated wickedness. Thus may we partially see the ground for the Saviour's awful warning.

13 And if so be that he find it, verily I say unto you, he rejoiceth more of that *sheep,* than of the ninety and nine which went not astray.

14 Even so it is not the will of your Father which is in heaven, that one of these little ones should perish.

15 Moreover if thy brother shall trespass against thee, go and tell him his fault between thee and him alone: if he shall hear thee, thou hast gained thy brother.

13 seek that which goeth astray? And if so be that he find it, verily I say unto you, he rejoiceth over it more than over the ninety and nine which have 14 not gone astray. Even so it is not [1] the will of [2] your Father who is in heaven, that one of these little ones should perish.

15 And if thy brother sin [3] against thee, go, shew him his fault between thee and him alone: if he

---

1 Gr. *a thing willed before your Father....* 2 Some ancient authorities read, *my....* 3 Some ancient authorities omit, *against thee.*

Comp. 25: 45.—V. 10. Despising Christians. 1) Why Christians are often despised. Many of them are ignorant; most are poor; they eschew fashionable vices; they will not defend their honor by brute force; their seriousness can be easily ridiculed; their humility can be regarded as mean spiritedness; their goodness can be represented as hypocrisy; their faults attract attention by contrast with general good conduct; they often incur reproach through unwise action when their intentions are good (Col. 4: 5). 2) Why Christians ought not to be despised. They are at least trying to do what all ought to be doing; many of them are without reproach and above suspicion, and some are the excellent of the earth; they render great service to society (5: 13 f.); all real Christians are children of God, who sends angels from his own presence to care for them; they will finally become free from all fault, and glorious forever (v. 14). Chrys.: "See by how many things he is urging the care of our mean brethren. Say not then, such a one is a blacksmith, a shoemaker, a ploughman, a fool—and so despise him."

18:15-35. How to Deal with a Brother who has Wronged us.

This is found here in Matthew only, though some of the expressions are paralleled on other occasions in Luke. The disciples having shown jealousy and selfish ambition (18:1), our Lord urged upon them humility and mutual kindness, and pointed out the great wickedness of causing the humblest Christian to sin. (v. 2-14.) He now proceeds to give directions as to what course one is to pursue towards a fellow-Christian who has sinned. This is divided into two parts, (1) efforts to win back such a brother, v. 15-20; (2) readiness to forgive great and often repeated offences, v. 21-35.

I. **15-20.** Efforts to Win Back a Brother who has Sinned. **If thy brother shall trespass,** or *sin.* The addition in the common text **against thee,** is wanting in several of the earlier documents,[1] and was doubtless brought in by copyists from v. 21, just as in Luke 17: 3, it was inserted from the next verse. In this general form the directions of the passage apply to all attempts to win back a brother from sin. (Comp. James 5: 19 f.; Lev. 19: 17.) To act quietly, and if possible privately, is hardly less important in other cases than when the sin was against ourselves. Still, the following context suggests personal offences, and that is still more plainly the case in Luke 17: 3 f. The word 'sin' was by Tyn. and followers translated 'trespass,' probably because that word is used in 6: 14; and they translate it likewise in Luke 17: 3 f. Notice '*thy* brother,' the following precepts being for individual action (v. 15-17), after which he returns to the plural. (Comp. on 6: 2.) In 5: 23 the injurer is addressed; here it is the injured. 'Brother' might mean any man (see on 5: 22), but here means a brother Christian, as shown by the reference to the church in v. 17. **Go and tell** (*show*) **him his fault.** 'And' after 'go,' is omitted by the correct text. The word means go right along, as in 4: 10; 5: 24; 13: 44, etc. 'Show him his fault' is, more strictly, convict him of his fault, as in John 8: 46; 16: 8; James 2: 9. To convince a man that he has erred, especially that he has wronged the person addressing him, is a difficult and delicate task. Some wise counsels were given in Ecclus. 19: 13–17. A famous Rabbi of later times said (Wün.), "I

---

1 Wanting in ℵ B, three cursives, Thebaic, Origen, Cyril, Basil. Internal considerations seem to settle the question. The words were easily introduced from v. 21, and agree well with the connection. We cannot conceive of a reason for their omission if originally present. So we must regard them as a spurious addition. In Luke 17: 3 the documents which omit are much more numerous.

16 But if he will not hear *thee, then* take with thee, one or two more, that in the mouth of two or three witnesses every word may be established.

17 And if he shall neglect to hear them, tell *it* unto the church: but if he neglect to hear the church, let him be unto thee as a heathen man and a publican.

16 hear thee, thou hast gained thy brother. But if he hear *thee* not, take with thee one or two more, that at the mouth of two witnesses or three every word

17 may be established. And if he refuse to hear them, tell it unto the [1] church: and if he refuse to hear the [1] church also, let him be unto thee as the Gen-

---

1 Or, *congregation.*

---

wonder whether there is any one in these times that accepts reproof'' (comp. above on 7 : 4). Another replied, ''I wonder whether any one nowadays knows how to give admonition.'' **Between thee and him alone.** Thus the injurer would be more likely to acknowledge his fault than if approached in company, so as to arouse his pride; and thus the difficulty if settled need never be known at all. **Thou hast gained thy brother,**[1] might mean only gained him for thyself, but probably means also (Ewald, Meyer, Weiss) gained him for God and salvation. (1 Cor. 9 : 19-22; 1 Peter 3 : 1.). **In,** or *at,* **the mouth of two or three witnesses.** It would seem to us more natural to say 'two or three witnesses,' but 'two witnesses or three,' is the Greek order, and so in 2 Cor. 13 : 1, both corresponding to Deut. 17 : 6; 19 : 15. Comp. John 8 : 17; Heb. 10 : 28. There is nothing to forbid the 'one or two more' from also helping to convince him. But with these as witnesses he cannot afterwards deny, or profess to have forgotten, what he had conceded. And if the matter has at last to come before the church, these witnesses can declare what passed in the private interview.

17. Only as a third step, when the two more private efforts have failed, must he **tell it unto the church.** As to the general uses of the word *ekklesia,* rendered 'church,' [2] see on 16: 28. In the present passage it cannot mean the Jewish synagogue (Calvin, Beza,

Fritz.); for it is impossible that v. 18-20 should have been spoken with reference to a Jewish synagogue. It must here mean one of two things. (1) It may be the body of Christ's disciples existing at the time he speaks, including the apostles. (v. 18.) It seems to be intimated by this passage, together with 16: 18, that as the end of his ministry approached, Jesus began to regard and speak of his followers as a sort of community or association, a thing which would in itself appear not unnatural. The twelve apostles seem to have been grouped in companies of four (see on 10: 2). Yet we can hardly suppose that they alone constituted the *ekklesia* here spoken of, since there is no clear analogy for applying the term to them, and since v. 19 f. refers, by common consent, to any gathering of believers, and not simply to a gathering of apostles. Upon this view, then, the word must denote a general community, including the apostles. The exact constitution of this supposed community cannot be determined. Some would liken it more to the Jewish synagogues, others to the churches described in Paul's Epistles; neither side can prove its point. (2) The word 'church' may be used by anticipation for one of the churches founded by the apostles. It might be taken for granted from the general analogy of the synagogues, that there would be some sort of assembly or congregation to which the person addressed in these instruc-

---

1 Wünsche, in his great desire to find Rabbinical parallels to the sayings of Jesus, quotes here from Pirqe Aboth, '' He that has won many for good, through him no sin is done.'' But the Heb. word *hamezakkeh,* means simply 'he that makes pure,' without any notion of winning or gaining; the similarity is greatly increased by the translation. There are other instances of the same sort in his useful collection.

2 The *English* word *church* comes from the Greek *kuriakon,* 'the Lord's (house),' so used to some extent by the early Greek Christians (Skeat). The Teutonic tribes, when converted to Christianity, adopted this Greek word for the house of worship, and it is found now in the German *kirche,* the Scottish *kirk,* Anglo-Saxon *cyrice, cirice, circe,* from which comes the Eng-

lish *church.* The use of the word was gradually extended to the assembly meeting at the church, an extension similar, though in the opposite direction, to that which has taken place in the words synagogue, parish, school, etc. (See on 4: 23). Those who wish to avoid the confusion which arises from applying the same word to the building and the assembly, would be keeping nearer to the *history,* at least, if they applied the term church only to the building. The Greek Christians themselves are not known to have ever used *kuriakon* for the assembly, and in modern Greek *ekklesia* is the only word in both senses. From this through the Latin form *ecclesia,* came the French *eglise,* our word ecclesiastical, etc.

18 Verily I say unto you, Whatsoever ye shall bind on earth shall be bound in heaven; and whatsoever ye shall loose on earth shall be loosed in heaven.

19 Again I say unto you, That if two of you shall agree on earth as touching any thing that they shall ask, it shall be done for them of my Father which is in heaven.

18 tile and the publican. Verily I say unto you, What things soever ye shall bind on earth shall be bound in heaven : and what things soever ye shall loose 19 on earth shall be loosed in heaven. Again I say unto you, that if two of you shall agree on earth as touching anything that they shall ask, it shall be

---

tions would belong. Perhaps the two ideas might be combined; 'the church' might mean at the moment the existing loosely organized community of Christ's followers, then after the Day of Pentecost the one organized assembly at Jerusalem, and still later the local assembly with which the persons in question should be connected ; *e. g.*, ' the church at Corinth,' 1 Cor. 5: 12. This question is of no great importance for the interpretation of the passage before us, whatever interest it may possess in general ecclesiastical theory. Tyndale, Cran., and Gen., correctly translated the word by 'congregation'; Wyc. and Rheims gave 'church;' and this was one of "the old ecclesiastical words" which, by direction of King James, his Revisers retained. The Rev. Ver. of 1881 has placed ' congregation' here in the margin, probably through recognition of the fact that the meaning of the original is in this case somewhat undefined ; for the word congregation has become gradually modified in meaning by usage, and can no longer be in general employed as the equivalent of church. **Let him be unto thee,** etc. The Rev. Ver. properly translates, *as the Gentile and the publican,* one with whom you have no communion or association, Rom. 16: 17 ; 2 Thess. 3: 14 (comp. on 5: 46 f.). This does not distinctly teach what we call excommunication, but contains the germs of that which Paul afterwards clearly taught. (1 Cor. 5: 3-5.)

18. Whatsoever ye shall bind on earth. He is directly addressing the disciples alone (18:1), probably only the Twelve; but he has just mentioned the action of a church, and so the reference here seems to be not to apostolic action, but to church action (Bleek, Keim). Whatever Christ's people, assembled in their organized congregation or church, may decide, is ratified **in heaven,** *i. e.*, by God— unless, of course, the decision be in itself wrong. The point is that the church has God's authority to decide. The reference here is especially to the settlement of a difficulty between brethren, but the statement is

a general one. The power some time before given to Peter (16: 19), is now clearly given to *others;* the only question being whether it is to the apostles or to a church.

19 f. This is closely connected with the preceding. The church expresses the view, not of an individual, but a number of Christians concurring in an opinion, and so is more likely to have the divine approval. He now adds that any *petition* in which two Christians unite, will be granted by God. **Agree.** The Greek word *sumphoneo* is used primarily of musical instruments that make the same sound, then of harmony, *symphony,* where the sounds agree, though not identical, then of agreement in general. Origen on this passage revels in the fancy of symphony in prayer. But it is doubtful whether more is here intended than the general idea of agreeing. **On earth,** as in v. 18. You pray "on earth," the "Father who is in heaven" answers. **As touching,** or simply 'about,' 'concerning.' **Anything that they shall ask,** not simply any decision that a church shall make (v. 18), but any petition which even two shall agree in offering. **It shall be done,** or 'shall come to pass,' 'take place,' see on 6: 10. **My Father which is in heaven,** as in 18: 10; he gives his assurance concerning his Father (see on 6: 9). This promise is of course understood as limited, comp. on 7: 7. The words ' in my name' are naturally reflected back from v. 20 upon the foregoing promise by the connecting ' for,' so that we have here an implied anticipation of John 16: 23. Men are more influenced by the united request of many persons than by the request of one; and this holds of requests to God. It applies also not merely to a large assembly, but to even two or three, when gathered in the Saviour's name, and agreeing in their petition. **In my name** is here in Greek a different construction from 18: 5, but without substantial difference of meaning (see on 28: 19). They are assembled with reference to Christ, and not to some other person or object—assembled according to his teaching, in reliance on him as their

20 For where two or three are gathered together in my name, there am I in the midst of them.
21 Then came Peter to him, and said, Lord, how oft shall my brother sin against me, and I forgive him? till seven times?
22 Jesus saith unto him, I say not unto thee, Until seven times: but, Until seventy times seven.
23 Therefore is the kingdom of heaven likened unto a certain king, which would take account of his servants.

20 done for them of my Father who is in heaven. For where two or three are gathered together in my name, there am I in the midst of them.
21 Then came Peter, and said to him, Lord, how oft shall my brother sin against me, and I forgive him?
22 until seven times? Jesus saith unto him, I say not unto thee, Until seven times; but, until [1] seventy
23 times seven. Therefore is the kingdom of heaven likened unto a certain king, who would make a reck-

1 Or, *seventy times and seven.*

Saviour, with desire to please him and to advance his cause. The pronoun **I** is not expressed in the Greek, and so is not emphatic, though commonly so uttered in English.[1] The point is not that *I* am there, but that I am *there*, in the midst of them. Theophyl.: "There, not far away to be sent after and waited for, but there." Our Lord here distinctly points forward to a time when he will be corporeally absent but spiritually present. So in some of the instructions in chap. 10, in the farewell discourse of John ch. 14–17, and in the parting words of Matthew 28: 20. Notice that the language is perfectly general. It is no longer 'two of you,' but in general 'two or three'; it is not 'there I shall be,' but 'there I am,' a general fact. And it holds, not merely of a large assembly, but of the smallest gathering in his name. He is there to give authority to their action as a church (v. 18), by making it his action, and to give efficiency to their petitions (v. 19), by adopting them as his own. It shall be done for them of my Father, for I am there. The Mishna (Aboth) has a similar expression: "Where two sit and occupy themselves with the law, the Shekinah is between them. Mal. 3: 16."

II. **21-35.** READINESS TO FORGIVE A BROTHER WHO HAS WRONGED US. Comp. on 6: 12, 14. Jesus had just been speaking of the proper way to act when a brother "sins," with special reference to personal offences. (v. 15.) This suggests to Peter a practical inquiry, which he approaches the Master to make. **Then** (v. 21) is therefore clearly to be understood strictly. (Comp. on 3: 13.) Jesus replies (v. 22), and then goes on to enforce the duty of forgiveness by a parable. (v. 22-35.)

Came, or approached, stepped forward from the group of disciples and came close to Jesus and asked him. Every person who at-

tempts to exercise a forgiving spirit towards those who do him wrong, will sometimes have occasion to feel that Peter's question was a practical one. We bring ourselves up from a sense of duty, to the point of forgiving; behold! very soon the same man commits an equal or greater wrong; and so, perhaps, again and again. How long are we bound to let this go on? **How oft shall my brother sin against me, and I forgive him?** The former clause is simply the basis of the latter; so in the much discussed passage, Rom. 6: 17, and so perhaps in Luke 24: 18. Tyndale, Cran., Gen., render, 'how oft shall I forgive my brother, if he sin against me?' This expresses the thought, but takes unnecessary liberties with the phrase. **Until seven times?** He probably thought this a very high number. Chrys.: "Peter supposed he was saying something great." The Talmud of Babylon says, "When a man sins against another, they forgive him once, they forgive him a second time, they forgive him a third time, but the fourth time they do not forgive him." 'Seven,' among its many uses, was sometimes a round number, Lev. 26: 21; Deut. 28: 25; Psa. 79: 12; Prov. 24: 16, etc. So our Lord, when speaking of this subject on a subsequent occasion, says, 'Seven times in the day.' (Luke 17: 4.) **Seventy times seven** is the natural meaning of the Greek. But it *may* mean (Rev. Ver. *margin*) 'seventy-seven times,' which some of the best expositors prefer (Origen, Bengel, Ewald, Keim, Meyer) because precisely the same expression is found in the Sept. translation of Gen. 4: 24, where the Hebrew can signify nothing else than 'seventy-seven times.' Comp. Moulton in Winer, 314, n. Either way it is a general expression, which practically removes all limit to the repetitions of forgiveness. (Theo-

---

1 The pronoun in the nominative is more frequently used in New Test. Greek than in classical Greek. Therefore its presence does not so certainly show em-

phasis, but its absence does even more certainly (if possible) than in classical Greek, show that there is no emphasis (comp. John 11:21, 32).

24 And when he had begun to reckon, one was brought unto him, which owed him ten thousand *a* talents.
25 But forasmuch as he had not to pay, his lord commanded him to be sold, and his wife, and children, and all that he had, and payment to be made.
26 The servant therefore fell down, and *b* worshipped him, saying, Lord, have patience with me, and I will pay thee all.
27 Then the lord of that servant was moved with compassion, and loosed him, and forgave him the debt.

24 oning with his 1 servants. And when he had begun to reckon, one was brought unto him, who owed
25 him ten thousand 2 talents. But forasmuch as he had not *wherewith* to pay, his lord commanded him to be sold, and his wife, and children, and all that
26 he had, and payment to be made. The 3 servant therefore fell down and worshipped him, saying, Lord, have patience with me, and I will pay thee
27 all. And the lord of that 1 servant, being moved with compassion, released him, and forgave him

---

a *A talent is 750 ounces of silver*, which after five shillings the ounce is 187 l. 10 s.....*b*. Or, *besought him*....1 Gr. *bondservants*....
2 This talent was probably worth about £240....3 Gr. *bondservant*.

---

phyl.) Of course all this rests on the supposition that we believe the man sincerely repents. (Luke 17:4.) Otherwise we are not bound to forgive even once, in the full sense of restoring to confidence and affection. (See on 6:14).
23. Therefore. Since the Messiah requires his followers to forgive, and no matter how often (v. 21 f.), *therefore* the Messianic reign resembles the story about to be told; under that reign men will be severely dealt with if they refuse to forgive (v. 35). **The kingdom of heaven,** see on 3:2. **Is likened,** or *has been likened,* see on 13:24. **Unto a certain king,** literally, *to a man, a king.* The action of the Divine King is illustrated by that of a human king. **Would take account,** (*wished to make a reckoning*). This and 'to reckon' in v. 24 are kindred expressions, and ought not to have been differently rendered. Besides, 'take account of,' is misleading, the idea being to settle accounts with. **His servants,** literally *slaves* (*doulos*), see on 8:6. It has always been common in the East to call the court officials the slaves of the king.—They are as dependent on his arbitrary will as a slave on his master, and with the servility which despotism engenders, they often seem even to delight in calling themselves by that name. This word *doulos* is similarly used in 23:2 ff., and in 1 Kings 1:47; the more common word in that sense is *pais* (see on 14:2). In a kindred but not degrading spiritual sense Paul delights to call himself a *doulos* of Jesus Christ, and so James, Peter, Jude. In the parable, therefore, the king's 'servants' are the great officers of government, who received his revenues and attended to their disbursement. It was quite possible in one of the great Oriental despotisms for a treasurer, or the satrap of a province, to embezzle as much as twelve millions of dollars. Our Lord purposely supposes a very strong case, in order the better to illustrate the vast disparity between what God forgives to us, and what we are called to forgive to others.
24-27. Ten thousand talents. Besides the difference between a talent of silver and of gold, the gold talent varied greatly in value for different countries and periods. Archæological exactness is here of no importance. According to *margin* of Rev. Ver., the ten thousand talents would amount to near twelve million dollars. We may see how vast the sum is by comparisons. The amount provided by David for building the temple was three thousand talents of gold, and seven thousand of silver, and the princes gave over five thousand talents of gold and ten thousand of silver (1 Chron. 29:4, 7), and the amount which Haman offered the King of Persia, for the destruction of the Jews, was ten thousand talents of silver. (Esther 3:9.) It is not necessary to suppose that the parable narrates a historical fact, but such things did happen. (Comp. on 13:3.) **To be sold, and his wife and children, and all that he had.** It is still common in Oriental countries to inflict all this upon a man of the highest station. The law of Moses allowed a man himself to be sold for theft (Exod. 22:3), or debt. (Lev. 25:39; 2 Kings 4:1.) **Worshipped,** the prostration before a monarch, see on 2:11; the Greek has here the imperfect tense, describing him as engaged in this lowly homage. The man only asked for indulgence, and he would pay. Perhaps he really hoped to do so; for men who go into vast fraudulent operations are usually of very sanguine temperament. **Loosed** (*released*) **him, and forgave him the debt.** 'Loosed' (Com. Ver.) would now imply that he had been bound or imprisoned, a thing not indicated nor probable; he was 'released' from arrest and from obligation. 'The debt' is here more exactly (Rev. Ver.,

28 But the same servant went out, and found one of his fellow servants, which owed him a hundred ^a pence: and he laid hands on him, and took *him* by the throat, saying, Pay me that thou owest.
29 And his fellow servant fell down at his feet, and besought him, saying, Have patience with me, and I will pay thee all.
30 And he would not: but went and cast him into prison, till he should pay the debt.
31 So when his fellow servants saw what was done, they were very sorry, and came and told unto their lord all that was done.
32 Then his lord, after that he had called him, said unto him, O thou wicked servant, I forgave thee all that debt, because thou desiredst me:
33 Shouldest not thou also have had compassion on thy fellow servant, even as I had pity on thee?
34 And his lord was wroth, and delivered him to the tormentors, till he should pay all that was due unto him.
35 So likewise shall my heavenly Father do also unto you, if ye from your hearts forgive not every one his brother their trespasses.

28 the ¹ debt. But that ² servant, went out, and found one of his fellow-servants, who owed him a hundred ³ shillings: and he laid hold on him, and took *him* by the throat, saying, Pay what thou owest.
29 So his fellow-servant fell down and besought him, saying, Have patience with me, and I will pay thee.
30 And he would not: but went and cast him into prison, till he should pay that which was due.
31 So when his fellow-servants saw what was done, they were exceeding sorry, and came and told unto their lord all that was done. Then his lord called him
32 unto him, and saith unto him, Thou wicked ² servant, I forgave thee all that debt, because thou be-
33 soughtest me: shouldest not thou also have had mercy on thy fellow-servant, even as I had mercy
34 on thee? And his lord was wroth, and delivered him to the tormenters, till he should pay all that was
35 due. So shall also my heavenly Father do unto you, if ye forgive not every one his brother from your hearts.

^a *The Roman penny is the eighth part of an ounce, which after five shillings the ounce is sevenpence halfpenny.* Ch. 20: 2.——1 Gr. loan....2 Gr. bondservant....3 The word in the Greek denotes a coin worth about eight pence halfpenny.

margin) 'the loan.' In his compassionate mood the king chooses to speak of it as a loan, not an embezzlement; afterwards, in v. 32, it is literally 'debt.'
28-30. One of his fellow-servants. One of the other court-officials; from the smallness of the debt we should think of him as an inferior officer. **A hundred pence,** or *shillings.* The Roman *denarius,* the word always used where our English versions have 'penny,' varied in value at different periods; if we take the estimate in *margin* of Rev. Ver., 'a hundred pence' will be seventeen dollars of our money. See, then, the disparity of the two debts—twelve million dollars, seventeen dollars. Or we could get the effect of round numbers by saying ten million dollars and ten dollars. This pictures the difference between the guilt of our sins against God and that of a fellow-man's sins against us. **Took him by the throat,** or more literally, *went to choking him.* **Pay that thou owest,** or *pay, if thou owest anything;* the debt is small and hardly amounts to anything, but he is determined to have it. The Roman law allowed a creditor to seize his debtor and drag him before the judge, and Roman writers repeatedly speak of a man's twisting the neck of his debtor till the blood flowed from mouth and nostrils. **Fell down** merely; **at his feet** being an unwarranted addition. **Besought** and **would not** (v. 29 f.) are in Greek in the imperfect tense, implying continued entreaty and refusal. **All,** at end of v. 29 in Com. Ver., was an addition by copyists from v. 26.

The similarity of the plea to that which had just availed for himself failed to touch the creditor's heart.
31-35. His fellow-servants, other court-officials, high and low, **saw what was done,** *what took place.* (See on 6: 10.) **Told** is in the Greek a very strong word, signifying that they gave a *clear* and *complete* account. **His lord,** etc.... **said, O thou wicked servant.** *Chrys.* : "When he owed ten thousand talents he did not call him wicked nor upbraid him, but had compassion on him; but when regarding his fellow-servant he was unforgiving, then he says, wicked servant." **Shouldst not thou also have had compassion** (*mercy*) .... **even as I had pity** (*mercy*) (v. 33), the same Greek word in both cases, and not that of v. 27, but that of 17: 15; 5: 7. **Tormentors** (v. 34), not simply 'jailers,' as Tyn., Cran., Gen , but strictly 'torturers'; he was to be not now sold into slavery (v. 25), but imprisoned, and from time to time tortured. This fearful punishment suggests the torments of Gehenna: comp. 8: 29; Luke 16, 23, 28; Rev. 14: 10 f. ; 20: 10. **So . . . unto you.** The comparison of sins to debts was a familiar idea to the Jewish mind. (See on 6: 12.) **From your hearts** comes in at the close with emphasis. **Their trespasses** is a useless addition by copyists, and so is **unto him,** end of v. 34. Nobody would have cared to omit either phrase if originally present, yet both are wanting in a number of the earliest documents. **Forgive,** see on 6: 12; 'hearts,' see on 6: 21.

CHAPTER XIX.

A ND it came to pass, *that* when Jesus had finished these sayings, he departed from Galilee, and came into the coasts of Judea beyond Jordan ;

1 And it came to pass when Jesus had finished these words, he departed from Galilee, and came into the

---

HOMILETICAL AND PRACTICAL.

V. 15 ff. How to deal with a brother who has wronged you. 1) Do not await his coming, but go right away to him. 2) Make loving, wise, and repeated efforts to gain him, by personal interview, by the help of other brethren, by the help of the church. 3) As soon (Luke 17: 3) and as often as he repents, forgive him (v. 21 f.); and when tempted to be unforgiving, remember how much is forgiven you (v. 35).—V. 15. CHRYS. : "He saith not, 'accuse,' nor 'charge him,' nor 'demand satisfaction,' but 'tell him of his fault.' " AUG. : (in Aq.) : "But why do you correct your neighbor? If you do it from self-love, you do naught; if you do it from love of him, you do most rightly." HENRY: "We should think no pains too much to take for the recovering of a sinner to repentance."—V. 16. CHRYS. : "The physician, in like manner, when he sees the malady obstinate, doth not give up nor grow impatient, but then makes the more preparation."—V. 19 f. United Christian prayer. 1) The prayer of many, even of two, is more likely to be for right objects. 2) The sympathy of common supplication promotes earnestness. 3) The Saviour himself is in the midst, making it *his* prayer to *his* Father. CYRIL: "For it is not the number of those coming together, but it is the power of their piety that will be effectual." HENRY: "If there be no liberty and opportunity for large and numerous assemblies, then it is the will of God that two or three should gather together. When we cannot do what we would in religion, we must do as we can, and God will accept us."

V. 23-35. God's unforgiving servant. 1) God forgives him an immense debt. 2) He refuses to forgive his fellow-servant some comparatively trifling debt. 3) God will punish him with terrible severity. All turns upon the 'if' of v. 35; a true servant of God will take warning and forgive. — V. 32. CHRYS. : "Let us hearken, the covetous, for even to us is the word spoken. Let us hearken also, the merciless and the cruel, for not to others are we cruel, but to our-

selves. . . . . Let us not thrust the sword into ourselves by being revengeful."—V. 35. Forgiveness. 1) Who must forgive ? 'Every one.' 2) Why must we forgive? (a) Fit in itself that they who wish to be forgiven should be willing to forgive. (b) Clearly taught that they who do not forgive are not forgiven; this parable and 6 : 14; James 2 : 13. (c) A great privilege that we can thus express to God our gratitude for his forgiveness, Col. 3 : 13. 3) How must we forgive? 'From the heart.' — BRUCE: "Obviously Jesus has no sense of incongruity between the Fatherhood of God and the strange work of stern judgment on the unmerciful. Neither was there room for such a feeling. Just because God is a Father, and because his inmost spirit is love, he must abhor a spirit so utterly alien from his own. It is only what we should expect, that under the government of a gracious God the spirit of mercilessness should have judgment without mercy."

Ch. 19: 1-12. DEPARTURE FROM GALILEE. INSTRUCTIONS AS TO DIVORCE.

The greater part of this section is found also in Mark 10: 1-12. Our Lord now leaves Galilee, and comes into Perea. Matthew and Mark make no mention of anything intervening, and a little later both bring us to the triumphal entry and the final Passover. But Luke, after completing his account, parallel to Matthew and Mark, of the ministry in Galilee, describes Jesus (9: 51-56) as going from Galilee not into Perea, but through Samaria on the way to Jerusalem. With this agrees John's account (7: 2-10) of his going in secret from Galilee to Jerusalem to attend the Feast of Tabernacles, six months before the final Passover. Then Luke goes on in 10: 1 to 18: 14, with a long account of the Saviour's sayings and actions, after which he again becomes parallel (18: 15) with Matt. (19: 13) and Mark (10: 13), and so continues to the end. We have heretofore noticed that Luke greatly condensed his narrative of the series of withdrawals from Galilee, giving to it only 9: 10-50, while Matt. gives 14: 13 to 18: 35, and

Mark gives 6: 30 to 9 : 50. It seems plain that Luke thus condensed in order to make room for the mass of matter in reserve, which for the most part is peculiar to him. Some of the miracles and discourses he goes on to narrate closely resemble several which Matthew and Mark gave during the ministry in Galilee before the withdrawals, and which Luke did not there introduce; *e. g.*, the blasphemous accusation in Luke 11 : 14-36 resembles Matt. 12: 22-45; Mark 3 : 19-30, and the discourse against temporal anxiety in Luke 12: 22-31 resembles Matt. 6: 25-34.   In the present state of harmonistic inquiry, we must choose between two theories.   (1) Luke in 10: 1 to 18: 14, must be supposed, with Robinson's Harmony and others, to give a loosely arranged mass of material, mainly falling between the last Feast of Tabernacles and the last Passover, but partly belonging in fact to the ministry in Galilee, where similar matters were given by Matthew and Mark.   This loose arrangement is unlikely in itself, particularly in the case of one who expressly undertook to write an orderly account. (Luke 1 ; 3.)[1] (2) Wieseler has pointed out ("Chron. Syn.," followed by Tischendorf's "Syn. Evang.," Ellicott's "Lectures on Life of Christ," G. W. Clark's "Harmony of the Gospels") that Luke in this large section three times speaks of Jesus as going to or towards Jerusalem (9 : 51-53 ; 13 : 22; 17 : 11), and has proposed to take the first of these three as parallel to our Lord's going up for the Feast of Tabernacles (John 7 : 2 ff.), the second to the journey for raising Lazarus (John 11 : 17 f.), the third as beginning the journey to the final Passover; and accordingly to arrange *all* this section of Luke, as belonging to the last six months of our Lord's ministry, and as located in Judea and Perea. It thus becomes a ministry distinct from that in Galilee narrated by Matthew, Mark, and Luke, and the similar events and discourses are to be regarded as not identical but repetitions, such as it is unquestionable that Jesus often made (see above, beginning of ch. 5). This view, well wrought out in Clark's Harmony, is followed in the present Com. as involving fewer difficulties than any other, and indeed as quite probably correct.   At any

rate, it is clear, from the comparison with Luke and John, that Matthew and Mark pass over nearly all the last six months of our Lord's ministry, just as both they and Luke passed over that early ministry of probably as great length in Judea which is recorded by John (see above on 4 : 12).   Matthew and Mark have in fact confined themselves entirely to the ministry in Galilee and vicinity, except the final Passover and a few incidents on the journey thereto.

1 f. Jesus goes from Galilee into Perea, and exercises his ministry. **Departed** is not simply 'went away,' but 'removed,' a rare word used in New Test. only here and in 13: 53.   It must not be here pressed to prove a permanent removal, for in 13 : 53 there was only a temporary removal across the lake. The statement that he departed from Galilee when he **had finished these sayings,** would most naturally mean that he left immediately upon completing the discourse of ch. 18; comp. the same phrase in 7: 28; 11: 1; 13: 53.   We should then take this departure as parallel to that of Luke 9 : 51 ff., viz., to attend the Feast of Tab., and the gap of nearly six months would have to fall between the two adjacent words 'departed' and 'came.' Wieseler holds that this departure was parallel to Luke 17: 11, where Jesus returns from Judea through Samaria and a portion of Galilee, and probably joins the pilgrims on the way from Galilee through Perea to Jerusalem. In this way 'departed' is followed naturally by 'came,' but 'when he had finished these sayings' has to be understood loosely.   Mark's expression (10 : 1) agrees best with Wieseler's view.   However much was to be omitted, we could not expect a break in the narrative; see remarks introductory to 4: 12.   It is well to observe that nothing in the interpretation of what follows will depend upon this nice question of chronology and harmony.

Matthew's account of the ministry in Galilee has continued since 4: 12.   That ministry appears to have lasted, if we take the feast of John 5: 1 to be a passover, nearly two years, the last six months, however, being nearly all spent in the series of withdrawals to adjoining districts. (14 ; 13 to 17 : 20.)   Matthew occupies him-

---

[1] Andrews has a copious discussion and a different scheme, on the same general principles as that of Robinson.   Farrar also (ch. 42) gives an independent scheme, which will reward examination.   A full discussion, or even statement, of the various theories would here be out of place.

2 And great multitudes followed him ; and he healed them there.
3 The Pharisees also came unto him, tempting him, and saying unto him, Is it lawful for a man to put away his wife for every cause ?

2 borders of Judæa beyond Jordan : and great multitudes followed him ; and he healed them there.
3 And there came unto him ¹ Pharisees, trying him, and saying, Is it lawful *for a man* to put away his

1 Many authorities, some ancient, insert *the.*

---

self especially with teachings concerning the kingdom of heaven, while most of the parables given in Luke ch. 13 to 18 refer only to individual piety, and would thus not come into Matthew's plan.

Into the coasts of Judea. *Borders* rather than 'coasts,' see on 2: 16; 15: 22. **Beyond Jordan.** The Greek construction is peculiar, but makes 'beyond Jordan' state the route by which he came into the borders of Judea. Mark (10: 1, correct text) has 'into the borders of Judea and beyond Jordan.' Copyists and early students saw that this differed somewhat from Matt., and so some omitted Mark's 'and,' others changed 'and' into 'through' (Com. Ver.). Mark's expression thus gives a twofold designation of the region into which he came, viz., the borders of Judea, and Perea. Matt. might seem to locate the following matters in Judea, after Jesus had passed through Perea; Mark refers them indefinitely to both districts; the Harmony (see 20: 17, 29) pretty clearly places the earlier portion, certainly 19: 1-15, in Perea. The region 'beyond Jordan,' *i. e.*, east of the Jordan (see on 4: 25), from its mouth to near the Lake of Galilee, was in the Roman period often called 'the beyond (district),' 'the Perea,' the Greek word for beyond being *peran.* The Galilean Jews preferred to go to Jerusalem by way of Perea, so as to avoid the unfriendly Samaritans (Luke 9: 52 f.); though the direct route through Samaria was sometimes taken (comp. Josephus, "Life," 52). Perea included the dominions of Sihon and part of those of Og, or the districts later called Gilead and part of Bashan. The Romans separated Decapolis (see on 4: 25) from this district, and accordingly Josephus ("War," 3, 3, 3) says that Perea extended from Machærus to Pella (nearly opposite the plain of Esdraelon and Bethshean). It was divided into a rougher and very beautiful northern portion, and a southern portion, which latter comprised the plain immediately east of the lower Jordan, and the high table-land beyond. So far as we can judge, our Lord here appears in Southern Perea, on his way to Jericho and

Jerusalem. (20: 29; 21: 1.) Many places of this region are of great interest in Old Test. studies, but none appear distinctly in the New Test. save Machærus (see on 14: 3), and 'Bethany beyond Jordan,' 'the place where John was at first baptizing' (John 1: 28 f.; 10: 40), and this last spot cannot be determined (comp. on 3: 13). We can therefore get no local coloring for 19: 3 to 20: 28. Like Galilee, Perea had so few Jews in the time of Judas Maccabaeus that he transferred them all to Judea for safe keeping (1 Macc. 5: 23, 45); but during the reign of Herod the Great the Jewish population of Perea evidently became considerable, which will account for the expressions in v. 2 and John 10: 40-42; and this district was an important part of the tetrarchy of Herod Antipas. For accounts of Perea, see especially Schultz in Herzog, Art. "Palästina," 4); Robinson's "Phys. Geog."; Tristram's "Land of Moab"; Merrill's "East of the Jordan"; but all are quite incomplete.

Great multitudes, see on 4: 25. Here, as so often in Galilee, vast numbers of the people throng and crowd around him. It is probable (see in Clark's "Harmony") that this was subsequent to the sojourn beyond Jordan mentioned in John 10: 41, 42, when "many resorted unto him," and "many believed on him there." It is not necessary to suppose a considerable stay in that region at this time, in order to account for the collection of great crowds, for they probably consisted in part of persons journeying to Jerusalem for the Passover. **And he healed them there,** as he had often done in Galilee. 'Them' of course means not all of the crowds, but such as needed healing. Mark says (10: 1), 'and, as he was wont, he taught them again.' Thus the Galilean ministry is reproduced in Perea —crowds, healing, teaching. And here is another instance of a general statement, which must be pondered in order to realize the extent of our Lord's work. (Comp. 4: 23; 9: 35; 14: 14; 16: 30.)

3. An inquiry as to divorce. Distinguish the original question of some Pharisees, v. 3; the answer, v. 4-6; an objection and his reply,

v. 7-9; a doubting remark by the disciples and his reply, v. 10–12. Mark's report (10: 2-12) omits the last portion, and gives the rest with slight differences of expression and order, but to the same general effect. **The Pharisees.** 'The' in Com. Ver., also in Mark 10: 1, was an addition by copyists, because 'the Pharisees' are generally spoken of as a class. In like manner, **unto him** after **saying,** and **unto them** in v. 4 are wanting in the earliest and best documents, and were very easily added by copyists. As to the Pharisees, see on 3: 7. **Tempting him,** as in 16: 1, putting him to the test, (Amer. Revisers preferred 'trying him'), and hoping he would say something they could use among the people to his prejudice, by representing his teaching either as intolerably severe, or as wanting in fidelity to the law of Moses. Perhaps they also hoped he would speak of divorce in a way offensive to Herod and Herodias. (See on 14: 3.) The place was not very far from Machærus, and they might have remembered the fate of the prophet John, the Baptizer. The opposition of the Pharisees to Jesus appearing in 12: 2, 14, 24, 38, and continued in 15: 1 and 16: 1, is here renewed towards the end of his ministry, and will be maintained until the end. See other cases of testing him with hard questions in 22: 17, 35. **Is it lawful,** or permissible, as in 12: 10; 14: 4. **For a man** is naturally suggested, and so was readily supplied by some early copyists, especially as it is genuine in the parallel passage of Mark 10: 4; while we could not account for its omission here in several of the earliest and best documents, if originally present. **To put away his wife** was understood as involving the right to take another—the Jews knew nothing of a mere legalized separation, without right of re-marriage.—Upon the general subject of our Lord's teachings as to divorce, see on 5: 31 f. These Pharisees in Perea probably did not know of that former teaching in Galilee. If the saying in Luke 16: 18 was distinct from this, it would appear to have been uttered in this same Perean district, and a little earlier than the present occasion (Clark's "Harm.," Edersh.) The reference is to Deut. 24: 1, "When a man taketh a wife, and marrieth her, then it shall be, if she find no favor in his eyes, because he hath found some unseemly thing in

her, that he shall write her a bill of divorcement," etc. The euphemistic Heb. phrase translated 'some unseemly thing,' has always been obscure. It is literally (as in margin of Com. Ver.), 'some matter of nakedness,' and appears to mean derivatively, something indecent, shameful, disgraceful, hateful. The Rabbis disputed much as to its exact meaning and limitations. The Mishna has a whole treatise on divorce, *Gittin,* but chiefly occupied with minute directions as to the preparation of the document and conditions of its validity. The last paragraph reads: "The school of Shammai says, no one shall put away a wife unless there has been found in her something disgraceful (a phrase exactly corresponding to that of Deut. 24: 1), as written, 'because he hath found something unseemly in her'; the school of Hillel says, even if she has burnt his food, as written, 'because he hath found something unseemly in her'; Rabbi Akiba says, even if he find another more beautiful than she is, as written, 'if she find no favor in his eyes.'" Maimonides explains (Note in Surenh. Mishna) that the school of Shammai rests on the term "unseemly"; the school of Hillel on the term "something." Rabbi Akiba took the phrase he quotes to mean in respect to beauty. Alas! with what perverse ingenuity men quibble to make the Bible mean what suits their wishes. We see the folly of this practice in others, but are all in great danger of doing likewise. Observe that in the Mishna the school of Shammai use simply the general phrase, something disgraceful or unseemly, as in the law. A late Midrash on Numb. 5: 30, quoted in Wet., and two passages in the Talmud mentioned by Edersh., state that the school of Shammai recognized no ground but unchastity. It is worth inquiry whether this was anything more than an incorrect interpretation afterwards put upon the language of the Mishna. Josephus, who was a Pharisee, gives ("Ant.," 4, 8, 23) a paraphrase of the law which uses essentially the same phrase as here: "If one wishes to be divorced from his wife for any causes whatsoever (and many such causes might happen among mankind), let him give assurance in writing that he will never more live with her," etc. It is evident that in our Lord's eyes the expression 'something unseemly' might extend to other faults

4 And he answered and said unto them, Have ye not read, that he which made *them* at the beginni;g made them male and female.

5 And said, For this cause shall a man leave father and mother, and shall cleave to his wife: and they twain shall be one flesh ?

6 Wherefore they are no more twain, but one flesh. What therefore God hath joined together, let not man put asunder.

7 They say unto him, Why did Moses then command to give a writing of divorcement, and to put her away ?

4 wife for every cause? And he answered and said, Have ye not read, that he who ¹ made *them* from the beginning made them male and female, and said,

5 For this cause shall a man leave his father and mother, and shall cleave to his wife; and the twain

6 shall become one flesh? So that they are no more twain, but one flesh. What therefore God hath

7 joined together, let not man put asunder. They say unto him, Why then did Moses command to give

---

besides unchastity, for otherwise there would have been no occasion for what he says in v. 8. The Pharisees, by holding up before him the Hillel view in its most extreme form, probably hoped to drive him to take the Shammai view, which was extremely unpopular. He did not side with either party, but (as in 22: 21) cut into the heart of the matter, reaching a fundamental and decisive principle.

4-6. Reply to the Pharisees. **Have ye not read,** comp. on 12: 3. The Scribes and Pharisees boasted of their acquaintance with the law, and he reproaches them with ignorance of it. He makes first a reference to Gen. 1: 27, and then a quotation from Gen. 2: 24. **That he which made them.** 'Created' (Rev. Ver. *margin*) is probably here the correct reading,¹ altered into 'made' to agree with Sept., with the word here immediately following, and with Mark 10: 6; but there is obviously no substantial difference. The words **male and female** have in the Greek an emphatic position. From the beginning, the race included the two sexes, and these were to be *united* in marriage. **And said,** viz., he who created them said, the words of Adam in that exalted mood being taken as expressing the will of the Creator. **Leave father and mother.** Even the important filial relation will give way to one higher still. **The twain** is given by the Sept., and several other versions of Old Test., and only expresses emphatically what the Heb. implies. **Shall be** (*or become*) **one flesh.** The union of soul is expressed, and therefore intensified,by a bodily union. Comp. Ecclus. 25: 26, "If she go not as thou wouldst have her, cut her off from thy flesh," break the bodily union;

Eph. 5: 28 ff., "to love their wives as their own bodies." In v. 6 the closing statement is repeated for emphasis. And there our Lord draws the conclusion that the two thus united into one ought not to be separated. **Joined together** is literally *yoked together* (so also in Mark), an image frequently employed among the Greeks for marriage. (Comp. 2 Cor. 6: 14; Lev. 19: 19.) Tyn., Cran., Gen., here render ' coupled.' **Let not man.** *Theophyl.*: "Showing what an interval there is between God who joined together, and man who puts asunder." Our Lord has thus laid down a broad general rule that the bond of marriage ought never to be broken. A little after (v. 9) he mentions, as if incidentally, an exception to this rule, about which there was no difference of opinion among his hearers, and which is in fact only apparently an exception, because in that case the essential bond has been broken.

7-9. The Pharisees raise an objection, very naturally suggested, and our Lord replies. Moses (in Deut. 24: 1) had certainly allowed divorce, and they held that he had *commanded* it; how could the prophet of Nazareth declare that divorce was contrary to the nature and divine design of marriage? The Talmud of Jerusalem even represents it as a peculiar privilege of Israel, not shared by the Gentiles. **A writing of divorcement.** The same phrase is rendered *bill of divorcement* in Com. Ver. of Mark 10: 4 and Deut. 24: 1, and there ought to have been no difference in translation. The Greek is slightly different above in 5: 31. **Moses . . . . suffered you.** Jesus speaks of the law in Deut. as coming from Moses. It is very hard to reconcile this with the fashionable theories as to a late date

¹ It is found in B, several cursives of singular excellence, Armenian, Origen (three times), and several other Fathers. It is much easier to suppose a change to suit the Sept., the following word here and Mark,

than an opposite change to suit the Heb., which means 'created,' for copyists and students of the text-forming period seldom knew Heb.

8 He saith unto them, Moses because of the hardness of your hearts suffered you to put away your wives: but from the beginning it was not so.

9 And I say unto you, Whosoever shall put away his wife, except *it be* for fornication, and shall marry another, committeth adultery: and whoso marrieth her which is put away doth commit adultery.

8 a bill of divorcement, and to put *her* away? He saith unto them, Moses for your hardness of heart suffered you to put away your wives: but from the

9 beginning it hath not been so. And I say unto you, Whosoever shall put away his wife, [1]except for fornication, and shall marry another, committeth

---

[1] Some ancient authorities read, *saving for the cause of fornication, maketh her an adulteress:* as in ch. v. 32.

---

of Deuteronomy, and indeed of the whole Pentateuch; it is necessary to maintain either that Jesus was mistaken, and this as to the word of God, or else that he used the phraseology of his time in a highly misleading fashion. Many similar expressions of his are given in the Gospels. (Comp. on 22: 43.) The Pharisees had said that Moses commanded; our Lord's reply puts it, 'suffered.' But in Mark 10: 3 f. he says 'command, and they answer 'suffer.' We learn then that the law did not *require* the wronged husband to put away his unfaithful wife; he might forgive her upon repentance, as the prophets so often declared Jehovah willing to do with his unfaithful spouse, Israel. The law *suffered* him to put away his wife, and *commanded* him in so doing to give the formal writing. **Because of the hardness of your hearts.** The preposition (*pros*) translated 'because,' signifies 'looking to,' 'considering,' 'having regard to.' It was wise not to attempt too much in these civil regulations for such a people. Remember that the Mosaic regulations as to marriage and divorce were civil enactments, though resting on an ethical basis. The nation of emancipated slaves whom Moses brought out of Egypt had no doubt fallen into great laxity concerning marriage, as slaves always do, and he was wise enough to know that it would be a slow and difficult task to lift them up to a high standard of morality in this important respect. Yet he placed serious restrictions upon the existing facility of divorce (see on 5: 31 f.), and even in this matter Jesus was only "completing"

the law by going further in the same direction (comp. on 5: 17). 'Hardness of heart' (Rom. 2: 5; Ecclus. 16: 10) denotes not merely lack of proper feeling, as we use the phrase, but lack of proper perceptions and will (comp. on 6: 21). The Israelites who received the law were not qualified for elevated ethical perceptions, dispositions, or conduct, and would fiercely break over a severe enactment; and their descendants were still too much of the same character. But the Messiah proposes to lift them higher; and in this matter to return to the original divine design of marriage. Our Lord thus recognizes the practical direction of the law of Moses in this particular respect fell short of perfection. But we must observe that he does not declare the Old Test. as a whole to be imperfect even in this respect, but simply goes back to its earliest teaching on the subject, its great fundamental principles. Mal. 2: 14-16 speaks of divorces as offensive to Jehovah; but the Rabbis quibbled, some saying that this only forbade a man's putting away his *first* wife. **And I say unto you,** solemnly calling their attention (comp. on 5: 18). Mark 10: 10 shows that this was said 'in the house'—we know not what house—where the disciples renewed the conversation. Matthew joins it without break to the foregoing, and it was really a part of the discourse on divorce. Our Lord gives his own authoritative statement on the subject, applying the principle of v. 6, and declares that divorce is not only not allowable 'for every cause' (v. 3), but not allowable at all—except of course for unchastity.[1] See the

---

[1] The reading of *margin* Rev. Ver. is evidently drawn from 5: 32. The first part 'saving . . . fornication' is pretty clearly a "Western" correction, being found in the characteristic Western documents D, Old Latin, Old Syriac, but found also in B, the two Egyptian versions, Origen, Basil. W H. have placed it in their margin, and so it is in margin of Rev. Ver. But is not this an instance of a "Western" alteration found in B, etc., like 27: 28? The next clause, 'maketh her an adulteress,' is also plainly taken from 5: 32. It is not given by D, etc., but is given by B, with C (first

hand), N, two cursives, and one or two mixed Latin copies, Memphitic, Origen, Aug. Here again B and Memphitic are clearly wrong, though not in this case "Western." The last clause 'and he that marrieth,' etc., is doubtful. It would be easily inserted from 5: 32, but it is here omitted only by the "Western" group with L and some other MSS., the Egyptian versions and Origen, most of which are clearly wrong just above; and its omission might have originally been accidental, through the similar ending of this clause to the foregoing. The confusion arising in the text of two such

10 His disciples say unto him, If the case of the man be so with *his* wife, it is not good to marry.
11 But he said unto them, All *men* cannot receive this saying, save *they* to whom it is given.

adultery: [1]and he that marrieth her when she is 10 put away committeth adultery. The disciples say unto him, If the case of the man is so with his wife, 11 it is not expedient to marry. But he said unto them, All men cannot receive this saying, but they

---

1 The following words, to the end of the verse, are omitted by some ancient authorities.

---

leading terms explained above on the similar statement of 5: 32. That was made in Galilee, and we are now in Southern Perea, a year or two later. It seems strange to modern readers that the highly important exception our Lord makes is so slightly mentioned, both here (v. 9) and in 5: 32, and that in Mark and Luke (on a somewhat earlier occasion, 16: 18) it is not recorded at all. The explanation is that among the Jews there was no question on this point. The strictest school of Rabbis, that of Shammai, allowed divorce for unchastity, if not for other disgraceful acts. So this matter did not need to be dwelt on, hardly needed to be mentioned, as it would be taken for granted by all parties. But the question is naturally asked, how could there be divorce for conjugal unfaithfulness, when the law punished that offence with death? It is evident that the law was not regarded as *compelling* the husband to bring forth his adulterous wife for the death penalty. Joseph was minded to put Mary away privately, and was prevented only by learning from the angel that her condition involved no guilt. (1: 19 f.) In the doubtless true story, though not belonging to Scripture, of the adulterous woman brought before Jesus (John 8: 3-11), the Scribes and Pharisees are represented as "tempting him" (just as here) with the question whether the law is to be enforced in her case, and he does not say that it must be. And in the Talmud it is perfectly plain that the Jews did divorce for adultery instead of stoning, and no one thought of condemning it.

In Mark 10: 12 the statement is expressly declared to hold of a woman also, who divorces her husband. Everywhere in Old Test., and everywhere else in New Test., only the case of a man divorcing his wife is presented, the opposite case being doubtless a very rare occurrence in Oriental life. We might take for granted that the same principles would apply to a woman divorcing her husband, and this saying expressly enjoins such an application. It had become quite

common for Roman women to divorce their husbands and marry again, and this custom had begun to affect the official and fashionable circles in Palestine—as when Herodias divorced her husband, Herod Philip, to marry Herod Antipas (see on 14: 3). This makes it natural that our Lord should once refer to that side of the question, and that Mark's Gospel should take pains to report the saying, as he wrote especially for Gentile, and perhaps especially for Roman readers.

10-12. A remark by the disciples and the Master's reply. The fact that this was 'in the house' (Mark), with only the disciples present, accords well with the delicacy of the subject. This naive remark shows that even they shared largely the popular views and feelings concerning marriage and divorce, and thought that as an indissoluble union, marriage was to be avoided. Similar (Plumptre) is the view of Milton's "Doctrine and Discipline of Divorce." **If the case be so,** and the form of expression implies that they accept the supposition as true. The word rendered 'case' is rendered 'cause' in v. 3. It seems here necessarily to mean 'case' or 'matter,' and this sense is very generally accepted, though it has not been established by other usage. The Latin versions have *causa.* Meyer's attempt to make it here mean cause is not successful. **It is not good** (or *expedient*) **to marry,** the term rendered 'it is profitable' in 18: 6; 5: 29 f.; see also in 1 Cor. 6: 12; 10: 23.

Our Lord's reply is that marriage is sometimes not expedient. **All men cannot receive this saying,** viz., the saying that it is not expedient to marry. What they have said is true in some cases, and for a special reason, quite different from the one intimated by them. To understand 'this saying' as his own saying, that marriage is indissoluble, would make the Saviour contradict his own argument, for he had argued from the divine purpose in the creation of man. 'Receive' does not here mean to accept as true, but the

---

notable parallel passages, is natural. It is not likely that the reading here has been affected by Mark 10: 11,

or the latter would have been itself likewise altered from Matt. in some copies.

12 For there are some eunuchs, which were so born from *their* mother's womb : and there are some eunuchs, which were made eunuchs of men : and there be eunuchs which have made themselves eunuchs for the kingdom of heaven's sake. He that is able to receive *it*, let him receive *it*.

12 to whom it is given. For there are eunuchs, that were so born from their mother's womb: and there are eunuchs, that were made eunuchs by men : and there are eunuchs, that made themselves eunuchs for the kingdom of heaven's sake. He that is able to receive it, let him receive it.

peculiar Greek word signifies to have space in one's nature for something—like a vessel holding so much, comp. John 21 : 25—sometimes in the sense of capacity to know (Lid. and Scott), here in the sense of capacity to act out. 'Not all men have room (capacity) for this saying.' The capacity depends on physiological constitution and general temperament, making it practicable to be happy and useful without marriage. Some men are naturally disqualified for marriage, and others have been disqualified by human action. Some voluntarily abstain from marriage **for the kingdom of heaven's sake,** for the sake of greater usefulness in proclaiming its truths and promoting its establishment. Some Rabbinical writers also use the phrase, "made themselves eunuchs," as a figure for voluntary and entire sexual abstinence. The phrase was, and would still be, natural enough in Oriental speech, however repulsive to us. It would probably never have been understood literally by any one, but for well-known practices among some heathen devotees in Asia Minor and elsewhere. Origen took it literally in his youth and acted upon it, but interprets it altogether spiritually in his commentary on this passage.—The Jewish feeling regarded marriage as universally desirable; Jesus says that for some persons it is best to abstain. He thus distinctly intimates that celibacy may give great advantages in promoting Christianity, as the Apostle Paul afterwards urged in 1 Cor. 7. Where a man feels deeply moved to engage in some form of religious work, with the prosecution of which marriage would greatly interfere, then it is well if he can be willing to remain unmarried. So John the Baptist, and Paul. But Paul by no means pressed celibacy upon all, recognizing natural differences in regard to it, and full liberty of personal decision. And so the Saviour did, even repeating, **He that is able,** etc. Observe that neither Jesus nor Paul nor Scripture anywhere favors the ascetic notion that marriage is impure, or essentially less pure than celibacy; on the contrary, "Let marriage be had in honor among

all" (Heb. 13 : 4, Rev. Ver.), and it was *false* teachers of the worst type who were in later times "forbidding to marry." (1 Tim. 4 : 1-3.) The question is not of a more or less holy state, but of greater or less *usefulness*, in promoting the kingdom of heaven. Among the apostles to whom Jesus said this, celibacy was not the rule, but the exception. Simon Peter was married (8 : 14), and when Paul wrote (1 Cor. 9 : 5 ff., R. V.), "the rest of the apostles," and "the brethren of the Lord," carried their wives with them in their missionary journeys. Paul himself remained unmarried for the sake of giving himself without hindrance to his work. (1 Cor. 7 : 32 f.)—The Romish rule of universal celibacy in the priesthood occasioned a Protestant reaction to the opposite extreme. Protestant public opinion almost demands that a minister shall marry. Yet how much missionary work, in savage or sickly countries, or in home fields that cannot support a family, could be far better done by unmarried men. How many a young minister cuts short his preparatory studies, or prosecutes them amid great interruption and hindrance, or is obliged to begin pastoral work in too exacting a field, for the sake of an unnecessarily early marriage. Every one must decide for himself; but he should decide in view of life as a whole, and of the life to come.

HOMILETICAL AND PRACTICAL.

V. 3. Tempting Jesus. 1) With hard questions, Luke 11: 16; Matt. 16: 1; 19: 3; 22: 18, 35. 2) By efforts to restrain him from going forward to death, 16 : 22 f., comp. John 12: 27 and Matt. 26: 36 ff. 3) By suggesting positive sin, 4: 1-11.

V. 6. God and man as to marriage. 1) All the fundamental relations of society are based on human nature as originally created. 2) Marriage was designed by the Creator to be a complete union of two into one, and indissoluble; the one sin that justifies divorce does so because it has essentially broken the union. 3) Wherever man has violated God's design, by separating the married for reasons which do not break the essential bond, there

13 Then were there brought unto him little children, that he should put *his* hands on them, and pray: and the disciples rebuked them.

13   Then were there brought unto him little children, that he should lay his hands on them, and pray: and

---

follow great and ever growing evils. In such cases re-marriage may seem to prevent adultery, but it is itself adultery (v. 9). 4) It is man's highest wisdom, interest, and duty—best for the parties concerned and best for society—to follow God's law of marriage, strictly and faithfully.

13-15. LITTLE CHILDREN ARE BROUGHT TO JESUS FOR HIS BLESSING.

Found also in Mark 10: 13-16; Luke 18: 15-17. Luke here again becomes parallel to Matthew and Mark, and continues so to the end, see above on 19: 1. The place of this occurrence appears to have been Southern Perea, in some house (Mark 10: 10), and the time a few days before the triumphal entry, see on 19: 1. **Then** is naturally, though not of necessity (see on 3: 13), understood strictly, as denoting the time of the foregoing conversation upon divorce. Mark has simply 'and.' **Were there brought.** Mark has 'they brought,' impersonal, like "they say"; Luke, 'they brought unto him their babes also,' which shows that the parents brought them. They were so moved by his teaching and healing as not only to seek a personal blessing, but a blessing upon their babes also. Mark and Luke have the Greek imperfect tense, *describing* them as engaged in bringing. And they have 'rebuked' in the same tense; while the parents were bringing and the disciples were rebuking, Jesus spoke. **Little children,** called 'babes' in Luke, and small enough to be naturally taken in one's arms (Mark). These terms forbid our understanding children old enough to exercise faith. **Put his hands on them, and pray.** The Jews had always valued the "blessing" of a father, a prophet, a great rabbi, or other venerable person. The Talmud says they brought their young children to the synagogue for this purpose. "After the father of the child had laid his hands on his child's head, he led him to the elders, one by one, and they also blessed him, and prayed that he might grow up famous in the law, faithful in marriage, and abundant in good works." (Buxtorf, in Geikie.) To lay hands on them, or (Mark and Luke) 'touch them,' was the symbol of invoking a blessing upon them, and seemed to es-

tablish a personal relation between the good man and the person blessed. See Gen. 48: 14; Numb. 27: 18; Acts 6: 6; 13: 3; comp. Matt. 9: 18, 20. They came to Jesus as a rabbi or a prophet; and he did what they desired, took the children in his arms and blessed them (comp. Mark 10: 16). **And the disciples rebuked them.** This in Matt. might mean rebuked the children or rebuked those who brought them; in Mark and Luke it is clearly the latter, which is obviously appropriate. Jesus had just been speaking of a highly important practical topic, viz., the propriety of divorce, and the expediency of marriage. The disciples had renewed the subject after leaving the Pharisees (Mark 10: 10), and the Master was pursuing it in private. Perhaps (Wet.) they were just thinking of other questions to ask on the subject. They did not want the privacy of Messiah the King to be interrupted, and these deeply interesting instructions stopped, by what they regarded as the mere trivial matter of bringing babes for the teacher's blessing. Comp. 20: 31; 2 Kings 4: 27. Our Lord not only spoke in opposition to their rebuke, but (Mark) 'was moved with indignation,' a strong word, the same as in 20: 24; 26: 8. Why was he so indignant? He warmly loved infant children. All good men ought to feel a tender affection for them, and it seemed that the disciples were in this respect deficient. This very scene has so taught the Christian world to love infant children that it is difficult for us to realize the apparent feelings of the disciples. They thought the infants and their parents unworthy of the Messiah's notice; and he was indignant at such a conception of childhood and of him. Moreover, while they were annoyed at the interruption of valued instruction, they were forgetting that some months before (18: 1 ff.) he had expressly used a little child as an object-lesson to give them a deserved rebuke for their selfish ambition and jealous strife. This was one of the lessons they most needed, and from that time forth they ought never to have looked at a little child without recalling the lesson and laying it to heart afresh. But no. They have forgotten the lesson, and behold little children

14 But Jesus said, Suffer little children, and forbid them not, to come unto me: for of such is the kingdom of heaven.

14 the disciples rebuked them. But Jesus said, Suffer the little children, and forbid them not, to come unto me: for [1] to such belongeth the kingdom of

1 Or, *of such is.*

without being reminded. In a day or two they will again manifest (20: 20 ff.) the ambition and jealousy he had used that illustration to correct. There *may* have been other grounds for the Master's indignation, and some of these may not have been correctly conceived. But we seem to perceive (a) a misapprehension of him, for he tenderly loved little children; (b) a defect in their own character, in that they did not love them as he did; (c) a grievous forgetfulness, and persistence in wrong dispositions he had taken such pains to correct; and it may also be that (d) he was displeased at their assuming the right to decide who should approach him, without waiting to know his wishes. More than once before he has sharply reproved them for not understanding or not remembering his instructions. (16: 8-11, 23; Mark 6: 52; Matt. 11: 25; 7: 21-23; comp. hereafter 20: 22; John 14: 9.)

14. The repetition, **suffer and forbid not,** is highly emphatic. It was vividly remembered, for Matthew, Mark, and Luke gave the same words, with a slight difference of order. 'Suffer' is aorist tense, expressing the simple action without the notion of continuance; 'forbid' is present tense, 'do not be forbidding', or 'do not make a practice of forbidding.' The distinction obtains in Matthew, Mark, and Luke; and the difference was felt, for the manuscript D has in Matthew and Luke altered 'forbid' to aorist. **To come unto me** is a general expression, not necessarily denoting either unaided locomotion or conscious spiritual approach, both of which are here forbidden by the terms 'babes' and 'were brought.' The disciples rebuked the parents and thus repelled the children they were bringing; but there must be free access to him. What follows may grammatically be a reason for their coming, or a reason why the disciples must let them come, and not forbid them. The latter seems to be the thought. **For of such is the kingdom of heaven.** Here, as commonly, Matthew has the Jewish phrase 'kingdom of heaven,' Mark and Luke, 'kingdom of God' (comp. on 3: 2); otherwise the phrase is identical in all three. For 'of such is,' the Amer.

Revisers give 'to such belongeth,' comp. 5: 3, 10; Luke 6: 20; James 2: 5. (So Meyer, Grimm, Jelf.) But the difference is not important. 'Such' evidently means *childlike* persons, as he had previously taught in 18: 3. The only question is whether it also means children. To understand it in both senses at the same time is very difficult. Morison argues that it means simply and exclusively children such as these, and not childlike adults at all. There is plenty of warrant in usage for so understanding the word 'such'; but does not the connection here in Mark and Luke absolutely require the sense of childlike persons? They both add, 'whosoever shall not receive the kingdom of God as a little child, he shall in no wise enter therein.' This is exactly what Jesus said on a former occasion (18: 3), when, as almost all commentators agree, he was using the little child only as an illustration. Morison's position is therefore untenable in this case. 'Such' certainly means childlike persons, and apparently does not mean children at all. So the Memphitic, "for persons of this sort, theirs is the kingdom of heaven." And the Peshito takes great pains, "for those who are like them, theirs is the kingdom of heaven." All the Greek commentators explain it as meaning the childlike, none of them mentioning children as included, and several expressly stating the contrary. Nor does any Greek commentator, so far as we can find, mention infant baptism in connection with the passage, though they all practiced that rite. *Origen* speaks only of the childlike; and so *Cyril:* "The new-born child is a symbol of innocence; for the babe is as it were a new creature. . . . . Christ does not wish us to be without intelligence when he says, 'For to such belongs (or, of such is) the kingdom of heaven,' but to be infants in evil, and in intelligence perfect (full-grown)." *Chrys.:* "Teaching them (the disciples) to be lowly, and to trample under foot worldly pride, he receives them, and takes them in his arms, and to such as them promises the kingdom; which kind of thing he said before also," *i. e.*, in 18: 3 f. *Theophyl.:* "He did not say 'these,' but 'such,' *i. e.*, the simple, the guileless, the innocent." *Euthym.:* "He did not say 'to these belongs the kingdom of heaven,' but 'to such,' those who imitate the simplicity of these." *Anon.* takes the occasion to exhort parents to bring their children incessantly to the priests, that they may put their hands on them and pray for them. Even the great Latin commentator, *Jerome* (followed by Bede), tells us: "He significantly said 'such,' not 'these,' in order to show that not age reigns, but character, and that the reward is promised to those who should have similar innocence and simplicity." But Tertullian and Augustine do mention, not this clause but that which precedes, in connection with infant baptism. *Tertullian* (on Baptism, 18) advises delay of baptism till there has been proper instruction, "delay according to each one's condition and disposition and even age; and especially as to the little ones. . . . The Lord does indeed say, 'Forbid them not to come unto me.' Let them come, then, while they are growing up; let them come while they are learning, while they are being taught whither to come; let them be made Christians when they have become able to know Christ. Why does the innocent age hasten to remission of sins?" He here shows, as throughout the treatise, that baptism is regarded by him and those he addresses, as securing remission and making persons Christians. So Cyprian ("Ep. to Fidus") and Origen (on Rom. ch. 5 and Homily 14 on Luke ch. 2.) give as the reason for infant baptism that the infants may receive remission of original sin, that the defilement of sin may be washed away through water and the Spirit, etc., but neither of them mentions this passage, nor does Origen mention infant baptism in his interpretation of this passage. He says (on Rom.), "The church received it as a tradition from the apostles, to give baptism to little ones also." *Augustine* ("Serm. 174") says: "No one passes from the first man (Adam) to the second (Christ) save through the sacrament of baptism. In little children born and not yet baptized, behold Adam; in little children born and baptized and therefore born again, behold Christ. . . . What is it that thou sayest, little children

have no sin at all, not even original sin? What is it that thou sayest, but that they should not approach to Jesus? But Jesus cries out to thee, 'Suffer the little ones to come to me.' " Aug. very frequently gives the same reason for infant baptism, constantly and vehemently assailing the Pelagians with the argument that there is no propriety in infant baptism unless infants are under the guilt of original sin, but we have found no other instance in which he associates with it this passage. Calvin says "both children and those who are like them." *Alexander* (on Mark): "More satisfactory is Calvin's explanation of the sentence as referring both to children (*i. e.*, to believing children) and to those who are like them in their childlike qualities." But *believing* children are in the same position as believing adults; so this is virtually admitting that there is here no reference to infants who are incapable of belief. *Alexander* adds, "The application of this passage to infant baptism, although scornfully rejected as absurd by its opponents, is entirely legitimate, not as an argument, but as an illustration of the spirit of the Christian system with respect to children." *Bengel* says: "Grant that such as are like infants are meant, then much more infants themselves, who are such, have the kingdom of God, and should and can receive it by coming to Christ." And he actually thinks it helps the matter to add: "Many of those who were then infants, afterwards when grown up believed on Christ Jesus." *Meyer:* "Not little children, but men of a childlike disposition, 18: 3 f."; and to the same effect Fritz., Bleek, Lutter., Keim, Godet. *Olsh.:* "Of that reference to infant baptism which it is so common to seek in this narrative, there is clearly not the slightest trace to be found. The Saviour sets the children before the apostles as symbols of spiritual regeneration, and of the simple childlike feeling therein imparted." *Geikie:* "Let the little children come to me, and do not forbid them, for the kingdom of heaven is given only to such as have a childlike spirit and nature like theirs." [1]

To sum up. (a) There is no good ground

---

[1] *Maldonatus:* "The Calvinists [*i. e.*, Reformed] have no other testimony by which to prove that infants ought to be baptized, than that Christ says, 'Suffer the little ones to come to me.' For that strongest and clearest testimony by which the church has always been led to baptize infants, 'except a man be born of water and of the Spirit he cannot enter into the kingdom of God,' they interpret not of baptism but of

15 And he laid *his* hands on them, and departed thence.

15 heaven. And he laid his hands on them, and departed thence.

---

for understanding 'such' as meaning children themselves, but only childlike believers (as in 18 : 3.) No question is here made that those dying in infancy are saved. They are saved through the atonement of Christ and the work of the Spirit, but this must hold true of all alike, without reference to any ceremony, and no matter whether their parents were believers, unbelievers, or heathen. The Messianic kingdom is always spoken of in connection with, and seems naturally to imply, persons capable of conscious submission to Christ's reign. It is here said to belong to, or consist of, the childlike, and (according to Mark and Luke) no others. If 'such' includes infants, it includes all infants, not only those dying in infancy, and those that live and become believers, but those that live a life of sin and are finally lost; in what sort of sense does the Messianic kingdom belong to (or consist of) these? (b) If it were supposed that 'such' does include literal children, it would not follow that infants ought to be baptized. There is here no allusion to baptism, and no one imagines that Jesus caused these little ones to be baptized. We know that at one period Jesus was baptizing (through his disciples) very many persons (John 3 : 22; 4 : 1 f.), but no one questions that they were baptized as penitent believers in the Messianic reign. Infant baptism seems to have arisen afterwards from the belief that baptism was necessary to salvation, being, in all the early references to it, associated with that belief, and only as an afterthought was ground for it sought in an inference from this passage. In like manner

Zwingli, in his controversies with the Anabaptists, introduced the argument from the Abrahamic covenant.[1]

15. Laid his hands on them, of course with the accompanying prayer (v. 13) that they might be blessed. Mark adds that he 'took them in his arms,' apparently from the arms of those who brought them, 'and blessed them, laying his hands upon them' ; he must then have been seated—we have seen that he was probably in a house. His blessing them means that he prayed (v. 13) that they might be blessed. We cannot possibly know what results followed to the infants from this benediction. He prayed that his crucifiers might be forgiven, and they were—if they repented and believed. **And departed thence.** Mark 10: 17 may perhaps indicate that he left sooner than was expected. Was it because of his indignation at the disciples?

HOMILETICAL AND PRACTICAL.

V. 13–15. Jesus and infant children. 1) Jesus tenderly loves infant children (comp. Mark 10: 16), for he has the same feelings now as when on earth. (Heb. 13 : 8.) 2) It is right for parents continually to seek the blessing of Jesus upon their infant children. 3) It is a great mistake and a great fault to take no interest in infants; they who do so are quite unlike Jesus, and forget one of his most impressive lessons. (Comp. 18 : 3.) 4) All followers of Jesus ought to be childlike, *i. e.,* teachable, loving, free from selfish ambition and jealousy, etc.; not only ought to be, but absolutely must be childlike. (Mark 10 : 15;

---

teaching; so it comes to pass that as long as they wish to be heretics and to resist the Catholic Church, they disarm themselves, and cannot withstand the Anabaptists [*i. e.,* rebaptizers], who deny that infants ought to be baptized." *Reuss :* "This word of Jesus, ' Let the children come to me,' is wrongly cited by those who attempt to establish the baptism of infants upon texts of the New Test. It can be used to that effect upon condition of forming a conception of baptism itself different from that of John the Baptist, Jesus, and the apostles, who demanded beforehand a conscious and thoughtful faith." *Plumptre :* " The words and the act have rightly been regarded, as in the Baptismal Office of the Church of England, as the true warrant for infant baptism. More than doubtful passages in the Acts and Epistles ; more than the authority, real or sup-

posed, of primitive antiquity ; more than the legal fiction that they fulfil the condition of baptism through their sponsors—they justify the Church of Christ at large in commending infants, as such, to the blessing of their Father. The blessing and the prayer of Christ cannot be regarded as a mere sympathizing compliance with the fond wishes of the parents, and if infants were capable of spiritual blessings then, why, it may well be asked, should they be thought incapable now ? " So "the true warrant for infant baptism " is found in a passage which very many of the ablest ancient and modern writers who have practiced it declare to have no connection with the subject.

[1] Dr. W. H. Whitsitt, Prof. of Ch. Hist., Louisville, knows of no earlier use of this argument.

16 And, behold, one came and said unto him, Good Master, what good thing shall I do, that I may have eternal life?
17 And he said unto him, Why callest thou me good? *there is* none good but one, *that is*, God: but if thou wilt enter into life, keep the commandments.

16   And behold, one came to him and said, [1] [2] Master, What good thing shall I do, that I may have eternal life? And he said unto them, [3] Why askest thou me concerning that which is good? One there is who is good: but if thou wouldest enter into life,

---

1 Or, *Teacher*....2 Some ancient authorities read, *Good Master.* See Mark x. 17; Luke xviii. 18....2 Some ancient authorities read, *Why callest thou me good? None is good save one. even God.* S e Mark x. 18; Luke xviii. 19.

---

comp. 18 : 3 f. ; 1 Cor. 14 : 20.)—This passage can hardly be used in addressing Sunday-school children as a proof that Jesus specially loves *them*, for they are deeply conscious of sin, and ought to ask from Jesus a new heart, forgiveness, and help to live as his followers. The lesson here is for adults, and the passage is often so misused as simply to promote in children a most hurtful conceit, to the effect that they are greatly better than grown people.

16-22. THE RICH YOUNG RULER.

Found also in Mark 10: 17-22; Luke 18: 18-23.

Jesus has left the house in which he blessed the babes (v. 15; Mark 10: 10), and is going forth into the road (Mark 10: 17), doubtless on the way towards Jerusalem (20: 17) for the last Passover. The place is still pretty certainly in Southern Perea. (19: 1; 20: 29.)

16. One came. 'One' may be taken loosely (see on 8: 19), as we in English often use it, to mean some one, a certain one; but is perhaps better taken strictly—not now a crowd (19: 2), only a single person, but a very interesting and important case. Matthew tells us that he was a young man (v. 20-22), Luke that he was a 'ruler' (18: 18), not probably meaning one of the Sanhedrin (John 3: 1), but a ruler of the local synagogue (Matt. 9: 18); all three state that he was very wealthy. The theory of Plumptre that this was Lazarus of Bethany, rests entirely upon certain resemblances, as wealth, high standing, and the fact that Jesus is said to have loved him, and it must be regarded as a pleasant homiletical fancy, rather than even a probable historical fact. The resurrection of Lazarus was almost certainly before this time. For 'came to him,' Mark says vividly, Rev. Ver., 'ran to him, and kneeled to

him.' Finding that Jesus had left the house, and eager not to miss the desired instruction, he runs to overtake him, and then kneels in profound reverence. **Good Master,** *i. e.*, teacher (*didaskalos*), see on 8 : 19. 'Good' is wanting in the earliest and best documents, and was manifestly brought in by copyists from Mark and Luke. The same early documents, with many others of great importance, read v. 17 as in Rev. Ver., which, especially as the meaning is not obvious, would be readily changed to agree with Mark and Luke.[1] **What good thing shall I do?** He has done many good things, what else? (v. 20.) **That I may have eternal life,** comp. on 25 : 46. He is sincerely and deeply desirous of gaining it, as he has shown by his conduct heretofore, and shows now by his eagerness to learn from the Galilean teacher who is passing by. Contrast the lawyer of Luke 10: 25, who quibbled. (v. 29.)

17. It is possible (Aug.) that Jesus used first the expression in Mark and Luke, and afterwards that in Matt. (Rev. Ver.) But the Evangelists often report a saying in different terms. (See on 3 : 17.) Both forms here express truth, and they substantially agree. To call him 'good' (Mark and Luke), was a sort of flattery to one approached only as a Rabbi, which he rebukes as improper; only God is perfectly good—keep that word for him. No religious teacher would really like to be accosted as "a good man." So here, to ask a teacher concerning that which is good, what good thing shall be done, must not be with the notion that any mere human teacher is of himself qualified to give the desired instruction. Only God is perfectly good; and lessons of goodness are not lessons of mere human ethical wisdom, but of divine instruction. This is a surpassingly important truth. Men

---

1 The other readings need not have been placed in the margin of Rev. Ver., for there can be no question that they are wrong. We cannot imagine any reason for changing an easy reading which agreed with Mark and Luke into an obscure one which strikingly differs, while the change into assimilation is precisely such as we constantly find in MSS. and versions. Origen expressly points out and dwells on the difference between the text of Matt. and that of Mark and Luke.

18 He saith unto him, Which? Jesus said, Thou shalt do no murder, Thou shalt not commit adultery, Thou shalt not steal, Thou shalt not bear false witness.
19 Honor thy father and *thy* mother: and, Thou shalt love thy neighbour as thyself.
20 The young man saith unto him, All these things have I kept from my youth up: what lack I yet?
21 Jesus said unto him, If thou wilt be perfect, go *and* sell that thou hast, and give to the poor, and thou shalt have treasure in heaven: and come *and* follow me.

18 keep the commandments. He saith unto him, Which? And Jesus said, Thou shalt not kill, Thou shalt not commit adultery, Thou shalt not steal, Thou shalt not bear false witness, Honour thy
19 father and thy mother: and, Thou shalt love thy
20 neighbour as thyself. The young man saith unto him, All these things have I observed: what lack I
21 yet? Jesus said unto him, If thou wouldest be perfect, go, sell that thou hast, and give to the poor, and thou shalt have treasure in heaven: and come,

in every age and country are prone to think of mere human instruction in morals and religion, and to forget that the highest religious wisdom must come from him who alone is perfect wisdom and perfect goodness. **But if thou wilt,** or *wishest to* (comp. on 15: 32; 16: 24), **enter into life** (comp on 5: 20), **keep the commandments.** *Bengel:* "Those who feel secure Jesus refers to the law; the contrite he consoles with the gospel."

18 f. Which, if strictly translated, would be what sort of, what kind of commandments, not inquiring as to particular precepts, but classes. Yet this Greek pronoun is used somewhat loosely in New Test., and may here mean simply which. In Modern Greek it has that meaning always. The ruler may have expected new commandments, or a special selection from those existing. The Rabbis would have prescribed stricter attention to traditional observances. Jesus did not propose new commandments, but a new spirit and motive. The sixth, seventh, eighth, and ninth commandments are given, then the fifth, and then Matt. alone adds the general precept (Lev. 19: 18) which sums up all the second table of the law; comp. on 22: 39. Luke quotes the same five commandments as Matt.; Mark, likewise, but inserting 'do not defraud,' equivalent to the tenth commandment. **Thou shalt do no murder** (Rev. Ver., *shalt not kill*). So also Com. Ver. in 5: 21; Mark 10: 19; Luke 18: 20; and Rom. 13: 9. The Old Test. Revisers, on the contrary, have changed 'thou shalt not kill' into 'thou shalt do no murder,' Ex. 20: 13; Deut. 5: 17. The Heb. and Greek verbs are frequently used for unlawful killing, murder, but not uniformly.

20. All these things has the emphasis here (according to the probable text) on 'all'; in Mark and Luke it is on 'these things.' **Have I kept.** Rev. Ver. gives *observed.* So

Tyn. and Gen. here, and all early English versions in Mark 10: 20, while all give 'kept' for the same word in Luke 18: 21. In v. 17 above, 'kept' represents a different word. **From my youth up** is spurious in Matt., but genuine in Mark and Luke, and so was really said.[1] The speaker was still a 'young man,' but it is quite common for young men to look back to their youth, viz., boyhood, and as a very remote period. He must have been sincere in his profession, and really blameless in outward conformity to law, for 'Jesus looking upon him loved him.' (Mark.) **What lack I yet?** Mark and Luke give as the beginning of the Saviour's reply, 'One thing thou lackest.' So the question here must not be regarded as a mere self-righteous expression. The only observance he had ever thought of was external and superficial; in regard to this, he had been very careful and correct. The Talmud repeatedly mentions persons as having kept the whole law, in one case "my holy ones, who have kept the whole law, from Aleph to Tau," like Alpha to Omega. The Great Teacher does not stop for distinctions between the external and the spiritual which the young ruler would have found it difficult to appreciate, but cuts through all his self-delusion and self-complacency by an extraordinary demand.

21. If thou wilt be, *wishest to be,* as in v. 17. **Perfect,** so as to *lack* nothing, see on 5: 48. **Go,** *go along,* go promptly, as in 4: 10; 5: 24; 13: 44; 18: 15. **Sell that thou hast** (comp. 13: 46), a comprehensive expression, strengthened in Mark by 'whatsoever,' in Luke by 'all.' **To the poor.** Here again (see on 5: 3; 11: 5) the notion of 'beggars' is quite out of place; the wisest giving is not always to beggars. The Talmud (Wet.) speaks of a rabbi as saying to some Gentiles who sought instruction,

---

[1] It was easily added in Matt. by copyists, just as in Mark some documents add to 10: 20, 'what lack I yet,' (which Mark really has just after in another shape),

and to 10: 21, 'if thou wishest to be perfect.' Such patent errors show the habits of copyists, and help us to group documents.

22 But when the young man heard that saying, he went away sorrowful: for he had great possessions.

22 follow me. But when the young man heard the saying, he went away sorrowful: for he was one that had great possessions.

"Sell all that you have, and moreover you ought to become proselytes."—This was a special test, exactly suited to the young ruler, as appears from his sorrowful failure to meet it. The principle involved is supreme devotion to Christ. The test of this is different for different people. Some find it harder to renounce hopes of wordly honor and fame for Christ's sake, than to renounce wealth; and for others the hard trial is to abandon certain gratifications of the various appetites or of taste. Abraham left his native country at God's command, but became rich and famous. Moses gave up the distinction and refined pleasures of court life, and tried patiently to rule a debased and intractable people. Elisha left his property at the call of God through Elijah. Paul abandoned his ambitious hope of being a great rabbi. All should be willing even to die for Christ (16: 24 ff.), though not many are actually required to do so. The Romanists build on this passage their theory that for all persons and times voluntary and absolute poverty is a chief means of securing the highest spiritual attainments. But there is no intimation that Jesus requires this of all his followers. He said nothing of the kind to any but the Twelve, and a few who, like them, were called to leave home and travel about the country with him. **Treasure in heaven,** see on 6 : 20. **And come, follow me,** see on 4 : 19. Many documents in Mark, and one or two in Matthew add 'taking up thy cross,' borrowed from Mark 8 : 34; Matt. 16 : 24.

22. He went away sorrowful. Mark prefixes 'his countenance fell,' 'he looked gloomy,' dark-faced ; comp. a similar expression in Luke 24: 17 (correct text). It was a painful disappointment; his eager longing and hope gave way to gloom—he *could* not give up his great possessions. Among all nations, but especially among the Jewish higher classes, the idea of falling from great wealth to utter poverty would be extremely painful. He went away, and appears no more in the history. One would incline to the hopeful persuasion that he afterwards became a true Christian, since Jesus loved him. But the story ends very sadly. And its lesson applies

very closely to many whose 'possessions' are by no means 'great.'

HOMILETICAL AND PRACTICAL.

V. 17-21. We need no new commandments, but a new motive, supreme devotion to Christ. So in Rom 8 : 1-17, there is presented the same old law, but a new revelation of forgiveness (v. 1), a new moral force (v. 2), a new motive (v. 15).—V. 16-22. The young ruler. 1) There may be much religious earnestness, and a lovable sincerity, without true Christian piety. 2) To become a thorough Christian requires no new precepts, but a new spirit. 3) A complete Christian character and life cannot exist without complete submission to Christ. 4) The tests of submission to Christ will be very different in different cases, but must in every case be squarely met. 5) Turning away from Christ with regret and gloomy sadness, is yet turning away.—V. 17 (latter part). If thou wishest to enter into life. 1) The wish. (a) None enter who do not wish. (b) None who wish to enter need fail. 2) The way. (a) The commandments must be kept not only outwardly, but inwardly, spiritually. (b) This can be done through help of Christ and of the other Comforter. (c) That help is received only where there is supreme devotion to Christ.—V. 20. What lack I yet ? 1) He might seem to others to lack nothing; he has wealth, honor, a blameless outward life, and a deep sincerity and earnestness. 2) He is conscious of lacking something, and eager to supply the lack. 3) He really lacks everything; for he has only kept the commandments outwardly, and thus altogether imperfectly. 4) He lacks one thing (Mark 10 : 21), without which all is inadequate, and with which all will work toward perfection and eternal life; and that one thing is supreme devotion to Christ.—V. 22. He went away sorrowful. 1) He went away *sorrowful.* 2) He *went away* sorrowful.

Ch. 19 : 23—20 : 16. HARD FOR THE RICH TO BE SAVED. REWARD OF SACRIFICES FOR CHRIST'S SAKE.

This section, except the parable, is found also in Mark 10: 23-31; Luke 18: 24-30. In both it is immediately connected as here with

23 Then said Jesus unto his disciples, Verily I say unto you, That a rich man shall hardly enter into the kingdom of heaven.
24 And again I say unto you, It is easier for a camel to go through the eye of a needle, than for a rich man to enter into the kingdom of God.

23   And Jesus said unto his disciples, Verily I say unto you, It is hard for a rich man to enter into the
24 kingdom of heaven. And again I say unto you, It is easier for a camel to go through a needle's eye,

the story of the young ruler. Luke tells us, 'And Jesus seeing him said'; Mark, 'Jesus looked round about, and said.' While the young man walked gloomily away, Jesus looked at him and at his disciples, and spoke to them the great lessons which follow. The section divides itself into v. 23-26, v. 27-30, and 20: 1-16.

I. **23-26.** HARD FOR THE RICH TO BE SAVED. Mark 10: 23-27; Luke 18: 24-27. **Verily I say unto you,** calling special attention, see on 5: 18. **A rich man shall hardly enter.** *It is hard for a rich man* (Rev. Ver.), was the rendering of Tyndale and followers. The Com. Ver. though more literal, would now suggest improbability rather than difficulty. The Jews inclined to think it much easier for a rich man than for a poor man. The former had in his very prosperity a proof of the divine favor; he was *prima facie* a good man, and might feel very hopeful about entering the kingdom. Our Lord had not long before this spoken a parable (Luke 16: 19), in which, contrary to what all Jews would have expected, the beggar Lazarus went to Abraham's bosom, and the rich man to torment. Much earlier (comp. on 5: 3) he had shown, that the kingdom of heaven belongs to the poor, if they have the corresponding poverty in spirit. **Kingdom of heaven,** see on 3: 2. He was far from meaning that all poor men will be saved, and all rich men lost; for Lazarus was carried to the bosom of Abraham, who in life was very rich, as were also Isaac and Jacob and Joseph, David and Solomon, Nicodemus and Joseph of Arimathea, and apparently the family of Bethany. On the perils of riches, comp. 13: 22; 1 Tim. 6: 9 f. The expression in Com. text of Mark 10: 24, 'for them that trust in riches,' must be omitted.[1] This strong statement our Lord now repeats (v. 24), in a hyperbolical form such as he so often employed to awaken attention and compel remembrance. (See on 5: 39.) **It is easier for a camel to go through the eye of a needle.** So also Mark and Luke. The camel was the largest beast familiar to the Jews, and the needle's eye was the smallest opening in any familiar object. So the expression denotes an impossibility, and it was so understood by the disciples, and so treated by Jesus just after. (v. 26.) A little later (23: 24), our Lord will again use the camel as the largest beast in another hyperbolical expression, "who strain out the gnat and swallow the camel." In the Talmud, for an elephant to go through a needle's eye is several times employed as an expression of impossibility, the Jews in foreign countries having now become familiar with an animal even larger than the camel. Our Lord may have been using a proverb (comp. on 7: 3), but there is no proof that such a saying was current in his time. The Koran (Sura VII, 38) borrows, as it often does, the saying of Jesus: "Those who say our signs are lies and are too big with pride for them, for these the doors of heaven shall not be open, and they shall not enter into Paradise until a camel shall pass into a needle's eye." The notion that the word means a cable, found in Cyril on Luke, and in a scholium ascribed to Origen (Tisch.), and mentioned by Theophyl. and Euthym. as held by "some," was merely an attempt to soften the incongruity of the image; and the statement of the late lexicographer Suidas and a scholium on Aristophanes that *kamelos* is the animal, *kamilos* a thick cable, probably arose from that attempt. (Liddell and Scott.) The Memph., Latin, and Pesh. versions give camel. Origen understands the camel, and takes the phrase as a figure for the impossible; so Chrys. and followers. Jerome explains likewise, but adds that as Isaiah declares (60: 6) that the camels of Midian and Ephah come to Jerusalem with gifts, and though curved and distorted they enter the gates of Jerusalem, so the rich can enter the narrow gate by laying aside their burden of sins and

[1] It is wanting in several of the earliest and best documents, and we readily account for its insertion as originally a marginal explanation of a difficulty, and by way of correspondence to the next verse, while we can see no reason why copyists should have struck it out.

25 When his disciples heard *it*, they were exceedingly amazed, saying, Who then can be saved?

26 But Jesus beheld *them*, and said unto them, With men this is impossible: but with God all things are possible.

27 Then answered Peter and said unto him, Behold, we have forsaken all, and followed thee; what shall we have therefore?

28 And Jesus said unto them, Verily I say unto you, That ye which have followed me, in the regeneration when the Son of man shall sit in the throne of his glory, ye also shall sit upon twelve thrones, judging the twelve tribes of Israel.

25 than for a rich man to enter into the kingdom of God. And when the disciples heard it, they were astonished exceedingly, saying, Who then can be saved? And Jesus looking upon *them* said to them, With men this is impossible; but with God all things are possible. Then answered Peter and said unto him, Lo, we have left all, and followed thee; what then shall we have? And Jesus said unto them, Verily I say unto you, that ye who have followed me, in the regeneration when the Son of man shall sit on the throne of his glory, ye also shall sit upon twelve thrones, judging the twelve tribes of

all their bodily deformity—which is only his loose allegorizing upon a point not brought into view by the Saviour. A gloss to Anselm (A. D. 1033–1109), given in Aquinas, says that "at Jerusalem there was a certain gate called the Needle's Eye, through which a camel could not pass, save on its bended knees and after its burden had been taken off; and so the rich," etc. This is to all appearance a conjecture suggested by Jerome's allegorizing remark. Lord Nugent many years ago (quoted in Morison, from Kitto) heard at Hebron a narrow entrance for foot-passengers, by the side of the larger gate, called "the eye of a needle." *Fish* (p. 165), speaking of the Jaffa gate at Jerusalem, says: "There is here a small gate in the large one, bearing the name Needle's Eye. My dragoman informed me of this, and said it had always been so called. I afterwards inquired of a Christian Jew, for thirty years a resident in Jerusalem, who verified the statement, and farther said that any little gate like that, in a large one, in both Palestine and Egypt, was called a needle's eye (a fact which I have since ascertained from other sources)." So far as this usage really exists, it probably arose from the saying in the New Test., the Talmud and the Koran, together with Jerome's allegorizing remark. It is perfectly evident that Jesus was understood, and meant to be understood, as stating an impossibility; and as to the incongruity of the image, it is no greater than that of 23: 24, and employed an animal as familiar to his hearers as the horse is to us.

25 f. The disciples **were exceedingly amazed,** for this was contrary to all the notions in which they were reared. Since everybody believed that a rich man was shown by his wealth to have God's favor, and could secure further favor by his beneficence, and since Jesus has declared that it is practically impossible for a rich man to enter the Messi-

anic kingdom, they very naturally asked, **Who then can be saved?** with emphasis on 'who' and 'can.' Their idea is that things being as the Master has stated (which is the meaning of the particle translated 'then'), nobody can be saved. And to this he assents. As a matter of human power, no one can be saved; but **with God all things are possible** (comp. Luke 1: 37; Job 42: 2; Gen. 18: 14), and the divine omnipotence may save even a rich man.

II. **27-30.** JESUS PROMISES REWARD TO THOSE THAT HAVE LEFT ALL FOR HIS SAKE. Mark 10: 28–31; Luke 18: 28–30. Peter speaks for his companions as well as himself (see on 16: 16), and the answer is addressed to them all, 'you' (v. 28). **Behold, we,** the word 'we' being expressed in the Greek, and thus emphatic; so also in Mark and Luke. **Have forsaken all,** as the rich young ruler had just refused to do. (19: 22.) **And followed thee,** comp. on 4: 19 f. Luke 18: 28 has (correct text) 'have left our own,' *i. e.*, property, while the young ruler would not leave his. Some had left their calling as fishermen, Matthew a public office, James and John their parents, Peter his home and family. **What shall we have therefore?** without any special emphasis on 'we.' This clause is not given by Mark or Luke, being obviously implied in Peter's foregoing statement. The apostle's inquiry may be easily stigmatized as self-complacent or mercenary. But Jesus evidently did not so regard it. They had made real sacrifices, and were following him in worldly destitution with dismal worldly prospects, for they were now near Jerusalem, where he would be rejected and put to death. (16: 21.) The situation was very serious. Jesus solemnly promises great reward to the Twelve (v. 28), and extends it to all who have left anything for his sake (v. 29); and then guards against all selfish and jealous

29 And every one that hath forsaken houses, or brethren, or sisters, or father, or mother, or wife, or children, or lands, for my name's sake, shall receive a | 29 Israel. And every one that hath left houses, or brethren, or sisters, or father, or [1]mother, or children, or lands, for my name's sake, shall receive [2]a

---

[1] Many ancient authorities add, *or wife :* as in Luke xviii. 29....[2] Some ancient authorities read, *manifold.*

---

claims of superior reward in v. 30, illustrated by the parable which follows.

28. He begins with a solemn assurance, as in v. 23, **Verily I say unto you,** see on 5 : 18. This special promise to the Twelve is found only in Matt., to whose Jewish readers it would be of special interest. **In the regeneration.** The Greek word here used (*palingenesia*) is found nowhere else in New Test. save Tit. 3: 5, where it denotes the spiritual new birth. Here it has a very different sense. Plutarch uses it for the appearance of souls in new bodies (Pythagorean doctrine of transmigration); M. Antoninus speaks, according to a Stoic conception, of "the periodical new-birth of the universe," viz., in spring; Philo, according to another Stoic conception, foretells a new-birth of the world out of fire; Cicero speaks of his "restoration to dignities and honors" as "this new-birth of ours"; and a late Platonist says, "Recollection is a new birth of knowledge." These uses will illustrate our passage, which has a kindred but profounder sense. When the Messianic reign is fully established, there will be a new-birth of all things, called also a "restoration of all things" (Acts 3 : 21, Rev. Ver.), "new heavens and a new earth, wherein dwelleth righteousness" (2 Pet. 3: 13; comp. Rev. 21: 1, 5), and the deliverance of the whole creation from the bondage of corruption at the revealing of the sons of God in redeemed bodies. (Rom. 8 : 18-23.) The Pesh. here translates 'in the new world,' or new age, period. (Comp. on 12: 32.) Understood thus, 'in the regeneration'[1] is manifestly not connected with 'ye that have followed me,' for it denotes not the beginning, but the consummation of the Messianic reign, **when the Son of man** (see on 8: 20) **shall sit in the throne of his glory,** comp. 25: 31; also 7: 22; 16: 27. All this high-wrought imagery of a universal restoration, a new birth, a new universe, must of course be inter-preted as imagery, and must not be so understood as to exclude other facts of the future which are plainly revealed, as in 25: 46. **Ye also shall sit upon twelve thrones,** is of course an image. It is idle to insist upon the exact number twelve (comp. Rev. 21: 12-14), and so to be troubled about the fact that while Matthias took the place of Judas, Paul made thirteen apostles. **Judging the twelve tribes of Israel** certainly does not mean that only Jews will be judged, or that one apostle will judge one tribe. The Oriental king, and the Roman emperor, was also a judge, and when he sat on his throne in public, it was usually for the purpose of hearing petitions or complaints and giving judgment. Such a monarch often had persons seated near him (called by the Romans "assessors"), to aid him in judging; comp. Rev. 4: 4; "round about the throne were four and twenty thrones." To this position of dignity and honor will the Twelve be exalted at the consummation of the Messianic kingdom; comp. 1 Cor. 6: 2, "the saints shall judge the world." Our Lord will use the same image again on the night before the crucifixion, Luke 22: 30.

29. Not only the Twelve are to be rewarded, but **every one that hath forsaken** (*left*) anything for his sake; 'every one' is in the Greek a very strong expression; every one whosoever. The enumeration is substantially the same in Mark and Luke. But Luke, while condensing some of the other expressions, has also 'or wife,' and this, as so often happened in parallel passages, crept early into many copies of Matt. and Mark. Being omitted by fewer earlier copies of Matt. than of Mark, the Rev. Ver. here places it in the margin. Though not belonging to either Matt. or Mark, we know from Luke that the word was spoken. The list of objects is not intended in any case to be complete; it mentions several principal things, and we under-

---

[1] On this term see Trench, Synonyms. It means not exactly a *new* birth, but a being born *again,* another birth. In 1 Pet. 1: 3, 23 the verb *anagennao* means 'to beget over again,' not a second begetting or birth, but going back and repeating the first process. So in John 3: 3, 'born anew,' over again. There is of course no *substantial* difference between this image and that of Tit. 3: 5. Other terms describe the same spiritual process as a 'renewing,' (2 Cor. 4: 16; Rom. 12: 2; Col. 3: 10; Tit. 3: 5; Eph. 4: 23.)

hundredfold, and shall inherit everlasting life.
30 But many *that are* first shall be last; and the last *shall be* first.

30 hundredfold, and shall inherit eternal life. But many shall be last *that are* first; and first *that are* last.

stand that the same is true of anything else. **Houses** may have been mentioned first because some of the Twelve, as Simon Peter, had left homes; **lands** last, because real estate among the Jews was specially valuable property, not to be alienated, comp. Acts 4: 34, 37. The most exactly similar case at the present time is seen in the foreign missionary, or in a converted heathen, who is cast out by his kindred, and finds compensation in the Christian affection and kind offices of the other converts, and in the joy of serving Christ, and hoping for eternal life. More remotely similar is the case of a worldly young person in a Christian land, who becomes converted, and forsakes worldly pleasures and companionships. **Shall receive a hundredfold.** It is doubtful whether we should read this as in Mark, or 'manifold' (Rev. Ver., *margin*), as in Luke. The question is of no practical importance.[1] We might in reading Matt. think only of rewards after death. Mark 10 : 30 says, 'a hundredfold now in this time. . . . and in the world to come eternal life'; and such a distinction seems to be intended in Matt. also. Jesus speaks of earthly rewards first, but does not mean literally similar things to those left, but equivalent things —blessings temporal or spiritual, that will compensate many times over for all that was abandoned. The expressions cannot possibly be understood literally, because that would be promising in Mark a hundred mothers, and comp. Luke.

30. But many that are first shall be last, etc. This enigmatical saying is given also by Mark 10: 31. In Matthew our Lord proceeds to illustrate it by a parable, at the close of which (20: 16) he repeats the saying. In the parable an employer pays, and asserts his right to pay, the same wages to laborers who began later in the day, as to those who began early. Then Jesus is here speaking of the rewards that will be given his followers, and declares that these will be given as a matter of sovereignty, without recognizing any claim to precedence. So the immediate application

of the saying to the Twelve is probably to the order in which they became disciples. In their disputes as to which should have the highest place in the kingdom (comp. on 18 : 1), now shortly to be renewed (20: 20), some of the disciples might naturally urge that the highest places should be given to those who first followed the Master. So far as we know, these were John and Andrew, next Andrew's brother Simon, and presently Philip and Nathanael. (John 1 : 35-51.) Now Simon and Andrew, John and his brother James, were afterwards together called to leave other employments and follow Jesus (4: 18-22), are repeatedly mentioned together as being in his company (Mark 1: 39; 13: 3), and constitute the first four in every list of the Twelve (see on 10: 2). Peter, James, and John were alone with Jesus during that night upon the mountain (17: 1), of which they would give the others no account (17: 9), as they had been on a former interesting occasion. (Mark 5: 37.) And presently James and John will ask through their mother (20: 20) for the two highest places. These facts make it not at all unnatural to suppose that the order of time entered into their disputes. Our Lord then means that he, or the Father (20: 23), will act as he shall think proper (20: 15) in respect to precedence, and *many* who entered his service late will receive greater reward than others who entered earlier; he will recognize no claim on any such ground. A notable instance would be the Apostle Paul. But while immediately designed to check disputes as to this question of time, the principle is stated generally and may have other applications. It is presupposed throughout, as already involved in 19: 28 f., that Christ's servants will be differently rewarded; we learn here that this reward will not be regulated by the mere outward conditions of the time spent in his service, or the results actually attained, but will be conferred according to his own judgment and sovereign pleasure. David, who meant to build, will be rewarded as truly, and it may be as richly, as Solomon who built;

---

[1] It has considerable scientific interest. The reading is certainly 'a hundredfold' in Mark (no variation at all), probably 'manifold' in Matt., and quite possibly 'sevenfold' in Luke, though this last is found only in the "Western" documents.

CHAPTER XX.

FOR the kingdom of heaven is like unto a man *that is* a householder, which went out early in the morning to hire labourers into his vineyard.

2 And when he had agreed with the labourers for a penny a day, he sent them into his vineyard.

3 And he went out about the third hour, and saw others standing idle in the marketplace,

4 And said unto them: Go ye also into the vineyard, and whatsoever is right I will give you. And they went their way.

5 Again he went out about the sixth and ninth hour, and did likewise.

6 And about the eleventh hour he went out, and found others standing idle, and saith unto them, Why stand ye here all the day idle?

1 For the kingdom of heaven is like unto a man that was a householder, who went out early in the morning to hire labourers into his vineyard. And

2 when he had agreed with the labourers for a [1] shilling a day, he sent them into his vineyard. And he

3 went out about the third hour, and saw others standing

4 ing in the marketplace idle; and to them he said, Go also into the vineyard, and whatsoever is right

5 I will give you. And they went their way. Again he

6 went out about the sixth hour, and did likewise. And about the eleventh *hour* he went out, and found others standing; and he saith unto

---

1 See marginal note on ch. xviii. 28.

James who was early slain, as truly as his brother who lived so long. The often repeated view of some Fathers that the reference was to Jews and Gentiles, is quite untenable. The equal reward of some who die early is set forth by a somewhat similar illustration in Talmud Jerus., Berach., ch. II, 8 (Schwab), designed to give comfort in regard to the early death of a rabbi. A king hired many laborers, and seeing one who worked remarkably well, took him apart after two hours to walk with him to and fro. At even he paid this man as much as the others, and when they complained, he said, 'This man has done more in two hours than you in a whole day.' In like manner the young rabbi knew the law better when he died at the age of twenty-eight than any other would have known it if he had lived to be a hundred. Thus the resemblance to our Lord's illustration is only partial, and the point of application quite different, while in itself very pleasing.

III. **Ch. 20: 1-16.** PARABLE OF THE LABORERS WHO RECEIVED THE SAME REWARD. Found in Matt. only. It is designed to illustrate the saying of 19: 30, which is repeated at the close, as the outcome of the illustration. (20: 16.) The terms of the parable itself are for the most part plain.

1-6. The kingdom of heaven, the Messianic reign (see on 3: 2) **is like,** in some respects resembles, the following story (comp. on 13: 24.) **Unto a man, that is a householder.** As the story is told in the past tense throughout, the *Amer. Revisers* very naturally wish to insert 'that was,' rather than 'that is,' as in 13: 22, where the present tense follows. 'Householder,' or *housemaster*, is

the same word as in 10: 25 (see note); 13: 27, 52, and below in 21: 33; 24: 43. He owns a house, and a vineyard. (v. 8.) **A penny,** *denarius*, about seventeen cents, see on 18: 28. This was the customary wages of a soldier or a laborer; Plin. XXXIII, 3; Tac., "Ann." I, 17; Tob. 5: 14; Talmud. **The third hour.** The Jews divided the day, from sunrise to sunset, into twelve parts. At the vernal and autumnal equinox these would be exactly as long as an hour with us, but at other seasons would be longer or shorter. The sixth hour would always be noon, the third and ninth would correspond loosely to our 9 A. M. and 3 P. M.; the eleventh hour loosely to an hour before sunset. **In the marketplace,** or public square, where people came together for business or conversation. **Go ye also,** 'ye' being expressed in the Greek and thus emphatic. **Whatsoever is right,** no definite bargain as with the first set. In the supposed actual occurrence this might result from haste, or from the fact that they would now be glad to find employment at all, and would trust the employer's justice without a definite arrangement. As to the illustration, this point prepares for the result, and the peculiar application. **About the eleventh hour.** Here 'hour' is not expressed in the correct Greek text, but naturally suggested. **Others standing idle.** The word 'idle' is here wanting in very many of the earliest and best documents, and was obviously drawn by copyists from v. 3 and the end of v. 6. **Why stand ye here all the day idle?** This is often used homiletically as representing persons who are slothful in neglecting to work in Christ's vineyard. But such application is unwarranted, and alien to the tone of the parable. The reason given by these men

7 They say unto him, Because no man hath hired us. He saith unto them, Go ye also into the vineyard; and whatsoever is right, *that* shall ye receive.

8 So when even was come, the lord of the vineyard saith unto his steward, Call the labourers, and give them *their* hire, beginning from the last unto the first.

9 And when they came that *were hired* about the eleventh hour, they received every man a penny.

10 But when the first came, they supposed that they should have received more ; and they likewise received every man a penny.

11 And when they had received *it,* they murmured against the goodman of the house,

12 Saying, These last *a*have wrought *but* one hour, and thou hast made them equal unto us, which have borne the burden and heat of the day.

13 But he answered one of them, and said, Friend, I do thee no wrong: didst not thou agree with me for a penny ?

14 Take *that* thine *is,* and go thy way : I will give unto this last, even as unto thee.

15 Is it not lawful for me to do what I will with mine own ? Is thine eye evil, because I am good ?

16 So the last shall be first, and the first last: for many be called, but few chosen.

7 them, Why stand ye here all the day idle? They say unto him, Because no man hath hired us. He

8 saith unto them, Go ye also into the vineyard. And when even was come, the lord of the vineyard saith unto his steward, Call the labourers, and pay them

9 their hire, beginning from the last unto the first. And when they came that *were hired* about the eleventh

10 hour, they received every man a ¹shilling. And when the first came, they supposed that they would receive more; and they likewise received every man

11 a ¹shilling. And when they received it, they mur-

12 mured against the householder, saying, These last have spent *but* one hour, and thou hast made them equal to us, who have borne the burden of the day

13 and the ²scorching heat. But he answered and said to one of them, Friend, I do thee no wrong: didst

14 not thou agree with me for a ¹shilling? Take up that which is thine, and go thy way ; it is my will to

15 give unto this last, even as unto thee. Is it not law-ful for me to do what I will with mine own? or is

16 thine eye evil, because I am good? So the last shall be first, and the first last.

---

a Or, have continued one hour only.....1 See marginal note on ch. xviii. 28....2 Or, *hot wind.*

---

is treated as valid, and they are paid for a full day's work.

7. Go ye also, 'ye' emphatic, as in v.4.¹ Obviously this employer of labor acts very peculiarly. (Comp. Bruce.) It is not neces-sary to seek parallel cases, nor wise to propose his course as a model in ordinary business (as Ruskin does in "Unto this last," the title being drawn from v. 12.) The thing is possible, and the story is meant as an illustra-tion of God's course, who is other and higher than man. (Isa. 55: 8 f.)

8-12. His steward, same word in Luke 8: 3; Gal. 4: 2, is natural in the story of a great employer; what good is done by saying that the steward represents Christ? (Comp. on 13: 3.) **Beginning from the last** was a special direction given, in order that those hired earlier might see that all were paid alike.

11. Murmured, a strong word, more ex-actly, *grumbled.* The Greek word, the Latin murmur, and the English grumble, are all ono-matopoetic. The tense is imperfect, *describ-ing* the grumbling as in progress.

12. Have wrought but one hour. *Spent* is the meaning, rather than 'wrought.' **The heat,** the same word as in Luke 12: 55; James 1: 11. The Rev. Ver. renders 'scorching heat' in this v. and Luke, and 'scorching wind' in James, and puts 'hot wind' in the margin of Matt. and Luke. The word means 'burner,'

and is applied sometimes to burning heat in general, but more frequently in Septuagint to the burning east wind. (See Grimm.) The order of the words, 'the burden of the day and the scorching heat,' (*kauson*), as well as its more frequent use in that sense, renders it likely that the hot wind is here intended. Mere heat is so common in Palestine that it would scarcely be worth remark; but the dry and scorching east wind is something terrible. Even in February (1871) this dry east wind, having come across the desert sands and lost all its moisture, in an hour so parched the mouth and nostrils as to make breathing pain-ful and speech difficult. The position of the article in the Greek makes it impossible to render, 'the burden and heat of the day' (as in Tyn. and followers.)

13-16. Friend, or 'comrade,' a familiar and kindly term, as in 11: 16; 22: 12; 26: 50. **14. Take,** *take up,* or 'take away.' They had received the pay, but perhaps had laid it down again, or stood holding it in the hand, unwilling to go off with it. **I will give.** The Rev. Ver., *It is my will to give,* con-veys the meaning well. The Greek is ex-pressed in English by 'will to' or 'wish to' (15: 32 ; 16: 24 ; 19: 17), according to the na-ture of the case; comp. v. 15; 1 Tim. 2: 4; 2 Pet. 3: 9. **15. Is it not lawful,** per-missible. (See on 14: 4.) **To do what I will with mine own?** The Saviour here illus-

---

¹ The final clause in the common Greek text, 'and whatsoever is right that ye shall receive,' is wanting in the earliest and best documents. We can easily

account for its insertion from v. 4, and cannot account for its omission if originally present; so there is no doubt that it is here spurious.

trates his *sovereignty* in the whole matter of rewarding his followers. *Or*, **Is thine eye evil**, here expresses jealousy and hate (Mark 7: 22; Deut. 15:9; Prov. 28:22), quite different from the meaning in 6: 23. 'Or' is in the correct Greek text. **16.** The latter clause of this verse in the common Greek text, **for many be** (*are*) **called, but few chosen,** is wanting in leading early documents, and evidently brought in from 22: 14, where there is no variation in the reading.[1] Our Lord here repeats the saying of 19: 30, which he introduced the parable to illustrate. It is very natural that it should be repeated in a general form, without the restrictive 'many' of the first statement. Some able writers (Meyer, Weiss, others) urge that the parable and this statement teach that in the consummated Messianic kingdom all will have an equal reward. But this is inconsistent with the first statement, and with the distinct intimation of 19: 28 f. that there will be difference of reward. The general thought of the parable is that the assignment of individual rewards will be a matter of divine *sovereignty*, precisely as in 20: 23, comp. Acts 1: 7. We have seen on 19: 30 that this had a special application for the disciples, but as a general principle may be variously applied. It is very true, as some commentators urge, and it may be properly recalled here, that God will reward men more according to aim and spirit than to time spent or results achieved: but the Saviour does not here say that, or distinctly imply it.

HOMILETICAL AND PRACTICAL.

V. 23–26. Salvation of the rich. 1) It is hard, v. 23. (a) Many peculiar sins connected with wealth, in procuring, loving, using, retaining it. (b) Men find it difficult to withdraw the heart from wealth (6:21), and give it in supreme devotion to Christ (comp. v. 21 f.); and without this there can be no salvation. 2) It is not only hard, but impossible, v. 24, 26; yea, it is impossible for any man to be saved, through human wisdom, power, or goodness.—V. 23. EUTHYM.: "If the rich man with difficulty, the covetous man not at all; for if he that does not give his own possessions is condemned, much more he that also grasps the possessions of others."—V. 25. Who then can be saved? HENRY: "Considering the many difficulties that are in the way of salvation, it is really strange that any are saved. When we think how good God is, it may seem a wonder that so *few* are his; but when we think how bad man is, it is more a wonder that so *many* are, and Christ will be eternally admired in them."—V. 27. Forsaking all. The all may not be much, yet it is much to forsake all. CHRYS.: "The forsaking was done for the sake of following, and the following was rendered easier by the forsaking."—V. 27–30. Forsaking and receiving. 1) Christ's servant must actually forsake many things, and be willing to forsake all things, for the sake of him and his work. 2) The negative forsaking must be accompanied by positive following. 3) He shall receive incomparably more than he has forsaken—both in time and in eternity. 4) The rewards received by different servants will be very different in degree, v. 28. 5) But Christ himself must decide what each one's reward shall be, v. 30, comp. 20: 1–16; we must make no claims and no complaints. —V. 28. They who follow Jesus in this world shall reign with him in the better world.—V. 29. CYRIL: "He does not say that they shall have many fathers or mothers in place of one, or many fields in place of few, but that all the earthly things will be incomparably excelled by the heavenly, and the things that are saved will be more valuable than those that are lost."—Ch. 20: 1–16. The laborers in God's vineyard and their reward. 1) Unlike many human employers, God cares as much for the good of the workers as for the amount of work done. 2) God's service is not repose in a "Castle of Indolence," but hard work in a *vineyard;* self-denial and toil in promoting our own piety and that of others. 3) God will reward his workers richly—in this life (19: 29, comp. Mark 10: 30), and in the life to come. (v. 8; ch. 19: 21, 28.) 4) He will give to none less than he had promised (v. 13), but he will give to some much more than he had promised; he will give as a sovereign (v. 15), and his workers must recognize that he does all things well. (v. 16, comp. 19: 30.)

---

[1] It is wanting in ℵ B, L, Z, 36, Thebaic, Memphitic, and a codex of the Æthiopic. We see at once how it could be inserted, and can see no sufficient reason for its omission if originally present.

17 And Jesus going up to Jerusalem took the twelve disciples apart in the way, and said unto them,	17 And as Jesus was going up to Jerusalem, he took the twelve disciples apart, and in the way he said
18 Behold, we go up to Jerusalem; and the Son of man s.iall be betrayed unto the chief priests and unto the scribes, and they shall condemn him to death,	18 unto them, Behold, we go up to Jerusalem; and the Son of man shall be delivered unto the chief priests
19 And shall deliver him to the Gentiles to mock, and to scourge, and to crucify *him :* and the third day he shall rise again.	19 and scribes; and they shall condemn him to death, and shall deliver him unto the Gentiles to mock, and to scourge, and to crucify : and the third day he shall be raised up.

Ch. 20 : 17-28. JESUS AGAIN FORETELLS HIS DEATH AND RESURRECTION. AMBITIOUS REQUEST OF JAMES AND JOHN.

Found also in Mark 10: 32-45; and (in part) in Luke 18: 31-34. This passage seems in Matt., Mark, and Luke to follow immediately upon the foregoing matters (19: 3 to 20: 16), and to precede by only a few days the triumphal entry. (21: 1.) The phrase 'going up,' 'we go up to Jerusalem,' does not prove that they had crossed the river, and were now ascending from its valley, as in Luke 19: 28. Since Jerusalem was reached by ascent both from east and west, it became customary to speak of 'going up' to Jerusalem from all parts of the country, Luke 2: 42; John 2: 13; 5: 1; 11: 55; Acts 15: 2; 25: 1; Gal. 1: 17 f.; 2: 1. It is after this that Jesus and his followers reach Jericho, 20: 29; Mark 10: 46. The scene is somewhat more likely to have been in Perea, than between the river and Jericho, which was only a few miles; but the question cannot be determined, and does not affect the exegesis. This section contains two parts, v. 17-19 and v. 20-28.

I. **17-19.** JESUS A THIRD TIME FORETELLS HIS DEATH AND RESURRECTION, comp. Mark 10: 32-34; Luke 18: 31-34. The two preceding recorded occasions were just before and just after the Transfiguration (16: 21; 17: 22), and at least six months earlier than this. We cannot judge whether he had spoken of it distinctly in the mean time, but there is in Luke 12: 49 ff., an indication that his own mind had been all the while turning towards what awaited him, turning with a feeling of constraint and pressure, but not of grief or discouragement. **Going up to Jerusalem.**[1] What follows was said **in the way,** on the road. Mark (10: 32) tells that his followers, here meaning more than the Twelve, were 'amazed' and 'afraid' as they walked after him along the road, probably because of what he had said about the difficulty of saving the

rich (19: 23 ff.), and about the Messianic rewards for sacrifices in his service (19: 28 ff.) ; perhaps also there was an absorbed and fixed look in the Master's face as he pressed on to his terrible baptism of suffering, that was new, and filled them with wonder and alarm. **Took the twelve disciples apart,** from the throng that were accompanying him to the Passover. (20: 29; Luke 18: 36.) Only the Twelve were in the least prepared to understand such predictions concerning the Messiah. Even at Jerusalem, some six months earlier, the people did not at all understand " Yet a little while am I with you, and I go unto him that sent me," John 7: 33-36, Rev. Ver. **We go up to Jerusalem,** etc. Origen remarks that Paul exactly imitated Christ when he went up to Jerusalem in full view of peril. Acts 21: 10-13. The prediction our Lord here gives is substantially the same as in 16: 21 (see notes). Some new particulars are now added, as is natural in the nearer approach to the event, and when their minds have been somewhat prepared by the previous predictions. The Sanhedrin will formally **condemn him to death ;** and not only will he ' be delivered into the hands of men,' as foretold on the second occasion (17: 22, with Mark and Luke), but **delivered to the Gentiles** (Mark and Luke also), **to mock, and to scourge, and to crucify ;** Mark and Luke add 'spit upon,' and Luke generally that he shall be 'shamefully treated.' Tyndale, Cran., Gen., King James, all here render the same word, 'betrayed' in v. 18 and 'deliver' in v. 19, a useless and misleading variation, comp. on 17: 22, and 10: 4.—Still, after this renewed and detailed prediction, the Twelve "understood none of these things." (Luke 18:34.) It was utterly contrary to all their ideas of Messiah and his work; these things *could* not be literally true of the king—what did it all mean? Notice how Luke dwells upon their inability: "and this

---

[1] W H. adopt the reading 'was about to go up,' from B, one cursive, Memph., Theb., Pesh , Origen (three times). This might easily have been changed into 'was going up' by way of assimilation to v. 18 and to Mark and Luke, and so is probably correct. There is of course no substantial difference.

20 Then came to him the mother of Zebedee's children
with her sons, worshipping *him*, and desiring a certain
thing of him.
21 And he said unto her, What wilt thou? She saith
unto him, Grant that these my two sons may sit, the
one on thy right hand, and the other on the left, in thy
kingdom.

20   Then came to him the mother of the sons of Zebedee with her sons, worshipping *him*, and asking a
21 certain thing of him. And he said unto her, What
wouldest thou? She saith unto him, Command that
these my two sons may sit, one on thy right hand,

---

saying was hid from them, and they perceived not the things that were said." Comp.
on 16 : 21. *Hanna :* " This only proves what
a blinding power preconception and misconception have in hiding the simplest things
told in the simplest language—a blinding
power often exercised over us now as to the
written, as it was then exercised over the
apostles as to their Master's spoken, words . . .
They had made up their minds, on the best
of evidence, that he was the Messiah. But
they had their own notions of the Messiahship. With these, such sufferings and such a
death as actually lay before Jesus were utterly
inconsistent. His expressions, then, must be
figurative, intended, perhaps, to represent
some severe struggle with his adversaries,
through which he had to pass before his kingdom was set up and acknowledged."

II. **20-28.** AMBITIOUS REQUEST OF THE
MOTHER OF JAMES AND JOHN. Mark 10:
35-45. Luke does not give this, though parallel to Matt. and Mark, just before and just
after ; but he gives similar teaching on
another occasion, Luke 22 : 24-30. Mark represents James and John as themselves saying,
in almost exactly identical words, what Matt.
ascribes to their mother. The case is precisely like that of the centurion (see on 8 : 5
ff.), and in accordance with the law maxim,
" He who does a thing through another, does it
himself." Our Lord so takes it, for he presently
addresses the sons as making the
request. ' ye ' v. 22 f. **Then came,** does not
necessarily (see on 3 : 13), but does naturally
indicate that this followed closely upon the
preceding ; Mark simply 'and,' as in 19 : 13.
The request seems to have been made privately, when the other ten apostles were not
present, v. 24. **The mother of Zebedee's
children with her sons.** Tyndale and followers rendered ' Zebedee's children,' probably to avoid the immediate repetition of
'sons;' but the effect is to suggest that there
were other children besides the sons. As to
Zebedee and Salome, and their sons, see on
10 : 2. We have no knowledge whether
Zebedee was in the company, or was still liv-

ing. It is clear that the mother here shares the
ambition of her sons, and so it is not unlikely
that from her it was inherited. If, as many
suppose (see on 27 : 56), she was the sister of
the Saviour's mother, that would explain her
boldness in personally approaching him and
preferring so grave a request. Comp. Bath-
sheba coming to David for Solomon, 1 Kings
1 : 11 ff. **Worshipping him** here evidently
means paying homage as to a king, (comp. on
2 : 2), for it is precisely as such that they approach him. ' Worshipping' and 'asking'
are in the singular number, but it is implied
that the sons united with her. **A certain
thing,** or 'something,' Wyc., Rheims, Bib.
Union, and so Meyer. Mark says they first
wished him to promise that he would do
whatsoever they should ask—which was presumptuous indeed. **Grant**—or *command,*
that, for the Greek construction see on 5 : 29.
She is thinking of the two highest places in an
earthly kingdom. Could not the solemn prediction of his death and resurrection which he
had just before made correct their unspiritual
conception? Nay, even after the death and
resurrection had actually occurred, the
Twelve retained the same expectation.
(Acts 1 : 6.) In fact the prediction seems on
several other occasions also to have been immediately followed by a dispute as to greatness in the kingdom; see on 18 : 1, and hereafter 26 : 2. (Luke 22 : 24.) They seem to have
lost sight of the suffering and death, and fixed
their minds only upon the thought that somehow or other the splendid Messianic kingdom
was about to be established ; comp. Luke just
afterward (19:11), "they supposed that the
kingdom of God was immediately to appear."
Our Lord had shortly before (Matt. 19 : 28), perhaps the same day, spoken of himself as the
Messiah who would 'in the regeneration sit on
the throne of his glory,' and had promised
that the Twelve should then occupy 'twelve
thrones.' Salome and her sons seem to have
fastened upon that thought. Why not ask
that her two sons may sit on the two chief
thrones? To place the most distinguished
persons on the right and left of a sovereign or

22 But Jesus answered and said, Ye know not what ye ask. Are ye able to drink of the cup that I shall drink of, and to be baptized with the baptism that I am baptized with? They say unto him, We are able.
23 And he saith unto them, Ye shall drink indeed of my cup, and be baptized with the baptism that I am baptized with: but to sit on my right hand, and on my left, is not mine to give, but *it shall be given to them* for whom it is prepared of my Father.
24 And when the ten heard *it*, they were moved with indignation against the two brethren.

22 and one on thy left hand, in thy kingdom. But Jesus answered and said, Ye know not what ye ask. Are ye able to drink the cup that I am about to drink?
23 They say unto him, We are able. He saith unto them, My cup indeed ye shall drink: but to sit on my right hand, and on *my* left hand, is not mine to give, but *it is for them* for whom it hath been prepared of my Father. And when the ten heard it,

presiding personage was common among the Greeks and Romans, as well as the Jews (Wet.), and is practiced among us at banquets, etc. As to the dignity of being on the right hand, comp. Psa. 16: 11; 45: 9; 110: 1; Mark 14: 52; Acts 7: 55 f., etc. Salome's two sons, with Peter, have already been treated with special distinction at the raising of Jairus' daughter and at the Transfiguration, and this might encourage their present high ambition. They had also shown a fiery and self-assertive nature in forbidding the man who followed not with them (Mark 9: 38), and in wishing to call down fire from heaven on the Samaritan village (Luke 9: 54); comp. above on 10: 2.

22 f. Our Lord treats the request as that of the sons themselves. **Ye know not what ye ask.** To ask that they might reign with him was asking that they might suffer with him; comp. 2 Tim. 2: 12; Rev. 3: 21; Rom. 8: 17. **The cup that I shall drink,** a familiar image for great suffering, as in 26: 39; John 18: 11; Psa. 75: 8; Isa. 51: 17; Jer. 49: 12. **Be baptized with the baptism that I am baptized,** to be plunged in the same sufferings, comp. Luke 12: 50, and see above on 3: 6. This comes from Mark 10: 38, and was added to Matthew here and in the next verse by many copies.[1] **We are able.** This was excessive self-confidence, but not mere arrogance. They were ignorant what the cup would contain, but sincere and resolute in their devotion, as they afterwards showed. Probably (Alexander) they thought of having to fight for the Messianic kingdom, and the ardent spirit of the "Sons of Thunder" would swell at the thought. Peter, the other of the three chosen disciples, made a like confident expression soon after, Luke 22: 33. Our Lord's reply is not severe, but kind. **Drink indeed of my**

cup, the particle rendered 'truly' in 9: 37, and there explained, indicating that this statement is placed in contrast with something to follow. **Ye shall drink indeed of my cup, . . . but,** etc. They were not appointed to suffer as profound mental anguish as the Master, nor would their suffering have any atoning character; but in his service James would die as the first apostolic martyr (Acts 12: 2), and John would as a living martyr suffer persecution (Rev. 1: 9), and sore trouble in conflict with error (Epistles of John). The legends that John was made to drink poison, and was plunged in boiling oil, are likely (Meyer) to have been suggested by this saying. **Not mine to give.** He thus lifts their minds away from the idea of a human sovereign bestowing earthly honors to that of divine gifts. He speaks of himself (comp. John 14: 28) as officially subordinate to the Father in his office as the God-man, the Mediator, in which he has derived all his authority and power from the Father (28: 18), and will at length return it to him. (1 Cor. 15: 28). Comp. 24: 36; Mark 13: 32. The *English* word 'but' might here seem to mean 'except'—"not mine to give except to those for whom it has been prepared," but the Greek word (*alla*) cannot have that sense. **For whom it is prepared of my Father.** All the arrangements of the Messianic kingdom have been already made by the Father, indeed made "from the foundation of the world," 25: 34, comp. Acts 1: 7.

24. When the ten heard it. They had not been present at the time, but heard, apparently soon after, what had occurred. **Moved with indignation against the two brethren,** not 'against' but *concerning*, about their whole course in the matter. Mark has the same expression. Their feeling is more easily accounted for from the fact

---

[1] It is here wanting (in both verses) in א B D L Z, two cursives, Old Syriac, most copies of the Old Latin, Vulgate, Memph., Theb., Aeth.; and the difference between Matthew and Mark is expressly mentioned by Origen. Such an enlargement of one Gospel from another is extremely common.

25 But Jesus called them *unto him*, and said, Ye know that the princes of the Gentiles exercise dominion over them, and they that are great exercise authority upon them.
26 But it shall not be so among you : but whosoever will be great among you, let him be your minister ;
27 And whosoever will be chief among you, let him be your servant :
28 Even as the Son of man came not to be ministered unto, but to minister, and to give his life a ransom for many.

25 they were moved with indignation concerning the two brethren. But Jesus called them unto him, and said, Ye know that the rulers of the Gentiles lord it over them, and their great ones exercise authority
26 over them. Not so shall it be among you : but whosoever would become great among you shall be your
27 [1] minister ; and whosoever would be first among you
28 shall be[2]your [2]servant : even as the Son of man came not to be ministered unto, but to minister, and to give his life a ransom for many.

---

1 Or, *servant*....2 *bondservant.*

---

mentioned by Matthew, that the request was made through Salome. Here was not only an ambitious attempt to gain the advantage over the rest, and to forestall matters by a promise in advance, but it may have seemed an unworthy thing to use a woman's plea ; all the more if she was near of kin to the future sovereign. So near the end, and they are still thinking of a worldly kingdom, and full of selfish scheming and unkindness.

25-28. What a sorrowful task for the loving Saviour, to repress these ambitions and asperities. **Called them unto him.** The two may have been still with him, or all may have been summoned together. He refers to the fact that high places of authority and dominion belong to worldly kingdoms. **It shall not be so among you,** or more likely, *not so it is among you.*[1] **Will be,** or *wishes to become ;* and so 'wishes to be.' For **minister** and **servant,** or more exactly 'bond servant'(Rev. Ver. margin), comp. on 8 : 6. Alas ! how easily human ambition can use these very words and yet retain its own spirit. The "great ones" in a kingdom are called "ministers." Even the Christian "minister" will sometimes 'lord it' over his charge (1 Pet. 5 : 3, same word as here) ; and the often arrogant despot in the Vatican calls himself "the servant of servants of the servants of God." **Even as the Son of man** (see on 8 : 20), the Messiah himself did not come to enthrone himself in an earthly kingdom, with higher and lower officials to wait on him. How different from all this his life had been they knew ; and he here declares that such was the purpose of his coming. Comp. Luke 22 : 27 ; Phil. 2 : 5 ; Rom. 15 : 3.

And now comes a phrase of the highest moment, such as the Saviour has not before employed. He has spoken repeatedly of his

approaching death (16 : 21 ; 17 : 22 ; 20 : 19 ; comp. John 7 : 33), but now it is added that his death will be redeeming and vicarious, and that this was the design of his coming. Mark 10 : 45 has precisely the same expression. This remarkable statement must have been quite beyond the comprehension of the disciples, till afterwards brought to their remembrance by the Holy Spirit (John 14 : 26). **His life,** comp. on 16 : 25. **A ransom** (Greek *lutron*). The Greek verb (*luo*) means to loose, release, *e. g.*, a prisoner, Acts 22 : 30. *Lutron* (termination—*tron*) is the means or instrument of releasing, and this in the case of a captive is naturally a ransom. The word is often used in the classics and the Sept. (Liddell and Scott, Cremer) to denote a ransom in money, and in corresponding figurative senses. So here Christ's life is given as 'a ransom,' serving to redeem men from captivity, from the power of sin and spiritual death. From this word *lutron* are formed the words translated in the New Test. 'redeem' and 'redemption.' Our English word *ransom* is the French rançon, contracted from the Latin *redemptio*, which we afterwards borrowed separately as redemption. The Old Latin and Vulg. here render *redemptionem* ; so Cranmer and Rheims, 'a redemption for many.' The preposition rendered 'for' (*anti*) necessarily means 'instead of,' involving substitution, a vicarious death. The preposition in Mark 14 : 24 and commonly employed by Paul in speaking of Christ's death for us (comp. John 11 : 51) is *huper*, which means 'in behalf of,' 'for the benefit of,' and derivatively 'instead of' wherever the nature of the case suggests that idea, wherever performing an action for one's benefit involves performing it in his stead. This derivative use of *huper* is frequent

---

[1] Several of the best documents here, and still more in Mark, read *esti*, 'is,' rather than *estai*, 'shall be.' It

is difficult to decide, for the former corresponds to what precedes, and the latter to what follows.

29 And as they departed from Jericho, a great multitude followed him.

29 And as they went out from Jericho, a great multitude followed him.

enough in the classics, and that Paul often employs it to mean 'instead of' is beyond all reasonable question. When objectors urge that that is only a secondary meaning of *huper*, and require us to prove otherwise that Christ's death was vicarious, then it is well to remember that here (and so in Mark) the preposition is *anti*, which no one can possibly deny to have, and necessarily, the meaning 'instead of'; and in 1 Tim. 2 : 6, while 'for' is *huper*, this same *anti* is prefixed to *lutron*, "who gave himself a *substitutionary* ransom for all." In 26 : 28 the preposition is *peri*, 'concerning.' **For many,** Christ's atoning death made it compatible with the divine justice that all should be saved if they would accept it on that ground; and in that sense he "gave himself a ransom for all" (1 Tim. 2 : 6), "tasted death for every man" (Heb. 2 : 9), comp. 1 John 2 : 2; but his death was never expected, nor divinely designed, actually to secure the salvation of all, and so in the sense of specific purpose he came "*to give his life a ransom for many.*" Comp. 26 : 28; Heb. 9 : 28; Rom. 5 : 15, 18; Isa. 53 : 12. *Henry:* "Sufficient for all, effectual for many." [1]

HOMILETICAL AND PRACTICAL.

V. 18. ORIGEN: "It is not proper that we should always avoid perils, or always advance to meet them; one must be wise in Christ to determine."—V. 19. ANONYM.: "All the salvation of men lies in the death of Christ." —Four discourses; Jesus predicting his passion (see on 16: 21); Jesus preparing for his passion (Luke 12 : 50; John 12 : 27 ff.; Gethsemane); Jesus enduring his passion (Matthew, Mark, Luke, John, comp. Heb. 12 : 2); Jesus looking back upon his passion. (Luke 24 : 26 f., 44-48; Rev. 1 : 18.) —V. 21 ff. CHRYS.: "Let no man be troubled at the apostles being in such an imperfect state. For

not yet was the cross accomplished, not yet the grace of the Spirit given. But if thou wouldst learn their virtue, notice them after these things, and see what manner of men they became by grace."—V. 20. f. HALL: "It is not discommendable in parents to seek the preferment of their children, so it be by lawful means, in a moderate measure. Oh, the madness of those parents that desire rather to leave their children great than good."—V. 22. Ye know not what ye ask. 1) To ask for special qualities of mind and character may be asking for the usually attendant faults and weaknesses, and the consequent perils and distresses; poet, artist, orator, financier,— beauty, wit, strength of will, passion, sanguine temperament. 2) To ask for worldly wealth and honor is asking for great toil and anxiety, asking to be envied and evil spoken of, asking often for disappointment and bitter sadness. 3) To ask even for eminent religious usefulness and reward is to ask for great suffering, Col. 1 : 24; 2 Cor. 11 : 28; Rev. 1: 9; 2: 10; Rom. 8: 17. Then let us always ask in subordination to God's will, 1 John 5: 14 f. . AUG.: "Give what thou bidst and bid what thou wilt." HENRY: "We know not what we ask, when we ask for the glory of wearing the crown, and ask not for grace to bear the cross in our way to it."—V. 26. Not so among you. 1) In worldly kingdoms ambition eagerly seeks for authority and dominion. 2) In Christ's kingdom the only greatness is usefulness, the only dominion is service. 3) Our King himself came to be a servant and a sacrifice. 4) Let these things be a check to religious ambition, and a cure for religious jealousy.

29-34. TWO BLIND MEN HEALED NEAR JERICHO.

Found also in Mark 10: 46-54; Luke 18: 35-43. Our Lord and his disciples and the

---

[1] Here the "Western" documents, D, Old Syriac, most copies of Old Latin and some Latin Fathers, add (details varying): "But do you seek out of little to increase and out of greater to be less. And when you enter in and have been invited to dine, do not recline in the prominent places, lest a more honored than thou come, and the host come and say to thee, Move still lower, and thou shalt be ashamed; but if thou recline in the inferior place, and there come one inferior to

thee, the host will say to thee, Get up still higher, and this shall be useful to thee." The latter sentence is obviously a mere traditional corruption of Luke 14 : 8-11. The former is likely enough based on a true saying of our Lord. For a collection of sayings ascribed to Jesus in early MSS. and Fathers, and not given in New Test., see Westcott's "Introduction to Study of Gospels," App. C.

accompanying throng on the way to the Passover, had crossed the Jordan, and were within one day's journey of Jerusalem. They had probably crossed by a ferry-boat several miles higher up the river than the point opposite to Jericho. Such a ferry exists there now, and existed in that vicinity at an early day. (2 Sam. 19: 18.) The river just before the Passover must have been comparatively high and swift, and only the more adventurous of the multitude would attempt to ford. As to the Jordan, see on 3: 6. Jericho, as flourishing and fortified with strong walls at the coming of the Israelites, and as destroyed by them, is well known from the Book of Joshua. The curse of Joshua (6: 26) was fulfilled against the man who rebuilt it (1 Kings 16: 34), and may have been regarded by some as exhausted in his case. The plain west of the Jordan is there some eight miles wide, the great fountain which bursts forth near the ancient site is so copious as to irrigate several square miles, there is another fountain northward and streams from the mountains lying west, while artificial irrigation from fountains higher up the valley could make all the lower plain richly productive. There were doubtless many dwellers in that plain at all periods. (2 Sam. 10: 5: 2 Kings 2: 1-22; Neh. 7: 36.) In the time of the Maccabees, about B. C. 160, a Syrian general "repaired the fort in Jericho." (1 Macc. 9: 50.) Pompey, B. C. 63, destroyed two forts that protected the entrance to Jericho. In speaking of this, Strabo (16, 2, 41) describes Jericho as a plain everywhere irrigated, filled with dwellings, abounding in the finest palm trees and other fruit trees, and says that here was "the paradise of balsam," a bush whose coagulated juice was highly valued as a medicine and the wood for its aroma, and which was found here only. The plain is so far below the level of the Mediterranean as to be extremely hot. Josephus says that linen clothes were worn at Jericho when there was snow in Jerusalem; and it may be added (from personal experience) that mosquitoes abound in the end of February. Accordingly the productions were tropical in character and in luxuriance. (Jos. "War," 4, 8, 3.) The Roman allies of Herod plundered the city in B. C. 39 ("War," 1, 15, 6),' finding "the houses full of all sorts of good things."

The great revenues of Jericho, especially from the balsam, were presented by Antony to Cleopatra (Jos. "Ant.," 15, 4, 2), and at a later period made the chief revenue officer notably rich. (Luke 19: 2.) Herod built a fortified palace and a new town northward from the old site ("Ant.," 16, 5, 2), and died there ("Ant.," 17, 6, 5). Eusebius says of Jericho ("Onom."): "Which our Lord Jesus Christ thought worthy of his presence. But when it also was destroyed at the siege of Jerusalem on account of the unbelief of the inhabitants, there arose a third time another city which is shown even now. And of the two former also the traces are even now preserved." We know not whether our Lord took any special interest in the fact that his own genealogy included Rahab of Jericho (1: 5); but we may be sure he delighted in the well-watered and verdant plain, with the spring flowers and fruits. "It was not the season of figs" on the Mount of Olives yet (Mark 11: 13, R. V.), but they were ripening at Jericho. The juicy green almonds were delicious to the taste. The "rose plants in Jericho" (Ecclus. 24: 14) were famous through the land. Every sense was gratified to the utmost as he and his followers came up the successive terraces from the river into this magnificent plain. And yonder precipitous rock mountain that overhangs the city on the west, was it indeed the scene of that forty days' temptation which began the ministry now so soon to end?

Jesus spent the night at Jericho, and may have stayed there longer. Luke gives a deeply interesting account (19: 1-28) of Zaccheus, at whose house he abode, and of a parable he spoke to modify the supposition that "the kingdom of God was immediately to appear," which parable in an altered form will be repeated a few days later. (Matt. 25: 14-30.)

As they departed from Jericho. So Mark. But Luke, (18: 35) 'as he drew nigh unto Jericho.' This celebrated "discrepancy" has not been explained in a thoroughly satisfactory way. The older explanations are very poor: as that he healed one man in drawing near and two others in leaving, thus making three in all; or that Matthew has thrown together the two cases described by Mark and Luke; that Jesus tarried some days, and the healing occurred while he was going in and out of the city; that 'draw

30 And, behold, two blind men sitting by the way side, when they heard that Jesus passed by, cried out, saying, Have mercy on us, O Lord, *thou* Son of David.
31 And the multitude rebuked them, because they should hold their peace: but they cried the more, saying, Have mercy on us, O Lord, *thou* Son of David.

30 tude followed him. And behold, two blind men sitting by the way side, when they heard that Jesus was passing by, cried out, saying, Lord, have mercy 31 on us, thou son of David. And the multitude rebuked them, that they should hold their peace: but they cried out the more, saying, Lord, have mercy

---

nigh' means simply to be near (which is not true), etc. Our choice at present must be between two possible views. (1) Calvin presents as his "conjecture," followed by Maldonatus, Bengel, Trench, Wordsworth, Ellicott, Hackett, Morison, that the blind man made his request as Jesus approached Jericho (Luke), but was not heeded, in order to develop his faith, as in 15: 23 ff., and in the closely similar case 9: 27 ff.; and that he renewed the application as Jesus was leaving Jericho, accompanied now by another, and they were healed. Then we understand that Luke, meaning to tell of Zaccheus and the parable and so pass on to the ascent to Jerusalem (Luke 19: 28), finishes the matter of the blind man in connection with his original application. Such prolepsis, or anticipation, is common in all histories. (2) Farrar quotes from Macknight the supposition, and Godet quotes it from a German periodical of 1870, that the healing occurred at a point between the old and the new city, and so could be described as occurring either when they went out from Jericho or as they drew near to Jericho. The same view presented itself independently on the spot a few years ago to Prof. H. H. Harris, D. D., of Richmond College, Va.[1] Each of these explanations seems labored, but either is entirely possible. It will not do to say that the accounts are irreconcilable, and therefore involve inaccuracy, if the apparent conflict can be explained in any reasonable way. These discrepancies in the Gospels show the independence of the narratives, and their verisimilitude, and thus do not diminish but add to their historical credibility, provided there be any reasonable explanation. It may nowadays be affirmed that nearly every case has received satisfactory ex-

planation. The present example, and a few others, would probably be plain enough if we knew some slight circumstances not mentioned; and may be fully cleared up hereafter, as some have been by the discoveries and researches of every recent generation. We must not nervously insist on the adequacy of our explanations in every case, nor arrogantly assume that the difficulty cannot be removed. **A great multitude followed him.** So also when he was approaching the city. (Luke.) They seem to have come with him from Perea, perhaps many of them from Galilee (comp. on 19: 1), *en route* for the Passsover.

30 f. Two blind men. Luke 'a certain blind man,' and Mark gives his name, 'the son of Timeus, Bartimeus.' Here, as in 8: 28 (see notes), we have to suppose that one of the two was more notable, and thus alone named by Mark and Luke. The supposition is somewhat difficult, but certainly by no means impossible, and on every account far more probable than that of a flat error. The balsam of Jericho was "a wonderful remedy for headache (neuralgia), and for incipient cataract, and dimness of vision." (Strabo 16, 2, 41.) But no balsam could open the blind eyes. **Sitting by the wayside,** Luke 'begging,' Mark 'a beggar.' **Heard that Jesus was passing by,** Mark and Luke 'Jesus of Nazareth,' a title by which the teacher and healer had doubtless been heard of throughout the land. **Thou Son of David,** so also Mark and Luke, meaning that he was the Messiah, comp. on 9: 27; 15: 22; 22: 42. We cannot tell how they reached this conviction. As to their particular request, they had doubtless heard of his healing the blind elsewhere, perhaps of cases in Galilee (9:27), more likely of the man born blind healed at Jerusalem six

---

[1] Dr. Harris writes in a private letter, Richmond, Virginia, September, 1885: "Suppose Jesus spent a night as he would likely do in the city of his foremother Rahab, and that Zaccheus had his office in the Roman town and his residence in the West End. Now locate the healing at a bank on the roadside about half way between the ruins of the two cities, where a beggar might naturally sit. Matthew and Mark speak of it as when 'he went out from Jericho,' *i. e.,* the old city. But Luke, a Gentile or Hellenist, and writing to a Gentile, says 'as he drew nigh unto Jericho,' *i. e.,* the Roman town, and going on to tell about Zaccheus adds 'he entered and was passing through Jericho.' " Dr. Harris says he was not aware that this idea had been suggested by others.

32 And Jesus stood still, and called them, and said, What will ye that I shall do unto you?
33 They say unto him, Lord, that our eyes may be opened.
34 So Jesus had compassion on *them*, and touched their eyes: and immediately their eyes received sight, and they followed him.

32 on us, thou son of David. And Jesus stood still, and
33 called them, and said, What will ye that I should do unto you? They say unto him, Lord, that our eyes
34 may be opened. And Jesus, being moved with compassion, touched their eyes: and straightway they received their sight, and followed him.

CHAPTER XXI.

AND when they drew nigh unto Jerusalem, and were come to Bethphage, unto the mount of Olives, then sent Jesus two disciples,

1   And when they drew nigh unto Jerusalem, and came unto Bethphage, unto the mount of Olives,

months before. (John 9 : 1 ff.) **The multitude rebuked them.** Luke 'they that went before,' Mark simply 'many.' They were vexed that mere blind beggars should disturb a procession, and annoy the principal personage, from whom they may have been eagerly expecting further teaching. (Comp. 19 : 13.) Beggars in the East are almost always offensive and often disgusting, and it is hard to feel compassion for them, even when blind. **Because,** or, *that* **they should,** for the Greek construction see on 5 : 29 ; so also, **that our eyes may be opened. Hold their peace,** an old English phrase, the Greek being literally *be silent.* As they were needy and hopeful, opposition only stimulated a louder cry. The Greek word denotes a harsh cry, comp. 8 : 29 ; 9 : 27 ; 15 : 23, and Mark and Luke have the imperfect tense, describing a continued crying.

32-34. Called them. Mark gives vivid particulars ; Jesus directed those near him to call ; they spoke cheeringly ; and Bartimeus, "casting away his garment (his loose outer garment, see on 5 : 40), sprang up, and came to Jesus." We easily suppose that the other and less noticeable blind man followed. **Jesus had compassion,** see the Greek word explained on 9 : 36. **Touched their eyes,** not mentioned by Mark or Luke, a sign to them that he was the healer, as in 9 : 29. Mark and Luke relate that Jesus said, "thy faith hath made thee whole," saved thee, healed thee, as above in 9 : 22, and comp. 9 : 29. **And they followed him,** Mark 'in the way,' Luke 'glorifying God.' They probably accompanied him to Jerusalem. Luke adds : " And all the people, when they saw it, gave praise unto God." (Comp. Matt. 9 : 8 ; 15 : 31.) Jesus here shows no desire to prevent his miracles from becoming generally known, as he did in 9 : 30 and often. The crisis of his ministry is now near at hand, and publicity will make no difference.

HOMILETICAL AND PRACTICAL.

V. 31. And the multitude rebuked them. 1) Men sometimes despise, as unfit to be Christians, those whose case afterwards brings great glory to God. 2) Religious decorum must sometimes give way to intense earnestness. 3) Attempted hindrance becomes for earnest souls a stimulus to greater exertions. 4) Christ's followers may hinder when Christ himself stands ready to hear. CHRYS. : "See how not poverty, not blindness, not their being unheard, not their being rebuked by the multitude, not anything else, impeded their exceeding earnestness." AUGUSTINE : " When any Christian has begun to live rightly, to be fervent in good works and despise the world, in the very novelty of his works he suffers blame and contradiction from frigid Christians. But if he perseveres, and overcomes them by endurance, and does not fail in good works, then they turn and begin to say, ' A great man, a holy man '—like that crowd that were with the Lord."—V. 34. The objects of Christ's compassion. 1) They were very needy. 2) They pleaded for pity. 3) They believed in his mission. 4) They persevered and grew more earnest. 5) They knew just what they wanted. 6) They followed him in gratitude and devotion.

Ch. 21: 1-11. THE TRIUMPHAL ENTRY. Found also in Mark 11: 1-11 ; Luke 19: 29-44 ; John 12: 12-19. John has heretofore been parallel to Matt. and Mark only at the early departure from Judea to Galilee (Matt. 4: 12 ; John 4: 1-4), and at the feeding of the Five Thousand. (Matt. 14: 13-21 ; John 6: 1-14.) He appears to have coincided with Luke several times in the last six months. (See above on 19: 1.) Here he once more becomes parallel to the others, and will be so at the Bethany supper, probably at the Paschal meal, clearly at the betrayal, and at certain points of the Passion and Resurrection. Matthew, Mark, and Luke continue from this time as generally and as closely parallel as they were during the ministry in Galilee.

We left our Lord at Jericho, Luke adding that he " went before, going up to Jerusalem." (Luke 19 : 28, B. U. Ver.) He doubtless climbed the Roman military road, carefully graded and paved with hewn stone, which came up from Jericho past Bethany and across the Mount of Olives to Jerusalem, and portions of which are still clearly marked by patches of pavement. There was no danger in this particular journey that one would fall " among robbers " (Luke 10 : 30, Rev. Ver.), since the multitude formed a protection ; but there was usually such danger, and one cannot safely travel that road to-day without a guard from the sheik of Lazariyeh (Bethany). The distance from Jericho to Jerusalem is about seventeen miles, or fifteen miles to Bethany; the difference in elevation is some three thousand feet. Matthew does not mention the arrival at Bethany (see on 21 : 17), which John describes as occurring "six days before the Passover" (John 12 : 1), probably on Friday afternoon. Here Jesus appears to have spent the Sabbath, and we may suppose him to have been the guest of Martha and Mary and Lazarus. Hearing of his arrival, many Jews came over from Jerusalem to Bethany to see him, and also Lazarus, whom he had raised from the dead (John 12: 9) ; the time of their coming may have been Saturday evening, or early next morning. Mark and Luke mention Bethany, in connection with Bethphage, as reached before the triumphal entry, but give no details of a sojourn at Bethany.

1-3. And when they drew nigh unto Jerusalem. The hills which form the site of Jerusalem are really the somewhat lower part of a space which gently slopes from the northwest, and seems elevated only because of the deep ravines which encompass it on the east and west and south. Seen from a real mountain five or six miles distant in the northwest, Jerusalem seems to be in a valley, with the high ridge of Olivet on the eastern and part of the northern side, and with another range of hills on the west and south. Seen from Olivet, the city rises on an opposite but lower elevation, with a deep and narrow ravine lying between them. Seen from another deep ravine on the south, the hill of Zion, or city of David, appears to be on a lofty and exceedingly steep hill, which Joab and his comrades found it hard to climb and capture the supposed impregnable fortress of the Jebusites. (2 Sam. 5: 6 f. ; 1 Chron. 11 : 5 f.) This central space, which slopes narrowing down from the northwest between its ever deepening ravines, is presently divided by a slighter depression, having the same direction, into somewhat separate ridges, the eastern ridge being the temple hill, two hundred feet lower than the other, which is Zion. The depression between them gradually deepens, containing the pool of Siloam near its southeastern end, and passing into the eastern ravine before that forms a junction with the other ravine which has come down on the west and south of Zion. The northern part of the temple elevation, higher than the site of the temple itself, and outside of the city, is recently with no small probability considered to be Golgotha or Calvary. (See on 27 : 33.) A considerable space north and south of the temple enclosure was occupied by dwellings, but the greater part of the city lay on Zion, and in the depression separating it from the temple. The eastern wall of the temple enclosure was part of the eastern wall of the city, and just north of that enclosure appears to have been the principal eastern entrance to the city, now called Saint Stephen's gate, from the tradition that Stephen passed through it to his martyrdom. Through this gate, Jesus and his followers probably entered in the triumphal procession, and were at once quite near the northern entrance to the outer court of the temple. And every morning, as he walked over the Mount of Olives from Bethany, he would enter the city and the temple the same way. In the northern and shallowest part of the depression between Zion and the temple ridge was doubtless, as now, the great northern gate of the city. Out of this it is most likely that our Lord was led to crucifixion, Golgotha being perhaps the elevation on the right after passing the outer gate. Pilate's official residence when visiting the city (27: 2) was doubtless on Zion, probably in Herod's palace. It would be hardly one-third of a mile from that place to the northern gate. Not far north of Herod's palace was the principal western gate, probably about

2 Saying unto them, Go into the village over against you, and straightway ye shall find an ass tied, and a colt with her: loose *them*, and bring *them* unto me.
3 And if any *man* say aught unto you, ye shall say. The Lord hath need of them; and straightway he will send them.

2 then Jesus sent two disciples, saying unto them, Go into the village that is over against you, and straightway ye shall find an ass tied, and a colt with her: 3 loose *them*, and bring *them* unto me. And if any one say aught unto you, ye shall say, The Lord hath need of them; and straightway he will send them.

the same place as the present gate leading to Joppa. The city at that time doubtless extended considerably farther to the northwest than now, but the whole space enclosed was quite small, as compared with modern conceptions of a great city. After allowing for the fashion in which Asiatics have always crowded together, as the Chinese do now, it is hard to see how the regular population in the time of Christ can have been more than two or three hundred thousand. But vast multitudes came to the Passover (Josephus talks of three millions), sleeping in the streets and public places, tenting in the surrounding fields, swarming over the suburban villages like Bethany for several miles around. **Were come unto Bethphage.** To mention the village and the mountain showed on what side they approached Jerusalem, and how near they were. Bethphage might seem from the order of Mark and Luke to have been reached before Bethany, but this inference is not necessary. The traditional site is between Bethany and Jerusalem, on the eastern slope of the Mount of Olives. The village is often mentioned in the Talmud, but not so as to show its location, nor are there any modern remains. It was at least near the mountain on the eastern side, and most likely on the Roman road from Bethany to Jerusalem. The name signifies 'house of figs.' **The Mount of Olives** (24: 3; 26: 30. 36; Zech. 14: 4), in Acts 1: 12 'Olivet,' is a low mountain or long and lofty hill, which begins north of Jerusalem and runs eastward, and then turning at a point nearly a mile northeast of the city, runs southward until interrupted by the outlet of the valleys which lie east and south of the city, and send off their united streams at the southeast in a deep ravine towards the Dead Sea. The mountain evidently took its name from its fruitfulness in olives. The valley which separates it from Jerusalem is "the brook Cedron" or Kidron, of John 18: 1. Looking from Jerusalem eastward across this deep and narrow valley (comp. on 26: 36), one sees that the central and highest part of the ridge is some three hundred feet higher

than the temple hill, and about one hundred feet higher than the hill of Zion; but that the summit line and face of the ridge are marked by three slight depressions, descending so as nearly to meet where they reach the valley of the Kidron. Up the northern depression, ascending northeastward, went David in fleeing from Absalom, "over the brook Kidron . . . . up by the ascent of Mount Olivet . . . . past the top," and so along a route still distinguishable east of the mountain in that direction. (2 Sam. 15: 23; 16: 1,) The central depression runs nearly east and much steeper, almost straight across the mountain and so towards Bethany (see on 21: 17), and is the direct way for walking between that suburb and the city. The southern depression ascends far southeastward, giving a better grade and crossing at considerably the lowest part of the summit-line; over this gap, and skillfully graded beyond it on the eastern slope of Olivet, is the riding way from Jerusalem to Bethany, still clearly indicated by patches of Roman pavement. Along this road came in the triumphal procession. **Then sent Jesus two disciples** (so also Mark and Luke); we know not which two, but very likely Peter and John, as hereafter in Luke 22: 8. **The village over against you** is not certainly known, but was probably Bethphage, fronting them as from Bethany they approached the eastern face of the Mount of Olives. **Straightway ye shall find;** the description is quite definite. **An ass tied and a colt with her.** Mark, Luke, and John mention only a colt, which here was the more important of the two. (Comp. on 20: 30.) The object was to have Messiah the King ride a young animal not previously used, "whereon no man ever yet sat" (Mark and Luke), as a matter of special honor (comp. Deut. 21: 3; 1 Sam. 6: 7); and the mother was probably led in front, to make the colt move quietly. Processions often include led animals, besides those ridden. **The Lord hath need of them.** We cannot tell whether this would be understood by the owners (Luke 19: 33) as meaning that they were

4 All this was done, that it might be fulfilled which was spoken by the prophet, saying,
5 Tell ye the daughter of Sion, Behold, thy King cometh unto thee, meek, and sitting upon an ass, and a colt the foal of an ass.

4 Now this is come to pass, that it might be fulfilled which was spoken through the prophet, saying,
5 Tell ye the daughter of Zion,
Behold, thy King cometh unto thee,
Meek, and riding upon an ass,
And upon a colt the foal of an ass.

---

wanted for the service of Jehovah, or definitely for the Lord Jesus; in the latter case we might suppose owners who knew of Jesus, and would gladly serve him, as in 26: 18. Doubtless the animals were restored that afternoon, as there was no further use for them; it could be easily done in returning to Bethany.

4 f. All this was done, etc.—better as Rev. Ver., *Now this is come to pass* (in the course of divine providence)—**that it might be fulfilled which was spoken by the prophet,** comp. on 1: 22. The Common Text has 'all this,' evidently altered by copyists so as to be like 1: 22 and 26: 56.[1] The quotation is from Zech. 9: 9, where the prophet predicts a righteous and divinely preserved king of Israel, coming to Jerusalem in peace and meekness. The Jews regarded the passage as Messianic. The Talmud of Babylon several times speaks of the Messiah as riding upon an ass (Lightf. and Wün.), and some Rabbinical commentaries apply this prophecy of Zechariah to the Messiah. (Edersh.) Matthew and John (12: 14-16) distinctly declare the passage of Zechariah to be Messianic, and Jesus so treats it; nor is there anything in the connection of Zechariah to forbid, but several expressions (Zech. 9: 10, 12) which are quite in keeping, while various other prophetic passages also represent the Messiah under the figure of a king of Israel. The Hebrew signifies (Toy), "Rejoice greatly, daughter of Zion, shout, daughter of Jerusalem. Behold, thy king comes to thee; just and saved is he, meek and riding on an ass, and on a colt the foal of an ass." The Sept. differs but slightly. Matthew omits 'just and saved,' as not important for his purpose, and abridges and modifies the opening clause without altering the substantial sense (comp. on 2: 6), as John does in another way. Some think that Matthew has combined this passage with Isa. 62: 11. **Daughter of Zion,** viz., Jerusalem, a common Hebrew figure by which a city was represented as the offspring of the locality. **Meek** (comp. 11: 29), not a fierce warrior. **Upon** is repeated before 'a colt' by the correct Greek text. In v. 5, **ass** the second time is literally (*an animal*) *under the yoke*, draught-animal, beast of burden, a more general term, but often used to denote the ass. (2 Pet. 2: 16, and Sept.) **Upon an ass, and a colt,** is a Hebrew parallelism of the peculiar kind in which the second clause more precisely defines the first; Rev. Ver. of Zechariah puts it 'upon an ass, even upon a colt.' The King does not come on a chariot or on a war horse, but riding as rulers did in time of peace. (1 Kings 1: 33; Judg. 5: 10; Num. 22: 23.) The trained mule and donkey of Egypt and Syria are very pleasant for riding, and have there no ludicrous associations. In the imagery of Rev. 19: 11 the Messiah appears again as a *conqueror* on a white horse. It seems clear that our Lord arranged to ride the young ass into the city, as an intentional fulfillment of the prophecy. The disciples quickly so recognized, though not fully understanding (John 12: 16), and communicated to the multitude the idea that this was a Messianic entry into the capital, as the shouts of v. 9 show that all understood. Jesus has heretofore carefully avoided (16: 20) any public declaration that he is the Messiah, because it would be misunderstood and lead to political agitation and fanatical disturbance, and because the disciples themselves were not yet sufficiently instructed as to the true nature of the Messianic reign. Only two or three days before this he had spoken a parable at Jericho (Luke 19: 11), designed to show that he must go away, and return at a later period to establish his reign. The time has now come (John 7: 6; 12: 23) for declaring that he is the king Messiah, but a lowly and peaceful king. (Comp. 26: 63 f.)

6-8. Mark here describes in detail (11: 4-6) the finding of the animal according to direc-

---

[1] B has this palpable error, and the "Western" documents, with many others, have the correct text. To 'prophet' a few copies add Zechariah, and two or three add Isaiah, which is mentioned as illustrating the ways of copyists.

6 And the disciples went, and did as Jesus commanded them,

7 And brought the ass, and the colt, and put on them their clothes, and they set *him* thereon.

8 And a very great multitude spread their garments in the way; others cut down branches from the trees, and strewed *them* in the way.

9 And the multitudes that went before, and that followed, cried, saying, Hosanna to the Son of David:

6 And the disciples went, and did even as Jesus appointed them, and brought the ass, and the colt, and put on them their garments; and he sat thereon.

8 And the most part of the multitude spread their garments in the way; and others cut branches from

9 the trees, and spread them in the way. And the multitudes that went before him, and that followed, cried, saying, Hosanna to the son of David: Blessed *is* he that cometh in the name of the Lord: Hosanna

tion. **And put on them their clothes** (*garments*). An animal to be ridden by a monarch was often covered with splendid cloths. Lacking these, the disciples took off their own loose outer garments (comp. on 5: 40), and put them as housings, not only on the colt but on the mother ass also, as that was to form part of the procession. **And they set;** *and he sat* is the text not only of the leading documents, but also of the majority.[1] **Thereon,** literally, *on them*, which naturally means on the garments. Of course the words could mean on the animals. Those who thus take them may understand the phrase generally, like "the postillion rode his horses hard," or " he sprang from the horses," when of course the saddle-horse is meant. (Winer, 175 [219], Olsh., Schaff.) [2] But it is much more natural to understand that he sat on the garments. We should not know from Matthew's expression on which of the two animals he rode, but the prophecy he has quoted shows, as do the other Gospels. **And a very great,** etc. *And the most part of the multitude*, is the only natural meaning of the Greek, and so Memph. distinctly. Tyn., Cran., Gen,, 'many of the people'; K. James followed Rheims, 'a very great multitude,' which quite overlooks the Greek article. The phrase indicates that a good many did not take part. Besides some who had joined them at Jericho and at Bethany, or had come over from Jerusalem (John 12 : 9) and were returning, there were doubtless persons among the crowd that had followed Jesus from Perea, and perhaps from Galilee, who did not yet believe him to be Messiah, and so were not prepared to treat him as a monarch entering his capital in triumph. Luke presently tells us (19 : 39 f., Rev.Ver.) that "some of

the Pharisees from the multitude" spoke to Jesus and complained of what was going on. **Spread their garments in the way,** having no magnificent carpets to spread on the road over which the King was to ride, as was often done in triumphal processions. Comp. 2 Kings 9 : 13. Wetstein quotes, from Greek, Roman, and Jewish writers, accounts of carpets and garments spread under the feet of some honored one moving in a procession. Robinson tells of the Bethlehem peasants as on a certain occasion spreading their outer garments on the road before the horse of the British Consul, and entreating his help against the exactions of the Turkish tax-gatherers. **And others,** must not be taken as meaning the rest of the multitude besides 'the most part' ; but simply as an additional number of friendly persons who offered another mark of honor to the king. This second class is mentioned by Mark also, though not by Luke. The tense of the verb 'spread' changes in Matthew to the imperfect, and with that of 'cut' *describes* these persons as engaged in cutting and strewing. Thus three things were done; the disciples placed their garments on the animal, most of the crowd spread their garments on the road, and some spread boughs of trees. The trees are naturally conceived of as mainly olive-trees, which have ample and accessible branches, and from which the mountain took its name, but also fig-trees and others. Mark's expression suggests rather leaves than boughs. The leaves were of course the main object, and they cast in the road only such smaller branches as would not embarrass locomotion for man and beast. So we scatter flowers.

9. The multitudes that went before and that followed, the honored King

---

[1] 'And they set him' (Com. Ver.) is not even found in Stephens' third edition, usually followed by King James' revisers ; Tyn. and followers had it, doubtless influenced by the Vulgate ; so also (Morison) the fourth edition of Stephens, and Beza, who so often influenced King James' men. Luke 19 : 35 has an equivalent expression.

[2] Strauss and some others have chosen to insist that Matt. represents his Master as riding both the animals. In this absurdly hypercritical fancy they were anticipated by the " Western " documents, which, with their usual free handling, changed 'on them' (both times) to 'on it' or 'on the colt.'

Blessed *is* he that cometh in the name of the Lord ; Hosanna in the highest.

10 And when he was come into Jerusalem, all the city was moved, saying, Who is this?

11 And the multitude said, This is Jesus the prophet of Nazareth of Galilee.

10 in the highest. And when he was come into Jerusalem, all the city was stirred, saying, Who is this?

11 And the multitudes said, This is the prophet, Jesus, from Nazareth of Galilee.

---

having an advance guard and a rear guard. John speaks of a great multitude that had come to the feast and went forth from Jerusalem to meet Jesus, bearing branches of palmtrees (comp. Lev. 23 : 40), and crying "Hosanna," etc. (John 12 : 12 f.) It is easy to suppose that they met the procession and turned back with those who preceded Jesus. From this statement in John comes the phrase "Palm Sunday." **Cried,** imperfect tense, were crying, kept crying. **Hosanna** is a word borrowed from the Hebrew, meaning 'save now,' 'O save,' in Psa. 118 : 25. The Hebrew form represented by Hosanna is a slight and natural alteration of that occurring in the Psalm. The Mishna (Succoth IV., 5) says that every day during the Feast of Tabernacles they encompassed the altar, repeating Psa. 118 : 25. The Talmud shows that this Psalm also formed a part of the series of Psalms sung at the Passover (comp. on 26 : 30), called by Jewish writers "the great Hallel," Psa. 113-118. It was thus very natural that the people should break out with this expression and the following verse. **To the Son of David,** recognized him as the Messiah, comp. on 20 : 30 ; 22 : 42. The grammatical construction, 'Hosanna to the Son of David' shows us that Hosanna had come to be a formula of congratulation or expression of good wishes, not unlike the English "God save the king." **He that cometh** (see on 3 : 11) **in the name of the Lord** (see on 28 : 18), from Psa. 118 : 26, quoted again by our Lord himself in 23 : 39. Luke has 'Blessed is the king that cometh in the name of the Lord,' distinctly declaring him the Messiah ; and Mark, 'Blessed is the kingdom that cometh, the kingdom of our father David.' Various other expressions are given by the four Evangelists, and in this case all may have been employed by different persons (comp. on 3 : 16). **Hosanna in the highest,** *i. e.*, in the highest (heavens), as in Luke 2 : 14. It is an

appeal to God in heaven that he will save and bless his people ; and it here implies a joyful recognition of evidence that he is about to do so. Luke alone here introduces (19 : 41-44) the pathetic account of the Saviour as seeing the city and weeping over it,[1] comp Matt. 23 : 37-39.

10 f. When he was come into Jerusalem. Mark adds 'into the temple,' and that he 'looked round about upon all things.' **All the city was moved,** a strong word, rendered 'quake' in 27 : 51 ; 28 : 4, Rev. Ver., 'shaken' in Rev. 6 : 13. The great procession and the loud salutations as to the King Messiah awakened general attention and agitated all the people. (Comp. 2 : 3.) **Who is this ?** It was plain that the multitudes who were applauding Jesus as 'the son of David,' as 'the king that cometh in the name of the Lord,' regarded him as being the Messiah. The citizens inquired simply who was the person thus regarded. **And the multitudes,** plural, as in v. 9, **said,** imperfect tense, kept saying, or said every time they were asked. **This is Jesus the prophet,** (Luke 7 : 16 ; John 6 : 14 ; 7 : 40 ; 9 : 17.) There could in their opinion be no doubt that he was a prophet ; their conviction that he was the Messiah they did not care to assert in so many words. **Of Nazareth of Galilee.** For Nazareth, see on 2 : 23 ; for Galilee, on 4 : 12. Certainly some, and probably many of the crowd had accompanied Jesus from Galilee (27 : 55), and would take special interest in stating that he was from that district. The Judeans insisted that the Messiah would not be from Galilee, and that in fact from Galilee arose no prophet. (John 7 : 41 f , 52.)

HOMILETICAL AND PRACTICAL.

V· 1-3. Co-workers with Christ. 1) Jesus needing the help of his followers. 2) Jesus giving full directions for their work. 3) Jesus promising them success (v. 3). 4) Jesus joy-

---

[1] The apparent contradiction in Luke between v. 37 and v. 41 is fully explained by Stanley, "Sinai and Palestine," whose beautiful description of the triumphal entry ought to be read by all. It may be worth while to mention that the present writer and a friend went over the ground in both directions with Dean Stanley's book in hand, and had no doubt remaining as to the correctness of his explanation. A patch of Roman pavement remains to determine within a few feet the point at which Jesus "saw the city and wept over it."

fully obeyed (v. 6 f.)—V. 3. The Lord hath need of them. 1) The Lord often needs the property of men. 2) The Lord's ministers must inform men of this need. 3) The Lord promises success in attaining what is needed. —V. 5. The peaceful King. 1) His character is peaceful. 2) His methods and surroundings are peaceful (comp. 12 : 19 f.) 3) His office is to bring men into peace with God and with each other. (Luke 2 : 14.) 4) His service may arouse the hostility of the ungodly (10 : 34 ff.), but its spirit and aim must still be peaceful. (Rom. 12 : 18.)—V. 7. Origen, Jerome, and other Fathers made the ass represent the Jews, accustomed to the yoke of the law, and the colt the hitherto untamed Gentiles. LANGE: "The old theocracy runs idly and instinctively by the side of the young Church, which has become the true bearer of the kingdom of Christ." It is somewhat dangerous to mention these conceits, even as a warning, for there are persons unwise enough to adopt them. Morison illustrates v. 8 by the famous story of Sir Walter Raleigh's cloak.—V. 8-11. Popular applause. 1) It may be sincere even when superficial. 2) It need not be despised because so often temporary. 3) It may awaken the attention of others, and thus do good (v. 10). 4) It must not prevent sorrow over the perishing. (Luke 19 : 41 ff.)—V. 10. HALL: "Christ's being amongst us doth not make us happy, but his welcome. Every day may we hear him in our streets, and yet be as new to seek as these citizens of Jerusalem, 'who is this?'" JER. TAYLOR: "O holy King of Zion, eternal Jesus, be pleased to enter into my soul with triumph, trampling over all thine enemies; and give me grace to entertain thee with joy and adoration, lopping off all my superfluous branches of a temporal condition, and spending them in the offices of charity and religion. Thou, to whose honor the very stones would give testimony, make my stony heart an instrument of thy praises ; let me strew thy way with flowers of virtue, and the holy rosary of Christian graces . . . and let us at last follow thee into thy heavenly Jerusalem with palms in our hands, and joy in our hearts, and eternal acclamations on our lips, rejoicing in thee, and singing hallelujahs in a happy eternity to thee, O holy King of Zion, eternal Jesus. Amen."

12-17. CLEANSING THE TEMPLE.

Found also in Mark 11 : 15-19; Luke 19 : 45-48. It appears from the order of Mark, who is nearly always chronological, that this did not occur on the day of the triumphal entry, but on the next day. Matthew, as so often before, has grouped topics, without stopping to indicate the time. Comp. on 21 : 20.

John (2 : 13-22) has described a similar cleansing of the temple, at the first Passover of our Lord's ministry. Of course the destructive critics at once assume that these are only conflicting accounts of the same event. But we have seen (on 15 : 38) that Jesus certainly did perform some very similar miracles, as he certainly repeated a number of sayings (see at beginning of ch. 5). To make the two cleansings the same is to treat either the Fourth Gospel, or all the other three, as grossly inaccurate in respect to historical order. Matthew, as we have seen, sometimes arranges topically rather than chronologically, but so far as can be judged, the others are as chronological as historians usually are. Certainly then we ought not to suppose that John has placed a striking event at the first of several passovers, and the other three have placed it at the final passover, unless it be impossible, or extremely difficult, to believe that the act was repeated. Now it is perfectly natural that the money-loving traders, who had been temporarily driven out by a prophet's stern rebuke, should quickly come back when he was gone. Their fathers had often returned to idolatry and gross vices very soon after the reformation wrought by a prophet. Nobody knew that the prophet from Nazareth would interfere with them again. And what he had done produced no great pecuniary loss, while the opportunity for gain in this business was enticing. After all, they might say, we were worse scared than hurt. The prophet does not kill nor imprison, nor impose fines, and the temple authorities make no objection ; why not go in again ? Nothing is more common than for reform, even when accompanied by severe penalties, to need frequent renewal on the part of civil as well as ecclesiastical authorities. Even the second cleansing doubtless had only temporary results. The chief importance of the act lies in the assertion of prophetic authority (21 : 23) and its recognition by all concerned, and in the symbolical lessons. There is thus no difficulty at all in supposing

12 And Jesus went into the temple of God, and cast out all them that bought and sold in the temple, and overthrew the tables of the money changers, and the seats of them that sold doves,

12 And Jesus entered into the temple [1] of God, and cast out all them that sold and bought in the temple; and overthrew the tables of the money-changers, and

---

1 Many ancient authorities omit, *of God.*

---

a repetition of the cleansing. The first would not be mentioned by Matt., Mark, and Luke, because they give no account of that early Judean ministry with which it was connected, and which John narrates; and the second would be omitted by John, who introduced very little already found in the other Gospels. There are numerous other cases in which one of the Gospels records a certain event or discourse, and omits the repetition of it which we find in another Gospel. On this second occasion of cleansing fewer details are mentioned —nothing of oxen and sheep, and nothing as to a scourge of cords.

12. Jesus went into the temple. The additional **of God** should probably be omitted (Rev. Ver., *margin*), but the question is difficult and the substantial sense not altered.[1] Though he had entered Jerusalem as the King Messiah, he did not seek the palace of Herod or the city of David, but we find him every day teaching in the temple (Luke 19: 47); for his Messianic reign was to be brought about through spiritual instruction. 'Temple' is here *hieron* (see on 4: 5), the general sacred enclosure. Jesus is nowhere said to have entered the *naos*, the sacred house, which none but priests were allowed to enter. (Comp. on 27: 5.) The sacred house was situated on the top of a hill, and surrounded by an enclosed space which, as enlarged for Herod's temple, seems to have been about six hundred feet square. The house on the summit was near the western side of this space. The large outer court, with its great wall and inner colonnades (see on 4: 5), was considerably lower down the hill. Into this, as more remote from the

sacred house and the altar, it had been customary to allow the entrance of Gentiles, and so it was called the Court of the Gentiles. From this court went up grand steps, in two flights with a landing between them, on the north, east, and south, to the next enclosure, called the Court of Israel, and a portion of it separated as the Court of the Women. The wall at the top of the steps had grand gates, one of which was known as "Beautiful" (Acts 3: 2), and was perhaps the same that Josephus glowingly describes in "War," 5, 5, 3. Along this wall were stone pillars, bearing in Greek and Latin the inscription, "Let no Gentile enter here under pain of death" ("War," 5, 5, 2); one of these is said to have been found a few years ago. Again steps, and gates at the summit, to the central Court of the Priests, lying east of the sacred house, with an enclosing wall of only two feet in height. Just within this court on the eastern side stood the great altar of burnt sacrifice— probably built on the large rock which the Mohammedans have enclosed in the Mosque of Omar. Thus the worshiper could bring his sacrifice up the steps and pass it in to the priests, and could see plainly when it was laid on the altar (5: 23); and looking beyond the altar could see into the eastern end of the sacred house, where the priests entered at certain times to burn incense. (Luke 1: 9 f.) As Gentiles were admitted into the large outer court, it was very easy for Jewish traders to conclude that they might properly sell here the animals to be used in sacrifice. Wherever purchased, these animals had to be led through the courts up to the altar. All that were brought in for sale would, it was hoped,

---

[1] Omitted by ℵ B L, several cursives, Memph., Theb., one copy of Old Latin, Jerusalem Syriac, Arm., Æth., and some Fathers. It is not found in the parallel passages of Mark and Luke, nor the similar passage of John (2: 14), but that fact, if observed by copyists, would have been a reason, as we may judge from their general practice, not for omitting it in Matt., but for inserting it in some of the others. The expression would not be intrinsically objectionable to any one, and so we cannot account for its omission on that ground. Some suppose it to have been omitted because the phrase is rare. The

Jews had little use for such a phrase, since for them 'the temple' could mean only one thing. But the addition would not strike a copyist as strange or unnatural. And a similar phrase does occur, even in 26: 61, and figuratively in 1 Cor. 3: 16 ff.; 2 Thess. 2: 4; Rev. 3: 12, etc., and 'temple of the Lord' in Luke 1: 9, the word in all these cases being not *hieron* but *naos*, which for our present purpose makes little difference. As the internal evidence is indecisive, it seems wisest to follow the documents which so generally give the correct text. (Comp. W H., App.)

13 And said unto them, It is written, My house shall be called the house of prayer; but ye have made it a den of thieves.

13 the seats of them that sold the doves; and he saith unto them, It is written, My house shall be called a house of prayer: but ye make it a den of robbers.

---

be purchased and sacrificed, and so they were in a certain sense already sacred, and quite as fit to be here as dogs of Gentiles. Worshipers from a distance would enter the courts, pass up toward the altar, and feeling moved to offer a sacrifice, would be glad to find a supply so conveniently near. Lightfoot says (from the Talmud) that they also sold "wine, salt, oil, and other requisites to sacrifices." It is natural that the practice of admitting traders, not mentioned in Old Test., should have arisen in a later time when so many Jews came from foreign countries to worship. Jerome suspects that the priests had a share in the profits; and probably (Morison) extortionate prices were charged. At any rate we know they derived gain from all sacrifices, and these would be multiplied by having the material convenient. *Plumptre:* "We must picture to ourselves, in addition to all the stir and bustle inseparable from such traffic, the wrangling and bitter words and reckless oaths which necessarily grew out of it with such a people as the Jews. The history of Christian churches has not been altogether without parallels that may help us to understand how such a desecration came to be permitted. Those who remember the state of the great Cathedral of London, as painted in the literature of Elizabeth and James, when mules and horses laden with market produce were led through St. Paul's, as a matter of everyday occurrence, and bargains were struck there, and burglaries planned, and servants hired, and profligate assignations made and kept, will feel that even Christian and Protestant England has hardly the right to cast a stone at the priests and people of Jerusalem." **Cast out.** We do not know whether as on the former occasion (John 2: 15), he used 'a scourge of small cords' as a symbol of authority and punishment. **Overthrew the tables of the money changers.** The Greek word signifies those who make small change. Comp. on 25: 27. One sees such men now in Jerusalem, with various coins piled in slender pillars on a table, ready for a small premium to change foreign money into such as would be more current. In our Lord's time there was much demand for this on the part of foreign Jews, whom custom forbade to put any but Jewish coins into the treasury of the temple. (Mark 12: 41.) As the change was thus needed in order to a sacred contribution, people easily persuaded themselves that it was proper to allow money-changing for the special purpose to take place in the outer court. **That sold doves.** These were appointed as sacrifices in various cases, and allowed in others as substitutes on the part of the poor. (Luke 2: 24.) There is here (and so Mark and Luke) no mention of oxen and sheep, as on the first occasion. It might be inferred that the traders had not again become bold enough to bring in these, but the inference would be somewhat precarious, as the account may have merely omitted them. Mark adds (11: 16, Rev. Ver.), "and he would not suffer that any man should carry a vessel through the temple." The word rendered 'vessel' denotes all sorts of utensils and implements (comp. above on 12: 29, 'goods'). It had probably become common to go through the courts for a short cut from the great eastern gate of the city towards the southern part of Zion, which was connected with the temple by arched bridges over the intervening depression.

13. It is written, in Isa. 56: 7. Luke quotes as here. Mark adds the prophet's concluding words, 'for all the nations,' which carry the emphasis in Isa., but are not necessary here. The meaning and application of this quotation are obvious. *But ye make it,* as in leading early documents, was easily changed to **ye have made it,** as in Luke (and Mark). **A den of thieves,** or, *robbers,* as in 27: 38. They were worse than 'thieves,' they openly plundered, making money out of the worship, in sight of the altar. The phrase is borrowed from Jer. 7: 11, where the prophet reproaches the people with having a superstitious reverence for the temple and its services, and yet living so immorally that they seem practically to regard the temple as 'a den of robbers.' The Jews whom Jesus reproached were reproducing (Toy) the superstitious reverence for the temple and the wickedness that dishonored it. On the former occasion (John 2: 16), Jesus had

14 And the blind and the lame came to him in the temple; and he healed them.

15 And when the chief priests and scribes saw the wonderful things that he did, and the children crying in the temple, and saying, Hosanna to the Son of David; they were ⹁ore displeased.

16 And said unto him, Hearest thou what these say? And Jesus saith unto them, Yea; have ye never read, Out of the mouth of babes and sucklings thou hast perfected praise?

14 And the blind and the lame came to him in the temple: and he healed them. But when the chief priests

15 and the scribes saw the wonderful things that he did, and the children that were crying in the temple and saying, Hosanna to the son of David; they were

16 moved with indignation, and said unto him, Hearest thou what these are saying? And Jesus saith unto them, Yea: did ye never read, Out of the mouth of

simply said, "Make not my Father's house a house of merchandise."—What led the traders to obey? There must have been in our Lord a look and tone of superhuman authority (21: 23; John 18: 5 f.) ; and then the traders knew in their secret heart that they were doing wrong.

14. This is mentioned by Matt. only. Many afflicted persons were doubtless to be seen in the temple courts, asking alms (Acts 3: 2), or seeking consolation in worship. The miraculous healings, then and there, served to establish Jesus' authority to cleanse the temple, and in some sense (Weiss) re-consecrated the courts which had been profaned.

15 f. The chief priests and the scribes were perhaps representatives of the Sanhedrin (see on 26: 59); comp. 21: 23; 26: 3, 47; Mark 11: 18. **Saw the wonderful things that he did,** not *terata*, 'prodigies,' usually translated 'wonders' (see on 12: 38), but the general term which means exactly wonderful things. This doubtless includes his cleansing the temple and his healing the blind and the lame. **And the children crying ;** *that were crying,* Rev. Ver., represents the Greek of the leading manuscripts. The words are masculine, meaning boys as in 2: 16, and not the general term children as in 11: 16. It would naturally be boys rather than girls, for comparatively few even of grown women went to the temple amid the crowds. These boys had heard the day before the cries of the triumphal procession, 'Hosanna to the Son of David' (21: 9), and readily understood it to mean the Messiah; now observing the authority with which he cleansed the temple and healed the blind and the lame, they recalled that cry and were loudly repeating it, even **in the temple.** The older people who had said the same on the Mount of Olives and in the streets of the

city might have shrunk from making the bold proclamation in this most public place and in the very face of their religious rulers; children are in such a case more ardent and more fearless. **They were sore displeased,** or, *moved with indignation,* same word as in 20: 24. They *ought* to have been led to earnest inquiry whether he who thus asserted authority and wrought miracles and allowed himself to be hailed as the Son of David was indeed the Messiah; and his purification of the temple might well have reminded them of Mal. 3: 1–4. They rejected the idea without inquiry, and were indignant at the apparent claim. He was altogether different from their notion of the Messiah, came from an obscure village in distant Galilee (John 7: 41 f., 52), had not asked the recognition of the Sanhedrin, but seemed to be relying on mere popular recognition (John 7: 49); and as the Messiah was of course to be a revolutionist and civil ruler, his claim and its popular support might provoke the Romans to crush out the "nation," and deprive these Jewish officials of their "place," as some of them had intimated not long before. (John 11: 47 f.) **Hearest thou what[1] these are saying?** They do not really doubt that he hears, but mean to intimate surprise that he does not stop a thing so improper as to call him Son of David. So during the triumphal procession (Luke 19: 39), "some of the Pharisees from the multitude" openly called on him to rebuke his disciples for language implying that he was the Messiah, but he refused. (Comp. above on 21: 9.) It is idle for critics to suppose this a mere inaccurate report of that former case, for the place is different, the persons making the outcry are here children, and the Saviour's reply is also entirely different, and adapted to the testimony of children. The Scribes complaining may have been different, or may have included some of the same persons, now still further outraged

---

[1] The simple interrogative in indirect question, here and in 10: 19; Mark 14: 36; Luke 17: 8, is occasionally used in classic Greek also, see Jelf, § 877, Obs. 2.

17 And he left them, and went out of the city into Bethany; and he lodged there.

17 babes and sucklings thou hast perfected praise? And he left them, and went forth out of the city to Bethany, and lodged there.

by the renewed hosannas. **Yea,** he hears it, and finds it unobjectionable and proper. **Have ye never read** (see on 12: 3), implying a blameworthy ignorance of what was meant by a very familiar passage of those sacred writings with which Scribes were supposed to be so thoroughly acquainted; so also in 19: 4; 21: 42; 22: 31. **Out of the mouth,** etc., from Psa. 8: 2 (3). Hebrew, 'out of the mouths of babes and sucklings thou hast established strength.' The Sept. has 'thou hast prepared praise'; in several other passages (Toy) it has rendered the word for 'strength' by 'praise.' Matt. follows the Sept., as he so often does where it expresses the Heb. sufficiently for his purpose. (Comp. on 3: 3 and 12: 14.) The Greek word means 'prepared' or 'completely prepared,' and so may be rendered 'perfected.' The first utterances of very young children, showing admiration of God's works, and ready recognition of his existence, are a strong testimony to his being and glory, and ought, the Psalmist adds, to silence the enemy and the avenger, all the "malignant railers against God." (*Alexander* on Psalms.) Suckling was sometimes continued among the Jews till the child was three years' old (2 Macc. 7: 27), and such a custom is still reported by some travelers in the East. What the Psalmist declared true of sucking babes was also and still more true of these boys crying hosanna. Toy says that the meaning in which the words are here used is "substantially the same as that of the Psalmist—God had shown these children a truth that the learned men did not see, and had thereby made them instruments of praise and strength." Our Lord's wise answer, while not provoking, yet failed to restrain, the purpose excited by the triumphal entry and his cleansing the temple, viz., to destroy him if possible; the popular recognition and enthusiasm made them fear him all the more, for they accounted him a dangerous rival to their own position as religious instructors and rulers. (Mark 11: 18; Luke 19: 47 f.)

17. And he left them, etc. Mark shows that this was not on the day of the triumphal entry, but on the day following. (Comp. above on v. 12.) Indeed, Mark tells us (11: 19, Rev. Ver.) that "every evening he went forth out of the city"; and Luke states in connection with the next day that "every day he was teaching in the temple; and every night he went out and lodged in the mount that is called the Mount of Olives." (Luke 21: 37, Rev. Ver.) This naturally enough means Bethany, which lay on a spur of the mountain. Thus the statements agree, and show us what course he took on the three days of his public appearance, probably the first, second, and third days of the week; he came "early in the morning" (Luke 21: 38) to the temple and taught, and went out at night across the mountain to Bethany. Many who had come to the feast sought nightly lodgings in the surrounding villages. Jesus would go out to seek repose in the home of his friends (comp. on 26: 6), and probably also to avoid an attempt to arrest him, such as was successfully made the first night he spent in the city. There is no occasion to suppose, as some have done, that he and his followers camped out near Bethany. His friends in the village were apparently wealthy.

In leaving Jerusalem by the eastern gate (comp. on 21: 1), Jesus and his disciples would descend the steep declivity into the narrow valley of the Kidron, and by a little bridge would cross over the dry bed of the stream, all covered with flat stones worn into rounded shapes by the torrents of the rainy season. Reaching the foot of the Mount of Olives, they found near them a garden called Gethsemane (see on 26: 36), doubtless occupied by olive-trees and fig-trees, with probably flowers, and less probably vegetables. It seems to have been a place open to the public, and "Jesus ofttimes resorted thither with his disciples" (John 18: 2), perhaps stopping to rest under shade and among flowers before climbing Olivet, or in the morning before entering the hot and crowded city; for in April it is extremely hot in Jerusalem in the daytime, though chilly towards morning. (John 18: 18.) Up the central depression in the slope of the Mount of Olives (comp. on 21: 1) the path is steep and toilsome, sometimes clambering up ledges of limestone rock, and gradually rising to a level with, and then above, the city on the hills behind. At the summit, from which could be seen the long

18 Now in the morning, as he returned into the city, | 18 Now in the morning as he returned to the city, he
he hungered.

---

eastern line of the high mountains of Moab, with glimpses of the Dead Sea in a deep cauldron between, they were half way to Bethany. Some distance down the eastern slope is a narrow neck of rocky soil between little northern and southern valleys. This neck of land connects with Olivet a small rounded outlying hill. Their path wound around the northern part of this hill, while the Roman paved road from Bethany to Jerusalem passed around its southern face. On the east this rounded hill slopes down in a tongue of land between two minute valleys, which presently unite beyond it and go deepening down towards the Dead Sea. On this little tongue of land and in these shallow valleys, amid olive trees, figs, almonds, vines, and apricots, and patches of small, bright-hued flowers, gleamed the white limestone dwellings of Bethany. The place is now called Lazariyeh, from Lazarus, or more exactly, in Arabic, el-Aziriyeh, from el-Azir. It is by the direct path a mile and three quarters from Jerusalem, corresponding exactly to the fifteen stadia (something less than furlongs) of John 11: 18. The name Bethany appears to mean either 'house of dates' or 'house of the poor.' There was another Bethany beyond Jordan (John 1: 28), and in John 11: 1 this Bethany is distinguished as "the village of Mary and her sister Martha."

HOMILETICAL AND PRACTICAL.

V. 12. THIEME (in Stier): "Once more he goes the way which he had loved as a child, up to the temple."—V. 13. A place of worship becoming a den of robbers. 1) When the worship is conducted by men who seek religious office for the money it yields. 2) When the worship is supported, or the house of worship erected, by such measures as extortion in "fairs," or covert gambling. 3) When persons join a certain church in hope of gaining custom, or otherwise promoting their worldly interests. 4) When men wrong others through the week, and try to atone for it by worshiping God on the Lord's Day. (Jer. 7: 9-11.) HENRY: "Lawful things, ill-timed and ill-placed, may become sinful things. That which was decent enough in another place, and not only lawful but laudable on another day, defiles the sanctuary and profanes the Sabbath." HALL: "Yea, thus it became thee, O thou gracious Redeemer of men, to let the world see thou hast not lost thy justice in thy mercy; that there is not more lenity in thy forbearances, than rigor in thy just severities; that thou canst thunder as well as shine."—V. 15 f. Children crying in the temple. 1) Would-be wise men often show folly by despising the young. 2) Children sometimes see religious truth more clearly than prejudiced adults. 3) The praise of children is thoroughly acceptable to God. 4) The piety of children ought to touch hard hearts, and silence malignant opposers of the gospel.

18-22. THE BARREN FIG-TREE.

Found also in Mark 11: 12-14 and 20-26. If we had only Matthew, we should suppose that all this occurred the morning which followed the triumphal entry and the cleansing of the temple. But Matthew does not at all contradict the fuller account of Mark, viz., that after the triumphal entry (probably on the first day of the week) Jesus returned to Bethany; the next morning (Monday) on his way to the city he pronounced a curse upon the fig-tree, and afterwards cleansed the temple; and the following morning (Tuesday) the disciples expressed their surprise that the tree had at once withered. Matthew has simply thrown together the whole matter of the fig-tree, just as in narrating the ministry in Galilee he often arranges topically rather than chronologically.

18. As he returned, or probably, *upon returning.*[1] **He hungered.** The first meal was usually taken about the middle of the fore-

---

[1] Aorist part. in א (first hand), B (first hand), L (followed by Tisch. and W H.), 'upon returning,' 'after returning,' 'having returned.' This, as the more difficult reading, easily changed by copyists into the other, has strong claims to adoption. The immediately following 'by the road' would show that the former expression is meant loosely, that though he had reached the city, he had not entered it. There is thus only an apparent contradiction between this and Mark, 'when they were come out from Bethany he was hungry.' It was less than two miles from one place to the other. Buttmann would here translate 'put off' as it means in Luke 5: 3 f., thus making it 'after putting off to the city.' But it can hardly be shown that the word has

19 And when he saw a fig tree in the way, he came to it, and found nothing thereon, but leaves only, and said unto it, Let no fruit grow on thee henceforward for ever. And presently the fig tree withered away.

19 hungered. And seeing [1]a fig tree by the way side, he came to it, and found nothing thereon, but leaves only ; and he saith unto it, Let there be no fruit from thee henceforward for ever. And immediately the

1 Or, *a single.*

noon. (Acts 2 : 15.) Comp. on 22 : 4. The case in John 21 : 12 is exceptional. Walking up and down the steep mountain in the early morning air would naturally awaken appetite, especially in one who had eaten moderately the evening before. There is no occasion for the supposition that he had spent the night in special prayer.

19. A fig-tree, or more probably, in the strict sense (Rev. Ver *margin*), '*a single* fig-tree' (comp. on 8 : 19), perhaps one that stood apart, or that attracted attention by the rich development of leaves which it alone presented. Pliny ("Natural History" XVI, 49) says of the fig-tree, "Its leaf comes later than the fruit, except a certain species in Cilicia, Cyprus, and Greece." Tristram says ("Nat. Hist. of the Bible") that in Palestine "the fruit appears before the leaves." Dr. Chambers (in Schaff) denies this, but the conflict of reports is accounted for by the statement of Thomson ("Land and Book") : "The fig often comes with, or even before, the leaves." Mark's expression, "seeing a fig-tree afar off, having leaves, he came," shows that the presence of leaves suggested the presence of fruit. They had perhaps eaten new figs in the deep plain of Jericho a few days before. And though "it was not the season of figs" (Mark 11 : 13, Rev. Ver.), here on the mountain, yet this appeared to be an exceptional tree, bearing fruit earlier than usual. Thomson says he has eaten very early figs on Lebanon in May, and that fruits are there a month later than in Jerusalem. So it was not impossible that in some warm nook of the Mount of Olives an exceptionally early variety might have figs at the beginning of April. To suppose that Jesus expected to find a few figs remaining from the fall and winter crop is entirely unsuitable. Leaves would be no sign

of such remaining fruit; there would be no occasion for finding fault, and no symbolical lesson. The artificial translation of Mark which some have proposed, "for the season was not a good one for figs," is without warrant in grammar, and a mere expedient to escape a difficulty.—To take from a fruit tree beside the road, or even to pluck ears of grain in passing, was entirely in accordance with law and custom, Deut. 23 : 24 f., comp. above on 12 : 1. See the thorough humanity of our Saviour — hungry from a mountain walk, seeking food from a tree beside the road, and disappointed in not finding figs when there was such a show of leaves. His human mind, which had grown in wisdom (Luke 2 : 52), which did not know the day and hour of his own second coming (Mark 13 : 32), was of necessity, as a finite mind, unable to contain all knowledge. We must beware of unchastened inferences from this fact that he did not know some things, remembering that in the unity of his person dwelt a divine as well as a human nature, and that the Holy Spirit was given him without measure (John 3 : 34) ; but we must not deny or becloud the fact, when distinctly set forth. This is indeed a necessary part of a real incarnation, and we must accept it as a mystery. Maldonatus holds that Jesus feigned to be hungry, and feigned to seek what he knew he would not find—which painfully reminds us that the great commentator was a Jesuit. **Let no fruit grow on thee henceforward forever.** So Mark, and this is what Peter called a curse. (Mark 11 : 21.) To suppose that Jesus angrily uttered imprecations against the inaninate object is not only irreverent, but gratuitous and silly. Our Lord sought illustration of religious truth from all sources ; from food and water, patching clothes and bottling wine,

that exact sense, unless the phrase were 'after putting off from Bethany.'—The Aorist part. in Acts 25 : 13, which Scrivener says is "manifestly false" though read by all uncials and some other good documents, and which Hort regards as an instance of "prior corruption" of the text, may perhaps be explained as meaning "they came down to Cesarea by way of greeting to

Festus," since the coming itself was a greeting as well as the words spoken on arriving. This would be like "You did well in reminding me" (*anamnesas*), Plato. (Comp. below 25 : 3 ; 26 : 12 ; 27 : 4.) The present part. would mean, "they came down while saluting." Comp. on 23 : 20, as to the general theory of the aorist.

20 And when the disciples saw *it*, they marvelled, saying, How soon is the fig tree withered away!
21 Jesus answered and said unto them, Verily I say unto you, If ye have faith, and doubt not, ye shall not only do this *which is done* to the fig tree, but also if ye shall say unto this mountain, Be thou removed, and be thou cast into the sea; it shall be done.

20 fig tree withered away. And when the disciples saw it, they marvelled, saying, How did the fig tree im-
21 mediately wither away? And Jesus answered and said unto them, Verily I say unto you, If ye have faith, and doubt not, ye shall not only do what is done to the fig tree, but even if ye shall say unto this mountain, Be thou taken up and cast into the sea, it

sowing and reaping, and changes of weather, birds and flowers, plants and trees, as well as the doings and sayings of men around him,— all were made to teach lessons. And here was an opportunity for a very striking lesson. The tree gave by its leaves a false sign of possessing fruit, and so would strikingly represent false professions of piety without the effects thereof, as so plainly seen in the contemporary Jews, and alas! not in them alone. By the curse pronounced it became a symbol and a warning to all who should ever hear the gospel. That withered fig-tree stands as one of the most conspicuous objects in sacred history, an object lesson forever (comp. on 18: 2). Its lesson corresponded exactly to that of a parable given some months earlier (Luke 13 : 6-9), and corresponds generally to the lamentation over Jerusalem the day before (Luke 19 : 42), to the cleansing of the temple which immediately followed, and to the long course of teaching on the next day. (Matt. 21 : 28 to 23 : 39.) There was among the Jews of the time great religiosity, and little religion. Witness the trading in the temple, the hypocrisy of the Scribes and Pharisees, their refusal to believe John the Baptist (21: 32), their rejection of the long expected Messiah. The fig-tree destroyed was of extremely little value, as it bore no fruit. It may be that standing ' on the road' it was not private property. The Talmud often distinguishes (Lightf.) between the fruit of trees that grew in commons, and the fruit of trees that grew in gardens or fields. But that a prophet, a "teacher come from God," should destroy a piece of property of trifling value for the sake of teaching a great lesson, would seem to the Jews no ground whatever of complaint; much less will it seem so to those who believe in his divinity. Comp. the destruction of the herd of swine, 8: 30 ff. *Theophyl.* remarks that our Lord's other miracles were all beneficent, and lest it should be thought that he cannot punish, he wrought two that were punitive: yet these were not upon men, but upon the tree and the swine, and really meant kindness toward men ; "he withers the tree that he may chasten men." **And pres-**

ently (Rev. Ver., *immediately*) **the fig-tree withered away,** does not necessarily mean that the withering was completed in a moment. And when Mark (11 : 20, Rev. Ver.) states that "in the morning they saw the fig-tree withered away from the roots," he indicates that the withering had previously occurred. So there is no contradiction.

20. And when the disciples saw it, which we learn from Mark was the following morning. Matthew does not mention the lapse of time, but does not deny nor exclude it. **How soon,** etc., better, as in Rev. Ver., *How did the fig-tree* immediately, etc. See Winer, p. 276 [345]. The Greek cannot mean ' how soon,' for the word is 'immediately,' just as in the preceding verse. The disciples inquire how the immediate withering occurred. The process was justly characterized as immediate, as there had been only twenty-four hours, and it was withered from the roots (Mark). The Master had not expressly said that the tree should wither at once, but only that it should never bear fruit. We learn from Mark (11: 21) that Peter, so often spokesman, mentioned the matter to the Teacher, but the answer was addressed to them all.

21 f. Our Lord indirectly answers their question by telling how they too may work not only such a miracle, but more wonderful ones, and may obtain in prayer all that they ask for, viz., through undoubting faith. **Unto this mountain** would naturally be the Mount of Olives, and **into the sea** would be the Mediterranean or the Dead Sea. Mark has both expressions the same. But the example is evidently presented, not as a thing likely or proper to be actually done, but as an extreme case of a conceivable miracle (comp. 1 Cor. 13 : 1), to illustrate more vividly the miraculous possibilities presented to unwavering faith. (Comp. on 17 : 20.) In a similar expression not long before he spoke of rooting up a tree and planting it in the sea. (Luke 17 : 6.) The Talmud of Bab. (Lightf.) frequently uses "rooter up of mountains" as a figure to describe some teacher who had great power in removing difficulties.—Christians of the pres-

22 And all things. whatsoever ye shall ask in prayer, believing, ye shall receive.

22 shall be done. And all things, whatsoever ye shall ask in prayer, believing, ye shall receive.

ent day have no reason to believe themselves commissioned to work miracles, and the attempt to do so is either irreverent trifling, or a fanaticism injurious to themselves and repulsive to thoughtful observers. Every true prayer of Christian faith is taught by the Spirit of God (Romans 8 : 26 f.), and he will never teach men a presumptuous prayer.

From the power which faith will give them to work miracles, our Lord passes to its more general power in prayer (v. 22). This in Matthew is merely added; in Mark (11 : 24) it is declared to follow as a *consequence* from what precedes. If faith could work miracles, it follows that faith can secure whatever we pray for (comp. James 5 : 16). **Believing, ye shall receive.** Of course this promise has limitations; we shall receive what we ask, or something which our Heavenly Father knows to be better (comp. on 7 : 7, 11). Mark has a yet stronger and quite peculiar expression, "believe that ye receive (Rev. Ver., *margin* received) them, and ye shall have them"; from the time of asking go on believing that your prayer was heard, that you virtually received when you asked, and you shall have the things in due season. Mark also adds (11 : 25) an injunction to forgive others when we are praying for God's forgiveness; which Matthew might omit from having recorded it as also given in connection with the "Lord's Prayer." (6 : 14.)

HOMILETICAL AND PRACTICAL.

V. 18 f. Nothing but leaves. 1) Profession without practice is worthless. 2) Profession without practice is offensive to God and man. 3) Profession without practice is in great danger of becoming perpetual. 4) Profession need not be laid down if practice be taken up. HALL: "That which was the fault of this tree is the punishment of it, fruitlessness. Woe be to that church or soul that is punished with her own sin."—V. 21 f. The power of Christian faith. 1) In the time of Christ and his apostles it could work miracles. 2) If we suppose it can now work any miracle, it ought to be able to work the greatest miracles. (John 14 : 12.) 3) Its power in miracle-working assures and illustrates its present power in prayer (comp. James 5 : 17 f. ; Luke 10 : 20).

4) We cannot be sure that miracles would now do good, but we know that the prayer of faith in every age brings the richest blessings. 5) It enhances the privilege of prayer to believe that God will give what we ask, or what he sees to be better.

23-32. THE RULERS QUESTION CHRIST'S AUTHORITY, AND ARE REBUKED.

Found also in Mark 11 : 27-33; Luke 20 : 1-8. It occurred on the third day of our Lord's appearance in the temple, which was probably Tuesday.

23. The chief priests and the elders. Mark, 'the chief priests and the scribes and the elders,' representing the three classes which composed the Sanhedrin (see on 26 : 59); it is not necessary to suppose a formal deputation. They had already begun seeking to destroy him (Luke 19 : 47 f.), and even some time sooner. (John 11 : 53.) **As he was teaching.** So Luke, Rev. Ver. ; Mark has 'as he was walking in the temple,' probably in one of the beautiful colonnades, as some months earlier in John 10 : 23. To teach while walking about was very common with the Rabbis, as it was at Athens, where the followers of Aristotle were from this specially called Peripatetics. To stop a teacher and ask him questions, was also common. (22 : 16, 23, 35.) The conversation between our Lord and the rulers now goes on for a long time in the temple court (21 : 23 to 22 : 46), the people thronging to hear, their usual keen interest in rabbinical discussions being heightened by the triumphal entry and other recent events. After that, he turns from the baffled rulers to address directly the multitudes and his disciples (ch. 23), and towards evening speaks to the disciples on the Mount of Olives. (ch. 24 and 25.) **By what authority** (see on 9 : 6), more exactly, *by what sort of authority ;* so also Mark and Luke. **And who gave thee this authority?** The first question asks the nature of the authority, the second asks its source. Did he claim prophetic authority (21 : 11), Messianic authority (21 : 15), or what? Did he claim authority from man, or from God? Any Jew was allowed to talk publicly about religious questions (as in our social meetings), but if he proposed to be a regular teacher (Rabbi), he must be authorized by other Rabbis or by

23 And when he was come into the temple, the chief priests and the elders of the people came unto him as he was teaching, and said, By what authority doest thou these things? and who gave thee this authority?
24 And Jesus answered and said unto them, I also will ask you one thing, which if ye tell me, I in like wise will tell you by what authority I do these things.
25 The baptism of John, whence was it? from heaven, or of men? And they reasoned with themselves, saying, If we shall say, From heaven; he will say unto us, Why did ye not then believe him?
26 But if we shall say, Of men; we fear the people; for all hold John as a prophet.
27 And they answered Jesus and said, We cannot tell. And he said unto them, Neither tell I you by what authority I do these things.

23 And when he was come into the temple, the chief priests and the elders of the people came unto him as he was teaching, and said, By what authority doest thou these things? and who gave thee this authority?
24 And Jesus answered and said unto them, I also will ask you one [1] question, which if ye tell me, I likewise will tell you by what authority I do these things. The baptism of John, whence was it? from heaven or from men? And they reasoned with themselves, saying, If we shall say, From heaven; he will say
26 unto us, Why then did ye not believe him? But if we shall say, From men; we fear the multitude; for
27 all hold John as a prophet. And they answered Jesus, and said, We know not. He also said unto them, Neither tell I you by what authority I do

---

1 Gr. *word.*

---

the Sanhedrin (comp. Edersh.). Jesus was not only making it his occupation to teach, but working miracles, cleansing the temple as if a prophet, and apparently justifying his followers in greeting him as the Messiah. It was proper for the Sanhedrin to inquire into his authority (comp. Acts 4: 7), if it had been done in a proper spirit. These rulers ought to have recognized his divine mission, as their associate Nicodemus had done two or three years before, just after the first cleansing of the temple. (John 2 : 18.)

24-27. Jesus answers by asking them a question. He did this not simply as a retort, or to escape from a dilemma, but (comp. Origen) because his question tended to show them the inconsistency of their position, and lead, if possible, to self-searching and a better mind (comp. 22: 41 ff.). If they would squarely answer his question, their own question would then answer itself. What sort of authority did John have, and who gave it to him? But John had testified to Jesus. **The baptism of John.** This striking rite, from which John was popularly called 'John the Baptizer' (comp. on 3: 1), represented in the popular mind his entire ministry, and our Lord so uses it here. Comp. Acts 1: 22; 10: 37; 13: 24. **From heaven,** was the same as to say 'from God' (see on 3: 2). **And they reasoned with themselves,** may mean either among themselves, or in their own minds. Their embarrassment in argument grew out of their practical misconduct, as often happens. John's ministry had made a great impression (comp. on 3: 5), and the people had very naturally recognized that it was from heaven, that he was a true prophet. This feeling was doubtless deepened by sorrow at his untimely death, so that the multitude would not now tolerate any expression

of doubt as to his being a prophet. But the rulers, after their first early interest (3 : 7), had turned away from his ministry, and declined his baptism (Luke 7 : 30); hence their present embarrassment. **Why did ye not then believe him?** John constantly testified that the Messianic reign was near at hand, and distinctly intimated to messengers from the rulers that the Messiah would very soon appear (John 1 : 19, 26 f.), and again in the presence of a Jew that Jesus was the Messiah. (John 3 : 25-30.) Long before, at Jerusalem, our Lord had recalled this embassy to John, and the testimony borne to himself. (John 5 : 32-36.) In the region of the baptizing this testimony was well remembered. (John 10 : 40-42.) So then to reject him, when by his actions and by popular acclaim declared to be the Messiah, was refusing to believe John; they saw this plainly, and knew that it would be said. (v. 32.) **We fear the people,** or *multitude.* Luke adds, 'All the people will stone us.' **For all hold John as a prophet.** So also Mark and Luke. Herod had long feared to put John to death for the same reason. (14 : 5.) In Galilee Jesus took for granted, and strongly encouraged, the popular persuasion that John was a prophet. (See on 11 : 7.) **We cannot tell.** *We know not,* is the literal and exact meaning. So Wyc. and Rheims. It was Tyn. that introduced 'we cannot tell.' **And he,** or *he also,* with a certain emphasis on 'he' (see on 1: 21.) **Neither tell I you.** So also Mark in Rev. Ver., and Luke. *Not* 'neither do I know,' as they had said; in fact even theirs was not *really* a failure to know, but to tell. He was released from all obligation to tell them on the ground of courtesy, by their declining to answer his question. He did not choose to answer, because he did not wish to make distinct and public proclamation of his

28 But what think ye? A *certain* man had two sons; and he came to the first, and said, Son, go work to day in my vineyard.

29 He answered and said, I will not; but afterward he repented, and went.

30 And he came to the second, and said likewise. And he answered and said, I *go*, sir; and went not.

28 these things. But what think ye? A man had two sons; and he came to the first, and said, [1]Son, go 29 work to-day in the vineyard. And he answered and said, I will not: but afterward he repented himself, 30 and went. And he came to the second, and said likewise. And he answered and said, I *go*, sir: and

---

1 Or, *Child*.

Messiahship till the moment of crisis came (26: 63 f.); while they probably wished to entrap him into some avowal for which he could be accused before the Sanhedrin, as in 22: 15 ff. And he did not need to answer, for they knew that John had testified to him as the Messiah, and that he had suffered the people to greet him as the Son of David. The principle involved in his refusal is the same as when he refused a sign from heaven (16: 4), viz., (*Alex.*) "that no man has a right to demand a superfluity of evidence on any question of belief or duty, and that as the call for such accumulated proof is a virtual rejection of that previously given, it is the law of that divine administration to refuse it even as a favor." (Comp. Luke 16: 31.)

Our Lord now rebukes the rulers by three parables, the first and second being pointedly applied to them, viz., v. 28-32, v. 33-46, ch. 22: 1-14. The first and third are given by Matt. only.

28-30. Two sons, literally, *children*. Perhaps we may suppose them to have been boys, to whom the conduct in the two cases would be especially natural. **Son,** *child*, as an expression of affection (see on 9: 2). **Go,** *go along*, said with a certain urgency, comp. 4: 10; 5: 24; 13: 44; 18: 15; 19: 21. **In my**

vineyard, *the*, not 'my,' according to the best text. The father speaks of it as pertaining to the family, not as distinctively his own. **I will not,**[1] a rough and curt answer. **Repented** is the Greek word (*metamelomai*) which expresses regret, and may or may not be followed by change of purpose and conduct (comp. 27: 3); quite different from the word (*metanoeo*) used to denote repentance unto life. (See on 3: 2.) It is rendered 'repented himself' in Com. Ver. of 27: 3, and it is better to give with Rev. Ver. the same rendering here and in v. 32. In 2 Cor. 7: 8, 10, the milder English term 'regret' is a sufficient translation. **I go, sir,** with emphasis on 'I,' as it is expressed in the Greek; a polite and pretentious reply. So the Jewish rulers professed that *they* served God, while others did not. The same fault had been illustrated that morning by the fig-tree, which made great show of leaves, but had no fruit. Some understand the 'I' as a Hebraistic expression without emphasis, comparing Acts 9: 10; Judg. 13: 11; but those cases are unlike this, and even in those the 'I' is really emphatic. —A somewhat similar parable is given (Wün.) in the Midrash (Jewish commentary) on Exodus, probably of the eleventh or twelfth century. A king wished to rent out some land;

---

1 There is here a famous and quite perplexing question of text criticism, though fortunately it does not materially affect the sense. W H. follow (as usual) B and certain other documents in transposing the order in which the conversation with the two sons is held, and then in v. 31 reading 'the latter'; thus getting the same sense as that of the common text. Lachm. and Treg. follow the "Western" documents in keeping the order of the common text and yet reading 'the latter.' They preferred this as the more *difficult* reading, readily accounting for the other two as alterations from it; but the difficulty here amounts almost to impossibility, for Jerome's supposition that the Jews purposely said 'the latter' through perverseness is excessively far-fetched. Those who prefer the "Textus Receptus" at all hazards, or who merely count authorities instead of grouping them, decide at once for the common reading. W H., on the other hand, declare B, the lost uncial represented by 13, 69, 124, and 346, with three cursives, the Memph., Jerusalem Syr., Arm., and some codices of the

Æth., and some rather late Fathers, to be "far the higher authority," which is surely far too strong a statement. It is not easy to say whether the common reading or that of B will best account for the others. Perhaps the most satisfactory conjecture would be that in some early copy of the "Western" type 'the latter' or 'the last' was substituted by a copyist's mistake, and propagated; and that then a corrector of the "Alexandrian" type (some such corrections we have already found in B) removed the difficulty by transposing the order of the two conversations, a transposition further recommended to him by the fact that it puts *first* the son who represents the rulers as opposed to publicans and harlots, and (upon the interpretation of Origen and other Fathers) the Jews as opposed to Gentiles, which might seem the more natural order, and would correspond to the order of allusion in v. 32. This theory is certainly not more finespun than that of W H. in the opposite direction. So far as it goes it will tend to support the common text.

31 Whether of them twain did the will of *his* father? They say unto him, The first. Jesus saith unto them, Verily I say unto you, That the publicans and the harlots go into the kingdom of God before you.
32 For John came unto you in the way of righteousness, and ye believed him not; but the publicans and the harlots believed him: and ye, when ye had seen *it*, repented not afterward, that ye might believe him.

31 went not. Whether of the twain did the will of his father? They say, The first. Jesus saith unto them, Verily I say unto you, that the publicans and the
32 harlots go into the kingdom of God before you. For John came unto you in the way of righteousness, and ye believed him not: but the publicans and the harlots believed him: and ye, when ye saw it, did not even repent yourselves afterward, that ye might believe him.

---

several farmers declined; one undertook it, but did not work the land; the king will be most angry with the last. This may have been an imitation of that given by Jesus.

31 f. The application is not (as Origen and other Fathers explain) to Jews in contrast to Gentiles, as in the next parable, but expressly (v. 31) to the Jewish rulers and outwardly correct persons, in contrast to some who had been grossly wicked. Comp. Luke's remark (7: 29 f.) on an earlier occasion. Here for the first time our Lord makes an open, personal application of a parable to the Jewish authorities. So also in v. 43 ff. The time has come for speaking out unreservedly to them, and also to the people concerning them, as he will do later in the day. (ch. 23.) **The publicans** were very unpopular, and often very wicked. (See on 5: 46.) To these he adds the class everywhere most despised, and too often regarded as beyond the reach of religious influence. The "woman which was a sinner" of Luke 7: 37 probably belonged to this class. *Bruce:* "Publicans and harlots! why, the phrase was proverbial to denote all that was vile, loathsome, and alien to the feelings of the pure, the respectable, and the patriotic. The analogous phrase in Corea, another Judea in exclusiveness, is 'pigstickers and harlots.' To tell the proud, self-satisfied zealots for righteousness that the moral scum of society was nearer the kingdom of God than they, was to offer them a mortal and unpardonable insult." **Verily I say unto you,** solemnly calling attention, see on 5: 18. **Into the kingdom of God,** the Messianic kingdom, see on 3: 2 and 11: 12. **Go before you** (as in 21: 9), or more probably 'lead you on' (as in 2: 9; Mark 10: 32, and so in 26: 32; 28: 7). You not only do not lead them forward, as you ought to do, but will not even follow their lead. **In the way of righteous-**ness, and not in any way of sin—a man of righteous behavior and righteous teaching. Comp. 2 Pet. 2: 21; Prov. 8: 20; 12: 28; Tobit 1: 3. You cannot excuse your failure to believe him by impugning his character or his instructions. John showed no lack of righteousness even as to the externals which the Pharisees so valued, for he practiced fasting (9:14; 11:18), and made formal prayers. (Luke 11: 1.) Olsh. and Bruce seem to go too far in making this last the sole thought. **And ye believed him not,** comp. on 3 : 7. They knew Jesus would charge this upon them. (v. 25.) **When ye had seen it,** or *saw,* saw that some of the vilest were believing John and entering the kingdom. **Repented not,** etc. Better, as in Rev. Ver., *Did not even*[1] *repent yourselves afterward, that ye might believe him.* This does not mean that they did not repent of their sins in general (*metanoeo*), but that they did not even after seeing the effect produced in others, repent (*metamelomai*) of their previous refusal to believe John and enter the kingdom. The terms 'repent yourselves' and 'afterward' are in the application borrowed from the parable.

HOMILETICAL AND PRACTICAL.

V. 24-26. A question answered by a question. 1) It is sometimes proper to silence captious inquiry by asking questions in return. (Comp. 12 : 27 ; 22 : 41, 46.) 2) We are frequently involved in logical and in practical difficulties by our previous wrong-doing; comp. Pilate. 3) One has no right to decide questions of truth and duty by considerations of safety and popularity. 4) Yet public opinion is often wiser than eminent rulers (comp. John 7: 48 f.).—V. 25. "From heaven or from men." 1) No religious teaching is authoritative unless it comes from God. 2) No relig-

---

[1] 'Not even,' *oude,* rather than *ou,* 'not' (com. text), is read by B, several cursives, the Latin and Syriac versions, Memph., Æth., and some Fathers. D and two copies of the Old Latin put it 'repented afterward because you did not believe,' which shows early confusion as to the text. 'Not even' would be readily changed to 'not,' by copyists who did not see the force of the argument, and is no doubt the correct reading.

33 Hear another parable: There was a certain householder, which planted a vineyard, and hedged it round about, and digged a winepress in it, and built a tower, and let it out to husbandmen, and went into a far country.
34 And when the time of the fruit drew near, he sent his servants to the husbandmen, that they might receive the fruits of it.

33 Hear another parable: There was a man that was a householder, who planted a vineyard, and set a hedge about it, and digged a winepress in it, and built a tower, and let it out to husbandmen, and went
34 into another country. And when the season of the fruits drew near, he sent his [1]servants to the hus-

---

1 Gr. *bondservants.*

---

ious ceremony is obligatory unless it is commanded by God. 3) All teachings from God should be believed, and all ceremonies appointed by him should be practiced.—V. 27. "We know not." 1) Men often shrink from knowing, because of a lurking fear that the knowledge might not please them. 2) Men often pretend they do not know, because it would be embarrassing to tell what they do know. 3) Men might often gain, by acting up to what they know, some blessed increase of knowledge.—V. 30. "I go, sir." 1) It is right to profess, if we also practice. 2) It is wrong in professing to assume superiority to others; comp. Peter (26 : 33). 3) It is abominable to profess, and that loudly, when one does not practice; comp. the fig-tree (21 : 19). 4) It is wise not to bring the profession down to the practice, but to bring the practice up to the profession.—V. 31 f. The decent and the vile. 1) The vile who believe God's message and turn from their sin are accepted; the Prodigal Son, Zaccheus, and the penitent robber. 2) The decent who refuse to believe God, are thereby guilty of great and ruinous sin; Eve, Caiaphas, Gallio. 3) The saved who were once vile should stir penitent shame and awaken new hope in the decent who have been unbelieving. "Moral" persons ought to set an example to the vicious of joyfully accepting God's mercy; but, alas! they are often self-righteous, and will not even follow an example. CHRYS: "It is an evil thing not at the first to choose the good, but it is worse not to even change afterwards. . . . Let no man then of them that live in vice despair; let no man who lives in virtue slumber. Let neither this last be confident, for often the harlot will pass him by; nor let the other despair, for it is possible for him to pass by even the first."

33-46. PARABLE OF THE WICKED HUSBANDMEN.
Found also in Mark 12: 1-12; Luke 20: 9-19.

33 f. Hear another parable. Jesus addresses the Jewish rulers. (21: 23.) Many of the people also were listening. (Luke 20: 9.) He had not called v. 28-30 a parable, but all perceived that it was such. As to the term, and the general principles upon which our Lord's parabolic discourses must be interpreted, see on 13: 3. In explaining certain points of the story itself, we may sometimes for convenience anticipate the application. The imagery here recalls Psalm 80: 8-16, and especially Isa. 5: 1-7. *Bruce:* "Our parable is but an old theme worked up with new variations. Every one who heard it knew what the vineyard with its hedge, winepress, and tower signified, and who the vine-dressers were, and who the servants sent for the fruits. These phrases belonged to the established religious dialect of Israel." **A certain householder,** see on 10: 25. **A tower,** in which guards stay to protect the vineyard against robbery. Pulpit interpretation should beware of separately "spiritualizing" the hedge, winepress, tower, etc. Origen here especially cautions against "torturing the parable," and then does it. These details simply show that the owner made all necessary arrangements, so that the vineyard ought to have yielded a good return (comp. Isa. 5: 4). **Let it out to husbandmen,** the general term 'agriculturists,' here applied to one particular department of agriculture. **Went into a far country,** literally (in our colloquial) *moved away.* Luke adds, 'for a long time.' **The time;** *season of the fruits* (as in v. 41), not 'time,' see on 11: 21. **His servants,** 'bond - servants' (Rev. Ver. *margin*), *doulous,* see on 8: 6; here they act as the master's agents. Mark and Luke mention only a single servant each time, but Mark adds 'and many others.' **To receive the fruits of it,** or, *his fruits.* The Greek may mean either; the connection favors the latter, and so Mark and Luke. The rent was sometimes paid in money (Edersh.), but in this case in a certain portion of the crop (see Mark 12: 2), which the agents

35 And the husbandmen took his servants, and beat one, and killed another, and stoned another.

36 Again, he sent other servants more than the first; and they did unto them likewise.

37 But last of all he sent unto them his son, saying, They will reverence my son.

38 But when the husbandmen saw the son, they said among themselves, This is the heir; come, let us kill him, and let us seize on his inheritance.

39 And they caught him, and cast *him* out of the vineyard, and slew *him*.

40 When the lord therefore of the vineyard cometh, what will he do unto those husbandmen?

41 They say unto him, He will miserably destroy those wicked men, and will let out *his* vineyard unto

35 bandmen to receive [1] his fruits. And the husbandmen took his [2] servants, and beat one, and killed another, 36 and stoned another. Again he sent other [2] servants 37 more than the first: and they did unto them in like manner. But afterward he sent unto them his son, 38 saying, They will reverence my son. But the husbandmen, when they saw the son, said among them- 39 selves, This is the heir; come, let us kill him, and take his inheritance. And they took him, and cast 40 him forth out of the vineyard, and killed him. When therefore the lord of the vineyard shall come, what 41 will he do unto those husbandmen? They say unto him, He will miserably destroy those miserable men,

1 Or, *the fruits of it.*...2 Gr. *bondservants.*

might then sell to the tenants or any one else, or might carry away with them. This is largely practiced at the present day in India and in Italy, and to a considerable extent in this country.

35. And beat one, more exactly, *scourged,* literally, '*flayed.*' *Goebel:* "For the bodily ill-treatment of the prophets, the example of Jeremiah may be compared (Jer. 20: 1 f.; 37: 15; 38: 6), and of Micah (1 Kings 22: 24); for the killing, the murder of the prophets in the time of Elijah (1 Kings 18: 4; 19: 10), and of Urijah by Jehoiakim (Jer. 26: 20 ff.); and for the stoning, the example of Zechariah. (2 Chron. 24: 21 f.) The killing of the prophets collectively is mentioned in Old Test. (Jer. 2: 30; Neh. 9: 26), and referred to by Jesus in 23: 31, 35, 37; Luke 13: 34; also in Acts 7: 52; Heb. 11: 36." **And stoned another** may well follow 'killed,' since it denotes a very wrathful and cruel way of killing. Stoning did not necessarily kill (Acts 14: 19), but was apt to do so. (Acts 7: 59.) However it is not necessary to find regular progression in a series of terms in a style so familiar as that of the Gospels.

36 f. Renewed and more urgent calls. Goebel urges that the word translated **more** (*pleionas*) here means more excellent (as in Heb. 11: 4), of higher dignity; but that use is quite rare, and does not seem to be here called for. **His son.** Mark and Luke add 'beloved.' **They will reverence my son.** Luke prefixes 'it may be.' This indicates a hope that was doomed to disappointment. Such a detail could be applied to God only by anthropomorphism, as when it is said that God repented. And we may add that although God's Son was slain, his mission did ultimately bring fruits from "other husbandmen."

38. Let us kill him, and let us seize on his inheritance. This was something not likely to occur in such a case, but entirely

possible, and that is enough for an illustration; the conduct to be illustrated was itself extraordinary. The owner in the story had been long absent, and seems to have had no other son; he might not return for years, might die in a distant land, and leave the vineyard permanently in their possession. The property of a continuous absentee is often very freely handled by the occupiers. The story shows serious defects in local government and outbreaks of popular violence, such as we know to have been not uncommon in Palestine at that period. *Alexander:* "It is incongruous to press the correspondence of the sign and the thing signified, although this proposition bears an evident analogy to the ambitious and absurd attempt of the Jewish rulers in the time of Christ to oust him from his heritage and make their own provisional authority perpetual. In every effort to continue the Mosaic institutions beyond the time prescribed for their duration, the Jews have been guilty of the usurpation here projected by the husbandmen."

39. And cast him out of the vineyard. *Alexander:* "The act of casting out denotes the whole rejection of our Lord, but perhaps with an allusion to the literal fact of his suffering without the holy city (Heb. 13: 11-13), which must not however be regarded as the whole sense." For six months past Jesus has been telling the disciples that the rulers at Jerusalem would kill him (16: 21; 17: 23; 20: 18), and now to the rulers themselves he intimates the same through a "parabolic veil" so transparent that they do not fail to see. (v. 45 f.) Doubtless some of those who heard these sayings were reminded of them a few weeks later by Peter's words on the Day of Pentecost, and all the more were pricked in their heart. (Acts 2: 23, 37; 3: 14.)

41. He will miserably destroy those

other husbandmen, which shall render him the fruits in their seasons.

42 Jesus saith unto them, Did ye never read in the Scriptures, The stone which the builders rejected, the same is become the head of the corner: this is the Lord's doing, and it is marvellous in our eyes?

and will let out the vineyard unto other husband-
42 men, that shall render him the fruits in their seasons. Jesus saith unto them, Did ye never read in the scriptures,
The stone that the builders rejected,
The same was made the head of the corner:
This was from the Lord,
And it is marvellous in our eyes?

---

wicked men. The Rev. Version preserves the verbal assonance of the Greek; but the Greek describes them as wicked—evil they are and evil shall be their fate. Instead of drawing out this reply from the rulers, so as to condemn them out of their own mouth (comp. Nathan and David), our Lord in Mark and Luke makes the statement himself. We may perhaps suppose (Mald.) that he *repeated* their statement, so solemnly and pointedly as already to indicate that it meant them; thus leading them to say " be it not so. " (Luke 20: 16, Rev. Ver., *margin*.) At any rate there is no substantial difference (comp. on 3: 17). *Goebel:* " On one side the rhetorical question (in Mark and Luke) is still an appeal to the assent of the hearers to the statement introduced by the question; and on the other, the acceptance of the answer of the Sanhedrists by the Lord (in Matt.) is equivalent in substance to a statement of his own of the same purport." In destroying the husbandmen, the owner acts as also a sovereign (comp. 22: 7).

42. Our Lord now pointedly and severely applies his illustration to the Jewish rulers, whom he has been addressing ever since 21: 23, and to the nation in general. (v. 42-44.) The nation of Israel, after being established by special divine act in the land of promise, and provided with everything necessary for righteous living, failed to render to God the fruits of righteousness, when called on by providential dealings and by inspired messages; they have insulted and sometimes killed his messengers the prophets, and are now on the point of slaying his Son (comp. Acts 7: 52.) Yet this will not end the matter. The rejected one is God's chief corner-stone for the temple of human salvation.

Did ye never read in the Scriptures? as in 12: 3; 19: 4; 21: 16. Mark's phrase (12: 10, Rev. Ver.) makes still more pointed the rebuke of their ignorance, 'Have ye not read even this Scripture'? The term 'Scriptures' or 'Scripture' (22: 29; 26: 54, 56, and throughout the New Test.) had a technical sense among the Jews of our Lord's time, (just as

among us), denoting a certain well-known group of sacred books. We learn from Josephus and the Talmud, from Melito and Origen (see works on The Canon), that this group comprised exactly our Old Test., neither more nor less, and was recognized as definite and fixed. The Talmud states, it is true, that in what must have been the latter part of our first century, some Rabbis questioned, on internal grounds, whether Ecclesiastes was sacred, and some others as to Solomon's Song; but the final decision supported those books, and there is no hint of any question as to the other books—so that the exception proves the rule. When therefore Jesus and the apostles spoke of 'the Scriptures' or 'Scripture' as sacred and authoritative, they knew that their hearers would understand them to mean that well-known group of books; and they have thus stamped their seal upon the entire Old Test.

Our Lord's quotation is from Psa. 118: 22 f., just preceding the words borrowed in the hosannas of the multitude during the triumphal entry (see on 21: 9). The quotation follows the Heb. and the Sept. without any noticeable difference. Mark has the same. The second couplet, 'This was from the Lord,' etc., is omitted by Luke, and also by Peter, who quotes the passage both in addressing the Sanhedrin (Acts 4: 11), and in his first Epistle. (2: 7.) Comp. in general Isa. 28: 16. **The stone which the builders rejected.** A few miles northwest of Jerusalem, on the Roman road to Gibeon, may now be seen in an old quarry a stone set on end, say 8 x 3 x 2 feet. As observed from the road it is a good stone, but on riding around you find a great flaw that destroys its value. This stone was quarried and offered, but when lifted up for inspection was rejected by the builders, and there it stands. Imagine such a rejected stone to become the chief corner stone in some grand building. The tradition sometimes repeated that such a thing actually occurred in building the temple, doubtless grew out of this passage and is worthless. The corner stones

43 Therefore say I unto you, The kingdom of God shall be taken from you, and given to a nation bringing forth the fruits thereof.
44 And whosoever shall fall on this stone shall be broken: but on whomsoever it shall fall, it will grind him to powder.

43 Therefore say I unto you, The kingdom of God shall be taken away from you, and shall be given to a nation bringing forth the fruits thereof. [1] And he that
44 falleth on this stone shall be broken to pieces: but on whomsoever it shall fall, it will scatter him as dust.

---

1 Some ancient authorities omit ver. 44.

---

of ancient buildings were often of enormous size, and therefore very costly, 'precious.' (1 Pet. 2: 6.) Thus even now at the southeast corner of what was the temple area is seen above ground a stone nearly 24 x 5 x 3 feet, and at the southwest corner one about 32 x 3 x 2 feet (comp. on 24: 1). **The same is become,** or simply *became*.[1] **The head of the corner** does not show clearly whether it stands as the foundation, or as the topmost stone, or elsewhere. It seems to be called 'head' simply from its prominence and importance. *This was* [2] *from the Lord*, is the literal translation. Tyndale's paraphrase, **'This is the Lord's doing,'** is very pleasing. In the Psalm, the date of which is uncertain, but probably after the captivity, Israel seems to be the stone, conquered, carried away, and flung aside as of no use, but divinely destined to a future of importance and grandeur. But there is a typical relation between the history of Israel and the Messiah (see on 2: 15), and our Lord shows us in this passage a prophecy at the same time of himself.

43. This is given by Matt. only, being of special moment to his Jewish readers. **The kingdom of God,** the Messianic reign (see on 3: 2), with its privileges and benefits. **Shall be taken away from you.** This was fulfilled partly in the destruction of Jerusalem and of the Jewish State, and partly in the fact that most Jews through their unbelief failed of the Messianic salvation. **And given to a nation** shows distinctly that it was to be

taken away not merely from the Jewish rulers, whom our Lord has been principally addressing, but from the Jewish people in general—though, as we learn otherwise, with many individual exceptions, and with a prospect in the far future (Rom. ch. 11), which our Lord does not here indicate. This other nation will be the spiritual Israel, called by Peter "a holy nation." (1 Pet. 2: 9.) Comp. Acts 13: 46; 18: 5. **Bringing forth the fruits thereof** (comp. 3: 8; 7: 16 ff.), living as is required of Messiah's subjects. The image changes from that of paying the owner's share of the fruits, to the more familiar one of producing the fruits. Or perhaps it is meant that the husbandmen were not only unwilling to pay the owner's share, but had failed to make the vineyard duly productive.

44 is here of doubtful genuineness,[3] as it is wanting in some documents, and might easily have been brought in from Luke 20: 18, where there is no variation at all, while, on the other hand, we can see no reason for its omission here if originally present. It is at any rate a real saying of our Lord on this occasion, as we know from Luke. The passage evidently refers to Isa. 8: 14 f., which is borrowed in 1 Pet. 2: 8, along with the quotation from Psa. 118, which has here just preceded. **Broken,** Rev. Ver., *broken to pieces*, the Greek being stronger than the mere 'broken.' **Will grind him to powder.** So Tyndale, Gen., and K. James. This would strike any one at first sight as being what the image calls for. But

---

[1] It is very doubtful whether the aorist passive of this verb is anywhere perceptibly different in force from the aorist middle.—'The stone' in Greek is an accusative, by an unusual, but not unnatural nor wholly unexampled form of attraction.

[2] 'This' and 'marvelous' are feminine in the Greek, and might grammatically refer to *kephale*, 'head' (Origen, Meyer); but Matt. only follows the Sept., and the feminine seems there a mere literal rendering of the Heb., which having no neuter, uses the feminine for general ideas, so that 'this' means this thing or this occurrence, as it would naturally be taken in English. There are other examples in Sept., as Psa. 26: 4; 102:

9; 119: 36; Judg. 15: 7. So our passage is understood by Buttm., Jelf, most commentators; Win. and Alex. hesitate.

[3] Wanting in D, 33, several copies of the old Latin, and passed without mention in Origen's copious commentary on this passage. Eusebius and Irenæus copy v. 33-43, and would hardly have failed to add so striking a concluding sentence. Yet as the authorities for omission are few, and represent mainly the "Western" group, which has so much arbitrary alteration of the text, the question must be left doubtful. The sentence is only *bracketed* in Lachm., Treg. (margin), and W H., and see margin of Rev. Ver.

45 And when the chief priests and Pharisees had heard his parables, they perceived that he spake of them.

46 But when they sought to lay hands on him, they feared the multitude, because they took him for a prophet.

45 And when the chief priests and the Pharisees heard his parables, they perceived that he spake of them.

46 And when they sought to lay hold on him, they feared the multitudes, because they took him for a prophet.

the Greek word nowhere has that meaning. By etymology and general use, it signifies to 'winnow,' to separate the chaff from the wheat; and derivatively to 'scatter,' like chaff or dust. Memph. and Pesh. both here render 'scatter.' There is doubtless an allusion to Dan. 2: 35, "Then was the iron, the clay, the brass, the silver, and the gold broken in pieces together, and became like the chaff of the summer threshing-floors, and the wind carried them away, that no place was found for them" (Rev. Ver.), in reference to which passage a little later (2: 44) the Sept. (Theodotion) uses the Greek word here employed by Matt. and Luke. The idea then is not simply that of crushing, but of scattering into nothingness. What then is the thought of our passage? He who in unbelief finds this stone an obstacle, smites against it and falls (comp. on 11: 6; 5: 29), will not only be bruised by the fall, but broken to pieces. (Isa. 8: 14; 1 Pet. 2: 8.) If he stumbles over Jesus as unfit to be a Saviour, all his religious hopes will be utterly destroyed. In the second clause the image is somewhat changed. The stone is here conceived not as the foundation stone, but as placed higher up in the corner, perhaps at the top, and some one tries to pull it down from its place; but it falls upon him, and scatters him like a puff of dust. Jesus came to be the Messiah; the Jews reject him, and thereby utterly lose the Messianic felicity. He is notwithstanding placed by God as the corner stone of salvation; the Jews try to pull him down, to defeat the divine plan by putting him to death, but in falling he will scatter like chaff their schemes and themselves. They will have not only the loss which comes from stumbling at him, but the terrible destruction which comes from pulling him down on their heads; while he, divinely replaced, will forever remain the corner-stone of human salvation.

45 f. The chief priests and Pharisees, correspond to the chief priests and the elders of 21: 23. The chief priests, certainly at this period, were for the most part Sadducees, comp. on 26: 57; 27: 62. As to the Pharisees,

see on 3: 7. **Had heard his parables,** this and that of 21: 28 ff., and perhaps others not recorded. Mark and Luke, having only given this one, say 'parable.' **That he spake of them,** not of them as distinguished from the people at large, but especially of them as being the leaders. (Comp. on v. 43.) **When they sought.** This would cover not merely actual efforts, but plans and wishes. The Sanhedrin had some weeks before formed the purpose to kill Jesus. (John 11: 47-53.) **They feared the multitudes,** just as with reference to John the Baptist. (21: 26; 14: 5.) **Took him for a prophet,** the expression being, in the correct text, a little different from that of 21: 26.

HOMILETICAL AND PRACTICAL.

V. 37. Reverencing the Son of God. 1) He deserves to be reverenced by all mankind. 2) He came to men, and his own chosen people (John 1: 11) rejected and killed him, v. 39. 3) He is now rejected and dishonored by many who ought most to admire and revere him. 4) He is crucified afresh (Heb. 6: 6) by some who have professed to show him reverence. 5) Yet, though rejected and slain, he is risen and ascended and reigning, and multitudes do reverence and serve him. 6) In the great day every tongue will confess that he is Lord. (Phil. 2: 9-11.)—V. 41. HENRY: "Many can easily prognosticate the dismal consequences of other people's sins, that see not what will be the end of their own."—V. 42. "Did ye never read in the Scriptures?" 1) If we had read the Scriptures aright, they would solve for us many a now perplexing question of truth and duty. 2) If we had read the Scriptures aright, we should clearly perceive that they condemn us. 3) If we had read the Scriptures aright, we should see in them Jesus Christ the corner-stone of human salvation.—V. 43. ORIGEN: "The kingdom of God is not given to any one that is reigned over by sin."—V. 44. Use and misuse of the corner-stone. 1) God gave his Son to be the corner-stone of salvation to all who will accept him. (Isa. 28: 16; 1 Pet. 2: 6; Eph. 2: 20.) 2)

CHAPTER XXII.

A ND Jesus answered and spake unto them again by
parables, and said,
2 The kingdom of heaven is like unto a certain king,
which made a marriage for his son,

1 And Jesus answered and spake again in parables
2 unto them, saying, The kingdom of heaven is likened
unto a certain king, who made a marriage feast for

Many stumble against that stone instead of building upon it (Isa. 8: 14; Rom. 9: 31 ff.; 1 Pet. 2: 8; Matt. 11: 6), and are broken to pieces by the fall. (a) Some believe nothing in the Bible. (b) Others do not believe that Christ is the foundation of salvation by his atonement. (c) Others think the vicious may build on Christ, but *they* can build on themselves. 3) On many that stone will fall and utterly destroy them. (a) He will destroy by his providence their plans of opposition to his kingdom. (b) He will destroy themselves to all eternity. (25: 46; Heb. 6: 2; 2 Thess. 1: 9.) CALVIN: "This teaching partly instructs us that with tender and flexible heart we may gently yield ourselves to be ruled over by Christ; partly also confirms us against the contumacy and furious assaults of the ungodly, for whom at last a fearful end is waiting."—V. 45. HENRY: "A guilty conscience needs no accuser, and sometimes will save a minister the labor of saying 'Thou art the man.' When those who hear the reproofs of the word perceive that it speaks of them, if it do not do them good it will certainly do them hurt."—V. 45 f. CALVIN: "The Evangelists show us how little Christ accomplished, in order that we may not wonder if to-day the gospel does not constrain all to obey God."

Ch. 22 : 1-14. MARRIAGE OF THE KING'S SON.

This is found in Matt. only, but the first part resembles a parable given by Luke as spoken some time earlier. (Luke 14 : 16-24.) Some critics at once assume that only one parable was given. But any man who ever went to and fro as a preacher will know that to *repeat* an illustration to a new audience with some modification is perfectly natural (comp. at beginning of ch. 5). So later in this same day, ch. 25 : 14 ff. will repeat Luke 19 : 11 ff. There are examples in the Talmud of a like repetition and reworking of an illustration by different Rabbis, and why not this be done by the same Rabbi? It has been held that a parable cannot have been spoken at this point, between the rise of the feelings described in 21 : 45 f. and the consultation of 22 : 15. But

why not? It required only a few minutes. And 21: 46 is a general statement, covering much that followed.—The supposed Rabbinical parallels to this parable (Wün., Edersh.) are in fact so little like it as not to be worth stating. To derive illustration from a feast would be a matter of course.

1. Answered, not to anything that had been said, so far as we know, but responded to the feelings and wishes (21 : 45 f.) which he knew were entertained. **And spake again by parables.** Only one is given; there may have been others, or this may have been regarded as comprising two (2-10, 11-13), or the plural may be (Goebel) only that of category, meaning that he spoke parabolically. This parable is not expressly applied, like the two foregoing, because the application is now sufficiently obvious, especially since 21 : 43. *Bruce :* "The parable of the vine-dressers exposes Israel's neglect of covenanted *duty;* this, her contempt of God's *grace.* The two are mutually complementary, and present together a full view of Israel's sin." For the term parable, and the general principles of interpretation, see on 13 : 3.

2 f. The kingdom of heaven, see on 3 : 2. **Is like unto,** see on 13 : 24. **Unto a certain king.** Note the leading differences between the present parable and that of Luke 14 : 16 ff. There it was simply 'a certain man,' here it is a *king ;* there merely a 'great supper,' here a *marriage feast* for the king's *son.* There he sent once to summon the invited, here twice. There they made excuse; here they make light of it, and some shamefully treat and kill the king's messengers, and the king destroys them and their city. Then in both parables other guests are invited wherever they can be picked up. It thus appears that this later parable brings out much more clearly the wickedness of the Jews in not simply rejecting God's general invitations of love, but dishonoring his Son, and killing his servants; and that difference exactly suits the change of circumstances. Very naturally the parable in Luke is oftenest used in our pulpits, as it does not so distinctively relate to the conduct of the

3 And sent forth his servants to call them that were bidden to the wedding: and they would not come.

4 Again, he sent forth other servants, saying, Tell them which are bidden, Behold, I have prepared my dinner: my oxen and *my* fatlings *are* killed, and all things *are* ready : come unto the marriage.

3 his son, and sent forth his [1]servants to call them that were bidden to the marriage feast: and they

4 would not come. Again he sent forth other [1]servants, saying, Tell them that are bidden, Behold I have made ready my dinner: my oxen and my

---

1 Gr. *bondservants.*

Jews. But this also, especially with the addition of v. 11-13, is full of solemn instruction for all times. **Made a marriage feast.** Some render this simply 'a feast,' because *gamos* 'marriage,' is used by the Sept. to translate the Heb. for 'feast' in Esther 1 : 5, comp. 9 : 22; and it may be added that Pesh. here translates back into the same word feast that is there employed in the Heb. But as there is no other known example of such a use of *gamos*, it is better to understand it here in the literal and common sense, especially since ' for his son ' means the Messiah (comp. 21 : 37), and the Messiah is elsewhere also represented as a bridegroom (25:1; 9 : 15; John 3 : 29; Rev. 21 : 2, 9; Eph. 5 : 25-32), just as in the prophets Israel is often the spouse of Jehovah. The Greek word is here in the plural, (*gamous*), and so in v. 3 and 4 (and Luke 12 : 36), while it is singular in v. 8, 11 f. The plural of a word denoting a festival was often used to indicate its several parts or stages (Buttm. p. 23); comp. our word nuptials. Wyclif here imitates the Greek plural, ' made weddings.' In modern English we could say, ' made a wedding,' but the singular is wanted for the Greek singular in v. 8, and so 'made a marriage feast' is our best translation. **His servants,** literally *slaves (doulous)*, see on 8 : 6 and comp. 14 : 2; 18 : 23; 21 : 34. **To call them that were bidden,** literally, '*to call the called.*' The guests were invited in advance and then, being close together in a crowded Eastern city, and not generally supplied with convenient time-pieces, they were notified when the feast was ready. Comp. Luke 14 : 17; Esth. 5 : 8 and 6 : 14.

4. Again he sent forth other servants. The king kindly renews the summons, and remonstrates, urging that he has prepared a grand entertainment, and they really ought to come. So in the foregoing parable (21 : 36) the householder sent others and more in number. **I have prepared,** or, *made ready*, the same Greek root as 'ready' just below. **My dinner,** *ariston,* found also in Luke 11 : 38, while *deipnon*, 'supper,' is found in 23 : 6 and often

elsewhere in New Test., and both occur together in Luke 14 : 12. The *ariston* seems to have been usually taken about the middle of the forenoon, sometimes earlier or later; the *deipnon* at the close of the day, often after dark. Josephus ("Ant.," 5, 4, 2) supposes that Eglon's guards (Judg. 3:24) were negligent about midday, "both because of the heat and because their attention was turned to dinner" (*ariston*). This would indicate that in Josephus' own time the *ariston* was sometimes taken as late as noon ; on the other hand in John 21 : 12, 15 it is taken shortly after dawn. *Vambery* (in Morison) says of the Turks at the present time, "There are only two meals during the day, the smaller one between ten and eleven o'clock in the morning, and the second and larger one after sunset." Grimm, Plump., and others seem to be wrong in supposing that the Jews of our Lord's time took a separate and slight meal on rising, as the later Greeks did, and some among the later Romans. There is no evidence that the Jews had more than the two meals. (See Smith's "Dict.," Art. "Meals.") In the time of Elizabeth and King James, the principal meal in England was taken some time before noon, and called 'dinner,' and the slighter meal taken at the close of the day was called 'supper.' Accordingly in the early English versions *ariston* is rendered 'dinner,' and *deipnon* 'supper,' which conforms to the time of day, but quite misrepresents the real importance of the two meals. In modern city life the words breakfast and dinner, the former occurring at 9 to 12 o'clock, the latter at evening, would correspond quite closely to *ariston* and *deipnon* in the New Test., but it is too late to make a general change (see Rev. Ver. of John 21 : 12, 15). The marriage feast mentioned in this parable is an *ariston*, curiously resembling the English "wedding-breakfast," while the feast of Luke 14 : 16 is a *deipnon*, as entertainments usually were. But here the feast is either protracted, or more likely delayed, until after night. (v. 13.) As new guests had to be summoned and must

5 But they made light of *it*, and went their ways, one to his farm, another to his merchandise:
6 And the remnant took his servants, and entreated *them* spitefully, and slew *them*.
7 But when the king heard *thereof* he was wroth: and he sent forth his armies, and destroyed those murderers, and burned up their city.
8 Then saith he to his servants, The wedding is ready, but they which were bidden were not worthy.
9 Go ye therefore into the highways, and as many as ye shall find, bid to the marriage.

5 fatlings are killed, and all things are ready : come to the marriage feast. But they made light of it, and went their ways, one to his own farm, another 6 to his merchandise: and the rest laid hold on his [1]servants, and entreated them shamefully, and killed 7 them. But the king was wroth ; and he sent his armies, and destroyed those murderers, and burned their 8 city. Then saith he to his [1]servants, The wedding is ready, but they that were bidden were not worthy. 9 Go ye therefore unto the partings of the highways, and as many as ye shall find, bid to the marriage

---

1 Gr. *bondservants.*

---

have time to assume festive apparel, it might well be night before the festival was actually in progress, and the king entered. Or the *ariston* may have been intended as a preliminary banquet, while the marriage would occur at night. (25 : 6.) In 1 Cor. 11 : 20, "the Lord's *deipnon*" seems to give the idea of a banquet to which the Lord invites. **My oxen and my fatlings,** beeves and fatted calves, as in 2 Sam 6 : 13 ; 1 Kings 1 : 9, where Adonijah made a royal feast. **Come** is the same strong and urgent word as in 11 : 28.

5-7. They made light of it, a great insult to a *king*, whose invitation was the highest honor, and who was celebrating an occasion of peculiar interest. These showed contempt by going off to their every-day employments, and those that remained showed even murderous hatred, a spirit of rebellion against the king and his son. (Psa. 2 : 2, 12.) **One to his farm.** *His own farm,* is the exact meaning of the Greek ; [1] he was caring exclusively for his own affairs. **Another to his merchandise,** his mercantile business. **The remnant,** rather, *the rest,* which is not only simpler but a more exact translation. **Took,** or, *seized,* a stronger term than in 21 : 35, 39. **Entreated them spitefully.** *Shamefully* (so Cranmer) is better than 'spitefully' ; we might say simply 'insulted them.' **But the king was wroth,** a strong word. **When . . . heard thereof,** is a spurious addition to the text. **Sent forth his armies.** Our word 'armies' now always suggests a large number of soldiers, which is not true of the Greek word; Plump. proposes 'troops.' **Destroyed those**

murderers. They were also rebels. *Goebel :* "The hitherto peaceful image of an invitation to a marriage feast is now changed into the warlike image of a military raid with fire and sword against murderous rebels." **And burned up their city,** which may be thought of as among the suburbs of the capital where the wedding feast occurred. There is no necessity for supposing that this order was *carried out* before the king sent forth to invite other guests. (v. 8.) An autocratic sovereign had but to give the order, and could then turn his attention to other things.

8-10. Into the highways.[2] Lit. *the partings of the highways,* colloq., 'the forks of the roads,' where the roads leading out from the city separated each into two or more roads. There the country people coming in from different directions could all be seen and invited. V. 10 has the simple term *highways,* which is enough without repeating the precise direction. It is surely over-refinement to say (Bishop Lightfoot on Revision), "In this change of expression we seem to see a reference to the imperfect work of the human agents as contrasted with the urgent and uncompromising terms of the command" ; but certainly the two phrases ought to be kept distinct in the translation, which was not done by Tyndale and followers, and imperfectly done by Wyc. and Rheims. In Luke 14 : 21 ff. the messengers were sent first into the streets and lanes of the city, and afterwards into the roads outside; here only the latter are mentioned. Meyer oddly concludes that the capital was the city burned, and none but

---

1 Winer, Buttm., Grimm, suppose that here and in 25 : 14, and some other passages *idios* loses its proper sense, and means not 'his own,' but simply his. But none of the passages *require* this weakened sense, and therefore it is not justified.

2 The term rendered 'partings' is not found elsewhere in the New Test. The frequent Sept. sense of 'outlet' would answer here, if the expression were

"*diexodous* of the streets," but not when it is "*diexodous* of the roads." Is there any clear instance of *hodos,* 'way,' 'road,' being applied to the street of a city ? The preposition *dia* here has its frequent force (in compound words) of division, from the primary sense of 'between.' Many have been misled, here and elsewhere, by supposing that *dia* must necessarily mean 'through.'

10 So those servants went out into the highways, and gathered together all as many as they found, both bad and good: and the wedding was furnished with guests.

11 And when the king came in to see the guests, he saw there a man which had not on a wedding garment:

10 feast. And those [1] servants went out into the highways, and gathered together all as many as they found, both bad and good: and the wedding was

11 filled with guests. But when the king came in to behold the guests, he saw there a man who had not

---

1 Gr. *bondservants.*

---

country people could now be invited; but 'their city' (v. 7), seems clearly to distinguish it from the city in which the king lived. **As many as they found, both bad and good.** They do not stop to discriminate as to social position or even moral character. This alludes to the fact that some very wicked persons would become Christians. The bad are mentioned first, so as to emphasize the king's grace. **And the wedding,** or, according to the more probable Greek text, *the bridal-hall* [1] **was furnished,** *filled,* the literal and exact meaning, **with guests,** *with persons reclining,* viz., at table. See on 8: 11.

The meaning of the parable up to this point is plain. The benefits and delights of the Messianic reign are represented under the image of a marriage feast in honor of God's Son. The Jewish people had long before been invited to enjoy the feast. God had sent his servants the prophets from time to time (we may include John the Baptist), to call them to the wedding. But many had been utterly indifferent, caring only for their worldly pursuits; and some had insulted and slain his messengers. These murderers God will most severely punish. Then his servants will go forth and bring in, no longer the chosen people originally indicated, but Gentiles, including some very wicked persons, and these will form the honored guests. If the destroyed city of v. 7 be supposed to point specially to the destruction of Jerusalem, then we may understand that the new messengers of v. 8 are the apostles, sent forth to the Gentiles. They began before Jerusalem was destroyed, but not before its destruction had been foretold as inevitable and near at hand. (23: 38; 24: 15 ff.) The very Greek phrase 'not worthy' of v. 8 is applied by Paul to the Jews in Acts

13: 46, and rendered 'unworthy.' Thus neglect and outrage on the part of the Jewish nation will not prevent the Messiah from having a people (John 6: 37), nor mankind from enjoying the Messianic benefits, the feast of salvation. This parable, therefore, repeats the idea of the foregoing that the Jews will be severely punished for slighting and slaying God's messengers, but brings out more fully the thought that *others* will enjoy the benefits they have lost. (Comp. 21: 41 with 21: 7-10.) Jesus here still looks sadly at the past and present, but also looks hopefully to the future.

11-13 present a new feature of the parable, having nothing like it in Luke 14: 16-24. V. 10 makes the *transition* from the main parable to this further lesson, as is shown (Goebel) by the phrase 'those servants,' whereas 'the servants' would have been natural in a mere conclusion of the foregoing narrative. The king's directions were carried out, and the bridal hall filled with persons reclining at the banquet; but they were not all suffered to enjoy the feast. **When the king came in to see the guests,** rather *behold,* not simply 'to see,' but to look at them as a pleasing spectacle. (6: 1; 11: 7.) This is not the forenoon meal originally intended or begun with, for it is now night. (v. 13.) **A man.** He represents a principle (Bruce), and therefore a class; comp. the one slothful servant in 25: 24. **Had not on a wedding garment,** a dress suitable for attending a wedding. We do not know of any specific *wedding* dress, as distinguished from that appropriate to other festive occasions; but the guests must come properly arrayed. Oriental monarchs now frequently present some elegant article of apparel to a visitor; and hence it has been widely supposed by commentators that in this case the king had

---

1 In א B (first hand) L the word is not *gamos* 'wedding,' but *numphon,* a rare word, meaning the place where the bride is, and found elsewhere only in the sense 'bride-chamber' (9: 15; Tobit 6: 14, 17). The obvious inappropriateness of that sense here would account for the change to *gamos* (from v. 8), while we could not explain the introduction of a word apparently so unsuitable. Etymologically it could easily signify 'bridal

hall,' the place of the wedding banquet, and so be entirely appropriate. Yet the mere fact that 'was filled,' suggests a room (comp. Luke 14: 23) would not account for a change from the sufficiently suitable term *gamos* to an apparently quite unsuitable term. Tisch., W H., and Weiss read *numphon,* and Treg. (who had not א) placed it in his margin.

12 And he saith unto him, Friend, how camest thou in hither not having a wedding garment ? And he was speechless.
13 Then said the king to the servants, Bind him hand and foot, and take him away, and cast *him* into outer darkness ; there shall be weeping and gnashing of teeth.
14 For many are called, but few *are* chosen.

12 on a wedding garment: and he saith unto him, Friend, how cames thou in hither not having a wed-
13 ding garment? And he was speechless. Then the king said to the [1] servants, Bind him hand and foot, and cast him out into outer darkness ; there shall be
14 the weeping and gnashing of teeth. For many are called, but few chosen.

---

1 Or, *ministers.*

---

furnished suitable apparel, and this man had refused or neglected to put it on. But the evidence furnished for such a custom (*e. g.,* by Trench) is not adequate; and if the supposition be here made, it must be grounded on the necessity of the case. There is, however, no intimation that the man was poor. This is not a charitable feast to the poor (Luke 14: 13), but a grand entertainment in honor of the king's son. A forenoon banquet was originally proposed and it is now night, so that there has been ample time for preparation. We may then suppose either that the man ought not to have come in at all if unable to dress himself properly, or that he might have sought help from the king under the peculiar circumstances if he had felt a proper anxiety to be attired worthily of the occasion. At any rate, his presence without proper dress was tacitly admitted by himself to be quite inexcusable, and was regarded by the king as a flagrant insult, deserving the severest punishment. No light is gained by supposing a reference to Zeph. 1: 6 f., where the imagery is quite differently used. **Friend,** or *comrade,* see on 20: 13. **And he was speechless.** This shows that he felt himself to be entirely without excuse ; he fully knew what was proper, and it was not beyond his reach. Our pulpit interpretation had better hold fast to this fact and not distract attention by discussing the question whether wedding garments were furnished. **Said to the servants,** the attendants (*diakonois,* see on 8: 6), including others besides his slaves (v. 3, 6); Rheims 'waiters.' **Bind him hand and foot, and cast him.** The inserted words *take him away and,* are wanting in the best manuscripts and nearly all early versions, and though really useless the phrase is not objectionable, so that it is clearly an addition of the copyists. The binding would prevent his return to the bridal hall, and would leave him helpless in the darkness. **Into** (*the*) **outer darkness** (see on 8: 12), which would be oppressively

dark by the contrast of the brilliantly lighted palace.

What now is the application? Those who repent and propose to be subjects of the Messianic reign must become righteous in character and life or they cannot enjoy its benefits. (5: 20; Heb. 12 : 14.) It is not enough for a man to place himself in outward relation to the kingdom ; he must also develop the corresponding character and conduct. There have always been persons who desired the temporal and eternal advantages which Christianity offers, without caring to be and to do what it requires. Those who accept God's bounty in the gospel, the salvation that is not by works but according to his mercy, must "be careful to maintain good works" (Titus 3 : 4-8) ; otherwise they insult God, and disgrace the feast of salvation, and will not be allowed to share it—yea, will be severely punished. The lesson here taught is thus seen to be of the greatest importance. But to bring in the Pauline conception of imputed righteousness, and understand the parable to teach that we must "put on the wedding-garment of Christ's righteousness," is altogether out of place, and turns attention away from the real lesson.

To leave no doubt as to what is meant by 'the outer darkness,' our Lord adds, **there shall be the weeping and gnashing of teeth** (see on 8: 12), the well known signs of wretchedness in Gehenna, the place of eternal punishment. (13 : 42 ; 25 : 30, 46, comp. on 5 : 22.) This clause cannot be taken as spoken by the king, and is easily understood as an addition made by our Lord, like that which immediately follows.

14. For many are called, but few are chosen. This is a general fact added as accounting for the particular fact described in the parable (notice 'for'). Many are called to share the Messianic benefits, but few are selected actually to attain them; a large portion of the called utterly refusing to accept,

15 Then went the Pharisees, and took counsel how they might entangle him in *his* talk.

15 Then went the Pharisees, and took counsel how

and some even of those who profess acceptance not developing the corresponding character and life. This selection of the actually saved may be looked at from two sides. From the divine side, we see that the Scriptures teach an eternal election of men to eternal life, simply out of God's good pleasure. From the human side, we see that those persons attain the blessings of salvation through Christ who accept the gospel invitation and obey the gospel commandments. It is doubtful whether our minds can combine both sides in a single view, but we must not for that reason deny either of them to be true.—This sentence is unwarrantably borrowed by many documents (and the common text) as an addition to 20: 16.

HOMILETICAL AND PRACTICAL.

V. 5. "They made light of it." 1) Many men acknowledge no obligation to honor the Son of God. 2) They take no pleasure in contemplating his character and showing him respect. 3) They are engrossed with their own worldly possessions and pursuits, and care for nothing that he offers. 4) They thus deprive themselves of the highest benefit, and offer him the grossest insult.—V. 7. HENRY: "Christ will have a kingdom in the world, though many reject the grace and resist the power of that kingdom."—V. 8. God's forbearance and wrath. 1) He is not repelled by refusal, but kindly urges the invitation, v. 4. 2) He chastises those who insult him and outrage his messengers, v. 7. 3) He condescends to call many whom the world would have thought unfit for such an honor, v. 8-10. 4) He punishes those who pretend to accept his invitation, but dishonor him by utter inconsistency, v. 11-13.—V. 12. CHRYS.: "Reverence the love of him who called you, and let no one continue to have filthy garments, but let each of you busy himself about the clothing of your soul."—V. 14. The called and the chosen. 1) The many are called in good faith, and it is their own fault if they do not have part in the feast. 2) There are various reasons why so large a number of the called fail. (a) Some turn away in contemptuous neglect, through worldly engrossment, v. 5. (b) Some hate him who calls and outrage even those who bring the call, v. 6. (c) Some profess to accept it, but take no pains to have the corresponding character and conduct, v. 11 f. 3) The few who are chosen give proof of it by accepting the call and behaving accordingly. 4) These enjoy the feast of salvation, gladly honor the Son of God, and humbly ascribe all to sovereign grace. JEROME: "He sums up all these parables in a brief sentence, to the effect that in working the vineyard, and in building the house, and in the marriage feast, not the beginning but the end is the great matter."

15-46. QUESTION AND ANSWER IN THE TEMPLE.

This is found also in Mark 12: 13-37; Luke 20: 20-44.

It was customary for any one who desired it to ask questions of a Rabbi in public, even interrupting him at pleasure. The Talmud gives many examples, and sometimes the Rabbi replied with further interrogation. So with the Athenian philosophers, especially Socrates, who reduced questioning to a science. The leading priests and Scribes felt themselves pointedly assailed by Jesus in the three parables just given, especially in 21: 28-32, 43-45. It was determined upon consultation to attack the Nazarene with hard questions before the multitude, hoping to extract from him some answer that would offend popular prejudice or provoke the Roman authorities, and at any rate hoping to show that he was not greatly superior to other Rabbis. Accordingly, three questions were successively proposed by representative persons, the first by Pharisees and Herodians united, the second by Sadducees, the third by a Lawyer. To all these Jesus made prompt and wonderfully wise replies, and then finished by asking them a question of the deepest importance, which they were unable to answer. These four instances of question and answer hang closely together in the narrative, being all given in the same order by Matthew and Mark, and all except the third given also by Luke. They occurred in the temple court, probably on Tuesday, three days before the crucifixion.

I. **15-22.** THE PHARISEES AND HERODIANS ASK ABOUT TRIBUTE TO CESAR. Mark 12: 13-17; Luke 20: 20-26. **Then** does not

16 And they sent out unto him their disciples with the Herodians, saying, Master, we know that thou art true, and teachest the way of God in truth, neither carest thou for any *man:* for thou regardest not the person of men.

16 they might ensnare him in *his* talk. And they send to him their disciples, with the Herodians, saying, 1 Master, we know that thou art true, and teachest the way of God in truth, and carest not for any one;

---

1 Or, *Teacher.*

---

necessarily (see on 3: 13), but does naturally indicate that this was on the same occasion as the foregoing (comp. on 14: 1); Mark and Luke have simply 'and.' **Went,** from where Jesus was teaching, to some other part of the temple courts. **The Pharisees,** see on 3: 7. **Entangle.** This literally means, to catch in a snare or trap. **Their disciples,** see on 5: 1; the leading Rabbis send some of their astute pupils, while they themselves stand aloof to watch the result, and so are not committed to any subsequent co-operation with the Herod party. **With the Herodians.** When Archelaus (see on 2: 22) was in A. D. 6 deposed from the ethnarchate of Judea and Samaria, and those districts were placed under a Roman governor (see at end of chap. 2), the Jews were much divided in sentiment. Secularists preferred the new arrangement, as giving security to business and property; and with these the Sadducees generally sympathized. Many Pharisees bitterly opposed it on the ground that Jehovah's people ought not to be subject to heathen rulers. Some persons insisted that another prince of the house of Herod ought to be appointed over Judea and Samaria, even as Herod Antipas was still permitted to rule over Galilee and Perea; and it was doubtless hoped that some prince of the family would one day regain all the dominions of Herod the Great, as was at length done for a few years by Herod Agrippa. (Acts 12: 1.) These persons gradually came to be known as Herodians, *i. e.*, partisans of Herod, comp. Pompeians, Cesarians, Christians (Acts 11: 26), the Latin termination — *anus* being used to denote a follower of a political leader. This political party probably had the sympathy of the less rigorous Pharisees, as offering the only available alternative to direct heathen rule; while the great body of the Pharisees hated them, since the Herod princes were, after all, only appointees and underlings of the Romans. (Comp. Smith's "Dict.") As Roman governors continued to rule over Judea and Samaria, the Herod party would gradually diminish, and accordingly it is mentioned only here (with Mark

12: 13), and in Mark 3: 6; not at all in Josephus, the Talmud, or elsewhere—whence it follows that the above or any other theory of their origin must be partly conjectural. When Herod Agrippa became king of all Palestine in A. D. 41, the lingering supporters of his family in Judea must have greatly rejoiced, but all men by that time saw that no political position was longer possible except submission or hostility to the Romans, and so it is natural that we should hear no more of a Herod party. When the Pharisees united Herodians with themselves in the effort to ensnare Jesus, it was obviously through the cohesive power of a common jealousy towards one popularly regarded as the Messiah; for if recognized as such, they were sure he would overthrow the Herod family everywhere, and depose the present Jewish officials. On the earlier occasion in Galilee, nearly two years before this, according to most harmonists (Mark 3: 6), the Herodians could be relied on to excite Herod Antipas against Jesus; here, they represent Roman sympathies, since on the Romans all Herodian hopes now really depended. Luke (20: 20, R. V.) does not mention Pharisees or Herodians, but says that the Scribes and the chief priests sent 'spies,' or in modern phrase detectives, 'which should feign themselves to be just'—which agrees with their attempt at flattery in Matt.—and wished to find an excuse for delivering him to 'the governor,' *i. e.*, Pilate—a design here represented by the Herodians. **Master,** or *Teacher* (*didaskalos*), see on 8: 19. **We know,** without emphasis on 'we.' They said it in a far different spirit from Nicodemus (John 3: 2); what they said was really true, but they meant it only as flattery. By this flattery they would embolden the teacher to speak out against the Roman rule, for they well knew in advance that only through the Romans could they compass his death. **The way of God,** the way in which God would have men walk; this would include the question whether the people of God ought to do so and so. **Thou regardest not the person of men.** This is one of several Greek phrases

17 Tell us therefore, What thinkest thou ? Is it lawful to give tribute unto Cesar, or not ?
18 But Jesus perceived their wickedness, and said,
Why tempt ye me, *ye* hypocrites ?

17 for thou regardest not the person of men. Tell us
therefore, what thinkest thou ? Is it lawful to give
18 tribute unto Cæsar, or not ? But Jesus perceived their
wickedness, and said, Why try ye me, ye hypocrites?

---

representing a peculiar Hebrew idiom, which probably signified originally (Morison) to lift up the face of a prostrate suppliant, and so to show him favor, and hence came to signify regard for a person in the good sense, or in the bad sense regarding the person rather than the justice of the cause ; in Hebrew and Greek the term ' face' was derivatively used for person. The flatterers meant that Jesus would follow principle and truth without fear or favor. (Comp. Gal. 2· 6; Rom. 2: 11.)

17. Is it lawful, or *permissible*, allowable (see on 14 : 4) ; there is no direct reference to law, whether Jewish or Roman. **Or not ;** they wish him to say yes or no, as when lawyers try to corner a witness. **Tribute.** The Latin word *census* is borrowed in the Greek of Matt. and Mark, while Luke has the general term 'tribute.' *Census* in Latin signifies a registration of persons and property (as we borrow it in English), and hence a tax on either. But here it signifies simply a poll-tax (comp. on 17 : 25), Pesh. Syriac ' head-money.' Of course the principle was the same, whether the question concerned poll-tax or tribute in general ; the former touched the poorest, and was, as it is among us, a matter of greater popular interest and complaint. **Cesar** is the general term for the Roman *imperator* or emperor, applied to Augustus in Luke 2 : 1, Tiberius in Luke 3 : 1; Claudius in Acts 17 : 7 ; Nero in Acts 25 : 8 ff.; Phil. 4 : 22. The family name of the great Julius thus became a title, and in modern times (Kaiser, Czar) is more honorable than even king. Paying the head-tax to Roman authorities was the most immediate and humiliating recognition of subjection to the heathen. Judas of Galilee (Jos. "Ant.," 18, 1, 1 and 6) headed a fierce insurrection against the first Roman governor (A. D. 6) for making a census with a view to taxation, saying that God was "their only Ruler and Lord," and that the census "was leading them right straight into slavery." He perished, and Gamaliel tells us that his followers "were scattered abroad." (Acts 5 : 37, Rev. Ver.) But the sentiment represented by that movement still burned in many bosoms.

Josephus says that Judas the Galilean was "the founder of a fourth philosophy," whose followers agreed in all other things with the Pharisees, but were fanatics for liberty, and that this led to the insurrection (in A. D. 66) which ended in the destruction of Jerusalem. At that later period they were called Zealots, and it is supposed that Simon the Zealot (10 : 4) had belonged to the party, and also perhaps Barabbas. (27 : 17.) We may therefore be sure that among the easily excited crowds who filled the temple courts when Jesus was asked this question, there were many who regarded paying the poll-tax as the very badge of slavery to the heathen, and as treason against Jehovah, the theocratic king of Israel.

18-22. Jesus perceived their wickedness, or as we should say, their villainy. With smooth, flattering words they came, asking a question which they thought would prove a hopeless dilemma. He was desired to say either yes or no. If he said yes, the Pharisees would loudly proclaim, through all the temple courts and every day, that the Nazarene said it was proper to pay tribute to Cæsar, which showed that all notion of his being the King Messiah must be ridiculous and that in fact he was neither patriotic nor pious. If he said no, the Herodians would go straight to Pilate. The Romans cared nothing for questions pertaining to the religion of a subject nation (comp. Acts 25 : 18-20), and interfered very little with local affairs, provided always the people kept the peace and paid the taxes. So confident were the Jewish rulers that this plea would be effectual before Pilate that three days later with flagrant falsehood they told him, " We found this man forbidding to give tribute to Cæsar, and saying that he himself is Christ, a king" (Luke 23 : 2, Rev. Ver.). **Why tempt ye me,** testing him with hard questions, in hope of drawing him to say something injurious to himself. (Comp. on 16 : 1 and 19 : 3.) **Ye hypocrites** (see on 6 : 2 and 15 : 7); they were pretending great admiration for him as a teacher, and pretending faithful allegiance to Cesar (John 19 : 15), and pretending a lofty patriotism and piety. Jesus

19 Shew me the tribute money. And they brought unto him a *ᵃ*penny.
20 And he saith unto them, Whose is this image and *ᵇ*superscription?
21 They say unto him, Cesar's. Then saith he unto them, Render therefore unto Cesar the things which are Cesar's; and unto God the things that are God's.
22 When they had heard *these words*, they marvelled, and left him, and went their way.

19 Shew me the tribute money. And they brought
20 unto him a ¹denarius. And he saith unto them,
21 Whose is this image and superscription? They say unto him, Cæsar's. Then saith he unto them, Render therefore unto Cæsar the things that are Cæsar's;
22 and unto God the things that are God's. And when they heard it they marvelled, and left him, and went their way.

---

a In value sevenpence half penny : ch. 20 : 2....*b* Or, *inscription.*——1 See marginal note on ch. xviii. 28.

---

showed them by this term (Bengel) that he was indeed 'true,' and ready to speak out. **Shew me the tribute money,** the coin used in paying the poll-tax. It was natural that the Roman coin should be commonly used in paying it, as there was no exact equivalent in other coins. Hebrew shekels, etc., from the days of the Maccabaean kings, and various Greek coins (17 : 24, 27 Rev. Ver. *margin*), were also in use. The Herod family and the procurators were allowed to coin only copper money (Lutter.); any new silver coins were of necessity Roman. The emperors, down to Vespasian, as a concession to Jewish feeling, had coins made for that province without the head of the emperor (Keim), which would have been offensive as a "graven image." But Roman coins from other provinces would of course come into Judea, especially at the festivals, and one of these happened (as we say) to be handed to Jesus. **A penny,** properly 'a denarius,' a Roman coin, equal to about seventeen cents of our money. (Comp. on 18: 28.) This was the price of a day's labor in the parable (20: 2), and the daily wages of a Roman soldier (out of which he paid for his food), and seems also to have been the poll-tax at this time. **Image and superscription,** or 'inscription.' The former translation might suggest something written *above* the image, whereas the Greek word means only something written (or graven) *on* the coin. (Morison.) Many such coins are still extant, bearing the head of some emperor, with words giving his name and the value of the coin. Lightfoot quotes from the Talmud that "if a king's coin is current in a country, the men of the country do thereby evidence that they acknowledge him for their Lord"; and there are various other testimonies to the same effect. Wünsche tries to show the existence of an expectation that the Messiah would declare the Roman coins uncurrent, which expectation would be an interesting illustration of this passage if its existence were better established.

Our Lord's reply is one of those great sayings of his which cut into the heart of things (comp. 15: 11; Mark 2: 27), clearing up difficulties that had long perplexed many honest and devout Jews, and occasioned vain wrangling without end. Under the theocracy, religious duties and civil duties were both duties to the same Divine Ruler, and men had little occasion to distinguish between them. There was, indeed, as Geikie reminds us, a somewhat similar confusion of religion and civil government among heathen peoples, as for example the Roman emperor was always chief priest. Now, however, that the Jewish civil government was administered by heathen rulers, the distinction between civil and religious duties was of great importance, but the people in general did not perceive that distinction. Jesus holds up the coin, which belongs to Cesar, which they use as furnished by him, and thus vividly shows that there are duties to the civil ruler which are distinct from duties to God, and do not necessarily conflict with them. In another sense, every duty to other men or to ourselves is at the same time a duty to God, but that is not here the point. Paul afterwards expressed the Saviour's teaching on the subject in definite precept, when writing to Christians at the capital of the empire (Rom. 13: 1, 5); comp. 1 Pet. 2: 13-17. This was another case of our Lord's giving an object-lesson, like the child (18: 2), the fig-tree (21: 19), the feet-washing. **Render** as in 16: 27; 21: 41, literally *give back,* translated 'pay' in 5: 26; 18: 25, 28; 20: 8. The idea here seems to be, "You got this from Cesar, pay it back to him." Chrys.: "For this is not to give (v. 17), but to give back." **The things which are Cesar's,** not merely the tax, but all that citizens owe the civil government, one matter here suggesting all. **The things that are God's,** not simply the

23 The same day came to him the Sadducees, which say that there is no resurrection, and asked him,
24 Saying, Master, Moses said, If a man die, having no children, his brother shall marry his wife, and raise up seed unto his brother.
25 Now there were with us seven brethren: and the first, when he had married a wife, deceased, and having no issue, left his wife unto his brother:
26 Likewise the second also, and the third, unto the ª seventh.
27 And last of all the woman died also.

23 On that day there came to him Sadducees, [1] who say that there is no resurrection: and they asked
24 him, saying, [2] Master, Moses said, If a man die, having no children, his brother [3] shall marry his wife, and
25 raise up seed unto his brother. Now there were with us seven brethren: and the first married and deceased, and having no seed left his wife unto his brother;
26 in like manner the second also, and the third, unto
27 the [4] seventh. And after them all the woman died.

---

a Gr. *seven.*——1 Many ancient authorities read, *saying.*...2 Or, *Teacher.*...3 Gr. *shall perform the duty of a husband's brother to his wife.* Compare Deut. xxv. 5.....4 Gr. *seven.*

---

temple revenues, but all ceremonial and moral duties. The notion that, like the coin, our souls are stamped with the image of God, and must therefore be yielded to his service (Tert., Origen, and many), is a mere fancy. **They marvelled.** With all their hostility they could not help seeing that he had not only escaped from the dilemma (comp. Luke 20: 26), but had wonderfully cleared up an important question. Yet when there was time to reflect, they could not fail to perceive that Jesus had distinctly declined the role of a political and revolutionary Messiah, and this would gradually alienate from him the popular heart. (Comp. Weiss, "Life.")

II. **23-33.** The Sadducees Ask as to the Resurrection. Mark 12: 18-27 ; Luke 20: 27-40. This is a second hard question from a new source. V. 25-28. **The same day** seems clearly to show the close connection with what precedes; Mark and Luke again have simply 'and.' **The Sadducees** (see on 3: 7). Omit 'the.' It was not 'the Sadducees' as a class, but some persons belonging to that party. **Which say.** The participle without the article here probably means indefinitely (Jelf, ? 451, Obs. 2) 'persons who say' (as Mark, and as Origen paraphrases Matt.), while with the article it would be 'those persons who say,' [1] as Luke. **That there is no resurrection,** not only doubting but denying. This particular negative tenet of theirs (Acts 23: 8) is named to explain what follows. It must have been well known that Jesus taught the resurrection of the dead. (John 5 : 29; Luke 13 : 28.) **Master,** *teacher*, as in 22: 16. These priestly aristocrats prob-

ably felt contemptuous; but they were gentlemen, and must be civil ; one seems to detect a tone of polished scoffing in their attack. **Moses said,** in Deut. 25: 5 f. The quotation is condensed but without important alteration. Mark and Luke have 'his brother shall take his wife,' etc., as in Septuagint. Matt., writing especially for Jewish readers, takes pains to translate more exactly the Hebrew, as Sept. does in Gen. 38: 8. The Hebrew has a peculiar verb representing this peculiar law, *yebamah yibbemah,* 'her husband's brother shall husband's brother her,' shall act the part or perform the duty of a husband's brother to her. (See *margin* of Rev. Ver. in Matt.) From the late Latin *levir,* 'brother-in-law,' this precept of Deut. is commonly called the levirate law. A like usage exists now in Arabia, the Caucasus, and elsewhere (Smith's "Dict." Art. "Marriage"). It was an old custom (Gen. 38:8), which Moses did not abolish, but regulated and restricted, as he did with divorce (see on 5: 32) and blood revenge. No actual case is recorded in Old Test., but the custom is alluded to in Ruth 1: 11-13, and a related practice in Ruth 4: 1 ff. In our Lord's time the law was but little observed, as there was then less concern about maintaining families and family estates. The right of the husband's brother to decline (Deut. 25 : 7 ff.) is declared in the Mishna (Edersh.) to take precedence of the obligation to perform, and there was a growing disposition to limit the practice. The case described here by the Sadducees need not be supposed to have actually occurred. As in a parable, they tell the story for illustration. Seven is natural in

---

[1] The article is omitted by ℵ B D M S Z, about fifty cursives, Æth., and some Fathers. The participle without it would at first sight seem to mean 'came to him, saying,' which would be an incongruous and improbable sense, though it is so understood by Old Syriac and Pesh. The difficulty would be easily removed

by copyists through the mere insertion of the article. The indefinite use of the participle after an indefinite noun, 'Sadducees, (persons) who say,' though infrequent is unquestionable. So with the reading of W H. in 23: 24.

28 Therefore in the resurrection, whose wife shall she be of the seven? for they all had her.

29 Jesus answered and said unto them, Ye do err, not knowing the Scriptures, nor the power of God.

30 For in the resurrection they neither marry, nor are given in marriage, but are as the angels of God in heaven.

31 But as touching the resurrection of the dead, have ye not read that which was spoken unto you by God, saying,

28 In the resurrection therefore whose wife shall she be 29 of the seven? for they all had her. But Jesus answered and said unto them, Ye do err, not knowing 30 the scriptures, nor the power of God. For in the resurrection they neither marry, nor are given in 31 marriage, but are as angels[1] in heaven. But as touching the resurrection of the dead, have ye not

---

1 Many ancient authorities add, *of God.*

---

such a story as a round number. One imagines they had often nonplussed the Pharisees with the question, **in the resurrection whose wife shall she be?** The Pharisees generally held that the resurrection life would be a mere reproduction of this life, with all its relations and conditions restored and made permanent. The Cabalistic book Sohar, written late, but with much early material, says, "The woman who has married two in this world is in the world to come restored to the former." Maimonides (twelfth century) taught that children would be produced in the world to come. Some Rabbis in the Talmud declare (Wet., Wün.) that in the world to come there would be no eating and drinking, no trading, no marriage and production of children. But it is evident that the other opinion generally prevailed.

29 f. Ye do err. He speaks with kindness and decision. **Not knowing the Scriptures, nor the power of God.** *Bengel:* "The resurrection of the dead rests on the power of God; and our faith in a resurrection rests on the Scriptures." These Sadducees were accustomed to deny that the Scriptures so taught, and doubtless also maintained, as skeptics in all subsequent times have done, that a resurrection of the body is impossible. But 'the power of God' can accomplish it, and that not by merely restoring the conditions of this life, but by exalting to a different and higher type of existence. **For** introduces the explanation of the difficulty. **In the resurrection,** in the state of things represented thereby, in the risen life. **They neither marry,** etc., viz., in the sense of earthly marriage, which under its physical aspects,

is necessarily an *exclusive* relation, so that a woman cannot here be the wife of several men at the same time. There is nothing in this statement to forbid the persuasion, elsewhere countenanced in Scripture, that the relations of earthly life will be remembered in the future state, the persons recognized, and special affections cherished with delight; and we can imagine that exalted and spiritualized conjugal affections may then and there exist towards more persons than one. The idea is hard to accept now, only because we do not realize how great changes of feeling will accompany existence in the glorified body (1 Cor. 15: 44; Phil. 3: 21.) In heaven, the love of two that were successive husbands may be as little mutually exclusive as the love of two children or two sisters, and yet be intense, peculiar, and delightful. This is another of those sayings by which our Lord at one stroke cut into the heart of some difficulty, and laid it open. Comp. on v. 21. **But are as the angels in heaven,**[1] viz., in being exalted above merely physical conditions and relations. Luke's expression, 'are equal unto the angels,' amounts to the same thing. There is nothing at all here to imply that the saints *become* angels (comp. on 18: 10). Our Lord at the same time teaches that the Sadducees are wrong in denying the existence of angels.

31-33. Having explained how they err through not knowing 'the power of God,' he now shows their ignorance of the Scriptures on this subject. (v. 29.) **Have ye not read,** comp. on 21: 42; 12: 3. **Spoken unto you by God.** God spoke thus to Moses (Ex. 3: 6), and presently (3: 15) bade him speak likewise to the children of Israel. Matthew

---

1 The addition 'of God,' *margin* (Rev. Ver.) is wanting in B D, two cursives, most copies of the Old Latin, Old Syriac, Theb., Arm., and repeatedly in Origen. We might regard this as a "Western" omission, followed by B. and Origen (as does sometimes happen), but for the fact that one sees nothing to cause the omission.

On the other hand, 'angels of God' would be a natural marginal note to explain 'angels in heaven,' and might then easily creep into the text. Several of the documents which add the words here add them in Mark also.

32 I am the God of Abraham, and the God of Isaac, and the God of Jacob? God is not the God of the dead, but of the living.

33 And when the multitude heard *this*, they were astonished at his doctrine.

34 But when the Pharisees had heard that he had put the Sadducees to silence, they were gathered together.

32 read that which was spoken unto you by God, saying, I am the God of Abraham, and the God of Isaac, and the God of Jacob? God is not *the Gou* of the

33 dead, but of the living. And when the multitudes heard it, they were astonished at his teaching.

34 But the Pharisees, when they heard that he had put the Sadducees to silence, gathered themselves

and Mark quote from v. 6, Luke from v. 15. Luke says, 'even Moses signified.' It was inferred from this by Tert., Origen, Chrys., Jerome, and has been often repeated, that the Sadducees recognized none of the sacred books as authoritative except the Pentateuch. But there is no proof of more than that they valued the Pent. more highly than the other books, which was true in some degree of all the Jews. Luke's expression is sufficiently accounted for by the fact that apparent proofs of the resurrection were familiar in the prophets. Jesus means to say, not only have the prophets shown it, but even Moses. **The God,** v. 32, is in italics in Rev. Ver.; it is naturally understood to complete the sense. The Sadducees denied a resurrection of the body and any existence of spirits (Acts 23:8), which position would exclude a separate immortality of the soul, and so there is no occasion to doubt the statement of Josephus ("War," 2, 8, 14) that "they do away with the continued existence of the soul, and the punishments and rewards in Hades." Indeed the idea of separate immortality of the soul was little present to the mind of the Palestinian Jews, and the question lay simply between a resurrection of the body, and no future existence; so also in 1 Cor. ch. 15. If the passage of Exod. be taken in the superficial sense, an objector might fairly deny that it proves a resurrection of the dead. It might mean simply, "I am he who was the God of Abraham, Isaac, and Jacob during their life, and this is a pledge that I will be the God of their descendants." We cannot insist on the present tense 'am,' as many have followed Chrys. in doing; for the verb is not expressed at all in Mark nor in the Hebrew, and therefore certainly cannot be emphatic. But our Lord is the authority (7:29) for understanding the passage in a profounder sense, even as he claimed to reveal God. (11:27.) God here speaks of his covenant with the patriarchs; and the Eternal One would not make and avow such a covenant save with those whose existence is permanent. Our Lord then does not so much argue from the passage

in its obvious meaning, as authoritatively expound it in a deeper sense. To explain in this way the difficulty which the passage represents is not entirely satisfactory, but it is certainly more natural and reasonable, on the very lowest ground, than to suppose that Jesus failed to see the fallacy which would otherwise lurk in the argument. The Talmud (Wün.) tells of Rabbi Gamaliel (not Paul's teacher, but a later Rabbi) as convincing some Sadducee by arguing from 'them' in Deut. 11: 9, "in the land which the Lord sware unto your fathers to give them"; and of another Rabbi as proving the resurrection from Exod. 6: 4, "to give them the land of Canaan," viz., (v.3) to Abraham, Isaac, and Jacob. These do not involve the profound thought of the passage used by our Lord, and even these (Edersh.) may have been only poor imitations of his teaching. **The multitudes . . . were astonished** as in v. 22; 7: 28; 13: 54, **at his doctrine,** lit. *teaching,* see on 7: 28. Luke says that some of the Scribes (not of the Sadducees) answered, "Teacher, thou hast well said."

The story of the woman taken in adultery (John 7: 53 to 8: 11), which certainly does not belong where the common text gives it in John, is placed after Luke 21: 38 by the lost uncial represented by the four cursives, 13, 69, 124, 346. This would put it on the day of these several attacks upon Jesus, which it strikingly resembles both in aim and in result. As the story is in all probability historically true (see Hovey on John), it may perhaps be supposed that the interview really occurred on this day. Lange ("Life") and Ellicott would place it at the point we have now reached, Hitzig before the question of the Sadducees, Weiss before the question about tribute to Cesar; which latter view suits the phrase "early in the morning." (John 8: 1.)

III. **34-40.** A LAWYER ASKS WHICH IS THE GREAT COMMANDMENT. Mark 12: 28-34. Luke does not give this, probably because he had given a similar teaching in connection with the parable of the Good Samaritan, some months earlier. (Luke 10: 25 ff.)

35 Then one of them, *which was* a lawyer, asked *him a question*, tempting him, and saying,
36 Master, which is the great commandment in the law ?
37 Jesus said unto him, Thou shalt love the Lord thy God with all thy heart, and with all thy soul, and with all thy mind.

35 together. And one of them, a lawyer, asked him a
36 question, trying him, [1]Master, which is the great
37 commandment in the law ? And he said unto him, Thou shalt love the Lord thy God with all thy heart,

---

1 Or, *Teacher.*

34-36. The rivalry between the Pharisees and the Sadducees (see on 3 : 7) here appears. The former, who had withdrawn (v. 22), were doubtless pleased to find the Sadducees beaten in argument, their perhaps celebrated and to the Pharisees very perplexing question solved, and the doctrine of the resurrection more firmly established in the popular mind ; but all the more was it important that they themselves should make a further attack upon the Nazarene, lest his followers should think him victorious over all. **When the Pharisees had heard.** This may refer to the leading Pharisees who had put forward the juniors. (22 : 16.) **Put the Sadducees to silence.** The passive of the same verb is rendered 'was speechless' in 22: 12. It signifies literally *to muzzle* (1 Cor. 9 : 9), then to silence. (1 Pet. 2 : 15.) **They were gathered together,** either for consultation as to their next move (comp. v. 15), or to give the weight of a large attendance to the new enquiry. **One of them . . . a lawyer.** Mark, 'one of the Scribes.' The Scribes, from being authorized copyists of the law, and thus minutely acquainted with the text, had come to be recognized as authoritative expounders of its meaning, (see on 2: 4). In this capacity they were called 'lawyers,' a term found also six times in Luke, and in Titus 3: 13, and which may have been applied only to such Scribes as were particularly noted for their interpretations of the law. Some of them acted as formal 'teachers of the law' (law professors), Luke 5: 17; Acts 5: 34; 1 Tim. 1: 7. As the law of Moses united civil and religious precepts, these lawyers must be described to the modern mind as half lawyer, half theologian, corresponding to the original and proper use of the title LL. D., a Doctor of Laws, *i. e.*, of both civil law and canon law. They were looked up to as great authorities. But their citations and interpretations of Scripture-law were often belittled by petty quibbling, and were loaded with references to former decisions (comp. on 7 : 29), both of these being vices not confined to the lawyers or theologians of any one age. **Tempting him.** (Comp. on 22: 18; 16: 1). Putting him to the test, with the hope that he would say something unpopular, or perhaps that he might be drawn into a bitter and wrangling discussion. This the lawyer does as representative, and apparently by request, of the many Pharisees assembled. Mark shows (12: 28), that the lawyer himself had been favorably impressed by our Lord's answer to the Sadducees, and was a man inclined to true devoutness. The apparent conflict between this and Matthew's statement is removed by the supposition just made. To understand 'tempting' here in the good sense (Plump., Morison), is contrary to the nearly uniform and very frequent use of the word in the New Test., and does not harmonize with the tone of Matthew's narrative. **Which is the great commandment in the law?** More literally this would be : *What sort of commandment is great in the law ?* And such is the exact sense in 19: 18; 21: 23. The Jews were fond of classifying the commandments as great and small, or weighty and light. (23: 23.) Wünsche thinks that the object of so doing was to decide rightly in case of conflict between several precepts and prohibitions, since the rabbis taught that there was the same reward for observing the light as the weighty. Some held (Talmud Jer.) that "the words of the Scribes surpass the words of the law; for the words of the law are weighty and light, but the words of the Scribes are all weighty." The special hope in asking this question may have been (Keim) that he would take position for or against the "oral law." Our Lord's reply (v. 38) shows that he recognized a difference in the importance of the commandments.

37 f. Jesus said. 'Jesus' is wanting in some of the best documents, and was readily inserted by copyists (comp. on 14: 14). **With all thy heart,** etc., literally, '*in all,*' the love dwelling in the heart. (Comp. on 3: 11). The Hebrew (Deut. 6: 4 f.) has heart, soul,

38 This is the first and great commandment.
39 And the second *is* like unto it, Thou shalt love thy neighbour as thyself.
40 On these two commandments hang all the law and the prophets.
41 While the Pharisees were gathered together, Jesus asked them,

38 and with all thy soul, and with all thy mind. This
39 is the great and first commandment. [1]And a second like *unto it* is this, Thou shalt love thy neighbour as
40 thyself. On these two commandments hangeth the whole law, and the prophets.
41 Now while the Pharisees were gathered together,

---

1 Or, *And a second is like unto it, Thou shalt love, etc.*

---

might. We have repeatedly observed that in Hebrew usage the heart is regarded as the seat of thought and volition, as well as emotion. (See on 6: 21). A kindred Greek use is found only in Homer and the tragic poets (Lid. and Scott); for late Greek prose some other expression might seem to be needed. Accordingly, in Sept. heart is here rendered by a word equivalent to 'mind'; though in 2 Kings 23: 25 it translates literally ' heart, soul, might,' and 'heart, soul' in Deut. 10: 12; 30: 6. Matthew retains ' heart and substitutes ' mind' for the general term ' might,' which of course here denotes mental and not physical power; Mark and Luke give both 'mind' and ' might,' and presently Mark (12: 33) has the Scribe stating it as heart, understanding, might. All these amount to the same thing, piling up different terms to show that all our faculties and affections must be occupied with love to Jehovah. **The first and great commandment,** [1] greatest in importance, and first in proper order of statement.

39 f. After answering the immediate question, Jesus further states what is **the second.** This is quoted from Lev. 19: 18, same in Heb. and Sept. **Like unto it,** viz., like in nature, as being a commandment to love, and perhaps like as being also very important. **On these two commandments hang,** etc. Literally, as in Rev. Ver., *hangeth the whole law,* the verb being singular in the correct Greek text. Like the peg on which garments hang, these great precepts upheld all the other precepts of the law, yes, and of **the prophets.** (Comp. on 7: 12.) Every thing commanded in the Old Test. may be included under one or the other of these (comp. Romans 13: 8 f.); and all the instructions and promises serve to help in fulfilling these great precepts. A Rabbi once said (Wün.), " Name a little saying on which all essential teachings hang.

'In all thy ways acknowledge him.' (Prov. 3: 6.)" Plutarch says (Wet.): "'Know thyself,' and 'Nothing in excess'; for on these hang all the others.'" We see from Luke 10: 27 that at least some of the 'lawyers' were wont themselves to combine these two great commandments, as together telling what must be done in order to "inherit eternal life"; yet we may be sure they took a far less broad and spiritual view of them than Jesus took. The two are quoted from different books, but our Lord declares them similar, and places them in close relation. Some religionists incline to dwell on the first and neglect the other, some unbelievers eulogize the second and care nothing for the first. But there is no earnest and intelligent love to God without love to our neighbor; and the love of our neighbor derives its fundamental and necessary sanction from love to God. The second precept cannot stand alone, even in theory. Why should I subdue egoism and lift altruism to a level with it? Certain skeptical philosophers say that natural sympathy by frequent exercise hardens into altruism. But suppose this has not happened with me; why should I feel it my duty to sacrifice my interest or inclination for the benefit of others? The true and only sufficient answer is, that supreme duty to God includes and authenticates duty to man.—Mark tells us (12: 32, 34) that the Scribe fully recognized the propriety of the answer, and the superiority of these great ethical duties to all religious ceremony; and seeing that he answered sensibly, Jesus said, " Thou art not far from the kingdom of God."

IV. 41-46. JESUS QUESTIONS THE PHARISEES AS TO DAVID'S SON AND LORD, Mark 12: 35-37; Luke 20: 41-44. Having answered all the questions so as to command the admiration even of his enemies, our Lord finishes the conversation by turning on the Pharisees

---

[1] This was changed by many documents from 'great and first' to ' first and great,' as smoother. We can see, upon reflection, that the phrase properly begins with 'great,' because that was the point of the inquiry; but copyists, like modern compositors, seldom had time to reflect.

42 Saying, What think ye of Christ? whose son is he? They say unto him, *The son* of David.
43 He saith unto them, How then doth David in spirit call him Lord, saying,

42 Jesus asked them a question, saying, What think ye of the Christ? whose son is he? They say unto him, *The son* of David. He saith unto them, How then doth David in the Spirit call him Lord, saying,

with a question which they cannot answer (v. 46; comp. 21: 27), and which ought to set them to thinking how defective are their conceptions of the Messiah. He knew that he would be condemned by the Sanhedrin for saying that he was "the Christ, the Son of God"(26: 63-66; comp. John 5: 18); and he defends himself in advance (Godet) by pointing out that the Messiah cannot be a mere man. He takes occasion for this **while the Pharisees were gathered together.** (Comp. v. 34.) **What think ye of** (*the*) **Christ?** What is your opinion concerning the Messiah? Pulpit interpretation of the Com. Ver. has often treated 'What think ye of Christ?' entirely according to our present use of the term 'Christ'; but with the article it evidently means 'the Messiah.' (Comp. on 2: 4.) This general question is then especially applied, if not restricted, to the added inquiry, **Whose son is he?** To this there could be but one answer, according to universal Jewish opinion and recognized Scripture teaching (comp. 9: 27; 12: 23; 15: 22; 20: 30; 21: 9, 15; John 7: 41 f.); in Mark and Luke our Lord refers to the fact that the Scribes so taught.

43-45. Jesus here quotes the first verse of Psalm 110 as said by **David in** (*the*) **spirit**, and said concerning the Messiah. Certain critics maintain that Psalm 110 was not written by David, and does not relate to the Messiah. Now, if this be really so, let us all recognize the fact, and modify accordingly our conceptions as to the teachings of Jesus, and as to inspired teaching in general; for here would be the Saviour asserting two things which are both untrue, and making them the basis of his argument. This psalm is oftener quoted in the New Test. as Messianic than is any other portion of the Old Test. Besides the quotation here, which is recorded by Matthew, Mark, and Luke, it is quoted by Peter in Acts 2: 33-35, by Paul in 1 Cor. 15: 25, in Heb. 1: 13; 10: 12 f.; and is distinctly alluded to as Messianic in Eph. 1: 20; Heb. 1: 3; 1 Pet. 3: 22; while v. 4 is made the basis of a Messianic argument in Heb. 5: 6 to 7: 25. The psalm is expressly ascribed to David by Jesus himself in all three Gospels,

and by Peter at the Pentecost, basing his argument on that fact; and 'David' certainly cannot be here understood, as some wish to understand it in several other passages, to mean merely the book of Psalms; for the argument both of the Saviour and of Peter refers to the man himself. The inscription, "A Psalm of David," at least shows that such was an early Jewish opinion. It was regarded as Messianic by Jewish expositors (comp. Edersh., App. IX.) up to the tenth century (Toy); the mediaeval Jewish writers doubtless began to deny it in order to escape the Christian argument.

On what grounds then do some assert that the psalm was not written by David, and does not refer to the Messiah? The matter is of such interest as to justify a detailed statement.

(1) It is urged that the psalm cannot have been written by David, because the writer speaks of David as 'my Lord.' Therefore some think it was written by a contemporary and addressed to David; so Ewald, Meyer. A divine oracle from Jehovah was given David, as in v. 1, and the poet started from this. But David may in high prophetic vision be speaking immediately of the Messiah. There is no certain example of this elsewhere in the Old Test., unless Moses' prediction of a prophet like himself (Deut. 18: 15) be thought an exception. It is always primarily David, or Solomon, or Cyrus, or Israel, etc., and then secondarily the Messiah. But our Lord says that Abraham saw his day and rejoiced (John 8: 56); and this being true, it is certainly possible that David may have done likewise. Jesus distinctly says that this is the case; that David does here address the Messiah as Lord. If prophecy involves supernatural knowledge of the future, this *might be* the meaning; if Jesus possessed supernatural insight into Scripture, this *is* the meaning. If the critic assumes, as many destructive critics really do, that neither prophet nor Saviour possessed any truly supernatural knowledge, then the argument may as well be dropped, or must be transferred to another department of inquiry. (2) *Toy:* "The psalm is an address to a king, whose capital was Jerusalem, announcing his

coming victories over enemies, and his establishment in the dignity of priest. There is
nothing on its face to indicate that it referred to
any other person than the one addressed; or
that this person was other than a contemporary of the poet; there is no such pointing
to a coming man as in Isa. 11, Mic. 5, and
other prophetic passages; it is a present monarch to whom the psalmist speaks." But if
there is any real Messianic prophecy in the
Old Test., then it is natural that such a
prophecy should draw imagery from a king
at Jerusalem. There may be nothing on
the face of the psalm which without assistance would have shown us that it is Messianic; but there is nothing to show that it is
not, and the Founder of Christianity informs us that it *is* Messianic. As to the
use of present tenses, many prophecies describe future events as present or even as past.
In this second case also, the whole argument
really turns upon the question whether there
was a supernatural element in the teaching of
Jesus. (3) It is objected that most of the
psalm describes a conqueror and a temporal
sovereign, and so it cannot be an immediate
prediction of the New Test. Messiah. But
the Messiah is necessarily described through
images, and is in various other prophecies
conceived of as a king and conqueror. We
need not suppose that David or Abraham
foresaw the Messiah's offices and experiences
in all respects. (4) It is urged that the idea
of a Messiah-priest is foreign to the Old Test.,
which knows only a Messiah-king, (Reuss).
But this is a Messiah-king, who is declared to
be also priest; and Jehovah recognizes that
there is no parallel in Israel by seeking one
in Melchizedek. (5) Some say that to find in
the actual history a priest-king, we must
come down to Jonathan the Maccabee. Yes,
farther still, to Alexander Jannaeus (B. C.
105 to 78); and even Alexander's is not a parallel case, for he was a priest becoming king,
while the psalm has a king made also priest.
Even without the supernatural, certainly
ideas might arise in literature before the facts
occur in life. Besides, David and Solomon

sometimes offered sacrifice, assuming temporarily the functions of priest; and the psalm
speaks of its king as a priest forever. So, the
idea is not impossible or unintelligible for the
men of David's time. And though supernatural prophecy usually drew its imagery from
the actual, it certainly might make new and
easy combinations of existing objects or ideas.
(6) The *language* has been held to show a far
later time than that of David. Some critics
have laid stress on this argument and afterwards silently abandoned it. Hitzig insists
that two words in the psalm clearly prove it
to have been written after the captivity.[1] But
Ewald says: "As also the language of the
song does not oppose, it is to be regarded as
certain that the king is David; for king and
kingdom appear here at the highest point of
nobleness and glory." Hitzig's proofs from
language cannot be very strong, when Ewald
brushes them so unceremoniously aside. In
fact, they amount to practically nothing.

These are all the objections that are known
to have been adduced. Only the first and
second have any considerable force, and certainly they are very far from being conclusive. Yet these are the grounds upon which
some even of reverent critics take the position
that Jesus has here based an important argument upon two downright errors. It is true
that the knowledge of our Lord's human
mind was limited (comp. on 21: 19); but that
is a very different thing from saying that it
was erroneous, and that he used error as a
means of instructing and convincing others.

In (*the*) **spirit.** The Greek expression, if it
stood alone, would be ambiguous, for it might
mean, as all the early English versions here
render, 'in spirit,' viz., in his own spirit (as in
John 4: 23). But the term Spirit soon became among the Christians equivalent to a
proper name, and so might be understood as
definite without an article, meaning the Holy
Spirit (as in John 3: 5). Now in the parallel passage of Mark (12: 36 R. V.), it is 'in the
Holy Spirit.' We cannot always determine
the exact meaning of language from a parallel
passage. But here the connection is precisely

---

[1] The word *yalduth*, 'youth,' is found elsewhere only
in Eccl., which it is taken for granted was written after
the exile. The word *mishchar*, 'morning,' is held to be
a late formation by addition, instead of the simple
shahar, like *mesar, migrash*, Ezek. 36: 5, instead of *sar*,
geresh. But the very word *migrash* is used as a noun in
Num. and Josh. And *mishhar*, though found only here,
is a regular *Hebrew* formation. not characteristically
Aramaic. So *mischak*, laughter, is found only in Hab.
1: 10; and *mishtar*, dominion, only in Job 38: 33.

44 The Lord said unto my Lord, Sit thou on my right hand, till I make thine enemies thy footstool ?
45 If David then call him Lord, how is he his son ?
46 And no man was able to answer him a word, neither durst any *man* from that day forth ask him any more *questions.*

44 The Lord said unto my Lord,
Sit thou on my right hand,
Till I put thine enemies underneath thy feet ?
45 If David then calleth him Lord, how is he his son ?
46 And no one was able to answer him a word, neither durst any man from that day forth ask him any more questions.

the same, and so Mark's expression may be taken as defining that of Matt. Comp. exactly the same Greek phrase in Rev. 1: 10; 4: 2, and nearly the same in Rom. 9: 1; 1 Cor. 12: 3. As to the idea here conveyed, comp. Acts 4: 25; Heb. 3: 7 (quoting a psalm), and 10: 15; also 9: 8, where the Spirit teaches through a type, and 2 Pet. 1: 21. These passages strongly assert that the Holy Spirit speaks through David in Psalm 2 and 110; also that he speaks in Psalm 95 and Jer. 31: 33; and that he speaks through the prophets in general. There is here no theory of inspiration; nothing taught as to the precise nature or *modus operandi* of that influence of the Spirit under which David spoke. But it evidently means a supernatural influence.

The Septuagint here exactly translates the Hebrew, and is closely followed in Luke, Acts, Hebrews. But instead of 'as the footstool of thy feet,' Matt. and Mark in the correct Greek text have simply 'underneath thy feet,' which was readily changed by copyists to agree with the Sept.[1] **The Lord said unto my Lord.** In the Hebrew, 'Jehovah (*Yahweh*) said unto my Lord.' The later Jews had a superstitious dread of pronouncing the proper name of the God of Israel, and when they came to it in reading would substitute, as the Jews do to this day, *Adonai,* the Lord. Accordingly the Sept. translators, who were Jews, rendered the proper name by *Kurios,* 'Lord.' When the Massoretic scholars, some centuries after Christ, undertook to write vowels under the consonants of the Hebrew words, they gave to the proper name, *J h v h* the vowels of the word *Adonai* which they were accustomed to substitute, with a slight modification of the first vowel which Hebrew

usage warranted. This has led to the modern pronunciation Jehovah. But there can be no doubt that the word was originally pronounced with other vowels; and its sound was probably *Jahveh,* or to represent it more exactly in English letters, *Yahweh.* Our English versions of the Old Test. have always in like manner represented this proper name by 'the Lord,' and it has become common to print 'the Lord' in capitals in those cases to distinguish it from *Adonai.* There would be great advantage in substituting Jehovah, as preferred by American Revisers, see Appendix, as showing that a proper name is really meant; and the mere matter of correctly representing the Hebrew vowels would be of little practical importance. The New Test. writers, being accustomed to read and often to quote the Sept., have followed its practice; and it is sometimes not easy to determine whether *kurios* means Jehovah, or simply Lord in the more general sense. **Sit thou on my right hand.** This was naturally the post of highest honor at the court, where one could be conveniently consulted by the monarch in judging his people, comp. 19: 28; Psa. 45: 9. **Make thine enemies,** etc., better as Rev. Ver., *put thine enemies underneath thy feet.* This is an image founded on the practice described in Josh. 10: 24; comp. Psa. 47: 3. The Messiah will share the divine reign and conquering power **till** all his enemies are completely subdued, and will then give back his delegated Messianic dominion (28: 18) to the Father. (1 Cor. 15: 28.)

The question repeated and pressed in v. 45 was no catch-question, such as the Phar. and Sadd. had addressed to him. (v. 17, 28.) It tended to show that the Messiah could not be

[1] 'Underneath,' *hupokato,* is here read by א B, D, L, several other uncials, and some cursives, the Egyptian and other versions. It was easily changed by copyists into *hupopodion,* 'footstool.' Nothing is more common in the manuscripts of the New Test. than to find a quotation altered in conformity with the Sept. In Mark *hupokato* is given by B, D, the Egyptian versions, etc. *Hupopodion* is read with slight variation in Luke, and without any variation in Acts and Hebrews. So it is

clear that 'underneath' is the true reading in Matt., and pretty clear in Mark, (Rev. Ver. *margin*). This 'underneath' is probably a mere simplification, but may have come (Toy) from the Sept. of Psa. 8: 7. The newspaper critics who have ridiculed Rev. Ver., in Luke, Acts, etc., for using such a phrase as 'footstool of thy feet,' did not know that they were ridiculing the originals.

a mere temporal sovereign, nor in fact a mere man.

46. No man was able to answer him a word. (Comp. Luke 14: 6.) According to their conception of the Messiah the question was unanswerable. It was afterwards answered by one who was at that time a young Pharisee, though we know not whether then studying in Jerusalem or absent at Tarsus. This Pharisee lived to gain such revelation of Jesus the Messiah, and such understanding of the Messianic Scriptures, as to perceive that he was " made (*born*) of the seed of David according to the flesh, and declared to be the Son of God with power, according to the Spirit of holiness, by the resurrection of the dead." (Rom. 1 : 3 f., comp. 9 : 5.) The fact that no one **durst from that day forth ask him any more questions** is also stated by Mark and Luke as the result of this same series of questions and answers. Mark (12 : 34) makes the remark at the close of the lawyer's question to Jesus, the last question of his enemies; and Luke (20 : 40) at the close of the question by the Sadducees, the last that he records. All the select wisdom and ingenuity of the learned and ruling classes, in both the great parties, had brought their most puzzling questions to the young teacher from Nazareth, who had never studied in any of the schools (John 7 : 15 ff.), and he not only gave in every case an answer of astonishing depth and clearness, which sent the wisest men away in wondering reflection, but at length retorted by a question which no one could answer, and which seemed plainly to indicate that their views of the Messiah were radically defective. Our Lord went right on discoursing, attacking the ruling classes with the most outspoken and unsparing severity (ch. 23), but they dared not any more interrupt or inquire. They were helpless in argument, and as usual with foiled and angry disputants who will not be convinced, they had no hope but in violence. At this point Mark says (12 : 37), 'And the common people heard him gladly.' The people who thronged the temple court had no position to lose, and no pride of learning; they were more hospitable to new truth, and were not sorry to see arrogant rabbis and priestly aristocrats put to shame.

HOMILETICAL AND PRACTICAL.

V. 15. CHRYS.: "'Then.' When? When most of all they ought to have been moved to compunction, when they should have been amazed at his love to man, when they should have feared the things to come."—V. 16. Jesus praised by his enemies. 1) Acute flatterers may show what reputation a person really desires. 2) What these flattering foes said of Jesus we know from other sources to have been thoroughly correct; (a) he was true, (b) he taught the way of God in truth, (c) and without fear or favor. 3) There are other recorded instances of unwilling testimony to Jesus. 4) The day is coming when every tongue shall confess that he is Lord (Phil. 2 : 11.)—Alexander: "Such adulation (as was here offered to Jesus) has blinded the eyes and warped the judgment of its thousands and its tens of thousands among human sages, and especially of those who glory in their insusceptibility of flattery."—V. 17. It is much to be desired that people shall often ask their religious teacher concerning questions of truth and duty. Even when questions are asked with evil motives, as a test or a snare, it is well to escape the snare by prudent answers (v. 46), and to silence the evil-disposed (Tit. 1 : 11), and better still to give answers that will clear up real difficulties (v. 21), and enlighten the well-disposed. (V. 22 ; Mark 12 : 7.) Human tempters may often be not merely overcome, but won to wiser judgments and kinder feelings.—V. 18. 'Jesus perceived their wickedness.' He knows to-day all that is in the hearts of those who are openly trying to injure his cause and dishonor his name, and of those who hypocritically pretend to be his friends.—'Hypocrites.' JEROME: "It is the highest excellence in one who replies to know the mind of the questioner."—V. 21. Civil and religious duties. 1) It is a religious duty to perform all real civil duties. 2) It is not a civil duty to perform religious duties. Laws as to Sabbath observance, etc., can be based only on public health and moral welfare, and the right of worshipers to be undisturbed. 3) Careful observance of the distinction between civil and religious duties is necessary to freedom of conscience, and greatly promotive of genuine piety. Here, as everywhere, liberty has its embarrassments and perils, but on the whole it is far best.—Civil duties may still be binding when the ruler is personally immoral and tyrannical; Cesar here was Tiberius, and when

CHAPTER XXIII.

THEN spake Jesus to the multitude, and to his disciples,

1   Then spake Jesus to the multitudes and to his
2 disciples, saying, The Scribes and the Pharisees sit

Paul and Peter urged obedience it was to Nero. CHRYS.: "But thou when thou hearest, 'render unto Cesar the things which are Cesar's,' know that he is speaking only of those things which are no detriment to godliness; since if it be any such thing as this, such a thing is no longer Cesar's tribute, but the devil's."

V. 28 f. Skeptics often have favorite catch-questions; but superficial and ridiculing inquiries are much better than silent neglect, and they should usually be met with a kind and thoughtful answer, and may sometimes be made the occasion of establishing positive truth. All skepticism as to Christian truth results in part from ignorance of the Bible, and of the divine attributes.—V. 29 ff. The resurrection of the dead. 1) It is taught in the Bible, (a) even in the Pentateuch, (b) in the Prophets, (c) in the New Test. (2 Tim. 1: 10.) 2) It puts great honor upon the human body. (Psa. 139: 14; Phil. 3: 21.) 3) It gives vividness to our conceptions of eternal existence and felicity. 4) It will exalt above much of the narrowness and exclusiveness of earthly relations and affections. CHRYS.: "Since then the resurrection is like this, come let us do all things that we may obtain the first honors there."

V. 36. All commandments of God are in one sense equally binding, and the spirit of obedience is tested by all; but some relate to matters intrinsically more important. Those commandments are greatest which are most spiritual, most opposed to selfishness, most comprehensive. Duty to God is in itself the highest duty, and comprehends all other duties.—V. 37. Love is the attraction of gravitation in the moral universe, binding moral creatures to each other, and all alike to God. Loving God and knowing God are mutually dependent. Pascal remarks that in other things we must know in order to love; in religion we must love in order to know. Sources from which we may gain knowledge of God—from nature—from human nature—from 'the image of the invisible God' ("God was made flesh, that flesh might see that God is love")—from revelation in general—from

observation of his providence, and communion with his Spirit. Reasons for loving God. 1) Because he is God. 2) Because he is our God. Means of increasing our love to God—think of him much—speak of him with reverence—cultivate delight in his worship—see him in history, and in our own life—obey his commandments—strive to bring others to love him too.—V. 39. 'Thou shalt love thy neighbor as thyself.' 1) Why should I love my neighbor as myself? 2) Who is the neighbor I must love as myself? 3) What is involved in loving my neighbor as myself?

V. 42–45. The Messiah. 1) To account the Messiah merely a man, is hopelessly inconsistent with Scripture. 2) The Jewish Messiah is also the world's Messiah. 3) The Messiah reigns now on the right hand of God. 4) Shall we live as the Messiah's enemies, to be trampled under foot, or as his loving subjects, to inherit the kingdom (25 : 34)?—V. 46. HENRY: "Many are silenced that are not saved, many convinced that are not converted."

Ch. 23: 1-12. WARNINGS AGAINST THE SCRIBES AND PHARISEES.

Partly found also in Mark 12: 38 f.; Luke 20: 45 f. This discourse probably belongs to Tuesday, three days before the crucifixion. The solemn intimations made early in the day that he knew the Jewish rulers would reject and kill him, and would be terribly punished for it (21: 23 to 22: 14), were followed by the sharp questioning of 22: 15-46; and now, having vanquished his opponents in question and answer, Jesus speaks out plainly about the Scribes and Pharisees, first warning the people against them (23: 1-12), and then denouncing upon them a series of mournful woes. (13-39.) After that he will speak no more in public, but will leave the temple, and give the final discourse to his disciples on the Mount of Olives. (chap. 24 and 25.) All these discourses follow each other in natural connection, and to all appearance were spoken on the same day. The attempts of some critics to scatter them upon different days are arbitrary and useless. Of these warnings and woes

2 Saying, The scribes and the Pharieees sit in Moses' seat:

3 on Moses' seat: all things therefore whatsoever

found in chap. 23, Mark and Luke give only a very small portion.

1. Then naturally suggests, though it does not necessarily mean (see on 3: 13), that the following was on the same day as the foregoing. **To the multitude and to his disciples.** His previous discourses during the day were addressed mainly to the rulers and the persons who came questioning—though in hearing of others. (Luke 20:9.) He now turns away from these leading persons and addresses himself to the people at large and to his immediate followers, the latter being specially addressed in v. 8-12. Luke has (20: 45, Rev. Ver.), "In the hearing of all the people he said unto his disciples"; which does not materially differ. A year before (comp. on 15: 7), Jesus had begun to censure the Scribes and Pharisees with outspoken severity; and within a few months, probably in Perea, clearly not at Jerusalem, he had denounced woes upon them and warned the people against them. (Luke 11: 37-54.) Now he does the same thing at Jerusalem, in the temple court, during the great feast of the Passover; and these denunciations form the climax and conclusion of his public discourses. It is natural that he should have thus spoken out earlier elsewhere than at Jerusalem during the feast; and it is much more reasonable to suppose such a repetition under these changed circumstances (comp. at beginning of chap. 5), than to suppose that either Luke or Matthew has utterly displaced these momentous teachings. Notice that Mark and Luke both report at this same quarter small portions of the discourse given by Matthew.

I. 2-4. The Scribes and the Pharisees do not Practice what they Teach. **The Scribes,** see on 2: 4; **the Pharisees,** see on 3: 7. **Sit in Moses' seat,** has in the Greek sentence an emphatic position. Literally the verb is *sat*, 'have sat,' have taken a seat there—which leaves it to be understood that they so remain; comp. Heb. 8: 1. Not

only the judge (Exod. 18: 13) but in later times the teacher, usually spoke in a sitting posture. (5:1; 13:2; Luke 4:20; Acts 22:3.) The Greek term for 'seat' is *kathedra*, and as borrowed into Latin gave the phrase "to speak *ex cathedra*," *i. e.*, "from the seat" of an authoritative teacher. The Rabbinical writers speak of a Rabbi's successor as sitting in his seat; so we, as to a professor's "chair," which word is our contracted form of *cathedra* (Skeat). Our Lord means, then, that the Scribes and Pharisees are in some sense successors of Moses, teachers of the law as he was. They claimed this, and to a certain extent the claim was just, since most of their explanations were substantially conformed to Scripture. The time had not come for turning away from their teachings to new and better teachers. **All therefore whatsoever they bid you** is set in contrast to **their works.** He meant in a general way to commend their *instructions* in religious duty as correct, and then to contrast strongly their *practice* as wrong. We know that he condemned the exaggerated importance they attached to their traditions (15:3,6), and their general spirit. (16:6.) The common Greek text has 'bid you observe,' but the authority against adding 'observe' is overwhelming. **Observe and do,** the verb being in the tense of continued action—continually observe. **They say, and do not.** So he had already declared in Galilee (15:7-9), and now repeats in Jerusalem on the most public cccasion. **For they bind,** *yea* represents the correct Greek text. **Heavy burdens** (comp. 11: 28), the strict requirements of tradition as to ceremonial observances and the details of moral duty; comp. Luke 11: 46. Peter substantially repeated this statement in Acts 15: 10. The image is of binding fagots of wood or bundles of grain; the idea is of combining many separate precepts or requirements until together they make a heavy load.

The term rendered **grievous to be borne** does not belong here, but was brought in by copyists from Luke 11: 46.[1] **Will not move**

---

[1] It is wanting in several early versions and some MSS., and Origen on Matt. expressly mentions that Luke adds this term. It might be easily inserted here from Luke, while on the other hand no one could have any reason for omitting it if originally present; so it is doubtless spurious in Matt. W H. place it in their margin here, apparently because B has it, and because the documents for omitting have an "Alexandrian" look.

3 All therefore whatsoever they bid you observe, *that* observe and do; but do not ye after their works: for they say, and do not.

4 For they bind heavy burdens and grievous to be borne, and lay *them* on men's shoulders; but they *themselves* will not move them with one of their fingers.

5 But all their works they do for to be seen of men: they make broad their phylacteries, and enlarge the borders of their garments,

6 And love the uppermost rooms at feasts, and the chief seats in the synagogues,

they bid you, *these* do and observe: but do not ye 4 after their works; for they say, and do not. Yea, they bind heavy burdens, [1]and grievous to be borne, and lay them on men's shoulders; but they them- 5 selves will not move them with their finger. But all their works they do for to be seen of men: for they make broad their phylacteries, and enlarge the 6 borders *of their garments,* and love the chief place

---

1 Many ancient authorities omit, *and grievous to be borne.*

---

them with one of their fingers does not mean that the burdens are easy to move, but that they will not make the slightest exertion to move them; far less will they take them on their shoulders.

II. **5-7.** THE SCRIBES AND THE PHARISEES ARE OSTENTATIOUS. Mark 12: 38 f.; Luke 20: 46. **To be seen of men,** 'with a view to be looked at by men,' the same phrase as in 6: 1. The desire for human praise was, and often is, a great hindrance to believing in Christ, and confessing him. (John 5: 44; 12: 42 f.) *For they make* is the correct Gr. text, and introduces the *proof* of the foregoing. **They make broad their phylacteries.** In Exod. 13: 16; Deut. 6: 8; 11: 18, it was said to Israel concerning the teachings of the law, that they should be bound "for a token upon thine hand, and for frontlets between thine eyes." Here an image seems to be drawn from the old Egyptian practice of wearing amulets; the Israelites were to keep the law always near them, always in mind. In the interbiblical period we find the Jews converting this figure into outward fact. They took four passages adjacent to the thrice repeated injunction, viz., Exod. 13: 2-10, 11-17; Deut. 6: 4-9; 11: 13-22, and writing them on strips of parchment, encased the folded strips in minute leather boxes. These four boxes were set on edge and fastened upon one leather base, which was placed on the middle of the forehead, and held there by a string tied round the head with peculiar knots, which had a mystical meaning. Four similar strips were placed in a smaller single box, which was worn on the palm of the hand by the Sadducees, apparently because the hand is mentioned in the figurative injunction, but by the Pharisees on the left arm near the heart, because of Deut. 6: 6, "and these words . . . shall be in (or *upon*) thy heart." They placed the box on the bare arm, as near the

heart as possible, fastening it with a mystically knotted string, and then covering it with the sleeve. These leather boxes must be made from the skin of a "clean" animal, and colored black. Phylacteries similar to those thus described by the Rabbinical writers are now worn by the stricter Jews, the details slightly varying in different countries; and those long used by some deceased Rabbi may be bought in the shops of Jerusalem. These little boxes with their contents are called by the Targum of Onkelos and by the Rabbinical writers *tephillin,* "prayers," because put on before praying (see Buxtorf); they were worn by men in general during public worship, but by the Pharisees worn continually. Matthew's term *phylactery,* found nowhere else in the Greek Bible, signifies in classical Greek a guarded post, then a safeguard, finally an amulet, as guarding against evils. The Rosetta stone speaks of "golden phylacteries" worn by the kings of Egypt. (Lid. and Scott.) The Rabbinical writings show that many Jews regarded the phylacteries as amulets; and it seems most likely that the Greek term was commonly employed among the Jews in that sense (so Jerome), and Matt. merely used it because it was common. The term might etymologically mean 'a place for guarding' the divine word (Schöttgen, Stier), but there is no usage for that sense. Justin Martyn tells Trypho (ch. 46) that Moses commanded the people to wear a phylactery, but does not throw any light in his connection upon the meaning of the term. The Pesh. here translates by *tephillin,* the Rabbinical word. The Council of Laodicea (fourth century) forbade clerics to make phylacteries, declaring (with a play upon the word) that they are prisons of their souls, and those who wear them must be expelled from the church. (Suicer.) Chrys. compares the fact that "many of our women now wear Gospels

7 And greetings in the markets, and to be called of men, Rabbi, Rabbi.
8 But be not ye called Rabbi: for one is your Master, even Christ: and all ye are brethren.

7 at feasts, and the chief seats in the synagogues, and the salutations in the marketplaces, and to be called
8 of men, Rabbi. But be not ye called Rabbi: for one

hung from their necks.'' Some modern writers have maintained that Moses intended these literal frontlets and armlets to be worn as a substitute for the superstitious Egyptian amulets. But how could Moses fail to see that they would themselves be worn as amulets? We find no evidence of their use until the latter part of the interbiblical period, and the general tendency to scrupulosity about externals would account for their appearance at that time. The Karaite Jews (who arose in the eighth Christian century) have always understood these passages of the law as figurative, holding that the hand represents precepts for action, and the head represents the mental and spiritual. Comp. Prov. 3: 3; 6: 21; Ezek. 24: 17. Making their phylacteries unusually broad would show every casual observer that the Pharisees were remarkably pious. The head being bare, or covered only with a cloth, this cube of some two inches on every side, projecting from the centre of the forehead, would attract great attention. **Enlarge the borders (of their garments).** These peculiar ' borders' were commanded to be worn (Num. 15: 38), and were worn by Jesus. (See on 9: 20.) It does not follow that he wore the phylacteries. Matthew's Jewish readers would at once understand 'enlarge the borders'; but many copyists thought it necessary for perspicuity to add, 'of their garments,' and this naturally crept into the Common text. **Love the uppermost rooms** (or *chief place*) **at feasts.** The feast is here *deipnon*, see on 22: 4. The guests *reclined* on couches, see on 8: 11. The place of highest honor for a guest apparently was to recline just in front of the host, so that the head could be laid back in the host's bosom. (John 13: 23-25; Luke 16: 22.) In general, the most honorable places were those near the host. Mark and Luke have the plural, 'chief places'; all three use the same Greek word, literally, *chief reclining-place.* The old ren-

dering, 'rooms,' really meant simply places, but would now suggest apartments. ' Uppermost' was probably used here by Tyn., Cran., K. J., because of the phrase 'come up higher' (Luke 14: 10), and the English expression, "the upper end of the table." **The chief seats in the synagogues** were the front seats nearest to the place in which the rolls of the law were kept. For 'synagogues,' see on 4: 23. **And greetings** (*salutations*) **in the markets,** that is, *the market places.* They were the general places of assembly, for men of all pursuits. Indeed, the Greek word denotes primarily a place of gathering or assembly, the thought of buying and selling being subordinate. The Asiatics have always attached great importance to profoundly respectful salutations in public intercourse. Not in Paris, but only in China, could one find such elaborate courtesy as in an old-fashioned sheik who meets you in Palestine, as he touches his lips and forehead and breast, each time bowing low, and saying, "Salaam to you!" **And to be called of men, Rabbi,** the common Jewish word for teacher. (See on 8: 19.) It means, etymologically, 'great one' or 'superior,' like master from *mag-ister*, and somewhat like "His Excellency," "Your Highness," etc. The office and its title were much coveted among the Jews in the time of Christ and afterwards. Statements of later writers make it probable (Herzog) that the use, or at any rate the frequent use, of the title began in the time of Hillel and Shammai, in the generation preceding the Christian era.[1]

III. **8-12.** CHRIST'S DISCIPLES MUST NOT BE LIKE THE SCRIBES AND PHARISEES. Jesus turns from his account of the inconsistent and ostentatious Jewish teachers to warn his disciples (comp. v. 1) against doing likewise. Keim thinks it impossible that in an address to the *people* (v. 1) Jesus should have introduced admonitions to the disciples con-

[1] The doubling of Rabbi (common Greek text) is against the earliest Greek MSS. and most of the early versions. Yet the doubling accords with a frequent Jewish practice (Lightf.), while to copyists, ignorant of that practice, it would be apt to seem superfluous; so we cannot, with entire confidence, reject it. 'Even (the) Christ' (v. 8), is no doubt spurious, added from v. 10; as also 'teacher' was here changed by some documents to 'guide,' the word in v. 10.

9 And call no *man* your father upon the earth: for one is your Father, which is in heaven.
10 Neither be ye called masters: for one is your Master, *even* Christ.

9 is your teacher, and all ye are brethren. And call no man your father on the earth: for one is your
10 Father, [1] *even* he who is in heaven. Neither be ye called masters: for one is your master, *even* the

1 Gr. *the heavenly.*

cerning their one Teacher the Messiah, and should then have launched 'woes' against the Pharisees, "as if he were speaking to them." But what strange criticism is here. With a heterogeneous crowd thronging around him, nothing was more natural than that an impassioned popular speaker should turn from one class of his hearers to another. After v. 12 it might even be supposed that some of the Scribes and Pharisees, hearing in the outskirts of the throng that he was warning the people against them, had pressed their way through and were just then drawing near with hostile looks, so as to furnish an immediate occasion for his addressing them.

Be not ye called Rabbi, with emphasis on 'ye,' as the Greek indicates. Do not crave the honor of being recognized as a religious teacher. **For one is your Master,** *teacher.* The Rabbis were independent, and any one of them might found a distinct school. But Christians are all pupils in one school of Jesus, and among them is no difference of dignity. So Ignatius addresses the Ephesians (ch. 3) as his "schoolmates." As Rabbi is equivalent to the Latin Doctor, 'teacher,' some literalists urge that to call a minister "Doctor" is here definitely prohibited. But the matter goes far deeper. What our Lord prohibits is desire for the distinction involved in being recognized as a religious teacher. A man who shows great desire to be "invited into the pulpit," or otherwise publicly treated as a minister, is exactly violating this command. The title of Doctor of Divinity is often so conferred, so sought, so borne, and sometimes so declined, as to come under this head, but it is the spirit involved rather than the phrase that should be condemned. It would be better to have no distinctive titles, seeming to set one minister above others, for there really is danger of forgetting that **all ye are brethren.** Yet (*Schaff*) "our addressing others by the usual titles is not forbidden; pride taking the form of want of courtesy cannot find shelter here." The folly of mere verbal and literalistic interpretation

is seen in the fact that persons who vehemently declaim against the use of "Doctor," as being prohibited in v. 8, are often fond of calling some venerable minister "Father," which is equally prohibited in v. 9. The Jews often addressed a religious teacher as 'Father' (Buxtorf, comp. 2 Kings 2: 12), even as the "sons of the prophets" and the "sons" of the Pharisees were their pupils. (Comp. on 12: 27.) Romanists habitually call a priest "Father," and the sovereign priest they call "Holy Father." So *Abbot* is derived from *abba*, 'father,' and *Pope* is the same word as the English *papa;* in the Greek Church *papas* is applied to any priest. In the Church of England a bishop is sometimes formally addressed as "Right Reverend Father in God." While earnestly condemning all this, we do well to remember that Stephen said, "Brethren and fathers, hearken" (Acts 7: 2); comp. also 1 Cor. 4: 15. **One is your Father, which is in heaven,** more exactly as by Amer. Revisers, 'even he who is in heaven,' literally 'the heavenly (one),' comp. on 6: 9.

10 ff. Master is here *kathegetes,* guide, instructor, see on 8: 19. **Even** (*the*) **Christ,** the Messiah, see on 2: 4. Jesus is not here distinctly saying before the hostile hearers that he is the Messiah. His disciples so understood him, but he did not publicly avow himself as such until he appeared before the Sanhedrin. (26: 64, comp. on 21: 16.) **He that is greatest among you,** etc., is repeated from 20: 26. 'Greatest' is here literally '*greater* (than all others),' as in 18: 1. In this matter also there may be loud professions without the reality. One who with strict and ostentatious literalness calls himself "servant of servants of the servants of God," yet claims to be sovereign of the Christian world. **Whosoever shall exalt himself,** seeking to attract human notice and praise. **Shall be abased.** The Greek has *humbled . . . . humble;* the early English versions, except Rheims, unnecessarily varied the translation, e. g., Com. Version. The saying of v. 12 had been given before, probably a week or

11 But he that is greatest among you shall be your servant.

12 And whosoever shall exalt himself shall be abased; and he that shall humble himself shall be exalted.

11 Christ. But he that is [1] greatest among you shall 12 be your [2] servant. And whosoever shall exalt himself shall be humbled; and whosoever shall humble himself shall be exalted.

1 Gr. *greater*....2 Or, *minister.*

---

two earlier, in Perea, Luke 18: 14. It is very natural that any saying uttered at a distance should afterwards be repeated in Jerusalem. The lesson of humility is one peculiarly needing to be often repeated. In one form or another, Jesus has taught it many times; comp. on 18: 4; and comp. Prov. 15: 33; 29: 23; James 4: 6; 1 Pet. 5: 5. The Talmud has similar sayings, especially one (Wün.), "Whoever humbles himself God exalts, and whoever exalts himself God humbles," which may have been borrowed from the Gospels, or may have been built on Ezek. 21: 26.

HOMILETICAL AND PRACTICAL.

V. 2-4. Teaching without practicing. 1) A very faulty man *may* give teaching that is Scripturally correct. 2) A man who utterly neglects his own duty is often very severe in laying down the duty of others. 3) We must often disregard a teacher's evil example, and heed his correct precept. 4) Yet how much better, for teacher and for hearers, when he that says, also does. CHRYS.: "For what can be more wretched than a teacher, when it is the preservation of his disciples not to give heed to his life." HENRY: "What greater hypocrisy can there be, than to press that upon others to be believed and done, which they themselves disbelieve and disobey; pulling down in their practice what they build up in their preaching; when in the pulpit, preaching so well that it is pity they should ever come out; but when out of the pulpit living so ill that it is pity they should ever come in."

V. 5. A man's aims determine the moral quality of his actions. The desire for popular applause may render a man very careful about outward religious observances or formal orthodoxy, but not about inward piety.—V. 5-12. Ministerial greatness lies 1) not in dress, or any outward display of pious punctilio; 2) not in social honors, or public recognition;

3) not in titles, or admiring followers; but[4]) in humble service of others.—V. 11 f. Humility. 1) Professed humility is often only covert pride. 2) Effort to be humble in hope of exaltation may impose on ourselves, and on many of our fellow-men, but cannot deceive God. 3) True humility has not time to think of self, because busy with serving others, by speech and action. 4) Genuine humility will lead to exaltation, in God's own good time and way. (1 Pet. 5: 6 f.)

13-39. WOES DENOUNCED UPON THE SCRIBES AND PHARISEES.

This is given by Matthew only. Luke records several similar woes (11: 37-54), which appear to have been pronounced some months earlier, comp. above on 22: 1 and on 19: 1. Our Lord now ceases to address his disciples and the people in general (23: 1), and turns back to the Scribes and Pharisees, pronouncing upon them a series of mournful woes, v. 13, 15, 16-22, 23 f., 25 f., 27 f., 29-36, closing with an apostrophe to Jerusalem, 37-39. In each case some special form of wickedness is made the ground of this stern denunciation, and the solemnly repeated address at the opening of the successive paragraphs gives them a rhythmical character, like strophes in an ode. *Keim:* "In the seven woes, the first place is given (first and second woes) to the judgment against the foes of the kingdom of God, whose proselyting zeal for their lost cause stands in sharp contrast to the hindrances to the progress of the kingdom of heaven. The third and fourth woes denounce their false teaching of the law; the fifth and sixth, the slovenly efforts after purity by the 'pure'; the seventh definitely reverts to the attitude of the Pharisees towards the prophets —the announcers and forerunners of Jesus —whose graves they build, and in doing so prove themselves to be the sons of those that murdered the prophets."

I. 13.[1] THEY SHUT THE KINGDOM. Woe

---

1 W H., and also Stephens' third ed., which in England is called the *Textus Receptus,* put this as v. 14. The spurious verse follows v. 12 in most of the documents which contain it. The early English versions probably followed the Vulgate in giving the other order.

13 But woe unto you, scribes and Pharisees, hypocrites! for ye shut up the kingdom of heaven 'against men : for ye neither go in *yourselves*, neither suffer ye them that are entering to go in.
14 Woe unto you, scribes and Pharisees, hypocrites! for ye devour widows' houses, and for a pretence make long prayer: therefore ye shall receive the greater ³ damnation.
15 Woe unto you, scribes and Pharisees, hypocrites! for ye compass sea and land to make one proselyte ; and when he is made, ye make him twofold more the child of hell than yourselves.

13 But woe unto you, scribes and Pharisees, hypocrites! because ye shut the kingdom of heaven 1 against men : for ye enter not in yourselves, neither suffer ye them that are entering in to enter.²
15 Woe unto you, scribes and Pharisees, hypocrites! for ye compass sea and land to make one proselyte; and when he is become so ye make him twofold more a son of ³ hell than yourselves.

---

1 Gr. *before*....2 Some authorities insert here, or after ver. 12, ver. 14 : *Woe unto you, scribes and Pharisees, hypocrites! for ye devour widows' houses, even while for a pretence ye make long prayers: therefore ye shall receive greater condemnation.* See Mark xii. 40 ; Luke xx. 47....3 Gr. *Gehenra.*

---

is a solemn warning and also an expression of pity—alas for you. (18: 7.) With these eight 'woes' (the eighth given by Mark and Luke), comp. six 'woes' in Isa. ch. 5, and five in Hab. 2: 6 ff. **Scribes,** see on 2: 4; **Pharisees,** see on 3: 7; **hypocrites,** see on 6: 2; **kingdom of heaven,** see on 3: 2. Our Lord implies that the Messianic reign has already begun, as he did even in 11: 12. **Ye shut.** These religious teachers ought to have set men in general the example of promptly and joyfully entering the Messianic kingdom, but they actually prevented others from entering. **Against men,** literally *before men* (Rev. Ver. *margin*), and so all English versions before K. James. The image is of the people at large as moving towards the open gate of the kingdom, and on the point of entering; but their religious leaders, heading the procession, refuse to enter themselves, and practically shut the gate in the people's face. (Comp. on 16: 19.) They do this by denying that the kingdom of heaven is at hand, and striving to turn the popular mind away from the rising persuasion that Jesus is the Messiah (21: 9, 15, 44 f.), and from entering the Messianic kingdom through penitent faith. They paraded themselves as leaders of the people, while really (Weiss) they were misleaders.

14. This verse of Com. Ver. is here spurious, ¹ but genuine in Mark 12: 40, and Luke 20: 47, so that it was actually spoken on this occasion, though not included in Matthew's report. Widows, being without a male representative in business, have always been in Asia specially exposed to fraud and other wrong. (Comp. Luke 18: 3; Acts 6: 1; James 1: 27.) To seize their property, even their homes, is in other parts of the world also a common practice of men who commend themselves by "making long prayers" (comp. 6: 7) as extraordinarily devout, and therefore trustworthy. The expression, "shall receive greater condemnation," suggests degrees in future punishment, a subject of very great practical importance. See the Commentaries on Mark and Luke.

II. 15. THEY PROSELYTE WITH WRONG AIMS. This saying is not elsewhere recorded. **Woe unto you,** etc., see on v. 13. **Hypocrites,** because they pretend to be zealous for the promotion of the true religion and for the religious benefit of men, when they are really aiming only to multiply partisans, and are making them not better, but worse. **Ye compass sea and land,** literally, *the dry (land),* as so often in Old Test. The hyperbolical expression shows how zealous and active they were in order that even a single Gentile might become a Jew. An interesting example of proselyting even beyond the Tigris, a few years after our Lord said this, may be seen in Jos. "Ant.," 20, 2, 2 ff. The same false zeal appeared afterwards in the Judaizers who followed Paul, Gal. 6: 13. The notion of Chrys. and others that Jesus reproaches the Pharisees with the small results of their immense activity, is quite foreign to the connection. He is speaking not of small results, but of bad results. **To make one proselyte.** This word is found elsewhere in New Test. only in

---

¹ It is wanting in the earliest and best Greek manuscripts, and several early versions, is evidently unknown here to Origen, and Eus. and Jerome, and was obviously brought in from Mark and Luke. Being written on the margin of Matt. by some student, and known by subsequent copyists to be a real saying of Jesus, it readily crept into the text, being placed in many copies after v. 12, but in some after v. 13. Such introduction of an addition at two different points in different copies is not infrequent, and sheds light on the treatment of parallel passages by students and copyists.

16 Woe unto you, *ye* blind guides, which say, Whosoever shall swear by the temple, it is nothing: but whosoever shall swear by the gold of the temple, he is a debtor!
17 *Ye* fools and blind: for whether is greater, the
gold, or the temple that sanctifieth the gold?

16   Woe unto you, ye blind guides, who say, Whosoever shall swear by the [1] temple, it is nothing; but
whosoever shall swear by the gold of the [1] temple,
17 he is [2] a debtor. Ye fools and blind: for whether is
greater, the gold, or the [1] temple that hath sanctified

1 Or, *sanctuary :* as in ver. 35.   2 Or, *bound* by his oath.

Acts 2 : 10; 6 : 5; 13 : 43, but very often in
Sept. It signified originally an immigrant, a
foreigner who had ' come to ' a community for
the purpose of dwelling there; this is its common use in Sept., English ' stranger.' By an
easy transition it denoted a Gentile who became a Jew, which is its use in New Test.
What is involved in ' make ' one proselyte?
To convince him that Jehovah the God of
Israel is the only true God (Deut. 6 : 4 f.), and
induce him to be circumcised and set out to
keep the law of Moses. (Exod. 12 : 48.) Those who
were convinced, but unwilling to submit to
this unpopular rite (Jos. "Ant.," 20, 2, 4),
were called " proselytes of the gate," as if not
fully entering the city and becoming citizens,
but merely sitting in the gate; the others
were called "proselytes of righteousness,"
righteous proselytes, who did their whole
duty. After the ceremony of circumcision,
the proselyte must of course give himself a
thorough purification, as he would after any
other thorough defilement, before approaching the altar with a sacrifice. In later times,
after the destruction of the temple by Titus,
and the consequent cessation of sacrifices, this
purification of the proselyte was the final act,
and came to be then regarded as a special rite,
which by modern writers is called "proselyte
baptism," see on 3 : 6. Tyndale and Gen.
have here 'to bring one into your belief,'
which is not a bad paraphrase. A picture of
a real proselyte to the true faith is given in
1 Pet. 4 : 2-4. Talmud Bab. says that a
heathen inclined to become a proselyte should
be told that "the Israelites are now enfeebled,
persecuted, and distressed." But this by no
means proves, as Wün. and others argue, that
the Jews were never much given to proselyting. The attempt in later centuries to check
the influx of proselytes by speaking of the
then depressed condition of Israel, implies a
previous contrary course. Tacitus ("Hist.,"
V., 5) says that the Jews grew because all the
worst men left their national religions and
became Jews. See Juvenal, "Sat.," 14, 96-
106, and other statements to the same effect in
Wet., and comp. Edersh. **And when he is**

made, Rev. Ver., *he is become so,* or 'is become (a proselyte),' as in 4 : 13; 13 : 32; 18 : 3;
'made' was here a bad rendering of the Greek
word, as it confounds this term with the term
'make ' that precedes and follows; it was an
imitation of the Vulgate. **The child,** *a son*
(Wyclif) is the exact translation, as in 5 : 9
Rev. Ver. and 8 : 12, etc. **Hell** is here *Gehenna,* the place of torment, see on 5 : 22. 'A
son of hell' would be one having a hellish
character, as a child is apt to resemble the
parent (comp. on 8 : 12), and so suited to
dwell in hell. This, then, was the ground of
the woe; not that they zealously made proselytes, which was entirely proper if rightly
done, but that they made them bad men like
themselves, yea, doubly as bad. These proselytes retained the essential faults of the
heathen, and took on the faults of the Pharisees. So some of our "civilized" Indians are
still savages, with the vices of civilization,
and comp. the heathen converts made by
some Jesuit missionaries. In these proselytes
the good was more superficial than in the
Pharisees—who often retained some roots of
old convictions—while the hypocrisy was not
less deep. Pupils in error and vice frequently
surpass their teachers. Very likely also some
became proselytes for the sake of gain. Yet
not all the proselytes of the time came under
the condemnation here uttered, for some of
them were among the early converts of the apos-
tles. (Acts 2 : 10; 6 : 5; 10 : 2; 13 : 43, 50; 16 : 14; 17 : 4. 17; 18 : 7.)
Other proselytes would naturally be very
bitter against Christianity; and Justin Martyr, after quoting this passage, says to Trypho
(ch. 122), "But the proselytes not only do
not believe, but twofold more than you they
blaspheme against his name." Proselytes are
often mentioned in the Talmud with suspicion
or contempt. *Plump.:* "The popular Jewish feeling about them was like the popular
Christian feeling about a converted Jew.
Proselytes were regarded as the leprosy of
Israel, hindering the coming of the Messiah.
It became a proverb that no one should
trust a proselyte, even the twenty-fourth
generation."

18 And, whosoever shall swear by the altar, it is nothing; but whosoever sweareth by the gift that is upon it, he is *a* guilty.

19 *Ye* fools and blind: for whether *is* greater, the gift, or the altar that sanctifieth the gift?

20 Whoso therefore shall swear by the altar, sweareth by it, and by all things thereon.

21 And whoso shall swear by the temple, sweareth by it, and by him that dwelleth therein.

18 the gold? And, Whosoever shall swear by the altar, it is nothing; but whosoever shall swear by the gift

19 that is upon it, he is [1] a debtor. Ye blind: for whether is greater, the gift, or the altar that sancti-

20 fieth the gift? He therefore that sweareth by the altar, sweareth by it, and by all things thereon.

21 And he that sweareth by the [2] temple, sweareth by it,

a Or, *debtor*, or *bound*.——1 Or, *bound* by his oath....2 Or, *sanctuary*: as in ver. 35.

III. **16-22.** BY FOOLISH DISTINCTIONS THEY EXCUSE THE VIOLATION OF OATHS. This is found in Matt. only. As to the general subject of oaths, comp. on 5: 33-37. Here the Saviour confines himself to one point, viz., that the Scribes and Pharisees wickedly encourage the people to violate oaths, by making untenable and silly distinctions between certain oaths as binding and certain others as not binding. **Woe unto you,** as in v. 13. **Ye blind guides,** see on 15: 14. A religious teacher who gives misleading instruction is strikingly represented by a blind guide. Our Lord does not in this case call them hypocrites, as in the other woes. **The temple** is here the *naos*, the sacred house, see on 4: 5. The oath by the temple would naturally be often used, and so would be often violated, until men did not feel very solemnly bound by it to speak the truth or keep an engagement. Then a new oath was invented, **by the gold of the temple,** and this as being new was felt to be more binding. This gold would mean the gold plates with which much of the temple was covered (Jos. "War," 5, 5, 3-6), and the golden vessels of the temple (6, 8, 3); probably also the coin from contributions. Jos. states ("Ant.," 14, 7, 1) that Crassus took from the temple eight thousand talents of gold, say ten million dollars. **It is nothing.** The Mishna on Vows (Nedarim, 1, 3) speaks of vowing, "This shall be to me as the lamb, as the wood, as the fire, as the altar, as the temple, as Jerusalem;" and adds "Rabbi Jehuda says, If one says 'Jerusalem' (*i. e.*, not 'as Jerusalem'), he has said nothing." (Comp. Wün.) The Scribes and Pharisees had conformed to popular custom and feeling by actually teaching that the old and common oath by the temple was not binding, but only the new-fashioned oath by the gold. The Saviour shows this to be an absurd distinction, since it was the temple that gave to this gold such sacredness as to make it the natural subject matter of an oath.

So as to the old oath by **the altar,** and the new oath by **the gift that is upon it.** It was only the altar that made the gift a holy thing, so as to render it natural that men should swear by the gift. He adds (v. 20) that to swear by the altar included swearing by the gift, for the former suggested and involved the latter. In like manner, the old and slighted oath 'by the temple' really involved swearing **by him that dwelleth therein,** who gives to the temple its sacredness. The Jews would avoid literally taking in vain any *name* of Jehovah their God, and when swearing only by things associated with him, as the temple, heaven, etc., they imagined that they would not break the third commandment in violating such an oath. The Mishna on Oaths (Shebuoth, 4, 13) says if one adjures others by heaven and by earth, they are not bound; but they are bound if he adjures them by *a d*, representing *Adonai* (Lord), or by *j, h,* representing *Jehovah*, or by *Sabaoth* (Jehovah of hosts), or by any divine attribute or divine name. The Gemara on this passage of the Mishna explains (Wün.) that this is because these terms must mean the divine being, while heaven and earth can be conceived of as mere objects, without reference to the Creator. This is exactly the notion that our Lord here condemns. Heaven and earth, when used in oaths, do suggest the Creator. So the Mohammedans will take many oaths without pretending to act accordingly, but an oath by the Koran they must keep. The Bohemian in "Quentin Durward" glibly utters many profuse oaths, but when required to swear "by the three kings of Cologne," and that with his face turned towards the east, he feels bound. Comp. above, "Hom. and Pract.", on 5: 33-37. **He is a debtor** (v. 16) means that he owes what he has thus solemnly declared or promised, and must pay it— he is *bound* by his oath (Rev. Ver. *margin*). The same Greek word is used in v. 18, but Com. Ver., as so often, must needs vary the translation, and

22 And he that shall swear by heaven, sweareth by the throne of God, and by him that sitteth thereon.

23 Woe unto you, scribes and Pharisees hypocrites? for ye pay tithe of mint and *a* anise and cummin, and have omitted the weightier *matters* of the law, judgment, mercy, and faith: these ought ye to have done, and not to leave the other undone.

24 *Ye* blind guides, which strain at a gnat, and swallow a camel.

22 and by him that dwelleth therein. And he that sweareth by the heaven, sweareth by the throne of God, and by him that sitteth thereon.

23 Woe unto you, scribes and Pharisees, hypocrites! for ye tithe the mint and 1 anise and cummin, and have left undone the weightier matters of the law, justice, and mercy, and faith: but these ye ought to have done, and not to have left the other undone.

24 Ye blind guides, who strain out the gnat, and swallow the camel.

a Gr. *anethon, dill.*——1 Or, *dill.*

give **he is guilty. That hath sanctified,** is in v. 17 the correct Greek text; in v. 19 it is **that sanctifieth.** The assimilation of the former to the latter was a characteristic act of copyists.[1] So with the addition of 'fools' in v. 19 from v. 17.

IV. **23 f.** SCRUPULOUS AS TO MINOR MATTERS, BUT NEGLECTING GREAT MORAL DUTIES. **Woe unto you,** etc., see on v. 13. The law required the Israelites to pay tithes of agricultural products, including fruits (Lev. 27: 30; Deut. 14: 22 ff.); and these punctilious Pharisees took pains to tithe every product that was edible and could be preserved. (Talmud.) Our Lord mentions as specimens, **mint and anise and cummin;** on the former occasion he gave 'mint and rue and every herb.' (Luke 11: 42, R. V.) Comp. the boast "I give tithes of all that I get." (Luke 18: 12, R. V.) Some even gave tithes of what they purchased for use. (Hausrath.) The Greek word here used for mint means 'sweet-smelling,' though the Greek also had the word *mintha;* our words anise and cummin are borrowed from the Greek. The leaves of mint and the seeds of anise (or dill) were

used both for flavoring food and as valuable carminative medicines; the seeds of cummin were used for the former purpose. **Judgment, mercy, and faith,** *i. e.,* good faith, fidelity (Rom. 3: 3), the common classical sense of the term. In Luke, it is 'judgment and the love of God.' Comp. Mic. 6: 8. The American Revisers properly urge that not 'judgment,' but 'justice,' is the correct translation here and in Luke, though the Greek word is correctly rendered 'judgment' in v. 33, and so rendered elsewhere. To render a Greek term everywhere by the same word is very desirable, but not always practicable. **The weightier matters of the law.** We have seen (on 22: 36) that the Rabbis called some commandments of the law weighty and others light. Jesus recognizes that such a distinction is legitimate, but draws the line very differently from their teachings, for he makes fundamental, ethical, and spiritual duties (comp. Luke) the weightier matters. Comp. 'one of these least commandments.' (5: 19.) As to the superiority of the ethical to the ceremonial, comp. on 9: 11 and 12: 7. **And not**

---

[1] 'He that sweareth' in v. 20, 21, 22 is the aorist participle, of which Meyer here gives a hopelessly artificial explanation, and which none of the grammars treat satisfactorily. It presents the simple notion of the action *without* any such idea of continuance or repetition or custom as the present participle would give. In general, the aorist tense (" second aorist ") is the original root of the verb, presenting the unmodified action. As various tense forms were devised, the present system, the perfect system, etc., to express particular modifications, the aorist continued to be used whenever no one of these others was distinctly wanted. This history appears to explain the use of the aorist in the subj., opt., imperative, infinitive, and participle; the aorist is in all these employed as a matter of course, unless the distinctive sense of the present or perfect tense be specially desired—because the aorist is the original verb. When the so-called "first aorist" form was subsequently invented, it came to be used in the same sense as the old aorist. Apparent exceptions to this theory of the aorist are believed to be only apparent.

If the aorist subjunctive is sometimes naturally translated by the Latin future perfect (as some would do in v. 16, 18), this is merely suggested by the nature of the case, just as when the aorist indicative is translated by the pluperfect. So when the aorist participle denotes an action antecedent to the time of the principal verb, this is only through a suggested contrast to the present participle, which would of necessity give an action contemporaneous with that of the principal verb; and in a case like that before us the suggestion of such a contrast is excluded by the nature of the case. Comp. on 21: 18. In the indicative mood the aorist bears the same relation to the imperfect that it bears in. the other moods to the present. If these views of the aorist be correct, there is no occasion for the various artificial definitions of that tense which are given by many grammarians and commentators.—In v. 21 the aorist participle for 'dwelleth,' given by many documents and editors, is probably an alteration of the copyists to make it correspond outwardly to the tense of 'sweareth.'

25 Woe unto you, scribes and Pharisees, hypocrites ! for ye make clean the outside of the cup and of the platter, but within they are full of extortion and excess.
26 *Thou* blind Pharisee, cleanse first that *which is* within the cup and platter, that the outside of them may be clean also.

25   Woe unto you, scribes and Pharisees, hypocrites! for ye cleanse the outside of the cup and of the platter, but within they are full from extortion and
26 excess. Thou blind Pharisee, cleanse first the inside of the cup and of the platter, that the outside thereof may become clean also.

---

to leave the other undone. The old English plural use of 'other' here creates momentary difficulty, as if referring to a singular, and there is no propriety in retaining it. Our Lord beautifully adapts his two expressions. They were strict as to the slightest externals, and left undone the ethical; he says that the ethical duties ought to be done, and the others not to be neglected. So Luke 11 : 42, and comp. above on 12 : 7. He does not *forbid* the tithing of herbs, but sets in strong contrast with this scrupulosity their neglect of great moral duties. **Ye blind guides,** as in v. 16, leading the people utterly astray by false teaching and bad example. The image in v. 24 expresses the same thing as v. 23. The Talmud speaks (Wet.) of straining wine in order to remove minute unclean creatures. (Lev. 11 : 41-43.) The Buddhists in Ceylon strain their wine for a similar reason. Gnats sip at wine, and so may fall into it. Trench (on Rev.) tells of a soldier in Morocco who always placed the end of his turban over the vessel from which he drank water, avowedly for the purpose of straining out the gnats, "whose larvae swarm in the water of that country." **The gnat** and **the camel** are put in contrast as extremes in regard to size; the latter is obviously a strong hyperbole, for the camel was the largest animal familiarly known to the Jews. (Comp. on 19 : 24.) Observe that it also was "unclean." (Lev. 11 : 4.) Thus these persons carefully strain out the smallest creature, and swallow the largest; they are very scrupulous about the minutest matters of ceremonial observance, and then neglect the highest ethical duties enjoined by the law. The translation **strain at** is generally supposed to have been a mere misprint, in the original edition of K. James' version, for 'strain out,' which had been given by Tyn., Cran., and Gen. The Greek means

'thoroughly filter,' thoroughly strain, applied to wine in Amos 6 : 6, and here to that which is removed by filtering wine. Alford thinks that the K. J. revisers purposely gave 'strain at,' meaning 'strain (the wine) at (the occurrence of) a gnat,' but this is highly improbable.

V. **25 f.** Caring for Outward Purification Rather Than for True Morality. Comp. what Luke gives (11 : 38 ff.), as spoken some time earlier. **Woe unto you,** etc., see on v. 13. Of all the requirements of the law, purification was that on which the Pharisees seem to have laid most stress; comp. on 15 : 2. There is here a regular progression, oaths, tithes, purifications. They were careful about not only the actual cleaning, but the ceremonial cleaning of **the cup and the platter,** Mark 7 : 4. 'Platter' is in the Greek a rare word, denoting a side-dish, some delicacy set on the side-table, and only handed to the guests, and derivatively the dish used for such dainties. **Full of from** (Rev. Ver.) **extortion and excess,** or 'intemperance,' in the original sense of that term. The *contents* of the cup and dish, namely the wine and food, are the product of extortion, and the cup and dish are *filled* in consequence of desire for excess in eating and drinking. The image seems to change slightly, the full cup and platter being due in one sense to extortion, and in another to excess.[1] **Thou blind Pharisee,** not now reproached as blindly leading others astray (v. 16, 24), but as blindly going astray himself. **Cleanse first that which is within.** Let the *contents* of the cup and dish be the fruit of honest industry and not of extortion, and be used temperately and not in excess; then your ceremonial cleansing of the vessels themselves, will be real, and acceptable to God. Comp. on 6 : 8. **May be clean;** Rev. Ver.

---

[1] This was not understood, and many manuscripts have 'extortion and iniquity,' and several leading early versions have 'extortion and uncleanness'; both are obviously changes to remove the difficulty, and, for once, the simplification did not pass into the Textus Receptus. So, also, some documents omit the preposition rendered 'from,' because it was not understood, and the early English versions fail to translate it, giving simply 'full of,' which is correct in Luke 11: 39, and below in v. 27.

27 Woe unto you, scribes and Pharisees, hypocrites! for ye are like unto whited sepulchres, which indeed appear beautiful outward, but are within full of dead *men's* bones, and of all uncleanness.
28 Even so ye also outwardly appear righteous unto men, but within ye are full of hypocrisy and iniquity.
29 Woe unto you, scribes and Pharisees, hypocrites! because ye build the tombs of the prophets, and garnish the sepulchres of the righteous,

27 Woe unto you, scribes and Pharisees, hypocrites! for ye are like unto whited sepulchres, which outwardly appear beautiful, but inwardly are full of dead men's bones, and of all uncleanness.
28 Even so ye also outwardly appear righteous unto men, but inwardly ye are full of hypocrisy and iniquity.
29 Woe unto you, scribes and Pharisees, hypocrites! for ye build the sepulchres of the prophets, and

---

may become clean is the exact meaning of the Greek and suits the connection.

VI. **27 f.** THEY ARE WHITED SEPULCHRES. Comp. Luke 11 : 44. The transition from outward and inward purity of vessels to outward and inward personal purity, is natural and immediate. **Woe unto you**, etc., see on v. 13. **Whited sepulchres.** Tombs of the better class about Jerusalem were caves, or artificial chambers cut in the limestone rock. (27 : 60.) The exterior of these was whitewashed, mainly to prevent persons from touching them unawares and thus becoming unclean (Num. 19 : 16), but also for agreeable appearance and perhaps for sanitary reasons. The Mishna states (Shekalim 1, 1) that on the 15 of Adar (roughly answering to our March, when the rains are over) people repair the roads, and public baths and other public works, and whitewash the tombs. The Jerusalem Gemara (tr. of Schwab) explains that this is because the rain may have washed off the lime. The Talmud also represents (Lightf.) that sometimes they whitened the whole tomb, in other cases made on it the figure of a bone or bones, and adds that as the leper said, "Unclean, unclean" (Lev. 13 : 45), so here "uncleanness cries out to you and says, 'Come not near.'" Our Lord is speaking at the Passover, when the recent whitening would be very noticeable. **Which appear beautiful outward,** not simply through the whitewashing, but architectural ornament, as seen in tombs still remaining. In Acts 23 : 3 Paul calls a hypocrite a 'whited wall.' **And of all uncleanness** is a delicate reference to the other products of the gradual decay besides the **bones.** These products according to the Mosaic law and Jewish feeling produced the highest degree of ceremonial uncleanness. In Luke 11 : 44, Rev. Ver., as spoken on a former occasion, the image is somewhat different, 'ye are as the tombs which appear not, and the men that walk over them know it not.' It is likely that the masses of the people buried in the ground, as we commonly do, and as is done with most of the Jews now dying at Jerusalem ; while the sepulchres in the rocks would correspond to our vaults and tombs above ground, though much oftener employed. The different Greek terms in Matthew and Luke do not suggest any practical distinction, for that of Luke is the same as the second term below in v. 29, and as in John 11: 28. In v. 28, **iniquity** is more exactly *lawlessness, anomia,* violation of law, as in 7 : 23 ; 13 : 41 ; 24 : 12. This word is not used by the other Gospels, but was a natural term for a gospel addressed especially to Jews and for Paul, while John particularly needs it in 1 John 3 : 4. *Adikia,* 'iniquity,' or 'injustice,' is not used by Matthew, but several times by Luke, Paul, and others, and Matthew has its adjective in 5 : 45, and its verb in 20 : 13. **Are full** here represents a different word from that of v. 25 and 27, but our language cannot conveniently express the difference, and it has no practical importance.

VII. **29-36.** THEY RESEMBLE THEIR WICKED ANCESTORS, WHO SLEW THE PROPHETS. Comp. Luke 11: 47-51, probably spoken some months earlier, see on 23: 1. **Woe unto you,** etc., see on v. 13. There is no practically important difference between the **sepulchres** and **the tombs.** The word rendered **garnish,** means literally, *adorn,* 'ornament,' as in 12: 44; comp. 25: 7. **The prophets, . . . the righteous.** (Comp. 10: 41; 13; 17). In 1 Macc. 13: 27-30, is described a grand tomb which Simon the Maccabee built for his father and brothers. Josephus tells us ("Ant.," 16, 17, 1) how Herod built a marble monument over the tombs of David and Solomon, to atone for his attempt to plunder them. It is very doubtful whether the elaborate structures on the lower slope of Olivet, southeast of the city, which are now called "tombs of the prophets," have any proper claim to that name; but they appear to date from the time of the Herods (Robinson, Thomson), and may thus give an idea of the tombs referred to. One of

30 And say, If we had been in the days of our fathers, we would not have been partakers with them in the blood of the prophets.
31 Wherefore ye be witnesses unto yourselves, that ye are the children of them which killed the prophets.
32 Fill ye up then the measure of your fathers.
33 *Ye* serpents, *ye* generation of vipers, how can ye escape the damnation of hell?
34 Wherefore, behold, I send unto you prophets, and wise men, and scribes: and *some* of them ye shall kill and crucify; and *some* of them shall ye scourge in your synagogues, and persecute *them* from city to city:

30 garnish the tombs of the righteous, and say, If we had been in the days of our fathers, we should not have been partakers with them in the blood of the prophets. Wherefore ye witness to yourselves, that ye are sons of them that slew the prophets. Fill ye up then the measure of your fathers. Ye serpents, ye offspring of vipers, how shall ye escape the judg-ment of [1] hell? Therefore, behold, I send unto you prophets, and wise men, and scribes: some of them shall ye kill and crucify; and some of them shall ye scourge in your synagogues, and persecute from

---

1 Gr. *Gehenna.*

---

them is now called the tomb of Zechariah, with evident reference to v. 35. A little later than our Lord's time, we have account in Josephus of several grand tombs, as that of Annas, the High Priest ("War," 5, 12, 2), of Philip, the Tetrarch ("Ant.," 18, 4, 6), and of Queen Helena, of Adiabene, and her son— with three pyramids ("Ant.," 20, 4, 3).

31. Wherefore, or more exactly *so that.* **Ye be witnesses unto,** or, *witness to* **your-selves,** *i. e.,* in this case (Winer) 'against yourselves,' it being a testimony to their hurt. (Comp. James 5: 3.) In the very self-excuse of v. 30, they acknowledge themselves the children of those who slew the prophets, and our Lord intimates that here, as is usual, the offspring resemble the parents (5: 45; John 8: 41, 44), though they pretend the contrary in their case. The rulers are already plotting to murder Jesus (21: 46.) They are minded to do as their fathers did in this very matter, and piously pretending to be altogether different. (Comp. Luke 11: 48.) "Ye are witnesses and consent unto the works of your fathers." (Comp. above on 21: 39 ff., and see Acts 7: 51 f., and 1 Thess. 2: 14, 15.)

32. Fill ye up then, or literally, *and do ye fill up,* the 'ye' being expressed in Greek, and thus emphatic, viz., 'ye,' as set over against your fathers. The expression is gravely ironical (Winer),[1] a thing natural in so impassioned and pointedly personal a dis-course, which has kept growing in earnest-ness. This generation ought to turn from their fathers' sins, but instead of that they were adding like sins, and the new divine warnings did not stop them. So with mourn-ful irony he bids them go on and fill the measure full. (Gen. 15: 16)

33. Ye serpents, ye generation (*off-spring*) **of vipers,** see on 3: 7; 12: 34. This corresponds to v. 31; they are like their an-cestors—they are serpents and the offspring of serpents. **How can ye escape,** or 'how are you to escape', implying that it is impossible to see any way. As they resemble their an-cestors, and are busily filling up the measure of their ancestors' sins, it is not possible that they should escape. (Comp. 11: 22; John 3: 19.) **The damnation** (*judgment*) **of hell,** *i. e.,* the judgment which condemns to punish-ment in hell, is a phrase also used several times in the Talmud (Wün.). 'Judgment' is the correct translation of *krisis;* it is *kata-krisis* that signifies condemnation, the idea formerly expressed in English by 'damna-tion.' This last word now denotes in English the eternal penalty resulting from judgment or condemnation, and *while often necessa-rily suggested,* this is not what the Greek terms themselves express. Accordingly, the words 'damn' and 'damnation' must now give way to 'judge,' 'condemn,' etc., leaving the punishment to be *suggested,* as it is in the Greek. (See Mark 3: 29; 12: 40; 16: 16; Luke 20: 47; John 5: 29; Rom. 3: 8; 13: 2; 14: 23; 1 Cor. 11: 29; 2 Thess. 2: 12; also (Greek meaning 'perdition') 2 Pet. 2: 1, 3.) The changes thus made in the Revised Ver-sion do not at all proceed from any change in exegetical views or in theological opinion, but are simply required by the altered mean-ing of an English word. (Comp. as to 'hell,' on 16: 18.) 'Hell' is here *Gehenna,* the place of torment, as in v. 15, see on 5: 22.

34-36. Wherefore, behold, I send unto you. The 'I' is expressed in Greek, and so is emphatic. Jesus speaks as the divine rep-

---

1 The ironical imperative was not understood, and by the change of one letter might be converted into a fu-ture, 'ye will fill up,' which is read in B and a very | few other documents. W H. cling to B, and place it in their margin, though plainly a correction.

35 That upon you may come all the righteous blood shed upon the earth, from the blood of righteous Abel unto the blood of Zacharias son of Barachias, whom ye slew between the temple and the altar.

35 city to city: that upon you may come all the righteous blood shed on the earth, from the blood of Abel the righteous unto the blood of Zachariah son of Barachiah, whom ye slew between the sanctuary

resentative (John 3:2), as having plenary authority in the whole matter of human salvation (28:18); he utters the divine decree, which in the similar passage of Luke (11:49) is referred to 'the wisdom of God.' 'Send' in the present tense, because the mission is arranged and on the point of beginning. *Wherefore*, or *therefore*, because they are like their fathers, and will treat God's messengers as their fathers did, he sends them messengers to be persecuted; it will thus become manifestly right that they should be held guilty for their ancestors' sin and their own. (v. 35.) God of course does not wish men to sin, but he tests them, so as to show to themselves and others their real character, and vindicate the justice of their punishment. **Wise men, and scribes** are Jewish terms, used because of what precedes (v. 29 and 23:2, 7), 'wise men' being a common appellation of the Rabbis. But they may be fulfilled in apostles and evangelists also (comp. 13:52). The distinction between them should not here be insisted on. The decree to send, and their treatment of the persons sent, may include all the divine messengers to that generation, from John the Baptist to the destruction of Jerusalem. (v. 36; 24:34.) Jesus intimates his knowledge that they will not only kill him (21:38), but also kill or maltreat his messengers hereafter sent (comp. 1 Thess. 2:15). **And crucify**, see on 27:35. This may include the case of Jesus himself. It is a tradition that Peter was crucified, and Simeon, a brother of Jesus. **Some of them shall ye scourge in your synagogues,** as he had already foretold to his followers. (10:17.) **And persecute them from city to city,** comp. 10:23; Acts 9:2; 13:50 f.; 14:6; 17:10 ff. **That upon you may come** is the divine purpose, not that of the Jews. (Comp. 2:23, and see on 1:22.) There here comes before us what recent philosophical writers are fond of calling "the solidarity of the race." *Plump.*: "Men make the guilt of past ages their own, reproduce its atrocities, identify themselves with it; and so, what seems at first an arbitrary decree, visiting on the children the sins of the fathers, becomes in such cases a

righteous judgment. If they repent, they cut off the terrible entail of sin and punishment; but if they harden themselves in their evil, they inherit the delayed punishment of their father's sins as well as of their own." The Jewish multitude afterward voluntarily took upon themselves and their children the blood of Jesus. (27:25.) Notice here the solemn threefold repetition of 'blood.' **Shed** is present tense; the totality of the righteous blood is conceived as in the process of being shed, the whole past and present thrown together.

Zacharias, the son of Barachias. There is here a well-known difficulty, which various theories have attempted to remove. (1) Some think that the prophet Zechariah is meant, who was son of Berechiah (Zech. 1:1); but we have no account of his being slain. (2) Some Fathers supposed Zachariah the father of John the Baptist to be meant, and had traditional stories of his being killed for asserting the perpetual virginity of the mother of Jesus; but all this is without historical foundation, excessively improbable, and very likely suggested by the present allusion. (3) Aug. and some others have supposed that our Lord is *predicting* the death of Zachariah son of Baruch, killed in the temple during the subsequent siege of Jerusalem, as described by Josephus. ("War," 4, 5, 4.) But the temple is there only *hieron*, which means the general enclosure, Baruch is quite a different name from Barachiah, and our Lord is evidently speaking of things already past ('ye slew'), while this event was forty years later. (4) In 2 Chron. 24:20-22, we read that a priest named Zechariah was stoned " in the court of the house of Jehovah." His dying words are quite in accordance with the reference our Lord here makes, "Jehovah look upon it and require it," and correspond to the other case of Abel's blood. (Gen. 4:10.) In the ancient Hebrew grouping of the books, as in Hebrew Bibles now, the Chronicles seem to have stood at the end; so that from Abel to this Zachariah would include all the cases from beginning to end of the sacred books. All these circumstances fit exactly. Both the Jerusalem

36 Verily I say unto you, All these things shall come upon this generation.
37 O Jerusalem, Jerusalem, *thou* that killest the prophets, and stonest them which are sent unto thee, how often would I have gathered thy children together, even as a hen gathereth her chickens under *her* wings, and ye would not!

36 and the altar. Verily I say unto you, All these things shall come upon this generation.
37 O Jerusalem, Jerusalem, that killeth the prophets, and stoneth them that are sent unto her! how often would I have gathered thy children together, even as a hen gathereth her chickens under her wings,

and the Babylon Talmud, as also some Midrashim (Lightf., Wün.), contain wild legends about the blood of this Zachariah as continuing to bubble for more than two centuries until the captivity—which go to show that his murder in the court of the priests was regarded as a notable event. But this Zachariah is expressly described as son of Jehoiada, the priest, whose kindness King Joash was thus ill requiting. Some make haste to say that Matt. has fallen into the error of confounding this Zechariah with the prophet who was son of Berechiah, while Luke gives no name of his father. (Luke 11: 51.) But we ought certainly to be very slow to remove difficulties by a supposition so improbable in the case of an inspired writer. There are several possible ways of explaining the matter. Zachariah's father, Jehoiada, may have had the surname of Berechiah, ' blessed of Jehovah,' a name borne by six or seven persons in the history, and which might have been given to the great priest for saving his country. Or, Jehoiada, who had just died at the age of one hundred and thirty (2 Chron. 24: 15), may have been the grandfather of Zechariah, and his father a Berechiah, not otherwise mentioned. So the prophet is in Zech. 1: 1, called " Zechariah, the son of Berechiah, the son of Iddo," while in Ezra 6: 14, he is called "Zechariah, the son of Iddo." Or it may be (Lutter.) that there was some other murder near to the time of Jesus, and known to his hearers. All these are unsupported hypotheses, but they are certainly possible, and so it is by no means necessary to suppose that Matt. fell into an error. Not a few cases that long appeared as difficult as this have been cleared up by the progress of knowledge within the present half century.[1] (Comp. on 20: 29.) **Whom ye slew,** viz., through your fathers. They are held guilty of their fathers' conduct because they have imitated it. **The temple** is here *naos*, the sacred house, as in

v. 17, see on 4: 5; **the altar** is the great altar of burnt offering, which stood in the Court of the Priests in front of the sacred house. ' Between the temple and the altar' would be a natural expansion of the statement in Chron., where Zechariah the priest stands "above the people," in the Court of the Priests. **Upon this generation,** comp. 11: 16, and see on 24: 34; the idea is kept up by v. 38 f. These are our Lord's farewell words to the Jews at large.

VIII. **37-39.** A MOURNFUL APOSTROPHE TO JERUSALEM. Our Lord's thoughts had been turning sadly toward Jerusalem for more than a half year, comp. on 16: 21; 20: 18 f. Now the conclusion of the series of woes having pointed directly to dreadful and speedy judgments upon the persons addressed, which would be connected especially with the destruction of Jerusalem, he breaks into a grieved and compassionate apostrophe. That such feelings should have taken this form when speaking of Jerusalem at a distance (Luke 13 : 34 f.), again when coming in sight of the city during the triumphal entry (Luke 19 : 41-44), and now again in closing his last address to the people, is in every respect natural; and there is not the slightest occasion for supposing that the saying has been displaced by one or the other Gospel. The doubled address, and the frequent changes of person, are also natural in the language of passionate emotion: "Jerusalem, Jerusalem—thou that killest . . . sent unto thee . . . thy children . . . your house . . . ye shall not see." **Thou that killest the prophets** gives the point of connection between this and the preceding paragraph. **And stonest them.** The Zechariah just before mentioned (according to the view preferred) was stoned to death. **How often** implies frequent visits to Jerusalem during his ministry, and special efforts to save her people, and this agrees with the Gospel according to John.

---

1 The omission of Barachiah in ℵ, and the change to Jehoiada, which Jerome found in the Gospel used by the Nazarenes, are obviously mere attempts to get rid of the discrepancy. W H, say (App. p. 282), " it is difficult to believe that all the words as they stand have apostolic authority." But conjectural emendation to remove a patent difficulty, would of course be extremely precarious.

38 Behold, your house is left unto you desolate.
39 For I say unto you, Ye shall not see me hence-forth, till ye shall say, Blessed *is* he that cometh in the name of the Lord.

38 and ye would not! Behold, your house is left unto
39 you [1] desolate! For I say unto you, Ye shall not see me henceforth, till ye shall say, Blessed *is* he that cometh in the name of the Lord.

1 Some ancient authorities omit *desolate*.

Others would suppose that he speaks of the frequent divine wish in past generations. **As a hen gathereth her chickens.** This beautiful comparison is the only passage of the Bible, except 26: 34, etc., in which barn-yard fowls are expressly mentioned, but see probable allusion in Psa. 17 : 8; 91 : 4; Jer. 48: 40; comp. Deut. 32: 11; Psa. 36 : 7, etc. Wilkinson says they are not represented in the old Egyptian paintings. Yet they are now extremely common in both countries, and must have been so from early times. There was simply no occasion for more frequent reference to them. Proselytes are spoken of in the Talmud (Wün.) as taking shelter under the wings of the Shechinah. **How often would I . . . and ye would not.** 'I' and 'ye' are not separately expressed in the Greek, and so cannot be taken as emphatic. The reference here is to the divine wish and not to the divine purpose. God's will of purpose is always carried out; his will of desire often fails, because the free will of men will not yield; comp. on 6: 10. **Your house is left,** present tense, 'is now being left.' The city, which is the house or dwelling of the people, is now in process of being left desolate, causes are in operation that must have this result.[1] Some think that 'house', means the temple rather than the city. **For** introduces the proof that this process of leaving them desolate is going on, viz., in the fact that the Messiah who has so often wished to gather and save, is now on the point of turning away. **Ye shall not see me henceforth.** After the resurrection he was not seen by the people at large, but only by chosen witnesses, Acts 10: 40 f. **Till ye shall say,** viz., at his second coming, of which he will presently speak fully to his disciples (ch. 24 and 25.) At the triumphal entry (21:9) some said this, but the people of Jerusalem in general did not. At the second coming all will sincerely, though some most unwillingly and sadly, recognize him as the Messiah, **that cometh in the name of the Lord,** 24: 30 f., comp. Rev. 1: 7; Phil. 2: 9-11. From Rom. 11: 25 ff. we may hope that among those who then joyfully recognize him will be many Jews.

HOMILETICAL AND PRACTICAL.

V. 14. ORIGEN: "Two faults. 1) They do not themselves enter the kingdom. 2) They do not suffer those that are trying to enter. These two sins are naturally inseparable; he who commits the one cannot refrain from committing the other; he who refrains from the one is sure to refrain from the other also." —What an evil thing it is by our teaching to shut the gate of salvation in men's faces; what a blessed thing to open the gate, and lead men to enter.—V. 15. False religious teaching is very apt to make the pupils worse than the teacher; 1) more extreme in opinion; 2) more sure they are right; 3) more unhesitating in action; 4) more uncharitable to those who think otherwise.—ORIGEN: "To the son of Gehenna, Christ's teaching gives the right to become the child of God." (John 1: 12.)—V. 16-22. Discrimination is an indispensable element of sound judgment, in the sphere of thought or of action; but false distinctions are one of the commonest means of self-deception. —The fact that oaths wear out is not a reason for inventing new ones, but for refraining from oaths, save when used on extraordinary occasions and in a reverent spirit; comp. on 5: 34.—V. 17. The Saviour calls these men 'fools,' notwithstanding what he said in 5: 22. He infallibly knows them to be fools, and he says it with perfectly right aims and feelings.

V. 23. The centre of gravity, even in the Mosaic system, lay in the ethical and not in the ceremonial, and still more is that the case with Christianity; but even apparently slight matters of external observance, if divinely

---

1 'Desolate' is omitted here by B, L, an Old Latin copy, and a quotation in Origen. In Luke 13: 35 it is omitted by most documents, and its chief supports are there " Western." It seems pretty clear that the word is spurious in Luke and genuine in Matt., as this sup-position accounts for all the phenomena. W H. omit it in Matt. also, placing it in the *margin.* But we have found various instances in which B, with some other documents, must be regarded as wrong.

CHAPTER XXIV.

A ND Jesus went out, and departed from the temple: and his disciples came to *him* for to shew him the buildings of the temple.	1 And Jesus went out from the temple, and was going on his way; and his disciples came to him to

enjoined, should by no means be neglected.—ORIGEN applies this to persons who neglect wholesome instruction, and care only for rhetorical ornament; comp. 1 Cor. 1: 17.—V. 24. Blind guides. CHRYS.: "For if for a blind man not to think he needs a guide be extreme misery and wretchedness; when he wishes himself to guide others, see to what a gulf it leads."—V. 25. Scrupulosity in religious ceremonial cannot atone for extortion in business or for indulgence of appetite to excess. Indeed, religious ceremonial is itself unacceptable to God when performed by the immoral. 1 Tim. 2: 8; Prov. 15: 8; 21: 27.— V. 28. ROCHEFOUCAULD: "Hypocrisy is a sort of homage that vice pays to virtue." POL-LOK: "He was a man who stole the livery of the court of heaven to serve the devil in."— V. 30 f. It is very easy to condemn severely the misconduct of others, while secretly guilty of essentially the same sin. But "God is not mocked," Gal. 6: 7. HENRY: "The deceitfulness of sinners' hearts appears very much in this, that while they go down the stream of the sins of their own day, they fancy they should have swum against the stream of the sins of former days; that if they had had other people's opportunities, they would have improved them more faithfully; if they had been in other people's temptations, they would have resisted them more vigorously; when yet they improve not the opportunities they have, nor resist the temptations they are in." —V. 32. Filling up the measure. 1) In one sense men are accountable only for their own sins; "the soul that sinneth it shall die," Ezek. 18: 4. 2) Yet all men suffer the consequences of the wrong doing of others—ancestors, present kindred, rulers, neighbors. 3) Human wickedness goes on increasing in lines of descent or of other relation till there comes a time of reckoning, till the full measure of guilt overflows in destruction. 4) The only escape is in really turning from the sin of wicked ancestors, so as to interrupt the transmission of wickedness and guilt; yea, in turning from all sin to the sin-hating and sin-pardoning God.

24: 1-36. DESTRUCTION OF JERUSALEM AND COMING OF CHRIST.

Found also in Mark 13: 1-32; Luke 21: 5-33. Our Lord's last *public* discourse has now been ended. The day is probably Tuesday of the Passover week (see on 21: 18, 23). He has been discoursing all day in the courts of the temple, and before turning away he draws instruction from the widow's touching gift to the sacred treasury. (Mark 12 : 41 ; Luke 21 : 1.) He then leaves the temple, and seems never to have entered it again. In this final departure it was very natural that his thoughts should dwell on the impending destruction of the temple and the city. Moreover, as there is no sufficient reason for departing from Matthew's order (comp. on 23 : 1, 13), we see that he had just before predicted the destruction of Jerusalem and his own future coming. (23 : 38 f.) Six months earlier (16 : 27 f.) he had declared that he would come again in the glory of his Father, as the sovereign Judge of mankind; and that some then present would live to see him "coming in his kingdom." We there found it necessary to understand that the particular coming to which this last phrase especially refers took place at the destruction of Jerusalem, which made Christianity completely and manifestly distinct from Judaism, and established the Messianic kingdom in its permanent present state. The prediction then briefly made by our Lord is now more fully unfolded. He first declares in leaving the temple that it is going to be completely destroyed (v. 1 f.); and then, sitting on the Mount of Olives, he gives the great discourse of ch. 24 and 25.

This discourse certainly foretells in the outset the destruction of Jerusalem (*e. g.*, v. 15-21, v. 34); and in the conclusion certainly foretells the final coming of our Lord, with the general judgment of mankind and the resulting permanent state of the good and the bad (25 : 31-46), in a way substantially equivalent to the predictive descriptions afterwards given by the apostles. To refer that closing passage to the destruction of Jerusalem is absurd and impossible. So then the discourse begins with the destruction of the temple and city, and ends with the final coming to judgment: how does it make the transition from the former to the latter topic? Every attempt to assign a definite point of division between the two topics has proved a failure. Place it after v. 28, saying that up to that point only the former topic is meant, and after that point only the latter, and at once we see that v. 34 must refer to the destruction of Jerusalem. Place it after v. 34 or 36 or 42, and we cannot resist the persuasion that v. 30 f. (and v. 36) must refer to the final coming for judgment (comp. 12: 41-43 ; 2 Thess. 1: 7-10). But if the destruction of Jerusalem was itself in one sense a coming of the Lord, why may we not suppose that the transition from this to the final coming is gradual? Then much in 24: 3-36 may be taken as referring *both* to the former and the latter topic, while some of the expressions may refer exclusively to the one or the other. In 24: 37 to 25: 13 the earlier topic is sinking out of sight; in 25: 31-46 it has completely disappeared, and nothing is in view but the final coming to judgment. (Luke and Mark are parallel only as far as 24: 42.) Similar cases occur in Old Test., where a prediction refers to some nearer event, and also, by typical relation, to a kindred event in the remoter future. This view does not rest on the crude notion of a "double sense" in Scripture words or phrases, but on the unquestionable Scripture use of types, prophetic as well as ceremonial. For example, in Isa. ch. 41: 8 to ch. 53, the predictions as to the "servant of Jehovah" make a gradual transition from Israel to the Messiah, the former alone being seen in 41: 8 ff., the Messiah also appearing to view in 42: 1 ff. (Matt. 12: 18-21), and Israel quite sinking out of our sight in ch. 53. (Acts 8:32-35.) Comp. above on 2: 15. All the Scripture predictions remained obscure till their fulfillment (comp. on v. 15). Accordingly we may expect here to see somewhat clearly the fulfillment in the destruction of Jerusalem, but the other and yet future fulfillment must remain still quite obscure, and we should be "contented (Alex.) with a careful explanation of the terms employed, according to analogy and usage, and a reverential waiting for ulterior disclosures by the light of

divine providence shining on the word." Some zealous students of prophecy have brought reproach on the Scripture by their lack of moderation and reserve in the interpretation. It should be frankly conceded that grave difficulties attend the interpretation of this discourse in any of the methods that have been suggested. The view above described is believed to involve fewer difficulties, and to yield better results, than any other theory.

1 f. The temple is here *hieron*, the general sacred enclosure, see on 4: 5. Jesus went into the Court of the Gentiles and the Court of Israel, but never into the central building (*naos*) and the surrounding Court of the Priests. (Comp. on 21: 12.) The clause 'from the temple' stands in the Greek (correct text)[1] between the participle rendered 'went out' and the verb 'was going,' and could be connected with the latter, as in Com. Ver., but is more naturally connected with the former, as in Rev. Ver. The preposition 'from' makes the temple the point of departure; the other expression, 'going out,' shows distinctly that he had been in the temple, which would be plain from the nature of the case. (Comp. on 3: 16.) *Was going on his way* (Rev. Ver.), doubtless returning towards Bethany, whence he had come that morning (21: 17 f.; Luke 21: 37); and the disciples interrupted his progress **to show him the buildings of the temple** (*hieron*). In Mark (13: 2) they are expressly called 'great buildings,' and in Mark and Luke special attention is directed to the vast "stones" employed. Josephus says ("Ant.," 15, 11, 3) that Herod built the sanctuary (*naos*) of stones that were "white and strong," probably meaning a hard variety of white limestone still much used in Palestine, and that they were about twenty-five cubits long, eight in height, and twelve in breadth, or in our feet about forty by twelve by twenty, which is even larger than the stones now found in the southern angles of Herod the Great's outer wall. (See on 21: 42.) In " War," 5, 5, 6, Josephus even says that some of the stones were forty-five cubits long (eighty-five feet). Doubtless the inner walls also, and pillars of the colonnades (see on 21: 12), presented very large and 'beautiful' stones.

---

[1] The earliest MSS. and nearly all the early versions give this order, and the internal probabilities are at least not against it; so there need be no question.

2 And Jesus said unto them, See ye not all these things? verily I say unto you, There shall not be left here one stone upon another, that shall not be thrown down.
3 And as he sat upon the mount of Olives, the disciples came unto him privately, saying, Tell us, when shall these things be? and what *shall be* the sign of thy coming, and of the end of the world?

2 shew him the buildings of the temple. But he answered and said unto them, See ye not all these things? verily I say unto you, There shall not be left here one stone upon another, that shall not be thrown down.
3 And as he sat on the mount of Olives, the disciples came unto him privately, saying, Tell us, when shall these things be? and what *shall be* the sign of

(Luke 21: 5, Bib. Un. Ver.) It is doubtful whether any other pile of sacred buildings on earth has been so vast or to contemporaries so imposing as Herod's temple. Talmud Bab. says: "He that never saw the temple of Herod, never saw a fine building." Luke's other expression, 'the temple was adorned with beautiful stones and offerings' (Bib. Un. Ver.), recalls Josephus' statement that "fastened all around the temple (*hieron*) were barbaric spoils, and all these King Herod offered up, adding whatever he took from the Arabians also." (Comp. Rev. 21: 26.) There were doubtless also many votive tablets, and other beautiful objects offered by the people, to adorn all the courts and colonnades, as well as the central sacred building. Tacitus says ("Hist.," V., 8, 12), that it was "a temple of immense wealth," and so constructed as to be "an excellent fortress." Our Lord seems to have been outside of the temple when his attention was called by the disciples, but this does not show that they were observing only the stones of the outer wall, for the central building rose high above the outer court and its wall, and was visible to a great distance, as Josephus states. ("Ant.," 15, 11, 3.) Our Lord's language in v. 2 shows that he is referring to the entire structure. **And Jesus said,** etc. *But he answered and said*, is the correct Greek text. The subsequent insertion of the name 'Jesus' is a thing of frequent occurrence in the manuscripts, comp. on 14: 14. **See ye not all these things?** This called their attention to the vast and solid mass of buildings, by way of preparation for the statement that all would be overthrown, a thing which then seemed in the highest degree unlikely; indeed, we know that Titus fully meant to preserve it. (Jos. "War," 6, 4.) **There shall not be left here one stone upon another.** So also in Mark and Luke. Some stickle at the fact that several stones of Herod's outer wall now remain *in situ, e. g.,* at the Jews' place of wailing, and at the southeast and southwest corners; indeed, at the southeast corner the recent English excavations reached foundation-stones supposed to have been laid by Solomon. Our Lord's language is of course popular, and such an objection is trifling. Comp. Jer. 26: 18. In fact, it is wonderful how literally the prediction was fulfilled, for very seldom was a great city so completely destroyed. Josephus says ("War," 7, 1, 1) that Titus finally ordered the whole city and the sanctuary to be razed to its foundations, except three towers and part of the western wall, and that all the rest of the city wall "was so completely leveled with the ground that there was no longer anything to lead those who visited the spot to believe that it had ever been inhabited."

3. Going on towards Bethany, our Lord climbs the steep base of **the Mount of Olives,** see on 21: 1, 17. Half way up the walking path one is apt to feel tired on a hot afternoon at the time of the Passover, and to seat himself on some ledge of limestone rock to rest. There he finds himself 'over against' (Mark) the site of the temple, at about the same height above the ravine of the Kedron. Our Lord may have sat here, or perhaps on the summit, where he would look down upon the whole city. The place at which some days before he "saw the city and wept over it" (Luke 19: 41. Rev. Ver.), was about half a mile further south, on the riding road from Bethany. The time was now towards night, and the evening sun kindled the white stone and gold of the temple buildings into splendor. **The disciples.** Mark says (13: 3), 'Peter and James and John and Andrew,' who were the first company of the Twelve (see above on 10: 2), and three of whom had been with the Lord on the Mount of Transfiguration. (17: 1.) This fact might have led these particular disciples to suppose that he would tell them what he would not tell the rest of the Twelve; and Matthew's general expression might be easily restricted to the four mentioned by Mark. Or it may be, as Euthym. suggests, that "they all came to learn, but four asked, as having greater freedom of access." **Privately,** so also Mark, as opposed to the public

4 And Jesus answered and said unto them, Take heed that no man deceive you.

4 thy [1]coming, and of [2]the end of the world? And Jesus answered and said unto them, Take heed that

---

1 Gr. *presence.*....2 Or, *the consummation of the age.*

---

discourses he had been giving all day in the temple. Jesus would of course refrain from speaking plainly in public of his future coming as the Messiah, when he had not yet publicly declared himself to be the Messiah. And it would have been dangerous (Mald.) to foretell openly the destruction of the temple (comp. John 2: 20), which in the case of Stephen was reckoned blasphemy. (Acts 6: 13 f.) **When shall these things be?** So Mark and Luke. The prediction that the entire temple would be thrown down reminded them of previous predictions that he would come again as the Messiah (16: 27 f.; Luke 19: 11; Matt. 23: 39), for they might well suppose such an utter destruction would occur only in connection with the establishment of the Messianic kingdom, which many Jews believed would be attended by mighty changes. So the disciples privately inquire as to the *time* of his promised coming, and the *sign* of it. **The sign of thy coming,** (*parousia*), *presence* (Rev. Ver. *margin*), as in 2 Cor. 10: 10, or 'arrival' as in the phrase 'by the coming of Titus,' 2 Cor. 7: 6; the idea is of not merely arriving but then remaining present, The word suggests (Ewald) that Jesus will come and *stay* with his people. This peculiar term is used for the second coming of Christ four times in the chapter (v. 3, 27, 37, 39), and repeatedly by James, Paul, Peter; also in 1 John 2: 28. Other terms used in the Epistles are manifestation, revelation, appearing, coming, day. The word 'thy' has a certain emphasis in the Greek. He has spoken of the *Messiah's* coming (23: 39; 16: 28); they are satisfied that this means *his* coming. **And of the end of the world,** or, as the Greek exactly means, *the consummation of the age* (Rev. Ver. *margin*), see on 13: 39 f. There is here no reference to any such idea as that of the destruction of the material universe (*kosmos*), but only the consummation and termination of the present *aion*, age, or state of things. A common Jewish conception was that the ap-

pearing of the Messiah would close 'this age,' and introduce 'the coming age'—these phrases often occurring in the Talmud. The disciples would easily transform the conception into that of a *future* appearance of their Master as the Messiah. Jesus had taught them that at 'the consummation of the age,' the end of the present state of things, the Messiah would destroy the wicked (13: 41, 49), and they were now fully convinced that he himself was the Messiah. Thus it was natural for them to ask these questions. It is not wise to distinguish sharply between the three clauses as if representing three entirely separate points. Evidently the disciples did not separate between his future coming and the end of the present period; nor has the Saviour done so in his reply. They also then supposed that the destruction of the temple would coincide with his coming and the end of the age; the reply did not clearly show that they would in fact be far apart, but it left the way open for what has in this respect turned out to be the case. The phrases 'coming' and 'consummation of the age' would be readily intelligible to the Jewish readers contemplated by Matt., but not to Gentiles; and accordingly Mark and Luke have simply 'and what is the sign when all these things are going to be completed' (Luke 'to come to pass').[1]

The Saviour's reply, so far as included in our present section, divides itself into v. 4-14, 15-28, 29-31, 32-36; and this last is very closely connected with what follows in the next section. Observe that the whole discourse is evidently designed, not to satisfy curiosity about the future, but to save from misconception, restrain impatience, and stimulate to perpetual watchfulness (24. 42) and faithfulness. (25: 14 ff.)

I. **4-14.** MISLEADING SIGNS. Found also in Mark 13: 5-13; Luke 21: 8-19. *Alexander:* "The divine wisdom of the Saviour and his knowledge of the perils which beset his followers

---

[1] Wünsche here quotes a good deal from the Talmud, and other Rabbinical writings, as to presages of the Messiah's coming (*i. e.* what we call his first coming), and descriptions of the Messianic time, but nothing that would really help in understanding this discourse. As to the wide difference between the Rabbinical conceptions of "the last things," and those of the New Test., see Edersh. II, 434, 445.

5 For many shall come in my name, saying, I am Christ: and shall deceive many.
6 And ye shall hear of wars and rumours of wars: see that ye be not troubled : for all *these things* must come to pass, but the end is not yet.

5 no man lead you astray. For many shall come in my name, saying, I am the Christ; and shall lead 6 many astray. And ye shall hear of wars and rumours of wars: see that ye be not troubled : for *these things*

---

are strikingly exemplified in this preliminary warning against error and delusion, this exposure of false signs before giving a description of the true. This method of proceeding is the more remarkable because the course suggested by fanatical excitement is the very opposite, and even wise men who devote themselves to such inquiries are too prone to look exclusively at what is positive in Christ's instructions, without heeding this preliminary admonition, or even observing that his purpose in this first part of his discourse is not to tell what are but what are not the premonitions of the great catastrophe to which he here refers, whatever it may be."

(a) False Messiahs and other false teachers, v. 4 f. ; also in Mark and Luke. **Many shall come in my name** (see on 18: 5), here means more than reliance on him, for they would claim to be what he really was. (Comp. v. 23–25 and Jer. 14: 14.) We have no account of any one who claimed to be the Messiah between this time and the destruction of Jerusalem. Yet there may very well have been such persons. As the Jews expected the Messiah to be a political deliverer, it was very natural that men who set up for political deliverers should pretend to be the Messiah; but as Josephus had interpreted the Messianic predictions as fulfilled in Vespasian,[1] and knew that any popular expectation of a native ruler would be highly unacceptable to the Romans, he would be likely to pass over such claims without mention. **Christ,** *the Christ,* with the article. (See on 2: 4.) Com. Ver. itself gives the article in 26: 63.

(b) Wars, famines, earthquakes, affecting the world at large, v. 6–8; so also Mark and Luke, the latter expanding. These extraordinary occurrences would become a false sign

by being misinterpreted, as such events often are. **Wars and rumors of wars,** which latter may turn out unreal. Both real wars and such rumors were abundant before A. D. 70, as well as often since. **Famines** (Acts 11: 28) are often mentioned in Old. Test., and are still frequent in Palestine ; **earthquakes** also frequently occur, and there are many signs of former volcanic activity. We read in Jos. and Tacitus of various famines and earthquakes in Palestine during the years preceding the destruction of Jerusalem. Persons caring to trace them out may refer to Alford or "Bible Comm." **Be not troubled.** Luke, 'terrified.' *Alexander :* "As if these commotions would necessarily imply the imminence of some great catastrophe, or of the final consummation. The necessity of this caution, not to the first disciples merely, but to their successors, is abundantly apparent from the well-known fact that pious men in every age have been continually falling into the mistake of looking on national commotions and collisions as decisive proof that the world is near its end. The meaning is not that such changes may not be immediately succeeded by the greatest change of all, but only that they are no sign of it, and ought not to be so regarded." **For all these things** (rather, *they*)[2] **must come to pass,** the latter term as in 5: 18. Why "must," or "must needs?" (Rev. Ver.) We might simply say (Meyer) that it was necessary according to the divine purpose, the thought of which might console the disciples, as it did the Saviour. (26: 54.) But does not the expression mean that in the preparation for the complete reign of the Messiah, conflict is unavoidable, not simply individual and domestic variance (10: 34 ff.), but conflict of the races and nations,

---

[1] See " War," 6, 5, 4, and comp. 3, 8, 9, with 4, 10, 7. The often quoted statement of Suetonius (" Claudius " 25) and Tacitus (" Hist." V, 13) as to an expectation " that persons proceeding from Judea would gain dominion," was to all appearance derived by them from Josephus, for they both make the same application that he does.

[2] Some documents inserted 'these things,' some 'all

things,' a few 'all these things;' the earliest MSS. and several early versions are without any such expression, and the various phrases mentioned are obviously additions made by students or copyists. In v. 7 'and pestilences' is added by many documents, but wanting in the earliest MSS., and plainly inserted from Luke 21: 11.

7 For nation shall rise against nation, and kingdom against kingdom: and there shall be famines, and pestilences, and earthquakes, in divers places.
8 All these *are* the beginning of sorrows.
9 Then shall they deliver you up to be afflicted, and shall kill you: and ye shall be hated of all nations for my name's sake.
10 And then shall many be offended, and shall betray one another, and shall hate one another.
11 And many false prophets shall rise, and shall deceive many.
12 And because iniquity shall abound, the love of many shall wax cold.

7 must needs come to pass: but the end is not yet. For nation shall rise against nation, and kingdom against kingdom: and there shall be famines and
8 earthquakes in divers places. But all these things
9 are the beginning of travail. Then shall they deliver you up unto tribulation, and shall kill you:
10 and ye shall be hated of all the nations for my name's sake. And then shall many stumble, and shall deliver up one another, and shall hate one another.
11 And many false prophets shall arise, and shall lead
12 many astray. And because iniquity shall be multi-

as afterwards depicted in the visions of John in Patmos? Meyer sees in v. 6 f., "the first, far off indirect prognostics of the second advent, like the roll of distant thunder." With the imagery of v. 7 comp. that of Isa. 19: 2. In v. 8, **the beginning of sorrows,** or, *travail,* and not the end, the consummation. 'Travail' is in the Greek a plural, meaning the pains of labor, the birth-pangs (1 Thess. 5: 3, and often in Old Test.); then any severe pangs (Acts 2:24.) These things will not be merely the beginning of distresses, but of labor-pains (comp. Rom. 8: 22); and the end of these will be the appearance of a better state of things (comp. "the regeneration," 19: 28.) *Edersh:* "Jewish writings speak very frequently of the so-called 'sorrows of the Messiah' [the word meaning labor-pains.] These were partly those of the Messiah, and partly—perhaps chiefly—those coming on Israel and the world previous to, and connected with, the coming of the Messiah." The particulars mentioned vary greatly, and the descriptions are quite fanciful. But they may generally be characterized as marking a period of internal corruption and of outward distress, especially of famine and war, of which the land of Palestine was to be the scene, and in which the people of Israel were to be the chief sufferers; yet none of them refers to desolation of the City and Temple as one of the 'signs' or 'sorrows' of the Messiah.

(c) Things directly affecting the Christians —persecution, false prophets, multiplied transgressions, v. 9-13. So Mark and Luke. But they here also give a prediction that the disciples will be brought before Jewish and heathen tribunals, with persecution and scourging (comp. Acts 22: 19; 2 Cor. 11: 24 f.); and that they will be taught by inspiration what to say in their defence, and need not be anxious in advance on that point. (Comp. Acts 4: 8-13.) Matthew has given a similar passage in the discourse to the Twelve on send-

ing them out (see 10: 17-22), and therefore (we may suppose) does not repeat it here. **To be afflicted,** better, as Rev. Ver., *to tribulation,* see the word explained on 13: 21. For instances of persecution, see Acts 4: 1; 7: 59; 12: 1; Rev. 2: 10, 12. **Ye shall be hated of all nations.** Comp. "as concerning this sect, it is known to us that everywhere it is spoken against." (Acts 28: 22. R. V.) Tacitus ("Annals" XV. 44) speaks of the Christians as "a kind of men hated for their acts of wickedness." **And then shall many be offended** (*stumble*), comp. 13: 21, 57, and see the term explained on 5: 29. **Shall betray** (or *deliver up*) **one another,** represents a peculiarly painful feature of the situation in times of severe persecution. Tacitus in speaking of the persecution of Christians by Nero in A. D. 64, says, "At first those who confessed were seized, afterwards upon their information a great multitude." **And shall hate one another.** Remember how Paul was hated by the Judaizers, and by various parties at Corinth.

11 f. is found in Matt. only. There shall be not merely persecution but false teaching. (Comp. Acts 20: 29 f.; 2 Pet. 2: 1; 1 John 4: 1.) **False prophets,** comp. v. 24; 7: 15; 2 Pet. 2: 1. **Shall deceive,** or *lead astray,* **many,** the same term as in v. 4 f. **Iniquity,** more exactly *transgression of law,* see on 23: 28. **Shall abound,** or *be multiplied,* as this word is everywhere else rendered. **The love of** (*the*) **many,** the general mass, excepting a few individuals. (Comp. Winer.) 'Love' here probably means love to Christ and to his people. The great increase of the violation of God's law among the wicked will gradually tone down and chill the zeal and love of the great mass of professed subjects of the Messiah. The Epistle to the Hebrews seems aimed at such a tendency, and similar periods have often existed in Christian history. Tyndale and followers greatly enfeebled this state-

13 But he that shall endure unto the end, the same shall be saved.

14 And this gospel of the kingdom shall be preached in all the world for a witness unto all nations; and then shall the end come.

15 When ye therefore shall see the abomination of desolation, spoken of by Daniel the prophet, stand in the holy place, (whoso readeth, let him understand :)

plied, the love of the many shall wax cold. B it he that
13 endureth to the end, the same shall be saved. And
14 1 this gospel of the kingdom shall be preached in the whole 2 world for a testimony unto all the nations; and then shall the end come.
15 When therefore ye see the abomination of desolation, which was spoken of through Daniel the prophet, standing in 3 the holy place (let him that read-

---

1 Or, *these good tidings*....2 Gr. *inhabited earth*....3 Or, *a holy place.*

---

ment by neglecting the article, and making it 'the love of many.'

13. He that shall endure unto the end, that through life endures persecution (v. 9-11) without flinching, and with multiplied transgression all around him maintains warm Christian love (v. 12); comp. Rev. 2: 10. Or 'unto the end' may mean not through life, but unto the end of these trials. Luke gives (21: 19) the kindred and remarkable expression, "in your patience ye shall win your souls" (correct text and translation), implying that men may gain possession of their own spiritual nature through patient endurance of the ills of life.

(d) A corrective to the false signs, v. 14; Mark 13: 10. Nothwithstanding the persecution from without and the false teaching and diminished love within, the gospel will be everywhere preached; then, and not till then, will the end come. **This gospel of the kingdom,** *the good tidings* (Rev. Ver. *margin*) that the Messianic kingdom or reign is near (see on 4: 23; 3: 2), which the Saviour was and long had been engaged in proclaiming. Comp. the beginning of our Lord's preaching in Galilee, Mark 1: 15. **Preached,** *kerusso,* see on 4: 17. **In all the world,** more exactly, *in the whole inhabited (earth),* as in Rev. Ver. *margin.* This term, *oikoumene,* is repeatedly used in Luke (and Acts), not elsewhere in the Gospels. From it comes the modern Popish phrase, "an œcumenical council," one whose members gather from all the inhabited earth. This statement, that the gospel shall be preached in the whole inhabited earth, and the following expression **for a witness unto all** (*the*) **nations,** could be regarded as a hyperbolical prediction of what was fulfilled before the destruction of Jerusalem, even as Paul wrote to the Colossians (about A. D. 63), concerning "the gospel which ye heard, which was preached in all creation under heaven." (Col. 1: 23, Rev. Ver.) It will evidently be fulfilled much more thoroughly before the second coming of Christ; yet Paul's phrase, and the apparent primary ref-

erence here to A. D., 70 as 'the end,' should restrain theorizers from insisting that the second coming of Christ cannot take place until this has been fulfilled with literal completeness. **For a witness,** or, *testimony,* in order that testimony may be offered them concerning the Messiah and his salvation, such as they may believe if they will.

II. **15-28.** ONE GREAT SIGN AT JERUSALEM; also in Mark 13: 14-23; Luke 21: 20-24. In v. 15-22 the Saviour states what they must do upon the occurrence of this sign, and in v. 23-28 warns against misleading pretensions and propositions.

(a) The sign, and what they must do, v. 15-22. **When ye therefore shall see.** What inference is expressed by 'therefore'? He has said that the end is coming (v. 14), and that those who endure to the end shall be saved (v. 13); when therefore they see a certain sign, let them promptly flee, in order to save themselves. (v. 16 ff.)

V. 13 f., apparently refers both to the destruction of Jerusalem and to the final coming of Christ; an inference from it in the former sense is that which here follows. **The abomination of desolation.** The Greek construction makes it the abomination characterized by desolation, which might be as a token or as a cause of desolation. This vague phrase is further described by adding **spoken of by** (*through*) **Daniel the prophet,** viz., spoken of by God through the prophet, comp. 21: 4, and see on 1: 22; 2: 5. This addition is wanting in the correct text of Mark (13: 14), having been added in the common text from Matt. It is stated in Daniel (9: 26 f.), that 'the anointed one,' the Messiah, 'shall be cut off,' and 'the people of the prince that shall come, shall destroy the city and the sanctuary. . . . and he shall cause the sacrifice and the meat-offering to cease; and upon the wing of abominations shall come one that maketh desolate,' or (*margin,* Rev. Ver.), 'upon the pinnacle of abominations shall be one that maketh desolate.' In

16 Then let them which be in Judea flee into the mountains:

16 eth understand), then let them that are in Judæa flee

this last sense it was understood by the Sept., which renders 'upon the temple (*hieron*) (shall be) the abomination of the desolations.' In Dan. 11: 31 and 12: 11 the Sept. has 'abomination of desolation,' as here. The writer of 1 Macc. (1: 54) applied this phrase to the heathen altar which in the time of Antiochus Epiphanes was set upon the altar of Jehovah. It is evident that our Lord interprets the prediction in Daniel as referring to the Messiah, and to that destruction of the city and the temple which he is now foretelling; and his interpretation is authoritative for us. What this predicted 'abomination of desolation' would be, was an obscure question. Many a prediction of human action was necessarily obscure till the fulfillment came, because otherwise it would have so influenced believers as to fulfill itself, and would have thus failed to be valid as a superhuman prediction to strengthen faith in him who spoke it. (John 14: 29.) Our Lord cites this obscure expression without explaining it, simply pointing out that it demands attention from the reader of Daniel—**let him that readeth understand**—and implying that if really understood it has the reference he is indicating. Some suppose the parenthetic remark to be that of Matthew, addressing the reader of the Gospel; but this is made improbable by the fact that Mark gives the same parenthesis *verbatim*, for although Mark (in the correct text) does not mention Daniel, yet the peculiar and well-known phrase would suggest its source in that book. Luke (21: 20), probably because the phrase was obscure and difficult, paraphrases it by an expression (or perhaps reports an additional expression, comp. Luke 19: 42), which suggests to us the interpretation: 'When ye see Jerusalem compassed with armies, then know that the desolation thereof is near.' Literally, it is 'being encircled by armies,' when you see the process going on, then flee. Notice that Luke retains the term 'desolation.' Now we cannot always interpret the phraseology of a passage from that of a parallel passage, but there is always a strong probability that their meaning is substantially the same. It is possible that Luke describes an occurrence without the city, and Matthew, some concurrent desecra-

tion of the temple, represented by the abomination of desolation. But it is much more likely that 'the abomination of desolation, standing in the holy place' means some object connected with the Roman army under Titus that encircled and captured Jerusalem, which object foretokened speedy desolation. The Roman military standard, with its eagle of silver or bronze, and under that an imperial bust which the soldiers were accustomed to worship, standing anywhere in the holy city. (4: 5) would be a violation of the second commandment, would be abominable in the eyes of all devout Jews, would in itself desolate the holy place, according to their feeling, and would foretoken a yet more complete desolation. **Holy place** cannot well mean distinctively the temple in this case, for when the Roman standards stood in the temple it was too late for fleeing to the mountain. One or two years before the Saviour thus spoke, Pilate had outraged the Jews by bringing into Jerusalem by night such military standards, having on them the emperor's bust, and only upon vehement and protracted entreaty did he consent to remove them (Jos. "Ant.," 18, 3, 1). The *masculine* participle for 'standing' used by Mark (13: 14, correct text) might refer to the emperor whose bust the standard bore, or to the general whose authority it represented. The term 'abomination' is oftenest used in Old Test. as denoting idols, or objects connected with idolatry. The horror of civil war in the temple (Jos. "War," 4, 9, 11 f.) would not so well account for this phrase, nor correspond to the connection in Daniel. Some prefer simply to understand the Roman power, as abominable and desolating.

16. Then. The signs previously mentioned will not show that the end is near; but when *this* sign is seen, then the followers of Christ must at once leave Jerusalem and the entire district of Judea. **Flee into the mountains** seems to be a general phrase, not denoting any particular mountains. In the Maccabean time the Jews had become familiar with the idea of hiding in ravines and caves of the mountains. Eusebius states ("Hist." III., 5, 2 f.) that at the time of the siege by Titus the apostles had gone to preach the gospel to all the nations, and that the people (laity) of the

17 Let him which is on the housetop not come down to take anything out of his house:
18 Neither let him which is in the field return back to take his clothes.
19 And woe unto them that are with child, and to them that give suck in those days!
20 But pray ye that your flight be not in the winter, neither on the sabbath day:

17 unto the mountains: let him that is on the housetop
18 not go down to take out the things that are in his house: and let him that is in the field not return
19 back to take his cloak. But woe unto them that are with child and to them that give suck in those days!

---

church in Jerusalem, in accordance with a certain divine communication given by revelation before the war, removed and dwelt in a city of Perea named Pella. Epiphanius has a similar statement. Merrill, "East of the Jordan," leaves no reasonable doubt that Robinson was right in identifying Pella with the ruins called Fah'l, lying just across the Jordan valley eastward from Bethshean, in a beautiful and healthy situation. The ruins indicate an important city. Epiphanius says that when Hadrian rebuilt Jerusalem, changing its name to Ælia (A. D. 135), the Christians a second time withdrew to Pella. It is not clear from Eusebius at what precise time the Christians withdrew from Jerusalem; it may have been (so Plump. and Edersh. think) in A. D. 68, but it seems to have occurred after Titus took command, which followed the death of Galba, A. D. 69 (see Jos. "War," 4, 9, 2). During the siege, in A. D. 70, Titus allowed many Jews to withdraw from the city ("War," 5, 10, 1), and the Christians may have left then. Such an abandonment of Jerusalem was not unprecedented, for after the affair of Cestius, in A. D 66, "many of the distinguished Jews left the city, as if swimming from a sinking ship" ("War," 2, 20, 1).

17 f. The flight is to be prompt, immediate. The top of an Oriental house is flat, with only slant enough to carry off the rain, and with a battlement or parapet to prevent persons from falling. (Deut. 22: 8.) This roof is usually reached by steps from the inner court. (Mark 2: 4.) In a city, where the houses adjoin, one might go along the roofs from house to house without descending to the court and the street. Josephus ("Ant.," 13, 5, 3) represents some Jewish soldiers as quelling a tumultuous rebellion in Antioch by going on the roofs of the palaces to cast down missiles upon the crowds in the streets, and then leaping from house to house and setting fire to the dwellings of the people. So here, he **which is on the housetop** (*e. g., Acts* 10: 9) will find it the shortest way to escape from the doomed city to pass from roof to roof, and must not go down **to take anything out of his house.**[1] In like manner, **neither let him which is in the field** at work, and has laid aside his outer garment (5: 40), return to the place where he laid it, but he must flee straightway. Origen understands return to the city, but that would take a long time, and the prohibition of it would not indicate great haste; besides that decorous persons would not leave the outer garment at home, but would wear it in going from the city to the field. These are strong expressions—such as the Saviour frequently used, see on 5: 39—to show that the flight must be extremely prompt, when the predicted sign appears.

19-22. Woe is here said compassionately, while in 23: 13 it was denounced as a thing deserved. A flight so prompt and hasty must involve great hardship and difficulty for delicate women, and for all if it should be **in the winter.**[2] So the traditional law as to a Sabbath day journey, that it should be not more than two thousand cubits, about ten hundred and fifty yards, would prove overwhelmingly inconvenient, if the flight should occur **on the Sabbath day.** Some (Wün.) held it

---

1 Literally ' *to take away the things that are out of his house,*' an abreviated expression for " to take out of the house the things that are in it." This is undoubtedly the correct reading here. The singular 'garment' (or 'cloak') is read by all the earliest MSS. and many others, and by nearly all the early versions; this must outweigh the probability of assimilation to Mark 13: 16.

2 It was a great mercy to the Southern people that the end of the Civil War (1865) came in April, when if the men hurried home and went immediately to work,

there was just time enough to plant corn, tobacco, cotton; this prevented disorder and violence, by engaging all in hopeful industry. So some Rabbinical writers (Wet.) speak of it as a special mercy that the destruction of Jerusalem by the Babylonians (2 Kings 25 : 3-9) occurred at a season of the year suitable for journeying and exposure. And, according to Josephus, the army of Titus reached Jerusalem in April (A. D. 70), and destroyed it in September.

21 For then shall be great tribulation, such as was not since the beginning of the world to this time, no, nor ever shall be.
22 And except those days should be shortened, there should no flesh be saved: but for the elect's sake those days shall be shortened.
23 Then if any man shall say unto you, Lo, here is Christ, or there: believe *it* not.
24 For there shall arise false Christs, and false prophets, and shall shew great signs and wonders; insomuch that, if *it were* possible, they shall deceive the very elect.
25 Behold, I have told you before.

20 And pray ye that your flight be not in the winter, 21 neither on a Sabbath: for then shall be great tribulation, such as hath not been from the beginning of 22 the world until now, no, nor ever shall be. And except those days had been shortened, no flesh would 23 have been saved: but for the elect's sake those days shall be shortened. Then if any man shall say unto 24 you, Lo, here is the Christ, or, Here; believe [1] *it* not. For there shall arise false Christs, and false prophets, and shall shew great signs and wonders; so as to 25 lead astray, if possible, even the elect. Behold, I

---

1 Or, *him.*

---

lawful to violate this when in peril of life; and such a course our Lord would certainly have approved (comp. on 12: 2 ff.); but it would be to any strict Jew a painful and embarrassing necessity. Moreover (*Hessey,* in "Bible Comm."), "it was no doubt considered wrong to assist the traveler, however urgent his errand, in his movements on the Sabbath day. All possible impediments therefore would be thrown in the way of the fugitives by those who were still zealous for the supposed requirements of the law." Our Lord seems to imply that his Jewish followers will be still scrupulous about the traditional mode of observing the Sabbath up to the destruction of Jerusalem. It was indeed this event that first made the Jewish Christians clearly understand the ceremonial law to be no longer binding (comp. on 16: 28). **Pray ye that your flight be not** is a non-final construction, see on 5: 29.

21. For, reason for the injunction of v. 16, which was expanded by v. 17-20. This reason is that the sufferings attendant upon the destruction of Jerusalem, will be without parallel in past or future history. (Comp. on v. 29.) We might regard this also as the hyperbolical language often used in prophecy (comp. Dan. 12: 1; Joel 2: 1); yet in this case it may be taken literally, for certainly no recorded distresses have been so vast, so prolonged, so terrible, as those described by Josephus in the "Jewish War." We are not surprised to find him saying (5, 10, 5), "no other city ever endured similar calamities, and no generation ever existed more prolific in crime." Comp. his Preface to the "War," § 4. **The elect** (v. 22) would seem to be the elect among the Jews (Isa. 65: 9), the Jewish Christians. If the destruction and desolation inflicted by the Romans during the siege and overthrow of

the city, and afterwards at various points, had been continued much longer, they would have swept away all Jews who were then Christians, and all who afterwards became Christians— yea, the whole Jewish race. **Should be shortened,** etc., Rev. Ver. *Had been shortened, no flesh would have been saved,* is the necessary meaning of the Greek; 'saved' means the saving of the life, 9: 21 f., comp. on 1: 21. Mark 13: 20 refers the shortening expressly to Jehovah. That others should also be saved for the sake of saving the elect, reminds of Gen. 18: 23 ff. Luke adds (21: 24, R. V.) 'and they shall be led away captive into all nations' (comp. Jos. "War," Book 7), 'and Jerusalem shall be trodden down by the Gentiles until the times of the Gentiles be fulfilled.'

We cannot say that v. 15-22 does not at all refer to the times just preceding our Lord's *final* coming; but no such reference shows itself. The *terms* of v. 22 might readily be so understood, but 'those days' can hardly mean anything else than the days of the flight from Judea. (v. 16-20.)

(b) False pretensions which must then be guarded against, v. 23-28; so Mark 13: 21-23; not in Luke.

23-25. Further cases of false Messiahs. (Comp. v. 5.) A *pseudo-christ,* one who falsely claimed to be Christ, must be distinguished from an *anti-christ,* an opposer of Christ (Epistles of John); compare the somewhat similar designation in 2 Thess. 2: 4. **Shall shew great signs and wonders,** comp. on 16: 1, and for the terms see on 12: 38. **Shall deceive,** or *lead astray,* same term as in v. 4 f., 11, and in 18: 12 f. (Comp. Deut. 13: 1 ff.; Rev. 13: 13.) *Alexander:* "This prediction, in its strict sense, is among the passages which seem to show that even real miracles are not sufficient of themselves to prove the truth of any doctrine, but only

26 Wherefore if they shall say unto you, Behold, he is in the desert; go not forth : behold, *he is* in the secret chambers; believe *it* not.
27 For as the lightning cometh out of the east, and shineth even unto the west; so shall also the coming of the Son of man be.
28 For wheresoever the carcass is, there will the eagles be gathered together.
29 Immediately after the tribulation of those days shall the sun be darkened, and the moon shall not give her light, and the stars shall fall from heaven, and the powers of the heavens shall be shaken :

26 have told you beforehand. If therefore they shall say unto you, Behold, he is in the wilderness; go 27 not forth: Behold, he is in the inner chambers; believe [1] *it* not. For as the lightning cometh forth 28 from the east, and is seen even unto the west; so shall be the [2] coming of the Son of man. Wheresoever the carcase is, there will the [3] eagles be gathered together.
29 But immediately, after the tribulation of those days, the sun shall be darkened, and the moon shall not give her light, and the stars shall fall from

---

1 Or, *them*....2 Gr. *presence*....3 Or, *vultures*.

---

one part of a complex demonstration, at once sensible, rational, and spiritual.''

26 f. The true Messiah's appearing will be sudden and visible to all. **The desert** or *wilderness* (4: 1), and **the secret chambers** (6: 6), are contrasted. He will not be known to have appeared elsewhere, and will not be found by searching in the wild, thinly inhabited regions, or in the private portions of some city house; his appearing will be visible to all, as a flash of lightning. (Comp. Luke 17: 23 f.) **The coming,** comp. on v. 3. **The Son of man,** the Messiah, see on 8: 20. Here 'the coming of the Son of man' answers to 'thy coming' in v. 3.

27 is closely connected by **for** with v. 26, which last points to the destruction of Jerusalem. Yet the language of v. 27 seems specially appropriate to the final coming; and it may perhaps be understood as referring to both. (Comp. on v. 3.) **Also** is an inadequately supported addition in the common text. **And shineth,** or *is seen*, as in 6: 5; not that the lightning goes to the west, as 'shineth' might suggest, but that its light is seen even that far. The thought therefore seems to be (Weiss) that the Messiah's coming will be alike visible to all, and so there will be no occasion for some to tell others where he may be seen.

28. Comp. Luke 17: 37, and the same image in Job 39 : 30. **Wheresoever the carcass is, [1] there will the eagles be gathered together.** As the eagle proper rarely feeds on carrion, the word probably here denotes a carrion-kite, which Pliny classes with eagles (Grimm), or a great vulture as large as the eagle, which now abounds in Palestine, and is called eagle by the natives (Thomson, III,

221). The meaning of the saying as here applied seems to be, that things will come to pass when the occasion for them exists. When Jerusalem is ready for destruction, the Roman armies will gather and destroy it; when the world lies awaiting the final appearance of Christ to judgment, he will come. Kendrick (in Olsh.) considers, with less probability, that it means the swarming of the false prophets to prey on the corrupt mass of Judaism. Calvin, after some Fathers, understands the children of God as gathering to Christ and feeding on him, an idea repulsive in itself, and out of harmony with the connection, in which ("Bible Comm.") Christ comes not in grace, but in judgment; yet many later writers have unwisely adopted this view. It is hardly possible, as formerly fancied by some, that our Lord meant an allusion to the Roman eagles.

III. **29-31.** SIGNS IN HEAVEN. Mark 13 : 24-27; Luke 21 : 25-28. **Immediately.** The phrase is not exactly 'immediately after'; the adverb 'immediately' is connected with 'the sun shall be darkened,' etc. The substantial sense is however the same. So far as this passage relates to the destruction of Jerusalem, we may suppose that the events it indicates were to follow immediately after those predicted in 15-28. As regards the ulterior reference to the final *parousia*, there may prove to be in like manner some close consecution, but only the fulfillment is likely to show. **After the tribulation of those days,** viz., the tribulation attending upon the destruction of Jerusalem, see especially v. 21. The English term tribulation is often regarded as interesting, from its supposed connection with the Latin *tribulum*, a threshing-sled with

---

1 'For' is wanting in the earliest MSS. and most of the early versions, and would be very easily inserted by students or copyists. The word meaning 'carcass,'

(or 'corpse') was here altered by some documents into the somewhat similar word meaning 'body,' which Luke has in 17: 37; comp. above on 14: 12.

30 And then shall appear the sign of the Son of man in heaven: and then shall all the tribes of the earth mourn, and they shall see the Son of man coming in the clouds of heaven with power and great glory.

31 And he shall send his angels with a great sound of a trumpet, and they shall gather together his elect from the four winds, from one end of heaven to the other.

heaven, and the powers of the heavens shall be 30 shaken: and then shall appear the sign of the Son of man in heaven: and then shall all the tribes of the earth mourn, and they shall see the Son of man coming on the clouds of heaven with power and 31 great glory. And he shall send forth his angels [1] with [2] a great sound of a trumpet, and they shall gather together his elect from the four winds, from one end of heaven to the other.

---

[1] Many ancient authorities read. *with a great trumpet, and they shall gather, etc.* .....[2] Or, *a trumpet of great sound.*

---

sharp teeth to beat the grain out of the straw. But the Greek certainly has no such association, and means simply pressure, oppression, affliction (*e. g.*, 2 Cor. 1 : 3-8). **Of those days,** is naturally but not necessarily the same period as 'those days' in v. 19 and 22. **The sun shall be darkened,** etc., comp. Joel 2 : 31; 3 : 15; Amos 8 : 9; Isa. 13 : 9 f. ; Ezek. 32 : 7; Rev. 6 : 12. These passages incline one to understand the expressions as a mere image. And so with the following expression, **the stars shall fall,** meaning not some stars, but the stars generally. Comp. Isa. 34 : 4. **The powers of the heavens,** the forces which dwell in the heavens and keep them stable; the shaking of which will disturb their stability (Meyer). Luke condenses all this into 'there shall be signs in sun and moon and stars,' and then adds some other striking imagery, as 'the roaring of the sea and the billows.' (Luke 21 : 25 f.,R. V.) Some Premillennialist or Adventist writers hold (Hanna) that with v. 29 begins the account of the introduction of Christ's personal reign on earth, extending to 25 : 30, and after that is described the general judgment at the end of the millennium. But it is extremely doubtful whether we ought to introduce into the Saviour's discourse such ideas supposed to be drawn from the Apocalypse.

30. The sign of the Son of man in heaven. The Jews had repeatedly asked for such a sign (16 : 1; 12 : 38; John 2 : 18), and the disciples had just inquired as to the sign of his coming. (v. 3.) He here tells the disciples when it will appear, but does not tell them *what* the sign will be, nor can we clearly perceive from the connection. Some Fathers fancied that it meant the appearance of a cross in the sky, as in the famous story of Constantine ; but this is quite unwarranted. It may be (Calvin) that the sign will be nothing more than the Saviour's

own coming on the clouds, as just afterwards mentioned, and as predicted in Dan. 7 : 13.

Then shall all the tribes of the earth mourn. (Comp. Zech. 12 : 10, 12 ; Rev. 1 : 7.) Not simply the Jews shall mourn, but all men. This may have been true in some partial sense at the destruction of Jerusalem. Is it not probable that many Jews who had heard the apostles preach, or who had read the Gospel of Matt., did then remember the rejected Jesus, how he predicted all this calamity and ruin, how they voluntarily assumed the guilt of his blood (27: 25), and did mourn bitterly ? But the prediction will doubtless be completely fulfilled at the second coming of Christ. **Coming in the clouds of heaven,** etc. (Comp. 16: 27.) Com. Ver. obscures the variation of this expression in different passages. The Greek has 'on the clouds' here, 26 : 64; Rev. 14: 14-16; 'in clouds' (Mark 13 : 26 ; Luke 21 : 27) ; ' with the clouds' (Mark 14 : 62 ; Rev. 1 : 7; Dan. 7 : 13.)

31. Send his angels (see on 13 : 41.), **A great sound of a trumpet.** *With a trumpet of great sound* (Rev. Ver., *margin*), i. e., with a loud-sounding trumpet (Buttm.), is the natural translation of the most probable text.[1] It might possibly be translated as in Com. and Rev. Ver., but not naturally, for so the word rendered trumpet would have in the Greek an emphatic position without any discernible reason (Weiss). The image is drawn from a herald sounding a loud trumpet to announce the approach of a monarch, or of his representatives, and to assemble the people that they may hear his commands. From this saying Paul probably derived the expressions of 1 Cor. 15: 52. **And they shall gather together his elect,** etc. Notice how often this term 'the elect' is used (v. 22, 24, 31), and so Mark in each case. (Comp. above,

---

[1] There is considerable documentary evidence for the other reading in the margin of Rev. Ver., 'with a great trumpet,' but only the "Western" documents support that in the margin of Com. Ver., 'with a trumpet, and

a great voice (sound)', which is a manifest alteration. The difference in any case is unimportant, as a great trumpet would make a great sound.

32 Now learn a parable of the fig tree; When his branch is yet tender, and putteth forth leaves, ye know that summer *is* nigh:
33 So likewise ye, when ye shall see all these things, know that it is near, *even* at the doors.
34 Verily I say unto you, This generation shall not pass, till all these things be fulfilled.

32 Now from the fig tree learn her parable: when her branch is now become tender, and putteth forth its
33 leaves, ye know that the summer is nigh: even so ye also, when ye see all these things, know ye that
34 1 he is nigh, *even* at the doors. Verily I say unto you, This generation shall not pass away, till all

---

1 Or. *it.*

22: 14.) **From the four winds,** a common designation of what we now call the four points of the compass. **From one end of heaven to the other,** a phrase drawn from the old conception of the earth as an oblong plain, bounded at each end by the sky, the horizon. Such familiar phrases are used in Scripture as they are among us, without becoming responsible for the conformity of the conception they involve to the physical fact. The meaning is that the elect will be gathered from every part ·of the earth in which they are found.

It is practically impossible to suppose that v. 30 f. relates *simply* to the destruction of Jerusalem. As the latter part of the discourse (25: 31-46) clearly refers to the second coming of our Lord, it seems unavoidable to suppose a similar reference here; see also the corresponding passage, 13: 41. But v. 34 will presently declare that 'all' the foregoing matter will occur during the existing generation. Then as we cannot believe (with Meyer and others) that the Saviour mistakenly expected his *parousia* to be within that generation, it follows that v. 29-31 must refer to the destruction of Jerusalem. The difficulty is relieved by understanding a typical relation between the destruction of Jerusalem and his final *parousia*, on the ground of which relation v. 29–31 really points in some sense to *both* events. (Comp. above on v. 3.)

IV. **32-36.** THESE SIGNS WILL SUFFICE TO SHOW. Mark 13: 28-32 (very nearly the same words); Luke 21: 29-33. **From the fig tree,** placed first in the sentence, and thus emphatic. He may have looked at some fig tree near them, just as in the same vicinity he had five days before used a fig tree for an object-lesson. (21: 20.) But the article, 'the fig tree,' does not necessarily indicate a particular tree, but may mean only that kind of tree, or that class of objects. **Learn a parable** (Rev. Ver., *her parable*), or simply 'the parable,' the one which the fig tree has to teach. Everything in nature has its moral

analogies; Jesus has set us the example of perceiving these and using them for religious instruction. The word parable (see on 13: 3) is here used in its general sense of an illustrative comparison, as in 15: 15, there being here no narrative such as we commonly mean by a parable. **When his branch . . . . leaves.** The 'his' is the old possessive of 'it,' which was originally '*hit*,' and is still often so pronounced by the vulgar. The possessive *its* was just beginning to be used when the K. James version was made. It is found in Shakespeare, though he generally uses *his*. (Schmidt "Shak. Lex.") *Its* is not in K. J. Ver., Ed. 1611, though now found, Lev. 25: 5. We find *his* as neuter repeatedly in Old Test. (*e. g.*, Psa. 1: 3; Exod. 25: 31; 36: 17, etc.), and several times in New Test. (5: 13; Acts 12: 10; 1 Cor. 15: 38.) The parallel passage in Com. Ver. of Mark has 'her branch,' which Rev. Ver. adopts here, personifying the fig tree as feminine (like the Greek), and so in Rev. 6: 13; comp. 22: 2. **Is yet tender.** The Rev. Ver., *Is now become tender*, gives the exact meaning. 'Is yet tender,' Tyn. and followers, suggests that the tenderness is about to cease, when the Greek means that it has just become complete. **When ye shall see all these things,** probably those of v. 15 and v. 29 f. **Know that it is near.** (v. 31.) The Rev. Ver. gives 'He is nigh,' or in margin, 'it is nigh,' viz., his coming (v. 27), or 'the kingdom of God is nigh' (Luke 21: 31), all obviously amounting to the same thing. The 'he' is most naturally suggested by what precedes, and is supported by James 5: 9. Edersh. thinks "it can scarcely be supposed that Christ would speak of himself in the third person"; but see in this very discourse v. 31 and 25: 31 ff.

34. Verily, I say unto you (see on 5: 18), calling attention to something of special importance. **This generation,** as in 23: 36, also 11: 16; 12: 41 f.; and compare Luke 17: 25 with 21: 32. The word cannot have any other meaning here than the obvious one. The attempts to establish for it the sense of

35 Heaven and earth shall pass away, but my words shall not pass away.
36 But of that day and hour knoweth no *man*, no, not the angels of heaven, but my Father only.

35 these things be accomplished. Heaven and earth shall pass away, but my words shall not pass away.
36 But of that day and hour knoweth no one, not even the angels of heaven, 1 neither the Son, but the Father

1 Many authorities, some ancient, omit, *neither the Son.*

---

race or *nation* have failed. There are some examples in which it *might* have such a meaning, but none in which it must, for in every case the recognized meaning will answer, and so another sense is not admissible. (Comp. on 3: 6.) Some of the Fathers took it to mean the generation of believers, *i. e.*, the Christians, etc., after the loose manner of interpreting into which many of them so often fell. We now commonly make the rough estimate of three generations to a century. The year in which our Lord said this was most probably A. D. 30, and if so, it was forty years to the destruction of Jerusalem. The thought is thus the same as in 16: 28; and comp. John 21: 22 f. **Till all these things be fulfilled,** or, more exactly, *take place,* 'come to pass,' see on 5: 18. The emphasis is on 'all.' All the things predicted in v. 4-31 would occur before or in immediate connection with the destruction of Jerusalem. But like events might again occur in connection with another and greater coming of the Lord, and such seems evidently to be his meaning. (See on v. 3.)

35. Heaven and earth shall pass away,

etc. (see on 5: 19), still further emphasizes the importance of what he is saying, which was introduced by 'Verily, I say unto you.' It was hard for the disciples to believe that their Master would come again and utterly destroy the temple and the holy city (v. 2 f.), and work such great changes as have been indicated by v. 29-31, within that generation; and so he asserts it very solemnly, comp. John 16: 7. We learn also in 2 Pet. 3: 7 f. and elsewhere that heaven and earth will pass away; not that they will cease to exist, but that they will be changed into something entirely new.

36. The predictions he has made will receive a fulfillment within that generation (v. 34), to be witnessed by some then living (16: 28); this much he solemnly declares, but the time he will not more exactly state, for indeed the precise time no one knows but the Father only. **Of** (*concerning*) **that day and hour.** It is mere quibbling to say that still we may ascertain the year and month. **No, not the angels of heaven,** comp. on 18: 10. The Rev. Ver. gives 'neither the Son.' It is difficult to decide whether these words are here genuine.[1] They are certainly genuine in

---

1 Though of little practical importance, the question is one of great interest to the science of text-criticism. The clause is given here by א B D, by the old uncial represented by 13, 124, 346, two other cursives, some codices of the Old Latin and a few of the Vulgate, Syriac of Jerusalem, Ethiopic, and Armenian, Origen (who carefully discusses the phrase in his commentary on Matt.), Chrys., Hilary, and the Anonymous Comm. on Matt. Now if B were absent from this list, the clause would be immediately rejected as a "Western" addition. obviously drawn from Mark. We know (W H., Int. § 159) that "in Origen, especially in some of his writings, Western quotations hold a prominent place," *e. g.*, see just after this, v. 41. The Ethiopic is well known to present "Western" readings in many passages, and the Armenian gives them in v. 2: 25: 1; Acts 8: 37; Eph. 5: 30, and elsewhere. It is of course possible (Tisch. and W H.) that the words were omitted because of the obvious difficulty they present; but then why are they omitted from Mark by no documents except X and one codex of the Vulgate? It is true that Matt. was more used than Mark, but the difference in this respect will bear no comparison with the immense difference between the documents for omission in Matt. and in Mark, even after we allow for the ready acceptance likely to be given to a form of text that would remove a difficulty. Various Fathers speak of the clause as wanting in Matt. and present in Mark, but they do not regard that as lessening the doctrinal difficulty. On the other hand, nothing would be more natural than the insertion of the clause in Matt. by transcriptional assimilation to Mark. Such assimilation of parallel passages occurs oftener than can be numbered; while alteration to avoid doctrinal difficulty is a thing of very rare occurrence. How then can W H. maintain that omission "can be no less easily explained by the doctrinal difficulty" than their insertion by "assimilation to Mark"? This seems to be only because they regard "the documentary evidence in favor" of the clause as "overwhelming"; and it is made overwhelming by the concurrence of B with the other documents. Now it is true that a group containing B very commonly presents the original text, as W H. have convincingly shown in their genealogical classification on the basis of internal evidence. But it is not true that such a group presents overwhelming evidence; for we have seen in this commentary a good many cases in which a group containing B is

Mark (13:32), and so were spoken by our Lord on this occasion. In fact, the thought they convey is implied in **but my** (*the*) **Father only,** for otherwise we should have expected 'but God only.' Comp. 20: 23; Acts 1: 7. The 'my' of the common text is spurious.

This statement of our Lord as to himself can be explained only by referring the ignorance to his human mind. We read of him at twelve years of age that he 'advanced in wisdom and stature' (or 'age'). If he then *advanced* in wisdom, he did not cease advancing at the age of twenty or of thirty. If his knowledge was incomplete at twelve, it was still incomplete at thirty. Indeed, a finite mind could not contain all knowledge. If there was to be a real Incarnation of the Eternal Word, then the body he took must be a real body, and the mind a real mind. How his divine nature could be omniscient, and his human mind limited in knowledge, both being united in one person, is part of the mystery of the Incarnation, which we need not expect to solve. (Comp. Phil. 2: 7.) But to be limited in knowledge, does not necessarily involve erroneous information or conceptions. The human nature of the Incarnate Deity was infallibly preserved from sin (comp. on 4: 1), and so, we may believe, from error of judgment.

So remarkable a statement seems much more natural if it relates not simply to the destruction of Jerusalem, but also, and mainly, to the second coming of which our Lord goes on to speak in the immediately succeeding verses; and we have seen that the passage as a whole appears to predict both events. This saying ought to repress all curious inquiry as to the precise time of his second coming, to prevent reliance on any arithmetical calculations, and also to foster confidence in him. The disciples greatly wished to know the precise time; in every age many have been eagerly seeking to determine, and some fancying they have ascertained it, only to be disappointed; but he expressly warned against this from the outset, and impliedly bade us be reconciled to an ignorance shared by the high angels, and (Mark) by the Son himself. The humiliating failures by so many well-meaning Christians in this matter, should bring no reproach to their Master, but cause him to be honored all the more. And if the God-man, the Mediator, left this and many other things (20: 23), to the Father alone, how cheerfully should we his followers rest in ignorance that cannot be removed, trusting in all things to our Heavenly Father's wisdom and goodness, striving to obey his clearly revealed will, and leaning on his grace for support. Whether this particular limitation upon the Saviour's knowledge was removed after his resurrection (28: 18), we cannot undertake to judge.

HOMILETICAL AND PRACTICAL.

V. 2. HENRY: "A believing foresight of the defacing of all worldly glory will help to take us off from overvaluing it."—V. 4 f. In times of great trial we must carefully avoid false guidance and comfort. GRIFFITH: "Men's first impulse under trouble is to catch rashly at every person who seems to promise relief."—V. 6. HENRY: "It is against the mind of Christ, that his people should have troubled hearts even in troublous times."

V. 12. Love waxing cold. 1) Through discouragement from apparently fruitless efforts to do good. 2) Through resentment at ingratitude and injustice. 3) Through general influence of evil example and environment. Happy the few who resist all such tendencies, whose love is warm even amid surrounding chill, for they shall be useful to men, shall honor Christ, shall themselves be saved. (v. 13.) —V. 14. Preaching the gospel. 1) It is the gospel of the kingdom. 2) It is adapted to all

---

certainly or probably wrong; and Dr. Hort himself states that B "has a few widely spread wrong readings in this Gospel" (App. on Matt. 13: 35.) For example, W H. do not follow groups containing B, some of them large groups, in 6: 22; 19: 9, 24; 20: 27; 27: 28, 49. Comp. above on 19: 9. In Mark 4: 21 ℵ B, the uncial represented by 13 and 69, with 33, and we may now add Σ, give a manifest clerical error, which Hort says is "due to mechanical repetition." There are various examples in the other Gospels which tend to the same result. So the B groups, and even the ℵ B groups (as in several of the above instances) do present a number of unquestionable errors, even in the Gospels, and W H. fully agree that B is repeatedly "Western" in the Epistles of Paul. Accordingly, the ℵ B group in this case does not constitute "overwhelming" evidence in favor of a clause wanting in the great mass of documents, and so readily accounted for by assimilation to Mark. We think that W H. ought to have confined it to their margin, and that Rev. Ver. ought not to have noticed it here at all. Comp. on 27: 49.

37 But as the days of Noe *were,* so shall also the coming of the Son of man be.

37 only. And as *were* the days of Noah, so shall be the

---

the world. 3) Christ commands his people to preach it to all. (Comp. 28: 19.) 4) Christ predicts that it will be preached to all. Are we personally receiving it, and busy in proclaiming it?

V. 16. HENRY: "In times of imminent peril and danger, it is not only lawful but our duty, to seek our own preservation by all good and honest means; and if God opens a door of escape, we ought to make our escape; otherwise we do not trust God, but tempt him."—V. 20. HENRY: "Though the ease of the body is not to be mainly consulted, it ought to be duly considered; though we must take what God sends, and when he sends it, yet we may pray against inconveniences."—V. 23. Faith is a characteristic of Christianity; but belief of truth involves stern refusal to believe in falsehood. HENRY: "There is not a greater enemy to true faith than vain credulity. The simple believeth every word, and runs after every cry."

V. 30 f. The final and glorious coming of Christ. 1) It will be sudden, v. 27. 2) It will be not in the form of a servant (Phil. 2: 7), but as the Divine King, with power and great glory. 3) It will cause mourning to all who have rejected him. (Rev. 1: 7; Heb. 6: 6.) 4) It will bring all his scattered people together in unspeakable and eternal blessedness, comp. 2 Tim. 4: 8. HENRY: "Sooner or later, all sinners will be mourners; penitent sinners look to Christ, and mourn after a godly sort; impenitent sinners shall look unto him whom they have pierced, and though they laugh now, shall mourn and weep in endless horror and despair."—V. 36. The great day. 1) There is a definite day on which Christ will come to judgment, comp. Acts 17: 31; 2 Tim. 1: 12. 2) The precise day is wholly unrevealed, and known only to God the Father; attempts to fix it by calculation are idle. 3) Our great concern is to be ready when that day comes, and we shall do this by constant and watchful service of Christ, v. 42; comp. 25: 1-14.

24: 37—25: 13. WATCH CONTINUALLY FOR THE COMING OF CHRIST.

Only the early part of this section has a parallel in Mark (13: 33-37) and Luke (21: 34-36); but Luke has more extensive parallels in earlier discourses. As to the general contents

and the divisions of this discourse on the Mount of Olives, see at the beginning of chap. 24. From the point we have now reached, the destruction of Jerusalem sinks rapidly out of view. The passage in v. 37-44 *might* be understood as having also a primary reference to that event, regarded as a coming of Christ, but it contains no expression *requiring* to be so understood. Still less indication is there of such a reference in the two illustrations of v. 45-51 and 25: 1-13. But throughout this section everything naturally suggests that final coming of Christ to judgment, which is alone brought to view in the closing paragraph of the great discourse, 25: 31-46. There would be no profit in working out a possible allusion to the destruction of Jerusalem in some parts of this section, and we may confine ourselves to its obvious and supremely important teaching as regards preparation for the final coming. Our Lord first declares that his coming will be unexpected, as illustrated by the coming of the flood and the coming of a thief, and bases on this an injunction to watchfulness (v. 37-44); he then further illustrates the same fact and consequent duty by the supposed case of a good and a bad servant (v. 45-51), and by the parable of the foolish and the wise virgins. (25: 1-13.)

I. **37-44.** WATCH, FOR HE WILL COME UNEXPECTEDLY. Comp. Mark 13: 33 and Luke in the earlier discourses he gives in 17: 26-35; and 12: 39 f.

(a) Illustration from the coming of Noah's flood.—37-39. **But as,** Rev. Ver., *and as.* But some of the best documents read 'for as,' which would easily be changed by copyists because somewhat obscure; it is therefore probably correct. (Lach., Treg., W H.) It does not exactly give the reason why the day and hour is unknown (24: 36), but a *confirmation* of the statement that no one knows: men will not even be thinking of it when it arrives. **Also** is genuine in Luke 17: 26, but not here, nor in v. 39. **The coming,** see on 24: 3. **The Son of man,** see on 8: 20. On a former occasion our Lord had added another illustration to the same effect from the times of Lot, Luke 17: 28-32. Here, as often before, the question arises whether we shall suppose that Jesus used these illustrations only once,

38 For as in the days that were before the flood they were eating and drinking, marrying and giving in marriage, until the day that Noe entered into the ark.
39 And knew not until the flood came and took them all away; so shall also the coming of the Son of man be.
40 Then shall two be in the field; the one shall be taken, and the other left.
41 Two *women shall be* grinding at the mill; the one shall be taken, and the other left.
42 Watch therefore; for ye know not what hour your Lord doth come.

38 [1]coming of the Son of man. For as in those days which were before the flood they were eating and drinking, marrying and giving in marriage, until the
39 day that Noah entered into the ark, and they knew not until the flood came, and took them all away; so
40 shall be the [1]coming of the Son of man. Then shall two men be in the field; one is taken, and one is left:
41 two women *shall be* grinding at the mill; one is
42 taken, and one is left. Watch therefore; for ye

---

1 Gr. *presence.*

---

and one or other Evangelist has made a dislocation; or that he repeated. To one who has had experience of itinerant preaching to popular audiences, the supposition that an illustration was repeated at some new place and time seems so perfectly natural that there is no occasion for the other hypothesis.—The coming of Christ will find men in general busy with the ordinary pursuits of life, as in the time of Noah; only those who are prepared as he was will escape the sudden and unexpected destruction. It follows that our Lord's coming certainly cannot be at the end of a thousand years of universal and perfect piety, for in that case all would know the exact time, and all would be devoutly and eagerly expecting the event. Comp. Luke 18: 8. **Took them all away,** with emphasis on 'all.'

(b) Persons most intimately associated will be separated by that unexpected coming.—40 f. **Two** (*men*). The Greek has only 'two,' but the connected words are masculine, as with the following 'two' they are feminine. **In the field,**[1] in the cultivated district appertaining to some supposed city. **One shall be** (lit., *is*) **taken,** taken along, perhaps by the angels sent to gather the elect. (24: 31.) The same Greek word is rendered 'receive' in John 14: 3; for the idea, comp. 1 Thess. 4: 17. The Greek has here the present tense, which is more vivid than the future would be. Some understand the term to mean taken along by the destroying agencies attending Christ's appearance, as the flood carried all away. In either view of this phrase the main thought of the passage remains the same; it shall be well with one and ill with

the other, and there will be no time then for preparing. **Two women grinding at the mill.** This domestic labor is still frequently performed in Palestine by women, and was observed there by the present writer. The lower millstone, say twelve inches in diameter, is placed on the ground and perhaps fixed in it; the upper stone is turned by a peg near the outer edge. One woman sits on the ground (Isa. 47: 1 f.), so as to have the mill steadied between her knees, the other crouches on the opposite side. Sometimes the stone is much larger, and each crouches on one side. One pulls the peg towards her through half a circle, the other seizes it above or below and completes the circle; or else both retain their hold, and one relaxes while the other pulls. With the free hand one now and then puts a little grain into the central orifice of the revolving stone. To the jerky motion of the stone they keep time by a low, wailing chant. "The sound of the grinding" (Eccl. 12: 4) may be only the rumbling and ringing noise made by the revolving stone, but more probably refers to this chant.[2] The two women are apt, in the nature of things, to be mother and daughter, or older and younger sister, or friendly neighbors, or slaves in the same house. Yet even these will be separated by the Lord's second coming, the prepared one being accepted, the other having then no time to prepare.—Some larger millstones were turned by an ass (18:6), and others by water, where this was available, as is now to be seen in many places. "The Greek Anthology" (Wet.) has a statement that "in ancient times" women used to grind, before the art of grinding by water was discovered.—A

---

[1] This expression was interpolated into the text of Luke 17: 36, and Luke 17: 34 was interpolated here, in both cases by the "Western" group of documents; the former interpolation passed into some "Syrian" documents, and so into K. James and the Elzevir, the *Tex-*

tus Receptus on the Continent, though not found in Stephens, the *Textus Receptus* in Great Britain.

[2] Dr. Robinson heard no such chant, but we heard it at El Jib (Gibeon). Laborers of many kinds all over the world have certain cries or songs to accompany and relieve monotonous work.

43 But know this, that if the goodman of the house had known in what watch the thief would come, he would have watched, and would not have suffered his house to be broken up.

44 Therefore be ye also ready: for in such an hour as ye think not the Son of man cometh.

45 Who then is a faithful and wise servant, whom his lord hath made ruler over his household, to give them meat in due season?

43 know not on what day your Lord cometh. [1] But know this, that if the master of the house had known in what watch the thief was coming, he would

44 to be [2] broken through. Therefore be ye also ready: for in an hour that ye think not the Son of man

45 cometh. Who then is the faithful and wise [3] servant, whom his lord hath set over his household, to give

---

1 Or, *But this ye know*....2 Gr. *digged through*....3 Gr. *bondservant*.

---

third illustration of the same kind is given in Luke 17: 34 as used on an earlier occasion, viz., that of two men on one bed.

(c) Application of these illustrations.—42; [1] Mark 13: 33. **What hour.** Rev. Ver., *on what day*. This is read by many of the best documents, and was easily changed by copyists into 'hour,' by assimilation to v. 44. Thus of the two words in v. 36, we have one in v. 42 and the other in v. 44, and again both in v. 50 and 25: 13. **Your Lord cometh.** Elsewhere he always says 'the Son of man cometh,' as in v. 44; comp. 24: 27, 30, 37, 39; Luke 12: 40; 17: 24, 26, 30; 21: 36. The expression 'your Lord cometh' connects itself closely with 'his Lord' in the illustration that presently follows, v. 45-50, and so in Luke. Probably this expression led to the phrase "our Lord cometh," which was so common a saying among the early Christians that Paul quotes it in the Aramaic, *Maran atha* (1 Cor. 16: 22); comp. Phil. 4: 5; James 5: 7; 2 Thess. 2: 2; 2 Peter 1: 16; 3: 10. Tyndale and Geneva use 'master' all through v. 42-50; Wyc., Cran., Rheims, have 'lord,' K. James 'Lord.' Wünsche says the Rabbis also declare that the Messiah will come when least expected; so every one must hold himself ready, and he who does not, will have himself to blame if he is shut out. Indeed, this is a principle applying to everything which is certain to come, but at an uncertain time. Hence it applies exactly to our own death, for which we ought to make ready in advance and to stay ready always.

(d) A further illustration and its application.—43 f.; comp. Luke 12: 39 f. This illustration was often repeated by the apostles, 1 Thess. 5: 2, 4; 2 Peter 3: 10; Rev. 3: 3; 16: 15. **Know this,** or *this ye know*. The Greek second plural has the same form in the indicative as in the imperative, hence occasional

ambiguities, as in John 5: 39; 14: 1. **The good man** (*master*) **of the house,** see on 10: 25. **In what watch.** The night, from sunset to sunrise, was divided by the Jews in earlier times into three, but under the Romans into four periods called "watches," comp. Mark 13: 35, and see above on 14: 25. **Broken up,** literally *digged through* (Rev. Ver. *margin*), implying walls made of mud or of sun-dried bricks, which are still common in many parts of the world, comp. on 6: 19. **Therefore** (v. 44), the propriety of the injunction being inferred from the foregoing illustration. **Be,** more exactly, *become*, get ready; **ye also,** as the householder must do if he would be ready whenever the thief comes. **The Son of man,** as in v. 37, 39; see on 8: 20.

II. **45-51.** LET HIS COMING FIND YOU A GOOD SERVANT AND NOT AN EVIL ONE. Mark 13: 34-37; Luke 21: 34-36; comp. an earlier discourse in Luke 12: 35-38, 42-46.

45-47. Servant, *doulos, slave,* see on 8: 6. **Wise** is not the general Greek word, but means more exactly prudent, discreet, shrewd, etc., with varying shades of good and bad meaning, as in 7: 24; 10: 16; 25: 2 ff.; Luke 16: 8. It here probably signifies prudent and judicious in the means and methods of faithfully serving the master; or possibly, prudent in subserving his own true interest by fidelity to his master. **Household.** The Greek word denotes the whole body of domestics. The servant in question is the head steward, charged with the special duty of regularly supplying all the domestics with food; along with that he exercised a general control, observe, **made ruler,** or *set over*, and sometimes assumed the right to punish (v. 49.). **Meat,** *food,* which was formerly the meaning of the English word 'meat.' **In due season.** To distribute the food regularly and promptly was

---

[1] Persons learning a Bible lesson, at this point, may find the connection traced on v. 37, and an outline of the whole discourse on 24: 3. Practical remarks on v. 42-51 will be found below, after 25: 13.

46 Blessed *is* that servant, whom his lord when he cometh shall find so doing.
47 Verily I say unto you, That he shall make him ruler over all his goods.
48 But and if that evil servant shall say in his heart, My lord delayeth his coming ;
49 And shall begin to smite *his* fellow servants, and to eat and drink with the drunken;
50 The lord of that servant shall come in a day when he looketh not for *him*, and in an hour that he is not aware of.
51 And shall *a* cut him asunder, and shall appoint *him* his portion with the hypocrites: there shall be weeping and gnashing of teeth.

46 them their food in due season ? Blessed is that [1] servant, whom his lord when he cometh shall find so doing.
47 Verily I say unto you, that he will set him
48 over all that he hath. But if that evil [1] servant shall
49 say in his heart, My lord tarrieth ; and shall begin to beat his fellow-servants, and shall eat and drink
50 with the drunken; the lord of that [1] servant shall come in a day when he expecteth not, and in an
51 hour when he knoweth not, and shall [2] cut him asunder, and appoint his portion with the hypocrites : there shall be the weeping and gnashing of teeth.

a Or. *cut him off.*——1 Gr. *bondservant.*....2 Or, *severely scourge him.*

an important point of good management in a steward. **Blessed** is more exactly *happy*, as in 5: 3 ff.; another beatitude. **His lord, when he cometh,** from some journey, or some other place of residence. **Shall find so doing,** faithfully and judiciously supplying the domestics with food, *i. e.*, performing the special duties of his position. **Verily I say unto you,** calling special attention, comp. on 5: 18. **Will make him ruler** (or *set him*) **over all his goods,** over all his property of every kind, and not simply over his body of domestics. Comp. 25 : 21; Luke 19 : 17, 26. Our Lord here puts honor upon those who serve him by comparing them, not to a menial or ordinary slave, but to the intelligent, faithful, and trusted head-slave of the household, like Joseph in Potiphar's house. Many have understood a specific reference to ministers, and from this notion has arisen a singular mixed text, widely current in the language of devotional meetings, "a workman that needeth not to be ashamed, rightly dividing the word of truth, and giving to each his portion (Luke 12 : 42) in due season" (but see Rev. Ver. of 2 Tim. 2: 15). That our passage really refers to all Christians is confirmed by Mark 13 : 37, "And what I say unto you I say unto all, Watch." The passage may be applied to ministers *a fortiori*, as having all the ordinary responsibilities of Christian life, and others that are extraordinary.

48-51. With the faithful diligence and happy reward of the good head-servant (in any supposed case) is now contrasted the behavior and punishment of the head-servant in case he turns out an evil one. **Evil** is opposed both to faithful and to prudent. (v. 45.) **But and if.** So also in Tyndale and all his followers. In Middle English *and* was used in the sense of 'if' (Skeat), afterwards distinguished from the

copulative *and* by writing it *an*, as in Shakespeare's "an it please you," "an thou lovest me," etc. When this conditional use of *and* grew indistinct to the mind it was strengthened by adding *if*, so as to make in Shakespeare 'an if,' and here, 'but and if'; modern usage omits the *and*, and the old phrase 'but and if' now looks very strange. Comp. Luke 12 : 45; 20 : 6; John 6 : 62; 1 Cor. 7 : 11, 28; 1 Pet. 3 : 14; in the three last passages Rev. Ver. unwisely retains 'and.' **Shall say in his heart,** comp. 'to say within yourselves,' in 3 : 9. The heart, as always in Scripture, is here the seat of thought as well as of feeling, see on 6 : 21. **Delayeth his coming.** *Tarrieth* expresses the correct Greek text. It contained a delicate intimation to the disciples that Jesus was not coming again in a very short time (comp. on 25 : 19). **Shall begin,** com. on 11 : 20. **And to,** rather, *shall eat and drink with the drunken,* carousing at the master's expense, instead of keeping the household in order and exercising a prudent economy. **In a day,** implies that he comes from some distance; **and in an hour,** amplifies and makes more impressive, as so often in Heb. parallelism. **Shall cut him asunder,** cut him in two. This is the exact meaning of the term, and no other has any support from Greek usage. The Old Latin translates by *dividet,* 'will divide,' or *findet,* 'will cleave'; Pesh. 'will divide'; and Memph. takes great pains, 'will divide him in his middle.' Such a severe punishment was practiced among the Hebrews (2 Sam. 12: 31; Heb. 11 : 37; Susanna 55); and Wet. gives various examples from Greek and Roman writers. Some think it must be here simply a hyperbole for severe scourging, because of the following phrase: **And appoint his portion with the hypocrites.** This makes a sudden transition from the illustration to the thing illustrated. 'Cut

CHAPTER XXV.

THEN shall the kingdom of heaven be likened unto ten virgins, which took their lamps, and went forth to meet the bridegroom.

1 Then shall the kingdom of heaven be likened unto ten virgins, that took their ¹ lamps, and went forth

1 Or, *torches.*

him in two' is the image, a severe temporal punishment; 'his portion with the hypocrites' is in eternity. That hypocrites (see on 6: 2) are grossly offensive in God's sight, and must be severely punished, was a thought familiar to the minds of the disciples (6: 2, 5, 16; 15: 7; 16: 3), and just freshened through the discourse of that same day. (23: 13-29.) The good servant will be exalted to the highest position a servant can have (v. 47); the bad servant, who drank with the drunken, shall dwell with the hypocrites. Now if 'appoint his portion' makes a transition from the earthly punishment to the punishment of hell (25: 41, 46), there is no occasion for objecting to the literal and only established sense of 'cut him in two,' and no ground for the alternative rendering of Rev. Ver., *margin.* **The weeping and the gnashing of teeth** (see on 8: 12.)

Luke having given a similar comparison to the good and bad steward in an earlier discourse (Luke 12: 42-46), does not here repeat it, nor yet wholly pass it by, but sums up the thought in the comprehensive and impressive sentences of 21: 34-36.

III. Ch. 25: 1-13. PARABLE OF THE TEN VIRGINS. Not found elsewhere. This beautiful parable is a further illustration of the variously illustrated injunction to 'watch' (24: 42, 44), which is repeated at its close (25: 13), in such a form as to recall also the great statement of 24: 36, and thus link all the discourse up to this point in the closest connection. Our Lord is still sitting on the Mount of Olives, late in the afternoon of his last day of public ministry (see on 24: 1, 3.)

1. **Then,** viz., at the time of the Saviour's coming (24: 42, 44.) **The kingdom of heaven,** the Messianic Dispensation (see on 3: 2.) **Be likened unto** (see on 13: 24.) The omission of certain details, and the desire of interpreters to prepare for this or that homiletical application, have led to much difference of opinion as to some points of this tender and beautiful story. But scarcely any of these seriously affect the main lesson of the parable, and they should not be allowed to occupy much space in an expository sermon or Sunday-school lesson. It was the custom to hold weddings after nightfall. The bridegroom and some friends went to the house of the bride, and after religious ceremonies there he set forth towards his own abode in a grand procession, which was illuminated by torches or lamps in the hands of the participants, and often preceded by musicians. In the utterly dark street of an Asiatic city, every one who goes forth at night is expected, and in modern Jerusalem is strictly required by the authorities, to carry a light. (Comp. Psa. 119: 105.) Other invited guests, who had not gone to the bride's home, could join the procession at any point, and enter with it into the bridegroom's residence, to share in the festivities. But without a burning lamp or torch they could not march in the procession, and so could not enter the house. In order to join the procession conveniently, such persons might assemble beforehand at different points along the proposed route, and wait for the bridegroom's approach. Some recent commentators urge that the bridegroom must here be conceived as on his way to the bride's house, to hold the festivities there, since in the application Christ comes from heaven to earth to establish his kingdom; but it is useless for the sake of a painful literalism, to imagine a departure from custom. In 1 Macc. 9: 39 only the bridegroom is mentioned as coming forth, with a grand procession and musicians; and yet just above (v. 37) we see that they were "bringing the bride." When the bridegroom came from a distance, the festivities were sometimes held at the residence of the bride, as in Gen. 29: 22; Tobit 8: 20 ff. In that case, however, the virgins would not have lighted their lamps till news came that the bridegroom was near, and after that the delay on his part would be unnatural, whereas according to the common view, the delay of the wedding procession in setting out from the bride's house is natural enough. In that case,

2 And five of them were wise, and five *were* foolish.
3 They that *were* foolish took their lamps, and took no oil with them :
4 But the wise took oil in their vessels with their lamps.
5 While the bridegroom tarried, they all slumbered and slept.

2 to meet the bridegroom. And five of them were
3 foolish, and five were wise. For the foolish, when
4 they took their [1] lamps, took no oil with them: but the wise took oil in their vessels with their [1] lamps.
5 Now while the bridegroom tarried, they all slum-

---

1 Or, *torches.*

---

also, not the bridegroom, but the father of the bride, would have decided whether the five should be admitted. It seems tolerably evident from v. 10–12 that the marriage feast is at the house of the bridegroom. Still, the general lesson remains the same in either view of this particular. The " Western " type of text has, with its usual free handling, made it read 'went forth to meet the bridegroom and the bride,' in order that the text might distinctly conform to custom. The bride is really not mentioned throughout the parable, doubtless because Christ's people in this image are represented by the attendants.

The story in itself considered has curious points of naturalness and verisimilitude. Young girls would be specially interested in a wedding, prominent in its ceremonies, and distressed at missing the festivities. Bridal ceremonies are very apt to be delayed beyond the time appointed. It is evident that great delay is here supposed, for otherwise the maidens would not themselves have been arrayed and assembled so long beforehand as to have time for all falling asleep while they waited.

Ten may be regarded as merely a round number, sufficiently large to show interest in the occasion. Comp. Luke 19: 13. We learn however from Lightfoot that the Jews "delighted mightily in the number ten. A synagogue must have at least ten present ; an order or ring of men consisted not but of ten at the least." Wün. adds that ten men must be present at a wedding, in order to utter the requisite blessings. Comp. Ruth 4 : 2. Josephus says (" War," 6, 9, 3) that not less than ten men must assemble to partake of a paschal lamb. Morison reminds us how these uses of the number might be suggested by the ten fingers, as was the decimal basis of numeration.

The word for **lamps** is different from that of 5: 15, and regularly means a torch (John 18 : 3 ; Rev. 8 : 10), and we know that the Greeks and Romans commonly used torches in marriage processions ; but here it seems to denote a lamp fed with oil, though it might be a sort of torch fed with oil (Rev. Ver. *margin*). In processions, such a lamp was borne on a wooden pole (Edersh.) ; and was doubtless protected from the wind, probably (as now) by a covering of wood, or of cloth supported by a wire frame (Smith's "Dict."). These lamps held but little oil, and would need to be replenished. As the lamp was indispensable, and the movements of a bridal procession were uncertain, prudent persons would carry with them vessels of oil, but these were very unpleasant for persons in festive apparel to carry, and the imprudent might conclude to risk it with the oil in their lamps. They would all set down the lamps and leave them burning, because they were constantly expecting the approach of the procession. If we conceive them as waiting at the bride's house, it would have been silly to leave the lamps burning, before there was any announcement of the bridegroom's approach ; especially as in that view he would be coming from a great distance. Goebel maintains that the foolish had empty lamps, the vessels being those which formed part of the lamps. This fancy is devised in order that the oil may mean divine grace, without any hitch in the interpretation ; but it makes the foolish virgins simpletons. **Wise**[1] is the word meaning prudent, etc., see on 24: 45. **Tarried** is the same word as in 24 : 48, and one of the links of connection between the two illustrations ; comp. also 25 : 19. **Slumbered and slept** is lit., *nodded and were sleeping.* Persons sitting up and overcome by drowsiness first nod and presently begin to sleep continuously.

---

1 In v. 2 the 'foolish' are named first in the best documents (and so in all English versions before K. James, which probably followed Beza). This would seem to copyists an unnatural order, but really accords with the whole tone of the foregoing passage, which makes

prominent the case of the unprepared. The change made here by copyists led to a corresponding change in v. 3 (almost exactly the same documents), which properly reads ' for the foolish,' introducing a proof of their folly.

6 And at midnight there was a cry made, Behold, the bridegroom cometh ; go ye out to meet him.
7 Then all those virgins arose, and trimmed their lamps.
8 And the foolish said unto the wise, Give us of your oil ; for our lamps are *a* gone out.
9 But the wise answered, saying, *Not so ;* lest there be not enough for us and you : but go ye rather to them that sell, and buy for yourselves.
10 And while they went to buy, the bridegroom came ; and they that were ready went in with him to the marriage : and the door was shut.
11 Afterward came also the other virgins, saying, Lord, Lord, open to us.
12 But he answered and said, Verily I say unto you, I know you not.

6 bered and slept. But at midnight there is a cry, Behold, the bridegroom ! Come ye forth to meet
7 him. Then all those virgins arose, and trimmed
8 their [1] lamps. And the foolish said unto the wise, Give us of your oil ; for our [1] lamps are going out.
9 But the wise answered, saying, Peradventure there will not be enough for us and you : go ye rather to
10 them that sell, and buy for yourselves. And while they went away to buy, the bridegroom came ; and they that were ready went in with him to the mar-
11 riage feast : and the door was shut. Afterward came also the other virgins, saying, Lord, Lord, open to
12 us. But he answered and said, Verily I say unto

a Or, *going out.*——1 Or, *torches.*

Go ye out, or, *come ye forth.* The latter is more probably the meaning than ' go ye out ' ; the Greek word oftener means come than go, which is usually expressed in New Test. by the word used in v. 9, comp. 3 : 5 ; 20 : 29 ; and the cry would naturally be made by persons in the street who saw the procession approaching, rather than by persons in the house ; nor would the latter have occasion for making a loud, clangorous cry, such as the Greek word denotes. **There was a cry,** or more literally *a cry has arisen,* a vivid expression which transports us into the midst of the scene. **Behold, the bridegroom !** like ' Behold, the Lamb of God ! ' (John 1 : 36) ; but many copyists added, as in Com. Ver., **cometh. Trimmed** is the word rendered ' garnish ' in 12 : 44 and 23 : 29, and denotes adorning, beautifying ; they poured in oil, trimmed and drew up the wick, wiped off the lamp, did everything that would make it beautiful and bright. **Our lamps are** *going* **out,** the Greek having the present tense and not the perfect ; correctly translated in Tyn., Rheims, and margin of Com. Ver. **Lest there be not,** Rev. Ver. says *peradventure, etc.* The wise kindly abstain from express refusal, and only imply it by the words, ' Peradventure there will not be enough for us and you, go rather, etc.' (Comp. Plumptre.) In attempting to buy oil at midnight, they would find few or no shops open, and would be much delayed. Bruce fancies that it was a second folly to go after oil, when if they had but remained they might have been admitted without it. But (1) the whole tone of the story, and all that we know of the wedding customs, implies that a burning light was necessary. Without it they would not have been showing honor to the bridegroom, and could not have been distinguished at the door from strangers

or other persons having no right to be admitted. (2) The advice of the wise to go and buy must, on Bruce's view, be taken as cruel mockery, or possibly as dictated by the unreflecting selfishness of persons hurried and disconcerted ; either of which would seem excessively incongruous and improbable. **To the marriage** (feast), as in 22 : 2 ff. **The door** was usually in the middle of one side of a house, leading by a passage under the second story to the inner court, upon which all the rooms of the house opened. When this outer door was shut, all connection with the outside world was cut off. Persistent knocking, and loud entreaty addressed to the bridegroom personally, might at length bring him to the door. **Verily I say unto you,** a solemn assurance, comp. on 5 : 18. **I know you not.** They have no claim to be received as guests ; he does not even recognize them as acquaintances (comp. 7 : 23).

The application of this beautiful parable is obvious, but is surpassingly tender and pathetic. It teaches the same lesson as 24 : 37-42, and 43-51, that the only way to be ready when Jesus comes is to be ready always. The term ' virgins ' must not be given a spiritual significance, as if denoting pure Christians ; for five of these represent persons not really Christians at all. The division into two halves must surely not be supposed to teach that at the coming of Christ half the people in the world or in any community will be ready to meet him, and half not ready ; it was simply the most natural division of the round number, there being no special reason for dividing otherwise. **The bridegroom tarried** might suggest to the disciples that their Lord would not come immediately. (Comp. on 25 : 19.) The fact that all the ten were sleeping should not be made a reproach to true Christians. It

13 Watch therefore: for ye know neither the day nor the hour wherein the Son of man cometh.

13 you, I know you not. Watch therefore, for ye know not the day nor the hour.

was not wrong for the virgins to sleep under the circumstances; they were neglecting no duty in so doing, provided they had thoroughly made ready for the bridegroom's coming. To understand it as meaning that the successive generations of mankind must fall asleep in death (various Fathers and some modern writers), is wholly unwarranted and seems strangely unsuitable. Whether the foolish virgins are to be considered as representing "church members," there is nothing to show; they are persons who profess, and honestly think that they are Christ's friends, and expect to meet him with joy. To take lamps and no lasting supply of oil, suggests that superficial and temporary interest in divine things which is so often witnessed; comp. Hosea 6: 4. The hurried and fruitless attempt, when the moment arrives, to make the preparation which ought to have been made in advance, is deeply pathetic, and touches a sadly common fault in regard to readiness for meeting Christ at his coming, or for meeting the messenger whom he sends to bear us away, even death. The inability of the prudent virgins to help the foolish in their extremity reminds us that piety involves personal conditions and relations to Christ that are not transferable. **I know you not.** This will not be rejecting persons who ask to be saved, but disowning persons who claim to have been saved, to have been ready and waiting for his coming.

To find some separate spiritual meaning in the lamps, the vessels, the oil, and the sellers of oil, etc., seems here worse than idle. (Comp. on 13: 3.) Maldonatus counts fifteen separate items having spiritual significance, and Keach thirteen. It is very unwise here to bring in the idea of the bride as meaning "the church." (Eph. 5: 25.) The bride is not mentioned in the parable, and, as already suggested, for the obvious reason that Christians here appear as friends waiting to join the procession. Bring in the bride as the church, and you introduce

inevitable confusion of idea through a mixture of distinct images. It ought to be everywhere carefully remembered that if "mixed metaphors" are bad for rhetoric, they are worse for exegesis.

Watch therefore, for ye know neither the day nor the hour[1] repeats the solemn refrain of 24: 42, 44, and 50. The whole passage from 24: 36 to 25: 13 should be read in worship as one, and this refrain brought out with special emphasis; just as one reads Psalms 42 and 43, with the refrain of 42: 5, 11 and 43: 5; or like the refrain in Psa. 80: 3, 7, 19, and various other Psalms. This is not saying that the passage before us is, properly speaking, poetical; it rather presents an oratorical repetition of the practical theme, after each separate illustration. "Watch" does not here mean keep awake, as opposed to the sleeping of v. 5, but be so heedfully expectant as not to be caught unprepared.

HOMILETICAL AND PRACTICAL.

Ch. 24: 37-39. The flood, as a picture of Christ's final coming. 1) Men knew not when it would be, and did not really believe it would ever be; comp. Luke 18: 8. 2) Men were too busy with ordinary affairs to stop and think about God's merciful warning. 3) Men in general were caught unprepared, and swept into destruction. 4) Those men who believed and made ready found themselves safe, and had a blessed future.—V. 40 f. The most intimate associations of this life will in many cases be severed, in a moment and forever, by the coming of Christ. And so death, though for none an eternal sleep, will be for many, alas! an eternal separation. — V. 42. The coming of our Lord. 1) We know not when he will come—need not know—cannot know —should not wish to know, comp. 24: 36. 2) We shall be ready when he comes if we are ready always, comp. v. 43 f. 3) We should watch, not in dread but in hope, for it will be *our Lord's* coming, comp. 2

---

1 'Wherein the Son of man cometh' is wanting in all the early versions and the leading Greek copies, and was easily added from 24: 44. In reality, the expression is more energetic without it, and amply perspicu-ous to one who has read what precedes, since 24: 36 The well meant but really enfeebling addition reminds one of that in 1 Cor. 6: 20.

Tim. 14: 8; Titus 2: 11–14. 4) Thus are we better prepared to serve him when he does come; (a) with patience under trouble, comp. James 5: 7; (b) with gentleness and forbearance towards others, comp. Phil. 4: 5; (c) with all holy living and piety, comp. 2 Peter 3: 11 f. ; (d) with efforts to make all men likewise ready to meet him, comp. 24: 14.—V. 45-47. A good servant of Christ. 1) He is aware that the responsibilities of Christ's service require not only faithfulness, but prudence, discretion, good sense. 2) He is conscious of duties to his fellow-men, and is exact and punctual in performing them, as being also duties to Christ. 3) He is always ready to meet Christ, because always busily engaged in Christ's service. 4) He will be rewarded for serving Christ here by better opportunities of serving him hereafter.—V. 45-51. The good and the bad servant contrasted. All men are in one or another sense Christ's servants, and will be held by him to account, comp. 2 Cor. 5: 10. 1) The good servant is faithful and wise; the bad servant is unfaithful and foolish. 2) The good servant is busy in serving Christ by benefiting others ; the bad servant is unkind to others, and engrossed with selfish gratifications. 3) The good servant will welcome the Lord at any moment; the bad servant will be caught unawares. 4) The good servant will be exalted to higher honors and wider usefulness ; the bad servant will be terribly punished, dwelling forever amid hypocrites, and filled with bitter but vain regrets.

25: 1-13. The Ten Virgins. 1) The coming of our Lord ought to be thought of as a joyful event. 2) The time of his coming is uncertain and may be delayed, so that preparation for it must be permanent. 3) Not all those who call themselves his friends, and nominally await his coming, will be found really ready when he comes. 4) Hurried attempts to make ready then, will prove a failure. 5) Oh the bitter grief and disappointment of having meant, and professed, and long appeared, to be his friends, and then encountering the closed door and the solemn voice of refusal.

"No light had we: for that we do repent :
And, learning this, the Bridegroom will relent.
'Too late, too late ! ye cannot enter now.'
No light, so late ! and dark and chill the night !
Oh, let us in, that we may find the light !
'Too late, too late ! ye cannot enter now.'"
Tennyson.

V. 8. HENRY: "Those will see their need of grace hereafter, when it should save them, who will not see their need of grace now, when it should sanctify and rule them."—V. 11. JEROME: "What does it profit to invoke him with the voice whom by works you deny ?"—V. 12. HENRY: "With regard to those that put off their great work to the last, it is a thousand to one that they have not time to do it then. While the poor awakened soul addresses itself, upon a sick-bed, to repentance and prayer, in awful confusion, it scarcely knows which end to begin at, or what to do first; and presently death comes, judgment comes, and the work is undone, and the poor sinner undone forever."—V. 13. We need not wonder at the frequent repetition, and fourfold illustration, of "Watch, for ye know not," seeing that human nature is so prone to heedless sloth or to preoccupation with worldly affairs.—All these exhortations to watch, and be ready, for the Lord's coming, will apply without material alteration to the duty of preparation for death, which will in an important sense summon us to meet Christ, and will leave fixed and permanent the relation in which we shall rise to meet him when he does come. (John 5 : 28 f.)

14-30. BE READY TO GIVE ACCOUNT AT THE COMING OF CHRIST.

This is found in Matt. only, though a quite similar parable is given by Luke (19: 11-27), as spoken at Jericho, some five or six days earlier. On that occasion it had a special design, to indicate that the consummated reign of the Messiah would begin only at his return after an absence, and that then he would reward and punish men according to their behavior during his absence; the illustration in that form exactly corresponded to the history of Archelaus. (See above, at close of chap. 2.) Here those peculiar traits are dropped, and we have not a returning king, but simply a master, who returns from a long journey to reward and punish. It must not be inferred that Jesus is here taking pains to avoid calling the Messiah a king, for he does so immediately afterwards. (25: 31, 34.) Some critics at once take for granted that Jesus spoke only one parable of this sort, and that either Luke or Matt. has reported inaccurately. But we have already remarked many times that such varied repetition on the part of a preacher who journeys about is perfectly

14 For *the kingdom of heaven is* as a man travelling into a far country, *who* called his own servants, and delivered unto them his goods.
15 And unto one he gave five *a* talents, to another two, and to another one: to every man according to his several ability ; and straightway took his journey.

14 For *it is* as *when* a man, going into another country, called his own [1]servants, and delivered unto
15 them his goods, And unto one he gave five talents, to another two, to another one; to each according to his several ability ; and he went on his journey.

---

a A talent is £187, 10s. ch. 18 : 24——1 Gr. *bondservants.*

---

natural. Meyer thinks it would be unnatural that the simpler should be the later form. It is amusing to watch the current propensity to explain every thing as an evolution from the simple to the complex. Certainly in preaching it is very common to produce a complex illustration adapted to certain surroundings, and on a second use in some other discourse to make it simpler and more general. Edersh. counts it difficult to believe that our Lord would give a parable in the presence of his disciples at Jericho, and then, a few days later, repeat it to the disciples in private; but theological instructors find frequent need of repeating to a class in an altered form what had been said in a sermon not long before.

14 f. For the kingdom of heaven is as a man, etc., Greek, lit., *for just as a man*, etc. The other member of the comparison is never formally stated, but it is understood without difficulty. Our Lord has given (since 24 : 37) a series of illustrations to show the importance of watchful preparation for his coming —the days of Noah, one taken and the other left, the thief coming unexpectedly, the headsteward and his returning master, the foolish and the prudent virgins. In the latter case he said expressly (25 : 1) that the Messianic reign shall resemble the case of these virgins and the coming bridegroom, so he here goes on without further stating the matter to be illustrated. It is important to watch (v. 13), *for* the Messiah's second coming is like the case of a man, etc. See a similar expression in Mark 13 : 34. **Travelling into a far country,** as in 21 : 33; 'took, or went on, his journey,' v. 15, is the same Greek term. **His own servants,** as in 22 : 6, those that belonged to him, *doulous, slaves* (see on 8: 6), from whom he might require and expect care for his interests. *Trench:* "Slaves in antiquity were often artisans, or were allowed otherwise to engage freely in business, paying, as it was frequently arranged, a fixed yearly sum to their master; or they had money committed to them wherewith to trade on his account, or with which to enlarge their business, and

bring in to him a share of their profits." A similar course was sometimes pursued in our Southern States, during the existence of slavery. **Five talents.** A talent of gold, see on 18 : 24, would be near twelve hundred dollars of our money, and with a purchasing power at least ten times as great. It was as if one should now put $60,000 in the hands of a dependent to preserve and increase. In the earlier parable (Luke 19) the sum stated is a "mina," about $17, so that ten minas would be one hundred and seventy, equal in purchasing power to say two thousand dollars. The sums used in the two illustrations are obviously round numbers. As talents in the parable represent whatever God gives us to use and improve, and as beyond comparison the most important of such gifts are our mental powers, so it has become common in English to call a man's mental powers his *talents*, and hence to speak of a man of talent, or a talented man. A more or less similar use is found in German and Dutch, in French, Spanish, and Italian, even in modern Greek. **To every man according to his several ability,** or 'his own ability,' viz., his capacity for preserving and increasing the funds intrusted to him. Comp. Rom. 12: 6; 1 Cor. 12: 11; Eph. 4: 11. In the earlier parable this distinction was not made, but to each was given the same sum. (Luke 19: 13.)

16-18. The trusted servants go to work. **Straightway** should most probably be connected with what follows, as in Rev. Ver., rather than with what precedes, as in Com. Ver. and Com. Greek text. In Matt. this Greek word (Weiss) always connects with what follows it. The good and faithful servant (v. 21), feeling his responsibility, went to work without delay. We naturally suppose that **likewise,** said of the second servant, includes this feature. **Traded,** literally *worked*, wrought (Wyc.), as in 21 : 28; 26: 10; then in a technical sense, 'engaged in *business*,' and so 'traded.' The men who conduct large business operations have to work indeed. One

16 Then he that had received the five talents went and traded with the same, and made *them* other five talents.

17 And likewise he that *had received* two, he also gained other two.

18 But he that had received one went and digged in the earth, and hid his lord's money.

19 After a long time the lord of those servants cometh, and reckoneth with them.

20 And so he that had received five talents came and brought other five talents, saying, Lord, thou deliveredst unto me five talents: behold, I have gained beside them five talents more.

21 His lora said unto him, Well done, *thou* good and faithful servant: thou hast been faithful over a few things, I will make thee ruler over many things: enter thou into the joy of thy lord.

22 He also that had received two talents came and said, Lord thou deliveredst unto me two talents: behold, I have gained two other talents beside them.

23 His lord said unto him, Well done, good and faithful servant: thou nast been faithful over a few things, I will make thee ruler over many things: enter thou into the joy of thy lord.

16 Straightway he that received the five talents went and traded with them, and made other five talents.

17 In like manner he also that *received* the two gained

18 other two. But he that received the one went away

19 and digged in the earth, and hid his lord's money. Now after a long time the lord of those [1] servants

20 cometh, and maketh a reckoning with them. And he that received the five talents came and brought other five talents, saying, Lord, thou deliveredst unto me five talents: lo, I have gained other five

21 talents. His lord said unto him, Well done, good and faithful [2] servant: thou hast been faithful over a few things, I will set thee over many things: enter

22 thou into the joy of thy lord. And he also that *received* the two talents came and said, Lord, thou deliveredst unto me two talents: lo, I have gained

23 other two talents. His lord said unto him, Well done, good and faithful [2] servant: thou hast been faithful over a few things, I will set thee over many

1 Gr. *bondservants*....2 Or, *bondservant.*

of the popular delusions is shown in speaking of "the working classes," as if brain-work were not often far more intense and severe than mere hand-work. But the term "business men" proceeds on a like assumption that no one else is really busy. In the other parable (Luke 19: 13-15) the Greek word used means directly 'engage in business,' which was expressed in Old English by 'occupy' (comp. Ezek. 27: 9, 22), used here also by Cran. and Rheims, while Tyn. and Gen. in Luke give 'buy and sell.' **Made.** It is hard to decide whether we should read this word or 'gained,' which has much better documentary evidence, but might easily here come from v. 17, 20, while 'made' is also found in Luke 19: 18, Rev. Ver. There is obviously no substantial difference. For **lord,** meaning *master,* see on 8: 19.

19-23. The master returns and demands an account. The two faithful servants. **After a long time.** This was necessary in the illustration for doubling the capital by any safe business. In the application it intimates that the final coming of the Messiah is remote, but still the phrase is quite indefinite. There was nothing in it to show that the coming would not take place in their day, but only enough to show that they must go on diligently serving Christ under present conditions. Bruce well compares the correction addressed by Paul to those Thessalonians who supposed the Lord was certainly coming immediately, and inferred that it was useless to engage any more in the ordinary duties of

life. (2 Thess. 3: 10-12.) **Well done** is a good translation, found first in the Geneva version; but stress cannot be laid on 'done' in contrast to the 'well doing' of Gal. 6: 9; for 'done' is not expressed in the Greek, but only implied in the word 'well.' Tyndale and Cran. translate simply 'well,' but this in modern English would be inadequate and ambiguous. **Over a few things . . . . over many things,** implies that the master had vast capital and many kinds of business to be managed. We can hardly suppose here a conception remaining from the former parable, where a king was speaking (Luke 19: 17) for there the reward was to be made governor over ten cities; the two parables seem to be consistently distinct throughout. **The joy of thy Lord** is in the story the rejoicing and felicity consequent on the master's return to his home (comp. Luke 15: 22 ff.). But here the application quite overpasses the limits of the illustration. The noblest and purest earthly delight could but dimly picture the joy which will follow the Saviour's final coming, for all that have been good and faithful servants, a joy unspeakably heightened by the fact that they will share in it with him; comp. Heb. 12: 2; Rom. 8: 17.

The rhythmical repetition in v. 22 f. of v. 20 f. reminds one of 7: 26 f., and of the parallelism which characterizes the Old Test. poetry. But what is more important, it commends and rewards the servant who has faithfully used the two talents in the same terms as the one who received the five talents.

24 Then he which had received the one talent came and said, Lord, I knew thee that thou art a hard man, reaping where thou hast not sown, and gathering where thou hast not strewed:
25 And I was afraid, and went and hid thy talent in the earth: lo, *there* thou hast *that is* thine.
26 His lord answered and said unto him, *Thou* wicked and slothful servant, thou knewest that I reap where I sowed not, and gather where I have not strewed:
27 Thou oughtest therefore to have put my money to the exchangers, and *then* at my coming I should have received mine own with usury.

24 things: enter thou into the joy of thy lord. And he also that had received the one talent came and said, Lord, I knew thee that thou art a hard man, reaping where thou didst not sow, and gathering
25 where thou didst not scatter: and I was afraid, and went away and hid thy talent in the earth: lo, thou
26 hast thine own. But his lord answered and said unto him, Thou wicked and slothful [1] servant, thou knewest that I reap where I sowed not, and gather
27 where I did not scatter; thou oughtest therefore to have put my money to the bankers, and at my com-

---

1 Or, *bondservant.*

There will doubtless be different capacities for sharing in the joy of our Lord, but every one will enjoy to the full. In the other parable the reward varies in exact accordance with the profit made upon the original trust, ten cities, five cities, as was natural in the case of a king appointing governors. Even here the wicked servant's talent is not divided between the two others, but given to the first. In v. 22 **received** is not expressed in the Greek, according to some of the best documents, but left to be understood; **beside them** rests on inferior evidence.

24-30. The wicked and slothful servant. **A hard man,** the Greek word for hard having metaphorical uses like our own. In Luke 19: 21 f. the Greek is substantially equivalent, being *austeros*, rough, harsh, etc., which we borrow through the Latin as austere, but now use in a somewhat more restricted sense. The image in **gathering where thou hast not strewed,** or *scattered,* is not exactly the same as in **reaping where thou hast not sown,** but seems to mean the gathering of wheat that after it was cut had been scattered, in order to become more dry and ripe; or else gathering up from the threshing-floor what another had scattered there to be threshed. The servant knew, he said, that his master was hard and grasping, drawing gain from the labor of others. He therefore pretends that he **was afraid** to invest the talent in business; for if he should make profit, the master would take it all (Goebel); and if he should lose the principal, he would be harshly treated, since one who so grasped after gain would have no patience under loss. So he returns the talent, as being all that would really have belonged to his master even if he had engaged in profitable business. He does not recognize his position and duty as a servant, and tries to excuse himself by attacking his master's character

and disposition. *Alford :* "The foolish virgins failed from thinking their part too easy; the wicked servant fails from thinking his too hard." **Hid thy talent in the earth,** comp. on 13: 44. In Luke 19: 20 the servant having a much smaller sum in charge simply kept it "laid up in a napkin." There is a sort of spiteful fling in the words **lo, there thou hast that is thine own,** or *thou hast thine own,* Rev. Ver.—implying that the master had no right to expect more. **Thou wicked and slothful servant.** He wickedly misjudged and slandered his master, and tried to make that an excuse for his slothful failure to do as he had been commanded. The master retorts that his own excuse established his guilt. Granting the master's character to be as represented, this would itself have indicated the propriety of at least lending out the money on interest. So also in the earlier parable, Luke 19:23. **Exchangers,** or *bankers.* The Greek word is derived from the word for bank or bench on which money used to be received and paid out. These bankers also changed money, but they were something much higher than the small-change men of 21: 12. *Plumptre :* It was in the servant's power "to take advantage of the banking, money-changing, money-lending system, of which the Phoenicians were the inventors, and which at the time was in full operation throughout the Roman Empire. The bankers received money on deposit, and paid interest on it, and then lent it at a higher percentage, or employed it in trade, or (as did the *publicani* at Rome) in farming the revenues of a province. This was therefore the natural resource, as investment in stocks or companies is with us, for those who had not energy to engage in business." The law of Moses forbade Israelites to charge interest against each other. (Ex. 22 : 25; Lev. 25 : 35-37; Deut. 23 : 19.) But Deut. 23: 20 allowed them to lend upon interest to Gen-

28 Take therefore the talent from him, and give *it* unto him which hath ten talents.

29 For unto every one that hath shall be given, and he shall have abundance: but from him that hath not shall be taken away even that which he hath.

30 And cast ye the unprofitable servant into outer darkness: there shall be weeping and gnashing of teeth.

28 ing I should have received back mine own with interest. Take ye away therefore the talent from him, and give it unto him that hath the ten talents.

29 For unto every one that hath shall be given, and he shall have abundance: but from him that hath not, even that which he hath shall be taken away. And

30 cast ye out the unprofitable [1] servant into the outer darkness: there shall be the weeping and gnashing of teeth.

1 Or, *bondservant*

tiles, and we may suppose this to have been a case of that sort, there being here no indication of nationality. Besides, the law was no doubt often disregarded or evaded in the dealings of Jews with each other, as we find in the time of Nehemiah. (Neh. 5: 10-12.) Our Lord draws his illustrations from the actual conduct of men, sometimes from their wrong conduct (*e. g.*, Luke 16: 1 ff. ; 18: 1 ff.). **Usury,** in Old English denoted simply what we now call interest, being the sum paid for the *use* of money, Latin *usura ;* but by degrees came to signify exorbitant interest, as so many words have from evil practices acquired an evil sense. Our word 'interest' derives its technical sense from the more general notion of profit. The Greek word here employed denotes what is born of money, what it brings forth or produces. The translation ought to be changed to 'interest,' throughout the Old Test. Psa. 15: 5 refers to the law of Moses above mentioned, which is not binding upon Christians.

28. "Bib. Comm": " God's gifts are not left unproductive, because one to whom they are intrusted neglects his duty. So far as such gifts are transferable, they are often, as a matter of fact, taken away from him who does not use them aright, and given to another. Thus the kingly power which Saul misused was taken from him and given to David. Thus the kingdom of God was taken away from the Jews, and given to a nation bringing forth the fruits thereof."

29. Comp. Luke 19: 26. See above on 13: 12. This is a principle of the divine government having many applications.

As some would make hiding the talent in the earth mean sinking the spiritual in the carnal, or what not, so some understand putting the money to the bankers to mean contributing to charitable associations, etc. This last might be suggested as one application of the principle that persons who timidly shrink from personal exertions may indirectly promote spiritual work; but a single practical

application of a general principle should not be put forward as an interpretation.

30. The unprofitable, or 'unserviceable,' in colloquial phrase 'of no use '; before called ' wicked and slothful.' If the man with one talent was blameworthy for making no increase, much more (Bruce) would that have applied to persons having two or five talents. Thus the guilt of uselessness holds true for high and low. Alas ! how many professed Christians are utterly useless. **Into** (*the*) **outer darkness,** etc., (see on 22: 13), while the faithful servants share their master's joy in his brightly lighted abode; the application of the image is to hell and heaven.

HOMILETICAL AND PRACTICAL.

V. 15. 'To each according to his ability.' 1) Inequalities of human condition necessarily result from the inequalities of human character and conduct. 2) To have more of property or of other talents than one can manage for God's glory, would be a burden and not a privilege. 3) The way to get a larger portion is to make wise use of what we have. 4) The best reward in eternity, will be the ability and opportunity to do grander work for Christ. 5) The faithful use of two talents will receive as hearty commendation as that of five ; and the cup of joy will in each case be full. Yea, it would have been the same with the servant who received one talent, had he faithfully used it.—V. 21. ' Enter thou into the joy of thy Lord.' 1) A joy unalloyed by sorrow. 2) A joy which is the reward of faithful service. 3) A joy which consists not in idle resting, but in higher and wider usefulness. 4) A joy shared with the Lord himself.—V. 23. Jewish comm. (Midrash) on Exodus (Wet.): "God never bestows great things on men till he has first tried them by little things; *e. g.*, Moses, David."—V. 24. Calling God a hard master. 1) Men are often hard masters, but that does not prove that God is. 2) God gives to every servant some talent to improve—only in pro-

31 When the Son of man shall come in his glory, and all the holy angels with him, then shall he sit upon the throne of his glory:

31 But when the Son of man shall come in his glory, and all the angels with him, then shall he sit on the

---

portion as he has really sown does he claim to reap. 3) It is the wicked and slothful servant who complains of having a hard master. 4) To excuse our lack of service by accusing him whom we ought to serve, is but adding insult to injury. 5) We may delude ourselves with flimsy excuses, but we cannot deceive God, nor escape aggravated punishment.—V. 25. The hid talent. 1) It is "his lord's money" (v. 18), entrusted for use and increase, and the servant has no right to hide it. 2) The reason for hiding may be professedly prudent fear, but is really sloth, disobedience, and lack of devotion to the master's interests. 3) The risks involved in doing anything whatsoever, form no sufficient reason for doing nothing. 4) To return the hid talent is not giving the master his own, for he has a right to expect increase. ANON.: "One who, receiving seed to sow, has at seed-time not sown it, inflicts loss upon his master; although he has not lost the seed, yet there is a loss in proportion as there might have been gain if he had sown at the fit time."—V. 29. CHRYS.: "He that hath a gift of word and teaching to profit thereby, and useth it not, will lose the gift also; but he that giveth diligence, will gain to himself the gift in more abundance; even as the other loseth what he had received."—V. 30. The unprofitable servant. 1) Unprofitable because slothful. 2) Unprofitable, and therefore wicked. 3) Unprofitable and inexcusable (v. 26 f.); if shrinking from one way, he might have been useful in some other. 4) Unprofitable, and for this severely punished.

V. 14-30. Parable of the Talents. 1) Christians should gladly recognize that they are Christ's "own servants," and must bend every energy to promote his cause in the world. 2) Christ commits to us as talents to be used in his service (a) our personal powers—of body—of intellect, imagination, passion, taste, conscience, will; (b) our attainments; (c) our possessions, and capacities for further acquisition; (d) our influence, through family, social, and business relations. 3) When Christ comes he will reward us for the faithful use of all these by admitting us into intimate and permanent intercourse with himself, and

by heightened resources for glorifying him. (v. 28.) 4) In the case of failure to improve our talents, many or few, complaints against Christ will be a poor excuse, only aggravating the offence. 5) To do no good in the world, to be simply useless and worthless, is to sin grievously against Christ; and only by incessant efforts to do good can we avoid doing positive evil. 6) The unprofitable servant will be punished by taking away his neglected resources for doing good (v. 28), and by grievous and abiding suffering. (v. 30.)

31-46. JUDGMENT SCENE AT THE COMING OF CHRIST.

The other Gospels have nothing at all parallel to this solemnly beautiful passage. Matthew has in various other instances given much more of a discourse than Mark or Luke, e. g., ch. 5-7, ch. 10, ch. 13, ch. 18; and so here ch. 25 is all peculiar to Matt., except that Luke has a parable given on a former occasion that closely resembles the parable of the Talents. The reference to the destruction of Jerusalem, with which this great discourse began, has now passed out of sight, and we think only of the final coming of Christ. (Comp. on 24: 3.) Our Lord had before intimated that he was to be the final judge of men (7: 22 f.; 13: 40-43; 16: 27; John 5: 25-29); he now describes the future judgment scene, in a way strikingly appropriate for the conclusion of his whole discourse on his coming. (Ch. 24 and 25.) Especially close is the connection with the foregoing parable of the Talents, in which the master returns to examine, and reward or punish.—Some expositors here introduce elaborate discussions as to the relation of this judgment to the "thousand years" of Rev. 20: 2-7. But whatever may be regarded as the meaning of that obscure and highly figurative statement in the visions of Patmos, it seems out of place to bring in the matter here, where there is no distinct room, and no occasion whatever, for its introduction. —The passage obviously divides itself into v. 31-33, 34-40, 41-45, and 46. *Alford:* "It will heighten our estimation of the wonderful sublimity of this description, when we recollect that it was spoken by the Lord *only three days before his sufferings.*"

32 And before him shall be gathered all nations: and he shall separate them one from another, as a shepherd divideth *his* sheep from the goats:

32 throne of his glory: and before him shall be gathered all the nations: and he shall separate them one from another, as the shepherd separateth the sheep

31-33. All men gathered and divided. **When,** Rev. Ver., *But when.* It is very doubtful whether the Greek particle ought here to be translated 'but,' or 'now,' or to remain untranslated. This depends on the relation of what follows to what precedes, which the particle itself does not at all determine. Only if the following passage stands in some sort of opposition to the foregoing, do we properly render 'but,' otherwise the Greek term is only a particle of transition, which we render by 'now' or 'and,' or often leave quite untranslated. This passage does not seem clearly opposed to the parable of the Talents, for that also, as we have seen, presents an examination followed by reward and punishment. It would therefore seem better to leave the particle untranslated, as in Com. Ver. **The Son of man,** the Messiah, as often in this discourse (24: 27, 30, 37, 39, 44), and previously; see on 8: 20. Nowhere in the discourse does Jesus say that this will be himself, but he is answering the question of the disciples, 'what shall be the sign of thy coming?' (24: 3); and indeed he had long encouraged the disciples in the belief that he was the Messiah. **Shall come in his glory,** comp. 16: 27, 'in the glory of his Father,' and 24: 30, 'coming on the clouds of heaven with power and great glory.' We have little further information as to the nature of this 'glory.' Just below is mentioned 'the throne of his glory;' and Paul speaks of 'flaming fire' (2 Thess. 1: 8), and 'the trump of God.' (1 Thess. 4: 16; 1 Cor. 15: 52.) Nothing earthly could furnish the images for an adequate description. **And all the holy angels with him,** like the splendid retinue of a king, comp. 13: 41; 16: 27. No longer will he be a homeless wanderer, with a handful of followers. As to the angels in general, see on 18: 10. 'Holy' (Com. Ver.) is a spurious addition.[1] **Sit upon the throne,** as a king (v. 34); comp. 19: 28. The Jews, including the Twelve, expected the Messiah to sit on a throne of temporal dominion. Our Lord here shows the disciples that at his second coming he will sit on a throne of judgment, making awards for eternity. He sits now already on the throne of mediatorial authority (28: 18), spiritually conquering and ruling. (1 Cor. 15: 25; Heb. 12: 2.)

All (*the*) **nations.** Not only Jews, but Gentiles, not only some nations, but all. The ancients all inclined to think that every nation must of course have its own deities; but there is only one God for all nations, and only one Mediator and final Judge (comp. 1 Tim. 2: 5). Though his personal mission was exclusively to the lost sheep of the house of Israel (15: 24), yet he was destined to draw all men unto him (John 12: 32), and the proclamation of his work was to be made to all nations. (28: 19.) *Bengel:* "All the angels, all the nations; how vast an assembly." Some commentators suppose that it means only the Gentiles, who are most frequently meant by 'the nations.' Plumptre finds a striking distribution: the parable of the Virgins refers to all Christians; that of the Talents to those "that hold any office or ministry in the church"; and this passage to the heathen. But the parable of the Talents does not admit of the proposed limitation; and here, certainly the blessed for whom the kingdom is prepared are Christians. Others, even Meyer, understand that this judgment relates to Christians only; but that is made highly improbable by 'all the nations,' and seems impossible in view of 'depart accursed'—strange Christians! **As** (*the*) **shepherd,** in any particular case, like 'the sower,' 'the good man,' etc. (12: 35; 13: 3.) **Divideth,** or *separateth* (Rheims), same word as in preceding clause. Com. Ver. follows Tyn., 'divideth,' an improper variation of the translation, comp. on v. 46. **From the goats.** The Greek word properly means 'kids' (Rev. Ver. *margin*), as in 'Thou never gavest me a kid,' Luke 15: 29. The Latin and Peshito versions have the distinctive terms for kids; Jerome expressly mentions that it is not goats but kids, and *Anon.* labors to show why the term kids is more appropriate. The difference is of course quite unimportant. Sheep and goats are often found in one flock (Gen. 30: 32 f.),

---

[1] It is wanting in the earliest uncials, and in nearly all the early versions. It was probably suggested by way of contrast to 'the devil and his angels,' in v. 41, or by "the Lord my God shall come, and all the holy ones with thee," Zech. 14: 5, Rev. Ver.

33 And he shall set the sheep on his right hand, but the goats on the left.

34 Then shall the King say unto them on his right hand, Come, ye blessed of my Father, inherit the kingdom prepared for you from the foundation of the world:

33 from the ¹ goats: and he shall set the sheep on his
34 right hand, but the ¹ goats on the left. Then shall the King say unto them on his right hand, Come, ye blessed of my Father, inherit the kingdom pre-

---

1 Gr. *kids.*

---

but sometimes do not feed well together, and are kept apart while grazing.[1] The Scriptures often employ sheep to denote those who trust in God, and so the goats or kids are here naturally taken to represent the worse side. Various Fathers and some modern writers proceed eagerly to trace minute analogies between the wicked and kids or goats, and between the righteous and sheep, in the way that has brought so much reproach upon the interpretation of Scripture. **On his right hand . . . on the left.** Wet. quotes Greek and Roman writers and the Talmud as putting the good on the right hand of the judge and the bad on the left hand. It is a perfectly natural symbolism, connected with our preference for the right hand in greetings, and in many ways. (Luke 1 : 11 ; Mark 16 : 5.) How far this predictive imagery of a judgment scene will be literally fulfilled by actual assembly in a locality, etc., no one can tell. All descriptions and conceptions of things unseen and eternal are necessarily dependent upon material analogies, even as our own mental action can be defined only in terms drawn from physical action. We may be very sure that the spiritual and eternal reality will be something far more solemn and instructive than any conception we are able to derive from the simplest or the most sublime images.

34-40. The King and Judge speaks to those on his right hand. **The King.** Our Lord has been constantly speaking, throughout his ministry, of the 'kingdom of heaven,' and 'kingdom of God' (4 : 17 ; John 3 : 3, etc.), the familiar Jewish designation of the Messianic reign (see on 3 : 2). In like manner "King Messiah" was a familiar phrase among the Jews. Had Jesus employed that expression in speaking to the people, they would have seized upon it as confirming their conception of a worldly sovereign, conquering and reigning in splendor at Jerusalem. So he has preferred to designate the Messiah by the phrase 'the Son of man' (see on 8 : 20), which would not encourage these popular misconceptions. In 16 : 28 he predicted 'the Son of man coming in his kingdom,' coming as king, and in 19 : 28 as sitting ' on the throne of his glory'; but in both cases he was talking with the Twelve. And so here—perhaps with only four of them (see on 24 : 3) ; the time is near when he will avow himself before the Sanhedrin to be the Messiah and will take the foreseen consequences. (26 : 63-68 ; 27 : 11.) Observe too that he distinctly speaks of his *future* coming, and not of any present and temporal reign. It must be remembered that an Oriental king, indeed any ancient king, often acted as judge. **Come,** in Greek the same emphatic expression as in 11 : 28 ; as now he strongly and warmly invites to loving trust and service, so hereafter to blessed reward. **Blessed,** not the word properly rendered ' happy ' (see on 5 : 3), but another which exactly means 'blessed,' persons whom God has blessed, who are in a blessed state ; as in 21 : 9 ; 23 : 39 ; Luke 1 : 42. **Blessed of my Father** means exactly ' my Father's blessed ones,' denoting not simply that they have been blessed by him, but that they are his. Tyndale unwarrantably, 'blessed children of my Father,' and this expression, though adopted by none of his followers, was introduced into the Burial Service of the Church of England. Our Lord delights to connect his work in many ways with that of the Father; see 10 : 32 f. ; 11 : 25-27 ; 15 : 13 ; 16 : 17, 27 ; 18 : 10, 19 ; 20 : 23 ; 23 : 29, 53 ; Luke 2 : 49 ; 22 : 29 ; 23 : 46, and exceedingly often in John. **Inherit,** because it is not merely theirs by gift, but theirs by inheritance (so Chrys. and followers), their Father's gift (Rom. 8 : 17 ; Rev. 21 : 7), designed from all eternity to be theirs. So the literal sense

---

[1] The morning after reaching Palestine, when setting out from Ramleh, across the plain of Sharon, we saw a shepherd leading forth a flock of white sheep and black goats, all mingled as they followed him. Presently he turned aside into a little green valley, and stood facing the flock. When a sheep came up, he tapped it with his long staff on the right side of the head, and it quickly moved off to his right ; a goat he tapped on the other side, and it went to his left. Thus the Saviour's image presented itself exactly before our eyes.

35 For I was a hungered, and ye gave me meat: I was thirsty, and ye gave me drink: I was a stranger, and ye took me in:

36 Naked, and ye clothed me: I was sick, and ye visited me: I was in prison, and ye came unto me.

37 Then shall the righteous answer him, saying, Lord, when saw we thee a hungered, and fed *thee ?* or thirsty, and gave *thee* drink?

38 When saw we thee a stranger, and took *thee* in? or naked, and clothed *thee ?*

39 Or when saw we thee sick, or in prison, and came unto thee?

40 And the King shall answer and say unto them, Verily I say unto you, Inasmuch as ye have done *it* unto one of the least of these my brethren, ye have done *it* unto me.

35 pared for you from the foundation of the world: for I was an hungred, and ye gave me meat: I was

36 thirsty, and ye gave me drink: I was a stranger, and ye took me in ; naked, and ye clothed me: I was sick, and ye visited me: I was in prison, and ye

37 came unto me. Then shall the righteous answer him, saying, Lord, when saw we thee an hungred,

38 and fed thee? or athirst, and gave thee drink? And when saw we thee a stranger, and took thee in ? or

39 naked, and clothed thee? And when saw we thee

40 sick, or in prison, and came unto thee? And the King shall answer and say unto them, Verily I say unto you, Inasmuch as ye did it unto one of these my brethren, *even* these least, ye did it unto me.

of the word seems appropriate here (comp. 1 Cor. 15: 50; Gal. 5: 21), and not the modified sense found in 5: 5, and perhaps in 19: 29. But this heirship is proven to exist by their manifesting a Christian character and leading a Christian life (2 Peter 1: 10); and particularly, as here set forth, by their kindness to Christ's people. **The kingdom** is here the Messianic kingdom (see on 3: 2) in its perfected heavenly state. **Prepared,** not merely destined, but made ready (Meyer); comp. John 14: 2; Heb. 11: 16; James 2: 5. Peter adds (1 Pet. 1: 4 f.) that it is preserved for the heirs, and they are guarded for the inheritance, so that neither shall fail of the other. The eternal fire also is 'prepared.' (v. 41.) **From the foundation of the world,** comp. John 17: 24; 1 Pet. 1: 20; Eph. 1: 4, and above in 13: 35. **For** introduces the proof that they are blessed of the Father, and entitled to inherit the kingdom, viz., that they have rendered service to the King's brethren, and thus virtually to him. **Ye took me in.** The Greek means *led me with (you),* viz., into your houses (Grimm.). **Naked,** imperfectly clothed. (Acts 19: 16.)—These tender and beautiful sentences are designed to impress the great thought that the Messiah would recognize himself as served in serving even the least of his brethren, and neglected in neglecting them, a thought for which the way has already been prepared in 10: 40 ff.; 18: 5 f.; comp. Heb. 6: 10; 1 John 3: 16. It would be a grave mistake to suppose that nothing will be regarded in the judgment, nothing help in determining a man's future, but the simple question whether he has been benevolent towards suffering Christians; we are taught elsewhere that each will "receive the things done in the body, according to what he hath done, whether it be good or bad." (2 Cor. 5: 10, Rev. Ver.) It is also a mistake to infer that only

actions will enter into the judgment. The essence of the passage is that the actions in question will be accepted as indicating *personal relation to Christ;* and it is really personal relation to Christ, as acted out in the life, that will fix eternal destiny. All this directly applies only to those who have had some knowledge of Christ's brethren and of him; the heathen who have had no such knowledge will be condemned for neglecting the light of nature, and the law of conscience. (Rom. 1: 18 ff.; 2: 12-16.)—Observe then that our Lord is not expressly speaking of benevolence to the poor and suffering in general, but of kindness to his poor and suffering 'brethren' for his sake. Yet he himself healed and fed many who were not truly his; and we are imitating and honoring him if for his sake we minister to any and all who are needy or distressed—provided always we minister wisely in a truly helpful way, and not so as to promote professional beggary or other imposition, nor the self-conceit of criminals in prison, etc.

37-39. The righteous answer in no self-depreciation, but in simple sincerity and humility; they have not personally seen the Saviour (1 Pet. 1: 8), and how (Mald.) can they have rendered him any personal service? They will, when actually brought to judgment, think and feel otherwise only in proportion as they have understood and remembered the lesson here given.

40. Verily, I say unto you, calling solemn attention. (Comp. on 5: 18.) With this reply of the King we may well compare 6: 4, Rev. Ver., "that thine alms may be in secret; and thy Father, which seeth in secret, shall recompense thee." He knows and remembers every act of modest charity, and is ready to accept it as done to himself. **One of the least of these,** or, *even these least.* Many of Christ's followers were poor and of little apparent

41 Then shall he say also unto them on the left hand, Depart from me, ye cursed, into everlasting fire, prepared for the devil and his angels:
42 For I was a hungered, and ye gave me no meat: I was thirsty, and ye gave me no drink:
43 I was a stranger, and ye took me not in: naked, and ye clothed me not: sick, and in prison, and ye visited me not.
44 Then shall they also answer him, saying, Lord, when saw we thee a hungered, or athirst, or a stranger, or naked, or sick, or in prison, and did not minister unto thee?
45 Then shall he answer them, saying, Verily I say unto you, Inasmuch as ye did *it* not to one of the least of these, ye did *it* not to me.
46 And these shall go away into everlasting punishment: but the righteous into life eternal.

41 Then shall he say also unto them on the left hand, 1 Depart from me, ye cursed, into the eternal **fire** which is prepared for the devil and his angels: for I was an hungred, and ye gave me no meat: I was thirsty, and ye gave me no drink: I was a stranger, 43 and ye took me not in; naked, and ye clothed me not: sick, and in prison, and ye visited me not. 44 Then shall they also answer them, saying, Lord, when saw we thee an hungred, or athirst, or a stranger, or naked, or sick, or in prison, and did not minister 45 unto thee? Then shall he answer them, saying. Verily I say unto you, Inasmuch as ye did it not 46 unto one of these least, ye did it not unto me. And these shall go away into eternal punishment: but the righteous into eternal life.

---

1 Or, *Depart from me under a curse.*

---

importance; only a few were otherwise. (John 7: 48; 1 Cor. 1: 26 ff.) He identifies himself not merely with the distinguished, but with those whom men would lightly esteem. *Morison:* "When the Judge, as it were, points to *these* his brethren, and then refers to the *least* of them, it is not needful that we should suppose that they are different from 'the sheep.' . . . In pronouncing sentence on each, he could point to surrounding brethren who had been loved and sympathetically helped."

41-45. Those on the left hand. **Depart from me,** substantially the same expression as in 7: 23; but the added words are here more awful. The participle rendered **cursed** lacks the article in some of the earliest and best MSS.,[1] and in that form it could not mean **ye curse**d, but *depart accursed*, 'depart from me under a curse' (Rev. Ver., *margin*), the curse resting upon them as a part of the sentence. **Everlasting,** or, *the eternal*, **fire,** the Greek having the article; that eternal fire which was a familiar thought to the minds of his hearers; see the same phrase in 18: 8, and comp. 3: 12, and Mark 9: 48, 'the fire is not quenched.' See on 5: 22, 'the Gehenna of fire,' and 13: 42, 50, 'the furnace of fire'; also on 3: 11, 'baptize . . . in fire.' (Comp. Jude 7; Rev. 20: 10 ff.) The term 'eternal' is used instead of 'everlasting,' merely to keep the translation uniform. (See on v. 46.) Whether eternal punishment involves any physical reality corresponding to fire, we

know not; there will be something as bad as fire, and doubtless worse, for no earthly image can be adequate. (Comp. above on v. 31–33.) **For the devil,** that is, Satan (see on 4: 1.) We might say that by analogy to the angels of God, Satan's attendants and helpers, the demons (see on 8: 31), are called **his angels.** But more than that appears to be true. The demons are fallen angels. (Jude 6; 2 Pet. 2: 4; Rev. 12: 7.) We must beware of confounding what little we know from Scripture concerning these dreadful beings with the ideas of Milton in Paradise Lost, or with popular traditions and nursery tales. (Comp. on 4: 1.) Notice (Origen) that while it is the kingdom prepared for you (v. 34), it is not the eternal fire prepared for you, but prepared for the devil and his angels; the wicked go to share the dreadful doom of the fallen angels, go of their own movement into that which was prepared for others. And they are not said to 'inherit' the eternal fire, but incur the punishment through conscious sin and through rejection of the Saviour.

42-45. This answers to 35-40, with the beautiful Hebrew circumstantiality and parallelism, comp. 25: 20-23; 7: 24-27. This passage presents a notable exemplification of *sins of omission.*

46. We find here a remarkable instance of that unnecessary and unwarranted variation in translation which so abounds in the versions from Tyndale to King James. The Greek here applies the same adjective to pun-

---

[1] The article is omitted by א B L, 33, 102, Cyril. One sees no ground for supposing it to have been struck out as an "Alexandrian" correction (such as these documents sometimes give), since the reading with the articles is good and unobjectionable, corresponding exactly to "come, ye blessed." But we can see obvious reasons for the *insertion* of the article by copyists, both because

of a certain obscurity without it, and from the desire to make the two corresponding clauses exactly symmetrical. Therefore the reading without the article is quite probably correct. Its distinctive meaning, though one that might not readily occur to a copyist, is thoroughly appropriate.

ishment and life. The Latin and other early versions translated both by the same word, and Wyc. and Rheims, following the Latin Vulgate, render 'everlasting' in both cases; but Tyn. and followers, 'everlasting pain . . . life eternal.' The English language, as being compounded of Anglo-Saxon and French (Latin), has an extraordinary number of words nearly synonymous; and this fact has probably fostered a passion for variety of expression. As a mere question of English literature, the early versions have no doubt gained a certain beauty of style by diversifying their renderings; and King James' translators, in their "Address to the Reader," have expressly defended themselves and their predecessors for this practice. But they have thereby seriously obscured the verbal connection throughout many a passage and between different passages. The careful student of the English Bible, using Concordance and References for comparing Scripture with Scripture, has been misled a thousand times, either imagining two passages to contain the same Hebrew or Greek word when they do not, because the English has the same word, or failing to learn, often in highly important cases, that two passages do contain the same word in the original, because the English has rendered differently. It is of course impossible to translate the same Hebrew or Greek word in every case by the same English word; but wherever this can be done with due regard to the meaning, it is a grave fault to neglect it merely for the sake of gratifying a certain fastidious taste in English style. Among the many examples of this fault which occur in the Common Version of Matt., see 5: 15 f.; 14: 24; 18: 33; 19: 20; 20: 20; 25: 32. For some examples in other parts of New Test., see Bp. Lightf. on Revision. As to whether eternal or everlasting should here be used in both cases, there is room for a slight difference of opinion. Noyes, Amer. Bib. Union, and Davidson give 'everlasting punishment . . . everlasting life' (comp. Dan. 12: 2); Darby, 'eternal punishment . . . life eternal.' Some would prefer to reserve the

term 'eternal' for that which is without beginning as well as without end; but that word is necessary in several passages of the New Test. to denote duration that is simply without end. Upon the whole, the Revisers are believed to have acted wisely in uniformly rendering this Greek word by eternal; there is a slight loss in some passages, but an important gain upon the whole. It is difficult to estimate how much would have been gained for the English speaking world in the exact apprehension of the present important passage, if the punishment and the life had been through all these centuries described, in English as in the Greek, not merely by substantially equivalent words, but by exactly the same word.

Eternal punishment . . . life eternal. It will at once be taken for granted, by any unprejudiced and docile mind, that the punishment of the wicked will last as long as the life of the righteous; it is to the last degree improbable that the Great Teacher would have used an expression so inevitably suggesting a great doctrine he did not mean to teach; those who deny the doctrine must establish here a difference of meaning, and with an overwhelming presumption against them. Attempts to set aside the obvious meaning have been made in several ways. (a) It is pointed out that the etymology of the term *aionios*, 'eternal,' has not been clearly ascertained. But it is now past question (Curtius, Lid. and Scott, Cremer, Skeat) that *aion*, originally *aiwon*, has the same root as *aiei* and *aei*, 'always'; the same as the Latin *aev-um*, from which came *ae(v)-ternus*, borrowed by us in the form eternal: the same as the Gothic *aiws*, *aiw*, the German *ew-ig*, 'everlasting,' 'eternal,' and the English *ev-er* in everlasting, forever, etc. And the words *aion* and *aionios* in the Greek as well as in the other languages mentioned certainly have the use in question, whatever may have been the primary sense of the root. You cannot persuade those who speak English that the meaning of everlasting is doubtful, simply because philologers have not determined the primary sense of the root *ev*.[1] (b) It is urged that *aion* and *aionios* are

---

[1] We do not know the original meaning of this root *aiw*, or *ev*, whether it meant primarily unlimited duration, and was then weakened to denote definite periods, or, more probably, meant a definite period, as a lifetime, an age, and was then extended to denote an in-

definite period, or unlimited duration. But there is no question that the Greek words formed upon the root do often actually denote unlimited duration; *e. g.*, *eis ton aiona*, 'forever,' *ap'aionos*, 'from everlasting,' etc., and *aionios*, as often applied to God.

in the Sept. frequently applied—following the Heb. word *'olam*,—to things finite, as "the everlasting hills," "an ordinance forever." Certainly, just as in English we say "to have and to hold, unto him and his heirs forever," or say "there is everlasting trouble in that church." In the one case we use a natural and perfectly intelligible hyperbole, in the other the possession or the law really *is* of unlimited duration, in a sense well understood, and not restricted save by the nature of things. Any terms that could possibly be employed to describe future punishment as unlimited would be equally subject to such processes of "explaining away." [1] (c) It is affirmed by some that while *aionios* here means 'eternal,' that is a wholly different idea from everlasting or endless. They say that 'eternal life,' as in John 3: 36, Rev. Ver.; 5: 39; 17: 3, Rev. Ver., does not mean 'endless life,' but simply the kind of life which is lived in eternity, for it really begins in this life whenever one becomes a Christian; and so they infer that 'eternal punishment' means simply punishment suffered in eternity and not necessarily endless punishment. But 'eternal life' *does* in all the cases primarily and distinctly denote the future and endless life, and it is simply an added thought that the believer becomes already in this world a partaker of its spiritual essence—this added thought not at all excluding or pushing out of view the primary sense. Of course then the inference as to eternal punishment falls away. Others turn attention to the Hebrew phrase 'this *'olam*,' and 'the coming *'olam*,'(see above on 12: 32), and urge that *aionian* punishment means only that which pertains to the coming *aion* (*'olam*), age or period, after the day of judgment, without saying that it is to be endless punishment. But the force of those Jewish phrases, whether as used by the Rabbis or in New Test., turned on 'this' and 'the coming,' which terms are wanting in the phrase *aionian* punishment. [2] Thus none of these at-

tempts have set aside or really weakened the plain meaning of the word *aionios*, 'eternal,' as here describing both the punishment and the life. Westcott and Hort suppose the expression to be derived by our Lord from Dan. 12: 2, 'some to everlasting life,' where the Greek has exactly the same phrase as here, 'and some to shame and everlasting contempt,' where the adjective is the same.

The term *kolasis*, rendered **punishment,** denotes primarily pruning (a tree, vine), and hence checking, chastisement, castigation, punishment. Aristotle says that this word is different from *timoria*, vindication, vengeance, revenge, "for punishment is for the sake of the sufferer, but revenge for that of the person inflicting it, in order that he may be satiated"; and Plato joins *kolasis* with admonition, as opposed to irrational vengeance (Trench "Syn."). So *kolasis* is the milder term, implying the absence of vengefulness. It is therefore naturally employed here to denote punishment inflicted by God, and so also in 1 John 4: 18, not 'torment' Com. Ver., but 'punishment' Rev. Ver., and the verb in 2 Pet. 2: 9; while the severer term *timoria* is used only in Heb. 10: 29, for the punishment of very aggravated sin. But that the distinction made by the philosophers was not absolute, that *kolasis* really meant penal infliction, is seen from the use of the verb in Acts 4: 21, "finding nothing how they might punish them," compared with Paul's use of the stronger term *timoreo* in Acts 22: 5; 26: 11, to describe the persecutions he had inflicted on the Christians; also from such classic phrases as "punish (*kolazein*) with death" and from the conjunction of the two words *kolazein timoriais* (Lid. and Scott). It is therefore vain to say that the use of this term here forbids us to understand the punishment as penalty, and without end.

With this passage agree the general teachings of Scripture on the subject, including even some corresponding expressions, as 'into

---

[1] Farrar says ("Mercy and Judgment,"p. 388) that *aei*, 'always,' "would have been regarded as decisive," and that *aneu telous*, 'without end,' "would preclude all controversy." Yet *aionios* has the same root as *aei*, and as *aidios*, which he mentions in the same connection: and Farrar himself, in quoting Ovid's expression, "Eternal civil wars," remarks (p, 390, n.), "So we say, 'It will be an endless business;' 'This led to endless trouble,' etc."

Thus we see that the term 'endless' could be explained away in the same fashion.

[2] Farrar even says (p. 395) that the phrase used here by the Peshito Syriac means 'the punishment of the world to come': whereas the 'to come,' is entirely wanting, and the Syriac plainly means 'the punishment that is forever,' using the same phrase as the Hebrew *le-'olam*, Greek *eis aiona*.

the eternal fire,' v. 41, Rev. Ver. (comp. Jude 7), 'into the unquenchable fire,' Mark 9: 43, Rev. Ver. (comp. Matt. 3: 12), and 'where their worm dieth not, and the fire is not quenched,' Mark 9: 48. This last phrase is obviously derived from Isa. 66: 24, but it does not follow that our Lord means by it only what the prophet had in view, for it is not a quotation, but a mere use of the prophet's terms. Comp. also John 3: 36, Rev. Ver., "He that believeth on the Son hath eternal life; but he that believeth not the Son shall not see life, but the wrath of God abideth on him," where the last phrases distinctly indicate a penalty without end; also John 5: 28 f., etc.

But certain more general objections are brought against the obvious meaning of our Lord's language.

(1) It is said (Farrar) that the Jews in our Lord's time did not believe Gehenna to be a place of eternal punishment, and that his hearers would understand him according to the common view, unless he stated the contrary. But this is an incorrect statement, see Wünsche, Edersheim (App. XIX.), and the Talmudic passages quoted in Surenh. Mishna, Vol. 2, p. 314. These make it manifest that the great Jewish schools about the time of our Lord did both believe in Gehenna as a place of perpetual punishment *for some persons.* And the Saviour here teaches that such will be the case with the persons of whom he is speaking.[1]

(2) A metaphysical objection is sometimes pressed, to the effect that suffering is necessarily destructive, and so the sufferer must sooner or later cease to exist. But this is not proven. And surely he who caused to exist could keep in existence. This is the most probable meaning of the Saviour's solemn word (Mark 9: 49), 'Every one shall be salted with fire.' Fire is usually destructive, but this unquenchable fire will act like salt, preserving instead of destroying. So Keble,

"Christian Year, Fifth Sunday in Lent," says of the Jewish race in their present condition:

"Salted with fire, they seem to show
How spirits lost in endless woe
May undecaying live.
Oh, sickening thought ! yet hold it fast
Long as this glittering world shall last,
Or sin at heart survive."

(3) There are also "moral arguments" alleged to show that the Saviour cannot have meant to teach eternal punishment. (a) Some maintain that it is inconsistent with the *goodness* of God. Thus John Foster said it was useless to occupy oneself with the discussion of texts, since the matter is decided by a great moral argument. But if we have a revelation from God, it is certainly our chief source of instruction concerning things unseen and eternal, and such lofty superiority to the discussion of texts is quite out of place. God is certainly a better judge than we are, as to what is consistent with his goodness. Perhaps we have not an adequate sense of the evil of sin, nor a full appreciation of the claims of justice. Perhaps the humanity for which our age is distinguished, has with many run into a sentimental humanitarianism, which weakly shrinks from the idea of suffering, and does not sympathize with stern moral indignation against wrong. Farrar argues that the doctrine of endless punishment has converted many men into infidels. But many have also declared themselves driven off by the doctrine of atonement, or that of regeneration, or of the divinity of Christ. Paul did not cease to preach the cross because to the Jews it was a stumbling-block. (b) Others say it is inconsistent with the *justice* of God to punish all alike, when their actual wrong-doing has been so different, and their advantages likewise so different. But it is expressly taught that the eternal punishment will *not* be the same for all. "That each may receive . . . according to that he hath done." (2 Cor. 5: 10.) "It

---

[1] The school of Shammai held there would be three classes on the day of judgment, the perfectly righteous, the completely wicked, and an intermediate class. The righteous are immediately inscribed in the book of life; the completely wicked "are inscribed and immediately sealed to Gehenna," according to (Dan. 12: 2). The intermediate class "go down to Gehenna, and moan, and afterwards ascend," according to (Zach. 13: 9). The school of Hillel held that in God's great mercy the intermediate class do not go down. Of the thoroughly wicked, some go down and are punished twelve months, and are then destroyed. But heretics, informers, Epicureans, persons who deny the resurrection of the dead, and persons who cause many to sin, like Jeroboam, "go down to Gehenna and are there punished unto ages of ages."

shall be more, tolerable for Tyre and Sidon, in the day of judgment, than for you." (Matt. 11 : 22, Rev. Ver.) Especially notice Luke 12: 47 f., Rev. Ver.: "And that servant, which knew his Lord's will, and made not ready, nor did according to his will, shall be beaten with many stripes; but he that knew not, and did things worthy of stripes, shall be beaten with few stripes." This teaching has been in many cases grievously overlooked. Taking images literally, men have fancied that the 'Gehenna of fire' (5 : 22) will be the same place and the same degree of punishment for all. But the above passages and many others show that there will be differences. The degrees of punishment must, in the nature of things, be exceedingly various, and the extremes of punishment must be as remote as the east is from the west. All inherited proclivities, "taints of blood," all difference of environment, every privilege and every disadvantage, will be taken into account. It is the Divine Judge that will apportion punishment, with perfect knowledge and perfect justice and perfect goodness. This great fact, that there will be *degrees* in future punishment—as well as in future rewards—ought to be more prominent in religious instruction. It gives some relief in contemplating the awful fate of those who perish. It might save many from going away into Universalism; and others from dreaming of "a second probation" in eternity, for which the Scriptures give no warrant (comp. on 12: 32); and yet others from unjustly assailing and rejecting, to their own ruin, the gospel of salvation.

HOMILETICAL AND PRACTICAL.

V. 32. Separation of the righteous and the wicked. 1) A necessary separation; (a) necessary to the vindication of God's justice; (b) necessary to the blessedness of the righteous; (c) necessary to the punishment of the wicked. 2) An accurate separation—no mistakes; self-delusion, hypocrisy, strangely mingled characters, nothing will prevent the assignment of each as he really belongs. 3) A separation leading to new companionships—the righteous with the Saviour and all the angels—the wicked with the devil and his angels. 4) A separation without hope of reunion, v. 46;

Luke 16 : 26.—V. 35–40. Charity. 1) Varieties of charity, v. 35; comp. James 1: 27. 2) Reasons for charity; (a) for the sake of humanity; (b) for Christ's sake. 3) Rewards of charity; (a) the joy of doing service to the Saviour; (b) the kingdom prepared.—V. 40. Christ identified with Christians. 1) Through them men may learn concerning him, and be convinced as to the divinity of his religion. 2) Inward union with Christ should be expressed, and thus strengthened, by an outward union with his people. 3) Benefits conferred on his people as such (comp. 10: 42), will be acknowledged and rewarded as benefits to himself. 4) Unkindness to Christians as such is insulting rejection of Christ.—V. 42. Sins of omission. 1) The neglect of any duty is in itself a great sin. 2) The omission of right-doing turns all our active powers towards the commission of wrong.—V. 40. LUTHER: "Whoever then is minded to do works of compassion to Christians, because he believes he has in Christ a faithful Redeemer who reconciles him to God; or himself suffers the opposition of the devil and the world because of his faith—let him be cheerful and joyous, for he has already received the joyous sentence, 'Come, ye blessed.'" CALVIN: "Whenever we feel slothful about helping the wretched, let the Son of God come before our eyes; to refuse him anything is a dreadful sacrilege."—V. 45. LUTHER: "What shall become of those who not only give nothing to Christ's poor, but by fraud and extortion rob them of what they have?" CALVIN: "Let believers be admonished; for as we need promises to incite us to zeal in living well, so also threatenings to keep us in solicitude and fear."—V. 31–46. The judgment scene. 1) The Judge—once a homeless wanderer, now enthroned in glory—once despised and rejected, now accepting or rejecting—once subjected to unrighteous judgment, now judging the world in righteousness. (Acts 17 : 31.) 2) The grounds of this judgment—the conduct of men to each other, as revealing their relation to God; (a) benefiting Christ's brethren is accepted by Christ as personal service to him; (b) neglecting them is regarded by him as personal neglect. 3) The results of this judgment—eternal punishment—eternal life.

CHAPTER XXVI.

A ND it came to pass, when Jesus had finished all
these sayings, he said unto his disciples,
2 Ye know that after two days is the *feast of the* passover, and the Son of man is betrayed to be crucified.
3 Then assembled together the chief priests, and the
scribes, and the elders of the people, unto the palace of
the high priest, who was called Caiaphas,
4 And consulted that they might take Jesus by subtilty, and kill *him*.

1 And it came to pass, when Jesus had finished all
2 these words, he said unto his disciples, Ye know
that after two days the passover cometh, and the
3 Son of man is delivered up to be crucified. Then
were gathered together the chief priests, and the
elders of the people, unto the court of the high
4 priest, who was called Caiaphas; and they took
counsel together that they might take Jesus by sub-

Ch. 26: 1-16. OUR LORD'S DEATH AP-
PROACHING. THE SUPPER AT BETHANY.

Found also in Mark 14: 1-11; Luke 22: 1-6;
John 12: 2-8.

Here begins what is commonly called the
history of our Lord's Passion. This is narrated by all four Evangelists, but the matter
given in the Fourth Gospel is for the most
part distinct from that given in the others.—
In Matt. 26: 1-46 everything is *preparation*.
Jesus prepares the disciples for the speedy
coming of the long predicted end (v. 1 f.); the
rulers lay their plans (3 f.); the anointing prepares Jesus for burial (6-13); Judas arranges
to deliver him up (14-16); Jesus further prepares the disciples, warns the betrayer, and
institutes a memorial of himself for the future
(17-30); he then warns them of the approaching trial to their own fidelity (31-35); and
finally he prepares himself by solitary prayer
for all that awaits him. (36-46.)

Our Lord has now ended his teaching in the
temple, and his great eschatological discourse
on the Mount of Olives, and goes on to Bethany (v. 6) to spend the night as usual. He
reached there probably late on Tuesday afternoon, or if it was after sunset, then in the first
hour of Wednesday. We have here his final
announcement to the disciples of his approaching death, with some account of the plans of
the Jewish rulers for killing him, v. 1-5; then
an account of the supper at Bethany, v. 6-13;
and finally of Judas' arrangement to deliver
Jesus for money, v. 14-16.

I. 1-5. OUR LORD'S DEATH APPROACH-
ING. Mark 14: 1 f.; Luke 22: 1 f. **Had finished all these sayings,** meaning the discourse of ch. 24 and 25, and perhaps also including the previous teaching on that day,
from 21: 23 onward. **He said unto his disciples,** probably all the Twelve, comp. on
24: 3. The three preceding recorded predictions of his death are in 16: 21 (comp. 17: 9);

17: 22 f.; 20: 18 f. **The passover,** see on
26: 19. **Is,** *cometh, occurs,* the word explained on 1: 22, and very often used; the
present tense signifies that the passover so occurs according to the custom and the law, as
the disciples **know.** **After two days** (so
Mark 14: 1) must mean less than forty-eight
hours, or it would have been called three days
(comp. on 27: 63); the festival began on
Thursday afternoon with the slaying of the
lamb. The words may be naturally regarded
as uttered after sunset on what we should call
Tuesday, but according to the Jewish reckoning, the beginning of Wednesday. (See
above.) **The Son of man,** the Messiah,
see on 8: 20. **Is betrayed,** strictly, *delivered
up* (see on 10: 4; 17: 22), stated in the present
tense because it is near and sure to occur.
His enemies are planning it, and he is preparing for it. Accordingly, the Latin versions translate by the future, and so did all
English versions before K. James. This
would from the construction of the sentence
be more naturally understood as a part of
what the disciples 'know,' but may be simply
appended to it. They knew that he was to be
crucified, and at Jerusalem (20: 18 f.), but we
are not informed of their knowing that it
would be at the Passover. **To be crucified,**
see on 27: 35. He does not in this case add
that he will be raised again, as he did in all
the previous announcements of his death.
Was it because his death would correspond
to the paschal offering (1 Cor. 5: 7), or because
the shadow of the cross was now on him, and
his thoughts went no further?

3-5. Then naturally, though not necessarily (see on 3: 13), means at the precise time
of what precedes. The night following his
great series of discourses in the temple
(21: 23 to 23: 30), which so defeated and silenced
the Jewish teachers, would have been the
natural time for this plotting; see 21: 45 f.

5 But they said, Not on the feast *day*, lest there be an uproar among the people.
6 Now when Jesus was in Bethany, in the house of Simon the leper,

5 tilty, and kill him. But they said, Not during the feast, lest a tumult arise among the people.
6 Now when Jesus was in Bethany, in the house of

The chief priests and the elders were two of the classes[1] constituting the Sanhedrin, see on 26: 57; also as to **the high priest who was called Caiaphas.** There is doubt whether we should translate **the palace,** or *the court, i. e.,* the inner court of the high priest's official residence, as in 26: 69, Rev. Ver., or whether it means in general the residence, palace, as rendered in this place by Grimm, Keim, Weiss, and so in 26: 58, and as often used in later Greek. It is perhaps better, with Rev. Ver., to use 'court' in all three passages, there being no substantial difference. **And consulted,** *took counsel together* (comp. Psa. 2: 2; Acts 4: 24 ff.), apparently not in an official meeting, but only an informal consultation. They had wished to apprehend him that morning in the temple court, but "feared the multitudes" (21: 46, Rev. Ver.); they had sent officers to seize him at the feast of Tabernacles, six months before, but the officers were awed by his teaching. (John 7 :32, 45 ff.) Now they propose to **take Jesus by subtilty.** Com. Ver. renders the Greek word by "guile" in John 1: 47, and by a still different word "craft" in the parallel passage of Mark 14: 1. *Weiss:* "Thus the rulers were obliged to resort to secrecy. It is not likely that they ever thought of assassination, for Jesus was so constantly surrounded by his disciples that such a deed must have been discovered, and the odium of it would have clung to the supreme Council. The respect entertained for him by his followers could only receive a fatal blow by a public and shameful execution carried through with all the forms of justice; and if he were once safely in confinement, ways and means for the execution would soon be found." *Not during the feast,* which lasted seven days. The rendering of Com. Ver., **on the feast-day,** is a mistake. The rulers say nothing as to the sacredness of the occasion, but are only concerned **lest there be an uproar among the people.** Of this there was always special danger when vast crowds were assembled for a great festival (comp. Mark

12: 12); and Pilate had taught them that a popular tumult could become with him the occasion of savage cruelties. The subsequent proposition of Judas (v. 15) led them to change their plan, and take the risk; and so the Saviour's death came at least a week earlier than they had calculated, and at the time he predicted. (v. 2.)

II. **6-13.** THE SUPPER AT BETHANY. Mark 14: 3-9; John 12: 2-8. **Bethany,** see on 21: 17. As to the *time,* no one of the three accounts gives any decisive statement. Mark agrees with Matt. in mentioning the supper immediately after the consultation of the authorities as to seizing Jesus; and Mark's narrative runs on without any break, so that it would be very difficult to remove his paragraph about the supper to an earlier chronological position. Luke does not speak of the supper, perhaps because he had described a somewhat similar anointing in Galilee (Luke 7 : 36-50), but he gives immediately after the consultation the proposition made to the authorities by Judas, which in Matt. and Mark follows in the same order, with the supper between. On the other hand, John mentions the supper just after telling of our Lord's arrival at Bethany before the triumphal entry, which would place it three or four days earlier. Either John, or Matt. and Mark, must be supposed to have given the event out of its chronological position. Several considerations support the opinion that it occurred where Matt. and Mark mention it. (a) The rebuke of Jesus to a suggestion about the poor which really came from Judas (John 12 : 4) would be the natural occasion of his deciding to carry out the design which may have been previously meditated, viz., to deliver the Master to the authorities; and this agrees with the order of Matt., Mark, and Luke. (b) The outspoken indication that our Lord's death is at hand (v. 12), agrees *greatly* better with a time following his intimations in 21: 38 f. and 23 : 39, his eschatological discourse in ch. 24 and 25, and his definite prediction here in 26: 2, than with a time preceding the triumphal

---

[1] The Com. text inserts also the 'scribes,' but this term is wanting in the earliest MSS. and versions, and was evidently interpolated by copyists from Mark and Luke.

7 There came unto him a woman having an alabaster box of very precious ointment, and poured it on his head, as he sat at meat.

7 Simon the leper, there came unto him a woman having [1] an alabaster cruse of exceeding precious ointment, and she poured it upon his head, as he sat

1 Or, *a flask.*

entry. (c) This also better accounts for the idea that the devout woman was preparing him beforehand for burial. (d) We can see a reason for John's mentioning the supper by anticipation, viz., because he has just spoken of Bethany, and he will speak of it no more. On the other hand, Mark at least has mentioned Bethany before the triumphal entry (Mark 11 : 1), and we see no reason why he should have dislocated the supper. John is in general more chronological than Matt., as some have here urged, but not more so than Mark; here Matt. and Mark exactly agree, and to a certain extent Luke also. John's expressions, 12: 2, 12, would naturally suggest that the supper occurred at the point of time at which he speaks of it, but they do not at all require that view. The great majority of recent writers follow John's order, usually without giving reasons. On the other side are Robinson, (but Riddle otherwise), Hackett, G. W. Clark, McClellan, Geikie, and others. It is impossible to settle the question, but the event seems to fit much better into the situation presented by Matt. and Mark. The notion of Origen and Chrys. that there were two different feasts of Bethany, with a similar anointing and conversation, only three or four days apart, is out of the question. The assumption of many that the anointing in Galilee described by Luke 7: 36-50 was the same as this, will not bear investigation. The only points of resemblance are (a) anointing by a woman, (b) at a feast, (c) in the house of Simon. But Luke is closely chronological in ch. 5 to 9, if not throughout, and he places his anointing at a much earlier time, and not at Jerusalem, but in Galilee. There the woman was "a sinner," here there is no such intimation, and in John's account it is the beloved Mary of Bethany. There the host scorned the woman, here (John) her brother is one of the guests, and her sister assisting the family. There we find nothing whatever answering to the complaint of the disciples and the Saviour's rebuke, justification, and wonderful promise; and on the other hand we find there the parable of the two debtors, and a very different assurance to the woman. The

distinct allusion to his death is possible only here, and there is nothing to account for Luke's removing the story so far away in time and place. An anointing might certainly take place more than once, being a very natural way, according to their customs, of exhibiting reverential affection. (Luke 7: 46.) The Talmud of Bab. reports it (Wün.) as a custom in Babylon at a wedding for women to pour fragrant oil upon the heads of the rabbis present. A feast where the guests reclined on couches, was a very natural occasion for anointing the feet. The name Simon was very common. Thus the differences between the two cases are many and serious, while the few points of resemblance are easily accounted for. This question is important; for to suppose that Luke had transported this story to Galilee, and so long before, would cut us off from all reliance upon his chronological order, and to suppose that the other Gospels have transformed the event in Galilee into the so different occurrence they here describe, would make the whole history unreliable. As to the occurrence of similar events in various cases, comp. above on 13: 54; 15: 38; 21: 12.

In the house of Simon the leper, (so also Mark), who is not otherwise known. Doubtless his leprosy had been healed (comp. on 8: 2), either by natural causes or by the Saviour's supernatural work, and he merely retained a distinctive name he had long borne; comp. Matthew the publican, Simon the zealot. It would have been a violation of the law of Moses for Jesus and his disciples to recline at table with an unhealed leper. **A woman.** Matt. and Mark give no name. John states that the woman who anointed was Mary, that Lazarus was one of the guests, and Martha "served," *i. e.*, took part with the women of the household in preparing and presenting the food. It seems clearly not true, as even Meyer holds, that John represents the supper as given by the well-known family; for in that case the expressions used in regard to Lazarus and Martha would be quite unsuitable. The notion that Simon was the deceased father of this family is idle. The sisters here present the same difference of

8 But when his disciples saw *it*, they had indignation, saying, To what purpose *is* this waste?

8 at meat. But when the disciples saw it, they had indignation, saying, To what purpose is this waste?

character as when Luke first mentions them (Luke 10:38-42), and at the raising of Lazarus (John ch. 11), the one showing love by bustling activity, the other delighting in unpractical and delicate manifestations of affection. True Christian piety does not alter one's fundamental type of character, but brings out its distinctive excellencies. It has been conjectured that the silence of Luke about Lazarus, and of Matt. and Mark about the whole family, was caused by the jealous hatred of the Jewish rulers, who might have revived their desire to put Lazarus to death (John 12:10), if the family had been brought to their notice in the oral and written accounts given by the apostles; but when the family had all passed away, and the Jewish State had been destroyed, John could speak of them without reserve. Comp. on 26:51. **An alabaster box,** or *cruse.* Some kinds of alabaster are of delicate and richly varied hues, and are extremely beautiful and costly.[1] The Jews, like all the other civilized ancient peoples, made much use of fragrant ointment, often rare and of great price; and the flasks which contained it were of great variety as to material and shape. John says this flask contained 'a pound,' viz., of twelve ounces. It was, with its contents, a tasteful and costly object, such as a woman would delight in possessing. **Very precious ointment.** Mark and John tell the kind of ointment, using the same terms. But one of the terms is of uncertain meaning, as stated in *margin* Rev. Ver. of Mark 14:3, "Gr. *pistic nard*," pistic being perhaps a local name. Others take it to mean *genuine;* others, *liquid.* Yet this uncertainty does not affect the substantial meaning; it was ointment of extraordinary value. Pliny ("Nat. Hist." XII. 26) tells of many kinds of precious nard. **And poured it on his head.** Mark says, (Rev. Ver.) 'she brake the cruse and poured it.' The flask, or cruse, probably had a long neck and a small mouth, to prevent evaporation, and the precious ointment was ordinarily extracted in small quantities. Being a thick, viscid mass,

it could not be made to flow freely through the opening, and so in her eagerness she 'thoroughly crushed' the cruse, and poured its contents lavishly upon one so honored and loved. A thin flask of delicate alabaster could be crushed by the pressure of the hands. **As he sat at meat,** lit. *as he reclined,* see on 8:11. John (12:2) describes it as a special entertainment in the Saviour's honor: "So they made him a supper there." John makes the apparently conflicting statement that she "anointed the feet of Jesus, and wiped off his feet with her hair." To anoint the head (Matt. and Mark) was the more common service of friendship or honor, but Mary went further and anointed even his feet. It is plain from the Saviour's expressions about the similar anointing in Galilee (Luke 7:44-46), that to anoint the feet was an act of greater humility and profound respect. Observe (Morison) that Matt. and Mark simply say 'poured upon his head,' without inserting 'it'; so there is no difficulty in supposing that she used a part of the contents otherwise, and even that much still remained in the crushed flask (see below on v. 10). John adds "and the house was filled with the odor of the ointment."—Upon this scene, see Tennyson, "In Memoriam," xxxi., xxxii.

8 f. Complaint as to such waste. **His disciples.** Mark says simply 'some.' John tells us that Judas Iscariot said, "Why was not this ointment sold," etc. It is easy to suppose that Judas first said this, and others of the Twelve approved and so repeated the saying (Mark), which was plausible, and might seem to them proper enough, though Judas himself had suggested the idea through very unworthy motives (John 12:6.) *Dickson* (Morison): "One murmurer may infect a whole company." Pliny remarks that indulgence in costly perfumes is more luxurious than in gems and garments, because the former perish in the moment of using. Most of the apostles had little familiarity with such costly luxuries, and the waste might seem to them frightful. The word 'ointment' is not pres-

---

[1] Suidas defines *alabastron* "an oil-vessel having no handles." Some think (Humphry) that the word meant primarily a flask without handles (*labe*) and was afterwards used to denote the material from which such flasks were often made. Hence the rendering a 'flask' in *margin* Rev. Ver.

9 For this ointment might have been sold for much, and given to the poor.
10 When Jesus understood *it*, he said unto them, Why trouble ye the woman? for she hath wrought a good work npon me.
11 For ye have the poor always with you; but me ye have not always.
12 For in that she hath poured this ointment on my body, she did *it* for my burial.

9 For this *ointment* might have been sold for much,
10 and given to the poor. But Jesus perceiving it, said unto them, Why trouble ye the woman? for she
11 hath wrought a good work upon me. For ye have the poor always with you; but me ye have not al-
12 ways. For in that she [1] poured this ointment upon

1 Gr. *cast.*

ent in the correct Greek text of v. 9, but is naturally suggested. **Might have been sold for much.** John: 'for three hundred denaries'; Mark: 'for above three hundred denaries.' The Roman denary, about seventeen cents (see on 18: 28), was the common price of a day's labor. (See on 20: 2.) So the ointment was worth more than three hundred days' labor, and omitting Sabbath and feast-days, this would be a year of labor. Pliny (XIII, 4), says that some unguents cost more than four hundred denaries a pound. We see at once that the sisters must have been wealthy. A poor young woman could not have possessed a flask of perfumery worth a man's labor for a whole year; or if by inheritance or extraordinary gift possessing it, she would have had no right to expend so large a sum in an utterly unpractical expression of affection. The inference that they were rich is supported by the fact that many of the Jews came out from Jerusalem to this suburban village to comfort the sisters after their brother's death (John 11: 19); and it explains the propriety of Mary's leaving Martha "to serve alone" (Luke 10: 40), which would have been wrong if they had been poor and unable to secure domestic helpers. The Talmud shows (Edersh.) that wealthy Jewish women often spent large sums for perfumery. **And given to the poor,** without article (in correct text) *to poor people.* It has the article in v. 11. Jerusalem abounded in poor people, and many others doubtless came to the passover, as they come now to Jerusalem at Easter, who were needy and dependent on assistance. Within two miles of the supper-table were thousands of the really poor.

10-12. Jesus rebukes the censurers, and vindicates the loving act. **When Jesus understood it,** or, *perceiving it,* exactly as in 16: 8, Rev. Ver. The complaints had doubtless circulated in a low tone. The Com. Ver. has given an unfortunate rendering, for it would suggest that a considerable time in-

tervened, and the Greek does not. **Why trouble ye the woman?** The Greek expression is quite strong; see in Mark also, and in Luke 11: 7; Gal. 6: 17. **She hath wrought a good work upon me,** is presently explained by saying, **she did it,** etc., (as in Rev. Ver.) *did it to prepare me for burial.* So Mark, Rev. Ver.: "She hath anointed my body aforehand for the burying.' John (12: 7), Rev. Ver., according to the correct text and most natural translation, has, 'Suffer her to keep it against the day of my burying,' which may mean that she had been interrupted, and much of the costly ointment still remained in the broken flask. See another possible translation in *margin* of Rev. Ver. of John. **Ye have the poor always with you.** And Mark adds, 'and whensoever ye will ye may do them good.' (Comp. Deut. 15: 11.) **But me ye have not always,** *i. e.,* in bodily presence; he would be with his people spiritually. (28: 20; John 14: 21-23.) Extraordinary occasions may justify extraordinary expenditures. We may suppose (Keim) that at an earlier period he would have declined the proposed service, and directed attention to the poor. But openings for ministry to the poor would never cease; while their opportunity for personal services to him would soon be at an end. And this apparently useless and wasteful service possessed in fact a special significance and timeliness in connection with that foreseen death which was now so near. (v. 2.) It was an interesting, gratifying, comforting token of affection, as a sort of anticipation (Mark) of the usual anointing when preparing a body for interment; comp. the large quantity of costly spices brought by Nicodemus for the actual interment. (John 19: 39.) To receive this loving preparation might help the Saviour to look forward with less pain to the suffering and shame which awaited him. It is not necessary to conclude that Mary so designed her action; but it is very natural to suppose she did, as they were all thinking

13 Verily I say unto you, Wheresoever this gospel shall be preached in the whole world, *there* shall also this, that this woman hath done, be told for a memorial of her.
14 Then one of the twelve, called Judas Iscariot, went unto the chief priests,

13 my body, she did it to prepare me for burial. Verily I say unto you, Wheresoever [1] this gospel shall be preached in the whole world, that also which this woman hath done shall be spoken of for a memorial of her.
14 Then one of the twelve, who was called Judas Is-

---

1 Or, *these good tidings.*

---

much of his intimations that he would soon die; at any rate, he so accepted it, and that must have been an unspeakable joy to her. "She hath done what she could" (Mark 14:8); and she finds that she had really done something extremely grateful to the Master. She could not prevent his approaching death, but she could manifest devoted love for him. Feminine intuitions, kindled by intense affection, might pierce through all preconceptions and accept it as a fearful reality that the Messiah was to be literally killed. This came as a new and startling announcement to her, without time for the mystical interpretations which the disciples appear to have placed upon it. (See on 16: 21.) Whatever fitly manifests, and by reaction strengthens, devout affection —true religious sentiment—is in itself acceptable to Christ and useful to us; for these sentiments are a necessary part of developed and symmetrical Christian character. Nor should they be hastily condemned as unpractical, for they stimulate to corresponding action. This unpractical gift, and the Saviour's commendation of it, have themselves caused richer gifts to the poor in all ages than the whole wealth of Jerusalem would have equaled. Twice did Mary incur human censure, and yet, for the same act, received divine commendation. (Luke 10: 40.) **Poured,** in v. 12, is not the ordinary word of v. 7, but means *threw,* cast, flung, a profuse and lavish pouring.

13. This gospel, the good news of the Messianic reign, as in 24: 14; and comp. 11: 5. **In the whole world.** He here anticipates the universal spread of his teachings and influence. (Comp. 28: 19.) This very remarkable promise concerning the woman was already in process of fulfillment when John wrote his Gospel, probably sixty years afterwards; for he distinguishes this Bethany from the one beyond Jordan (John 1: 28) by calling it (John 11: 1 f.) the village of Mary (placed first) and her sister Martha; and then makes all definite and clear by adding, "it was that Mary who anointed the Lord with ointment," etc. He has not yet in his Gospel told the story of the anointing, but he assumes that it is familiar to all Christian readers. *Chrys.:* "For lo! what he said is come to pass, and to whatever part of the earth thou mayest go, thou wilt see her celebrated." *Alexander:* "One of the most glorious distinctions ever conferred upon a mortal, a distinction which instead of fading with the lapse of time, grows daily brighter, and to which, as one has well said, even unfriendly critics and interpreters contribute, as it were, against their will and in the very act of doubt or censure."

III. **14-16.** JUDAS PROPOSES TO DELIVER JESUS TO THE CHIEF PRIESTS. Mark 14: 10 f.; Luke 22: 3-6. **Then** does not necessarily (see on 3: 13), but does naturally indicate that what follows in the narrative occurred immediately after what precedes. Mark and Luke have simply said 'and,' but place the matter in the same connection as Matthew. The rebuke Judas had received (see on v. 6), may have brought to a crisis those wrong feelings towards the Master which he had more or less consciously entertained for a long time. (John 6: 70 f.) Even after this, when he had made the bargain, and was awaiting an opportunity, Satan took still stronger possession of him upon its becoming manifest that Jesus understood him. (John 13: 27.) **Judas Iscariot,** see on 10: 4 and 27: 3. **One of the twelve** is a phrase given by all four Evangelists, doubtless because this fact showed how peculiar was his wickedness. **The chief priests,** see on 2: 4. **What will you,** etc. *What are you willing to give me,* is the exact translation. This was expressed in old English by 'what will you give me,' but that is now understood as a mere future tense, as in the following words. **And I will deliver him,** the Greek making the 'I' emphatic. He knows they wish to get Jesus in their hands, and *he* will gratify them if they are willing to give enough. 'Deliver' is here correctly translated in Com. Ver (see on 10: 4; 17: 22), but in v. 16, and in Mark and Luke, they translated it 'betray,' with that passion for variety in rendering which marks

15 And said *unto them,* What will ye give me, and I will deliver him unto you? And they covenanted with him for thirty pieces of silver.
16 And from that time he sought opportunity to betray him.

15 cariot, went unto the chief priests, and said, What are ye willing to give me, and I will deliver him unto you? And they weighed unto him thirty
16 pieces of silver. And from that time he sought opportunity to deliver him *unto them.*

the early English versions. Comp. on 25 : 46. **They covenanted with him.** Rev. Ver., *weighed unto him.* The word means literally *placed* (*in the balance*), and is used for weighing money in the classics and the Septuagint, *e. g.,* Zech. 11 : 12, "So they weighed for my hire thirty *pieces* of silver." The word in Matt. might be translated, 'appointed unto him,' or 'covenanted with him,' and these were preferred by the early English versions because Mark says they ' promised,' Luke ' covenanted,' to give him money. But Mark and Luke use other terms, and there can be little doubt that Matt. is referring to Zechariah. Coins had certainly been in use from the time of Simon the Maccabee, B. C. 140 (1 Macc. 15 : 6) ; but it may have been still not uncommon to weigh the coins, being of variable value, and this especially on the part of religious functionaries, who usually retain old customs. Matthew's expression does not require us to understand that they paid it at the moment of his proposition, but that they paid it in advance. Some have plausibly suggested that this sum was only earnest money, and more was to follow. A traitor is seldom trusted with his entire reward in advance. The **thirty pieces of silver** were probably shekels, worth in our Lord's time something over sixty cents, comp. on 17 : 24. Thirty shekels was appointed by the law as damages for the killing of a slave by an ox. (Exod. 21 : 32.) **He sought opportunity.** Luke adds "without a throng." This plan Judas skillfully carried out, finding him at night, and without the city. *Jerome:* "Unhappy Judas! the loss he thought he had incurred by the pouring out of the ointment, he wishes to make up by selling his Master."

HOMILETICAL AND PRACTICAL.

Ch. 26. 1. HENRY: "So Christ's witnesses die not till they have finished their testimony." V. 8, 9. EDERSH.: "It is ever the light which throws the shadows of objects—and this deed of faith and love now cast the features of Judas in gigantic dark outlines against the scene. He knew the nearness of Christ's betrayal, and hated the more; she knew of the nearness of his precious death, and loved the more." HENRY: "It is no new thing for bad affections to shelter themselves under specious covers; for people to shift off works of piety under color of works of charity."

V. 10. "Why trouble ye the woman?" 1) A woman's love will sometimes be wiser than a man's judgment. 2) A devout heart will often build better than it knew. 3) An act plausibly censured at the moment may be destined to everlasting honor. HENRY: "It is a great trouble to good people to have their good works censured and misconstrued; and it is a thing that Jesus Christ takes very ill."— A good work. 1) A good work, though due to the unaided promptings of a loving heart. 2) A good work, though severely censured by some good men. 3) A good work, though wholly unpractical. 4) A good work, though under ordinary circumstances it would have been wasteful and wrong. 5) A good work, which gained the Saviour's approval, and will be honored for evermore.—It has been remarked that the only two persons Jesus is recorded as commending for their gifts were women, one poor, the other rich.—V. 11. Jesus and the poor. 1) By helping the poor we may always honor Jesus. 2) By honoring Jesus we do always help the poor.—Charity to the poor. 1) Charity is not our only duty. 2) Charity must not be made an excuse for neglecting other duties. 3) Charity is greatly promoted by loving devotion to Jesus.—V. 14-16. CHRYS.: "Hearken, all ye covetous, and beware of the calamity. For if he that was with Christ, and wrought signs, and had the benefit of so much instruction, because he was not freed from this disease, was sunk into such a gulf; how much more shall ye, who do not so much as listen to the Scriptures, who are constantly riveted to the things present, become an easy prey to this calamity, unless ye have the advantage of constant care."— V. 15. BISHOP HALL: "If Judas were Christ's domestic, yet he was Mammon's servant; he could not but hate the Master whom he formerly professed to serve, while he really served that master which he professed to hate." HENRY: "The greater pro-

17 Now the first *day* of the *feast of* unleavened bread the disciples came to Jesus, saying unto him, Where wilt thou that we prepare for thee to eat the passover?
18 And he said, Go into the city to such a man, and say unto him, The Master saith, My time is at hand; I will keep the passover at thy house with my disciples.

17 Now on the first *day* of unleavened bread the disciples came to Jesus, saying, Where wilt thou that we make ready for thee to eat the passover? And he said, Go into the city to such a man, and say unto him, The [1] Master saith, My time is at hand: I keep

1 Or, *Teacher.*

fession men make of religion, and the more they are employed in the study and service of it, the greater opportunity they have of doing mischief, if their hearts be not right with God."

17-35. THE PASSOVER MEAL AND THE LORD'S SUPPER.

Found also in Mark 14: 12-31 ; Luke 22: 7-39; comp. John 13: 1 to 18: 1. Mark is here quite closely parallel to Matthew; Luke adds a good deal. John introduces the feet-washing, and the great farewell discourse, which belong to this same evening, and present several not very distinct points of contact with the narrative of the other Gospels. Our Lord seems to have remained in seclusion at Bethany from Tuesday evening (beginning of the Jewish Wednesday) to Thursday afternoon; comp. on 26: 1. Judas would naturally go the morning after the supper at Bethany to Jerusalem, and make his arrangement with the rulers. Jesus stays away from Jerusalem till his "hour is come." It was proper for every devout Jew to eat the passover, and Jesus was careful to "fulfil all righteousness" (see on 3 : 15). So he returned to Jerusalem for this purpose, though foreseeing the consequences (v. 31 f. ; John 13 : 1) ; and he sent two disciples in advance to prepare for the feast. This section may be divided into v. 17-19, 20-25, 26-30, 31-35.

I. **17-19.** THE DISCIPLES PREPARE FOR THE PASSOVER MEAL. Mark 14: 12-16; 22: 7-13. **On the first day of unleavened bread.** Mark adds, Rev. Ver., 'when they sacrificed the passover,' which Matthew's Jewish readers would not need to be told. The law required the Jews to begin to use unleavened bread with the fifteenth day of the month Nisan. (Lev. 23 : 6; Num. 28 : 17.) But Exod. 12: 18 suggested that all leavened bread be removed in the afternoon of the fourteenth day; and the Talmud (Lightf. on Mark 14 : 12) says they removed it at noon. Accordingly Josephus in one place puts the beginning of the feast on the fifteenth ("Ant.," 3, 10, 5), and in another place on the fourteenth ("War,"

5, 3, 1), and elsewhere says ("Ant.," 2, 15, 1), "We keep a feast for eight days, which is called the feast of unleavened bread." With all this Mark agrees, and Luke is equivalent. In Exod. 12: 6 ; Num. 9: 3, they were directed to *kill* the lamb 'between the two evenings' (Rev. Ver. *margin*), which the Jews of our Lord's time understood to mean the middle of the afternoon, beginning at 3 P. M. ; and they would continue killing lambs till the going down of the sun. (Deut. 16: 6.) Josephus ("War," 6, 9, 3) says, "they slay the sacrifice from the ninth hour to the eleventh," from 3 to 5 P. M.,and mentions the number of lambs slain on some occasion as 256,500. After the fifteenth day began, *i. e.*, after sunset, they ate the paschal lamb. (Exod. 12 : 8 ; Num. 33 : 3.) So the disciples probably went to the city about noon, to procure a room, take a lamb to the temple court and slay it, roast the flesh with bitter herbs (Exod. 12 : 8 f.), and provide bread and wine for the meal. **The disciples came to Jesus,** at Bethany. **Prepare,** or, *make ready* same Greek word as in v. 19. It may very well be that the lamb had been procured the day before, as was common ; what they inquire about is the *place.* **And he said, Go into the city.** Mark says (Rev. Ver.) 'he sendeth two of his disciples and saith unto them, Go into the city' ; and Luke, 'he sent Peter and John,' who from this time are frequently mentioned together (John 13 : 24 ; 18 : 15 f. ; 20 : 2 ff.; Acts 3 : 1 ; 8 : 14, etc.) ; even as they and James were the only disciples accompanying the Master on several occasions. **To such a man.** This may mean that Jesus indicated who the man was, but Matthew does not give the name. Some however suppose that Jesus gave no name because he did not wish Judas to learn the place in advance, being aware of his treacherous designs, and desiring to remain uninterrupted till a later hour. With this agrees the fact that Mark and Luke tell how they were to find the person in question. In the city they will meet a man bearing a pitcher of water, and following him home they must deliver a message to the goodman

19 And the diisciples did as Jesus had appointed them ; and they made ready the passover.

19 the passover at thy house with my disciples. And the disciples did as Jesus appointed them; and they

---

of the house, substantially the same as that recorded by Matthew. All this would seem to involve supernatural knowledge, like the prophetic direction in 1 Sam. 10: 1-8; but some think that Jesus had arranged with the householder for such signs. **The Master saith,** shows that this man would prove to be a disciple of Jesus, if not in the full sense, yet so far that he would gladly render him this service; comp.· Nicodemus and Joseph of Arimathea, and comp. above on 21: 3. ' Master' is *didaskalos*, 'teacher,' see on 8: 19. **My time,** *kairos*, set time, special time, season, see on 11: 25, meaning here the time of his death ; comp. the use of ' hour' in John 12: 23; 17: 1, and often. **I will keep,** or, *I keep*, the present tense[1] indicating an intention about to be carried out. **At thy house,** has in the Greek an emphatic position. The householders at Jerusalem were accustomed to receive into their houses without charge such family groups as wished to eat the paschal lamb (Edersh. and others); but they would of course exercise some choice. In Mark our Lord adds, "And he will himself show you a large upper room furnished and ready "; the householder would show respect by going himself, the room would be large, and in all respects prepared for use. It is still common in Oriental houses to have the principal rooms in the second story (comp. Acts 1: 13). **And they made ready the passover,** as described above; and at even Jesus came and ate it. (v. 20.) So also Mark and Luke.

Thus Matt., Mark, and Luke distinctly state that Jesus ate the paschal meal, and that would place his death at 3 P. M. on the fifteenth of Nisan. But there are several passages in John which at first seem inconsistent with the idea that he ate the paschal meal. If John really meant that he did not, then there is a hopeless conflict between him and the other three Evangelists, one side or the other being in error; unless, indeed, we adopt the highly artificial supposition of some writers that Matt., Mark, and Luke refer to an anticipation of the paschal meal twenty-four hours in advance. But this we cannot do; for besides the difficulty of supposing that the Saviour would thus violate the law in the act of observing it, who can believe that temple authorities would have knowingly allowed the slaying of the paschal lamb before the time, or that Peter and John would have slain it clandestinely? A number of recent writers contend or assume that John's language does forbid our believing that Jesus ate the passover. Most of these writers, it should be observed, are quite willing to recognize errors in the Scriptures as to matters of fact; and some of them are anxious to point out such errors upon every possible occasion. Others of us are very unwilling to admit the existence of such errors, and earnestly strive to remove the appearance of contradiction in the sacred writers, whenever it can be fairly done. Neither side in such a case can claim superior exemption from the influence of theoretical prepossessions; and it becomes every writer to state his views with due respect for those who differ with him.

There are five passages of the Fourth Gospel which have been regarded as showing that Jesus did not eat the passover. (Comp. especially Robinson's "Harm.," Clark's "Harm.," Andrews, Milligan.) Do these passages really thus teach ? (1) John 13: 1, Rev. Ver., " Before the feast of the passover, when Jesus knew," etc. This is held to show that the supper described in John 13 occurred before the paschal supper, and consequently twenty-four hours before it. But observe that 13: 2 is not ' supper being ended,' but (in the correct text) ' during supper.' Then may we not understand that ' before the feast' refers to the feet-washing, which occurred after they had reclined for supper, but before they actually partook of the feast? Is not this more probable than that Matt., Mark, and Luke are in downright error? (2) John 13: 27, "That thou doest, do quickly." It is added that some thought this meant, " Buy what things we have need of for the feast," Rev. Ver. But if the pas-

---

[1] This is one of the cases as to which it used to be said that in New Test. Greek, the present tense is used for the future. Comp. 26; 2, 45; John 10: 32; 11: 47. Accordingly, Tyndale and followers here render ' I will keep!' But no one now talks about present for future. See Winer and Buttmann.

2" Now when the even was come, he sat down with the twelve.

20 made ready the passover. Now when even was come, he was sitting at meat with the twelve [1]disciples;

chal feast was twenty-four hours off, what possible propriety would there have been in hastening out that night to make purchases for it? It is much easier to suppose that they thought of hurried purchases to complete the feast then in progress. But the new difficulty arises that upon this supposition there had already begun the first day of the paschal festival, and this being a holy day, purchases would not have been lawful. Now the Mishna, "Sabbath," 23, 2, says that if the day before the passover be a Sabbath, one may buy a lamb, even leaving his garment in pledge, and then settle after the feast. From this Edersh. and others fairly argue that if a purchase of something needed for the feast could be made even on the Sabbath, much more on the first day of a feast when not a Sabbath. (3) John 18: 28, Rev. Ver., "They themselves entered not into the Praetorium (palace), that they might not be defiled, but might eat the passover." This seems at the first glance distinctly to show that the paschal supper was yet to come when our Lord was before Pilate. But in fact the passage furnishes an argument in the other direction. If this had been the morning before the paschal meal, then the defilement incurred by entering a Gentile's dwelling could have been removed at sunset by washing with water. (See Lev. 15: 5-11,16-18; 22: 5-7.) *Edersh. :* "In fact, it is distinctly laid down (Jerus. Talmud, Pes. 92 b.) that the 'bathed of the day,' that is, he who had been impure for the day and had bathed in the evening, *did* partake of the Paschal Supper, and an instance is related (Pes. 36 b.), when some soldiers who had guarded the gates of Jerusalem 'immersed,' and ate the Paschal Lamb." It is not necessary to explain with certainty the meaning of the phrase 'eat the passover' as here employed. It may be a general expression for observing the paschal festival, or may refer to the *Chagigah*, or feast-offering which was offered on the morning of the first paschal day; and various other suggested meanings are possible. If the passover festival had already commenced, the rulers would wish not to be cut off from its privileges during the day upon which they had entered. At any

rate this passage as a whole agrees best with the idea that the paschal meal was not still in the future. (4) John 19: 14, "Now it was the Preparation of the passover." This was the day of the crucifixion, and many argue that the day of the crucifixion was not on the first day of the paschal festival, as Matt., Mark, and Luke represent, but on the day of preparation for the passover. But "the Preparation" was already an established phrase for "the day before the Sabbath," as distinctly shown by Mark 15: 42, Matt. 27: 62; and the Greek term here employed has from an early period been the regular word for Friday in the whole Greek speaking world. This passage of John may therefore easily mean that it was the Sabbath eve, or Friday, of the passover week; and observe that John himself so uses the term Preparation in 19: 31, 42. (5) John 19: 31, "For that Sabbath day was a high day," has been supposed to mean that the first day of the passover festival on that occasion coincided with the weekly Sabbath. But the weekly Sabbath during the great annual festival would have been without that a notable occasion, "a great day."

It thus appears that no one of these five passages at all requires us to understand that Jesus did not eat the paschal supper on the night before his crucifixion, and the second and third distinctly tend in the contrary direction. Grant that the first impression produced by reading these passages in John would be as claimed; grant that some of the explanations above given are not obvious nor certainly correct,—yet how can one say that the total result is to furnish sufficient ground for accusing the other three Gospels of uniting in a definite error? Among the writers who hold that John's expressions do not contradict the express statements of the other Gospels are Robinson, Andrews, Wieseler, Tholuck, Ebrard, Clark, Milligan, Plumptre, McClellan, Schaff, Morison, Edersheim. On the other side are Neander, Ewald, Bleek, Meyer, Ellicott, Alford, Pressensé, Godet, Farrar, Westcott, Weiss.

II. **20-25.** WHILE EATING THE PASSOVER, JESUS DECLARES THAT ONE OF THE TWELVE WILL DELIVER HIM UP. Mark

21 And as they did eat, he said, Verily I say unto you, that one of you shall betray me.

21 and as they were eating, he said, Verily I say unto

14: 18-21; Luke 22: 21-23; John 13: 21-30. **When the even was come,** after sunset (see on v. 17); no particular hour of the evening was fixed by the law or by custom. **He sat down,** etc., Rev. Ver., *he was sitting at meat, reclining,* as in 26 : 7, see on 8: 11. It was originally directed (Exod. 12: 11) that the passover should be eaten in a standing posture, "with your loins girded, your shoes on your feet, and your staff in your hand; and ye shall eat it in haste," representing the circumstances of its first observance. This posture and haste had been disused, probably because the circumstances no longer seemed to call for it. The Talmud of Jerusalem says, "It is the manner of servants to eat standing, but now let them (the Israelites) eat reclining, that they may be known to have passed out of slavery into liberty." We have to conclude that the matters of posture and haste really were of no importance, and so Jesus conformed to custom. Reclining at table at all was an indolent practice, but it was not necessarily wrong; and in this, as in dress and various other matters, Jesus was content to follow custom. **With the twelve** *disciples.* 'Disciples' was omitted by some early and many later documents, probably by way of assimilation to Mark 14: 17; the word is implied if not expressed. Twelve made a party of about the usual , size. Josephus says ("War" 6, 9, 3), that the company partaking of a paschal lamb consisted of not less than ten men, and sometimes reached twenty. It was necessary to have a good many, in order to consume the entire lamb. (Exod. 12: 4, 43-46.) On the several steps in the observance of the Passover, as described in the Rabbinical writings, see Lightf., Meyer, and a highly interesting account in Edersheim. It is not certain how far this round of observances already existed in the time of Christ. Nor do they throw any clear light on our Lord's appointment of bread and wine. Though instituted on the occasion of the paschal meal, and out of its materials, the Christian ceremony is in no way dependent, for its meaning, importance, or proper observance, upon the Jewish ceremony.—Luke reports (22: 14-16), our Lord's expressions of gratification in eating the passover with his disciples. He also states

(Luke 22: 23-30, R. V.), that "there arose a contention among them, which of them is accounted to be greatest," as above in 18: 1; Mark 9: 34. Our Lord rebukes this spirit, in terms similar, *first* (Luke 22 : 23-27) to that uttered after the ambitious request of James and John, Matt. 20: 25-27; Mark 10: 42-44, and *secondly* (Luke 22 : 30), to that recorded by Matt. alone in 19: 28. It is thus possible that Luke, who has no record of those sayings, gives here what was spoken then. But it is much more likely that on a new occasion Jesus rebukes the same fault in similar terms, as we have often found him doing (comp. on 21 : 12). The contention as to who was greatest might have been suggested in this case by questions of precedence at table, about which Orientals and even Europeans show an outspoken solicitude which in America we can hardly imagine. The Mishna ("Sabbath" 23, 2) speaks of drawing lots to determine the place at table, even among the members of a family. Luke passes at once from the opening paschal cup to tell of our Lord's institution of the memorial bread and wine; then narrates the allusion to Judas, the contention among the disciples, and so arrives at the warning to Peter. This contention also suggests a very natural occasion for the feet-washing of John 13: 1-17, as another object-lesson in humility, answering exactly to that of Matt. 18: 2. **As they were eating** (v. 21 and 26), two things occurred: Jesus (a) foretold that one of them would deliver him up, and (b) established the ordinance of bread and wine.

21 f. The strong expression **betray me,** seems to be necessary to our feeling throughout this passage (v. 21, 23, 24), partly because we are accustomed to it; yet the Greek really means simply *deliver me up,* precisely as in Rev. Ver., 26: 2, 15 f. The Evangelists speak with compassionate moderation of Judas, comp. on 17: 22. **Began** is not mere Hebrew circumstantiality (comp. on 11: 20), but suggests that the process of inquiry was continued by one after another. **Lord, is it I?** with an interrogative particle in the Greek which strongly implies expectation of a negative answer, as in 7: 9 f.; 9: 15; 11: 23 R. V. The nearest English equivalent would be, 'It is not I, Is it?'

22 And they were exceeding sorrowful, and began every one of them to say unto him, Lord, is it I?
23 And he answered and said, He that dippeth *his* hand with me in the dish the same shall betray me.
24 The Son of man goeth as it is written of him: but woe unto that man by whom the Son of man is betrayed! it had been good for that man if he had not been born.
25 Then Judas, which betrayed him, answered and said, Master, is it I? He said unto him, Thou hast said.

22 you, that one of you shall betray me. And they were exceeding sorrowful, and began to say unto 23 him every one, is it I, Lord? And he answered and said, He that dipped his hand with me in the dish, 24 the same shall betray me. The Son of man goeth, even as it is written of him: but woe unto that man through whom the Son of man is betrayed! good 25 were it [1] for that man if he had not been born. And Judas, who betrayed him, answered and said, Is it I,

1 Gr. *for him if that man.*

Jerome : "The eleven, believing the Master more than themselves, and fearing their own weakness, sadly ask about a sin of which they had no consciousness." The answer in v. 23, **He that dippeth,** or *dipped* (Rev. Ver.), **his hand with me in the dish** (so also Mark), might seem only a general description, as doubtless all the Twelve did so. Knives and forks were not used in eating, and any person would help himself from the dish before him. Our Lord might appear here not to be identifying Judas, but merely showing the enormity of his offence : the man that ate from the same dish with me will deliver me up. (Comp. Psa. 41: 9; John 13: 18.) 'He that dipped' does not necessarily mean before the time of speaking, but just as well before that of delivering up. So it does not materially differ from 'he that dippeth' in Mark 14: 20, Rev. Ver. It is thus possible to regard this saying as different from the identification described by John; see below on v. 25. **The Son of man,** our Lord's common designation of the Messiah, see on 8: 20. **Goeth,** present tense because the going is certain and near at hand; so with **is betrayed. As it is written of him,** apparently not a reference to any particular prediction, but to the general tenor of Messianic prophecy, viz., that he should die. Some compare Isa. 53: 7-9; Dan. 9: 26; see also Luke 24: 46. Luke has here (22: 22. Rev. Ver.), 'as it hath been determined,' viz., in the divine purpose. *Plump.:* "It was appointed that the Christ should suffer, but that appointment did not make men less free agents, nor diminish the guilt of treachery or injustice. So, in like manner, as if taught by his Master, Peter speaks of the guilt of Judas in Acts 1: 16-18, and of that of the priests and Scribes in Acts 4: 27, 28." **Woe unto** may express not only wrath (23: 13 ff.), but at the same time compassion (24: 19.) **By,** or *through,* **whom,** the person through whose action a thing comes to pass. It does not seem proper

to find here (with Winer) a hint that Judas was merely the instrument of other men. He appears to have acted of his own motion. Origen thinks it represents him as the tool of Satan. **Betrayed,** *delivered up.* (See on v. 21.) **It had been good for that man,** etc. This is a popular expression. If he had never lived, then, while losing all the good of life, he would have escaped the dreadful guilt he is incurring, and the horrors of future retribution. For him life was not "worth living."

25. Judas, see on 27: 3. **Answered.** He had not been directly addressed, but he felt himself concerned in the pointed sayings just uttered. (v. 21-24.) As all the others were asking, he probably thought it necessary to ask also, lest silence should betray him. **Master, is it I?** with the same interrogative particle as in v. 22, implying the expectation of a negative answer. He does not say 'Lord,' like the others, but literally, *Rabbi,* and so in 26: 49; but the difference must not be pressed, for the disciples often addressed Jesus as Rabbi. (Comp. on 8: 19.) **Thou hast said,** *i. e.,* hast said what is true. This was a common form of affirmative reply, found also in 26: 64, and occurring in the Talmud. It here solemnly repels the suggestion of a negative answer, and treats his question as a virtual confession (Lutter.) This is the moment represented in Leonardo Da Vinci's fresco of the "Last Supper," of which everybody has seen some engraving; Judas has just received the affirmative answer. Of course we must not think of the guests as *sitting,* according to that picture, for we know that they reclined. See an ingenious representation of the probable scene, with a plan of the table, in Edersh., II., 494. This question of Judas and the answer in Matt. (not found in Mark or Luke) is recorded in terms so general as not to show whether the answer was also known to others. John has a full account of apparently the same matter, differing in form, but not in sub-

26 And as they were eating, Jesus took bread, and *a* blessed *it* and brake *it* and gave *it* to the disciples, and said, Take, eat; this is my body.

26 Rabbi? He saith unto him, Thou hast said. And as they were eating, Jesus took [1] bread, and blessed, and brake it; and he gave to the disc ples, and said,

a Many Greek copies have, *Gave thanks.* See Mark 6: 41.——1 Or, *a loaf.*

stance, from Matthew's summary statement. He says the disciples were at a loss whom Jesus was speaking about, and that Peter beckoned to John, who was reclining in the bosom of Jesus, to inquire who it was. Then Jesus replied, apparently in a low tone, that it was he for whom he would dip a sop and give it to him; and presently he dipped, and gave it to Judas, who immediately went out into the night. In connection with this sign to John, our Lord may have given an oral answer to the question just asked by Judas, as in Matt.; or the facts may be harmonized in other ways.

According to the order in Matt. and Mark, Judas went out *before* the memorial of bread and wine was instituted. Luke seems to place things otherwise; but we have seen that he appears to relate the institution of the bread and wine immediately after mentioning the first paschal cup (Luke 22: 17-20), and then to return to speak of the false disciple; if so, Luke does not teach that Judas was present at the institution, and partook of the loaf and the cup. The case is not certain, but this is the most natural way of combining the accounts. So there is no propriety in understanding that here a flagrantly wicked person was knowingly admitted to take part in the ordinance.

III. **26-30.** The Lord's Supper. Mark 14: 23-26; Luke 22: 19, 20; 1 Cor. 11: 23-25. John gives no account of the institution of the Lord's Supper. Paul says, "I have received of the Lord,' and judging from his similar expressions elsewhere, we understand him to mean by direct revelation, which would make this an independent account. It resembles that of his companion Luke,[1] and Matt. and Mark form another pair. The place is an upper room in the house of some friend (v. 18), and the time apparently some hours after sunset, on the evening before the crucifixion. **As they were eating,** comp. v. 21; this is the second thing described as occurring in the course of the meal; so Mark 14: 18, 22. **Jesus took bread,** or *a loaf* (Rev. Ver. *margin);* the common Greek text has an article, but wrongly. The word is singular in all four accounts. It is sometimes employed collectively for bread in general (4: 4; 6: 11; 15: 2, 26), but more commonly for a loaf or cake of bread (4: 3; 12: 4; 14: 17, 19; 15: 33 ff.; 16: 5-12), and probably so here. This is more likely to have been what we should call a cake than a loaf (see Smith's "Dict.," *Bread);* such flat cakes the Jews at Jerusalem now eat at the passover. It was unleavened, of course, as required by the law at the passover (Exod. 12: 15; 13: 3, 7; Deut. 16: 3); but our Lord makes no reference to this, and it is not wise to insist on using only unleavened bread in the Lord's Supper. **And blessed,** naturally means blessed the loaf, that being the object of the preceding and the two following verbs. Luke and Paul, however, have 'gave thanks,' viz., to God, as below, v. 27;[1] and so some would here understand it to mean blessed God. But in Luke 9: 16 it is distinctly 'he blessed them,' viz., the loaves and fishes. This shows that the idea of blessing the loaf is not repugnant to Scripture, and as the connection naturally indicates that idea here, it should be preferred. Comp. 1 Cor. 10: 16, "The cup of blessing which we bless." To bless a loaf is of course to invoke God's blessing upon it, to ask that God will make it a means of blessing to those who partake. **And brake it.** Hence the observance of this ordinance came to be described as ' the breaking of bread.' (Acts 2: 42, 46; 20: 7; comp. 1 Cor.

[1] If indeed W H. are not right in holding that all in Luke, after 'body,' being absent in the "Western" group of documents, is really an interpolation from Paul; and that v. 17 f. is Luke's account of our Lord's giving the cup, the order of the cup and the loaf being simply transposed. The question of text is very difficult, but the arguments for exclusion seem to grow upon one with renewed consideration. The omission of that portion of Luke would, however, take away nothing from the total information possessed by us, as it is all given in Paul.

[2] The reading 'gave thanks,' in v. 2', mentioned in *margin* Com. Ver., is supported only by later documents; the earliest uncials, and nearly every one of the early versions, give 'blessed,' and the change to the other is at once explained as an assimilation to v. 27, and to Luke and Paul.

10: 16.) **And gave,** is according to the most probable Greek text[1] in the imperfect tense, which *may* mean that he went on giving, himself breaking a piece for each one, to be passed on to those out of his reach; while as to the cup it is aorist, since he simply gave the cup, and they passed it to each other. But the imperfect in such a case might only *describe* him as engaged in giving, and so would not substantially differ from the aorist. **Take, eat.** Mark has simply 'take'; Luke and Paul in Rev. Ver. have neither. **This is my body.** 'This' is neuter, while the masculine would be needed to agree with 'bread'; it means, this object represents my body. Paul (1 Cor. 11: 24, Rev. Ver.) has 'This is my body, which is for you,' where 'broken' was early inserted, probably suggested by 1 Cor. 10: 16. The phrase current among us, "broken for you," is thus not a Scripture expression. 'That is for you' means 'for your benefit'; we should lovingly take what represents the body that is for us. Luke, Rev. Ver., has 'this is my body which is given for you,' which amounts to the same thing. *Weiss:* "Not as a dark fatality were they to regard the death which he was now to meet, but as the way by which God would make them sharers in his greatest gift of salvation; and that gift was not to be for mere contemplative purposes, but for personal appropriation."

Four different views as to the meaning of the phrase, 'this is my body,' now prevail in the Christian world. Two of them take the expression literally, the others figuratively. (1) Transubstantiation, which represents the Roman Catholic view, mean that the bread ceases to be bread, and its substance is changed into the substance of the glorified body of Christ. This notion arose from combining the expression before us with John 6: 48-58, the images there used being taken literally. In Justin Martyr, "1 Apol." 66, Irenæus, 4, 18, 5, and even in Ignatius, Sm. 6, are expressions which do not in fact mean transubstantiation or real presence, but which tend in that direction, and doubtless helped to prepare the way for the doctrine subsequently developed. There is nothing of the sort in the "*Di-*

dache." The question need not be here argued. The language seems evidently figurative, as in "I am the door," "I am the vine," "and the rock was Christ," "the field is the world," etc. We must remember that in Hebrew or Aramaic the copula 'is' would not be expressed at all. (2) Consubstantiation, the term invented by Luther, and still used by some of his followers, means that with the unchanged substance of the bread is united the substance of the glorified body of Christ. *Luther:* "What is now the sacrament of the altar? Answer: It is the true body and blood of the Lord Christ, in and under the bread and wine, which we Christians are through Christ's word commanded to eat and to drink . . . but how the body is in the bread, we know not." His followers have compared it to iron, with heat superadded, or more recently to iron magnetized. But the whole notion is obviously a mere makeshift of persons unwilling to give up the literal sense of 'is,' and the mystical notion of Christ's real presence. And how could the glorified body be invisibly dwelling in the bread, and the blood of that same glorified body be separately dwelling in the wine? They could be symbolized separately, but how could they exist separately? (Comp. Meyer.) (3) The view of Calvin, now held by Presbyterians, Methodists, and many Episcopalians, appears to be that to the partaking of the bread is attached by divine appointment a special spiritual blessing, which is received by all who take the bread in faith, and which cannot be had without taking it. Hence, they sometimes feel aggrieved that other Christians who do not invite them to partake of the bread and wine are denying them the opportunity of a spiritual blessing, not to be otherwise enjoyed at that time. Some High Churchmen have receded from the Calvinian view, and maintain the "Real Presence" of Christ in the Sacrament, without undertaking to explain in what way or in what sense it exists. (4) The view of Zwingli, now almost universally held by Baptists, is that the bread is simply appointed as the symbol or memento, which we take in remembrance of the Saviour's body,

---

[1] The aorist (participle) here is read by א B D L Z, some important cursives, and the Memphitic, strong evidence. But we see at once how the imperfect might have been changed into correspondence with the aorist of v. 27, and of the parallels as to the loaf in Mark and Luke, and we see no reason for the counter change; therefore the imperfect is probably correct.

27 And he took the cup, and gave thanks, and gave *it* to them, saying, Drink ye all of it:
28 For this is my blood of the new testament, which is shed for many for the remission of sins.

27 Take, eat; this is my body. And he took [1] a cup,
28 and gave thanks, and gave to them, saying, Drink ye all of it; for this is my blood of the [2] covenant,

---

1 Some ancient authorities read *the cup*.....2 Many ancient authorities insert *new*.

---

and that the natural effect of such a memento or symbol in vividly reminding of the Saviour, and kindling grateful affection toward him, is blessed to the devout participant. A memento of the departed may be a very simple thing, and yet deeply move the heart. But the blessing thus receeived is not supposed to be essentially different in kind from other spiritual blessings, or to be associated by mere divine appointment with this particular means of grace. Hence no spiritual loss is necessarily inflicted by failing to invite to this ceremony persons who have made a credible oral profession of faith, but have not yet submitted to the prerequisite ceremony.

27. Took the cup; *a cup*, is the correct text in Matthew and Mark, while it is 'the cup' in Luke and Paul. There was a cup on the table for drinking wine according to the custom of the paschal meal; 'a cup' does not say there were others. The paschal wine was usually mixed with a double quantity of water (Edersh.). **Gave thanks.** From the Greek word thus translated comes 'the Eucharist,' *i. e.*, 'the Thanksgiving,' as a phrase for taking the bread and wine. It is used by Ignatius and the *"Didache"* to denote the taking of bread and wine in connection with an *agape*, or 'love-feast' (Jude 12), just as Paul seems to use his phrase 'the Lord's Supper.' (1 Cor. 11: 20.) But the connection with a regular meal in common

is not made a duty by Paul, nor the connection with the passover by our Lord. What he directs is *not* to eat the passover, or to eat a supper, *not* to eat in the evening, or at a table, or in a reclining posture, but to eat bread and drink wine. Protestants unite in declaiming against the Romish practice of withholding the wine from the laity, because the Saviour enjoined both the eating and the drinking; and exactly what the Saviour enjoined we should do. So as to baptism, there is no command to baptize "in living water," as the *"Didache"* declares preferable, or in any particular place, time, circumstances, or manner; the thing enjoined is to baptize (28: 19), viz., in water (3: 11), and we should insist on nothing but water and the baptizing. (Comp. on 3: 6.) **Drink ye all of it.** It would seem unnecessary to say that this means all of you, and not all of it, as the Greek places beyond question; yet some have misunderstood. Mark records, not the command, but the performance, 'and they all drank of it.' **For,** what follows being a reason for drinking. **This is my blood,** *i. e.*, this wine represents my blood, like 'this is my body.' **Of the new covenant;** the correct reading here,[1] and in Mark, does not contain "new." It was added by copyists from Luke and Paul. (Comp. Jer. 31: 31: Heb. 8: 8.)[2] Moses at Mount Sinai "took the book of the

---

[1] 'Covenant,' without 'new' in ℵ B L Z, 33, 102, Thebaic, Cyril; in Mark, ℵ B C D L, Theb. and Memph., and k of the Old Latin. We see at once that the 'new' might have been interpolated in Matt. and Mark from Luke and Paul (and comp. v. 29), while we see no reason why it should have been omitted if originally present. So the internal evidence supports this important group of documents. Notice the constant correspondence in this narrative between Matt. and Mark, and between Luke and Paul.

[2] The word *diatheke* signifies both covenant, an arrangement between (*dia*) two parties, and testament, an arrangement of things *at intervals* (*dia*), each in its proper place, a *disposition* of one's affairs. The former is clearly the sense in most passages of the New Test., but the two ideas are blended in Heb. 9: 15-20, because the new covenant was made in and through Christ's *death*, and its benefits are, as it were, an inheritance from him. This sense of *testament* early took hold of

the Christian mind. The Old Latin and Vulgate versions everywhere translate *diatheke* by *testamentum*, which in many passages is flagrantly inappropriate (as Luke 1: 72; Acts 3: 25; Heb. 8: 8 etc.), and nowhere needed except in Heb. 9: 16 f. The Old Covenant and the New Covenant thus gave names to the two great divisions of the Bible under the form of Old Test. and New Test., which names cannot now be shaken off, though Covenant would be far more expressive. The domination of this idea made it hard for early English translations to break away from the rendering 'testament.' Wyc. and Rheims of course follow the Vulgate, and give testament everywhere. Tyn., Cran., Gen., and K. J., all give testament in the four passages pertaining to the Lord's Supper, in 2 Cor. 3: 6, 14, and throughout Heb. 9: 15-20 (Gen. has covenant in 9: 15 only); and all give covenant in Luke 1: 72; Acts 3: 25; 7: 8; Rom. 9: 4; 11: 27; Tyn. and Cran. have testament, but Gen. and K. J. covenant, in Gal. 3: 15, 17; Eph. 2: 12; Heb. 8: 6-

29 But I say unto you, I will not drink henceforth of this fruit of the vine, until that day when I drink it new with you in my Father's kingdom.

29 which is shed for many unto remission of sins. But I say unto you, I shall not drink henceforth of this fruit of the vine, until that day when I drink it new with you in my Father's kingdom.

---

covenant and read in the audience of the people," and they promised to obey. Then he "took the blood" of oxen just slain, "and sprinkled it on the people, and said, Behold the blood of the covenant." (Exod. 24 : 3-8 ; comp. Heb. 9 : 19 f.) So the new covenant predicted by Jer. 31 : 31-35 is about to be ratified by the Saviour's own blood as the "blood of the covenant." (Comp. Heb. 10 : 29 ; 13 : 20.) For world-wide symbolism of blood as sealing a covenant, and its participation as denoting vital union, see Trumbull : "The Blood Covenant," especially p. 271–286. **Which is shed,** present tense (in Mark also), expressing what is near and certain, on the point of taking place, like 'is delivered,' 26 : 2, Rev. Ver., and 'I keep,' 26 : 18, Rev. Ver. **For many,** so Mark. In Luke, if v. 20 be genuine, it is 'for you.' The 'many' (comp. 20 : 28) is simply a general expression (probably derived from Isa. 53 : 12, "he bare the sin of many," comp. 52 : 15), not necessarily indicating that some are omitted. In one sense, Jesus "gave himself a ransom for all" (1 Tim. 2 : 6), and to "taste death for every man" (Heb. 2 : 9 ; comp. 1 John 2 : 2), making salvation objectively possible for all; in another sense, his atoning death definitely contemplated the salvation of the elect. Euthym. understands that whereas the blood of the sacrifices was shed for Jews only, *i. e.*, few, this blood is shed for many, *i. e.*, for Gentiles also. The preposition here rendered 'for' means 'concerning' (*peri*), and so 'for the benefit of,' as in John 16 : 26 ; 17 : 9, 20 ; Heb. 5 : 3 ; 11 : 40. This preposition would not of itself suggest the idea of substitution. That idea would be readily, though not necessarily, suggested by Mark 14 : 24, *huper* (which copyists easily changed by assimilation to Matt. ; and so the common Greek text of Mark has *peri) ;* and substitution is necessarily the meaning of *anti*, see on 20 : 28. **For,** or **unto,**

remission of sins, in order that sins may be remitted. (Heb. 9 : 22.) This is the natural and most probable meaning of the preposition and its case, and is here entirely appropriate. (Comp. on 3 : 11.) The bread and wine symbolize objectively the Saviour's body and blood ; our eating and drinking these symbolizes our personal union with Christ, and feeding our spiritual nature upon him ; and our doing this together with others will, from the nature of the case, like any other action in common, promote Christian fellowship and unity where these already exist. Yet this last is a subordinate and incidental effect of the ceremony, and the presence of some in whose piety we lack confidence should not prevent our eating the bread and drinking the wine in remembrance of Christ. The Lord's Supper is often called "the Communion," through a misunderstanding of 1 Cor. 10 : 16, where the word communion really means 'participation,' as in Rev. Ver., *margin.* This wrong name for the ordinance has often proved very misleading. (See T. G. Jones, "The Great Misnomer," Nashville, Tenn.) Few have ever questioned that the apostles had all been baptized before this ordinance was established ; some urge that being the baptism of John, this was not Christian baptism, and so they curiously infer that Christian baptism is not a prerequisite to the Lord's Supper. But if John's baptism was *essentially* distinct from Christian baptism, then how as to the baptism administered by Christ himself (John 3 : 22. 26), *i. e.*, through his disciples (John 4 : 1 f.), at the same time with John, and upon the same general teaching (Mark 1 : 15) ? If the baptism performed by Christ was not Christian baptism, then what was it? (Comp. on 11 : 11.)

29. I will not drink, should be, 'I *shall* not drink,' as preferred by Amer. Revisers. **This fruit of the vine.** One of the prayers

---

10; 9 : 4 ; 11 : 16, 29 ; 13 : 20 ; Tyn., Cran., and K. J., have testament, though Gen. has covenant, in Heb. 7 : 22 ; Rev. 11 : 19 ; Tyn., Cran., and Gen., testament, but K. J. covenant, in Heb. 12 : 24. Coming out of all this confusion, Bib. Un., Noyes, Darby, Davidson, and Rev Ver. give covenant everywhere except in Heb. 9 : 16 f.,

and all but Darby there explain in the *margin* that Greek word means both ; Rev. Ver. also puts testament in the *margin* of several other passages, including those relating to the Lord's Supper, but the American Revisers rightly desired to omit this marginal alternative rendering.

30 And when they had sung a hymn,*a* they went out into the mount of Olives.

30   And when they had sung a hymn, they went out unto the mount of Olives.

a Or, psalm.

---

used at the Passover was (Lightf.): "Blessed art thou, Jehovah our God, who hast created the fruit of the vine." **Drink it new with you in my Father's kingdom.** He has gradually succeeded in making it plain to them that he will not establish a temporal kingdom, such as the Jews expected the Messiah to found. He is going to die, will soon leave them. But there will be a future kingdom of God, not a temporal but a spiritual kingdom, in which all things will be new. (Rev. 21:5.) In that *new* kingdom, founded on the New Covenant, he will meet them again, and drink with them a new kind of wine (Lutter.) This can hardly be understood otherwise than as a figure, even by those who expect a quasi-temporal reign of our Lord at Jerusalem after his second coming. (Comp. Luke 22:16, 30.) In his present state of submission and suffering, our Lord does not speak of his own kingdom (as in 16:28; 25:31, 34), but of his Father's kingdom, in which he, as the Son, will rejoice with his friends. Yes, and all who shall have believed on him through the word of the apostles, will be with him there. (John 17:20. 24.) Matthew and Mark have not stated that the taking of the bread and wine was established by Jesus as a permanent institution. But Paul makes it clear by recording the words, "this do ye, as oft as ye drink it, in remembrance of me," and adding, "For as often as ye eat this bread, and drink this cup, ye shew the Lord's death till he come." And we see the apostles practicing it in Acts 2:42; 20:7.

30. When they had sung a hymn, literally, if our idiom would allow, *after hymning.* The Greek word *humnos* was properly a song of praise; and with this agrees the Sept. and New Test. use of the word, Acts 16:25; Heb. 2:12. We learn from the Talmud that the Jews were accustomed in connection with the paschal meal to sing Psalms 113 to 118, which Psalms they called "the great Hallel" (praise); it was sung in two parts, 113, 114, and 115 to 118; the singing here was probably the second of these parts, or possibly 136, which the Jews now sing at the close of the passover meal. It is interesting to read these Psalms in this connection, remembering that Jesus himself took part in the singing. The psalms were written in the *Hebrew* form of poetry, viz., parallel clauses; to translate them into metre, which is the ordinary *English* form of poetry, is therefore appropriate. The term 'hymn' must not be here taken in our common sense as differing from a psalm, nor is there any radical distinction between the two in Col. 3:16; Eph. 5:19. The music was a very simple chant; something probably quite similar may now be heard in an old-fashioned (not "reformed") Jewish synagogue. **They went out,** viz., out of the house and the city. There was light in many dwellings, and movement in the streets, till long after midnight, at which hour the feast was required to end. — Before leaving the house, our Lord must be supposed to have given the great farewell discourse, and the prayer of John ch. 14-17. It is not unlikely that ch. 14 was spoken before singing the latter part of the great Hallel; then Jesus said, "Arise, let us go hence" (John 14:31), and after making arrangements for leaving the room, they sung the psalms, and he went on with ch. 15, 16, and the sweet and solemn prayer of ch. 17, after which we read (John 18:1. Rev. Ver.), "When Jesus had spoken these words, he went forth with his disciples over the brook Kidron, where was a garden," and hither Judas came, with the soldiers and officials. This answers to the present sentence of Matt., and the parallels in Mark and Luke. **Into the mount of Olives,** see on 21:1. They would naturally go through the eastern gate north of the temple area, which is now called St. Stephen's Gate; then down the steep declivity into the valley, presently crossing the bed of "the brook Kidron," probably on a low bridge as now, and in not many steps further would reach the foot of the mountain. It was late, perhaps midnight or later; but the city gates were open all night during the great feasts. The paschal full moon shone upon them from exactly overhead, lighting up the bottom of the deep ravine.

IV. **31-35.** Our Lord Foretells the

31 Then saith Jesus unto them, All ye shall be offended because of me this night: for it is written, I will smite the Shepherd, and the sheep of the flock shall be scatter. d abroad.
32 But after I am risen again, I will go before you into Galilee.

31 Then saith Jesus unto them, All ye shall be [1]offended in me this night: for it is written, I will smite the shepherd, and the sheep of the flock shall 32 be scattered abroad. But after I am raised up, I will

---

1 Gr. *caused to stumble.*

DISPERSION OF THE TWELVE, AND THE FALL OF PETER. Mark 14: 27-31; Luke 22: 31-38; John 13: 36-38. The passage occurs in Mark in the same order as here, but neither of them compels us to understand that the warning was given after leaving the room. That recorded by John is distinctly placed by him just after the commencement of the farewell address—for that address really begins with John 13: 31. Luke seems also to put the warning *before* they left the house (22:39), but his order in 22: 21-38 is, as we have seen, pretty clearly not chronological. It is more difficult to suppose the report in John to be out of its chronological position than those of Matt. and Mark. Clark's "Harm." supposes two distinct warnings, that given in Luke and John occurring before they left the house, and that of Matt. and Mark after they went out. This is an improbable supposition, though presented by Greswell and Oosterzee, and by Riddle in Robinson's "Harmony." Different as are the terms employed in Luke, we more naturally understand the warning as the same in all four Gospels, for its repetition during the same evening is highly improbable. It is therefore best to suppose, with most harmonists, that Matt. and Mark have here introduced the warning a little later than its chronological position, in order to avoid breaking the connection of v. 20-29. It is likely that more was said than any of the Gospels give, or all of them together; as in the Sermon on the Mount, and often. **All ye shall be offended because of** (*in*) **me,** or *shall find in me occasion of stumbling,* as in 11: 6, and see on 5: 29. They will find in him some obstacle to continued devotion, and so will turn away and forsake him. **This night.** He has during more than six months repeatedly foretold that he should be put to death in Jerusalem and rise again; see 16: 21; 17: 22 f.; 20: 18 f. At the close of his public teaching, he declared that he should at the passover be delivered up and crucified, 26: 2. Now he is perfectly definite as to the time. **For it is written,** stands on record, a common formula of reference to the Old Test. Scriptures, as in 2: 5; 4: 4, etc. Neither our Lord nor the Evangelist says that this was *fulfilled* in the present occurrence, and it might be enough to understand that our Lord merely borrows the language to indicate that he will be killed, and the disciples will leave him and disperse. Still, his introducing the quotation by 'for' (so also Mark 14: 27), indicates it as proving or as requiring that which he has just foretold; and it is entirely possible to understand Zech. 13: 7 as really pointing forward to this event. As to the form of the quotation Matt. and Mark follow the Hebrew, except in changing 'smite' (singular) into 'I will smite'; while the Sept. (B and א) is quite different, 'smite (plural) the shepherds and draw forth the sheep.' This is a clear case of Matthew's following the Hebrew rather than the Sept. (Comp. on 3: 3.) To take the passage as referring to the Messiah, corresponds to the idea of the Messiah as king, since kings were often described as shepherds. Then the flock will here be Israel, and the prediction is that Israel will be scattered, the first stage of which was the scattering of the Twelve when the Shepherd was smitten. It is, however, difficult to connect Zech. 13: 7, thus understood, with what there precedes. (v. 1-6.) There is of course no absolute necessity for supposing such a connection. But the idea may be that in the coming time (v. 2 ff.), idolatry and false prophets shall cease (which was true just before the coming of Christ), and yet there shall be great wickedness, and the Shepherd shall be smitten and Israel scattered, and only a third (v. 8, 9) finally purified and saved. Many writers insist that the idea of a shepherd here must be essentially like that of Zech., chap. 11, so that this is a bad shepherd, *i. e.,* a bad king of Israel, whom God will remove. That is a possible interpretation, if we leave the New Test. out of view, but not at all a necessary one.

32. After I am risen again, or *raised up.* He has in every case, except 26: 2, promised that after being killed he would rise again.

33 Peter answered and said unto him, Though all *men* shall be offended because of thee, *yet* will I never be offended.

34 Jesus said unto him, Verily I say unto thee, That this night, before the cock crow, thou shalt deny me thrice.

35 Peter said unto him, Though I should die with thee, yet will I not deny thee. Likewise also said all the disciples.

33 go before you into Galilee. But Peter answered and said unto him, If all shall be [1] offended in thee, 34 I will never be [1] offended. Jesus said unto him, Verily I say unto thee, that this night, before the 35 cock crow, thou shalt deny me thrice. Peter saith unto him, Even if I must die with thee, *yet* will I not deny thee. Likewise also said all the disciples.

---

[1] Gr. *caused to stumble.*

I will go before you into Galilee, literally, *will lead you forward,* see on 21: 31; possibly with reference to the figure of a shepherd here just preceding. So Mark, and below, 28: 7. His chief appearance to them was to be in Galilee (28: 16), which had been the principal field of his ministry.

33-35. Though all. . . . I never. The peculiar Greek construction (two indicative futures) implies the assumption that all will. Here is the beginning of that self-confidence which led step by step to Peter's dreadful fall. And here is the distinct assumption that he loves the Master "more than these" (John 21:15), indeed more than any one whatsoever loved him. When bitter experience had chastened him, he made no more comparisons, but said only, "Thou knowest that I love thee." **Verily I say unto thee,** calling attention to something solemnly important (see on 5: 18). **This night,** as in v. 31. **Before the cock crow.** Mark (14: 30, 72) has 'before the cock crow twice.' The cock was apt to crow about midnight, and again a few hours later. The second crowing was the one more apt to be observed as indicating the approach of morning; and so this alone is mentioned by Matt., Luke, and John. *Alexander:* "The difference is the same as that between saying 'before the bell rings' and 'before the second bell rings' (for church or dinner), the reference in both expressions being to the last and most important signal, to which the first is only a preliminary." The minute recollection of this reference to the first cock-crowing also would be natural in Peter, and there are many things in the second Gospel to support the very early tradition that Mark wrote

down what he heard Peter say. (Comp. 1 Pet. 5: 13.) Some have made a difficulty of the fact that one passage of the Mishna forbids rearing fowls in Jerusalem, because the worms they scratch up would be Levitically defiling. But Wün. and Edersh. show that the cock-crow is repeatedly mentioned in the Talmud, and produce from it a story of a cock stoned to death in Jerusalem because it had killed a child. So the Rabbinical rule did not exist in the time of Christ, or else was not strictly observed. Palestine seems particularly well suited to fowls, and they are very numerous there now. **Deny,** see on 16: 24.[1] *Even if I must die,* is the exact translation; that of Com. Ver., **Though I should die,** is inadequate. Peter is so extremely self-confident through consciousness of real and honest attachment, that even the Master's own warning cannot make him think it possible that he would do such a thing. And encouraged by his ardor and positiveness the other disciples make similar assurances. Comp. the proposal of Thomas some weeks before (John 11: 16), "Let us also go, that we may die with him." We have no reason to believe that any of the ten did formally deny their Lord, though they all left him and fled, Peter and John presently returning. (26: 56.) All four of the accounts of the warning to Peter include the cock-crowing and 'deny me thrice.' But in Luke and John the confident expressions of Peter are called forth by sayings of our Lord quite different from each other, and from that recorded by Matthew and Mark. In John, Peter wishes to go with the Master *now,* and asserts that he has no fear of perils: "I will

---

[1] In 1885 was published, see "Theolog. Literaturzeitung," 13 June, a papyrus fragment in Greek, brought from Egypt to Vienna, which forms a shorter parallel to v. 31-34, and Mark 14: 27-30. As completed and translated, it reads, "[And after] eating, as they were going forth: I will smite the [shepherd and the] sheep will be scattered. Upon Peter's [saying], even if all, no[t I, he

said to him], the cock will crow twice, and thou first (*i. e.* before that) wilt thrice deny me." Harnack thinks this shorter account is from a gospel earlier than Matt. and Mark. But it is easier to suppose, with Warfield and Hort, that this is a mere abridgement of the gospel story, given from memory in some homily or practical treatise. The reasons cannot be here presented.

36 Then cometh Jesus with them unto a place called Gethsemane, and saith unto the disciples, Sit ye here while I go and pray yonder.

36 Then cometh Jesus with them unto [1] a place called Gethsemane, and saith unto his disciples, Sit ye

---

1 Gr. *an enclosed piece of ground.*

---

lay down my life for thy sake." In Luke, Jesus speaks of Satan's asking for the disciples that he might sift them; he says he has made special supplication for Peter, and adds an injunction that after turning again he must stablish his brethren. Peter repels the implication that he will go wrong and have to turn, saying, " Lord, with thee I am ready to go both to prison and to death," Rev. Ver. In each case, our Lord replies by substantially the same warning as in Matthew and Mark. It is not necessary for us to consolidate or concatenate all these distinct occasions for the warning. Probably the conversation was more extended than any of the narratives would indicate. And a few missing points of information might harmonize all the accounts.

HOMILETICAL AND PRACTICAL.

V. 17-19. The externals of religious service. 1) They should be observed with forethought and propriety. 2) They are a proper subject of request for the Lord's guidance. 3) They offer many opportunities of honoring the Lord with our substance, v. 18. 4) Yet, alas! they are sometimes shared by one whose heart is set on worldliness and wickedness, v. 21; comp. Phil. 3: 18.—V. 21-25. The betrayal foretold. 1) Consciousness of good intentions cannot always save us from fear of committing great sin, v. 22; 1 Cor. 10: 12. 2) The most affecting associations and solemn warnings may not prevent desperate wickedness. 3) One whose heart is set on the darkest crime may sometimes talk calmly and with affected modesty, v. 25. 4) A bad man may be unintentionally accomplishing some exalted purpose of God, v. 24; (comp. Psalm 76: 10). 5) The fact that an evil action is overruled for good does not lessen its guilt and penalty, v. 24. 6) It is possible for human wickedness to make human existence a curse, v. 24.—V. 26-28. The bread and wine. 1) Jesus has bidden us commemorate, not his birth, his miracles, his triumphal entry, but his *death.* 2) His death sealed a covenant of salvation (comp. Heb. 9: 19 f.), making atonement for sin, and purchasing forgiveness for sinners. 3) To eat and drink these simple emblems of his body

and blood should awaken grateful remembrance of him (1 Cor. 11: 24 f.), and stir the strong desire to live for him who died for us.—V. 28. HENRY: " 1) 'It is my blood of the covenant.' 2) It is shed for many. 3) Unto remission of sins."—V. 33. HENRY: "Those are often least safe that are most secure."

36-56. THE AGONY IN GETHSEMANE AND THE ARREST OF JESUS.

Found also in Mark 14: 32-52; Luke 22: 39-53; John 18: 1-12. The time of this section is between midnight and morning. Gethsemane is here called **a place,** Rev. Ver., *margin, an enclosed piece of ground ;* comp. the same word in John 9: 5. The name Gethsemane means ' oil-press.' But the place was not simply an oil-press, for John calls it a garden or orchard, probably containing fruit trees and flowers, as well as vegetables. Gethsemane is now shown as a small enclosure lying just where the three roads across the Mount of Olives branch off at its base (see on 21: 1), and between the central and southern roads, both of which lead to Bethany. This enclosure is of somewhat less than an acre, and contains several very old olive trees, looking at a distance like large old apple trees. These identical trees appear to be traced back for many centuries. But they cannot have existed in our Lord's time, for Josephus tells us ("War." 6, 1, 1), that the Romans, in order to build their mounds about the walls, cut down all the trees for ten or twelve miles around the city, so that the region that had been so beautiful with trees and gardens (paradises) was now desolate on every side, and a pitiable, mournful spectacle. And even before this (" War." 5, 12, 2), they had drawn around the city a wall which is described as passing south along the foot of the Mount of Olives to a point opposite Siloam, and must therefore have passed exactly where the present enclosure stands. The real Gethsemane was probably quite near this enclosed place. As " Jesus oft-times resorted thither with his disciples," so that Judas "knew the place" (John 18: 2), we naturally think of it as near the way to and from Bethany. If not a small public garden or park, it was owned by a

37 And he took with him Peter and the two sons of Zebedee, and began to be sorrowful and very heavy.

38 Then saith he unto them, My soul is exceeding sorrowful, even unto death: tarry ye here, and watch with me.

39 And he went a little further, and fell on his face, and prayed, saying, O my Father, if it be possible, let this cup pass from me: nevertheless, not as I will, but as thou *wilt*.

37 here, while I go yonder and pray. And he took with him Peter and the two sons of Zebedee, and

38 began to be sorrowful and sore troubled. Then saith he unto them, My soul is exceeding sorrowful, even unto death: abide ye here, and watch with me.

9 And he went forward a little, and fell on his face, and prayed, saying, O my Father, if it be possible, let this cup pass away from me: nevertheless, not

---

public-spirited man who allowed visitors to enter at will, particularly during the great festivals, or else by some friend of Jesus, like the owner of the house in which he had eaten the passover.—In 1871, a party of Americans went forth from Jerusalem one night at Easter to visit Gethsemane. Passing through what is traditionally called St. Stephen's Gate, we went along a winding path far down the steep descent into the narrow valley of the Kidron (which has there no water except in the rainy season), and crossing, were almost immediately at the modern stone wall which encloses the old olive trees. The paschal full moon for us too shone bright on the scene. It was late at night, and all was still; and at several different points we kneeled, a little company from a distant land, and one or another of us prayed with choked utterance, for we knew that we could not be far from the spot at which the Saviour kneeled down, and fell prostrate, and prayed in his agony.

This section divides itself into two parts, the Agony and the Arrest.

I. **36-46.** The Agony in Gethsemane. Mark 14: 32-42; Luke 22: 40-46. John does not record this, but he records (Alf.) a somewhat similar utterance on the previous day, John 12: 28-33, and other passages which reveal mental suffering, John 13: 21; 16: 32. **Sit ye here,** apparently outside of the enclosure. **Peter and the two sons of Zebedee.** These three belong to the first group of four among the Twelve (see on 10: 2); they alone had accompanied Jesus when he raised Jairus' daughter to life, and up into the Mount of Transfiguration. **Began,** and continued for some time (see on 11: 20). **Very heavy;** *sore troubled* is a better translation than 'very heavy.' Mark has the same peculiar Greek term. **My soul is exceeding sorrowful.** The phrase, which resembles Psa. 41 (42): 6 in Sept., can only denote a real human mind; comp. John 12: 27. The ancient fancy which some are trying to revive, that in the Incarnation the divine nature

took the place and fulfilled the functions of a human soul, is incompatible, not only with this scene and the temptation of 4: 1 ff., but with the whole history of Jesus. Whatever anthropomorphic expressions may be necessarily used in speaking of God, it is evident that the divine nature could not, in any proper sense of the term, suffer agony. How his human soul could suffer apart from his divine nature, is a part of the mystery of the Incarnation, like his temptation, his increasing in wisdom (Luke 2: 52), and his not knowing the day nor the hour. (Mark 13: 32.) Nor is it wise to make trichotomist distinctions between 'soul' here and 'spirit' in v. 41; see on 16: 25. **Even unto death.** Comp. Isa. 38: 1. The time is now nearer than on the occasion described in John 12: 27, and his suffering is more intense. *Alford:* "Our Lord's whole inmost life must have been one of continued trouble of spirit—he was a man of sorrows, and acquainted with grief—but there was an extremity of anguish now, reaching even to the utmost limit of endurance, so that it seemed that more would be death itself." **Tarry ye here.** He had brought the three to some point removed from the other eight. **And watch with me.** The idea seems to be that they were to guard his season of exceeding and deadly sorrow from intrusion, and also to give him the support of knowing that sympathetic friends were close by. In any season of extraordinary sorrow, one likes to be much alone, and yet to have some dear friends near, so that he may go to them when the craving for sympathy becomes uppermost. *Alford:* "He does not say pray with me, for in that work the Mediator must be *alone*."

39-41. He withdraws the first time. **He went a little further.** Luke says 'about a stone's cast,' say fifty yards. This might be from the eight disciples, as Luke does not mention the special three; but from comparing his whole connection we see that it more likely means the three. Jesus doubtless sought the most secluded spot in the enclo-

40 And he cometh unto the disciples, and findeth them asleep, and saith unto Peter, What, could ye not watch with me one hour?
41 Watch and pray, that ye enter not into temptation: the spirit indeed *is* willing, but the flesh *is* weak.

40 as I will, but as thou wilt. And he cometh unto the disciples, and findeth them sleeping, and saith unto Peter, What, could ye not watch with me one hour?
41 [1]Watch and pray, that ye enter not into temptation: the spirit indeed is willing, but the flesh is weak.

---

1 Or, *Watch ye, and pray that ye enter not.*

---

sure, and probably withdrew from the light of the full moon to the shade of trees. **Fell on his face.** Luke says 'kneeled,' which would naturally be followed, in an agony of distress, by complete prostration. **And prayed,** the tense (in Mark and Luke also) denoting continued action. The Saviour evidently spent much time in prayer, and particularly on any special occasion. At his baptism (Luke 3 : 21), before choosing the twelve (Luke 6 : 12), when the multitudes wanted to make him king (Matt. 14 : 23 ; John 6 : 15), when the disciples were just becoming satisfied that he was the Messiah (Luke 9 : 18), when on the Mount of Transfiguration (Luke 9 : 28), and upon other occasions, there is special mention of his praying, sometimes for many hours, even a whole night. So his praying here, long and repeatedly, is no new thing in his experience. **O, my father.** Mark gives the Aramaic word *Abba*, which our Lord doubtless actually employed, and then adds the Greek word, making 'Abba, Father'; so Paul in Rom. 8: 15. **If it be possible,** *i. e.*, morally possible, consistent with the Father's purpose of saving men. The God-man speaks according to his suffering human nature, referring all to the Father (comp. 20: 23 ; Mark 13: 32). In Mark (14: 36) the expression is stronger, 'All things are possible unto thee . . . . but what thou wilt'—he refers it to the Father's *will*. **This cup,** a common image for great suffering, like some allotted bitter draught. See on 20: 22. **Let this cup pass from me.** So Mark. But Luke, in the common and probably correct text, 'If thou art willing to let this cup pass away from me'—the sentence remaining unfinished, an aposiopesis, as in Luke 13: 9; 19: 42; Acts 23: 9 (Winer, 599 f. [750]). We have seen that the words spoken from heaven at the baptism and the Transfiguration (3 : 17; 17 : 5) are not reported in precisely the same terms by the different Evangelists, which conclusively shows that they did not undertake to give in all cases the exact words spoken. But there is no substantial difference.[1] **Not as I will, but as thou wilt.** Comp. John 5 : 30; 6: 38; Phil. 2: 8. Many months earlier, when he first spoke to the disciples of his approaching death, he indicated that such was God's thought and purpose. (16: 23.) **He cometh unto the disciples,** the three. **And findeth them asleep.** Luke adds 'for sorrow.' They felt a dull, depressing sorrow at the intimation that their Master was about to leave them, was about to be killed. They saw nothing to be done by themselves, and could not realize that the danger was so imminent and perilous as the result showed. Such a state of mind often superinduces heavy sleep; and it was now long past midnight. These same three disciples were "heavy with sleep" during the Transfiguration. (Luke 9 : 32.) **And saith unto Peter,** who was the recognized leader, in some sense, of the Twelve, see on 16 : 16. Notice that the following verbs are all plural ; he addresses all three through Peter. **What, could ye not,** is a good English equivalent to the peculiar phrase of the original, 'were ye thus unable,' were ye as unable as this? **Watch with me one hour.** The expression is doubtless only general and not to be pressed, but it shows that he had been alone no little time. 'Watch' refers primarily to keeping awake, but also suggests mental alertness. It

---

1 After v. 39, the old uncial represented by 13, 69, 124, some Greek lectionaries, and the Syriac of Jerusalem introduce the account of the bloody sweat and the angel's appearing, taken from Luke 22: 43 f., and, of course, not genuine here. A number of important documents *omit* that passage from *Luke*. But the omission can be more easily accounted for than the insertion. All the Gnostic heretics of the second century would dislike the passage intensely, and many orthodox people might think it derogatory. Epiphanius remarks that "orthodox persons removed the passage, because they were afraid, and did not understand its design and extreme importance." We think, therefore, that it ought to be retained in Luke. In combining the Gospels, this passage is more naturally connected with the first season of prayer, than with the second or third, when his agony seems to have been less severe.

42 He went away again the second time. and prayed, saying, O my Father, if this cup may not pass away from me, except I drink it, thy will be done.

42 Again a second time he went away and prayed, saying, O my Father, if this cannot pass away, except I

became a favorite term with the apostles; comp. 24: 42; 25: 13; 1 Thess. 5: 6; 1 Cor. 16: 13; Rom. 13: 11; Col. 4: 2; 1 Peter 5: 8. **That ye enter not,** may be connected with both 'watch and pray,' or with only 'pray,' as in Rev. Ver. *margin*, and so Origen ("On Prayer," page 557, Migne), Chrys., Theophyl., Euthym. In Luke 22: 40 it is simply 'pray that ye enter not,' etc.; and in 22: 46 Rev. Ver., 'rise and pray lest ye enter into,' the latter connection is much the more natural of the two.[1] **Temptation,** comp. on 4: 1. Observe that it is not merely "that you may overcome temptation," or "that you may be supported under temptation," but "that you may not come into temptation," may avoid being tempted. Comp. on 6: 13, and see Luke 22: 31. The Com. Ver., through oversight or in its passion for variety (see on 25: 46), translates by 'lest ye enter' in Mark and Luke. In the following clause it gives in Mark, 'the spirit truly is ready,' but in Matt. where the Greek has exactly the same words, it translates, **the spirit indeed is willing,** the word 'indeed' being used to translate the Greek word *men*, a particle which merely indicates that to its clause something else will presently be brought in contrast; comp. on 3: 11 or 9: 37. The emphasis is on 'spirit,' not at all on 'indeed.' This is given as a general proposition, suggested by their case. **The flesh** means not simply the body as opposed to the mind, but the body as representing our sinfulness, being so used because bodily sins are patent; while the spirit represents what is better in us, regarded as produced by divine influence. Comp. a similar contrast between body and spirit, or flesh and spirit, frequently occurring in Paul's Epistles. This statement was not added by way of excuse, as some have imagined, but of warning and incentive. The fact that while the spirit is willing the flesh is weak forms a reason why we should watchfully and prayerfully strive to keep out of temptation, lest it take advantage of our weakness and overcome us. *Eu-*

thym.: "Do not look to the soul's readiness and be bold, but look to the flesh's weakness and be humble."

42-44. He withdraws the second and third times. **He went away again the second time.** When one is in very bitter grief, and, after being for some while alone, comes back to his friends, it is natural, especially if they do not seem very sympathetic, that presently a great wave of sorrow should come afresh over his soul, and he must again seek to bear it alone. **If this cup may not pass away.** Correct text omits 'cup.' The Rev. Ver. has more literally *cannot*. 'May not' is a quite different and feebler expression, the question being not merely as to the permissible, but the possible, as in v. 39. Mark (Rev. Ver.) says, 'and prayed, saying the same words.' They are, as given by Matt., substantially the same as the first time, and yet we note a certain progress. He does not now begin by asking that the cup may pass away, and afterwards attain resignation; he begins with the assumption that it cannot be otherwise (which the Greek phrase implies), and at once expresses resignation. The third time, Matthew also has, 'saying the same words.' This was very different from the "vain repetitions" condemned in 6: 7. Impassioned feeling sometimes makes repetition natural. **Thy will be done,** the same phrase as in the model prayer, 6: 10. **Asleep again.** Alas! not even from ardent Peter, and the impassioned "disciple whom Jesus loved," could he find sympathy in this terrible time. Mark adds (Bib. Un. Ver.), 'and they knew not what to answer him.' Their minds were confused at the thought of the Messiah dying, of the miracle-worker slain, of the Master forsaking the disciples, and this increased their dull drowsiness. Luke does not mention his withdrawing three separate times, but makes one general statement (Luke 22: 40-46), substantially equivalent to the more detailed narrative of Matthew and Mark. **Again.** The Greek word for this (*palin*) occurs twice in v. 44, ac-

[1] If connected with both terms, the dependent clause is final; if taken only with 'pray,' it is non-final, see on 5: 29. Origen, Chrys., etc. use the infinitive (and so Luke 22: 40), which is the classical construction to con-

vey the idea often expressed in 'later' Greek by *hina* non-final; and the infinitive in this connection could not be taken with 'watch.'

43 And he came and found them asleep again: for their eyes were heavy.
44 And he left them, and went away again, and prayed the third time, saying the same words.
45 Then cometh he to his disciples, and saith unto them, Sleep on now, and take *your* rest: behold, the hour is at hand, and the Son of man is betrayed into the hands of sinners.
46 Rise, let us be going: behold, he is at hand that doth betray me.
47 And while he yet spake, lo, Judas, one of the twelve, came, and a great multitude with swords and staves, from the chief priests and elders of the people.

43 drink it, thy will be done. And he came again and found them sleeping, for their eyes were heavy.
44 And he left them again, and went away, and prayed
45 a third time, saying again the same words. Then cometh he to the disciples, and saith unto them, Sleep on now, and take your rest: behold, the hour is at hand, and the Son of man is betrayed unto the
46 hands of sinners. Arise, let us be going: behold, he is at hand that betrayeth me.
47 And while he yet spake, lo, Judas, one of the twelve, came, and with him a great multitude with swords and staves, from the chief priests and elders of the

cording to the best documents. **The third time.** Yet again the wave of sorrow came rolling over his soul. It must have been something awful and overwhelming, if Jesus found it so hard to bear. Was this dread cup merely the bodily pains and the shame of approaching crucifixion? Was it merely the interruption of a good man's course of self-denying and loving usefulness? Why, many of his followers have faced impending death, even at the stake, without once praying that they might, if possible, be spared the trial; have in the very midst of the torturing flames been found "rejoicing that they were counted worthy to suffer" all this for him. Were they sustained by conscious innocence? He alone was perfectly innocent. Were they supported by the remembrance of good already done, by unselfish devotion to human welfare and to God's glory, by the indwelling Spirit? In all respects, he much more. The agony of Gethsemane, and the cry of the forsaken on Calvary, can be accounted for, in one of strong and sinless character, only when we remember how it is said, "Him who knew no sin he made to be sin on our behalf." "He was wounded for our transgressions, he was bruised for our iniquities"; "Who his own self bare our sins in his body on the tree." (2 Cor. 5: 21, Rev. Ver.; Isa. 53: 5; 1 Pet. 2: 24, Rev. Ver.) The effect of these agonizing supplications is referred to in Heb. 5: 7-9, Rev. Ver. He was "heard for his godly fear," and while the cup did not pass away, he became through suffering completely fitted to sympathize and to save. (Heb. 2: 18; 4: 15; 5: 7 ff.) We need not then be surprised that our prayers also are often answered by granting, not what we at first asked, but something better.

45 f. His final return. **Sleep on now, and take your rest.** This is a "permissive imperative." (Winer, 311 [391], Ellicott, "Hist. Lect."). He has no further need of their keeping awake; his struggles in the soli-

tude close by are past. So far as concerns the object for which he desired them to watch (v. 38), they may now yield to sleep without any effort to resist. But the close of his season of struggle is promptly followed by the approach of a new experience for him and for them. It may be (Hackett) that just after saying 'sleep on now,' his eye caught the gleam of the torches descending the steep declivity beyond the ravine of Kidron and coming towards them. **Behold,** calling attention, as so often in Matt. **The hour is at hand,** *has come near,* the same expression as in 3: 2; and so in v. 46. **The Son of man,** the Messiah, see on 8: 20. **Is betrayed,** present tense, because just on the point of occurring. The word really means 'is delivered,' comp. on 26: 23. **Into the hands of sinners.** The Greek has no article, but means, 'into sinners' hands,' indicating not the particular persons, but the kind of persons. The reference is not to the mere officials sent to lay hands on him, but to the wicked authorities, the Sanhedrin. **Rise, let us be going,** looks to what is just beginning, as 'sleep on now,' based itself on what had just ended. He does not propose to go away and avoid those who are approaching, but to go forth from the enclosure and meet them. (John 18: 4 ff.) Other proposed explanations of the apparent conflict between v. 45 and v. 46 may be found copiously discussed in Morison.

II. 47-56. JESUS DELIVERED UP BY JUDAS, AND SEIZED BY THE SOLDIERS. (Mark 14: 43-52; Luke 22: 47-53; John 18: 2-12.) **And while he yet spake.** So Mark and Luke, and comp. John 18: 4. He foresaw not only 'the hour,' but the moment. **Judas,** see on 10: 4; 27: 3. He had probably gone to the house where the supper was eaten, and not finding them there, had come on to the well-known garden. (John 18: 1 f.) **A great multitude, with swords and staves.** So Mark. John (Rev. Ver. *margin*), says that

48 Now he that betrayed him gave them a sign, saying, Whomsoever I shall kiss, that same is he; hold him fast.

49 And forthwith he came to Jesus, and said, Hail, Master; and kissed him.

50 And Jesus said unto him, Friend, wherefore art thou come? Then came they, and laid hands on Jesus, and took him.

48 people. Now he that betrayed him gave them a sign, saying, Whomsoever I shall kiss, that is he:

49 take him. And straightway he came to Jesus, and

50 said, Hail, Rabbi; and ¹ kissed him. And Jesus said unto him, Friend, *do* that for which thou art come. Then they came and laid hands on Jesus, and took

---

1 Gr, *kissed him much.*

Judas received 'the cohort' of soldiers, which, if full, would be several hundred men, and the extreme solicitude of the Jewish rulers lest the Galilean crowds attending the feast should rescue Jesus might well account for so large a force; but the word may be used generally for a 'band' of men. The article suggests the particular cohort or band then garrisoning the temple. It was commanded by a chiliarch, or military tribune, a rank higher than our colonel. (John 18: 12; comp. Acts 21: 31 ff.) Edersh. suggests that so large a force and so high an officer commanding would hardly have been furnished without the knowledge of Pilate, and this might account for the anxious dream of Pilate's wife. (27: 19.) It was common to strengthen the garrison of the Castle of Antonia at the time of the great feasts, in order to restrain the throngs in the city and in the temple courts (Acts 21: 31 ff.), just as the Turks do now at Easter. This 'band' cannot have been Jewish soldiers, for the Romans would not have allowed bodies of armed natives in what was now a regular Roman province. The 'great multitude' may have included many followers through curiosity, as people were moving about through the whole of the passover night. Whatever was the number of soldiers, there was at any rate a military force to support the officials sent to make the arrest, which was not the case at the attempt of six months earlier. (John 7: 32.) Besides the weapons, John says the party had 'lanterns and torches.' The moon was full, for the passover came at the middle of the month, and the month began with the new moon, but the officials might expect to have occasion for search in dark places, and for assured identification. **From the chief priests and elders.** Mark adds, 'the Scribes,' thus showing more plainly that the Sanhedrin is meant, see on 26: 59. We learn presently from Luke 22: 52 that some of these dignitaries were themselves among the multitude. So there were soldiers (John), temple officials (Luke, John), at least one servant of

the high-priest (Matt., Mark, Luke), and some of the chief-priests and elders (Luke); altogether 'a great multitude' (Matt., Mark, Luke).

48-50. Jesus is pointed out and seized. **Gave them a sign,** gave it when they set out together. All the better instincts of human nature revolt at the treacherous disciple's kiss. The kiss was a common form of salutation, but only between friends. And Judas seems to have pretended a very marked friendliness; for both Matt. and Mark, in saying 'and kissed him' (v. 49), do not use the simple verb as before, but compound it with a preposition, so as to mean kissed frequently, eagerly, warmly. (Rev. Ver., *margin.*) There is the same change from the simple to the compound verb in Luke 7: 45 f., where the latter denotes warm affection; comp. also the prodigal's father (Luke 15: 20), and Paul's friends. (Acts 20: 37.) The distinction is recognized by Meyer, Ellicott, Grimm, Alford, Morison, Edersh. Comp. Prov. 27: 6, Rev. Ver. "The kisses of an enemy are profuse." **Hold him fast,** *take him,* the same word as in v. 4, 50, and 55, and the translation ought not to be varied. Our Lord is described by John as coming voluntarily forward to the multitude and avowing himself to be the person they were seeking; and this while Judas was standing with them. We may perhaps suppose that Judas, to fulfill his contract and earn his reward, stepped forward notwithstanding and gave the appointed sign. And the occasion for this may have been afforded by the fact that the multitude, overawed by the calm majesty of the Saviour as he avowed himself, "went backward and fell to the ground." (John 18: 6.) Moreover, the Roman officer might not know but that some other person was pretending to be the one whom he sought, and would naturally wait for the sign agreed upon. **Master,** or *Rabbi.* This term was often used by the disciples in addressing Jesus, comp. on 8: 19. **Friend** is not the common Greek term, but signifies *compan-*

51 And, behold, one of them which were with Jesus stretched out *his* hand, and drew his sword, and struck a servant of the high priest, and smote off his ear.

52 Then said Jesus unto him, Put up again thy sword into his place: for all they that take the sword shall perish with the sword.

53 Thinkest thou that I cannot now pray to my Father, and he shall presently give me more than twelve legions of angels?

51 him. And behold, one of them that were with Jesus stretched out his hand, and drew his sword, and smote the [1] servant of the high priest, and struck off his ear.

52 Then saith Jesus unto him. Put up again thy sword into its place: for all they that take the

53 sword shall perish with the sword. Or thinkest thou that I cannot beseech my Father, and he shall even now send me more than twelve legions of angels?

---

1 Or, *bondservant.*

---

ion, 'comrade,' as in 20 : 13. He had long been an every-day associate, and Jesus reminds him of this fact. (*Do that*) *for which thou art come.* This is the natural meaning of the Greek, and not, **Wherefore art thou come?** The Greek pronoun used is not an interrogative, but a relative, which as very often in Greek and Latin suggests its antecedent, '(that) for which thou art come.' We then have to supply a verb, which might be 'tell' (Morison, 'say'), 'mind' (Meyer), or better 'do.' (Euthym.) This accords with the saying given by Luke, 'Judas, betrayest thou the Son of man with a kiss?' and with John 13 : 27, Bib. Un. Ver., 'What thou doest, do quickly.' 'Wherefore,' in Com. Ver., would imply that Jesus did not know, and would seem to conflict with Luke. '(What is that) for which thou art come,' is also a possible way of supplying the gap.[1] **Laid hands on Jesus and took him.** The binding (John 18:12) seems to have occurred a little later, when they were about to lead him away.

51-54. The disciple's rash attempt at defence. **One** is the numeral, not simply 'some one.' John tells (18:10) that it was Simon Peter, and gives also the name of the man smitten, Malchus. The names were perhaps omitted by Matt., Mark, and Luke because Peter was still living when they wrote, and might have been seized on this pretext in any season of special persecution by the Jews (comp. Acts 21 : 27); while when John wrote, Peter was dead. Comp. on 26 : 7. **Stretched out his hand and drew his sword,** details all the circumstances, as in 5 : 1 f. and often. Luke says (22 : 49) that others of the Twelve in sympathy with Peter united with him in asking, 'Lord, shall we smite with the sword?' And one of them (rash Peter) did not wait

for the answer, but smote. **A** (*the*) **servant of the high priest.** The word is *doulon,* 'slave,' see on 8: 6. But a slave of the high-priest would have, under the circumstances, a sort of official character. All four Evangelists mention this, for it was an important circumstance, greatly increasing the peril of Peter's position. His invincible self-confidence had made him fall asleep notwithstanding the Master's warnings. Now, suddenly awakening, he saw the new comers laying hands on the Master, and with a sudden impulse he attacked and wounded a person having official importance. **Smote off his ear,** having evidently intended to smite his head a deadly blow. Peter came very near (Alf.) being like Barabbas and his followers, "who in the insurrection had committed murder." (Mark 15 : 7.) Luke and John mention that it was the right ear, and we can see exactly how the blow missed. **Return thy sword into his place.** 'His' is the original possessive of it (hyt), see on 24: 32. Notice that Jesus does not bid him throw away the sword. **All they that take the sword,** etc. Comp. Rev. 13: 10. Christ's followers are not to carry on his work with carnal weapons. *Lutter.:* "Christ has no other sword than the sword of his mouth. (Rev. 2 : 16.) Those who wish to fight for him must in like manner have no other." Even as a matter of general human prudence, men who carry weapons in a civilized country are on the whole in much greater danger than men who do not. **Thinkest thou,** etc., lit., or if this consideration does not restrain you, take another view of the matter (comp. on 7 : 9), *thinkest thou that I cannot beseech my Father,* is the exact translation, not simply 'pray.' **Now** (rather *even now*), in the common Greek text is connected with 'beseech,'

---

1 Winer, Buttm., and Grimm, and many commentators, take the pronoun as used interrogatively, being influenced by a traditional interpretation (from the Vulgate). But there are no clear examples of such a use of the relative *hos* (comp. Meyer), and it is highly im-

probable in itself. The examples collected by Moulton in his Winer, 207 f., are all readily explained as relative with the antecedent understood, or as attracted relative.

54 But how then shall the Scriptures be fulfilled, that thus it must be?

55 In that same hour said Jesus to the multitudes, Are ye come out as against a thief with swords and staves for to take me? I sat daily with you teaching in the temple, and ye laid no hold on me.

56 But all this was done, that the Scriptures of the prophets might be fulfilled. Then all the disciples forsook him, and fled.

54 How then should the scriptures be fulfilled, that thus it must be? In that hour said Jesus to the multitudes, Are ye come out as against a robber with swords and staves to seize me? I sat daily in the temple teaching, and ye took me not. But all this is come to pass, that the scriptures of the prophets might be fulfilled. Then all the disciples left him, and fled.

---

but in ℵ B L, and most of the early versions it is connected with 'shall send' as in Rev. Ver. **Give,** or supply, furnish. **More than twelve legions of angels.** To protect twelve men (himself and the eleven), he might have twelve legions and more of defenders. If a cohort seemed formidable, he might have legions. A full Roman legion at that day contained some six thousand men. Of course the expression is general, a round number, and stated strongly. He is not helplessly submitting through lack of strength and of protection (comp. 2 Kings 6: 17), but is voluntarily yielding himself to those who design putting him to death. He could easily avoid all that is coming, but **how then shall the Scriptures be fulfilled, that thus it must be?** viz., that the Messiah must be despised and rejected, must suffer and die (comp. Luke 24: 25 f.). 'The Scriptures,' a technical term among the Jews, denoting the collection of books which we call the Old Testament, see on 21: 42. Only Matt. gives here the reference to prophecy, a matter in which he took peculiar interest, as writing especially for Jewish readers; but Mark also gives the parallel to v. 56. John (18: 11) records another expression in harmony with v. 52-54, "The cup which my Father has given me, shall I not drink it"? Just after, or just before, thus speaking to Peter, he spoke also (Luke 22: 51) to the persons who were arresting him, "Suffer ye thus far"; suffer the resistance of the mistaken but well-meaning follower to go thus far without punishing him. Then immediately healing the ear by a miraculous touch, he induced them to let the rash disciple alone.

55 f. Having rebuked the disciple, and conciliated the persons immediately engaged in arresting him, Jesus now turns to **the multitudes** that thronged around. Luke shows (22: 52) that among them were chief priests and captains of the temple and elders, who might naturally enough, in their extreme solicitude, come along to see that the perilous

arrest was surely and safely made. **In that same hour** (comp. 18: 1), viz., at the time when they were engaged in arresting him; but it is not easy to see why this more emphatic expression is used instead of the simple 'then.' Perhaps the following words were well known among the Christians to have been spoken by Jesus, and Matt. means to say that this was the time of their utterance. Mark and Luke have a simple 'and.' **Are ye come out as against a thief,** etc. Better as in Rev. Ver., *as if against a robber are ye come out with swords and staves to seize me?* Not a 'thief,' but the quite different Greek word meaning 'robber,' see on 27: 38. A thief would try to escape by flight, a robber was likely to resist, and they must bring weapons to apprehend him. 'Seize' is in the Greek a stronger term than that of v. 48, 50, and end of 55; Mark makes exactly the same distinction. Jesus reproaches the multitudes with coming against him as if a man of violence. There had been abundant opportunity of arresting him without difficulty. **I sat,** imperfect tense, continued or habitual action. This posture, which was common for a teacher (5:1), would have made it easy to seize him, and also indicated quiet innocence. **Daily,** for several days of the preceding week; possibly it points back also to earlier periods of teaching at Jerusalem, recorded only in the Fourth Gospel. **With you,** is wanting in some of the best documents. **In the temple,** *hieron,* the general sacred enclosure and edifices (see on 4: 5); he taught in the Court of the Gentiles and the Court of Israel; not being of the tribe of Levi, we may be sure he never entered the *naos,* nor the Court of the Priests. **And ye laid no hold on me.** He thus reminds them that he had given no occasion for their treating him as violent and dangerous. nor for their arresting him at all. **But all this was done,** *is come to pass* (comp. on 1: 22), still the Saviour's words, as clearly shown by Mark 14: 49. In the course of Providence this plotting and arresting had all taken place, **that the Scriptures might be fulfilled;** though the human actors had no such design. **The Scriptures of the prophets,** because the reference is especially to the predictive portions of Scripture, the Messianic prophecies; comp. at the crucifixion, John 19: 28. Luke records the additional saying, in harmony with that given here, "But this is your hour, and the power of darkness." The purpose of redemption now permitted that great wrong, which was to be wonderfully overruled for good. **Then all the disciples forsook him and fled.** In judging them, we must remember that the Master had forbidden all resistance, and had distinctly said he was about to leave them. Mark adds (14: 51 f.) an account of a certain young man who left his solitary garment when he was seized by the captors, and fled. The mention of this slight incident may be sufficiently accounted for by the fact that it shows how great was the terror felt by the followers of Jesus. Some think, however, that it is to be regarded as a personal reminiscence, the youth being Mark himself, whose mother is found living at Jerusalem a dozen years later (Acts 12: 12); and it is suggested (Weiss, Edersh.) that the youth had followed Jesus and the disciples from the house in which they had eaten the passover, and so that the hospitable householder was Mark's father. There is very slight ground for this conjecture, or for the notion that it was Lazarus of Bethany. We find afterwards that Peter and John must have speedily returned. (26: 58; John 18: 15.) They might be regarded as exceptions to the general statement that all fled; but the Saviour had also made a general prediction (26: 31, R. V.), 'All ye shall be offended because of me this night.'—So the officials and the soldiers led Jesus away (John 18: 13); and mean time (*Weiss*, "Life"), "Jerusalem slept in peace, and did not know what had happened."

HOMILETICAL AND PRACTICAL.

V. 37. The three disciples in Gethsemane. 1) How hard to realize the significance of great crises in life. 2) How imperfect is all human sympathy with the Divine Redeemer. 3) How readily does human infirmity weigh down the willing spirit. 4) How watchful we should be in all times of special trial. 5) How great the privilege of praying that we may not come into temptation.—Three witnesses of three scenes. 1) Their Master's power, Mark 5: 37. 2) Their Master's glory, Matt. 17: 1. 3) Their Master's agony.—V. 39. Three prayers of Jesus. 1) The prayer he taught his disciples to pray. 2) The prayer he offered in behalf of his disciples, John 17. 3) The prayer he made in his own behalf. ALFORD: "All conflict of the holy soul is prayer; all its struggles are continued communion with God. When Abraham's faith was to be put to so sore a trial, he says, 'I and the lad will *go yonder and worship.*' Our Lord (almost on the same spot) unites in himself (Stier) as the priest and victim, Abraham's faith and Isaac's patience."—The three gardens, Eden, Gethsemane, Paradise. The fall of man in Eden made necessary the agony of man's Saviour in Gethsemane, and this made possible the admission of man into the Paradise on high.—V. 40 f. Even in this season of special suffering he has time to counsel his disciples; so on the cross he prays for his murderers; provides for his mother, and answers the request of his companion in suffering.—V. 41. Safety as regards temptation. 1) Temptation is dangerous because the flesh is weak. 2) Our only real safety is in *avoiding* temptation. 3) In order to this, let us be watchful and prayerful.—V. 42. PRESSENSE: "Not thy will but mine be done, changed Paradise into a desert; not my will but thine be done, changed the desert into Paradise, and made Gethsemane the gate of glory."— V. 43. Their eyes were heavy. BENGEL: "Such slothfulness often holds the pious when it is least becoming."—V. 45 f. Rest and arise. It is often the case that when one cause of anxiety has ceased and left us a moment's rest, in the next moment some new trouble comes, and we must arise to face it.— V. 47-54. The betrayal of Jesus. 1) The traitor's kiss, and the Saviour's calm response. 2) The rash disciple's blow, and the Saviour's mild rebuke. 3) The Saviour's determination, though he could escape in a moment, to fulfill the Scriptures and work out the world's salvation.

57-68. JESUS SENTENCED BY THE SANHEDRIN.

This is found also in Mark 14: 53-65; Luke 22: 54, 63-65; John 18: 12-14, 19-24.

57 And they that had laid hold on Jesus led *him* away to Caiaphas the high priest, where the scribes and the elders were assembled.

57 And they that had taken Jesus led him away to *the house of* Caiaphas the high priest, where the

---

The trial of our Lord may be divided into two main parts, the Jewish and the Roman trial. Each of these must be subdivided. (1) The Jewish trial comprises (a) The examination before Annas, John 18: 12-14, 19-23; (b) The sentence by an informal session of the Sanhedrin, Matt. 26: 57-68; Mark 14: 53-65; (c) The formal trial before the Sanhedrin, which sends him to Pilate for sentence, Matt. 27: 1 f.; Luke 22: 66-71. (2) The Roman trial includes (a) The first examination before Pilate, 27: 11-14; John 18: 28-38; (b) The reference to Herod, Luke 23: 6-12; (c) The final appearance before Pilate, 27: 15-31; John 18: 39-19: 16. It is noticeable that John gives a good deal as to the Roman trial that is not found in the other Gospels, particularly as to Pilate's private inquiries. Mark continues to resemble Matt. Luke has some matter not found in the others.

Our present section contains the trial before an informal session of the Sanhedrin. It may be divided into v. 57 f.; 59-63a; 63b-66; 67 f.

I. **57 f.** Jesus is brought before Caiaphas and the Scribes and Elders. Peter follows and looks on. (Mark 14: 53 f.; Luke 22: 54; John 18: 15, 24.) **They that had laid hold on Jesus,** at Gethsemane. **Led him away to Caiaphas, the high priest.** The appended 'where' implies that this means to the house of Caiaphas, and that is distinctly stated in Luke. Caiaphas was the son-in-law of Annas, Ananus, or Hanan, who had long before been high priest himself, and among the numerous changes of the time, was succeeded by five sons and this son-in-law (Jos., "Ant.," 18, 2, 1 f.; 20, 9, 1.) The family were all Sadducees (Jos., Talmud), and were specially odious to the Pharisees, the "house of Annas" becoming a by-word (Talmud). Joseph Caiaphas was deposed shortly after Pilate lost the procuratorship, A. D. 36 ("Ant.," 18, 4, 2 f.) The time when he was made high priest depends on an obscure statement of Jos. ("Ant.," 18, 2, 2.) His expressions leave hardly more than four years between Annas and Caiaphas. Either Annas officiated about A. D. 7-21, and then Caiaphas A. D. 25-36, or Annas A. D. 7-14, and then

Caiaphas A. D. 18-36. The son Eleazar came between Annas and Caiaphas; Jonathan and Theophilus (Keim) A. D. 36 f.; Matthias A. D. 42 f.; Annas, junior ("Ant.," 20, 9, 1) A. D. 63. This makes the last a different person from the high priest Ananias of Acts 23: 2; 24: 1, A. D. 58. The character of Caiaphas appears from John 11: 49-52, and from the trial of Jesus, to have been shrewd, self-seeking, and unscrupulous. **Where the scribes and the elders were assembled.** Mark mentions also (14: 53) 'all the chief priests,' and these are expressly mentioned just after by Matthew, v. 59. These were the three classes composing the Sanhedrin (see on v. 59.) Instead of 'were assembled' (Com. Ver.), it is better to translate *were gathered together*, for the former would indicate a formal session of the Sanhedrin, while the Greek term is neutral on that point. Mark's phrase is simply 'there come together with him,' and the fact seems to be that this was an informal gathering before dawn, whereas, a formal session could not be held till 'morning was come.' (27: 1.)

It was apparently while the dignitaries were gathering at that unseasonable hour, that Jesus was first questioned by Annas. (John 18: 12-14.) Annas and Caiaphas were both regarded as high priests (Luke 3: 2), the former still in popular estimation holding the office as long as he lived, while the latter only was recognized by the Romans. So in 1 Kings 4: 4, Zadok and Abiathar are mentioned as priests, it having been stated in 2: 35 that the king put Zadok in the room of Abiathar. An action would be valid in the eyes of both the people and the Romans if known to have the approval of both Caiaphas and Annas. This was easier from the fact that Caiaphas was son-in-law to Annas; and the supposition (Euthym. and various recent writers) that Annas at this time lived with Caiaphas in the high priest's official residence, each having his own reception room, will account for all the statements in the several Gospels. It is also a plausible conjecture (Wieseler, Ewald), that Annas may have been at this period president (Nasi) of the Sanhedrin. John distinctly states that they "led him to Annas first; for he was

58 But Peter followed him afar off unto the high priest's palace, and went in, and sat with the servants, to see the end.

58 scribes and the elders were gathered together. But Peter followed him afar off, unto the court of the high priest, and entered in, and sat with the officers,

---

father-in-law to Caiaphas, who was high priest that year." (Rev. Ver.) Then after mentioning some things about Caiaphas and about Peter, John states that "the high priest" questioned Jesus "of his disciples, and of his teachings" (Rev. Ver.); but the Saviour declined a response, saying that he had taught publicly, and those who had heard him could be asked. Then John adds (correct text, Rev. Ver.), "Annas therefore sent him bound unto Caiaphas the high priest." This seems to leave no doubt that the high priest who first vainly interrogated Jesus was Annas. Many of the ablest recent writers have taken this view, while not a few still think otherwise.[1] Thus understood, this was not a trial, but a mere personal interrogation by an aged ex-high priest. John gives no account of the trial before Caiaphas and the Sanhedrin, that having been fully described by the earlier Gospels. Indeed, it may be (Weiss, "Life") that John mentions this preliminary examination only because of its connection with the first of Peter's denials.

But Peter followed him afar off, viz., followed him from Gethsemane (comp. on 26 : 56). Really attached to the Master, and still self-confident, he was yet alarmed by the probable consequences of his smiting the high priest's servant, and so he took a middle course; John went along with the party who conducted Jesus; the other disciples fled; Peter followed at a distance. *Alexander:* "However unexpected the fact here recorded, there is probably no reader who, as soon as it is stated, does not feel it to be perfectly in keeping with what he knows already of the character of Peter, who would scarcely seem to be himself if he continued in concealment, and whose re-appearance on the scene, and subsequent performance there, exhibit just the strength and weakness which together constitute the native temper of this great apostle." **Unto the high priest's palace,** see

on 26 : 3. The building was doubtless four-square, surrounding an open court. Upon this court opened the rooms, one of which formed the audience room of the high priest, and probably another that of Annas. John gives the further details that Peter reached the house only after the procession had all entered and the gate was closed; and that he (John), being "known unto the high priest," . . . . . went out "and spake unto her that kept the door, and brought in Peter." **And sat with the servants,** or *officers.* Tyndale, etc., 'servants,' Greek *huperetes,* see on 8: 6. John adds (18 : 8) that "the servants (*douloi*) and the officers stood there, who had made a fire of coals; for it was cold." At the time of the passover it is quite hot in Jerusalem at mid-day, but frequently grows cold towards morning. As to the fact that Matt. says 'sat,' and John 'standing,' it is easy to meet so trifling a difficulty by remembering that they would be likely to change posture. **To see the end.** He was anxious as to the matter, and determined to see it through, but not humble, watchful, and prayerful (26 : 40 f.), or he would not have become involved in such difficulty. The further account of Peter see below in 26 : 69-75. Bengel: "Here mid-way between courage (v. 51) and cowardice. (v. 70.)"

II. 59-63 a. Vain attempts to convict Jesus by false witness. Mark 14: 55-59. Luke does not mention this informal gathering of the Sanhedrin, but only the formal session "as soon as it was day." (Luke 22: 66; comp. Matt. 27:1.) Many expositors identify the two meetings; but the supposition of a previous informal meeting is natural in itself, as many of the rulers would be anxiously awaiting the result of Judas' expedition, and this supposition accounts for all the phenomena of the narrative; accordingly it is adopted by Wieseler, Alford, Godet, Keim, and various other recent writers. Edersh. insists that neither of these was a regular session of the

---

[1] Vedder ("Bibl. Sac.," Oct. 1882), calls it a "clumsy and improbable hypothesis," and says, "There is something ludicrous in the statement, 'Now Annas sent him away bound to Caiaphas,' if the sending away consisted in a removal from one apartment to another in the same house." But he has laid an unwarranted stress upon

the *apo,* failing to notice that *stello* is not used in New Test. (except twice in the middle voice), and *apostello* is frequently employed where there is no distinctive notion of sending *away.* Moreover, sending from one audience room to another, across a large court, was not a trifling removal.

59 Now the chief priests, and elders, and all the council, sought false witness against Jesus, to put him to death ;
60 But found none: yea, though many false witnesses came, *yet* found they none. At the last came two false witnesses,

59 to see the end. Now the chief priests and the whole council sought false witness against Jesus, that they
60 might put him to death; and they found it not,

Sanhedrin, and there was no formal condemnation of Jesus by that body ; but his line of argument is far from convincing. Geikie adopts the same view from the Jewish writer Jost. **Chief priests, and elders, and all the council,** or Sanhedrin. The phrase suggests that the chief priests formed a part of the Sanhedrin, and that this was a full meeting. While no exception is here mentioned, we know from Luke (23 : 50 f., R. V.) that Joseph of Arimathea "had not consented to their counsel and deed," and we infer the same as to Nicodemus from the accounts in John. It would not be an improbable supposition that the rulers had avoided informing Nicodemus of this meeting (comp. John 7 : 50-52). A quorum of the Sanhedrin was twenty three (Lf.), but this was "all the Sanhedrin," a very full meeting.

The Sanhedrin was in the time of our Lord the highest court of the Jews. Our knowledge of its constitution and functions is but fragmentary. It arose during the Greek or the Maccabaean period. The very name is a mere Hebrew spelling of the Greek *sunedrion* ('sitting together'), the *h* of *hedra*, lost in the Greek compound, being restored in the transliteration, as has frequently happened. The Mishna supposes that the Sanhedrin was a survival of the council of seventy formed by Moses (Num. 11 : 16), and infers that it also must have contained seventy members, or adding one for Moses, then seventy-one. It is probable that this was the number, but we cannot certainly determine. The constitution of the body is not described by the Talmud, but the New Test. shows (27 : 1 ; Mark 15 : 1 ; Luke 22 : 66) that it consisted of chief priests, elders, and scribes, though we know not in what proportions, nor what sort of elders were included. As to the chief priests and the scribes, see on 2: 4. The chief priests are usually mentioned first, and would naturally be the ruling section of the body. They were for the most part Sadducees, while the scribes were probably all Pharisees. The presidency of the body seems to have been elective, but the high priest was commonly the person elected. The Sanhedrin tried (Schürer) all the more important secular and religious, civil and criminal causes, the less important being tried by inferior local tribunals. It seems highly probable, though not certain (see the difficulties well stated by Vedder, p. 666 ff.), that the Sanhedrin's death-sentence could at this period be executed only by the procurator's permission. In John 18: 31, the Jews say to Pilate, "It is not lawful for us to put any man to death." Some argue that the Romans had taken away this power when Judea first became a province, as they are known to have done in some other provinces. The Jerus. Talmud says (Sanh. i, 1 ; vii, 2), "Forty years before the destruction of the temple, judgments upon life and death were taken away from Israel." This date is probably given (Schürer) in a round number, as was natural three hundred years later. The crucifixion was probably in the forty-first year before the destruction of the temple. The stoning of Stephen was a tumultuary proceeding, and probably occurred at a time when there was no procurator. The regular place of meeting of the Sanhedrin was at a hall either in or near the temple area (Jos. and the Mishna differ). It is stated in the Talmud that forty years before the destruction of the temple the Sanhedrin ceased to meet in its hall, and met in shops; these may have been in the outer court of the temple, which the Saviour more than once cleansed. At any rate, a special meeting at the high priest's residence would not be surprising in such an emergency as the trial of Jesus, when in various ways they were departing from custom. Moreover, it may have been only the informal meeting that was held at the high priest's house; the formal session of 27: 1, may have been at their hall—notice especially 'led him away' in Luke 22: 66 (Rev. Ver., correct text).

Sought false witness, imperfect tense, describing them as engaged in seeking. **To,** or, *that they might,* **put him to death.** They must have sufficient evidence for sentencing him to death, in order that they might gain the Roman governor's authority to execute

61 And said, This *fellow* said, I am able to destroy the temple of God, and to build it in three days.
62 And the high priest arose, and said unto him, Answerest thou nothing? what *is it which* these witness against thee?

61 though many false witnesses came. But afterward came two, and said, This man said, I am able to destroy the [1] temple of God, and to build it in three 62 days. And the high priest stood up, and said unto him, Answerest thou nothing? what is it which

---

1 Or, *sanctuary:* as in ch. xxiii. 35; xxvii. 5.

---

the sentence. **Though many false witnesses came.**[1] This was easy to bring about through the continued exertions of influential men comp. Acts 6 : 11; in fact, they had no doubt been for some time hunting up witnesses. (26:4 f.) Anywhere in Asia, not to speak of other countries, there are hangers on about the courts ready to sell testimony. Mark explains (14:56) that 'their witness agreed not together.' The Sanhedrin could not afford to disregard the ordinary forms of judicial procedure. Their proceedings could not be permanently kept secret. The law expressly forbade the death penalty upon the testimony of a single witness. (Num. 35:30; Deut. 17:6.) Here there were many witnesses, each making a separate accusation, but not two to the same count. It is vain to conjecture what were the various and conflicting false testimonies. **At the last** (*afterward*) **came two.** The Com. text adds 'false witnesses,' from the preceding verse. We might suppose that these two agreed in their testimony; but Mark (14:59, Rev. Ver.) says, "and not even so did their witness agree together," probably meaning that it did not so agree concerning the circumstances and terms of the alleged statement to be credible. The Mishna, treatise 'Sanhedrin,' gives detailed directions concerning witnesses, one of which is ("Sanh.," V., 1) that each witness must be asked seven questions as to the alleged offence, viz., in what period of seven years (counting from the Sabbatical year) it occurred, in what year of the period, in what month, day of the month, day of the week, hour of the day, and at what place; and the limits are indicated within which two witnesses may differ upon one or another question, without invalidating their testimony. (Comp. Wünsche, or "The Criminal Code of the Jews," London, 1880.) Observe that in Mark (14:58) the witnesses declare, "We heard him say," etc., with emphasis on "we"; and so they could be required to give time and place. We of course do not know how far these strict rules were actually observed two centuries before the Mishna was written down. But while the Sanhedrin was bent on conviction, it would for that reason be all the more careful to observe customary forms. Notice that there seems to have been no call for evidence in Jesus' defence, though he had intimated to Annas (John 18:20 f.) that such evidence might be easily found. The mediæval Jewish fables tried to remove this obvious injustice by declaring that heralds made proclamation for forty days, and no witness appeared in Jesus' behalf. It is hardly necessary to say that Jewish writers do not now claim any respect for these fables, though some of them try to soften the guilt of the Sanhedrin. **This fellow** (rather, *man*) **said.** The Greek for 'this' does not in itself carry such contempt as Tyndale, etc., expressed by 'fellow.' **I am able to destroy.** Mark has 'I will destroy,' substantially equivalent; and so as to the other slight differences between Matt. and Mark. 'Destroy' is literally, 'pull down,' same word as in 5: 17. **The temple,** is here *naon*, the central house, see on 4: 5. **In three days,** or, more correctly, *after three days*, literally, 'with an interval of three days,'[1] as in Acts 24: 17; Gal. 2: 1. This alleged statement was evidently a perversion of what Jesus had said at the first passover of his ministry (John 2: 19), "Destroy this temple, and in three days I will raise it up." He did not even suggest

---

[1] The common text here presents an interesting example of a "conflate reading." True text, 'and they found it not, though many false witnesses came.' Rev. Ver., some documents, 'and though many false witnesses came they found it not.' Conflate text, 'and they found it not, and though many false witnesses came they found it not.' Any body can see that the last was formed by combining the other two; and there are many such readings in the Common Greek text (comp. W H., Int. § 132 ff.).

[2] Meyer and many are here misled by taking *dia* in the sense of 'through,' and overlooking its primary sense of 'between,' from which one derivative sense was that of interval. In 27: 40 and John 2: 19 the phrase employed literally means 'in three days."

63 But Jesus held his peace. And the high priest answered and said unto him, I adjure thee by the living God, that thou tell us whether thou be the Christ, the Son of God.

63 these witness against thee? But Jesus held his peace. And the high priest said unto him, I adjure thee by the living God, that thou tell us whether

the idea of himself destroying the temple, which the Jews would naturally call impious; and we know, as the Sanhedrin might have learned from him if they had desired, that he meant the expression in a merely figurative sense. But we find the same conception still cherished among the Jews in Acts 6: 14. It might be (Edersh.) a good pretext to use with Pilate, that Jesus would encourage popular violence against public and sacred buildings. The Egyptian of Acts 21: 38 promised his followers that from the Mount of Olives they would see the walls of Jerusalem fall at his command, and could march in. But this could hardly be seriously treated as a ground for sentence of death; so the high priest eagerly urges Jesus to answer the accusation, hoping that thus he will somehow criminate himself. This eagerness is indicated by the fact that **he arose,** or *stood up,* Mark likewise, and also by the second question, **what is it,** etc., by which he seeks to arouse the accused into attention and response. It is much more natural to understand the Greek as two questions than as one. **But Jesus held his peace,** literally, *was silent,* comp. Isa: 53: 7. He knew that no explanation or self-defence would be heeded, that his condemnation and sentence was a foregone conclusion; comp. on 27: 14. He was fully prepared for the foreseen result (26: 42), and now awaited it in calm silence. Origen remarks that the utter failure, notwithstanding diligent effort, to find anything against Jesus, shows that his life was most pure and wholly irreprehensible.

III. **63b-66.** Jesus is condemned upon his own testimony. Mark 14: 60-64. Luke, who gives no account of the informal meeting, presently introduces much the same matter into his account of the formal session held "as soon as it was day." (Luke 22: 66-71.) It is very improbable that this was *all* repeated in the formal session (Clark's "Harmony"), and very easy to understand that Luke has thrown all the examination together, while some portions of it would very likely be repeated.

The only matter of great practical importance was that Jesus was condemned by the Sanhedrin, and upon his own confession.—Finding that the false testimony does not suffice for a conviction, and that the accused will not discuss it, the high priest essays a bold stroke. He demands a categorical answer, upon oath, to the question whether Jesus is the Messiah. **And the high priest answered and said unto him.** The Com. text seems to be here right in its reading.[1] The 'answered' means responded to the situation presented by the persistent silence of Jesus (comp. on 11: 25). **I adjure thee,** means exactly 'I put thee on oath.' See the same Greek term in Gen. 24: 3, 'I will make thee swear by the Lord,' and comp. Lev. 5: 1 (Rev. Ver.), where it is declared to be a sin if one who has witnessed a matter "heareth the voice of adjuration" and does not tell what he knows. Comp. also 1 Kings 22: 16. The high priest used the most solemn form of oath, **by the living God.** If one answered after such an adjuration, he answered on oath; the mere ceremony of putting on oath is conventional, as in some parts of our country men take an oath by pointing to heaven, in other parts by kissing the Bible. So then Jesus spoke on oath before a court of justice, which shows conclusively that he did *not* mean to condemn all such oaths when he said, "Swear not at all" (see on 5: 34); that he spoke of oaths familiarly used in conversation. **That thou tell us.** The peculiar Greek construction is explained on 5: 29. **Whether thou be the Christ,** the Messiah, see on 2: 4. Here (Mark and Luke also) K. James rightly inserted the article, though Tyn., Cran., Gen., had simply 'Christ,' as K. J. has in many other places. Luke here gives only 'the Christ'; Mark adds 'the Son of the Blessed'; Matt., **the Son of God.** It is evident from John 19: 7 that 'the Son of God' was understood to mean the Messiah, and that claiming to be the Son of God was considered blasphemy. But it does not follow that the Jews used or understood the phrase as denoting di-

---

[1] Answered' is omitted by ℵ B L, Memph., Origen, Cyril, and various documents; but it may well be an "Alexandrian" alteration due to the apparent incongruity of answering one who was silent.

64 Jesus saith unto him, Thou hast said: nevertheless I say unto you, Hereafter shall ye see the Son of
man sitting on the right hand of power, and coming in
the clouds of heaven.
65 Then the high priest rent his clothes, saying, He
hath spoken blasphemy: what further need have we
of witnesses? behold, now ye have heard his blasphemy.

64 thou be the Christ, the Son of God. Jesus saith
unto him, Thou hast said: nevertheless I say unto
you, Henceforth ye shall see the Son of man sitting
at the right hand of power, and coming on the
65 clouds of heaven. Then the high priest rent his
garments, saying, He hath spoken blasphemy: what
further need have we of witnesses? behold, now ye

---

vinity, since they spoke of blasphemy quite loosely (see on v. 65), and there is no indication in the Jewish books that the Messiah was expected to be divine.—According to our ideas and legal usages, very different from those prevailing in many other countries, it is unjust to call on an accused person to give testimony against himself; and so it is often said that the high priest dealt unjustly in calling on Jesus to testify. The law of Moses provided that in some cases of uncertainty the accused should take an oath upon the matter; see Exod. 22: 10 f.; Num. 5: 19 ff.; 1 Kings 8: 31 f. Thus the high priest's course was not formally illegal, though in spirit and intent it was unjust. It is of late coming to be provided in our laws that an accused person may testify in his own behalf, but cannot be required to criminate himself.

64. Jesus knew that the question was designed to secure a ground of conviction. But he was no longer silent. Now that the crisis had arrived, that his 'hour' was come, he would not decline to say distinctly, before the highest Jewish tribunal, that he was the Messiah. He had long urged the disciples to "tell no man that he was Jesus the Christ," or the Messiah (see on 16: 20), because the crisis must not be precipitated before his work of teaching and healing in every district of the Holy Land was completed. Only a few days before the end he had quietly avoided saying to the rulers that he was the Messiah, while allowing the people to think so (see on 21: 15 f.). But he will not pass to his death as "despised and rejected" without having borne distinct public testimony that he is the Messiah. **Thou hast said,** viz., hast said what is true, a formula of affirmative answer found also in the Talmud (comp. above on 21: 4 f.). In Mark it is directly 'I am.' In Luke (22: 67 f.) the answer is preceded by a censure of their unbelief and unfairness. **Nevertheless.** Although they now scorn his claim to be the Messiah, and reject all the evidence in his teachings and his works, yet they will henceforth see his Messiahship indubitably

manifested. **Hereafter,** *henceforth* is the real meaning. So Luke 22: 69, the Greek in both cases being literally 'from now.' The word refers to something that would be true onward from the time of speaking. The Saviour's death, resurrection, and ascension, the miracles wrought by his apostles and other gifts of the Spirit, the spread of the gospel and its beneficial effects, would go on manifesting him to be the Messiah, **sitting on the right hand of power;** and finally they would behold his second coming **in,** *on,* **the clouds of heaven.** For the phrase, 'the Son of man,' see on 8: 20. This expression would remind the rulers of Dan. 7: 13. By this title Jesus had long virtually claimed to be the Messiah, though not distinctly asserting it in public. 'Power' (so Mark and Luke) is the abstract for the concrete (Meyer); Talmud and Midrash (Gill, Wün.) sometimes use the term 'power' to denote God, as "The Ten Commandments came from the mouth of power." In 22: 42-45 Jesus had spoken of sitting on the right hand of God as a definitely Messianic phrase, and derived from Psa. 110. As to 'coming on the clouds of heaven,' comp. on 24: 30; that was said to the disciples in private; this to the Sanhedrin.

65 f. The high priest has accomplished his object and proceeds to make much of the confession. **Rent his clothes,** the usual expression of grief, horror (Acts 14: 14), or other violent and uncontrollable emotion. The custom, which existed also among the early Greeks and Romans, doubtless originated (Bengel) in the fact that excited emotions often cause one's garments to seem confining. 'Rent' is a compound verb, thoroughly rent to pieces; comp. 2 Kings 18: 57; 19: 1. Mark has the more specific term which denotes the under-garments, of which several were sometimes worn; see on 5: 40. The Talmud directs (Lightf.) that when the judges in a case of blasphemy rend their garments, they must not be sewed up again. Maimonides shows that at least in his time even this expression of uncontrollable emotion was

66 What think ye? They answered and said, He is guilty of death.
67 Then did they spit in his face, and buffeted him; and others smote *him* with the palms of their hands,

66 have heard the blasphemy: what think ye? They
67 answered and said, He is [1] worthy of death. Then did they spit in his face and buffet him: and some smote him [2] with the palms of their hands, saying,

---

1 Gr, *liable to*....2 Or, *with rods*.

formulated by custom; a man rent all garments except the innermost and outermost; and rent from the front of the neck downwards to the length of a hand. The high priest was forbidden in the law (Lev. 10 : 16; 21 : 10) to rend his clothes; but this was in mourning for the dead, because such mourning unfitted him for the performance of official duties, and it was not understood as prohibiting the practice on other occasions; see examples in 1 Maccabees 11: 71; Jos. "War," 2, 15, 4. **He hath spoken blasphemy.** It is not entirely clear, but seems probable, that the high priest here understood the phrase 'the Son of God' as claiming divinity; comp. Luke 23: 70. At any rate Jesus had distinctly claimed it in the added words about sitting at the right hand of power, etc. In John 5: 18, R.V., he was accused of "making himself equal with God," because he "said God was his Father," and in John 10: 50, for saying "I and my Father are one," the Jews sought to stone him, "because that thou, being a man, makest thyself God." It is very hard to determine how much the Jews really meant by these charges, as accusatory expressions are apt to be stronger than would be used in calm declaration. Nor is the question important to us, since the Saviour left no doubt as to the meaning of his answer, and the New Test. as a whole teaches that Jesus Christ is the Son of God in the highest and fullest sense. And certainly, if Jesus had only been a human teacher, he would surely now have explained himself to that effect. **What think ye?** This was the regular Greek phrase for putting any question to the vote. **They answered and said.** They took no formal vote, but decided by acclamation. **He is guilty of death,** or *liable to death* (Rev. Ver. *margin*), as in 5: 21 f., 'in danger of.' So Tyn., Cran., Gen., 'worthy to die'; K. James followed Wyc. and Rheims, 'guilty of death,' comp. Num. 35: 31. The same term is here used in Mark. Death was the legal punishment of blasphemy. (Lev. 24 : 16.)— The Mishna requires ("Sanh." v, 5) that where a vote would condemn to death, the matter

must be postponed to the next day, when after the night's reflection any of those who voted to condemn may change, but not contrariwise. If this rule existed in the traditional law at the time of our Lord, we can image the Sanhedrin evading it by construing that they had virtually voted to condemn Jesus some time before (John 11 : 47-53), or that the meeting after dawn (27 : 1) was virtually another session, with a portion of night for reflection —which would have been a device quite after their fashion. It is, however, probable, as Edersh. and Schürer remark, that these were largely ideal regulations, expressing what the Rabbis thought ought to be done, and by no means strictly followed.

IV. **67 f. Jesus** spit upon, buffeted, and mocked. Mark 14: 65; Luke 22: 63-65. Observe that while Luke has transferred the examination and condemnation to the regular session after dawn, he puts this outrage and mocking first, in the same order as Matt. and Mark. **Then did they spit in his face.** This would most naturally mean the members of the Sanhedrin, mentioned in the preceding sentence, but might mean (comp. 27 : 2) the subordinate officials who had Jesus in custody, and so Luke has it (22 : 63), "the men that held Jesus." Mark's statement (14 : 65, Rev. Ver.) "some began to spit on him . . . . . the officers received him with blows of their hands," explains that some members of the Sanhedrin joined the subordinates in these outrages. (Comp. Acts 7 : 57; 23 : 2.) They would be encouraged (Keim) by finding that they could with impunity smite him whose reported miracles had often made them tremble. **Buffeted him,** smote him with the fist. So Tyn., Cran., 'buffeted hym wyth fistes.' **Smote him with the palms of their hands,** as in 5: 39, and so Latin Versions, Memph., and Gothic; or perhaps (Rev. Ver. *margin*), 'smote him with rods,' as Geneva. The same two terms occur in Mark 14: 65. Luke says (22 : 63 B. U. Ver.) they "mocked him, beating him." **Prophesy,** meaning, speak by divine inspiration, not necessarily, nor even most commonly in Scripture, involving a predic-

68 Saying, Prophesy unto us, thou Christ, Who is he that smote thee?

68 Prophesy unto us, thou Christ: who is he that struck thee?

---

tion. Here, with his face covered (Luke and Mark), he would need superhuman knowledge to tell who smote him, and such knowledge the Messiah might be expected to have. Matt. alone gives the taunting address, **thou Christ,** or simply ' Christ.' Luke adds, Rev. Ver., "And many other things spake they against him, reviling him." Here the *Jews* mock Jesus as a pretended *prophet;* in 27: 27 ff., the *Romans* will mock him as a pretended *king.* Amid all these insults of word and deed he was still silent. Comp. 1 Peter 2: 23.

HOMILETICAL AND PRACTICAL.

V. 58. JEROME: "Following afar, on the road to denial." BENGEL: "Sat with the officers, inopportune good-fellowship."—'To see the end.' HENRY: "It is more our concern to prepare for the end, whatever it may be, than curiously to enquire what the end will be. The event is God's, but the duty is ours."—V. 59. Jesus condemned, but righteous. After the failure of false witnesses, he could be condemned only through his confession of what should have been a reason for reverencing him. The traitor confessed him to be righteous. (27:4.) Pilate found no fault in him. (Luke 23: 14.) The centurion at the cross declared him righteous. (Luke 23: 47.) The day is coming when every tongue will confess that he is Lord. (Phil. 2: 11.)—V. 61. BENGEL: "By no great change of words is often made a great calumny."—V. 63. ORIGEN: "We learn from this passage to despise the utterances of calumniating and false witnesses, not holding them worthy of reply or of resistance, when by their contradictions they resist each other. It is a greater thing to maintain a brave and self-respecting silence, than to defend oneself to no purpose."—V. 64. HENRY: "He thus confessed himself, for example and encouragement to his followers, when they are called to it, to confess him before men, whatever hazards they run by it."—V. 66. HALL: "O Saviour, this is not the last time wherein thou hast received cruel dooms from them that profess learning and holiness. What wonder is it, if thy weak members suffer that which was endured by so perfect an head."

69-75. THE FALL OF PETER.

Found also in Mark 14: 66-72; Luke 22: 56-62; John 18: 15-18, 25-27.

Peter's three denials of his Lord evidently occurred during the progress of the Jewish trial, which seems to have lasted two hours or more. (Luke 22: 59.) We see from John (comp. above on 26: 58) that the first denial was made while Annas was questioning Jesus; and it is clear from comparing all the narratives that the second and third were made while Jesus still remained at the high priest's house and Peter in the court, and probably during the trial by the informal meeting of the Sanhedrin. (26: 57-68.) Now Matt. and Mark do not record the examination by Annas; accordingly they only mention at the outset that Peter followed Jesus afar off and entered the high priest's court, and then, after narrating the trial by the informal meeting, they describe Peter's three denials. Luke does not give either the examination by Annas or the informal trial; accordingly, as soon as he brings Peter into the high priest's court, he at once tells of the three denials. John has no account of the Jewish trial except the examination by Annas; so he gives the first denial in connection with the appearance of Jesus before Annas, and then, after narrating the interrogation and telling how Annas sent Jesus to Caiaphas, he speaks at once of the second and third denials. Thus the apparent dislocation of this narrative in the several Gospels is satisfactorily accounted for. Minute discrepancies as to the exact place and time of the different denials need not surprise us. The accounts are extremely brief, the numerous persons in the court were moving about and much excited, the questions addressed to Peter may in one case or another have been repeated by several persons, and the denial variously made to each of these (comp. on 'began' in v. 74), while yet there were three distinct and separate denials, as indicated in each of the Gospels. It is not even necessary to suppose that they all give the three in the same order. To make out (McClellan and some others) five or six separate denials, and thereby harmonize the details, is to diverge from the Saviour's express prediction, "thou

69 Now Peter sat without in the palace: and a damsel came unto him, saying, Thou also wast with Jesus of Galilee.
70 But he denied before *them* all, saying, I know not what thou sayest.
71 And when he was gone out into the porch, another *maid* saw him, and said unto them that were there, This *fellow* was also with Jesus of Nazareth.
72 And again he denied with an oath, I do not know the man.
73 And after a while came unto *him* they that stood by, and said to Peter, Surely thou also art *one* of them; for thy speech bewrayeth thee.

69 Now Peter was sitting without in the court: and a maid came unto him, saying, Thou also wast with
70 Jesus the Galilæan. But he denied before them all,
71 saying, I know not what thou sayest. And when he was gone out into the porch, another *maid* saw him, and saith unto them that were there, This man
72 also was with Jesus the Nazarene. And again he
73 denied with an oath, I know not the man. And after a little while they that stood by came and said to Peter, Of a truth thou also art *one* of them; for thy

shalt deny me thrice," and to disregard the stress laid by all four narratives upon three denials. Surely much more is lost than gained by such painful harmonizing.

FIRST DENIAL. **69 f. Peter sat without in the palace,** or *court,* viz., in the court of the high priest's house (26:58); 'without' is said in contrast with the audience room in which Jesus was appearing before the authorities. Peter was not in this room, but out in the open air of the court; and this was 'beneath,' on a lower level than the audience room. **A damsel,** viz., *maid-servant;* and literally,[1] 'one maid,' as distinguished from 'another,' in v. 71. So, Mark 14: 66, 'one of the maids of the high priest.' **Came unto him,** as he sat in the court, beside the fire of charcoal; so Mark and Luke. John says that the maid, who was the doorkeeper, and who was induced by John to admit Peter, asked him the question; and this might seem in conflict with the other accounts. But John's brief statement does not necessarily mean that she asked him at the moment of admitting him. She would very naturally close the door and return to the fire herself, and might then ask the question. **With Jesus of Galilee,** a very natural expression in the high priest's servant, feeling everything at Jerusalem to be immeasurably superior to the provinces. Mark, B. U., 'with Jesus the Nazarene,' and so Matt. in v. 71, Rev. Ver. We have often seen that the Evangelists do not undertake in all cases to give the exact words spoken; we are concerned only with any such discrepancy of statement as might

seem to impair credibility. **I know not what thou sayest.** So Mark; Luke 'I know him not'; in John she asks if he is one of this man's disciples, and he answers 'I am not.' There is here no substantial conflict.

We must remember Peter's situation. Over-confidence in himself, notwithstanding the Master's warning (26:33-35), had led to lack of watchfulness (26:40 f.); suddenly awaking, he committed a rash action (51), which he might very reasonably fear would be avenged if he were discovered; so when suddenly asked, he was startled, frightened, and hastily denied. Then he was deeper in trouble than ever. We are not called to extenuate his conduct, but only to observe that it was psychologically not unnatural.

SECOND DENIAL. **71 f. When he was gone out into the porch,** the open gateway passing under the middle of one side of the house into the court; Mark calls it 'the forecourt.'[2] Luke gives at this point no note of place. John gives the second denial as made while Peter was standing and warming himself. Possibly the first and second denials are by him given in reverse order. Observe that he here says generally 'they said,' while Matt. has 'another' (feminine), Mark 'the maid,' Luke 'another' (masculine), *i. e.,* another person. The terms of address and denial slightly differ as before.

THIRD DENIAL. **73 f. And after a while.** Mark says 'a little after,' while Luke says more definitely, 'about the space of one hour after.' **Came they that stood by, and said to Peter.** So in effect Mark, but Luke says,

---

[1] It is not certain that 'one' ever becomes in New Test. a mere indefinite article; the most likely examples in Matt. are 8: 19; 21: 19, (Rev. Ver. *margin*). In the present passage the Latin versions and Gothic have 'one,' Memph. 'a,' Pesh. ambiguous. Rönsch holds that *unus* is sometimes a mere indefinite article; but many of his examples are clearly forced, and none of them (including this passage) seem conclusive.

[2] The statement in Com. text of Mark at this point, 'and the cock crew,' is probably spurious, as it is wanting in א B L, one Evang., Memph., and one copy of the Old Latin, and might be very naturally placed on the margin here (and creep into the text), as explaining 'twice' in Mark 14: 30, 72, and 'the second time' in 72. See a very interesting discussion in W H., App. § 323.

74 Then began he to curse and to swear, *saying*, I know not the man. And immediately the cock crew.

74 speech bewrayeth thee. Then began he to curse and to swear, I know not the man. And straightway

'another (person),' and John, Rev. Ver., ' one of the servants of the high priest, being his kinsman, whose ear Peter cut off,' which would be a specially alarming fact, especially when he asked, "Did I not see thee in the garden with him?" Now we may either suppose that a question asked by one person was taken up and repeated by others, which would be very natural, or that the three denials are given in different order by the several Gospels. Matt. and Mark have (a) a maid in the court, (b) another maid in the court, (c) the bystanders, apparently in the court. Luke has (a) a maid as he sat by the fire, (b) another (person), place not indicated, (c) some other (person), place in the court, as indicated by Luke 22: 60 f. John has (a) the maid that kept the door, (b) plural, apparently the persons with whom he was standing and warming himself (John 18: 18, 25), (c) one of the servants of the high priest, place not indicated. It may be that John has mentioned the second denial first, because suggested then by his account of the admission of Peter, or on the other hand, that Matt. and Mark have changed the order. John's (b) agrees as to the *plural* with the (c) of Matt. and Mark. The vague 'another person' and 'some other person' of Luke, treat the details as comparatively unimportant. We need not insist on any particular theory for exactly harmonizing the several statements. There is nothing in the group of details to weaken the credibility of the narratives, but their evident independence strengthens their credibility, as persons accustomed to compare the testimony of several witnesses will readily see; and we may be content to notice one or another possible mode of combining all the facts. In preaching or Sunday-school teaching, it would be better to pass lightly over the mere harmonizing of details, and dwell on the general facts which are the same in all the Gospels, and which yield lessons of so great importance.

This third denial was the most vehement of all. Peter had involved himself by the first in the apparent necessity, so sadly familiar to human observation and experience, of adhering to an initial falsehood. Now the bystanders insist and argue. **Surely,** *of a truth, i. e.,* **thou also art one** of them. They are sure of it. **For thy speech bewrayeth thee,** literally, *makes thee manifest* (*evident*). The English word bewray meant primarily to accuse, and is of Teutonic origin. The entirely distinct word betray is connected with traitor, of French and Latin origin. (See Skeat.) Mark and Luke have 'for thou art,' (Luke ' he is') a Galilean.' Mark would be more exactly 'for even thy speech,' or 'for thy speech also,' as in 8: 9. Perhaps (Plump.) his excitement and confusion made the local peculiarities of speech more marked.[1] **Then began he** (see on 11 : 20), suggests that it was continued some time, as does the tense of the verbs 'to curse' and 'to swear.' This implies various expressions of denial, perhaps addressed to different persons (comp. on v. 69). He had already used an oath in the second denial. (v. 72.) Cursing would, in such a case, be invoking a curse upon himself if he were speaking falsely, and so would be even stronger than an oath. The Jews were much given to a careless use of oaths (see on 5 : 33), and it may be, as Alexander supposes, that Peter relapsed under the excitement into an early habit, which he had abandoned through the Saviour's teaching. Alas! for human nature; the Word made flesh was rejected by the great mass of his own people, was betrayed by one of his own followers, and by the very leader of them was basely denied, again and again, with oaths and curses. See 1 Cor. 10: 12. **And immediately,** *or straightway,* **the cock crew.** Mark, Rev. Ver., and John Rev. Ver. 'straightway': Luke 'immediately, while he yet spake.' The Greek noun has no article; it does not mean some particular

---

1 Galilean peculiarities of speech are repeatedly mentioned in the Talmud. They consisted of (a) interchange of the gutturals Aleph and Ayin, or Cheth and Ayin, which cannot be illustrated from our language; (b) Interchange of the palatals Kaph and Qoph, a little like the negligent fashion in which some now pronounce quote, quota, quorum, as if written with a k; (c) interchange of s or sh and th, like our lisp, and the French change of our th to s or z; (d) difference of some vowel sounds, like English home, Scotch hame, etc. Examples are given from the Talmud in Wetstein, Buxtorf, etc. As early as Judges 12: 6, the local change of shibboleth to sibboleth was marked and invariable.

75 And Peter remembered the word of Jesus, which said unto him, Before the cock crow, thou shalt deny me thrice. And he went out and wept bitterly.

75 the cock crew. And Peter remembered the word which Jesus had said, Before the cock crow, Thou shalt deny me thrice. And he went out, and wept bitterly.

---

fowl, and our English article only denotes the well-known sign of coming day. Mark, 'a second time,' comp. above on 26: 34; see there also as to the Talmudic statement that barn-yard fowls were not allowed in Jerusalem. **And Peter remembered.** Luke prefixes "and the Lord turned and looked upon Peter." The Saviour may have been in the high priest's audience chamber, either undergoing the informal trial, or kept there till the dawn should allow a formal session. This chamber might be open to the inner court : and the lights in the room, and the fire in the court, would make the pitying Master and the fallen disciple visible to each other. Otherwise we may suppose that the attendants were just then leading Jesus across the court. See Mrs. Browning's two sonnets, "The Look," and "The Meaning of the Look." **And he went out,** into the great entrance as before, or more probably, quite out of the building. At such a moment one would naturally long to be alone. **And wept bitterly.** So Luke; comp. Isa. 22 : 4.—Peter is seen no more in the history till after our Lord's resurrection, but seems to have sojourned with his friend John (John 20 : 2, 10). Some of the early Latin hymns allude to a legend that through life he never heard a cock crow without weeping.

HOMILETICAL AND PRACTICAL.

Peter's fall and rising again. (1) Steps downward. (a) Self-confidence, and loud professions, 26 : 33; (b) Lack of watchfulness, v. 40 f.; (c) Taken off his guard, he does a rash deed, v. 51; (d) Alarmed, yet still self-confident, he takes a middle course and follows at a distance, v. 58; (e) Courageous enough to venture into danger, though wanting courage to overcome it, v. 58; (f). Suddenly asked, he denies; (g) Feeling bound by this denial, and frightened by the repeated inquiry, he denies again and again, with oaths and curses. Alas, alas! (2) Climbing upward, through God's help. (a) The Lord had prayed for him (Luke 22 : 32), and now looked upon him (Luke 22 : 61), and he felt genuine grief and shame; (b) The risen Lord

appeared to him alone (Luke 24 : 34), a most touching occasion of confession and forgiveness; (c) The Lord afterwards delicately reminded him of his loud professions, and while no longer claiming superiority to others, he earnestly avowed his love, John 21: 15 ff.; (d) Helped by the Pentecostal Spirit, he boldly confessed Christ before the Sanhedrin and the nation, Acts 4: 10.

CALVIN: "The fall of Peter is a mirror of human infirmity, and a memorable example of God's goodness and compassion. Peter acted inconsiderately in entering the high priest's court. It was proper to follow the Master, but he had been warned of his coming defection, and he ought to have avoided the occasion. Often thus under the appearance of virtue do believers fling themselves into temptation. Conscious weakness should not hinder us from going whithersoever God calls us; but it ought to restrain rashness and stimulate to prayer."—V. 69. CALVIN: "He who has thrown away the fear of God, may tremble at the fall of a leaf. . . . The more eminent one is, the more should he be careful; because he cannot fall from his high place without damaging others."—V. 70. WEISS ("Life"): "When Peter vowed so confidently that he would go with his Master to death, he was thinking, no doubt, of a solemn testimony to him for whom he was ready to sacrifice everything. But a great deed of heroism is often easier than loyalty in small things."—V. 74. Contrast Peter in his great confession (16 : 16), wishing to stay on the Mount of Transfiguration (17 : 4), and making grand promises only a few hours before this (26 : 33).—V. 75. (1) Seeing that Peter fell, let him that thinketh he standeth take heed lest he fall, 1 Cor. 10 : 12. (2) Seeing that Peter was forgiven and became so useful, let him that knows he has fallen rise up in earnest repentance. LUTHER: "No article of the Creed is so hard to believe as this : I believe in the forgiveness of sins. But look at Peter. If I could paint a portrait of Peter, I would write on every hair of his head forgiveness of sins."

CHAPTER XXVII.

WHEN the morning was come, all the chief priests and elders of the people took counsel against Jesus to put him to death:
2 And when they had bound him, they led *him* away, and delivered him to Pontius Pilate the governor.

1 Now when morning was come, all the chief priests and the elders of the people took counsel against
2 Jesus to put him to death: and they bound him, and led him away, and delivered him up to Pilate the governor.

Ch. 27: 1-10. JESUS FORMALLY SENTENCED AND DELIVERED TO PILATE. SUICIDE OF JUDAS.

This section divides itself into v. 1 f., and v. 3-10.

I. **1 f.** The formal meeting of the Sanhedrin. Mark 15: 1; Luke 22: 66-71. It seems greatly best to suppose, as we have been doing, that while the real trial and condemnation of Jesus had already occurred (26 : 57-68), a formal session of the Sanhedrin was held after daybreak, **when the morning was come.** So Mark 'in the morning,' and Luke 'as soon as it was day.' The Mishna ("Sanh." IV., 1) expressly provides that criminal cases can be decided only in the day time, and that while a sentence of acquittal may be made the same day, a sentence of condemnation must be postponed to the next day. We have seen (on 26: 66) how the latter provision might have been evaded, but the former seems to have been here regarded, being in fact harder to evade. Luke has not described the informal meeting and sentence, but he has just before mentioned the indignities offered to Jesus, which we know from Matt. and Mark to have followed that sentence. It is natural that Luke, in describing the formal session should include some things that occurred in the previous investigation, since this made no difference as to the general result; nor can we tell how far the formal meeting would repeat the processes of the other. Whatever view may be adopted as to the several examinations of our Lord by the Jews, we see clearly that it was public action, on the part of the highest national authorities, and was afterwards approved even by the popular voice. (27 : 25.)—The place of this session may have been the high priest's residence, as before, but more probably was the regular hall for meetings of the Sanhedrin (see on 26 : 59); notice especially that Luke

22: 66 says, "they led him into their council," the Sanhedrin.

Took counsel against Jesus to put him to death. They had already voted that he *deserved* to die (26 : 66), and would only need to repeat that vote in the formal session. But there was a further question as to how they could actually put him to death, as the Romans had taken from the Sanhedrin (see on 26 : 59) the right to inflict capital punishment, and this could be managed only through Pilate the governor (see on 27: 11), who had come from his usual residence at Cesarea to Jerusalem, in order to insure order at the great feast, and attend to any administrative points that might come up. They probably then agreed to make before Pilate the accusations they actually did make, viz., that Jesus claimed to be a king, and forbade payment of tribute to Cesar (Luke 23 : 2), and that he stirred up the populace. (Luke 23 : 5. 14.) The further charge of blasphemy (John 19 : 7) they would hold in reserve. The Com. text has 'Pontius Pilate,' as in Luke 3: 1; Acts 4: 27; 1 Tim. 6: 13; but 'Pilate' alone is probably correct, according to some of the best documents.[1] As to Pilate, and the term 'governor,' see on 27: 11. **When they had bound him.** So Mark. He had also been bound when they arrested him at Gethsemane, John 18 : 12, 24, but the bonds would naturally be at least in part removed while they kept him in the house. The persons who bound Jesus and led him away are naturally understood to be not the chief priests and elders (v. 1), but the officials who did their bidding. The Mishna directs ("Sanh.," VI., 1) that sentence shall be followed by leading away to execution, while the court remain in session so as to hear any new evidence that may be brought in the criminal's behalf, or any reasonable appeal he may make, while on the way, for a new trial. But here "the whole

[1] א B L Σ, 33, 102, Memph., Theb., Pesh., Origen. We might suppose Pontius struck out here because wanting in the other Gospels; or inserted because familiar to the early Christians; but then why not likewise insert it in Mark, Luke, and John? In the absence of decisive internal considerations, it is safest to follow documents so generally right.

3 Then Judas, which had betrayed him, when he saw that he was condemned, repented himself, and brought again the thirty pieces of silver to the chief priests and elders,
4 Saying, I have sinned in that I have betrayed the innocent blood. And they said, What *is that* to us? see thou *to that.*
5 And he cast down the pieces of silver in the temple, and departed, and went and hanged himself.

3 Then Judas, who betrayed him, when he saw that he was condemned, repented himself, and brought back the thirty pieces of silver to the chief priests 4 and elders, saying, I have sinned in that I betrayed [1] innocent blood. But they said, What is that to us? 5 see thou *to it.* And he cast down the pieces of silver into the sanctuary, and departed; and he went away

1 Many ancient authorities read, *righteous.*

company of them rose up, and brought him before Pilate.'' (Luke 23 : 1, Rev. Ver.) He was not yet on the way to execution, and they need not keep the Sanhedrin in session.

II. **3-10.** The sad fate of Judas. Not found in the other Gospels, but comp. Acts 1 : 16-19.

(a) Judas returned the money and hanged himself. (v. 3-5.) **Judas, which had betrayed him,** see on 10 : 4 as to his earlier history. **When he saw that he was condemned,** viz., that Jesus was condemned by the Sanhedrin. Perhaps he literally saw the procession to Pilate's abode, and understood it to mean that the Sanhedrin had condemned him. This must have occurred before the crucifixion, as only the condemnation is mentioned. It is most natural to follow Matthew's order, placing it before the trial by Pilate. Yet that is not a necessary view, since Matt. might record the scene here to avoid a break in the subsequent narrative. The chief priests and elders in general went with the procession to Pilate (Luke 23 : 1), but some of them may have gone at once to the Court of the Priests, in order to oversee the morning preparations for worship. **The chief priests and elders** are mentioned in v. 3, with one article for both names (correct text), probably because the two classes were closely associated in the Sanhedrin and otherwise. In v. 1 the article in the original is repeated because of the added words ' of the people.' **Repented himself,** deeply grieved over and regretted his conduct, the word being *metamelomai,* quite different from *metanoeo,* which is used for repenting unto salvation, see on 3 : 2; 21 :

29. **Brought again the thirty pieces of silver,** see on 26 : 15. **In that I have be-trayed,** *delivered up,* as in v. 2, see on 10 : 4 and 17 : 22. **Innocent blood.** The Rev. Ver., *margin,* ' righteous blood' [1] is probably correct, but there is no important difference. The reply of the rulers was scornful. Comp. Acts 18 : 15. **In the temple,** Rev. Ver., *into the sanctuary.* But the Com. text, ' in the sanctuary' is more probably correct.[2] The sanctuary is *naos,* the central building or temple proper, see on 4 : 5 and 21 : 12. Some have attempted to establish an occasional loose use of *naos* for the whole sacred enclosure, but without success. Not being a priest, so far as we have any reason to believe, Judas had no right to enter this building, or even the Court of the Priests that surrounded it. He must have felt desperate and reckless, so that he rushed into the Court of the Priests, or into the building itself, and flung the coins ringing on the floor of the sanctuary. If we read ' into,' he must at any rate have entered the court, which was equally forbidden. **And went and hanged himself.** See the same word in 2 Sam. 17 : 23; Tobit 3 : 10. As to the further statements in Acts 1 : 18 f., see below.

In connection with what has been said of Judas in 10 : 4; 26 : 14, 24, it may be remarked that our Lord gave Judas a position for which he appears to have been by nature specially fitted. That is for any man the best providential assignment, and can only turn out otherwise through his own grievous fault. (Comp. Edersh.) Some modern critics and literary men, in view of Judas' remorse and suicide, have tried to construct for him a noble char-

[1] It is read by B (second hand) L, Memph., Theb., Old Latin, and Vulg., Syriac of Jerus., Arm., Æthiopic, Origen, and other Fathers. The Sept. has ' innocent blood' fifteen times, ' blameless blood' three times, ' righteous blood' four times; but in only one of these is that expression found in the Hebrew. So 'righteous blood' is a rare expression, and more likely to have been changed into the common ' innocent blood' than

contrariwise. In New Test. ' righteous blood' is found only in Matt. 23 : 35; ' innocent blood' not at all.

[2] ' In ' might easily be changed to ' into,' by persons who knew that Judas had no right to enter the sanctuary. It is probably an " Alexandrian " alteration, being found in א L, Origen, Eus.: and W H. would doubtless call it such but for its being found also in B.

6 And the chief priests took the silver pieces, and said, It is not lawful for to put them into the treasury, because it is the price of blood.
7 And they took counsel, and bought with them the potter's field, to bury stangers in.
8 Wherefore that field was called, The field of blood, unto this day.

6 and hanged himself. And the chief priests took the pieces of silver, and said, It is not lawful to put them into the [1] treasury, since it is the price of blood.
7 And they took counsel, and bought with them the
8 potter's field, to bury strangers in. Wherefore that field was called, The field of blood, unto this day.

1 Gr. *Corbanas*, that is, *sacred treasury.* Compare Mark vii. 11.

acter—being apparently influenced partly by love of paradox, partly by pity and charity, and partly, it is to be feared (Olsh.), by a low estimate of sin. They say that Judas, like the other apostles, was expecting Jesus to set up a worldly kingdom, in which, whoever was otherwise greatest, he might hope to be Treasurer. This hope would feed at once his ambition and his covetousness. Seeing that the Master shrank from establishing a worldly kingdom, he is supposed by these writers to have resolved upon a diplomatic stroke; he would betray him to the rulers, and then Jesus would be obliged to deliver himself by force, perhaps by miracle, and would no longer delay to assume the Messianic throne. It was the unexpected and mortifying failure of this high scheme that wrought in him such intolerable remorse. Now that such alone was the aim of Judas, is a fancy forbidden by the express statement of John that he was "a thief" (John 12:6); and of Jesus, long before, that he was "a devil" (John 6:70); and by the Saviour's awful words (26:24, Rev.Ver.), "Woe unto that man through whom the Son of man is betrayed! Good were it for that man if he had not been born." One may sometimes incline to think it possible that, along with the low avarice which accepted a small reward for treachery, there may have been connected in his mind vague hopes that somehow Jesus would escape, and it would all turn out well. See an excellent article in this direction by Park in Smith's "Bib. Dict.," Amer. Ed., vol. 2, page 1498 ff. But it is difficult to suppose the elevated aims above indicated to have been cherished by a thief and a traitor; and most of the critics in question have felt it necessary for their theory to disparage the Gospel statements. It seems much more probable that, taking literally the Saviour's predictions that he would be crucified, and perceiving the growing enmity and fixed purpose of the rulers, Judas was minded to save what he could out of the wreck, as the end of his course of petty peculation, and as some consolation for blasted hopes in regard

to the kingdom and its treasury. It may also be that he was angered by the rebuke during the supper at Bethany (see above on 26:10 f.), and long before dissatisfied at gradually perceiving how Jesus proposed self-renunciation and cross-bearing instead of worldly self-aggrandizement. As to his end, we know that men often lay plans for some vile act in a dreamy, or a moody, sullen fashion, and when it has been consummated, awaking to realize what they have done, are filled with vain regret and remorse. It might easily have been so with Judas, and thus his remorse and suicide are not in the least inconsistent with his having been a low thief and a shameful traitor.—What mournful scenes of evil encompass the awful tragedy of the crucifixion,—Caiaphas and Pilate, Peter and Judas. Let these help us to understand the sinfulness of human nature and the dreadful guilt of sin, and we can better appreciate the necessity, significance, and power of the cross.

(b) How the money was disposed of. (v. 6-10.) **To put them into the treasury,** the *korbanas* (Hebrew word borrowed in the Greek), where every *korban* (see on 15:5) or consecrated article was deposited. (Comp. Jos. "War," 2, 9, 4.) **It is not lawful . . . . because it is the price of blood.** This is supposed to have been inferred from Deut. 23:18. The money had already dishonored the temple by being thrown on its floor. **And they took counsel,** probably some hours or even days later, when they had more time to think of so small a matter. **The potter's field,** spoken of as known by that name. **To bury strangers in.** This was a contemptuous charity, probably referring to Gentiles who died at Jerusalem, as they would have been unwilling to bury any Jew in a place having a taint of desecration. **The field of blood.** Acts gives also the Aramaic term Aceldama. The tradition fixing the place of Aceldama in the side of the valley of Hinnom, on the south of Jerusalem, goes back as far as Jerome ("Onom."), while Eus. seems

9 Then was fulfilled that which was spoken by Jeremy the prophet, saying, And they took the thirty
pieces of silver, the price of him that was valued, whom
they of the children of Israel did value;

9 Then was fulfilled that which was spoken through
Jeremiah the prophet, saying, And [1] they took the
thirty pieces of silver, the price of him that was
priced, [2] whom *certain* of the children of Israel did

---

1 Or. *I took*....2 Or, *whom they priced on the part of the sons of Israel.*

---

to locate it on the north. Comp. Robinson,
" Bibl. Res.,'' and a striking description in
Hackett's " Illustrations of Scripture.'' **Unto
this day,** shows that this Gospel was written
a good many years after the crucifixion ; it
would be much more natural in A. D. 60 than
in A. D. 40.

The account in Acts 1 : 18 f. differs in various points from that here given. (1) Matt.
says the chief priests ' bought the field ' ; Acts,
' this man purchased (acquired) a field.' The
latter is a high wrought expression, perfectly
intelligible — all that he acquired by his
treachery was a field. The money bought
him a burial-place ; that was to him the sole
financial outcome of the iniquitous transaction. (2) Matt. says he 'hanged himself';
Acts, 'falling headlong, he burst asunder in
the midst, and all his bowels gushed out.'
Why should these be called inconsistent statements? Suppose that he hanged himself in
the potter's field—probably an unenclosed
spot, from which potter's clay had often been
obtained, like a brickyard, and therefore not
costly ; and suppose that the rope, or a limb
of a tree, broke ; and the statements are all
accounted for. (3) Matt. ascribes the name
field of blood to the fact that it was bought
with the price of blood ; Acts, to the fact that
his own blood was poured out there. All the
circumstances (McClellan) must have become
known to the Christians, who resided at Jerusalem for years after their occurrence, and
would feel a painful interest in the entire
story. One of the reasons for that name does
not exclude the other.—These several explanations are artificial, but not highly so, and are
certainly all possible ; and therefore it cannot
be fairly said that the accounts are incredible
because contradictory, nor that the writers
were erroneously informed.

9. Then was fulfilled. For the term
'fulfilled,' see on 1 : 22; and for the phrase
'then was fulfilled,' instead of 'that it might
be fulfilled,' comp. on 2 : 17. It was natural
to shrink from referring so horrid a crime in
any sense to the divine purpose. **Spoken by,**
through, **Jeremiah,** viz., 'by God through

Jeremiah,' see on 1 : 22; 2 : 17. **Price . . .
was valued . . . did value.** The same word
is used throughout in the Greek ; the repetition being painfully impressive. Com. Ver.
must of necessity vary the translation, 'price,'
'valued,' ' did value '; but it did better than
Tyn,, Cran., Gen., which had ' price,'
'valued,' 'bought.'

The prophecy is evidently derived from
Zech. 11 : 13, and yet is here referred to Jeremiah. There can be no doubt as to the text.
Augustine already remarks that the few
(Latin) copies which omitted the name (as
also Peshito does), or substituted Zechariah,
were evidently trying to remove a difficulty.
This difficulty has been the subject of immense
discussion. The principal theories are as follows : (1) Error on the part of Matthew. This
is apparently a very easy solution of Luther,
Beza, etc., and is popular now with many,
even Keil and Wright (on Zechariah), but
some have surely failed to consider the consequences involved in such an admission. Persons who earnestly seek another solution, or
who admit they cannot find one and are
quietly recognizing an unsolved difficulty,
may be just as honest and truth-loving as
those who with reckless bravery cut the knot.
(2) Origen and Eus. suggested, and many
have repeated, that it might be a mistake of
an original copyist, which is of course a mere
assumption, but quite as likely as a mistake of
the Evangelist. Morison ingeniously compares "strain at a gnat " in 23 : 24, which
appears to have been a slip of the pen or a
typographical error in the original edition
of King James. (3) The notion (Origen, Jerome, Ewald, and others), that it was taken
from some Apocryphal writing ascribed to
Jeremiah, is arbitrary and hardly worth discussing. (4) Mede suggested, followed by
Turpie, Wright, and others, that Jeremiah
may have been the author of Zech. ch. 9-11.
This would partly fall in with the recent
theory as to a divided authorship of that book ;
but the theory holds, for internal reasons,
that the author must have belonged to the
time of Micah and Isaiah. Mede's view is

barely possible. Morison well says that it would be "a critical anachronism" to suppose Matthew indicating in this fashion the composite authorship of the book. (5) Lightfoot quotes the Talmud as saying that, in the ancient order of the prophetic books, Jeremiah stood first. So he thinks Matthew has quoted from the general prophetic collection as the Book of Jeremiah; comp. the Psalms of David, the Proverbs of Solomon. This is very ingenious. But no similar quotation is found in New Test. Hengstenberg and Cook ("Bib. Comm.") notice the fact that only Jeremiah, Isaiah, and Daniel are quoted *by name* in the Gospels, Zech. being several times quoted or referred to in the Gospels, and many times in New Test., but never named. (6) Hengstenberg thinks that as the later prophets often reproduce earlier predictions, so Zech. was here really reproducing Jer. 18: 2 and 19: 2, and Matt. intentionally refers to the original source, though adopting mainly the later form. This theory is ably argued in Hengst.'s "Christology," and Kliefoth has a similar though distinct theory (see Wright). Besides the above-mentioned fact that Zech. is so often quoted but never named, Hengst. notices also that Mark 1: 2 f. refers to Isaiah what comes partly from Malachi, giving the older and greater prophet credit for the whole, the two predictions being akin.—On the whole this last seems the most nearly satisfactory theory; but some of the others are possible, even plausible. If not quite content with any of these explanations, we had better leave the question as it stands, remembering how slight an unknown circumstance might solve it in a moment, and how many a once celebrated difficulty has been cleared up in the gradual progress of Biblical knowledge. Comp. on 20: 29; 23: 35.

In Zechariah 11: 13 the prophet in vision is a representative of Jehovah acting as shepherd of Israel. The flock so misbehave that the shepherd calls for his wages to quit. The people (flock) show him contempt by valuing him at thirty shekels, the price of a slave. Jehovah says to the shepherd, "Fling it to the potter, the glorious price at which I was priced by them." The prophet adds, "And I took the thirty pieces of silver, and I flung it, in the house of Jehovah, to the potter." In like manner, Jesus is contemptuously valued

by the representatives of Israel at thirty shekels, and this is flung away in the house of Jehovah, and goes to a potter for the purchase of his field. The two cases are similar internally as well as in striking external points, and the Evangelist declares them to have a prophetic relation. Comp. on 1: 23; 2: 17 f. —Ewald, Bleek, Meyer, and others, hold that the Hebrew does not mean 'potter,' but 'treasury.' They change the vowels, and make an unknown word, and think that this is required by the subsequent words 'in the house of Jehovah.' It is enough to say that the money flung in the temple did go to the potter. Some have suggested the artificial but not impossible hypothesis of a potter who had a shop in the temple courts and supplied the temple, and who owned the piece of land that was bought.

As to the form of the quotation, Matt. here leaves the Sept. and makes considerable changes in the expressions of the Hebrew, but only such as bring out more clearly the meaning which, if we consider the passage as prophetic, is really conveyed by the Hebrew. Comp. on 2: 6.

HOMILETICAL AND PRACTICAL.

V. 3. Downward course of one who began as a teacher and an apostle. 1) Avarice, 2) Thievery, John 12: 6, 3) Betrayal, 4) Remorse, 5) Suicide, 6) His own place, Acts 1: 25.—Peter and Judas. 1) They both, and they only, are called Satan, 16: 23; John 6: 70. 2) They both, and they only, turned openly against the Master at the end. 3) They both sorrowed deeply, but in one it was remorse, in the other it was humble and loving repentance. 4) One committed suicide, the other found forgiveness and lived a long life of usefulness.—How the traitor was treated. 1) Eagerly welcomed, and promptly paid, 26: 15. 2) Solemnly warned, but in vain, 26: 24. 3) Diligently assisted, 26: 47; John 18: 3. 4) Scorned and slighted, 27: 4. 5) The price of his treachery made a monument of his ignominy forever.

V. 4. "I have sinned." Spurgeon has a sermon that introduces seven different persons in Scripture, each saying, "I have sinned." "What is that to us?" It was really much to them; for if Judas had betrayed a righteous man, *they* had condemned him. They could

10 And gave them for the potter's field, as the Lord appointed me.

11 And Jesus stood before the governor: and the governor asked him, saying, Art thou the King of the Jews? And Jesus said unto him, Thou sayest.

10 price; and [2] they gave them for the potter's field, as the Lord appointed me.

11 Now Jesus stood before the governor: and the governor asked him, saying, Art thou the King of

---

1 Some ancient authorities read, *I gave.*

---

not shift their guilt upon Judas, as Pilate could not shift his upon the Jews. (27:24.) HENRY: "It is folly for us to think that the sins of others are nothing to us, especially those sins that we are any way accessory to, or partakers in. . . .' Sinners, under convictions, will find their old companions in sin but miserable comforters. It is usual for those that love the treason to hate the traitor."—V 5. How often does gain gotten by crime become a torment.—V. 6. Scrupulosity and injustice. 1) They would pay the price, but would not put the price of blood in the treasury. 2) They would not enter the governor's abode for fear of defilement (John 18:28), but they would manœuvre and lie to make the governor murder the righteous. 3) They were horror-struck at a claim to be the Messiah (26:65f.), and they would bribe Roman soldiers to a false report to prevent the claim from being believed. (28:12.)—V. 10. EUTHYM.: "Let the money-lovers consider how Judas 1) committed the sin, 2) did not enjoy the money, 3) lost his life." LUTHER: "In Judas we see two things; how sin at first easily slips in, but afterwards makes such a horrible end."

11-31. JESUS TRIED BY PILATE.

Found also in Mark 15: 2-20; Luke 23: 2-25; John 18: 28-19: 16. Luke here gives a good deal, and John still more, of matter not found in Matt. and Mark; while Matt. has two remarkable points not found in the others, viz., v. 19 and v. 24 f. This section in Matt. divides into v. 11-14, 15-18, 19, 20-23, 24 f., 26, 27-31.

I. **11-14.** Pilate finds no grounds of condemnation. **And Jesus stood before the governor,** viz., Pilate. (27:2.) The time was early morning. (27:1; John 18:28.) The place was either in the Castle of Antonia, at the northwest corner of the temple area, or at the grand palace of Herod the Great, on the western side of the city, near the present Jaffa gate; it does not seem possible at present to decide between the two localities. The Greek word translated "governor" is a general term signifying leader, ruler, governor in

general, as in 10: 18; 1 Peter 2: 14, and frequently applied to a Roman procurator, as throughout this and the following chapters, and in Acts ch. 24-26; so sometimes in Josephus.

When Archelaus was banished in A. D. 6 (comp. above, end of ch. 2), Judea and Samaria were made a Roman province, governed by a procurator, who resided at Cesarea as the political capital, and visited Jerusalem upon occasion, especially at the time of the great feasts. The sixth procurator, A. D. 26-36, was Pontius Pilatus, who, besides New Test. and Jos., is mentioned by Tacitus ("Ann.," 15, 44), "Christus, in the reign of Tiberius, was executed by the procurator Pontius Pilatus." We know nothing of Pilate's history before entering upon office. In the probably four years he had now been holding it, he had made himself very odious to the Jews, by disregarding their religious convictions and feelings. We find mention of four instances, all apparently belonging to this early period. (a) In removing his army from Cesarea to Jerusalem for winter quarters, he sent in by night some ensigns bearing busts of Cesar, while former governors had used other ensigns in entering Jerusalem, out of regard for Jewish feeling against graven images. Multitudes of the people went to Cesarea and continued for five days and nights their incessant entreaties for the removal of these images, which he refused because it would seem an insult to Cesar. On the sixth day he let in soldiers threatening the suppliants with slaughter; but they prostrated themselves and bared their throats before the drawn swords, saying that they would gladly die rather than allow transgression of the law; so he yielded, and ordered back the images (Jos., "Ant.," 18, 3, 1; "War," 2, 9, 2-4). (b) Philo, in urging upon Caius Caligula the example of Tiberius, tells that Pilate once offered up in the palace of Herod some golden shields, without figures, but inscribed, and after long obstinately refusing the entreaties of the people, received orders from Tiberius at Rome to remove them.

12 And when he was accused of the chief priests and elders, he answered nothing.
13 Then said Pilate unto him, Hearest thou not how many things they witness against thee?

12 the Jews? And Jesus said unto him, Thou sayest. And when he was accused by the chief priests and 13 elders, he answered nothing. Then saith Pilate unto him, Hearest thou not how many things they wit-

---

See that curious work, written soon after A. D. 40, Philo's "Embassy to Caius," ¿ 38. (c) He used the sacred treasure called Corban (Mark 7: 11), to build an aqueduct near fifty miles long. On his return to Jerusalem the people gathered about his tribunal with loud clamors, and he sent among them soldiers, who beat them savagely with staves, killing many, while others were trodden to death in the flight; and so in that case he triumphed (Jos. "War," 2, 3, 9). (d) He slew certain Galileans while engaged in offering sacrifices at the temple, so that their blood mingled with the blood of their sacrifices—to Jewish feeling a horrible combination of cruelty and profanation. (Luke 13: 1.) We need not wonder that Jos. has no account of this, for Philo speaks of Pilate's "successive murders without trial," declaring that he feared any appeal to Tiberius, lest the embassy should also accuse his "acceptance of bribes, plunderings, outrages, and wanton insults, continual and most grievous cruelty," and characterizing him as "unbending, self-willed, harsh, and malignant." These facts and statements will prepare us to understand the relations of the accusers and the judge in the trial of Jesus before Pilate. It should be added that six years later the proconsul of Syria, who was the procurator's superior, upon complaint of his cruelty towards certain Samaritans, ordered him to Rome, where he arrived after the death of Tiberius ("Ant." 18, 4, 1 f.). Eusebius says ("Hist." II, 7), that "in the time of Caius (A. D. 37-41) Pilate fell into so great misfortunes that he committed suicide." It is stated by Justin Martyr, Tertullian, and Euseb., that Pilate made an official report to Tiberius concerning his trial of Jesus; but this is now represented only by unquestionably spurious writings.

John relates how Pilate came out from the prætorium, because the rulers were unwilling to enter, and inquired "What accusation bring ye against this man?" They replied that he was an evil-doer. Upon Pilate's bidding them take him and judge him themselves, they said "We (emphatic) are not permitted to put any one to death"; and so

Pilate knew that they designed a grave accusation. He must have repeatedly heard of Jesus during the last three years, of the great crowds that followed him, and the reported miracles, but also that he seemed to have no political aims. Luke (Rev. Ver.) tells that they said, "We found this man perverting our nation, and forbidding to give tribute to Cesar, and saying that he himself is Christ, a king." They kept the purely religious question in reserve (John 19: 7), and put forward political accusations, such as alone properly concerned a Roman governor (comp. Acts 18: 12-17), and these of the most serious kind. Now, in Roman trials (Keim), great importance was attached to a confession by the accused. Accordingly, Pilate asked the question given by Matt., Mark, and Luke, and John, **Art thou the king of the Jews?** This in Matt. and Mark requires something said by the Jews as accounting for it, which John and Luke afford. 'Thou' is emphatic, being separately expressed in the Greek. **Thou sayest**, viz., sayest what is true (comp. on 26: 25). John shows that this question and answer were spoken in private within the prætorium (John 18: 33), and that Jesus explained, "My kingdom is not of this world." We have seen on 25: 34 how our Lord had of late been speaking of himself to the disciples as king, and on 26: 64 how before the Sanhedrin he avowed himself the Messiah, and thus a king. It is probably to this confession that he was the king of the Jews that Paul refers in 1 Tim. 6: 13, Rev. Ver.: "Christ Jesus, who before Pontius Pilate witnessed the good confession."

When he was accused, or, 'while he was being accused.' **By the chief priests and elders,** first one speaking, and then another. This was probably both before and after Pilate's private interview with him. **To never,** or, *not even to one word*, is the literal translation. Pilate's remonstrance (v. 13) appears to have been kindly meant. The utter silence of the accused seemed wonderful. (v. 14). A Roman writer says, "Silence is a kind of confession." Did Jesus mean thus to confess the charge as true? There was something about

14 And he answered him to never a word: insomuch that the governor marvelled greatly.

15 Now at *that* feast the governor was wont to release unto the people a prisoner, whom they would.

16 And they had then a notable prisoner, called Barabbas.

17 Therefore when they were gathered together, Pilate said unto them, Whom will ye that I release unto you? Barabbas, or Jesus which is called Christ?

14 ness against thee? And he gave him no answer, not even to one word: insomuch that the governor marvelled greatly. Now at ¹the feast the governor was

15 wont to release unto the multitude one prisoner,

16 whom they would. And they had then a notable

17 prisoner, called Barabbas. When therefore they were gathered together, Pilate said unto them, Whom will ye that I release unto you? Barabbas, or Jesus

---

1 Or, *a feast.*

---

him which disinclined the governor to think so. **How many things.** The Greek may mean either how many or how great, indeed may include both—what a mass of things. Can we see reasons for this remarkable silence, before the Roman as well as the Jewish tribunal (26:63)? (1) He has already been condemned by the Sanhedrin for blasphemy. His death is a foregone conclusion with them, and Pilate is fettered by his own past wrongdoing, and must yield to their wishes. It will do no good to speak; it would be casting pearls before swine. The only charge that needed explanation to Pilate he did explain to him in private. (2) The crisis of his ministry has arrived, his 'hour' is now come. For two years he has prudently avoided exciting the hostility of his enemies, and the fanaticism of his friends. But there is no occasion for further delaying the inevitable collision. He has finished his work of teaching, his life of humiliation, and the hour is come that he should be glorified. (John 12:23; 17:4.) (3) His death is not only inevitable, but necessary, and he now voluntarily submits to it. (John 10:17 f.) One prayer to the Father might stop it, but he will not so pray. (John 12:27; Matt. 26:53.) The thought of this hour has long been a burden to his soul (Luke 12:50), and last night its approach cost him a long and painful struggle in the garden; but now he is ready to endure the cross, despising the shame, for the joy that is set before him. (Heb. 12:2.)

Luke and John here relate that Pilate declared he found no fault in the accused. (Luke 23:4; John 18:38.) So the trial before him was thus far a failure. But the Jewish rulers (Luke 23:5, R. V.) "were the more urgent, saying, He stirreth up the people, teaching throughout all Judea, and beginning from Galilee even unto this place." Thus Pilate learned that the accused was a Galilean. He seized upon this fact as affording a prospect of an escape from this unpleasant trial, and at the same time of conciliating Herod Antipas, the tetrarch of Galilee, with whom he had been at enmity. So he sent Jesus to Herod, who had come to Jerusalem for the feast. (Luke 23:7-12.) This formed the second stage in the Roman trial. But while he succeeded in conciliating Herod, the governor failed to escape the responsibility of the investigation. Jesus was utterly silent before Herod also, and was sent back, nothing having been accomplished.

II. **15-18.** Pilate attempts to release Jesus. Mark 15:6-10; Luke 23:13-16; John 18:39 f. Summoning the rulers and the people, the procurator declared (Luke) that he, and likewise Herod, had found no fault in this man concerning the matters of accusation. So he proposed a sort of compromise, "I will therefore chastise him, and release him." He hoped that this amount of punishment might satisfy the hostility of the accusers. **At that feast,** Rev. Ver., *the feast,* feast by feast, whenever a feast occurred; but the reference is probably to the passover, and not all the feasts. **The governor was wont to release unto the people,** *multitude.* This was more likely a Roman than a Jewish custom, but its origin is quite unknown. Despots have often found some release of prisoners to be popular with the many. **A,** *one,* **prisoner.** This is clearly a numeral, and not an indefinite article, comp. on 26:69. **They had,** viz., the governor and those associated with him in such matters. **Barabbas.** The insurrection against the Romans when a procurator was first appointed had left some popular robbers, who were regarded as patriots (comp. on 22:17). It is not unlikely that Barabbas was one of those. He was not only "a robber" (John 18:40), but had excited an insurrection in the city, during which he and his followers had committed murder. (Mark 15:7; Luke 23:19.) These facts account for Matthew's calling him **a notable prisoner,** or 'a prisoner of mark.' It is also probable that the two robbers crucified with Jesus were Barabbas' followers, so that the

13 For he knew that for envy they had delivered him.

19 When he was set down on the judgment seat, his wife sent unto him, saying, Have thou nothing to do with that just man: for I have suffered many things this day in a dream because of him.

20 But the chief priests and elders persuaded the multitude that they should ask Barabbas, and destroy Jesus.

18 who is called Christ? For he knew that for envy 19 they had delivered him up. And while he was sitting on the judgment-seat, his wife sent unto him, saying, Have thou nothing to do with that righteous man: for I have suffered many things this day in a 20 dream because of him. Now the chief priests and the elders persuaded the multitudes that they should

---

Saviour literally took his place. Jesus was falsely accused of sedition, and a man really guilty of sedition was released. The name Barabbas occurs frequently in the Talmud, and signifies 'son of Abba,' or 'son of a teacher,' it being common to call a rabbi 'father.' (23:9.) Comp. Barjonah (16:17), Bartholomew. (10:2.) The name might mean simply 'son of his father,' but not so probably. A few documents give in v. 16 and 17, or in v. 17 alone, 'Jesus Barabbas.' Every one feels this to be an interesting reading, but the evidence is too slight to warrant accepting it, as is done by Fritz., Meyer, Farrar, and others. Tregelles has shown how it might have arisen through a mistake in copying; see also Tisch. and W H., App. **Whom will ye that I release unto you?** John also states, and Luke implies, that Pilate suggested the release of Jesus. Mark (15:8) at first seems to make it come from the people. But he only states that the thronging multitude at that point reminded Pilate of the custom, a very natural thing upon coming before the tribunal early on the first day of the feast, and Pilate took up the idea and asked whether they wished him to release Jesus. **For envy they had delivered him.** Mark carefully distinguishes —Pilate addressed "the multitude," and "perceived that for envy the chief priests had delivered him up," R. V. Their jealousy arose from the fear that a person claiming to be the Messiah would interfere with their popularity and power. Pilate might well enough suppose that the multitude would have little sympathy with this feeling. **Or Jesus, which is called Christ.** We usually find 'the Christ,' the Messiah, see on 2:4; but here, as in 1:1, 16, and probably in 16:20, it is simply 'Christ,' a proper name.

III. **19.** Message from Pilate's wife. This is found in Matt. only. **The judgment seat** was a special chair, often carried about by a Roman official of rank, and placed as a seat of justice in front of his tent or house, upon an elevated 'pavement,' tesselated or mosaic.

The Romans were ostentatious of publicity in trials, as opposed to secret investigations. Comp. (Keim) the case of the procurator Florus, who in A. D. 66, after spending the night in Herod's palace, "the next day placed in front of the palace a judgment seat, and sat down; and the chief priests and men of power and all that was most distinguished in the city stood beside the judgment seat." (Jos., "War," 2, 14, 8.) This curious interruption from Pilate's wife gave time for the rulers to move about among the crowds and persuade them to ask for Barabbas. (v. 20.) It is suggested by Edersh. (comp. above on 26: 47) that so large a force as a cohort, commanded by a chiliarch, could not have been furnished to the rulers for the apprehension of Jesus without authority from Pilate. This would account for the fact that Pilate's wife knew what was going on, and felt distressed and anxious. **Have thou nothing to do with that just man;** the same Greek construction as in 8: 29; John 2: 4. **This day** in the Jewish sense, beginning at sunset. There is nothing here to indicate a divine influence in connection with the dream, and it can be accounted for by natural causes. The message would naturally increase the governor's reluctance to condemn the accused. A tradition, with but slight support, gives to Pilate's wife the name of Procla, or Claudia Procula. In like manner, the two robbers, the centurion, etc., have received traditional names, which interest some minds, but are of no real value. In A. D. 21, it was proposed in the Roman Senate that no provincial magistrate should be accompanied by his wife, as had been growing common; but the motion failed. Tacitus ("Ann.," III., 33-35) gives a summary of arguments on both sides.

IV. **20-23.** The people choose Barabbas rather than Jesus. Mark 15: 11-14; Luke 23: 18-23; John 18: 40. **The chief priests and elders persuaded the multitude,** while Pilate was occupied with the message from his wife. Notice that *great throngs* of

21 The governor answered and said unto them, Whether of the twain will ye that I release unto you? They said, Barabbas.

22 Pilate saith unto them, What shall I do then with Jesus which is called Christ? *They* all say unto him, Let him be crucified.

23 And the governor said, Why, what evil hath he done? But they cried out the more, saying, Let him be crucified.

24 When Pilate saw that he could prevail nothing, but *that* rather a tumult was made, he took water, and washed *his* hands before the multitude, saying, I am innocent of the blood of this just person: see ye *to it.*

21 ask for Barabbas, and destroy Jesus. But the governor answered and said unto them, Whether of the twain will ye that I release unto you? And they

22 said, Barabbas. Pilate saith unto them, What then shall I do unto Jesus who is called Christ? They

23 all say, Let him be crucified. And he said, Why, what evil hath he done? But they cried out ex-

24 ceedingly, saying, Let him be crucified. So when Pilate saw that he prevailed nothing, but rather that a tumult was arising, he took water, and washed his hands before the multitude, saying, I am inno-

---

people were gathered in front of the prætorium. The Jews have always been skillful politicians. The popular zeal about Jesus as the Messiah had evidently cooled, and probably because now for five days since the triumphal entry he had done nothing towards establishing himself as king. The wily demagogues could say that the highest court had tried Jesus, and found him an impostor and a blasphemer, who deserved to die, and they hoped Pilate would crucify him. If Barabbas was associated with patriotic traditions, as we have supposed (on v. 16), it was easy to excite popular good-will towards him. Comp. the modern Greek robbers under Turkish rule. Mark, Rev. Ver., says, "the chief priests stirred up the multitude," a strong term, indicating that they roused them to excited feeling, for Barabbas or against Jesus, or probably both. 'Persuaded that they should ask', is a non-final construction, explained on 5 : 29.—*Alexander:* "This deliberate preference of a bad man to a good one, of a justly condemned criminal to one whom even Pilate recognized as innocent, would have been enough to brand the conduct of the priests with infamy. But when to this we add that they preferred a murderer to the Lord of life, a rebel and a robber to a prophet, to their own Messiah, nay, to the incarnate Son of God himself, this perverseness seems almost incredible and altogether irreconcilable with rectitude of purpose and sincere conviction." Comp. the striking statement by Peter in Acts 3 : 13-15. —In consequence of this skillful persuasion from the rulers, the multitudes 'cried out' (Luke and John), shouted the request. **What shall I do then with Jesus which is called Christ?** He wishes them to observe (Alex.) that the effect of their choosing Barabbas is to leave Jesus in danger, hoping that this thought may lead them to change the request. **They all say unto him, Let him be crucified.** The hint to this effect had probably

been given the crowd by the rulers. They could thus make his death ignominious, so as to break his hold on popular admiration; and could also have an excuse for saying in future, if complained of, that it was not their act but that of the Romans—as some Jews anxiously maintain now. They knew not that under an overruling Providence they were bringing about a form of death most suitable to atonement, as involving "shedding of blood," and causing wounds that would be marks of identification after resurrection, without the distressing mutilations caused by stoning. As to the term, '*crucified,*' see on 16 : 24, and 27 : 35. **Why, what evil hath he done?** Pilate had no liking for the rulers, and understood their jealousy of Jesus. (v. 18.) And where his own interests or passions were not involved, he had some sentiment of Roman justice. So he remonstrates with the crowd. Luke tells us that he declared, "I find no cause of death in him," B. U. Ver., and a second time proposed (Luke 23 : 16, 22), as a sort of compromise that might satisfy the enemies of Jesus, "I will therefore chastise him and let him go." All this, as Chrys. says, was weak and unmanly conduct; see below on v. 24. **But they cried out the more,** or *exceedingly.* An excited throng is often more boisterous in proportion as it has less reason. Comp. Acts 19 : 34.

24. Pilate tries to shift the responsibility, and the people assume it. This is recorded by Matt. only.—**Saw that he could prevail nothing,** that he did no good by his suggestions. Why was the man of power thus powerless? Why could he not say, *Fiat justitia, ruat caelum? Let justice be done, if the heavens fall.* He was evidently very anxious to avoid condemning the innocent, for he made in all six distinct efforts to escape the difficulty: (1) sending Jesus to Herod; (2) suggesting that he might be released according to the custom; (3) proposing to compro-

25 Then answered all the people, and said, His blood *be* on us, and on our children.

26 Then released he Barabbas unto them: and when he had scourged Jesus, he delivered *him* to be crucified.

cent [1]of the blood of this righteous man: see ye 25 *to it.* And all the people answered and said, His 26 blood *be* on us, and on our children. Then released he unto them Barabbas: but Jesus he scourged and delivered *him* to be crucified.

---

1 Some ancient authorities read, *of this blood ; see ye, etc.*

---

mise by scourging and releasing, Luke 23 : 22 f.; (4) washing his hands and disclaiming responsibility; (5) proposing to turn the case over to the Jewish rulers, John 19 : 6; (6) appealing and remonstrating before he pronounced judgment, John 19 : 14 f. Pilate was not a man of heroic mould, but he was "self-willed and obstinate." Why could he not do what he so greatly desired? He was entangled by his own previous wrong-doing, see on v. 11. He had made rulers and people hate him thoroughly, so that they would be glad of an excuse for reporting him to Tiberius; and he knew that the suspicious and jealous emperor would be slow to pass over the charge that he let go one who claimed to be king. Pilate was weak now because he had formerly been wicked. Like many a politician, his record was in the way of his conscience. **A tumult was made,** or, *was arising.* The Romans desired two things in the provinces, tribute and peace. A successful governor was one who kept everything quiet, and popular tumult was greatly disliked, as being troublesome and expensive, if not dangerous. **Washed his hands before the multitude.** The law of Moses had directed this ceremony in a peculiar case of real innocence (Deut. 21 : 6-9); an image was drawn from it in Psa. 26 : 6. Pilate might easily become acquainted with this Jewish custom, which was in itself a very natural symbol. **Innocent of the blood of this just person,** or *righteous man.* The shorter text of *margin* Rev. Ver. is quite probably correct, 'innocent of this blood'; there is no important difference, for Pilate elsewhere declares him to be righteous, Luke 23 : 14; John 19 : 4. But the governor was *not* innocent. *Plump.:* "One of the popular poets of his own time and country might have taught him the nullity of such a formal ablution—

'Too easy souls, who dream the crystal flood
Can wash away the fearful guilt of blood.'
Ovid, '*Fast.*' ii. 45."

And he himself felt that he was not inno-

cent, for it was afterwards that he made the two new efforts in John 19: 4-16 to overcome the opposition of the Jews. **Then answered all the people.** Not simply some; it was a general cry. **His blood be on us and on our children.** *Jerome:* "A fine inheritance the Jews leave to their children." Josephus tells that in the insurrection against Florus, about A. D. 65, "many of the Jews were apprehended and brought before Florus, who first scourged and then crucified them." And Titus, during the siege, A. D. 70, caused many captured fugitives, sometimes five hundred a day, to be "scourged and tortured in every form, and then crucified in front of the ramparts. . . . And so great was their number that there was no space for the crosses, nor were there crosses for the bodies." ("War," 2, 14, 9; 5, 11, 1.)

VI. **26.** Jesus delivered to be crucified. Mark 15: 15; Luke 23: 24 f.; John 19: 1. **Scourged.** The terrible Roman scourging carried with it into the provinces the Latin word, which is here borrowed into the Greek of Matt. and Mark, and so into the Syriac (Pesh.) and Coptic (Memph.) Jerome here remarks that it was according to the Roman laws that one who is crucified shall first be scourged. Wet. quotes Greek, Roman, and Jewish writers as showing that it was common to scourge before crucifying; comp. Jos. above. The sufferer was stripped and bound to a pillar or post, bending forward so as to expose his back completely; the heavy whip or strap often contained bits of bone or metal, and tore the quivering flesh into one bloody mass. The law of Moses had provided (Deut. 25: 3), that a scourging should not exceed forty stripes, and Jewish custom made sure of this by stopping at "forty save one" (2 Cor. 11: 24); but the Roman scourgers were restricted by nothing but strength and inclination. We ought to feel a shuddering gratitude at our inability to conceive the consequences of this cruel infliction. **Delivered,** to some of his soldiers. (v. 27.)

VII. **27-31.** Jesus mocked by the soldiers,

27 Then the soldiers of the governor took Jesus into the *common hall, and gathered unto him the whole band *of soldiers.*
28 And they stripped him, and put on him a scarlet robe.
29 And when they had platted a crown of thorns, they put *it* upon his head, and a reed in his right hand: and they bowed the kn e before him, and mocked him, saying, Hail, King of the Jews!
30 And they spit upon him, and took the reed, and smote him on the head.
31 And after that they had mocked him, they took the robe off from him, and put his own raiment on him, and led him away to crucify *him.*

27 Then the soldiers of the governor took Jesus into the [1] Prætorium, and gathered unto him the whole
28 [2] band. And they [3] stripped him, and put on him a
29 scarlet robe. And they plaited a crown of thorns and put it upon his head, and a reed in his right hand; and they kneeled down before him, and
30 mocked him, saying, Hail, King of the Jews! And they spat upon him, and took the reed and smote
31 him on the head. And when they had mocked him, they took off from him the robe, and put on him his garments, and led him away to crucify him.

a Or, *governor's house.*——1 Or, *palace.*...2 Or, *cohort.*...3 Some ancient authorities read, *clothed.*

and led away to be crucified. Mark 15: 16–20; John 19: 2–16. **The soldiers of the governor,** the Roman soldiers in immediate attendance. These were seldom Italians (Acts 10: 1), but drawn from all parts of the empire. They may in this case have been Syrians, or may have been Germans. **Took Jesus into the common hall.** In Rev. Ver., *palace* was used by English Revisers. This is not the word rendered 'palace' in Com. Ver. of 26: 3, 58, 69, but another term, the Roman prætorium (borrowed in the Greek), denoting the prætor's tent or abode, the general's head-quarters. The American Revisers wisely preferred to render *prætorium.* The trial and the scourging had taken place in front of the prætorium, in a broad open space where the judgment seat was placed and the crowds assembled. The mocking that follows occurred within the prætorium, and afterwards the sufferer was again led out by Pilate, for another appeal to the people. (John 19: 5, 13.) **And gathered unto him the whole band,** or 'cohort' (*margin,* Rev. Ver.), comp. on 26: 47. The expression (Meyer) is of course popular, not necessarily implying that every soldier of the cohort was present; but it was a large number. **And they stripped him.** There can be little doubt that this is the correct text; that of *margin,* Rev. Ver. (differing in the Greek by only one letter) would mean that having previously stripped him for the scourging (Acts 16: 22), they now replaced his garments and then put round him the scarlet cloak. **A scarlet robe.** Mark and John, 'purple.' The ancients did not so carefully discriminate colors as we do, and royal purple is believed to have included all tints from sky-blue to crimson. The term here rendered 'robe' denotes a short red cloak worn by Roman military and civil officials. The soldiers would naturally take this as a mocking substitute for a king's purple robe; indeed, a Roman emperor might wear it. **A crown of thorns.** So Mark and John. The crown would simply be a garland. The plant employed cannot certainly be determined, but was most probably the *nubk* of the Arabs, "a tree which is found in all the warmer parts of Palestine, and about Jerusalem. . . . The flexible boughs are tough, and well suited to form a garland, and the thorns are numerous and sharp" (Tristram, "Nat. Hist."). The thorns were of course unpleasant to the brow, but not excessively painful, and were probably used more in derision than in cruelty. **A reed in his right hand,** as a mock sceptre. **Hail, King of the Jews!** The Jews had mocked him as a pretended *prophet* (26: 68); here the Romans mock him as a pretended *king.* **Spit upon him** (Mark likewise), as the Jews had done in their mocking. (26: 67.) **And took the reed and smote him on the head.** So Mark. The tense of 'smote' is imperfect, a continued smiting, and so in Mark as to the spitting also. Then restoring his own garments, they **led him away to crucify him.** So Mark, Luke, John. John interposes an account not given by the other Evangelists, of a renewed effort made by Pilate once and again, to excite popular compassion and change the result. But the wily Jewish rulers knew his weak point and their advantage, and said (John 19: 12), "If thou let this man go, thou art not Cesar's friend: whosoever maketh himself a king speaketh against Cesar." We have seen (on v. 24) why Pilate felt helpless in presence of this thought. And so his last efforts had failed.

HOMILETICAL AND PRACTICAL.

V. 11 f. HENRY: "Many oppose Christ's holy religion, upon a mistake of the nature of it; they dress it up in false colors, and they

32 And as they came out, they found a man of Cyrene, Simon by name: him they compelled to bear his cross.

32 And as they came out, they found a man of Cyrene, Simon by name: him they [1]compelled to go

---

1 Gr. *impressed.*

---

fight against it." GRIFFITH: "So always a true heart will speak out boldly, indifferent to circumstances,—will not endeavor to clip and tear and file the form of its utterances, in order to avoid collision with misconception and prejudice."—V. 14. There is a time to speak and a time to be silent.—V. 19. HENRY: "It is an instance of true love to our friends and relations to do what we can to keep them from sin."—V. 21. Barabbas. 1) The son of a religious teacher sometimes becomes very wicked. 2) People often choose some evil person or thing in preference to Christ. 3) A man guilty and condemned may escape death because of Christ's dying in his place. —V. 22. Alas! for the fickle multitude who shout "Hosanna" to-day, and ere a week has passed cry out, "Crucify him." The *vox populi* is sometimes *vox diaboli.*—V. 23. HENRY: "The Lord Jesus suffered as an evil-doer, yet neither his judge nor his prosecutors could find that he had done any evil."—V. 25. CHRYS.: "Passion and wicked desire suffer not men to see anything of what is right. For be it that ye curse yourselves; why do you draw down the curse upon your children also?" CALVIN: "There is no doubt that the Jews felt secure in devoting themselves, supposing their cause to be just in the sight of God; but inconsiderate zeal drives them headlong to cut off from themselves all hope of pardon for their wickedness. Hence we learn how anxiously in all judgments we should avoid headlong rashness."—V. 26. Lessons from the case of Pilate. 1) Skepticism and superstition often go together— "What is truth?" and the dream. 2) Skepticism will sometimes turn away from the richest sources of instruction and the amplest evidence. 3) A man feebly anxious to do right may be sorely embarrassed by previous wrong doing. 4) A man cannot make a decision and evade the responsibility of it. 5) Others may voluntarily share a man's guilt, and not lighten it.—The greatest of all instances of God's bringing good out of evil is the fact that because of Judas, Caiaphas, Pilate, and Barabbas, the Divine Redeemer

was lifted up that he might draw all men unto himself.

32-56. CRUCIFIXION OF JESUS. Found also in Mark 15: 21-41; Luke 23: 26-49; John 19: 17-37. In their accounts of the crucifixion, Matt. and Mark most nearly agree in the selection and order of the material, as they have been doing since 19: 1. Luke gives much that they do not contain, and John's narrative is nearly all additional to the other three. Matthew's account divides itself into v. 32-34, 35-38, 39-44, 45-50, 51-56.—The *time* of the crucifixion was beyond question from about 9 A. M. to 3 P. M., and probably A. D. 30; if so, the day of the month was probably April 7 (Wieseler, p. 355, Clark's "Harm." p. 291). As to the *place*, see below on v. 33.

I. **32-34.** He is led to the place of crucifixion, and refuses the stupefying draught. **And as they came out,** not out of the prætorium, but out of the city, as shown by the statement of Mark and Luke that Simon was "coming out of the country." It was customary and natural to go out of the city for executions. (Num. 15 : 35 f.; 1 Kings 21 : 13; Acts 7 : 58.) **A man of Cyrene.** Cyrene was an old Greek settlement on the coast of Africa, immediately south of Greece, and west of Alexandria. Being a place of much trade, it contained many Jews; the second Book of Maccabees (2: 23) was originally written by one Jason of Cyrene. The city is mentioned in Acts 2: 10; 6: 9; 11: 20; 13: 1, all going to show that Cyrenean Jews were numerous; and often seen in Jerusalem and vicinity. **Simon by name.** The name shows that he was a Jew. Mark adds, "the father of Alexander and Rufus," who must for some reason have been well known among the Christians at the time when Mark wrote. We cannot say whether this was the Rufus of Rom. 16: 13, the name being very common. Mark and Luke state that Simon was "coming out of the country," just entering the city as the procession went out of the gate; there was no objection to journeying on the feast-Sabbath (see on v. 39). **Com-**

33 And when they were come unto a place called
Golgotha, that is to say, a place of a skull,

33 *with them*, that he might bear his cross. And when
they were come unto a place called Golgotha, that is

pelled, more exactly *impressed* (Rev. Ver. margin), a peculiar word employed by Mark also, and explained above on 5: 41. **To bear his cross.** We have seen on 16: 24 that it was customary to make the condemned carry his cross to the place of crucifixion. Meyer shows that this was usually the upright post, the transverse piece or pieces being carried separately and fastened on after reaching the place; in some instances (Keim) the accused bore the transverse portion, perhaps in rare instances the whole. John says (19: 17, R. v.) that Jesus went out, bearing the cross for himself. So we must suppose that the burden proved too great for one who had spent a sleepless and troubled night, including the supper and farewell discourse, the agony in Gethsemane, the apprehension and series of trials; the repeated mockings and terrible Roman scourging; and when he fell under the burden or walked too slowly for their convenience, the soldiers used their power of impressing the first stout man they met. Luke says they "laid on him the cross, to bear it after Jesus." Some think this means that Simon walked behind Jesus, bearing one end of the piece of timber; but the more obvious view is probably correct.—On the way, Jesus was accompanied (Luke 23: 27-32, R. v.) by "a great company of the people, and of women," who were bewailing him; and in tender compassion he broke his calm silence to say, "Daughters of Jerusalem, weep not for me, but weep for yourselves, and for your children," and went on with an intimation of coming national calamities, which we now readily understand as referring to the destruction of Jerusalem.

Unto a place called Golgotha, that is to say, A place of a skull. In Hebrew *gulgoleth* is 'skull,' from a root meaning to roll, indicating the globular form of a skull. This in Aramaic would be *gulgoltha*, which is found in the Syriac of Jerusalem, and easily contracted, by omitting either *l*, into

gugoltha (Syriac Pesh., and Hark.), or *golgotha*, the form found in most documents. Thus the word means simply skull, and so Luke (23: 33, Rev. Ver.) says, "unto the place which is called The skull," while Matt., Mark, and John have literally 'skull-place.' The notion was early suggested (Jerome) that this denoted a burial-ground, or a place of execution, marked by a skull or skulls lying on the surface.[1] But the Jewish law did not allow bones to remain unburied, and this would have been carefully observed near the city. So it must have been (Cyril of Jerus.) a round hill or rock, somewhat resembling a skull in shape. Mark, Luke, and John all have the Greek definite article, 'unto the place,' indicating that it was known by this name. It is common among us to call a rounded mountain-top or hill-top a head, as "Cesar's Head" in the Blue Ridge; comp. headland.

It was suggested in the last century (Herzog), and has been fairly established by Robinson ("Biblical Researches") and others, that this cannot have been the place discovered at the request of Helena, the mother of Constantine, and now covered by "the Church of the Holy Sepulchre." Golgotha was "without (or outside) the gate" (Heb. 13: 12), while "nigh to the city" (John 19: 20); but the Church of the Holy Sepulchre is far within any probable position of the city wall at the time of the crucifixion. The reverence many feel for whatever has been believed for fifteen hundred years has caused earnest resistance to this conclusion, but in vain; see results of recent English explorations in Conder, I, pages 361–371.—The site of Golgotha has for a generation and more been apparently quite unknown. But Thenius, A. D. 1849, and independently Fisher Howe, pamphlet on "The True Site of Calvary" (New York, Randolph, 1871), suggested a theory which has of late been adopted by many. The northern extension of the Temple Hill, beyond

---

[1] Accordingly, Tyn., Cran., Gen., rendered 'a place of dead men's skulls,' though the Greek is singular, 'a place of a skull.' So they did also in Mark. But in Luke (23: 33) this rendering was impossible, and so they fell back upon the Latin translation *Calvaria*, which meant skull, and gave us Calvary. Tertullian already began to treat this *Calvaria* as the name of a place. Jerome mentions the notion of some that Adam was buried in Golgotha, and Christ's blood dropped upon his tomb; and says the people liked to hear it.

34 They gave him vinegar to drink mingled with gall: and when he had tasted *thereof*, he would not drink.
35 And they crucified him, and parted his garments, casting lots: that it might be fulfilled which was spoken by the prophet, They parted my garments among them, and upon my vesture did they cast lots.

34 to say, The place of a skull, they gave him wine to drink mingled with gall: and when he had tasted 35 it, he would not drink. And when they had crucified him, they parted his garments among them,

the walls, rises into a rounded hill resembling the top of a skull, and some sixty feet above the level of the surrounding ground. A cut across the ridge to protect the wall from being commanded by an enemy's military engines, gives to this rounded hill a perpendicular southern face, in which is the entrance to a cave called the Grotto of Jeremiah. Seen from the Mount of Olives and other points of good view, this hill looks strikingly like a skull, with a great eyeless socket. The cut across the ridge must have been ancient, from military necessity, and the cave is probably ancient too. The theory is that this hill was Golgotha or Calvary. The site fulfills all the conditions. It is outside the great northern gate, and near. The hill rises beside, and its summit is in full view of, the great northern road, which accounts for passers by (v. 39, Mark 15 : 29); and the Romans were accustomed to crucify in a conspicuous place, to make the lesson more notable. It is in a region abounding in ancient tombs, which accounts for Joseph's garden and tomb. And this site accounts for the tradition of a hill, "Mount Calvary," which is traced back to the fourth century. A Jewish tradition points to this hill as "the place of stoning," *i. e.*, the regular place for executions. And a Christian tradition makes it the scene of Stephen's death, afterwards by tradition located elsewhere. — This theory was adopted by the late Bishop Gobat of Jerusalem, by General (Chinese) Gordon, "Reflections in Palestine," 1883, and by Professor Sir J. W. Dawson, "Syria and Palestine," 1885. It is favored by Schaff, "Through Bible Lands," and Conder, both publishing in 1878, and is advocated by Edersh. Dr. Selah Merrill, Amer. Consul at Jerus., in "Andover Review," Nov. 1885, says that "for some years past there has been a growing conviction" to this effect and that "hundreds of Christian tourists visit the place every year, and few of them go away unconvinced that both the arguments and the strong probability are in favor of" this view.
Gave him vinegar (or *wine*) **to drink,**

mingled with gall. Mark, 'wine mingled with myrrh.' The correct text in Matthew is clearly 'wine;' it was probably changed in many documents to agree with v. 48 below; and with Psa. 69: 21. Talmud Bab. says (Lightf.) that to criminals on the way to execution was given a drink consisting of wine mixed with a bit of frankincense to stupefy them, and that according to tradition, the noble women of Jerusalem furnished this at their own expense. This may be connected in our minds with the "daughters of Jerusalem," who had sorrowfully accompanied the procession. (Luke 23: 27.) The term 'gall' in Matt. must be used generally to denote any bitter and nauseous substance, which in this case would be some bitter vegetable narcotic. It would seem (Keim, Plump.), that Matthew's word sometimes denotes wormwood; see Sept. of Deut. 29: 18; Prov. 5: 4. Keim: "The drink might have been prepared from poppies or wormwood. Simpson, the discoverer of chloroform, thought of hashish, the Indian extract of hemp." Dr. A. Coles, "Life of our Lord in Verse," (New York, Appleton), suggests mandragora, mandrake, "which is said to have been employed by the ancients as an anæsthetic in surgical operations."
II. **35-38.** He is crucified between two robbers. Mark 15: 24-27; Luke 23: 32 f.; John 19: 18-22. **And they crucified him.** For the different kinds of cross, see the Bible Dictionaries. There can be no doubt that the Saviour's cross was of the shape with which we are familiar, an upright post with a transverse piece some distance below the top, the inscription being placed "above his head." But the cross was not so high as the ordinary representation, the person being usually but a foot or two above the ground, and this would especially be the case in Palestine, where timber was scarce. The hands were nailed to the transverse beam. This sometimes extended across the post at right angles; but in other cases consisted of two parts sloping upward from the post, so that the body seemed to hang by the hands, though it was really supported by a projecting peg. The feet were

36 And sitting down they watched him there;
37 And set up over his head his accusation written,
THIS IS JESUS THE KING OF THE JEWS.

36 casting lots: and they sat and watched him there.
37 And they set up over his head his accusation writ-

usually nailed to the post, we do not know whether together or separately; but more probably the latter. They were sometimes drawn up so that the soles rested against the post, but in other cases stood upon a projection. It has been maintained by Paulus and others that the feet of Jesus were not nailed, but bound to the post or left loose. But the risen Saviour identified himself by showing "his hands and his feet" (Luke 24: 39 f.), and certain supposed ancient evidence that only the hands were nailed in crucifixion is indistinct, and far out-weighed by contrary statements. (See Meyer, Smith's "Bib. Dict." Amer. ed., "Crucifixion," or Keim). It cannot be determined whether the sufferer was fastened to his cross before or after its elevation; the method appears to have varied.—The physical suffering produced by crucifixion was fearful. The constrained and immovable posture of the body and arms would gradually produce violent aching and cramps; the pierced limbs became inflamed, producing fever and thirst; the circulation of the blood being hindered, it gathered in the head and lungs, causing great distress; the body would gradually grow stiff, and the vital powers sink from exhaustion. (See Richter in Schaff.) Our Lord's mental suffering (v. 46) must have been greater still; but we should not under-rate the physical.

A cross mark of various shapes appears as a symbol in several ancient religions. But this has really nothing to do with Christianity, into which the cross did not enter as a symbol, but as a historical fact. Persons interested in the doubtful symbolisms referred to may find an account of them in Baring-Gould's "Mediæval Myths," and a condensed statement in "Homiletic Review," Jan., 1886, p. 76 ff.

Mark tells us (15: 25) that the crucifixion began at "the third hour," which soon after the equinox would be almost exactly 9 A. M. John 18: 14 long seemed hopelessly to contradict this, by saying "it was about the sixth hour" when Pilate was ending the trial. But the view of Wieseler and Ewald is now widely adopted, that the Fourth Gospel counts the hours as we do, making the sixth hour 6 A. M., and we could easily suppose that the preparations consumed the intervening three hours. This view is strenuously opposed by Farrar (App. to "Life of Christ"), but he is answered by McClellan, p. 737 ff.; see also Westcott on John. All the passages of John in which hours of the day are mentioned may be readily understood in this way, and it seems to be necessary for John 20: 19, when compared with Luke 24: 29, 36.—At this point Luke mentions (23: 34) that Jesus said, "Father, forgive them; for they know not what they do." Every one feels that these must be words of Jesus, and they are most probably genuine as a part of Luke's Gospel, though it is hard to account for their absence from some important early documents.

And parted his garments among them, casting lots. John explains in detail that they "made four parts, to every soldier a part," there being a quaternion or group of four soldiers detailed to crucify and guard each prisoner (comp. Acts 12: 4), who naturally took his clothing as their perquisite. John also adds that his 'coat,' or tunic, the undergarment (see above on 5: 40), "was without seam, woven from the top throughout," apparently a costly garment, and no doubt a gift of affection, and that being unwilling to "rend" this, they cast lots for it; and that this occurred in the course of providence "that the Scripture might be fulfilled (comp. above on 1: 22), which saith, **They parted my garments among them, and upon my vesture did they cast lots.** This quotation from Psa. 22: 18 was introduced by some copyists into Matt., being given in v. 35 by documents of no great value. Jewish feeling required (Mishna, Sanh., VI, 3) that the person of one stripped when about to be stoned should not be left wholly exposed; and though the Roman custom for crucifixion was otherwise, we may perhaps suppose that Jewish feeling was in this case regarded.

And they set up[1] over his head his accu-

---

[1] Some grammarians and commentators have earnestly discussed the question whether this aorist ought to be rendered like a pluperfect, 'had set up,' because they think the inscription must have been put up be-

38 Then were there two thieves crucified with him; one on the right hand, and another on the left.
39 And they that passed by reviled him, wagging their heads,

38 ten, THIS IS JESUS THE KING OF THE JEWS. Then are there crucified with him two robbers, one on the 39 right hand, and one on the left. And they that passed by railed on him, wagging their heads, and

sation written, it being common to put over a crucified man a statement of his crime. We know not whether in this case, as in one described by Suetonius, the title was borne before the criminal in the procession. John says (19: 20, correct text), "it was written in Hebrew, and in Latin, and in Greek." The first (Aramaic) was the language of the people, the second that of the civil rulers, the third that of general intercourse throughout that part of the world. A pillar was dug up at Jerusalem not many years ago, bearing an inscription in these three languages. The inscription on the cross is given in different terms by the four Gospels. We have seen that the same is to some extent true of the words spoken from heaven at the baptism and the transfiguration, so as to show beyond question that the Evangelists are not solicitous to give always the exact words. It is very likely that the inscription was verbally different in the three languages; and it has been ingeniously suggested (Westcott, "Int." p. 328) that John, who says carefully, 'and it was written,' etc., gives the exact Greek form, 'Jesus of Nazareth, the King of the Jews,' of which Mark gives only the special point of accusation, 'the King of the Jews'; and that then Matt. has the Hebrew, and Luke the Latin form. This is possible, but the matter is of little importance, as the inscription is substantially the same in all the forms. John adds that Pilate himself wrote the inscription, and curtly refused to alter it it when requested. He had been compelled to yield the main point, and he was determined not to yield here; see as to his character on 27: 11.

Then were there two thieves (*robbers*) **crucified with him.** It is quite likely that these were comrades of Barabbas (27: 16), who would have been here between them had not Jesus taken his place. Our Lord had said the night before (Luke 22 : 37), "This that is written must yet be fulfilled in me, And he was reckoned among the transgressors." (Isa. 53 : 12.) This was substantially fulfilled by

punishing him as if for transgression; but all the more strikingly by associating him with actual transgressors. Wetstein gives passages of ancient writers which show that crucifixion was the regular punishment for robbery. The Greek language has two words, *kleptes* 'thief,' and *leistes* 'robber,' differing very much as our words do. The former occurs sixteen times in New Test., and in Com. Ver. is always correctly rendered 'thief'; the latter is four times correctly rendered 'robber,' but eleven times rendered 'thief'; including all the references to the two persons crucified with Jesus, and also Matt. 21: 13; 26: 55. In John 10: 1, 8 the distinction is observed in Com. Version. One evil result of this irregular translation has been that people would read "Barabbas was a robber" (John 18: 40), and it did not occur to them that these two were like him. Besides, a robber would be more likely than a thief to exhibit the character shown by the penitent on the cross. Rev. Ver., and other recent versions, observe the distinction throughout, as there is no difficulty whatever in doing. Luke has here a general term, 'malefactors' or evil-doers; John simply 'two others.'

III. **39-44.** On the cross he is mocked and reviled. Mark 15: 29-32; Luke 23: 35-43. Crucifixion itself was the most disgraceful punishment in use, being appointed by the Romans for slaves, and expressly forbidden for Roman citizens—while the law of Moses (Deut. 21: 23) declared one "accursed" who even after being killed was hanged on a tree. In this case all that could be thought of was done to aggravate the disgrace. Several different classes of persons joined in railing and mocking at Jesus. We must remember the similar treatment when he appeared before the Sanhedrin (26: 67 f.), before Herod (Luke 23: 11), and before Pilate. (27: 27-31.)

(a) **They that passed by,** probably along a road leading into and out of the city, which according to the above-stated theory concerning Golgotha (on v. 33) would be the great

---

fore they parted the garments. This is mere learned trifling. Any animated writer, in narrating a series of occurrences, would consult convenience as to taking

up this or that point. Besides, who knows that the soldiers would nail up the title *before* they divided the plunder?

40 And saying, Thou that destroyest the temple, and buildest *it* in three days, save thyself. If thou be the Son of God, come down from the cross.

41 Likewise also the chief priests mocking *htm*, with the scribes and elders, said,

42 He saved others: himself he cannot save. If he be the King of Israel, let him now come down from the cross, and we will believe him.

43 He trusted in God ; let him deliver him now, if he will have him: for he said, I am the Son of God.

---

40 saying, Thou that destroyest the [1] temple, and buildest it in three days, save thyself: if thou art the Son

41 of God, come down from the cross. In like manner also the chief priests mocking *him*, with the scribes

42 and elders, said, He saved others; [2] himself he cannot save. He is the King of Israel; let him now come down from the cross, and we will believe on

43 him. He trusteth on God: let him deliver him now, if he desireth him: for he said, I am the Son of God.

---

1 Or. *sanctuary*....2 Or, *can he not save himself?*

---

northern road. Some have inferred that this must have been a working day, and not the first day of the passover, which would be a Sabbath ; but Edersh. says that "traveling, which was forbidden on Sabbaths, was *not* prohibited on feast-days," adding that "this is distinctly stated in the Talmud." **Reviled him.** The Greek word is borrowed as 'blasphemed' in 9: 3; 26: 65, and explained above on 12: 31. Com. Ver. translated it 'railed on him' in the parallel passages, Mark 15: 29, Luke 23: 39. **Thou that destroyest the temple,** etc. This accusation (see on 26: 61) the rulers had probably spread while persuading the crowds to prefer Barabbas. **Save thyself.** The word is used (see on 1: 21) both of bodily and spiritual saving. **If thou be the Son of God,** as in 4: 3, 6. The form of expression assumes that he is the Son of God, but their whole tone and manner showed that they meant the contrary. It is not clear that the Jews understood this expression to carry the idea of Deity (comp. on 26: 63) ; they certainly understood that one who assumed it claimed supernatural power.

(b) **The chief priests . . . with the scribes and elders.** Of these three classes the Sanhedrin was constituted (see on 26: 59); so all classes of the rulers took part in the mocking. While the other mockers all address Jesus, the rulers do not condescend to speak to him, but speak contemptuously about him in his presence. Notice Mark 15: 31, R. V., "mocking him among themselves"; and Luke has the same difference. The rulers make three distinct taunts. (1) **He saved others,** probably refers to bodily healing. The other clause may be either an assertion or a question (*margin*, Rev. Ver.), as the Greek in this class of expressions makes no difference; the substantial meaning is the same either way. (2) **If he be the King of**

Israel. This is said in irony, derision. He had that morning claimed before them to be the Messiah (26 : 63 f.), and the Messiah was of course to be king; the inscription also declared him to be the King of Israel. *Euthym.:* "For as they could not change the inscription, they try to prove it false." The irony not being understood, 'if' was inserted, like v. 40, and passed into most documents, but is wanting in some of the earliest and best.[1] **And we will believe him,** or, *on him.* They would have done no such thing. He had wrought miracles even more wonderful, and upon learning it they were only the more determined to kill him. (John 11 : 47-53.) Our Lord never responded to any demand for signs of his mission. (3) **He trusted in God,** properly perfect tense, *has placed his trust on God* and keeps it there. 'Trusted,' past tense, Com. Ver., is an erroneous translation ; 'on' here and in v. 42 is the literal meaning of the Greek preposition. The similar words of Psa. 22: 8 probably occurred to the rulers through general familiarity as expressing their thought—a sort of unconscious Messianic quotation (comp. below on v. 46), like the unconscious Messianic prediction of Caiaphas in John 11: 51 f.—*Edersh.:* "These jeers cast contempt on the four great facts in the Life and Work of Jesus, which were also the underlying ideas of the Messianic Kingdom : the new relationship of Israel's religion and temple ('thou that destroyest the temple and buildest it in three days') ; the new relationship to the Father through the Messiah, the Son of God ('if Thou art the Son of God' R. V.); the new all-sufficient help brought to body and soul in salvation ('He saved others'); and finally, the new relationship to Israel in the fulfillment and perfecting of its mission through its King ('He is the King of Israel, R. V.')."

---

1 Wanting in א B D L, 33, 102, Theb. If originally present there would have been no objection to it.

44 The thieves also, which were crucified with him, cast the same in his teeth.
45 Now from the sixth hour there was darkness over all the land unto the ninth hour.

44 And the robbers also that were crucified with him cast upon him the same reproach.
45 Now from the sixth hour there was darkness over

(c) Luke states (23:36) that "the soldiers also mocked him," offering him the sour wine they were drinking. At a later period, this was given him in kindness. (John 19:29.)

(d) **The thieves also ;** better as in Rev. Ver., *the robbers* (see on v. 38) *also that were crucified with him, cast upon him the same reproach*, viz., that he had professed to trust in God and claimed to be the Son of God, and yet was not now delivered. **Cast the same in his teeth,** is a vigorous image of Com. Ver., but not presented by the Greek. Mark makes a similar statement, 'they that were crucified with him reproached him.' But in Luke we find a striking difference. There (Luke 23:39-43), "one of the malefactors railed on him," as pretending to be the Messiah, while the other believed that he *was* the Messiah ; yea, more discerning than the Twelve, he believed that though now despised and rejected he would come again as king, even as he had of late been teaching (Luke 19: 11 f.; Matt. 25:31; 16:28), and in humble petition said, "Jesus, remember me when thou comest in thy kingdom," R. V. How he learned so much, and understood so well, we do not know ; but the Saviour, who made no response to taunts and revilings, from whatsoever source, answered the first word of petition, and promised more than he had asked. Not merely shall the penitent robber be remembered when the crucified comes again as king, but "To-day shalt thou be with me in Paradise."—Now the question has been much discussed, and cannot be solved with certainty, how we are to reconcile Luke's account with that of Matt. and Mark. The prevailing view is that both the robbers at first reviled, and afterwards one of them, impressed by the Saviour's aspect and his prayer for the crucifiers, and perhaps recalling earlier knowledge of his teachings and miracles, became now convinced that he was indeed the Messiah. This makes it all the more wonderful that he should understand so thoroughly, though of course not impossible under special divine influence. But Matt. and Mark may be understood, with many expositors, as merely including in general the Saviour's fellow-sufferers among the different classes of revilers, without distinguishing between the two, which would have required a full account of a matter they did not undertake to narrate. If it be asked how they could omit this, the same question arises as to their giving only one of the seven words on the cross, and so in many other cases. In this view the penitent robber may have become a believer in Jesus as the Messiah on some earlier day, since his crime, yet hardly since his sentence, for among the Jews that was quickly followed by execution (see on 27: 1).—However this may be regarded, we must remember the general and impressive fact that Jesus was reviled by many classes of persons, by the people at large, the rulers (all sections of the Sanhedrin), the soldiers ; and even participation in suffering did not prevent reviling. This mocking and railing probably began when he was first lifted on the cross, and continued from time to time. Observe that all the verbs here, 'railed,' 'said,' (v. 41), 'reproached' (v. 44, Rev. Ver.), are in the Greek imperfect tense, denoting continued or repeated action.—At some point during the first three hours occurred the pathetic incident of John 19: 25-37, "Behold thy son," and "Behold thy mother." Thus the Saviour spoke three times that we know of during the first half of the crucifixion.

IV. **45-50.** He cries out in the darkness, and dies. Mark 15: 33-37; Luke 23: 44-46; John 19: 28-30. **From the sixth hour . . . . unto the ninth hour** (comp. on 20: 3), from twelve o'clock to about three P. M. **Darkness,** supernatural. It cannot have been an eclipse of the sun, because the Passover was at the middle of the month, and the month always began with the new moon, so that the moon was now full, *i. e.*, on the opposite side of the earth from the sun. Thus all the long discussion about the account of an eclipse said to have been given by Phlegon, a writer of the second century, is beside the mark, for this was *not* an eclipse. 'The sun's light failing,' Rev. Ver., Luke 23: 45 (correct text), need not mean what is technically called an eclipse, but simply states that the sun failed, without

46 And about the ninth hour Jesus cried with a loud voice, saying, Eli, Eli, lama sabachthani? that is to say, My God. my God, why hast thou forsaken me?
47 Some of them that stood there, when they heard *that*, said, This *man* calleth for Elias.

46 all the [1] land until the ninth hour. And about the ninth hour Jesus cried with a loud voice, saying, Eli, Eli, lama sabachthani? that is, My God, my God, [2] why hast thou forsaken me? And some of them that stood there, when they heard it, said, This man

---

1 Or, *earth*....2 Or, *why didst thou forsake me?*

---

indicating the cause. All men feel alarmed by any sudden and great darkness. The Rabbis said (Wün.) that such an occurrence was a bad sign for the world, and was to be expected upon occasion of certain great crimes or misfortunes. Wetstein has many passages from Greek and Latin authors showing a similar feeling. **Over all the land,** viz., of Palestine. The word might mean 'earth' (*margin* Rev. Ver.), comp. on 5: 5; but it was dark, naturally, over half the earth, and a miraculous darkness over all the enlightened half is improbable, seeing that so large a proportion of the persons involved would not know its meaning, and so it would be a useless miracle. The supernatural darkness was an appropriate concomitant, and may be regarded as a sort of symbol of the Saviour's mental suffering, which at last found expression in his loud cry. Through nearly all this period he seems to have continued silent. He must have been enduring a dark sorrow, a crushing grief, even greater than in Gethsemane, seeing that he speaks here in more impassioned distress; and here, as there (see on 26: 44), it can be explained only by the fact that "he was wounded for our transgressions," was "made sin for us," "gave his life a ransom for many" (comp. on 20: 28). **Cried with a loud voice,** showing great suffering. **Eli, Eli, lama sabachthani.** The original words are given, because *Eli*, explains the supposition of 'some' (Mark likewise) of the bystanders, that he was calling for Elijah. The first words are here given in the Hebrew, like the Psalm, but by Mark in the Aramaic *Eloi*, which Jesus had doubtless spoken. The last word is given by both in the Aramaic (so in the Targum, Buxtorf), the Hebrew having another term [1] of the same sense. Our Lord's borrowing the phraseology of Psa. 22: 1, does not show that Psalm to be Messianic; comp. his borrowing in Luke 23: 46 from Psa. 31: 5, and his answering each of Satan's three special temptations by quoting from Deut.

chap. 6–8. Still, as Psalm 22: 13, was a Messianic prophecy (John 19: 24), we may suppose that 22: 1 was designed by the Spirit of inspiration to be used by the Messiah on the cross. It is commonly said that Psa. 22 was not regarded by the Jews as Messianic. Edersh. (App. IX) gives two references to it (v. 7, 15) as applied to the Messiah in a collection made in the thirteenth century, but believed to consist of ancient material. Tertullian thought that Psa. 22 "contains the whole passion of Christ." **Why hast thou forsaken me?** A more literal translation would be, *Why didst thou forsake me* (*margin* Rev. Ver.), but it would amount to the same thing. 'Why' is not here 'for what cause,' but 'to what end'; yet the distinction must not be pressed (comp. 9: 4). If the question be asked in what sense the Father forsook the Son, the answer is that we really do not know. In himself the Saviour was still well-pleasing to the Father, in voluntarily laying down his life that he might take it again (John 10: 17 f.); it must have been as our substitute, because he "bare our sins in his own body on the tree," that he was forsaken. If it be asked how he could feel himself to be forsaken, we must remember that a human soul as well as a human body was here suffering, a human soul thinking and feeling within human limitations (Mark 13: 32), not psychologically unlike the action of other devout souls when in some great and overwhelming sorrow. Comp. W. N. Clarke on Mark 15: 34. *Hanna:* "It was the sensible comfort only of the divine presence and favor that was for the time withdrawn; the felt inflowings of the divine love that were for the time checked. But what a time of agony must that have been to him who knew, as none other could, what it was to bask in the light of his Father's countenance; who felt, as none other could, that his favor indeed was life! On us—so little do we know or feel what it is to be forsaken by God—the thought of it, or sense of it, may make but a slight impression, produce

---

1 Hebrew *'azavthani*, which some "Western" documents have endeavored to reproduce here by changing into *zaphthani* and similar forms; so also in Mark.

48 And straightway one of them ran, and took a sponge, and filled *it* with vinegar, and put *it* on a reed, and gave him to drink.
49 The rest said, Let be, let us see whether Elias will come to save him
50 Jesus, when he had cried again with a loud voice, yielded up the ghost.

48 calleth Elijah. And straightway one of them ran, and took a sponge, and filled it with vinegar, and
49 put it on a reed, and gave him to drink. And the rest said, Let be; let us see whether Elijah cometh
50 to save him.[1] And Jesus cried again with a loud

1 Many ancient authorities add, *And another took a spear and pierced his side, and there came out water and blood.* See John xix. 34.

but little heartfelt misery; but to him it was the consummation and concentration of all woe, beyond which there was and could be no deeper anguish for the soul."

This man calleth for Elias, or *Elijah.* The grand figure which Elijah made in the history, and the promise of his coming in Mal. 4:5 f., caused him to stand out in the Jewish mind as the greatest of the prophets. There was a general expectation, derived from Mal., that he would work various wonders (comp. on 16:14). It is not easy to determine whether this utterance was a mocking misrepresentation by Jews, or a misunderstanding by Roman soldiers. Jews can hardly have really misunderstood, for the opening vowel of Eli has to the Oriental ear a very different sound from that of Elijah. Soldiers, if long resident in Palestine, might have become acquainted with the popular expectations concerning Elijah. **Gave him to drink,** is imperfect tense, probably describing the kindly soldier as repeatedly applying the sponge to the sufferer's parched lips. **The rest said,** imperfect tense, describing them as engaged in saying. *Bengel:* "After the dreadful darkness they returned to scoffing." **Let be,** let things stay as they are; do not give him any aid or comfort—see if Elijah will hear his prayer; for if so, all his wants will be supplied. They seem to have amused themselves with the thought that this pretended Messiah was in his helpless extremity calling on the predicted forerunner of Messiah to come and help him. **Whether Elias,** or *Elijah,* **will come,**[1] or *is coming.* As to spelling Elijah, instead of Elias, see on 1:2.

The **reed** probably means in general a staff for walking, which we in like manner call a cane. From John 19:29 it appears to have been made from a stalk of hyssop; and Tristram ("Nat. Hist.") says that the caper, which is probably the Biblical hyssop, would furnish a stalk three or four feet in length. The **vinegar** was probably a sort of sour wine, though vinegar itself (no doubt diluted with water) was used as a cooling drink. (Ruth 2:14.) It was given mercifully, to refresh the sufferer's parched mouth. John shows (19:28) that it was done in consequence of his saying "I thirst." He had refused the stupefying draught at the beginning, but asked for this slight refreshment when near the end. Then he uttered a third word (John), "It is finished," and finally a fourth (Luke), "Father, into thy hands I commend my spirit." So there were four sayings close together, and near the end; and with the three uttered during the first three hours, we find in all seven sayings on the cross, of which one is recorded by Matt. and Mark only, three by Luke only, three by John only.

Cried again with a loud voice, Mark likewise. This seems to denote great bodily suffering. The sayings just quoted from Luke and John can hardly be here meant, for they were not of such a nature as to be uttered in a loud voice; it must have been a cry of pain or distress. This great outcry in the moment of dying was not a natural result of mere death by crucifixion, which would produce gradual exhaustion. Taken in connection with the blood and water brought forth by the soldier's spear (John 19:34), it has been

1 The addition in *margin* Rev. Ver., 'And another took a spear and pierced his side, and there came out water and blood,' must be regarded as an insertion from John 19:34. It is found in ℵ B C L U Γ, a few cursives, and less important versions, Chrys., Cyril. This only shows, as we have seen in several other cases (comp. on 24:36), that ℵ B, even with other support, present some distinctly erroneous readings. It might be urged that the words were omitted because they represent the piercing as preceding the Saviour's

death, whereas John makes it follow; but that difference would only have been a reason for removing the passage to the close of v. 50 or 54 or 56, or else there would have been some tampering with the position of the passage in John, which is not the case. The passage of John was written by some student on the margin of Matt. from memory, and by a copyist awkwardly introduced into the text. No critic would question this, but for the persuasion of some that B ℵ C L "can do no wrong."

51 And, behold, the vail of the temple was rent in twain from the top to the bottom; and the earth did quake, and the rocks rent;

52 And the graves were opened; and many bodies of the saints which slept arose,

53 And came out of the graves after his resurrection, and went into the holy city, and appeared unto many.

51 voice, and yielded up his spirit. And behold, the veil of the [1]temple was rent in twain from the top to

52 the bottom; and the earth did quake; and the rocks were rent; and the tombs were opened; and many

53 bodies of the saints that had fallen asleep were raised; and coming forth out of the tombs after his resurrection they entered into the holy city and

---

1 Or, *sanctuary.*

---

thought to show that our Lord died from a bursting of the heart. This is argued with great force by Stroud, "Physical Cause of the Death of Christ," republished in New York, and by Hanna, App. to "Life of Christ." The question possesses a certain kind of interest, but cannot be settled. Let us beware of spending too much thought upon the surroundings and physical conditions of our Lord's death. The great matter is that he "died for our sins," "tasted death for every man."—**Yielded up the ghost** (*spirit*). The closing expiration seems a natural indication of letting the immaterial in us, which is oftenest called spirit, go forth from the body "unto God who gave it." 'Gave up the ghost' was good in old English, but we do not now use 'ghost' in that sense.

50-55. Portents following his death, and the effects. Mark 15: 38-41; Luke 23: 47-49. **The vail of the temple** (*naos*, see on 4: 5), was a richly wrought and heavy curtain which hung between the "Holy Place" and the "Holy of Holies." (Exod. 26: 31-35.) There are some Talmudic statements to the effect that this vail was double in the second temple, but that is a matter of no consequence; nor have we anything to do here with an outer vail (Grimm), which hung between the porch and the Holy Place. Once a year the high priest lifted a corner of this heavy curtain and passed into the Holy of Holies, carrying sacrificial blood which he sprinkled on the mercy seat, and made supplication for the forgiveness of his own sins and those of the people. (Heb. 9: 7.) The sudden rending of this vail **from the top to the bottom** (Mark likewise, showing that it was not done by human agency) symbolized the complete opening for all of a way of access through Christ to the throne of divine mercy. Christ, our high priest, has entered the true Holy of Holies in heaven, offering once for all the all-sufficient atoning sacrifice of his own blood (Heb. 9: 11-28); and now in his name we may look without

dread upon the very throne of God, and come with boldness to the throne of grace. (Heb. 4: 16; 10: 19.)—The other portent is mentioned by Matt. only. Earthquakes are common in Palestine, and this earthquake need not be thought supernatural. The earthquake might naturally rend rocks and open tombs—not graves like ours, but tombs in the rock. (Comp. on 27: 61.) But the rising of the dead was of course supernatural. Notice that they were **bodies of the saints.** The clause **after his resurrection** is ambiguous, as it may be connected with what precedes or what follows. It is more naturally connected with what follows; then we understand that they rose at the time of Christ's death, when the earthquake opened the tombs, but appeared only after he appeared. It may be that they appeared only to believers, who knew that Jesus had risen. The conjecture of Plump. concerning this matter is of some interest. He holds that the tombs opened by the earthquake were near Jerusalem, and as the term "saints" was almost from the first applied to Christians, he thinks that these saints were believers in Jesus who had died before his crucifixion. On this supposition, we see some reason for their appearing to Christian friends and kindred, in order to show that they were not shut out from a share in the kingdom. (Comp. 1 Thess. 4: 13 f.) "The statement that they did not appear till after our Lord's resurrection, is from this point of view significant. The disciples were thus taught to look on that resurrection, not as an isolated phenomenon; but as the 'first fruits' of the victory over death (1 Cor. 15: 20), in which not they themselves only, but those also whom they had loved and lost were to be sharers."—**The holy city,** comp. on 4: 5.

Our Lord's death is described as specially impressing three classes of persons. (a) The Roman centurion, or as we should say, captain (see on 8: 5), and also his soldiers who conducted the crucifixion, were convinced that

54 Now when the centurion, and they that were with him, watching Jesus, saw the earthquake, and those things that were done, they feared greatly, saying, Truly, this was the Son of God.

55 And many women were there, beholding afar off, which followed Jesus from Galilee, ministering unto him;

56 Among which was Mary Magdalene, and Mary the mother of James and Joses, and the mother of Zebedee's children.

54 appeared unto many. Now the centurion, and they that were with him watching Jesus, when they saw the earthquake, and the things that were done, feared exceedingly, saying, Truly this was [1] the Son

55 of God. And many women were there beholding from afar, who had followed Jesus from Galilee,

56 ministering unto him: among whom was Mary Magdalene, and Mary the mother of James and Joses, and the mother of the sons of Zebedee.

1 Or, *a son of God.*

Jesus was what he claimed to be. **When . . . they saw the earthquake, and those things that were done,** *were taking place* (correct text), or coming to pass (comp. on 1: 22), apparently referring to the long-continued supernatural darkness, and perhaps also to the Saviour's aspect and expressions, they *feared exceedingly.* (Rev. Ver.) Well they might fear; for they had been engaged in putting to an ignominious death one who, as they now felt sure, was not a criminal, not an impostor nor a fanatic, but **truly the Son of God. Was,** because his life had ended. Mark has the same expression as Matt. Luke gives "Certainly this was a righteous man." If so, he was what he claimed to be, and he had claimed to be the Son of God. So the difference is only apparent, and in fact we may in this case suppose that he used both expressions. The Greek might mean 'a son of God,' and some suppose that the heathen centurion thought only of one among many demigods. But this Greek phrase is very often used as definite, determined by the connection, and here it is easy to suppose that he had borrowed the phrase from the Jews, and understood it in their sense, which was more or less vague. (Comp. on 26: 63.)

(b) "All the multitudes that came together to this sight," the throngs of Jewish spectators (Luke 23: 48, Rev. Ver.), "returned smiting their breasts," satisfied that a great wrong had been done, and fearing that they would suffer for it.

(c) Many of his own followers beheld his death, with the deepest grief. **Many women.** But Luke mentions also men—"all his acquaintances" (Luke 23: 49), nominative plural, masculine. **Beholding afar off,** through timidity, and through delicacy. The only women of his following who *came near* the cross were his mother and her sister, Mary the wife of Clopas, and Mary Magdalene. (John 19: 25.) **Ministering unto him.** They personally bought and prepared food; and they also furnished money wherewith to purchase food and to pay for cooking it—all this being suggested by the term and circumstances, comp. Luke 8: 2 f.

Mary Magdalene, *i. e.,* from Magdala, probably the place now called Mejdel, on the western shore of the Lake of Galilee (see on 15: 39, where the correct text is Magadan.) Mary Magdalene has received scant justice in Christian literature and art. The heavy affliction of being possessed by "seven demons," from which it was doubtless Jesus that delivered her, does not prove that she had been exceptionally wicked. A late tradition identified her with the "woman that was a sinner," in Luke 7: 37 ff. This tradition is first mentioned in Jerome and Ambrose, was probably nothing but an inference from the severe demoniacal possession, and was never received in the Greek Church. The identification is not only unsupported by anything in Scripture, but rendered highly improbable by the way in which Luke just afterwards mentions Mary Magdalene as a new personage. (Luke 8: 2.) Next, it was taken for granted that the "woman that was a sinner" had been guilty of unchastity, and upon this foundation only, this highly improbable tradition, and this uncertain supposition, it long ago became common to call an abandoned woman a Magdalen. The celebrated paintings of the Magdalen are *historically* an abomination, and religiously quite hurtful. There is at Dresden a painting "of the School of Titian," which represents her as a woman of middle age, once very beautiful, with deep lines of suffering in her face but over it all a look of gentleness, peace, and unutterable gratitude. This conception is historically reasonable. Christ did save persons of the class to which she is usually referred (21: 32), and will save such persons still if they repent and believe him; but that is no reason for involving this special friend of his in undeserved dishonor. The usage about Mary cannot now be wholly corrected, but it may be personally avoided. With this list of three women, 'Mary Magdalene, and Mary the mother of James and Joses, and the mother of the sons of Zebedee,' comp. Mark's three (15: 40, Rev. Ver.; 16:1), "Mary Magdalene, and Mary the mother of James the Little, and of Joses, and Salome." This leaves little doubt that the mother of Zebedee's sons was Salome. Again, in John (19: 25), the women present are "his mother, and his mother's sister, Mary the wife of Clopas, and Mary Magdalene." Here his mother's sister might be Mary the wife of Clopas. But it is not likely that two sisters would be named Mary ; and if we understand that here are four distinct persons, then they fall into two groups, the first group being two unnamed persons, the second two named persons—and this rhythmical form of statement (Westcott on John) resembles the style of the Fourth Gospel. Now it is generally agreed that John's "Mary the wife of Clopas" is the same as "Mary the mother of James the Little and of Joses" in Mark and Matt. (Comp. on 10: 3.) Leave aside then the mother of Jesus in John's list, with Mary Magdalene, who is the same in all, and it becomes highly probable that Salome, the mother of Zebedee's sons, was the sister of our Lord's mother. This theory helps to account for the prominence of James and John, and for the ambitious request of their mother in 20: 20. Then also John's omission of his mother's name would be (Westcott) exactly like his constant omission of his own name. These devout and loving women, and (Luke) some men with them, saw for themselves that the Master really died, and where he was buried. (v. 61.)

HOMILETICAL AND PRACTICAL.

Sermons and devotional books often give overwrought descriptions of the crucifixion. The feelings excited by contemplating it ought to be natural and genuine, and not galvanized. It is better to imitate the reserve and simplicity of the Evangelists, making our narration and description quiet and inelaborate. Any other course is injudicious, in questionable taste, and really irreverent.

V. 32. Simon of Cyrene. 1) A man sharing undeserved reproach. 2) A man rendering involuntary service to Christ. 3) Yet, let us hope, learning to walk voluntarily after Christ, bearing his own cross (16: 24), as we know that his two sons did. (Mark 15 : 21.) CALVIN : "In the sight of men, this task brought him to the lowest degradation ; but God turned it into the highest honor."

> "Shall Simon bear thy cross alone,
>   And other saints be free ?
> Each saint of thine shall find his own,
>   And there is one for me."[1]

V. 33. Because of Gethsemane and Golgotha, we sinners may hope for Paradise.— V. 35. SHAKESPEARE :

> "In those holy fields
> Over whose acres walked those blessed feet,
> Which fourteen hundred years ago were nailed,
> For our advantage, on the bitter cross."

V. 40. "Save thyself." How easily he could have done so ! But his object was still to save others (v. 41); he was dying that men might live.—V. 42. EUTHYM. "And he would have come down, if it had been true that they would believe. Like them are many now who propose their own conditions of believing, but really would not believe on any condition." CALVIN : "It is too common with the impious to measure the power of God by present appearances, so that whatever he does not do, they think he cannot do." V. 46 1) He is my God, yet he has forsaken me. 2) He has forsaken me, yet he is my God.— MRS. BROWNING :

> "Yea, once Immanuel's orphaned cry his universe
>   hath shaken.
> It went up single, echoless, 'My God, I am forsaken !'
> It went up from the Holy's lips amid his lost creation,
> That, of the lost, no son should use those words of
>   desolation."

V. 47. HENRY : "It is no new thing for the

---

[1] Recent hymn books have :

"Must Jesus bear the cross a'one," etc.
Having in youth heard it sung with "Simon" instead, we have long been satisfied, on principles of text criticism, that this was the original form. A friend who has given much attention to hymnology, recently stated that the stanza in the above-quoted form is taken from the "Penitential Cries" of Rev. Thomas Shepherd, of Braintree, Essex, England, published in 1692. The hymn in its now common shape has borrowed only this one stanza from the original. It is credited in some collections to Prof. G. N. Allen, 1852, who wrote the familiar tune, and may have made the changes and the additions.

57 When the even was come, there came a rich man of Arimathea, named Joseph, who also himself was Jesus' disciple:

57   And when even was come, there came a rich man from Arimathæa, named Joseph, who also himself

---

most pious devotions of the best men to be ridiculed and abused by profane scoffers."— V. 50. JER. TAYLOR: "O holy and immaculate Lamb of God, who wert pleased to suffer shame and sorrow, teach me to apprehend the baseness of sin, in proportion to the greatness of those calamities which my sin made it necessary for Thee to suffer, that I may hate the cause of Thy sufferings, and adore Thy mercy, and imitate Thy charity, and copy out Thy patience and humility, and love Thy person to the uttermost extent and degrees of my affections."—Through the cross of Christ may the world be crucified unto us, and we unto the world (Gal. 6: 14.)—V. 51. Our "great High Priest, Jesus the Son of God," has passed through the vail of the heavens into the true sanctuary, and there ever lives to intercede; let us therefore come with boldness. (Heb. 4: 14-16; 7: 25.)—V. 54. If men will but look candidly at the life and death, the teachings and claims of Jesus Christ, must they not acknowledge him to be more than a mere man?—V. 55. CALVIN: "When the disciples had fled hither and thither, yet some women from their company had been kept by God as witnesses; more brightly then shone out their piety towards the Master."

57-66. JESUS BURIED AND REMAINING IN THE TOMB.

Found also in Mark 15: 42-47; Luke 23: 50-56; John 19: 31-42.

Before the interment comes the proposition of the Jews (John) to break the legs of the three crucified persons, which was usually followed (Edersh.) by giving them a death-stroke. The object of the proposition was that they might die and be removed before sunset, when the great Sabbath of the Passover week would begin. The soldiers were surprised to find Jesus dead already, as persons usually remained alive on a cross more than twenty-four hours, and sometimes even for three days; and one of them pierced his side with a spear, bringing out blood and water. John appeals to this as seen by himself, probably because it proved that Jesus had a real human body, in opposition to the Docetic notions referred to in 1 John 4 : 2; 2 John 7, and that he was really dead.

I. **57-61.** The burial. *Luther:* "From this conclusion of the history of our Lord's passion we see what the death of our dear Lord Christ has effected, both with his friends and his enemies. The enemies become unquiet and fearful, and evidently fall deeper into sin. But those who love the Lord Christ, although they are feeble, fearful folk, are yet through the death of Christ consoled and confident, and venture now upon what before they would not have dared to think about." We see that the Father, who appeared to have "forsaken" Christ, is exercising a special providence over his death and interment, with reference to his speedy resurrection. His bones were not broken like those of the robbers, nor his body flung into a public receptacle, but while "numbered with transgressors" he "was with the rich in his death" (Isa. 53 : 9-12); his tomb was in a conspicuous place, was occupied by no other body, closed with the government seal and guarded by Roman soldiers.—**When the even was come,** towards sunset, which at that season would be about 6 P. M. **A rich man of Arimathea,** a place not otherwise known. The name is obviously formed upon Ramah, 'high place,' dual Ramathaim, the name of several cities in Palestine. Luke says it was "a city of the Jews," which probably means of Judea. Eusebius and Jerome ("Onom.") held it to be the Ramathaim of 1 Sam. 1: 1, which was Samuel's birth-place, apparently a few miles northward from Jerusalem; the Sept. calls this place Armathaim, and Jos. ("Ant.," 5, 10, 2) Armatha. The fact that Joseph was rich explains his owning grounds near the city, and also adds importance to the marks of respect he paid to Jesus. Mark and Luke say he was "a councillor," *i. e.*, a member of the Sanhedrin, and Luke adds "a good man and a righteous—he had not consented to their counsel and deed." John says, "in the place where he was crucified there was a garden, and in the garden a new tomb." Joseph may have stood in his garden, which perhaps occupied a slope of the hill on whose summit the crosses stood (see on 27: 33), and his eye falling on the unoccupied tomb, he determined upon his course. **Who also him-**

58 He went to Pilate, and begged the body of Jesus. Then Pilate commanded the body to be delivered.
59 And when Joseph had taken the body, he wrapped it in a clean linen cloth,
60 And laid it in his own new tomb, which he had hewn out in the rock : and he rolled a great stone to the door of the sepulchre, and departed.

58 was Jesus' disciple: this man went to Pilate, and asked for the body of Jesus. Then Pilate com-
59 manded it to be given up. And Joseph took the
60 body, and wrapped it in a clean linen cloth, and laid it in his own new tomb, which he had hewn out in the rock: and he rolled a great stone to the door of

---

self was Jesus' disciple (comp. on 5:1), John adding "but secretly, for fear of the Jews." He the more readily became a disciple because (Mark) he was "looking for the kingdom of God." **Went to Pilate,** Mark adding "boldly." It required courage to offer so much honor to one whom his associates of the Sanhedrin had sentenced for blasphemy, and who had died an ignominious death. He had shrunk from declaring himself a disciple, but now, when all the world had turned against Jesus, he came out boldly. As the execution was by the Roman authorities, their permission was naturally required in order to take charge of the body. The Romans often left the bodies of crucified persons on the cross till they decayed or were devoured by birds of prey, just as in England and the American colonies bodies used to be hung in chains; but the law of Moses required that a dead body hung on a tree should not remain over night, as it would defile the land. (Deut. 21: 23.) Jos. says ("War," 4, 5, 2), "The Jews are so attentive to the rites of sepulture as to take down even those who have undergone the sentence of crucifixion, and inter them before sunset." **Begged.** *Asked* is the exact meaning, not 'begged,' as in Com. Ver. Mark relates that Pilate wondered if he had died so much sooner than was common with the crucified, and sent to ask the centurion in charge. This message (though the distance was small), and the various purchases, took a considerable part of the time between three and six o'clock, and made it needful to act promptly, and fortunate that "the tomb was nigh at hand" (John). **Commanded the body to be delivered,** not requiring money, as was so common when favors were asked from the Roman governors. (Acts 24:26.) Mark says in effect, "made a present of the corpse to Joseph." 'The body,' after 'commanded,' is wanting in several of the best early documents, and was easily added from the preceding sentence. —It was, perhaps, some little comfort to Pilate to see respect shown the remains of one

whom he had so reluctantly yielded to an undeserved punishment.
Took the body, Mark and Luke 'took down,' which was the "descent from the Cross," so often represented in pictures. They of course washed off the stains of blood. **Wrapped it in a clean linen cloth,** which Mark mentions his purchasing. John adds, "There came also Nicodemus, he who at the first came to him by night, bringing a mixture of myrrh and aloes, about a hundred pound weight." The hundred pounds (probably of twelve oz. each) could be easily borne by two servants. In the funeral procession of Herod the Great, five hundred domestics and freedmen bore spices (Jos. "Ant," 17, 8, 3; "War," 1, 33, 9). A rabbinical writing says (Wet. on John) that at the funeral of Gamaliel the elder, a proselyte burned more than eighty pounds of balsam.—Nicodemus doubtless recalled with deep emotion, as he aided in taking down the body, what Jesus had said in their conversation of three years before (John 3:14): "As Moses lifted up the serpent in the wilderness, even so must the Son of man be lifted up."—The linen cloth in consequence of their haste, was probably not torn into many narrow strips, as in the case of Lazarus (John 11:44), but into several pieces, and these are called cloths (plural) in John 19: 40; 20: 5-7; Luke 24: 12. There was also a napkin, or as we should say, handkerchief (John 20:7), probably put under the chin and tied over the head, so as to keep the features in position (comp. John 11; 44). **In his own new tomb.** It was a special honor to occupy a new tomb, like riding the ass's colt, "whereon no man ever yet sat," see above on 21: 2; and all the more that it was the tomb of a wealthy member of the Sanhedrin. Comp. Isa. 53: 9. **Which he had hewn out in the rock** (Mark and Luke likewise), a better kind of tomb than a cave (John 11:38), less subject to dripping water, and to decay of the walls. The rock tombs now found around Jerusalem usually present a number of recesses in the walls, each large

61 And there was Mary Magdalene, and the other Mary, sitting over against the sepulchre.
62 Now the next day, that followed the day of the preparation, the chief priests and Pharisees came together unto Pilate,
3 Saying, Sir, we remember that that deceiver said, while he was yet alive, After three days I will rise again.

61 the tomb, and departed. And Mary Magdalene was there, and the other Mary, sitting over against the sepulchre.
62 Now on the morrow, which is *the day* after the Preparation, the chief priests and the Pharisees were
63 gathered together unto Pilate, saying, Sir, we remember that that deceiver said, while he was yet

---

enough to hold one body. **Rolled a great stone,** too large to lift; comp. Mark 16: 3, and below 28: 2. This was designed to keep out beasts and birds of prey, and petty thieves. The Talmud (Keim) often mentions the *golal*, 'roll-stone,' in describing interments. One large tomb now exists, half a mile or so north of the city, which has a circular stone, like a millstone on edge, cut from the solid rock, with the channel in which it revolves (see engraving in Clarke on Mark, or Hovey on John), and originally furnished with a secret fastening, doubtless in the hope of keeping out robbers, who might plunder the spices, costly linen, jewelry.—**Mary Magdalene, and the other Mary, sitting over against the sepulchre;** comp. 27: 56. Luke adds that they "beheld the tomb, and how his body was laid," so that they knew whither to go on the next morning but one. They would naturally keep at some distance (27:55) while the body was preparing for the tomb, and thus might not know how amply Nicodemus had anticipated them in providing spices; or, they may have wished to complete a process which they knew had been hastily performed. —Com. Ver. quite confounds two Greek words, both signifying a tomb. The difference is of no great practical importance, but they ought to be kept distinct, as in Rev. Ver., which consistently gives 'tomb' in v. 52 f., 60, and so in 8: 28; 23: 29, and 'sepulchre' in v. 61, 64, 66 and 28: 1, and in 23: 27, 29; so in the other Gospels.

II. **62-66.** The sepulchre sealed and guarded. This is narrated by Matt. alone. **Next day,** etc.; Rev. Ver., *the morrow, which is the day after the Preparation.* The Preparation usually meant the day of preparation for the Sabbath. This curious circumlocution for the Sabbath may have been used (Plump.) because the term 'Sabbath' would in this case have been ambiguous, as the day of the crucifixion was itself observed as a Sabbath, being the first day of a feast. **The chief priests and Pharisees.** The chief priests were at this time mostly Sad-

ducees, and so the two parties were uniting in the matter. Comp. 21: 45; 22: 16, 23, 34. **We remember,** literally, *we remembered*, at some time since the crucifixion. **That deceiver.** They can now assume that he was a deceiver (comp. John 7: 12), since he has been put to a disgraceful death. The world is much disposed to judge character by circumstances and outward results. **After three days I will rise again.** The present tense (Rev. Ver.) gives an assured fact, comp. 2: 4; 26: 2. There is record of his predicting this in 16: 21; 17: 23; 20: 19. We do not know how the rulers learned that he had made such a prediction; possibly from Judas, when he first came to them. (26:15.) How can we account for the fact that the rulers remembered, while the disciples seem to have forgotten the prediction? It is probable that the latter regarded the whole idea of the Messiah's being killed and rising again as something figurative. Peter, James, and John, being directed to tell no man of the Transfiguration "save when the Son of man should have risen again from the dead," were accustomed to "question one with another what the rising from the dead should mean." (Mark 9:9 f.) They could not believe that the glorious King Messiah would be literally killed and literally rise again. Comp. on 17: 9. Men are much disposed to "interpret spiritually" when the literal sense conflicts with their fixed opinions. If taken as only meaning something figurative, the prediction would be more readily forgotten, till the literal fulfillment brought it to mind. So the angels said to the women (Luke 24:6), "Remember how he spake unto you when he was yet in Galilee, saying that the Son of man must . . . the third day rise again." The rulers, on the other hand, when they heard of such a prediction, would think of it only in a literal sense, and so they remembered it.

After three days has been insisted on by some as showing, here and in Mark 9: 31 (correct text), that Jesus must have lain seventy-two hours in the tomb, which they sup-

64 Command therefore that the sepulchre be made sure until the third day, lest his disciples come by night, and steal him away, and say unto the people, He is risen from the dead: so the last error shall be worse than the first.
65 Pilate said unto them, Ye have a watch: go your way, make *it* as sure as ye can.
66 So they went, and made the sepulchre sure, sealing the stone, and setting a watch.

64 alive, After three days I rise again. Command therefore that the sepulchre be made sure until the third day, lest haply his disciples come and steal him away, and say unto the people, He is risen from 65 the dead: and the last error will be worse than the first. Pilate said unto them, [1] Ye have a guard: go, 66 [2] make it *as* sure as ye can. So they went, and made the sepulchre sure, sealing the stone, the guard being with them.

1 Or, *Take a guard*....2 Gr. *make it sure, as ye know.*

pose to be confirmed by ' three days and three nights' in Matt. 12: 40. But the only natural way to understand 'after three days' in the mouth of Jew, Greek, or Roman, would be (comp. on 26: 2) to count both the first and the last day, so that it would mean any time on the third day. The phrase ' on the third day' is employed in seven independent statements about our Lord's resurrection; (1) in 16: 21 (and Luke 9: 22) ; (2) in 17: 23 (and Mark 9: 3, common text) ; (3) in 20: 19 (and Luke 18 : 33) ; (4) in Luke 24: 7; (5) in Luke 24: 21; (6) in Luke 24: 46; (7) in 1 Cor. 15: 4. There is then an apparent conflict between these seven statements and Matt. 12: 40, while the other expression, 'after three days,' distinctly sides, according to known usage, with the former, and is indeed parallel in Mark 9 : 31 (correct text) to the former in Matt. 16: 21; Luke 9: 22, and in Mark 10: 34 to Matt. 20: 19 and Luke 18: 33; comp. here also v. 64 with 63. Now 'the third day,' so often used, *cannot possibly* mean after seventy-two hours, while the single statement 'three days and three nights' *can* be understood as meaning three *onahs* or night-day periods of twenty-four hours, any part of such a period being counted, according to the Talmud, as a whole *onah* (see on 12: 40). There is therefore no propriety whatever in saying that our Lord remained in the grave seventy-two hours. And the narratives show that it was in fact a very small portion of one day, all of a second, and less than half of a third day.—**Lest his disciples come. By night** is given in none of the earliest manuscripts and few of the early versions, and was obviously added from 28 : 13. **Ye have a watch,** or, *take a guard* (*margin,* Rev. Ver.). The Greek is ambiguous, and either the indicative or the imperative idea will suit the connection, the former being somewhat more probable. **Make it as sure as ye can.** *As sure as ye know* (how to do), is a more literal translation (*margin,* Rev. Ver.), and would indicate such measures as they understood and actually proceeded to take. **So they went,** not prob-

ably a Sabbath day's journey, though in their present mood that would not have restrained them. **Setting a watch,** or as Rev. Ver., *the guard being with them.* The guard were present and united with the rulers in sealing the stone; and then of course remained to watch the sealed tomb. (Comp. 28: 11.) To break a seal fixed by government authority would be a high crime, bringing condign punishment. (Comp. Dan. 6: 17.) A cord was probably drawn across the stone which closed the door, and its ends were fastened by seals to the walls This labor was contrary to all the Jewish ideas of Sabbath observance, and would be performed by the chief priests and Pharisees only in some extraordinary emergency, even as they had on the first day of the feast condemned the Saviour and secured his execution. We may suppose ("Bib. Comm.") that they had expected Pilate himself to take all these steps, and when he simply authorized *them* to do so, they could not draw back. It is difficult to suppose they did the sealing after sunset, when the Sabbath was ended, for that would not be ' on the morrow' (**v. 62**) after the crucifixion and interment.

HOMILETICAL AND PRACTICAL.

V. 57. Joseph of Arimathea. 1) A member of the Sanhedrin, who had refused to go with the current. 2) A man of high official and social position, who at a crisis was ready to risk all. 3) A wealthy man, whom the governor would listen to, and who could offer the most honorable burial to the body of the crucified. 4) A man who looked for the kingdom of God and knew it when he found it. 5) A disciple of Christ, whose timidity we must not judge harshly, since he came out so grandly at last.—HENRY: " Worldly wealth, though it is to many an objection in religion's way, yet in some services to be done for Christ it is an advantage and an opportunity, and **it** is well for those who have it, if withal **they** have a heart to use it for God's glory.'

CHAPTER XXVIII.

IN the end of the sabbath, as it began to dawn toward the first *day* of the week, came Mary Magdalene and the other Mary to see the sepulchre.

1 Now late on the sabbath day, as it began to dawn toward the first *day* of the week, came Mary Magda-

---

"R ·sting from his work to-day,
In the tomb the Saviour lay;
Still he slept, from head to feet
Shrouded in the winding-sheet,
Lying in the tomb alone,
Hidden by the sealed stone.

"Let me hew thee, Lord, a shrine
In this rocky heart of mine,
Where, in pure embalmed cell,
None but thou may ever dwell.

"Myrrh and spices will I bring,
True affection's offering;
Close the door from sight and sound
Of the busy world around;
And in patient watch remain
Till my Lord appear again."

T. WHYTEHEAD, 1842.

V. 66. CHRYS.: "They who seized him when living, are afraid of him when dead. And yet if he had been a mere man, they had reason to have taken courage. But that they might learn, that when living also he endured of his will what he did endure; behold, both a seal, a stone, and a watch, and they were not able to hold him."

Ch. 28: 1-15. THE RESURRECTION OF JESUS.

Found also in Mark 16: 1-11; Luke 24: 1-12; John 20: 1-18. Comp. 1 Cor. 15: 1-8. The five narratives of our Lord's resurrection and appearances differ much as to the details, but only in the way common when there are several independent and brief accounts of the same series of events. If the narratives are found to agree substantially, then the differences of detail show them to be independent, and really strengthen their credibility. The details in this case can all be harmonized by reasonable suppositions. If at some points the only explanations thus far offered seem artificial and strained, we must remember that the total information given on the subject is quite limited and yet embraces a great variety of distinct matters, and it could not be expected that the relations between these would be everywhere made perfectly clear; also that the progress of research is in every generation clearing up some question that was long con-

sidered difficult. The sacred writers do not treat their Lord's resurrection as a doubtful point, needing to be established by their statements, but as an unquestionable fact. Each of them gives such information concerning it as bears upon the design of his particular writing. Thus in Matt. the earthquake connects itself with that of 27: 51; the report of the guard bears upon a story current among the Jews; the prominence given to Galilee accords with the large space occupied in this Gospel by the Galilean ministry; and the Great Commission shows the true nature of the Messianic reign, as spiritual, and destined to be universal.

This section of Matt. divides itself into v. 1-4, 5-7, 8-10, 11-15.

I. 1-4. Certain devout women find the stone rolled away from the sepulchre.—**In the end,** etc. The Rev. Ver. begins with *now,* the Greek *de,* the usual particle of transition. It might here be rendered 'but,' expressing an opposition between the precautions of the rulers and the events which here follow. **End of the Sabbath,** (Rev. Ver., *late on the Sabbath day,*) **as it began to dawn toward the first day of the week.** This opening expression is not easy to interpret. 'Late on the Sabbath day' is the only natural and well-supported meaning. But the Jewish Sabbath ended at sunset, while Matthew's account indicates, and the other Gospels distinctly declare, that our Lord's resurrection occurred in the early morning. The other expression, 'as it began to dawn,' might refer to the beginning of the new day after sunset, as it apparently does in Luke 23: 54. There are three ways in which Matthew's opening phrase may be understood, so as not to conflict with the other Gospels. (a) It may perhaps mean 'after the Sabbath,' and many insist that this is made necessary by what follows and by the other accounts. It is not clearly made out, but is maintained by such authorities as Fritzsche, Grimm, Godet, and others, that the Greek phrase can have this meaning. (b) 'Late on the Sabbath day' may perhaps reckon the following night as a part of the

2 And, behold, there *a* was a great earthquake: for the angel of the Lord descended from heaven, and came and rolled back the stone from the door, and sat upon it.
3 His countenance was like lightning, and his raiment white as snow:
4 And for fear of him the keepers did shake, and became as dead *men*.

2 lene and the other Mary to see the sepulchre. And behold, there was a great earthquake; for an angel of the Lord descended from heaven, and came and
3 rolled away the stone, and sat upon it. His appearance was as lightning, and his raiment white as
4 snow: and for fear of him the watchers did quake,

---

a Or, *had been.*

Sabbath, departing from the Jewish usage. This interpretation is given by Meyer, and vigorously stated by *Morison :* "The difficulty vanishes if we suppose that the method of adding diurnally the night to the day, rather than the day to the night, had got more or less into common use among the Jews, so that there were two ways of reckoning complete astronomical days; namely, first by night-days, and secondly by day-nights. Here the Evangelist was thinking of day-night (see next clause), and hence 'late in that day-night' would mean about the end of the night that followed the day of the Sabbath." This explanation is possible, but is certainly strained. (c) 'Late in the Sabbath' may be taken in its ordinary sense of before sunset, and we may understand, with McClellan and Westcott on John, that Matt. here mentions a previous visit by the two women, quite distinct from the visit of next morning. This also is possible, but difficult; for 'the women' of v. 5 are almost necessarily understood to be those of v. 1; and after seeing the guard, if not the seal, on the previous visit, how could they expect admission into the tomb? Thus no one of the explanations is easy, and entirely satisfactory; but as each of them is possible, it will not do to say that Matt. is here in irreconcilable conflict with the other Gospels. If compelled to select, we should prefer (b), and understand that Matthew's opening statement refers to the morning dawn. Mark has it, 'very early on the first day of the week. . . . when the sun was risen,' which may mean only the first rays of morning light, which really come from the sun; Luke says, 'at early dawn'; John 'while it was yet dark.' The Orientals have always been accustomed to early rising. The gates would be closed at sunset, and opened at dawn. **The first day of the week** is, in Greek, a peculiar expres-

sion, answering to a well-known Rabbinical phrase (Lightf.), but there is no doubt as to its meaning. **Came Mary Magdalene and the other Mary;** *the mother of James the Little and of Joses,* 27: 56; Mark 15: 40. Mark adds (16:1) Salome; Luke (24:10) adds Joanna (comp. Luke 8: 3), and indicates that there were yet others. There may have been two different parties, that of Joanna and others coming later; so Westcott, Edersh. **To see the sepulchre.** The verb means to behold, as a spectacle; so in 27: 55, and a kindred term in 6: 1. They designed also, if it should appear practicable and appropriate, to 'anoint him' (Mark 16:1), and brought with them spices (Luke 24:1) which they had provided the evening before, when the Sabbath was past. (Mark.) As they went (Mark 16:3, Rev. Ver.), they were concerned about the question, "Who shall roll us away the stone from the door of the tomb?" for they knew from observation of the interment that "*it was exceeding great*" (Mark 16:4, Rev. Ver., comp. Matt. 27:60), and a man's strength would be necessary.

And behold. Matthew often thus introduces matter of special wonder; and here it was peculiarly appropriate. The account in v. 2-4 is found in this Gospel only. The great earthquake is here distinctly supernatural, but that does not prove that the same was true in 27: 51.[1] As to angels, see on 18: 10. The comparison of the angel's appearance to **lightning** and his raiment to **snow,** recalls the Transfiguration. The general term rendered "appearance" (R. V.) was unwarrantably restricted by Tyn. and successors to the countenance, perhaps from comparison of Dan. 10: 5. **The keepers,** or *watchers,* same word as in 27: 54. **Shake,** *quake,* same Greek root as in the word rendered 'earthquake.' Matthew's language would allow, but does not require us to believe, that the women saw the angel

---

[1] The margin of Com. Ver. here gave 'had been' for 'was' to indicate that the earthquake, etc., preceded their coming. But Matthew's connection leaves that doubtful. There should be great caution about trans-

lating the aorist by the pluperfect. It is only the *connection* in the Greek that shows one action to be prior to the other, and the connection can show it in English.

5 And the angel answered and said unto the women, Fear not ye: for I know that ye seek Jesus, which was crucified:
6 He is not here: for he is risen, as he said. Come, see the place where the Lord lay.

5 and became as dead men. And the angel answered and said unto the women, Fear not ye: for I know 6 that ye seek Jesus, who hath been crucified. He is not here: for he is risen, even as he said. Come,

roll away the stone;[1] Mark shows the contrary, for while discussing, as they approach, the question who shall roll it away, 'looking up,' they see that it is rolled back (perfect tense), they see the result, not the process; and so Luke and John. They "were perplexed" (Luke) by finding the sepulchre open, but it does not occur to them that the Lord has risen. See below v. 5 f.

The Fourth Gospel, which gives an account of the movements of Mary Magdalene, says that seeing the stone taken away she ran to Peter and John and said, "They have taken away the Lord out of the tomb, and we know not where they have laid him." Observe that 'we' accords with the statement of Matt. that she had gone in company. She had evidently no idea that the Lord had come to life. (Comp. also John 20: 13.) Peter was probably at John's place of residence in the city. (John 19: 27.) They appear to have been old friends (comp. on 26: 17); John had secured Peter's admission to the court of the high priest, where the mournful fall occurred, and now received Peter, penitent and ashamed, to his own abode. So Peter and John set forth, running towards the tomb (John 20: 3 f.), followed by Mary Magdalene.

II. 5-7. An angel tells them that Jesus is risen. (Mark 16: 5-7; Luke 24: 4-8.) **The angel** is here obviously the one that had rolled away the stone. Mark, who has not told how the stone was rolled away, says that "entering into the tomb they saw a young man sitting on the right side, arrayed in a white robe," Rev. Ver. As this young man said what Matt. ascribes to the angel, we understand that he was the angel. Luke says "two men stood by them in dazzling apparel," Rev. Ver., and gave them the same information. Some understand that this was at a later point, and that is possible. But we have had several instances of one person mentioned in a narrative, and two persons in another narrative of

the same event. (Comp. on 8: 28; 20: 30.) We have only to suppose here, as in those cases, that one of the two was more conspicuous and acted as spokesman, and the variety of statement becomes natural. John also tells that Mary Magdalene presently saw "two angels in white sitting, one at the head, and one at the feet, where the body of Jesus had lain." The images used in the several narratives to describe the appearance of the angel or angels, differ precisely as at the Transfiguration. The different positions and postures mentioned are readily understood as obtaining at different times during the rapid series of events. Such slight points of disagreement only add to the naturalness and verisimilitude of the total report.

Answered (comp. on 11: 25), responded to their look of perplexity, amazement, and fear (Mark and Luke). Luke says that in affright they "bowed down their faces to the earth," Rev. Ver. **And said unto the women.** We know from John that Mary Magdalene had now left, but we have seen that Salome and Joanna, and apparently others, were present with 'the other Mary.' **Fear not ye,** with emphasis on 'ye,' as it is separately expressed in the Greek; not so in v. 10. The guard might well be alarmed (v. 4), but these who came to seek Jesus had no cause for fear. **For I know.** This gives a remedy for fear by telling the great reason they have for joy; comp. v. 8. **Jesus, which was crucified,** or simply '*Jesus the crucified.*' **For he is risen, as he said.** In Luke (24: 6 f.) they are bidden to remember how when still in Galilee he predicted that he would be crucified and rise again the third day. **Come, see the place where the Lord lay.** 'Where he lay' (*margin,* Rev. Ver.) is probably correct.[2] John vividly describes (20: 5 ff.) the appearance of the tomb, as seen (a little later) by himself and Peter; and intimates that the orderly disposition of the linen cloths and the hand-

---

[1] 'The stone' stands without addition in א B D, several cursives, Old Latin, and Vulg., Æth., Origen. Many documents added 'from the door,' and some also added 'of the tomb,' by assimilation to Mark 16: 3.

[2] It is found without 'the Lord' in א B, 33, 102

Memph., Arm., Æth., Origen, and some other Greek Fathers. 'The Lord' would be easily inserted from some student's marginal note, but was not likely to be omitted. The addition is what W H. call "Western and Syrian."

7 And go quickly, and tell his disciples that he is risen from the dead; and, behold, he goeth before you into Galilee; there shall ye see him: lo, I have told you.

8 And they departed quickly from the sepulchre with fear and great joy; and did run to bring his disciples word.

9 And as they went to tell his disciples, behold, Jesus met them, saying, All hail. And they came and held him by the feet, and worshipped him.

7 see the place [1] where the Lord lay. And go quickly, and tell his disciples, He is risen from the dead; and lo, he goeth before you into Galilee; there shall ye 8 see him: lo, I have told you. And they departed quickly from the tomb with fear and great joy, and 9 ran to bring his disciples word. And behold, Jesus met them, saying, All hail. And they came and

---

1 Many ancient authorities read, *where he lay.*

---

kerchief, showing that here was no work of robbers, nor removal of a dead body to another tomb, caused him to "believe," viz., that the Master was alive again. This same impressive situation the women beheld. **And go quickly, and tell his disciples.** "Quickly," so that they may the sooner have opportunity to rise out of their distress and despair. **And behold,** same word as 'behold' in v. 2 and v. 9. **He goeth before you into Galilee,** as Jesus had promised in 26 : 32; and the same verb is used here as there, meaning 'he goes before and leads you,' as a shepherd his flock. (John 10 : 4.) The present tense represents the action as sure and near. **There shall ye see him.** This does not necessarily exclude the possibility of their seeing him elsewhere, before or after, and we know from Luke and John that they saw him in Jerusalem and vicinity, both before going to Galilee and after returning. But the emphasis here laid on their seeing him in Galilee accords well with the view (comp. below on v. 16), that on a certain mountain in Galilee was to be the *great* meeting, where many disciples should receive the Great Commission, thus differencing this coming event from the appearances on that same day at Jerusalem to a comparatively small number. Notice Luke's statement (24 : 9, R. V.) that the women "told all these things to the eleven, and to all the rest." Did they not then understand a message to 'the disciples' as not merely to the eleven but to all the known disciples then present at Jerusalem? Now most of these had come from Galilee, and when the feast of the Passover was over it would be natural that they should 'depart into Galilee.' (v. 10.) Remember, too, that already on the evening before the crucifixion Jesus had promised to meet them in Galilee. (26 : 32.) There is also force in the suggestion (McClellan) that in Galilee their minds might be more rapidly weaned away from the notion of a temporal kingdom, which partially reasserted itself afterwards when they returned to Jerusalem before the ascension. (Acts 1 : 6.)—**Lo, I have told you.** Here Mark, who has agreed with Matt. almost word for word through several lines, has 'even as he told you.' Some "Western" documents changed Mark to be like Matthew.

IV. **8-10.** Jesus meets them as they hasten away. Mark 16: 8. **Quickly,** as the angel bade them, v. 7; **and did run.** The word **sepulchre,** Rev. Ver., *tomb*, changes from that of v. 1 (comp. on 27 : 61), though there is no important difference in substantial meaning. **With fear and great joy.** The fear (v. 5) has not ceased, but it has become mingled with great joy. Mark (16 : 8. R. V.) says strongly, "for trembling and astonishment had come upon them." He adds, "and they said nothing to any one; for they were afraid," *i. e.*, they spoke to no one they met on the way, being too much occupied with the fear produced by what had occurred. **To bring his disciples word.** The most of the disciples were not at the same place as Peter and John. It has been suggested that they probably retired to Bethany, as they and the Master had been wont to do every evening. (Luke 21 : 37.) **Jesus met them saying, All hail.** This is simply the common Greek salutation, rendered 'hail' in 26 : 49; 27 : 30, and there is no reason for rendering it otherwise here. The 'all' was introduced by Tyndale. The common text prefixes 'as they went to tell his disciples,' but this is a mere explanatory addition brought in from the margin. **Held him,** literally, *seized* or 'grasped,' the action showing great humility and veneration. This was not censured, and yet the Saviour said to Mary Magdalene (John 20: 17, Rev. Ver., *margin*), "Take not hold on me; for I am not yet ascended unto the Father." The most probable explanation of the difference is that **Mary** supposed this was only the Master's "spirit,"

10 Then said Jesus unto them, Be not afraid: go tell my brethren that they go into Galilee, and there shall they see me.
11 Now when they were going, behold, some of the watch came into the city, and shewed unto the chief priests all the things that were done.

10 took hold of his feet, and worshipped him. Then saith Jesus unto them, Fear not: go tell my brethren that they depart into Galilee, and there shall they see me,
11 Now while they were going, behold, some of the guard came into the city, and told unto the chief

---

as the disciples did the same evening (Luke 24: 37), and was proposing to test the reality of the bodily appearance, which experiment Jesus rebuked. **Worshipped.** *Bengel:* "Jesus before his passion was worshipped by others rather than his disciples." **Go tell my brethren.** It was special kindness thus to speak of them (comp. 12: 50; 25: 40; John 20: 17), when they were likely to feel special humiliation at the thought that they had all forsaken him, and one of them denied him. It was apparently for the same purpose that the angel had expressly added the name of Peter (Mark 16: 7), lest the sadly fallen one should fear to think that a message to the disciples of Jesus could any longer be regarded as a message to him.

Meantime Peter and John arrived at the tomb, saw it empty, and returned home. (John 20: 3-10.) Mary Magdalene remained behind, standing without, weeping. And presently Jesus appeared to her, in that affecting interview which John describes in 20: 11-18. If the expression ' he appeared first to Mary Magdalene ' (Mark 16: 9) be regarded as genuine and chronological, then it may be thought that as she departed to tell the disciples (John 20: 18), Jesus also departed, and overtook the other women. As he suddenly appeared that evening in a room with closed doors (John 20: 19), there was already, from the resurrection onward, something supernatural in his bodily condition and movements, and so it may be that he overtook them, though they were running. But if Mark 16: 9-20 be considered spurious,[1] or if 'first' be there understood to mean simply the first of the three appearances which that passage describes, then we can dispense with the supposition just made as to locomotion, and suppose that Jesus ' met' the other women a few moments after their departure, and then, returning to the tomb, appeared to Mary Magdalene.

The question has been frequently discussed,

why these angelic appearances, and first appearances of the Lord himself, were made only to women. The women went early, and being the first believers present, gained the first knowledge of what had occurred. But why did neither the angels nor the Lord appear to Peter and John? If we adopt the simpler view as above, that Jesus appeared first to the women on their way (perhaps to Bethany), and then returning appeared to Mary Magdalene, it might be enough to suppose that he did not reach the tomb till after Peter and John left. As to the angels, it would be a question whether the women received the angelic communication because of their faith, or needed it in order to faith. John believed, merely from observing the order that prevailed in the empty tomb; and Peter was the first person to whom the Lord afterwards appeared in the course of the day. (Luke 24: 34.)

V. **11-15.** False report by some of the guard. This is found in Matt. only. It was natural that he, rather than the other Evangelists, should give it, because he wrote especially for Jews, among whom this report had spread. (v. 15.) **When they were going.** The events were exciting, and nobody delayed. **Some of the watch came into the city ;** perhaps the rest remained until officially authorized to leave. **And shewed unto the chief priests.** These had taken them out to the sepulchre (27: 65 f.), and very likely stated their fear that the disciples of the buried one would come and steal him away. At any rate, the chief priests had stationed them, by Pilate's permission, and to the chief priests they reported. According to Roman discipline, they were liable to very severe punishment for losing what they guarded. They thought that an account of the angelic appearance and the stone rolled away would have influence with the Jewish authorities, and so their crime as soldiers might somehow be for-

---

[1] This is a question which, in the present state of knowledge, it is very hard to determine. But the external and internal evidence against the passage is so strong (see W H., Appendix, p. 28-51), that we think it should not now be appealed to for proof texts, nor insisted on in harmonizing the Gospels at this point.

12 And when they were assembled with the elders, and had taken counsel, they gave large money unto the soldiers.
13 Saying, Say ye, His disciples came by night, and stole him *away* while we slept.
14 And if this come to the governor's ears, we will persuade him, and secure you.
15 So they took the money, and did as they were taught: and this saying is commonly reported among the Jews until this day.

12 priests all the things that were come to pass. And when they were assembled with the elders, and had taken counsel, they gave large money unto the sol-
13 diers, saying, Say ye, His disciples came by night,
14 and stole him away while we slept. And if this [1] come to the governor's ears, we will persuade him,
15 and rid you of care. So they took the money, and did as they were taught: and this saying was spread abroad among the Jews, *and continueth* until this day.

1 Or, *come to a hearing before the governor.*

given. Accordingly, they told the chief priests **all the things that were come to pass.** The story must have excited great surprise and alarm, but it wrought no repentance. Alas! for these bad men, they were now, like Pilate, so entangled by previous wickedness, that it seemed they must go forward. They had said, "Let him now come down from the cross, and we will believe on him" (27: 42; Rev. Ver.); behold, he has done something still more wonderful, yet they do not believe, no, nor make further inquiry, but simply bribe the witnesses to report a stupid falsehood. **Large money,** or 'quite a number of silver (pieces),' which would most naturally mean shekels, 26: 15. **His disciples . . . stole him away while we slept.** The statement is absurd on its face, for if asleep they did not know it, and if one of them knew, he could have awaked the others. It also confesses on their part a criminal breach of discipline. **If this come to the governor's ears ;** so Tyn., Cran., and K. James. It much more likely means, with Geneva and *margin*, Rev. Ver., 'come to be heard before the governor,'[1] be tried before him. (See Buttm., p. 336.) **We will persuade him** ('we' being emphatic), not simply by argument and personal influence, but by the consideration they had just brought to bear upon the soldiers themselves. Wet. gives several passages of Greek authors in which mention is made of *persuading* men by means of money. Philo expressly states (see on 27: 11) that Pilate was a bribe-taker, as we know was true of Felix. (Acts 24: 26.) **And secure you,** literally, *and make you to be without anxiety,* the same root as in 6: 25 ff. **And did as they were taught.** The rulers, doubtless, kept quiet until after Pentecost, when the disciples began to declare and to prove that Jesus was risen, and then made the soldiers tell their false story. **Until this day,**

the time when Matt. wrote his Gospel, comp. on 27: 8. *Justin Martyr* says to the Jew Tryphon (ch. 108), "You (the Jews) selected men and sent them into all the world, proclaiming that a certain atheistic and lawless sect has arisen from one Jesus, a Galilean deceiver, whom we crucified, but his disciples stole him by night from the tomb, and deceive men by saying that he has risen from the dead and ascended into heaven." The absurd and blasphemous mediæval Jewish legend called "Toldoth Jeshu" expands this allegation.

Attempts are still made, by men whose theories cannot be otherwise maintained, to set aside the fact of our Lord's resurrection. No intelligent critic now holds that Jesus did not really die, or that he died, but his resurrection was a mere imposture on the part of his disciples. The now common theory of unbelieving critics is that it was a vision, or, in some way, an illusion, on their part. These men are not mere disinterested inquirers after truth, as they sometimes assert; they have to account for Christianity, as having in it, according to them, nothing supernatural, and yet as a great power in the world; as affording the noblest ethical teachings, and presenting the unrivaled character of Christ, and as unquestionably based by its propagators on belief in a risen Saviour. Of course, men so ingenious will make some plausible show of explaining away the evidence, or flinging around the subject some appearance of doubt, as skillful lawyers know how to do with the weakest case. See an examination of their theories in Milligan, Lect. III, and brief and vigorous discussions in Godet, Weiss ("Life"), and Edersh.; see also a curious and powerful refutation of these skeptical theories by Keim, on grounds as rationalistic as their own.—The great fact stands. *Westcott* ("Gospel of the Res."): "It has been shown that the resur-

1 B has here a "Western" reading, found in B D, and Latin versions, *hupo* instead of *epi*, making it mean   'be heard by the governor,' which was manifestly introduced for simplification.

rection is not an isolated event in history, but at once the end and the beginning of vast developments of life and thought; that it is the climax of a long series of divine dispensations which find in it their complement and explanation; that it has formed the starting-point of all progressive modern society, ever presenting itself in new lights, according to the immediate wants of the age." Then after restating the evidence, he adds, "Taking all the evidence together, it is not too much to say that there is no single historic incident better or more variously supported than the Resurrection of Christ." And let it be remembered how much this great fact carries with it. The resurrection of Christ establishes the divine origin of his mission and teachings; it gives God's sanction to all his claims, and he claimed to be the Messiah, to speak by divine authority, to be one with God. Rom. 1: 4. *Hanna*: "Jesus had publicly periled his reputation as the Christ of God, on the occurrence of this event. When challenged to give some sign in support of his pretensions, it was to his future resurrection from the dead, and to it alone, that he appealed. (John 2: 20; Matt. 12: 38-41.) Often, and that in terms incapable of misconstruction, had our Lord foretold his resurrection. It carried thus along with it a triple proof of the divinity of our Lord's mission. It was the fulfillment of a prophecy, as well as the working of a miracle; that miracle wrought, and that prophecy fulfilled, in answer to a solemn and confident appeal made beforehand by Christ to this event as the crowning testimony to his Messiahship."

HOMILETICAL AND PRACTICAL.

V. 5. Seeking the Crucified, finding the Risen One.—V. 7. "Go quickly." 1) Religious excitement should prompt to religious exertion. 2) Where others are sorrowing, we tell twice if we tell quickly, the news that will cheer them.—"Lo, I have told you." HENRY: "Those messengers from God, that discharge their trust faithfully, may take the comfort of that, whatever the success be. Acts 20: 26 f." —V. 8. EUTHYM.: "With fear, at the strange things they saw; with great joy, at the good news they heard."—V. 9. It was while they were hastening to honor the Saviour and rejoice his disciples, that he met them.—V. 10. The Saviour recognizes the importance of

repetition in giving instruction. (Comp. v. 7.) —"My brethren." 1) This suggests humility, at our utter unworthiness of the honor. 2) It encourages return if we have forsaken him. 3) It stimulates to diligence in doing the will of God, 12: 50. 4) It reminds us that we can serve him by serving the least of his brethren, 25: 40. HALL: "Beloved Jesus, how dost thou raise the titles of thy followers with thyself! At first they were thy servants, then disciples, a little before thy death they were thy friends; now, after thy resurrection, they are thy brethren."—V. 11-15. The chief priests and the guard. 1) No multiplication of evidence will convince those who are stubbornly resolved not to believe. 2) Think of religious teachers serving God by a purchased lie. 3) Bribery required further and heavier bribes; first a trifle to Judas, now large money to the soldiers, and presently, perhaps, the governor. 4) A falsehood will be long-lived if it suits men's prejudices. (v. 15.) 5) Efforts against the truth sometimes help its progress; the seal and the guard only make it more clear that the Saviour rose from the dead.—V. 13. SCHAFF: "Men in the infatuation of unbelief will believe any story, however improbable." —V. 15. CHRYS.: "Seest thou again the disciples' love of truth, how they are not ashamed of saying even this, that such a report prevailed against them."

The resurrection of Christ is not only a pillar of Christian evidence, but has important theological and practical relations. (a) It *completed* his work of *atonement*, and stamped it with divine approval; Rom. 4: 24 f.; 8: 44; 2 Cor. 5: 15. (Rev. Ver.) Accordingly, to believe that God raised the Lord Jesus from the dead is to believe the gospel; Rom. 10: 9. See Milligan, "Lect." IV. (b) It is the ground and pledge of his people's resurrection (1) Of their spiritual resurrection, to walk in *newness* of life; Rom. 6: 4; Col. 2: 12 f.; 3: 1-4. See Westcott, "The Gospel of the Resurrection"; Liddon, "Easter Sermons," 2 vols., 1885, (treating numerous aspects and relations of our Lord's Resurrection). (2) Of the resurrection of the body; 1 Cor. 15: 20; 1 Thess. 4: 14; Phil. 3: 10 f. See Candlish, "Life in a Risen Saviour" (Lectures on 1 Cor. 15); Liddon. (c) It is represented in baptism; Rom. and Col. (as above). (d) It is celebrated on the Lord's Day.

16 Then the eleven disciples went away into Galilee, into a mountain where Jesus had appointed them.

| 16 But the eleven disciples went into Galilee, unto the mountain where Jesus had appointed them.

16-20. JESUS APPEARS TO THE DISCI-
PLES AND GIVES THEM A COMMISSION.

Found also in Mark 16: 9-20; Luke 24: 13-53; John 20: 19 to 22: 25; 1 Cor. 15: 1-8. Combining the four Gospels and Paul's account we find recorded ten appearances of our Lord between the resurrection and the ascension; comp. the Harmonies of Robinson and Clark, and that of Augustine, III, § 83; also Westcott on John, beginning of chap. 20. (1) To the women; in Matt. (2) To Mary Magdalene; in John [and Mark]. (3) To Simon Peter; in Luke and Paul. (4) To the two going to Emmaus; in Luke [and Mark]. (5) To the apostles, except Thomas; in Luke, John [and Mark]. — These five appearances were on the day of the resurrection, and at or near Jerusalem. (6) To the apostles, including Thomas, a week later at Jerusalem; in John and Paul. (7) To seven disciples at the Sea of Galilee; in John. (8) To the apostles, and probably at the same time to above five hundred brethren, on a mountain in Galilee; in Matt. and Paul. (9) To James; in Paul. (10) To the apostles, just before the ascension; in Luke; (Acts) and Paul.—Then comes the Ascension; in Luke, Gospel and Acts [and in Mark].—Of these ten appearances Matt. records but two, viz., 1 and 8; Luke records four; John four; Paul five; Mark (if 16: 9-20 be genuine), three. Thus the events following the resurrection are to be sought much more in the other narratives than in Matt. But the one appearance and commission here given must be regarded as of very great interest and importance.

As to our Lord's appearances in general, certain points may be noted. (a) He appeared under a great variety of circumstances; as to places, times of day and night, number of persons. This seemed to leave no doubt of the fact that he had risen, and to make his followers thoroughly familiar with it. (b) He took great pains to show that here was a real body, of "flesh and bones," not "a spirit"; and that it was the same body, with the marks of crucifixion. (c) Yet he appeared only ten times that we know of, in forty days. And he never remained long in their company. He was thus preparing them to live without him. See Hanna and Geikie. (d) He ap-

peared suddenly in a room with closed door (John 20: 26), so that sometimes he was not at first recognized. (Luke 24: 16; John 21: 4.) With this agrees the expression of Mark 16: 12, "in another (that is, in a changed) form." It would seem that his body was already partially transformed, as it were beginning to be glorified. This, with the foregoing, would prepare his followers for thinking of him aright after his ascension; comp. Ellicott, Hanna. Yet he was not, as some have thought, fully glorified, completely changed into a "spiritual body," at the resurrection, for he afterwards ate food. (e) He appeared only to his disciples, though once to above five hundred of these. (1) Perhaps they were alone able to appreciate the change in him; comp. Westcott, "Gosp. of Res."; Milligan, "Lect. I." (2) Had he appeared to others, we can see that the multitude would have blazed with fanaticism, worse than ever; and the rulers would have furiously sought to slay him afresh, as they proposed with reference to Lazarus. (John 12: 10.) It was necessary to lift friend and foe to the thought of his spiritual work; and this would have been defeated by his bodily appearance to the multitudes at this time.

Then, or *but*, in opposition to what the soldiers and the chief priests did, the eleven disciples carried out the Saviour's direction. The Greek could be rendered "now," as a particle of transition, though the connection here indicates the other idea of opposition; but 'then,' as in Com. Ver., would suggest a notion quite foreign to the Greek. **The eleven disciples went.** Matthew gives no means of judging how soon. But we see from John 20: 26 that it was more than a week after the resurrection, and from Acts 1: 3 that it was within forty days thereafter. It is commonly taken for granted that the commission of v. 19 was given shortly before the ascension, and hence the arrangement of the Harmonies as above indicated. But this is by no means certain, for in John 20: 22 ff., we find a commission given on the very day of the resurrection. So we cannot decide at what point in the four weeks preceding the ascension the appearance recorded by Matt. occurred. And if Matthew's record seems to suggest that the disciples went promptly to

17 And when they saw him, they worshipped him: but some doubted. | 17 And when they saw him, they worshipped *him:* but

---

Galilee (after the week required by John 20: 26), and that this appearance and commission came not many days after their arrival in Galilee, there is nothing to forbid the adoption of that view. If we suppose that above five hundred were present, it would require several days to circulate the private invitation. **Into Galilee.** See description of the district on 4: 12, 23. Matthew's account of our Lord's ministry, except the last week or two, is confined to the ministry in Galilee. (4:12-18:35.) That is probably the reason why he seized with exclusive interest upon the direction to go to Galilee (28:7, 10; comp. 26:32), with the appearance and commission which followed accordingly. Comp. on 28: 7. Luke tells only of appearances in Jerusalem and vicinity; John gives appearances both in Jerusalem and in Galilee. When it is said that Matt. appears to exclude all other appearances than those he has described, it may be answered that from Luke, ch. 24, one might understand our Lord's Ascension to have taken place on the day of the resurrection, while from Luke's statement in Acts 1: 3, we know that forty days intervened.

Into a (*the*) **mountain where Jesus had appointed them.** We have not been told of a mountain, or other particular place in Galilee, as appointed for the promised meeting. But Matt. (R. V.) speaks of it as '*the* mountain,' one definitely appointed or assigned; and there is nothing in the other accounts to conflict with this representation. We have no means of judging what particular mountain it was, and conjecture is idle. A very late and very silly tradition makes it mean the northern part of the Mount of Olives, said to have been called 'Galilee'; such a meaning in v. 7, 10, and in 26: 32, is out of the question. The selection of a mountain, which would be a retired place, and the formal appointment of the meeting at that place, suggests something more than a mere meeting with the eleven, such as we know from John to have been held once and again before leaving Jerusalem. Now Paul (1 Cor. 15:6) says that Jesus appeared to "above five hundred brethren at once," the greater part of whom remained as living witnesses some twenty-seven years later. The supposition that this

appearance is to be connected with the one in Matt., accounts for the retired place and the formal appointment. It also helps to explain why this meeting was to be in Galilee, both because Galilee contained a larger number of pronounced and trustworthy disciples of Jesus than Judea or Perea, and because it was farther from the watchful jealousy of the rulers at Jerusalem. This accounts also for the stress laid at the outset on going to Galilee and there seeing him; *there* was to be the great meeting with many disciples, and the giving of the Great Commission (comp. on v. 7). These two appearances are placed together in the Harmonies of Robinson and Clark, and by many very able recent expositors, including Ellicott, Godet, Weiss. **They worshipped him.** This was not merely homage to a king (as in 2 : 2; 9 : 18, and often), but probably involved the conviction that he was divine. Thomas had already expressed his personal conviction to this effect. (John 20 : 28.) Even the Saviour's bodily appearance seems to have been, since the resurrection, so altered and spiritualized (see above), that they felt more inclined than formerly to worship him, besides the awe with which he was invested by the fact of having raised himself from the dead. (John 10 : 18.) **But some doubted.** The peculiar Greek construction is the same as in 26: 67. The subject of doubt must have been whether this was their Lord really come to life. From Matt. alone we should naturally understand that the doubters were some of the eleven, and this is in itself entirely possible, even as at first they "disbelieved for joy" (Luke 24 : 41, R. V.), or from previous despondency. (Luke 24 : 21; John 20 : 25.) Such continued doubt is more intelligible if we suppose this to have occurred in the early part of the forty days. The accounts all go to show that the apostles were by no means swift to accept the great and amazing fact of their Master's resurrection, and that they became all fully convinced at last only because of multiplied and varied evidence—a fact which makes their final conviction and testimony all the more valuable to us. *Jerome:* "Their doubting increases our faith." If we suppose the "above five hundred" to have been present on the same occasion, then 'some doubted' may mean

18 And Jesus came and spake unto them, saying, All power is given unto me in heaven and in earth.
19 Go ye therefore, and teach all nations, baptizing them in the name of the Father, and of the Son, and of the Holy Ghost:

18 some doubted. And Jesus came to them, and spake unto them, saying, All authority hath been given
19 unto me in heaven and on earth. Go ye therefore, and make disciples of all the nations, baptizing them into the name of the Father and of the Son and of

some of the five hundred, though not of the eleven. We should in that case suppose Matt. to be writing simply as an eye-witness, mentioning persons whose presence his narrative has not accounted for. Whoever the doubters were, we may feel confident that their doubts were removed by the words that follow, and by the ascension and the Pentecostal gift. Some take the phrase, **and Jesus came,** as suggesting that he suddenly appeared at a distance, and the doubting continued only until he came near. **And spake unto them.** We may well suppose that he first said many other things. What is here given divides itself into three parts; (a) The assertion of authority, v. 18; (b) The commission, v. 19 f.; (c) The promise, v. 20 b.

(a) 18. **All power.** Jesus claims universal authority. We have seen on 9 : 6 that the Greek word denotes permission, privilege, right, authority, and it sometimes suggests the power naturally attendant upon authority, or necessary to enforce it. In this passage '*authority*' is the correct translation, and the idea of corresponding power is suggested. **All power** (*authority*) **in heaven and in earth,** evidently denotes complete and universal authority. *Calvin:* "He must have supreme and truly divine dominion, who commands eternal life to be promised in his name, the whole world to be reduced under his sway, and a doctrine to be promulgated which is to subdue every high thing and bring low the human race. And certainly the apostles would never have been persuaded to attempt so arduous a task, had they not known that their Protector and Avenger was sitting in the heavens, to whom supreme dominion had been given." But by the very fact of saying 'in heaven and in (or *on*) earth,' the Saviour showed that he did not mean the authority of a temporal king, such as even the disciples so persistently believed that the Messiah would be. **Is given,** more literally, *was given*, without saying when, and leaving

it to be understood that the authority thus given is still possessed. We might suppose a reference to the councils of eternity, but more likely the gift was at his incarnation, as in 11 : 27, Rev. Ver., "all things have been delivered unto me of my Father," and perhaps was consummated at his resurrection. Comp. in general Dan. 7 : 13 f. The giver was God the Father; comp. especially John 13 : 3 and 17 : 2, also Matt. 9 : 8; 20 : 23; 21 : 23; John 5 : 27; 12 : 49. We learn elsewhere that this authority given to the God-man, the Mediator, is a temporary gift. When he shall have subjected to himself all opposing authority among men, then he will deliver up this delegated authority of the King Messiah to God, even the Father, and his special mediatorial dominion will be re-absorbed into the universal and eternal dominion of God (1 Cor. 15 : 24–28). It is on the basis of this mediatorial authority, in heaven and on earth, that the Saviour issues his commission to his followers. **Go ye therefore.** This 'therefore'[1] should never be overlooked when we think of the commission (comp. 'therefore,' in Heb. 4 : 16). It was a despised Galilean, a wandering and homeless teacher, that gave this audacious command; but it was a teacher just raised from the dead, and endowed by God with universal authority. *Hanna:* "When Jesus said, 'Go, make disciples of all nations,' he announced in the simplest and least ostentatious way the most original, the broadest, the sublimest enterprise that ever human beings have been called upon to accomplish."

(b) **19 f.** Jesus gives direction that all the nations shall be discipled unto him, and taught to keep his commandments. If the "above five hundred" were present (see above on v. 16), then this commission was not addressed to the Eleven only; and it is plain from Acts 8 : 2, 4, that the first Christians all set themselves to carry it out. Judaism in general was not a missionary religion. It was willing for Gentiles to come, as the prophets

[1] The reading is not certain; the word is omitted by many documents, and may have been inserted to bring out the relation between this and the foregoing clause. But that relation evidently exists, whether expressed by a particle or not.

had predicted they would, but it had no thought of going. The later Judaism had developed a zeal in proselyting, which in itself would have been commendable; but it proselyted to mere formalism and hypocrisy; (comp. on 23: 15). Christianity is essentially a missionary religion, analogous to the great conquering nations, the Romans, English, Russians. It must spread, by a law of its nature; it must be active at the extremities, or it becomes chilled at the heart; must be enlarging its circumference, or its very centre tends to be defaced. We learn from Luke (24: 47-49) that they were not to go immediately, but to tarry at Jerusalem for the promised gift of the Holy Spirit's power. This came in a very short time, and yet they tarried long, apparently several years; for the great Pentecost was probably in A. D. 30, and the death of Stephen in A. D. 36 or 37. It required persecution at last to scatter them, and then they "went about preaching the word." (Acts 8: 4, Rev. Ver.)

Teach, Rev. Ver., *make disciples of*, or more exactly, *disciple*. We greatly need an English verb 'disciple,' for this passage, and for 13: 52 and Acts 14: 21. In John 4: 1, the literal translation is 'makes disciples.' The Syriac (Pesh.) here exactly reproduces the Greek, by means of a causative form, probably devised for the purpose, and quite distinct from 'teach' in v. 20. The Latin and the Coptic were unable to make the distinction, and the Latin failure extended itself to the early English and German translations. Some later Germans have rendered 'make disciples of,' as in several recent English versions. The verb 'disciple' is found once in Shak. ("All's Well," 1, 2, 28), once in Spenser's "Faery Queene," b. iv., c. 1), also in Hammond (d. A. D. 1660); it is called obsolete by Webster, but recognized by Richardson, Worcester, Stormonth, etc. There may be doubt as yet about introducing it into a popular version, though employed here by Am. Bib. Un. and by Davidson, but it may be used in religious discourse with great advantage. 'Teach,' in all early English versions, was a very imperfect translation, confounding this term with that in v. 20, which really means 'teach.' To disciple a person to Christ is to bring him into the relation of pupil to teacher, "taking his yoke" of authoritative

instruction (11:29), accepting what he says as true because he says it, and submitting to his requirements as right because he makes them. Towards a mere human and uninspired teacher we can properly feel and act thus only within narrow limits; but the Great Teacher has perfect wisdom and unlimited authority. We see then that Christ's intimated authority (v. 18) is not only the basis of our duty to disciple others, but the basis of all true discipleship. His teachings and requirements are perfectly wise and righteous and good, and we may see this to some extent at the outset, and more and more as we go on in the disciple's life; but we accept them at once, and set about conforming to them, because he has a perfect right to be believed and obeyed. As to the noun 'disciple,' see on 5: 1. We know from other Scriptures that in order to men's becoming true disciples to Christ, there is needed, not merely human instruction and influence, but a special work of the Holy Spirit of God.

All (*the*) **nations,** the Greek having the article. Not merely the contiguous, or the kindred nations, not merely the most cultivated, but all the nations. Discipleship to Christ is possible to all, necessary to all. Our Lord has already predicted that the good news shall be preached in the whole world (26:13), and that when he finally comes for judgment "before him shall be gathered all the nations." (25:32.) So in the latest commission, given just before the ascension, "and that repentance and remission of sins should be preached in his name unto all the nations, beginning from Jerusalem." (Luke 24:47, R. V.) And if Mark 16: 9-20, R. V., be accepted as genuine, the commission there given reads, "Go ye into all the world, and preach the gospel to the whole creation." In Matt. 10: 5, Rev. Ver., the Twelve were forbidden to go "into any way of the Gentiles"; but that was a temporary and limited mission; the final and permanent mission made them begin with the Jews (Luke 24:47), but go into every way of the Gentiles, disciple all the nations. The idea of one religion for all the world then seemed very strange. *Liddon* (II, 247): "No existing religion could aim at it, since the existing religions were believed to be merely the products of national instincts and aspirations; each religion was part of the furniture of a nation, or at most of a race. Celsus, looking out on Christianity in the second century of our era, with the feelings of Gibbon or of Voltaire, said that a man must be out of his mind to think that Greeks and Barbarians, Romans and Scythians, bondmen and freemen, could ever have one religion. Nevertheless this was the purpose of our Lord."

Baptizing them. See the term explained on 3: 6. It is here the present participle,[1] as is 'teaching' in the next clause. This construction might grammatically mean, if called for by the natural relation between the actions, or by the connection here, or by the known relations as elsewhere set forth, 'disciple by baptizing . . . by teaching'; and so many understand it. But the general teachings of Scripture do not allow us to think that discipling can be *effected* by a ceremony and a subsequent course of instruction in Christ's precepts. We must therefore understand that the present participles give baptizing and teaching as in a general way concomitants of discipling, the ceremony attending it promptly and once for all, the instruction in precepts beginning immediately, and continued without limit, from the nature of the case.

In the name, but *into* (Rev. Ver.) is the most obvious and commonest translation of the Greek phrase (*eis to onoma*). The same preposition and case are found after baptize in Acts 8: 16; 19: 5; 1 Cor. 1: 13, and (with other nouns) in Gal. 3: 27; Rom. 6: 3 (twice); 1 Cor. 10: 2; comp. also Matt. 10: 41 f.; 18: 20. Now if we take this obvious sense 'into,' the question will arise whether the ceremony actually brings the person into the name, into Christ, into Paul, Moses, etc., or whether it only represents, symbolizes, the relation thus indicated. Those who believe in baptismal regeneration, or in baptism as constituting regeneration, will of course take the phrase in the former sense; others will understand that the ceremony only *represents* the person's introduction into the name, into Christ. In either case the idea denoted by 'into' seems to be a highly *important,* and with those who believe in baptismal regeneration, etc., an *essential* element in the signifi-

cance of the ceremony. Now it is to be observed that Luke in Acts, while twice using 'into the name' (*eis to onoma*) (as above cited), in 2: 38 has *epi toi onomati* (so also in Matt. 18: 5; 24: 5), 'upon the name,' upon this as basis or ground of the ceremony, and in 10: 48 *en toi onomati*, 'in the name,' within the limits of it, with relation to it and it alone. If then the idea attached to 'into' be highly important, or even essential, how do we account for the fact that Luke uses these other expressions, which may with some effort be construed as equivalent, but will quite fail to indicate the important conception in question? It would seem clear that Luke, when recording the action of the apostles in carrying out the commission, did not regard the distinctive notion of 'into' as essential or highly important, or he would not have used that phrase twice, and twice the other phrases. And those who insist on the most obvious translation of *eis* by 'into,' must beware of treating any particular interpretation of the expression as very important, in the presence of Luke's usage. The question may also arise whether it is not better, with the great grammatical commentators Fritzsche and Meyer (comp. also Weiss) to understand *eis to onoma* as meaning in all these cases 'unto the name,' with reference to the name, as that to which the ceremony is restricted. Then it becomes plain at once that Luke's other phrases give substantially the same sense, and we see why he has varied the expression at will. This rendering is felt by all to be necessary in 1 Cor. 10: 2, 'baptized unto Moses,' which only Davidson ventures to translate 'into Moses.' Noyes says 'into the name,' but 'to Moses'; Darby 'to the name' and 'unto Moses.' And in Gal. 3: 27; Rom. 6: 3, 'unto' gives a thoroughly appropriate conception, 'baptized unto Christ,' with distinct and exclusive reference to him; *i. e.*, the ceremony does not refer to Moses, or to Paul, but to Christ. And note especially the appropriateness in Rom. 6: 3, "all we who were baptized unto Christ Jesus were baptized unto his death." Our baptism in referring to Christ Jesus referred especially to his death. "We were buried therefore with him through the

---

[1] The aorist participle is read by B D, without other support, and in obvious assimilation to the aorist participle and verb which precede.

baptism unto death," etc. We believe then that it would be a decided improvement to render baptize *eis* everywhere by 'unto.' If this be not done, it would be less misleading to retain the customary baptismal formula 'in the name,' and thus avoid suggesting a conception which Luke's usage clearly forbids.[1] Or if 'into' be employed as the most obvious translation, then we should beware of treating the distinctive notion it suggests as essential or important, when Luke has evidently not so considered.

In Hebrew thought and feeling, the *name* of God was peculiarly sacred, as representing him. It must not be spoken irreverently, and later Jewish feeling exaggerated this into a rule that the proper name Yahweh must not be pronounced at all, but another word substituted. (Comp. on 22: 44.) The name of God must not in an oath be taken in vain, but the oath by that name must be solemnly taken and sacredly kept. In numerous passages of the Old Testament, the name of God solemnly represented himself; to perform any action with express reference to his name gave the action a sacred character. And so in the New Testament use, 'hallowed be thy name,' 'did we not prophesy by thy name,' 'in his name shall the Gentiles hope,' 'where two or three are gathered together in my name,' 'many shall come in my name,' etc. In such phrases a great variety of specific ideas will arise according to the natural relations of the particular objects and actions, and the connection of the statement; but in all cases the name is a sacred representative of the person. Thus 'baptized unto the name of Paul' is an impressive way of saying 'baptized unto Paul,' like 'baptized unto Moses'; 'baptized unto the name of the Lord Jesus' (Acts 8: 16 ; 19: 5) and 'baptized on (in) the name of Jesus Christ' (Acts 2: 38; 10: 48), are an impressive equivalent for 'baptized unto Christ' (Gal. 3: 27 ; Rom. 6: 3) ; and 'baptize unto the name of the Father and of the Son and of the Holy Spirit' is a solemn way of saying 'unto the Father, and the Son, and the Holy Spirit.'

Baptism then is here enjoined as to be performed with express reference to the Holy Trinity. Comp. 2 Cor. 13: 14. From this, no doubt, arose the quite early practice of baptizing three times, a practice still maintained in the Greek Church, and in Germany and America by the Tunkers or Dunkards, and some others. It is not an unnatural conception, and, not in itself particularly objectionable, but it has no warrant in Scripture; and indeed, the form of expression here employed, 'unto the name' being used only once, is distinctly unfavorable to that practice. It should also be discouraged as tending to exalt the ceremonial element, while New Test. Christianity has the minimum of ceremony.

It is very natural that Christians should everywhere employ in baptizing this phrase, 'unto (into, in) the name of the Father and of the Son and of the Holy Spirit,' and we see no reason for departing from it. But it is of doubtful propriety to call this a *law*, and to insist that baptism would not be "valid" without the use of this particular phrase. For it must be remembered that baptize is nowhere else in the New Test. associated with this particular expression. In Acts and the Epistles we find only 'the Lord Jesus,' or 'Jesus Christ,' or simply 'Christ.' We may well enough understand that this is a compendious expression, which touches the main point or peculiarity of the great Christian purification. We could not wisely infer from that usage that it is improper or undesirable to employ the full expression given by Matt., but we are bound to understand that it is not indispensable. There would be nothing gained in practice by using one of the shorter phrases given in Acts and Paul, but there is something gained in just conception if we abstain from regarding the expression in Matt. as having the character of a *law*, about which we should then have to suppose that Luke and Paul had been strangely negligent. Plumptre fancies (after Cyprian, "Ep. 73," c. 17, 18) that it was enough for *Jewish* converts "to be baptized into the name of Jesus as the Messiah," while heathen converts, who "were without God in the world," and had not known the Father, needed the other and fuller formula. But Paul has not used it,

---

[1] Tertullian gives *in nomen*, but the Latin versions in all forms, and numerous Latin Fathers quoted by Sabatier, give *in nomine*. The Memphitic seems to be equivalent to *in nomen* ; the Syriac cannot well make the distinction.

20 Teaching them to observe all things whatsoever I have commanded you: and, lo, I am with you alway, *even* unto the end of the world. Amen.

20 the Holy Spirit: teaching them to observe all things whatsoever I commanded you: and lo, I am with you [1] alway, even unto [1] the end of the world.

---

1 Gr. *all the days....*2 Or, *consummation of the age.*

---

and his converts were mainly heathen.[1]—It was probably this passage and the great benediction of 2 Cor. 13: 14 that made the English Revisers unwilling to adopt the suggestion of their American associates, and change 'Holy Ghost' into 'Holy Spirit' (comp. on 1: 18). The former will, no doubt, long continue to be employed in certain phrases of devotion; but it would be a gain to uniformity and clearness of rendering, if the latter were everywhere used in the translations.

The *design* of Christian baptism seems to be indicated as threefold. (1) The element employed represents purification; "arise, and be baptized, and wash away thy sins, calling on his name."(Acts 22 : 16, R. V.) This meaning it has in common with the Old Testament purifications of every kind, being a very impressive kind of purification, because "the putting away of the filth of the flesh" (1 Pet 3: 21) is in this case so complete. (2) The action performed symbolizes burial and resurrection, the actual burial and resurrection of Christ, and the spiritual death and resurrection of the believer in union with Christ. (Rom. 6: 3 ff.; Gal. 3: 27.) (3) To have this ceremony performed upon ourselves in the name of Jesus Christ, or in the name of the Father and of the Son and of the Holy Spirit, is a sort of oath of allegiance or pledge of devotion to him as our Saviour, and our God; we are not baptized unto Moses or unto Paul, but unto Christ, unto the Trinity. Hence it was a pleasant fancy of the early Latin Christians to call baptism a *sacramentum*, the Roman soldier's oath of absolute devotion and obedience to his general; though the word sacrament afterwards came to be gradually employed in applications and senses quite foreign to the New Testament.

Teaching them to observe all things whatsoever I have commanded you. Baptism is a mere ceremonial and initial act of obedience to Christ, which should be followed by a lifelong obedience to all his commandments.

The person who is discipled and baptized is only started in a course of Christian living. Notice that it is not simply teaching them the commandments of Christ, but teaching them to observe his commandments. They who disciple and baptize men must teach them the duty of obeying Christ in all things; and the Christian instructor has still fallen short of his task unless those whom he is called to instruct have both learned what Christ's commandments are, and have learned to observe them. Notice also the emphatic and comprehensive terms, 'all things whatsoever I have commanded you.' The risen Redeemer looks back upon his now finished work of teaching and speaks of it all in the past tense, as he already often did in the prayer of John 17, on the night before the crucifixion. These completed commandments would be hereafter brought fully to the remembrance of the disciples by the new Paraclete who would soon take the Saviour's place as their instructor and counsellor (John 14: 16, 26), and this whole mass of sacred instruction and duty, without omission or alteration, they must teach those whom they disciple to observe. *Liddon:* "This is not the least noteworthy feature of our Lord's words, that he does not foresee a time or circumstances when any part of his teaching will become antiquated or untrue, inappropriate or needless."

How vast is the range of thought presented or suggested by this saying of our Lord. (1) Theology, the doctrine of the Trinity, and the Mediatorial authority of Christ. (2) Discipleship, and the work of discipling others. (3) The great missionary idea, 'all the nations.' (4) The ceremonial element of Christianity. (5) Christian ethics. (6) Christ's perpetual spiritual presence with those who serve him. (7) Christ's final coming.

(c) **20 b.** Jesus gives assurance of his perpetual spiritual presence with all engaged in discipling others and in observing his commandments. Obedience to the Great Com-

---

[1] In the "*Didache*," ch. 7, and in Justin Martyr, "Apol. I," chap. 61, the formula of Matthew is given, as if a matter of course. There was no little dispute among the Fathers as to whether baptism in the name of Jesus would suffice. See Herzog, "Taufe," 4).

mission is based on his universal and complete authority (v. 18), and encouraged by the promise of his unfailing and sustaining presence. And this clearly applies, not merely to the apostles, but to disciples of every period, even to the end; comp. 18: 20. True Christian workers may be despised by skeptical philosophers and some pretentious men of science or men of letters; but history has shown that they are a power in the world, and that power is explained by the perpetual presence of their Lord and Redeemer.

Many things in this Gospel have been introduced by **lo** or **behold,** calling attention to what follows as wonderful; but surely none more fitly than this its marvelous and blessed closing word. I is separately expressed in the Greek, and is therefore emphatic. **Alway** is literally (*margin,* Rev. Ver.), *all the days;* days of strength and of weakness, days of success and of failure, of joy and of sorrow, of youth and of age, days of life and day of death—all the days. (Comp. Westcott, "Revelation of the Risen Lord.") **The end of the**

world is literally (*margin,* Rev. Ver.), *the consummation of the age,* or of the world-period (comp. on 13: 39; 24: 3), viz., of that world-period which was introduced by the Messiah's coming, and will be consummated by his second coming. Then his spiritual presence will become a visible presence, but none the less spiritual, sustaining, and delightful; then we shall see him whom not having seen we love, and shall know even as also we were known.

> Jesus, the very thought of thee
>   With sweetness fills my breast;
> But sweeter far thy face to see,
>   And in thy presence rest.
>
> May every heart confess thy name,
>   And ever thee adore;
> And seeking thee, itself inflame
>   To seek thee more and more!
>
> Grant me, while here on earth I stay,
>   Thy love to feel and know;
> And when from hence I pass away,
>   To me thy glory show.
>
> BERNARD OF CLAIRVAUX, TR. BY CASWALL

AUTHOR INDEX

DEMOPHILUS, a Greek Pythagorean philosopher, date unknown.

DELITZSCH, Franz (born 1813). Germany. "A Day at Capernaum," 1873.

DE WETTE (1780-1849). Germany. Exegetical Hand-book to New Test. (in German).

DIDACHE. The so-called Teaching of the Twelve Apostles, written in the Second century (probably latter part).

DIOD. SIC., Diodorus Siculus (flourished about Christian Era). Universal History (in Greek).

DÖLLINGER, I. Germany. "Old Catholic." The First Age of Christianity and the Church.

DOUAY version, *see* Rheims.

DYKES, J. Oswald. London. Presbyterian minister. "The Manifesto of the King." (Sermon on the Mount).

EBRARD, John Hen. Aug. (born 1818). Germany. Criticism of the Gospel History, 1842, 1850.

ECCE HOMO. Anonymous work on Life of Christ, but written by Prof. J. R. Seeley, London.

ECCLUS., Ecclesiasticus, Wisdom of Jesus the son of Sirach, a book of the Old Testament Apocrypha, written about B. C. 190.

EDERSH., Edersheim, Alfred. Church of England. Life and Times of Jesus the Messiah. Sketches of Jewish Social Life. The Temple.

EGYPTIAN VERSIONS: (1) Memph., or Memphitic, in Lower (Northern) Egypt. (2) Theb., or Thebaic, in Upper (Southern) Egypt. Both were probably made late in the Second, or early in the Third century.

ELLICOTT, Chas. John. (1819). Bishop of Gloucester and Bristol. Historical Lectures on Life of Christ. On Revision. Commentaries on Galatians to Philemon. New Test. Commentary for English Readers, *edited* by Ellicott, *see* Plumptre.

EPICTETUS (flourished A. D. 90). Stoic Philosopher. Discourses, etc.

2 ESDRAS, one of the Old Test. Apocryphal books.

EURIPIDES (B. C. 480-406).

EUS., Eusebius (about A. D. 260-340). Greek Father. Ecclesiastical History. Commentary on the Psalms.

EUSTATHIUS (died A. D. 337). Bishop of Antioch.

EUTHYM., Euthymius Zygadenus (Twelfth century). Byzantine Greek writer. Commentaries on the Four Gospels.

EWALD, Henry Geo. Aug. (1803-1876). Germany. History of Christ and His Times. Three first Gospels. 1830.

EXPOSITOR, The, monthly. London.

FAIRBAIRN, Patrick (1805-1874). Scotland. Presbyterian minister. Hermeneutical Manual.

FAIRBAIRN, A. M., England. Independent College principal. Studies in the Life of Christ.

FARRAR, F. W., Church of England. Life of Christ. Mercy and Judgment.

FISH, H. C. (1820-1877). New Jersey. Bapt. minister. Bible Lands Illustrated.

FRITZ., or Fritzsche, Karl Fred. Aug. (1801-1846). Germany. Commentaries on Matthew, 1826, and on Mark, 1830 (both in Latin).

GEIGER, Abraham (1810-1874). Germany. Jewish rabbi. Judaism and Its History. Sadducees and Pharisees. (Both in German).

GEIKIE, C. Church of England. Life and Words of Christ.

GEN., or Geneva, an English version of the Bible (1557).

GILL, John (1697-1771). London. Bapt. minister. Commentary on the Bible. Body of Divinity.

GLOAG, P. J., Scotland. Presb. minister. Exegetical Studies.

GODET, Frederic (born 1812). Switzerland. Commentaries on Luke and on John. New Testament Studies.

GOEBEL. Germany. The Parables of Jesus.

GOODWIN, W. W., Prof. of Greek in Harvard University. Greek Moods and Tenses.

GOTHIC, Version of New Test., made in Fourth century.

GREAT BIBLE, an English version in a large volume (1539), second ed. with preface by Cranmer, and hence often called Cranmer's Bible.

GREG. NAZ., Gregory Nazianzen (A. D. 330-390). Greek Father. Works (in Greek and Latin).

GRIFFITH, Thomas. Church of England. Studies of the Divine Master.

GRIMM, C. L. Wilibald (born 1807). Germany. Lexicon of the Greek Test. (in Latin), 2d ed., 1879. (Thayer's Lexicon, 1886, translates Grimm entire, and makes valuable additions.)

GROTIUS, Hugo (1583-1645). Holland. Annotations upon the Old and New Testaments (in Latin).

GUÉRIN. France. Description of Palestine (in French). 7 volumes.

HALL, Bp. Hall (1574-1656). Joseph Hall, Bishop of Norwich. Contemplations upon the New Testament.

HANNA, Wm. (1808-1882). Scotland. Presb. minister. Life of Christ.

HARRIS, John (1802-1858). England. Independent minister. The Great Commission. Mammon.

HASE, Karl Aug. (born 1800). Germany. Life of Jesus. (Fifth ed., 1865, in German.)

HAUSRATH, Adolph (born 1837). Germany. History of New Testament Times. 3d ed., 1879.

HENGSTENBERG, Ernest Wilh. (1802-1869). Germany. Christology of the Old Testament.

HENRY, Matthew (1662-1714). England. Independent minister. Exposition of the Old and New Testaments.

HERMAS (Second century). Book called "The Shepherd"; among the so-called Apostolic Fathers.

HER., Herodotus (B. C. 484-420). History.

HERZOG, John Jacob (1805-1882). Germany. Theological Encyclopædia (in German). Second Ed. chiefly used, 18 volumes out.

HERVEY, Lord A. England. The Genealogies of our Saviour.

HESIOD. Early Greek poet, date unknown.

HESSEY, Jas. Aug. (born 1814). On the Lord's Day, Bampton Lectures, 1860.

HILL, General D. H. North Carolina. Presbyterian layman. The Sermon on the Mount.

HILLEL (died about Christian era). Jewish Rabbi. Sayings preserved in Talmud.

HOMILETIC REVIEW, monthly, New York, 10 Dey Street.

HORT, see Westcott and Hort; also articles in periodicals by F. J. A. Hort.

HOVEY, A. Massachusetts. Baptist President Theological School. On John. 1885. On the Scriptural Law of Divorce. Both published by the Amer. Bapt. Pub. Soc.

HUMPHRY, Wm. Gilson (1815-1886). Church of England. Commentary on Rev. Ver. of New Test. (explaining changes).

IGNATIUS. Greek Father. Martyred about A. D. 110 (Bishop Lightfoot). Seven Epistles.

ILIAD.

INDEPENDENT, THE, weekly religious paper, New York.

IRENÆUS (flourished Second century, latter half). Greek Father. "Against Heresies."

IRVING, Edward (1792-1834). Scotland and England. Minister. Sermons on John the Baptist (in Works).

JELF, W. E. Church of England. Greek Grammar, two volumes, fourth edition.

JEROME (about A. D. 340-420). Latin Father. On Matthew. Latin Translation of Eusebius on Names of Places, see Eusebius.

JONES, Tiberius G. Virginia. Baptist minister. "The Great Misnomer" (Communion), Nashville, Tenn.

JOSEPHUS (born A. D. 37 or 38, died after A. D. 100). "Ant.", Antiquities (Ancient History) of the Jews; "War," History of the Jewish War; "Life," Autobiography; "ag. Ap.", Against Apion.

JULIAN (A. D. 331-363). Roman Emperor, called "the Apostate." Works (in Greek).

JUSTIN, Martyr (flourished Second century, middle). Greek Father. Two Apologies. Dialogue with Trypho.

KEBLE, John (1792-1866). Church of England. The Christian Year.

KEIL, Karl Fried. (born 1807). Germany. Commentary on Matthew (in German).

KEIM, Theodore (1825-1878). Germany. Jesus of Nazara.

K. J., or K. James, the English version made for King James, published 1611. The Com. Ver. as now printed, differs in many slight details.

KIMCHI (1160-1240). France. Jewish Rabbi. Hebrew Commentaries.

KIRTLEY, J. A. Kentucky. Baptist minister. On the Design of Baptism. Cincinnati.

KITTO, John (1804-1854). English Layman. Daily Bible Illustrations. Cyclopædia of Biblical Literature.

KÖHLER. Germany. John the Baptist (in German).

LACHMANN, Karl (1793-1851). Germany. Professor of Philology. Text of Greek Testament. 1831, 3 ed. 1846.

LAP., or a Lapide, Cornelius a Lapide (1568-1637). France and Rome. Roman Catholic. Commentary on the Gospels.

LANDOR, Walter Savage (1775-1864). English Man of Letters.

LANGE, John Peter (1802-1880). Germany. Commentary on Matthew. Life of Christ.

LATIN VERSIONS: (1) Old Latin version or versions, made first in Second century, and new or revised versions in several following centuries. (2) Latin Vulgate, made at end of Fourth century.

L. and S., or Lid. and Scott. H. G. Liddell and Robert Scott. Church of England. Greek-English Lexicon, sixth and seventh editions.

LIDDON, H. P., Canon of St. Paul's. Easter Sermons.

LF., or LIGHTF., John Lightfoot (1602-1675). Church of England. Works.

BP. LIGHTF., J. B. Lightfoot, Bishop of Durham. "Rev.", on a Fresh Revision of the English New Testament. Commentaries on Galatians, Philippians, Colossians; also on Clement of Rome, and on Ignatius and Polycarp. Articles in Contemporary Review.

LORIMER, G. C. Chicago. Baptist minister. Jesus the World's Saviour.

LUTHER, Martin (1483-1546). Exposition of the Gospels, collected from his works. (In German).

LUTT., LUTTER., Lutteroth, Henri. France. Exposition of the Gospel according to Matthew (in French).

LYNCH, W. F. (1801-1865). American naval officer. U. S. Expedition to the River Jordan and the Dead Sea.

MACCABEES, First, Second, Third, Fourth. Among the Old Test. Apocryphal books.

MAIMONIDES (1135-1204). Jewish scholar in Spain, etc. Commentary on the Mishna.

MAL., Maldonatus (1533-1583). Spain and France. Jesuit. Commentary on the Four Gospels (in Latin).

MANSEL, Henry Longueville (1820-1871). Church of England. Commentary on (part of) Matthew, in "Bible Comm."

MARGOLIOUTH, Moses. Church of England. The Lord's Prayer.

MAUNDRELL. English. Traveler in Palestine about 1690.

McCLELLAN, J. B. Church of England. New Test., with Notes, etc., Vol. 1.

McGARVEY, J. W., Kentucky. Disciples, or Christians. Minister and Professor. Lands of the Bible.

MEMPH., Memphitic, *see* Egyptian versions.

MERRILL, Selah. American Consul at Jerusalem. Congregational minister. Galilee in the Time of our Lord. East of the Jordan.

MEYER, Hein. Aug. Wilh., (1800-1873). Germany. Commentary on New Testament. His own latest edition on Matthew has been used, not that edited by Weiss, whose views have been taken from his own works.

MIDRASH, plural, MIDRASHIM. Jewish Commentaries on several books of Old Test. Usually later than Talmud.

MILL, W. H. Church of England. On the Mythical Interpretation of the Gospels.

MILLIGAN, Wm. Scotland. Presb. Theolog. Prof. Articles in Contemporary Review for Aug. and Nov., 1868. Lectures on the Resurrection of our Lord.

MISHNA, Jewish traditions written down towards end of Second century. Latin Translation by Surenhusius; English translations of some portions by Barclay, and by Sola and Raphall.

MONTET, Ed., France. Origin of the Pharisee and Sadducee parties (in French).

MOULTON, W. F. English Wesleyan Theolog. Prof. Translation of Winer, with copious footnotes.

MULLACH, F. W. A. Germany. The Speech of the (modern) Greek Common People (in German).

NICODEMUS, Gospel of. An apocryphal writing of the Second or Third century.

NICOLL, Wm. Robertson. Scotland. Presb. minister. Editor of the Expositor (1885). The Incarnate Saviour.

NOYES, G. R. (1798-1868). Prof. in Harvard University. Unitarian. New Test. translated (1868).

ODYSSEY.

OLSH., or Olshausen, Hermann (1796-1839). Germany. Commentary on New Test.

ONOM.,Onomasticon, *see* Eusebius and Jerome.

OPTATUS, (Fourth century). Donatist. On the schism of the Donatists.

ORIGEN, (about A. D., 185—about 254). Greek Father. On Matthew. On Luke. On Prayer. Other works, and extracts in Cramer.

PARKER, Joseph. London. Independent minister. "These Sayings of Mine." Inner Life of Christ.

PASCAL, Blaise (1623-1662). France. Roman Catholic (Jansenist). Thoughts.

PHILO, Philo the Jew (an old man in A. D. 40). Alexandria. Works.

PIRQE ABOTH, *see* Aboth.

PLATO (about B. C., 428-347).

PLINY (A. D., 23-79). Natural History.

PLUTARCH (flourished latter part of First century). Greek. Parallel Lives. Morals, or Miscellaneous Writings.

POLLOK, Robert (1799-1827). Scotland. The Course of Time.

PORTEUS, B. (1731-1808). English Bishop. Works.

PSALMS of Solomon, so called, probably written about B. C. 45.

PYTHAGORAS (Sixth century B. C.). Greek philosopher. Fragments.

QUESNEL, Pasquier (1634-1719). France. Roman Catholic. New Testament, with moral reflections.

QUINTILIAN (about A. D. 40—118). Roman writer on Rhetoric.

RABANUS (about 776-856). French abbot. Quoted from Aquinas.

RAWLINSON, George (born about 1815). Church of England. Seven Great Empires.

RECOVERY OF JERUSALEM, see Warren and Wilson.

REFLECTIONS. Practical Reflections on every verse of the Gospel. By an English Clergyman. 1881.

REUSS, Ed. Strassburg, Germany. Synopsis of the three first Gospels.

REYNOLDS, H. R. England. Independent College President. On John the Baptist.

RHEIMS, a translation of the New Test. into English (1582), made from the Latin Vulgate by Roman Catholics at Rheims in France. The Old Test. in 1609, at Douay, called Douay Version.

RIDDLE, M. B. Connecticut, Presb. Theological Prof. New Editions of Robinson's Harmonies.

RITTER, Karl (1779-1859). Germany. On the Geography of Palestine.

ROBINSON, Edward (1794-1863). New England and New York. Presb. Theological Professor. Greek Harmony of the Gospels, and English Harmony (new editions by Riddle). Lexicon of New Test. Greek. Biblical Researches in Egypt, Arabia Petraea, and the Holy Land. Physical Geography of Palestine.

ROBINSON, Thomas. England. The Evangelists and the Mishna (1859).

ROCHEFOUCAULD (1613-1680). France. Moral Maxims (in French).

RÖNSCH. Hermann. Germany. The Italic (Old Latin), and the Vulgate; a grammatical treatise (in German).

ROST AND PALM. Germany. Greek lexicon (in German).

RUSKIN, John (born 1819). England. The Lord's Prayer. Other works.

SCHAFF, Philip. New York. Presb. Theolog. Prof. Commentary on Matthew. Companion to the Revised Test. Church History (second ed.) On the Person of Christ. On Revision (including the treatises of Ellicott, Lightfoot, and Trench).

SCHNECKENBURGER, Matthias. Germany. How old is the Jewish Proselyte Baptism? (in German). 1828.

SCHÖTTGEN, Christian (1687-1751). Germany. Horæ Ebraicae et Talmudicae (Illustrations of the New Test. from the Talmud). (In Latin.)

SCHÜRER, Emil, Germany. History of the Jewish People in the Time of Christ.

SCHWAB, M. French Jew. Talmud Jerusalem translated into French, nearly finished; into English, begun.

SCRIVENER, F. H. A. Church of England. Introduction to the Criticism of the New Test. (Third ed., improved).

SENECA (died A. D. 65). Roman Stoic. Works.

SEPTUAGINT, the familiar Greek translation of the Old Test., made by different persons, probably between B. C. 285 and 130.

SHAKESPEARE (1564-1616).

SIRACH, *see* Ecclus.

SKEAT, W. W. Prof. in Cambridge University, England. Etymological Dict. of the English language.

SMITH'S DICT., or Smith, Bib. Dict., Smith, William. Church of England. Dictionary of the Bible; American edition, enlarged by Hackett and Abbot. Dict. Chr. Ant., Dictionary Christian Antiquities.

SMITH, Philip. Church of England. Manual of New Testament History.

SPURGEON, C. H. Sermons.

STANFORD, Charles. (1823-1886). England. Baptist minister. The Lord's Prayer.

STANLEY, A. P. (1815-1881). Dean of Westminster. Sinai and Palestine.

STEINMEYER, F. L. Germany. The Miracles of our Lord.

STIER, Rudolph. (1800-1862). Germany. Words of the Lord Jesus.

STRABO (flourished about Christian Era). Geography (Roman Empire). (In Greek).

SUETONIUS (flourished early part of Second cent.). Roman. The Twelve Cæsars.

SUICER (1620-1684). Ecclesiastical Thesaurus (in Latin).

SUIDAS (probably Tenth century). A Greek Lexicon.

SYMMACHUS (Second century, latter half). Samaritan, Jewish proselyte, or Judaizing Christian. Translated Old Test. into Greek; fragments remain.

SYRIAC versions: (1) Old (Curetonian) Syriac, probably made in Second Cent. (2) Peshito, a revision in the Third cent. (3) Harklean, made in the Sixth cent., and revised in the Seventh. (4) Jerusalem Syriac, Gospel "Lessons," of unknown date, but with an early form of text.

"SYRIAN" text, according to the theory of Westcott and Hort, see their Introduction.

TACITUS (flourished about A. D. 100). Roman. Annals. History.

TALMUD OF JERUSALEM (Third century, compare Mishna). Quoted from Schwab, or at second hand.

TALMUD OF BABYLON (Fifth century, compare Mishna). Quoted at second hand, or from German translation by Wünsche.

TAYLOR, Jer., Jeremy Taylor (1613-1667). English Bishop. Life of Christ.

TENNYSON. Alfred Lord (born 1809). England.

THEB., Thebaic, *see* Egyptian versions.

THEOD. MOPS. Theodore of Mopsuestia (about A. D. 556-429). Greek Father. Fragments of Commentary on Gospels.

THEODOTION. (Second century, middle). Greek, Jewish proselyte. Translated Old Test. into Greek; fragments remain.

THEOPHYL., Theophylact. (Eleventh century). Greek Commentator. On the Gospels.

THOLUCK, Friedrich Aug. (1799-1877). Germany. The Sermon on the Mount. Commentary on John.

THOMAS, D. English Independent minister. Homiletical Commentary on Matthew.

THOMSON, W. M. Amer. Presb. minister and missionary to Syria. Some references to first ed., "Land and Book." Others to enlarged ed., by pages of Volumes I., II., III.

TISCH., or Tischendorf, L. F. C. (1815-1874). Germany. Greek Testament (Eighth larger edition). Synopsis Evangelica (Harmony of the Gospels).

TOY, C. H. Prof. in Sou. Bapt. Theol. Sem., now in Harvard University. Quotations in the New Testament. Articles in periodicals.

TREG., Tregelles, Samuel P. (1813-1875). England. Plymouth Brethren. Greek New Test.

TRENCH, R. C. (1807-1886). Archbishop of Dublin. On a Revision. Synonyms of the New Test. Miracles of our Lord. Parables of our Lord. Studies in the Gospels. Translations of Augustine's Harmony of the Gospels, and Sermon on the Mount.

TRISTRAM, H. B. Church of England. Natural History of the Bible. The Land of Moab.

TYNDALE, William (1484-1536). New Test. translated into English (1525).

TYREE, C. Virginia. Baptist minister. "The Living Epistle."

TURPIE, D. M. Scotland. Presb. minister. The Old Test. in the New.

ULLMANN (1796-1865). Germany. The Sinlessness of Jesus.

UPHAM, F. W. New York. The Wise Men.

VAN DE VELDE. Officer in Dutch Navy. Map of the Holy Land, and accompanying Memoir (1858).

VEDDER, H. C. New York. Baptist minister. Article on "The Trial of Christ," in Bibl. Sacra, Oct. 1882.

WARFIELD, Benj. B. Pennsylvania. Presb. Theolog. Prof. Articles in periodicals.

WARREN. English Captain of Engineers. Excavations at Jerusalem (in "Recovery of Jerusalem").

WAYLAND, Francis (1796-1865). Baptist. President Brown University. University Sermons.

WEISS, Bernhard. Germany. Life of Jesus. The Matthew-Gospel (in German).

WELLHAUSEN, Julius (born 1844). Germany. Pharisees and Sadducees (in German).

WESTCOTT, B. F. Church of England. Commentary on John (in Bible Comm.). Introduction to Study of the Gospels. The Gospel of the Resurrection. Revelation of the Risen Lord. Articles in Smith's Dict. Bib. See also W H.

W H., or Westcott and Hort. Church of England. Greek Testament, Vol. I, Greek text; Vol. 2, Introduction and Appendix. Int. by Hort.

"WESTERN" text, according to the theory of Westcott and Hort, see their Introduction.

WET., Wetstein (1693-1754). Holland. Greek Test., with numerous extracts from

Greek and Roman, and from Jewish writers. (In Latin and Greek).

WIESELER, Karl. Germany. Chronological Synopsis of the Life of Christ.

WILLIAMS, Wm. R. (1801-1884). New York. Baptist minister. The Lord's Prayer.

WILSON. English Captain of Engineers. Survey of Jerusalem and Sea of Galilee. (In "Recovery of Jerusalem.")

WIN., or Winer, Geo. Benedict. (1789-1858). Germany. Grammar of the New. Test. Diction ; the references are to the pages of Thayer's translation, with those of Moulton's translation added in square brackets; where no page is given, the student can find it by consulting Winer's Index of Passages. Bible Dictionary (in German).

WISDOM OF SOLOMON. An apocryphal book of the Old Test., written at Alexandria, probably not long before the Christian era.

WOOLSEY, T. D. Congregational minister, formerly President of Yale College. On Divorce.

WORDSW., or Wordsworth, Christopher (1807-1885). Bishop of Lincoln. The Holy Bible, with Notes.

WRIGHT, C. H. H. Church of England. Zechariah and his prophecies. (Bampton Lectures, 1879.)

WÜN., or Wünsche. Germany. Illustration of the Gospels from Talmud and Midrashim (in German). One volume of German translation of Talmud of Babylon.

WYC., or Wyclif, John (about 1317-1384). Roman Catholic and Reformer. English translation of the Bible (1380).

YOUNG EDWARD. (1684-1765). Church of England. Night Thoughts.

ZWINGLI. (1484-1531). Switzerland. Works.

Information as to text-criticism may be had from any of the following: (1) More elaborate works. Scrivener's "Introduction to Text-criticism of the New Test.," third edition (conservative). Westcott and Hort's "Introduction," in Vol. II (progressive). (2) Shorter works. Mitchell's "Critical Hand-book." Schaff's "Companion to the Revised Version," or Schaff's "Introduction" to Westcott and Hort, in Vol. 1 (American ed.) (3) For readers not acquainted with Greek, Scrivener's "Six Lectures." Milligan and Roberts, "The Words of the New Test." (progressive).

TOPIC, TERM, PERSON & PLACE INDEX